Roger Casement
Imperialist, Rebel, Revolutionary

Roger Casement
Imperialist, Rebel, Revolutionary

Séamas Ó Síocháin

THE LILLIPUT PRESS | DUBLIN

d'Etaín, Cearbhall agus Iseult

First published 2008 by
The Lilliput Press
62–63 Sitric Road, Arbour Hill
Dublin 7, Ireland
www.lilliputpress.ie

Copyright © Séamas Ó Síocháin, 2007

ISBN 978 1 84351 021 5

A CIP record for this title is available
from The British Library.

10 9 8 7 6 5 4 3 2 1

Set in 10 pt on 13 pt Hoefler by Marsha Swan
Printed in England by Athenaeum Press Ltd, Tyne and Wear

Contents

Illustrations

Frontispiece: Portrait of Casement in Germany by Juliet Brown (1869–1943), from a private collection

I

The following plates are between pages 200 and 201.

The infant Roger David Casement with his parents, Roger and Anne (*née* Jephson), no attribution

Casement and dog with Emma Dickie and Mrs Young, © The National University of Ireland Maynooth

Magherintemple, the Casement home in Ballycastle, Co. Antrim, no attribution, © The National University of Ireland Maynooth

Casement with close Congo friends, Edward Glave, W.J. Parminter and Herbert Ward, © The National University of Ireland Maynooth

Joseph Conrad (1857–1924), courtesy of Art Media / Heritage-Images

Monument in the cataract district of the Lower Congo to the carriers on the Matadi–Leopoldville caravan route, no attribution, © The National University of Ireland Maynooth

Photographed in Calabar, Niger Coast Protectorate, during Mary Kingsley's 1895 journey. Kingsley is seated between Lady MacDonald and Sir Claude MacDonald. Casement is at back right, © Derek Holt West African Collection; reproduced with the permission of the Cambridge University Library

Leopold II (1835–1909), no attribution

Congo Free State. Flogging with the *chicotte* (hippopotamus hide whip), © Anti-Slavery International

Congo Free State. Mutilated boy – Epondo, © Anti-Slavery International

The following plates are between pages 424 and 425.

Upper Igaraparaná River, Indostan Station, © The National Library of Ireland

Young boy on Putumayo showing scars from flogging, © The National Photographic Archive, Ireland

'Volley on departing'. Group departing from rubber station on march, © The National Library of Ireland

Indians on Putumayo, © The National Photographic Archive, Ireland

Casement and Juan Tizon at La Chorrera during the Putumayo investigation, © The National Photographic Archive, Ireland

Muchachos de confianca; armed Indians on a Putumayo rubber station, with a Barbardian, © The National Photographic Archive, Ireland

William Rothenstein's portrait of Arédomi and Omarino, the two youths whom Casement brought from the Putumayo to England to draw attention to the campaign. From the collection of Rupert Sawyer and reproduced by permission of Lucy Dynevor

Casement and the Putumayo Commissioners. From left to right: Juan Tizon, Seymour Bell, H.L. Gielgud, Walter Fox, Louis Barnes, Roger Casement, no attribution

Youth posing in front of wall. Photograph possibly by Casement, © The National Photographic Archive, Ireland

Two stylish young men photographed by Casement (his shadow is visible in the foreground), © The National Photographic Archive, Ireland

Alfred Emmott (1858–1926), © Nuffield College Library, Oxford

Emmeline and William Cadbury with parrot and children, c.1909–10, reproduced by kind permission of the William Adlington Cadbury Trust' and Birmingham City Archives

John Holt (1842–1915), Liverpool trader and humanitarian campaigner, no attribution

Sir Arthur Conan Doyle (1859–1930), courtesy of Art Media / Heritage-Images

Sir John Harris (1874–1940) Congo missionary and campaigner, later secretary to the Anti-Slavery and Aborigines Protection Society, © The Bodleian Library, University of Oxford

Travers Buxton (1873–1944), honorary secretary of the newly amalgamated Anti-Slavery and Aborigines Protection Society, in 1909, © The Bodleian Library, University of Oxford

Casement in consular uniform, in his forties, no attribution, © The National University of Ireland Maynooth

Casement with John Devoy (1842–1928) in New York, August 1914, reproduced with the kind permission of The National Museum of Ireland

Postcard portrait of Eoin MacNeill (1867–1945), © The National Photographic
Archive, Ireland

Senator Colonel Maurice Moore (1854–1939), © The National Photographic
Archive, Ireland

Postcard portrait of Joseph Mary Plunkett (1887–1916), © The National Photographic Archive, Ireland

Adler Eivind Christensen (b. 1890), © The National Photographic Archive, Ireland

The Irish Brigade in Germany, c.1915, reproduced with the kind permission of
The National Museum of Ireland

Count Rudolf von Nadolny of the German Army General Staff, © The Political
Archives of the Federal Foreign Office, Germany

Captain Robert Monteith, no attribution, © National University of Ireland
Maynooth

Richard Meyer of the German Foreign Office, © The Political Archives of the
Federal Foreign Office, Germany

Sir Roger Casement having tea with Mr and Mrs St John Gaffney and other
friends in Munich (September 1915). Gaffney is second from left; Mrs
Gaffney is seated centre, © The National Library of Ireland

Casement during his trial, 1916, no attribution

Serjeant Alexander Martin Sullivan (1871–1959), no attribution

Postcard of the leaders of the 1916 Rebellion; Casement's portrait on the wall
suggests his peripheral position in the proceedings, no attribution, © The
National University of Ireland Maynooth

Editorial Note

In transcribing Casement's despatches, letters and private writings, I have made a number of changes. In places, paragraphs have been amalgamated and minor changes made in punctuation, in the interest of comprehension. Within sentences, Casement frequently used upper-case letters and, on occasion, these have been retained, to give a sense of his usage. Similarly, he alternated regularly between 'and' and '&' (the ampersand); I tried to retain the latter, particularly when used in the diaries. Names of individuals and places vary in Casement's writings, e.g. Glenariffe/Glenariff, Ohumbele/Ohumbela, Komatipoort/Komati Poort, Chinkakassa/Shinkakassa, Kassai/Kasai etc. I have, generally, chosen one variant. To add emphasis to words, Casement used single or double underlinings, for which I have substituted italics. I have also employed italics for non-English words, the names of ships and the titles of books, where he used inverted commas. I have occasionally changed spellings, such as 'employes' to 'employees'. In general, I have tried to retain a sense of his idiosyncratic usage in the diaries. Where published editions exist (Curry, Mitchell, Ó Síocháin and O'Sullivan, Sawyer, Singleton-Gates and Girodias), I have drawn on them, giving page references. However, at times I have made modifications, based on the original manuscripts.

Acknowledgments

Though a study of this length takes many hours of labour on the part of the writer, one learns in the course of doing it how generous and indispensable is the contribution of the many archivists and librarians who facilitate the work, be they in the larger institutional settings or the smaller, more intimate, collections. To all staff in the following institutions I express sincere thanks and admiration. In the Republic of Ireland: the National Library of Ireland; the National Archives of Ireland; the Allen Library; Farmleigh House Library; the University of Limerick Library; Clare County Archives; the National Museum of Ireland; the Natural History Museum; Trinity College Archives and Rare Books; the Archives Department of University College Dublin. A special word of thanks is due my own university library, that of the National University of Ireland, Maynooth, for the constant support of its staff. In Northern Ireland thanks go to the Public Record Office of Northern Ireland; the Linenhall Library; Belfast Central Library; Ballymena Library and the Ulster Museum.

In England I am indebted to the following institutions: the National Archives (Public Record Office), Kew, which houses the largest collection of Casement-related material in Britain and whose staff have always been most helpful; the British Library of Political and Economic Science (LSE, archives and general); the British Library (general, manuscripts and newspapers); the National Register of Archives; the Foreign Office Library; Hatfield House Library; the Bodleian Library Oxford; Rhodes House Library Oxford (Anti-Slavery Papers); Regent's Park College Oxford (The Baptist Missionary Society archives); Nuffield College Oxford; Birmingham University Library; Birmingham Central Library; Central Library, Liverpool; the Plunkett Foundation for Co-operative Studies; Berkshire Libraries. In Scotland the work was facilitated in Edinburgh University by the Library and by the Centre for the Study of Christianity in the Non-Western World, by the National Library of Scotland and by the National Register of Archives (Edinburgh). The Farquharson family of Invercauld were also gracious in facilitating a visit to the family archives. Among those overseas who responded to postal queries were the Berlin-Branderburgische Akademie der Wissenschaften; the Political Archives of the German Federal Foreign Office; New York Public Library; the Sanford Museum (Sanford, Florida); the Archive of the American Baptist Missionary Union; the Disciples of Christ Historical Society; and the South African Library (Cape Town).

During the many personal interactions engaged in during the course of this work, friendships have grown with some and debts of gratitude to many. From the beginning, Roger Sawyer has been warm in his friendship and rapid in his responses to my various requests; he also read sections of the manuscript. Eunan O'Halpin read the whole manuscript and made many useful suggestions. Patrick and Anne Casement in Ballycastle have lent quiet encouragement throughout and Hugh Casement in Munich has made a range of contributions, not least in his invaluable genealogical notes. Jeff Dudgeon has been an enthusiastic correspondent and a generous host. Michael O'Sullivan became a close collaborator and his premature death was a personal loss and deprived us of a promising young Casement scholar. Angus Mitchell facilitated an early stage of the research in London when he and I shared our research enthusiasm in long conversations, exchanging much information about sources. A particular debt goes to Jim Keenan, cartographer in Maynooth, whose skills turned my rough sketches into professional maps. Gerard Lyne of the National Library of Ireland has always been available to encourage and offer support.

Many other individuals helped by facilitating access to materials and by discussing and sharing information. These include the late Seán Ó Lúing; the late Ann Byrne; Eamonn Moffett; Noel and Adrienne Molloy; members of the Casement Foundation; Brian Ó Catháin; Joachim Lerchenmueller; Professor W.J. McCormack for organizing a series of very useful symposia in London; Thomas Kabdebo; the staff of the Maritime Institute of Ireland; the Wilkinson family; Seamus Ó Cléirigh (Ballycastle); Oliver McMullan (Cushendall); Brian Walker; Noel McGuigan; Winifred Glover; Andrew Porter; John Hartford; Jeremy Coote (Pitt Rivers Museum, Oxford); Barry McLoughlin; Barbara Coudenhove-Kalergi; Rheinhard Doerries; Christhard Hoffmann; Daniel Vangroenweghe; the late Jules Marchal; Lucy McDiarmid; John O'Loughlin; Wyatt MacGaffey; William A. Christian Jr.; and Jim McKillop. Deirdre Dunne and Jacqui Mullally of the Anthropology Department in Maynooth also helped in numerous ways. The National University of Ireland, through its Publications Fund, has made a generous financial contribution to meet production costs.

Despite the frustrations of a long delay in getting into print, I owe a great deal to Antony Farrell and the board of The Lilliput Press for undertaking publication. Fiona Dunne of The Lilliput Press has contributed many hours of work and made substantial improvements to the text. My thanks, too, to Nicola Sherwell, Marsha Swan, Brendan Barrington, and to Gloria Greenwood for the index.

Preface

The life of Roger Casement (1864–1916) continues to fascinate for his many-sided activities: campaigner for the rights of indigenous inhabitants in Africa and South America; Irish nationalist leader of his day, associated with the Irish Volunteers and the Easter Rising of 1916; traitor to Britain during the First World War, hanged for his actions; author of homosexual diaries or, for some, innocent victim of an insidious deed of forgery. Opinions about him, both in his own day and in ours, have varied widely. In England, while Casement awaited execution, he was described, on the one hand, as a 'moral degenerate', and 'cold traitorous dog', but as 'a man of fine nature and chivalrous disposition' on the other. In our day, some of those who have studied him, while giving due credit to his humanitarian contributions, have also described him, varyingly, as 'a walking fluke', a 'schizoid personality', or as having a mind 'suspended between two worlds'. Rebecca Solnit, with perhaps a degree of overstatement, has remarked that 'most of his biographers have openly disliked him in a way almost unique in the genre'.[1]

How are we to make sense of him? The predominant focus of the present work is on Casement's public life. He lived through and actively participated in one of the most remarkable series of historical episodes any human could imagine playing a role in. The almost twenty years he worked in Africa, between 1884 and 1903, coincided with that momentous phase of European colonialism known as the Scramble for Africa, the last major episode of European imperialism whose earliest phase is frequently dated from the Berlin Conference of 1885–6. Casement served, successively, in the emerging Congo Free State (1884–92), in the nascent British colony of the Niger Coast Protectorate (1892–5), in the Portuguese territories of Lourenço Marques (1895–8) and St Paul de Loanda (1898–9) and, once more, in the Congo (1900–3). From 1895 on, he was a career British consul, responsible to the Foreign Office in London. In late 1899, at the outbreak of the Second Anglo-Boer War, he travelled to South

Africa and was both participant in and observer of events there. When mounting criticism of the increasingly serious abuses against the indigenous population in the Congo forced the hand of the British Foreign Office, Casement undertook an investigative journey on the Upper Congo River (1903) and the official report which followed (1904) substantiated earlier accusations of systematic abuse and proved to be a landmark event in the campaign against atrocities. For his services he was awarded the CMG (Companion of the Order of St Michael and St George). He then helped found the Congo Reform Association (CRA) and continued to offer warm emotional support to its key activist, Edmond Morel, until the dissolution of the CRA in 1913.

After a career break of over two years, which followed the publication of the Congo Report, he was posted to South America. Having served in Brazil (1906–9), he was chosen by the Foreign Office to investigate another situation of alleged atrocities, this time in the Putumayo region of the Upper Amazon and once more connected with the exploitation of rubber. His investigation in 1910 demonstrated courage and balance of judgment and for this he was rewarded with a knighthood in 1911. He remained active in the Putumayo campaign until 1913, collaborating with officers of the Anti-Slavery Society and with Charles Roberts MP, chairman of the Parliamentary Select Committee set up to investigate the issue.

Though a nationalist in orientation since his youth, from 1904 onwards a major shift began to manifest itself in his political loyalties and in the direction he sought to give to his life. He became enraptured by the Irish cultural revival and immersed himself in Irish literature, particularly in works of history. The movement for the revival of the Irish language captured his heart and he associated himself fully with its goals and with its foremost organization, the Gaelic League (Conradh na Gaeilge). His political attitudes also evolved and when, almost a decade later, the Liberal government introduced a Home Rule Bill for Ireland (1912), arousing the vehement opposition of the Unionist community in Ireland and in Britain, Casement's commitment to Ireland found a direct political outlet in support of Home Rule. He expended considerable energy in helping to organize the Irish Volunteer movement (1913–14), founded to protect Home Rule, and was active in a scheme to import arms for the Volunteers. In mid 1914 he travelled to the United States to raise funds for that organization.

The First World War began while Casement was in the United States. Probably in anticipation of a German victory, he resolved to go to Germany to seek official support there for the cause of Irish independence. The consequences of such a bold step, of his associating with a country with which Britain was at war, must surely, even then, have been clear to him. After a year and a half there, most of it spent in deep misery, he returned to Ireland by submarine in April 1916 and was captured and taken to London, where he was tried for treason, found guilty and hanged.

We know comparatively little of the first twenty years of Casement's life. The second twenty cover his career in Africa, ending with his Congo investigation and report. The last twelve include his reawakening interest in Ireland, his South American postings, the Putumayo investigation, the growing crises in Ireland and in Europe, culminating, in the one case, in the Easter Rebellion and, in the other, in the First World War. While the latter phase of his life merits and is accorded detailed treatment, the present work devotes more attention than has hitherto been accorded to Casement's twenty years in Africa. As well as the significance of the events of these years in themselves, analysis of his writings during the period yields many clues to his thinking on such topics as the characteristics of indigenous societies, the duties and the weaknesses of colonialism, the patterns of European trade – German trade included – the natures of agriculture, of land concessions and of capitalism. There is evidence, too, of the early stages of his anti-Englishness. In two places in the text, the narrative of Casement's life has been interrupted to allow a fuller focus on African issues. At the end of Chapter 6, which discusses his Boer War service, a section is devoted to tracking his changing loyalties towards British rule in Africa between 1900 and 1909. In similar fashion, after his professional consular contribution had ended with his Congo Report of 1904, his contribution to the cause of Congo reform between then and 1913 is dealt with ahead of the general narrative of his career, in order to make its contours more visible.

Despite the length of Casement's first stint in the Congo, 1884–91, and its strong formative influence, this period has been comparatively neglected by previous biographers. B.L. Reid, for example, suggested that 'precisely what Casement was *doing* in Africa, especially in the first eight years, is still not easy to say'.[2] As a result of this neglect, up to now one could only imagine what Joseph Conrad, who had stayed with Casement in 1890, might have been alluding to when he wrote to R.B. Cunninghame Graham in 1903, saying: 'He could tell you things! Things I've tried to forget; things I never did know.'[3] But it is possible to piece together a detailed picture of Casement's activities during these years. Admittedly, he was still a virtually unknown young man and had not yet begun that voluminous correspondence, consular and personal, which was to mark his later career. Nevertheless, through the eyes of others and to a lesser extent through his own words (some of them later recollections), considerable flesh can be put on the bones of this early phase of his career. Greater attention to the historical and geographical context contributes to making the surviving records more meaningful.

For a significant portion of his adult life, the world of Roger Casement was that of the consular official in late Victorian and Edwardian Great Britain. His first professional appointment as consul came in 1895 in Lourenço Marques and he retired from the service in 1913. Adding the Niger years (1892–5), some of the duties of which were consular in function, the span is two decades. During all of this time, he devoted his professional energies to the various tasks associated with the role. In addition to the staff of the Foreign Office in London, the British Foreign Service comprised two main divisions, the Diplomatic Service and the Consular Service, the latter very much the subordinate and later termed the 'Cinderella Service'.4 For much of its existence, the Consular Service employed both professional salaried officials and honorary consuls, unpaid men, generally involved in trade. As Casement liked to point out, he was a consul *de carrière*.

The Consular Service was a neglected and underfunded one. It was, essentially, an assemblage of separate posts, each with its own allocated salary, and there was no real career structure. Salaries were low and, frequently, had to be supplemented from private means; putting money aside was not easy. Despite this, there was no shortage of applicants, as secure positions bringing a degree of status were not easy to come by for members of the gentleman class. Working conditions tended to be poor. Consular buildings were often non-existent or inferior in quality; basic furnishings had to be provided by each successive incumbent; archives were often poorly maintained. Many consulates were identified as 'unhealthy posts', being located in tropical areas where health risks were a major threat. Finally, the work included a great deal that was repetitive and mechanical, which could have been done by clerical staff, had they been available.

These limitations brought frustrations to serving consuls, which are clearly in evidence during Casement's career and are reflected in letters to him from consular colleagues. He, however, appears to have been more forthright than others in making his Foreign Office employers aware of the deficiencies, as he did in his correspondence with London. And it was he who was selected to give evidence to the Royal Commission on the Civil Service in 1914, when it was investigating conditions in the Consular Service. All of Casement's postings were in 'unhealthy posts' and, over the years, he declined from being a strong and athletic man to one racked by fevers and arthritis. Despite all of this, and despite his increasing testiness over conditions, he was an energetic, efficient and conscientious official for the most part.

The content of consular work can be divided into three sections: representing the interests of British subjects; trade and commercial functions; political and intelligence functions. With regard to the first of these, Casement registered the births, marriages and deaths of British residents; he looked after the welfare of British citizens and subjects, providing both immediate relief for what were called Distressed British Subjects (DBSs) and monitoring and making quasi-legal interventions where litigation was involved. In the Congo Free State, his knowledge of Leopold's regime came to a degree from the protective work he exercised for black West African British subjects working in the Congo. Regarding the second function, in all of his postings he produced annual reports on trade and responded to routine queries from the Department of Trade and individual exporters. He also monitored and acted as troubleshooter for British shipping.

Under the third function, he provided intelligence reports on a range of topics, from the cargoes of ships (including the movement of arms) to details on the Congo fort of Shinkakasa; from the affairs of the Delagoa Bay Railway in Lourenço Marques to those of the Madeira–Mamoré Railway in Brazil. Political work was normally the prerogative of diplomatic missions, where these were present. But in certain parts of the world they were not. When Casement served in Lourenço Marques, for example, the British diplomatic representative was located in far-off Lisbon. Consequently, there was an important political component to his consular work there. This was even more so with regard to the Congo Free State. On the other hand, a degree of Casement's frustration in Brazil was due to the presence of a British Legation in Petropolis and the reduction of his own duties, therefore, to more mundane consular tasks.

It is not possible to reach a measured judgment of Casement's contribution to the Congo or Putumayo campaigns, or more generally, without devoting adequate attention to the content of his consular despatches to the Foreign Office. The present work attempts to reflect the broad content of his communications with the Foreign Office in each of his consular postings. In Africa, his despatches comprise the largest part of his written output. They not only reveal the major concerns of a British consul of the time, they also give clues about the development of certain patterns in Casement's thinking.

His systematic interaction with the officials of the Foreign Office in London certainly coloured Casement's view of the workings of the British establishment. He had friends there – Henry Foley, Sir Martin Gosselin, Harry Farnall and Sir William Tyrrell – but he had a poor opinion of others, Sir Constantine Phipps, Francis Villiers, and Rowland Sperling, for example. But, in the years leading up to the outbreak of the First World War, criticism of what was taken to be the non-democratically answerable 'secret diplomacy' of the Foreign Office spread in radical circles in Great Britain, one prominent critic being Casement's close friend, Edmond Morel. In parallel with the change in Morel, Casement gradually grew more critical of the influence on foreign policy of what he called the 'permanent gang' – the professional officials. This negative attitude reached its height when Foreign Office policy manifested clear anti-German signs in the years preceding the War.

Of the volume of consular work he complained to his cousin Gertrude (also known as 'Gee'), that 'I write, write, write', while a Foreign Office clerk was to complain that the extent and detail of his despatches 'make one's head whirl'. And his literary output was not, of course, confined to his consular despatches. He also produced a huge outpouring of written material during his life, which falls into different categories. There were letters to family, friends and acquaintances, few in the early years, but mounting to a crescendo later. There were articles and letters for publication, generally anonymous while he was still a public servant, but signed after his retirement. There was his poetry. And there were the diaries. Throughout, this study attempts to present a detailed narrative of the life of Casement, drawing on the full range of his writings: despatches, diaries, private correspondence, public writings and poetry. For the earlier part of his career, he must be largely viewed through the eyes and observations of others; but the volume of his own writing increased considerably as time went by. Where possible in the present study, Casement's own words are used, in all their variability.

In addition to what it tells us of Casement's professional and personal activities, the corpus of his writing reveals certain patterns of thought with which he interpreted the world around him. One can identify more-or-less systematic ideas on a wide array of topics: on the growth and decline of societies and empires; on the colonial mission of bringing the three Cs – Christianity, civilization, commerce – to less favoured parts of the world; on the Irish nation as an ancient and precious creation and nationalism as the necessary means to defend the value of freedom; on the origins of freedom in northern countries (Teutonism); on the gentlemanly values of 'chivalry' and 'manhood' or 'manliness' and the negatives of 'sin', 'evil', 'lies' and 'greed', references to which pepper his writings; on miscegenation or fears of racial mixture. One theme, for example, which runs like a thread through his writings, surfacing again and again throughout his life, is that of the land: in his youthful concern with the Irish Land War; in his comments on his uncle's productive farming; in his praise for enterprising Danish small farming; and in his opposition to landlordism, concessionaire systems, commodity exporting (he dubbed the system of rubber extraction in Brazil 'vegetable filibustering'), and mining, all of which, at some point or another, he criticized as being not in keeping with a healthy economy.[5]

The interconnections that Casement made between some of these themes, as well as the romantic cast of his mind, can be captured by a passage in an essay he published in 1914. In it he identified the activities of the early Irish bands of warriors, the Fianna, with the values of chivalry and the defence of freedom against imperialism. He saw such ideals as models for the Irish youth, the 'manhood' of his own day.

> Chivalry dies when Imperialism begins. The one must kill the other. A chivalrous people must respect in others what they strive to maintain in themselves. Hence it comes that when the age of empire begins the age of chivalry dies. So it has ever been. Rome the Republic, Rome the Nation, had her knights and knighthood, and the ideals of knighthood are the laws of chivalry. But Rome the Empire lost her ideals as she extended her frontiers, and when an Augustus or Claudius replaced a Cincinnatus or Horatius, Rome, the emporium of the world, had all things but knighthood and chivalry ... Rome was the first great illustration, but not the last in history, that where wealth accumulates men must decay.[6]

Where in all of this lies Casement the man? While the present study is in no sense a psychological one, adequate evidence is included to enable an assessment of his personality. Casement was certainly a man of emotion: he could be tender and solicitous; courageous, loyal and tenacious; humorous and sarcastic. He could also be boastful; testy and resentful; given to anger and even rage; subject to deep depressions. After his execution, one Irish observer described his propensity to anger:

> If I understand aright, Sir Roger was at times capable of hot-rages; a one-time editor of the *Irish Review* gave me a most amusing account of the 'Black Knight's' frenzied letters denouncing him over the mangling of a sonnet horribly misprinted in that luckless magazine. Sir Roger was made to appear as an Etna vomiting a most devastating lava of boiling-hot abuse. But editor and mangled contributor remained very good friends: Sir Roger could indulge his rage but could not bear long malice ...7

On the other hand, Fred Puleston, who spent time with Casement in his early years in the Congo, described his disposition as 'the gentlest imaginable', always 'sweet-tempered, ready to help'; when his dog was injured by a wild hog, he was 'unable to control his feeling and wept like a girl'.8

B.L. Reid, whose accomplished psychologically-orientated biography set out to try to reveal 'the character of the man behind the famous events', argued that the focus of earlier biographers on Casement's public life failed to make the man himself knowable or credible. Yet, his own interpretations seem overdrawn: Casement was 'hazardously rooted in the real world'; and his 'nature was divided to a depth just short of real pathology, of disastrous incoherence'.9 Reid took his cue from Joseph Conrad's judgment that Casement

> was a good companion; but already in Africa I judged that he was a man, properly speaking, of no mind at all. I don't mean stupid. I mean that he was all emotion. By emotional force (Congo report, Putumayo, etc.) he made his way, and sheer temperament – a truly tragic personality: all but the greatness of which he had not a trace. Only vanity. But in the Congo it was not visible yet.10

Though Reid distanced himself, somewhat, from Conrad's view, the judgment provided a basic orientation for his analysis: Casement was a man dominated by emotion, with 'strong feeling overriding expression and orderly thought'. For Reid, Casement was not only a bad writer, wordy and given to 'meretricious forms of true feelings'; for him, 'Casement and a pen made a dangerous combination in any crucial situation'.11 While one recognizes Casement's tendency to rant, the judgment lacks balance. Towards the end of Casement's life, when the flaws in his personality were more pronounced, the influential German academic Eduard Meyer noted them, but in a more sympathetic light:

> Casement was a typically sanguine character, full of projects and the most far-reaching hopes. When the inevitable disappointment then set in, he could fall into a deep depression, but new plans and hopes always broke through, which were just as unlikely to achieve the objectives. This was associated with unshakeable optimism, especially with regard to his belief in his fellow human beings. This led him to completely trust everyone he met. He told us how, in Africa, he demonstrated complete trust in young people – including sailors – who had fairly serious matters on their consciences, and how this trust (for

example in money matters) drew them to him and prevented them committing new crimes. There is no doubt that this trust was not always justified; thus his relationship with Adler Christensen seems to have been quite problematic ... Nevertheless, when in Berlin or elsewhere in Germany he always observed the necessary caution with regard to his statements and behaviour, however hard this was. In a manner which was unique but possibly typically Irish, he was a combination of two people: a person living in the midst of bold far-reaching projects, and a naïve and trusting optimist.[12]

Casement's homosexuality and the content of what are generally called the 'Black Diaries' have cast a long shadow over interpretations of his personality. While, in common with virtually all recent biographers, I am convinced, on the available evidence, of the authenticity of the diaries and of the record therein of a robust sexual life, I am less convinced that they provide the evidence of a 'pathological' or divided personality, as is sometimes claimed. But rather than hope, as some would have it, that if only the diaries could be proven false then the true Casement would re-emerge unsullied, I would echo the words of one commentator that 'an integrated picture ... necessarily has to include both black and white, as well as what lies in between'.[13]

However one assesses his personality and sexuality, Casement's historical contribution was considerable. The historian Roger Louis wrote of him that '[t]he history of the Congo, unlike the history of his native Ireland, was profoundly influenced by Roger Casement'.[14] His biographer, Roger Sawyer, spoke of him as an 'exceptional man', drawing attention to his defence of indigenous peoples: 'Within the context of the department of an imperial power which, towards the end, he came to despise, he marshalled world opinion behind helpless primitive peoples and argued for recognition of their human rights.' In Sawyer's view, Casement was 'probably the bravest, most selfless, practical humanitarian of his day, one whose acts of emancipation have seldom been surpassed before or since the Edwardian era, the period of his most effective activity'.[15] Mansergh has suggested that while his role in Ireland is subject to debate, 'it would be legitimate to co-opt him as a forerunner of Ireland's independent foreign policy tradition'.[16]

Casement's life has already attracted the attentions of a number of biographers. In the words of Lucy McDiarmid,

Casement could easily be said to be over-remembered. He has received more biographies than any other figure of 1916, and he can be found, in one form or another, in poems, plays, orations, memoirs, songs, legends, jokes, allusions, anecdotes, paintings, monuments, documentaries, film-scripts, and – by the thousands – letters-to-the-editor. The ubiquitous subject of an unendable argument or long national dream, Casement has proved disturbing, entertaining, irresistible. The sheer quantity of material about him defies measure.[17]

It is hoped that the present addition to that expanding corpus will be found to have its merits.

Abbreviations

ABIR	Anglo Belgian India Rubber Company
ABMU	American Baptist Missionary Union
AOH	Ancient Order of Hibernians
APS	Aborigines Protection Society
ASG	Alice Stopford Green
ASS	Anti-Slavery Society
BBAW	Berlin-Branderburgische Akademie der Wissenschaften
BCB	*Biographie Colonial Belge*
BL	British Library
BLO	Bodleian Library Oxford
BMS	Baptist Missionary Society
BMSA	*Baptist Missionary Society Archives*
CBM	Congo Balolo Mission
CS	Congo State (=CFS/CIS)
CO	Colonial Office
CRA	Congo Reform Association
DB	Delagoa Bay
DBSs	Distressed British Subjects
EDM	Edmund Dene Morel
FO	Foreign Office
Gee	Gertrude Bannister
GFO	German Foreign Office
HH	Hatfield House [see SalP]
HO	Home Office
IAA	International African Association
LIM	Livingstone Inland Mission

LSE	London School of Economics
MP	Morel Papers
NLI	National Library of Ireland
NLS	National Library of Scotland
PAC	Peruvian Amazon Company
PRO	Public Record Office, Kew (National Archives)
PRONI	Public Record Office of Northern Ireland
r.	received (of letters)
RDC	Roger David Casement
RHO	Rhodes House Library, Oxford
RIA	Royal Irish Academy
RIC	Royal Irish Constabulary
SAB	Societé Anonyme Belge
SEE	Sanford Exploring Expedition
SanP	Sanford Papers
SalP	Salisbury Papers, Hatfield House [see HH]
Tel.	Telegram
TCD	Trinity College Dublin
UCD	University College Dublin
UE	University of Edinburgh (Archives)

Roger Casement

Imperialist, Rebel, Revolutionary

PART I

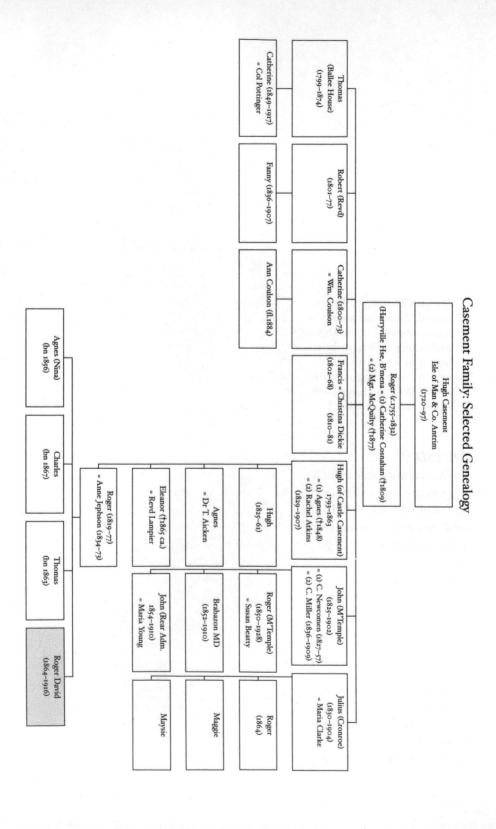

Casement Family: Selected Genealogy

Hugh Casement
Isle of Man & Co. Antrim
(1720–9?)

Roger (c.1755–1832)
(Harryville Hse, B'mena = (1) Catherine Cosnahan (†1809)
= (2) Mgt. McQuilty (†1877)

Thomas
(Ballee House)
(1799–1874)

Robert (Revd)
(1801–77)

Catherine (1800–73)
= Wm. Coulson

Francis = Christina Dickie
(1802–68)   (1810–81)

Catherine (1849–1917)
= Col Pottinger

Fanny (1836–1907)

Ann Coulson
(fl.1884)

Hugh (of Castle Casement)
1793–1863
= (1) Agnes (†1848)
= (2) Rachel Atkins
(1829–1907)

John (M'Temple)
(1825–1902)
= (1) C. Newcomen (1827–57)
= (2) C. Miller (1836–1909)

Julius (Cronroe)
(1830–1904)
= Maria Clarke

Roger (1819–77)
= Anne Jephson (1834–73)

Eleanor (†1865 ca.)
= Revd Lampier

Agnes
= Dr T. Aicken

Hugh
(1825–61)

Roger (M'Temple)
(1850–1928)
= Susan Beatty

Brabazon MD
(1852–1910)

John (Rear Adm.
1854–1910)
= Maria Young

Roger
(1864)

Maggie

Maysie

Agnes (Nina)
(bn 1856)

Charles
(bn 1867)

Thomas
(bn 1863)

Roger David
(1864–1916)

1: *Early Life*

My 45th Birthday ... Just think of it! I was born in 1864 in that wee cottage we passed, Nina you and I, last December – Christmas Day – on the way to Sandycove in dear old Dublin. I think of Ireland in 1864 – full of people, brave and strong – Fenians in every county, preparing for the great fight they all hoped to have within two years – a land poor and oppressed indeed, but still with its own brave native heart and resolute belief in its own right arm – and today! What a change! Talk, drivel, lying and sham – taken the place of self-belief and self-reliance.[1]

Ancestry

About a century and a half before the birth of Roger David Casement in 1864, his great-great-grandfather Hugh Casement (1720–97), of Ramsay on the Isle of Man, had crossed to Ireland and settled in Co. Antrim, where the Casement family became 'a leading county one'. They were landowners and local officials, and some held respected positions in the British army and navy and in imperial administration.[2] Roger Casement was to refer proudly to this family background during the campaign against atrocities in the Congo, when the supporters of King Leopold II of Belgium questioned his impartiality:

Here in this County four of my father's uncles owned – and the family still own it – 8387 acres with a rentroll of £5300 a year. Part of this estate was my grandfather's – and if my father had not been so extravagant I should have been well off. As it is I am without a penny.[3]

Roger David Casement's father, also Roger, born in Belfast in 1819, was the eldest son of Hugh Casement of Holywood, Co. Down, grandson of Hugh of Ramsay. The younger Hugh was a grain importer and shipowner in Belfast, whose fortunes declined after he suffered shipping losses and who was 'considerably in his father's debt at the latter's death'.[4] Hugh died in 1863 in Melbourne,

Australia, where he had business interests. The elder Roger was sent on the Grand Tour as a young man, and then sailed for Calcutta on his father's ship in November 1840. In 1841 his father purchased a commission for him in the Third Light Dragoons in India, where he is said to have fought Afghans and Sikhs and become a lieutenant.5 In 1848 he sold his commission and took the remarkable step of returning to Europe to assist Louis Kossuth and the Hungarians, then fighting the Austrians.

The events that followed were described in Kossuth's memoirs. Following defeat at Világos, Kossuth and his supporters found refuge at Widdin, in Turkish territory on the Danube. Fearing that pressure from Austria and Russia would lead to their extradition, it was suggested that Kossuth should send a letter to the British Prime Minister, Lord Palmerston, appealing for England's intervention. The difficulty was in ensuring the letter's safe and rapid delivery. At this point – September 1849 – an unknown 'Englishman' appeared, announcing that he had 'come from India to fight for Hungarian freedom'. After a brief consultation, the letter was entrusted to him, a dramatic journey made, and the letter placed in the hand of Lord Palmerston. British intervention eventually did save the Hungarian patriots.6

In the autumn of 1850 the elder Roger Casement visited the United States, which he termed 'the great land of "Liberty"' and in which he had a chance encounter with Kossuth.7 Some years later, in 1855, he married Anne Jephson, twenty-five years younger than him, in Belfast.8 Anne Jephson's maternal grandfather was Adam Ball, postmaster general for Dublin. On the paternal side she seems to have been a member of a distinguished Irish family whose ancestral home was Mallow Castle, though she belonged to a very junior branch. While Roger David Casement would come into contact on a number of occasions with individual Jephsons, the maternal side of his family was to play virtually no part in his life, with the important exception of close links with his mother's sister, Grace Bannister, and her family in Liverpool. The only occasion we are aware of on which he tried to probe his maternal descent stemmed from a meeting in 1892 in Las Palmas with Miss Louisa Jephson-Norreys. He wrote to her three years later from Ballycastle for help in determining the link between his mother's family and the Jephsons of Mallow Castle. 'She died when I was quite a child and I only know she spoke of being related to Jephsons of Mallow, in my hearing, when a boy and since her death I never met with anyone whom I might make enquiry from.' He continued:

> As far as I know my mother's father was James (or John) Jephson, and he died somewhere near Dublin from a fall from his horse when hunting about 1840. He lived in the County of Dublin – and I *think*, but here I am groping in the mists of early recollections – that he was the son of a Lorenzo Jephson of Tipperary Co. One of them I believe married a Martin of Co. Galway – my grandfather James Jephson's mother I think was a Miss Martin.9

Miss Jephson-Norreys obviously replied, as Casement sent her a second letter on 10 June in which he thanked her for her help and was more forthcoming about his maternal grandfather:

> I think you have helped me – for with the information about the Dublin Jephsons I may be able to do something. All you so kindly told me was very interesting, and what you say about them being dissipated, reckless and brave, induces me to tell you that I believe my grandfather Jephson (my mother's father) broke his neck as the result of a wager that he would jump the Grand Canal on his horse. He tried and came to the not unnaturally to be expected fate of those who do these things. As the story is another of my childhood's days, I have, in these hard practical years of prosaic people, and railway trains, come to regard it as a myth, and so I never mention the belief that lies deep in my heart, but I say he was killed 'hunting' as being the more respectable method of coming to one's death from horseback; but your statement about your ancestors inspires me with the belief that my grandfather's neck did go for a wager, and as to his property, *that* I know went in some such a way.[10]

James Jephson married Anne Ball, daughter of Adam Ball. Of Casement's mother's personal history virtually nothing is known. The Jephsons of Mallow had the idea 'that Casement's mother ... was a music teacher in Dublin, but chapter and verse for this has not been traced'.[11]

Roger Sr. is described in family records as 'an insinuating idler who lived on his debts'. He seems never to have secured paid employment after his departure from the army and to have lived off family allowances and the expectation of a settlement from his father's will. He was clearly under financial pressure when, writing from London in January 1871, he explained to his uncle John, at Magherintemple, Co. Antrim, that

> for nearly four years, I have not received so much as a single penny from my father's legacies. Indeed it was owing to the stoppage of all income that my kind Uncle Thomas made me the allowance of which I told you. I shall not worry you with any sad details, but I shall add that I am quite able to prove that my troubles since my father's death have been brought on by incapacity and devilry, chiefly the latter, on the part of those who had charge of his affairs, including the lawyers.[12]

In the almost two decades between their marriage and Anne's death, the pattern of family movements is very unclear. According to the reminiscences of Roger David Casement's cousin Gertrude (Gee) Bannister, during his youth the family moved frequently, living in France, in Italy, and then in England and Ireland. Some time was spent on the island of Jersey, near St Heliers, where Roddie (Roger David) showed his first prowess at swimming. Some of the movement was likely caused by Roger Sr.'s search for a mode of livelihood, but some addresses seem to be holiday destinations – poverty for one of minor gentry background was likely to have been relative. There are indications that they lived in Ireland in the late 1860s and in London in the early 1870s.

Four children were born to Roger and Anne Casement. Agnes (Nina), the eldest, was born on 25 May 1856, presumably in Ireland, as her father was a captain in the North Antrim Militia from 1855 to 1858. Charles (Charlie) was born on 5 October 1861, in Westminster; Thomas (Tom) on 3 January 1863 (the year of their grandfather's death), in Boulogne sur Mer; and Roger David, the youngest, was born on 9 September 1864 in Doyle's Cottage, Sandycove, Dublin.

On 5 August 1868, when Roddie was almost four, his mother had the children baptized secretly as Catholics when on a holiday in Rhyl, North Wales.[13] While Casement was later to claim 'My mother was a Catholic and I am one at heart', Fr James McCarroll, one of the prison chaplains who attended Casement in Pentonville Prison prior to his execution, reported him as saying that 'he was brought up a Protestant or as he said himself he was brought up really nothing'.[14] This is corroborated by Nina, who wrote: 'Mother was not *actually* a Catholic, but as she always had strong leanings towards the Catholic faith we were all baptised into the Catholic Church when children by her.'[15]

Significantly, Roger Sr. seems to have had sympathies with the Fenian movement, which was founded in 1858 and organized an abortive rebellion in 1867. Nina recollected their mother crying in 1867 or 1868 when her husband wanted 'to go out' with the Fenians. 'Remember your wife and young children', she pleaded – and prevailed. In 1870, during the Franco-Prussian War and the Siege of Paris, Casement Sr. composed a letter of support to Leon Gambetta, 'the great French republican leader', together with a draft plan for the provisioning of the besieged city and two draft letters to English newspapers. The latter show him to be strongly supportive of France against what he termed the 'aggressive designs' of Prussia. His republican sympathies are evident from the following remarks in the Gambetta letter:

> Owing to the hostile jealousy by all great European governments of Republicanism – the Prussian being the chief hater – I apprehend, in spite of the noble attitude of France, the stifling for some years longer of human freedom; but there remains a grand consolation to your patriots and philanthropists, in extracting the greatest hope for the future, from a temporary increase of repression and even barbarism. But for a time only. Heaven will then no doubt ordain that the very evils, which the enemies of freedom may multiply in Europe, shall so horrify the world, that the masses of the people will be joined by the majority among the middle classes, and a few aristocrats, in hailing universal republicanism as a harbour of refuge.[16]

In a postscript, he apologized to Gambetta for his 'inability to leave my family and give my sword even in the interests of France'.

Childhood and Schooling

The family lived in London for some of the early 1870s and there Roger received part of his primary education. When in prison at the end of his life, he told his counsel that he was 'educated in Ireland and in England'.[17] Two childhood books of his have survived, prizes he won for performance in school. One, Anna Bartlett's *Casper*, 'a tale for the young', is inscribed 'Roger Casement from Miss Haynes for best answering in French in Third Class, Christmas 1873'. The following year a similar inscription from A.E. Haynes was 'for second answering in Latin in Second [*sic*] Class Christmas 1874'. The prize in this case was *The Grey House on the Hill; or 'Trust in God and do the right'*, by Louisa L. Greene (1874).[18]

His cousin Elizabeth Bannister described visiting the Casement family in London when she was about three years old and Roger seven or eight. She recalled a dining room with mahogany furniture and Roddie being given the task of getting drinks for the guests; it was he, not Nina, Charlie or Tom, who made a vivid impression on her mind. She remembered Anne Casement as 'a tall graceful woman' and that 'we stayed some little time in London and I was made much of by my uncle Roger'.[19]

Gertrude, the younger Bannister sister, told of later conversations between herself and Roger about his childhood. 'He talked much about his mother, whom he adored, and who died in childbirth a few days after I was born. He told stories of his father who was stern and harsh with his children, but who nevertheless inspired Roddie with affection. Uncle Roger visited any breach of discipline with sound thrashings.' On one occasion Roddie fled to his room, wrongfully accused, while 'his irate father pursued him with a rod'. '[N]othing would induce him to submit', commented Gertrude, if he believed he was in the right. Nina described their father as an 'irascible' man, feared by all the children, except Roddie.[20]

The influence of a strict upbringing was reflected in Casement's own attitudes later in life. 'Brazil', he wrote, 'wants a severe attack of discipline – beginning in childhood and enduring into old age ... The children are brought up entirely lawless ...'[21] He expressed a similar attitude to 'Ulster' lawlessness. 'Sometimes the only thing to bring a boy to his senses is to hide him – and I think "Ulster" wants a sound hiding at the hands of her that owns her – Ireland's hands. Failing that – I pray for the Germans and their coming.'[22]

Roddie's childhood seems to have been generally happy. According to Nina he was a healthy child. On his fifth birthday he was given a box of paints, with which he drew animals, forests and wild men. Later, there were 'concerts' in the boys' room. He had a beautiful voice and was a member of the church choir, though he fled on one occasion at the prospect of solo singing. Roddie and Nina loved history – Greek, Roman, French – and she remembers questions to her mother on 'Irish history'.[23] A close relationship developed between Roddie and his sister. Nina recalls him, the youngest, rushing to defend her from 'attacks' by Charlie and Tom. In his highly emotional letter to her from his condemned cell in 1916 he imagines standing beside her, 'just as I did as a little boy when you comforted me and took me by the hand'. And he added: 'Now that I have only these few days to live – that a cruel fate has brought me to the grave so far from you I bow my head in your lap, as I did when a little boy, and say Kiss me and say Goodnight.'[24] Their father, too, taught the children to be kind to animals, putting a splint on a blackbird and keeping a 'beautiful hyacinth-blue macaw', named Polybius, who would sit on his shoulder and nuzzle him.[25]

Anne Jephson Casement died on 27 October 1873 at the age of thirty-nine. Roger was nine. Later in life, according to Gertrude, he constantly spoke of her 'gentleness, beauty, bright disposition and religious feeling', while from prison he wrote: 'I felt the loss of my mother more than I have felt anything in my life.'[26] But the story that she died in childbirth may no longer be tenable: a recent discovery indicates that she died in a lodging house in the town of Worthing, of cirrhosis of the liver, complicated by asthma.[27] Not long afterwards, Roger Sr., in clear distress, wrote again to his uncle John in Magherintemple, recounting his ill fortune, including Anne's death. Arrears of rent and other financial pressures meant that he had not been able to afford the type of medical help he would have liked during his wife's illness. He had not yet got permanent lodgings, 'landladies having so much aversion to boys generally'.

> I am trying *very hard* indeed to get something to occupy me, even slightly remunerative, just to supplement Uncle Thomas's allowance, finding it always impossible to gain the very smallest competence, or promise of it for my proffered labours or services, and the War Office still shows no sign.[28]

Another of Elizabeth Bannister's early memories is likely to date from this time, soon after the death of Anne Casement. She recalled Roger Sr., her uncle, coming to visit them, 'tall and striking' in his 'long military cloak'. Roddie she remembered 'with the same rather grave manner, and thoughtful look in his deep-set grey eyes'. There is some indication that Roger Sr.'s thoughts focused on religious matters, specifically Spiritualism, at this time. A manuscript essay of his survives, fourteen foolscap pages entitled: 'A Review of the Extraordinary Spiritual Phenomena of Modern Times, in America and Europe, and their Connexion with Science, Religion and human needs generally, traced and explained.' Its author is described as 'a former officer of the British Army in India', and an editorial note adds: 'In the English and Hindustani Languages and intended chiefly for gratuitous circulation in Hindustan.'[29]

Roger Sr. was to die in 1877, less than four years after his wife, apparently in a Ballymena hotel. He was in his late fifties and Roddie was twelve. It is easier to assess the influence of Casement's father on his son than that of his mother. It seems likely that his mother's loving gentleness had a formative effect and that her muted Catholicism influenced her son's religious identity. In the case of Roger Sr., there is a consistent thread in his commitments: leaving India to fight for Hungary in the 1848 revolution; his support for the republican Gambetta in France and for the Fenians in Ireland; his efforts as a writer. Despite the general loyalty of the Casements to the Empire, there are examples of liberal dissent within the family, clear in the case of Roger Sr. [30] In this respect his son was to follow in his footsteps.

Orphaned

After the deaths of Anne and Roger Casement Sr., close relatives assumed responsibility for the future of the children. These included the Bannisters in Liverpool and a range of Casement family members in Ireland.[31] One version of what happened is that in 1874, soon after the death of their mother, the children were sent to live at Magherintemple, Co. Antrim, and that the cost of their education 'was borne by poor Katie Pottinger, Anne Coulson, and doubtless John Casement'.[32] Elizabeth Bannister's recollection was that the older boys spent much time with their father's people, 'but Roddie was most of his time with us'. Gertrude Bannister, in contrast, recalled that, after his father's death, Roddie lived with his father's stepbrother and his wife and 'with an old friend of the family who lived in Ballymena', as well as with her own family in England.[33] Casement developed warm ties with the Bannisters; his maternal aunt, Grace, was married to Edward Bannister, who traded in West Africa and was British vice-consul in the Congo for some years. They had four children (Edith, who died young, Elizabeth, Gertrude and Edward) and lived in the Liverpool suburb of Anfield.

The legacy of Hugh Casement of Holywood, which Roger Sr. had complained about some years previously, was distributed in 1877, shortly after the latter's death. Hugh had left £1000 to Roger Sr., and this was passed on to Nina and the boys, with an additional £222. Hugh had also left English, Irish and Australian properties. A quarter of the relevant sum went to Nina, now twenty-one. She and the Revd Lampier were made guardians of the three younger children. When Lampier died soon afterwards, Nina was made sole guardian, a responsibility she is believed to have relinquished to John Casement of Magherintemple in January 1880.[34]

According to Nina, it was after his father's death that Roddie was sent to the Ballymena Diocesan School.[35] There had been a strong Casement branch in Ballymena and this may have been a factor in the decision to send Roddie to the Diocesan School there. The Revd Robert King was principal of the school and was said to be the head of a happy household.[36] Roddie 'was a happy boy those years of study', according to Nina, while she herself spent months at a time in Ballymena in the house of a great-aunt, strict, but of the 'best'. Perhaps this was the wife of the Revd Robert Casement, referred to by Nina when discussing Roddie's schooling: 'The only relatives he had while at school in Ballymena as a boarder were his great uncle, Revd Robert Casement, Harryville, [and] his daughter Fanny. He *never lived* with any relatives in Ballymena, as he was a *boarder*, but spent holidays with Mr and Mrs Young and with his great uncle and aunt in Ballycastle.'[37] Mrs Young ('Mrs Johnnie') remained a friend to be visited in later years.[38] In later life he maintained links with another Ballymena family, the Dickie sisters. The RIC file opened on Roger Casement in 1914 states that he had been adopted by a Dickie family in Ballymena.[39] Christina Dickie (c.1810–81) had married Francis Casement (1802–68), Roddie's grand-uncle; Roddie was quite close to her two nieces, Emma and Harriette. Harriette was to marry into the Wilkinson family at Baronstown, Tara, Co. Meath, and Emma too lived there for some time. Roddie visited the Wilkinsons regularly afterwards.[40]

Details of his time in the Ballymena Diocesan School are not available. He himself later claimed that he 'went off into the world straight from my old schoolmaster's house in this county, a boy of 15'.[41] If Nina's suggestion that he went to the Diocesan School after his father's death is correct, then he would have spent about three years there. Elizabeth Bannister recalled that King 'prepared boys for the army and various professions' and that Roddie did well in his work (gaining prizes for Classics) and was popular both with master and boys.[42] It is clear that he received a solid education. His later writings reveal, for example, his knowledge of English literature – from Shakespeare to the Romantic poets (Keats, Shelley, Tennyson) – and of French literature, Latin and history, especially classical history.[43]

Some accounts suggest that Casement gained a love for things Irish at the Ballymena Diocesan School from Dr King, who was, indeed, a recognized Gaelic scholar. But his own later observations do not bear this out. Responding, in 1912, to an appeal for a subscription to the school from the then Head, Mr W.A. Fullerton, he replied:

> Now from my own recollection of the old Diocesan School and from what I know of similar establishments in Ireland, their aim is not so much to fit a boy to live and thrive in his own country as to equip him for export from it. I was taught nothing about Ireland in Ballymena School – I don't think the word was ever mentioned in a single class of the school – and all I know of my country I learned outside the school.[44]

And he did learn outside of school, as Nina recalled: 'He learned much of the history of our country during those years. Long walks and visits to historic remains of antiquity, talking to the kindly Ulster folk who could tell many a tale of '98 and the horrors perpetrated by the brutal soldiery of George the Third of England.'[45] There are hints here and there in his correspondence and diaries about his friendships with neighbouring families, not least in his letter from Brixton Prison to his cousin Roger at Magherintemple: 'I hope you are well and all around you flourishing – land and people. If ever you see John Brown – up Glenshesk – give him my regards – and the McAllisters too – and the McCarrys of Murlough.'46

At fourteen Roddie acted in amateur theatricals and played youthful games, such as 'Hare and Hounds', ending up in a manure heap on one occasion after a spectacular leap over a wall, following which he hid his ruined suit. Gertrude recalled him picking music out on the piano, and he was to develop a fine baritone voice with which he would sing his favourite songs, such as 'Oft in the Stilly Night', 'Let Erin Remember', 'The Wearing of the Green', 'The Snowy-Breasted Pearl' and 'Silent O Moyle'.47 She also describes his youthful crush, at the age of seventeen, on his cousin Eva, daughter of the Lampiers, when the two wrote to one another every day.48 Elizabeth Bannister recalled:

> He spent many of his holidays with us, and we came to look on him more as an elder brother than a cousin. He was devoted to my mother, who, unlike his own mother, was very small. He always spoke and wrote of her as 'Dear Wee Auntie'. During his holidays he would play games with us and entertain us for hours. I never remember him to lose his temper, nor to become rough in his play, as occasionally the two older boys would do in their exuberant high spirits. He was always fond of painting and of inventing stories and I believe if he had seriously cultivated these gifts he would have made a name for himself.49

Nina recalled the Bannister family's mirth at the 'African Robe' incident, when Roger, aged sixteen or seventeen and six feet tall, dressed in a chief's grass robe with huge headdress and, armed with spear and shield, 'attacked' an elderly citizen of their staid Liverpool suburb on a moonlit night. Local police went looking for a madman.50

Writing poetry became part of Roger's life around the age of seventeen and he produced a steady flow of poems from 1882 onwards. Not surprisingly, his early verse was marked by a mixture of classical and nature themes, the latter in the manner of the English Romantics. He showed a strong attachment to the North Antrim countryside in poems on the glens of Glenariff and Glenshesk, and on the island of Rathlin. A link developed, too, between his growing love for the Irish countryside and his sense of Irish history. Local landmarks had been the scenes of dramatic and tragic encounters. Quite a few of the poems treat romantically Ireland's resistance to the English conquest of the sixteenth and seventeenth centuries and, in particular, of events in Ulster. Dunluce Castle ('Dunluce Castle', 1883) had been the location, in the late sixteenth century, of the resistance of Sir Randall MacDonnell and Sorley Boy MacDonnell to Sir John Perrott. 'O'Rorke's Warning' (1882) dealt with an incident in the saga of the Spanish Armada of 1588. 'Song of Tyrconnell' (1883) celebrated Red Hugh O'Donnell's dramatic escape from Dublin Castle in 1592, while 'Triumph of Hugh O'Neill' dealt with the Battle of the Yellow Ford in 1598. 'Rory O'More' was an Ulster leader in 1641; 'Benburb' told of a famous victory of Owen Roe

O'Neill in 1646, and the subject of 'Oliver Cromwell' came to Ireland in 1649. The author of these poems was clearly immersed in the reading of Irish history from a romantic nationalist perspective.[51]

'Rory O'More' can provide an illustration. Speaking of the English conquerors, one verse proclaims:

> They came as robbers, with swords in their hands,
> To ravage and spoil us of house, home and lands;
> And as robbers we treat them, and God send the day
> We drive or we fright them, the bodachs away.
> O! our hearts and our swords they are both made of steel,
> And to strengthen them both to the Virgin we kneel:
> Then let if he will the false traitor deplore,
> Sure *our* trust is in God and in Rory O'More.[52]

Virtually the only hint in his poetry of a non-nationalist viewpoint comes in 'Portglenone'. But it is a burlesque poem and, I believe, not necessarily to be taken as a reflection of Casement's own political views.

> And if a Home Ruler should be such a fool or
> Ass as to come with his preachin' up here –
> He'd get a back hander from Bob Alexander
> Would lave him a black eye for many a year.[53]

Casement's nationalist sympathies were not confined to Ireland's past. Gertrude recalled:

> In his school days he begged from the aunt, with whom he spent his holidays, for possession of an attic room which he turned into a little study, and the writer remembers the walls papered with cartoons cut out of the *Weekly Freeman*, showing the various Irish Nationalists who had suffered imprisonment at English hands for the sake of their belief in Ireland a Nation.[54]

One surviving item exemplifies this practice. Pasted into the inside cover of a copybook containing his early poetry are some newspaper cuttings giving details of a Land League meeting in Ballycastle, Co. Antrim, regarding debates in the House of Commons on the introduction of a Coercion bill and a Land bill, and of the arrest of Michael Davitt, the Land League leader. This would date them to the early months of 1881, when Casement was sixteen.

The Irish Land War dominated Irish public life in the years 1879–81. The 1870s were years of agricultural depression, with prices for agricultural products falling. In addition, bad weather and the failure of two successive potato crops towards the end of the decade meant that a disaster on the scale of the Great Famine of the late 1840s threatened. Inability to pay rents led to a jump in the number of evictions. In this context, Davitt, who had earlier spent a term in prison for Fenian activities, began organizing tenants in the west of Ireland and the Irish National Land League was formed in 1879. It stood on a platform of 'the land of Ireland for the people of Ireland' and organized opposition to landlords, as well as aid for farmers. Charles Stewart Parnell, a rising constitutionalist, agreed to become president of the organization. There followed the land war of 1879–92. Emotions were inflamed and evictions and retaliatory actions increased in number. Gladstone's government responded with a mixture of coercion and agrarian reform. Casement was later to express his admiration for Davitt, while Parnell was one of his heroes.[55] He was to express a concern over access to land, in various contexts, throughout his life, from concessions in various parts of Africa to *latifundismo* in Latin America.

A few months before his seventeenth birthday he was confirmed in the Anglican church of St Anne's, in the Liverpool suburb of Stanley, where he was staying with the Bannister family. His comment many years later, when responding to an invitation to be present at the launch of a Church of Ireland Irish Language Society, suggests some measure of discomfort with his Anglican background:

> I was brought up in the Church of Ireland, but its aloofness, to use no harsher word, from things that should be dear to all Irishmen, repelled me even as a boy. What seemed to me worthy of study, examination, and often of love I was told to regard as foolishness. Where as an Irishman, I asked for bread I was offered a stone.[56]

First Employments

In 1880 Charlie and Tom, Roger's brothers, left to seek a life overseas. Tom recalled in 1917: 'When we were boys the last time I saw him was in 1880. He came down to the Waterloo Dock to see us off.'[57] Charlie, the eldest, would have been about nineteen and Tom, a year older than Roddie, seventeen. Both spent time in Australia, where Charlie was to work as a clerk at the Melbourne Tramway and Omnibus Company, marry, and raise a family. Tom, more flamboyant, married twice and separated twice, tried a succession of occupations in Australia and South Africa, including seafaring, mining and running a mountain lodge, before returning to Ireland in 1920. Nina wrote:

> My elder brothers had both gone abroad, detesting the notion of a stool and pen, one to South Africa, the eldest, Charles, to Australia. Roddie and I were then left behind with our aunt and cousins. He was strongly opposed to the proposed stool and pen, saying, 'I must have an open-air life or I will die.'

The 'stool and pen' refers to a period Roger spent as clerk in the Liverpool offices of the Elder Dempster Company after he completed his schooling. Elder Dempster was headed by Sir Alfred Jones and, when Casement later felt he was being exploited in the Congo, he accused 'that cad Jones' of doing the same 'when I was a boy of sixteen'. He appears to have spent about two years with

Elder Dempster in the early 1880s. His escape from a desk job came when he was offered the position of purser on one of the Elder Dempster boats and, according to Nina, 'made one or two passages to West Africa', returning dangerously ill with fever.[58] Captain H.G. Harrison, of the *Bonny*, with whom Casement sailed, wrote of him after Casement's capture in 1916, recalling his anti-English sentiments at that time and at subsequent meetings. 'He is tall and quiet. I have seen stories that would indicate him as a noisy, talkative character. He is anything but that, and no one who knows would ever call him a "mouther". But when he does talk he generally finds an opportunity to denounce England.'[59]

Between voyages, during a sojourn in Magherintemple, Casement met a woman who was to have a significant influence on him. Ada MacNeill lived in Cushendun, on the east coast of Antrim, and was a little older than Casement, having been born in 1860.[60] John Casement of Magherintemple had married Charlotte Miller, a cousin of the MacNeills, and the families visited one another across the mountain. 'I was very fond of this cousin,' wrote Ada, 'and she was hospitality itself. They kept open house.'[61] Many years later, she recalled her first meeting with Roger, when she was twenty-four years of age.

> He was disturbed at his work and came into the dining room, his hand full of papers. Tall and slight and handsome ... he looked untidy and his hair was dishevelled as if he had been writing for hours and had had no time even for breakfast. I think he was home from Africa. He walked about the room talking delightfully, about what I forget ... I seemed to be meeting a friend of a long time ago, not a stranger.

Friendship developed and, according to Ada, whenever Roger was at Magherintemple he rode over to see them.

> We were both great walkers and strode over the hills and up the Glens and we both discovered we could talk without ceasing about Ireland. This was a great joy to me, because there was no one to talk to on that subject, except the country people who had sworn to make of me a red-hot Republican and Fenian like themselves ... Roger had the history of Ireland at his fingers' ends and influenced me till it became a passion with me to see Ireland free.
>
> I remember rainy days in the dark old library there [Magherintemple] – which were anything but grey for me – with the open doors of the big bookcases and Roger refuting my arguments with quotations upon which he could always lay his finger ... Then there were more walks at home over the moors and along the Tor road and life seemed to hold only Ireland.[62]

Religion, too, was discussed in these meetings between the two, and Ada's observations suggest its importance in Roger's life.

> I remember a long walk with Roger up the Glen. As we turned home he talked eloquently and earnestly against scoffing at religion. I listened – actually paid attention and listened. His enthusiasm was as great as my own and he was far more earnest and simple. There was something always very young and boyish

and yet so very true and earnest about his character, that he made you pause and think. I remember at a picnic at Murlough his actually sitting on the rocks and talking so earnestly about Faith and Religion that we all listened and bicycling home that night we agreed that no one could have done it but Roger.

On 20 June 1884 Casement wrote from Liverpool to his great uncle John at Magherintemple. He had, he said, when in Madeira, received a reply from the International African Association regarding his application for a position with them. He had approached the Elder Dempster Company on the previous day for a testimonial and Mr Jones, who knew Colonel Strauch, the Brussels head of the Association, felt sure he would get an appointment.

> Of the objects of the Association you know something I suppose. They have several Corps expeditions up the River Congo in South West Africa, of which Stanley the great explorer is at the head. At present they are merely exploring and opening up the country by establishing stations along the River and getting small steamers up on its higher waters but ultimately I believe they will trade with the natives.

He might, he felt, receive £150 per year to begin with, and the prospect of higher appointments existed. Since the *Bonny* was due to sail on the 28th, he was unsure what to do if an appointment came late and he sought his uncle's advice on the matter.[63] He did receive an offer but, since the Elder Dempster had no one to replace him, 'rather than inconvenience them' he had remained with the *Bonny*. Colonel Strauch, in fact, had only offered him £72 per annum, but Casement hoped that the offer would be renewed, and at a higher salary, on his return in October. They were due to return via Hamburg, whence he would travel to Brussels and make contact with the Association.[64] The offer was, indeed, renewed and Roger Casement commenced his long association with the Congo late in 1884.

PART II
Africa

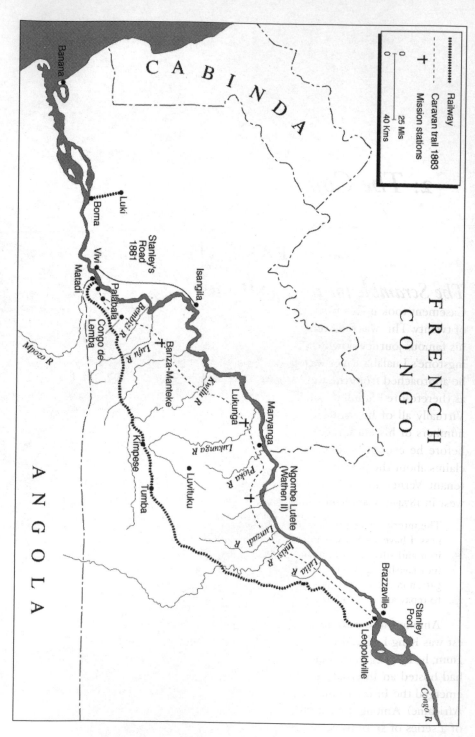

Map 1: Lower Congo (Cataract Region)

2: *The Congo Free State, 1884–91*

The Scramble for the Congo

Casement took up his first employment in the Congo in 1884, a raw young man of twenty. This was only ten years after Henry Morton Stanley had commenced his famous journey down the Congo River, a journey that established that Livingstone's Lualaba River was, in fact, the Congo and that Central Africa might be approached from the west coast rather than from the Arab-dominated east, as theretofore.[1] Stanley's journey had taken 999 days, lasting from 1874 to 1877. Virtually all of his white companions died during it, as well as considerable numbers of his entourage and of the peoples among whom the party passed, before he eventually emerged in Boma on 9 August 1877. Stanley reinforced claims about the potential great wealth of Central Africa, made earlier by Lieutenant Verney Lovett Cameron, who had crossed the continent from east to west in 1874–5. Cameron had written:

> The interior is mostly a magnificent and healthy country of unspeakable richness. I have a small specimen of good coal; other minerals such as gold, copper, iron and silver are abundant, and I am confident that with a wise and liberal (not lavish) expenditure of capital, one of the greatest systems of inland navigation in the world might be utilized, and from 30 months to 36 months begin to repay any enterprising capitalist that might take the matter in hand ...[2]

Among those who noted Cameron's and Stanley's journeys with great interest was King Leopold II of Belgium.[3] Long interested in a colonial role for Belgium, he had begun to focus his attention on Central Africa. Already, in 1876, he had hosted an International Geographical Conference in Brussels from which emerged the International African Association (IAA/Association Internationale Africaine). Among the aims discussed for the Association was the establishment of a series of stations across Central Africa. The Association proved to be the first of a number of organizations, ostensibly with scientific and humanitarian goals, which were, in reality, tools for Leopold's economic ambitions. They were to lead directly to the founding of the Congo Independent State.4

Leopold made every effort to persuade Stanley to lead his Congo enterprise, but the explorer was won over only when it became clear that there was no strong British interest in the region. The two men met in 1878 and Stanley agreed to direct an expedition to investigate the possibility of opening a direct link between the Lower and Upper Congo (Map 1).5

Between Stanley Pool and the sea, the river dropped 1000 feet and was funnelled through a narrow channel in the Crystal Mountains. To reach the anticipated wealth of the Upper Congo, therefore, colonizers had first to negotiate this unnavigable stretch of over 200 miles of rapids and cataracts, some of them awesome. 'They thunder through narrow gorges and ravines, boil up in vicious yellow waves 30 to 40 feet high, crash over giant boulders, rip giant trees and islands of sod from the river's banks, twist and turn and whirl around to create terrifying whirlpools and dreadful, fathomless holes.'6 The last of the cataracts, some 100 miles from the sea, was named the Cauldron of Hell, and downstream from it were established the European settlements of Noki, Matadi and Vivi. To bypass the cataracts a caravan road had to be built, and this became Stanley's task. Two of Casement's friends have left descriptions of the terrain over which the road had to pass. Of one stretch, Edward Glave wrote some years later: 'Our journey led through long stretches of stifling valleys, plunged us into the heat of the tropical jungle and spongy quagmire, and took us over deep, swift streams, which had to be crossed in rickety canoes.' And Herbert Ward told of paths less than one foot wide, of steep hills, deep swamps, and swollen rivers crossed by bridges of vines.7

In the employ of the IAA, Stanley returned to the Congo in 1879 and founded the first station at Vivi, on the north bank of the river. This was the starting point for the new road to Stanley Pool, the gate to the Upper Congo, on which work commenced early in 1880. The first stretch was to be from Vivi to Isangila (83 km), where the second station was established; a middle section of the river was navigable, from Isangila to Manyanga (120 km), where the third station was built; the final section of 152 km, again overland, was from Manyanga to the Pool. Work progressed quickly and the fourth station, named Leopoldville, was established in December of 1881.

Meanwhile, Leopold had quickly replaced the IAA with another purportedly philanthropic and scientific but, in reality, commercial organization called the Comité d'Études du Haut-Congo. Its secretary was Colonel Maximilien Strauch, a loyal servant of Leopold's. The Comité, in turn, was replaced before the end of 1879 by another mysterious body, the Association Internationale du Congo. Leopold became its sole stockholder. By now, unknown to himself, Stanley was working directly for Leopold. So secretive were the changes that little was known of the differences between the organizations; both the International

African Association and the International Association of the Congo were called 'The Association'. After completing the onerous task of opening the road to the Pool, Stanley returned to Europe; but he was again persuaded to return to the Congo, where he began establishing stations on the Upper River and making treaties with native chiefs. The Equator station was built and, in November 1883, another was built at Stanley Falls. Having returned to Leopoldville in January 1884, his contract with Leopold completed, Stanley was replaced by Sir Francis De Winton.[8]

International interest in the Congo was intensifying. The French explorer de Brazza, having approached the river by a more northerly route, reached the Pool and made a treaty with a local chief; thus began France's claim to the northern Congo Basin, to become Congo Français. Portugal, an ancient colonial power in the region but now weak, tried to have her claims accepted. Britain was unwilling to see France go unchallenged and Germany, not long united under Bismarck, was trying to establish herself as a colonial power. To address these rivalries in the Congo and elsewhere, Bismarck convened a conference in Berlin, which lasted from November 1884 to February 1885 and was attended by fourteen nations.

Adroitly, Leopold played each of the Powers off against the others. With the help of 'General' Henry Sanford, a wealthy and influential American entrepreneur with strong connections in Belgium, he had already succeeded in getting President Chester Arthur, and later the US Congress, to recognize the blue flag of the International Association of the Congo.[9] This was done by stressing the philanthropic mission of the Association and by arguing that the treaties made with Congo chiefs were to be the basis of a Confederation of Free Negro Republics, similar to the American-supported state of Liberia. Leopold had similarly worked on France, which was worried about the likelihood of an Anglo-Portuguese treaty on the Congo. In return for certain assurances, France recognized the sovereignty of the Association on 23 April 1884. At Berlin, confrontation was avoided by granting recognition to Leopold's Association rather than to any of the established Powers. On 26 February 1885 the General Act of Berlin was signed. Under its terms, the Free State was recognized, giving Leopold some one million square miles of territory.

When Casement arrived in the Congo in 1884, Stanley's road had been completed and was being used by agents of the Association, by commercial companies and by missionaries. All were intent on reaching the Upper Congo and, while some ivory was being exported, most energy was expended in establishing stations and other infrastructure for the later exploitation of the interior. Maintenance of the transport system on the Lower River, crucial to the development of the Upper River, was a complicated task and one that grew increasingly difficult as demand intensified. Goods were transported on the caravan road by African carriers; a standard load, one that could be carried by a single porter, weighed 65 lbs and was paid for in cloth ('handkerchiefs') or brass rods. Some porters were Zanzibaris, others came from Cabinda, but most were recruited locally, in the cataract region, with chiefs of villages often expected to provide a quota of men. The volume of loads carried increased enormously during the 1880s; one estimate had 1000 in 1882, 12,000 in 1885, 50,000 in 1887 and 80,000 by 1893.[10]

The State resorted to an increasing use of force in acquiring porters. While this became most marked in the 1890s throughout the Upper Congo, it certainly existed in the 1880s along the Lower River. One authority notes: 'The recruiting effort was backed by several hundred African mercenary troops and the liberal use of appalling violence. Many people fled to remote forests to escape it; all villages near the new transport routes were abandoned.'[11] One form the violence took was the 'punitive expedition', as in the following graphic account:

> The Swedish lieutenant, Posse, conducted an expedition to the villages Tundua and Lufundi in 1884, as both villages were not prepared to provide porters. Just after midnight, the expedition surrounded the sleeping villages, where none of the villagers suspected their presence. Lieutenant Posse led the attack, and seven men were killed, six were taken prisoner, but many succeeded in escaping. Ten women were taken prisoner, the huts were set alight and the villages sacked. The prisoners were taken to Vivi and then to Banana. The punishment did not produce the desired effect, and the people still offered opposition, and therefore, a new punitive expedition was sent out to the region to burn more villages to the ground.[12]

Casement and the International Association of the Congo, 1884–6

Casement commenced employment with the International Association of the Congo on 1 November 1884, the month in which the Berlin Conference opened.[13] All indications are that from the end of 1884 until he transferred to the Sanford Exploring Expedition on 1 September 1886, Casement worked for the Association and its successor, the Congo Independent State, in the Lower Congo, as part of a team responsible for the storage and transportation of goods through the cataract region to the Upper Congo. Exploration on the Upper River was still in progress and the economic exploitation of that river and its tributaries was in its infancy. It seems likely that Casement's duties were only in the stores at Vivi, though it is possible that he helped with transport on the road itself.

Despite the modest starting salary offered by Colonel Strauch, he had very positive feelings towards the administrator general of the Congo State, Sir Francis De Winton, who 'was always my close friend up to his death' and had 'formed the highest opinion of my worth and always expressed it'.[14] Francis De

Winton had replaced Stanley in January 1884 and would have been responsible for all Association personnel, Casement included. On 1 July 1885, as first administrator general, in a letter from Vivi, he proclaimed the Constitution of the Congo Independent State. With the founding of the State all of the Association's staff automatically transferred to the new entity.

During this first phase of his Congo career, Casement developed a number of friendships with Englishmen serving there. One of these was his immediate superior, Major W.G. Parminter.[15] Parminter had taken up a position under Stanley in September 1883 and had responsibility for the Lower Congo, particularly for finances and transport. Casement developed a strong loyalty to him, and retained positive memories after Parminter's death in 1894. In 1899, when trying to help Parminter's nephew Alfred, Casement wrote: 'His uncle, Major Parminter (now dead) was a very dear friend of mine, and for his sake if not for the man's own, I should always keep a very kind corner in my heart for him.'[16]

A second friend was Edward Glave, who, like Parminter, had arrived in 1883. Glave first joined Stanley at the Pool and was then assigned to the Upper Congo, where he had responsibility for building a station at Lukolela. He worked, too, at Bolobo and at the Equator station, where Casement was to spend some time with him in 1887, when the two worked for the Sanford Exploring Expedition.[17] Third, and closest of all to Casement, was Herbert Ward. He, like Casement, was engaged in the autumn of 1884 and for a similar salary.[18] Years later, Ward was to write of Casement in his book, *A Voice from the Congo*:

> The first name I would mention of all the European pioneers who were connected with the opening up of the Congo is the name of my friend and companion since 1884, Roger Casement. Imagine a tall, handsome man, of fine bearing; thin, mere muscle and bone, a sun-tanned face, blue eyes and black curly hair. A pure Irishman he is, with a captivating voice and a singular charm of manner. A man of distinction and great refinement, high-minded and courteous, impulsive and poetical. Quixotic perhaps some would say, and with a certain truth, for few men have shown themselves so regardless of personal advancement.[19]

Nina Casement later recalled the friendship between the two. Ward, she wrote,

> was a distinct type, always immaculately groomed and turned out. Roddie would chaff him unmercifully, saying: 'Do you know, Herbert used to shave, or try to, every day on the Congo, when we were obliged to eat, with our dogs, native food, *quanga* (pounded root and coconut milk).' He would retaliate: 'Yes, what about you, old man? I assure you ... you never saw such a ruffian as your distinguished brother used to look. I can see him now, tramping ahead of his bearers ... a beard half way down his chest, clothes in ribbons and patched beyond repair, on his feet a piece of bark from a certain tree, tied on with string and to bring up the rear a couple of the most villainous dogs you ever saw.'[20]

A final friend was Fred Puleston, who, like Glave and Ward, was also to publish a record of his time in the Congo. Puleston worked in Africa in four stints between 1882 and 1896, most of it in the Congo and adjacent territories. He ended what he called a 'chapter of portraits' in his book *African Drums* by attempting 'to do justice to the memory of Sir Roger Casement' in the following words:

> Casement's disposition and make-up was the gentlest imaginable; he was always sweet-tempered, ready to help, condemning cruelty and injustice in any form. Indeed, he was so emotional, tender, and sympathetic that, when his fox terrier (Spindle, I think he named it) got at cross purposes with a wild hog and had his stomach ripped open, Casement was unable to control his feeling and wept like a girl. Jimmy Glave and I picked Spindle up, washed his intestines as well as we could, and then I, with ordinary needle and thread, after pushing the intestines back into the abdominal cavity, sewed him up. Casement, through the whole operation, acted like a mother alarmed over her child.
>
> I knew him to be a most ardent Irish Nationalist, but his nature was so distinctly honourable and loyal that his defection from England was a shock to me. His philosophy of life was somewhat strange, always a little of a mystic, and apparently looking on death as a relief, for I often heard him say, 'The finest thing God put into this earth is Death.'[21]

Puleston tells us of two native names given to Casement, *Swami Casement* and *Monafuma Casement*, 'Woman's God' and 'Son of a King', adding: 'He deserved both, for a more charming, loveable man never lived.'[22]

Many years later, writing from the Eden Hotel in Berlin during the First World War, in response to a letter and an article sent by Dr U. von Dandelman, Casement reminisced about his early years in Africa:

> I knew Vivi well. I was there in 1885 – July and later – and in 1886 – and I remember your name. Wissmann and his party passed through in 1886 and he gave me his greyhound 'Guerra' ... I spent five years on the Congo then 1885 to 1889 travelling over much of the country, and learning to love and pity the natives, and it was this earlier knowledge of them and of the things that went to their undoing that enabled me to look for light in 1903 when I visited the Upper Congo as a public 'avenger'...
>
> Stanley, too, I knew well – and I share your opinion of him to the full. The Pocock Falls at Manyanga I know very well and how they came to find that name. I am the only whiteman alive (I think) who ever *swam* the Nkissi River. You may remember it's the biggest river on the caravan road between Manyanga and the Pool. I used to swim all those rivers, *plein des crocodiles*, Kwilu, Lukungu, Mpozo, Lunzadi, but the greatest of these was the Nkissi, about 100 metres broad, and swift at the canoe crossing, because the great fall of the Nkissi was not far below ...[23]

Casement again thought back to his early days in Africa, when advising a friend about the climate: 'I went to Africa as a *boy* – strong, thin, clean-limbed and very sound. I had an exceptionally healthy and vigorous constitution – the proof of that is that I spent twenty years in those awful climates and am still what you know – but I was, in truth, a great exception ... I took quinine constantly as a boy out there – but I bathed, I swam, I ran, I jumped and walked often forty to even fifty miles in the day under those blazing skies.'[24]

Sanford Exploring Expedition, 1886–8 and Railway Survey, 1888

The Sanford Exploring Expedition (SEE) was established by Henry Shelton Sanford and a group of associates in June 1886.[25] The purpose of the new company was to trade in the Upper Congo, mainly in ivory, but also in other commodities such as gum-copal, rubber, palm oil and copper. Almost all the investors were Belgian, but Sanford was the chief shareholder and became the effective administrative head. Baron Louis Weber de Treunfels became the financial comptroller. In recognition of Sanford's services in helping to bring about recognition of the State, the company was granted important concessions by Leopold, which, on paper, gave it important advantages over potential rivals. The State promised storage of SEE goods on government stations and tracts of land at key locations, and offered to facilitate the transport of goods on State steamers and by State porters.

In late 1886 virtually all the foreigners working for the Congo State transferred to the Sanford Exploring Expedition, as more and more positions of responsibility in the State system went to Belgians. Sanford had already engaged key staff. Emory Taunt, a lieutenant in the American navy with prior experience in South America and Africa, was granted leave to lead the Expedition and became administrator in Africa. Major W.G. Parminter was recruited from the State as second in command with responsibility for local finances. Anton Swinburne, formerly secretary to Stanley, was to head the station at Kinshasa and Glave that at the Equator station.[26] Two elephant hunters, Bailey and Deane, were also hired to begin providing ivory. Among those who transferred from the State, though in more junior positions, were Casement and Ward.

The experience of the new company did not live up to the promise. The State did not supply the necessary porters and SEE goods began to pile up in Matadi. Valcke, minister of the Department of the Interior, wished to impose an arbitrary charge for each load, thereby bringing profit to the State. Other impediments to trade were also put in place. Added to these were the shortcomings of certain personnel, together with injuries and illness caused by climate; shortage of, and disputes with, carriers; and the general difficulties of transport over rough terrain and tropical conditions.

The Expedition could not expect to recoup its investors' money until it began serious trading on the Upper Congo. To do this it needed a steamer, which would have to be disassembled and carried from Matadi to Stanley Pool, before being reassembled and launched for work. A 20-ton stern-wheeler was manufactured by Forrestt and Son in England and shipped to the Congo, where it arrived in Matadi in February 1887. Sanford named her the *Florida*. There were major delays in transporting her to the Pool, shortage of carriers being a major problem. Each load had to be no more than 65 lbs; but the shaft weighed nearly 1000 lbs and no one had ordered its dismantling. It was transported in one piece, on a cart, with over 100 men engaged in the task, supervised by Ward and Casement. Then, when the *Florida* was reassembled on the Pool, but before the arrival of the shaft, Stanley requisitioned her for the Emin Pasha Relief Expedition.[27] While she was in use by Stanley, between May and August of 1887, considerable damage was done to the hull, which had to be repaired. All in all it was months before the *Florida* was ready for trading.

It became clear, after a year's operations, that the company would not be successful without considerable additional capital. Yet, existing investors were unwilling to risk more and all of Sanford's attempts to woo new investors came to nothing. Discussions were opened with a Belgian company and a decision was taken to merge. In December 1888 the Société Anonyme Belge pour l'Industrie et Commerce du Haut Congo was formed and the assets of the SEE transferred to it.

Casement's contract with the SEE began on 1 September 1886. Emory Taunt, the chief agent, wrote to Sanford:

> The Ad[ministrator] Gen[era]l has permitted me to take over from the State two white Agents, Messrs Ward and Casement (English). They are by far the best men I could get and I don't want any more white men until the affair assumes larger proportions. Mr Ward at [£]170 per year, Mr Casement at [£]150. This is an increase of 40 for Mr Ward and 20 for Casement – Ward had applied and was going home, he would not come for less. I consider he is well worth it, if only to transport our Steamer to Stanley Pool but he is a valuable man in every particular. And when the transport work is once well started, I shall place him in charge of a station on the Haut Congo or take him with me on board the Steamer.
>
> These are all the men I want – I neglected to mention that Mr Casement will be placed at Matadi – it is an absolute necessity that we have an Agent there. The present man is careless and inefficient; if properly furnished with wine etc. etc. he will do for us but otherwise not. I know Casement to be an upright honorable gentleman, and he will carefully look after our interests ...[28]

Not long after his appointment, Casement was taken along on what would have been termed a 'punitive expedition'. Taunt, again, described the events to Sanford:

> Mr Janssens asked me, just as I was leaving Boma, to aid Capt. Roget in his fight at Congo de Lemba. As you may imagine I was only too glad to avail myself of the opportunity to aid the State and thus place them in our debt. I took with me 14 Zanzibaris, Mr Casement, and gave the State 11 Kabindas for porters, *all for nothing*. You must make as much capital out of it as you can and impress upon

H[is] M[ajesty] the fact that we will aid them on all occasions. The fight was a complete 'fizzle'. We left camp at 3 am and did not reach the Main Village until 5.30 am. We ought to have had twenty prisoners. We got but one. The chief was killed and about ten others but I fancy the State will keep it quiet ...[29]

Two weeks later, on 24 September, Taunt again wrote to Sanford, this time from Boma:

Mr Casement is at Matadi attending to the accounting and forwarding of our loads and also building our store there ... It is with this rain that I am taking Legat up the Kasai and if things prosper I shall move Mr Casement up country at the end of *our* year, say June 1887, and put Matadi in charge of some good Belgian. These Belgians are jealous to the *very last degree* and I must try and nurse them up a bit. They are not competent to hold responsible positions and work as we want the work done. But I can give them minor positions and make them think they are doing it all ...[30]

In October Valcke, for the State, demanded that all SEE stations and men 'should be under the orders of the State, that any carriers they recruit should be paid for by the SEE at the same rate as if engaged by the State'. Parminter complained:

The reason why Matadi was founded, Casement and Ward engaged, and our own transport system inaugurated [was] because the State cannot alone and unaided do our transport work; and we also desired, by paying our own carriers, to diminish the expenses of State carriage. We are now well on to 12 weeks here and the State has not sent up 50 loads![31]

Swinburne, based at the other end of the caravan trail, in Kinshasa, shed further light on the same problems a month later. In two months he had received only sixty-eight carriers, instead of the 400 contracted for with the State.

After having been given Manyanga station as a depot for carriers and placing an agent there, our carriers sent down by him to Matadi for our goods are quickly informed on arriving there that they must carry for the State and go to Lukunga, of which place many have a pious horror, and also of its chief, Mr Dannvelt. Our agent Mr Casement at Matadi, on expostulating, is told by Mr Valcke that our goods will be thrown out of the State stores and on his further questioning the right of the State to take our carriers in this manner, Mr Casement, being perfectly willing to take our goods over, suddenly finds that the door of the Matadi store is locked against him, and he is not allowed even to take out cloth enough to pay his own men (he being an authorised agent of the Expedition).

Lieut. Taunt leaves instructions at Matadi for all goods and loads of steamer to come up on the south Bank and *not* to risk them in the cataracts by the North bank. Lt. Valcke quietly informs Mr Casement it is neither his business nor that of any member of the SEE to dictate to him how *any* loads shall go up. He then threatens to throw up the transport of our goods entirely.[32]

By the following February, Taunt was reporting from Boma on what appears to have been a major blow-up between himself and Casement.

Mr Casement was at Boma for men but I regret exceedingly to say the station was not satisfactory – *everything in confusion* – only 43 loads had he attained – He was in a continual fight with the State people and the *man is Lazy* ... After I told this young man my idea of work and duty he claimed the balance of 6/- per day subsistence in case *he could not eat his full 6/- per day*. I said 'under no circumstances would I, for a moment, consider such an absurdity' – he then replied he would resign. My reply was – '*do so I will accept this morning*'. He didn't, I wish he had ... This young fellow *must* have one month's pay kept in reserve by Weber and Co. in case he *does resign*, we will inform them. He has written for legal advice on the 6/- per day case to London. If it is in his favour I will simply place trade rates 200% on our food and he will find he will then draw about 2 ½% of food he has now ... These men think they are paid to sleep and eat. *Work doesn't enter into their calculations* but as long as I am here that will never answer ...33

Taunt's outburst has to be assessed in the light of his own troubles. Under the pressure of circumstances, he had developed a severe drink problem and, in March 1887, shortly after his disagreement with Casement, he deserted the Expedition, returning to Europe on a pretext. There Baron Weber declared, on 23 April, that 'Taunt is a lost man, if he can get enough drink it will not last 6 days for him to have delirium tremens and be locked up'.34 He was discharged in May and, later, in August, he was court-martialled by the US navy for being absent without leave and for intoxication.35 Taunt engaged a replacement, Baron Rothkirch, who seems to have taken over not only some of Taunt's duties, but also his negative attitude towards Casement.

Before leaving, Taunt had redeployed Casement to assist Ward with the transport of the *Florida* and, specifically it would seem, the crankshaft, from Matadi to Stanley Pool. Casement and Ward were close friends and, when Casement was awaiting execution in 1916 he recalled:

When I think of him it is of earlier days when the good things of life were all contained for him and me in a Huntley and Palmer biscuit tin, and we were lugging the crankshaft of the *Florida* over Mazambi Hill, down to the Bumbizi and up again, to the night camp where red ants came.36

This would seem to be the same occasion recalled by Ward when he wrote: 'In company with Roger Casement on one occasion I camped in a wood, and in the evening while sitting in front of our camp fire, we discussed that great work of Schweinfurth, *The Heart of Africa*, a book that we had both recently read.' He went on to describe how, as they talked of ants journeying, an army of red ants appeared.37

In the middle of transporting the shaft, Ward suddenly abandoned the SEE for the Emin Pasha Relief Expedition, causing some bitterness and a practical problem for those who remained. Because of the defection of Taunt and Ward, Parminter informed Sanford on 15 March that the transport of the *Florida* was in 'immense peril of completely breaking down'. For once the State came forward to help: Valcke made an arrangement with Rothkirch to transport 400 loads per month, including heavy pieces. A long letter from Rothkirch to Parminter illustrates the complexities facing the agents on the ground. He had, he wrote, just received a letter from Casement, who was at Mazambi, abandoned by Ward; the cart used for carrying the shaft was broken, and the party in need of food. Rothkirch sent off five bags of rice and ordered Casement to continue the journey with the other loads, leaving the shaft and other large pieces for Rothkirch himself to deal with.[38]

While Casement was engaged in the task of transporting the *Florida*, the Emin Pasha Relief Expedition passed on its way to the Upper Congo. Two of its members have recorded meeting Casement's caravan, travelling in the same direction. A.J. Mounteney Jephson camped at the Ngoma River on Thursday, 14 April and left the following description:

> After I had been in camp about a couple of hours Casement of the Sanford Expedition came up and camped by me. We bathed and he gave me a very good dinner – he is travelling most comfortably and has a large tent and plenty of servants. It was delightful sitting down to a *real* dinner at a *real* table with a table cloth and dinner napkins and plenty to eat with Burgundy to drink and cocoa and cigarettes after dinner – and this in the middle of the wilds – it will be a long time before I pass such a pleasant evening again.[39]

Two days later, Edmund Musgrave Barttelot, having reached and crossed the Nkissi River, described how they 'encamped on the other side, just the far side of a camp of Casement, an uncommon nice fellow belonging to the Sanford expedition'.[40] On the 17th both Jephson and Barttelot lunched with Casement and on the 18th Barttelot noted that 'Stanley and Casement came up in the afternoon and camped with me. We dined together.' On the 19th all reached the Luila River and Casement helped Barttelot's men to cross late in the day, while he and Jephson waited to do so until the following morning.[41]

Further meetings followed on the 20th and 21st. Jephson was becoming ill and his progress slowed:

> I travelled slowly, each step being painful, and got about half through the march when I came upon Casement who was camping for breakfast in a deserted village. I could go no further for I felt the fever had me and I was fain to lie down in an old hut, whilst Casement got his bed made up and put me on it. For a couple of hours I tossed about in a half sleep dreaming that Stanley was far ahead and that I was struggling to catch him up with the boat and couldn't overtake him. Casement gave me ten grains of quinine and when it got a little cooler put me in a hammock and sent four men to carry me into camp. Stanley became anxious when the boat arrived and the men reported that I was not well. As I did not turn up he sent six chiefs back to fetch me in and they met Casement's men on the way and carried me into camp.[42]

Stanley was soon to commandeer the *Florida* for the Emin Pasha Expedition and he invited Casement, whom he considered to be 'a good specimen of the capable Englishman', to a champagne breakfast to celebrate her launching.[43]

Casement recorded his own reflections on the Expedition years later, in 1915. He told of meeting the Expedition at the Nkissi River:

I was there at that crossing in 1887, when Stanley came up river with the Emin Pasha 'Relief' Expedition – and there are references to me in the Life of poor Major Bartellot [sic] – one of that ill-fated, ill-led and fraudulent Expedition, whose object was not the relief of Emin at all, but the capture of Emin and his ivory [army?] and the district he controlled for the British Empire. I was invited to join the Expedition by a cable from London from Sir Francis de Winton – and although this adventure appealed to me, then a very young and very adventurous Irishman, my instinct as to the motives and aims led me to refuse what was intended as a flattering invitation. I was indeed glad, later on, when Stanley returned to assail and defame his dead comrades, that I had not yielded to de Winton's wire.44

The first evidence of Casement's active intervention in defence of the native population comes from an incident which took place at this time. In 1904 he recalled the incident, which involved an agent of the State, Lieutenant Francqui:

I often met Lieutenant Francqui during 1886 and 1887 and twice saw him responsible for barbarous acts (once for an act of mutilation carried out (in September 1886) under his eyes). On one occasion (April 1887) I complained personally at Boma to the judicial authority of his brutality and was informed that I had no right of intervention on behalf of the people he had injured ... Lieutenant Francqui was then acting as Commissaire of the Cataract Region: the nice natives he had so brutally flogged were poor Portuguese natives from S.E. Africa – all of them Government servants.

One of them, who had been so cruelly flogged by this officer's direction and under his eyes that he was literally cut to pieces, I had to have carried in my own hammock for over fifty miles when taking him to Boma to the State Doctor to have his wounds dressed and in order that I might lodge a complaint on his behalf ... I was laughed at for my pains ... Lieutenant Francqui was never punished.45

There were other problems, too, during these months. Brief references in the correspondence of Baron Weber and Swinburne suggest that the SEE was under organizational and financial pressure and that employees might have to be let go. On 17 April Weber wrote: 'Casement may be a good man but decidedly in an inferior position having been storekeeper and purser ... If we go on engaging men not knowing if our steamer gets up at all we shall be very quickly eaten up without results.' On 6 July he was admitting: 'Casement we probably shall have to send away.'46 Part of the problem was a clash between Swinburne and Casement. On 30 May Swinburne had stated: 'While I am on my voyage with the *Florida* I intend to have Mr Casement in charge of Kinchassa Station.' In mid July he stressed the importance of having three good intelligent agents for Matadi, Luebo and the Upper River, but had serious reservations about Casement's ability for such posts: 'Mr C. is I am sorry to say utterly useless as a trader, and I shall have to try and get rid of him.' Later, he repeated his judgment: 'Mr

C. I am sorry to say is little or no good, far too much of a boy; however, I have no one else, so must use him for Kassai.'[47] But, as with the case of Taunt, the fault may not have all been on one side. In his letter of 6 July, Weber had commented: 'You must now clearly see that Swinburne is not worth much.'[48]

Whatever the tensions, Casement was kept. After the *Florida* was transported and finally made available to the Sanford Expedition, he spent some time on the Upper Congo with Edward Glave, who used the *Florida* for trading purposes. Writing to Morel in 1904, Casement stated, with regard to the SEE: 'I never bought or sold anything for it – I simply organised its transport on the Lower Congo – and made one journey in the interior with the late E.J. Glave – as his guest – when he went up the Maringa River. The whole thing was an honourable and *by no means* lucrative period of some years of roughing it and working with Natives.'[49] From comments of his in 1903 and 1904 it appears that Casement joined Glave by travelling on a small steamer for over two weeks in August and September 1887 with Captain van Kerkhoven. According to Casement, Captain van Kerkhoven told him that he paid 'his cannibal soldiers' five brass rods per human head they brought in.[50] On the journey from Stanley Pool to the Equator Station they passed through places which were later to be of great significance to Casement: Bolobo, Lukolela, the Irebu area and, finally, the Equator Station (later Coquilhatville), where Glave was based.[51]

Glave wrote of Casement in a letter to Sanford on 30 December 1887:

Casement – I have always found this gentleman most willing and obliging in everything at the Equator. He had very little to do as I never received goods enough to keep myself employed in trading. But on the *Florida* he rendered me great assistance and was very disappointed that, upon leaving the Equator, I was not able to leave him there as he would have been very successful there. I have heard him spoken badly of but I think myself he is a scapegoat for every one's faults. But all agree that he displayed great energy whilst on the road transporting loads.[52]

With insufficient work on the Upper Congo, Casement presumably returned downriver. By the following February he was again in trouble and this time he did resign. He was on his way to Luebo on the Kasai with Swinburne, to take charge of the station there. Baron Weber referred briefly to the resignation in two letters. In one, undated, he stated: 'The *Florida* started from Kinchassa on the 3rd February having on board as relief for Luebo, Mr Casement. On the 4th this agent returned to Kinchassa by canoe having, it appears, had some words with Mr Swinburne at Kimpoko, and having left the steamer with that gentleman's consent.'[53] Casement's recollection of the incident some years later is rather opaque: 'I left the Sanford Expedition (again in a perfectly correct way – I resigned rather than go up to Luebo in an invidious position) to go off elephant shooting in 1888.'[54]

Casement's next employment was for the Compagnie du Chemin de Fer de

Congo. '[F]or some months I commanded the Congo Railway Company's advance expedition in its survey – finally coming home still a complete freelancer in 1889 – when merely 25 years of age.'[55] The building of a railway between Matadi and the Pool, to bypass the cataracts, had been discussed in the earliest plans for opening up the Congo region. The need became more pressing as the demand for carriers far outstripped supply. Preliminary studies in preparation for the construction of the railway began in June 1887 and were completed by 1889. Construction began on 15 March 1890. The first section, from Matadi to Nkenge, was opened in 1893; by 1896 Tumba was reached; and the first locomotive reached Leopoldville on 16 March 1898. The railway covered a distance of 435 km.

Casement's involvement was confined to a short period when the terrain on which the railway would be built was being surveyed. In a long letter to Sanford dated 27 August 1888, he gave details of the survey activities and provided further clues about his resignation from the SEE and about the earlier contretemps with Taunt. Writing from the Nkissi Valley, he commented on the circumstances of his resignation:

> I thank you for the good wishes contained in your first letter when you believed me to be at Luebo. I regret that circumstances have so arranged matters that I am no longer a member of your Expedition – but the fact of my being so was brought about against my wishes although at the end I quitted the Expedition willingly. However, I do not wish to reopen that question now – for, unfortunately, it involves personalities.

He drew Sanford's attention to the fact that arrears in salary were being withheld from him by Messrs Weber & Co., adding that he found it 'scarcely courteous' that they seemed to have ignored a letter from him on the matter, written in May. He went on to describe his current work with the railway company. They had spent two months surveying the relatively unknown valleys of the Lukunga, Kwilu and Ngongo rivers and had now reached the Nkissi; progress had been rapid and, should it continue, they hoped to reach Stanley Pool by November. Reflecting, however, on his own experience of the Congo over three years, he doubted that a railway was necessarily the most suitable means of communication for the region.

> A good road with bullock and mule teams would meet every requirement of Congo commerce for the next twenty years, I think. The difficulty here is not that the country is not fertile but that the people do not work and that there is nothing like systematic labour to be found among the natives in any part of the good [?] country. For instance, a man lives in his house until it falls to pieces and then necessity urges him to build another; a woman cultivates just enough ground, and no more, to yield sufficient sustenance for her household; a carrier when he feels inclined goes to some market and takes a Kapita's [captain/labour contractor] rations for the road and he fulfils his contract with that Kapita more or less according to his own inclinations while the Kapita on his part carries out his engagement with the Whiteman pretty much according to his own fancy

and so all things march home in a general happy-go-lucky manner and all's well that ends well, but anything like systematic or organised labour – save in the white factories on the Lower Congo below Matadi – does not exist here.

Much is spoken of the State's *system* of Transport – but there is no State System of Transport. The State transport – like that of the trading houses – depends entirely upon the willingness of the natives and that may be stimulated or depressed by a good whiteman or a bad, by suitable cloth or otherwise, by a superabundance of *malafu* [palm wine] or a paucity of sunshine – in fine, by a hundred petty circumstances – and I think here in this very fact – the general disinclination of all the Congo natives to anything like disciplined labour or to encountering present hardship for some ulterior benefit – lies the great obstacle at present to the proper development of the country or the interests of trade. No doubt, in time, the people will learn the value of useful and diligent lives and then something may be hoped from the Congo – but until that time I do not believe there is anything like sufficient produce to keep a railway going, and pay for its construction. The money so spent would be better employed if used in organising a more extended and suitable administration of just laws – and ideas of Government among the people – quickening their good instincts (and they have many) and repressing their bad – relieving those on the Upper River from the terrible misery of Arab robbery and oppression – and in general, by showing the natives that there is more to be gained by regular labour and honest lives – than by idling in their villages – or occasionally carrying a whiteman's load.

The country I have recently passed through affords a fine field for increased transport to the Pool, for the people here are quite untouched by any other State or trading house recruiting agents – and yet they are born carriers and would be glad of opportunities to earn cloth. Something could be done here I am sure and the road too down to Matadi is more direct than by the ordinary caravan road.[56]

In his book *Five Years with the Congo Cannibals*, published in 1890, Herbert Ward indirectly shed further light on his friend's participation in plans for building a railway between Matadi and Stanley Pool.[57] The first phase of the surveying, Ward stated, proved very difficult and little progress was made. 'With the commencement of the second campaign, in the summer of '88,' Ward continued, 'the work advanced more rapidly. The following descriptions I gathered from a friend who was attached to the surveying column.' Undoubtedly this friend was Casement, and the four pages of description that follow were surely derived from him. It tells of surveying first through an area of grassy plains, where the burning of the long grass by the surveyors angered the local people and where the party had regular encounters with herds of elephants. 'On arriving at the Nkissi River, which is the largest of the southern tributaries of the Congo from the sea up to the mouth of the Kassai, the expedition quitted the game country, and entered a broken land of ravines and forest, extending for fifty miles or so to near Stanley Pool.' Here, again, the local people, in this well-populated area, were suspicious of the strange intruders with their red and white painted poles. The expedition finally emerged onto the level plain below Stanley Pool.

Baptist Mission Station, 1888–9

After his work with the railway survey, Casement took employment for a short period as a lay helper with the English Baptists, who were one of a number of missionary organizations in the process of establishing themselves in the Congo. The Congo Free State and associated commercial companies were not alone in being attracted to the Congo Basin; there was, in addition, a 'missionary scramble'.[58]

Livingstone's work in East Africa had many admirers and Stanley's celebrated passage down the Congo turned missionary minds in that direction. In 1877 Robert Arthington, dubbed 'the miser of Leeds' because of his ascetic lifestyle, offered £1000 to the Baptist Missionary Society (BMS) if they would start a mission in the Congo. In the same year, Dr Grattan Guinness of the Livingstone Inland Mission (LIM) initiated a mission in the Congo.[59] George Grenfell and Thomas Comber of the BMS made their first journey to the Congo in January 1878 and both missionary groups were soon heavily engaged in setting up mission stations in the Lower Congo, with the dual purpose of carrying out missionary work in the area and of acting as way stations for the passage of personnel and goods to the Upper River. In 1879 the LIM established the stations of Palabala and Banza Manteke. The BMS station of Wathen, first founded in 1881 at Manyanga, was moved in 1883 to the more convenient location of Ngombe Lutete, on the south bank caravan route. They were provided with a site on Stanley Pool in 1882 and proceeded to build Arthington Station there in 1883. The LIM also established themselves at the Pool in that year. In 1884 the BMS placed a steamer, the *Peace*, on the Upper River, as did the LIM with the *Henry Reed*. Beginning in 1884, George Grenfell started a series of seven exploratory voyages in the *Peace* on the Upper River and its tributaries, journeys which 'opened up the main waterways of the Congo basin to European knowledge'.[60]

The early days of missionary work had a heavy secular content, which involved the enormous task of transport, but also the construction of buildings and the provision of food for members. The death rate was high, as it was among State employees on the Congo. In the first part of 1887, the BMS had six deaths among its staff.[61] Those who acted as transport agents negotiated with neighbouring chiefs to engage the required number of porters.

Travelling up and down the route between Matadi and Stanley Pool, as he had regularly done since 1884, Casement inevitably came to know the missionaries. The Revd A.D. Slade of the BMS, stopping at Banza Manteke on his way back from England, made the following entry in his journal in June 1888:

> I must not forget Mr Casement in my mention of Banza Manteke. He is, I believe, or was, in the service of the Free State and was stopping there a few weeks. A tall (6ft. 3in. I should say) thin, gentlemanly fellow, of affable manners and a very pleasant face, I took to him at once. He was kind enough to lend me his mosquito curtain, as mine is gone to Ngombe, and already I have found it

very serviceable. He is a good fellow, too, and Christian and it's possible he may join one of the missions. I sincerely hope he may.[62]

More than two months later, Slade again mentioned the possibility of Casement's coming to work for the mission:

I do wish my proposition for a business man at this station met with more favour, for I am convinced it would be a right step in every way. But W.H.B[entley] does not take kindly to it, although in a long talk we had on Thursday night, he would not object to our engaging Mr Casement if we could get him for the post, after my telling him that I heard that Casement would probably join us if invited. He would be a great acquisition to our staff – a Christian man, and an exceedingly pleasant man, and withal a competent man.[63]

It did come about, and on 29 November 1888 William Holman Bentley wrote to Alfred Baynes, the secretary of the Baptist Missionary Society in London, explaining that they had made an arrangement with Casement that he would come to work for the mission for a short period as a lay helper.[64] Ratification from England was sought and Bentley tried to assure London by giving details of Casement's career to date.

He was ... engaged by the State to manage the transport & shiftings of camp of the Railway Surveyors; & had just finished that business & was adrift again when I made the arrangement with him. It was no sudden move however; for you know how much talk and writing there has been about the collateral work & the advisability of employing a 'lay helper' or two ... When going down country with my wife I learned from Mr Hoste of Lukunga (A.B.M.U.) that Mr Casement had been recently led to Christ. I was specially glad to hear it, for Casement is very highly esteemed by every one out here; a perfect gentleman & very good & patient with the natives ...
... he would like to have some employment for a few months. At the same time it was a great pleasure & gratification to him that we should think of asking him to come to our assistance. He would like to be doing something really useful in the country. I feared that we would scarcely be able to offer him anything worth while in the way of salary; our single missionaries received an allowance of £120 per ann[um] & boarded themselves out of that. He said that would be sufficient for him; so all such details were arranged; & he agreed to join us as lay helper or whatever the position may be called, for 3 or 4 months at a remuneration identical in every way with the allowance to single men in our mission ... So far I am sure that we could not have done better either in terms or type of man. He is an Irishman I believe & well connected. Mr Bannister the vice-consul at Loanda married his aunt. Jefferson [sic, Jephson], who bought a position in Stanley's expedition & is with him now if they are alive, is his cousin.[65] His general bearing & all that I have learned mark him as a gentleman. His treatment of the natives is all that could be desired so far as I can learn; I managed very delicately to get an assurance also that there had been nothing in his manner of life out here which would cast reflection on us did he become identified with us. I do not think that we have any ground of apprehension on those lines. Then as to his religious convictions & experience. He speaks very definitely of his conversion & faith in Christ, which he dates from the early part of this year

& attributing much to the influence & conversation of Mr Hoste ... Mr Casement will free Mr Slade at once or at least as soon as he returns from the coast & Mboma [Boma]. He will manage the transport, building, planting, accounts & correspondence & the general work of the station.[66]

Casement arrived to take up his position on the evening of 30 December 1888.[67] Details of his work during his sojourn at Wathen are sparse, but a few specific references have survived. As early as 6 January 1889, he and one of the missionaries, Oran, went on a circuit of neighbouring villages for a purpose unspecified.[68]

There is evidence of another trip of Casement's in the vicinity of the station during his stay. An undated note from him in the Bentley correspondence for the period reads:

Stream between Makweke and Mission, 11 am.

Dear Bentley,
Can you send a hammock for me; I am not well and fear the hill beyond this stream in the burning sun. I shall lie here in the shade until the hammock comes – very sorry trouble you, but it might mean being seriously ill, instead of only unwell, to go on now on foot.
Yrs. R. Casement[69]

On 29 April, Bentley set down his reflections on Casement's tenure.

I have to thank you and the Committee for endorsing our action in reference to Mr Casement. The time which he had engaged to stay with us has expired and he is on his way down country. He served three months at £10 p. month paying his own board as we do. On leaving he presented the church here with £3.10. We do not, of course, pay his passage home. He came to us most opportunely and by his assistance the work of the Station was not in any way hindered by the death of our Brother Slade ... He will try to enter the service of the East African Co. and that failing will perhaps return for the Railway Co.

The question of lay assistance or whatever it may be called has been much thought of and discussed by us out here. We have made the experiment with a very good man; well used to the life out here and in full sympathy with the work, genial and in every way a most agreeable fellow. He is very good to the natives, too good, too generous, too ready to give away. He would never make money as a trader.

Of course, he kept up our prices of barter stock, but left entirely to himself would have lowered them, and would rather give 20 rods for a thing than bargain and beat down to 12 rods, the proper price. Of course such haggling is a great nuisance, but unless we keep firm to prices they would run up no one knows where to. If he sold a fathom of cloth he would wish to give 6 inches more than a fathom and so on. There is far too much of this throwing away of money out here on the part of State men, and we in the Missions have great difficulty in keeping prices down. A man travelling who has no meat for dinner will give a very long price for a fowl.

I only mention this to show you how free, generous and good hearted he is. His work was well done and the books well kept.[70]

Home Leave, 1889–90

After his three months at the mission station, covering the months of January to March 1889, Casement left for home, presumably arriving in early summer. In his own later recollection, he arrived home a very young man 'with all the love of Africa upon me – but no wish to continue in the service of what was clearly becoming a Belgian enterprise'.[71] His overall summing-up for Morel in 1904 was: 'Now all that service in Congoland was honourable and reflected only credit on me – I had no enmities only friendships – no man ever said a word against me – I did a great deal in the way of exploring and making friends with the natives – and I liked them poor souls – and they me!'[72] If this seems somewhat misleading, in the light of some of his experiences with the Sanford Expedition, it must be interpreted as a defence of his integrity in Africa in the light of the attacks directed at him for his 1904 Report, by Leopold's supporters.

One can only presume that he spent his leave relaxing and socializing in Ireland and England. 'Gado Hill', an emotional poem on the death of someone close to him, he wrote on 9 June.[73] The first extant letter of his to Gertrude Bannister, written in October, mentions the possibility of his leaving for Africa on 6 November 'for some special work'.[74] In the event, the trip was postponed and instead we find him travelling to the United States with Ward and Glave. During 1890 and 1891, Herbert Ward engaged in an extensive lecture tour about his African experiences, the American part of which was arranged by the J.B. Pond Lyceum Bureau.[75] Casement accompanied him for part of the time and was in the United States from December 1889 to March 1890. When back in New York in 1914, fundraising for the Irish Volunteers, he strolled down Broadway 'in the thought of perhaps locating old points of view, like Pond's and the Hotel I lived in in 1890'.[76] Emory Taunt, still in contact with General Sanford, was monitoring their movements and wrote twice about them to Sanford on 13 November: 'It is certain that Ward and Glave are now in America and Casement is to follow – *the Agent saw them sail*. It is reported that they are to lecture – but I think it must be about the new company they talked – they say they expect to return to the Congo – Parminter knows all about it I am sure and you must look out for that fellow ... Keep your eye on Parminter and the other Englishmen.'[77] Parminter was now working for the Société Anonyme Belge, which had assimilated the assets of the SEE, and Casement was soon to join him; one detects a measure of commercial rivalry in Taunt's comments to Sanford. Back in London after this interlude, Casement and his sister Nina went to hear Stanley lecture in St James's Hall on the day before he left for Brussels and Africa. And he had a formal photograph taken on 8 May for Harriette Dickie (Wilkinson) of Baronstown, Co. Meath, to which the caption reads 'For Harriette, with Roddie's best love, sailing for Congo tonight'.[78]

Transport on the Lower Congo, 1890–1

Casement's return to the Congo, despite his wish to distance himself from 'a Belgian enterprise', was at the urging of Major Parminter, who 'begged me to return with him'.

> The SEE, which I had been a foundation member of, had since, chiefly under Parminter's able direction, become the big Société Anonyme Belge of today. Parminter was returning as Director in Africa of this company – and they badly wanted me to go out to undertake the organisation of Native transport in the Cataract Region – especially to open up a new road inland of the ordinary caravan route.79

Casement agreed, mainly, he claimed, from friendship with Parminter, but 'refused to join definitively the SAB – pointing out clearly to Albert Thys, at a personal interview, that I had no wish to become a "trader" and no desire to remain in Belgian service on the Congo'. He had promised Parminter in September 1889 that he would help establish a 'proposed new carrier route via Luvituku' and he told Thys that he would carry out that promise and no more. He refused the usual three-year contract, promising one year *at the outside*'. Thys consented. 'I went out in May 1890,' wrote Casement, 'to open Luvituku road and make friends with the Natives – and I founded the transport section as I promised – and came home in May 1891.' Again, reflecting accusations of being a resentful failed trader, he commented: 'During no period was I a trader or had I the slightest direct interest in trading', though he admitted that from May 1890 to May 1891 he served a commercial company.80

Almost immediately after Casement's return to the Congo, a brutal crime was perpetrated there. The Belgian officer in charge of the station at Manyanga, De Ghillage, participated in a native celebration, during which he became hopelessly drunk, dancing naked in the station square. Having gone to bed later, he awoke and asked his servants to make tea for him. Then, thinking the tea poisoned, he attacked the three servants. His cook fled to the bush, but he beat the remaining two boys with his rifle stock until it broke, whereupon he ordered a Zanzibari employee to continue with a bamboo staff. Casement's friend, Reginald Heyn, was awoken by the screams and rushed out to witness the scene. He pointed his revolver at the Zanzibari and threatened to shoot if he did not desist. One of the boys was already dead. The other died soon after and the bodies were dragged to the river and thrown in. One of the victims, Casement later pointed out, 'was a little native boy of 13 years of age'.

Casement learned of the crime a few weeks later, when visiting Heyn at Manyanga. What Casement described as a 'mock trial' occurred some time after that; the culprit remained in his post and was merely fined 500 francs. Casement and Parminter both wrote to protest to Major Coquilhat, the governor of the State. The first letter brought no reply, but Parminter was informed verbally by the governor that no private accusations would be tolerated. When Casement wrote again, word was sent to him that he might find himself 'in prison if I did not look out'.[81]

Not long afterwards Casement met Joseph Conrad, then in his early thirties.[82] Conrad arrived at Matadi on 13 June 1890 and his diary entry reads: 'Made the acquaintance of Mr Roger Casement, which I should consider as a great pleasure under any circumstances and now it becomes a positive piece of luck. Thinks, speaks well, most intelligent and very sympathetic.'[83]

In a letter to John Quinn, written during Casement's trial in 1916, Conrad recalled this period:

I met Casement for the first time in the Congo in 1890. For some three weeks he lived in the same room in the Matadi Station of the Belgian Société du Haut-Congo. He was rather reticent as to the exact character of his connection with it: but the work he was busy about then was recruiting labour. He knew the coast languages well. I went with him several times on short expeditions to hold 'palavers' with neighbouring villager-chiefs. The object of them was procuring porters for the Company's caravans from Matadi to Leopoldville – or rather to Kinchassa (on Stanley Pool). Then I went up into the interior to take up my command of the stern-wheeler *Roi des Belges* and he, apparently, remained on the coast.[84]

On 24 June, Conrad wrote, 'Gosse and R.C. gone with a large lot of ivory down to Boma', and, on the 28th, when Conrad left Matadi for the overland trek to Leopoldville, 'Parted with Casement in a very friendly manner.' They had known one another for two weeks in all, during which Casement made the short journey to Boma and back. Casement's departure for Boma seems to provide the only possible factual basis for Conrad's best-known description of Casement, which was made in Conrad's letter to Cunninghame Graham in 1903, when Casement was trying to interest influential people to campaign on the Congo issue. Conrad congratulated Graham on his recently published book, *Hernando de Soto*, and while complimenting him on his insight into the souls of the conquistadores, introduced Casement to him:

I send you two letters I had from a man called Casement, premising that I knew him first in the Congo just 12 years ago. Perhaps you've heard or seen in print his name. He's a protestant Irishman, pious too. But so was Pizzaro. For the rest I can assure you that he is a limpid personality. There is a touch of the Conquistador in him too; for I've seen him start off into an unspeakable wilderness swinging a crookhandled stick for all weapons, with two bull-dogs: Paddy (white) and Biddy (brindle) at his heels and a Loanda boy carrying a bundle for all company. A few months afterwards it so happened that I saw him come out again, a little leaner, a little browner, with his stick, dogs, and Loanda boy, and quietly serene as though he had been for a stroll in a park.[85]

What Conrad is likely to have witnessed is Casement, a strong walker, leaving Matadi some time after the rest of his load-bearing caravan had gone on ahead. The account, which has contributed to a romanticization of Casement's African activities, exaggerated the duration of the journey, its solitariness and the nature of the terrain – hardly 'an unspeakable wilderness'.[86]

In a letter to Gertrude from the village of Luvituku, Casement gave an account of his peregrinations between early July and early September 1890. Though 'I have not been as much on the tramp as usual this time', he had, he told her, walked from Matadi to Kimpese (75–80 miles), from Kimpese to Manyanga (65 miles), from Manyanga to Bwende and back (50 miles), from Manyanga to Kimpese (65 miles) and, finally, from Kimpese to Luvituku (25 miles). All of this was since 2 July and did not include, he told her, the 'walking in between ... These 280 miles represent 17–18 days real walking – the rest of the time I have been squatting some where or other'. He contemplated going down to Matadi 'if I can induce a sufficiently large number of natives to go in one caravan. It is a long journey down to Matadi – nearly, if not quite, 100 miles'. In the meantime there were local activities. 'I shall be off tomorrow and next day on the tramp round here to find a nice place to build on – and as soon as that turns up I move out my whole brigade and we commence running up grass houses.' And:

> I have had several chiefs of the country interviewing me today and there is to be a mass gathering of them on nKenge (next Sunday). The Konjo week is of only four days, nKonzo, nKenge, nSona, nKandu, each of them being market days in different parts of the country. For instance the market in this neighbourhood is held every nKonzo and some miles off there will be nKenge markets, nSona and nKandu – so that every day there is a market somewhere within reach in different directions and to suit the surrounding villagers. The market near this is a big one – and is attended from far and near.[87]

Though details of this last phase in Casement's early employment in the Congo are sketchy, his work was in keeping with what he had been doing up to then – facilitating the process of transport over the difficult cataract region of the Lower River. This employment for the Société Anonyme Belge was Casement's greatest responsibility to date, and his record is summed up in *Biographie Coloniale Belge*: 'During this, his third term, Casement accomplished significant work: he established a station at Kimpese, then one at Luvituku, he organised transport in the cataracts region and he was deemed by the directors of the Society to be an "exceptional agent".'[88]

Home Leave, 1891–2

Leaving the Congo in May 1891, he would have arrived home by early summer. He visited Donegal and later wrote: 'I walked thro' Donegal – and for 26 miles of the road from the Poisoned Glen down to almost within sight of Letterkenny heard more Irish than English.'[89] While in Ireland he clearly indulged in some poetry writing, as several pieces are dated between August 1891 and April 1892. The Antrim landscape was again a theme ('To Sarah of Glens of Antrim', September 1891; 'Glenariff Bay', August 1891), but he was moved, too, by the death of Charles Stewart Parnell on 6 October 1891 to write a sonnet, part of which went:

> Hush – let no whisper of the cruel strife,
> Wherein he fell so bravely fighting, fall
> Nigh these dread ears; fain would our hearts recall
> Nought but proud memories of a noble life.

He was to comment during his trial in 1916 that, while always an Irish nationalist, he had lost interest when Parnell died.[90] Two further poems, on Montreux at the eastern end of Lake Geneva in Switzerland, written in March 1892, suggest that Casement holidayed in the area during the winter.[91] In May Herbert Ward wrote from Brussels, announcing the impending wedding of Miss Heyn, presumably Reginald Heyn's sister. The groom was Major Parminter ('I know he also is your attached old friend'), and Ward was to be best man.[92] The joy was to be followed by sorrow, as Reginald Heyn himself died in the Congo on 2 June, still in his early thirties. Casement must have left England again for Africa early in the summer of 1892, as the next indication we have of his movements comes from his voyage out.

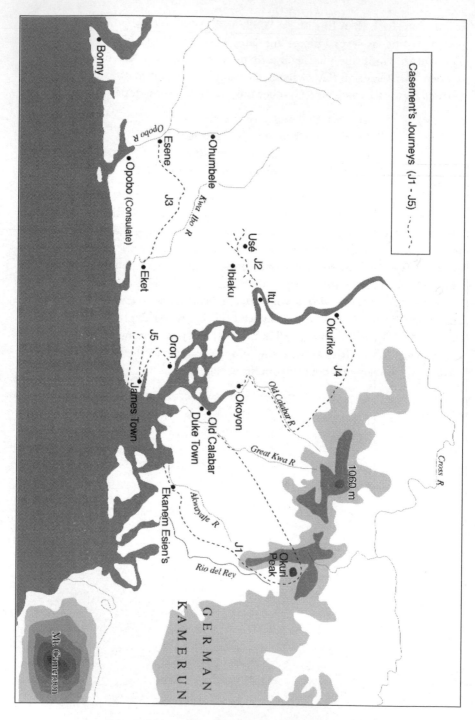

Map 2: Niger Coast Protectorate (Eastern Section)
(Data taken from contemporary maps; not to scale)

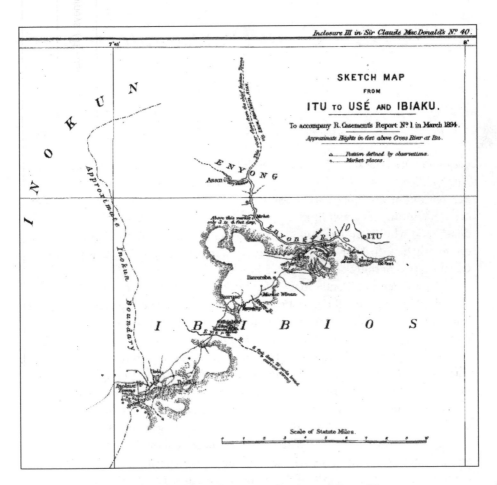

SKETCH MAP

FROM

ITU TO USÉ AND IBIAKU.

To accompany R. Casement's Report Nº 1 in March 1894.

Approximate Heights in feet above Cross River at Itu.

Position defined by observations.
Market places.

Scale of Statute Miles.

Map 3: Map by Roger Casement: Opobo and Cross Rivers

3: *The Niger Coast Protectorate, 1892–5*

Casement was appointed to the staff of the Niger Coast Protectorate on 1 August 1892.[1] It was his first employment as an official of the British Foreign Service and he attributed his appointment to the recommendation of Sir Francis De Winton, 'my chief in 1884–5', who 'was always my close friend up to his death' and who 'introduced me to MacDonald as being by my Congo service eminently qualified for our own service'.[2] Casement's stay in the Niger region falls into two periods, separated by a home leave.

Major (later Sir) Claude MacDonald was appointed first commissioner and consul general to the Oil Rivers Protectorate in 1891 in a new initiative aimed at implementing a policy of 'peaceful penetration' of the area following the controversial actions of earlier British consuls. During the nineteenth century, in the area of the Niger Delta, the Atlantic slave trade had been replaced by trade in palm oil.[3] This new trade, which had reached substantial proportions by the latter part of the nineteenth century, had led to the emergence of a new class of middlemen on the coast. On the one hand, they began to control the supply of oil from inland areas and, on the other hand, they organized themselves into strong city states. In the last decades of the century, competition between Delta and British traders, who generally had the support of consuls and the Royal Navy, led to the defeat and collapse of the indigenous states. The Berlin Conference of 1884–5 recognized the Delta area as a British protectorate, relying on a distinction between annexation and protection. The latter involved 'the recognition of the right of the aboriginal or other actual inhabitants to their own country, with no further assumption of territorial rights than is necessary to maintain the paramount authority and discharge the duties of an occupying power'.[4] Under this system, British consuls were intended to be 'arbitrators', but in practice consuls such as E.H. Hewett and Harry Johnston acted virtually as governors, siding with British against local traders. Indeed, in 1887 Johnston precipitated a crisis when, illegally and without sanction from London, he organized the overthrow and deportation of King JaJa of Opobo, who had built up a substantial trading network. His action has been described by one authority as 'one of the shabbiest incidents in the history of Britain's relations with West Africa'.5

In 1889 the British government, perturbed by events in the region, sent a special commissioner to make recommendations on the best form of administration. Claude MacDonald was chosen and, having submitted his report in 1890, was selected to implement the plan. A diplomatic man, tactful and patient, he had consulted widely with local leaders in drawing up his report. He recommended the establishment of an administrative unit separate from the Royal Niger Company, whose sphere of influence stretched inland from the Delta to the confluence of the Niger and Benue rivers and beyond. Thus, the Oil Rivers Protectorate came into being (to be renamed the Niger Coast Protectorate in 1893). The tasks of the unit included general administration, the establishment of fortified stations and small mobile military units, and the development of communications (roads and rail, steamboats, telegraph). Revenue was to be raised in the territory, chiefly by levies on imports.

MacDonald's first task was the recruitment of staff, not without its difficulties in an area known as 'the white man's grave'. A team of vice-consuls was put together. The vice-consul was to be a jack-of-all-trades, responsible for general administration, travelling to open up friendly relations, assessing resources, signing new treaties, collecting intelligence reports, levying import duties, organizing the postal service. Referring to the Old Calabar area, Sir Claude MacDonald wrote to the Foreign Secretary, Lord Rosebery, in 1893: 'This is undoubtedly the most important district in the Protectorate and one most capable of development.'6 To this he added: 'I am of opinion that the Old Calabar district will within a few years yield a revenue almost double the present one. The future wealth of this country would appear to lie in the direction of plantations of cocoa, coffee, rubber, landolphia etc.'7 Later, in his Annual Report for 1894–5, when discussing the Constabulary report he commented: 'The establishment of the military posts, mentioned by Captain Boisragon, is a source of considerable expense to the Protectorate, though doubtless, in time, it will lead to an increase of trade owing to the greater security of life and property in the regions where these posts are established.'8

Customs Official, 1892–3

We first hear from Casement towards the end of his voyage out, just as he arrived at the Niger, when he wrote to his cousin Gertrude describing his journey: 'I have been having a queer time of it up on the Kroo Coast roughing it among the naked savages of that region – until I got quite ill from bad food and exposure to cold and damp through sleeping on the earthen floors of the native houses.' He had travelled on eleven different steamers since leaving Antwerp, and was due in Bonny the following day. After one final steamer change, he would be in Old Calabar in a week or so, where he expected to 'settle down for a year or two at good hard work'. There appeared to be an element of openness in his plans, judging from his comment that, 'I think it is likely I shall remain up in this district and not go down to the Congo at all. I like the Congo better in all respects save that there I have only Belgians to associate with – while here my companions will be Englishmen – and mostly gentlemen'.9

Records show that Casement was attached to the Survey Department, though during his stay in the protectorate he also served in the Customs Department and as an acting vice-consul. There is no evidence of his engaging in surveying journeys during his first stint in the protectorate. Rather, his early duties seem to have been in the customs division, where his superior was T.A. Wall, director of customs. In his report for 1891, MacDonald stated that customs stations had been established at Old Calabar, Opobo, Bonny, Brass, Benin and Warri.10 The last two of these were to the west of the Niger Delta, Brass lay on the Delta, and the remaining three were to the east. Casement's career in the protectorate was spent in the eastern section, particularly in Opobo and Old Calabar. On 10 October 1892 he issued two public notices from the Customs Department, Old Calabar, one of which reads:

> Notice is hereby given that Bakana on the New Calabar River, is the Port of Entry for the same river; and that from and after the first day of October 1892, all Customs and other Regulations in force in the Oil Rivers Protectorate will be applied to the aforesaid port of Bakana; and furthermore that from the Introduction of this notice all vessels for New Calabar need not call at Bonny to enter and clear as formerly.

The second notice repeats a similar formula for 'Idu on the Orashi River between New Calabar and the Niger'.11

With the exception of these notices, Casement's activities in relation to customs have to be inferred from the general reports of his superior, Wall, to Sir Claude MacDonald, commissioner and consul general, and, ultimately, to the British government. The general reports on customs by Wall and MacDonald gave detailed lists of imports, exports and duties for the six ports mentioned above. They also referred to general customs regulations. The principal exports included palm oil, palm kernels, india rubber, ebony and ivory, while imports included a range of European manufactured goods.12 Clearly, maintenance and supervision of a system involving such detailed data absorbed a great deal of time.

Early in 1893, Casement wrote to his 'Uncle John' in Magherintemple (actually his great-uncle), telling him that Tom was in difficulties in Australia and asking if John would be prepared to send a sum of money to pay off his debts. He,

Roger, would then pay this back in monthly instalments. It is the first record of what was to become his regular financial support for his siblings during the course of his life. He went on to say that he had sent some 'curios' for the wedding of his great-uncle's son and his own cousin, Jack, to Mya Young and that he 'saw from a *Belfast Newsletter* sent to me by Mrs Young that you were all at Galgorm for the wedding'. 'I was', he said, 'delighted at the news of Jack's marriage to pretty, good tempered, kind hearted Mya Young and I don't candidly think there could be a better match. Both are old enough to know each other's minds.'[13]

During his first phase of his stay in the Niger, Casement interacted with the local Protestant missionaries. The Qua Iboe Mission, based in Belfast, had two missionary couples in the area, S.A. and Gracie Bill, and H. and Martha Bailie. Casement visited the Bills from 24 to 28 October and made a positive impression: 'He seems to be a nice kind of man', remarked S.A. Bill in his diary. Bill had just got a steam saw set up and, as he later reported for the benefit of supporters at home, 'We have tried the saw, and found it very satisfactory, all except the wooden table, which is not strong or so steady as we would wish. Mr Casement, the Vice-Consul, was here when we were trying it. He was highly pleased with it, but saw the defect in the table and gave me a guinea to help in getting a metal one.' Before leaving, Casement also 'gave the baby 10/- as a birthday present.[14] The missionaries were again in contact with Casement in late December, when Mrs Bailie became seriously ill and depressed after the loss of a baby in childbirth. Messengers were despatched to Casement, asking that he send a doctor. On 22 December Bill recorded, 'Today brought no doctor – but Momo and Kamanda came back by the sand and brought very kind letters from Mr Casement.' He also sent plum pudding for Christmas and news that boxes of theirs were safe. He was to help again in January 1893, when he provided the missionaries with a surfboat and crew of five to enable them to return to the mission station from Old Calabar.[15]

He had some contact, also, with the Scottish United Presbyterian Mission. On 21 September 1892, the Revd William Marwick of that mission noted in his diary that 'Commander Rolleston and Mr Casement called for Dr Meek, who had been here'.[16] And, on St Patrick's Day, 17 March 1893, Mrs Elizabeth Marwick wrote: 'Had visit of Mr Casement and Mr Menzies. The former got a loan of books (Mr Marwick's *Revolution of* ...[?] and *A City without a Church*).'[17] A month later, on 24 April 1893, Casement sent a note to William Marwick from Creek Town: 'I am sorry to have again missed you at Creek Town. I now return you two of the books you have lent me – and with many thanks. Hoping your trip to Okoyon will have done you good.'[18] And on 26 June, an entry in Mrs Marwick's diary states: 'Had visit of Mr Walls and Mr Casement. The latter is going to England in *Cameroon*, which is overdue now. May be in any day.'[19]

Home Leave, 1893

Precisely when Casement took his leave is not clear, nor are his movements while at home, but on 2 September he wrote to Gertrude from Evesham, Worcestershire, to thank her for her congratulations on his twenty-ninth birthday, saying: 'I am down here until Monday with a Congo friend, Alfred Parminter.'[20] On 10 October he wrote to Magherintemple from Chiswick, in London, to say that he had got through his course at Greenwich and should have been sailing for Calabar on the 28th. While no details are available on the nature of the course, given that on his return to the Niger he was to embark on a series of journeys of exploration, which entailed taking positional measurements and map-making, it is likely that the Greenwich course involved training for this survey work. He also told John Casement in his letter that he had to undergo an expensive surgical operation, costing fifty guineas, and would have to lie up until November. 'The operation is consequent upon my journeys down the West Coast of Africa last year when the exposure to damp and bad food ... brought on an attack of piles which now call for this immediate remedy.' He had thought to postpone it until next year but the surgeon, Mr Dean, thought that unsatisfactory – even dangerous, 'especially as I have rough work in my next year's service in the Protectorate'. He requested a loan of £30 until November.[21] The operation for piles is the first of a number over the years; Dr H. Percy Dean, of Harley Street, was to treat Casement from time to time and a friendship seems to have developed between the two.

This letter was followed by another on 11 October, informing his uncle that he was going that day to St Thomas's Hospital at Westminster for the operation, and should be there for three weeks.[22] On 6 November Casement wrote to Gertrude from London to tell her that he was going to Brussels to stay with the Heyns. While in Brussels, he was to meet his friend Major Parminter – for the last time, as it turned out.[23]

We get an insight into his thinking from a poem he wrote before leaving England, 'To Lobengula', on the recent destruction of one of the last independent African kingdoms. Lobengula, the Ndebele king, had been playing a cat-and-mouse game for several years in the effort to protect his kingdom from concession hunters associated with Cecil Rhodes. He commanded a formidable army of some 15,000 warriors, though he was aware that it was no match for modern weapons. Eventually, in late October 1893, hostilities broke out and the king's army was routed in a number of encounters with a small force led by Rhodes's associate Leander Starr Jameson.[24] The king fled and, after his warriors had surrendered, took poison in December 1893. Casement's poem is subtitled 'In his flight after the slaughter of his *impis*', to which is added the note, 'Written before the news of his death reached England'. The tone is remarkably similar to that of his youthful poems on Irish historical themes in that it praises gallant resistance and attributes base motives to England. It is, perhaps, the first evidence of a parallelism between his thinking on Africa and on Ireland:

> Weep not the dead who fell in hopeless fight
> To save their land and thee:
> In desert lone to dwell – in hunted flight
> Your heart will long with those brave dead at rest to be!
> Tho' England brave blood shed in that far field,
> Her heart is sick with lust:
> The gold she wins is red nor can it shield
> Her name from tainted league with men of broken trust.[25]

En route to Africa he wrote to Magherintemple from Grand Canary, quite recovered from his operation: 'the wound is almost healed'. He was due in Old Calabar by 31 December and promised to send the borrowed £30 at the beginning of the new year.[26] A quick visit he made to the island of Fernando Po is likely to have taken place shortly after arrival; he crossed the ninety miles from Old Calabar in a six-oared gig. There he ascended a volcano to its peak, accompanied by 'an old Bubi hunter' and an old Bubi lady to carry his cooking gear. According to Casement's later account, his companions wouldn't go to the top, 'fearing ... the demons that roared (in the high winds) on those ultimate slopes of an ascending world that here went out of sight'. He left behind him a note scribbled in a bottle.[27]

'Travelling Commissioner', 1894–5[28]

Casement was intensively involved in survey activities for the greater part of 1894. The need for surveying was reflected in the observations Claude Mac-Donald made on 12 January 1893 in a report to Lord Rosebery: 'The Cross River has not been properly surveyed, indeed has not been surveyed at all, the present map of the River being an eye sketch done without instruments. Arrangements are now in progress to send out a properly equipped surveying party for this purpose.'[29] And, in a report on the Bonny district, Vice-Consul Campbell wrote: 'The part of this district which can be called *known* to the white man, consists almost entirely of mangrove swamp. The region north of Okrika from whence the waters of the Bonny River come, are as yet totally unknown.' MacDonald himself had to turn back during an attempted expedition on the Cross River, late in 1893, when the water level dropped too low.[30] Clearly, then, knowledge by white staff of large parts of the protectorate was confined to rivers and coastal strips. MacDonald was anxious to change this and Casement played a key surveying role during the year 1894.

MacDonald had spent the early part of 1893 in London and in Berlin (negotiating with the German authorities about the borders between the Oil Rivers territory and the German colony of Cameroon to the east). He did not return to West Africa until mid June of that year. Casement himself was back in post in January 1894. The only other official listed as attached to the Survey Department, Arthur Bourchier, was appointed on 18 March 1894. There followed an intense burst of exploratory activity, involving at least five journeys, some of it carried out jointly by Casement and Bourchier. MacDonald's plans, it seems, were now coming to fruition.

The first surveying journey took place in January, on the borders between British territory and the German Cameroon. Casement was accompanied by Horace Billington, curator of the Botanical Gardens at Old Calabar (for these journeys see Map 2). It began at a place known as Ekanem Esien's, on the Akwayafe River, and swung westwards to the rapids on the Kwa River and Old Calabar. It is the only journey of the five for which no written report by Casement has been located, though some textual corroboration exists. The second was led by Casement on his own. It was an attempted journey from Itu, on the Cross River, to the Opobo River, and took place between 4 March and 26 March 1894. The third journey was undertaken with Arthur Bourchier, from 16 to 29 April, between Esene, on the Opobo River, to Ikorosan on the Kwo Ibo River. The fourth, again with Bourchier, was from Okoyon on the Calabar River to Okurike on the Cross River; it took place between 15 and 30 May. Journey five was an attempt to travel from Oron on the Cross to Eket on the Kwo Ibo. It was undertaken in the company of Captain James Lalor of the Protectorate Force and lasted from 18 to 26 June.

The maps for these five journeys add an extra dimension to our understanding of Casement's activities in the Niger. The maps exist in two forms: a set of three sketch maps, prepared by Casement, and a set of lithograph versions, prepared in London. The sketch maps, each with notes in Casement's hand, are the cruder in form. These would have been drawn in the protectorate and submitted to MacDonald, who forwarded them to the Foreign Office. These three maps outline the routes of four journeys (one of the maps contains the routes of two journeys, journeys two and five above). The second set of three maps was lithographed in London in the Intelligence Division of the War Office in October 1894. This set shows the routes of five journeys. Four of the journeys correspond to the four in the sketch versions, for which textual reports have also been identified. But the lithograph set also includes a map of journey one, above, that made in January 1894 to the boundary with the German Cameroons, for which no sketch map or written report by Casement has been found.[31]

All the maps include the routes of Casement's marches; the locations of villages and towns passed (with population estimates); streams and rivers crossed, with their direction and size; plateaux, slopes and mountains; vegetation, including crops, trees, scrub and forest. Miscellaneous other information is also included such as trade paths crossed, or orally-derived information on regions immediately beyond those traversed. Readings were taken on all the routes to check longitude and latitude in relation to readings on existing Admiralty maps. Casement found a discrepancy between his and the Admiralty readings on latitude, his estimates putting locations six or seven miles further east. While allowing for the possibility of chronometer error, the consistency of his and Bourchier's findings over a number of trips and readings led Casement to believe that his readings were the correct ones. At the end of his report on journey three he writes: 'I hope to be able to furnish you with a map of the eastern portion of the Protectorate, embodying the changes in the direction I have suggested, and containing all fresh information we have been able to gather.'[32]

Though the first journey had an added, strategic purpose, all shared a common set of goals: to explore areas inland hitherto little known to whites; to map these areas as accurately as possible; to learn as much as possible about the character of the people, the nature of the terrain and the local economy; to assess the potential for trade; to identify likely routes for roads; to win the acquiescence of the local population to the new order and its priorities. All of these Casement's surveys accomplished more or less successfully.

The mechanics of the journeys were similar in all cases. Local native leaders were looked to for help in providing guides and in 'opening doors' by giving assurances to their allies at various points along the route. The total entourage might number forty persons, mostly carriers employed locally, but also consular servants. Stores carried would have included tents and sleeping equipment, mapping instruments (e.g. chronometers), books and (presumably) European food, and, very importantly, cloth and tobacco as gifts and payments for passage.

Casement wrote home to Magherintemple on 2 January 1894 to tell of his arrival and to repay the money he had borrowed. He anticipated the first surveying journey:

> Sir Claude is expected round here in his yacht from Bonny at any moment, and he has ordered me to be ready to start with him at once to make a short reconnaissance of our frontier line with the German colony of Cameroons – our neighbours to the South. The frontier has not yet been delimited, and my journey will be the first visit made by either side to the scene. A botanical man is to accompany me – to report upon the timber etc. of the country we pass through – my duties being chiefly to take observations *en route*, up to a certain point – and to roughly establish the general frontier line and make a rough map of all the country we traverse. I expect to get off tomorrow or next day.[33]

The 'botanical man' was Horace Billington, and a botanical report on this journey was submitted by him. He gave a general sense of the terrain covered: 'After leaving the mangrove swamps of the lower part of the Akpayafe, the whole of the country traversed by the expedition was forest, with the exception of the small amount that has been cleared from time to time by the natives for farming purposes.'34

The second surveying journey began on 4 March.35 Casement set out without a European companion, but with an entourage of forty carriers (Krooboys and Calabar natives) and three guides supplied by King Koko Bassy. On the first day's march, Casement remarked that the natives, 'while not unfriendly', were 'marked by a certain surliness and dislike to the presence of a white man'. Gifts of cloth and tobacco were made and ensured their passage. They were not to be so lucky on the second day. On the borders between the Ibibio and Inokun territories, Casement caught up with his carriers to find them surrounded by an armed and angry crowd of Ibibios. A swarm of bees was let loose on them, gifts failed to mollify the crowd and, when Casement gave the order to his party to move on, pandemonium broke loose. The crowd descended on them, knocked the porters and tried to drag them away, and seized the loads. Since 'we were quite unarmed and at the mercy of the natives', the situation was only retrieved when sympathizers sent to the Inokuns for help. The Inokun young men quickly arrived, putting the locals to flight.

The party now had to wait while the stolen loads were gradually recovered, but also while negotiations got underway to ensure a safe passage on to Esene, on the Opobo River. An insuperable barrier, however, presented itself, in the form of the hostile Anang people. The march to Esene was estimated by the natives to be one of three or four days, through Anang lands. The guides would not proceed without Anang consent: 'you'll be killed and eaten, and I shall die too', said the chief guide, Etun. A series of palavers got nowhere. The King of Anang stated that he would come to a final decision when they 'chopped new yam', that is, as Casement wryly commented, about the following July.

The attempted journey was clearly over and the party returned to Itu, arriving on 26 March. But the three weeks in waiting had not been wasted. The second half of Casement's report consisted mainly of ethnographic observations that, presumably, he made while negotiations were taking place. The Inokuns were 'a branch of the great Ibo family', and he outlined the region to which the name applied, and also that of the Inokun sub-branch in whose territory he now was. He spoke of the dress of Inokun women, of marriage rites, of the severity with which adultery was treated, and of burial practices. 'Cannibalism', he went on, 'prevails both among Ibibio and Inokun, but is much commoner among the latter. It forms a part of the funeral ceremonial at the funerals of all great men; and prisoners are eaten in wartime, to give, as one of my guides said, "a strong, fierce heart". At the death of a king many slaves are killed; some of these are eaten, while others are buried with their masters to accompany him to the next world.'

The third surveying trip, undertaken with Arthur Bourchier, went from west to east, starting where Casement had intended to end the second journey and finishing on the Kwo Ibo River, which lay between the Cross and Opobo Rivers.[36] The initial task, again, was to secure guides, and the surveyors investigated two possible routes. Their inquiries about a more southerly route took them to a chief's yard, where a crowd awaited them. 'They appeared to be a wild set, all of them with filed teeth, and many had their foreheads smeared with yellow ochre, believed to be an infallible charm against any evil influences exercised by the white men in their capacity of "devils".' The party decided to take a more northerly route.

Soon, it looked as though the experience of the previous journey was going to repeat itself. Cloth and tobacco offered to a crowd in a town where they stopped did not satisfy the recipients; 'we hastily locked our trunks and hurried off at full speed, leaving the "dash" of discord to cover our hasty retreat'. Fearing they were being followed, 'our walk became a run'. The remainder of the journey continued in this nervous manner. Later in the same day, hearing drums being beaten, 'our walk once more became a run'. They continued travelling in darkness, in order to reach the sanctuary of Chief Akpania, known to their guides. The following morning, 'the Chief insisted on our active participation in a ju-ju celebration of our arrival, and to insure our mutual esteem'. A goat was slaughtered and Bourchier and Casement 'underwent a plentiful impression of bloody fingers on our foreheads and chests' and had to render the same service to a crowd of men, women and boys. Akpania requested that the whites come and trade with him, and his mother 'wept when she looked at us, and said that now she could die in peace, as her son had got white men to come to his country to make him a great man, and that she had prayed for this all her life'.

After a ceremonial farewell from Akpania, they left for the Kwo Ibo. At two points they were accosted by men 'wearing hideous masks and head-dresses used in the various ju-ju ceremonies'. In one of these cases the masked man rushed into the town 'crying shrilly with the peculiar cry that proclaims a fight'. Elsewhere, loud drumming was heard, but they avoided trouble by the speed of their march and reached their destination without incident.

At the core of this journey was a rapid two-day march, during which the party covered, on Casement's estimation, about thirty-two miles. A return trip by the same route had been envisaged, but the white men were persuaded by their guides not to attempt this, on the grounds that it was unlikely that their luck in traversing dangerous territory would hold out a second time.

On the fourth surveying trip, which took place between 15 and 30 May, Bourchier was Casement's companion again.[37] The party travelled northwards up the Calabar River from Okoyon before turning westwards and crossing to Okurike on the Cross River, which they descended a little by canoe, before retracing their steps, ending up where they had started at Okoyon. Guides had been obtained from a Calabar native, Efium Otu Ekom. Most of the journey was through forested country, with a sparse population of farm dwellers. The many river crossings were not made any easier by recent heavy rains. The people were friendly, but poor; in one small village 'we were unable to obtain more than two small yams as food for twenty-eight people'. Another village comprised 'a collection of a half-dozen huts built of bark and pieces of old wood lashed together'. The largest town they visited had a population of four to five hundred people.

The reception at Okurike itself was a little tentative, not surprisingly in the light of recent events. Sir Claude MacDonald had written to the Foreign Office on 12 October 1893 informing them of 'disturbances' (a favourite word in communiqués) at Okurike. A chief of the Akuna tribe, Akpotem Akpan, had killed five Ibos, and MacDonald had subsequently attacked Okurike and burned the town. Akpotem was hanged.[38] When Casement's party arrived the following May 'the town was in course of being rebuilt, most of the houses were still in ruins, and piles of bamboos were stacked all over the sites of the burnt buildings'. The chiefs were very friendly, wrote Casement, 'but expressed themselves doubtful of our good intentions coming upon them from the back. Hitherto, they said, they had only looked for the white man by the river, now they must expect him from the land as well, and if they should have trouble with the Government again, where were they to run away to'. Casement hastened to reassure them regarding the government's intentions, but one can sympathize with the chiefs.

Casement and Captain Lalor on the fifth surveying journey tried to survey some of the same territory that was the focus of the second and third trips.[39] The starting point was back at the Cross River, but this time at a point further south than Itu. And, rather than aiming again for the Opobo, their goal was the more modest one of Eket on the Kwo Ibo, just south of Ikorosan, where Casement and Bourchier had ended their march. Leaving their porters and loads at Oron on the Cross River, the likeliest starting point for a road to Eket, the leaders withdrew to James Town to try to obtain guides and information. Having failed in this, they returned to their men, travelling inland by means of a long creek and then marching back eastwards to where the men were camped, thereby surveying a little of the path the whole party was due to travel. But with no local guides or help, the party, when it did set out with them, had not travelled more than a mile and a half 'when we found the natives unwilling to help us to go beyond that point'. The porters were unwilling to risk introducing white men to the area on their own. This attempt was abandoned and all returned to James Town.

Another path was tried, this time starting from James Town itself. Westwards lay a tract of swampy forest, about twenty miles from east to west and six to eight miles from south to north. The forest was rich in wildlife, but passable only in the dry season and frequented then only by 'stray Eket hunters'. Casement wrote that it was 'hard to say to which of the divisions of water known to geography it belongs', since it was fed both by rivers and by tidal creeks. The proposed path took them to the northern fringe of this forest. In one village they passed through the people were friendly but very poor – 'although the farms are fertile'. They begged for a white man to come and trade with them. Further on, the party entered a village 'enclosed in a network of palisades and stout wooden fences, some of which were seven or eight feet high'. The people were uneasy and ready to fight at first. Pushing on, the surveying party came to the next village, Ntaenan, at 7 pm 'in rain and darkness ... after wading for fully half a mile nearly neck deep in water'. Here the headmen begged them to abandon the attempt, partly because of the flooded terrain and partly because of the hostile reception they would receive were they to proceed unannounced. The territory ahead was that of the king of Anang. Casement and Lalor reluctantly agreed to halt.

They set out at 10.30 the following morning to return to James Town by a creek south of Ntaenan. They descended the slopes and soon the path was completely flooded:

> Wading for half a mile in water up to the shoulders and waist, we found it rapidly deepening, until it rose over our heads. Those of the men who could swim pushed on, floating their loads in front of them and resting by climbing into branches of the trees that stretched all around, or, wherever at intervals they could touch the bottom and wade; but the non-swimmers had to be floated along on rafts of some old fishing stakes we fortunately found and lashed together. We did not get down to the beach until 5 pm although the distance could not have been more than a mile and a half from the beginning of the water, and even then several of our men were left behind and had to climb into trees (tying their loads to the branches), where we were forced to leave them all night. We swam back several times, and tried up to 8 o'clock to get them off, but in the darkness could not find them and they were not reached by a relief party until 8 o'clock next morning when they had been nearly twenty hours clinging to the trees, exposed to pitiless rain and without food.

It must have been an exhausted and chastened group that arrived back in James Town not long afterwards, on 26 June.

One of the major purposes of Casement's journeys was to advise on the most appropriate routes for building roads. For this task Casement had his Congo experience to draw on. The fifth surveying trip had shown 'the proven impossibility of the low-lying district behind James Town offering the physical features necessary to the construction of a roadway required to be kept permanently open and free from stoppage ... We have proved the necessity of Oron being chosen as the starting point'.[40] A further reason for the inland route, argued Casement, was that it would run through a populated area:

> if we seek for a route down near the sea, we shall only have human beings on one side of us, – and the inland people, whose present boast is that we dare not come near their country, will only see, in our clinging to the neighbourhood of the seashore, a fresh proof of their view that the whiteman has no power or wish to go beyond the guns of a man-of-war.

All of the reports commented on the potential for trade. Observations on population density, on the size of towns and villages, on the intensity of farming, on the presence of palm trees or on the potential economic value of forest trees – all were included, to some extent, with trade in mind. Other passages referred more directly to trade. The locations of local market places were given, both on the maps and in the texts. Casement registered the complaints of those who said they were impeded from travelling to trade by hostile or difficult neighbours. His comment that one Calabar trader was astonished at the survey party's arrival at his trading beach from the landward side ('a country that to Calabar men ... is as much of a *terra incognita* as is the Soudan') indicates that the mobility of Calabar traders was severely constrained by local rivalries and feuding. Price competition between traders was also in evidence. Surprised at the twofold cost of food and the cheapness of cloth at Itu compared with Duke Town or Old Calabar, he wrote:

> This, I believe, is due to the extravagant and irresponsible trading of young Calabar natives in the Itu markets ... who, having no expensive establishments to keep up as the Chiefs and old traders of Duke Town have, are content with a smaller profit, and are able to overbid their Chiefs in purchasing produce. The margin of profit may be sufficient for their smaller wants, and as their European goods are obtained from the merchants on trust, they feel that if their purchases of palm-oil leave an insufficient margin even for them, they may always repudiate their debt to the white man by pleading trouble with the natives, or a bad debt in an up-country market.

Casement was hopeful for the future development of the region:

> I have no doubt the Inokun will prove friendly to the white men when once their country is opened up, and will welcome the presence of any official with power to open to them the markets of their neighbours, now closed, and strong enough to enable them to use the paths and trade routes now barred by the hostility of other branches of their own race.

An experience during the course of the fourth surveying trip led Casement into an extended and revealing statement on what he took to be the 'native mind'. He had discovered that the local people, instead of tapping the rubber-bearing vines, were cutting through them, destroying them in the process. The cutting was done in ignorance and the natives seemed quite willing to adopt better practice, if instructed. Casement continued:

> Much might be done through the example of such men as Efium Otu Ekon, whom the people of Uyanga follow in many things, and were several of the more intelligent Calabar traders induced to plant rubber in their districts, and to distribute some of the plants among natives they had confidence in, I believe a considerable quickening would thereby be given to the slowly dawning conception in the native mind that there are other means of making money than by relying solely on palm-oil and other products to be drawn by labour from the soil besides yams and food-stuffs.

The native African seems to regard the cultivation of scanty patches of food-bearing soil as the only labour the earth requires at his hands; all else – the trees and vines of the forest, the oil and wine palms, come unsown and unworked for. If they thrive, well and good; if they die, they have only gone back to Nature who gave them, and what can feeble man do to arrest her hand or take back her gifts? To remove this belief in the growth of centuries of a life little better than animal, and to show the natives that the timber on the hills, and the vines in the forest, and even that most freely bestowed of all their possessions, the palm-oil tree, can not only repay care and attention as surely as the yam-field does, but that these lavish gifts of their soil and climate require at their hands, as surely as the yam-field does, care and labour and forethought – is a part we can play by such instruction and example as that I have ventured to indicate.[41]

Protest at German Atrocity, February 1894

On 7 February 1894, following his first surveying trip on the border between the Niger Coast Protectorate and German Cameroon, Casement wrote to H.R. Fox Bourne of the Anti-Slavery Society (ASS) about a German atrocity.[42] He recounted how the Germans had trained a group of Dahomean men as soldiers for their colony in Cameroon. In the absence of the German governor, his substitute, a judge named Lyst, had ordered that the wives of some of the Dahomeans be flogged, which immediately led to an outraged backlash. The Dahomeans came to Government House and shot a man sitting where Lyst usually sat, upon which the Germans fled to two small steamers. The Dahomeans shot up the place, but touched no goods and did not interfere with either English or German trading establishments. They later tried to surrender to an English trading ship, which was unable to help them.

A German man-of-war duly arrived and the Dahomeans were driven into the bush; weakened by hunger, they eventually surrendered in twos and threes. 'As promptly as they surrendered without form of trial, and only the delay necessary to rig up a ... rope they were hanged, men and women alike.' The total to date, wrote Casement, was twenty-seven hangings. 'I trust you may do something to raise a protesting voice in England against this atrocious conduct of the Germans. Altho' the men were their soldiers, we all on earth have a commission and a right to defend the weak against the strong – and to protest against brutality in any shape or form.'[43]

Opobo: Acting Vice-Consul, 1894–5

Towards the end of 1894, Casement served as acting vice-consul in Opobo. In this capacity he exercised responsibilities of a kind different from those with customs or as a travelling commissioner. In November and December 1894 he played a role in an incident involving the practice of human sacrifice in the town of Ohumbele, situated about thirty miles up the Opobo River. Ohumbele, in the words of Sir Claude MacDonald, had 'been inclined to give trouble, notably with regard to the practice of human sacrifice, to which they were supposed to be addicted'. MacDonald had spoken twice in the past to the chief of the town saying the practice would not be tolerated.44

Casement visited Ohumbele on 16 November to arrange a hearing on a dispute between Ohumbele and another community. He learned that human sacrifices were planned following the recent death of a chief, Wankwanto. In his own words:

> I clearly and emphatically pointed out that the custom of human sacrifice was one opposed to the interest of the community, as well as being cruel and wicked, and that on these grounds it was one the Government was resolved to suppress, and those persisting in it would be punished with a strong hand if warnings failed to bring about its discontinuance.45

Casement relayed this information to MacDonald, who visited Opobo on the 19th. He determined that it was time for a show of force and despatched a hundred men and three officers from Old Calabar upon his return there. It was too late, however. In his letter of the 24th, Casement informed him that three slaves had just been sacrificed, one female and two males. Casement held the brother and son of Wankwanto primarily responsible; he proposed arresting them and, since his warning had been given publicly, in the presence of the town's leaders, he proposed levying a fine on the town and holding its king and the chief men 'as securities for its speedy payment'. In fact, he had been informed by them that 'the practice of sacrificing slaves at the death of a chief was one they had no intention of giving up'.

Force, he pointed out, would be required to effect the arrests and armed resistance was possible, so that 'the destruction for the time being of Ohumbele might necessarily result'. But he would do all in his power to avoid such an outcome.46 On 4 December, he reported complete success to MacDonald. The troops, under Captain Boisragon, had arrived and paraded in the town, producing the intended effect. The inhabitants 'have amply apologised for their past disregard of Government authority, offering to pay any fine I might inflict – and they have further agreed to surrender the person implicated in the late sacrifice of human beings on the occasion of Chief Wankwanto's burial'.47

This direct encounter with human sacrifice undoubtedly influenced Casement's overall attitude to Niger society. In a draft article he gave free vent to all his negative feelings in overblown language.48 'British Africa,' he opened, 'probably presents in all its diversified extent, whether from Cape to Cairo, or the Gold Coast to Uganda, no more interesting district than that of the Niger Delta – officially termed the Niger Coast Protectorate.' He gave a page of physical description, on the 600 miles of coastline, the connecting creeks running twenty to thirty miles inland, the mangroves and forests. Here, he continued, we find a race of people as 'far from our ways of thought as the most hopelessly unrecallable days of antiquity, and yet almost within the sound of the mail steamer's whistle'. The region 'offers the contradictory spectacle of a soil but little less fertile than that of Egypt, possessed by a people as remote from our civilisation as were the earliest inhabitants of the Nile Delta, and yet administered in accordance with the latest method of Foreign Office control'.

An illustration of Foreign Office control was the Consular Court, and he cited a few examples of its operation. One case involved a dispute between 'the chief James Egbo Bassi II' and his 'under chiefling' Esukwa Akpan. The former had fined the latter, who, 'having turned himself into a shark, had in this guise eaten and disposed of divers persons of the household of the aforesaid James II'. The court decision, carefully arrived at, would be, suggested Casement, 'to the satisfaction of all parties – till next time'.

It may then reappear in the sterner and more familiar aspect of a large weed-grown crocodile wherein the aforesaid Esukwa Akpan, having transported himself by night, had nightly caused himself to be encased that he might live off the mouth of the town creek, wait for the smaller canoes of the fisher folk, or the dawn visit to the river bath of some extra early female riser. Routed from this – one of its favourite strongholds – the spirit of superstition has not far to go to seek other living or inanimate agent for the carrying out of its bloodstained behest of sacrifice and death.

On this ominous note, he went on to describe various circumstances in which human sacrifice was practised. In one district, he suggested, mother and newly-born twins must be put to death before cockcrow. The termination of a bloody conflict between neighbouring villages, which had closed the trade road, was 'consummated by a fresh act of carnage ... frequently the crucifixion of a young girl – a *virgo intacta*' – on a tree and under a blazing sun. The death was protracted, 'for the greater the agony of the crucified one and the longer under it life can be prolonged the mightier is the "ju-ju" guarding the sanctity of the treaty thus sealed'.

The tone of his third example was even more condemnatory:

Another and more diabolical mode of procedure (designed possibly to bring rain, or to ensure plentiful crops) is to peg the selected victim out upon the earthen floor of his own house so that in cooler shadow the death struggle may endure perhaps many days – while the priests of evil with strange eyes in yellow ochre and red painted upon their clay-smeared bodies point out the dying agonies to the feverishly exultant crowd as the approving tremors of an acceptant and appeased spirit.

His final example was the burial alive of slaves after the death of a chief. He concluded: 'These beliefs, as their tribal possessors stoutly assert, in the face of consular exhortations and punitive expeditions, have endured "since the world began".' Appropriately, perhaps, in view of the high emotional tone of his descriptions, he finished by summoning up the prophet Ezekiel:

Here, if anywhere in Africa, is to be found the realisation of Ezekiel's terrible vision. 'Then will I make their waters deep, and cause their rivers to run like oil, saith the Lord God' – 'her princes in the midst thereof are like wolves ravening the prey, to shed blood, and to destroy souls, to get dishonest gain ... and they shall be an execration, and an astonishment, and a curse, and a reproach'. But if that part of the prophecy be indeed fulfilled in horrible truth – the ending of the inspired denunciation is already in sight, for: 'In that day shall messengers go forth from me in ships to make the careless Ethiopians afraid, a great pain shall come upon them as in the day of Egypt: for, lo, it cometh.'

One sees in all of this not only a standard sense of European social and technological superiority but also a religiously-driven viewpoint, presumably reflecting Casement's Christian upbringing and the later influence on him of missionaries in the Congo.49

A further view of Casement at this period is provided by A.C. Douglas in his memoirs.50 When Douglas arrived in the protectorate as a young recruit, Casement was away on a 'political trip' to the Kwa Ibo River. On his return, Casement reported that Opobo traders had been causing trouble at some of the markets further inland. 'They have been looting at the market, assaulting and beating the women, and causing an uproar amongst the Quas [Kwa Ibos].' The offending traders were men from the trading house of Chief Ogolo, one of the principal Opobo chiefs, with, it was said, over a thousand slaves in his house. Casement invited Douglas to attend court on the morrow, when he would supervise a hearing. Enquiring about Casement of Mr Digan, due to replace Casement once he left, he was told:

> We call old Roger the Black Man's Friend; I don't know that I personally agree entirely with his policy, it is what some people call pro-native, but he is a very good chap, and he can go anywhere amongst them. By all means attend his Court tomorrow; it will do you good to learn how to hear a native palaver; you want a great deal of patience and of that you will get a perfect object-lesson from Casement.

Casement had taken steps to hear both sides of the story and had brought over, with considerable difficulty, several Qua witnesses. The following day the court met. Douglas continued:

> During a patient hearing of many hours the sordid tale was slowly unfolded by two interpreters, one representing the Opobo Chiefs and the other the Quas. Casement listened most attentively, and took down nearly everything in writing; very little seemed to escape him. It was a kind of Court with Native Chiefs as assessors, and the Chiefs addressed the Court at the end, in defence of the conduct of their boys.

A decision was reached and punishments imposed which, in Douglas's recollection, involved 'a beating ... where it was proved that theft with violence had been committed'. Chief Ogolo gave an undertaking that the chastisement would be carried out, and the Corporal of Police was despatched to see that this would be done 'in a humane and proper manner'. Casement offered some general advice to Douglas for dealing with the local population:

[A]lways remember that they are only children; never promise them anything that you or the Government are unable to give them, and never threaten them with any punishment that you cannot enforce. I don't know that I think a legal training to be the best for an Administrator in this part of the country. What you really want is sound common sense, sympathy and considerable courage and perseverance.

Douglas summed up his impressions of Casement:

[T]here was nothing about the man at that time to give the slightest indication of his subsequent extraordinary lapse from normality and sanity, and there is no doubt that at that period Casement was a very able and loyal administrator and a fine example of devotion to the Service. Moreover, of handsome prepossessing appearance, he had a personal attractiveness to which many, and it must be confessed, Nemo [Douglas], succumbed. Certainly no braver man ever existed in Africa; he would go about unarmed amongst the wildest cannibals in the Niger with what another equally distinguished Administrator had laid down as the only equipment necessary, namely, 'a white umbrella and a pleasant smile'.⁵¹

It was at this time, towards the end of Casement's protectorate career, that Mary Kingsley visited, in the company of Sir Claude and Lady MacDonald. This was Mary Kingsley's third visit to West Africa and the date would have been February or March of 1895.⁵² Shortly before Casement left, he and Douglas attended a number of feasts. One was hosted by Chief Cookey Gam, for what the guests termed 'palm oil chop': in Douglas's description, 'a rather hot dish made of fowl, fish, shrimps, and so on, stewed up with Chile pepper, and covered with this rich palm oil, which, if eaten in small quantities is quite wholesome, and when one is hungry and used to the dish, is not unappetising. But, like caviare and suchlike luxuries, it is an acquired taste'.

Finally, as 'a kind of valedictory carouse to celebrate Casement's departure', a huge dinner party was held at the vice-consulate.

He was very popular with the traders and they were very sorry he was leaving, so out of regard for him the whole of them turned up to dinner ... What was lacking in quality ... was made up for in abundance of beer, whiskey and mess champagne. This particular gathering was a festive one; and the West African merchant, who is not averse to a little post-prandial oratory, was seen at his best, and many toasts were drunk.

Departure and Home Leave, 1895

In his 'Brief to Counsel' at his trial in 1916, Casement stated that he 'resigned' from the protectorate service. Why might he have done so? William Maloney, intriguingly, makes the following suggestion: 'When the British service seemed to him incompatible with his duty he withdrew from it: first, in 1895, when he was a Vice-Consul in the Niger, and the English shelled the native villages there ...'53 Though Maloney provides no primary source for the shelling story, it is difficult to imagine it not having some basis. 'Punitive expeditions' were a normal part of colonial operations and we have seen that Casement sometimes felt they were justified. His attitude was later to change, and he reflected on it in 1912 when he sent a copy of an old letter of his from 1901 to William Cadbury.

> In 1901 I was much more of an Imperialist than today! I should not today – or for years now – have willingly expressed the opinion put forward in my last paragraph of this letter. 'Punitive' expeditions are rarely justified – sometimes they become inevitable – and possibly this Bende and Aro-Chukwu Expedition in 1901 was necessary. I had then long left the Niger Coast Protectorate.54

If there is basis to Maloney's claim, I believe it could be linked with the departure of MacDonald from the protectorate and his replacement by his deputy, Ralph Moor.55 Moor followed a more aggressive 'forward policy' than MacDonald and this manifested itself in his relations with local African leaders. In 1894, while MacDonald was on leave, Moor precipitated conflict with Nana, governor of the Benin River. Hostilities broke out in August and Nana's capital, Ebrohimi, was destroyed in September. He was tried and exiled to Accra. And in 1895, following a conflict with the Royal Niger Company, King Koko of Brass was defeated, his centres destroyed and the power of Brass totally broken.56

According to Casement's own later account, he returned home via the Congo. 'I then went down to the Congo ... I here met a missionary whom I had met there before and who had a great influence over me at that time. I met him at the mouth of the Congo on his way home. I came home with him with absolutely nothing to do.'57 At any rate, he seems to have arrived home in the late spring of 1895. When home and with some leisure, he turned once more to poetry. The dates and content of his poems also allow us to trace Casement's movements that summer and to make some assessment of his moods. The first is entitled 'Lines in a London Square' and was dated May Day. Others followed on the scenery of the north Antrim coast, especially Rathlin Island. In June, the *New York Ledger* sent a copy of an issue in which his lines 'A Song of Tyrconnell' had appeared.58 In May and June, too, he wrote to Gertrude from Ballycastle, telling of his activities and being solicitous about her affairs. One assumes that he stayed at Magherintemple with his ageing uncle, John, now in his late sixties, and his wife, Charlotte, who was in her late fifties. According to Reid, 'He loafed and swam and walked and scribbled and began to think seriously of putting together a volume of verse.'59

Another link with the Congo was broken in May, with the death of his friend Edward Glave. Casement wrote the following biographical note:

First went to Africa in 1883, to the Congo. Served there with distinction until 1889. Undertook two journeys to Alaska 1890–93. Returned to Africa to East Coast end of 1893. Crossed the Continent from Indian Ocean to Atlantic, 1894 to May 1895. Died at Matadi on May 12th 1895 – and buried in the little Mission Cemetery at the foot of Tunduwa Hill close to the banks of the Congo (in sight of the last foam-covered rush where it sweeps through the last gap in the hills before widening out to the Atlantic) where many other Englishmen lie, who like him had turned their feet to the great 'realm of Congo' whence, alas, like him, they returned not – on the morning of the 13th May.60

The death of Glave followed those of a number of other Congo friends. Reginald Heyn had died in June 1892 and Charles Ingham was killed in November 1893. A deeper blow was the unexpected death of his friend, Major Parminter, not long married, on 24 January 1894. Clearly, Casement received word of the death of three friends, including Ingham and Parminter, early in 1894, and he wrote, in response, to Herbert Ward: 'Poor Leslie [?]. I am grieved greatly at his loss, altho' he was not all to me that the dear old Major was. I shall never have another friend like him. His poor wife – and dear old Mrs Heyn – what a fearful blow it is to them.' He had, he said, left Parminter in Brussels on 22 November and, though the latter was suffering from his liver, no one dreamt he was so near a critical illness – he had died in Nice. 'I grieve over his untimely death as much as I should over the death of a brother ... We are all going adrift my dear Ward – all going adrift in this world, and we shall soon think of all Congo chums only as a pleasant and sad memory – nothing more of them left – but I shall think of none of them as I do of Parminter.' He went on to say he was glad Ward was doing so well – and benefiting from Paris. And he had had a long account from Mrs Troup about his godson No.1 (Ward's was No. 2 and 'the dear old Major's', No.3). 'I write this from Opobo,' he continued, 'having come round here to get in a bit on this side – although I shall not succeed in doing more than one or two miles – the people are so savage and jealous of letting the whiteman in.' He then mentioned the death of Ingham – killed by an elephant, when his rifle jammed: 'Alas, another of the dear old friends gone.'61

In June, his correspondence with Louisa Jephson-Norreys began, in which he enquired about his mother's links with the Jephsons of Mallow Castle. He first wrote on 1 June, saying that a cousin of his on his father's side was 'compiling a sort of family history for our own amusement and interest', hence his query. Having introduced his Jephson links, he went on to say that he was 'very busy writing up some account of my recent journeys in Africa for the British Association Meeting in the Autumn' and that he expected 'to go to Uganda on a Foreign Office mission next – if I am lucky'. On the 10th he wrote again saying he hoped to be in Dublin in July and wondering whether he might visit her in Mallow. But then, on the 29th, he sent a hurried note from London to say that he had 'got orders from the Foreign Office last night to hold myself in readiness to go very soon ... The resignation of the Ministry has caused this alteration and hurry in my plans – and I *may* have to sail for the Cape in a week or ten days.' He still had hopes, though, of a quick visit to Mallow.[62]

Casement's service in the Niger coincided almost exactly with a period in government by the Liberals. After a general election in July 1892 the Liberals, under Gladstone, had come to power with the aid of the Irish Nationalists. They were to remain in office until 1895 and, during this term, the second Home Rule Bill was defeated by the Lords. Gladstone stood down at the age of eighty-four, and the new administration under Lord Rosebery had a troubled time, until Rosebery resigned in June 1895. In July the Unionists – a combination of Conservatives and Liberal Unionists – won a majority of 152 in a general election and were to remain in power until December 1905.

Casement's appointment to Lourenço Marques was made in the last days of the outgoing Liberal administration. His term in the protectorate reveals a maturing Casement in his late twenties, taking on greater responsibilities than had been his in the Congo. His activities clearly impressed his superiors sufficiently to be offered a full consular posting. And his judicial work would be built on later in his consular work for Distressed British Subjects and in his advocacy work in the Congo and the Putumayo. We get a hint as to the personal factors in his appointment from his later correspondence. To his consular colleague Francis Cowper he wrote in 1901:

> When I want anything at the FO – which thank goodness is not very often for myself – I prefer stating my wants officially – or if it must be by private channel then I go to [Henry St George] Foley – whom of all the nice good natured men of the FO holds I think to be the nicest. I hold him as my personal friend, and I don't mind sometimes telling him privately that I should like so and so. It was through Foley's friendship I first entered the Consular Service – thro' him I came again to Congo last year ...[63]

And, writing to Foley himself, in June 1901, he expressed his sorrow on reading of the death of Armine Wodehouse. 'To his kindness – as to yours, my dear Foley – I think I owed much when, thanks to you both, I was chosen for Lourenço Marques; and I had looked forward to seeing him do something distinguished in Parliament.'[64]

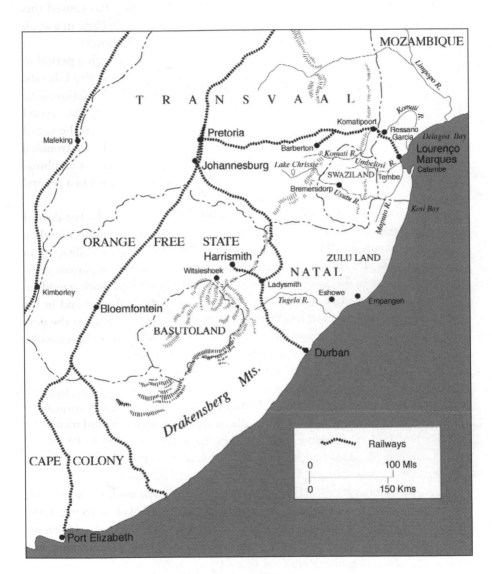

Map 4: Southern Africa

4: *Lourenço Marques, 1895–7*

In his 1916 'Brief to Counsel', Casement recalled that in June of 1895 he had received a telegram from Lord Kimberley offering him the post of consul at Lourenço Marques, in Portuguese East Africa.[1] The record of the time shows that, on 27 June, he received a letter of appointment as consul for the Portuguese Province of Lourenço Marques, at a salary of £600, with an office allowance of £200 and an outfit allowance of £200.[2] On the following day, he received word that he was to be exempted from examination. He proceeded to Lourenço Marques without delay and on 9 September the Foreign Office received a telegram stating: 'Took charge of Consulate today.'[3]

Delagoa Bay, in which Lourenço Marques – now Maputo – is situated, was reputed to be the finest harbour on the east coast of Africa. Yet it was geographically peripheral to the rest of Portuguese East Africa (Mozambique), its natural hinterland being Natal to the south and the Transvaal (the South African Republic) to the west. Because of its strategic location and its importance as a port, Lourenço Marques had become the focus of considerable interest for a number of parties – Britain, Germany, France, the Transvaal and the British South Africa Company of Cecil Rhodes.[4] During the Scramble for Africa, at its height in the last decade of the nineteenth century, each colonizing country rushed to gain maximum territorial advantage. Metropolitan Portugal was financially and politically weak; she was deeply indebted to financiers in other European countries, and governments fell when trying to reduce the debt by introducing taxes. Portugal's rivals felt that her empire might collapse at any time and were ready to compete for the spoils. Germany was anxious to expand her nearby colony in East Africa. Cecil Rhodes was actively carving out territory in Shona and Ndebele lands to the north-west and manoeuvered also within the traditional Portuguese sphere of influence. It was felt that Portugal might be prepared to cede Delagoa Bay if the transaction helped her in her difficulties. Interested parties initiated secret financial dealings, usually concealing their real identities, while rivals watched every move carefully. For the Transvaal, whose access to the sea had been mainly through Cape Town or Durban, a more independent rail line through Lourenço Marques held considerable attraction.

This was the context into which Casement arrived on his first consular posting. What were his functions to be? Drawing on a phrase from Ernest Hambloch, Roger Sawyer has suggested that consular functions can be broadly reduced to two: to protect British subjects and to further British interests.⁵ The range of functions summed up under these two headings was dealt with in a number of British government publications for consuls. Firstly, there was the *General Instructions for HM's Consular Officers*, relevant editions of which, as far as Casement was concerned, appeared in 1893 and 1907. Secondly, there was the *Instructions to Consuls relating to matters affecting the British Mercantile Marine, under the Merchant Shipping Act, 1894*, a new edition of which appeared in 1905. Where the manuals failed to help, guidance on specific questions was regularly sought directly from the Foreign Office.

With consulates frequently located in ports, the system was strongly focused on the protection of British commercial interests. Registers of shipping were kept; consuls mediated in cases of accident and of dispute with local authorities; an annual trade report was sent to the Board of Trade via the Foreign Office; commercial queries from individual companies were answered. In addition, a great deal of a consul's time was taken up with helping what were known as DBSs, Distressed British Subjects, many, but by no means all of them, seamen. The consul, too, was a marriage officer and kept a register of births and deaths. A greyer area concerned the political functions of the consul. The Consular Service was subordinate to the Diplomatic Service and the political sphere was the proper concern of diplomats, based in the appropriate legation. But, where the legation was a considerable distance away – in Lisbon in the case of Lourenço Marques – the consul could perform important political and intelligence functions.

Politics: Portugal, Germany and the Transvaal

Lourenço Marques, being the natural port for the Transvaal, figured prominently in British–Transvaal economic and political relations. It was also a natural listening post for the British government in relation to the Transvaal, and Casement's reports reflect this function.

Established in 1852 by Boers who had trekked from the Cape to the interior, the Transvaal was a poor state until the discovery of diamonds in Kimberley in 1867. There followed an influx of non-Boer residents in a series of diamond rushes, giving rise to jurisdictional disputes and a gradual encircling of the two Boer republics of the Transvaal and the Orange Free State. The First Anglo-Boer War (1880–1) followed the failure of British and Boer attempts to resolve their differences. Though defeated, the Boers were granted complete self-government; Boer national sentiment grew steadily.

In an attempt to retain political control, the Boers severely limited the franchise for non-Boers, a major point of grievance for the latter (the *Uitlanders*, as they were called). Mostly British, they looked to Britain for support and, though London demurred, the belief grew that if the *Uitlanders* rebelled, outside support would be forthcoming. In late 1895, Leander Starr Jameson, an associate of Cecil Rhodes's, assembled a force of some 500 men and waited on the Bechuanaland border for the expected rising. They made their move on 27 December and rode towards Johannesburg, 180 miles away. The *Uitlanders* in Johannesburg, divided, produced no real rising. Jameson's force was surrounded and quickly surrendered; all were in jail by 2 January 1896. The four principals of Jameson's organization were sentenced to death, a sentence commuted to fines by President Kruger. The overall effect of the Jameson Raid was a heightening of British–Boer tensions and the beginning of a steady build-up of arms by the Boers for the coming struggle with Great Britain, now felt to be inevitable.

Casement began his consulship in late 1895, not long before the Jameson Raid. His period of tenure was, therefore, a sensitive one, leading up to what was to be the Second Anglo-Boer War of 1899–1902. He was away in Durban when the Jameson Raid took place, having been granted a week's leave starting on 20 December. He did not return until 6 January, being delayed in his return from Durban due, he wrote, 'to the outbreak in the Transvaal'.[6] During the crisis the Revd J. Bovill, acting consul in his absence, had telegraphed him in Durban to say that the British warship *Thrush* had arrived and that the German *Seeadler* was reported to be landing guns at night. What specific action Casement took during the crisis is unclear, but when he wrote early in March to Magherintemple there was an air of self-importance in his tone:

> There was of course great excitement over the Transvaal affair. I may as well tell you in confidence, that I was the direct cause of the German 'scare' early in January: as I have every reason to believe it was in consequence of information I wired from this and Durban, that the Govt. took such prompt steps to mobilise the Flying Squadron – and to send ships here to counteract German designs.[7]

Following his return from Durban, having consulted the captain of the *Thrush*, Casement assured the FO that no landing of arms had taken place and that Portuguese warships were watching the Germans 'well prepared to guard the neutrality of the port'.[8]

When, three months later and after a renewed bout of fever, Casement took another leave, he spent time in Pretoria and Johannesburg. From the Rand Club in Johannesburg, on 3 April 1896, he sent a long letter to Henry Foley in which he commented at length on the political situation. He had come to the Transvaal, he said, 'feeling more or less general sympathy for the Boers, and a want of sympathy for Johannesburg', but left feeling the reverse. He had met many of the members of Jameson's Reform Committee and found them 'earnest and principled men'. The charge of high treason against the leaders was a 'put up job' and the death sentence and commutation a humiliation to Englishmen. He sensed everywhere Boer antipathy towards England and favouritism toward Germany. 'I feel so strongly that England is the rightful and wisest ruler of South Africa, I cannot bear to think of her influence in this country being in any way weakened ... The Boer is like a native in many ways. He thinks now we are afraid of him (the native, I may add, thinks so too). He believes himself invincible – and in this belief lies the danger.' Casement advocated taking a firm line, including sending troops to protect Natal and Cape Colony. He went on to suggest that Joseph Chamberlain, the colonial secretary, whose understanding and handling of the situation to date he strongly approved of, should insist that the just claims of the *Uitlanders* be met, for 'this persistent refusal of just rights to the majority of the population of the Transvaal must inevitably lead to further outbreaks and breaches of the peace in South Africa'.[9]

A different attitude to events in the Transvaal was taken by Count Pfeil, German consul in Lourenço Marques. In a conversation with Casement, he stated himself pleased with the 'sentences on the four Reform leaders' and spoke of the 'artificial immigration' of Englishmen and the need for a 'policy of exclusion' on the part of the Transvaal government. He would, he informed Casement, welcome the decline of British and the increase of German influence in the Transvaal.[10] The day after he had relayed details of this conversation, Casement, in another despatch, reported a visit to the Orange Free State capital, Bloemfontein, by two Transvaal representatives, Dr Leyds and General Joubert, 'to try and induce the Orange Free State to hitch on to Germany'.[11] Count Pfeil's dislike of England was again manifested when, on 'Majuba Day', he hoisted the German flag – the only other consulate to do so being that of the Transvaal.[12] It was ironic, then, that, mistaken for the British consul, Pfeil should have been jostled and knocked on the railway platform at Lourenço Marques.[13]

Following the Jameson Raid, the topic of the importation of arms into the Transvaal by the Boers was given regular attention in communications between Casement and the FO. By mid June 1896, first in a telegram and then in a full despatch, Casement gave details of arms importation: '104 cases of Maxim guns weighing 27,000 lbs, 65 cases of rifles weighing 28,000 lbs and 4,000,000 cartridges have passed through this to the Transvaal since March 11, and 4,000,000 more cartridges are arriving this week.' These figures were derived from the despatching notes of the Lourenço Marques Railway and Casement believed them to be accurate. He was confident that no shipments took place through Lourenço Marques before 11 March. He also gave details, derived from an English resident in Johannesburg, of men under arms in the Transvaal, including a significant minority of Germans.[14] On 26 June he reported on having been told that 28,000 guns had been sold to Transvaal burghers, the fiercely independent-minded Boer citizens, 500 of them given free to poor burghers. He also wondered about arming in the Orange Free State and among the Dutch in the Cape Colony. On 20 March of the following year, 1897, he was to quote the *Johannesburg Star* as saying that a German steamer, the *Kaiser*, brought 1650 cases of artillery material for the Transvaal to Lourenço Marques on the 14th.[15]

Between November 1896 and February 1897, Casement wrote four more times to Foley and gave further assessments of the situation in the Transvaal. He stressed the danger of underestimating the Boers:

> ... there seems such a large body of the public in England who will persist in regarding the Boer patriot as a simple peasant only desirous of governing himself and of being left alone. He's nothing of the kind. He is scheming, plotting and planning night and day, back door and front door, how to become the undisputed master of South Africa as a whole.

For Casement the future of the Transvaal lay with the English-speaking people there – 'the Government of the country must some day fall into their hands'. He hoped they would remain well disposed to England and observed that, at present, 'most Englishmen in the Transvaal strike me as being loyal'. He was less sure of the support of the 'big men' of Johannesburg, i.e. the businessmen and mine owners. 'They are a poor lot as politicians and are selfish to the core – and too rich. They will only follow the British Government – they won't give her a lead as they might do.' He believed, though, that they were suffering from the 'ruinous exactions of the Transvaal Government – chiefly exercised through the Railway Company'.

His letter to Foley of 3 February 1897 was written from Johannesburg, where he had gone after another bout of illness, and he was clearly assessing the mood he found. There was, he said, a danger of the cooling of the patriotism of Englishmen here, if they lost faith in Britain's 'earnestness to maintain her supremacy in South Africa'. What was needed were firm signals from England. Such a signal he found in a speech given by Chamberlain in the House of Commons.

> Mr Chamberlain's speech has given widespread satisfaction to the English – I might say the general South African – community ... [It] has struck the right keynote – it implies a calm, earnest, strong determination not to abandon Englishmen or British rights in South Africa – and if persisted in it will win to our side the waverers and the weakly of this great community. I cannot tell you how I long – how all good Englishmen here long – for the honest clear rule of a Government that represented the people of the country, and not the ignorant privileged few who now hold the destinies of the Transvaal in their hands.[16]

Trade and Economic Issues

Casement's reports about the port, the railway, concession granting and customs and taxation policies reflect the close interrelationship between political and commercial affairs at Lourenço Marques. Conditions at the port were a matter of concern. Despite the natural advantages of Delagoa Bay, the entry to the port was treacherous and several despatches refer to the damage done to ships.[17] The Portuguese authorities addressed the problems and Casement reported on improvements, including the introduction of mandatory pilotage and the buoying of the port.[18] More serious were conditions on the quayside itself. Not only were berthing facilities inadequate, but storage conditions and the general management of goods were appalling. In a long despatch on the port and the railway, Casement stated the condition of both to be very bad, with blockages, goods lying exposed and a real danger of fire.[19] Again, during the course of his stay improvements were noted, including the appointment of new and more efficient directors of port and railway.

Despite the advantages of nature and Portuguese attempts to improve facilities, Casement, drawing on analysis of shipping returns, pointed out that Lourenço Marques was losing out to other ports in the region, notably Durban. While the trade of Lourenço Marques had increased by 20 per cent between November 1895 and June 1896, that of Durban increased by 900 per cent. And Lourenço Marques seemed to be 'becoming more and more a timber and rough goods port', while fine goods were routed through Durban.[20]

Despite the deficiencies, there was considerable rivalry between competing European nations for the growing trade in the region. While Britain had a traditional dominance, German trade was expanding. As early as November 1895 Casement had concluded that the Germans might be attempting 'to obtain the chief carrying trade of the port'. They had purchased several square kilometres of land, sought permission to build a private pier, purchased two new steamers, and sent a man-of-war to visit.[21] Later, Casement was to refer to the growing popularity of the shipping company, the German East Africa Line, even for people from Natal.[22]

The Lourenço Marques Railway, which ran to Pretoria and Johannesburg, was competing with lines running there from both Durban and Cape Town. The railway was completed in 1894 and ceremonially opened in June of 1895, shortly, that is, before Casement's arrival. Its history was steeped in controversy.[23] The Transvaal had begun to attempt to develop a rail link between the capital, Pretoria, and Lourenço Marques after 1875. Finance was difficult to come by and an arrangement was entered into with a Colonel McMurdo, a US citizen, to build the section that passed within Portuguese territory, using American and British capital. There were considerable delays and, eventually, as allowed for in a clause in the agreement, Portugal took over the McMurdo enterprise in June 1889 – McMurdo having died in May. The US government, on behalf of his widow, and the British government, on behalf of British shareholders, challenged the Portuguese takeover, and an agreement was reached that a tribunal, located in Berne, would adjudicate on the matter. While its decision was expected at any time after 1892, it was not delivered until 1900. For bankrupt and politically volatile Portugal, the prospect of an award against it (expected to be between £600,000 and £1,000,000) was very serious and other interested parties (Germany, the Transvaal, Britain, Cecil Rhodes and private financiers) used this threat to try to further their interests in the area.

One of the first requests to Casement from the FO was for detailed information on the railway in relation to the negotiations at Berne. Those parties with an interest in a large settlement were suspicious that efforts might be made in Lourenço Marques to maintain the railway at a low level of efficiency, thereby contributing to a lower valuation, and Casement's despatch of 25 October 1895 was directed at such suggestions. While admitting that serious problems existed – poor piers, old cranes, inefficient handling methods – he concluded:

> I am of opinion that no impediments in the power of the local authorities to remove have been allowed to exist, or any others created by them; but that, on the contrary, by every means their very limited powers have permitted, the Governor of Lourenço Marques and his subordinates have done what they could to advance the utility of the port and railway.[24]

In February 1896, Casement made a train journey on the Lourenço Marques Railway to Ressano Garcia, the border post with the Transvaal, in the company of Colonel Aranjo, director of the railway, and Senhor Lança, the Governor General of Mozambique. During the journey, Colonel Aranjo, himself involved in the Berne tribunal, made negative comments to Casement about a section of line laid down by a British company.[25] Afterwards, Casement submitted to the FO an annotated map of the railway, indicating features along its course, and the state of the railway remained a topic of communication between Casement and the Foreign Office for the rest of his tenure in Lourenço Marques.

The pursuit of land concessions was another matter connected with the railway and with the interest of outside parties in the territory of Lourenço Marques. A great deal of the territory of Mozambique had already been granted out in concessions, mostly in the north of the colony.[26] As hopes of major deals in the surrounding territories vanished, attention began to focus on the port and on industrial concessions in the immediate vicinity of Lourenço Marques. Some of the same players were involved – private capital, the Transvaal and Germany (the latter two themselves often camouflaged behind private financiers). Casement reported regularly on movements concerning concessions, particularly one such, the Catembe Concession, felt to be particularly sensitive because of its location adjacent to the port and railway. Britain now moved to block the Catembe Concession, making use of an agreement between Portugal and herself, ultimately dating back to the McMahon agreement of 1875, that neither would alienate land to a third party. Crown law officers argued that the granting of concessions, leases, etc. would lessen the value of territory and was, therefore, against the spirit of the earlier agreement.[27]

Production of an annual trade report was one of the more important duties of the British consul and in early 1897 Casement applied himself to writing one for the year 1896. While so doing, he wrote to Henry Foley suggesting that it was like 'trying to make bricks without straw, and evolve a future for British manufacturers with no past statistics to go upon'.[28] He submitted it to the FO at the end of March, apologizing for the delay on the grounds that statistics for the Transvaal only reached him in the middle of the month.[29]

Many of the trade-related issues discussed by Casement in despatches reappeared in his trade report. He was impressed by the professionalism of the Germans in trade matters. The sale of kerosene lamps was one example:

Here, too, Germany and the United States seem to have adapted their goods to their customers more readily than the British producer. At any rate many of the lamps employed in this part of the world come from the former country. They are made of apparently cheaper material, with lighter framework, and with burners, it is said, of stronger make than our own lamps, but none the less are of attractive appearance, give a good light and can, it is probable, be sold by the dealer at a larger profit than English-made lamps. Quite recently a local restaurant, formerly lit by wall lamps of British make, has replaced these, to the satisfaction it must be owned of all its frequenters, with shapely and brilliant hanging lamps of German origin.

A second idea running through his trade report was that it was unwise to neglect agriculture for either mining or the mere shipping of goods:

This increase in the importation of foodstuffs, which it might be thought the Transvaal itself was eminently capable of producing, was, no doubt, due to the famine caused by drought and locusts. Apart, however, from scarcity due to such causes there can be little doubt that in all this part of South-Eastern Africa an insufficient attention is paid to the soil or its capabilities of production. The gold fever would seem to drain the earth, not only of its precious metals, but of much of that necessary labour upon its surface which yields returns more vital to mankind than any to be gained from exploiting its depths ...

As if to emphasise the force of the remarks already made upon the neglect of agriculture, it may not be out of place to notice here that while such large sums can be spent by the native labourer at the mines upon clothing and South African rum, and while mealies and Kaffir corn, the chief articles of his diet, were imported from abroad in 1896 to the value of £512,987, a sum of only £1529 was expended last year by the entire Transvaal upon such necessary native agricultural implements as Kaffir picks and shovels. It is true that in Swaziland, where the native owns the soil he cultivates, ploughs are now often used on native farms.[30]

The Rights of British Subjects

Throughout his stay in Lourenço Marques, Casement was assiduous in monitoring, reporting on and intervening in cases involving the rights of British citizens. Virtually all of these cases involved discrimination or harassment connected with trade. In communications between himself and the FO, regular reference was made to the possibility that the Portuguese authorities were discriminating against British goods destined for British South Africa by imposing higher duties on them than on goods destined for the Transvaal. Individual British traders, who were exploring alternative routes to Swaziland, British Tongaland and Zululand via the Maputa/Pongola Rivers, also found barriers placed in their paths.

From the middle of 1896 onwards, Casement was more and more concerned with a number of cases of what look like clear harassment and intimidation of British citizens, all involving the courts. On 18 May he stated: 'I have hitherto refrained from drawing attention to even graver faults in a branch of the public service more vitally affecting the interests of the community, namely the administration of justice.' [31] In this instance he was referring to two cases. The case of Frank Sheppard, an English storekeeper, was one of a number, all of which had the same general characteristics. Sheppard was arrested on charges of gun-running, charges which were then changed several times. His trial was delayed and, since he lived at a great distance from Lourenço Marques, he incurred considerable losses due to absence from his business. After a delay of seven months, he was tried and acquitted. According to Casement there was no evidence against him and the judge acted impartially. But, were it not for the kindness of a friend who advanced the bail money, he would have spent the seven months in jail. There was considerable anger among foreign residents.[32]

The case of Mr McNicholas, another storekeeper, was even worse. McNicholas's main business, according to Casement, was at Komatipoort, the Transvaal border settlement on the railway line between Lourenço Marques and Pretoria, but he also had a store just across the frontier at the Portuguese border settlement of Ressano Garcia. It was here, in Portuguese territory, that the events took place. His store was attacked and ransacked and two of his employees, an Italian and an American, beaten up, one of them badly. The perpetrator, Senhor Noqueira, was not arrested. McNicholas incurred losses and received no satisfaction from the authorities. Since 'five old useless guns' had been found on his premises, he himself was arrested, tried, found guilty and given the choice of a jail sentence or a fine. He paid the fine but, intent on defending his good name, pursued the matter. Legal advocates, however, were reluctant to act for him against Portuguese officials. Casement, clearly angry at the frivolity of the charges and the general facts of the case, protested to the governor. The latter would not help. Later, McNicholas's store was 'accidentally' burned down. It was suggested that the motivation for the harassment was Noqueira's desire to acquire the store for himself.

The case illustrates the pains Casement was prepared to take where he believed a serious injustice was taking place. He reported regularly on developments in the case between May and November of 1896; his letter of 5 September was over twenty pages long and included all the preceding correspondence between McNicholas, himself and the governor. As 1896 progressed, his comments on the administration of Portuguese justice grew more negative. He raised the general question 'as to whether the Portuguese law affords protection against such acts as those complained of; or whether British settlers in this province must submit themselves not to well-defined and readily obeyed laws but to the good disposition or otherwise of practically irresponsible military commandants'.[33] When lack of confidence in the courts caused aggrieved individuals to approach him, as consul, he increasingly found that his representations to the authorities got nowhere.[34] He reported that the present governor wouldn't intervene in legal issues, unlike his predecessors, and that, since the Sheppard case, he had 'a deepening conviction' that his intervention was only making the petitioners' situations harder than before. His German and French colleagues agreed. He appealed to the Foreign Office to make representations, but FO minutes reflected a sense of helplessness.[35]

Clearly, the accumulation of such cases placed some strain on his relations with Portuguese officials. He shared his frustrations in a private letter to Henry Foley at the end of November 1896. He was sorry, he said, to be forced to kick up rows with the Portuguese, though he was 'on the best of terms with them ... It is only our official intercourse has become strained over the strange ways of the local authorities, to which I feel obliged to take exception'. This derived, he thought, from a belief that 'foreigners must be put in line'; there was an 'evil spirit', which came, he believed, from Mousinho de Albuquerque, the conqueror of the Gaza chief Gungunhana. Now the Royal Commissioner for the Province of Mozambique, he was 'suffering from swollen head of the largest type known'. Casement was tiring of his post: 'I wish to goodness you could create me a kind of Central African Consul to go up the Congo and get to Wadelai or something like that – where I should be in my element out among the natives, and every day doing something instead of being boxed up in this prison.'[36]

Native Peoples

Consuls were not directly concerned with the affairs of indigenous populations, but, given the European scramble for territory in East and Central Africa, and British concerns in the region, some discussion of such matters was to be expected in Casement's consular reports. Poultney Bigelow, an

American correspondent who visited southern Africa at this time where he met and became friendly with Casement, was impressed with his local knowledge. 'It is not saying more than the truth,' he wrote, 'when I testify that Mr Casement knew more of the natives between Basutoland and the shores of Mozambique than any other white man.'37

Casement's posting to Lourenço Marques coincided with the overthrow of the Gaza kingdom, the last great independent state in southern Africa.38 From the mid nineteenth century its capital had been in the foothills of the Chimanimani Mountains, between the Zambesi and the Limpopo rivers. In 1885 Gungunhana succeeded as chief, after the death of his father, Umzila. An intelligent man, related to Lobengula by marriage, Gungunhana set about defending his independence by a combination of military and diplomatic means. He affirmed his military dominance over neighbouring peoples while attempting to gain diplomatic recognition from both the Portuguese and the British. With rapidly increasing European penetration of the region, this was to prove difficult. Suddenly, in 1889, Gungunhana moved south with 60,000 people to a new capital, Manhlagazi, not far north of the Limpopo. Freedom for manoeuvre had become increasingly constrained in the old capital, given the presence of the concessionary Mozambican Company and the nearby British South Africa Company. Demoralization was increasing, caused in part by the widespread introduction of cheap alcohol. Finally, the Gaza economy depended more and more on the returns from migrant labourers working in the South African mines. It may have been that Gungunhana felt he could better control the flow of labour from a more southerly location.

If Gungunhana was intent on maintaining his independence, for the Portuguese the presence of a strong African kingdom was a barrier to their own control of land – much of it quickly allocated to concession hunters – and the cheap labour necessary to exploit it. The belief grew that Gaza could only be incorporated into the colony by military conquest. Meanwhile, Gungunhana sought British protection, sending emissaries to Natal and to London. While in London in 1891, the two Gaza representatives were informed that Britain could do nothing, since she accepted that Gaza territory lay within the Portuguese colony. The location of the new Gaza capital led to conflict with the Portuguese of Lourenço Marques and southern Mozambique. In 1894 there was a minor revolt by one of Gungunhana's dependents, Mahazul, close enough to Lourenço Marques to cause considerable concern to its inhabitants. When António Ennes arrived as Royal Commissioner in January 1895, he was intent on the military defeat of Gaza and began an invasion in August. This was the context into which Casement arrived in September 1895.

Casement's first despatch of significance concerned Portuguese–native relations. On 9 September he wrote to reassure London about a reported threat to the safety of Lourenço Marques due to a native rising. They should treat newspaper accounts guardedly, as 'there is no cause for anxiety here'. Though it was difficult to get reliable information, there had been, he said, a clash at Maraquin between a local chief, Nhlahla, and the Portuguese, who lost sixteen men. On 21 September he gave further details. Reports were conflicting: in the Portuguese version, two hundred natives had been killed, while, according to reports circulating among members of the foreign community in Lourenço Marques, the Portuguese had been no match for the natives. Numbers of Portuguese dead varied from five to sixteen, and a lighter had carried the wounded down the Inkomati River. It was also being said that the houses of British Indian traders had been looted by Portuguese soldiers, though no complaints had been received at the consulate.[39]

Of much greater local and international significance was the sequence of events leading to the defeat and capture of Gungunhana himself. Casement reported receiving a message from Gungunhana, via a British messenger, to the effect that Gungunhana only wanted peace with Portugal, 'but a peace confirming him in all his native rights and sovereignty which he had never, by treaty or verbal promise, surrendered to Portugal'. He would only make over his country and people to the Queen. Casement's reply, clearly reflecting Foreign Office briefing, was that Great Britain recognized the rights of Portugal and that Gungunhana's best step was a 'timely submission to the Portuguese authority'. He later received approval for this reply from the FO.[40] In what proved to be a final effort to invoke British support against mounting Portuguese pressure, Gungunhana also sent messengers to the British authorities in Natal. Casement reported their return through Lourenço Marques, which they then left by rail, 'bearing a safe conduct back to Manslagasa [Manhlagazi], Gungunhana's kraal', given at Casement's request.[41]

Six weeks later the governor called on Casement to inform him of the defeat of Gungunhana in what the Portuguese official called a 'serious engagement'. Casement in his report doubted the Transvaal newspapers' claims that the natives lost 2000 men, suggesting that Gungunhana would have only put up 'that show of resistance necessary to sustain his *prestige* among a savage people' and aimed at getting better terms by not seriously fighting. Gungunhana's whereabouts were unknown and it was said that many natives were joining the victors.[42] Four days later Casement, together with his French and German colleagues, called on Senhor Ennes 'to offer our unlimited congratulations on the victory over Gungunhana'. They were given a detailed account of the battle. The encounter had taken place seven miles from Manhlagazi, and the Portuguese square was repeatedly attacked by several thousand natives, carrying guns and spears. The attacks were beaten off, with the loss of only five dead and twenty-five wounded. The royal kraal of 700 huts was then burned. Foodstuffs had been abandoned, but Gungunhana had fled with his cattle and other valuables. Ennes thought that matters might rest thus until the next dry season.[43]

In fact, the end came rapidly. On 7 January 1896 Casement telegraphed the FO, saying: 'Gungunhana brought here a captive on 4th and publicly exhibited yesterday in town. Believe he surrendered himself. His wives and son are with him.'[44] Greater detail of Gungunhana's surrender and subsequent public humiliation were given later, in a regular despatch. He had been captured in his kraal, with 3000 men, by Captain de Albuquerque and forty-six men. He had voluntarily surrendered; his two head councillors (indunas) were shot 'then and there'. The rebellious chief, Nhlahla, had been delivered into Albuquerque's hands some days previously.

On 6 January, Gungunhana, six or seven wives, two sons and Nhlahla, with his family, were exhibited for three quarters of an hour on a wooden stand outside Government House to the populace of Lourenço Marques and to public functionaries. Consular officers had been invited, but Casement was clearly not present, since he states that 'I understand from those who were present ... that the Chief and his son Godide appeared to be overcome with shame at their exposure in this manner.' Casement had been on sick leave in Durban and only arrived back on the day of the exhibition itself. Whether he availed of this as an excuse for not attending or was genuinely unable to, one cannot tell. One can, however, sense in his language his discomfort with the treatment of the prisoners. On succeeding days, the prisoners were kept in the town jail, exposed to curious eyes, before being sent to Lisbon. This, noted Casement, was the fate of 'this last of the Zulu Chiefs of South East Africa'.

Casement felt that the surrender of Gungunhana was due as much to representations from HM Government as to the achievements of Portuguese troops. In other words, given the clear message that Britain would not intervene, conveyed earlier by himself, among others, Gungunhana had elected to the 'surrender of power and liberty rather than to plunge by resistance his people and country into a bloody war with the whiteman'.

In the aftermath of the Portuguese campaign against Gungunhana, accusations were made that Protestant missionaries had incited the rebellion and given ammunition to the natives. Two were later charged. Casement was approached by M. Junod, head of the Swiss Mission, after one of their members, Dr Liengme, was accused. Junod's reading of the whole episode was that Gungunhana never desired to fight, that the actual engagement was very small, and that there was no evidence of missionary guilt.[45] Liengme, a medical missionary, had been in Gungunhana's kraal until a few days before the entry of the Portuguese troops but, lacking guarantees of protection, he left. His house was looted and destroyed by the troops and the cartridges he had for his own gun seem to have been the basis for accusations against him. A missionary couple working in Tembe district, Mr and Mrs Loze, were also asked to leave, being 'inconvenient' to the authorities.

Casement seemed most upset at the deportation of a young Wesleyan native teacher, Robert Mashaba. 'It is probable that he, with all the natives, sympathised with Mahazuli and Mantibiane in their struggle against the injustices and tyranny of the Portuguese administration at that date.' Mashaba was accused of knowing of the planned attack and of not telling the authorities. 'Mahazuli and Mantibiane', Casement continued, 'took up arms on account of the illegal seizure and deportation of their young men for enforced military service or labour in Angola' – one of the chief causes of trouble, according to white and black alike. Robert Mashaba's punishment, Casement felt, was disproportionate to his offence, and his loss was keenly felt by the natives, 'who profited by his teaching'.[46] When asked, about this same time, whether he could confirm reports about a German Catholic missionary group (Trappists) being sent to Mozambique, Casement could not, but welcomed the possibility, arguing that 'it would seem to be an eminently desirable thing that Trappists of any nationality should settle in a district so much needing the example of good men, and of steady persistent labour for unselfish ends'.[47]

One issue relating to Portuguese–native relations threatened to spill over into Portuguese–British relations. This concerned the border between Natal and Mozambique, south of Lourenço Marques. Not long after he took up his post, Casement had a conversation with Senhor Ennes, the Portuguese Royal Commissioner, in which Ennes suggested that the real boundary between Portuguese territory and British Amatongaland, which lay in the northern portion of Natal, was twenty-five miles further south than appeared on War Office maps. He claimed that natives had intimated that they did not wish to be divided between two jurisdictions and raised the possibility of an exchange of territory. Casement wondered what lay behind the suggestion and informed the FO and the governor of Natal, Sir W. Hely-Hutchinson. The FO response was firm on the correctness of the boundary, and Casement was instructed to 'keep the Governor of Natal and Zululand informed of anything affecting the British Protectorate in Amatongaland'.[48]

Contrary to Ennes's contention, the existence of two jurisdictions was soon to prove very valuable to one Temne chief. Not long after the Portuguese issued an edict stating that they would not be held liable for the losses of traders due to disturbances, Chief Nguanasi, whose kraal was located about twenty miles south of Lourenço Marques, sent armed bands around demanding tribute (*saguati*) of traders – ten sacks of mealies each. Casement received complaints from one of the traders thus affected, Von Wissell, who was a British subject. Unfortunately for himself, Nguanasi also tried to levy tribute from Portuguese officials. Casement reported the sending of an expedition comprising an officer and thirty-five men against the chief, and his imminent capture was anticipated. But Nguanasi, whose territories lay on both sides of the border, crossed over into British Amatongaland. The result was a flurry of diplomatic despatches and a period of increased attentiveness to border sovereignty.

The Portuguese acting Governor General, Senhor Lança, sounded out Casement on the possibility of settling the matter quietly on the spot – by the British
either handing over Nguanasi or turning a blind eye to a Portuguese raid across
the border. Casement was firm; he was sure HM Government would prevent
Nguanasi from stirring up trouble across the frontier. And he suggested to the FO
that Nguanasi's actions – blackmailing and killing people and taking cattle – were
contrary to both white and native interests. Following FO instructions, Casement
kept in contact with Hely-Hutchinson, the governor of Natal, who, in turn, sent
messages to Nguanasi, instructing him not to act across the border.49

During their conversation on 7 January 1896, Senhor Lança had outlined to
Casement the Portuguese policy of breaking the power of large chiefs, who,
according to him, came into conflict 'not only with Portuguese sovereign rights,
but with the imperative demand of civilisation and humanity', as well as that of
commerce. They were to be replaced with men of lesser power, chiefs only over
their own communities, and with Portuguese Resident Magistrates.50 Since
1894 they had put down the revolt of Mahazuli and Mantibiane, overthrown
Gungunhana and his subordinate Nhlalha, and neutralized Nguanasi. However,
Casement observed that the role of the Portuguese military was not confined
to breaking the power of native leaders; the civil administration, too, was dominated by military men.51

On 9 April 1897 he reported news of a renewed outbreak of hostilities in
Gazaland, brought by fugitive Indian storekeepers who claimed that ten soldiers had been killed and the commandant taken prisoner. Thirty to fifty soldiers had been sent as reinforcements a few days previously, and one hundred
left that day. But, if the natives were determined, they could withdraw into the
interior of the area, harass and 'ultimately exhaust the efficiency of any possible Portuguese system of transport'. The trouble was between the military governor and Gambul, uncle of Gungunhana, and at its source, according to Casement, was the levy, or mode of levy, of a hut tax. He felt that the amount
collected from the hut tax would not have been excessive in itself, if properly
collected. But Portuguese control was only effective in part of the area and, as
a result, collecting was limited. Neither did they collect regularly, and in collecting more than one year's tax at a time they left the people with a sense of
grievance. Finally, the collection was done by military men and almost all expenditures were of a military nature. The justification for extra fines (*visitas*) was
questioned, since there was 'no provision ... for public works of any kind – such
as roadmaking in particular, a necessity be it said of effective occupation as of
civilising influence ... and no provision ... for an administration of justice to
determine native offences'. Only a small amount was spent on public health.52

The changing nature of political and economic life led to a considerable
amount of native migration. Some of this was to urban centres, such as
Lourenço Marques; more was to the mining areas of South Africa. In a report

on the port and railway at Lourenço Marques, transmitted on 6 March 1896, Casement commented negatively on the native labour situation:

> No control is exercised over the natives working in the town to force them to obey a contract they voluntarily may enter into, or to compel natives, as is done in Durban, to work if they come to town at all. Here, every native is a 'loafer', not only by 'right divine' but also by right of Government sanction and approval. He only works while he feels inclined, or until he has earned enough to go and get dead drunk at one of the far too numerous native canteens, which, even in the chief thoroughfare, and right in front of the Governor's official residence, lie open to him.

The government seemed indifferent to drunkenness; it continued issuing liquor licences.[53]

The abuse of alcohol was an issue Casement returned to several times. In Lourenço Marques, with an official population of 2779, eighty-two houses were listed as licensed to sell liquor (and that was an underestimate). Liquor was also available in kraals. On a Sunday walk in early August 1896, in a kraal twelve kilometres from Lourenço Marques, his native guide was able to buy a 'coarse Portuguese wine'. Both local and imported alcohol were sold, the latter from Germany (though sold as local). Casement himself found and moved a boy of fourteen, lying naked and comatose on the street, while, on another occasion, a man was left dying with his head bashed in, and only later dragged away. And writing of the revolt of Gambul, Casement noted the presence in Gazaland of 600 Indian traders, not an unmixed blessing, he says, as the 'article most in evidence there is undoubtedly alcohol, in one or other of the villainous forms it takes when intended for the African native'. So much so, that the result of the switch from Gungunhana's rule to Portuguese was that 'while bad gin has become cheap, good roofing straw has been made dear'.[54]

Life in Lourenço Marques

Apart from the range of issues dealt with by Casement as consul, day-to-day living in Lourenço Marques provided its own pleasures and frustrations. He was to experience a good deal of the latter in his first days, as he recounted to the Royal Commission on the Civil Service in 1914:

> I went out to Delagoa Bay in 1895, a young man with no knowledge of the Consular Service at all and entirely untrained. They had built a consulate there at an expense to the Office of Works and to the tax-payer here of £7000 or £8,000 – a large house. The man I was to relieve was being transferred to some other post. I received a telegram from him at Cape Town, asking me if I would buy his furniture for a fixed sum; if not, he would sell it. Well, I was a poor man. The sum he named was quite beyond my means; I could not have bought his furniture. I wired back and said: 'Will you not wait until I arrive', and I got a reply at Natal,

'Either buy now or I sell.' I wired then from Natal at a point nearer Delagoa Bay on my way: 'Regret cannot buy but beg that you will await my arrival.' I arrived at Delagoa Bay and he told me he was leaving by the steamer that had brought me. I arrived at 10 o'clock and the steamer went out at 2. He had sold every stick in the consulate. There was not a table, a chair, a pen, a bottle of ink, or a sheet of paper or a single thing. I took over a roof and bare walls. I had to sleep on the floor for three days. I had absolutely nothing with which to discharge my public functions. I had to furnish the house. I am not complaining of the absence of beds and chairs, but of the absence of public furniture for me as a public officer to discharge my public duties. He had sold everything. That occurs nearly every time that a consul is transferred, and it goes on to-day.[55]

The quality of consular offices in all of Casement's postings, beginning with Lourenço Marques, left a lot to be desired and added to the strain of the work. It reflected the haphazard organization of the Consular Service. Casement was to sum up his feelings after his return to England in 1897, when he suggested to the FO that they build a new consulate: 'The present condition of HM's Consulate in Lourenço Marques is little less than a scandal.' The most irritating problem came from iron ceiling plates, which dropped rust-damp that he described as 'metallic rain', enclosing a rust-spotted page as proof.[56]

The roof was not the only problem. Shortly after his arrival the FO asked him to investigate the possibility that, during a predecessor's tenure, a constructor had failed to put in a damp-proof course, diverting the materials for his own use. And in mid 1896, Casement suggested a thorough set of improvements instead of ad hoc repairs, which would be more expensive in the long run.[57]

The volume and range of Casement's workload is evident from the number and varied content of his despatches, and he made reference in his private correspondence to the pressures of work. Explaining, in early March 1896, to his great-uncle John the difficulty he had in keeping up with personal correspondence, he described his practice:

I have at present a mass of official matter to deal with that will keep me hard at work until the end of March; and I was looking forward to then getting on to my private letters. When one is writing from 7 am (as I am now since the 8th January) until 5.30 or 6 pm at trying reports, adding up figures – and interviewing people on business in the intervals – one has not much mind or mental activity left after dinner to write to one's friends.

I have no secretary or anyone to help me – and last year 230 British steamers & sailing ships entered this port – all making claims upon my time – while distressed British subjects asking for relief are of daily regularity. To these miserables I have advanced more than £60 since I came here (out of my pocket) [and] as the regulations on the subject are so strict my chances of recovering anything of this from the FO – if the people themselves or their friends don't pay me back – are most remote.[58]

He told Gertrude in October: 'I don't write any letters now I can help – as I'm writing, writing, writing all day and every day in my office.'[59] His work was much more onerous than that of his German and French counterparts: during his term, 268 British ships had visited the port, while a total of only fifty-seven German and French ships had called. Official correspondence had increased markedly between 1894 and 1896: from 196 to 566 (in) and from 169 to 523 (out).[60] The lack of professional staff added to the strain:

> At Delagoa Bay I could not afford a secretary or clerk. I was bottle-washer and everything else. I had to sit in an office for two years and open the door to anyone who came in. You would be insulted. You have no means of keeping yourself apart from any drunken individual who would come in. There is absolutely no staff appointed, no equipment, and no means of discharging your duties.[61]

This did not mean that the consul was completely without assistance. When negotiating with the FO on an increase in his own salary and on the appointment of his Congo friend Alfred Parminter as vice-consul, he detailed his outgoings on African staff. This included a Mauritian coloured clerk, an office messenger, a garden boy, three house boys (all Zanzibaris) and a refuse cleaner (presumably local). His Zanzibari servants cost £114 p.a., 'a fifth of my official income being thus spent in retaining the services of two boys, whose intrinsic domestic worth should be apprised rather in cowries, or other worthless form of savage currency, than in hard-earned sterling'. The cost of living was high, he pointed out, and he had had to dismiss his cook and eat in local hotels and restaurants, where the bad food undermined his health.[62]

A run of ill health beginning in November 1895, which gave rise to the leave of absence that coincided with the Jameson Raid, was followed by a more serious illness in March 1896. The FO received a telegram from Casement saying that a doctor had advised an immediate change, due to a bad fever, that he was leaving for the Cape on the morrow and that he was appointing the local English clergyman to act in his place.[63] Details followed later, including a certificate from a Royal Navy surgeon diagnosing 'extreme anaemia and debility, the result of a prolonged attack of malarial fever'. Casement told of the ill health of residents of Delagoa Bay, of the unsanitary conditions of dwellings and of the 'neglect by the authorities of the elementary duties of municipal control'. Refuse was thrown around 'by careless servants or dirty natives'; the body of a native shot by police had been left for two days in the heat; the smell was a 'continual martyrdom'.[64] On this occasion he stayed away for a month, visiting Johannesburg and Pretoria as well as the Cape. Almost a year later, in an application for leave, he explained that in his year and a half as consul he had had two fevers, one serious, as well as suffering from the dampness of the consulate.[65]

Despite his illnesses and the pressures of routine office work, Casement was not a prisoner of the consulate. On long Sunday walks he combined pleasure with information gathering.[66] Aside from the official travels already referred to, Casement made three journeys that seem to have been concerned with gathering information on activities on the Mozambique–Transvaal border. The briefest was to the south of Delagoa Bay, in June 1896, when he went on 'a brief journey up the Tembe River ... as far as the head of navigation at Tembe Drift'. Here, on the old Swaziland wagon road and twenty miles inside Portuguese territory, he found evidence of an incursion from the Transvaal – the wagon of Abel Erasmus, the 'notorious Native Commissioner of Lydenburg District', who had raided the area the previous year.[67] He made a longer trip towards the end of July, which he described as follows:

> On the 24th and 25th ultimo, while making a journey on foot up the western side of the Inkomati River from Komatipoort to the junction of the Umlomati River, and thence eastwards to the Lebombos in a line with Moveni, over a tract of possibly 20 sq. miles of open country within Transvaal territory, I found many native kraals deserted, and on inquiring the cause, was told that, to avoid the hut-taxing visits of the Lydenburg Commissioner, it was now customary for many natives to drive their cattle over into Portuguese territory at the time of year when such visits from 'Abel' ... might be expected.

Casement also reported plans in Pretoria to attempt to gain access to the sea, avoiding Portuguese control, by developing a route through Swaziland and the Umbelosi River.[68]

The final and longest excursion he undertook as consul in Laurenço Marques was in October 1896. 'I have recently completed a long journey on foot through Swaziland and a part of the Transvaal,' he wrote in a personal letter to Foley, 'which was delightful and reminded me of my tramps up in central Africa.' He mentioned the journey in a despatch to the FO, when discussing the possibility of war and of the Boers trying to capture Lourenço Marques. 'I have myself walked from near Lake Chrissie in the Transvaal across Swaziland to Lourenço Marques in five days – a distance of about 160 miles.' Boer horsemen could do it, he believed, in three days, and large numbers of men and ammunition could be sent swiftly to fortify the port.[69]

Casement had a circle of friends, too, in Laurenço Marques which included the Austrian aristocrat Count Richard Coudenhove, who had a warm regard for Casement; the two were to meet occasionally in later years and to correspond.[70] When their mutual friend, Count Gebhard von Blücher published his memoirs, long after Casement's execution, he included the following assessment of the latter by Coudenhove:

> All I can say from personal experience, and long friendship, is that I always found him sympathetic, clever, and fascinating, and that I have met very few men during my whole life who had such an exceptional personality. He possessed an absolutely genuine though somewhat exaggerated idealism: nothing whatever would stop him assisting the weaker against the stronger, because he simply could not help it.[71]

Casement talked of Blücher to Henry Foley: 'Together we called on the great Kruger ... in April last: and together we have been about a good deal in

South Africa ... He is a Blücher – a Count G. Blücher, of the Waterloo family, who often goes to Ireland to hunt, I think, and I have found him the brightest spot in my South African existence ... he is a most delightful companion and sympathetic.'[72] Two young Irish peers, Lords ffrench and Ennismore, were also numbered among Casement's friends at this time. Of the former he wrote to Foley: 'I have spent some time with ffrench (an Irish peer) out here (he is as desperate a "rebel" as any of the 59 sentenced Africaners ...).'[73] Then there was Casement's own brother, Tom, still seeking a niche in life, who seems to have arrived in South Africa from Australia about the time that Casement took up his position in Delagoa Bay. A more passing acquaintance was made with James Bryce, who passed through Delagoa Bay in October 1895; their paths were to intersect in several contexts in subsequent years.[74]

The closest friend, also one of the German-speaking community, was the trader Fritz Pincus, with whom Casement was to maintain a correspondence for the rest of his life. The warmth of the relationship is evident from Casement's later letters: 'I shall not ever forget you, or Delagoa ... dear old Dirty Delagoa. I could make you laugh if we met with stories of it ...' Again, he nostalgically expressed a wish to be back with Pincus, 'on your best sofa, looking over the lamplit table at the bookcase and drinking a glass of your wine. I'm *very* sorry in many ways when I think of you all at Lourenço Marques that I ever left it'. He wondered, 'When shall we meet again? ... to return you in some way the many kindnesses you have lavished on me and which are by far the pleasantest recollections I have of Lourenço Marques.'[75]

Casement, spending more than he earned, borrowed money from Pincus. At times, too, he stayed at Pincus's house when the latter was away.

> I am stopping over at your house still. I have allowed the Bovills to stay on at the consulate until they get a house – and I am living in your room and messing with Clark, who is a nice quiet chap. I am going off shooting in a few days until the end of the month. The weather is delightful and cool and the climate glorious. Lots of people in town, band three times a week and heaps of gaiety ... Get over to Germany and rest ... don't stay in London and get sick ... Go and get fat and strong – eat and drink like a Zulu and come back to Delagoa with the colour of apples in your cheeks.[76]

And in May 1897 he wrote saying he proposed to stay with Pincus at a rate of £25 a month, 'until I go home two months hence. I'm quite tired of the town and those restaurants ... I shall have Mr Parminter with me for some little time I expect, as a guest ...'[77]

On 5 March 1897 Casement applied for home leave from as early a date as possible after the end of June, to which the FO communicated its agreement in mid April. On 24 April he followed this up, suggesting Alfred Parminter as his substitute. Parminter 'has come to stay with me, on what I hope may be a prolonged visit', and was willing to enter the Foreign Service. He was the son of an English clergyman; thirty-one years old; wrote and spoke French fluently; had long experience of tropical Africa (the Congo) and had 'experience of men'. With an eye to easing the burden of his own work, Casement suggested making him a consular agent or vice-consul at £250. This stimulated a flurry of FO minutes; there was a worry about creating a precedent, but there was also sympathy for Casement.[78]

On 7 June he telegraphed, 'Urgent private affairs recall me immediately' and asked if Parminter was sanctioned. The FO reply came immediately: 'Leave approved. Proposed arrangement approved.'[79] There is no record of Casement's activities during his home leave. He arrived back in Lourenço Marques on 1 November, having travelled via Durban, Johannesburg and Pretoria (where he consulted with HM's Agent, Conyngham Greene). On the 2nd he asked if the FO would pay Parminter for work through the end of September, even though his own leave had ended officially on the 9th of that month. And on 3 November, just two days back, he telegraphed the FO: 'Much regret compelled to ask sick-leave of absence to have operation performed.' 'Flaringly armadillo', minuted the FO, but sanctioned the leave.[80] On 23 November Parminter telegraphed the FO with the message that 'Casement left today via Zanzibar.'[81]

He began this second extended leave by visiting friends. Herbert Ward was living at the time in Lambourn Place, Berkshire, from where, on 18 January 1898, Casement wrote to the FO informing them that he had reached England on the 6th and requesting four months' sick leave.[82] Two months' leave was granted, though Casement's sudden departure from Lourenço Marques, just days after his return there, was queried.[83] From Lambourn Place he wrote his first extant letter to Richard Morten, who was to become his closest friend in life and who provided him with warm hospitality on many occasions.[84]

In mid February Casement wrote to the FO, this time from the Wilkinson home, Baronstown House, Tara, Co. Meath, to advise on the sale of the consular buildings in Lourenço Marques and on the site for a new consulate, and also to request a further three months' leave from 6 March. In support he submitted a medical certificate from a Dr P.M. Laffan, whom he described as 'the resident medical man of this district'. Laffan's certificate stated that 'Mr Roger Casement is suffering from the effects of recent malarial fever, neurasthenia, haemorrhage and weak circulation.' He advised prolongation of leave and strongly opposed a return to a malarial area.[85]

Casement wrote from Baronstown House on 12 March to thank the FO for the extension to his leave.[86] In early March he wrote again to Richard Morten: 'Did you read Lord Roberts' speech? Exactly my argument re. the N.W. Frontier – and almost word for word in places ... only we're both Irish old Bob and I.' He added, 'The cold is killing here.' He told Morten that he had got his leave extended and didn't expect to be in England until Easter, when he would go to Salisbury. 'I'm very busy writing – and rather enjoying Dublin ... How are you getting on with Gibbon? There are some fine second-hand book shops here – with old students' books from Trinity.'[87]

In mid March he travelled north, visiting old friends. On the 16th he wrote to Gertrude from Lisdoron, Ballymena, Co. Antrim, which he gave as his address until the end of May. Ballymena was, of course, the location of his old school, of a branch of the Casement family, and of family friends and relations. Lisdoron was the home of one of these friends, Mrs Young. At the end of March he wrote to the FO, advising on the topic of concessions in Portuguese Africa. He was negative about the influence of Royal Commissioner Albuquerque in Mozambique, believing it to be prejudicial to British interests. On Lourenço Marques in general, he wrote:

> What that port needs above all else is honest and simple administration in the interests of its trading community; and this, were the needs of the inhabitants generally, and not the wants of a few only of their number, the first care of the authorities, could be speedily brought about without extraordinary powers, Royal Decrees ... by attention on the part of each official to his own duty, and a strict enforcement by the executive that this should not be exceeded in behalf of any man, or fallen short of in behalf of any other.[88]

On 27 May he again wrote from Lisdoron, requesting a further two months' leave. His health, he claimed, was now 'almost restored', but 'urgent private affairs' and 'other and pressing causes' made an extension of his stay at home desirable. The leave was granted.[89] On the same day he wrote to Richard Morten to say that he would probably go to England in early July ('it is still Erin go Bragh!'). He had, too, he continued, heard a lovely piece of music some evenings previously, called 'Trois Moments Musicaux' by Moskowski, and he hoped Morten would get it.[90]

Subsequent communications with the FO came from Ballycastle (June) and London (July). Discussions in July concerned a reorganization of the consular system in Mozambique, from which it would appear that Casement was intended to return there at the end of his period of leave. But on 29 July the FO informed him of the appointment of A. Carnegie Ross as consul at Lourenço Marques. The decision to redeploy Casement must have been taken around this time.[91] In July, too, Casement made representations on behalf of his friend from Lourenço Marques, Count Blücher. Writing to Francis Bertie at the FO, he said he wished to draw his attention, as his 'official chief' to the planned project of the Mossamedes Company in Portuguese S.W. Africa. Count Gebhard Blücher 'who is trying to work the scheme here' had British sympathies and resided often in Britain. There would be British money and control and Blücher could 'disarm Portuguese distrust'. Casement knew him well 'both in Lourenço Marques and the Transvaal, where his sympathies were always on the British side ... I formed there a high opinion of his abilities and integrity.' He believed in Blücher and his plan. Bertie forwarded the letter to Lord Selborne,

Undersecretary at the Colonial Office, asking if anything could be done for Blücher 'the concession hunter'.[92]

On 5 September, from Ballycastle, he wrote excitedly to Gertrude: 'Only this morning the Irish papers have the news of the capture of Omdurman and the Khalife's defeat ... I've been cheering all thro' breakfast over the Soudan news ...' And, annoyed that the Belfast papers, preoccupied with the North Down election, had been late in reporting the news, he blurted: 'Belfast is really I think a very stupid ill-bred town.'[93]

5: *St Paul de Loanda, 1898–9*

His leave over, Casement set sail for Africa to take up his new appointment. He had already begun his journey to St Paul de Loanda, in the Portuguese colony of Angola, when he received his formal appointment. He left England on 5 November and he acknowledged his appointment from Las Palmas, in the Canaries, on the 12th. The appointment was a triple one – to Angola, to the Independent State of the Congo and to the Gaboon.[1] On the voyage out he recorded composing 'The Dream of the Celt': 'Begun 5.30 am on SS *Accra* Nov. 10th 1898 on way to Grand Canary going to St Paul de Loanda'.[2] Another poem, 'The Nameless One', was written on 29–30 November 'outside Lagos Bar on the *Gretchen Bolen*'.[3]

He broke his journey to Loanda in the Congo. Having arrived in Boma on 13 December, he called on the acting Governor General, Félix Fuchs, who returned his call the next day.[4] On the 16th he crossed to Matadi, where he called on the French vice-consul, St Ange. He reported to the FO, from private sources of information, that French officers and men had recently gone by rail from Matadi for the Bahr-al-Ghazal in the Upper Nile region, carrying ammunition including shells for quick-firing guns and a consignment of valuable presents for native chiefs. Two related sets of circumstances lay behind this report. One was the opening of the railway between Matadi and Leopoldville. Casement, as we have seen, had been involved in the land survey undertaken prior to the construction of the railway. The opening of the railway, which bypassed the unnavigable cataract region of the Lower Congo, shifted colonial attentions firmly to the Upper River. The second set of circumstances concerned the little settlement of Fashoda, far away on the Upper Nile. Anglo-French tensions over Egypt had simmered for some years and led to French resolve to send an expedition to the Upper Nile. One was despatched from West Africa in 1896, led by Captain Jean-Baptiste Marchand; it eventually reached Fashoda on 10 July 1898, and Marchand claimed the settlement for France. The small French party, threatened by the Dervishes, held on until confronted by General Kitchener, fresh from the victory of Omdurman on 2 September. Kitchener and Marchand faced one another in Fashoda on 17 September; when news of events arrived in Europe, tensions increased almost to the point of war. Finally, the French government backed down and decided that Marchand should withdraw.

Casement's appointment followed hard on these events. The opening of the Matadi–Leopoldville railway meant that a new path to the Upper Nile and the Great Lakes area was now available, one that was likely to be used by all interested parties. From Britain's point of view France was the player to be most carefully watched, but King Leopold, too, had considerable ambitions for the Upper Nile area. The monitoring of movements through the Lower Congo would clearly be among the responsibilities of any British official in the area.

As he passed on his journey, Casement noted improvements in Boma and Matadi from his earlier days there. Boma had become the state capital and from here construction had begun on the Mayumbe railway, to tap timber and ground-nut resources. Matadi had become 'quite a town' and lay 'upon the rocky slope of the river shore where only a few years ago stretched a pitiless waste of bare sunburnt rock showing but scant traces of vegetation and none of humanity'. The improvised town had a population of 2500 to 3000 persons, including a large number of British subjects (from Lagos, the Gold Coast and Sierra Leone). He noted houses built of pieces of iron, old lids, provision cases, grass and cast-off apparel; the haphazard building, overcrowding and poor sanitation had contributed to the outbreak of smallpox and many deaths.[5]

In Boma, too, he learned that the vice-consul there, Mr Underwood, wished to stand down. Both the FO and Casement recognized the need for a vice-consul, given the numbers in the Congo of 'British native subjects' from West Africa, but there was no one to replace Underwood.[6] On 21 December Casement telegraphed the FO to say that he had arrived in Loanda and had taken over the archives. He informed them that Arthur Nightingale in Loanda would accept the vice-consular position at Boma if permanently appointed.[7]

From Loanda he wrote to Fritz Pincus in Lourenço Marques on 9 January 1899, saying that he liked the town. 'I am here three weeks tomorrow. It is a city of sleep after Lourenço Marques – not even of dreams. Commercially it is dead – but I hope it may be resurrected and I mean to try. The country is a good one, with possibilities that don't exist even at Lourenço Marques.' And he enquired about people he knew: 'Do you hear anything of my brother Tom? I can never get word of him – or of Lord ffrench – or any old friends ...' He added, too: 'I hope to be up the Congo as far as the Upper Nile this year.'[8] In another letter he reported that the cost of living in Loanda was lower than in Lorenço Marques. 'We have of course a lot more Portuguese here. This is solely a Portuguese town – there must be 2000 of them at least – probably more – and a lot of *Degradados* – convicts, mostly murderers ... I have rather a pretty little house here. Beautifully situated with fine views and a lessening number of mosquitoes. They were bad at first, but they are going now.'9

On 29 January he walked six miles to Kakuako, around Langosta Point, bought some sole and sent them to four young Englishmen at the Cable Station at Loanda. On the same day, having watched some young Portuguese naval sailors hauling nets on the sand, he wrote a poem entitled 'Youth', which he signed on 4 February: 'His heart was ever tutor to his hand. R.C.'10

He was all the time thinking of the Congo. On 15 January, in one of his despatches to the FO, he proposed a journey to the Upper River, during the dry season from May to October. He hoped to reach Stanley Falls, visiting Bolobo on the way and the Lulongo River, if possible. He added:

> This river and its chief feeder, the Malinga, I visited in 1887 when it had not yet been explored and it would be of interest to compare the recollections of that time when the banks still stretched for hundreds of miles the haunts of remote tribes of cannibals with the evidence of governmental and missionary improvement that a ten years' subjection to both influences should today afford.
>
> The Balolo tribe is one of the most interesting of Central Africa. The name Balolo implies the Iron People – not by reason of their hardihood of temperature [*sic*, temperament?], for the Balolo are among the gentlest and least offensive of the Congo population, but from the skill this people has displayed in the manufacture of iron weapons and instruments of agriculture. The Balolo country has, or had up to the period of my visit in 1887, provided the greater number of the slaves used in the neighbouring territories and the raiding canoes of the populous native towns at the mouth of the Lulongo were constantly returning to the lower reaches of the river with a full human freight.

The first government posts had been established in 1889 and were followed by the suppression of the slave trade. He was interested, then, in observing the changes over a ten-year period, 'in a district I knew when sunk in its own profound native misery brought about, be it observed, mainly by the natural instinct of the African savage to enslave principally for his own domestic uses his fellow savage and not as is so often assumed chiefly with an eye to a profitable export trade in him'.11

Casement had first expressed this wish to go to the Upper Congo to Henry Foley, when he was still in Lourenço Marques. During 1899 he repeated the wish a total of eight times – to the FO in this and later despatches and, in his private correspondence, to Fritz Pincus and to his cousin, Roger. The FO refused permission, as they had just authorized a British officer, Major Pulteney, to travel and make enquiries for them in the region and it was felt that the two men 'should not be roaming up and down the river at once'.12 News of a revolt among native soldiers on the Upper Congo led Casement to pass on the opinion of George Grenfell, given in a letter, that the execution of Charles Stokes had had a profoundly negative effect on the natives, as it convinced them that Europeans didn't respect their own kind. Charles Stokes, a British (Irish-born) trader, was arrested in the Congo State and immediately executed in January 1894 for, allegedly, trading in guns on the eastern frontiers of the State. The case caused a furore in Britain, contributing to the growing sense that arbitrary terror was widespread in the Congo State.[13]

In mid February Casement left Loanda for the first of two routine one-month visits northward to Boma in the Lower Congo. He telegraphed on the 17th to say he was on his way to Boma, and on 23 March announced his arrival back. He repeated the process from mid May to mid June. From these visits came a number of despatches, in which we see the beginning of Casement's systematic criticisms of the Congo State. Since his first period in the Congo, the State's activities had become a cause of deep concern to humanitarians, as reports of the ill-treatment of its inhabitants had begun to increase in number. Indeed, concern over them by the Foreign Office may well have been the major factor in their decision to move Casement from Lourenço Marques to Loanda.

The Congo Atrocities

During Casement's first period in the Congo, from 1884 to 1891, King Leopold's interests there were still widely believed to be humanitarian. In addition to the general 'civilizing' mission which he claimed to be undertaking, he masked his real intentions behind the mantle of engaging in a campaign against Arab slavery to the east of the Congo. In November 1889 he convened an Anti-Slavery Conference in Brussels, and in May 1890 he announced the launch of an anti-slavery crusade. In reality, his goal was to establish control over the Congo Basin and to install the infrastructure necessary to exploit the resources of the area. In order to do so he completely overturned two of the key dimensions of the Berlin Act, those guaranteeing free trade in the Congo Basin and the protection of the rights of the indigenous population.[14]

But, bringing the Congo to a point where it made a profit for its new sovereign required a heavy investment, in this case from an individual and not a colonizing country. While Leopold had borrowed substantial moneys from the Belgian government for his Congo project, the administration of the Free State was independent from that of Belgium. It had its own ministries in Brussels with subordinate structures in its Congolese capital of Boma, all tightly controlled directly by Leopold himself. The wealth of the area was in the Upper Congo; to exploit it, the caravan road past the cataract region had had to be built, a fleet of steamers placed on the Upper Congo and a series of stations constructed. Leopold had expended a large portion of his personal fortune on the enterprise and needed to see a return. In the first years he spent £80,000 per annum; this later rose to £120,000. Income was only a tenth of that; Leopold was forced to borrow. Using the cover of paying for his anti-slavery campaign, one of his first moves to recoup money was the introduction of a 10 per cent tax on all imports to the Free State – a clear breach of the agreed free-trade principle. The agreement of other countries was reluctantly given and a new General Act was signed in Brussels in July 1890.[15]

Leopold was fortunate that circumstances provided his saviour – a rapid increase in the demand and price for rubber on the world market, a product to be found in abundance in the forests of the Congo Basin. The demand stemmed from the development of the pneumatic bicycle tyre in the 1890s, from the increase in the industrial uses of rubber for hoses, tubes, washers and for wiring insulation, and, soon afterwards, for expanding automobile production.[16] The focus in the Congo shifted from ivory to rubber. Production soared: from 250 tons in 1892 to 1200 in 1896 and to 1500 in 1897. So did profits, which reached 700 per cent. The Congo Free State became the most profitable colony in Africa.[17]

Widescale abuses, which became apparent in the 1890s, were linked to Leopold's need to generate income. Anxious to make his colony pay as soon as possible, he had put in place, largely in secret, a series of administrative mechanisms needed for the task. From the time of the Berlin Conference, all land not in immediate cultivation by Africans was deemed to be 'vacant land', to be disposed of by the State. In decrees of September 1886 and June 1887 the State spelled out its control not only of land but of forests and minerals. Elephant hunting without state licence was prohibited in June 1889; the object of this was to monopolize the ivory trade. The exploitation of rubber was nationalized in October of the same year.[18] In January 1887 land rights granted to the Compagnie du Congo pour le Commerce et l'Industrie foreshadowed the arrangements made later with concession companies. Gradually, independent trading companies were squeezed out and the exploitation of the Congo's resources confined to enterprises either directly under the king's control or, as with the concession companies, in which he had a substantial holding. Further restrictions on free trade came in 1892, with the establishment of the Domaine Privé, an area reserved for direct state exploitation, from which private companies and traders were excluded. In 1892 two key concession companies came into being, the Ango-Belgian India Rubber Company (ABIR) and the Société Congolaise-Anversoise. To these was added a large territory under the direct control of the king himself, the Domaine de la Couronne. Virtually all the land of the State was parcelled out by the beginning of the twentieth century.[19]

The exploitation of land and resources, including rubber, was not realistic without the control of local labour and Leopold took the steps necessary to compel the Congolese to provide the labour for the colony. A labour-contract system was introduced in 1888, with a maximum service period of seven years.

In theory, cases of ill-treatment could be appealed to the courts but, in practice, this option was not available to Africans. In the 1880s, the State's main preoccupation was with the Lower Congo and the establishment and maintenance of overland links with Stanley Pool and the Upper Congo. As the volumes of cargo increased, the pressure on the local population intensified. In 1888 the Force Publique, an armed force of native troops under the command of European officers, was established. The Force Publique, whose soldiers generally served in areas distant from those of their birth, was to become a major weapon in a campaign of terror directed at the native population, especially in areas of rubber exploitation in the Upper Congo. The ordinary Congolese provided all the labour to maintain the colonial system: this included provision of foodstuffs; provision of commercial commodities, such as rubber and gum-copal; provision of labour – for building housing, piers, cutting firewood for steamers, cutting and maintaining paths, for paddling canoes, and (in the case of women) for service at white posts. Force was an integral part of the system and included the standard placement of 'forest guards' or sentries in native villages, armed punitive expeditions, the keeping of women and children as hostages to ensure the work compliance of husbands, the confiscation of canoes and other objects of value (e.g. brass rods/money), fines on villages, flogging and imprisonment, shootings and beatings, and the cutting-off of hands and other mutilations.

The elements of the repressive regime to which the native inhabitants of the Congo were subjected, then, were: denial of ownership of the land and of products of the soil; taxation in labour or in kind, with minimal regulation and collected by any means chosen; punishments enforced at the whim of State or concession functionaries, with protection by the State for such personnel; the payment of bonuses to functionaries for the amount of produce collected, which provided an incentive to maximum exploitation. In the 1890s the flow of atrocity stories began to reach the ears of European and American audiences; they told of hostage-taking, of floggings, of bodily mutilations – including the cutting-off of hands – of the destruction of native villages, and of indiscriminate killings.

At first the concern of the Foreign Office in London was with abuses against British subjects, mostly workers from West African colonies such as Sierra Leone. Gradually, reports of atrocities against the Congolese themselves became more pervasive. Among the first to draw attention to cases of ill-treatment was Edward Bannister, Casement's uncle by marriage, who had been appointed vice-consul for the Congo in 1892. He became convinced that British subjects from West Africa were being cruelly treated and, as a result of his representations, the Colonial Office laid down stricter terms for their recruitment to work in the Congo.[20] In 1894 and 1895 came the Stokes affair, with its attendant publicity. British missionaries, though, were cautious and, while some made private complaints to their parent bodies at home, they refrained from publicly criticizing the State. However, in late 1895, an American Baptist, J.B.

Murphy, gave a graphic description in an interview with Reuters of mutilations caused during the collection of rubber. The story received publicity in the English papers, causing a stir.[21] Before he died in 1894, Casement's friend Major Parminter had criticized the regime; in 1896 the major's nephew, Alfred, also gave an interview to Reuters, criticizing the brutality of the system.[22] The FO, too, was getting reports directly from its own consular officials. Vice-Consul Leonard Arthur indicted an official whose path he and Casement had crossed previously. He wrote:

> I have also ascertained, from a purely private source of information, that Captain Francqui was in the habit of sending out small parties of troops under a non-commissioned officer to the villages and neighbourhoods for the purpose of demanding ivory and rubber. If these articles were not forthcoming, he would dispatch another armed party to attack the natives. On the return of the party the non-commissioned officer in charge would report that so many natives had been killed. This, however, would not satisfy Captain Francqui, who demanded proofs in the form of human hands that the number stated had been killed, and the armed party would again be sent out for this purpose, returning in due course with the right hands of the natives who had been killed, and having seized whatever ivory and india-rubber that could be found in the village.[23]

Stung by the mounting criticism, Leopold reacted by setting up a Commission for the Protection of the Natives in September 1896, consisting of three Catholic and three Protestant missionaries (including George Grenfell and William Bentley). With its members, however, stationed far apart and not given any transport or administrative support, the Commission remained a paper reform. The atrocity stories continued. A Swedish missionary, the Revd E.V. Sjöblom, made a public statement for the Aborigines Protection Society in May 1897, while Fox Bourne of that society published an account left by Edward Glave during his journey through the Congo in 1893. And in April 1897 Charles Dilke MP, an active member of the Society, raised the matter in Parliament, calling for a new conference of the Powers who had met in Berlin in 1884–5.[24]

Casement's Congo Despatches, 1899

In his despatches on the Congo in 1899, Casement began to address aspects of its system of administration. He reported on trade in the Congo, on State transport policy, on the proposed new consulate, on the affairs of British subjects, on massacres in the Upper Congo and on his projected journey to the Upper River.

Some of his thoughts he communicated in a *Report on Congo River, Rail and Road Traffic*, which he built around two transport tickets, submitted with the report.[25] One of the tickets is a one-franc state charge on the American Baptist Missionary Union for the short rail journey from Matadi to Mpalabala. He drew attention to the significant rise in costs, recalling his earlier days in the Congo, before the railway, when the state charge for transporting a load from Matadi to Lukungu was one franc. Such charges had brought in substantial government income, but the carriers and employers got little in return, as 'the bridges over the streams and the tracks travelled were both of the rudimentary native kinds and were in general in existence long before the coming of the Congo State'. The State, 'in the fury of its desire to be first in the rich field of spoil, placed difficulty after difficulty in the way of the free recruitment of porters by kindred but more legitimate trading associations'. His argument continued:

> When executive hostility, and direct intimidation by its officials in the cataract region still failed to deprive these bodies of the confidence of their native clients, the Government invented both the *peage sur les routes* and the *tax sur le portage* under pretext of assisting by their exactions the trading firms and missions in the engagement of porters and the transport of goods to Stanley Pool.

The charges were actually designed to control carriers and the freedom of movement, and he quoted what he called a remark of 'unreflecting frankness' once made to this effect by Captain van Doop, then commissaire of the Cataract District. Such arbitrary measures, introduced in 1890–3, had been defended as being justified by 'State needs', which was equated with the 'public good'. He wryly commented that State needs were, firstly, the acquisition of fresh territory on the Upper Nile and, secondly, 'a trading monopoly in the richest part of the Upper Congo', in evidence of which he instanced the output figure of 10,200,000 francs from the Domaine Privé in that year's budget: 'The illegalities on the Lower Congo in the years 1890 and 1891, at the inception of the scheme, were but the faint counterpart, I fear, of the atrocities its development to life on the Upper Congo called into being.'

The atrocities he was referring to were recent killings at Lake Mantumba and at Coquilhatville – well authenticated, not by 'malevolent missionaries and dismissed employees of the State', as Stanley had asserted, but by 'straightforward' and 'very simple-minded' English missionaries, who had been witnesses to them.

In an appendix to the report he analysed the balance sheet of the Société Anonyme Belge for the year 1897, commenting that he knew the society from its birth and had followed its fortunes until the death of its director, Major W.G. Parminter, who died in Nice early in 1894. The SAB had initially tried to fight State competition, but only prospered when it threw in its lot with the State. Another despatch on transport, this time on the Boma–Mayumba railway, followed on 10 April, in which he summarized the concessions granted the railway company in a convention agreed between it and the government in Brussels on 21 September 1898.[26]

Casement devoted much attention during 1899 to defending the rights of British subjects in the Congo. This reflected the priorities of the Foreign Office and was consistent with the duties of consul. One case in particular occupied him through most of the year. On 16 March, while visiting Matadi, ten 'British colonial natives' from West Africa approached him with their story. Seventeen of them had gone to the Kasai on a two-year contract. During that period, one of their number, Cobla Ayenso, had been bludgeoned to death in a canoe by a M. Bloemen, in the presence of the others. The rest were then dismissed, without pay or food, and sent back to Stanley Pool. In considerable straits, ten of them succeeded in reaching Matadi, on foot, and there sought justice. Casement immediately made representations to the local authorities on their behalf; their case was sympathetically received and compensation agreed. Since Casement had to leave early next morning, he sent two letters to Major Emile Wangarmée, vice-governor of the State, outlining the details of the case and enquiring about the investigation of the charge of murder against Bloemen.[27]

By 25 April, when he reported again, Bloemen had still not been brought to justice, though it was now five months since the murder had taken place. There was a note of suspicion in Casement's despatch about Major Wangermée's assurances:

> the fact remains that these wretched men were harshly dismissed from their employment under the eyes of one State official, that they spent several days at Stanley Pool in a destitute condition within the knowledge of another; that all along the route to Matadi they passed many State posts in charge of white men, and at Tumba, when half-way on their weary journey, they were under the eyes of a Commissaire-General himself; and that, finally, they had been ten days at Matadi, within the knowledge of all the officials there, and yet no one of the numerous agents of the protecting authority had moved a finger on the men's behalf until their case was taken up by one of Her Majesty's Consular officers.[28]

When Casement again questioned Major Wangermée in September, there had been no further progress in the case. Finally, on 9 October, shortly before his own departure on leave, he reported that he had received a letter from Wangarmée, informing him that Bloemen was to be tried for murder.[29]

Trade Report for Angola

On 1 September 1899 Casement submitted his trade report for Angola for 1897–8.[30] The following month he mentioned the report to Dick Morten: 'Look out for my Trade Report on Angola which ought to be public property in November ... if you see any comment in the *Morning Post* (it gave me a very nice review in '97 on Delagoa Bay report) send them to me. As a Trade Report I felt it to be a dead failure as I wrote it – for I don't know enough about the commerce of Angola yet to point the British merchant out his narrow path of profit. I, therefore, went into [the] more general question of West African trade – the India Rubber in particular and tried to make the subject interesting ...'[31]

Focusing in the report on the potential for economic development in Angola, Casement argued for the need for European investment: 'Without capital ... nothing can be done in Angola. The individual seeker of work, whose chief object is the bare means of existence, will find here no market for his muscles or means of earning his daily bread. The foreign labourer could only hope to come in the train of the foreign capitalist, and so far but little capital has been tempted into this part of Africa.' Despite its riches, the country had had little European influence and '[f]ar the greater extent of the country remains in the hands of its tribal possessors, subject to the rule of their native chiefs, and adopting only the rudest methods of extracting from the soil the bare necessaries of life'. Estimating the total value of goods traded as worth £5 million, Casement commented:

> The produce representing this sum, it should be borne in mind, is practically the outcome of waste land, and such time as its native gatherers care to spare from the more engrossing occupations of mutual slaughter, drinking bouts, and interminable witchcraft 'palavers', varied with the frequent hunt and sale of human beings, or the more leisured chase of wild animals. The vast majority of the people of this continent ... cultivate the ground only for their own immediate needs. All else the earth gives them for little labour beyond that involved in gathering it; and yet this is worth £5,000,000 to the white races of the earth. It should not be forgotten, moreover, that where a native gathers 1s. worth of, say, india rubber, he wastes probably 2s. worth, and where he gathers for one day he sleeps for two and loafs for four.

European influence had not been all that it might be. The major form of labour recruitment had been for plantation work on the islands of São Tomé and Principe, where forced labour was employed. Casement's assessment of the consequences of forced labour was oblique:

> From this it comes that most of them who work in the service of white men are engaged under a system not altogether of their own choosing, leaving them but few chances of carrying to their homes the lessons of obedience learned during their term of service. From the years 1887–96 inclusive it is stated officially that 22,140 contracted *servicaes* left the ports of Angola for the two Portuguese islands of San Thomé and Principé to work on the plantations there. The same document shows that during 1897 1,919 labourers (1063 males and 856 females) were so sent to those places. It is not stated how many of these *servicaes*, whose contracted term of labour is for five years, returned to Angola.[32]

If Europeans could have encouraged native dedication to labour, they could also have established a system of education. This hadn't happened either. One European influence directly undermined the ability to labour: the trade in alcohol. Far from being an inducement to labour, this trade 'on the contrary ends by killing all worthy desire, and in rendering those subject to its influence incapable of either sustained work or sudden effort'. Casement then painted the sad picture of the contrast between the West Coast Kruboys, the steadiest of West African workers, who spurned alcohol while on terms of service, and the Cabindas, once regarded as the Kruboys of the south-west coast, but now demoralized by alcohol.

The Cabindas, as a tribe, have retrograded since 1874, not only in physical characteristics, but morally, and above all in actual numbers. A visit to Cabinda and a week's sojourn there would convince any unprejudiced observer that the deterioration is due very largely to drink.

These views were not, he claimed, those of 'temperance reformers', but were held by those very traders involved in the liquor trade itself, who recognized that the natives would be better traders without the alcohol.

European influence could also be brought to bear on the plague of sleeping sickness devastating the region: 'This fearful malady is responsible for the deaths of more people than any other of the many ills to which African flesh is heir.'

The disease exists in its most virulent form in the district traversed by the Congo railway to Stanley Pool, and in some parts of that country it has proved so fatal that the dwindling survivors of quite recently flourishing villages have themselves assured the writer that their country is a 'land of death'. Old and young, men, women, and children seem equally liable to attack, and when once attacked by sleeping sickness, ultimate recovery is unknown.

Casement suggested that the newly-established School of Tropical Medicine in Liverpool 'should find in a study of sleeping sickness a work of as great importance to the future of Africa as in anything that malarial fevers may offer to special research'. Should a remedy not be found, 'entire districts of South-West Africa will be either stripped of their present inhabitants or kept in a perpetual state of under-population'.33

In the course of analysing trade figures for Loanda itself, Casement devoted several pages to a systematic treatment of the growth of German trade in Angola. What emerges is that Britain, which began from a position of being 'paramount', was faced by stiff German competition. While Britain still maintained a greater percentage of trade with Angola, Casement suggested that this dominance could be misleading: a significant proportion of British imports was made up of coal, used for British men-of-war, while, of the rest, a large percentage was in traditionally dominant British textiles. In other products, Germany had taken over. Complacency seemed to be the problem:

The truth of the matter lies in the fact, so far as facts can be adduced from observation or general conclusions, that the individual German is a better trader than the individual Englishman. He may not make as good wares – although many think he does – but he knows better how to sell them. Where the British trader with unconcern waives aside a small market as a thing to be attended to later on when more worth his while, the German quietly sets about understanding the specially small needs of that market and the best way of meeting them; and in the end he will no doubt make it a bigger one, and the result profitable to himself. So, too, in satisfying his customers the German supplier will take more pains to be agreeable and, strange as it may sound, he will more cheerfully adapt himself to and overcome certain difficulties before which the Englishman with his uncompromising humour will recoil.

For Casement, these developments raised the role of British consuls with regard to the promotion of British trade and, specifically, the production of trade reports.

> British Consular Officers have been resident in Loanda since early in 1840; and trade reports have been issued by them for the last 25 years. Germany had only this year appointed a Consul to Angola, and, so far, I am not aware that any official German account of the trade of the province has ever been published.

Despite this, British trade had declined and German expanded. For Casement, it was not enough to circulate consuls with trade brochures: 'The local consumer will not be caught either by persuasive Consuls or circulars. He wants something more; he wants to see and finger, and first try to sell the new thing offered him before he buys it.' A more concrete presence was needed: visits from experts to determine the needs of the trade; visits from salesmen (in 1892, Consul Brock had reported the visits of five commercial travellers to Loanda – all German); and samples of the goods themselves.34

Looking Beyond Loanda

In a letter to Fritz Pincus in April, Casement commented on his Congo responsibilities. 'I have just returned from the Congo where I had to go on business (consular) early last month. It was terribly hot there ... I shall soon be off again up the coast on another tour of inspection and then later on my celebrated Congo journey must be pulled off altho' I doubt greatly that I shall reach the Nile. That is *entre nous*.'35 Early the following month he again wrote to Pincus, reporting that he was going on another trip to the Congo, from 10 to 20 June, on the gunboat *Rambler*. He also hoped to pull off his 'long journey in that part of the world'.36

Casement became increasingly disenchanted with Loanda and with Africa generally. After his second trip to the Congo, the strain was evident. He wrote to Dick Morten: 'I am just back from 6 weeks in the Congo and north of this. Beastly hole! I've had about enough of Africa. I got fever there – and chiggers in my feet and am lame.'37 In another letter to Morten he observed: 'I shall be glad this time to leave Africa – it seems to me one can have quite enough of a good thing – and I can now say "Enough" to the Dark Continent ... I have a new Vice-Consul here – Major Pulteney, who was in Uganda for some years ... We shall probably all meet at the Paris Exhibition next year. If I can afford it I mean to go home to that Entertainment.'38

Later in the year he went further:

> I've come to the conclusion that I'd like to conclude Africa – I'm sick of the place – it isn't the Early Paradise I once felt it – or rather I'm no longer the bird

of that Paradise. I've grown old and grey – and now I want peace and music – and nice people round me – and old friends – and not any more truculent savages – and dirty bad servants – and worse food – and no single civilised distraction in life. I shall try for some nice healthy post when I get home from this ... and shake the dust and chiggers of Africa off my feet for ever I hope – save perhaps an occasional winter in Egypt or somewhere up there.39

In September he wrote for the first time to his cousin Roger in Magherintemple. Roger, eldest son of Casement's great-uncle John, had gone to Canada in 1886; in 1899 he came home as his father weakened.40 He received a long letter from Loanda:

... I hope to get away from this early in December – but before getting home on leave I shall probably be forced to visit the Congo; and that may mean a long journey into the interior.

One year here without change is enough – and on 19 December I complete a year in this city of Sleep. On the 1st September I was 35! Still quite a boy you see – although I distinctly remember once, in talk with you alluding to 'old men of 40'. That was when I was 27 or thereabouts; you grimly chuckled – and said 'wait Mr David till you're 40, and see if you think it old'. As a matter of fact I intend celebrating my first childhood in my 40th year – and beginning a second youth from that date. Only this will have to be in a happier climate than that of West Africa. Between ourselves Africa after so many years of it is enough – and a feast – and provided England settles the Transvaal, and I settle the Congo state before the end of next year – I'm going to move the kindly powers of the FO to settle me somewhere else.

Speaking of a birthday telegram from his brother Tom, he continued:

Its coming from Durban instead of Johannesburg looks bad – as if the exodus from that place had really been general. Tom would certainly not have thrown up his work & quitted Johannesburg unless compelled to – so I am thinking (here in my City of Sleep, a month behind the world) that things must have marched ahead (or backwards, as you look at it) in S. Africa since the date of my last newspaper 16th August – just 40 days old!

I want you, please, to try and get me two books, if you are in touch with Belfast or any old Dublin bookstalls. They are Hills' *MacDonnells of Antrim* – and a *complete* edition of the 'Four Masters' (*not* the latter an Irish or Celtic text – *that* wd be too much for my limited reading, but a complete edition in the *sacsanach* (that's a fine word!) rendering). Perhaps Rose Young would take pity on me and help you to find where such a book is. The one at Magherintemple is only a part of the Annals I fancy – and I want the whole thing ... Your copy (Jack's) at Churchfield – I fear I rather ill used in taking away to South Africa in '95 – however, I brought it back and a little paste would repair the ravages of a Delagoan climate.

Referring to the healthy appetites of other family members, he continued:

Fish is our main diet here – that with bread, sweet potatoes & Bananas. Fowls (of course!) and goat. Cattle we had which gave Beef early in the year, but since the Rinderpest swept our herds the residuum gives old boots. I have become a terrible house bird the last few months – and hardly ever go out – but write, read and 'think long' as the old folk say up your way. It isn't good for one so I welcome the prospect of change – and ructions in the Congo State – or anywhere else.

He went on to refer to the new county councils in Ireland, asking if Roger was a county councillor and poking gentle fun at a local Antrim man he had discussed the matter with when last at home. He continued:

It is 'though – joking aside – a very interesting Experiment in Irish history – and I hope will do much in the future for the people. It's like the Hut Tax in Sierra Leone – calculated to bring home a sense of individual responsibility which in the end must tell for good. There we see the African savage being brought to individual participation in the public affairs of his country and despite all the turmoil and uproar that has been made over the Hut Tax I am sure – from my knowledge of Africa – that Col. Cardew and Mr Chamberlain are right – and that the tax is one will in the end prove a blessing not merely in the increase of revenue – but in the necessity of work, for one thing, it will create – and in the sense of ownership in the thing paid for, and, therefore, of responsibility for what goes on under that roof – it will induce in the native mind.[41]

The tensions in South Africa began to dominate his letters in the latter part of the year. Anglo-Boer relations had deteriorated since Casement had left Lourenço Marques. In the aftermath of the Jameson Raid, Sir Alfred Milner had been appointed high commissioner by Chamberlain as a firmer administrative hand representing the British government. But the Transvaal would not be cajoled and the *Uitlanders* were still denied the franchise. Milner, who believed in federation for South Africa, supported the *Uitlanders* as an element likely to help bring that about. In an attempt to find a negotiated settlement, a conference was called in Bloemfontein in May 1899. Before it was held, the *Uitlanders* collected over 21,000 signatures calling for British intervention. Milner and Kruger, the latter supported by J.C. Smuts, met but failed to reach agreement on the franchise question. War seemed closer. On 8 September a cabinet meeting in London ordered that 10,000 troops be sent to South Africa. Troops already in South Africa were sent to the Transvaal border in Natal. Kruger issued an order on 10 October demanding their withdrawal. When the ultimatum was ignored, Transvaal commandos crossed the border on 12 October and war began.

Casement watched these developments carefully. In July he expressed his thoughts at length to Dick Morten:

We shall have to send about 60,000 to South Africa, and good men at that, and more than men even, we shall have to make quite sure we've got a leader who can use them. 60,000 men not well led won't keep South Africa British – but less than that number might entirely suffice if we had a proper General. The Boers – if war comes, as to me seems very likely – will play the old game of good positions *chez eux* and leave us to attack these well-chosen and ably-defended sites. If our generals don't know what they are going to do then that will spell disaster, and I'm sorry to say, my dear D., with all my admiration for *your* race (the English) they seem in their history to have persistently shown a remarkable aptitude at the start of every crisis, of not knowing what they were going to do, or what they quite wanted. To me the South African question is in a nutshell. It is *either* Boer or Briton. It can't be both. There isn't room for a divided rule; one or other must be Boss. Now the Uitlander question is not so much getting the franchise for a certain large number of our own folk whom we think – rightly – ought to have it, as a final showing *who* is Master in South Africa. If we fail to get the rights (and I use the word advisedly) of the Uitlanders extorted from or granted by the Boers, then you may rest assured South Africa will recognise, if England doesn't, that the power of Yea and Nay lies at Pretoria and not in London, or Cape Town. The end of that would inevitably be that South Africa would as a whole turn to Pretoria more and more, and to the strongmen sitting there who know their own minds and their right strength – and that British paramountcy in South Africa would become as idle a phrase as the integrity of China or the policy of the 'open door' – to say nothing of Taliemoan!

I believe Chamberlain and Milner both know what they want and the way to get it, but I doubt greatly if England at large is prepared to back them up to the bitter end, for that very possibility will mean war – a war not against the Transvaal so much, I fear, as against the Dutch in South Africa.

And his solution?

... we have the ships, the men and the money, and the grievance, and I say have it out once and for all with the Boers and South Africa generally. Send Kruger an ultimatum, and if he doesn't come to straightforward terms, then make him. That means war, of course, and it's better that than give up South Africa to Kruger, or let things drift – the latter a fairly damnable way of going to hell, much in vogue with British Ministers.

He ended on a lighter note: 'Dear Dick, please shut me up – go to your bath, if I won't go to mine. I'm very dirty – in pyjamas – waiting for the sun to rise, funking the cold shower bath.' He would like to be at the Savoy, with its lawn, strawberries and tennis. 'I've got a dog named "Rags", a bobtailed English sheepdog – but he is dying poor old thing.' Rags, like his master, had got fever at Banana.[42]

Writing around the same time to Pincus, he referred to the possibility of war. 'It is not, of course, the franchise that is at issue between us: it is the whole position of the Transvaal in South Africa and its studied belittlement of its duties to England. Those claims of England it will have to recognise – sooner or later – and I hope peacefully.'[43]

On the day war commenced, but before he had got the news, Casement was writing to Morten: 'I fear it's war with old Kruger – ain't it? It looks mighty like it – and I suppose it *has* to be – but I'm sorry it cannot be settled otherwise.'[44] He was clearly immersed in the issue and it would seem that the leave he had planned to take in Europe he now decided to spend in South Africa. At any rate the FO telegraphed on 17 October, granting him permission to travel to South Africa on a man-of-war for two months leave.[45] He left five days later.

6: *The Boer War: Special Commissioner, 1899–1900*

Casement left Loanda for Cape Town on 22 October 1899 and went on from there to Durban, arriving on 19 November. From Durban he travelled to the front in Natal, where for two weeks he experienced the war at close quarters. His fortnight in Natal coincided with the lowest point in British fortunes during the war. After hostilities had opened, the Boers attacked and surrounded Mafeking and Kimberley in the west and Ladysmith in the east. All three were desperately defended and early British efforts were aimed at their relief. In the third week of December – 'Black Week' as it came to be dubbed in England – these efforts ended in disaster, with defeats at Stormberg (10 December), Magersfontein (11 December) and, in the attempt to relieve Ladysmith, at Colenso (15 December). As a result of these defeats, Generals Wolseley and Buller were superseded by Roberts, as commander-in-chief, and Kitchener, as his chief of staff. Casement was in Natal at the time of General Buller's defeat at Colenso. It is probably this event which his sister, Nina, was to recall years later: 'He told me: "I saw one of our Irish regiments, just before a disastrous battle, kneeling reverently, each man, and receiving the Holy Sacrament from the Catholic chaplain. It made a very deep impression upon me, for", as he said, "not one man survived that terrible day".'[1]

He talked of his visit to Natal and of the war in a letter to Henry Foley, written on his return to Cape Town on 25 December:

> I have returned from nearly a fortnight with the Naval Brigade in Natal up at the front. I left Frere just before the advance to Chievely for the unhappy attack on the Tugela. It struck me then Buller could not possibly succeed in a frontal attack on the Boer position.

In a postscript to the same letter, he added:

I greatly fear Buller will not be able to relieve Ladysmith. I have in my heart looked on it as lost since he shot his bolt at Colenso and failed. If so, we must strengthen our hearts, and meet the Boer in his own way.

He was very conscious of the size of the theatre of war and of the advantage the Boers had in familiar territory. South Africa, he pointed out, was 'big enough to swallow up ten Army Corps'.

The area of the war field here is as large as Central Europe – and our utmost strength in men, I take it, would be, say, 200,000 men. I verily believe that if the Boers can keep the field in food and war material for a certain time – say six months longer – they will succeed in baffling the direct offensive attacks of this or even a larger force. The nature of the country is entirely in his favour – which it is as surely against both our tactics, our troops (infantry) and our means of communication.

The British, therefore, should concentrate on cutting off Boer food and other supplies and on harassing communications, which would be 'better than any such terribly purchased victories as those of Belmont, Enslin and Modder River'. The question of supplies brought Casement to discuss Lourenço Marques, a major Boer access route. Thirty tons of foodstuffs were passing through Lourenço Marques every day. He summarized possible courses of action the British might take with regard to Lourenço Marques: diplomacy, which was not very promising; seizing the port, which would 'raise an awful flare-up in Europe' and was, therefore, unlikely to be tried; using money to 'buy over Boer operators', thereby, presumably, undermining their operations; finally, blowing up the railway line in Transvaal territory.

He suggested that 'in this crisis we should remember we are being fought by an enemy entirely unscrupulous in such things, who leaves no stone unturned to achieve his objects', such as destroying private property and forcing British subjects to fight at risk of court martial or ruin. He was not, he assured Foley, grumbling at the soldiers, 'but we are opposed by an enemy cleverer than ourselves in the game of war as played in South Africa', and 'money will often win what bullets won't for us'. At this point he put forward a scheme that was to preoccupy him for the rest of his involvement in the war:

I have already suggested out here (at Government House) that we should try to raid, through British territory and Swaziland, the Delagoa Bay line to Pretoria in Transvaal territory. Were we to cut that and blow up two of the bridges (those over the Komati and Kaap Rivers) we should effectively smash the Boer Commissariat through Lourenço Marques.

Even if the military authorities wouldn't do it, it could be done by what he termed 'adventurous men'.[2]

Special Mission: Lourenço Marques

In the meantime, Casement's role was being addressed in a series of telegrams between the Colonial Office in London and the high commissioner's office in Cape Town. On 20 December a telegram from Chamberlain, the colonial secretary, to Milner, the high commissioner, read:

> It being deemed essential that there should be full investigation of continued reports of contraband of various kinds passing through D[elagoa]B[ay] to the Transvaal, the Portuguese Government has been informed that Her Majesty's Government propose to send Casement, formerly Consul at DB, who is now at Durban, to inquire, with the friendly assistance of the Portuguese authorities, and arrive at the truth. The Portuguese Government has been invited to give authorities at DB confidential instructions to facilitate Casement's task. He will be instructed as early as possible by telegraph. His mission need not be official, and will not be announced.3

On the 22nd, Milner informed Chamberlain that a Mr S. Evans was also being sent to Delagoa to investigate smuggling: 'Casement should also be useful, working separately, but must be well supplied with money to do anything.'4 On the 24th, the Colonial Office forwarded detailed instructions for Casement's mission:

> Please communicate following Confidential instructions from Lord Salisbury to M. R. Casement:
>
> Her Majesty's Government hear that recruits and munitions of war reach the enemy through Delagoa Bay under incorrect descriptions, or perhaps through Limpopo River, Inhambane, or Kosi Bay. Her Majesty's Government wish you to go as soon as possible to Lourenço Marques, as Special Commissioner, to investigate and report to them ... You should treat your stay as due to a desire to revisit your former post at Lourenço Marques, and you should act throughout in secret concert with Mr Ross and with Commanders of Her Majesty's ships. Open co-operation should be avoided as far as possible.
>
> Ascertain independently – 1. What munitions of war. 2. How many and what kinds of recruits and military adventurers. 3. What amounts of ordinary food-stuffs have passed since the commencement of war, and still pass, to the enemy's territory. 4. Whether there is greater transit of food-stuffs than in normal times. As regards 2, you should endeavour to ascertain nationality; to what arm of the service they belong; and whether they bring arms on shore and uniforms in baggage. Munitions of war includes articles which presumably will be used to facilitate directly the prosecution of hostilities. Such are food-stuffs especially designed for the use of troops, components of explosives, equipment, transport, oxen, mules, &c., railway and bridging material, barbed wire.
>
> You should observe whether the search by Portuguese authorities for munitions of war is thorough, or whether there has been bribery to avoid it. Orders have been received by Portuguese officials to permit no munitions of war to pass to the enemy. On your arrival at Lourenço Marques you should communicate these instructions to Mr Ross for his confidential information. Telegraph home any other points for enquiry which you may think of.5

In his letter of 25 December to Foley, Casement mentioned that he had seen Milner that day and received the Foreign Office telegram; he was glad of the chance to be useful. On the same day, a Colonial Office telegram instructed him to send his telegrams from Lourenço Marques in Consul Ross's name and series, with his own signature in cypher: 'Spend what is requisite to obtain information. Draw for your travelling expenses and inform me what subsistence allowance you require.' On the 26th Milner confirmed to the CO that Casement had seen his instructions and would start as soon as possible. On the 29th the CO telegraphed to warn Casement about the chief of custom house, Senhor Everard, said to be pro-Boer and anti-English; and also the governor's secretary Cabreal, 'who is suspected of endeavouring to facilitate the passage of military supplies in league with Cohen'.[6] Casement left Cape Town that day and arrived in Lourenço Marques on 8 January.

In a telegram dated 1 February he stated that there was no proof that war munitions had passed through Lourenço Marques to the Transvaal since the outbreak of war. Smuggling probably existed, due to the laxity of Portuguese customs supervision. Military adventurers had also passed through Lourenço Marques – they came and went as ordinary travellers. He realized quickly that he could do little in Lourenço Marques and concluded: 'My continued stay in Lourenço Marques will not I fear materially assist HMG. While I say one thing to local authorities my acts contradict the confidence I express.'[7]

He later explained his experience in detail in a letter to the FO from HMS Racoon as he travelled back from Lourenço Marques at the beginning of March. He had found his hands tied because, on the one hand, he was a 'Special Commissioner whose duty it was to work in secret harmony with the Portuguese', while, on the other hand, he was publicly known as an official returning to visit 'his former post on a pleasure trip (which no one believed)'. If he were active in seeking out the weak points in Portuguese administration, he could be said to be contradicting his words of trust. He had found it difficult to act either openly or secretly. Upon his arrival in Lourenço Marques, his letter continued, he immediately got in touch 'with two of the oldest resident merchants in the community – men in whom I had every confidence, and whose judgment, common sense, and means to arrive at just conclusions' about the affairs of the Customs and Railway Departments he trusted. He offered large rewards – in one instance £500 'for such evidences as might lead to the detection of munitions of war for the Transvaal being smuggled through the port'. Despite getting daily reports, however, he had learned nothing, and locals doubted the stories circulating of large-scale smuggling. He considered trying to bribe Senhor Albero, Director of Rail, known to be strongly pro-Boer, believing him 'not averse to being bribed by both parties', but 'Your Lordship's view upon this point did not accord with mine' and, therefore, this was not pursued.[8] Coming quickly to believe that neither he nor Consul Ross could do more, and seeing no advantage in continuing present strategies, he made two suggestions: the reorganization of rail and custom administration to bring them under British control; or 'a more able intelligence department than any Mr Ross or I could organise should be at once established at Lourenço Marques'.

Milner had cabled Chamberlain on 17 February, saying that 'the question of Delagoa Bay causes me increasing anxiety' and suggesting that the Boers would increase their efforts at smuggling:

> ... and the latest reports from the Consul [Ross] show that he has not confidence in the efficiency of present measures to prevent this. His efforts have drawn forth an angry letter from the Governor-General and I must express my conviction that the Consul, though very active and zealous, has neither the tact nor the status to cope with the present situation.

He went on to state that Lord Roberts had recommended the appointment of one man of ability 'to control all questions on Delagoa Bay'. On 6 March the Colonial Office informed Milner that 'it has been decided to appoint Captain Crowe R.N. to be Consul General at Delagoa Bay with superintendence over all other British Consular officers in Portuguese East Africa'.9

Casement meanwhile had been pondering his scheme for blowing up the railway. On 5 February he telegraphed the FO:

> My conviction is that best course for HMG's Govt. to ensure stoppage of German route and contraband of war for the Transvaal is for the military authorities at Natal to send expedition through British territory and Swaziland to seize and to hold or else destroy Netherlands railway. I am prepared to give personal assistance and to bring several useful helpers from Lourenço Marques.10

He repeated the message on 24 February: 'I have scheme I am sure would succeed effectually if my plan is strictly carried through. May I proceed to Cape Town to lay details before the proper Authorities? ... As at present engaged here I am little use ...' To which the FO minute commented, perhaps wearily: 'He might just as well be at Cape Town? Tell him he may go.'11

From the SS *Norham Castle* on 5 March he told the FO of reports of attempts being made at Pretoria, 'through a Transvaal detective of Irish birth, to seduce the prisoners of war there belonging to Irish regiments to go to the front with the Boer army'. He believed the story to be true:

> They tally with frequent allusions to 'downtrodden Ireland' which appeared from time to time in the *Standard and Digger News* in connection with the so-called 'Irish Brigade' with General Joubert's forces – a runlet of Johannesburg tapsters and cornerboys, swelled by driblets of Continental ruffianism.

He went on to refer to the

> methods of those in power at Pretoria to leave no weapon untried, whether commandeering or cajolery to induce men loyal to their Queen to be false to their allegiance – to be false to themselves, and to dishonour their oaths on

behalf of a cause which claims to be, above all else, the soul of simple loyalty to a high ideal of truth and independence.[12]

In the light of his later activities in trying to organize an Irish Brigade in Germany, one imagines that Casement would have come to deeply regret penning these words.

Cape Town and Kosi Bay

From the time he arrived back in Cape Town in March until he finally left South Africa in July, Casement's attention continued to focus on his scheme to sabotage the Delagoa Bay Railway. He gave a complete overview in a long letter dated 5 July, addressed to Lord Salisbury and written just before he returned home:

> On 31 March I drew up at Cape Town a memorandum embodying my views, and the means I suggested to their attainment, which was despatched to Lord Kitchener. In April I gathered that, in consequence of representations originating with Your Lordship, steps were being taken, under the direct orders of Lord Roberts, to put into execution the project against Komatipoort, practically as I had proposed.[13]

Casement's memorandum suggested sending a force of 500 mounted men to Komatipoort either through Zululand or, if feasible, from Kosi Bay through Swaziland. He was exultant when he wrote to Henry Foley on 24 April:

> The military people have – at last! – taken up the proposal about the D.B. Railway. If that thing had been done in December – as it easily could have been – we should long ere this have had complete control of the line – and should have been able effectually to block the Boers from the sea. Now Sir A. Milner tells me it is being seriously taken up, and he has asked me to stay on to advise when the matter comes up for discussion and preparation ... I hope the military people may ask me to go with the Expedition.[14]

In his letter to the FO of 5 July, he related how the matter had been approved in early May and had Milner's support. His version is supported and supplemented by that given in Lord Milner's published papers:

> Mr Casement, Consul-General at Lourenço Marques, had reported that it was possible to destroy the line by a raid on the Transvaal side. Buller had opposed the project, but on April 6, HM Government instructed Sir Alfred to consider the question 'most seriously' with Roberts. Prolonged consultations were held by the High Commissioner with the Commander-in-Chief, General Forestier-Walker, Colonel Trotter, Chief Staff Officer, Admiral Harris, Mr Casement, and Mr David Forbes, Jun., who had suggested this step so far back as January.[15]

On 25 May Casement had been informed that plans were complete. Where he had outlined two alternative routes to Komatipoort, both would now be used. The Canadian Strathcona's Horse, 540 strong, under Lieut. Col. Steele, would divide into two groups. The larger, numbering 340 men and the heavier equipment, would travel the longer route overland from Eshowe through Zululand. A smaller party, with light equipment, would be landed at Kosi Bay, moving rapidly through Swaziland, to take and hold Komatipoort until the arrival of the main party. Steele was to command the Kosi Bay party and Casement would accompany it. Both parties set out and Casement's reached Kosi Bay on 2 June, accompanied by Rear Admiral Harris.

From this point on everything went wrong. When landing arrangements were underway, word came through that a concentration of Boer forces seemed to be taking place at Komatipoort. After consultation, Steele decided that it would be unwise, under these circumstances, for the smaller party to proceed to Komatipoort. They would return to Durban, join with the larger group at Eshowe and proceed as a single body. This they did, though Casement dissented, judging that it would have been better for the Kosi Bay party to remain and reconnoitre the area while awaiting the arrival of the larger force.

Casement's group arrived in Durban on 4 June to find that the larger party was only at the Tugela River, not Eshowe, and that its officers had been ordered to Pietermaritzburg, where Steele was also immediately ordered to go. Casement telegraphed the high commissioner in Cape Town twice, urging that, if the project was to continue, Steele must go to Eshowe at once. Orders to this effect were given and the Kosi Bay group left Durban on Friday, arriving at the Tugela on 9 June. The united force proceeded to Eshowe and were preparing to move north on the 13th when they were ordered from Pietermaritzburg to return to Durban, whence Strathcona's Horse joined General Buller's forces.

Casement shared his reflections on all of this with Lord Salisbury in his letter of 5 July. First of all, he argued, the surprise element and the overall impact of the action would have been greater if it had been carried out when first proposed, when there were few Boers at Komatipoort. Secondly, he attributed the arrival of Boers to their withdrawal from areas further west, following reverses, rather than to any intelligence about the expedition; even with their presence, he judged the task possible. Thirdly, 'if worth doing at all it was worth doing well, and the fact that it was not well done should be attributed to others than those who made the recent abortive attempt'.[16] Clearly, Casement had invested a lot of his ego in the scheme and he felt he had been denied his moment of glory. It would seem from the available evidence that, despite the support from London, Milner and Roberts, the scheme was undermined by General Buller, who used his authority in Natal to recall the expedition. Casement hinted at this in his letter, saying that 'it should never have been interfered with at the very moment when plans ... were being pushed into actions'.[17]

The delay from March until the expedition actually left at the end of May Casement had found wearying and he told Henry Foley that he had been on the point of going home three times; he had actually almost embarked twice. While he waited in Cape Town, he wrote poems dealing with the war situation. 'The Fingo stand at Mafeking' was written in May and shows sympathy with a marginalized group of Africans, the Fingo people; a note in one of his poetry collections identifies the occasion: 'Written on news of killing of the Fingoes [sic] at Mafeking'. Some Fingos had been armed by the British in Mafeking and had helped in the defence, but, on one occasion, some starving members of the group were executed and others flogged for stealing food.

They say ye went to rob a kraal – The men who still would keep you thrall,
Who see no good in black at all
Except to brand the slave.[18]

He thought, too, of the Boers and wrote 'Briton to Boer', which was published in the *South African News* on 26 May. It began:

Come brother, come: this was not of our seeking,
We each have stood from each too far apart,
And listening each to hostile prompter's speaking
Neither hath heard the beating of his heart.
Peace – be at peace: they were an earlier race
Who held it only noble to shed blood:
Man hath a higher calling in his face
Than aught he oweth to that old-time mood.[19]

While Casement was still in Lourenço Marques in February, the fortunes of war shifted and British forces began to have important successes. At the end of February, just as he returned to Cape Town from Lourenço Marques, Ladysmith was relieved. He wrote to Pincus on 5 March from Durban: 'The rejoicings here over Ladysmith were tremendous. I went out with the Governor and a party to the *Terrible* on Saturday night and stayed over yesterday. We had a good time. Durban has been quite *en fete*.' He also referred to the surrender of Cronje and asked that Pincus get him copies of the *Standard & Diggers News*: 'I want to see how the "J'burg Liar" gets out of Cronje and Ladysmith.'[20]

During his period of enforced leisure in Cape Town before the Kosi Bay episode, further letters to Pincus followed. On 21 March he wondered when they would meet again, so that he could 'return you in some way the many kindnesses you have lavished on me – and which are by far the pleasantest recollections I have of L.M.'.[21] He wrote again on 18 May to say that he was waiting for the relief of Mafeking. 'My brother', he told him, 'is off fighting in the Free State with his squadron of Irish Horse.' The end of the war was inevitable, he felt. The Boers should look to 'the kind heart of the British people':

... they could not be spared the ideal of their 'independence'. That must go in the republican form they have built it – but they will not lose their true or individual independence. I am sorry to think of their being killed in defence of a principle that at root is wrong – for their 'independence' implies the subjection of others. They are fighting not for freedom but for intolerance.[22]

During this time Casement was also receiving news from the Congo. He told Foley: 'I get terrible private letters from the Congo of the continued violence and barbarities practised by the Congo State soldiery. I believe they are true; and when I get back to that part of the world I mean to put in some time on the Upper Congo.'[23] On 30 April he wrote to Sir Martin Gosselin about affairs there, referring to German press reports calling for an International Conference to deal with Belgian brutalities. He hoped that 'it may be found possible to join Germany or any other Power interested in putting an end to the veritable reign of terror which exists on the Congo, so far as the natives of that unhappy region are concerned'.[24]

One source of his information about abuses was, he said, an unnamed missionary friend, nineteen years in the Congo, a moderate man and universally respected. The specific abuses concerned the rape and attempted rape of women, in one case mission evangelists, and the imprisonment and ill-treatment of their husbands or relatives. The perpetrators in each of the incidents were native State soldiers. Punishment of these individuals would not suffice, argued Casement, the evil lay deeper:

> The vast majority of the native soldiers and police are absolute savages but recently withdrawn from the most barbarous surroundings, to be placed in positions often of untrammelled authority over large and populous districts. Their white officers can exercise only a slight supervision over them, and I fear I must add that in nine cases out of ten their white officers, by temperament as by official tendency, are indisposed to trouble themselves in anything that does not make for profitable returns of native produce from their districts. I will say nothing of the cases, I fear still far too numerous, where the white officials themselves directly instigate, and even direct outrages upon the native surroundings, in pursuance of their paramount duty of 'tax gatherers'.

Casement had also received a letter from a 'high official of the Congo Government', who was leading a large expedition engaged in laying a telegraph line from Lake Tanganyika to Stanley Falls. This man had been part of the campaign, in the same territory, to break the power of the Arab slave traders. Now he had come to reflect on the changes brought about. The Arabs, 'a superior race', had done far more good than they were given credit for, though the only physical signs of their occupation now were the profusion of fruits growing – mangoes, oranges, guavas, lemons, limes, pomegranates and onions. But, though the Arabs had now been defeated, slavery still existed and he could buy as many 'women, men and children as I might care for'. Casement's informant continued: 'For the native I believe the change has been for the worse, as they certainly haven't the same respect for a dirty native chief as they had for the powerful Arab, always clean, and even the worst of them with the manners of gentlemen.'[25]

Casement's conclusion from this was that he feared 'the barbarism they claimed to be suppressing was by their success only the more firmly, but perhaps to the Belgian-Congo exchequer more lucratively, established. Where ivory and slaves formerly swelled the trade income of Zanzibar, they were now diverted to the markets of the Middle and Lower Congo':

> The root of the evil, to my mind, lies in the fact that the Congo Government is first of all a trading concern – that everything else is subordinated to the lust of gain – and that, only when its claims in this respect are attended to, does it become an instrument of reform. If a European Conference could indeed put an end to the State in its trading capacity, curtail its military expenditure, and bring about effective supervision of the present methods of 'tax collecting', the boon would be not less grateful to hundreds of thousands of central Africans than beneficial to the true and lasting interests of the Congo Government itself.
>
> I have written you a long letter, but I know that you are interested in the welfare of our native subjects residing there. The simplest way to secure their well being is, perhaps, to strive for that of all natives of the Congo. It is difficult to obtain a special recognition of and favourable treatment for one class of black men, when the whole practice of executive obligations towards natives is so wilfully wrong as it is upon the Congo today.

After Casement had written to Salisbury on 5 July to explain the affair of the railway bridge, he had no further role in South Africa and he must have sailed for home immediately afterwards.

Disenchantment with British Rule in Africa, 1900–9[26]

While he was in South Africa during the Boer War, Casement's loyalties were decidedly on the side of the Crown. In the years that followed he became increasingly disaffected with the Empire, and one of the causes of his disaffection was British conduct in South Africa. He became perturbed by a number of matters, significantly the treatment of Boer prisoners in the later phases of the war, the use of Chinese indentured labour, and the rapacity of the mine owners. In addition, it seems likely that the more personal cases of the treatment of his brother Tom, and of his close friend Fritz Pincus, added to his growing disenchantment. Later, he was further outraged by events in Natal and Egypt.

After their initial successes, the Boers were soon unable to match their opponents in open military encounters; the war took on the character of a guerrilla campaign and became increasingly nasty. To counteract the fast-moving Boer commandos, British forces had recourse to the destruction of crops and farms, the forced movement of women, children and the elderly into 'concentration camps', and the ringing of the countryside with miles of barbed wire and blockhouses. Opposition to these methods grew in Britain, especially when disease and death spread rapidly in the camps. These events seem to have affected

Casement also, though the transition can only be dimly traced and there is a danger that his later recollections were coloured by his changing loyalties.

A change of attitude is not yet reflected in his letter to Henry Foley of 3 August 1900, when he wrote:

> I may only hope the surrendered Boers will be treated as prisoners-of-war, i.e. deported – and not as men on parole whose oaths of neutrality will secure them restoration to their farms. That acceptance of oaths, and permission to return *chez eux* will, to my mind, if persisted in, simply mean an indefinite prolongation of hostilities of sorts long after definite resistance has broken down – and entailing now far more loss of life to us than commensurate political gain in South Africa.[27]

In his 'Brief to Counsel' in 1916, he reflected back to his South Africa days, saying:

> I arrived home in July of 1900 and I was then becoming a pro-Boer as a result of what I had seen in South Africa. I went home to Ballycastle and this visit and the lessons of the Transvaal brought my thoughts back to Ireland for, though always a strong Nationalist, I had lost interest when Mr Parnell died and had come to look on myself as an African until my stay in the Cape.[28]

And, writing to Alice Stopford Green in 1907, Casement expressed regret at his political position during the Boer War, but also hinted at why his attitude had begun to change:

> I had accepted Imperialism – British rule was to be extended at *all* costs, because it was the best for everyone under the sun, and those who opposed that extension ought rightly to be 'smashed' ... Well the War gave me qualms at the end – the concentration camps bigger ones – and finally when up in those lonely Congo forests where I found Leopold I found also myself – the incorrigible Irishman![29]

The rising doubts in his mind about the colonial world of South Africa can be detected much earlier than this, in his letters to Fritz Pincus. The treatment of Pincus himself was a factor. As a German based in Lourenço Marques, attempting to make his living by trading into South Africa, Pincus fell under the suspicion of the British authorities in the latter stages of the war, perhaps in the light of German support for the Boer cause. Inevitably, he turned to Casement for help. Back in England in September of 1900, Casement expressed his pain at the accusations of Pincus's anti-Britishness and promised to write to the FO if the matter developed. It did, and in June of 1901, now in the Congo, Casement sent a flurry of supporting letters to all his influential acquaintances. In addition to an official letter to the FO, he wrote personally to Lord Lansdowne[30], to William Tyrrell[31], to Henry Foley, to Milner in South Africa, and to Reuters.

He knew Pincus better than anyone else, he claimed to the FO, having been close to him since his very first days in Lourenço Marques in 1895. 'I do not give my friendship by halves, and I make his case my own. As Mr Pincus is found guilty or innocent so shall I hold myself to have failed in or done my duty.' To Tyrrell he suggested that Pincus was the victim of

> some trading competitor at Lourenço Marques who had the ear of the military – or else of the stupidity of these latter – who many of them are incapable of distinguishing friend from foe – honest man from rogue. But I am aware of the enormous areas of littleness in some military minds. I had occasion more than once during my stay in South Africa to rub against the barbed wire fencing of these tenantless wastes.

He had no intention of letting 'the poor bald-headed, Wagner-loving, fiddle-playing Pincus' be buried by them.[32]

Casement's letters to Pincus between 1901 and 1904 articulate a mounting critique of British rule in South Africa:

> That country wants less Milner I fancy and more white workingmen. I'm not a believer in the Chinese scheme – I fancy the natives could be got allright if there was any real desire to recruit and pay them properly. The crux of the difficulty out there is, to my thinking, the over-influence of the rich mine magnates. Those individuals control the Government in their individual interests – and the country is less independent and much less prosperous than under the benighted (!) rule of Kruger.
>   I should bring in a Millionaire-cum-British-Officer-Exclusion Bill and I think you would find South Africa would right itself – but what between greedy capitalists, always hungering for more, and brainless noodles of ultra-English 'society' officials, you have been having a pretty severe visitation. I saw enough during the war to convince me that the average British officer official of the Milner type of young man would dish any country under the Sun.[33]

Later, the affairs of his brother Tom, who had been living in South Africa for some years, might also have had some bearing on Casement's growing disaffection with South Africa under British rule. Tom wrote in January 1904 to say that he had lost a job because of the jealousy of his boss. At the end of the same year, in December, he wrote to say that he had been refused leave with pay, and complained that Milner had pushed someone else's case: 'They are far more corrupt than ever poor old Kruger could be.' The cover comment to this, in Casement's hand, is 'Milnerism at work'.[34]

The 'Chinese scheme' was much more significant. The South African mines were soon restored to working order after the war, but, despite an arrangement with Portugal allowing native migration from Mozambique, a labour shortage developed by 1903. In desperation, Milner approved a scheme for the importation of indentured Chinese labour. In the words of one historian:

> This brought the required results, for productivity immediately improved, but it turned out to be a political bombshell. Attacked by the Liberal party in England as a new form of slavery, it was instrumental in causing the fall of the Unionist Government in 1906.[35]

The Liberal opposition denounced the scheme, Campbell-Bannerman calling it 'the biggest scheme of human dumping since the Middle Passage was adopted'. Conditions of life for the Chinese workers were degrading: 'They were confined in compounds for three years without their families, forbidden to take skilled work, prevented from mixing with the rest of the population, and subject to harsh punishment if they tried to escape.' In the course of time it also became known that Lord Milner had approved flogging as a disciplinary measure. And the sexual behaviour of the men – wives had not been allowed to accompany husbands and even visits to local prostitutes were not allowed – had led to the issue of 'sodomy' becoming an element in the controversy.36

Casement was opposed to the use of Chinese indentured labour. In an incomplete letter to Dick Morten, written at the very beginning of 1905, he discussed it in the wider context of the relationship between labour and the circulation of money:

> Your argument seems to me to be this: that the character of the labour or the product *in kind* of the toil doesn't signify very much – the thing is that men are employed, earn wages, and money circulates. The rich man is simply the medium of circulation and all his money goes back, at once, into the crowd.

With this last point he agreed, but went on to suggest that 'very much does depend on the character of the work and the nature of the output'.

> If the labour be unhealthy, demoralising and only possible in a compromising environment the character of the labourer and therefore of the nation to which he belongs is deteriorated. Second, if the product of his labour be in itself undesirable, although he earns wages by his work, he is not contributing by the output of that work to the sum of human happiness – but to the contrary.

In illustration of this latter point he adduced the production of drink in Ireland, equal to the value of nearly all the tillage product, but producing 'no healthy gain at all'. He illustrated the deficiencies of the productive system with the historical examples of Roman slave society, Spanish exploitation of South American gold through Carib slave labour, and Leopold's exploitation of rubber by Bantu slave labour. Suggesting that there were lessons in all of this for Britain in India and South Africa, he turned to the Chinese labour question. The case against it rested, he argued, on moral and economic grounds:

> As to the moral aspect – no man who has travelled but knows that Chinamen hold views on sexual intercourse not in favour in Europe since the days of Greece and Rome. They come from their country without their women-folk – and they are enclosed in compounds for three years. It is not difficult to imagine that, with such men, with such natures, the results are not entirely healthy and charming to contemplate.37

Another series of events, beginning in 1906, contributed to the change in Casement's attitudes. The introduction of a poll tax in 1905 on unmarried Zulu adult males had increased tensions between the black population of Natal and their white rulers. After some disturbances and murders in early 1906, martial law was introduced. When the Colonial Office in London tried to intervene to modify the severity of punishments, there was a storm of protest in white South Africa, and the Natal government resigned. London backed down. The Zulu revolt, led by a minor chief named Bambata, was crushed and at least 3000 shot down for the loss of a few dozen whites.[38] Casement was outraged. His first comment was to Gertrude:

I think the Natal business an abominable cowardly butchery – and deliberately provoked too. They wanted the natives to 'rebel' in order to have a little 'healthy blood-letting' – followed later by ample confiscation of native land and compensation for the poor panic-struck 'Loyalists'. God's wrath upon all 'Loyalists' – the brand is always the same.[39]

To Edmond Morel, the following month, he wrote: 'We see already in Natal, the same devilish theories at work and how they have already cost a pyramid of human bodies and a tale of murder and pillage that the British name will not get rid of for some time.' Word of the flogging of a native pastor 'for offering up prayers of a seditious character' led him to suggest that the Natal colonists had eclipsed Leopold and, with regard to British rule, that 'the Tables of its Law are kept at the money changer's office – which is also its Temple'. But he added an immediate qualification: 'While I say these things of the British public – I think the British Government is about the most high-minded and earnest on Earth and if anyone is going to bring the Leopold devil to account, it will be that Government.'[40] He felt he could have had a role to play himself: 'Why, if I had been in Natal instead of McCallum I could have saved all that hideous massacre there.' And to Alice Stopford Green he suggested that the Zulus were to play the same part as the Irish did in the extension of the Empire, being first enchained themselves before going on to help bring yet untamed people into the prison life.[41]

Following the unrest in the Natal in 1906, the Natal authorities came to believe that Dinizulu, head of the Zulu royal house and son of Cetshwayo, was behind the disturbances. In December 1907 he was committed to trial: 'The case attracted wide publicity in Britain, deeply embarrassing for the Liberals.' In 1909, Dinizulu was found guilty on three charges of harbouring rebels, given a four-year prison sentence and sent into exile.[42]

At the time of Dinizulu's arrest, Casement shared his indignation with Morel:

They will doubtless allow poor Dinizulu to be 'tried' (God save the mark!) by the Natal colonists who covet his country – and deported. *His* crime, of course, is that he is the Son of a King – that he is Dinizulu – Chief of a People doomed to lose all in order that a band of greedy shopkeepers (I know the Durban and Maritzburg heroes well) may have more lands for their growing whelps and more cheap labour for their mercenary pursuits. And this accursed thing calls itself Civilisation! The Zulu people in their native state were one of the finest, noblest, cleanest and most *moral* people on Earth – but they must give place to the knock-kneed loafing swab who calls himself the British Empire and whose chief aim is to rob at the least cost to himself.[43]

Several years later, writing from Rio, he reflected on the role of Sir Edward Grey, not long Foreign Secretary at the time, in the Dinizulu incident and in the execution and flogging of allegedly riotous Egyptians at Danishway in 1906:

Sir Edward Grey is not a Liberal in any real meaning of the word. Can you imagine a *real* Liberal carrying out the Egyptian massacre – 'executions' they called it – three years ago, when the pigeon shooting officers were avenged of a whole rural population by widespread *public* floggings and hangings. Can Liberalism be one thing in England and another in Egypt? It evidently can ... If these things dare not and could not be in England – public hanging and floggings – how then can a great Englishman approve them in Egypt? Only to 'strike terror'. But does injustice first, and brutality next strike terror or plant hate?

Moreover, if it is legitimate to strike terror in Egypt by such methods – that are criminal methods, remember, say what you will – then it is equally legitimate for Leopold or Belgium to strike terror in the Congo in their own approved fashion. There is also the case of Dinizulu – also under this 'Liberal' regime – to say nothing of the case so much nearer home of Ireland – where Grey has followed the recreant traitor Rosebery into not so open but none the less effective apostasy. Can a man be false to one pledged word – to one great question and true on another?[44]

A month later, the incidents continued to exercise his mind.

I judge them by their treatment of Ireland; their shameful cowardice in Natal and Zululand; their cowardly abandonment of Dinizulu; their hangings in Egypt and floggings in Egypt; their 'deportations' by secret tribunals and '*lettres de cachet*' in India – and, now by their faithless, fainthearted retreat on the Congo. The people, who, all powerful with a mechanical majority of 300 votes could permit a paltry handful of Natal shopkeepers and farmers to publicly flog men and women and children in Natal; to fire down by the hundred naked Zulus ... for a 'rebellion' deliberately provoked; to drive in the relatives, women and mothers, sons and daughters, fathers and even grand-fathers to *witness* the execution of their sons and husbands and fathers; to be guarded by the troops of civilisation at the point of the bayonet so that they might sniff the bold and see the last agonies of those they loved – this was a supreme devildom that even Leopold never exceeded.[45]

In September, he told Morel: 'No great man is ever afraid ... You don't fear – when you see straight and believe strongly and know in your heart and soul that the thing is right.' He had seen this quality of courage in Morel at their first meeting. 'I have something of it too,' he continued, 'but not to the same extent as you – and I could tell you the reasons only they concern me only.'[46]

PART III
Ireland and Congo Reform

7: *The Congo Free State, 1900–2*

Home Leave, 1900

Casement arrived in London from South Africa on 26 July 1900.[1] On 3 August he wrote a personal letter to Henry Foley at the Foreign Office apologizing for not having called earlier, due to illness which

> proved to be an attack of jaundice plus my general condition of rundownness. The doctor would not hear of my going about – so I spent the greater part of the time in bed ... My surgeon (who has known me for years and my ailments) tells me an operation will be required, and that the general state of my health calls for a spell of good climate, food and rest.

He was enjoying 'this genial Europe ... which is a very delightful land to return to after the drawbacks of Africa'.[2]

On 7 August he wrote two letters to the FO, announcing his arrival and proposing to delay his return until his health improved. The second letter enclosed a medical certificate from Dr Dean, dated the 3rd, which stated: 'Mr Roger Casement was operated upon by me for *fistula-in-ano* some 5 years ago. A few days ago he came to me to be examined and I found that he had developed a form of piles which is often contracted by those living in Equatorial regions.' This was best treated by an operation. Casement was also run down and Dean advised that he not return at present.[3] On the first of these letters the FO minuted: 'he is to be transferred to Kinchassa'. On the 14th they agreed to grant two months' sick leave. On 20 August, the FO announced his appointment 'for the Independent State of the Congo, to reside at Kinchassa' as a full-time consul. His salary was to be £1000 a year, with an allowance of £300 and £165 for outfit.[4]

On 11 August he wrote to Fritz Pincus, who was on his way to Germany, to announce: 'I'm off to the Continent tomorrow to Switzerland – and then to Italy.' And, on 8 September he wrote to say that he was back from a month in France, Switzerland and Italy. Italy he described as 'my eternal joy and delight

... I frankly love Italy – don't you? Rome is a joy to me – I love every inch of it – and life and air – and sea and sun at Naples are beautiful ... I shall be here – at these my charming rooms until the end of September. My sister will be with me till 22nd from Ireland – you will like to meet her.' While public opinion in Britain was hostile towards Germany, Casement hoped that 'we shall all (English and Germans) get to understand and like each other better'.5

From 17 to 23 August Casement had stayed in an Alpine chalet belonging to Francis 'Sligger' Urquhart, where William Tyrrell, Blücher and Gertrude Bell were also guests.6 Presumably, he travelled on from there to Italy.7 Back home, he submitted to the FO his claim for expenses incurred 'by me upon the public service in connection with the special mission to Lourenço Marques entrusted to me by your Lordship's despatches of 24 and 25 December last year'. Charged at £2 per day ('a strictly just charge'), the total came to £385.8 A week later, he requested a further four weeks' extension – his health was improved, he said, but he would like it to be completely so.9

Interviews with Leopold and the Journey Out

On 10 and 11 October, Casement visited Brussels, where he was received by King Leopold for two separate discussions; he incorporated the contents of these into a long despatch to the FO. The conversations began with Leopold stating that the chief of his desires for the Congo was 'the well being and good government of the natives', an object that was continually impressed upon his officers. But progress was slow and the natives 'must learn to appreciate the value of work'. In response to this, Casement approvingly instanced the imposition of a hut tax in the British colony of Sierra Leone, which he believed would both profit the administration and induce responsibility and enlightenment, since 'what a man had to pay for he would naturally come to regard as worth taking good care of'. To this Leopold replied that he had not wished to levy direct taxes on the natives, 'but to induce them to develop their country, by working its india rubber, to their own benefit and to the profit of the companies interested. This was not forced labour, although it was necessary to insist that the natives should work'. Leopold became defensive when Casement commented on the difficulties in ensuring good government over territories so extensive. They were by no means too large, the king suggested, when compared with those of other European nations. And when Casement hinted that the pace of expansion in the Congo was too rapid compared with the more methodical development of British colonies, Leopold again defended the need to establish order to the limits of his territories.

The second interview, which lasted an hour and a half, focused for a time on issues concerning the eastern borders of the Congo, where Britain, Germany and France, as well as Leopold, all had competing interests. By suggesting that England had not been justly supportive of him in the past, Leopold seemed to Casement to be angling for English support 'on questions which might yet arise between His Majesty and ourselves'. Had Britain, for instance, supported Leopold's aspirations in the Nile region, the French might never have reached Fashoda. On the topic of reported outrages Leopold feared that, at times, they were well founded, 'since it was impossible to have always the best men in Africa; and indeed the African climate seemed to frequently cause deterioration in the character of men previously deemed of the highest standing'.

Turning to the question of trade, Casement reported Leopold as asserting that:

> There was complete equality of trade ... upon the Congo save only that the Congo Government reserved under the name of *Domaine Privé* certain districts of the country whence a revenue for public purposes was derived. This revenue did not at all – as was sometimes most untruthfully asserted – enter into His Majesty's pocket, but was essentially devoted to the public service.

To this, Casement had responded 'that public opinion, which was so powerful a factor in our affairs, was greatly interested in unrestricted commerce, and that any measures tending to facilitate trade dealings on the Congo would be welcomed in England in influential commercial quarters'.

Leopold asserted his desire to adhere to his agreement with the Great Powers, but stressed that he was also responsible to Europe to maintain order at home: 'There must be here no outbreak of disorder, no recurrence of the Commune of Paris.' With two million workmen in the population, he could maintain peace only by finding an outlet for the work of these men. Finally, he pleaded, as a small people, for a few of the crumbs 'that fall from your well stocked English table'.[10]

On 15 October the FO sent two messages to Loanda, the first confirming Nightingale as consul there and the second stating: 'Casement, appointed Consul at Kinchassa, sails for Loanda in a fortnight. He wishes his servants and house retained to await his arrival at the end of next month.'[11] In London, Casement sent two further communications to the FO. On the 17th he suggested that it would be more logical for the British consul at Kinchassa to have jurisdiction over inland areas of French Congo and for the consulate at Loanda to look after maritime sections. The suggestion was positively received and referred for consideration. On the 20th he reported that he was leaving for his post that day, but was unlikely to arrive until December. He proposed taking all Congo-related matter from the archives at Loanda and suggested that the FO send mail in sealed bags. He would reside in Boma, since there was no house at Kinchassa.[12]

Having enjoyed his Italian sojourn in September, Casement now decided to indulge himself further by beginning his long journey to the Congo with still more travel in Europe. From Taormina in Sicily he wrote to Francis Cowper, consul in Lisbon, to say that he would 'not have the pleasure of making your acquaintance' on this journey, since he could get to Cape Verde more easily on an Italian steamer from Genoa and therefore would not be coming to Lisbon.[13] In the event, a change of plan took him from Italy to Barcelona and then on to Lisbon via Madrid, so he probably met Cowper after all. During his subsequent voyage to the Congo he shared his impressions of Spain with Dick Morten. His host in Barcelona was the consul there, 'an old friend of mine – a former colleague when I was in the Niger Coast Protectorate'. The consul was J. Frederick Roberts and with him Casement saw the city (which impressed him with its fine avenues), a game of *peloto* ('a very manly, fine game'), and a performance of *Siegfried*.[14]

His experience of a bullfight drew words of wrath. 'All that I had ever read of bullfights pales before the dirty, shoddy, cowardly, base and contemptible reality ... It is a paltry exhibition of bad butchery carried on in the bloodiest and most revolting manner possible to conceive.' His negative feelings led him to a condemnation of Spain generally. He was glad the Americans had 'licked these hounds' (a reference to the Spanish-American War). 'I know now why the Inquisition flourished in Spain – it was not the will of King or Pope – but the bloody lusts of the people.' Becoming conscious of his own vehemence, he shifted to more pleasant matters and enclosed two songs 'for your musical mind' and reminisced about wild strawberries and Swiss hilltops. He listed, too, the capital cities he had by now visited or not visited and talked warmly of his recent trip to Naples:

> I love Naples – it is the most human town in Europe. People there do what they think – and, as they are in the privacy of their own rooms (if they are among the fortunate Neapolitans who possess separate rooms), so they are in the street. It is a last link with the outdoor life of the ancient world, when men were quite natural. Whether it is better to hide our hearts – to muffle up our lives – and to live the truer part of our lives in secret as we do today, the future only knows – for my part I cannot help feeling that the world lost something when discretion became the first of the ten commandments.

He spoke of the ancient admiration 'of the lovely forms around him', while we 'are constrained by our upbringing and all the weight of our surroundings to stifle that admiration – or if we give it vent, it takes a sensual course. Are we really more virtuous than the Greeks? Perhaps, but I often doubt it ... give me rather the nudity of the temple steps, in the eyes of all men – than the portico of the midnight music-hall, or the gas-lit gutter of the closing "pub".' He believed that 'a different training of the youth – a greater frankness in dealing with the relations of man to woman, would I verily think do away with the necessity for some of our laws – and make the grown-up race a purer and a happier one'.[15]

Matadi, 1901

Casement arrived in the Congo at the very end of 1900 and immediately began setting the routine procedures of the post in order. He requested copies of recent despatches, of the general instructions for consuls, a register for correspondence, and registration forms for births and deaths; he acknowledged receipt of seals; he submitted a list of services for which fees were levied; and he accepted temporary responsibility for US interests in the area.[16] If the provision of consular offices had been far from ideal in his previous two postings, there was none at all in the Congo. His appointment specified 'for the Independent State of the Congo, to reside at Kinchassa', but he had already informed the FO, before leaving London, that he would reside in Boma, since there was no house at Kinchassa.[17] In the event, he got rooms at the Hatton & Cookson factory at Nkalakala, Matadi, across the river from Boma. While Boma was the capital of the Congo State, Matadi had the advantages of being its major shipping port and the starting point of the railway to Stanley Pool and, as such, was a good vantage point for observing the flow of goods and personnel in and out of the State. In addition, the factory may have provided British company for Casement. On the negative side, he was neither in the capital nor in as good a position to assess happenings in the Upper Congo as he would have been had he been based at Stanley Pool. For most of 1901, his despatches to the FO came from either Boma or Matadi.

His first foray out of Matadi was to the Pool, where he went at the beginning of February in search of a site for a consular residence. The most detailed account of his journey came from a letter he wrote to his cousin Susan Casement at Magherintemple early in March:

> I have been up to Stanley Pool – but everything on the Congo is so changed – and I am not less changed, that it is no joy to be here now ... I went up to Stanley Pool by rail – the distance is 240 miles – the train takes 2 days – sleeping the night at a halfway Station. There are two classes for passengers – 1st and 2nd – 1st class fare is 500 frs = £20; 2nd class fare is 50 frs = £2. All Europeans go first class – even the poorest – & it is not so good as the worst European 3rd class. The so-called 2nd class is only for blacks, and would in an ordinary European community be held cruel for the transport even of hardy animals. I went 2nd class to the Pool!
>
> It created excitement: the idea of HM Consul going 2nd with 40 dirty 'niggers'. I did it on purpose as a protest against the gross robbery of the 1st class fare – & also as an example to all my countrymen out here – who think it *infra dig* to go 2nd with black. Since I set the start, many whites are now going – and I hope the railway Swindle Coy will have to reduce its 1st class fares.
>
> Coming down from Pool I walked 140 miles to Ngombi Mission Station to Mr Bentley an old friend of mine – & on to Ntumba & took the train back to Matadi from there, the halfway Station. I had to go 1st class unfortunately – the 2nd Class only 'seats' 40 people & there were over 50 – chiefly naked savages from Upper Congo – & even my free & easy way of travelling could not stand making the 51st in such a crowd. The ticket for the 187 Kilometres = 110 miles,

say, from Tumba to Matadi, was £9.8/– !!! & excess luggage is charged 1 franc per kilogramme, or 2 lbs. Can you conceive a more outrageous public theft?[18]

At Ntumba he observed the advance party of a large French expedition, which, he told the FO, was destined to occupy territory between the Oubangi and Lake Chad. The advance party comprised eighteen French officers and 450 Senegalese, marked by spirit and discipline; the main expedition would have 1500 to 2000 men with field pieces.[19]

Back in Matadi, despatches began to flow, and each cast its own, mostly critical, light on the broader State system. At the root of that system lay the State's approach to land, particularly the granting of concessions, whereby the State granted exclusive rights of exploitation to commercial companies over vast tracts of land and, indeed, people, in return for a percentage of the revenues. In one despatch, he drew attention to the 'rather outspoken' letters being sent by Richard Edward Dennett for publication in England on the question of French concession companies, which had been modelled on those of the Free State. Dennett's letters years earlier against the Congo State resulted in his having to leave – he now lived in the French Congo. While an 'amiable man', 'liked and respected', the danger was that he 'may give more offence to the French authorities than assistance to the cause of himself and friends in their possibly legitimate protests against the concessions policy of those authorities'. Casement went on to say that the government of the Congo State was the 'vastest Concessionaire in all Central Africa' to the exclusion or extinction of other trade interests. He had recently learned that M. Gresholt, director of the Dutch House on the Upper Congo, had had to withdraw agents from two bases because he couldn't compete with the concessionaires.[20] A new decree, reported in the *Bulletin Officiel*, even limited the use of wood without government permission, barring direct trade with the natives in this product.[21]

He described the problems being experienced by the Westcott brothers, independent English missionaries who were having difficulties with the State in getting land for their mission. The case raised two issues, said Casement, that of State policies in general and that of the different treatment of Catholic and Protestant groups. The State would not sell land, but only lease it, and Casement was inclined to believe that this policy was driven by its need for a steady income. This, in turn, was driven by the possibility of its having to repay the Belgian government a loan of 25 million francs, should that government decide not to annex the State at the end of the loan period, as it was entitled to, in accordance with the terms of a convention of 1890.[22]

Casement detected a difference in policy towards a Belgian Catholic mission and an English Protestant one from his reading of the State's *Bulletin Officiel*. In June 1897 the Catholic Scheutist Fathers had been given a grant of land at Boma, whereas when the English Baptists at Matadi sought a grant of land, they had to surrender another patch twice as large.[23]

Another key aspect of the system analysed in his despatches was that of imports to and exports from State territories. Rubber, for example, was a key export. He had been told in January that there were 3000 tons of rubber on the Upper Congo awaiting transport to Leopoldville. Governor Wahis had told him that 5000 tons were exported the previous year, which at £250 per ton gave a total of £1.2 million, 'a very considerable amount to be derived from one article of export only'.[24] And on 27 July, while at Banana, he reported that the *Philippeville* was soon to leave, said to be taking home almost 1000 lbs of rubber, equivalent to £240,000 in value. This 'will constitute the biggest cargo of rubber that has ever been taken from Africa in one vessel, and probably the largest single consignment of that commodity ever made from any country'. The greatest part of it, as with every consignment, came from the Domaine Privé:

> I think it is not likely that as long as these very profitable results to the present system of Government upon the Congo can be looked for there will be any serious effort made to substitute for it a Belgian colonial or any form of local administration likely to clash with the measures of arbitrary restriction which today confer upon their originators such financial benefits.[25]

In another despatch he suggested that, despite its denials, the State paid its officers a premium for 'trade products shipped from their districts'. There was good evidence, for example, from a returning officer who confessed in Brussels to having got a *joli cadeau* over and above salary for having made his district profitable.[26]

Ivory was a second major export and a despatch of 11 July was devoted to this. Casement had given the local authorities copies of the *East African Game Preservation Regulations* and they professed great interest. A large part of State revenue came from ivory, he reported, most from the Domaine Privé, and he worried that it came from young animals: 'a very considerable part of this ivory consists of small tusks called *scrivelloes*, coming within the limit of weight prohibited by the regulations adopted in East Africa'. The Congo government, he believed, must export many tons of this immature ivory. Of the Hatton & Cookson exports of ivory between January and June of 1901, he estimated that one third was the product of 90–100 young elephants. Extrapolating to the State as a whole, this would give a figure of 4500 young animals.[27]

In the same despatch, Casement reported that the last Antwerp steamer had imported guns, gunpowder, elephant guns and caps for its agents in the Domaine Privé, but only a relatively small amount of 'ordinary articles of legitimate commerce'. Indeed, stimulated by requests from the FO, he regularly monitored the cargoes of vessels coming from Antwerp.[28] In February, from Stanley Pool, he had reported on the advance party to the French expedition. On 25 June, he reported that ammunition and ten cannon had been sent by the State to the Upper Congo a short time before. The previous week, two field pieces and forty tons of ammunition went to Stanley Falls. Generally, however, the arms shipped were not sophisticated; most were the 'cheap variety of African trade gun', not rifled weapons, and were destined for the Domaine Privé.[29] The pattern of exporting large quantities of rubber and ivory, while importing mainly arms, had obviously impressed itself on him:

[I]t has been more than once brought to light that natives of one Congo district, having been armed in a superior manner by the authorities, have been let loose, chiefly as revenue agents, in districts whose population could protest only through the ineffective, six-foot muzzles of the antique type of gun known as the 'Long Dane'. The Congo State Government must have an armed establishment of some 20,000 men, drawn principally from the wilder and more vigorous savages of the Upper Congo, by a system of compulsory service.[30]

One danger of arms in the Congo, he suggested in a subsequent memo, lay in the fact that 'the natives are not slow to learn – and a rule that rests chiefly on the rifle is one that may any day pass into the hands of those who know the rifle only as the source of authority and the sole arbiter'. He recounted an incident, which took place in April and May of the previous year, when the native garrison of the fort of Shinkakasa, which had cost £300,000 of public money to build, captured the fort one evening and turned the guns intended to defend Boma on the town itself. The men, mainly Batatela from the Upper Kasai and Sankuru rivers, complained of 'immoral acts committed upon the persons of their womenfolk by Belgian officers'. Though they fired 168 shells, the vast majority were aimed too high and little damage was done. After two days they fled. Many were caught and hanged; most got back to their own home territories. The moral for Casement was that 'as things are now on the Congo, there is little else but a teaching to appeal to force – and that lesson once well-learned by the Congo tribes, they will apply it, I fancy, more vigorously than these Batatelas did to the men who wronged them'.[31]

The concerns of British subjects living in the Congo occupied a good deal of Casement's time, as usual, and from his account of the trial of one of these, Cyrus Smith from British West Africa, we get further glimpses of how awry things were in the Congo. Smith and several white men, all employees of the Société Congolaise-Anversoise under Major Lothaire, were sentenced for their part in atrocities in the Mongala district of the Upper River. They had been imprisoning natives, chiefly women and children, to force their villages to provide quotas of labourers and produce. In this case, many of the prisoners, for whom no food was provided, had died of starvation. Lothaire, one of the leaders of the anti-Arab campaign and the man who had executed Stokes, on being informed that arrests were imminent and that he might be implicated, left the Mongala, took a train to Matadi and boarded the Antwerp steamer on the eve of its departure. Casement's anger is evident:

It should ... be borne in mind that the Société Congolaise-Anversoise is, sweeping all subterfuges aside, as much a part of the Congo State machinery of Government for india-rubber as any branch of the Executive. The Sovereign granted it its Concession in his own domain; he reserved it a large and wealthy region, from which, by direct Decree, he excluded independent trading Companies along with the light of public opinion; he lent it, again and again, large bodies of his soldiers – that Force Publique – organised, so it was said, to combat the Arab slaver, and to protect the Congo native against the horrors of the slave trade; he placed a large force under State Officers, and under Lothaire, to assist the 'operations' of this latter in his Directorship of that region; he permanently supplied this criminal Company with a force of soldier-police, recruited from barbarians, to be directed by such agents as this judgement reveals the employers of the Société Congolaise-Anversoise to have in many instances been; and his treasury at Boma undertook many of the financial obligations of this company. [32]

As an illustration that 'the rule of the rifle still continues', he noted that the last steamer from Europe carried thirty cases of rifles and fifteen cases of cartridges for the Anglo-Belgian India Rubber Trading Company (ABIR) and would bring home to Europe a 'record' cargo of 600 tons of rubber and sixty tons of ivory. 'What wonder', he continued, 'that the irreverent among the subjects of that Sovereign speak openly ... of the india-rubber raised by this association of ruler, ruled and rifle as "red".'[33] He concluded: 'The only hope for the Congo, should it continue to be governed by Belgians, is that its Governors should be subject to a European authority responsible to public opinion, and not to the unquestioned rule of an autocrat, whose chief pre-occupation is that this autocracy should be profitable.'[34] This is the first reference by Casement to what was to be called 'the Belgian Solution', later advocated by reformers, whereby the Congo State would cease to be a personal colony of King Leopold and come under the control of the Belgian government.

During 1901 the Commission for the Protection of the Natives, first set up in 1896, was reappointed by royal decree. The names, Casement informed the FO, were those of the original members, including three English missionaries and two Belgian priests; 'It is perhaps well to point out that this Commission, as thus constituted, cannot exercise any united control whatsoever.' Its members lived far apart and there was no occasion on which they could meet. In fact, there was no single occasion on which they *had* met, and Dr Sims, one of the members, had been absent since the summer of 1898.[35]

In addition to assessing and criticizing general public policies, Casement also gave his opinion of individual Belgian officials. He reported that Colonel Wahis, the Governor General, had gone to Europe, leaving Casement with the impression that he was not returning. Rumour had it that he might be made Secretary of State in place of Van Eetvelde. While this would be a valuable appointment for the Congo State, Wahis was not 'a friend to or admirer of those principles of free dealing and equal opportunity identified with our treatment of colonial affairs'. The very restricted form of participation by traders 'not affiliated with the Congo Government trade ring' was unlikely to be modified under him.[36] Casement's opinion of the vice-governor, Major Wangermée, who was to take over from Wahis, was much more positive. He was a sympathizer with English methods, and when he first met Casement in 1899 he expressed satisfaction at England's success at Fashoda. Having attended the sixteenth anniversary celebrations of the founding of the State, Casement attributed the very good atmosphere prevailing to the character of Wangermée, 'an honest, single-minded and capable administrator'.[37]

Apart from his visit to Stanley Pool, shortly after his arrival, and an escape to Loanda in April, the only other journeys he seems to have made were two to Banana at the mouth of the Congo. The first was to make sure a despatch to the FO made it onto the next day's mail boat. The need to do so revealed the fragility of the communications system with the FO. He had just received a FO telegram, after almost a month – it had had to be re-routed and posted by the superintendent of the West African Telegraph Company, who told him that the land lines to Brazzaville were 'continually interrupted' and the delivery of telegrams so uncertain that he had posted it.[38] His second journey to Banana was made in late July. He explained to the FO that he had business in a mission station and also wished to learn the rules of pilotage and navigation. While in Banana he sent a copy of the ordinances dealing with navigation and shipping on the Lower Congo and questioned the rights of the Congo State to treat those waters – an international highway – as territorial waters.[39]

On several other occasions during 1901 he reported telegraphic problems and advised on alternative routes. More sensitive, though, were incidents when FO bags were opened at the Boma post office. In one such case, the label of the bag from the FO to Casement had been cut and resealed. He drew this to the attention of the secretary general of local government, Van Damme. Was it the 'outcome of momentary inattention'? Assurances were received. But the label was again cut some time later, although an investigation determined that the perpetrator was not a post-office employee.[40]

Daily Life and Friends

Casement's arrival had almost coincided with the onset of the hottest season and the climate soon began to tell. Already, by the beginning of March, he informed his cousin Susan:

> ... it is *very* hot – too hot for words, or for work – or for sleep. I am not well – altho' not ill – the heat is too great & the sleepless nights – night after night panting for air like a hot dog – are too much for us all. I am going to go down to Loanda for a change of air in the next English steamer – & shall not return to Congo until April.[41]

And he told Francis Cowper, not well himself, that the 'Congo is an ideal

Hell!' The heat was 'truly infernal!' – it had been 111°C in the shade a few days previously. Of 'food there is nil; society nil; life nil; nothing thrives here but disease, death and mosquitoes'. Two small fevers and uninterrupted heat for two months 'with almost sleepless nights as consequence have pulled me down greatly'. He estimated that he must have lost a stone since he saw Cowper in Lisbon.[42]

He left for Loanda on 3 April and returned on the 25th. The week he had left Matadi there had been four European deaths out of a total population of 130, and a similar number had died in Boma. He had not wasted the trip to Loanda, as, while there, he had 'travelled into the interior a distance of 300 km and obtained some information chiefly upon the railway line and the plantations of that province'.[43] The weather should change by mid May, he told the FO, and be 'cool' from June to September. It did improve and in June he told Henry Foley that he was thanking God for cloudy skies and lower temperatures. 'I intend avoiding the fearful heat from January to May next – another season of that would finish me, I think.'[44] As early as March he had told Susan:

I do not think I shall stay very long out here as Consul – I shall try for a transfer. I did not ask to come here – it was Govt. sent me, and so I am the more free to ask for a removal. The place is not nice; *very* unhealthy; no society at all except my dog; and nothing to Eat. My food today has been three slices of toast (2 ozs each) for breakfast; three tinned sardines & a plateful of Congo Beans for Luncheon; tonight only the Cook knows what is coming – but it is generally uneatable. This is a fairly typical day's feed.[45]

With Cowper indisposed in Lisbon and expecting to retire, the possibility of being appointed his successor had clearly begun to enter Casement's thinking. He shared his thoughts with Cowper: 'I think if you are still your own successor when I get home (D.V. this year) and the other man has got a nice billet elsewhere, I should, if you were still of the same mind too, and FO approved, like to be your later successor.' But he had a 'strong aversion to seeking a place – and hanging around the purlieus of the FO ... Mine is a very independent Irish soul, and I positively loathe the little advances of the kind often called for if one wants to bring one's claim forward'.[46]

Casement's response to the death of Queen Victoria, of which he received confirmation on 2 February 1901, reveals that he remained a loyal British subject:

We held (at my request) a Memorial Service in the Mission Church on 3 February – it was one of the biggest European gatherings I should think there has ever been in Central Africa – all the Congo State officers came in full uniform (about 50 of them) and I went (knowing they were to be in uniform) also in my uniform. The clergyman who officiated, died five days ago! He had just come out from England with his wife – they only arrived there on 25 January – both got ill together ten days ago & he died after 5 days – she poor soul is going home at once to her children ... It was sad news – but after all the Queen had lived her life – lived it splendidly and beautifully every day of it – and she has left a memory I suppose no other Monarch in the World ever left before.[47]

To Cowper he added further reflections:

Now that the Great old Lady is gone, one readily realises how vast was her place not only in the history of our country, but even in the daily lives of each of us. I cannot think of an England without 'the Queen' ... the German Emperor has come out splendidly; what now are all his Kruger wild-oats – he has gone home to the hearts of all of us, I think, by his prompt and manly coming to the poor old Lady's dying bed.[48]

With Susan he shared more homely remarks and concerns. He sent the boys stamps and was glad they liked the game he had sent; he had also heard from Aunt Charlotte. And he had had news from Tom on 19 October of the previous year, from Pretoria, where he had been sent on a mission by Lord Roberts and promised a 'good billet in the Administration if he got back all right', but, 'I've not heard a line since from him – or of him – and as there has been so much sniping by brother Boer, & so many night attacks & captures, it's quite possible I never may again.' He finished: 'Well I've yarned enough to you – I think I told you I had got Hills' *MacDonnells of Antrim* before I left home. The Isle of Man books are the ones I want now, but they will wait until I get to a better climate. Here the cockroaches eat one's books to pieces.'[49]

Home Leave, 1901–2

On 22 August Casement sent a telegram to the FO to say that he was in ill health, that he would be returning home soon and that he was appointing Underwood as acting consul. He added: 'existing dwelling arrangements unsatisfactory'.[50] Some days later he wrote to Gertrude to say that he was recovering from illness: 'I shall be *awfully* glad to get away from Congo – it is a horrid hole – worse than Nina's surroundings.'[51] Having asked permission to return home, he sailed and announced from San Thomé that he expected to reach Lisbon on 6 October. He arrived in England on the 12th.

Once home, he made contact with friends to apprise them of his movements. He told Gertrude he was off to Ireland. He tried, unsuccessfully, to meet Foley. He wrote from the North Western Hotel, Liverpool, to Fritz Pincus [52] and made a further representation on his behalf, this time a two-page tribute to the managing director of Reuters in London, in which he stressed Pincus's upright character and how he had served British interests.[53]

Meanwhile, he sent several missives to Cowper in Lisbon, where he had left his dog, Rags. Agricultural officials insisted on having Rags quarantined for three to six months, despite Casement's arguments: 'The truth is they have no jurisdiction over Ireland – for the Act applies only to "Great Britain" – and Ireland is no part of that geographical or political term.' He asked that Mr Parkinson in Lisbon keep the dog for the moment. As for himself, the home climate was none to his liking; he got a bad cold in London and 'fled from that horrid place after one brief visit to the Foreign Office', but Portrush didn't seem 'much better'. The weather was killing him and he longed for 'the sun and warm breeze of the South!'[54] Dick Morten got the same story from him – his cold was better, 'but this climate is worse and worse, I think every time I come home'.[55]

In November he heard a speech by Sir Edward Grey, the future Liberal foreign minister, which Casement was to recall with bitterness when in Germany in 1915. In an article published in *The Continental Times* in October 1915, he attacked Grey for his role in leading Britain into war and recalled that Grey was 'the man who subscribed in my hearing, in November 1901, to Lord Rosebery's abjuring of his Home Rule pledge to Ireland – at Chesterfield – and declared that in those perjured words the Liberal Party had a lead of statesmanship to follow'.[56]

He wrote to the FO on 13 November asking that leave be given, 'on account of impaired health, for a possibly somewhat prolonged period'. He enclosed a statement from Mr H. Percy Dean, 'a most distinguished surgeon', who 'has had me under treatment for a long time for the complaint referred to'. He felt he needed a complete change, because of 'the continuous undermining of strength a residence in West Africa, even under comfortable conditions, necessarily entails'. He was willing to forego salary if necessary, but would go back if asked. Dean's letter, from 69 Harley Street, stated that a return would be bad both for Casement's general health and for his 'local condition', which consisted of 'a weak and irritable state of the mucous membrane of the lower bowel together with an associated loss of tone in the muscular action of that region'. His patient should rest until the lower bowel had regained normal health – a period of at least six months. The FO reply granted four months from 12 December; he was to be on half pay from 13 to 31 December, on full pay in January (his 1902 leave of absence) and on half pay again from 1 February until he returned to his post.[57]

During his leave, he kept up contact with the FO on Congo matters. On 23 November he informed them that he had learned of the return to the Congo of Lothaire, which had been thought unlikely due to his 'alleged implication in the Mongala outrages of last year':

> Mons. Lothaire, I am told, has more than once declared that the Congo authorities were not in a position to call his acts in question, owing to the character of documentary orders he held from his superiors, and which he should publish if attacked, issued to him at the period of his illegal action in the Stokes affair.

Lothaire was said to have a 'free pass' from the King, and, to Casement, it seemed 'a scandalous shame that this man, who has perpetrated untold of atrocities, and who laughs at the laws of God and man, should be allowed to do anything he likes, and go unpunished ...'.[58]

He was active, too, on another front. By now he had produced such an accumulation of poems that he approached T. Fisher Unwin with a view to having a volume published. He submitted a collection divided into three parts, the first on Irish topics, the second on other areas, such as Africa and Sicily, and the third made up of personal and love poems. Fisher Unwin responded on 19 November: 'I think I ought to say at once that I do not look forward to a remunerative sale.' Poetry books seldom covered expenses. 'I note', he continued, 'your reference to those poems that have a political interest; now to speak frankly these poems are the ones we should think are least likely to be successful.'[59] Fisher Unwin sent on his readers' notes, and their critical comments added further to Casement's sense of injured pride.[60]

Casement saw to it that he had some organized leisure during his leave. 'I go down to Cork to hunt with God's help in a few days,' he told Cowper, 'if I can shunt the FO and Congo Consulates aside for some time.' But he hoped to get away altogether 'from these distressful islands' to the Continent at the end of November. He loathed, he said, the sound of the Congo name and believed he would be excused from purgatory because of it.[61] Towards the end of November he wrote again, expressing his concern that Cowper 'had a second bad heart attack'. He himself was leaving for Paris that night for a week and hoped to travel on to Lisbon. He had applied for an extension 'on strong medical authority', which 'will allow of my spending a good long time in the sunny south'. He hadn't, he said, sought a transfer.[62] His holiday took him to Italy rather than Lisbon and he stopped in Paris to visit the Wards. Paris, he wrote to Dick Morten on 9 December, was cold but dry. He was leaving the following night to go to Sicily: 'I have been longing to see it, and now I've got a chance.'[63] Back home in the new year, he brought a present from Naples to Gertrude and, a little later, he told Cowper of the change in holiday destination. He had intended going to Portugal, 'but fate took me to Italy instead!' Now he was back, much better in health, but facing snow and slush and piercing cold. He hoped to go to Madeira with his sister and, if so, would call on Cowper. He had done nothing regarding a transfer from the Congo.[64]

The possibility of transferring to Lisbon was becoming a persistent theme in his correspondence with Cowper.[65] From Ballycastle he forwarded to the FO contributions collected in the Congo for a Victoria Memorial. He had called a meeting in Matadi the previous June 'of coloured British West African natives', at which a local committee was formed. Despite their low wages, there had been great enthusiasm. He now sent £32–4–0 from 'coloured natives of three West African Colonies and £16 from ten Europeans, all but one of them missionaries'.[66]

He left for the Congo again on 28 March, before the expiration of his leave, because Vice-Consul Underwood was in 'impaired health' and wished to return to Europe.[67] From Cadiz, where he took ship for Tenerife, he wrote to Cowper. Cadiz was a 'ghastly hole'; Seville was better, but

> greatly overrated – and as far as the beauties of Andalusia! ... the fable of the
> lovely women of Seville – is grotesquely absurd when one sees them face to face.

Both sexes seem to me almost inhumanly ugly. How these people ever had the audacity to drive out the Moors and to put themselves in their place, beats me. The sense of their own unloveliness should have steeped them in humility ... They are hard, cruel, blood-letting beings – with none of the northern kindliness of their Gothic ancestors – and none of the warm softness of the Southerner in their desert natures.

The Portuguese were nicer, as were their trains.[68]

When he reached Las Palmas, Grand Canary, he wrote to his cousin Roger in Magherintemple, following up on the topic of the Casement name, which they had discussed during his leave. 'While waiting here for the Congo steamer to take me on (I came here from Lisbon) I am sending you the extract I promised, from Moore's *Names of the Isle of Man* upon Casement.'[69]

From Sierra Leone he wrote to Cowper and to Eric Barrington at the FO.[70] He was, he told Cowper, finally within one week of the Congo on the *Anversville*. He had arrived at Tenerife on the 9th and stayed at Tenerife and Grand Canary until the 24th, 'going a good deal about the island and enjoying myself greatly'. Croker – their colleague at Tenerife – was a 'very nice chap' and gave Casement a bulldog named John to take to the Congo. Rags, he said, would be jealous. Croker had nine children and was an invalid 'and has a hard time of it – beyond conceiving – between his health, his large family – and only £500 a year of consular salary'.[71]

In a long letter to Eric Barrington he responded to a suggestion made by Barrington to have the Congo discussed at an international conference. 'I fear', wrote Casement, 'I have not much faith in international conferences – they finally end in agreements which it is nobody's business to see maintained.' Rather than 'indicting the Congo State for its career of atrocities against the natives', it would be better to call it to account 'for its systematic commercial breaches of the Convention to which it owes its existence'. He believed the atrocities occurred, but it was difficult to get reliable witnesses to prove them. 'Moreover, the atrocities are the natural outcome of the monopolist system which has created the Domaine Privé and all its attendant illegalities against both European and native African alike.' It ought to be easy, he felt, to prove the Congo government false to its promises to the Powers under the Berlin Act. An agent of the State itself had said to him that 'this is indeed the most gigantic act of piracy that has been ever brought to a successful end'.

There is no free trade on the Congo today; there is, it might be said, no *trade* as such at all on the Congo. There is the ruthless exploitation at the hands of a savage and barbarous soldiery of one of the most fertile regions of Africa in the interest of and for the profit of the sovereign of that country and his favoured concessionaires.

The danger was that, if not checked, it would end 'in a widespread upheaval some day, of the native African against his European despoiler'. This would affect not only the wrongdoers, but 'all men of white race in tropical Africa', and he instanced the spread of disorder to the French Congo. He ended his letter to Barrington by stating his fears about being able to stand more than a year of the Congo: 'it is such an unhealthy climate ... but I do hope that before I may be forced to give it up I shall see its rotten system of administration either mended or ended'.[72] He was to express, more graphically, his apprehensions about the climate in a letter to Sir Martin Gosselin, shortly after arriving back:

> I hope I may last out to the end of the year, but I must say when I saw the Congo again, when its waste of gaunt waters broke on my view, and the blaze of its intemperate sun made me close my eyes in sheer physical pain, I felt like turning tail at the mouth of the river, and not drawing breath till I saw the peak of Tenerife.[73]

Boma, 1902

He arrived in Boma on 6 May and took over consular duties on the 8th. The first news to greet him was of death: five Europeans of a total of fifteen based at Luki, on the Boma–Mayumbe railway, had died in ten days.[74] During 1902 he maintained his link with Hatton & Cookson, but this time basing himself in their Boma factory rather than in Matadi. He informed the FO in June that it was not very comfortable, 'but it is far better than going to one of the two so-called "Hotels" of Boma, which are simply dirty ill-kept shops frequented by beer-drinking Belgians and rum-drinking natives'. He was renting three rooms, two for dwelling (each 14' x 14') and the third as consular office, in a different building. He was paying £72 per year for this, but H.A. Shanu, a native of Lagos and a successful businessman in the Congo, was looking for £180 per year for a small one-storeyed building of wood and zinc. Hatton & Cookson was cramped and it was bad to associate with a trading firm. What was needed was a consulate, though the price of land was exorbitant; the minimum required would be 6000 square metres, with the house separated from servants' quarters for privacy.[75]

Meanwhile, the international campaign against abuses in the Congo State had again been mounting, especially in Britain, now that the excitement of the Boer War had begun to fade. A consistent opponent of the regime, the American Presbyterian missionary William Morrison, had written directly to Leopold in October 1899 about conditions on the Kasai, where he worked. His reports circulated in the US and in Britain, where he visited and spoke; in consequence, a question was put in the House of Commons. The most important figure for the campaign now appeared, in the person of Edmond Dene Morel, a young clerk in the Elder Dempster Company in Liverpool. An idealist, brimming with energy, Morel had earlier been a defender of the Congo State; between 1897 and 1900 his attitude changed. Careful analysis of trade figures and the statistics supplied by the State showed that, while increasingly valuable quantities of rubber and ivory were leaving the Congo, few trade goods were being imported, only large quantities of guns. Morel concluded from this that the inhabitants were not being paid for their labour, but were in virtual slavery. He published his first findings in 1900, in a series of unsigned articles and later severed his connection with Elder Dempster and began his crusade against the State. In May 1902 he spoke at a public meeting of the Aborigines Protection Society (APS). Later in 1902 he began to seek detailed evidence of atrocities from missionaries working in the Congo.[76]

Casement's despatches during 1902 reflected the growing criticisms of the State. One of the more important themes was the growing importance of concessions. Among his first despatches were two on the newly-formed Compagnie du Kasai, which had a reported territory of 36 million hectares ('considerably greater in extent than the United Kingdom'):

> The great extent of this Concession, embracing as it does much of the richest and probably the most densely populated regions of the C[ongo] S[tate], and the fact that the newly-formed Company swallows up what was until its formation supposed to be a free-trade region as opposed to the monopoly of the Domaine Privé, justify a close scrutiny of the reasons for this amalgamation of interests and the objects it has in view. It is true that although nominally a region in which all comers were supposed to have equal trading rights the Kasai territory has, for some time, in reality been closed to all would-be traders whose presence was not desired by the authorities.

The method of exclusion was simple: the State refused to sell land to newcomers, and 'squatting' was illegal or impossible. Moreover, the government controlled the administrative council and the permanent committee of the Compagnie du Kasai, so that it was, except in name, 'an executive branch of the Congo State Administration' aimed at ensuring the production of india rubber 'and anything else that can be got out of them for the sole profit of their monopolist masters'.[77]

On 30 June he forwarded a map, published in the Belgian journal *Mouvement Geographique*, showing concessions on the Upper Congo. The largest was the Compagnie du Katanga, approximately the size of France. Again, Katanga 'for all practical purposes' was a portion of the Domaine Privé, exploited either by agents of government or of the Comité Speciale du Katanga, 'which may be regarded as merely a subordinate branch of the Congo Executive'. The Compagnie du Kasai, he reported, followed the Katanga model and one of its chiefs was Alexandre Delcommune, delegate of the Conseil d'Administration and one of the administators of the Compagnie du Katanga. The foundation of the Compagnie du Kasai, he continued, had forced the withdrawal of a Portuguese company intending to open operations on the Kasai.[78] In October, returning to the issue, he relayed the contents of a conversation with Mr Van der Most, chief agent of the

Dutch House, and also Dutch consul. The Dutch had virtually been forced to go in with the monopolistic Compagnie du Kasai. Leopold was reported to have stated that the independents didn't have to do so but, if they didn't, 'let them see what they will make of it!' The Dutch felt they had no option.[79]

The State undermined the position of independent traders in a variety of ways. It made the acquisition of land for trading stations almost impossible, and it imposed a series of taxes – personal, property, import and export. On 22 July, Casement reported on an increase in import tax on goods from 6 per cent to 10 per cent, with virtually no notice. 'Already many local houses in Boma and Matadi are closed, failing, or bankrupt; the effect of this increase in the import duties can only have the effect of accelerating the collapse of the independent trade organisations established in the Lower Congo.'[80]

He returned to the theme on 10 August and began by showing how 'direct and personal taxes' affected the various Protestant missionary groups, including the small and poor Westcott Brothers mission. He gave similar details for the Hatton & Cookson factory in Boma. Such taxes had been originally introduced to help finance the fight against the Arab slavers, now long over; they were only to be in effect until import duties were put in place, also long done. He cited the case of the Lagos trader Shanu, who had to pay 40 per cent on the cost of firewood and then, when he wished to build a house, he was taxed on stones collected from waste land in Matadi, the very name of which meant 'stones' and was 'itself simply one huge piece of rock'. Duties were also imposed on the rubber the independent traders exported, while state exports of rubber were exempt. The effect was to drive the independent trader out of the rubber business.[81] For example, Hatton & Cookson had had twenty-seven trading posts in the district of Ponta da Lenha in the 1880s, but 'today this firm has only one trading house in that district, and the head establishment, that of Ponta da Lenha itself, has long since reverted to the encroaching waters of the Congo, and not one stick stands today to mark that once flourishing depot'.[82]

While independent traders were going under, state profits were 'considerably more than double the entire revenues of any of our established and flourishing West African colonies'.[83] A great deal of this increase came from the Domaine Privé, as Casement demonstrated from figures provided by a French report:

Year	Total State Revenue	Revenue from DP
1896	8 million francs	3 million francs
1901	30.75 million francs	17.42 million francs[84]

At the same time as the general public was being heavily taxed and State income increasing, what State services were given in return? 'The public who contributed it have had neither lights, nor roads, nor wharves, nor sanitation, nor hospital accommodation, nor – I would unhesitatingly assert – any single one of the essential concomitants of civilised rule.' He continued:

Although Boma and Matadi are, for West tropical Africa, fairly large and important commercial centres, there exists in neither any form of municipal authority or communal control. No provision whatsoever has been made for increase of population; no allotment of lands for public purchase or even lease; no public roads or streets in the proper sense of the word exist (save a few hundred yards at Matadi); no public bridges over streams or ditches; no public lamps; and what is even more essential, no public latrines are to be found; and for 'police' – a gang of sturdy savages, armed with cutlasses, dragged from the interior by a system of forced labour ...[85]

What they did get was the fortress of Shinkakasa, commanding the River Congo on the seaward side of Boma. 'That fortress, which is a threat to civilised men only, and which can serve, by no possibility, any useful purpose in the government of this country or contribute to the welfare of its native populations, has eaten up, it is believed, some £300,000 of public monies.'[86] The State's 'drilled and officered cannibal army' was now larger than that of any of the European Powers on African soil.[87]

Commenting on a report by Captain Burrows, Casement referred to forced recruitment to the Force Publique, which was stipulated to be for a minimum of three years' service but often stretched to seven:

The drain upon the already sufficiently scanty native population of the Lower Congo the military system has created has completely upset the ordinary life of the natives, and has caused large numbers of them to migrate into the neighbouring Portuguese territory ... and has certainly brought about the partial extinction of the only trade the Lower Congo possessed, i.e. that in palm oil and kernels and ground-nuts.[88]

The results of the use of compulsion in the general administration of the State were disastrous for the native population:

[T]he native of the D[omaine] P[rivé] became a serf, not in theory only but in fact, ground down, exploited, forced to collect rubber at the bayonet's point, compelled to pay onerous tribute to men whose salaries depend upon the produce returns from their respective stations – the punishment for disobedience, slothfulness, or inability to comply with the demands, ever growing in extortion, being anything from mutilation to death, accompanied by the destruction of villages and crops.[89]

In a despatch on 16 May he gave a graphic instance of the type of lawlessness widespread in the Congo. In September 1899 a group of eight men and four women were taken to a state post by the chief of a village where they were preaching the Gospel. They were tied, beaten, stripped and otherwise ill-treated. Most were then released, but two young women were detained and repeatedly raped, before being set free. Casement went on:

There would have been no inquiry into the complaint of these unfortunate people at all had it not been for the energetic representations of the missionaries at Mbanza Manteke; and after weeks of detention at Matadi (50 miles from their home, over a very fatiguing and stony route – I know it too well! –

which they had to traverse each way on foot), and some months of delay in coming to a decision, the satisfaction the injured women obtained was to be told that the cost of the food they had eaten during the course of the trial would be the penalty inflicted on their brutal ravishers!90

Casement did not attribute all loss of life to state exploitation; he was aware of the effects, for example, of sleeping sickness. But, even here, the state was deficient:

The unchecked and, so far as the CS [Congo State]is concerned, wholly unstud-ied ravages of sleeping sickness have carried off more able-bodied men than even the recruiting sergeant. In a Report I drew up at Loanda in 1899, atten-tion was drawn to the extent of the ravages of this terrible disease. The Por-tuguese Government have since that date made serious effort to study the nature of this malady; but, although sleeping sickness causes greater havoc in the CS than in Angola, no effort has been made by this Government either to study it or to combat it.91

An agent of the State, an Italian gentleman named Rossi, told Casement that 'at least 40% of the Belgian firms on the Congo were dishonest', that things would get worse and that a complete change of system must take place. Casement learned that Rossi had visited the ABIR Concession on the Upper Congo and was visiting a mission station 'at the very moment when some of the fearfully wounded or mutilated natives, victims of the ABIR's method of obtain-ing a dividend, were brought in for medical or surgical help'.92 In the light of all of this, Casement was beginning to see another side to at least one of the three Cs: 'I think if the *civilisation* offered the negro in the CS were somewhat less profitable to those who compel its acceptance by force of arms and more ben-eficial to those who are forced to sustain its chief burthen by their "taxes in kind", the opposition to its spread would be of a less pronounced character.'93

Little wonder that there was some resistance. He described Lothaire's cru-elty – shooting a man in the legs and cutting off his lips, nose and ears – in sup-pressing 'the so-called "Budja revolt" (which was simply an uprising of the tor-tured natives against their murderous spoilers)'. And, referring to persistent rumours of a native rising in the Stanley Falls district, he felt that it was 'quite impossible here to sift the true from the false in the stories that filter down coun-try', but that there was 'always an inherent probability' about native resistance.94 The natives had lost much. He quoted information given by a local trader:

By an Ordinance dated the 1st July, 1885, all vacant lands were to be considered as belonging to the State. Concluding that certain lands were ownerless, although having a long-established native population upon them with a clearly-defined system of land tenure and an existing trade in the products of the soil, the State prohibited the exploitation of rubber by private individuals in the basins of the Rivers Inbomu and Uele, Mongala, Itimbiri and Aruimi, Lopori and Malinga, and in a zone near the meeting of the Bussera and Ichuapa.95

Referring to the circumstances in which the state capital at Boma was established (he himself remembered its transfer from Vivi), he wrote:

> The sites of the Government buildings now standing here were acquired by bargain and purchase from the native Chiefs of Boma, who, in no case that I am aware of, ever understood by these friendly transactions with the white men that they were irrevocably parting, not only with their lands but with their sovereignty, with their personal freedom, their right of trading in the products of their soil, and their right of dwelling on and dealing with, as their tribal customs dictated, the other lands they had held from time immemorial. The vesting, by a stroke of the pen, of the 'unoccupied' lands of this country in the hands of the King-Sovereign of the Congo State was an act of deliberate theft, and one the wickedness of which I believe will yet be startlingly demonstrated by the retaliation of the natives who have been robbed of their rights.[96]

Resistance to such oppression wasn't confined to the Congo; during 1902 he informed the FO about revolts in neighbouring Angola. The first of his reports came at the end of June, when he reported a serious revolt in two Portuguese districts. This was the likely outcome, he suggested, of the 'forced labour system', whereby 'under the term of contracted labour', 'large numbers of natives are annually exported from Angola to Sao Thomé & Principé'. Bands of armed Portuguese and half-caste *afilhados* had been slave-raiding within Congo territory, but had been defeated.[97]

On 18 July, Casement submitted to the FO a densely documented dossier on the case of British colonial subjects dismissed by the Mayumbe Railway Company at Luki, eighteen miles from Boma. A group of these men had been arrested as vagabonds and jailed, and seven of them died in prison:

> It is with sincere pain that I approach this subject, but I cannot but feel that seven deaths out of eleven men arrested but little more than a month ago is very regrettable; and to be quite frank, I think many more of those poor men might have been alive today had it not been for their arrest and imprisonment.

The several hundred pages of documentation Casement submitted include his correspondence with the governor of Sierra Leone, the Governor General of the Congo and the Procureur d'État, as well as his notes on individual cases. Among his enclosures were case-by-case details under the title of 'Entries in a Memorandum Book, begun by his Majesty's Consul at Boma on 28 June 1902, noting Cases of Complaint and other Cases concerning British Colonial Natives there reported at Consulate'. His description of conditions at the jail (the men were confined in neck and leg chains) and hospital elicited shocked minutes from FO officials: 'This despatch shows a very terrible state of things'; 'The account of the condition of the prisons and the hospital is terrible'; and, from Lord Lansdowne, 'It is a terrible story.' Casement's intervention *did* have an effect: 'The whole of the official world on top of the hill has been considerably disconcerted by my intervention on behalf of these poor men.' The details of the case were even more complicated than he then realized and were to occupy him into 1903.[98]

During this stay, Casement only left Boma on a few occasions. The longest absence was from 29 May to 15 June, during which he visited Loanda and Cabinda. Regarding the latter location, he submitted a memo supporting the plea of the local Hatton & Cookson agent for a scheme to clear the waterways of the Chiloanga River system, which would facilitate the export of palm oil.[99] He crossed the river to Matadi for business on a couple of occasions and went downriver to Banana to view the new telegraphic station. With the Banana station and one almost completed at Ambrizetta (Angola), it should, he claimed, be possible to send a telegram to Europe via Loanda in one day.[100]

He reported, as well, on road and rail developments. A reduction of fares on the Congo Railway must have brought him satisfaction and he felt that it should facilitate movement. Nevertheless, when he compared the Sierra Leone Railway (built, he claimed, in the public interest) with the Congo Railway (built in the interests of shareholders), his judgment was negative. In a six-month period, the Sierra Leone Railway had carried over 60,000 passengers and the Congo Railway only some 7000, but the income from the latter was much higher.[101] A new automobile road, he thought, might be of interest to the Intelligence Division of the War Office. This was a 150-km stretch from Nsongololo, a station on the Matadi–Leopoldville railway.[102]

Significant, too, in the light of earlier European attitudes (including his own) to the African practice of cutting down rubber vines, was a copy of a decree from Brussels concerning rubber cultivation, which he sent, with comment, to the FO. The decree, he said, required those exploiting india rubber to plant 500 feet (versus 150 feet formerly) of rubber plants for each ton of rubber exported. The methods of collecting sap, too, were to be changed. Hitherto it was held that the vines should be tapped and not cut through, for which heavy penalties were imposed on native owners. Now, experience was showing that to cut down the vine was the most profitable and was wisest for the plant. A plant wounded by incisions weakened and died, soon giving no sap. A plant boldly cut sent up fresh vigorous shoots, which after ten years were again at their best. They should be cut when ten to twelve years old, after which they would go to wood. Cut vines should be crushed immediately for every drop of fluid. This method (a crop every ten years) would ensure the best yield.[103]

He told Cowper that he was busy with 'lots of local "palavers" ' – defending British interests – 'our coloured West African natives'. The previous day, for example, there were coronation festivities at which about 400 West African natives 'ate and drank ... till they could no more and gave hearty cheers for the King and Queen (as also for your humble servant)'. It was not cheap: he had, he said, provided '360 bottles of ginger beer, 200 loaves of bread, butter and jam in immense quantities, 50 tins of Huntley & Palmer's dessert biscuits, 1 case of cakes, 30 tins of plum puddings and 3 cases of chocolates (for wives and children)'. He expected a bill of £60 or £70, 'but I don't grudge it as it does good to keep these black folk in touch with their Government – and is in marked contrast with the way the Congo Government treats its own black people'.

He went on to consular talk. Sir Martin Gosselin was to succeed Sir Hugh McDonnell at Lisbon. 'He is a charming man – kind and nice, and with the pleasant manners that are not an external gift only, but the outward and visible sign of a fine inner nature. I like him immensely ...' He intended to complete the work he had mapped out to do, and six months should see him well on. He was getting a man to act for him and hoped to go upcountry on a long journey 'if my health will allow it'. In the margin, he added: 'There is a dire revolt of natives in Benguela, Nightingale writes me – with fearful atrocities on the whites.' This letter was rapidly followed by another, in which he reported that his bulldog was almost dead; the state doctor had had to give him two enema injections. As for himself, 'I am breaking up already. I only exist on quinine and tennis and my Bulldog.'[104]

At the end of September he wrote to Fritz Pincus, hoping all had improved with him at Lourenço Marques and Johannesburg. 'I wrote you a long letter last year – the 27 October – containing a copy of the letter I wrote Reuters about you', but it had been returned 'unclaimed'. He sent his love to Coudenhove and Tom, should Pincus see either, and to friends at Delagoa, especially the Budds.[105]

Home Leave, 1902–3

His stay in the Congo during 1902 lasted five months. During this period, on several occasions, he reiterated his wish to undertake one or more journeys on the Upper River. He mentioned it to Cowper in June, and in July he told the FO that he hoped to go to Matadi, Leopoldville and the Upper Congo, to register all British subjects. Then, in August, he asked permission from the FO to go in October or November. Permission was granted.[106] Suddenly, however, on 5 September he announced by telegraph that he intended to return home by the mail of 10 September. The existing consular accommodation, he said, was most uncomfortable and the work, accordingly, difficult. He believed that it was better to hasten the plan for a consular house than to undertake the journey into the interior. While granting permission, the FO reaction was puzzled: 'I really think the poor man must have gone off his head', wrote one official. 'He is a good man, has had fever, and would not telegraph like this unless it was really necessary,' wrote another. At Cabinda, he clarified his reasons for wishing to return home. He had decided to defer the Upper River journey because of the priority of building a consular residence at Boma and because 'there are other needs of the Consular district I control which it would seem desirable to have discussed at home at an early date'. The journey home, he stressed, was not a health trip or a leave of absence.[107]

He had left Loanda on 10 September for Lisbon, but stopped in Cabinda to deal with important despatches. While there he lost his pocketbook (a present from Nina for his birthday on 1 September), with his tickets, visiting cards, money, letters and official passport. He told Cowper that he had to call at Gaboon, which was in his French Congo consular district.[108] In Tenerife he found a minder for his ailing dog.[109]

He arrived in Plymouth on 19 November, having suffered a malaria attack on the last leg of the voyage. He had gone down with fever twelve days previously – eight of them he had spent in bed 'with flesh and *complexion* all gone!' He hoped to be up and about the following week. 'I think I shall go for Lisbon', he added, offering to go and help out if Cowper wanted a rest or a change for Christmas, though he, himself, was behind in the work he had brought home to finish.[110]

In December Casement sought advice from the FO on an approach that had been made to him, just as he had left for England, from the Revd William Morrison, an American Presbyterian working in Luebo on the Kasai. This was the first formal approach to him as acting US consul. Morrison's allegations of man-catching raids, the burning of villages and the taking of women and children as hostages, had the ring of truth, he informed the FO.[111]

Early in January he suggested that the Commission for the Protection of the Natives was a dead letter. Its three English members were Dr A. Sims and the Revds George Grenfell and Holman Bentley: 'I know these three gentlemen well, and have known them for years, and I cannot recall an instance where any one of them attempted to exercise his supposed protective functions under this Commission.'[112] Early in January, critics of the Congo Free State were shocked when the Baptist Missionary Society, with attendant publicity, presented an address of thanks to Leopold, praising the enlightened rule of the State in the process. Casement took issue with the address, claiming that it did not represent views of Baptist missionaries on the ground. Referring to the Baptist Missionary Society authorities, he stated: 'I suppose they say here it is their duty to keep in with the Government at all costs – so that no difficulties may be put in the way of their work on the Congo, but, personally, I prefer the outspoken criticism of the, perhaps, less-cultivated American missionaries on the Kasai.'[113]

The most significant, detailed, and cogently presented despatch he wrote during his home leave was a memorandum on the question of concessions in the French Congo dated 15 February.[114] French concessions, he pointed out in the memo, were modelled on those of the Congo Free State; to judge them and their effects on English traders, one must first look, therefore, at the model. The Congo State had been brought into being at the Berlin Conference of 1884–5; while it sought to guarantee free trade in the Congo Basin, the Powers also 'asserted an equal care for the well-being and future interests of the native inhabitants of the regions affected by their deliberations'. At the first sitting, Casement continued, Sir E. Malet, the British representative, stated:

> I cannot forget that the natives are not represented amongst us, and that the decisions of the Conference will, nevertheless, have an extreme importance for them. The principle which will command the sympathy and support of Her Majesty's Government will be that of the advancement of *legitimate commerce*, with security for the equality of treatment of all nations and for the well-being of the native races.

This led Casement to two considerations. Firstly, governments in the Congo Basin had no inherent right to the tracts of land they had arrogated to themselves. This was implicit in the need to enact legislation, as was done in the Congo, to create the Domaine Privé and the *terres domaniales*. 'If it can be shown', he continued, 'that not only the interests of legitimate commerce have suffered, but that the well-being and advancement of the native races have been seriously retarded by reason of this legislation, then it is hard to deny that such legislation is a violation of the principles and contrary to the terms of the Berlin Act.' Secondly, if such a Power then grants concessions, it 'remains to be shown that such exercise of the sovereign right is in harmony with the anterior rights and well-being of the native races and the advancement of legitimate commerce'. In the Congo State, the native inhabitants alone were the subjects of the State. The concessionaires were, in fact, aliens:

> Moreover, it should never be lost sight of that since the Congo State claimed recognition as a Sovereign State upon the validity of Treaties entered into by its agents with the native Chiefs of the Congo basin, it can claim no greater development of sovereign rights than those Chiefs had themselves to cede. The Chiefs could not grant what they did not possess; and in no part of Central Africa can a claim be maintained by any native Sovereign to sole possession of the land, the products of the soil, or the labour of the inhabitants. The Chief is only the trustee of the tribal family, and his public rights are well defined and strictly limited by popular control.

The claim by the Belgian king, therefore, to be sole owner of nearly one million square miles of African soil and of its products and occupants, Casement believed to be preposterous and a form of 'legalised piracy'.

On the pretext of suppressing the Arab slave trade, the Congo State introduced personal and import taxes. These remained, yet 'so, too, do the slaves, they only serve other masters'. The sole return from the income derived from taxes and monopolies were such as, on the one hand, the fort of Shinkakasa, 1800 miles away from the former Arab slavers' strongholds, or, on the other, the Force Publique. As to the native, 'his lands are no longer his own – he may neither sell nor let them; their produce he may no longer dispose of in open market; neither is the work of his own hands his'. The lands now belonged to the State or to the concessionaire, who could pay him a pittance for products and labour exacted by force.

Casement had heard concessionaires in French Congo lamenting the lack of armed forces to compel native labour and requesting rights similar to those of their Congo counterparts. 'Without compulsion they now admit the native will not bring them the india-rubber, the ivory, the ebony, and the various "products of the soil", which they own, but which, strange to say, the native, who was there before them and who has all the labour of gathering and bringing to purchase, thinks he owns.'[115]

The Foreign Office took this despatch seriously, though with reservations. Harry Farnall wrote: 'For Ld. Lansdowne's perusal ... I fear the argument is not of use in French Congo. We have no brief for the natives. We have recognised that they are under French sovereignty.' And, again,

> It would be out of the question to limit the powers of a civilised government to those of the native chiefs. The State of Pennsylvania could not be worked if the powers of the Executive were limited to those of the Red Indian chiefs from whom the land was taken over. The British crown claims the right to dispose of vacant land both in colonies and in Protectorates. The question is: 'Were the lands treated by the French as vacant, really vacant?'

Lord Lansdowne added: 'This is a valuable and interesting paper, even if it be admitted that it peeves [proves?] too much, and that the language is here and there unusually strong – but Mr Casement's indignation is natural and justified.'[116]

While at home, Casement kept in touch with his cousin Gertrude. They talked mostly of family matters, but, just before he left on his return voyage and conscious of the mounting public campaign on the Congo, he told her that he would welcome her sending any cuttings on Congo affairs.[117] In mid February he prepared to set off for the Congo again. He apprised Cowper of his movements. He had, he said, been very busy – only four days in Ireland, eight outside London and the rest with his nose to the grindstone. 'The FO has treated me very well and kindly – and they do not hunt me back to Congo – but I am going "off my own" ... I have applied for a transfer to a healthier post and they are quite agreeable. I may say, privately, I quoted your letter about Lisbon and your intention to go on leave on 31 March. I think there is little doubt I shall get Lisbon when you go.' He expected to reach the Congo on 17 March – 'Patrick's Day – more Power to him!'[118]

From 14 February until the end of 1903 Casement's personal diary allows a more detailed view of his movements (and sometimes thoughts) than can be gained from his FO and personal correspondence. The day-to-day entries are short, staccato, mnemonic rather than reflective.[119] Those from 14 to 21 February, when Casement sailed on the *Jebba*, are what one would expect for someone preparing to make a journey. He purchased his tickets from the Elder Dempster Company, paid his bills at his lodgings in Aubrey Street, organized his money, stored items at Peacock's in Ebury Street, wrote up material for the FO, and engaged in a last round of social activities. His companions in these latter included Nina, Herbert Ward and the Mortens, the Cuibonos, the Tyrrells, and Baron Nisco.[120] He went to *Aladdin* ('awfully stupid piece') with Nina and to *La Bohème* with a number of friends on the following night. From the diary, too, we begin to get the first clear evidence for Casement's sexual longings and actions, generally directed towards youths and young men with comments often focused on penis size ('enormous'). 17 February was a typical day:

> Left Denham. 9. Uxbridge 9.32. Saw in paper 'Saxonia' arrived Queenstown 16th & proceeded immediately. Back to pack up at Aubrey. Lovely weather. Sharp frost – but at 11 bright glorious sunshine. Lunch with Nina. Then both of us to Park & saw Troops from Parliament. Then to H.W. studio & then home. Letter from G. Blücher to Mrs Tyrrell with it at 8. Then Club dinner with H.W. Then walk. Papers. Saw (enormous – youthful). Home – letter from G.B. of 6 Feb at New York – & from Parkinson about 'Rags'.[121]

He went by train from London to Liverpool on the 20th, his friends seeing him off at Euston Station, and he sailed from Liverpool on the 21st, having visited his aunt and his cousin Lizzie before leaving. The first leg of his journey, from Liverpool to Madeira, took a week. The weather was rough and the *Jebba* an 'awful tub, very uncomfortable indeed'. They arrived on 28 February and Casement began a two-and-a-half week sojourn in Funchal. The entry for the 28th catches the mood:

> In to Funchal at 7.30. Perestrello – as in Sept 1897, on 'Scott' with photos – grown tall – eyes beautiful. Down on lip. Curls. On shore with Reid to Carmo. At Café in square, coffee & carro offered – Lunched with Hon. A. Bailey. They off at 3. 'Jebba' 3.30. Walked Almadea [sic, *Alameda*] types. Dark, distressful. Then gardens at 4. Band of 'Majestic' – Prowse R.N. of 'Jupiter' came up & spoke. Squadron goes on Monday. Dinner very stupid. Hotel Carmo bad. Out at 8 to old town – same place as in Feb. 1885!!! 18 years ago. Then to Square. Two offers. One doubtful. The other got cigarettes – same I think as in Alameda in afternoon. Whiskey drunk by waiters, 8/- bottle – 16/-; a day at Carmo far too dear. Went Casino at 5. 1 milreis on Roulette lost.[122]

He divided his time in Madeira between daily visits to the Casino, meeting and dining with friends and acquaintances, and walking and visiting local sights. Some of the walking was done with an eye for approachable young men. Mostly it was mere eyeing, at a distance ('many beauties there – exquisite eyes'), but with one, Augustinho, mentioned on six different days, the entry for 13 March records: 'Augusthino – kissed many times'. His social rounds included the British consul (Spence), Dr Connolly, Will Reid (of Reid's Hotel) and John Hughes from Ireland.[123] There were more casual acquaintances, too: Miss Rolland, Laura Lady Wilton, Mrs Stanford, Lady Edgecumbe and the Duke of Montrose. Mrs Raglan Somerset gave him a hymnal. He collected and paid for photographs, 'Got shamrock' on St Patrick's Day, 'smoked too much y'day', and had one of his regular periods of indisposition ('Stayed in all day, not feeling well. Lay down in afternoon with 3 overcoats on, so cold').

On 18 March he left for the Canary Islands ('on the worst ship I've been on yet. Vile Germans on board'). After a day in Las Palmas, he moved on to Tenerife. He wrote to Cowper, telling him of a book just out, *The Curse of Central Africa*, with two photos of his dog, Rags, in it. Rags was not the 'Curse', he reassured Cowper, but was a Congo celebrity. Consul Croker, he continued, was 'very seedy'; the colony at Madeira was 'most objectionable ... a narrow-minded greengrocer community ashamed to be seen drinking its own wine'. He had met 'young McDonnell' the previous day on his way home from Liberia, also very seedy. 'Africa needs special types of character as well as men – and unless a man is of the peculiar type required he might as well go to the churchyard at once.' He, himself, hoped to go upcountry in May. 'I trust this will be my last journey to that part of Africa – if I am happy to keep my life and to do the things I want to do this time it will certainly be my last journey.'[124]

On the evening of the 21st, the diary records: 'Home by Plaza de Constitucion at 10.30. Sat down and then to waste ground. Came X. not shaved – about 21 or 22. Gave pesetas 13. about. To meet tomorrow.' It would seem, too, that at times phrases of Kikongo helped created the intimate mood of sexual encounters for him, as on the 25th: 'Pepe 17 bought cigarettes – mucho bueno – diaki diaka – moko mavelela mu mami mucho bueno – fiba, fiba, x. p.16.'[125] His health deteriorated, too, as we learn on the 24th:

> Not well. Went Paco's house to 11 Breakfast. Back lay down – then to Laguna feeling very seedy. Got 'John'. Dined with Croker and Mrs C. at Tenerife. Drove back in carriage at 9 pm arriving about 10. To bed. To WC 11 times – awfully bad attack, half dysentry – 'John' barked all night – Charlie's fault leaving him out. Feeling very ill – lots of blood passing.[126]

He finally set sail for Africa on 26 March on the *Anversville*, one of those ships whose cargoes he had monitored for the FO. He was given 'the best room on board' by the captain but was still feeling quite 'seedy': 'Bleeding badly aft as in Santa Cruz.' He rested and read a lot, mostly light material: Loti's *Mon Frère Yves*, *Les Carnets du Roi* ('stupid exposition of a beast king'), Henri de Régnier's *La Double Maîtresse* and M. Corelli's *The Soul of Lilith*. There was time, too, for a rapid sexual encounter: 'Monrovian ... Down and oh! oh!, quick, about 18.' On the morning of 6 April he noted 'Congo water', and they reached Banana that day at 4.30. After an overnight stop the ship continued to Boma, from which, after a brief meeting with Underwood, he left again for Loanda. Following more short consultations with Nightingale, the two of them sailed back north for Cabinda (Nightingale, presumably, on his way home), arriving on the morning of 12 April, Easter Sunday. Here Casement stayed for two and a half weeks and, once again, began his regular consular correspondence.[127]

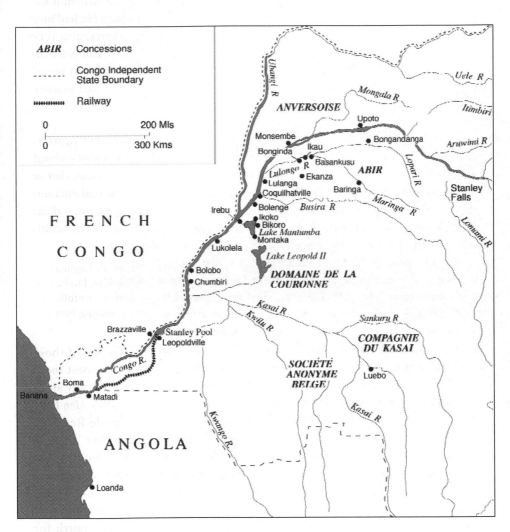

Map 5: Congo Free State, Upper Congo

8: *Congo Investigation, 1903*

Cabinda

'Cabinda quite dead, like Loanda and Boma too', Casement commented in his diary at the beginning of his last and most momentous stint of service in Africa. The climate was oppressive. On 29 April he wrote in his diary: 'Fever on me – all thro' night. First attack since I came out. Took 16 grains of quinine and lay down till 3 pm.' In his spare time he played snooker or read – Conan Doyle's *Mystery of Cloomber* and, a present from Gertrude, Somerville and Ross's *Some Experiences of an Irish RM*. He availed of an opportunity to buy six bottles of Irish whiskey from a passing ship and four suits from the local Hatton & Cookson store. To Gertrude he wrote: 'I am now back on my way to Boma where I go to the Upper Congo I hope in May ... Charlie my Kruboy servant is with me – but he will go home to his own people soon for a visit.' He thanked her for the Somerville and Ross book. 'I wish I had more books by the same authors – I fancy one of them is a woman – don't you?'[1]

In Cabinda came news of the death of Sir Hector Macdonald, a distinguished officer who had committed suicide in Paris when returning to Ceylon to face charges of homosexuality: 'The most distressing case this, surely, of its kind and one that may awaken the national mind to saner methods of curing a terrible disease than by criminal legislation.'[2]

Boma and Matadi

On 30 April he packed up and left Cabinda for the Congo. After an overnight stay in Banana, he arrived in Boma on 1 May. From the tone of entries in his diary, one gains the impression that his thoughts were already on his planned journey to the Upper Congo. In the three weeks he was to remain in Boma, he quickly busied himself with the preparatory arrangements for constructing a new consulate; masons began work on 11 May. Routine consular business kept him busy – complaints from British West African subjects, monitoring of ships' cargoes. All the time, he was preparing for his forthcoming investigation. On 8 May he telegraphed the FO: 'Leaving for interior end May closing Boma office'. The FO minute to his telegram was that he be instructed to wait, to deal with the question of wrongs to British subjects.[3]

When he telegraphed on 22 May, suggesting that 'report of cases mentioned will be sent soon but may delay intended journey to interior', an exchange of views took place among FO officials. Farnall felt that the completion of the report on abuses against British subjects was more important than a journey into the interior. Another thought the trip ought not to be delayed too long. It was also felt that Brussels would be angry over the House of Commons debate on the Congo which had just taken place and that, therefore, the FO must be sure of its facts. 'His Majesty's Government are anxious to obtain authentic information.'[4] Pressure from the humanitarian lobby, with the support of many Liberal MPs, had forced the British government to hold a major House of Commons debate on the Congo on 20 May. Among the speakers who castigated the State system were Sir Charles Dilke and Alfred Emmott. A resolution was passed, which had been moved by Herbert Samuel, stating:

> The Government of the Congo Free State having at its inception guaranteed to the Powers that its native subjects should be governed with humanity, and that no trading monopoly or privilege should be permitted within its dominions, and both these guarantees having been constantly violated, this House requests His Majesty's Government to confer with other Powers, signatories of the Berlin General Act by virtue of which the Congo Free State exists, in order that measures may be adopted to abate the evils prevalent in that State.[5]

Casement left Boma on 22 May and travelled across the river to Matadi, where he lodged with Dr Sims. The stay was intended to be short – on his second day he jotted in his diary: 'Hope to get up country now in a few days.' While waiting for FO approval, he got through a substantial amount of writing, mainly on cases concerning the affairs of British West Africans. One of his walks took him past the local prison, where the Luki men had been held the year before: 'Went out for walk to Prison. Just the same as last year; no change save whitewash. No beds. Looked in one of the three cells. Bare cement – blankets rolled upon it – saw no jailor. Three police in yard at back.'

The FO focus on State abuses at this point still rested firmly on the maltreatment of black British subjects in the Congo rather than on that of the general population. In one of his despatches, Casement addressed the FO question of why abuses against British subjects seemed concentrated in a short period. The answer, he pointed out, lay in the sporadic consular presence in the Congo. For example, the Mayumbe rail dismissals had started in January 1902, but he had only returned to his post in May after home leave. He suggested that the British authorities were much to blame for the frequent unavailability of consuls – and he included himself and his predecessor in the criticism: 'It was only with the advent of the Luki cases in June of last year that I took anything like forcible action to recall the Congo authorities to a sense of their duty.' He went on to point out the connection between abuses against natives of the Congo and against black British subjects:

> ... the Congo Administration has deliberately set up a system of government in this country which, for its financial success, has to depend upon criminal methods towards the subject native population. Officials accustomed to dealing with Congo-born natives without the slightest regard for native rights or even for common decency could not, in the case of another black skin, alter their mode of dealing, so that British colonial natives, despite the supposed safeguards of International Conventions and a consulate generally conspicuous by its absence, often suffered as grievously as the native-born victims of oppression.

The problem was the pervasiveness of the Congo State. If one was engaged in litigation with a trade company, this was tantamount to litigation against the State; if one took a steamer, this was almost certain to be a State steamer; if one wished to engage native workmen, State corvée had a higher claim; if one wished to build a house, all land was State-owned; if one wished to buy rubber, ivory or even firewood, the strong arm of government interposed.[6]

While in Matadi he gave the details of one case, from 1901, which he now recounted to underline the importance of British West African subjects having proper contracts before leaving West Africa to work in the Congo. On the morning of 17 July 1901 he had been awoken by a crowd of men outside his bedroom door. He had put them in line, ninety-six in all, and discovered that they had come on a one-year contract with the Congo Railway, the cost of repatriation to be covered by the employer. Now, their contracts expired, they had been refused permission by railway officials to board a ship, due to sail. Having determined that their contracts were in order, Casement instructed them to gather their belongings and go to the ship. He went with them and spoke to the ship's captain before proceeding, with their two headmen, to the offices of the railway company. After spurious excuses, the men were paid and got their passage tickets.[7]

On 4 June his diary recorded: 'The Debate in Commons has been terrible attack on Congo State. Morrison to lecture too!' He wrote privately to Farnall, saying that he hoped not to be in the Congo when the FO made representations to the Congo government:

> It will make my position highly disagreeable – for I am on friendly terms with the individuals whose official acts I feel at times compelled to very harshly criticise ... and I have no colleague to support me – so that all the burden of attacking the misdeeds of this Government falls on the one Consul. The Congo Government here look on me with no friendly eye as you may imagine ...

The problem was that 'in so small a circle we have to meet so often'; thus he would hope either to be in the interior or 'in some position of retirement', when the FO acted: 'I wish very sincerely, from a personal point of view, I were out of this horrid country – it is a nightmare – and I may die of morphia like Rabinek – or become a drunkard like all the people who put themselves in antagonism to the amenities of Congo civilization.' In a first reference to his future friend, he asked if Farnall could help Morel with 'his new paper': 'I don't know the man but I'm told he is honest and his articles on Congo misrule have appealed to me – they are so singularly well-informed.'[8]

He had time in Matadi for a last busy round of social calls. He read some Irish magazines and got some literary inspiration: 'Dreamed splendid plot of Novel. Got up at 3 am, sketched it out. Wd. make splendid story.' He tried to make arrangements to have his 'lunatic bulldog' looked after while he was away on the Upper River, but John, who had been alternatively sick or troublesome (he arrived 'very badly burnt on nose, brutally burnt by Underwood over some dirty pig of his'), continued to cause problems. An attempt to send him home by ship from Matadi failed after John took over the captain's cabin 'and refused to give way', so Casement prepared to keep him for his upriver journey.[9] Casement also alerted his cousin, Roger, to the arrival in Magherintemple of a consignment of furniture: 'I hope you will pardon my making Magherintemple a sort of dumping ground for old curios – the present things consist of a Table & a (very much broken) chest of Drawers in a dark Brazilian wood called *jacarandá*.' In a postscript he announced: 'I got the South African War Medal (of 1900) day before y'day – sent me by the Sec. of State! Three years old, but better late than never.'[10]

Stanley Pool

On Thursday, 4 June he received a number of FO wires, one of which must have carried the awaited approval to proceed and he jotted: 'To go to interior as soon as possible, and to send reports soon.' He telegraphed back immediately: 'I proceed Stanley Pool tomorrow'.[11] He left Matadi by train on 5 June on the two-day journey to Leopoldville. At Kimpese he commented: 'The country a desert, no natives left.' When he called on the local commissaire, the latter estimated that there were five women to one man in the country, suggesting sleeping sickness as the cause – 'I said also Transports!' The second day took him past familiar terrain to Leopoldville: 'No signs of improvement, save a few broader paths to the water where we swam of old.'[12]

He was to spend almost a month in the Leopoldville area, the time probably being needed to make travel arrangements for his upriver investigation. His diary shows a reasonably intense range of activities, including those concerning his onward travel. He was able to make arrangements with the Société Anonyme Belge to take him on the first leg of his journey, as far as Chumbiri. Since State regulations did not allow the Société to carry passengers, permission had to be sought; it came on 27 June. The rest of his journey would be more sensitive, and he was intent on avoiding dependence on State transport, with its attendant risk of obstruction and monitoring. He consulted with local missionaries regarding use of a boat and a crew, in particular with the Revd T. Hope Morgan of the Congo Balolo Mission, with whom he was staying.

Since the French Congo was part of his responsibility, he took the opportunity of twice crossing to Brazzaville to make diplomatic calls. He liked Brazzaville: 'It is the beginning of a town – not as at Leo only a Great Govt factory.' In Leopoldville, too, there were diplomatic calls. Casement had several meetings with the Italian consul, Dr Villa: 'Dr Villa told me of a recent visit he made to a village near Madimba and the people seeing a white man all ran away.' Villa, he reported to the FO on 30 June, gave it as his opinion that the only focus of the Congo State was in money-making and he regretted the involvement of Italians. The judiciary was only nominally independent and could be denied transport, for example. The State had adopted and used those very means of oppression which it was created to abolish. If force ceased to be used, then exports would decline.[13]

While waiting to proceed upriver, Casement spent a good deal of his time carrying out his normal consular functions. In one despatch he referred to the case of a West African, S.C. Bentill:

> Bentill first drew my attention to his situation and begged for my intervention by letters addressed to me in June 1899, when I still resided in Loanda. Despite nearly two years of inquiry and of hearings carried on at Matadi and at Boma which resulted in a wholly illogical finding of the Court, it is only now, nearly two years after Bentill's departure from the Congo and four years after the case was first brought by Bentill to the official cognizance of the *Ministère Public* at Matadi that a judgement in his favour has been obtained.
>
> It has taken almost four years, during which period I must have written and received nearly fifty letters in connection with the case and repeatedly interviewed Bentill and others, to obtain a settlement of a simple claim for wages between master and servant which should have been easily settled on the spot, had there been a competent authority to decide such cases, within a week.[14]

Several other despatches continued the sad story of the men arrested as vagabonds at Luki in May 1902. By his persistence in following up the case, Casement was discovering further injustices. The Mayumbe Railway Company, for whom the men had been working, finding it was not doing as well as expected, decided to reduce its personnel. It began to dismiss men, though the Sierra Leoneans had two-year contracts, drawn up before an official of the Congo government. Now they were simply cast adrift at Luki, where the company had its headquarters.

The men's situation was known locally by officials of the State, but no effort was made to intervene on their behalf.[15] On the contrary, because of the increasing number of idle men – and there were some 'bad characters' – the State took rapid repressive measures. A raid was made in the neighbourhood of the railway station, during which the men for whom Casement later intervened were arrested. So, too, were other West Africans, to whose cases Casement devoted considerable attention. Of the twelve men he knew of, seven died in prison, one escaped and he repatriated four. He had been told by one of the four whom he repatriated that Judge Beekman had found in their favour but, because of the man's 'imperfect English', Casement could not determine the grounds of the judgment.[16]

Some days later he reported again on the case of these men, after receiving from London the draft of the Foreign Office's proposed instruction to its representative in Brussels, Sir C. Phipps, on the subject of hardships caused to British subjects in the Congo. He had just got a copy of the judgment from Judge Beekman, who also told him, referring to another mistreated British subject, that he (Beekman) had 'tried to obtain reparation for Mrs Meyer, but had found himself powerless in face of the opposition of the Governor-General'. Casement commented:

> If the Law Officers of the Congo Government themselves admit their inability, without the intervention of His Majesty's Consul in the country, to render a measure of justice to British subjects – and it is apparent from these cases that that intervention has been absolutely essential to obtain adequate inquiry or redress – it cannot well be sustained that His Majesty's Government have not indeed, as your Lordship states, very good grounds to consider whether one of the measures to be adopted should not be the eventual resumption of their extra-territorial jurisdiction.[17]

At the Pool, too, he continued to monitor the importation of arms. Numerous arms had been imported in 1901 and 1902, he reported, but there had recently been a falling-off. Many Albini rifles had been imported, which were 'in the hands of the large, loosely-organised masses of natives who compose the public force of the Congo State', and some of these would have passed into other hands.[18]

While at Leopoldville he mixed a good deal with the local missionaries and members of the commercial and administrative establishment. In his diary he noted getting a copy of *Punch*, with a satirical poem on the Congo. He wrote to Gertrude some days later, thanking her for the cuttings and for Congo news from England.[19] Replying to a letter from Pincus in Lourenço Marques, he said that he was sorry to learn that 'you are still without satisfactory prospects ... I sometimes wish I were there again – but this place too has its attractions and here I am quite free from red tape and officialism – the latter of which is insupportable to one of my (too) independent views'. He asked Pincus to pass on his

greetings to Tom, 'young Parminter', Blücher and Coudenhove ('I owe both letters – especially the latter'), the Budds and Sievwright.[20]

The Thieves' Kitchen: Journey to the Upper Congo

On 1 July he informed the FO that he was 'on the point of leaving for
Chumbiri'.[21] He got away on 2 July on what was to be a two-and-a-half month
journey, one of momentous significance for himself and for the Congo campaign. He sailed on the *P. Brugmann* as far as Chumbiri, a voyage of four days.
As he left, he noted: 'Beautiful Dover cliffs – lovely view. Camped on island in
Pool at 6.30 about. Hippo down stream. Saw three pelicans feeding – close to
us. Also saw a beautiful Egyptian Ibis. Black body & white wings – a lovely fellow in full flight over us for his Home in the woods below Dover Cliffs – white-
winged too.' He had talked to the Revd Hope Morgan about Rabinek and now
he got physical reminders. On the 3rd the diary had: 'Passed Rabinek's grave at
11', and on the 4th: 'Black River: 9.38. where Rabinek died. 1st September 1901,
the day I left Congo for Loanda, I think the last time!'[22]

On the 6th he arrived at Chumbiri, where he spent four days. In his Congo
Report, submitted in December and published the following February, he contrasted the Chumbiri of 1903 with that he remembered from 1887: 'I had visited
this place in August 1887 when the line of villages comprising the Settlement
contained from 4000 to 5000 people. Most of these villages to-day are entirely
deserted, the forest having grown over the abandoned sites and the entire community at the present date cannot number more than 500 souls.'[23]

While recognizing the role of sleeping sickness as a factor in the decrease
in population, Casement focused on State impositions on the local population.
The heaviest of these was the compulsory supply of food to the government
post and to the local woodcutting post. 'The staple food of the entire Upper
Congo', he explained, 'is a preparation of the root of the cassava plant, steeped
and boiled, and made up into loaves or puddings of varying weight.' Despite the
decline in population, the demands for this food, called *kwanga*, remained constant, even increased. Local people complained, 'How can we possibly plant and
weed our gardens, seek and prepare and boil the cassava, make it into portable
shape, and then carry it nearly a day's journey to the post?' On top of this, they
were compelled to give free labour in clearing the path of the telegraph line that
passed through the area. Moreover, the State recompense for *kwanga* was only
about a third of the price paid by missionaries.

There was evidence, too, of force, in the form of armed expeditions, being
used to extract food. 'Very specific statements as to the harm one of these
recent expeditions worked in the country around Chumbiri were made to me
during my stay there,' he reported. He referred to an expedition in 1900, which

left fifteen dead and others taken prisoner. While, in this case, some compensation was paid following complaints, the officer in question still remained in the neighbourhood. Not all Casement's comments were negative and he warmly welcomed the termination of the 'open selling of slaves and the canoe convoys'. But other trade had disappeared, too.

> While the suppression of this form of slave dealing has been an undoubted gain, much that was not reprehensible in native life has disappeared along with it. The trade in ivory has to-day entirely passed from the hands of the natives of the Upper Congo, and neither fish nor any other outcome of local industry now changes hands on an extensive scale or at any distance from home.[24]

He did not like Chumbiri; the weather was hotter, the food monotonous, and he suffered from headache. From Chumbiri he was to travel in the *Henry Reed*, a steamer belonging to the American Baptist Missionary Union. His diary for 10 July recorded: 'Leaving about 8 am this morning. Delayed in starting by the Infallible Cause of all Delay & Every Miscarriage since Eve first ... upset Adam's apple cart – woman!' After a day's steaming, the steamer arrived in Bolobo at 6.55 pm.

He spent ten days in Bolobo, from 10 to 20 July, as a guest at the Baptist Missionary Society station, while the *Henry Reed* was prepared for the voyage ahead. Meanwhile, he interacted with the local Baptists: he visited Miss de Haile's hospital; he joined the Clarkes for a meal: 'a blessed gathering – all silent and all diligently damned like Wordsworth's or Justin McCarthy's tea party'. And, on Sunday: 'At Church about 400 there – mostly males.' His bulldog was with him, creating his usual havoc: ' "John" caught Fataki's goat by forearm – choked him off.' On the 14th, he wrote: 'This must be Auntie's birthday. Poor wee soul. I will send her a present.'

On the 16th he wrote a long letter to the FO in which he suggested that regulations for the control of arms had long been flouted by officials, many of whom sold guns to the natives, until the capture of gun-wielding intruders from Angola had brought about a tightening up of procedures.[25] In a separate letter he informed the FO that, since returning to the Congo in April, he had met sixteen Baptist missionaries, and all had expressed their disapproval of the BMS deputation that visited Leopold in January. On the following day, the 19th, he forwarded a copy of a letter that the six missionaries at Bolobo had sent to the BMS secretary in London, Mr Baynes, protesting at the deputation. It stated: 'We are deeply pained that our beloved Society should be so grossly misrepresented as to be made to appear satisfied with the methods employed by the Congo Government in the collection of rubber, or with its general administration.' They went on to make a vigorous protest, denouncing the system of administration in the country and deploring the unhappy condition of the natives: 'The whole country between our station and the Lake [Leopold] is in a state of unrest, and the timidity of the people painful to witness.'[26]

In his Congo Report Casement would describe the changes that had taken place around Bolobo:

Bolobo used to be one of the most important native Settlements along the south bank of the Upper Congo, and the population in the early days of civilised rule numbered fully 40,000 people, chiefly of the Bobangi tribe. Today the population is believed to be not more than 7000 or 8000 souls. The Bolobo men were famous in former days for their voyages to Stanley Pool and their keen trading ability. All of their large canoes have today disappeared, and while some of them still hunt hippopotami – which are still numerous in the adjacent waters – I did not observe anything like industry among them.

The reasons, which he then summarized, were the same as those described for Chumbiri – the exacting of food and labour taxes.[27]

Arrangements concerning the *Henry Reed* were now being finalized. On the 18th, his diary noted: 'Everything ready on *Reed* ... I am responsible for compensation if she is wrecked! How much I don't know.'[28] He reported to the FO that he felt justified in chartering the ABMU steamer, at the cost of £45 per month, 'for the sake of the objects I have in view on my present journey – viz. to place before your Lordship, so far as it lies in my power to do so, an account and faithful representation of the state of affairs prevailing in this country – more especially in the less frequented districts lying off the main river'.[29]

Having heard that there were refugees from the Lake Leopold II region living in some inland villages not too far away, he set off on the 20th to investigate. Since the lake was the centre of the Domaine de la Couronne and thus more directly under the control of King Leopold than the concession areas, it was the first of the rubber-collecting areas that Casement investigated. He steamed upriver from Bolobo, collected the Revd A.E. Scrivener and camped for the night on the riverbank, before journeying inland the following morning. He was impressed by the industriousness of the refugees in Mpoko, but their story was harrowing. One recounted:

It used to take ten days to get the twenty baskets of rubber – we were always in the forest and then when we were late we were killed. We had to go further and further into the forest to find the rubber vines, to go without food, and our women had to give up cultivating the fields and gardens. Then we starved. Wild beasts – the leopards – killed some of us when we were working away in the forest, and others got lost or died from exposure and starvation, and we begged the white man to leave us alone, saying we could get no more rubber, but the white men and their soldiers said: 'Go! You are only beasts yourselves, you are *nyama* [meat].' We tried, always going further into the forest, and when we failed and our rubber was short, the soldiers came to our towns and killed us. Many were shot, some had their ears cut off; others were tied up with ropes around their necks and bodies and taken away. The white men sometimes at the posts did not know of the bad things the soldiers did to us, but it was the white men who sent the soldiers to punish us for not bringing in enough rubber.

Casement wrote:

I then asked them through Scrivener and Lusala – the native interpreter – to tell me why they had left their homes. Three of the men sat down in front of me, and told a tale which I cannot think can be true, but it seemed to come straight from their hearts. It was translated to me almost word for word by Scrivener and Lusala, and I repeatedly asked certain parts to be gone over again while I wrote in my note book. The fact of my writing down and asking for names etc. seemed to impress them, and they spoke with what certainly impressed me as being great sincerity.[30]

Any doubts about the veracity of the depositions had been dispelled by the time Casement returned downriver in September. While he had been continuing his journey on the Upper Congo, the Revd Scrivener made a six-week journey to the shores of Lake Leopold II and, as Casement's report put it: 'This journey had carried him through the homelands of some of the very refugees I had seen and spoken to at Mpoko. He found the truth of their statements made to me amply confirmed, both by his own observations on the spot and statements made to him by the present Government officer in charge of the district.' Scrivener put his findings in writing and his letters were incorporated into Casement's report.[31]

On the morning of the 22nd, Casement and Scrivener left the village of Mpoko and returned downstream to Bolobo. George Grenfell's steamer, *Goodwill*, had arrived and Casement and Grenfell had a long conversation. Next day Casement continued his progress upriver, reaching Lukolela on the 25th. Here he was met by the Revd John and Mrs Whitehead of the BMS and spent two days looking at Lukolela and neighbouring villages. The local population had declined from about 5000 people in 1887 to less than 600. The reasons given were as elsewhere: 'sleeping-sickness, general ill-health, insufficiency of food, and the methods employed to obtain labour from them by local officials and the exactions levied on them by State soldiers'. The villages he visited were 'ill-kept and tumble-down', a great decline from times past.

Lake Mantumba

Lukolela was near the entrance to Lake Mantumba and Casement stopped at the settlement of Irebu, which lay 'at the mouth of the channel connecting the Congo with Lake Mantumba'. Formerly a flourishing community, the village had 'entirely disappeared'. In its place was a military station – one of four such on the Upper Congo, providing recruits for the Force Publique. He estimated that there must be not less than 18,000 members of the Force distributed throughout the State.[32]

From Irebu he travelled into the lake to Ikoko, an ABMU mission station. 'Rather like Ikoko', he noted the following morning, the 29th, 'the situation is splendid and the lake a delightful feature – no mosquitoes to speak of.' He remained seventeen days, investigating the villages around the lake and some further afield. His Congo Report set the scene:

> Lake Mantumba is a fine sheet of water about 25 or 30 miles long and some 12 or 15 miles broad at the broadest part, surrounded by a dense forest. The inhabitants of the district are of the Ntomba tribe, and are still rude savages, using very fine bows and arrows and ill-made spears as their weapons. There are also in the forest country many families or clans of a dwarf race called Batwas, who are of a much more savage and untameable disposition than the Ntombas, who form the bulk of the population. Both Batwas and Ntombas are still cannibals, and cannibalism, although repressed and not so openly indulged in as formerly, is still prevalent in the district.

The inhabitants had also been successful fishermen and traders, before State rule, but were no longer so. Casement cited testimony about the confiscation of the best canoes by State officials at Irebu. When he suggested to one man that he should lay the matter before the local official, the man 'pulled up his loin cloth and, pointing to where he had been flogged with a chicotte (a whip of hippopotamus hide), said: "If I complained I should only get more of these" '. The worst atrocities and the start of the decline in the area dated from 1893, when a rubber levy was introduced; 'for some four or five years this imposition could only be collected at the cost of continual fighting'. The rubber levy was finally removed, and was replaced by levies of food, baskets or gum-copal.

On 31 July the party crossed the lake to the state post at Bikoro, where they were received by Mr Wauters, the government official in charge of the Equator district, stationed at Bikoro. Casement recorded: 'M.M. Wauters & Van Dele met us & showed the Station and plantation of 800 hectares 400 workmen – Part of the exploitation of the *Domaine Privé*. A Horrid business.' He also noted how few goods there were in the store to pay for the labour and goods extracted from the natives. There seemed to be no more than '200 to 300 pieces of coarse cotton cloth', visibly old and worth no more than £15. Conditions had been much worse in the past, but a mood of fear still pervaded all the local communities. When the *Henry Reed* approached, the inhabitants ran away and only returned when they were assured that the visitors were mission and not State. In a letter to the FO on 3 August, Casement gave a flavour of conditions under the former regime and its then chief, Léon Fiévez. The Revd Joseph Clark had been at Ikoko then, as had two other missionaries, Sjöblom and Banks (both now dead). All had lodged protests:

> A young man, whose hands have been both hacked off, made a statement to me three days ago, which I have taken down in writing, as to how he came to be thus mutilated, which, were it published, would shock the world. It is only one of many such dreadful recitals I have heard.

Fiévez's deeds, which included ordering the hacking- or beating-off of the hands of many men on the edges of canoes, were confirmed to Casement by Mr Wauters at Bikoro. Fiévez had killed 'thousands of the natives at the back of Bikoro'. Casement believed this to refer to the suppression of a revolt brought on by outrages committed. Those days were now gone, claimed Wauters, but the legacy remained. Fiévez had never been tried or punished.[33]

Casement included in his Congo Report a long account by Clark of the rubber wars that started in 1893, along with detailed depositions taken by Casement from five young women who had been orphaned during the wars and were now living at the mission. Bikela, one of the young women, told of how the soldiers came to her village and killed a lot of people, while she and others hid in the bush:

> After that they saw a little bit of my mother's head, and the soldiers ran quickly towards the place where we were and caught my grandmother, my mother, Nza-ibiaka, and another little one, younger than us. Several of the soldiers argued about my mother, because each wanted her for a wife, so they finally decided to kill her. They killed her with a gun – they shot her through the stomach – and she fell, and when I saw that I cried very much, because they killed my mother and grandmother, and I was left alone.[34]

As recently as five months before Casement's visit, a punitive raid had taken place when the village of Mwebi was in arrears with its supply of fish to the camp at Irebu. An armed force took over the village and captured ten men and eight canoes. The captives were taken back to Irebu, 'tied up with native rope so tightly that they were calling aloud with pain'. The men were detained at Irebu until the village brought in a supply of fish and paid a fine. Two died on their release and two more soon afterwards. Of the canoes captured only the old ones were returned.[35]

The pressure on the local community was brought home to Casement when he tried to hire men for woodcutting on the *Henry Reed*:

> More men offered than I needed, and I selected six. The State Chief of the village hearing of this at once came to me to protest against any of his people leaving the town, and said that he would have all the youths I had engaged tied up and sent over to the Government official at Bikoro ... The Chief's argument, too, was perfectly logical. He said, 'I am responsible each week for 600 rations of fish which must be delivered at Bikoro. If it fails I am held responsible and will be punished. I have been flogged more than once for a failure in the fish supply, and will not run any risks. If these men go I shall be short-handed, therefore they must stay to help in getting the weekly tax.' I was forced to admit the justice of this argument, and we finally arrived at a compromise. I promised the Chief that, in addition to paying wages to the men I took, a sum representing the value to him of their labour would be left at Ikoko, so that he might hire extra hands to get the full quantity of fish required of him.[36]

While staying at Lake Mantumba, Casement caught up on his correspondence. On 3 August he sent a long despatch to the FO in which he reported on the meeting he had had at Bolobo with the Revd George Grenfell, the senior BMS missionary in the Congo and an original member of the Commission for the Protection of the Natives. Grenfell had told him that the Commission was 'unworkable and a dead letter'. Members lived hundreds of miles apart and there had been only two meetings since 1896. It had 'no machinery of inquiry nor means of obtaining evidence'. Its members were not consulted prior to their reappointment in 1901 and they were never informed of it nor did they receive any subsequent instructions. Grenfell was stimulated to make this statement following Lord Cranborne's remark in the House of Commons that the Congo State 'had created a Commission for protecting the natives which had sat repeatedly and reported repeatedly and had appointed an inspector'. None of these statements was true, Grenfell stated. The FO found Grenfell's statement of great interest and help, but was unsure if it could be used – it would make his position difficult.37

On 4 August Casement reported to the FO that a considerable force of troops had recently been sent up to the Upper Welle districts – 300 native soldiers and ten or eleven new Italian officers. When he asked Captain Hansen why there were no new Belgian officers, he was given two reasons: the stoppage of a percentage payment on rubber collected and 'the coming of the judges'.38 On 5 August he addressed a letter to Farnall: 'I am going about a good deal. In this lake district things are pretty bad – they have been much worse, but they are to-day very bad.' He went on to compare what he was now seeing with his memories of 1887, the year of his earlier upriver journey:

> Whole villages and districts I knew well and visited as flourishing communities in 1887 are today without a human being; others are reduced to a handful of sick or harassed creatures who say of the Government: 'Are the white men never going home, is this to go on for ever?' I can only outline the sad state of affairs prevailing. I have got a good deal of evidence and testimony, apart from my own observation, and contrast of the state of things today with what I knew formerly, and I am trying to put it into a comprehensive report. But you won't get this for some months, as now I am busy going about and noting, and I cannot well sit down to a report on my tiny steamer with a lot of natives to look after. So far as I can see I shall be months up here. There is very much to see, and it were useless to rush round getting only superficial impressions; much better, now that I am here to see one district thoroughly and get at the bottom of things, than merely run from district to district.39

'The fact', noted the FO minute to this, 'that what Mr Casement knew in 1887 as flourishing communities are today without a human being is worth as evidence against the CS a ton of the vague rumours and hearsay reports which he has been sending us.'

Casement made time, too, to keep in contact with friends. To Gertrude he wrote from 'Interior parts of the Country', thanking her for her letters and musing, once more, about the *Irish RM*. 'The last Irish book I like immensely but not so much as the *RM* – the immortal *RM*! Philippa's foxhunt was delightful. I have lent them out here and everyone likes them.' Going on to Congo matters, he revealed some of his frustrations and uncertainties:

> I am sick of the wilderness and its wild beings and long for the paw of civilised man once more *chez lui* ... I am travelling a good deal on a small steamer over lakes and broad stretches of Upper Congo – and shifting my view continually ... write soon to your poor misinformed cousin who knows nothing of what is going on under his eyes and is deaf as well as blind and cannot form an opinion – not anything like a full opinion – upon anything but Bullpups ...40

Cowper was treated to a more racy and partly tongue-in-cheek account:

> I am far away in the interior now – travelling about in my huge Consular dominions ... I write this from a small steam launch in which I am crossing a delightful lake about 20 to 25 miles of open water communicating with the Congo by a deep channel ... The people round this are all cannibals – you never saw such a wild looking lot in your life. There are also Dwarfs (called Batwas) in the forest – who are even worse cannibals ... They eat man flesh *raw*! It's a fact. Both lots go armed with bows and arrows and in war time the arrows are poisoned. I bought a lovely bow (7 ft. high) yesterday for a handful of coarse salt – but the savage owner wouldn't sell the arrows. He needed them he said to bring down a dwarf or two on the way home for the marital cooking pot. The dwarfs, as I say, dispense with cooking pots and eat and drink their human prey fresh cut on the battlefield while the blood is still warm and running. These are not fairy tales my dear Cowper – but actual gruesome, daily reality in the heart of this poor, benighted, savage land.
>
> The missionaries do enormous good here ... these savage lives once brought under the kindlier influence of the Missions frequently develop into gentle, earnest, quiet creatures who seek to live wholly reasonable, decent lives. The more I see of Mission work here in Central Africa the more convinced I am of the vital need for such agencies of human love and brotherhood to beat the life out of the inhuman hate and devildom of this world of savage men ...41

It was while Casement was on Lake Mantumba that the British government finally took some action on the Congo issue. Arising from the motion passed in the House of Commons on 20 May, Britain sought the cooperation of the other signatories to the Berlin Conference in bringing about reform in the Congo. A memorandum from Lord Lansdowne was sent to all the British representatives in those countries that were signatories of the Berlin Act. The memorandum dealt with two issues: the ill-treatment of natives and the existence of a trade monopoly. Lord Lansdowne referred to repeated allegations against the Congo State on both these issues and to the recent debate in the House of Commons. While individual instances of cruelty had been proved by court prosecutions, more serious was the accusation that ill-treatment was systemic:

> It is reported that no efforts are made to fit the native by training for industrial pursuits; that the method of obtaining men for labour or for military service is often but little different from that formerly employed to obtain slaves; and that

force is now as much required to take the native to the place of service as it used to be to convey the captured slave. It is also reported that constant compulsion has to be exercised in order to exact the collection of the amount of forest produce allotted to each village as the equivalent of the number of days' labour due from the inhabitants, and that this compulsion is often exercised by irresponsible native soldiers uncontrolled by any European officer.

Most of the abuses were said to be taking place in the Upper River, in lands of the State or of concessionaires but, the document continued with a reference to Casement and his work:

His Majesty's Government have further laboured under the disadvantage that British interests have not justified the maintenance of a large Consular staff in the Congo territories. It is true that in 1901 His Majesty's Government decided to appoint a Consul of wide African experience to reside permanently in the State, but his time has been principally occupied in the investigation of complaints preferred by British subjects, and he has as yet been unable to travel into the interior and to acquire, by personal inspection, knowledge of the condition of the enormous territory forming his district. His reports on the cases of British subjects, which have formed the basis of representations to the Government of the Independent State, afford, however, examples of grave maladministration and ill-treatment. These cases do not concern natives of the Congo State, and are therefore in themselves alien to the subject of this despatch; but as they occurred in the immediate vicinity of Boma, the seat of the central staff, and in regard to British subjects, most of whom were under formal engagements, they undoubtedly lead to the belief that the natives, who have no one in the position of a Consul to whom they can appeal and have no formal engagements, receive even less consideration at the hands of the officers of the Government.

Despite, then, the lack of conclusive proof, 'there is a feeling of grave suspicion, widely prevalent among the people of this country, in regard to the condition of affairs in the Congo State, and there is a deep conviction that the many charges brought against the State's administration must be founded on a basis of truth'.

In these circumstances, His Majesty's Government are of opinion that it is incumbent upon the Powers parties to the Berlin Act to confer together and to consider whether the obligations undertaken by the Congo State in regard to the natives have been fulfilled; and, if not, whether the Signatory Powers are not bound to make such representations as may secure the due observance of the provisions contained in the Act.

Regarding trade, Lansdowne went on to observe that 'no one other than the agent of the State or of the concession-holder has the opportunity to enter into trade relations with the natives; or if he does succeed in reaching the natives, he finds that the only material which the natives can give in exchange for his trade goods or his money are claimed as having been the property of the State or of the concession-holder from the moment it was gathered by the native'. Therefore, the time had come again for the Powers to consider whether the system of trade and the practice of concession-granting prevailing in the Congo were in harmony with the provisions of the Berlin Act.[42]

Coquilhatville and the La Lulonga Company

From Lake Mantumba, Casement returned to the Congo and turned upstream once more. At Bolenge the party stopped at a mission station run by the American Christian Mission, its only station in the Congo, and met the three missionary couples there, 'Dr Leyton, Mr Faris and Mr Eldred – with their wives.' 'They have done much good in the district', he commented in his report, 'and Dr Leyton, the medical missionary, is making a special study of sleeping sickness, which disease has of late years invaded the district, coming up from the Lower Congo.'[43] In the five days he spent in the villages around Coquilhatville, he focused, again, on the oppressiveness of the food exactions, going into great detail on the amounts of *kwango* required. He offered to buy one amount for ten brass rods or ten times what the man was going to receive at the government post, but '[h]e refused my offer, saying that, although he would like the 10 rods, he dare not be a bundle of his ration short'.[44] Population in the area was much reduced: 'Today, they are broken up into isolated settlements, each much reduced in numbers, and with (in most cases) the houses badly constructed. There were no goats or sheep to be seen, whereas formerly these were very plentiful, and food for the crew was only obtained with difficulty.'[45] This area had special poignancy for Casement: it was here that his friend Edward Glave had been based in the 1880s and that the two had spent some time together in 1887.

On 20 August he arrived at the Congo Balolo mission station of Lulonga, where he was met by 'Messrs Gilchrist, Whiteside and Bond'. Some letters awaited him, including one from Underwood, 'who congratulates me on my appointment to Lisbon!' And, with a sense that his investigation was nearing its end, he reported to the FO: 'I have ample corroboration ... of the systematic maladministration in regard to the natives of the Congo State.' He would, he continued, reach the territory of the Anglo-Belgian India Rubber and Exploration Company (ABIR) on the following day and wouldn't send a report until his return to Stanley Pool around 31 October.[46]

On 22 August he left Lulonga, entered the Lulonga River and, after seven and a half hours' steaming, arrived at the CBM mission station of Bonginda, where he was met by 'Armstrong and Walbaum & 2 ladies'. He had now reached one of the key areas for his investigation, a major rubber-producing region and one of the major concessionary areas, as he later outlined in his report:

> With my arrival in the Lulonga River, I was entering one of the most productive rubber districts of the Congo State, where the industry is said to be in a very flourishing condition. The Lulonga is formed by two great feeders – the

Lopori and Maringa Rivers – which, after each a course of some 350 miles through a rich, forested country, well peopled by a tribe named Mongos, unite at Bassankusu, some 120 miles above where the Lulonga enters the Congo. The basins of these two rivers form the concession known as the ABIR, which has numerous stations, and a staff of fifty-eight Europeans engaged in exploiting the india-rubber industry, with head-quarters at Bassankusu.47

Before he reached the confluence of the Maringa and Lopori and the beginning of the ABIR Concession, he had to pass through the territory of the La Lulonga Company. The region had been exploited, earlier, by two concession companies that 'only abandoned it when, as one of their agents informed me, it was quite exhausted, the stock of rubber vines in it today is drawing to an end, and it is only with great difficulty that the natives are able to produce the quantity sufficient to satisfy their local masters'. The La Lulonga Company, now operating here, had been charged with 'gross offences', including murder and mutilation.48

Casement visited two communities in the La Lulonga Company territory. The first was Bolongo and, again with 1887 as a yardstick, he noted the general decline in the town ('which had only a few years ago been a large and populous community, filled with people and well stocked with sheep, goats, ducks, and fowls'). Because Bolongo was on the main river, he chose a second village on a tributary, where his arrival would not have been anticipated. He spent part of 26 and 27 August in this village, Ifomi, and, 'in an open shed built at the landing-place, I found two sentries of the La Lulonga Company guarding fifteen native women, five of whom had infants at the breast, and three of whom were about to become mothers'. Most of the women were being held to compel their husbands to bring in the required amount of rubber.

> I found that the two sentries at Ifomi were complete masters of the town. Everything I needed in the way of food or firewood they at once ordered the men of the town to bring me. One of them, gun over shoulder, marched a procession of men – the Chief of the village at their head – down to the water side, each carrying a bundle of firewood for my steamer.

When he tried to interview the chief, the sentry 'peremptorily broke into the conversation and himself answered each question put to the Chief'. When night came, 'the fifteen women in the shed were tied together, either neck to neck or ankle to ankle, to secure them for the night, and in this posture I saw them twice during the evening. They were then trying to huddle around a fire'.49

ABIR

From Ifomi, Casement moved on to the ABIR station of Bongandanga, some 120 to 130 miles up the Lopori. He arrived on 29 August, having passed the

ABIR headquarters of Bassankusu on the 28th. The impact of his first day can be gleaned from his diary: '12.10 arr. Bongandanga. Went Abir called on Lejeune. Saw Rubber "market" nothing but guns – about 20 armed men – some with … Albinis – most with cap guns. The people 242 men with rubber all guarded like convicts. To call this *"trade"* is the height of lying. Lejeune a gentlemanly man.' During his stay of five days he observed the high degree of militarization in the station and he reflected in his subsequent report on the importation of arms and on State regulations governing their use. 'There is also', he commented, 'a considerable import by the ABIR Company, I believe, of cap-guns, which are chiefly used in arming the sentinels – termed "forest guards" – who, in considerable numbers, are quartered on the native villages throughout the Concession to see that the picked men of each town bring in, with regularity, the fixed quantity of pure rubber required of them every fortnight.'[50]

He had, as his diary noted, arrived on the day of a 'market', i.e. the day when the men of one village, Nsungamboyo, about twenty miles away, had to bring their rubber to the station.

> There were everywhere sentries in the ABIR grounds, guarding and controlling the natives, many of whom carried their knives and spears. The sentries were often armed with Albini rifles, some of them with several cartridges slipped between the fingers of the hands ready for instant use. Others had cap-guns with a species of paper locally manufactured for charging this form of muzzle-loader. The native vendors of the rubber were guarded in detachments or herds, many of them behind a barricade, which stretched in front of a house I was told was the factory prison, termed locally, I found, the *maison des otages*.

In his conversations with ABIR officials, Casement queried the contradictions in the system: 'trade' in which participation was compulsory and in which one was imprisoned for failing to match targets laid down; a state tax in labour, which was implemented by a private concession and the profits of which accrued to the company; the imprisonment of women and children, who were not themselves responsible for labour. Needless to say, the answers did not satisfy.

While in Bongandanga he stayed in the local mission, immediately beside the ABIR station. On the day after he arrived, a Sunday, some mission boys rushed in to say that a group of women prisoners was being taken through the mission grounds by ABIR sentries. 'In afternoon saw M. Lejeune at Abir. 16 men women & children tied up – from a village Mboyo close to the town. Infamous! The men were put in the prison; the children let go at my intervention. Infamous! Infamous shameful system.' The missionaries told him that they regularly saw such caravans, and, he noted in his report, 'I gathered from the same quarter that the cries of men being flogged have been clearly heard in the Mission, which lies only some 300 yards from the *maison des otages*.'[51] The torment of the missionaries was increased by the fact that they were not allowed to obtain food directly from the local population, but received it from the ABIR, associating them with the oppressive system by which it was obtained.

Casement saw more of the same in outlying villages during the remaining days of his stay. Lejeune, the ABIR agent, suggested that the regime was, in fact, comparatively mild:

> He added that it was not the few guns he disposed of at Bongandanga which compelled obedience to this law, but the power of the Congo State Force Publique, which, if a village absolutely refuses obedience, would be loosed on the district to compel respect for these civilised rights. He added that, as the punishment inflicted in these cases was terribly severe, it was better that the milder measures and the other expedients he was forced to resort to should not be interfered with.⁵²

Casement's thirty-ninth birthday came on 1 September, while he was at Bongandanga. The evening before, Lejeune had organized a dance in Casement's honour: 'all the local Chiefs and their wives &c. came (at L's orders) to it. Poor souls I am sorry for it – of all the forced enjoyment I ever saw this took the cake'.

Downriver

From Bongandanga he turned downriver, clearly considering that he had amassed the evidence needed to indict the State. He had investigated a range of communities, rubber-producing and non-rubber-producing, concessionary territories and those of the Domain de la Couronne. He had analysed food and labour exactions, the quality and quantity of goods given in return, the role of arms used in controlling local populations; he had listened to the testimony of many members of local communities and assessed the general state of their communities. He was now ready to shape his notes into a report.

He left Bongandanga at 8.45 on the morning of 3 September. That night, having surrendered his cabin to a missionary couple, he slept, or tried to, on the roof of the cabin. Earlier in the day he had begun writing to the Governor General 'about ABIR exactions'. On the evening of the 5th the *Henry Reed* again reached the CBM mission station of Bonginda.

From Bonginda he sent off a long despatch to the FO (probably one of those he had been writing on the steamer). His tone had become more indignant since his last letter to them. He began by referring to Captain Guy Burrows's book on the Congo, *The Curse of Central Africa*. Though he felt that the facts recounted by Burrows had the ring of truth, he believed the FO should be cautious: 'Captain Burrows during his later residence on the Congo was not distinguished by temperate habits, and I doubt not the local authorities would be able to bring damaging charges of a more or less personal nature against him, did they so wish, during the course of the pending libel action the publication of his book has given rise to.' Casement had met him at Matadi in the spring of 1901 and 'he did not impress me favourably'. Taking his cue from Burrows, he focused on the effects of the unjust system of food 'prestations':

The effect of these impositions is that, while the natives themselves are often underfed and invariably badly housed and suffering from many ailments, the Government posts maintained by their unremunerated or scarcely remunerated industry are flourishing and prosperous.

Nearly everything necessary for the upkeep of these stations is levied in kind each week from the natives of the immediately surrounding districts, which may or may not be paid for at a figure averaging one-third or one-fourth of its market value. Natives further afield contribute very valuable weekly or fortnightly yields of rubber, gum-copal, ivory, or other natural products of the 'Royal domain', for which a wholly inadequate payment is made.

The punishments inflicted for non-compliance with or failure to complete the tally of these exactions are out of all proportion to the offence, [and] are, I believe, quite illegal, and are often shocking violations of every humane and decent instinct of civilised society. The most specific evidence upon these points possible for one in my position to obtain has been laid before me – sometimes by the sufferers themselves, and I have kept careful record of these statements, so that, if desirable, their truth might later on be tested.

In his judgment, the sixteen years of state rule between 1887 and 1903 'have been, for the native inhabitants, more materially disastrous than the preceding century of savagery – slavery, witchcraft and internecine strife'.

Today these towns have often entirely disappeared, or are, often, only wretched collections of ruinous and ill-kept hovels, wherein a panic-stricken remnant of fugitives (there is no other word to apply to the average Congo householder I have interviewed for the last six weeks) toil, under ever-present dread of the rifle, the lash, or the chain-gang, to satisfy the unremitting demands of the local tax collector, who appears in the guise of a local 'trader' to whom they and their labours have been made over, just as often as in that of a Government official.

Many were killed; others fled to French Congo or to remote and unhealthy forest regions. Casement believed conditions to have been worst between 1893 and 1900, i.e. between the time the decrees for exploiting the Domaine Privé began to take effect and the 'coming of the Judges'. The decline in the reign of terror, which began to take effect in 1900, had less to do, he felt, with the 'coming of the Judges' than with the fact that the resistance of the native population had been broken. Disarmed and 'overawed by the most powerful military organisation in central Africa', they had 'not even the right to die like men defending their homes'. He concluded that slavery was 'today the corner-stone of the edifice raised by Belgian Administration on the Congo – a slavery more degrading and debasing than that of the earlier dealers in human wares'.

He was aware that the FO would need proof:

In making these statements I am aware of the responsibility I incur, and of the necessity which lies upon me to support them by proof. Proof amply sufficient for all impartial minds I believe I have obtained since entering Lake Mantumba on the 28th July; and that proof I hope to lay shortly before your Lordship, and possibly to supplement it by the personal testimony of some of the cruelly outraged individuals who have appeared before me. I have almost finished my investigation, although I hope still to continue my journey to Stanley Falls.[53]

On the following day, 6 September, he forwarded to the FO a copy of a letter he had sent to the Governor General of the State. Since one of Casement's responsibilities was for British subjects, the letter to the Governor General focused on the effects of the state system on members of the Congo Balolo mission.

> By being forced to owe their daily and weekly food supplies to it, the English missionaries dwelling within the ABIR Concession are made participators in a systematic breach of the laws of this country as well as sharers in a method of dealing with the natives, which is contrary to the dictates of humanity, and which must fatally compromise their teaching in the eyes of the community they seek to instruct and lift up.

This system, he said, he had no hesitation 'in denouncing as entirely illegal'. And, 'it is clear to me that the situation thus created is not only prejudicial to the prior rights secured to missionary enterprise in the Congo State by the terms of the Berlin Act, but is in direct conflict with the common law of this country'. He insisted that the missionaries had not requested his intervention and, likewise, that his complaint was not against persons; Mr Lejeune, the ABIR agent, had been exceedingly kind to Casement during his visit.

In his covering letter to the FO he described 'a certain aspect of the illegal system of control of the natives established in the ABIR Concession, in so far as it affects British subjects residing in the territory administered by that Society':

> I am aware that it is asserted by the Congo State authorities that the ABIR society has no administrative powers, but possesses merely proprietorial rights over the soil and its products. As a matter of fact, the ABIR Society exercises absolute authority over every human being, save the English missionaries and some native members of their households dwelling within the basins of the Lopori and Maringa Rivers.

He described how the two rivers, each between 300 and 400 miles long, drained a forest region rich in natural products – rubber, gum-copal and timber. The native population of Mongos numbered possibly 1,500,000 and were 'among the most docile and tractable of all the Congo races'. They 'possess many excellent natural qualities, and under a just or ordinarily humane administration they would quickly respond to civilised teaching':

> They have been ... handed over, bound hand and foot to a gang of unscrupulous plunderers, and are reduced to a condition of servitude and unhappiness in the interest of these privileged scoundrels I could not have believed possible had I not seen it with my own eyes. I have spent only a few days in the country of this interesting race, in touch with one only of the ABIR factories, and that I gather from all sides unquestionably the best managed of any within the Con-

cession, and yet I have seen enough in that brief period to make me sick at heart for the lot of these people and ashamed of my own skin and colour, where to be a white man means to be a greedy and pitiless oppressor.54

The Case of Epondo

In his diary for 6 September, while at the CBM station of Bonginda, Casement recorded: 'In eveg. Bompoli came with wounded boy – hand off. Awful story. Decided go to Ekanza.' Greater detail is given in the Congo Report. The boy, it was reported, had been shot by a sentry of the La Lulonga Company and, as he lay unconscious, the sentry cut off his hand to take it to the director of the company at Mampoko. Casement decided to visit the boy's village, Ikanza-na-Bosunguma, the following morning.55 But, on the morrow came a stream of visitors, local people bringing their stories to the British consul. A delegation from the village of Lobolo brought three individuals 'shockingly wounded by gunfire' and a small boy of six or seven, whose right hand had been cut off. The chief and sub-chief of Bosombongo came with a man and a small boy, both with limbs shattered by gunfire.

Then came a number of people from Mpelenge with a boy of seven, whose right hand was gone; and a group from Bokotila, telling their story. Casement took the details, in all cases involving the La Lulonga Company. 'Other people were waiting,' he wrote, 'desirous of speaking with me, but so much time was taken in noting the statements already made that I had to leave, if I hoped to reach Ikanza-na-Bosunguma at a reasonable hour'. He left with Armstrong and Danielson in two canoes. They reached Bosunguma and '[a]fter some little delay a boy of about 15 years of age appeared, whose left arm was wrapped up in a dirty rag. Removing this, I found the left hand had been hacked off by the wrist, and that a shot hole appeared in the fleshy part of the forearm. The boy, who gave his name as Epondo, in answer to my inquiry, said that a sentry of the La Lulonga Company now in the town had cut off his hand'. They searched for and found the sentry, Kelengo, who blamed another sentry for the deed, but the villagers were adamant in accusing Kelengo. Realizing that he did not have time to visit other villages in the area, Casement decided to make a test case of this.

> In that one case the truth of the charges preferred was amply demonstrated, and their significance was not diminished by the fact that, whereas this act of mutilation had been committed within a few miles of Mampoko, the headquarters of a European civilising agency, and the guilty man was still in their midst, armed with the gun with which he had first shot his victim ... no one of the natives of the terrorised town had attempted to report the occurrence.

Fear, he believed, was the main reason that events such as this were not reported. Their stories had carried the conviction of truth.

That everything asserted by such a people, under such circumstances, is strictly true I should in no wise assert ... In spite of contradictions, and even seeming misstatements, it was clear that these men were stating either what they had actually seen with their eyes or firmly believed in their hearts. No one viewing their unhappy surroundings or hearing their appeals, no one at all cognizant of African native life or character, could doubt that they were speaking, in the main, truly; and the unhappy conviction was forced upon me that in the many forest towns behind the screen of trees, which I could not visit, these people were entitled to expect that a civilised administration should be represented among them by other agents than the savages euphemistically termed 'forest guards'.[56]

The following day, 8 September, Casement spent writing. He decided to lay a charge against Kelengo in the Epondo case and left the mission at Bonginda on the 9th, arriving in Coquilhatville on the 10th. His diary records: '8.30 Arr. Wangata. Stevens [sic]. Charged Kelengo with his abominable crimes. Told Steevens. I denounced the System which permitted armed savages to go about the country.'[57]

He was approached that night by a chief from Monsembe, fleeing from the State, who begged Casement to take him as far as Lukolela and leave him on the French side; he could no longer meet State food demands. The State demanded goats, but there were none left in the neighbourhood; some could be bought in inland areas, for 3000 brass rods, but the State only paid 100 rods. The price for default was the 'chain gang' and probable death. Though not in a position to take the man with him, Casement wrote to the Revd John Weeks in Monsembe, who corroborated the man's story in a letter on 7 October.[58]

Leopoldville

The rest of the return voyage downriver was rapid – past Lukolela, Bolobo and Chumbiri. He reached the Pool on 15 September, going first to Brazzaville and then across to Leopoldville. He telegraphed the FO from Brazzaville:

I have returned from the Upper Congo State today with convincing evidence of shocking misgovernment and wholesale oppression. I ought to place facts of the case before your Lordship before submitting these to any party and pretended local investigation. I would return to the Consulate without visiting Boma where the Congo State authorities by means of verbal intercourse will try to diminish the significance of my disclosures.

One FO minute to his telegram suggested that it was better for him to remain where he was, as he would be of no use in London, but of some use in the Congo.[59] On the same day, the 15th, he began another despatch, in which he explained the immediate circumstances of his return:

From far and near people were coming in to beg that I would help and protect them. On Monday, the 7th ... there must have been close on 100 wild forest savages on the mission beach at Bonginda waiting or hoping to see the

'Bonkunzi' (i.e. the chief of the English), to pour out their tale of wrong. This within a few hours only of my arrival at Bonginda ... I was rapidly ceasing to be a Consul travelling in a foreign country, and had become a Criminal Investigation Department.

When he asked the people why they had not appealed to the local commissaire, they replied, 'Why it is the Commissaire – it is Bula Matadi who does these things. It is he who lets loose the sentries on us for rubber; and burns down our towns if we fail.'

After helping Epondo to bring a charge against Kelengo in Coquilhatville, Casement had returned quickly to Leopoldville:

I do not think I shall go again up-river unless your Lordship desires it. I have seen enough. My Report will take time to complete. I have a great mass of statements and notes which require to be put into shape. They constitute an extraordinary case for inquiry, seeing that I have been away from Stanley Pool only since the 2nd July, and in the regions where atrocities are very profitable not more than six weeks.

He thought it best to leave for home quickly, without calling at Boma.

The truth is, I have broken into the thieves' kitchen, and they will not willingly let the information go out of the place intact. I am very tired, having travelled about 1600 miles in a small steam-launch, and all my regular Consular work is in arrears, and I hope it may soon be found possible to send out a Vice-Consul.

In a postscript he added that he was sending a personal letter to Fuchs, the Governor General, about the mutilated boy; it would doubtless 'give great offence', but 'I cannot help it, it is the sad truth, and then people want the truth more badly even than, in another sense, they want rubber.'[60]

On the following day, 16 September, he forwarded to the FO copies of two letters which the Revd John Whitehead had sent from Lukolela to the Governor General. Together they comprised further indictments of the State system. Whitehead's first letter, written on 28 July, was a response to a State questionnaire on sleeping sickness. As well as answering the questions asked, Whitehead suggested that high mortality derived in part from the weakened condition of the people because of the exactions of the State. The population of Lukolela had dropped from 6000 in 1891 to 719 in 1896 to 352 in July of 1903, Whitehead reported.

If something is not soon done to give the people heart and remove their fear and trembling (conditions which generate fruitfully morbid conditions and proneness to attacks of disease), doubtless the whole place will be very soon denuded of its population. The pressure under which they live at present is crushing them; the food which they sadly need themselves very often must, under penalty, be carried to the State post, also grass, cane string, baskets for the *caoutchouc* [rubber] (the last three items do not appear to be paid for); the *caoutchouc* must be brought in from the inland districts; their Chiefs are being weakened in their prestige and physique thorough imprisonment, which is often cruel, and thus weakened in their authority over their own people, they are put into chains for the shortage of manioc bread and *caoutchouc*.

State officials made not the least effort to help the people to prevent sickness or to provide relief. As a result of all this, the people saw the State as their enemy.

Some have already sworn to die, be killed, or anything else rather than be forced to bring in *caoutchouc*, which spells imprisonment and subsequent death to them; what they hear as having been done they quite understand can be done to them, so they conclude they may as well die first as last. The State has fought with them twice already, if not more; but it is useless, they will not submit.

The second of Whitehead's letters, written on 7 September, was more forceful still.[61]

Casement spent ten days around Stanley Pool. 'I am wondering what to do,' he noted in the diary. Stress and exhaustion probably contributed to an uncharacteristic outburst: 'Gave "John" a fearful hiding, broke my stick over him.' He made arrangements for the return of the *Henry Reed*, now leaking, and paid off the crew. He walked and he socialized – with members of the business community, with the missionaries and, on several occasions, with Dr Villa, with whom he discussed his findings. But, most of all he wrote. Finally, on the 25th, he departed by train: 'Left Kinchasa at 7 am Billington, Gordon, Williams & Villa came to see me off – Beastly journey down in dirty foul smelling smoke.' After a night's stop in Tumba, he reached Matadi on the 26th.

He was met by a group of friends, but only lingered in Matadi long enough for essential tasks. He arranged the hire of a steam launch for the trip to Banana and 'sat up late writing out fresh plain copy of my letter to Gov. General of 12 Sept on condition of the country in interior. Will leave it at Boma to go up'. On the 27th, his diary opened: 'Finished the letter to Gov. Tired after writing most of night.' He left early and took the launch down to Boma, arriving late. Early next morning he sent the letter and travelled on to Banana.

Cabinda, Loanda and Home

En route next day to Cabinda, he wrote a long, explanatory despatch to the FO, enclosing the second letter he had sent to Fuchs. Having summarized some of his observations for Fuchs, regarding the ABIR and La Lulonga areas, he wrote:

The things I have seen in those parts of the district of the Equator I have recently visited, accompanied, too, as these have been by the most specific statements it was possible for the rude beings relating them to make, have left me in bewilderment as to what my duty as a civilized man should be. I am not a private individual, and my position in this country as the Consular Representative of a foreign Power places me in an exceptionally difficult position. A heavy responsibility lies upon me.

For I cannot conceal from your Excellency that to me the responsibility for the dreadful state of affairs prevailing in many parts of the country I have visited is not to be attributed to the meaner instruments of crime and the savage agents of extortion I have seen at their dirty work, but to the system of general exploitation of an entire population, which can only be rendered successful by the employment of arbitrary and illegal force. That population is supposed to be free, and protected by excellent laws: those laws are nowhere visible; that force is everywhere.

I am amazed and confounded at what I have both seen and heard; and if I, in the enjoyment of all the resources and privileges of civilized existence, know not where to turn to, or to whom to make appeal on behalf of these unhappy people whose sufferings I have witnessed, and whose wrongs have burnt into my heart, how can they, poor, panic-stricken fugitives, in their own forest homes, turn for justice to their oppressors? The one dreadful, dreary cry that has been ringing in my ears for the last six weeks has been, 'Protect us from our protectors.'

He assured the Governor General that he had been personally received with great courtesy by local officials; his criticisms were not directed at individuals: 'I do not accuse an individual; I accuse a system.'[62] He informed the FO that he was conscious of the implications of his letter:

I was, and am, fully aware of the personal responsibility I incurred by the employment of such language – even in the guise of a personal appeal – to the Head of the Government of the country, where I must exercise, by friendly intercourse, my Consular functions; and I fully realised that with the dispatch of this letter, if I decided on sending it, I probably severed my connection with the Consular representation of my country in the Congo State – if not, indeed, my entire connection with His Majesty's Consular Service. I finally decided that my duty was to serve the persecuted beings who had far and wide appealed to me for help, even at the risk of incurring your Lordship's displeasure.

Casement believed that he had only touched on the fringe of the abuses, but to have pursued them further would have led to intervention on the part of the State to prevent his investigations. Already, he claimed, he was being 'shadowed' wherever he went. What was needed, though not likely to be agreed to, was an international commission, completely independent of the Congo State, and endowed with supreme authority, which the natives could trust. The results from the work of such a commission would, he believed, be 'astonishing'.

His despatches from the Upper River produced varying assessments from Foreign Office officials. 'Something no doubt in reading these despatches must be allowed for the rather exuberant diction for which Consul Casement has a weakness,' one wrote. '[B]ut ... they seem to me to provide us with a far more effective weapon of attack on the Congo State than any which we have hitherto had in our hands.' The official drew attention to Casement's repeated use of phrases such as 'most specific evidence' and suggested that Casement would write a much better report 'in the quieter atmosphere of London' and with someone from the Office to help in drafting. He believed that if Casement could substantiate a half or a third of the cases, then the FO should drop weaker ones.

A second official was somewhat more biting, suggesting that Casement should come home for drafting and assistance 'in the direction of the elimination of violent diatribes against the Congo State which he has no evidence to support'. He agreed with Casement 'that his residence in the CS is no longer of utility'. And, 'he has – perhaps not unnaturally after all he has heard and seen – got the "system" of administration on the brain, and has come to regard the whole matter as a personal one between himself and the CS; and we ought to have as British representative someone not harder hearted, but harder headed'. Lord Lansdowne himself was more discriminating: 'making every allowance for the strength of his feelings these papers are a terrible indictment', and, 'he speaks as an eye witness upon many of the points'.[63] With regard to the possibility of Casement's staying on to acquire further information, one official addressed the question of whether Casement was in any danger: 'It is inconceivable ... the Congo people would never be so mad as to make away with a British Consul at the present moment.'[64]

On 2 October, having bought tickets for himself, his three servants, Charlie, Masamba and Mawuku, and, of course, his bulldog, John, Casement set out on the *Benguela*, arriving in Loanda late on the 3rd. On Sunday morning, the 4th, he went ashore, made his way to the consulate and '[g]ot in all right over wall and so installed'.[65] He was to remain in Loanda for over a month, in part, presumably, because he and the FO were uncertain how to proceed and in part because he thereby avoided the awkwardness of being in Boma.

The month alternated between periods of intense writing and others of lassitude. At times he was indisposed; on the 17th he wrote: 'Not well ... Turned in in fearful sweat feeling very seedy.' But for the most part he was busy. On 15 October: 'Wrote a little to clear up back work – got rid of several outstanding things. Then to FO corr[espondence].'

While he was in Loanda, the FO telegraphed to say that Grenfell's comments on the Commission for the Protection of the Natives were of great importance 'and we should like to publish them. Do you see any objections?' Casement warned that there could be problems for British missionaries and asked that they wait while he contacted Grenfell himself. He followed with another telegram saying that it would take a month to communicate with the missionary.[66] During his stay, too, news came of the British government's Note to the Powers: 'Got big mail from Congo by her with papers up to 24th September – The British Note to the European Powers published – I am referred to as a "Consul of Extensive African Experience". Well, we'll see.' On 20 October he received a letter from Edmond Morel; on the following day he noted in his diary: 'Wrote to Morel about Congo also writing Poulteney Bigelow on the same subject & to Joseph Conrad – & telling E.D.M. to send his pamphlet to them.' Several days later he got further letters, this time from Morel and Herbert Ward. In his letter to Morel, Casement recommended Joseph Conrad for help in the Congo campaign:

> Another man who might be of help (in a literary way) is Joseph Conrad the author of some excellent English – a Pole, a seaman and an ex-Congo traveller. I knew him well – and he knows something of the Congo – indeed one or two of his shorter stories – such as *The Heart of Darkness* deal with his own view of Upper Congo life. Send him one or two copies of the pamphlet ... and I will drop him a line to say I had asked them to be sent ... Conrad is a charming man – gentle, kind and sympathetic and he will, I hope, move his pen when I see him at home.[67]

After Arthur Nightingale failed to arrive back in the Congo when expected, Casement commented in his diary: 'I suppose he is being kept by FO over the Congo palaver to advise them. They need an adviser but A.N. knows but little on the subject. Still it is good to have even him – but he will give them wrong advice I fear. He is not very pro-native & is after all a trader at heart.'

The FO moved to bring Casement home. On 20 October they telegraphed: 'If you are now in possession of all such facts and evidence as you are likely to be able to obtain, you had better come home, and prepare your detailed report here.' On the following day he wrote in the diary that he was 'not decided. Shall wait till FO wire me what they think of my private letter to Gov-General'. Perhaps the issue was whether it was now possible for him to return to Boma at all.[68]

During all of this time there was a fair amount of socializing – games of tennis, listening to band recitals, walking and meals with friends and associates. He saw much of the British vice-consul, W.S.R. Brock, and even more of the German consul, Paul Dorbritz, with whom he discussed the Congo on a number of occasions. According to Dorbritz, 'wholesale butcheries' and 'mutilations' were not unknown in (German) Cameroon, from his own experience, and he presumed they were present in British colonies. Better to focus, he suggested, on commercial rights rather than on injured human rights.[69]

He reported to the FO that the ABMU had refused to accept payment for the use of the steamer. He had fulsome praise for all involved and suggested a donation of £25 to the ABMU and one of £20 to the Congo Balolo mission for the services of Mr D.J. Danielson, the Danish engineer. He had time, while in Loanda, to write to Fritz Pincus: 'I have been on a long journey up the Congo. I am having hard times of it in some senses – and fighting the great fight against injustice and oppression – and I think I shall win the day yet – The public mind of the world is being moved – and light *shall* break in on the horrid thing I have been battling against now for years.' He asked, as usual, for his friends. 'Do you ever see my dear old Coudenhove? I have not written to him for years – it is all my fault.'[70]

On 31 October he telegraphed the FO to say that he might return to the Congo State on 7 November 'for the acquirement of further facts but, if so, local authorities will certainly obstruct my movements'. The FO telegraphed on 3 November, repeating that his information 'should be in the hands of HMG and that your report should be prepared asap'. He should return to London, therefore, unless he could clearly get further information. Casement replied on the following day that he would leave for Europe on Friday and should reach Lisbon on 26 November.[71] He paid off Masamba, Mawuku and Charlie, dined with friends and, finally, boarded the *Zaire*. The diary entry for 7 November read: 'Steaming splendidly. Did 191 miles to noon – *Zaire* very pleasant.'

The *Zaire* reached Lisbon on the 24th. There he met Cowper, had lunch with the Gosselins at the legation and left his dog with Parkinson once more. Leaving on the 26th he reached Liverpool late on the 30th and took the night train to London.

9: *Congo Report and Congo Reform,*
1903–13

Casement arrived in London on 1 December.[1] On the same day Joseph Conrad wrote to invite Casement to visit him at his home, Pent Farm, in Hythe, Sussex. He joked about the spartan conditions: 'I have always had a great opinion of your courage ... If you are the man I knew in Africa you shall not shirk coming all the way here to see a more or less lame friend ... I need not tell you there is no more ceremony than if we asked you to step under a tent on the road to Kinchassa. I am glad you've read the *Heart of Darkness* tho' of course it's an awful fudge.' He was now married, with a child, and living a frugal life with few acquaintances.[2]

Harry Farnall dropped Casement a note to say that Lord Percy, the new Parliamentary Undersecretary of State, would like to see him. The diary recorded their meeting, on the 2nd: 'Went & saw him & had a long talk. Think I gave him some eye openers.' Then Eric Barrington wrote informing him that Lord Lansdowne wished to see him also. He did so on the 3rd: 'Went Lansdowne House – Saw Barrington & then H.L. [His Lordship]. He was very nice & after hearing my dire tale said "Proof of the most painfully convincing kind, Mr Casement." '

He also wrote to Cowper on the 3rd to let him know that he had arrived, after a rough journey over the Bay of Biscay, and that he was busy writing his report: 'I saw Eric Barrington today who spoke of Lisbon again – and of ME as the man for it – so that seems to be quite decided on ... Personally I hope you will hold on longer – for I want to put in another spell on Congo to *convict* that abomination of all its shortcomings and excesses. My whole life seems now to be run into that and I feel I'd sooner die tonight than leave that duty undone.'[3]

Work on producing the report commenced in earnest on 5 December: 'Typer came & hard at work all day – began dicting [*sic*] my Report. Got 4500

words of it typed & wrote more.' The press was courting him, looking for interviews. On the 10th he met the missionary organizer, Harry Grattan Guinness[4]
and, for the first time, E.D. Morel: 'Dined at Comedy together late – & then to
chat till 2 am. M. sleeping in study.' Sir Arthur Conan Doyle, later an active participant in the Congo campaign, would describe this first meeting of Casement
and Morel as 'the most dramatic scene in modern history'.[5] Morel described the
meeting in his *History of the Congo Reform Movement*:

> In Ward's empty house in Chester Square ... Casement and I met for the first
> time, the Foreign Office having given Casement its sanction to that meeting. It
> was one of those rare incidents in life which leave behind them an imperishable
> impression. I saw before me a man, my own height, very lithe and sinewy, chest
> thrown out, head held high – suggestive of one who had lived in the vast open
> spaces. Black hair and beard covering cheeks hollowed by the tropical sun.
> Strongly marked features. A dark blue penetrating eye sunken in the socket. A
> long, lean, swarthy Vandyck type of face, graven with power and withal of great
> gentleness. An extraordinarily handsome and arresting face. From the moment
> our hands gripped and our eyes met, mutual trust and confidence were bred and
> the feeling of isolation slipped from me like a mantle.

Casement talked Congo into the small hours,

> crouching over the fire in the otherwise unlighted room ... unfolding in a musi-
> cal, soft, almost even voice, in language of peculiar dignity and pathos, the story
> of a vile conspiracy against civilisation ... For hours he talked on, with now and
> again a pause, as the poignancy of recollection gripped him, when he would
> break off the narrative and murmur beneath his breath, 'Poor people; poor,
> poor people.' At intervals he would rise, and with swift silent steps, pace the
> room; then resume his crouching attitude by the fire, his splendid profile
> thrown into bold relief by the flames.

Despite his vigorous campaigning, Morel admitted to having been beset by
occasional nagging doubt. Now the doubts were set aside. He and Casement
discovered that their analysis coincided on all points. They needed each other:

> It was long hours past midnight when we parted. The sheets of his voluminous
> report lay scattered upon the table, chairs and floor. And it was with the debris
> of that Report around me, that Report which was to brand a reigning sovereign,
> allied by family connections to half the Courts of Europe, with indelible infamy;
> that Report which, finally and for all time, was to tear aside the veil from the
> most gigantic fraud and wickedness which our generation has known, that I
> slept in my clothes upon the sofa; while its author sought his bedroom above.[6]

On the following day, 11 December, Casement completed his report. The
period between then and mid February, 1904, when the report was finally published, was mainly taken up with checking, clarifying and redrafting. It also
marked the beginning of the fightback by the forces of the Congo State. On the
very day he completed the report, Casement wrote to Edward Clarke at the FO,
having learned of the Belgian intention to challenge the Epondo case. 'Before

this controversy ends,' he wrote with sarcasm, 'you will be astonished to find how very good they really are – how sordid the motives of those impeaching their humane administration!'7 He wrote to Poulteney Bigelow on 13 December, presumably as part of his effort to enlist sympathetic acquaintances to the campaign, which he foresaw were needed. He took the occasion to reflect on the nature of his inquiries on the Upper Congo:

> There are two ways of seeing the interior of the Congo State – either blind-folded or looking for the facts affecting the social condition of the natives underlying the veneer of European officialdom which had imposed itself upon them. I chose to look for the facts. I said: he who goes to a foreign country to see the people of it and form a just conclusion of their mode of life does not confine his investigations to museums, picture galleries and public buildings, or to the barracks and reviews of soldiers or State-conducted enterprises: he goes also into the villages of the people, he speaks with the peasant and the shop-keeper and enters sometimes the dwellings of the very poor: he watches the growth of crops and how the fields are tilled and seeks from the country producer to understand how his agricultural industry rewards him. He does not confine himself, for all the information he desires, to the statistics published in official bulletins – or seek for the main springs of national economy in the routine statistics of Government offices. If he wants to see how a people lives and how they are affected by the laws they must obey and the taxes they must pay, he goes, if he goes for truth, to the homes of the people themselves. This is what I have, *very inadequately, been striving to do on the Upper Congo during the last few months* ...8

Having submitted the report, he remained in London about another week. There were still consultations with the FO, from which one can discern his impatience with officialdom: 'Saw Villiers who again gave me impression of being abject piffler'; 'Busy again at additions to report & then with them at 4 to FO to Farnall who seemed very desponding. Villiers again at his "indecisions". My report not likely to come out until February now when Parliament meets!' Apart from Congo work, there was time for some relaxation and social calls. He made regular calls to the Sanfords, presumably the parents of Herbert Ward's wife, Sarita. He even attempted, without success, to get Mr Sanford to support Morel's struggling *West African Mail*, established earlier that year. He saw Casement relatives, young Bertie and Jack, then in London: 'Bertibus called & we dined together at Club & then to King Richard II at H.M's. Not good.' He dined, too, with the Cuibonos and met Miss Louie Heath.9 He got an invitation from Lord Ennismore to visit him at his home at Convamore, Co. Cork, which he was to take up the coming February. In the evenings he regularly cruised the streets in search of sexual partners, recording the results in his diary: 'Dusky – depredator – Huge. Saw 7 in all. Two beauties' and, 'strolled. Dick West End – biggest & cleanest *mu nua ami*'.

There were two more letters from Conrad. The first was in response to a query Casement was addressing to a number of Congo associates, regarding a claim by the Congo State authorities that the lopping-off of hands was an indigenous custom. 'During my sojourn in the interior,' wrote Conrad, 'keeping my eyes and ears well open too, I've never heard of the alleged custom of cutting off hands amongst the natives; and I am convinced that no such custom ever existed along the whole course of the main river to which my experience is limited.' He thanked Casement, too, for a copy of Morel's pamphlet: 'There can be no doubt that his presentation of the commercial policy and the administrative methods of the Congo State is absolutely true. It is a most brazen breach of faith as to Europe. It is in every aspect an enormous and atrocious lie in action.'[10]

On the 21st Conrad sent another long supportive letter:

It is an extraordinary thing that the conscience of Europe which seventy years ago has put down the slave trade on humanitarian grounds tolerates the Congo state to day. It is as if the moral clock had been put back many hours ... That precious pair of African witch-men seem to have cast a spell upon the world of whites – I mean Leopold and Thys of course. This is very funny ... And the fact remains that in 1903, seventy five years or so after the abolition of the slave trade (because it was cruel) there exists in Africa a Congo State, created by the act of European Powers where ruthless, systematic cruelty towards the blacks is the basis of administration, and bad faith towards all the other states the basis of commercial policy. I do hope we shall meet before you leave. Once more my best wishes go with you on your crusade. Of course You may make any use you like of what I write to you.[11]

After a rapid visit to the Mortens at the Savoy, he crossed over to Ireland on 21 December: 'Bad crossing to Dublin. At North Wall. Went Bray. Francis Naughton not there – Back to Westland Row. At Harcourt Street J.B. Grown greatly in all ways. £1.6/- Xmas Dinner at Dolphin. Home to Hotel nice fire. In bed & off to sleep. J.B. 1/8/- Enormous – came handled & also came.' On the following day he took the train for Belfast and, after an overnight there, he travelled on to Ballycastle on the 24th. 'No one to meet me. Cold & black. I will not go there again. Aunt C[harlotte] up & all well. House changed but not improved at all – on the contrary.'

Circumstances had now changed in Magherintemple. His Uncle John had died in 1902 and 'Aunt Charlotte' was his widow. Casement's cousin, Roger, his wife, Susan, and their children were now the householders. He did not enjoy his stay. On Christmas Day: 'Miserable day – Did not go out till afternoon with Roger. Busy on my Report revising it which I found here from Farnall.' And on the following two days: 'Again in bed till lunch at Report – but not finished. The additions came from Farnall with excellent opinion of my report – "could not be better – admirable both in style and substance"... Miserable place to stay in this.' On the 28th he finished the report, posted it to the FO and left Magherintemple for Portrush and his sister Nina. Together, they spent a couple of enjoyable days. On the 30th they seem to have travelled to Newcastle, Co. Down, where they stayed in the Slieve Donard Hotel, leaving the following

morning for further social calls in Ballymena. On 1 January 1904 Casement sent
Morel a Slieve Donard postcard ('View from Slieve Donard Hotel, Newcastle,
Co. Down. An Ideal Health and Golfing Resort'), with this message: 'A grand
place this! We came down last night, and leave for Belfast at 2 to-day. It is quiet
and beautiful, and one can think. A glorious green sea opposite. I must bring
you here – and to Portrush.'[12]

On 28 December Casement wrote to Farnall from Ballycastle to say that revisions had been delayed, as 'I have been in bed mostly since getting here'. He
added further clarification on the administration of the ABIR area and mentioned
awful stories coming from further up the river, e.g. that the entrails of seventy
killed on a punitive expedition had been festooned around the village palisades.[13]

Meanwhile, with Casement in Ireland, Conrad had not forgotten the
Congo issue. On 26 December he wrote to R.B. Cunninghame Graham to enlist
his support. Having congratulated him on the publication of *Hernando de Soto*,
he introduced the Casement he had known in the Congo. Conrad saw traces of
the conquistador in Casement, but something, too, of the great Spanish missionary defender of the Amerindians, Bartolomé de Las Casas:

> I have always thought that some particle of Las Casas' soul had found refuge in
> his indefatigable body. The letters will tell you the rest. I would help him but it
> is not in me. I am only a wretched novelist inventing wretched stories and not
> even up to that miserable game; but your good pen, keen, flexible and straight,
> and sure, like a good Toledo blade would tell in the fray if you felt disposed to
> give a slash or two. He could tell you things! Things I've tried to forget; things I
> never did know. He has had as many years of Africa as I had months – almost.[14]

Three days later Conrad wrote to Casement to let him know that Cunninghame Graham had responded positively and wished to meet him in person:
'The man is able and more than willing to help in your noble crusade; and you
may safely give him your confidence ... Do not let his reputation for socialism
influence your judgment upon the man. It has never been anything but a form
of his hate for all oppression and injustice.'[15]

An accumulation of letters and papers awaited Casement in London on
New Year's Day, including an article about him in the *Morning Post* by Poulteney
Bigelow – 'It is a rummy one.' He called on Cunninghame Graham, and on the
2nd he submitted a memo to the FO, discussing possible steps to be taken
regarding the Congo. He would support the call for an international commission only if it were to be 'supreme in its functions', which he felt was unlikely.
If it were not independent, the effect would be negative, as Britain would be
seen to have called for it. The dangers lay in the members chosen and in its freedom of enquiry. He still felt that the best option lay in the exercise of British
extraterritorial rights on the Congo, which, he believed, would 'paralyse Congo
wrongdoing upon the native at large' by showing up the contrast between the
two systems of justice.[16]

He spent Sunday 3 January with Conrad at Pent Farm. On Tuesday he went to Liverpool to meet Morel: 'Talked all night nearly. Wife a good woman.' On the train back to London on the following day, he met Lloyd George: 'We talked much of it [Congo] – & other things.'[17] Meanwhile, there were daily meetings with Farnall and Villiers, as the report was being finalized. The last entry in the 1903 Diary, that of Friday 8 January 1904, reads: 'At Final Revise, I hope, of my Report, taking out the names of Wauters & Lejeune &c. Decided to go Ireland again tomorrow. Left final Revise with Farnall at 5 pm & yarned about Ireland.'

He had followed up his visit to Cunninghame Graham in writing. A review of *Hernando de Soto* had dubbed the author the 'Apostle of Failure': 'It is only by constant failures,' wrote Casement, 'that men have ever grown better; and I suppose the most gigantic personal failure humanity has known ended on the Cross.' He then tried to interest Cunninghame Graham in the Congo issue:

> I wish you'd make yourself the apostle of that failure – and devote your pen for a spell to pointing the gaze of literary England on that dreadful picture. Those wretched Congo people are *far* worse off than they were 18 years ago before the Belgians came upon them with their civilising agencies – these civilising agencies I saw recently on the far-upper Congo communities I knew 16 years ago as strong, brave-hearted savages – killed and raided by their savage neighbours often, it is true, but able to give back blow for blow and wound for wound – and at any rate to die like men, spear in hand defending their village stockades.
>
> Today these people – or the cowering remnant I found cringing at the frown of some gutter-sweep ... of Antwerp or Liege who holds over them *droits de police* – can no more defend themselves than they can satisfy the insatiable greed of their masters. They said to me – when I asked them whether they were not after all better off today seeing that the Congo Government had suppressed intertribal wars and neighbourly raids – 'No – it is true what you say that we had to fight continually to guard our homes, but we were *men* then and could fight – now can we fight?' Disarmed as they are and overawed by the most powerful military organisation in central Africa every courageous instinct of their manhood points only to a hopeless end.

He told Cunninghame Graham of his visit to Conrad: 'I have got him hot on the trail – but I feel scruples pressing Conrad. He has so much to do on his book that to obtrude this Congo abomination on his imagination seems unjust.' He concluded with the wish that 'some able pen' would take up the Congo issue: 'I do so wish to enlist friends on behalf of these wretched people whose wrongs have burnt into my heart.'[18]

Towards the end of January, the FO reflected on the appropriate course of action to take next with regard to the Congo. Acknowledging that Casement's report had confirmed maladministration, the choice lay between publishing it and circulating it to the signatories of the Berlin Act, or withholding it pending the establishment of an international commission to investigate abuses. Arguments were assessed carefully, including the danger of giving the appearance of placing Casement on trial by appearing not to find his evidence and that of others trustworthy. A second issue which emerged was whether or not to include in the report the names of State and concession officials, missionaries, natives and place names. The FO listed the arguments pro and con, at one point drawing on Casement's view that it was the system that was on trial and not individuals.[19]

Casement had departed again for Ireland in mid January, where he was to remain for several months, mostly in Portrush and Ballycastle, Co. Antrim. His reasons for doing so were probably several: he had been under sustained pressure with the investigation and report and may have desired a period of withdrawal; Ireland itself was an attraction as he was beginning to become captivated by Irish issues. He may have wished to distance himself somewhat from the FO and the process of editing his report. All his communications on revisions to the report came from Ireland. The FO decisions were to publish the report but to withhold names. By the beginning of February, Casement, who cannot have been displeased at the first decision, was registering his objections to the second, arguing that when he last met Farnall and Villiers, it had been agreed that the names of missionaries and natives were all to stay in. On the 7th, he commented: 'I think the report without names and with indications of locality withdrawn or obscured will be a very ineffective document.'

On the 11th, immediately before the report was released, he strongly urged that the names issue be reconsidered. For example, to conceal the identity of the two ABIR agents at Bongandanga, one would have to suppress or change the place name – making the report worthless. Farnall seems to have shared Casement's view on the names. 'Now we have taken out officials' names, natives' names and geographical names and have tried to hide whence you got the missionary information. I think however that it will be labour lost – it is perfectly well known where you went and a little trouble would discover whom you saw.' He hastened to add that these were his private sentiments.[20] On 20 February, after the report had appeared, Casement sent Farnall a long letter of protest. The presentation was 'calculated ... to rob what I had written of much of its value'. None of the changes made really concealed the identity of individuals and made confusion or distortion by the Congo government more likely. In addition, 'several of my remarks are altered or suppressed' and a statement by the missionary Clark had been attributed to him. 'I am clearly not responsible for a Report so issued.' More ominously, he suggested that

> it renders my position in regard to the FO a somewhat difficult one. I am not clear as to what my course should be – but it would seem to me that my resignation is called for. I cannot well continue to serve a department which has so little confidence in me and so little regard for my opinion as to give to the world as mine statements made by another, and to make such vital changes in face of my strong protest.[21]

The Congo Report was published as a White Paper on 15 February. The immediate public impact of publication was disappointing and could have contributed to Casement's mood. Only the *Morning Post* gave detailed coverage, including an editorial; the treatment given it by *The Times* was much more cursory.[22] Its longer-term effect was, however, to be crucial.

On 21 March, his leave having expired at the end of February, Casement requested an extension until 30 April. This was granted. On the same day, however, he wrote to Barrington, offering to resign, if necessary, uncertain perhaps of his position. Barrington responded on the 27th: 'Nobody wants you to resign. I never heard of such a thing. As to your temporary return to the Congo I think it is very unlikely, but it has always been intended to appoint you to Lisbon when the time came. The present incumbent will go I am assured, at any moment.'[23]

On 16 April Casement asked for a further two months, 'in view of the fact that my immediate return to duty is not contemplated'. This, too, was granted, despite a minute from the chief clerk noting that Casement had exceeded his leave but that 'the circumstances are peculiar and I am under the impression that he will not return to the Congo'. Casement had written to Cowper the day before he wrote to the FO, sympathizing over a harsh winter and reiterating that he believed he would be going to Lisbon. At any rate, he was not going back to the Congo – the Congo State wouldn't have him. Later in April, Lord Ennismore, who had obviously heard of the pending appointment, congratulated him on getting Lisbon.[24]

The Founding of the Congo Reform Association, 1904

In the two meetings between Casement and Morel, the germ of the idea of founding an organization to campaign exclusively on the Congo must have formed. Morel recalled Casement's role: 'His suggestion was concrete. If Leopoldianism was to be overthrown, an organisation would have to be created, and I must be the creator. He would help. But necessarily under the restrictions which his official position imposed upon him.'[25]

Morel hesitated. A struggling young journalist, his livelihood precarious, he was suffering due to the time and energy already devoted to Congo campaigning. It was Mary, his wife, who gave him the determination:

> As frequently happens in such cases of mental conflict, woman proved the stronger vessel. Casement's plan found fervid support in my wife, and if I crossed the Irish Channel that night to meet him, convinced that Fate must do with me as Fate might choose, it was very largely owing to the influence of one without whose unswerving courage and faith in the blackest of future days these pages would not now be written.[26]

He went on to describe the meeting itself:

It was at the foot of ... [blank in manuscript] on that Irish soil which has given birth to so many generous emotions and whose soil has been fertilised by so many human tears, that Casement and I conspired further to disturb the equanimity of the blameless Monarch: discussed ways and means and drew up a rough plan of campaign. To unite in one body the various influences at work against Leopoldianism; to appeal to a wide public on a single issue; to incorporate all men whose hearts were touched, whatever their standing, profession, political opinion and religious beliefs, in a common aim – that was the task.[27]

The missing words in Morel's manuscript are, undoubtedly, 'Slieve Donard'; the meeting took place an 24 January in the Slieve Donard Hotel in Newcastle, Co. Down, which Casement had visited at the end of December. 'Idea Conceived, Ireland, 24 January, 1904', says a marginal note on a 'Preliminary Announcement' for the Congo Reform Association.[28] On a number of occasions in subsequent years, Casement was to refer back to that momentous meeting. On 23 March 1908, for example, when consul in Pará, Brazil, he wrote to Morel:

Who could have predicted it all? Do you ... remember the coffee room in the Slieve Donard Hotel, at Newcastle, Co. Down, Ireland, in January 1904? How we planned and plotted – and I said that if the Congo question was to be made a living one, it must be taken out of the hands of the Foreign Office and Government and made a people's question – and how I said to you 'Thou art the man'! For it has been entirely one man's work – and you have done it.[29]

The day after their meeting, Casement wrote to Grattan Guinness, to the journalist W.T. Stead, a supporter of Morel's, and to Morel himself; in this last, he outlined the ingredients of a programme:

Sporadic meetings and occasional lectures – articles in the press from time to time are not sufficient. They do good of course, but they are not systematic. The defenders of the monstrous regime we are each individually attacking in our separate paths, are all banded together in one powerful and wealthy league, with a sovereign state for execution [*sic*, for executive] and a King for chairman. They are systematic – and only systematised effort can get the better of them ...The one clear way to me seems then to found now and at once a Congo Reform Committee – or call it by any name you will so long as it is born.

With this letter Casement enclosed a contribution of £100 towards the work, work he acknowledged would have to come from Morel.[30] On the 26th and 27th, Morel wrote to Grattan Guinness; Stead, to the Liberal Party supporters, Alfred Emmott and Sir Charles Dilke, and to Fox Bourne of the Aborigines Protection Society, mentioning his meeting with Casement and seeking support for the new organization.

On 1 February, from Kingsbridge Station in Dublin, Casement telegraphed Morel: 'You have done splendidly ... heartily approve your action. Bourne's movement is absurd and cannot influence any large section – go on and rely my fullest support.'[31] And, on the 13th, he again commented on Dilke's and Fox

Bourne's objections to the new organization, saying that their opposition stemmed from 'jealousy on behalf of the Aborigines Protection Society. They fear its role will be taken from it by the new organisation, or at least that it will be injured. In that they are right'. He believed that they would give only moral support. Morel and Casement believed that the situation in the Congo was a special evil and could not be treated on a par with other situations where natives were abused. 'All round philanthropy won't meet the Congo evil at all,' said Casement. 'The Congo evil is a gigantic infamy – a fundamental invasion of primitive humanity and its rights.' He believed that the Aborigines Protection Society was 'incapable of *directing* the movement for Congo reform'.

Casement worried about the impact of organizing a new movement on Morel's health: 'Are you equal to this task? I mean physically equal. I fear for you.' Both men engaged in a flurry of activity in trying to attract prominent patrons for the organization. Casement worked through friends: Theodore Hoste (who was approaching the Duke of Hamilton), Lord ffrench and the Duke of Norfolk; Cunninghame Graham had recommended the radical journalist, Henry William Massingham, to Casement 'as a man to approach for his powerful pen'. And he praised some of Morel's catches, being delighted about John Morley, for instance, 'the truest of the true, the Champion of the weak'.32

An active member of the Congo Reform Association from the beginning was Alice Stopford Green, already an associate of Morel's. Green was an Irish scholar heavily involved in African affairs. Now, she was to become one of Casement's closest friends. To her he was able to stress the Irish dimension of his Congo involvement:

> I think it must have been my insight into human suffering and into the ways of the spoiler and the ruffian who takes 'civilisation' for his watchword when his object is the appropriation of the land and labour of others for his personal profit which the tale of English occupation in Ireland so continually illustrates that gave me the deep interest I felt in the lot of the Congo natives. Every argument by which King Leopold and his aiders seek to justify the merciless oppression of the Central African today was stereotyped in the 'Laws' and measures of the past in this country. We had it all, even to 'moral and material regeneration' ... the more we love our land and wish to help her people the more keenly we feel we cannot turn a deaf ear to suffering and injustice in any part of the world.33

The inaugural meeting of the Congo Reform Association was set for 23 March, though as a public servant (even if on leave) Casement felt it wiser to keep away: 'I think it is my duty to hold myself aloof as much as I can.' He wrote on the 24th to say he was back from Donegal and had got a telegram announcing the public birth of the Association the previous night. 'The CRA is yours – yours in every way – you toiled and wrote and laboured while I merely made a bare suggestion and backed it with a few pounds I could spare.'34

The Developing Battle[35]

The publication of Casement's report in February and the foundation of the Congo Reform Association in March were critical landmarks in the history of the Congo reform movement. The historian W.R. Louis has suggested that the campaign fell into three distinct phases.[36] The first ran from the publication of Casement's report and the foundation of the Congo Reform Association, in early 1904, to the publication of the report of Leopold's Commission of Investigation in November 1905. Throughout this first phase, Casement was effectively on leave and in a position to contribute to the campaign, allowing for the limitations of being a public servant. He played a key role in organizing an important public meeting held in Holborn Town Hall in June 1905, which saw the public adoption of what was known as 'the Belgian Solution'. The second phase ran from November 1905 to August 1908, when the Congo State was annexed by Belgium. The third phase ran from August 1908 to the dissolution of the CRA in June 1913. Casement left for Santos in September 1906 and was at home, therefore, only for the early part of the second phase. For the entirety of the third phase, he was either in Brazil or immersed in the affairs of the Putumayo. In one sense he had made his contribution with the publication of his report. Yet he was a constant voice of encouragement for Morel until the dissolution of the CRA in 1913.

For most of 1904, after the publication of his report, Casement was preoccupied with Ireland. During that time, significant developments took place in Congo affairs. In March, against advice, King Leopold decided to answer Casement's charges. The response was contained in a set of observations on Casement's report, which were transmitted through Constantine Phipps in Brussels.[37] Two of the major ones, depopulation and mutilations, could be explained, the counter-argument went, by factors other than those put forward by Casement. Depopulation was primarily caused by sleeping sickness, while the practice of mutilation, including the cutting-off of hands, was a native custom. In the case of the boy Epondo, the damage had been done not by a sentry but by a wild boar. 'It is only natural to conclude', stated the reply, 'that if the rest of the evidence in the consul's report is of the same value as that furnished to him in this particular case it cannot possibly be regarded as conclusive.'[38]

Having impugned the reliability of Casement's facts and judgments, Leopold's reply went on to state that 'the authorities will of course look into the matter and cause inquiries to be made'. This was a mistake; the FO jumped at the opening and welcomed 'the announcement that a searching and impartial inquiry will be made'. While this was unlikely to have been Leopold's intention, the pressure of public opinion grew in Britain, the United States, Italy and even within Belgium. Meanwhile, the CRA was increasingly active in Britain and floods of petitions arrived at the FO. CRA pressure also led to a Commons debate on 9 June. Members of the Liberal opposition were prominent among the speakers: Emmott, Dilke, Grey[39], Fitzmaurice[40] and Samuel all spoke. The Congo State was roundly condemned and the British government urged to take stronger measures. This allowed the FO to make stronger demands for a full and impartial inquiry. Shortly afterwards, Leopold acquiesced and announced the establishment of a commission of inquiry. Its members were to be the Belgian judge Emile Janssens, the Italian judge Baron Nisco (already serving in the Congo), and Dr Edmund de Schumacher, head of the Department of Justice in the Swiss canton of Lucerne. Casement had doubts, he told Morel, not about the integrity of individual members but about the mandate of the commission. Its method of investigation would yield nothing and allow the FO to re-establish normal relations with Belgium, which was in Britain's strategic interests. The members of the commission left Antwerp for the Congo in September 1904 and were to return in March 1905. The FO had supplied them with a full copy of Casement's report; in the Congo, they followed his footsteps.[41]

While all of this was happening, the supporters of the Congo State were waging a propaganda campaign. Some of the darts were aimed at Casement himself. One that found its mark was that launched by Colonel James J. Harrison, who had been to the Congo on a big-game hunting expedition. On 10 June 1904, the day after the Congo debate in the Commons, he wrote a letter to several English papers, including *The Times*. He strongly defended the Congo State and, in the process, wrote: 'Personally, I think it was a great mistake that Mr Casement was chosen to act. As a trader, whether he was biased or not, he got the reputation of being so.'[42] Harrison's charge that Casement resented the Belgians because he was frustrated as a 'trader' in his early career in the Congo prompted a long letter to Morel in which he rebutted the charge. A letter of refutation for the newspaper was drafted but not sent. Harrison he dubbed 'an honest fool' and a 'pigmy intellect' and opponents in general become 'Harrison and the pigmies'. When Lady Margaret Jenkins, another of his new associates in the Congo campaign, suggested a meeting between the two, Casement refused.[43]

Throughout 1904, Morel had laboured assiduously in building up the CRA.[44] Nevertheless, towards the end of 1904 prospects for the reform campaign looked poor. Leopold's commission had gone to the Congo and the FO was content to await its findings. Pending this, it was difficult to arouse public enthusiasm. Finances, too, were perilous, since hoped-for subscriptions from influential supporters had not materialized. In mid December, Casement wrote to Morel complaining that '*interest* in the Congo question is practically dead. No one cares a d – – n about it'. It was more and more difficult to get press coverage. People were silent, he believed, partly because the government was supposed to be handling things diplomatically. And Morel, himself, he gently chided, was getting people's backs up by lecturing them too much.[45]

To make matters worse, at this point what became known as the 'Benedetti scandal' erupted, casting a cloud over the CRA. Antonio Benedetti, a police commissaire at Boma, had made contact both with H.A. Shanu and Arthur Nightingale in the Congo, offering damaging information against his employers in exchange for funds to make a fresh start in Europe. Though aware of the possible dangers, Morel agreed, Benedetti travelled to England and a contract was signed. Benedetti, however, went straight to Brussels and, on 1 December, the *Independance Belge* carried the story of the attempted bribing of a Congo official to give false evidence against the regime. Though Morel explained the circumstances in a letter to *The Times*, the episode was deeply embarrassing.[46]

Casement tried to reassure Morel in his letters. Benedetti was a 'rascal', had 'turned traitor' and was a 'thoroughgoing blackmailer'. He advised caution and promised to contact the editor of *The Times*, privately. He was able to reassure Morel that *The Times*, the *Morning Post* and Stead were all aware of the details of the case.[47] Casement worried, too, about the repercussions for Shanu if the State retaliated for his links with Morel. He was, said Casement, in danger and needed protection – he could be prosecuted, his business ruined.[48] Others were conscious of the need to protect Shanu; in January 1905 Nightingale wrote: 'You may be sure I won't allow the State to harm Shanu' and, anyway, Shanu was 'capable of fighting his own battles out here'.[49] In the event the State did retaliate, harassing Shanu and withdrawing all custom from his business. After a period of humiliations, he committed suicide in July 1905.[50]

Neither did Casement forget the fragility of Morel's financial circumstances. The latter's work for the CRA depended on his source of income, the *West African Mail*, remaining in business. Its future, however, looked doubtful. Casement, Alice Stopford Green, and Colonel Stopford, Mrs Green's elder brother, came up with the proposal to get the *Morning Post*, always supportive of the Congo issue, to take over Morel's paper.[51] Nothing came of the idea.[52] On another front, aware that Morel was the butt of constant attacks from the supporters of Leopold, Casement chided Congo missionaries for not defending him. Lawson Forfeitt replied to say that he had preached on the Congo question, as did Bentley a little later. Only the younger BMS men were strong and good, Casement remarked to Morel.[53]

Interventions of partisans from either side were constantly monitored and commented upon. One of the hostile critics was Mrs French-Sheldon, a London publisher and travel writer, judged a serious threat by Casement because 'she will – as a woman who has been there "à la Mary Kingsley" count for much with the popular point of view'. He later commented that he was sorry for her as she had been 'got at'.[54] She went to the Congo, travelled on State steamers and was chaperoned by officials. The Revd John Weeks reported to Morel that State agents even 'pulled down an old prison, and levelled the ground, and made it all nice, because she was coming'.[55] Another critic referred to in Casement's letters to Morel was the young Lord Mountmorres, who also visited the Congo and returned with glowing accounts. Nightingale told Casement that he was 'a rabid

Catholic' and 'sure to discredit everything the Protestant missionaries say'.[56] Henry Wellington Wack, Casement said, was, 'doubtless, engaged at a cost'.[57] Finally, A.L. Jones, by far the most active of Leopold's advocates in Britain, was a 'cad', a 'poisonous serpent', 'a snake second only in size to Leopold'.[58]

When an issue in one of Leopold's pamphlet series *La Vérité sur le Congo* published what he called a 'scurrilous' attack on him, Casement felt that an appropriate counter would be to draw attention to his background and, specifically, to his father's exploit in helping Kossuth in 1848. He suggested to Morel that 'the most fitting way to reply would be if the *West African Mail* were to insert the enclosed reference to my father's ride thro' Hungary. Not a word more than I have put – and *no reference* to *La Vérité*'s attack on me ... It speaks for itself – and is, I think, the nicest refutation of their low-down method you could employ ... My father's act speaks for itself'.[59]

By the end of 1904 the accumulation of pressures left Casement feeling distinctly fragile. First, there had been his chagrin over the exclusion of all names from his report; then there had been the Leopoldian counter-attack, including personal attacks on himself; there was what seemed to him to be an unenthusiastic and foot-dragging FO, unwilling to press for action. His financial situation was becoming precarious; he had been appointed to Lisbon but, after two brief visits there, turned it down and decided to take a period of unpaid leave from the Consular Service from the end of 1904. Added to all of these must be the degree of vanity and insecurity that marked his personality. 'It has practically ruined me – this Congo business', he moaned to Morel, '... injured in health – most depressed in spirit and nerves – and with a hard struggle before me.'[60]

What continued to rankle most was the perceived failure of the Foreign Office to defend him during the Congo controversy:

> They *know* the truth and yet deliberately, for the sake of paltry ease, prepare to throw over an honest and fearless official they deliberately thrust forward last year when it then suited their book. They are not worth serving – and what sickens me is that I must go back to them, hat in hand, despising them as I do – simply to be able to live.[61]

It was not Lord Lansdowne he blamed, but 'the permanent gang'.[62] He believed that Villiers and Constantine Phipps, the British ambassador in Brussels, controlled the Congo question and that they regretted how far Lansdowne had gone in December. Phipps was playing a 'low-down game'; he was a 'cur' and 'I'd like to lay that same contempt on with a good thick Irish blackthorn'.[63] Likewise he had a low opinion of their political masters and little sympathy regarding the wider political considerations that FO policy makers faced. But, the FO had to assess the support it was likely to receive from other countries for any measures it proposed regarding the Congo, and there were few signs that the other Powers were prepared to support Britain in forceful action. Given that Leopold had despatched a special commission to the Congo and that it could be expected to report soon, Britain was prepared to wait. There were also the diplomatic considerations of Britain's relationships within Europe. In April 1904, striving to end her tradition of isolation and wishing to avoid the danger of conflicts (in Egypt and the Far East, for example), she signed the *entente cordiale* with France. In the shifting power relations within Europe, Germany began to be perceived by Britain to be the most significant and growing threat to the balance of power and to peace. In this context Belgium could play a part and Lansdowne, who had been central in negotiating the *entente*, did not wish to alienate her.

Casement saw an important parallel between the plight of the Congo people and that of Ireland: 'The Congo question is very near my heart – but the Irish question is nearer ... it was only because I was an Irishman that I could understand fully, I think, the whole scheme of wrongdoing at work on the Congo.'[64] Inevitably, then, the response of MPs of the Irish Parliamentary Party to the Congo campaign became a matter of increasing concern for him. From 1903 on, Leopold consciously tried to use Catholic influence to defend the Congo State; there developed a tendency among Catholics internationally to see criticism of the Congo State as emanating from Protestant missionary hostility to Catholic Belgium. The English *Catholic Herald* led a vehement campaign in support of Leopold. A similar campaign emanated from the United States, in which Cardinal Gibbons played a part. If one adds the extra ingredient of anti-Englishness, it is little wonder that Irish Catholic leaders reacted similarly.[65]

In one House of Commons debate, when an Irish MP made 'another bid for fame by defending Leopold', Casement remarked that 'such men represent nothing of Irish intelligence'.[66] Douglas Hyde, with whom he was in contact regarding the Irish language, drew his attention to a Catholic priest 'writing about the Congo in the *Freeman* about three days ago, saying it was all a Protestant slander on the Catholic missionaries!!'[67] With these sensitivities in mind, he took Morel to task both for referring to the presence of three Catholic priests at the head of the funeral cortège for Paul Costermans – the acting Governor General of the Congo State who committed suicide after receiving a preliminary report from Leopold's commission – and for terming them 'Roman'. 'I only point this out to you – because I find, wherever I go, that the Catholics are profoundly suspicious – and all, almost, believe that the Congo campaign is instigated by anti-Catholic partisans.'[68]

A wiser view was held, he felt, by another Irish Catholic, Lady ffrench. 'I heard from old Lady ffrench yesterday – Lord ffrench's mother,' he told Morel. 'She writes, "I am very sorry the religious element has been imported into the Congo affair ... I think it a very great pity that any section of the press should have been hoodwinked into supporting a system which every Catholic *worthy of the name* must conscientiously condemn." These are cheering words from a very good Catholic – as dear old Lady ffrench is.'[69]

Partly through Alice Stopford Green, Casement worked at approaching and influencing Irish MPs. He had begun this in April 1904 but it wasn't until a year later that he set to it earnestly.[70] In early April 1905 he hoped to meet Hugh Law to arrange a meeting with Irish members 'to hear the Congo story from myself'. Law, he claimed, was different from those Irish MPs who had signed the *Catholic Herald* address to Leopold. He was going to try to detach them from Leopold's cause and, if they would not help the CRA, he hoped at least that they would 'not ... help the oppression of the defenceless Africans'.[71] And, he wanted 'for a thousand reasons, to prevent them from backing up that scoundrel in his hideous oppression of his people – they should be the foremost champions of a poor people against misrule'.[72] While the Irish Party had always fought for Ireland first, he said, 'they have always fought for liberty wherever it was oppressed throughout the world and always will'. He enclosed a quote from a speech by John Dillon, suggesting that Morel incorporate it into a plea to Irish MPs.[73] The problem was that Irish members tended not to associate the British government with humanitarian motives, but with 'the old predominant lust and grab'.[74]

The meeting with Hugh Law was a success. The two met for lunch on 12 April; afterwards, Casement appealed to Law for the support of Irish members on the Congo issue:

> Our country ... above every other civilised land is called on to give sympathy and support to a movement of this nature. In the light of our past history and of all that the native Irish suffered at the hands of exploiters and Exterminators we should be the last people on earth to take part, today, with those who are playing the same old game, by the same old methods on a hapless multitude of subject people. That those people are savages does not lessen their claim on our sympathies; it should rather quicken our activities and sharpen our faculty of intelligent insight into their relation to those who, while growing rich on their labours, are libelling them as idle and worthless.

He concluded by turning to the importing of religious differences into the Congo debate, a sensitive issue for Irish members: 'As a matter of fact I do not know that there are any Catholic Mission Stations in the districts chiefly exploited by the rubber adventurers – there are none in the ABIR territory or in the Lac Leopold II region.'[75]

Holborn Town Hall Meeting, 7 June 1905

As early as September 1904 Casement was in contact with members of the family of Lord Norbury, several of whom became staunch supporters in the Congo campaign and played a part in bringing about the Holborn Meeting.[76] This large public meeting, held on 7 June 1905, was attended by public figures of some standing and adopted the Belgian Solution, whereby responsibility for the Congo would be taken out of Leopold's hands and vested upon the Belgian government. The Congo State would thus be answerable to the Belgian Parliament and, ultimately, people. The Belgian Solution was subsequently adopted by the British government and, eventually, accepted with reluctance by Leopold.

The idea of a public meeting seems to have emerged when Casement spent a week at Carlton Park, Market Harborough, home of the Norburys. He wrote to Morel on Thursday, 27 April 1905 to say that he was travelling to Carlton Park on the morrow for a week. On Saturday he again wrote to Morel, suggesting holding a public meeting on the Congo issue with Morel as the main speaker. [77]

During May, Casement launched himself into frenetic organizing activity for the meeting. Colonel Stopford had proposed having a prestigious chairman – Sir Harry Johnston was suggested – and, on the 4th, Casement told Morel that Harry Johnston had 'jumped at it', when the idea was put to him; Grattan Guinness would work in the background, and would contact churches. There was to be a ladies' committee to work on publicity and getting an audience; there would be 500 reserved seats for smart folk, expected to come after dinner. Casement envisaged an opening address of eight minutes from Johnston, followed by fifty minutes from Morel (he was to prepare a 'masterly address') and another fifty minutes devoted to presenting resolutions. Money was not to be a worry – Casement proposed to contact William Cadbury, who had contributed £1000 to the *West African Mail*,[78] and John Holt, another Morel supporter.[79] When the organizing committee of Emmott, Samuel, Grattan Guinness, Mrs Green, Colonel Stopford and himself met, he wrote to Morel to say that he had got his way. A few days later he proclaimed that 'I shall have to take the meeting on my shoulders. I am coming out strong as an organiser.'[80]

Holborn Town Hall was chosen as the venue; it would take 900 seated and 100 standing. Music had to be arranged and pamphlets prepared for sale (Morel's *Red Rubber*, Mark Twain's *King Leopold's Soliliquy*).[81] In mid April he announced that he was going to stay with Colonel Stopford until the meeting. By then the outlines of the programme were clearer. Sir Charles Dilke, Howard Samuel and Seaton-Karr[82] would be speakers; on the platform, he hoped to have Poulteney Bigelow, Joseph Conrad, F.C. Selous,[83] Colonel Stopford and Mrs Green, and he would also try the Revd Scott-Holland, John Burns[84] and Lord Beauchamp, president of the CRA.[85] He gave advice on the content of Morel's address, suggesting a quotation from Edmund Burke on the dangers of being manipulated by 'designing men', which he believed had a 'singular application' to the Congo question. They should 'avoid personalities' and 'stick to the first principles at issue – the virtual enslavement of a whole people'.[86]

Of most concern to Casement were Johnston's likely performance and the content of the resolutions. Johnston's speech should suggest that Belgium must take responsibility for the Congo. There was no such thing as an international conscience, only a national conscience, accountable to popular opinion and ultimate control. Early in May he felt that Johnston's line was 'strong and clear and emphatic'. On the 26th, he believed that Johnston's suggestion 'that Belgium should take over the Congo under strict guarantees' was 'a sound proposal', if not the ideal solution. Yet, in an undated letter, he worried that Johnston 'is a wobbling man' and 'I have to keep him up to the mark'. On 1 June: 'If Johnston piffles too much I'll take the Chair – by force if necessary!' By this time, too, having expended a great deal of energy, he was 'very tired of "flying round"'.[87] Shortly before the meeting itself, he made his first contact with John Holt. He was, he said in a letter to Holt, sorry to hear that he was ill and unable to come to the meeting, or to meet Lord Norbury and his sisters, 'who have taken so lively an interest in Congo affairs'. He hoped the meeting would show the untruth of the claim 'that in attacking it [the rubber regime] we necessarily attack Belgium'.[88]

The day after the meeting Casement sent an enthusiastic report to Holt. It had been a 'great success', though a scurrilous leaflet attacking Holt had been handed out at the doors. On the platform had been Lords Aberdeen, Beauchamp and Norbury 'and a good gathering of Members of Parliament'. Sir Harry Johnston was effective as chairman and 'paid a glowing tribute to Mr Morel', whose address was 'splendid'. A lot of well-known people were present, 'a body of keen sympathisers and aiders'. Perhaps the only downside was the newspaper coverage afterwards, 'but then we knew last night that it would be crowded out by the King of Spain – and still more by the deposition of King Oscar by the Norwegian Storthing'.[89]

The Holborn meeting was significant for two reasons. Firstly, the co-option of Harry Johnston has been described as a 'masterstroke', because of his prominence.[90] With considerable African experience, he had been a supporter of the Congo regime, only latterly coming round to accept the reformers' point of view. His own sense of self-importance was reflected in his letter to Casement on 18 May: 'I am one of the few living Englishmen who knew the upper Congo before the birth of the Congo Free State, who has discussed the questions affecting its inception with the King of the Belgians, Sir Charles Dilke, Stanley, and the principal Belgian pioneers.'[91] His public identification with the reform movement had an important effect. The meeting was even more important because the resolution passed at it, which was then accepted by the CRA, advocated the transfer of the Congo State from Leopold's personal rule to the Belgian government's. Annexation by Belgium, with guarantees that the system of exploitation would be changed, became the key goal of the reform movement. Morel had been lukewarm to this proposal; Johnston's influence was significant.[92]

Leopold's Commission of Investigation

While Casement was busy lobbying Irish MPs and organizing the Holborn meeting, everybody was awaiting the report of King Leopold's Commission of Investigation. While it was in the Congo, during the winter of 1904–5, accounts of its work began to filter back. Missionaries who were being interviewed sent details of their testimony to Morel, who published them. Casement, meanwhile, was getting regular word from Nightingale in Boma. The commission, the latter wrote, had interviewed missionaries on the Lower Congo: 'But it is further up that the "Music" will begin to play – up by Baringa and Monsembe, and both Harris[93] and Weeks appear to be in good fighting trim.' Some time later, Nightingale said that he had heard good reports of the commission, especially of the Swiss, M. de Schumacher. He worried, however, about what Leopold would cut from the report and of the effect of his 'long purse'. By mid February he was able to announce that the commission's findings had vindicated Casement. Phipps, he felt, would 'squirm'.[94]

Though the members of the commission were back in Europe by March 1905, their report was not published until November. The long delay fuelled suspicions regarding Leopold's intentions. The reformers kept up the pressure; between February and August, sixteen Parliamentary Questions were put down and on 3 August another Congo debate took place, with contributions from Dilke, Emmott and Fitzmaurice. In August, the star witnesses at Baringa, the Revd John Harris and his wife Alice Seeley Harris, returned to England and threw their energies into the campaign, speaking at meetings up and down the country.

When it finally appeared in November, the commission's report was 'generally recognized as a severe blow to King Leopold', though he tried hard to soften its impact.[95] The more graphic and damning detailed evidence taken by the commissioners was not published with the report. Moreover, a distorted and greatly watered-down English summary was released to the press before the report itself by a bogus 'West African Missionary Association'. Coinciding, too, with its publication, Leopold announced the formation of a commission for reform. Despite such attempts to water down the effect of the report, the accusations of Casement and of the missionaries had been confirmed. Its publication renewed the cries in Britain for reform .[96]

From the Commission Report to Belgian Annexation

The report of Leopold's commission ought to have brought a measure of satisfaction to Casement and lessened his sense of grievance. But by the time it came he was suffering serious financial worries. At the end of 1905 he was forced to appeal to friends for assistance and he was also in contact with the journalist and businessman T.L. Gilmour about the possibility of employment in East Africa.[97] Around the same time, there was a suggestion that Casement ought to go to the Congo as an 'independent' investigator for the CRA. His immediate reaction was to reject it. He was not 'independent', he stated, and would damage the CRA. He urged them to get a fresh man. But the possibility was kept open and, by early July of 1906, with no offer of a post in sight from the FO, he was considering the matter seriously. On 4 July he gave a definite yes, saying he was now finished with the FO. He began estimating costs of the different components: carriers 'are the most costly mode of conveyance of any in existence'; he would not use any of A.L. Jones's steamers. On the 17th, he responded in detail to proposals that had been made by Morel and Harris. He offered to do it for about £50 per month with an extra payment of £500 in the case of his death, so that his loans could be paid off and an allowance provided for his sister. The total cost he estimated would be between £1000 and £1600 for a year, a big sum. In order to keep his arrival secret, he would take French steamers, then travel from Angola to the Kasai. 'The Lomami', he added, 'is another nest of Devils, I believe, and the Ruki – if one could get in there one could find them "at home".'[98]

At the end of 1905 British focus on the Congo had been diverted by the collapse of the Conservative government. A number of factors contributed to this. One was the failure of the government to introduce adequate social legislation, particularly in the face of increasing unrest among the working classes and women. Overseas, with the decline in the fervour generated by the Anglo-Boer War, criticism of how it had been managed and of the 'methods of barbarism' employed in its later stages had steadily mounted. Then, the use of Chinese labour in the South African mines became an important campaign issue. The most significant factor in Conservative decline, however, arose from Joseph Chamberlain's campaign for tariff reform, which he had waged for several years. He believed that in order to strengthen the Empire, Britain's traditional policy of free trade should be abandoned in favour of protection, with preference being given to products from within the Empire.

His campaign split the Conservative Party, helped unite the Liberals and alienated many voters, who feared higher food prices would result. Balfour resigned in early December 1905, Sir Henry Campbell-Bannerman formed a Liberal cabinet, and a general election was called. The result, when declared in early February 1906, was a Liberal landslide. They won 377 seats, the Irish Nationalists 83, Labour 53, while the Conservatives and Liberal Unionists together had 155 (down from 401).[99]

Disillusion with the Conservatives had begun to manifest itself in Casement's comments and in those of some of his associates in the year 1905. His friend Cuibono agreed in January that 'Balfour & Co.' were 'played out'; Stead felt that Balfour had 'but a short tether now'.[100] Casement himself was more forthright in his language and his disillusion stemmed both from his Irish and

The infant Roger David Casement
with his parents, Roger and Anne
(*née* Jephson)

Casement and dog with
Emma Dickie and Mrs Young

Magherintemple, the Casement home in Ballycastle, Co. Antrim

Casement with close Congo friends, Edward
Glave, W.J. Parminter and Herbert Ward

Joseph Conrad (1857–1924)

Monument in the cataract district of
the Lower Congo to the carriers on the
Matadi–Leopoldville caravan route

Photographed in Calabar, Niger Coast
Protectorate, during Mary Kingsley's 1895
journey. Kingsley is seated between Lady
MacDonald and Sir Claude MacDonald.
Casement is at back right

Leopold II (1835–1909)

Congo Free State. Flogging with the *chicotte* (hippopotamus hide whip)

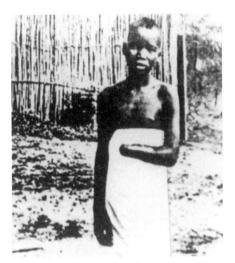

Congo Free State.
Mutilated boy – Epondo

Casement at Boma, Congo, unknown formal event, *c.*1903

Congo Free State.
Mutilated boy – Mola Ekulite

Edmond Dene Morel (1873–1924),
Congo campaigner

The American
Baptist Missionary
Union steamer
Henry Reed, used by
Casement for his
Congo investigation

Postcard from
Casement to Morel,
looking south to the
Mourne Mountains
and Newcastle,
Co. Down, from
the Slieve Donard
Hotel, where the
two first discussed
the formation of
the Congo Reform
Association

VIEW FROM SLIEVE DONARD HOTEL, NEWCASTLE, CO. DOWN.
AN IDEAL HEALTH AND GOLFING RESORT.

Studio portrait of Casement in his forties

Historian Alice Stopford Green
(1847–1929) 'taken by Elsie Brunton at
Pondtail Lodge Fleet about 1898'

Ada (Íde) MacNeill (1860–1959)

Francis Joseph Bigger (1863–1926)

Group outside Ardrigh, Antrim Road, Belfast, *c.*1912.
From left on steps: Casement, Fr Kelly, Lord Ashbourne,
Francis Joseph Bigger, Alice Stopford Green

Colonel Robert Gordon John
Johnstone Berry (1870–1947)

Bulmer Hobson (1883–1969)

At the Irish College in Cloghaneely, Co. Donegal: front, Professor Séamus Ó Searcaigh and Roger Casement; middle, Professors Éamonn Ó Tuathail and Agnes O'Farrelly; back, Pádraig Carr (Mac Giolla Chearra) and Brother Malachi

Julio César Arana (1864–1952), *cacique* and rubber baron, founder of the Peruvian Amazon Company

Casement instructed Travers Buxton to caption this: 'Sir Roger Casement at home on Torry [*sic.*] Island, off the Donegal Coast, Ireland'

Chiefs of Putumayo sections

The camera Casement bought to take to the Putumayo and with which he took several of the photographs in this volume

The Peruvian-Amazon Company's steamer *Liberal*

La Chorrera Station, headquarters of J.C. Arana and Co. on the Igaraparaná River

Congo concerns. To Gertrude, in March, he lashed out: 'This d – – nable conception of Joe Chamberlain – Imperialism plus the cynical disregard of all things fair and true of Balfourism shall not destroy our ideal – nor our race. These things shall not take root in Irish hearts – our ideal of civilisation does not build on the robbing of other people of their rights or nationality.' In a letter to Morel in September he believed there would be no progress on Congo affairs 'until Balfour (dishonest) and Lansdowne (weak) go' and were replaced by the Liberals. In an undated draft article from this period, in which he dealt with Irish history, he again attacked Chamberlain: 'These State papers are really charming reading. You get the British mind in all its majesty revealed in them, long before Mr Joe Chamberlain began to think Imperially.' He made specific reference to a speech made by Chamberlain in Parliament, in which he had mocked the Irish, including John Redmond.[101]

The new Liberal government contained a number of members who had been prominent in raising the Congo issue in Parliament. It included Herbert Samuel, Alfred Emmott, Lord Beauchamp and Lord Edmond Fitzmaurice, who became Parliamentary Undersecretary of State for Foreign Affairs; it also included Sir Edward Grey as Foreign Secretary. One of Grey's first actions in relation to the Congo was to replace Phipps in Brussels. Things looked more promising for the reformers. Casement, though, was unsure, both for the Congo and for himself. He told Morel he was sorry that Grey had gone to the Foreign Office: 'He will be, more or less, a friend of Leopold I fear. These Imperialists are not to my heart.' In a later letter he added that he distrusted the Whig family tradition of Grey and his stance during the Boer War. Apart from his suspicions about Grey, he had heard nothing about his own future from the FO, which now contained a new team and had new thoughts and new friends: 'I really cannot hear of anything, or meet anyone who wants a Consul out of work.'[102] Despite his reservations, he wrote to Grey on 12 December requesting a return to active employment after his secondment of one year.[103] On 24 January 1906 he told Morel that he was going to start pulling strings regarding a Foreign Office job.[104] But a new consular posting was not to come for several more months, influenced, perhaps, by the change in government, some pique in the FO at his turning down Lisbon, and the need to await a suitable vacancy. He expressed interest in serving on a mooted South African Labour Commission, but nothing came of it.[105]

Following the publication of the Congo Commission's report in November 1905, opposition to Leopold's regime grew within Belgium itself. There was a major five-day debate in the Belgian parliament in February–March 1906, which called for annexation. In June, Leopold announced a Congo reform package, which was generally recognized as leaving the State system intact, despite some measures of amelioration. Simultaneously, he released a 'Royal Letter', effectively a gesture of defiance, in which he opposed annexation, unless adequate compensation were granted to concessionaires. The letter alienated many and over the following months pressure on him mounted, especially in the United States, until, in December 1906, he gave way and accepted the inevitability of annexation.[106]

The publication of the reforms and of Leopold's 'Royal Letter', was followed by a full debate in the British House of Commons. During the debate, Grey asserted that, now that the Belgian parliament and people had begun to play a positive role on the matter, they ought to be given time to act. Lord Fitzmaurice, Grey's Parliamentary Undersecretary, took the opportunity to praise Casement's role in the Congo affair. Casement, said Fitzmaurice,

> had an exceedingly difficult task, and was subject to all those perils of flood and fire which a man who has work to do in the interior of Africa has to encounter. He had, moreover, to carry on an inquiry which could not fail to be more or less disagreeable to those concerned, and to make him an object of suspicion and dislike to them. It is, as has been pointed out, unfortunate that the Report of the first Commission was not accompanied by the evidence, but the report is sufficient to vindicate Mr Casement.[107]

Given Casement's deep sense of hurt at the way he had been treated by the FO since the publication of his report in February 1904, these references to him acted as a partial salve. From Ballycastle he wrote to Morel on 4 July to say that, while there was little detail in the Irish papers, he was aware that Fitzmaurice and Lansdowne had both spoken. Lansdowne's intervention did not impress him: 'What a swindle! Fancy him saying that things are worse than ever – that he trusts only the British Consular officers and their reports – and that we have an efficient agency of reform in asserting our Consular jurisdiction! How characteristically dishonest! ... Lansdowne laughed at our Consular jurisdiction when I put it forward in December 1903 – in a well-reasoned memorandum.' He would not, he said, approach the FO again and his friends were not to do so – he had been 'humiliated, insulted and deserted for performing "invaluable services".'[108] But friends were writing to congratulate him. William Tyrrell wrote on the following day, the 5th, expressing his delight at Fitzmaurice's comments. Emmott and Gilmour were also positive. Dick Morten sent a letter and cuttings, to which Casement responded with thanks, adding: 'The Times gave Lord FitzM[aurice]'s words in full – and it was a generous tribute of esteem he paid me – for which I am very grateful to him.'[109]

The tone of his comments remained mixed during the following days. He had written to thank Lord Fitzmaurice 'for his generous references to myself', he told Morel. 'As regards myself the speech makes no difference. Soft words butter no parsnips – and I want to be up and doing – not loafing or waiting in demoralising idleness.' He had heard nothing from the FO, and had forfeited pension rights. He now chafed while awaiting a suitable appointment.

Leopold's acceptance that annexation must take place was anything but the end of the contest. Between December 1906 and the actual date of annexation in August 1908, he intrigued to bring it about on terms favourable to himself. A battle now raged within Belgium, and the CRA in Britain worked hard to influence the outcome. Morel's output at this time was extraordinary:

> In the first half of 1906, for example, he mailed over 15,000 pamphlets and wrote 3700 letters accompanying various pieces of propaganda in addition to handling the voluminous daily correspondence of the Association. When Morel moved the headquarters of the movement from Liverpool to London in October 1908 he estimated that his files contained over 20,000 letters about the Congo. He frequently worked up to sixteen or eighteen hours a day.[110]

Meanwhile, during the summer of 1906, Casement's long period without a post and without an income finally came to an end: he received an appointment to the Brazilian port of Santos, where he was to serve from October 1906 until July 1907. Congo matters continued to occupy him up to his departure. In his last letter to Morel, days before leaving, he informed his friend that he was seeing Hoste, whom he would get to approach the Duke of Hamilton again about supporting the CRA.[111] In his first letter from South America, he announced that he had talked Congo to some merchants and would try to get a branch of the CRA established.[112] In November he expressed delight at the news that Leopold ('crowned robber') had made Prince Albert of Flanders 'the heir of all his rights in the Congo Free State'. In response to receiving a copy of a pamphlet by Harris, he not only criticized it but also the missionaries in the Congo: 'they were silent for years – they took everything the Congo authorities gave them – often even shared in the plunder' and didn't act until his report was issued. From this criticism he excepted Weeks and the 'brave man' at Lukolela.[113]

Pressure of public opinion had increased in America during 1906 and, towards the end of the year, Leopold was dealt a blow when it became known that he had been paying lobbyists to influence Congress. In December President Roosevelt indicated his wish to cooperate with Britain regarding the Congo. In Belgium there was a three-week debate in Parliament on the terms under which the Congo would be handed over to the Belgian state. The reformers in England became increasingly concerned over the likely terms of that annexation; guarantees of genuine reforms were needed and not a mere continuation of the Leopoldian system. Watching these events, Casement told Morel, in January 1907, that the Belgian debate had been a sham.[114] In April 1907 he felt that Leopold's draft 'annexation' bill was 'the most impudent document that rascal has yet given to the world ... the fight with Belgium will be as hard, I fear, as the fight with Leopold'.[115]

Home again in August 1907 he admitted to being 'quite out of touch with the later developments of the Congo fight and don't think it is possible for me to do anything to help it. I have my hands full of other fights'.[116] Nevertheless, a week later he made his first move regarding a testimonial for Morel, whose finances were precarious. Some supporters wished Morel to take the (paid) CRA secretaryship, but Casement preferred the idea of a testimonial 'to demonstrate in the most public and effective way the gratitude and respect (and financial support) of all in Great Britain who have been moved by you to a sense of the great Congo Crime ... Would you still be disposed to let that idea go forth?'[117] In September, however, having taken soundings, he decided that the moment was not opportune.[118] He still encouraged Morel to keep up the fight to ensure that annexation took place on acceptable terms: 'It will take a big lift by Bishops, and Churches, and humble common-place man, above party and politics ... You are moving the mass of the people, however, and that is in the end, the way to win.'[119] In November, the FO approached Casement to inquire if he were willing to document the case against Leopold. But, out of touch to a degree and with his mind now on other matters, he told Morel that he couldn't undertake the task and asked if his friend could (confidentially) recommend someone to take it on.[120]

Annexation and After

Casement, stationed in Pará, had become seriously ill and was in Barbados, recuperating and out of touch, when Belgian annexation took place in August 1908. After Pará, he was promoted to be consul general in Rio de Janeiro and arrived there in March 1909. At this point the Congo campaign in Britain was focused on the question of the terms under which Britain should recognize the annexation. Belgium had proceeded with annexation without having reform measures in place. Grey withheld recognition and there ensued a long process of pressuring the Belgian government to introduce acceptable changes. Morel and other humanitarian campaigners attempted to cajole Grey and the FO to follow a more vigorous policy, but Grey, conscious also of growing tensions within Europe, was content to allow the Belgians the time to introduce their own measures, withholding recognition in the meantime. Morel's relations with Grey became increasingly strained. From Rio, on 29 June 1909, Casement launched into a strong criticism of Grey and of British foreign policy on the Congo since 1883. They had, he claimed, been following events rather than shaping them:

> You got up the parliamentary following and I got up the Congo. I went up river, remember, off my own bat, not as a result of any order of theirs. I had started and was already at Stanley Pool with all my measures prepared when they telegraphed out suggesting that in view of the debate of May 1903 I might start.

He added a postscript, apologizing for his harsh and sweeping comments on Grey.[121] When Morel publicly criticized Grey, Casement disagreed strongly with his friend's tactics.[122]

Religious leaders were giving strong support to the CRA and a large meeting, a 'Protest of Christian England', chaired by the Archbishop of Canterbury, was held in the Albert Hall on 19 November. Casement rejoiced.[123] When news of its success arrived, he was ecstatic: 'Indeed you *have* won! Never was anything like it, I think.' He referred to the illness of Leopold, the death of A.L. Jones, but especially the astonishing campaign in England leading to the Albert Hall meeting: 'We all owe a debt of gratitude to the A.B. of Canterbury ... a noble part.'[124]

Leopold died in December, and by Christmas Casement was positive about King Albert's speech from the throne, which showed a complete change in attitude to the Congo.[125] Proof of Congo reform, however, would come in the Belgian budget and Belgium 'must foot the bill and not the poor Congo "taxpayers"' – the 'needed revenue must be provided by Belgium for the colony, and not by the colony for Belgium'. Responding to news of Harris's departure from the CRA, he continued: 'I am glad you are losing Harris – I never trusted him over much. I think he took up the Cause when he saw it was on the road to success – but there I won't say harsh things. He did his share to help on the good cause.'[126]

Back in Ireland after his Rio stint, he noted Teddy Roosevelt's visit to Britain, his criticism of England in Egypt and his lack of comment on the Congo ('The more I see of Americans the less I believe in them'). Britain and the US 'both are materialistic first and humanitarian a century after'. He contrasted them with France: 'France is really a more humane people and one with a greater power of imagination – but she has not had the same reasons to call her feelings into play as England, with her enormous world interests, has had – hence the smaller relative role she has played in these matters.' And he reflected more broadly on Europe's relations with Africa:

> For the fight of the future must be against the degrading and paralysing effort to 'Anglicise' (just the word for collective Europeanising) a native people into a sham likeness of wholly different conditions. What Europeans have to do in Africa is to render easier and speedier the task of the African himself in bringing his race and land into the stream of gentler humanity – but always by himself – developing on native lines. For that reason I think that Mohammedan teaching may conceivably be better adapted for him than the doctrines of Christianity – as Christianity has developed in Western lands.[127]

The British government was still withholding recognition of Belgian annexation, though there were indications that improvements were taking place in the Congo. The CRA was uncertain how to proceed and convened an executive meeting for 14 July 1910 to decide what course to take. Casement's advice to Morel was to 'welcome what has been won – but insist as firmly as ever on what has to be won'. The Belgian government was a friend, but an embarrassed friend. The day after the meeting Casement was 'burning with desire to hear what went on', but he was already immersed in the Putumayo atrocities: 'I write from my desk at FO *up* to the *Eyes*.'[128]

During the summer of 1910, upon his return from Rio, Casement reopened the matter of a testimonial to Morel. One of the first to whom he turned was Arthur Conan Doyle. In 1909, Doyle had thrown his weight behind the work of the CRA.[129] He and Morel met in the summer of that year and, when the latter provided the materials, Doyle produced *The Crime of the Congo*. 'I finished my book today,' he wrote to Morel, '45,000 words in eight days, one of which I spent in London. I think it is about a record.'[130] He followed this up with numerous campaigning letters (including to President Roosevelt and the Kaiser) and a whirlwind lecture tour, which attracted huge audiences. 'Conan Doyle's intervention at that time', Morel wrote later, 'exercised a decisive influence on the course of events ... I do not think that any other man but Conan Doyle could have done for the cause just what Conan Doyle did at that time.'[131]

Casement and Doyle now renewed their acquaintance. 'To dine with Conan Doyle. Morel there & to *Speckled Band* after', his 1910 Diary recorded for 24 June. 'I like him greatly,' he told Gertrude, two days later. He told Morel about Doyle and about a talk with Emmott ('still the good, honest type of the best his country breeds'), and he expressed delight at the news that Britain was going to start free trade on the River Congo.[132] Casement and Doyle arranged a second lunch meeting on the 30th. A few days later Doyle wrote to Casement discussing details of a public appeal towards a Morel testimonial, arrangements for which were clearly well underway.[133] The appeal was to begin with a letter from Lord Cromer to *The Times*, after which a committee would look after the details. Lord Beauchamp wrote on 1 July, saying he had sent a subscription to Cromer and asking Casement to come and see him. Casement approached John Holt, long a supporter of Morel's and a likely key contributor. Shortly afterwards, Cadbury advised against phrasing a public appeal in terms of the 'hardship endured in the past or anxiety for the future'; it should, rather, be made 'on the simple grounds that this one man had done a great national service and that the public had a right to share in a national thanks offering'.[134]

Lord Cromer's letter appeared on 11 July, formally launching the appeal. Casement noted its appearance in his diary and, on the following day: 'Splendid leader in *M. Post*.' But, for Casement, the Putumayo affair intervened and he was soon to leave once more for South America. He wrote to Holt suggesting names of possible Liverpool supporters for the testimonial, adding: 'Alas! I can help but little. All my plans are changed. I was leaving for Ireland on Wednesday, when I was sent for and find I must leave almost at once for Brazil.' He maintained his involvement with the testimonial before leaving and met Doyle again on the 21st, when his diary recorded the amount of £350 already in, plus £217 from associates of his own. Two days after setting sail for the Putumayo, he was still 'writing many letters about EDM testimonial'.[135]

Casement arrived back in England from the Putumayo on 4 January 1911, after which he divided his time between working on reports for the FO and visiting Ireland. As the date chosen for the testimonial function, 29 May, was fast approaching, from the end of March he began to devote some of his attention to the event. He wrote to John Holt and spent a day with Alice Stopford Green. Holt replied to his letter on 30 March, saying that he shared Casement's disappointment about the response; there were fine words and great men, but a poor financial return: 'I wish we could have had your fire and enthusiasm in the hearts and minds of those who have been working this testimonial matter. What has been lacking has been an appeal to the hearts of the people of this country. The appeals have been cold and passionless. Far too much respectability; without any meaning; in other words, a lack of real enthusiasm.' He now offered to pledge £1000, if the rest of the fund reached £9000. He concluded by expressing an interest in Putumayo events:

> I should like to hear what you found in the Amazon ... It is appalling to get these accounts of misdoings of white people towards natives, all over the world, wherever the white man has a helpless creature to deal with, and can make money out of cruelty and wrong doing. It makes one fear for the future of the world, when we have, at this period of its history, so much unnecessary misery caused by mere greed and power.[136]

On 3 April Casement recorded: 'To London to E.D.M., Forfeitt & then Parry. Latter gave £40 to E.D.M. testimonial.' Preparing to leave the Mortens, with whom he had been staying, he noted on 6 April: 'Wrote 30 letters, packed & up to London to leave tomorrow morning for L'pool.'[137] He took the train to Liverpool on the 7th and spent the next two days there, working for the testimonial. He wrote twice to Alice Stopford Green, keeping her up to date with the response; the clergy and ordinary people were interested, he said, but 'the commercial class are selfish and ignorant too'.[138] On the 10th he went on to Manchester, where he again spent a few days trying to interest people.[139]

On Good Friday, 14 April, he crossed over to Belfast, where he and Mrs Green were to spend Easter with Francis Joseph Bigger. After a few days with Bigger, he left Ardrigh on Easter Tuesday, the 18th, for 105 Laburnum Terrace, a rooming house of Mrs Elizabeth Thomas, which was to become a regular lodging for him in Belfast. While in Belfast he noted: 'Very busy all morning writing E.D.M. testimonial business. Sent out 750 circulars.' He returned briefly to London on the 30th: 'To visit many people today on Morel Testimonial. Went H. of C. and then to Sir Richard Staples.' On 4 May, after this short sojourn in England, his 1911 Cash Ledger noted: 'Return to Ireland today'. He now spent another fortnight in Belfast and its surrounds before leaving for England, once more, arriving on the 17th.[140]

The testimonial was now less than a fortnight away and, in the intervening period, he kept in touch with his collaborators, Cadbury, Holt and Mrs Green. On the 25th, he lunched with Nina for her birthday and then went to Mrs Green to discuss the testimonial. A letter to Holt, written on the same day, showed his disappointment at the amount raised: 'All told I don't think my personal advocacy, so far as it went (which was not far) brought in much over £500. That was always something – but it fell so lamentably short of what I hoped for & of the needs of the case.' They had quite failed to get £9000; the fund stood at £3600 and they would be lucky, he felt, to get £4000. The rest of the letter was virtually an appeal to Holt to produce an eleventh-hour donation.[141]

On 29 May, after calling at the FO, Casement went to the Morel function. The printed programme contained tributes from overseas, including one from prominent leaders in Lagos and one from the Comtesse de Brazza. Also included were warm wishes from a large number of British dignitaries, clerical and lay, who were unable to be present; among them were the Archbishop of Canterbury, the Bishop of Liverpool, Lord Fitzmaurice, Sir George Goldie and John Holt. But the ranks of those actually present, presided over by the Bishop of Winchester, were equally distinguished. Included were many associated with the CRA: Lord Cromer, Alfred Emmott, Ramsay Macdonald, the Revd Silvester Horne, Arthur Conan Doyle, Alice Stopford Green, the Cadburys and Herbert Ward. There were press supporters: Gardiner, Strachey, Fabian Ware. There were over a dozen speakers, among whom were prominent overseas supporters of the Congo campaign, Emile Vandervelde, of the Belgian Labour Party, Anatole France, Pierre Mille and Felicien Challaye of France, René Claparède of Switzerland, and Robert Whyte of the United States. As an additional gesture a 'fine Statue of a Congo Chief by Mr Herbert Ward' was presented together with a pledge by William Rothenstein to paint a portrait of Morel, as a remembrance for Mrs Morel.[142]

Casement, though in the hotel, did not attend. A few days before, he had written to Morel, saying that he hoped to be at the lunch, but that he hated functions.[143] Afterwards, he talked of the occasion to Mrs Holt. Everyone, he said, had been delighted at the function; Morel himself was

> overwhelmed at it all ... Your husband's splendid generosity saved the situation! We were able to present Mr Morel with a fairly good sum and Liverpool, after all, had the honour of contributing the lion's share ... I was not in the luncheon room – that is why we did not meet. I was in the Hotel at the time – but did not come into the room and saw none of you.[144]

While preparations were underway for the testimonial, Morel came to Casement for advice on another matter; the proposal by Lever Brothers to open a factory in the Congo. William H. Lever, the soap-manufacturing magnate, had approached Morel in July 1910 to seek his advice on a proposal to build a palm-kernel crushing-mill in Nigeria. After his first discussions with Morel, Lever switched the plan to the Congo, where he was granted permission for the mill together with a concession. Morel found himself in a difficult position and, in April 1911, sought Casement's advice.[145] He was worried about the effect on indigenous landownership of certain clauses in Lever's agreement. On the other hand, Lever could be an 'enormous power for good', if steered. Morel saw a role for Casement: 'There is no man on this earth that can make him see the heart of things as you would do, because you have a power of persuasion and a personality, an individuality, and a way of putting things which I altogether lack.'[146]

From the SS *Heroic*, on his way to Belfast, Casement replied. He felt that Morel should talk to Lever and advise him; there was a danger that, with an evil administration in the Congo, Lever's enterprise might go astray, especially with regard to native land rights. Morel should handle Lever gently, offering friendly help and friendly criticism. His Congo experiment

> may prove *far* better than anything yet set up on the Congo and change is good, and improvement can only come through change and trial of new courses there. The best thing to do is to get him deeply interested in the country and its *people* and their future ... and who knows but *his* land concessions might not be the beginning of a true rooting of the people in their soil. Lever might create the Congo peasant proprietor and on his big tracts ... In fine I'd help Lever *all* I could if I were you until you were sure that good could *not* come out of his trial.[147]

A week later he offered further advice. He agreed with Morel on the question of the nationalization of land, 'but I don't approve of *attacking* all who differ from me on that point'. It was important to separate essentials from non-essentials, 'and there are diversities of view on every question that must endure as long as human nature endures'. The concessionaire system was not the best, but there were good concessionaires; similarly, the Irish landlord system was not the best, but there were good landlords: 'In dealing with primitive peoples, like the Congo natives, you are dealing with people a very long way behind the Nigerian Muhammendans or Yoruba nations – and it may very well be that Lever's going there will prove a great blessing.' Attacking non-essentials brought the risk of creating enemies and weakening one's hold on 'a large circle of men and women'. Casement instanced the liquor trade, religion and polygamy: 'My opinion, for instance, is that the liquor trade in Africa is not a good trade. I'd like to see no trade liquor imported by Africans – and I sympathise a great deal with Temperance crusaders.' But it was non-essential beside the question of 'oppression, slavery and cruel misgovernment'. He continued,

> You regard these matters as all branches of one tree – I don't think they are – they are separate plants ... I should stick to my tree – which is to fight slavery ... I feel just as strongly as you do on most things, for instance, the Irish question, which to me is of supreme importance and far transcends African landownership or human slavery even. But I have to work with the material I find – and influence the human nature I am in contact with by suasion and not by attack.[148]

Early in 1912 Morel consulted Casement on his projected history of the CRA. Casement advised Morel to wait.[149] In June, recognizing that Morel was committed to writing the history, he reflected: 'I do not attach the same interest that you do to the written word. I much prefer the acted thing.'[150] Two days later, he wrote:

'One thing is clear to my mind. The Congo Reform Movement is dead. Its work is done – so far as the public interest and political effort to attain the public will are concerned ... Once annexation is recognised the CRA must shut down.' Morel should think seriously about how to wind up the CRA, which must be 'a full and formal and deliberate termination in the eyes of the world of what was a great world task' and it would be a positive wrong and injury to continue it, lending strength to the 'taunt that you are oiling and running a toy'.[151] When, Morel wrote an encomium in the *Daily News* on 20 July 1912, with Casement's contributions on the Putumayo and the Congo in mind, and with an accompanying photograph, Casement's response, while overtly angry, seemed just slightly pleased. He had had, he said, a 'stand up fight with the Intelligence Bureau', who had published his photo, and he made them recall all photos of him throughout the country and apologize. 'I object very strongly to publicity and the idea of one's photo in the papers is nauseous to me.'[152]

Meanwhile, signs of improvement in the Congo continued through 1911 and 1912, until the CRA held its last executive meeting in April 1913 and recommended recognition of annexation and the dissolution of the organization upon recognition. On 29 May 1913, Grey opened the parliamentary debate on recognition, supported by the CRA's parliamentary followers. When the end of the CRA finally came in June 1913, Casement was in Dublin. Writing on the 5th, he told Morel that he would be in Dublin till near the end of the month and that he could not be in London on the 16th, the day of the formal winding-up, 'but I will write you a valedictory letter to read, if you care, at the final meeting. I am glad you are closing down – I think it is a wise act'.[153] On the 11th he proclaimed: 'Here is my Epistle to the Meeting!' It was written, he said, 'as I so often do, rather, on an impulse of the heart than a direction of the head ... It is a word of friendship and farewell from one who has never been with you in the body, but very often in the spirit and in the heart of your work'.[154]

Morel, Casement's statement read, had earned the gratitude of the whole world, 'first of the black peoples of the Congo basin and next, if I may say so, of the Belgian people'. It continued: 'I am convinced that when the whole story of the Congo has passed into history, the Belgian people will feel that the work of the Congo Reform Association was a work of friendship and enlightenment in their behalf, no less than a struggle in the interest of those distant Africans whose welfare has been committed to their trust.'[155]

10: *Ireland: A New Commitment, 1904–6*

While he devoted considerable energies to Congo affairs between his return from Africa in late 1903 and his departure to take up a consular post in Santos in late 1906, there also occurred during this period a remarkable transformation in Casement's attachment to Ireland. He later claimed that 'when up in those lonely Congo forests where I found Leopold I also found myself – the incorrigible Irishman'.[1] As part of the process of transformation, he made the acquaintance of a considerable number of talented women and men involved in the Irish cultural revival, most of them Protestant and most from the north of Ireland.

During the last decades of the nineteenth century a great vibrancy entered into Irish intellectual life and popular culture. In 1884, the Gaelic Athletic Association was formed to promote native games. The Association gradually helped to generate enthusiasm and deep attachment to locality and to country, as well as antipathy to foreign games. In 1893, the Gaelic League (Conradh na Gaeilge) was founded with the aim of arresting the decline of the Irish language, Douglas Hyde and Eoin MacNeill being among its most prominent founding members. Hyde argued for recognition of the language as a unique mark of nationality and for 'the necessity of de-Anglicising Ireland'. The League, too, spread and, with 600 branches early in the twentieth century, fostered local attachments and a new national consciousness. The popular language movement was complemented by the scholarly interest in Irish, which encompassed historical, philological and literary researches, and the publication of folklore, poetry and songs. Important contributors to the former included German-speaking scholars such as Rudolf Thurneysen, Kuno Meyer and Rudolf Pokorny.

At the same time an Anglo-Irish literary revival was being spearheaded by such authors as Standish James O'Grady, Lady Augusta Gregory, William Butler

Yeats and John Millington Synge. These writers were inspired by the rediscovery of ancient Ireland and of the hidden culture of the Irish country folk (especially in the Irish-speaking west), the materials for which were being made available through the translations of scholars. The Irish Literary Society was formed in London in 1891, followed by the National Literary Society in Dublin in 1892. From this literary movement emerged the Abbey Theatre in 1904.

The enthusiasm for language, literature and games fed into the political current. The fall and death of Parnell in 1891 led to a split in the Irish Parliamentary Party, followed by a decade of bitter internal strife. The internal bloodletting, combined with the large Conservative majority in the UK Parliament, left the Irish Party powerless. The factions did not reunite until 1900, when both sides accepted John Redmond as leader. Only then did the party begin to regain its credibility.

One of the new forces which was to emerge from the ferment was the Sinn Féin ('Ourselves') movement, brought into being by Arthur Griffith.[2] A campaigning journalist, Griffith had established *The United Irishman* in 1899, opposed the Boer War and, in opposition to royal visits, established two nationalist organizations, Cumann na nGaedheal ('Society of the Irish') and the National Council. In 1903, following the Hungarian example of winning a measure of independence by boycotting the parliament in Vienna, he began to enunciate his 'Hungarian Policy' in a series of articles. The material was published as a pamphlet in 1904 as *The Resurrection of Hungary: a Parallel for Ireland*, and was widely influential

Meanwhile, the Irish Republican Brotherhood, heir to the physical force tradition, was also stirring. In 1905 two northern members of the IRB, Bulmer Hobson[3] and Denis McCullough,[4] established the first of the Dungannon Clubs, which aimed at educating the rising generation in the ideals of independence. The Dungannon Clubs were open and legal, while the IRB was a secret organization. Another member of the IRB, the veteran Fenian Tom Clarke, returned to Ireland in 1907 and, in the years following, the organization began to increase its membership and influence.

It was to this Ireland that Casement was converted in 1904. In the period of enforced leisure, if it can be called that, which he experienced from 1904 to 1906, Casement read widely in the literature of the Irish cultural revival. He was friendly or acquainted with many scholars and writers associated with the movement. His reading over the years was wide and eclectic: poetry, drama and other literature by William Butler Yeats, Stephen Gwynn, Seosamh Mac Cathmhaoil (Joseph Campbell), Alice Milligan, Canon Hannay (the novelist, George A. Birmingham); the literature of early Ireland, available to him through the works of friends like Mary Hutton, Margaret Dobbs and Kuno Meyer, but also through the modern versions of Standish James O'Grady; Gaelic literature, from such as Douglas Hyde, George Sigerson and an tAthair Peadar Ó Laoghaire. But, most of all, he read works on Irish history.

These ranged from general works by R. Barry O'Brien and A.M. Sullivan; to the biographies of Owen Roe O'Neill by Taylor and of Patrick Sarsfield by Todhunter; to regional studies, such as Hardiman's history of Galway and Hill's on the McDonnells of Antrim. A special place was held by the writings of his friend, Alice Stopford Green, which he greatly admired. More passionate were the works of John Mitchel. The Tudor and Elizabethan periods, which saw the final overthrow of the Gaelic order, seem to have had a central place in his thinking, and here he drew directly on State papers as well as on secondary sources. His approach conformed to and was, presumably, partly shaped by the growth in nationalist historiography, itself a reaction to the hitherto dominant Ascendancy and unionist historiography. Concerning one of the latter, Richard Bagwell, he wrote: 'I maintained that his point of view was radically wrong and, after all, the writing of history means always a certain point of view.' Of another: 'I can't read that awful Froude – altho' his facts are often good – but he uses them to such bad ends.' Of the most prominent historian of them all, W.E.H. Lecky, Casement judged that he had failed to grasp the Irish mind.5

In a letter written on 5 March 1904, he informed the recipient, John Hughes, whom he had met in Madeira in 1903, that: 'I had not much acquaintance with the gaelic movement in Ireland until last month when I was fortunate enough to come across, at two country houses (one in Cork, the other in Antrim) I was visiting, ladies in touch with the movement, and from them I learned how deep was the interest growing in this effort to keep alive and extend Irish influences and thought.'6 The two ladies in question were the Hon. Louisa Farquharson and Ada MacNeill. Casement met Louisa Farquharson when visiting his friend from Lourenço Marques days, Lord Ennismore, in February 1904. This was at Convamore, Ballyhooly, Co. Cork, the home of the latter's father, Lord Listowel.7 Of Louisa Farquharson, Casement later told Dick Morten that she had 'come to Ireland with the Cadogans as Lady Cadogan's Lady-in-waiting'. She came, he said, a Unionist, but she told him 'that she had not been a year in Ireland before she perceived the necessities of the case. But she came without prejudices, without an axe to grind, or self interests to "preserve".'8 A passionate lover of Scotland, Louisa Farquharson became a member and later chief of the Gaelic Society of London. She and Casement corresponded during 1904 and 1905 on language and literary matters. Casement was to acknowledge her influence on him in his 'Brief to Counsel' in 1916.9

Casement renewed contact with Ada MacNeill shortly after he returned north. On 3 March he wrote as follows to John Clark, owner of a hotel in Glenarm: 'Miss M'Neill gave me your address, and I send you the enclosed which perhaps you may care for your *Fear an Gleanna* ['The Glensman']. I saw your paper at Cushendun, and I admired it greatly.' What he enclosed was a short poem on the decline of the Irish language:

It is gone from the hill and the glen
The strong speech of our sires;
It is sunk in the mire and the fen
Of our nameless desires.
Like the flicker of gold on the whin
That the spring breath unites
It is deep in our hearts and shall win
Into flame where it smites.[10]

He informed John Hughes in his letter of 5 March that:

I was present a few days ago at a meeting in Cushendall in the Glens of Antrim
called for the purpose of organising a *feis* of the Glens in the summer. The *feis*
has been fixed for 30th June in Glenariffe – and I trust it may do something to
knit together in that part of Antrim the growing sentiment of love for the
ideals and hopes of Ireland.[11]

His purpose in writing was to encourage Hughes to use his influence to get
the *Irish News*, with which Hughes was connected, to restore its weekly contribution in Irish. Though his own knowledge of Irish was minimal, the language
had become for him one of the key indicators of nationality. He was successful
with Hughes to the extent that a letter of his on the language revival was published in the *Irish News* shortly afterwards.[12]

Eoin MacNeill's sister, Mrs Annie McGavock, also a supporter of the first
Feis, wrote to her brother on 8 March about the plans being made and telling
him of Casement's involvement:

Mr Clarke [*sic*] told me that at the meeting on Sunday week in Cushendall he
said a few words about the movement and when he had finished a tall sol-
dierly looking man came over to him and said: 'I agree heartily with all you
have said; these have just been my own thoughts for years.' Mr Clarke thought
no more of the incident but on Friday last he got a letter from the gentleman
telling him he had heard of the little manuscript paper that had been started
and enclosing a couple of verses on the Irish language for the March number.
He is greatly interested in the *Feis*, hopes he will be here at the time, but as
he is going to South Africa soon he fears he may have to leave before 30 June.
He subscribes £5. Mr C. says that he can hardly believe that a Casement of
Ballycastle (they were considered tyrants in the the old days) could hold such
views.[13]

The first meeting of the Feis committee had taken place on 28 February.
Miss Barbara MacDonnell of Cushendall was elected president, Ada MacNeill
secretary, Francis Joseph Bigger and Joseph Duffy (Cushendall) treasurers, while
committee members represented the Nine Glens of Antrim.[14] The 1904 Feis na
nGleann (Feis of the Glens), the first, was to be held in one of the glens, Glenariffe. Casement spent most of the spring in Ballycastle and was active on the
organizing committee, representing Glenshesk. Competitions were planned in

language, music, industry, sport; sponsorship for prizes and adjudicators for the competitions had to be found.

Casement's letters to Gertrude in the first half of 1904 hint at his enthusiasm. On 9 March he wrote: 'I should like to stay in this beloved country till I die – I like it better every day – and I cannot think of England!!!' Later in the month, he sent her an Irish play, presumably his own work, which he modestly referred to as 'not a particularly good one – the speeches are too long for the stage – but the intention is good, and a second effort may go better'. And on 2 May he told her: 'I am very busy in Ireland learning Irish and helping in that movement there – It is a delightful study.'[15]

He also found time and scarce money to help the distress calls of a local woman, Mrs Dunlop-Williams, now in difficulties in the United States, communicated to him by Miss Margaret Causton. He had first responded to her plight in 1902, but the tone of her calls now in 1904 became desperate. In a series of letters to Miss Causton, Casement sent help and sympathy ('I fear I cannot send more than £2 or £3 for Mrs W. I have given so much to the Congo natives of late – all I could spare').[16]

That spring he established other contacts in the Irish cultural field. In April he seems to have visited Sligo and met Douglas Hyde there, while in March he visited Donegal, giving gifts of books to two teachers, which drew letters of grateful response.[17] One of the teachers, J.C. O'Boyce, of Portsalon, told Casement that he believed Irish to be safe in Donegal, as it was spoken by the bulk of the people. He was also positive about improvements in teaching, particularly the new bilingual programme introduced by the Commission on National Education.[18]

In April Casement first introduced himself to Alice Stopford Green. His immediate purpose was to enlist her support in the Congo campaign, but to her he was able to stress the Irish dimension of his Congo involvement. Also involved in the preparations for the Feis na nGleann was Francis Joseph Bigger, and Casement came to know him at this time.[19] He lived in his family home, a large house on the Antrim Road, which he christened *Ardrigh* ('High king') and where he frequently held *céilís* or musical evenings. Casement was to be a frequent visitor. While awaiting execution in prison, he wrote fondly of these evenings to Brigid, Bigger's housekeeper:

> Do you remember the 'Cradle Song' I liked so much? Get Cathal to sing it for me, and give him my love and thanks from my heart, also to Colm if he is ever near you and Dinny and Seaghan Dhu, whenever they come to you and the old room again. I dreamt last night I was lying before the fire in it, and the boys were telling stories, and you standing at the door with the pipes.[20]

Another record of those evenings in Bigger's house was left by the poet Joseph Campbell:

Bigger loved youth, and once a week round the hearth in his library at 'Ardrigh' collected his 'young bloods' as he called them, to read Fionn MacLeod's *Sin-Eater* and the *Washer of the Ford* ... Brigid his faithful housekeeper would entertain us to supper in the dining-room, where his mother's vacant chair was kept, shrouded and inviolate; then we would go upstairs, and until 11 o'clock sit spellbound under his infectious leadership. Distinguished guests would sometimes join us. Roger Casement was there at a Samhain festival, and I remember a cryptic utterance of his (cryptic, in the light of after events), as he lay stretched at full length on the Irish-made hearthrug: 'Ye are all broken reeds!' Nothing, at the time, registered momentarily; but it has held me pondering ever since.[21]

Feis na nGleann

Casement was due to take up the consular post in Lisbon on 1 July. He wrote to Cowper to say that he could not be there by the 1st, requesting the 15th instead: 'Things have arisen to detain me somewhat ... I have a big meeting on 30 June and have various things to get through.' The 'big meeting' was, of course, the Feis.

The 1904 Feis na nGleann in Glenariffe was a key event in focusing Casement's Irish attachments and in bringing him new friendships and acquaintances. Among those listed as attending, adjudicating at competitions or offering prizes were many who became important friends or acquaintances of his in later years: Ada MacNeill, Bigger, Eoin MacNeill, John Clark, Bulmer Hobson, Colonel R.G.J.J. Berry,[22] Margaret Dobbs,[23] Alice Milligan[24] and Stephen Clarke. In addition, Casement came to know Stephen Gwynn[25], Horace Plunkett[26] and Evelyn Gleeson, though his relations with these were less close.[27] Casement's brother, Tom, was also present, home from South Africa.

Proceedings were opened by Barbara MacDonnell. Plunkett spoke on the importance of Irish industry, while Eoin MacNeill spoke on the language. There were short-story competitions, history essays, poems, songs, notes on ruins, plays, compilations of Gaelic names and craft competitions.

Stephen Gwynn later recalled this, his first meeting with Casement:

What remains now in my mind is chiefly the impression of his personal charm and beauty ... Figure and face, he seemed to me to be one of the finest-looking creatures I have ever seen; and his countenance had charm, distinction, and a high chivalry. Knight-errant he was; clear-sighted, cool-headed, knowing as well as any that ever lived how to strengthen his case by temperate statement, yet always charged with passion.[28]

Alice Milligan also met Casement here for the first time. She described him 'listening eagerly to the competitions in Song and Language in which the schoolchildren took part, or cheering on the boys at their hurling and their games. It was his way to be candid of speech, and one felt after very brief acquaintance, that here was a man whose desire it was to serve Ireland at any sacrifice.'[29]

John Clark ('Benmore'), who was on the organizing committee, wrote this shortly after Casement's execution in 1916:

> And the man who sleeps in that far off grave was with us: a man of splendid physique, well-built, towering conspicuously above many of average height, keen grey eyes that mirrored a living soul of great force within commanding appearance, with strength of character stamped on an extraordinary countenance, a beard raven black and pointed, with curls of loosely arranged black hair covering the brain of a man of genius.[30]

Lisbon

On 29 June the FO had sent a telegram, stating that HM Consul at Lisbon had been granted leave until his retirement on 1 January 1905 and instructing Casement to 'take charge of the Consulate from the date of Mr Cowper's departure'. The full salary of the post was £800. Casement took a steamer on 7 July and arrived in Lisbon on the 10th.[31]

We catch a brief glimpse of him in Lisbon, from a letter to Bigger on 15 July. He was house-hunting and enjoying the sun and heat. He hoped, soon, to meet the Count O'Neill.[32] He received several letters from Louisa Farquharson, who congratulated him on the Feis, spoke of a course in Irish she had just completed, and of going to Braemar for the summer. She sensed his unhappiness at being away from his passions: 'Portuguese and Gaelic – they are far apart.' And: 'Your poor blacks. I expect they haunt you always and make you wish to be back helping, but be patient a little and you may be allowed to help later – It may be you are helping now more than you think.'[33]

Cowper proposed to transfer duties to Casement on 31 July, but it did not happen. In mid August Casement wrote to the FO explaining: 'On 21st July I became ill and this illness had developed into a somewhat severe attack of dysentery from which I have not yet recovered.' He proposed returning to the UK. Cowper was agreeable to remain at his post and Casement looked for an extension of leave until the end of September. On the same day he wrote two more letters to the FO. To Cockerell he said that he was ill and couldn't possibly do the work. Besides, Cowper had much improved and 'Entre nous, I think he does not wish now to retire so soon as he first said – his health has improved so much.' A similar message went to Barrington, with the further information: 'It is a complication – my old African complaint for which I have been operated on, aggravated by dysentery.' He didn't think he would get well in a Lisbon hotel and wished to go to a quiet place. Leave was granted.[34]

Casement had actually spent very little time in Lisbon itself. After a short stay there, he travelled south to Andalusia; on 27 July, just over two weeks after he had arrived in the Portuguese capital, he wrote to Cowper from the Hotel Reine Cristina, Algeciras, to say that he was sick. He had come to Seville and spent two days there, but the journey had made him ill. He dreaded the train journey back from Seville; he had been told that steamers went from Lisbon to Malaga but found that it was only cargo boats – and the same was true from Gibraltar. He couldn't face trains and was stuck until he improved. It was a 'delicious locality' and a 'delightful hotel', if only he could enjoy them. He asked Cowper not to let others know he was ill. Two days later he was 'horribly weak and in pain ... I have never had an attack like this in my life'; he had lost over a stone in weight.

On 4 August he tried to arrange a transfer of money, with Cowper's help, in order to travel. He noted that he felt better at night, but in great pain in the morning, and that he spent the whole day without eating a scrap. He did return to Lisbon by mid August, from where he sent his telegram to the FO suggesting his return home. On the 22nd he dropped a note to Cowper, mentioning practical matters in preparation for leaving. On the same date, O'Neill wrote to Bigger to say that he was delighted to make Casement's acquaintance. But he had only learned of his arrival on the previous day and Casement was leaving on the morrow. He was sorry not to have met him earlier, as he could have helped with medical advice.35 On the 26th Casement reported to Bigger on his meeting with The O'Neill: 'I have seen O'Neill. His English is perfect and his manner charming. He is a very well-known man here – in Court and town – and is very wealthy, I believe, having large interests in various companies.'

Casement's letters to Bigger from Lisbon mainly concerned Irish literature and history: books (*Red Branch Crests* and *Songs of Uladh*); membership in the Irish Texts Society; praise for Bigger's answer to critics on a massacre at Island Magee during the bitter revolt of 1641.36

He left Lisbon in early September and on the 5th wrote to Cowper from the Exchange Station Hotel in Liverpool to say that he had got in the day before after an excellent voyage. He was feeling much better and going to London to see an old doctor and 'abide by his advice'. He enclosed money for the bootmaker, who had made him four pairs, two black and two of yellow leather. On 17 September he reported to Cowper that he needed two operations, one for fistula ('not serious') and one for his appendix ('chronic disease'). He was asking the FO for extended leave up to 30 December and feared the need of a long spell of nursing: 'I may go off the books.'37

The West of Ireland

After his return from Lisbon, Casement went on a rapid visit to the west of Ireland, calling first to the Aran Islands. His visit was recalled by Tom O'Flaherty, older brother of the writer Liam O'Flaherty. Back on a visit after many years, O'Flaherty wrote:

My most treasured recollection of Oatquarter national school is the memory of Roger Casement, tall and thin, his black beard accentuating the pallor of his countenance. I believe he was British Consul at Lisbon at the time. He visited the school house and told the teacher he would like to know if he had a pupil who could grind his way through Eoghan Ó Neachtain's column in the *Cork Examiner*. The teacher fondled his luxuriant brown beard and smiled. 'Indeed I have,' he said. I was called to the front and came out of the test with drums beating. Sir Roger gave me half-a-crown, and afterwards sent me three books: *The Story of Ireland*, by A.M. Sullivan; *Séadna*, by Father O'Leary; and *Fairies at Work*, by William P. Ryan, then the editor of the *Irish Peasant*. The two latter books were in Gaelic. Later Sir Roger planned to send me to Summerhill College, Sligo, but fate intervened and the project fell through.[38]

During a second sojourn in Lisbon, Casement was to remark to Mary Hutton: 'I am not settled in Lisbon yet – and the Aran boy must wait till I get a house first.'[39] The teacher, Daithí Ó Ceallacháin (David O'Callaghan), wrote in January 1905. 'Tomás', he said, 'was very sorry for your illness.' Ada MacNeill, too, reported on O'Flaherty to Casement in an undated letter from Aran. He was, she said, working hard with his father, but she would ask him what sort of books he would like.[40]

After Aran, Casement went on to the small community of Tawin (Tamhain), near Clarinbridge, Co. Galway. He later wrote to Douglas Hyde from Sligo about his experiences in these two Gaeltacht areas. He had, he told Hyde, first heard of Tawin in an article in *An Claidheamh [Soluis]* some weeks before. He had then met the Tawin Company in Galway with their play *An Dochtúir* ('The Doctor'). He had gone to Tawin with the play's author, S. O'Beirne, and stayed as guest of O'Beirne's mother. He had also met the manager of the local school, Fr Kean, and learned of their problem.[41] They had lost their teacher and the school was in disrepair; the National Board would only pay two-thirds of the cost of repair, which left some £80 to be made up, an amount beyond the resources of the local community. Casement appealed for support. He went on:

> I have not anywhere seen or heard of such a brave true spirit as beats in that handful of poverty-stricken Irishmen and women. They are Irish to the heart, and it did me more good than all else I have seen in Ireland to find them so fiercely trying, in the face of the utmost difficulty, to keep their own language ... Only in Tawin, in all that coast strip, do the parents insist on the children having the language, and they are often being jeered and laughed at by the bigger neighbours round.

He contrasted Tawin with Kilronan on the Aran Islands:

> In Kilronan I heard the fathers and mothers speaking a vile attempt at English to their children – and they with a rich splendid speech of their own. But there it is! Nowhere did I find the language cared for, and, with the exception of Tawin, every Irish-speaking home I entered tabooed the tongue of the parents to the children. It is shameful, and almost inexplicable to a man who has

travelled as I have among peoples who each and all respect and love their own language. My own countrymen alone are contemptible! For it lies with the people themselves, and if they wished or cared for their country really they could keep her language here in the West, where it is still known and spoken. Although I nearly despair of the future (I hope I am wrong and only temporarily depressed) of the language, still I feel the very urgency of the situation calls for all the braver effort, and I should be a traitor, if I allowed my fears to stay my hand or chill my heart.[42]

Hyde, responding, asked permission to publish Casement's letter in *An Claidheamh Soluis*, the Gaelic League paper, edited by Patrick Pearse.[43] Both Pearse and Casement agreed.[44] Casement, simultaneously, opened a private appeal among friends. Foremost among these was Mary Hutton, to whom he sent a copy on 1 November, suggesting that Douglas Hyde's appeal would not reach people whom he would like to reach.[45]

In early November, he discussed with Mary Hutton the possibility of initiating an Irish-language scholarship scheme. He would, he said, when settled in Lisbon the following week, draft a scheme and put it to Mrs Green, with a view to seeking help in the US; 'before this day year we shall have *at* least one scholarship for Irish in the land'. It was probably while thinking on these lines that he drafted, though never published, an outline of such a scheme, in commemoration of John Mandeville. Mandeville, a landowner active in land agitation, had died in 1888 following brutal treatment in prison. Casement took as his cue the proposal to erect a statue to Mandeville in Mitchelstown, Co. Cork. Rather than put up a monument of stone, he suggested that Mandeville would have supported him in advocating a living monument, the 'John Mandeville Scholarship for the National Language of Ireland'. Quoting the well-known language scholar Fr Dineen and the Bishop of Killala, he argued that the key problem was to save the language in the west of the country. A scholarship scheme – to pay fees for colleges of higher education – would have an important inducement value. An endowment of £700 would produce £25 per year. He went on: 'Ireland will be dead if the soul of the race, which was Ireland for 3000 years, passes away ... no after-growth of prosperity, material wealth, instruction or commerce – no conquest of things of the body – can make this soulless land Ireland.'[46]

Earlier, towards the end of September, when his leave was drawing to a close, Casement had applied to the FO for an extension and was granted leave until 31 October. He kept Cowper apprised of his condition; he was much better and 'may not have to undergo the operation for appendix after all. The surgeon and doctors I have seen think it would be wiser I had it done', but he was worried over the long lying-up and felt that the cost might be unnecessary. He was, though, not fit for Lisbon, with all its Distressed British Subjects and 'rush of work'.[47]

On 9 October Casement sent a card to Cowper stating that he was sending a paper or two for The O'Neill. 'The Language Movement is steadily progress-

ing and I am in the thick of it – God bless it! (You see I use Irish post cards!)'
On 3 November he said that he was leaving for Lisbon on the 9th or 10th,
though it was still clear that he had the operation on his mind.[48]

He did return to Lisbon during November but his stay was brief. On 24
November he informed the FO that he needed longer leave and wished to
abstain from duties he was not, at present, 'prepared to adequately fulfil'. He
requested to retire temporarily from active service and be seconded from duties
for a year from 1 January. He followed this up the next day with a letter to Cockerell: 'I have arrived at this decision only after long doubt as to the best course
to adopt.' He was granted permission to return from Lisbon immediately, leave
being granted until 31 December, from which point he would be on secondment. No salary was to be paid while he was unemployed, and 'your return to
the service will be governed by the occurrence of a suitable vacancy'.[49] Back in
England, he wrote somewhat nostalgically to Cowper:

> I go to FO today to bid them adieu for a time and then into Hospital for
> Christmas ... I shall always keep a very vivid recollection of your kindness to me
> during my various visits to Lisbon – I owe you much more than thanks and fear
> I shall never be able to repay you ... I retire from the service from 1st January
> ... and my return to it seems very unlikely I fear.[50]

Towards the end of 1904, he heard from some of his Lourenço Marques
friends. Ennismore had written from Convamore on 8 October, hearing that
Casement wasn't well, but also to announce that he had got engaged. He wrote
again in late November to thank Casement for his 'valuable present ... I shall
value the volumes not only for themselves, but as a remembrance of one of my
best friends'.[51] Blücher wrote from Vienna at the end of December: 'I am sorry
and wish I were there to cheer you up. I also have my time of travail and trouble ... You and I won't be happy until in a "happy union" ... Richard C[ouden-
hove] joins me in wishing you all imaginable happiness for the next year.' In January Blücher wrote again to say that he was glad of Casement's recovery. 'I do
hope you will benefit by it.'[52] Another who showed solicitude for him at this
time was The O'Neill in Lisbon, who wrote, warmly, on 6 January enquiring
about his health and praising his poetry: 'You *are* a poet!'[53]

He had told Cowper that he was going into a hospital-cum-nursing-home
in Belfast on 4 January; the operations duly took place in Fitzroy Avenue and,
on 10 January, Casement wrote to Morel 'from bed and bandages', rejoicing:
'getting on splendidly – much better that could ever have been expected. I shall
be up and all right by end of month'.[54] Mary Hutton visited him while he was
recuperating and they kept up their correspondence about literary matters.[55]
He was on the mend by the end of the month. 'Here I am now,' he told Morel,
'in my fourth week of bed – and getting very tired of it – I may be up next week
– but it will take a long time, I fear, before I go about again with freedom.'[56] On
1 February he told Hutton he was leaving the nursing home for Bigger's house,

Ardrigh, and again thanked her for her visits.[57] By mid February Casement was in Ballycastle with Nina. He wrote to Cowper: 'I hope to go to South Africa very shortly on a long voyage – and on to New Zealand where I have a share in some property left by my grandfather. If all goes happily with me I shall spend a considerable time out there.'[58]

Kossuth's Irish Courier and the Hungarian Model

On his return to Ireland after his abortive posting to Lisbon, the story of his father's ride in 1848 in aid of Kossuth came to have new significance for Casement. The episode was called up by two independent stimuli. The first was the appearance on 15 October of the following notice in the English periodical, *Notes and Queries*: 'Roger Casement: Is anything known about him? It was he who, in 1849, travelled from Widdin to London to deliver to Lord Palmerston Kossuth's letter, wherein the latter called for England's help to save him from Austria and Russia, who demanded his extradition from Turkey.'[59]

A friend from early Congo days, J. Rose Troup, wrote to him about the entry, asking if this man was any relation of Casement's.[60] The second stimulus came from the writing of Arthur Griffith's pamphlet *The Resurrection of Hungary*. On 15 December Casement wrote to Mary Hutton of his father's Hungarian intervention, and continued: 'He used to tell me this story when I was a little boy – and then, long ago I came across it in a Review of Kossuth's book in a London paper. So the *Resurrection of Hungary* has a special interest to me.' Further statements in his letter reflected his mood at the time: 'I may some day do something for my country. Yes, any man – or woman – who loves Ireland would gladly go to the scaffold – or to any shameful end – to strike such a blow for Ireland's honour and right as the Hungarians did in '48.'[61]

Early in 1905, while convalescing after his operation, he pursued the Hungarian theme. He enlisted former Africa friends to get a copy of Kossuth's book. In February Blücher reported: 'Coudenhove begs me to tell you that one volume of Kossuth's memories only is out, but he can get it in French or German only, there is no English translation – let me know.'[62] Casement wrote up the details of his father's adventure and it was published as 'Kossuth's Irish Courier', under the name 'x', in *The United Irishman* on 25 February 1905.[63]

As a model for Irish imitation, Arthur Griffith had put forward the strategy of Francis Deak, who represented the 'peaceful' alternative to Kossuth's 'forceful' ways. The notion of non-violent resistance excited Casement. To Gertrude he wrote that England 'will find we can play a more dangerous game than any we have yet attempted – Passive Resistance on a gigantic, national scale. No taxes, no recruits, no public service in any department the passive resistance can influence – such shall be the reply of Ireland'.[64]

He responded, too, in late January, to the massacre by the Russian czar's troops of unarmed people in St Petersburg. In a draft letter on 23 January he called for the severing of official relations with Russia, drawing a parallel with the withdrawal of British ministers from Belgrade after the assassination of the Sovereign's Consort.[65] He must have sent a copy to Lady Margaret Jenkins, for she responded on 1 February, agreeing that the events were 'too horrible' and that she looked on the czar 'with the profoundest contempt'. But she was glad he hadn't sent the letter for the CRA's sanction: 'Such red hot socialism would discount your Congo verdict terribly. All the same what you say is very true.'[66]

While he recuperated from his operation, he maintained his steady involvement in language matters. Alice Milligan later reminisced:

> In the winter following my first meeting with him, he organised a series of five lecture entertainments for me along the Antrim coast, and I vividly recall how we drove past the foot of Glenariffe, the scene of that delightful summer *Feis*, in a snowy blast which swept down from the mountain heights. Just as we passed under the sandstone Arch at Red Bay, the Irish travelling teacher of the district rode by us on his bicycle, and we could scarcely hear the greeting he shouted to us, for the roaring of wind and sea. The house of a kinswoman and friend of his was our headquarters, and there we had talk till late in the nights, about how the cause of Ireland might best be served and the old tongue revived.[67]

Deepening Engagement, 1905

Casement's financial situation deteriorated steadily the longer he remained on unpaid leave. In February 1905 he talked of plans to go to South Africa, where his brother Tom lived, but in early March he announced that the trip was off – he couldn't raise the money. 'I am practically at the end of my resources – indeed I think I have about £20 in the world – and when that is finished I shall be in the workhouse!' He had lent money that he could not get back.[68] In May he wrote to Morel: 'I am going to sell a splendid Tusk of Ivory I have in Ireland – nearly 7 feet long.' He still had it in August, however, when he again expressed interest in selling: 'I want for the money badly.'[69]

Meanwhile his engagement with Irish issues intensified. He devoted a considerable amount of his time to writing of various sorts. Some was on his new-found love, the Irish language. He published a pamphlet entitled *The Language of the Outlaw*, in which he set out to answer the contention that Irish was useless in the Ireland of his day. Giving examples, he suggested that this argument had been used from the days of the English conquest. He devoted most space in his pamphlet, however, to summarizing a speech by the late Irish journalist John F. Taylor, who projected the argument back to the time of the Hebrew captivity in another empire, that of Egypt. Referring to Hebrew but with Irish in mind, Casement concluded: 'The language of the outlaw gave the Law of

God to man: The tongue of those who made bricks without straw was chosen for the shrine of Divine utterance on Earth, while the speech of Pharoah lies smitten, silent as the stones of his Pyramids.'[70]

A second piece on the Irish language appeared in *Uladh* in May. Again he blended the contemporary with the historical. He instanced the prosecution of a Donegal man for having his name painted in Irish on his cart, the *Morning Post*'s comparison of Irish to 'kitchen kaffir', and the *Daily Mail*'s comment on letters posted with addresses in Irish as being 'in the uncouth characters of a barbarous language'. Turning to history he pointed out that the bill making Henry VIII King of Ireland as well as of England was proclaimed in 1541 'in Irish and English'. The Irish-speaking city of Galway was second only to London in trade, beautiful buildings and general wealth around the same time. Its Irish-speaking inhabitants, however, were ejected in the middle of winter by the Cromwellian government in the mid seventeenth century. Speaking of himself, he concluded:

> I bethought me that a people's language was a living thing, and that it was a shameful thing for an Irishman to stand by and see the soul of his country being dragged out through its lips. I accordingly gave up my club in London, and devoted the amount of the annual subscription thus saved to a training college in Munster where Irish teachers are perfected in a fuller knowledge of, and more scientific methods of imparting 'kitchen Kaffir'.[71]

The references in these articles indicate acquaintance with a range of historical sources. He commented to Morel in March: 'I amuse myself and serve my country by compiling a string of healthy arguments in favour of the capacity and character of my Irish nation – I am writing an article on Irish commerce and trade in the middle ages which is an untouched and vastly interesting subject.' He told Morel that he was not brooding, 'but very busy on Irish things – writing and moving about and speaking. It is only when I cease from these that sometimes my heart goes down to my boots'.[72] Among his published articles of a historical nature were 'A Forgotten Nationalist' in *The United Irishman* in April 1905 and 'The Irishman as Soldier' in the *Freeman's Journal* in September. In the latter Casement developed the theme of Irish bravery and the superior physique of Irish soldiers.[73]

Associated with his interpretation of Irish history, and with the centrality of the Irish language in his thinking, are ideas about national character, not only of Ireland but of Ireland's oppressor, England. The literature of early Ireland revealed the national character of Ireland. 'Every people has a national character,' he claimed. In a lecture on the Irish language he tried to identify what the Irish national character entailed:

> I will now try to point out to you what I mean by those distinctive characteristics of our Irish nationality and why it is I think we should be loath to see them slip from us. And remember that a Nation is a very complex thing – it never does consist, it never has consisted solely of men of one blood or of one

single *race* – It is like a river, which rises far off in the hills and has many sources, many converging streams before it becomes one great stream.74

The world of early Ireland, reached through Irish literature, held great significance for him, as it did for most revivalists of the day. He told his listeners:

> Now I want to try and take you back tonight to a far country just with themselves and their own voices to tell what they *did* do ... just what those old Irish men and women thought and did – just what their view of life was, just what the motives were which inspired their actions, just what it was they loved and admired, just what it was they despised and scorned.

The question was not whether the heroes of the early Irish sagas, Finn, Ossian or Cuchullain, really lived, 'the point of real significance is that these stories reveal to us very clearly the mind and mental stature and moral code of the people who composed and of the people who loved these old tales'. What was being presented was what was admired and 'held worthy of imitation' and 'held up to popular imagination' down through the generations. The listener 'was ever shown that the supreme test of manly character was not in *getting* things ... but in *doing* and in *giving* ... All the great men in these stories who were exalted by the poets were those who kept their troth, who never broke their words, who were staunch in their friendships, firm and abiding in their love – and faithful unto death'.75

A number of his poems were also published in 1905. Mostly his theme was Ireland, but in one poem, 'Life', published in *Uladh* in May, the treatment is personal:

> O Hearts that meet, and hearts that part,
> The world is full of sorrow;
> Men love, and die – th'almighty mart
> Put up new hearts to-morrow.
> Was this Creation's scheme at start
> Oh! then I little wonder
> That Lucifer's proud, human heart
> Preferred to God his thunder!76

In the spring of 1905 he contributed an article entitled 'Redistribution' to *The United Irishman*, again signed 'x'. He admitted he was the author to Gertrude: 'Yes – Redistribution was also mine barring the misprints. Only you must not let on or peach on me – It is nothing to what I am up to.'77 The article dealt with a proposal, touched on in the king's speech on the opening of Parliament, to reduce the number of Irish representatives in Westminster by thirty-seven. The proposal was being justified in terms of 'electoral anomalies' and the movement of population.

> 'Ireland', stated Casement with irony, 'has no blessings of increased population to justify "electoral anomalies"; she has only a "movement of population" to account for them. The Irish people have moved across the Atlantic, that is all

... The thing is simplicity itself. The same happy process of removal need but continue for another sixty years, at the existing rate of drain, and the Imperial Parliament of great Britain and Ireland will have eliminated the kingdom of Ireland as effectually from the Imperial problem, as an unkind fate has withdrawn the erstwhile Kingdom of France from the Royal Arms.'

Turning to the Act of Union of 1800, he sarcastically suggested that its two benefits for Ireland were 'that those who legislate for it know less about the moral condition and temper of the people than they do about the races in Central Africa' and that the population of Ireland had been removed across the Atlantic in many millions.[78] The decline in Irish population he attributed to the effects of the English colonial system and involved a draining away, as he put it later, of men, mind, food and money. This reading of history contributed to a regular mood of pessimism, which was evident in this letter to Gertrude:

> It is a shameful thing that a whole race should be slowly and relentlessly done to death and refused the right to heal themselves. First stricken to the dust, drained of their wealth – their industries destroyed, their land entirely confiscated – their religion, their laws, their language banned – until too weak to resist they gave up all and sank in despair – and now to be chucklingly regarded as a fair green isle that can, all in good time, be replaced with the dregs of English City life.
>
> The history of civilisation offers no more shameful picture than the persistent agony of Ireland ... and ... no parallel ... to the steady, persistent clinging to their own lofty generous ideal of kindly humanity as the Irish people present.[79]

His education and, crucially, his life experience had already added a wider level to Casement's thinking about the decline of societies and empires.

One of the clearer statements of his view of the decline of societies, indeed empires, comes in a letter to his close English friend, Richard Morten, written at the beginning of 1905. The letter also reveals the strongly moral character of his thinking. He wrote:

> If you would study history more attentively you would see this. Rome centralised the wealth of the ancient world in herself – Italy became a beautiful garden filled with the villas of the rich, maintained by the labour of millions of slaves. And Rome fell. Spain, in her pride, exploited the mines of the Indies by Carib slave labour – just as, identically as, Leopold is exploiting the india rubber mines of the Congo by Bantu slave labour – and sent the wealth of Peru, Mexico and the Caribbean sea to Madrid. She had a monopoly of the gold of the world – but she did not know how to use it wisely – and Spain fell.
>
> Read Montesquieu's *Considerations sur* the decline and fall of Rome ... and you will ... find considerations in it which will make you tremble when you look at South Africa – and India.[80]

This theory of the decline of empires, of Rome and Spain, had a definite moral for the British Empire in Casement's thinking. The accumulation of wealth, if based on the exploitation of labour, would bring a fall. There is a strong moral content (the vices are aggression, venality, perhaps the debilitation of wealth itself). In the passage, Casement drew on Montesquieu's *Consideration sur les causes de la grandeur des Romains et de leur decadence*, written in 1731–3.[81]

He concerned himself, too, with the economic aspects of nationalism. In March he wrote from Ballycastle to T.P. Gill, secretary of the Department of Agriculture and Technical Instruction.[82] As well as telling Gill about some of his own doings, Casement expressed a wish to meet Gill on the latter's forthcoming visit to the area with Bigger. In particular, he wanted Gill to meet some 'local folk', especially R.P. Woodside, 'a good soul' and a 'good kindly man (a Unionist of course) with many undeveloped but latent Irish sympathies'. Two days later he again urged Gill to meet Woodside to discuss fishing, for example in Ballintoy:

> It was once fairly successful – and Woodside can tell you how it was sat upon. Like everything else in this unfortunate country it paid the toll to that damnable fraud the British Empire. Absentees who cared more for rents that they might have 'a good time' elsewhere – and a system of education which has brought up Irishmen and women to know more of and care more for England in the world than their own – a system of benevolence which rests on the same basis as burglary and which, not content with abstracting everything of saleable value in Ireland, has also abstracted the soul and intelligence of her people – that is the British Empire as it has revealed itself to this country.[83]

At the end of June, Casement learned from the Foreign Secretary that he was to be made a Companion of the Order of St Michael and St George, 'to recognise your services in the Congo State'.[84] This was followed by a letter from the Duke of Argyll, chancellor of the Order. Casement received the news at Cushendall, Co. Antrim, where, together with Bulmer Hobson, he was spending the day with his cousin, Jack Casement RN. According to Hobson, Casement was for turning down the honour, but his companions tried to convince him otherwise. 'I reminded him', recalled Hobson, 'that it was a mistake to make a hasty decision. I pointed out that if he refused it, that would be tantamount to sending in his papers and resigning from the foreign service. Did he really want that, I asked him. Casement paced up and down the sands in agitation for over an hour, before he sighed and reluctantly agreed to accept the honour.'[85]

The only direct record of his thoughts comes in a letter he wrote on 20 July to Edward Clarke of the FO. He told Clarke of 'my oft uttered contempt (that's a nasty word – but I fear it expresses literally my feeling) for distinctions and honours and principalities and powers,' a view of his that was well known, he felt, in the FO. In addition, there was the specific embarrassment to him as an Irish nationalist. 'You know,' he said, 'I am a confirmed Home Ruler ... and I shall now be regarded askance in every respectable quarter of Ireland.' On the assumption that Clarke had played a key role in forwarding his case, he concluded: 'To you, my dear Clarke, I reserve the full and unreserved thanks of one who is not a formalist, but your very sincere and grateful friend.' Clarke, in response, suggested that he deserved no great credit for Casement's honour, though 'I did what I could'. 'But,' he continued, 'in deed there was small need for me or any one else to "push" the matter since it was the general feeling that you deserved some small recognition' for 'what you had done and what you had gone through'.[86]

Casement was still vacillating when he was contacted by Sir W. Baillie-Hamilton with an invitation to the presentation in Buckingham Palace on 24 July. He was, he replied, unable to appear. A second invitation followed in November, which he again declined, citing a problem with his hand as the reason.[87] He approached William Tyrrell on how to handle the situation. Tyrrell advised him to write to Baillie-Hamilton explaining that his recovery from an operation was not as rapid as expected, that a second operation might be needed, and to express his hope that the King would dispense with his presence and that the decoration be forwarded.[88] Since the next investiture would be the following June, Baillie-Hamilton suggested that it could be sent by post, with which suggestion Casement concurred.

Casement attended the 1905 Feis na nGleann at the end of June. On 3 July he wrote to Morten from 'the heart of the Glens of Antrim' saying, 'The Feis was first rate'. He enclosed a cutting, asking Morten to forward it to Louisa Farquharson, 'a subscriber to it and a warm well-wisher'. Though badly described in the newspaper, 'the gathering of people ... was an encouraging thing – and the Hurling was splendid!' He was staying with Ada MacNeill, who was 'a delightful person and keeps open house with a vengeance'.[89]

In mid 1905, too, in response to the introduction of a new Militia Bill, which would have made it compulsory for militia regiments to serve abroad, Casement, Bulmer Hobson and Alice Stopford Green wrote an anti-enlistment pamphlet called *Irishmen and the English Army*. The authors averred that militias were intended for the defence of one's own land: 'It is the glory of soldiers to stand as the unconquerable defence of the land where they were born, and where their fathers' graves lie; but the Irish must learn to forget their own homes and the relics of their fathers.' They went on to criticize the calculated use of Irish soldiery since Tudor times for fighting England's wars of aggression outside of Ireland, in Scotland, in France and in the Boer War, for example. In the meantime Ireland was reduced to being 'a hungry, idle, uneducated and depopulated country'. The pamphlet concluded, rousingly:

> Let England fight her own battles – we have done it long enough. Let her arm and drill the sickly population of her slums; the men of the hills and the country places in Ireland will go no more. Let her fight for the extension of her empire herself, for the men of the Gael are not going to be bribed into betraying themselves and their country again at the bidding of England.[90]

There was an aftermath. Stephen Clarke of Ballycastle was arrested in July for distributing the pamphlet. Undoubtedly, this is what lay behind Casement's enigmatic message to Richard Morten on 8 July, after he had had to leave England suddenly: 'My wild rush over has its equally wild departure ... I am terribly rushed and bothered – something I am dearly interested in has gone wrong in Ireland – and I must return there to see it through – until it is settled I cannot interest myself in anything else.' Casement helped pay for the defence and Clarke was acquitted.[91]

At the end of July, Casement spent a weekend in distinguished company on Lord Monteagle's estate, at Mount Trenchard, Co. Limerick. Horace Plunkett's diary entry for 29 July read: 'Mt Trenchard ... Interesting party. Hon. Bertrand Russell and William Russell, Douglas Hyde, Emily Lawless, Mrs J.R. Green, Casement and others.' And, for the following day: 'A delightful Sunday. My work was to convert Douglas Hyde and the Gaelic Leaguers to my domestic economy views. I think I succeeded. I had long talks with Mrs J.R. Green and R. Casement with a view to ascertaining their real political opinions. They are so predominantly anti-English that I fear there is nothing constructive in them.'[92]

On 3 August, shortly after Casement's visit to the Limerick area, an exchange of letters began with the Revd Lucius O'Brien, Dean of Limerick and son of the Young Ireland leader, William Smith O'Brien. O'Brien wrote to Casement from Adare Rectory, thanking him for a copy of a pamphlet by Barry O'Brien, which he would 'read with interest'.[93] Lucius O'Brien did not believe in 'the learning of an ... obsolete language, dancing at the crossways, and ever talking of a past history'. On the contrary, he believed in 'more circulation of money', the 'breaking up of ranches', Horace Plunkett's work and in 'a strenuous effort to be part of the Great Empire' while retaining national sentiment. Casement might consider him a 'West Britainer', but 'I am just as much interested altogether in my country as you are in your views'.[94]

Casement, responding on 22 August, defended his own approach to Irish affairs, stressing the cultural as against the economic emphasis of O'Brien and Plunkett:

> I believe that the Gaelic people are still the matrix of the Irish people – and that whatever tends to strengthen the Gaelic element in Irish life must be for the good of the modern race ... 'The passionate aspiration for Irish nationhood will outlive the British Empire,' said John Mitchel – I would put it otherwise. The passionate aspiration for Irish nationhood should be, if not opposed, the strongest support of the British Empire.[95]

In August, too, he was in Dublin for the Oireachtas, the annual national cultural gathering of the Gaelic League. 'I was delighted with the Oireachtas', he wrote to Mary Hutton, whom he had met there,

> and came away from Dublin really cheered for once – for the language is *not* dead that can inspire so many people and provoke such enthusiasm. The Ard Fheis, too, was cheering – to hear so much Irish spoken in business makes one think that it cannot be very long to wait before all Gaelic League functions and gatherings will be held only in Irish.[96]

From Dublin he wrote to Hobson: 'Just at present I am trying to get some representative Irishmen interested in "foreign policy" – and if we can succeed in getting a commercial agency into existence it will be a beginning.' Indicating a lack of sufficient interest, he continued: 'This country needs men of leisure, who would love her for herself, and who would give to her service what the English aristocracy are trained to give to English public life. All our men of leisure, with scarcely an exception, are English at heart, or by training.' The Irish Parliamentary Party members, he believed, should establish a cabinet, with a prime minister and ministers for foreign affairs, agriculture, home affairs and education. And they should *act* instead of wasting energy in Westminster.[97]

While spending some time with the Mortens in September, Casement met Henry Wood Nevinson for the first time. Nevinson described the occasion in his diary:

> Journeyed to Uxbridge and drove to the Savoy, a lovely old house by the Colne near Denham. Has been rented by the Mortens for six generations. Met Casement there – large, dark, blue-eyed, very handsome and soft-voiced Irishman from N. Antrim. Talked well but never listened. Spoke much about the Congo and the shame of our Government in allowing a Commission to enquire into its official's report. Thought nothing could be done under Balfour. Lansdowne was good, Percy harmful. Told me true story of his return, rapidly through Boma and Banana, for fear the Governor should detain him for investigations. Thinks Schumacher, the Swiss, is standing for full publication of Rept. of Commission. Of Angola and San Thomé he knew nothing.[98]

Towards the end of 1905, obviously unhappy with Irish press coverage on national and international matters, he took an initiative on the establishment of an Independent News Agency. An undated and partial letter of his suggested that such an agency might establish a link with the *Freeman's Journal* to supply Irish publications with Irish material – thereby circumventing the controlling clique in the *Freeman*, which, he suggested was often obscurantist (he gave an article on the Congo as an example). He envisaged a mediating agency or individual, mentioning Stephen Gwynn.[99]

A proposal was clearly put to the newspaper since, early in 1906, he had a response informing him that the idea of a detachable supplement, carrying information on industry, language, temperance and 'other progressive movements', had not been well received by the board or the editor.[100]

Beastly Idleness

Casement had never quite turned his back on the prospect of returning to the Foreign Office. In September 1905 he told Morel that he had no *locus standi* with the FO; he was only 'on the list', like hundreds of others: 'I think it highly probable they will not want me back very much – for they must know pretty well how

I feel toward them – and the fact that I refused Lisbon and came away was an unusually independent step to take, for which I must expect to pay.' He felt that if he didn't hear by the end of the year, he would have to find other work. Early in November he reported positive noises from FO friends about a vacant post.[101]

By the end of 1905, having gone without pay since the beginning of the year, Casement was out of money. He turned to his friends. In late December, Theodore Hoste responded to a request for £150: 'Please dear Casement regard me as a friend who will share everything he has got. Your friendship for me has been one of the brightest things in my life ... I am burning your letters so there is no record that might be seen by others; this is a private affair between us.' A few days later he forwarded a cheque for £50.[102]

A request for help to Herbert Ward brought about a strain in their relations. On 28 December Casement sent a six-page letter to Ward remonstrating because Ward, on the one hand, had failed to reply to an appeal from him for money and, on the other, had breached confidence in mentioning, and distorting, the issue to Dick Morten. Casement elaborated on his very strong views on the obligations of friendship. In turn, he explained to Morten that he had told Ward he would make no further appeals to him: 'I want no money from you – what you told me on 23 December has more than surprised me.' He continued to Morten: 'the whole proceeding of that other person has been such a violation of friendship and confidence that I do not like to touch upon it'. Ward's behaviour had been 'unfriendly, ungenerous and untruthful'. Morten remonstrated with him: 'I don't believe in your methods of drawing conclusions, only looking on one side and ignoring or abusing any one who does not think as you do – allow that the other side may be as honest as yourself, and don't be a crank ... my dear Roddie, so I mean to read you a lecture.' He was, he said, five years Casement's senior and had lent money spontaneously and not 'as an agent of any one else'. He did not know what grievance Casement had against Ward, but was sure it was a misunderstanding.[103]

Casement's contacts with Thomas Lennox Gilmour offered some promise of a position. Gilmour had been involved in the Congo reform movement since the previous year and had become editor of the *Morning Post*. On 11 November 1905, he informed Casement that he was to be the London manager and one of four directors (one of the few non-Portuguese officials) of the Mozambique Company. He envisaged the possibility of a position for Casement, as inspector general of exploitation. By the following day, however, it had emerged that this was not a possibility and he tried to interest Casement in an opening in the Niger Basin. He had contact with a 'financially very powerful group' and the first step would be a small expedition to spy out the land: 'How would the organisation and conduct of such an enterprise meet your views?' He felt Casement was the 'right man' and could 'do something for the further development of Africa on right lines'.[104] Casement told Morel in March 1906 that he was trying to get out to East Africa 'for a Company having large interests there', but that it was hard to get one's foot on the first step of the business ladder.[105]

Meanwhile, relations with the FO were fraught. On 5 January 1906 the FO responded to Casement's letter of 23 December inquiring about a resumption of active service:

> Sir Edward Grey regrets to state that there is at present no post vacant in the service to which you could be appointed, and it is therefore necessary that you should still remain *en disponibilité*. In these circumstances I am to inform you that your request to be seconded for a further period of six months from the first instant is granted.[106]

In April 1906, presumably following another query from Casement, Barrington responded rather curtly:

> I am afraid from what I hear that the Secy. of State will not be able to offer you one of the present vacancies in the Consular Service, though he recognises your claim to re-employment when a suitable opportunity presents itself. It was in my opinion most unfortunate that you shd. have so hastily resigned Lisbon which is one of the nicest posts in the Service & was given you in recognition of your work in Africa.[107]

Stung, Casement sent an angry letter to Tyrrell on the following day challenging Barrington's interpretation of his motives in resigning from the Congo consulate and in not accepting Lisbon. The real reason, he stated, was to allow him the freedom to speak and write on the Congo, because the FO had seemed to wash its hands, leaving the court open for Leopold's commission. His health had also been a factor.[108] More of the same was shared with Morel: 'Barrington's rudeness was certainly intentional – and whether that was so or not I cannot go on waiting in beastly idleness.'[109] Tyrrell had responded soothingly:

> A line to say that you need not be alarmed as to your case not coming before Sir Edward Grey and on its merits. Nobody would accuse you of being an 'officeseeker'. There must have been a serious misunderstanding between you and Barrington who at present is away. You may rest assured that the matter will be thoroughly cleared up. You must have received an absolutely wrong idea of your position.[110]

Perhaps Casement's pressure did have an effect, for at the end of May Tyrrell asked Casement to come and see Lord Fitzmaurice. He reiterated that he felt Casement was wrong to see Barrington as an enemy. The latter intimated that he had spoken to Casement 'quite frankly as a friend' – there had been a misunderstanding. In any event, the meeting with Fitzmaurice took place and Tyrrell again wrote to say he was glad that the interview had gone well and that Casement was now happy.[111]

But by the summer of 1906 his financial situation was precarious. Writing from Ballycastle in June, he confided to Morel that 'Here in Ireland I live in cheap rooms (25/– a week all found) and I have to write where I can – generally in the neighbouring hotel – as I have only a bedroom here.' He was borrowing money to pay his way and help his sister. In the same month he admitted 'I owe now over £300 and every month adds some £20 to my borrowings – and there must be an end of *that*.' His earnings for the last nineteen months had been £3 for an article and £1-1-9 from a tea company. A stark indication of his straitened circumstances was that he had borrowed £50 from Morel, himself surviving on the edge. 'I pile up a load of debt,' he moaned, 'this long spell of idleness is killing soul and body.'[112]

Time hung heavily. 'I am loafing as usual', he told Morten, 'and trying to kill time. But one does want an occupation badly – and after having worked all my life I feel this long spell of idleness as very depressing.' His six months' further secondment had ended and he worried about loss of pension. It was 'really very bad for me to be so long idle. I shall not be fit for work soon if I loaf much longer ... The truth is when one gets past 40 it is very hard to get anything decent to do – people don't want middle aged men but young men.'[113] On 31 May, he wrote to Gertrude: 'I see Michael Davitt is dead and gone. Alas, mavrone, mavrone.' His was the greatest loss since Parnell, he claimed, and left no leader for Sinn Féin.[114] The following day Nevinson noted in his diary: 'Casement ... lunch at Club. Fairly good. Casement chiefly on Ireland and Davitt.'[115]

On 25 July Louis Mallet wrote to inform Casement that the consul at Bilbao had died and to ask if he was interested in the post.[116] Mallet wrote again on 30 July mentioning both Bilbao and Santos and adding, soothingly: 'Sir Edward is glad to hear that you have decided to return to the fold and that the FO will have the benefit of your assistance.'[117] Tyrrell joined in; he was glad that Casement had accepted Sir Edward Grey's offer and that 'you are actively "one of us" again'. When Casement chose Santos, after consideration (the Bilbao salary had been reduced), Tyrrell wrote to say he had chosen wisely. He wrote again to say that Grey would like to see Casement.[118] The salary at Santos was to be £600 per annum plus non-pensionable local allowance of £200 per annum, an additional temporary allowance of £100 per annum, and an annual office allowance of £500.

After a visit to London in mid August, he returned to Ireland towards the end of the month: 'I want, if possible, to spend my 42nd birthday, 1st September, in the old land.' He told Morel on 19 September that he was sailing from Southampton that Friday. 'I don't suppose I shall be for ever at Santos – in spite of its name I fancy it is neither holy, saintly nor healthy.'[119] On the 21st, on board the RMS *Nile*, he sent Gertrude a postcard of Euston Hotel, with a Union Jack on the card blacked out.[120] On the same day he wrote to the FO to say he was leaving that day on the *Nile* and was due to arrive in Santos on 9 October.[121]

From Vigo he wrote to Gertrude on 23 September, asking her to send cuttings on Irish and Congo affairs – he was not going to get any English papers at Santos, only *Sinn Féin*. 'I am a queer sort of "British" Consul, alanna, it strikes me, and I ought really to be in jail instead of under the Lion and Unicorn. I must say, Gee, I *can't* stand Anglo-Saxons or Imperialists.' He encouraged her to

> get A.M. Sullivan's *New Ireland* and read his account of the Manchester Martyrs in 1867 – God bless them – I read it last night – and it made my heart on fire and the tears from my eyes and heart. That one little incident should be taught in every Irish school – just as to the Greeks the tale of Thermopylae meant a living fire of patriotism burning in every boy's heart, so the tales of the dauntless loving, sacrificing young Fenians of 1867 should point each Irish boy's footsteps on the upward path.

More neutrally, he suggested reading Horace Plunkett's *Ireland in the New Century* – 'and his pages on the Gaelic movement are full of truth and patriotic insight'.[122]

PART IV
South America

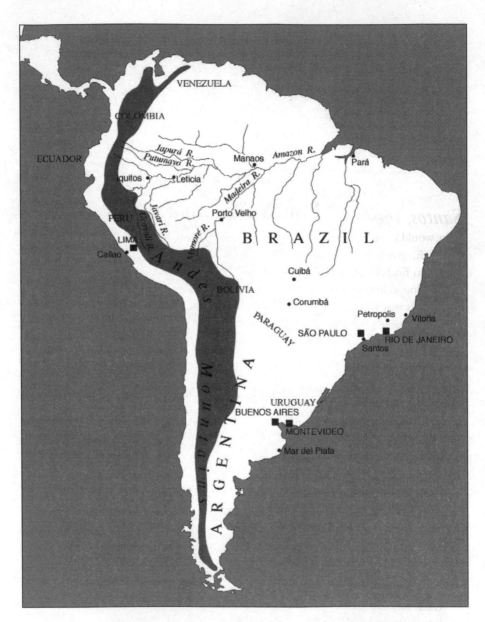

Map 6: South America

11: *Brazil, 1906–9*

Santos, 1906–7

How would Casement react to his new posting? He was in an unfamiliar continent, although, given his experience in Portuguese territories, one where he might expect to find certain things familiar. Having been deeply immersed in the affairs of the Congo and Ireland, he was now to be far removed from his associates in both. This was his first posting in a country where there was also a British legation responsible for diplomatic affairs and to which he was, to a degree, answerable.

He arrived in Santos in October, the height of the coffee season. Coffee, he was to write in his trade report, formed 47 per cent of the total export trade of Brazil, and the year 1906 'was the most prosperous one Brazil as a whole has enjoyed'. Santos was the chief coffee-exporting port and, as a port, second only to Buenos Aires in all of South America.[1] His consular district embraced the southern Brazilian states of São Paulo and Paraña, but communication between them was possible, effectively, only by sea. He was to point out that 'owing to the difficulties of communication and the superior claims of the more populous and highly developed State in which the Consul resides, little or no attention can be given by this Consulate to commercial or other questions in Paraña'. Santos had a population of some 45,000 and the city of São Paulo, 34 miles inland at 2800 feet, had a population of some 300,000.[2]

His letter to Gertrude on the day he arrived revealed a state of mind that was not to change for the duration of his stay:

> I am a fool to come here – this place looks abominable – inhabited by lepricauns [*sic*] and satellites of evil ... I ought never to have come to South America – after Africa and the life there I fear I shall not be able to stand this life ... send me news of Congo and Ireland – nothing else counts. Ireland first and ever – and poor old Congo too for the sake of the dark skins and all they have suffered and all the brave indomitable Morel has done to free them.[3]

A few days later he wrote to Morel:

Frankly I am greatly disappointed – both at Santos and in Brazil. Place and country are uninteresting in the extreme so far as I can see. Everything in Brazil is imported – including the inhabitants. There is nothing Brazilian – nothing natural, native and inevitable ... I cannot imagine such a thing as Brazilian 'patriotism' because none of the patriots have anything of this country in their blood. The population is of all variety of colour – and here in the south mostly Italian. All come here to get money and bolt.

Nothing was talked of but coffee. Only a trading consul was needed, not a *consul de carrière*. The post promised 'interest none, conversation none, society none, exercise none and I really don't know how I am going to get through my time'. In sum, he concluded, 'Santos is a *Hole!*' Contributing to his unease was the high cost of living.[4]

Towards the end of the month he wrote to Mary Hutton in Belfast. He enclosed a cheque for £3-5-0 for Dáil Uladh, the Ulster Gaelic League committe (collected from friends around Ballycastle), and promising £5 for the Rathlin School for Christmas: 'It hangs on my heart to think of Rathlin so close to our doors and nothing being done for the language which so many of the elders still speak so well and which so little real energy would give to their children.' He went on to describe Santos and São Paulo for her. Santos was very rich and would probably export £20 million sterling in coffee that year, but everyone was working 'at highest pressure' and life was 'supremely uninteresting'. Currency fluctuated wildly, even hourly. He added:

It is naturally a wonderfully rich country – with a very inert and vicious native population and worthless administration – yet in spite of evil government the prosperity of the country increases – so great are its natural resources and the fertility of its soil. It needs a big immigration of healthy European blood – preferably Italians – to swamp the indolent half-caste Indian-Negroid Brazilian native – and I think it will get it. Some day in this State of Sao-Paulo the Italians will be supreme.

Santos was, he said, not without irony, the 'most democratic spot in democratic Brazil'. He was addressed by local authorities as 'Citizen Roger Casement, most worthy consul', though 'it is rather a joke as the next door "citizen" is a coal black darkie perhaps'. As for his consular work: 'I am kept busy with British Shipping, trying to maintain discipline on board – an impossible task as the men get drunk and come ashore and desert in shoals and the place is a pandemonium.' While there were no Irish in Santos, one figure in São Paulo clearly reminded him of home: 'The Protestant Chaplain at São Paulo is a Mr Macartney – an awful stick – a typical music-hall variety Parson of the unctuous, oily, spirit-catching kind. I've really never seen in real life such a caricature of stage personation.'[5] When he wrote to Cowper on 7 November, he was staying in São Paulo and travelling up and down to Santos daily by train. He had come for a change, having suffered from a daily fever for three weeks: 'There is a lot of this melancholy recurrent malaria here – not of the virulent African type, but simply a heavy slow discouraging temperature which slowly pulls you down and yellows your skin.'⁶

To Morel he wrote of the futility of his position: 'My whole duties consist in chucking out a few beach-combers and deserters – day in, day out – there is *absolutely* nothing to do.'⁷ On the same day he sent a long and revealing letter to Emmott. Brazil was uninteresting 'apart from the beauty of the hills and vegetation'; the life of the people was 'dull and soulless and uncouth ... The lower classes are coarse and brutal, without any redeeming quality I have yet encountered, callous and cruel to animals and coarse and nasty in manner to men – and the richer ranks (there are no true 'upper classes') are extravagant, empty-minded altho' quick-witted and with few warm or real sympathies.' Everyone was after money, but there was little comfort and much pretence and ostentation:

> The rich want money chiefly for trips to Paris and for the keeping of strange women (there is a positive mania for this form of fast life and it is the pride and ambition of all the youths to imitate their seniors in this respect) and the poorer classes want money to get out of Brazil – back to Italy, Spain or Portugal. There is no *native* or national Brazilian mind or type that I can yet feel sure of as being Brazilian. A coal-black darkie is a 'Brazilian' – a native Indian is a 'Brazilian' and all the intermediate stages of type and colour from the old time Inca of Peru, or conquistador, to the darkest son of Africa are all equally Brazilian.

Two recent murders caused Casement to assess negatively the nature of law and morality in the country. The first was the murder of a priest-senator some days previously. The Senate had been adjourned out of respect for the murdered member ('a disgrace to our civilisation'). The murder was committed by three youths, sons of a doctor who had himself been assassinated some time before. Their friends and the press congratulated the youths; the relatives of the priest-senator vowed vengeance. Everyone assumed that the senator had assassinated the doctor. But an enquiry? Proof? 'Nobody knows and nobody cares – they laugh and turn to the coffee gamble ... The law of Brazil is a fiction.'

The second murder had happened the previous day at 4 pm outside the consulate in the busiest part of Santos. An official of the municipality stopped a cart loaded with coffee – three times its maximum weight. The driver stabbed the official 'right under my window'; everyone laughed, saying the most the driver would get was 'a week in the lock-up':

> Brazil wants a severe attack of discipline – beginning in childhood and enduring on into old age. Possibly some time or other Uncle Sam, when he is fully grown up and has quite given over lynching, may administer it. The children are brought up entirely lawless – they are even taught to be vindictive and rebellious by their parents and encouraged in 'tempers' and selfishness. Passion is regarded as Virtue.

Blazing tempers, leaving off steam, drawing knives or revolvers (everyone carried them, even the Senator), were taken as examples of 'manhood', of true 'Brazilian' blood. Lord Salisbury had been right in his comment on the 'savage hordes' of South America. In support of his own view and that of Salisbury, Casement quoted the comment of a Kerry boy working for him, 'a poor Irish lad I picked up out of the street here', who had said, 'Sir, they're savages – look at the way they beat the mules.' Casement wrote: 'All the traffic, and it is enormous – is accomplished by mules – poor patient hardworking splendid little creatures – and they are shamefully and horribly flogged with whips as thick as your wrist. The Irish boy spotted this at once – and his kind heart came to the same just conclusion as the old Premier arrived at.'[8]

Though Casement found the consular work in Santos not to his liking, he nevertheless threw himself energetically into it. After his arrival, he wrote to the FO to comment on the condition of the consular files. While his predecessor, F.W. Mark, had been popular, despatches had not been registered since 1894. He found FO circulars 'in blotting pads, old books or pigeon holes'; many couldn't be found at all. Thomas Thornton, Mark's temporary replacement, had been busy with his own work, but was adequate.[9] Sometime later, however, he discovered and drew attention to the fact that Mark had been acting improperly in officially attending and registering marriages outside his official consular residence.[10] Casement appears to have rectified the anomalies. He also directed attention to the situation of vice-consulates within his jurisdiction. That at Parañaque he suggested abolishing – the present incumbent didn't answer letters and didn't speak or write English (the FO agreed). In the case of other vice-consulates he negotiated their terms of leave and embursement.[11]

Before the end of the year, he had drawn up a printed petition and subscription list for the relief of British Distressed Subjects, directed at the British community in Santos and São Paulo. He opened the subscription himself with a donation of $100; Mr J.J. Keevil, of the London and River Plate Bank, added $500. In opening the petition, he was consciously fulfilling consular duties, as part of the appeal text indicates:

> It is nearly always possible for this Consulate to deal with seamen who may be in distress, but for distressed British subjects who are not seamen there is no readily provided official means of relief. Many of those who come to the notice of His Majesty's Consulate as destitute belong to the latter category and in dealing with them it becomes the Consul's duty to show 'that every effort has been made, by recourse to local charitable agencies or other available sources' before he is permitted to incur any expenditure which may fall upon public funds.[12]

When he reported to the FO on the appeal in mid January 1907, he was disappointed at the amount raised – £125, as against the hoped-for £500, the interest on which would have provided a permanent fund of £40–50 per annum, administered by the consul and a committee of local residents. In addition to welfare work for

British subjects, Casement devoted attention to a central consular function, keeping a register of British shipping and dealing with other shipping matters.[13] And in May 1907 he submitted an intelligence piece on the State of São Paulo, in which he talked of the composition of the population, the Brazilian federal system, the separatist mood in São Paulo and the military and police systems.[14]

Casement was assiduous in attempting to recoup all expenses he had incurred performing FO duties. At the end of January, citing expenses incurred, he pleaded for a common consular stationery. The request, which had been turned down previously by the Treasury, evoked mixed responses from the FO. Campbell retorted sharply: 'Ever since his arrival at Santos Mr C. has been trying to give as much trouble as he can. Some of his grievances are childish.' Rowland Sperling defended Casement: he had never had a post of this kind before and had had to make up for Mark's deficiencies.[15] When Casement announced on 9 March that he was taking a short leave to go to Buenos Aires, it is perhaps not surprising that Sperling should have minuted: 'Santos evidently does not agree with MrCasement.'[16] Leaving Thornton in charge, he was away for two weeks, including six days in Buenos Aires, remarking to Gertrude afterwards that 'the Argentines are bright, intelligent, go-ahead people'.[17] He told Cowper: 'Buenos Aires I liked greatly – it is a splendid place – full of life and people and a tremendous contrast from the gloomy melancholy mind of Santos.'[18] His colleague from Lourenço Marques days, Carnegie Ross, was now consul in Buenos Aires and probably Casement's host.[19] He wrote to the FO on the 24th, to inform them that he was back in Santos, and to the minister in Rio, William Haggard, on the 26th, to let him know that he had been away![20] For some of his time, too, he resided in the fashionable and salubrious island community of Guarujá, some distance outside of Santos. He wrote to Berry to say that he was 'staying out at a Hotel 8 miles from Santos on a lovely sea beach – and come in every morning'. He travelled in and out to the consulate each day by train.[21]

His Santos trade report for the years 1905–6 was the shortest of all his trade reports, consisting mostly of detailed tables of imports and exports, culled from local sources. But the document does reveal dimensions of his thinking. He began by stating that since little of Santos's coffee went to Britain or her colonies, he felt that the chief British interest lay in the carrying trade and imports. With regard to the former, he reported: 'It will be noted that British carrying lines still lead the list of carriers, although if "tramp" steamers be taken away the two principal German lines would represent a larger export trade from Santos than the two leading British lines.'[22]

Germany also threatened on the import front: 'British imports easily head the list, but their superiority is more apparent than real from the point of view of manufacturing industry, for if coal and specie are subtracted it will be found that imports from the United Kingdom in 1906 do not greatly exceed in value those from Germany.'[23] In keeping with his now heightened sense of his Irishness, he devoted some space to specifically Irish exports. These included Guinness stout from Dublin, and Belfast mineral waters, linens and steamships, though he pointed out that such items were listed as of British origin and were difficult to identify from the methods of statistical reporting.[24]

Finally, he drew attention to what he called 'invisible exports' from Brazil, namely the considerable amount of money earned by foreign workers – mainly from Italy, Spain and Portugal – which was either taken back home with them at the end of their contracts or was sent home as remittances. 'No account', he commented, 'is taken in Brazilian commercial statistics of these "invisible exports". That they constitute a steady export of the wealth of the country cannot be doubted – how great a drain it would be impossible to say.' In addition, many such workers left immediately after the coffee harvest, either going home or moving to nearby Argentina, where 'food and the necessities of life are fully 40 per cent cheaper'. This, too, represented a drain on the Brazilian economy.[25]

Throughout his stay in Santos, Ireland was close to his thoughts. Writing to Alice Stopford Green, he first criticized Charles Lever, whose biography he had been reading, because he 'knew nothing about his country's past'. He then asserted, quoting Michael Davitt, that 'I have no belief in Englishmen', before admitting to having almost become an Englishman at the time of the Boer War. The concentration camps there and, later, in the Congo, had begun to change him. He had remonstrated with the British missionaries in the Congo, whose attitude was 'why bother?' He continued:

> I realised then that I was looking at this tragedy with the eyes of another race – of a people once hunted themselves, whose hearts were based on affection as the root principle of contact with their fellow men and whose estimate of life was not of something eternally to be appraised at its market 'price'. And I said to myself, then, far up the Lulongo River, that I would do *my* part as an Irishman, wherever it might lead me to personally.

Despite the horrors of the Congo regime, he felt the future of Ireland to be even more perilous.

> Africa can wait – for centuries and centuries. She will still be Africa. Leopold might murder millions but nothing could destroy or efface the ineffaceable negro – his ways, his colour, his mind, his stature and all that makes him the negro. No matter how cruel the persecution he might suffer the negro will remain unchanged and unchangeable and Africa could *always* be reconstituted by her own sons and the waves of European misgovernment ebbed back leaving no trace upon her shores or native character.'

Not so with Ireland.[26] In another long letter he reflected on the topic of national character, beginning with the English: 'Their one view of life is to make – to get – to have – to possess. Ireland is a bit of real estate belonging to them ...' Lecky, whom he had been reading that morning, failed to grasp the Irish soul. And in a passage contrasting sharply with his view expressed to Morel some months earlier, he talked of Brazilian nationality.

I see this same process at work here in Brazil – the Portuguese and others coming here quickly become 'Brazilians' – no man could define Brazilian 'nationality' – and as to race – it is made up of a great many different stocks – but the *thing* is here and is turning them all – Italian, Portuguese, Spaniard, German or *Negro* – into a Brazilian people – and the type that will ultimately evolve will more and more assimilate itself to the old Indian stock of the land, altho' these are willingly exterminated.[27]

His thoughts about nationality may have been heightened by his reflections at the time on the Irish language; he drafted an eleven-page essay on the headed paper of the consulate on the distribution of Irish in the north of the country, including among the Protestant community.[28] To Bulmer Hobson he commented: 'The Birrell Bill and its almost unanimous rejection in Ireland will clear the air. It should show the Irish people how much faith to put in the "Imperial" Parliament.' The Irish Party, he commented, was 'growing old'.[29] Somewhat earlier, he had elaborated to Gertrude on his attitude to the Irish Party. Noting Stephen Gwynn's success in being elected Nationalist MP for Galway, he added:

I don't know if it is good or not. I know him well – but then I don't believe anymore in the Irish Parliamentary Party – I think they are shams and that the movement has lost all vital force – and that Ireland can be regenerated only from within – not by any action or talk in England or from England ... I tell everyone I'm an Irishman here and they are beginning to understand the meaning of the word.[30]

His growing identification with Ireland heightened his sense of isolation in Brazil: 'The worst ... is the loneliness and expense of life here ... no congenial companions'. The 'British' colony, he remarked, comprised 'the shop-keeping class of Englishmen, without patriotism, belief or any charm or idea at all. The Brazilians one does not meet ... No one cares about anything beautiful or nice – and the *population* at large consists of the lowest *class* of Latin races – dirty, noisy, coarse and turbulent'. His attachment to the young Kerry youth is understandable in this context: 'I've a very decent Irish boy from Kerry in my Office – Patrick by name and a real Pat by nature too. He is a great friend of mine and altho' only a poor boy I find I can talk to him on any subject.'[31]

On 4 March 1907 Casement addressed himself to the Foreign Secretary, Sir Edward Grey, on the subject of Santos:

Santos is not a nice place – indeed it is quite the nastiest place I've ever been in ... in this dreary, melancholy coffee ring where no one smiles – Africa was a very happy land, since the African natives, despite all the evils they suffer under, are a happy-hearted, bright-faced people – but the Brazilians are the gloomiest, most demure savages posing as civilised men and saddened beyond endurance by the burden which they have assumed of exotic clothing to support the pose. If they'd only go naked they might be happy and smile too – they'd certainly be natural.[32]

It was clear to the FO that Casement was unhappy, and steps were taken to find him an alternative posting. Tyrrell wrote in February 1907 to say that there was some prospect of consular moves and that he was recommending Casement's name.[33]

Home Leave, 1907–8

'Here I am back again', he announced to Gertrude on 22 July, after arriving in England on the 20th. Her father had died and he extended his sympathies. The Bannister family soon left for a holiday in Brittany and Casement travelled on to Antrim, staying at the Antrim Arms Hotel in Ballycastle.34 His arrival in Ireland coincided with the worst tensions of the Belfast dock strike of 1907. James Larkin had come to Belfast early in that year to organize the dock workers, attracting both Catholic and Protestant labourers to the movement. In May they had been locked out by the employers and blacklegs introduced in their place. Tensions increased and other categories of workers joined in – iron-moulders, firemen, sailors and carters. When the police themselves joined in and began disobeying orders, nine warships and an extra 2550 English and Scottish troops were sent to Belfast. The police mutiny quickly collapsed at the same time as the dock strike was settled, with the virtual capitulation of the workers. But the existing tension and the arrival of the troops led to rioting on the Falls Road on 11 August, involving cavalry charges and the deaths of some civilians.35 Not surprisingly, Casement reacted angrily: 'Belfast', he wrote to Gertrude on the 14th,

> is in the hands of the English soldiery and battles are raging in the streets. D..n them from the bottom of my heart ... The whole thing has been an abominable piece of the usual sort – the 4000 troops were absolutely unneeded and were only sent to Belfast to provoke bloodshed. Everyone who knew the town and the people said it could only have the one ending. I go up there tomorrow and please God I'll take a gun and if it comes to shooting I know who I'll shoot.

The strike may have been the catalyst for another of Casement's pessimistic comments to Edmund Morel: 'there is work here for an Irishman to do – and when one's country is going downhill so fast as Ireland is it is the duty of all who care for her to make her lot theirs'.36 He told Gertrude that he hoped to go to the Irish college in Cloghaneely, Co. Donegal, on the 22nd or 23rd.37 Before leaving Antrim, he also hoped to meet the novelist George Birmingham (The Revd J.O. Hannay), who was visiting the area: 'Mr Hannay of Westport is up at Runkerry with Mrs H. – I am hoping he will come over to me on Wed. to see Ben Mór and Murlough.'38

When he got to Donegal, he sent bulletins to friends. To Gertrude he sighed: 'I wish I knew as much Irish as I do French.'39 To Bulmer Hobson:

> It is a grand neighbourhood – all Irish ... It has made me mad to think how easily Irish could have been saved over widespread districts – within my lifetime – if only there had been any effort. The language was all over N. Co. Donegal thirty years ago – in fine vigorous life, spoken probably by 90,000 people at least in this one county ... it is now like bringing medicine to the lips of a dying man – yet who knows but that God may be the physician.

The school needed organizing still and 'a strong resolute *head*, a Man! ... the thing needed is a strong firm man to enforce discipline' and to look after build-

ings and correspondence. Una O'Farrelly, he continued, was going on an organizational motor tour through the county and he might join her.⁴⁰ He did so,
as he told Mary Hutton:

> I saw a lot of her in Donegal – and we motored together with her brother and
> Aodh Ua Dubhthaigh, the Gaelic League Organiser – from Letterkenny to
> Bundoran via all the West & Carrick & Slieve League. There is still plenty of
> Irish spoken if only it could be systematically spoken – There must be nearly
> half – certainly over a third of the whole population of Donegal Irish speakers
> – but English has supplanted it terribly in their *thoughts* I fear.

He signed himself 'Ruaidhrí MacAsmund'.⁴¹ It was after this experience of the
college in the summer of 1907 that Casement began to make regular financial
contributions to it, most substantially for the building of a new hall. His
chequebook stubs show such payments from 1908 to 1910.⁴²

He had already, shortly after his arrival in Ireland, submitted an article on
the forthcoming Olympic Games, which he hoped Hobson would publish in
Uladh. It challenged the English tendency to claim all good things Irish as 'English' or 'British' (Duns Scotus and Columcille, for example). He gave historical
references to Irish athleticism in history, citing Spenser, Captain Cuellar of the
Spanish Armada and Arthur Young. Three of the major winners in the 1906
Olympics had been Irish, he pointed out. His proposal was to have Ireland recognized as a country for the Olympics to be held in London in July of 1908 and
to organize a committee that would help select an Irish team.⁴³ During his leave
and particularly after his return from Donegal to Antrim, he expended a good
deal of energy trying to improve the uncertain employment prospects of Bulmer Hobson. The employment he envisaged for him was in a cooperative in
Cushendall, involving the production of eggs. He advised Hobson on how to
apply for a managerial job and may well have interceded on his behalf. Hobson
got the job and Casement advised him to work and impress: 'you can prove to
Unionist and Parliamentarian alike that Sinn Féin means what it says – the
material uplifting of our country by her own effort'.⁴⁴ But the omens were not
good from the beginning, and by November the head of the project, Miss Barbara McDonnell ('dear fighting, sincere Miss Barbara'), was sending warning signals. Shortly after he arrived in Pará in March, he learned that Hobson had left:
'Rude letter from Miss Barbara – you and she at loggerheads?'⁴⁵

The prospect of Casement's going to Pará after Santos had not been on the
cards when he returned home from South America. Rather, he had been offered
the post of consul general in Haiti, which had the attraction of a low cost of living, little shipping and something akin to diplomatic functions. Towards the end
of August, Emmott congratulated him on the promotion, even if, he added, Haiti
was a 'devilish' place.⁴⁶ A.G. Vansittart, the retiring consul for Haiti, began sending long letters of advice on the conditions of the position and on travel.⁴⁷ But
the FO then changed its mind, wishing instead to give Haiti to a former army

officer, wounded in the Boer War; they appealed to Casement to surrender the post. His anger was evident when he wrote to Gertrude:

> I came home from Santos last July, intending to leave the Foreign Office for good and all. I had been offered an excellent post out in East Africa by a big undertaking – good pay and *most interesting* duties, far more useful than a consul's. The FO, on my landing, promoted me to be Consul-General for Haiti and San Domingo, one of the six first class, top-rank posts in the whole Consular Service. I accepted this after some hesitation, and declined the good African offer. Well, in November, when I went over from Ireland to London to get final instructions to go out to Haiti, and to be gazetted, they had the audacity to *appeal* to me and my good nature to make room for another man; to resign Haiti and wait for another Consulate General some time next year when a certain post (Rio de Janeiro) would be vacant.

'I have told them', he concluded, 'pretty frankly what I think of them, their methods, and their Consular so-called "Service". It is no service at all, but only robbery and corruption, and an enormous fraud on the public.'[48] As an alternative to returning to Santos the FO offered Pará, which the existing consul, C.B. Rhind, was anxious to leave, having earlier, indeed, suggested a swap with Casement.

He had gone to London for these negotiations early in November. When the FO broke the news to him, he drafted but did not send a sharp letter to Tyrrell. Instead he communicated his feelings verbally to Lord Dufferin, who, he reported, was very sympathetic.[49] The appointment followed in December, to the states of Pará, Amazonas and Maranham.[50] He returned to Ireland in mid November, going straight to the Berry family at Richhill Castle, Co. Armagh. His mood was probably bleak, because of the FO fiasco. It was unlikely to have improved when, a little later, he heard from W.A. Churchill, who had also been consul in Pará. Churchill gave him detailed information about Pará – the office, hotels, climate and work. It was dearer than Santos, he informed him: 'I could not afford to employ a clerk, and was therefore a prisoner at my post, and never went away.' He agreed with Casement's view of the consular system as 'the most idiotic branch of the public service'.[51]

Apologizing for his silence to Mary Hutton, he wrote to her that in London he had 'got a bad chill which confined me to bed' and that 'as soon as I was able I fled back to Ireland arriving at Greenore on Thursday and coming on here to Major Berry on Saturday'. He had received a copy of her translation of the *Táin*, plus one he had ordered for a friend. Since he hadn't finished reading it, he would, he said, reserve his opinion until later. But he liked her treatment; the blank verse was easy, 'gives charm ... One thing is clear. The interest in Irish literature is only beginning. It will grow each year – and so, too, will the band of those who seek their knowledge in the Irish materials'. These readers would not accept Anglicized spelling of Irish names, such as she had employed. 'They will accept and prefer the original spelling, and the symbol created in their minds by that spelling will become a part of the tale told.' Therefore, usages such as

'Faylim', 'MouWee' or 'Ooaha' were distasteful. But he offered her hearty and sincere congratulations.[52]

Early in December he left Richhill Castle and travelled to the outskirts of Dublin, joining Nina at the Spa Hotel, Lucan. Here he stayed from mid December through the first week in January. 'Lucan', he told Gertrude, 'is very nice in winter – the air is good and the Dublin hills are shining to the South. I like the place.' But to Hobson he commented, with Hutton's *Táin* and the heroism of ancient days on his mind: 'Here the whole world is either hunting or cattle driving. There's mighty little Nationality in these parts.'[53] Nationality was something he was constantly thinking of. His comments to Hobson show that he was regularly reading *Sinn Féin*, and at this time he had his first meeting with Arthur Griffith: 'I saw A.G. the other day – for the first time – and he wants me to go with him on Sunday to Æ's [George Russell] house where there is to be a gathering of *Sinn Féin* men. I'll go.' A fortnight later he met him again: 'I saw Griffith yesterday and he is cheerful of feeling and hopeful too – which is more than I am! The only hopeful thing is the Gaelic League and the Sinn Féin idea between them – but there is a long ridge to hoe yet.'[54] He told Gertrude, 'I dine with Mr Green on Thursday next to meet two Fenians of charm and distinction.'[55] One of the key expressions of lack of freedom in Ireland was, he believed, the power of the Catholic clergy over the people, a theme that ran through his letters at this period. He expressed his opinion, for example, on clerical influence during the campaign to have Irish recognized in the education system; on the new Birrell Universities bill he commented to Hobson: 'all the Cawtholics [*sic*] are on the sniff – and scent Cawtholic meat at last. We want to make it National however'.[56]

From Lucan, Casement crossed to England and stayed with the Mortens until he left for Pará on 18 January 1908. He took a leisurely route back to Brazil, spending some days with Herbert Ward in Paris, continuing by way of Vigo and Lisbon before stopping over for ten days in Madeira.[57] He reported back to Dick Morten from Paris on his stay with their mutual friends the Wards. Paris was 'gay and lively and streets full of a cheerful life one never sees in London'. The previous night he and the Wards had gone to the Folies Mariguy, to an Italian play – Gabrielle d'Annunzio's *La fille de Jorio*; the acting had been strong, but the play was 'a bit too much unmitigated tragedy for me'.[58]

Pará, 1908–9

The outgoing consul, Rhind, in bad health and clearly anxious to hand over, reported to the FO to say that Casement had arrived in Pará on 22 February, having been expected on the 10th. Casement's first communication home was to Morel, to whom he wrote on the 23rd. 'It is pretty hot, rather pretty and *very* expensive', rather like Lourenço Marques in the balmy days before the Boer

War, he suggested.[59] On the 27th he sent a card to Gertrude: 'I like Pará so far ... It is pretty, clean and not too hot and is a very agreeable change to Santos. The people, too, look far nicer and I think I shall like it much better than that Southern Wapping.'[60] Pará (the city of Belém), where he had arrived, was located at the mouth of the Amazon close to the equator. It was the capital of Pará State and chief port of the lower Amazon, owing its commercial importance to the expansion of Amazon trade, especially that in rubber, in the late nineteenth century.

He took over consular duties from Rhind on 29 February, and his mood quickly deteriorated, upon discovering the conditions facing him.[61] Rhind was 'a complete morbid – scarcely able to walk – he could only just sign his name and all else was done by the clerk – and he had to be nursed and cared for as if in Hospital'. Casement felt sorry for him, but the consulate was 'simply so many bundles of stray paper'.[62] Rhind, too, it seems, had taken to drink, another factor in the deterioration of consular business. He survived only a short time after the move to Santos, dying later that same year, on 17 August.[63]

Rhind's incapacity had determined his living and office arrangements. Casement gave the details in one of his replies at the hearings of the Royal Commission on the Civil Service in 1914:

> In Pará ... I arrived after a decrepit consul who could not work and had to be carried away. He had a hired house up in the town. There was no other consulate. He hired a furnished house which I either had to take or go to a hotel. The house was a very unsuitable one. It suited him because he was in bed the whole time and unable to move. It did not suit as a consulate. I had to hire two rooms first to have a consular office, and I lived in the hotel. The two rooms were in the [London and] Brazilian Bank – a British bank – and I paid £120 a year for those two small rooms. After I had had them for three months the bank directors here, in London, notified their manager that they did not wish a consular office established in the bank because it attracted undesirable people – which is quite true – sailors, and other people, and distressed British subjects – and they would be much obliged if the manager would get rid of the consul.[64]

The furnishing and running of the office also posed difficulties:

> The same thing applied to Pará in 1908, and I took over a consulate there in exactly the same circumstances, without a bottle of ink, a pen, or a sheet of paper. I furnished the Pará consulate at my own cost. Nearly all the office allowance paid to me went to my secretary, and when I left to be transferred to Rio my successor took my furniture that I had bought and refused to pay me for it.[65]

Casement's arguments about office and furnishings were reasonable. He didn't help his case, however, by sending a number of emotional private letters to the FO in which he questioned the need for the expense of maintaining a full-time consul in Pará at all – contrary to the view expressed in his official despatches. Foreign Office minutes drew attention to these contradictions, spurring one exasperated comment that 'Mr Casement is like the late General

Gordon. His recommendations are wild, vague and contradictory, and his other statements are no doubt exaggerated.' This is hardly a fair assessment and it would seem sufficient to suggest that Casement's statements about the post reflect his view that, 'if it is worthwhile having a Consulate at all there should be a proper Office with proper equipment'.[66]

A further worry was the state of the archives, which he set to putting in order. He was later to describe the situation in more detail. Material that was 'Separate and Secret' was filed with ordinary correspondence. Everything was in three wooden boxes, loosely nailed and kept in an outhouse accessible to servants and friends. Much of what they contained was 'worm-eaten and spoiled by damp, cockroaches and dirt, so as to be almost illegible'. The safe was too small for confidential documents. He made suggestions, reorganized things and was able to report on 13 April that he had bought some cheap furniture and that 'as it stands today I could hand over the records of the post in a fairly satisfactory state'.[67]

One source of Casement's tension – and here the Foreign Office was sympathetic – was that his income was not adequate, given the expense of the location. He had a salary of £600, a local allowance of £200 and an office allowance of £500. From the office allowance he had to pay his clerk £350; rent of the consular offices came to £114. In addition, he had to furnish the office completely. He estimated to the FO that these 'unavoidable expenses' amounted to £750–£800 a year, leaving him a sum of £500 to live on – 'just the salary of a newly arrived Commercial Clerk'.[68] Casement's own clerk was 'a highly untrained specimen of Londoner who cannot write or speak Portuguese', who left for home at the end of May, finding that £350 was inadequate for his needs.[69] Casement reported in October that the clerk had later returned to Pará, in private employment as an assistant accountant, at £720 per annum plus a house allowance of £108 per annum.[70]

Only a fortnight after his arrival, he sent two broadsides to Lord Dufferin, stating his intention to resign shortly. The people and the cost of living were his main targets. The former were rude, uncouth and arrogant:

> They are nearly all hideous cross-breeds – of Negro-Portuguese with, up here in the Amazon, a very large admixture of native Indian blood. Altogether the resulting human compost is the nastiest form of black-pudding you have ever sat down to. The native African is a decent, friendly, courteous soul – the Indian, too, I dare say, is a hardy savage *chez lui* – but the 'Brazilian' is the most arrogant, insolent and pig-headed brute in the world I should think.[71]

The cost of living outstripped his income, he complained, and this made his living conditions intolerable:

> ... and then I go out to hunt for a dinner in one or other of the cafes at night. The great majority of the population of Pará is negroid-Indian – a yellow race. So I must either continue the present haphazard and very uncomfortable way of living – if 'living' it can be called – or try to join one of the trading messes

and chum up with them. They are decent kind-hearted folk many of them – but I like some freedom and privacy and the prospect of a common mess life of this kind is not very attractive.[72]

After the initial frustrations and outbursts, his equanimity seems to have returned somewhat. He told Cowper that he liked Pará more than Santos: 'This is a civilised town and the whole community are far nicer – both natives and Britishers.' The streets and squares were charming, the electric tram service was excellent, there was a splendid theatre (not open often), some fine buildings and beautiful gardens and squares. He was, he told him, going to join a household of Britishers: 'The British community is a sociable friendly one ... The only drawback I find is the excessive rainfall – it has poured every day since I came – and the almost impossibility of getting out of Pará' – there were no suburbs, no surroundings, only the river on one side, forests on the other, no sea beach or bathing place – 'one is *inside* the town always'. And there was a lot of death from yellow fever – five to six fatalities each week, including some in the British colony.[73] In mid May he wrote to Milne Cheetham at the legation in Petropolis:

The people are too good-natured and cheerful to make trouble. It is quite a different people from the Rio and Santos lot. These folk are amiable, gentle and even caressing in their manner with much passive goodness of disposition. Thus they are lively and vivacious and take real pleasure in their Amazon city. To them it is Paris – every one walks about and at night the streets are quite lively and full of people up to midnight – like a Spanish town rather than one drawing its civilisation from Portugal.

'The town', he continued, 'is pretty and beautifully laid out and the people are the most charmingly immoral in Brazil. All Brazilians I believe are bad moralists, but these Paranenses do the thing nicely and are clean, pretty and graceful.' Everyone bathed two or three times a day.[74] In July he wrote to Gertrude: 'The people of Brazil are very charitable and kind hearted I must say – in their own ostentatious way. Socially they are not interesting and one never sees the inside of a Brazilian house any more than of a Portuguese.'[75]

At the beginning of April, Casement proposed making a journey up the Madeira River, a southern tributary of the Amazon: 'It would seem to me desirable that HM's Consul in these northern States of Brazil should seek to become acquainted with the conditions of commerce and industry in the fertile state of Amazonas, the centre of the rubber production of the world.' On the 10th he sent another message, telling them that he would go up the Madeira River 'to the beginning of the construction works of the Madeira–Mamoré railway ... The journey will not exceed one month in duration, and will probably not extend beyond three weeks.'[76]

He does not seem to have written any letters while on the journey. On his return, he wrote to the FO expressing gratitude for the trip to the shipping company, Booth's, and enclosing a copy of his letter of thanks to Captain Benjamin Crimp, the local Booth representative, for the 'invitation to accompany you on your recent journey to the falls of the Madeira river'.77 He wrote to some of his friends, too, when he returned; 'I was away up the Almighty Amazon for 1600 miles and only got back last Sunday,' he told Gertrude.

> I've got an extraordinary beast from the Upper Amazon – a childish imp the Indians call an *iguati* – it is half mongoose and half Heavens-knows-what with a snout on it like an ant-eater and it laughs and chuckles and fights and climbs and plays the imp generally with a puppy dog – or a big macaw – or the servants or anything that comes to hand. I've christened it *Manoel* – and please God it shall go home to the Dublin Zoo when I go.78

On 11 May he submitted a report to the FO on the Madeira–Mamoré Railway and on his voyage up the Madeira River, and he was to include further observations in his trade report for Pará.79 The Madeira River was the gateway to Bolivia and to the Brazilian state of Matto Grosso. The huge commercial potential of both was blocked by '240 miles of difficult and dangerous waterway, interrupted by frequent cataracts, where unloading and porterage are needed'. The railway project, attempted and abandoned at various times since the 1860s, aimed at bypassing the cataract region. It was estimated that a workforce of 3000 would be needed and outside labour would have to be imported, since the local supply was insufficient. Casement estimated that white labour could not stand the unhealthy conditions: 'I would put the working value of the best white labourer at not more than six months, and for the majority at less than this period.' Chinese labourers, he felt, were unlikely to be much better:

> My own impression is that the Company should look to Africa or the Africans, for the completion of their task. The 'darkie', and I mean the pure article, not the nigger, mongrel or half-caste of Brazil, but the pure-blooded, vigorous native African is the only type of humanity that can successfully grapple with hard work, hot sun and Malaria at the same time. I should say the Company should try to get in a large contingent of Kru-boys from Liberia. These men, too, would come for lower wages and less expensive food, and if well treated, the first batch repatriated would give the place a good name and ensure future supplies.

In fact, he continued, the Madeira–Mamoré Railway Company was seriously addressing the health problem. At Candelaria, just upriver from their headquarters at Porto Velho, hospital buildings and a medical headquarters had been set up, and 'it is hoped shortly, when the number of labourers has been increased, to have a perfectly equipped building capable of accommodating 350 invalids'. But his own observation showed him that many of the staff were either in hospital or showing signs of malarial fever. Another dimension of the labour problem was that of discipline. Desertions, he had been informed, had been frequent – some at Pará, before ever reaching the Madeira, but more at the company site itself. At San Antonio, the settlement at the foot of the cataracts (and just above the company's headquarters at Porto Velho), 'I saw a lot of men who had been workmen of the Company, but who preferred to desert the line and loaf around that den of thieves.'

Although the project was under the control of the Brazilian federal government and though considerable revenues flowed from the region, no investment whatever was made in local facilities: 'neither the Federal nor the State Governments seem to care whether it is ever finished or not. As for the individual officials, whether Federal or State, they are thinking only of what they may make out of the irregularities or petty mistakes of the Company's agents on the spot, and where they do not actively annoy they can hardly be said to help'. What the government could do, as the Congo government had done, was to intervene positively, for example in helping maintain worker discipline:

> Either the Brazilian Government must effectively police the line, in the interest of the Company, or it must grant the Company police rights. The Congo Government gave the Congo Railway Company full *droits de police* and then itself supplied the necessary force and did everything to maintain an effective discipline.

Casement recorded a wide range of observations during the course of his Madeira journey. He discussed banana flour (commercially produced on a fazenda 300 miles above Pará) as a potential food supply for tropical countries. He noted the decline in turtles and the export of turtle oil; the haphazard cultivation of cocoa trees, once a significant export crop; the lack of 'organised agricultural life' – he had seen only one plough, at a fazenda owned by an American at Itacoatiara; and the unused potential of forest timber.

Casement began his trade report shortly after his return from the Madeira in May. By 13 June, he told Gertrude that it was almost finished and that 'it will be a corker'. His last trade report, from Santos, he boasted, 'gave "intense indignation" to the loyal British Community', because of its references to the trade of Great Britain *and Ireland*.[80]

The Amazon region, he pointed out in the report, was 'far and away the most productive region of Brazil'. The rubber exports of the Amazon surpassed the coffee exports of the states in the south of the country and were, in fact, produced 'by a comparatively small band of *seringueros* and their workers distributed along the banks of the main waterways'. Having sketched the growth of the trade in rubber in the latter part of the nineteenth century, he speculated on the future of the product:

> When it is reflected that almost the whole of this great quantity represents a production from non-cultivated sources it is legitimate to speculate as to the future of the world's rubber trade when cultivated rubber begins to play an important part in the sources of supply. Tropical America contributes 63 per cent of the world's total – all of it wild rubber gathered in swamp and forest from virgin soil; Africa comes next with 31 per cent, collected by even more primitive methods in still wilder regions; leaving to Asia the modest cultivation, supported by capital and scientific application of labour. That this agricultural outlay in Ceylon, Malaya and elsewhere, where rubber plantations are being systematically extended, must in future years largely influence the supply of rubber cannot, I think, be disputed. In the entire absence of agricultural effort,

and in relying solely upon a wild forest growth, it cannot be maintained that the Amazon Valley, great as are its natural resources, is playing the part in this great industry assigned to it by so lengthy and so pre-eminent a lead.

He went on to note the drop in the price of rubber during 1907 and to state his belief that it must continue, depressing the purchasing power of the region as a consequence. The depression was not unconnected, he argued, to two characteristics of the Brazilian economy:

About five-sixths of all Brazilian trade, import and export, is carried on with four countries – the United States, the United Kingdom, Germany and France – and fully as large a proportion of all Brazilian exports is made up of two vegetable products, one of them cultivated, the other a wild growth, viz. coffee and rubber ... A country that depends on four foreign markets for the bulk of its overseas trade and on two sole commodities for fully 80 per cent of its export trade is especially liable to sustain, at unforeseen moments, serious sets back [*sic*] to its prosperity.

Criticism of Brazilian agriculture lay close to the surface in much of this report. It was suggested in his references to rich, but untapped, natural resources; to reliance on wild as opposed to plantation rubber; to the haphazard cultivation of cocoa. Referring to 'rubber estates', Casement pointed out that the term 'estate' should not be taken as 'a property of scrupulously defined limits, exactly defined area and clearly established title deeds'. He argued that

no legislation could have possibly conferred individual rights of ownership over the vast tracts of desolate swamp and forest. The *seringuero*, who today works a certain district of Upper Amazon forest, does so by a right that is not challenged rather than by one that is not challengeable. It is the right of the first comer, or, indeed, not of him but of the stronger first comer. The native Indian owned the lands under recognised tribal rights up to the beginning of the last century.

He returned to the topic when writing to Cheetham shortly before he finally left Pará. The context was the introduction of a new law on agriculture, which he called 'this Tom-fool law of the local Chambers':

Aviadore might be termed a 'banker'. It is hard to define him. He advances cash and goods against rubber which in turn he sells to the export houses. The idea of the Law is that *aviadore* and *seringuero* represent the great 'agricultural industry' of rubber production. As a matter of fact there is no agriculture about it. It seems to me absurd to found such associations of simple traders and middlemen on a decree clearly established to advance *agriculture*. There is no agriculture in the Amazon – not even the cocoa is grown on an estate or by any system.

He told Cheeetham that he called this 'vegetable filibustering' in his report, 'but the FO funked that and struck out some of my most truthful statements'. Despite the toning down, the locals were furious about his comments.[81]

During his tenure at Pará, Casement carried out the usual duties regarding the supervision of vice-consuls, trade and shipping, and helping Distressed British Subjects, though in comparison with his earlier postings the number of despatches on these seems small. In addition he reported on a couple of incidents on the frontiers of Brazil, one of which was a presage of future events. On 4 June, he relayed reports about an incident involving Colombians and Peruvians in disputed territory, though he thought the local press might have been exaggerating the clash:

> A party of Colombians, described quaintly enough as 'missionaries desirous of converting the Indians' were recently reported in the Pará papers to have been massacred (save one wounded man) by a surprise of the very Indians they set out to 'convert'. As the telegram stated they were armed with guns as well as Bibles, I fancy the repugnance of the Indians to such attempt at conversion was not illegitimate. The Julio Arana referred to in the present telegram is a big merchant at Manaos where I think he is Peruvian Vice-Consul. He travelled out from Europe on the steamer by which I came to Pará in February. The *'terrivel syndicato' Peruviano* which has reduced the Indians to slavery is doubtless modelled on extinct exemplars of the same kind of Brazilian 'trust'.[82]

This is Casement's first reference to events on the Putumayo, which were soon to be of major significance in his life.

While devoting considerable energy to his official duties, he never lost sight of Ireland. It was a regular theme in his letters to Gertrude. 'Ireland is not going to be bought,' he said in one, 'we shall see the blue sky yet.' He reacted dismissively towards Rudyard Kipling, recent winner of the Nobel Prize. His 'rubbish', declared Casement, was getting worse and worse: 'all his yarning now about "the breed" makes me ill. One would think the "Anglo-Saxons" owned all the morality and worth of the world'. He asked Gertrude to get him a copy of the *Irish Year Book*, just out; he got a copy of Mr Hannay's *Benedict Kavanagh* for his forty-fourth birthday.[83] He explored, too, the tradition of possible links between Ireland and Brazil, in the legends of 'Hy Brasil', the tales of 'isles of the blessed', and of St Brendan's voyages.[84]

He reacted enthusiastically to the publication of Alice Stopford Green's *The Making of Ireland and its Undoing*: 'Her magnificent mind has grasped many things and she shows how great was the industry of the Irish in the old days – ere the pious Tudors and their pilfering pirates came to destroy all in the name of the Lord.'[85]

He commented to Bulmer Hobson on a range of other happenings in Ireland. Since he had left, Sinn Féin had participated for the first time in a parliamentary election. C.J. Dolan, a former Irish Parliamentary Party MP, had resigned his seat in Leitrim and then recontested it on a Sinn Féin, abstentionist ticket. Not unexpectedly, he lost, but with a creditable vote. 'So North Leitrim (of course),' Casement wrote, 'elected the spouter – anyhow it is the first blow.' He talked, too, of the 'bust-up' between Hobson and Miss McDonnell in Antrim, and of Miss M'Neill and Stephen Clarke; he sent a subscription for Hobson's new paper; he followed the details of a controversy between F.J. Bigger and O'Riain in *The Irish Nation and Peasant* [*The Peasant*]; and he enquired about Robert Lynd, now in London and doing well. Despite the expensiveness of Pará, he began, once more, to send sums of money home: quarterly allowances of £25 for Nina, for example, and a generous donation of £25 to Aodh Ó Dubhthaigh for the college at Cloghaneely.[86]

In September 1908, he wrote at length to Hobson on the implications for the British Empire of reforms in Turkey: 'This Constitution of Turkey, if it works and the Sultan is sincere and can be kept now by his Parliament within bounds, will spell strange things for John Bull in India – and in Egypt too.' As for the British in India:

> They count on the Mussulman there to pit him against the wild Hindu – but the Mussulman will soon say that the Head of his Faith has granted free Government to the faithful – and how is it that the Mussulmans of India are still ruled from without. In Egypt the lesson will come quicker – for Turkey is the Suzerain of Egypt just as England was of the Transvaal. In international law Egypt is still a dependency of the Sultan and the Khedive must be installed by Imperial firman from Constantinople. With a free Turkey, is it long, do you think, ere the Turkish Parliament will begin to [take] stock of the affairs of Egypt or the Egyptians to take stock of the State of Turkey? How *can* John Bull refuse to allow to the Egyptians – he the 'Lover of Liberty' etc. – what the autocrat and despot of the Ottomans has granted his hereditary dominions. I believe the Emperor William has inspired the Sultan ... Germany will win in Morocco – from the very first I saw and said that – and now with this great change in Constantinople her influence for good in the world will be enormously increased ...

He foresaw an end to the occupation of Egypt followed by more rapid developments in India: 'The transporting of Tilak for "sedition" is the trial and packed jury of John Mitchel over again – with this difference that whereas poor John had only a people of seven millions, swept to the grave by famine behind him, Tilak has a continent of 300 millions, growing in reason, swelling in strength and knowledge behind him.' Would Ireland, he wondered, be the only nation left behind?[87]

By mid May, Casement was complaining of ill health. Churchill had warned him that the rainy season lasted from January to June and that it was very disagreeable. The climate began to tell, and he reported to Morel: 'Personally I am not well – neither in body nor mind. I have been more or less seedy since I landed here.' He was also suffering from an 'eczematic attack of scrofula or some other devilish thing' between the toes of his feet, which led to scratching at night and made work difficult. Writing on the same day to Cheetham he announced: 'I am two stone lighter since I landed in Pará in the middle of February.'[88] On 16 July he telegraphed the FO: 'Seriously ill. When possible begin to move will leave short leave if you approve. Please telegraph if approved.'[89] On 25 July E.A. Kup informed Rio that Casement had been seriously ill since the beginning of that month and had been confined to bed until the day before.

He was sailing that day for Barbados and would be absent for four weeks. Kup was to be acting consul.

News of his unhappiness about Pará reached Sir Edward Grey via Emmott, who relayed Grey's comments back to Casement: 'Casement went to Pará on the understanding that he should have the reversion of the Consulate General at Rio – one of the best in the service – as soon as it became vacant, and he appeared to be quite satisfied with the arrangement at the time it was made.' Emmott granted that the Consular Service was underpaid, but said it was not possible to change things at that point. Don't, he pleaded with Casement, 'leave me in the lurch by jibbing at Rio'; if he did, he could not say another word for him. Showing insight into his man, Emmott continued: 'You have spent all your spare cash on other people and if I may I should much like to be allowed to loan you something if you are in temporary difficulty. You can replace, if you wish, when you get Rio.' And, coming at Casement from another angle – with a reference to King Leopold – he suggested that for him to chuck the service 'would be a sweet morsel for that old brute, and all of the Congo regime'.[90]

On the voyage to Barbados, Casement wrote to Gertrude: 'I am a loathsome sight – blotches and sores and eruptions – a sort of blood poisoning.' It was cheaper, he said, to go to Barbados than to stay in Pará.[91] Several weeks later he described his illness to Hobson:

> I have shrunk to a shadow and neither eat, sleep nor walk but lie on my back all day sitting in bed or on a sofa ... The whole thing is ghastly – I've had bad fevers etc. on the Congo – but I always pulled up from them and felt each day of recovery a bit better – now, on the contrary I feel no recovery and each day dawns finding me within just the same – or a little bit weaker and more apathetic and dull.[92]

His doctor in Pará, Dr Karl Ornstein ('of Vienna University'), provided a diagnosis: 'He was suffering from an *urticaria erythemie* in consequence of an "acute gastritis" and "blood impurities".'[93] On 18 September he was still confined to bed in Barbados under the medical supervision of five local doctors. Dr Clarke had advised him to stay on for a further six weeks and 'fears that my return to Pará will only prelude a complete break down'. Dr Messies, the chief doctor of the Royal Mail, 'declared that I was suffering from a malarialised condition of the internal organs and a general breakdown and advised that I should seek a cold climate with as little delay as might be'. But, contrary to doctors' advice, he intended returning to Pará by the steamer of the 23rd. He went on to comment that this had been an unusually unhealthy year in Pará, especially for the 'small British colony' of about eighty, roughly a quarter of whom had been invalided out or left during the first six months of 1908. This letter drew the anxious FO minute that it was 'stupid to disregard the doctor's advice. He must be moved from Pará soon'.[94]

Despite his illness, he was able to rouse himself to complain to Gertrude about Barbados, a British colony. It had been

built up thro' centuries of slavery and forced to end in pauperism and universal cheating and begging. Everyone here begs. So truly Anglo-Saxon, isn't it? ... You cannot walk 50 yards from the door but you are accosted by paupers – and the whites are nearly as bad as the blacks. The place is a Congested District – 200,000 stagnant paupers on 180 sq. miles! and a poor soil over a great part of the island. It is a marvel how they live at all. And with it all the whites are ignorant, petty-minded and bigoted – and the wretched pauper negro multitude of 180,000 lives a life of real servitude – slaves to hunger, low wages and no future.[95]

He arrived back in Pará on 29 September and resumed duties on the 30th, but on 4 November he again telegraphed the FO, asking for leave due to ill health. He proposed asking the US consul, Pickering, to act for him. On the same day he informed Cheetham in Rio of his intentions:

I have been and am ill and find it very hard to take interest in anything ... The doctor says I must get away from Pará or I shall break down ... I am some hundreds of pounds out of pocket since coming to Pará and I have suffered far more pain and had far worse health than in Central Africa. My eight months have been a dreadful nightmare, and I shall never get my strength back again. It is a loathsome place – and people.

On 17 November he handed over to Pickering and sailed for home.[96]

Home Leave, December 1908–March 1909

He arrived in Liverpool on 4 December and dropped a note to Morel, informing him of his return and expressing satisfaction at Morel's planned move to London. He, himself, was crossing to Dublin that night. The change in climate was affecting him: 'I feel it already in my bones'; he was not, he said, in 'robust health'.[97] He let Gertrude know he was back on the 7th: 'I am back in dear Dirty Dublin', adding that he had visited her mother's grave in Anfield. Nina was already in Dublin and he told Gertrude a few days later that her house was 'in the nicest, most fashionable, most Loyalist, most Protestant part of Dublin'.[98] Gertrude came to visit and the three of them arranged to meet Evelyn Gleeson for lunch at the Dún Emer Guild.[99]

From Nina's address, 7 Upper Mount Street, he wrote to the FO on 7 December and enclosed a certificate from Dr Ornstein which stated that the local conditions had been 'most injurious to him ... and that as he is already greatly reduced in health and strength his speedy departure from these surroundings is imperative ... He is moreover in need of undergoing an operation of no magnitude, which can be best performed in Europe'.[100]

He was greatly moved by the poverty he saw both in Liverpool and Dublin: 'I never saw so much poverty and sheer hunger staring out of the eyes of the poor as this winter. It is shameful to think of it – hunger and dirt and misery in the heart of the Greatest Empire in Christendom – and nobody save a handful caring a rap.' The impact of seeing the poverty of Liverpool and Dublin led him to exclaim that 'one is not called on to respect the British Empire or its social frameworks. The whole thing is wrong – from top to bottom – and until we can get more equal conditions of livelihood it is little short of criminal to be "expanding" and campaigning abroad and overtaxing a degraded and wholly demoralized population.'[101]

He remained in Dublin for a good deal of his leave and immersed himself in Irish affairs. His letters to Hobson give a good idea of his activities and pre-occupations: he was dining with the Gills; he saw Robert Lynd and P.S. O'He-garty about raising funds to keep *The Peasant* going; he talked of the energy of Ó Riain (W.P. Ryan) and O'Beirne; he appointed Hobson as proxy for his eighty £1 shares in *The Peasant*; he asked for copies of it and *Sinn Féin* to be sent to Lis-bon. Responding to an election result in Glasgow, he expressed satisfaction that the candidate had got his comeuppance; he was, he said, a 'fraudulent Home Ruler of the United Irish League of T.P. O'Connor & Co.' The result was a nail in the coffin of trust in Liberal England and Liberal Scotland and the Irish should learn from it.[102]

A debate on the place of the Irish language in the universities was in progress at the time and he wrote to Mary Hutton about it:

> I saw Mr Fisher and he will 'cordially support' optional Irish ... also I meant to try to get an endowment fund for an Irish Chair ... John [Eoin] MacNeill's lec-ture at Belfast will do much good – so, too, his fine pamphlet. Everyone here seems very confident of winning in spite of the Bishops. Indeed their pro-nouncement has done good on the whole – and there is a fine, decent, healthy spirit abroad – not anti-clerical, but strong and sincere and determined to argue the matter out fairly.[103]

On 31 December 1908, not long after he arrived home, Casement was appointed consul general 'for the States of Rio de Janeiro, including the Federal District, Espirito Santo, Minas Geraes, and Matto Grosso, to reside at Rio Janeiro'. The appointment was effective from 1 December 1908 and carried a salary of £1000 per annum, a local allowance of £300, an office allowance of 24,000 milreis, temporary allowance of £200 and outfit allowance of £250. Casement's letter of acceptance was sent from Mount Street, Dublin, on 30 Jan-uary 1909.[104] On 2 February he wrote to Tyrrell pointing out that there was a discrepancy between the salary originally offered and the official offer, made on 12 November 1908. His point was accepted and the offer emended to £1100 salary and £200 local allowance, a change that had pension implications.[105] The promotion, with its higher salary, had one immediate result: Casement was able to repay loans he had taken. He repaid Emmott £100 and Ward £50. He was also able to increase his support for Irish activities and took out eighty £1 shares in *The Peasant* and, some time later, £50 in *Sinn Féin* shares.[106] Casement had already requested an extension of leave for January and February and, at the end of January, asked for five days in March, stating that he intended to leave the UK on 6 or 7 February, spend 'the remainder of my leave abroad' and sail to Rio from Lisbon.[107] He spent five days with the Wards in Paris before arriving in Lisbon on the 21st. There he intended to stay a week, as he told Cowper, whom he invited to lunch.[108] On 27 March he wrote from Rio to say that he had arrived on the 22nd and was starting work that day.[109]

Consul General, Rio de Janeiro, 1909–10

As consul general, Casement now had an office staff to whom he could delegate some of the more humdrum consular functions. V.H.C. Bosanquet was his vice-consul and he had the services of Charles Pullen as chief clerk.[110] He inherited, too, a fully functioning office, with none of the archival or furniture problems of his earlier postings.[111]

A good deal of Casement's consular correspondence for the years 1909 and 1910 dealt with shipping matters: the steep rise in dock and shipping charges in Pará; British shipping at Rio for 1908; lack of reciprocity regarding inspection of foreign vessels by Brazilian consuls; the treatment of foreign vessels by Brazilian authorities. Other despatches dealt with commercial affairs: he reported on companies engaged in diamond dredging; on the failure of a British company with a tender for a naval dock; French–German trade rivalry; even on the level of duty on Cerebos salt, depending on whether it should be classified as a foodstuff or a chemical.[112] There were also matters of military intelligence: he reported on 1 May on the Brazilian fortification at Obidos on the Amazon and, on 6 December, gave details of the proposed composition of the Brazilian fleet.[113]

In June 1909 came word of the death of Youle, vice-consul at Victoria, in the state of Espirito Santo. Casement informed both the legation and the FO that he intended visiting Victoria to find a replacement for Youle. He left Rio by ship on 6 July and arrived in Victoria on the 8th, but couldn't leave again until the 28th, due to transport limitations. 'I took advantage of this enforced delay,' he reported, 'to journey over a good deal of the interior of the State of Espirito Santo and acquire material for a report upon that State which is now being prepared.'[114] His choice of vice-consul, he informed Grey, was Brian Barry, born in Castleblayney, Co. Monaghan, who was fifty-five years old and 'one of the leading members of the commercial community of Victoria'.[115]

Casement acquired and forwarded some photographs of indigenous people in the state of Espirito Santo, which the FO subsequently sent to the Anthropological Institute in London. Casement's covering letter reflects on the contact situation:

I transmit herewith a series of photographs of the native Indians of the State of Espirito Santo, a branch tribe of the Botocudo family who are among the most debased of the aboriginal inhabitants of Brazil. This tribe is termed locally the Bugre, and inhabits chiefly the left bank of the Rio Doce, a large river of the State of Minas Geraes ... The photographs ... illustrate a type of humanity which, outside of Brazil, is not anywhere else to be found in close touch with, yet entirely untouched by, modern civilisation.

The Australian bushman may be cited by some, but there is really no parallel between the relation he occupies to, say, the Queensland settler of white blood and that which the Brazilian Indian occupies to the Brazilian properly so termed. The bushman in Australia is a man apart, with whom the European has never had any relations save those of hostility, loathing and contempt, whereas the Indian in Brazil is the foundation stone of its national citizenship. His blood mingles in the highest families in the land, and the facial characteristics these photographs of the Bugres offer are to be met with every day in the streets, cafes, reception rooms and even Departments of State of the Brazilian Capital.

Yet this tribe (one of many) inhabiting a region that for centuries has been colonised by a European race, within a few miles only of long established European settlements, the people of which have freely mixed their blood with that of these Indians, have retained within view of their 'civilizers' the rude habits of a social existence that dates from the most primitive era of humanity. I found, in my recent journey up the South bank of the Rio Doce, constant reference in conversation to this tribe of Botocudo Indians as 'just across' that narrow river, yet no attempt seems to have been made during centuries of Portuguese and Brazilian rule to modify their environment, instruct or in any way humanise this primitive people. They remain exactly as they were on the first day that the Portuguese invader landed on Brazilian soil, although the incomers have freely intermarried and are even proud of their connection with this and other native Indian tribes.

So little intellectual (or even ancestral) curiosity exists among Brazilians that until a German photographer quite recently visited Victoria I believe no photograph could be procured of a people who constitute the basis of the claim to separate nationality that Brazilians are so proud of asserting over their European motherland.[116]

It is difficult to assess Casement's relations with the British legation in Petropolis.[117] William Haggard took over the legation from Colville Barclay on 19 December 1906, not long after Casement's arrival in Santos. Haggard was head of the legation from that point on, but was on leave from May 1908 to August 1909, after which point Casement's legation despatches are once more addressed to him. In Haggard's absence, Milne Cheetham was in charge. In January 1910 Haggard wrote requesting copies of commercial despatches, which Casement had sent to the Foreign Office for the attention of the Commercial Intelligence Board of the Board of Trade. Consular instructions required that copies of despatches 'of interest' be sent to the legation, but Casement justified his procedure by claiming that he did not consider the despatches to be 'of interest'. Who was to decide what is 'of interest'? If it was the legation, then everything would have to be sent there. Moreover, he cited an increasing demand for reports, but no increase in resources to meet those demands. He had been without a vice-consul for over five months and without a correspondence clerk since the previous August, and had 'no type machine until I bought one from my private means'.[118]

If Haggard felt he had to lay down a marker with Casement, so, too, did the Foreign Office when, on one occasion, he overstepped the mark. In a FO despatch, Casement enclosed a letter of his to be sent to the *Southampton Times & Hampshire Express*, correcting an inaccurate account the newspaper had carried about an incident involving the innapropriate opening of a postal parcel in Pernambuco. The FO minuted that it was 'no business whatever of Mr Casement's to address himself to a Southampton newspaper on a matter that is forming the subject of correspondence between the Minister in Brazil and the Brazilian Government'. Haggard was instructed 'to inform Mr Casement privately' that his letter had not been forwarded to the newspaper and that his action was 'quite irregular'. It was also suggested that the next edition of consular instructions might be amended to cover the point. 'Of course Mr Casement – as usual – *meant* extremely well,' commented one FO official, perhaps condescendingly.[119]

Ernest Hambloch, who became Casement's vice-consul towards the end of his year in Rio, was to quote Casement's response to a commercial enquiry: 'Oh, that's not really any part of our job at all. A consul's real functions are diplomatic.'[120] The comment probably reflects what Casement valued in the post, if not what actually required his attention from day to day. The society of businessmen bored him and he sought more cultured surroundings whenever possible. His posting at Rio allowed him some interaction in diplomatic circles, which Santos and Pará had not allowed. Accordingly, Casement made regular visits to Petropolis, situated in a pleasant elevated position above Rio and the location, not only of the British legation, but of other diplomatic missions in Brazil.[121]

In one submission to the FO, he recorded having visited the US ambassador in Petropolis, the late German minister and the Japanese minister and consul general. Hambloch later commented that the German minister, Baron Ferdinand von Nordenflycht 'was the only colleague whose acquaintance Casement cultivated'.[122] He was to maintain friendly relations with the Nordenflycht family subsequently, especially when he went to Germany.

Despite being quite busy with his consular duties, Casement was not a happy man in Rio. In a letter to Gertrude a week after his arrival, he lamented the expense and the hotel life: 'No home; no privacy; no comfort; no friends; no social life or pleasant friendly intercourse ... My bedroom is exactly 12 ft. broad and 14 long – a small iron bedstead just broad enough for the human body flat, not long enough for me – grass stuffing to mattress: a shower bath in an outhouse ...'[123]

After a month in Rio, he told Cowper that it made an agreeable change after Pará but, 'I do not think, however, it will last.' The heat was greater than in Pará for a good part of the year. The food was atrocious ('a filthy luncheon of garbage that makes you ill') and dearer. There was nothing to do after the office; distances were great and trams slow, so that 'visits are few and far between'. 'However,' he concluded, 'I won't growl.' In June, he even sounded perky: 'weather delightful in the extreme at present and everything *looks* delicious'. He went often, he said, to Petropolis 'and find the change most agreeable ... I am pretty busy but not too much overworked and have a good staff who relieve me of most of the routine work and *all* the unpleasant work'.[124]

But the deeper unhappiness remained. This he expressed to his cousin Roger in mid August:

> I cannot say I like Rio de Janeiro but then I knew that before coming. I refused the place (and promotion) two years ago, and only took it in the end to escape from Pará, which was intolerable. I *loathe* Brazil – it is an abominable country and the towns are disgusting. I do not hope to remain in Rio but will try to exchange to some smaller post out of South America, which is the least attractive of all earth's continents. It is meant for the yellow races – and, faith! it has got them, for the Brazilians are yellow when not black!
>
> I am now over fourteen years a Consul and this post, Rio de Janeiro, ranks with five others as the first in rank of all the Consular Service; yet I'd gladly exchange it for one of the fourth class away down the scale if it could be in a nice country. No one of my colleagues likes Brazil and the Govts. have difficulty in getting anyone to stay in this beastly country.[125]

His views were even more forthright to Gertrude a few weeks later:

> The country is a paradise – and the people await the great descending birch rod of some strong handed Power to teach them to be men and women. Were it not for that abominable Monroe Doctrine the rod would long since have been applied by Germany and Italy – but England, for her own ends now, backs up the United States in support of that absurd doctrine. South America needs European immigration, and European government too – but because the USA want to keep it as a Sub-Continent under their tutelage until *they* are ready (200 or 300 years hence) to overflow into it & swamp these Barbarian hordes dressed to look like Parisians, so the whole world must be kept back from realising its rights over this vast unoccupied, misused earthly Paradise. Someday Europe will challenge this pretence of the USA and put it to the arbitrament of battle, and I sincerely hope Germany will win and erect a Great German State with honest clean laws and institutions here under the Southern Cross.

Contemplating the effect such words might have locally, he begged Gertrude not to quote him or he would be expelled 'with a howling mob of these pie-bald half-castes pelting me from the quays. Give me the real black – not this mongrel half black, half white, half Portuguese, half Jew mongrel Indian mestiço'.[126] In this sort of mood he clearly contemplated resigning, but Alfred Emmott once more pleaded with him not to, unless health forced him to it: 'think twice and thrice', he begged, before stepping down in rank.[127]

He missed congenial society and gracious living. 'I hardly ever feel in the mood for writing,' he told Dick Morten, 'I've only a bedroom with a *tiny* table –

in a bad lodging house where I can't even get a meal! I often go to bed without dinner – from sheer weariness rather that go out for miles to a dirty eating house to eat Brazilian garbage costing 6/– or 7/– a filthy meal of uncooked horror ... *slung* at you by cataleptoid brutes.' He joked that the epitaph on his carcass would be, 'He died of Brazilian food.' He had started his letter to Morten in mid September, but got ill and didn't finish it for almost a month: 'I got seedy on 20th September, had to clear out of house and home and take to bed with gout, rheumatism and Water on the Knee. I was 10 days laid up with that.'[128]

Casement commented on Irish matters, too, and writing to Hobson, he was critical of Arthur Griffith: 'I've never felt confidence in him as a leader I may tell you but I did not like to say a word to anyone that would weaken their faith. The meeting I attended in Dublin in December last convinced me of his narrowness – and that we cannot stand in our far too narrow Ireland.'[129] He criticized *The Peasant*, edited by W.P. Ryan (Ó Riain): 'The paper itself I fear is not better. It is dull still as ever – too much Christian Socialism – not enough Irish nationalism' and 'Rian's [*sic*] socialism exceeds his nationalism almost altho' I never doubt the depth of the latter.'[130] He sent a piece for Æ's *Homestead* and ordered copies of *The Gaelic American*.

He appointed Hobson as 'commission agent', arranging that he send supplies of Irish-made office supplies to him at Rio – envelopes, paper, dye, a typewriter and even an embossing seal with the Royal Arms of Great Britain and Ireland. He constantly enquired about friends: P.S. O'Hegarty (who had had a breakdown), Robert Lynd, Sean McDermot, Dick Bonner, Francis Joseph Bigger and Dinny McCullough. When the Catholic bishops dismissed Fr Michael O'Hickey from the Chair of Irish in the National Seminary at Maynooth, for his intemperate public utterances on the place of Irish in the university system, Casement was angered:

> We must try to help the O'Hickey Memorial by the way. That is a disgraceful thing the dismissing him from the Chair of Irish in the Irish College because he stuck up for the language he is paid to teach. The Bishops, too, I see mean well to Ireland in this action – only for her own good and the discipline of her clergy ... It would be a very excellent thing if Ireland could relapse into brilliant Heathendom for a year or two – when she got "converted" again the Bishops would all be gone anyhow.[131]

This and other aspects of the Irish situation led him to a broader reflection on national character:

> It is hopeless to think you can free Ireland when she licks her chains ... every people in Europe – save only ourselves – has not been afraid to die and shed its blood and, when needed, to treat its priestly enemy as it treated its secular foe. It is the Church has kept Ireland tied to England and will do so ... The Irish Catholic, man for man, is a poor crawling coward as a rule. Afraid of his miserable soul and fearing the Priest like the Devil ... freedom to Ireland can come *only* through Irish Protestants because these are not afraid of any Bogey (except

the Pope, and their fear of him is after all a bit of playacting – he'd have a damn bad time of it in Lurgan if he showed up there!).

Revolutions, he felt, needed men and women prepared to die, as had been the case in Italy, in Paris in '48 and Ireland in '98:

All since '98 has been *ráiméis* – or at any rate has been put out of action by a mere Bogey – the Priest. The priest slew O'Connell's soul of a man – and the priest slew Smith O'Brien – and the Fenians – and Parnell – and the Irish Language – and now the priest will slay the Gaelic League and Sinn Féin ... I am very sick sometimes and quite despair of ever seeing a *real* people in that lovely old land again.[132]

On 1 September, his forty-fifth birthday, romantic nostalgia swept over him, as he evoked the year of his birth in a letter to Gertrude:

I think of Ireland in 1864 – full of people, brave and strong – Fenians in every country, preparing for the great fight they all hoped to have within two years – a land poor and oppressed indeed, but still with its own brave native heart and resolute belief in its own right arm – and today! What a change! Talk, drivel, lying and sham – taken the place of self-belief and self-reliance.[133]

And, responding to news of Lieutenant Ernest Shackleton's return to England after an epic journey to the South Pole, he reflected:

Lt. Shackleton, by the way ... is a Home Rule Irishman – his Uncle is the owner of Shackleton's Mills at Lucan and is a Sinn Féiner. His family have been for over 100 years against England – one uncle was with the Young Irelanders in '48 and an earlier man against the Union. Its funny to find him acclaimed as an 'Englishman' by all the London gangs! If he had cut a cow's tail off instead of gone near the South Pole of course he would have been an Irish man right enough. He too is to blame. Had I come home from that journey I'd have gone straight to Dublin without one hour's halt en route from the Continent and to all English invitations etc., I'd have sent the polite reply that after I had completed my visits in my own country I should be very happy to address foreign gatherings ...[134]

Two sequences of events more significant for Casement and for Ireland than Shackleton's expedition, however, were taking place during 1909. One was the confrontation between the Liberal government and the House of Lords, the other the increasing tension between Great Britain and Germany. Since the signing of the *entente cordiale* between Britain and France in 1904 and another between Britain and Russia in 1907, Germany had begun to feel encircled. She tried to prise Britain away from France and, in one such incident, the German emperor, Wilhelm II, challenged French claims to Morocco, landing at Tangier on 31 March 1905 and making a speech in support of Moroccan independence. In the ensuing international crisis Britain supported France. A conference was convened to mediate the conflicting claims, which opened on 6 January 1906 at Algeçiras in Spain. A few months later it reached its conclusions, which favoured France and angered Germany. In February 1906, German–British tensions were stimulated on another front, when the British navy launched HMS *Dreadnought*, the first of a new and powerful type of battleship. During the following months naval rivalry was much in the air as *Dreadnought* trials and British naval exercises took place. In 1908 the Germans countered with the first of their dreadnought-class ships and in March 1909 there was panic in the House of Commons when the First Lord of the Admiralty, Reginald McKenna, declared that Germany might soon overtake Britain in naval might, giving details of the German building programme.

The confrontation between the Liberal government and the Lords had its catalyst in Lloyd George's 'People's Budget' of 1909, which, in order to pay for an increased social welfare programme and the new costly naval expansion, proposed a steep increase in taxation, mainly on the propertied classes. The budget was unpopular in some sectors of the population and it was generally so in Ireland. In Parliament it provoked a fierce Tory attack and, at the end of November, was thrown out by the Lords. A constitutional crisis followed, Parliament was dissolved and an election called. Should the Liberals be re-elected, limiting the power of the House of Lords was on the cards. For the Irish Party the prospect emerged that, in return for their support for the Liberals, including on the budget, they could gain a pledge of Home Rule legislation, in the knowledge that it might no longer be subject to the veto of the conservative House of Lords. In the event, the election of January 1910 saw 275 Liberals and 273 Conservative and Unionist candidates elected; the balance of power lay with the 84 Irish Nationalist and the 4 Labour MPs.

Casement watched these events. His reaction to the budget was in keeping with his predominant one on Irish affairs: 'That Lloyd George budget is an infamous swindle,' he wrote to Gertrude. To Morten he dismissed as 'fraudulent claptrap' the suggestion of gains by Irish nationalists or of 'Home Rule in sight'. The Lords, he claimed, cost twice a dreadnought and were 'a far greater terror'. As for the Irish Party, 'They've long since ceased to be Irish at all – and are merely Westminster sparrows.'135 He used even less polite language when writing to those who shared his own biases: he talked of Irish duffers and deadheads, of 'Tay Pay' (T.P. O'Connor) and of the three Johns (Redmond, Dillon, John Bull). Regretting the closure of the daily *Sinn Féin*, he felt the only '[g]ainers will be the wretched "Party" – with all their Libirral [sic] twaddle'. During the election, he dubbed Redmond and Dillon 'a tail of the Liberal Party'.136 'I see the elections are on,' he wrote to Cowper, 'and the Thugs are thugging away at each other. A plague on both their houses – so far as Ireland is concerned – Neither of them cares a *thraneen* for that poor old land and of the two I think the Unionists are perhaps the better.'137 And should Arthur Balfour be elected, he worried that 'it would be a queer Government he'll have and I expect it would "go for" Germany – what a tragedy that will some day be'.138

Departure

As 1910 opens, Casement's diary for the year allows us other glimpses of his thoughts and actions at the end of his Rio tenure. The first entry, for 13 January, chronicles sexual encounters: 'Gabriel Ramos – Last time – "palpito" at Barca at 11.30. to Icarsby "precisa muito" – $15 or $20. [margin] X *Deep to hilt*. Also on Barca the young caboclo (thin) dark gentleman of Icarsby – eyed constantly & wanted – would have gone but Gabriel querido waiting at Barca gate! Palpito – in *very* deep thrusts.'139

Towards the end of January 1910, Casement wrote to Lord Dufferin saying that he would like to escape the hot season, which had just begun with a temperature of 100°C in the office the previous day. He was very seedy, as Bosanquet, his vice-consul, would testify. Ernest Hambloch, Bosanquet's successor, had been appointed and was expected to arrive soon. Hambloch duly took up post on 4 February. On the 16th, Casement applied for two months' leave, proposing Hambloch to act in his place. He left on 1 March, travelling to Buenos Aires, where he remained for some weeks. On the 31st he wrote from Buenos Aires, thanking the FO for his leave; he added that he 'came down here largely on business and partly on a visit to friends' and that he intended continuing his leave in the UK, where he hoped to arrive at the end of April.140

The diary corroborates the pattern of his movements as communicated to the FO. Casement left Rio on 1 March and journeyed to São Paulo and to Santos and nearby Guarujá. There were sexual encounters in Rio before he left and in São Paulo. On 8 March he left Guarujá for Buenos Aires, arriving on the 11th. On Sunday the 13th he met William Warden at the Hurlingham Club and they lunched. For the rest of his stay, he moved around between Buenos Aires, Mar del Plata and San Marco. Throughout, there are regular references to meetings with 'Ramon', including on the day before his voyage home: 'Last time *Ramon* at Tigre. At Hurlingham & then to Tigre with Ramon from Belgrano. Saw last time at Belgrano. Never again.'141

He sailed on 4 April, and arrived at Las Palmas on the 23rd. Here he met Katie Moule, daughter of Charles Stewart Parnell and Kitty O'Shea, and they shared the voyage back to England. On the 30th, he recorded: 'Approaching Lands End & in *Irish Sea*. Saw Ireland & Lugnaquilla & pointed it out to Katherine Parnell.'142 He arrived in Liverpool on Sunday 1 May and took the train to London. He remained in the London area for over two weeks, staying with Miss Emma Cox at 110 Philbeach Gardens and making his usual round of calls. He saw Alice Stopford Green and her brother the day after he arrived and Tyrrell, Morel, the Mortens, Selous, Robert Lynd, and Nina and Gertrude during the weeks that followed. And there were social occasions: visits to the theatre (*Tales of Hoffman*, for example), to Kew Gardens and to exhibitions. On Wednesday 18 May he crossed to Dublin, and his diary entry for the following day read: 'In *Dublin* at Miss Ffrench's & at Irish Opera *Eithne*. Rotten. *Stayed at Gresham*.

Very comfortable.' While in Dublin he visited the zoo, from which he sent a postcard to Ramon; he attended the theatre with a group that included the Hydes, Agnes O'Farrelly, Arbuthnot and the Wilkinsons.[143]

On Thursday, the 26th, he travelled north, where he moved around from place to place, visiting friends and acquaintances. One such was Joseph Millar Gordon, with whom he spent the 28th:

Left for Warrenpoint with *Millar*. Boated and *Huge* Enjoyment. Both Enjoyed. He came to lunch at G Central Hotel. [In margin: 'Turned in together at 10.30 to 11 – after watching billiards. Not a word said till – "wait – I'll untie it" & then "grand" X Told many tales & pulled it off on top grandly. First time – after so many years & so deep mutual *longing*.'] Rode gloriously – splendid steed. Huge – told of many – '*Grand*'.[144]

There were further social calls: to Mrs Berry at Richhill; to Bigger and Hobson in Belfast; to Mrs King and others in Ballymena; to Nina and the Pottingers in Coleraine and Portrush; to the Dobbs family at Castle Dobbs. He spent a lot of time in Ballycastle, staying at Brannigan's Hotel, and visiting Roger and Susie at Magherintemple. While he was there, word came of Rear Admiral Jack's sudden death in Cushendall and he attended the funeral. Afterwards he visited Shane O'Neill's Cairn with Ada MacNeill. He took the time, while in Antrim, to write to the *Northern Whig* on 'Irish in Ulster'. Douglas Hyde wrote shortly afterwards, commending him on 'your really splendid letter to the *Whig*'. Hyde spoke of successes in the campaign to have Irish recognized in the university system: 'We enjoyed', he ended, 'our evening with you ever so much that night you took us to the theatre. It was very good of you.'[145] Casement spent a day on Rathlin Island and made contributions to island funds.

His diary recorded that, when at Magherintemple on 17 June, he received a letter 'from Anti-Slavery People about Putumayo River & the Amazon Rubber Coy. Answered by wire at once and wrote also'. He got a further letter from them on the following day and jotted: 'Going to London on Wednesday morning.'[146] In London he met a number of people associated with the Anti-Slavery Society and began to learn of the developing scandal in the rubber-producing area of the Putumayo in the Peruvian Amazon. Talks followed with the FO and Casement agreed to travel to the Putumayo to investigate allegations of atrocities. Before leaving in mid July he busied himself with arrangements for the Morel testimonial (Chapter 9) and engaged in a rapid round of social calls.

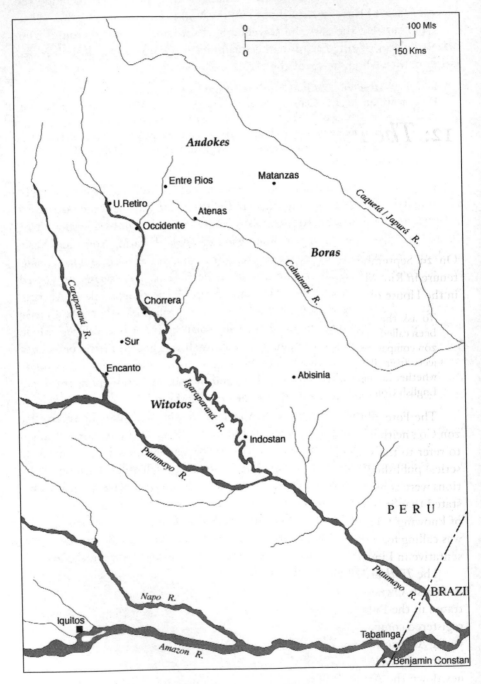

Map 7: The Putumayo Region

12: *The Putumayo Investigation, 1909–10*

On 29 September 1909, when Casement was roughly midway through his tenure in Rio, Mr Hart-Davies MP asked the following Parliamentary Question in the House of Commons:

> To ask the Secretary of State for Foreign Affairs, whether his attention has been called to the proceedings of an English company called the Peruvian Amazon company; whether any report as to the alleged ill-treatment of British subjects from Barbados has been made by the English Consul at Iquitos; and whether he will call for a report on the doings of this company from the local English Consul at Iquitos.

The Foreign Office minuted: 'We know nothing about the Peruvian Amazon Co.; neither do the Commercial or Consular Depts.' The minutes went on to refer to the source of Mr Hart-Davies's question – an article (the first of a series) published in the London periodical *Truth* on 22 September. The allegations were considered 'most serious', in the words of one official, while another stated that 'it is a horrible account, whether it is a true one we have no means of knowing'.[1] The answer to be given Hart-Davies's question was that the FO was calling for a report; meanwhile they set about contacting the British representative in Lima, Mr Des Graz,[2] and the consul in Iquitos, David Cazes.[3]

The *Truth* article was startling. Entitled 'The Devil's Paradise' and subtitled 'A British-Owned Congo', it told the horrific story of atrocities being perpetrated in the Putumayo region of the Upper Amazon by the staff of a British-registered company, the Peruvian Amazon Company (PAC), as witnessed by two young Americans and reported on in local newspapers on the Amazon. The two Americans, Walter E. Hardenburg and W.B. Perkins, had left Colombia to journey down the Amazon. Their arrival at La Union on the Putumayo in January 1908 coincided with the brutal capture and murder of a group of Colombian rubber workers in the area at the hands of PAC personnel, who were intent on acquiring control of the territory. The two were temporarily detained by PAC men, roughly treated, lost all of their possessions and, during an enforced stay at a company station, El Encanto, Perkins witnessed the appalling treatment of the native population of the area – the enforced labourers of the company.

Hardenburg, who travelled on to Iquitos, the company headquarters, showed extraordinary courage and tenacity in not walking away from the situation he had stumbled upon. He remained in the Amazon region, at some danger to himself, making systematic enquiries in Iquitos and Manaos about the Peruvian Amazon Company. He collected affidavits from witnesses, wrote an account of what he found and eventually went to London to try to get some response to his story. Having tried a number of publishers unsuccessfully, he approached the Revd John Harris, still at that point with the Congo Reform Association. Harris described the meeting:

> ... a young man walked into my office, and placing a budget of documents on my desk rather peremptorily remarked – 'Please read these, I will call again in about a week to hear what you think.' ... The documents, which included the MS of a book, were of the most appalling nature. The horrors they depicted exceeded in bestiality even those with which we had been acquainted in Central Africa.4

Their meeting occurred in August or September of 1909. Harris referred Hardenburg to Travers Buxton of the Anti-Slavery Society and to *Truth*. The story was soon in print. Harris collaborated privately with Buxton and, in March 1910, himself took up a post with the Anti-Slavery Society. The society pursued the matter with the Peruvian Amazon Company, which would not cooperate in enquiries, and with the Foreign Office.5

Following Hart-Davies's question, the FO began to piece together the elements of the story. Des Graz in Lima informed them that a British officer, Captain Thomas W. Whiffen, had travelled recently in the Putumayo. Contacted by London, Whiffen provided a report in mid October that confirmed the stories of atrocities – of Colombians shot in their canoe, of the forced labour of the Indians, of floggings and sexual depravities. Despite attempts to hide barbarities from him (prisoners were released, flogging ceased, stocks and whipping posts were hidden), he did find the evidence. In particular, he commented on the 'unbridled lust' in evidence, which, he considered, even overshadowed the collection of rubber. Many chiefs of station, he was led to believe, became nymphomaniacal and 'the satisfaction of his appetites without restraint becomes his one ambition'. Agents had twenty to thirty concubines and one, Aguero, boasting of his sexual dominance, bragged that no female – child or woman – was ever allowed to pass his door.6

From Washington, James Bryce, British ambassador since 1907, reported in November that Hardenburg and Perkins were to receive $500 from the Peruvian Treasury in compensation for their ill-treatment, an act which lent credence to their story.7 By the end of November, following enquiries in Lima, Bogotá, Barbados, Washington and Britain, the Secretary of State was convinced of the 'substantial accuracy of a great part of the narrative'.8

Casement, when in Pará, had admitted that his map of the Putumayo region was deficient; all concerned were soon to get to know its geography and history in great detail. The Putumayo River, which gave its name to the area, was a northern tributary of the Upper Amazon, flowing south-east from the Andes. The region was on the borders – all of them disputed – of Peru, Colombia and Ecuador. Parallel with the Putumayo and a little further north was the Caquetá or Yapura, beyond which lay undisputed Colombian territory. The rubber area of the PAC actually lay mainly on three smaller rivers, the Igaraparaná and the Caraparaná, both tributaries of the Putumayo, and the Cahuinari, a tributary of the Caquetá. The Igaraparaná and the Caraparaná flowed parallel to one another for some 300–400 miles, before flowing into the Putumayo some 200 miles apart. The area comprised some 10,000 square miles with an Indian population of perhaps 40,000 to 50,000.

The Putumayo had remained remote from European settlement until the very recent past. Colombian rubber collectors or *caucheros* had travelled down the Caquetá and established settlements among the Indians, 'conquering' them. Since communications across the mountains with the rest of Colombia were difficult, rubber was exported and stores obtained downriver. In about 1896 the firm of Arana Brothers had begun trading with the Colombian settlements and, gradually, the Aranas either bought out or forced out almost all the Colombians. The firm was re-formed in 1903 as the Peruvian Amazon Company; its four key players were Julio Arana, his brother Lizardo and his brothers-in-law Pablo Zumaeta and Abel Alarco.9 In 1904 Abel Alarco, as managing director, recruited in Barbados the first batch of Barbadian workmen, partly to help establish the stations, but increasingly to help control the Indian population. In 1907 the company was registered in London, with a share capital of £1,000,000, though the majority of shares was still controlled by the Peruvian directors. The four British directors, who joined the PAC at varying points after this, were H.M. Read, J. Russell Gubbins, Sir John Lister Kaye and J.F. Medina. By 1910 a well-defined system was in operation in the Putumayo for the exploitation of rubber. While the general Peruvian headquarters of the company was in Iquitos, there were also two regional headquarters on the Putumayo, the principal one at La Chorrera, on the Igaraparaná, and a second at El Encanto, on the Caraparaná.

The question, now, for the British government, was what to do. The matter concerned a British-registered company and Barbadian workmen who were British subjects. It was recognized that Parliament wouldn't allow the matter to drop. Two lines of action suggested themselves: firstly, that the FO should request of the PAC what it proposed to do and, secondly, that the US government might be persuaded to join the FO in raising the issue with the Peruvian government.[10] Neither path looked promising. The FO believed the company to bear responsibility and the most important question was whether it had taken any steps once the allegations came to the knowledge of the present directors. But the PAC response had been defensive and uncooperative. How, then, could pressure be brought to bear on them? One suggestion was that a consular officer should be sent to the Putumayo, with the company bearing half the expense. Alternatively, the company might be asked to send a commission, to which a consul might be attached.[11] With regard to US involvement, the FO realized that Peru would resent representations being made and that the US was hardly likely to wish to increase its unpopularity in Latin America. In addition, the US was involved as mediator in boundary disputes and was reluctant to lose Peruvian goodwill over this issue. The FO stalled. Meanwhile, public pressure grew and Parliamentary Questions were put down at regular intervals. The Anti-Slavery Society was pressing, too, both directly on the FO and by campaigning throughout the country. Resolutions began arriving at the FO, stimulating one FO minute to note that 'public interest into "Putumayo atrocities" is increasing'.[12]

The company at first denied the charges. Responding to the Anti-Slavery Society on 11 April 1910, H.L. Gielgud, as PAC secretary and manager, declined to give credence to the *Truth* allegations: 'Mr J.C. Arana, the founder of the business in the Putumayo, a man in whose integrity the Board have the utmost confidence, asserts most positively that the allegations in *Truth* are gross misrepresentations.' He went on to refer to his own visit to the Putumayo during the preceding year, suggesting that he had seen no evidence of atrocities.[13] A similar reply had gone from Gielgud to the FO on 8 March: 'My Directors place absolute reliance on the statement made by their Co-Director, Señor Julio C. Arana, in his letter to the shareholders of the Peruvian Amazon Company, dated 28th December 1909: "The alleged atrocities related in *Truth* are entirely unfounded, our employees being incapable of committing such cruelties, which, if perpetrated, the Peruvian authorities would certainly not allow to go unpunished." '[14]

The London directors of the PAC did eventually agree to send a commission to the Putumayo. On 8 June 1910 they gave the FO an indication of its composition and terms of reference. Its members were to be: Colonel the Hon. R.H. Bertie, a personal friend of the PAC director Sir John Lister Kaye; Mr L.H. Barnes, tropical agriculturist; Mr W. Fox, rubber expert and botanist; Mr E.S. Bell, merchant; and Gielgud.

Walter Hardenburg advised the Anti-Slavery Society on what was needed from such a commission on the Putumayo. It would need to watch the company at every turn, lest witnesses be bribed. He suggested that the Indians were likely to be the best witnesses, but, again, care was needed, as interpreters could be bribed.[15] Members of the society had interviews with Sir Edward Grey on 1 June and on 1 July, trying to 'find a way into the question'. Casement's name was suggested at these meetings as a suitable consular representative to accompany the commission. After receiving two letters from the society, Casement travelled to London immediately and had his first meetings on the Putumayo issue on 23 June: 'To Anti-Slavery and H of C. Dilke, Wedgwood[16] & other MPs – Splendid talk – Noel Buxton.'[17]

Casement recorded in his diary for 11 July: 'Wrote to Tyrrell saying had heard I was to go to Putumayo & was ready if Sir E. Grey wished it.' Tyrrell replied the following day, asking him to come to the FO. This he did, on Wednesday 13 July, where, having been informed by Tyrrell that he was being sent, he had a 'long talk' with Grey. On the 13th and 14th he worked at the FO on the Putumayo papers[18] and lunched with Gerald Spicer of the FO American Department.[19] Since arrangements had been made that the PAC commission would leave on the 23rd, Casement had little time left. After a short break in Ireland, he returned one final time to the FO, on 20 July, before sailing from Southampton on the 23rd. He was seen off by Mrs Green, Morel, Harris and Will Reid.[20]

On the 13th Tyrrell had written to the Anti-Slavery Society to say that 'Sir Edward Grey ... has decided to employ Mr Casement on the mission suggested by you on July 1.'[21] On the 21st the FO wrote to the PAC to express satisfaction about the commission, to inform them of Casement's role and to request that they assist him in that role. It was unlikely to have improved the mood at the company. The Colonial Office was confident that an officer as experienced as Casement would adequately represent the interests of Barbados and required no additional nominee.

The brief that Grey had given Casement related primarily to the circumstances of the Barbadian employees of the PAC; from a consul's point of view they were Distressed British Subjects. Probing into the wider dimensions of the Putumayo system was a delicate matter and could have led to accusations of interference. Accordingly, the formal brief given to Casement in July 1910 was a limited one: 'you will endeavour to ascertain whether any British subjects have suffered or are in distress, and if so from what causes, and whether they stand in need of relief'. However, when the Blue Book on the Putumayo was eventually published in 1912, a second dimension to his brief had been added: 'you should also report, in a separate despatch, any facts which may come to your knowledge in the course of your enquiry, in regard to the methods of rubber collection and the treatment of natives by the employees of the Company in the district which you visit.'[22] This second dimension had, in fact, been discussed when Casement and Grey met in July 1910. Casement later recounted their conversation:

> Sir Edward Grey next pointed out that in addition to the specific charges alleged against the employees of the Company in which British subjects and their interests might be involved there would arise facts connected with the general rubber regime in the country visited that it might be well to note and report on separately. It would be necessary to exercise great caution in this respect – as indeed throughout the enquiry – so as to afford no ground for possible objection being raised by the governments of the territory visited.[23]

Towards Iquitos

During the voyage, Casement seemed to wish to keep his distance from the commission members, even at some inconvenience to himself: 'No meals because "Commission" at my table.' There was a brief sojourn in Madeira, where he sought out sexual satisfaction: 'Splendid testemunhos – soft as silk & big & full of life – no bush to speak of. Good wine needs no bush.' The voyage was uneventful and they reached Pará on Monday, 8 August. From Pará he wrote to Gertrude, wishing her well in Cloghaneely, and to Hobson, with the very generous offer of £150 to purchase a farm, if that were deemed by Hobson and his father to be the best option. There were social meetings and shared meals – with George Pogson, his successor as British consul, whom he didn't think highly of ('Pogson *is* an ass!'), and with his old American colleague Pickerell. He visited familiar spots, on the lookout for available men, mostly young.[24]

He took time to write to Morel, saying that the commission member R.H. Bertie had been trying 'to get me to regard myself as one of his party. I know his feelings, but I've got nothing to do with them and I intend to keep aloof as much as can be done with regard to politeness'. He was pessimistic about the chances of success in the mission: 'the good will be in a general cleaning up and more care for the future'. He wrote, too, to Spicer to say that, whatever the differences between himself and the members of the commission, he would keep on good terms with them: 'I fully realise that the surest hope of getting permanent good for the people of the region we are visiting is to convince the Commission and carry it with me so far as possible.' Already the journey was taking its toll. He and Bertie were 'off colour'. His eyes were 'weakening and trouble me a bit'; he was writing on his knees 'in a dark cabin – mosquitoes have been at us day and night'. One positive piece of news came from Brazil, where there was evidence of an improvement in the approach to indigenous affairs: 'A Rio telegram stated that the Government had chosen Lieut. Col. Rondon as "Chief of the Service for the Protection of the Forest Indians". This refers to Brazilian Indian tribes – and Rondon is a very capable man, I believe. It is a good thing to see that one of the Republics is beginning to realise its duties and responsibilities toward Indian tribes.'[25]

From Pará the party continued its journey on Friday 12 August; their ship, the SS *Hilary*, was going upriver to Manaos. Casement was worried about his health, especially about his eyes: 'My eyes have got very bad – that is why I write in pencil, they have shown signs of weakness just before I came away, but had improved at home. On arrival at Pará the bad symptoms returned and the ship's doctor says I am threatened with chronic opthalmia.' He feared a 'complete breakdown of the eyes in the wilds of the Amazon forests'.[26]

They reached Manaos on the 16th. Bertie had decided to abandon the project due to ill health. Casement wrote to Grey, informing him that Bertie was doing so on doctor's advice and was handing over the leadership of the commission to Barnes: 'I am proceeding to Iquitos by the Booth steamship *Huayna* tomorrow afternoon, due to arrive there 29th or 30th instant.' The commission members were to travel on in the *Urimaguas*, a launch provided by the company. While Casement was able to maintain a certain distance at this stage, he was conscious that, once they reached the Putumayo, he would be dependent on the PAC for transport and would lose his independence of movement.[27]

Casement transferred to the *Huayna*, which left Manaos ('a horrid town!') on the following day. On board with him was Victor Israel, a Jewish trader with rubber interests in Peru. 'He is', commented Casement, 'the only passenger on board the *Huayna* who speaks English well, and with whom I find anything in common.' In a long discussion, Casement drew him out on the conditions of labour in the rubber business, specifically regarding the treatment of local Indians. Israel began to show his hand and admitted, finally, 'Oh! ... there is fighting of course. They resist and often kill parties and burn the houses – but in the end they are reduced.' When Casement revealed his own hand, by describing 'British methods of colonisation and the legal safeguards that had been and were being set up by our Colonial govt. to protect natives and above all their rights over their lands' and by indicating how he might behave in the Peruvian situation, both men realized the gulf between them and the conversation ended.[28]

A reported sighting of another PAC launch, the *Liberal*, led him to a series of reflections on the likely conflict of interest the Peruvian government got itself into by its dependence on the company for transport in the Putumayo area.[29] And, reminiscent of his consular work in the Congo, he asked the captain to see the ship's manifest. There were rifles for Ecuador but he wanted 'to see just what the Peruvian Amazon Company imports to pay its labour and its rubber. Forty-five tons of rubber in West Africa would cost (except on the Congo) in actual payment to the natives fully 2/– a pound or say some £11,000 worth of goods. In some aspects this thing is worse than the Congo – altho' it affects a very much smaller population'.[30]

Iquitos

On the night of 28 August the *Urimaguas*, with the commission members on board, caught up with the *Huayna* and came alongside. Casement transferred the following morning and they set out for Iquitos, arriving on the 31st. He stayed with David Cazes, while the commission members stayed at the house of the PAC. He now saw, for the first time, the commission's terms of reference, which he felt were 'sufficiently clear and general to cover the ground of a full and fair enquiry into the actual state of things on the Putumayo'. As with Pará and Manaos, Iquitos thrived during the rubber boom:

The second most active port in Peru, Iquitos had resident consuls from ten foreign countries. The wireless telegraph provided communications with Lima and a cable laid in the Amazon River linked the city with Europe and the United States. The population of Iquitos grew to more than 25,000 persons who were famous for their extravagance. The city imported almost everything, from common foodstuffs, champagne and caviar, to the Malecon Palace, a luxury hotel transported from Paris in pieces and reassembled on the banks of the Amazon. Its ballroom boasted performances by Sarah Bernhardt and the French Grand Opera.[31]

Casement's reaction was less positive: 'The town is very well situated, but horribly neglected & dirty. The "streets" atrocious, the houses poor. Hundreds of soldiers in blue dungaree – splendid looking Indians & Cholos. Nearly all are Indians – a conquered race held by *blancos*. They are finer men than the *blancos* & with gentle faces, soft black eyes with a far off look of the Incas.'[32] Mainly with the help of Cazes, he established contact with key Iquitos residents to talk about the Putumayo. He met Dr Paz Soldan, prefect of the Department of Loreto, whom Casement thought 'straightforward' but ignorant of Putumayo affairs; Soldan thought the atrocity stories 'fables' and Arana's contribution to the state worthy of distinction. He talked to a French trader and former consular agent, M. Vatan, whom Cazes held in high regard; Vatan described the regime on the Putumayo as one of slavery. However, when the two notaries who had witnessed the depositions made to Hardenburg were interviewed before Casement and the commission members, they 'knew nothing' about the men who had given the depositions published in *Truth*.[33]

Cazes had arranged to have a number of Barbadians present for Casement, who quickly proceeded to interview them. Their depositions provided the first direct evidence of his investigation, that of Frederick Bishop, a twenty-nine-year-old, being the most damning. Bishop gave graphic evidence, on the one hand, of the ill-treatment of Barbadians and, on the other, of their active participation in the enslavement of the Indians. He told of forced labour, of flogging, of confinement in stocks (the *cepo*), of virtual starvings and of killings. Casement, clearly impressed by Bishop, offered to take him with him to the Putumayo, as 'servant-interpreter'; Bishop agreed.[34]

He made every effort to acquire an interpreter who was independent of the PAC and competent in Huitoto and Bora, the major native languages of the Putumayo area. Having heard, through Vatan, of such a man, working on the Napo River, several hundred miles from Iquitos, a launch was sent to see if he would come. After days of waiting, the launch returned without him. Casement did succeed, however, in getting an interpreter for the commission and himself, and he could also use Bishop, who 'knows a "bit" of Huitoto, but no Bora to speak of'.[35]

While in Iquitos, Casement dined and played bridge with commission members; he read a little; he bathed in a forest pool. On occasions such as the latter, his sexual instincts were active: 'I walked Punchana 9–10.30 am. Wretched. No plantation or life at all. Women bathing in stream. 2–4 Cholo soldiers discharging *America* in blazing sun. Almost all Indians & a few half-castes, all fine, splendid youths. One half-white muchacho magnificent display & a young Cholo with erection as he carried heavy box. Down left leg about 6–8'. They are far too good for their fate.' His health caused him worry: '*Very* seedy all day, altogether quite unable to do anything. Running blood last night and left me weak & faint & my head aching dreadfully ... I spent a truly *awful* night. Mosquitoes like drops of fiery poison all over me – pale yellow beasts & horrors.' 36

He made a diplomatic gesture by hosting a dinner to which were invited Lizardo Arana and Pablo Zumaeta, Cazes and the four commission members. Casement told Tyrrell about it afterwards: 'I gave a dinner the other night to two of the principal criminals and drank their health in Iquitos champagne and said nice things! The dinner cost me £12 – but I fancy the toast will cost me dearer some day. They nearly choked me – but it was wise to do it, for I know they were awfully suspicious and their seeming show of being hoodwinked has helped a little.'37 Arana and Zumaeta were not the only ones to be suspicious. When it came to posting his letters to the FO before leaving for the Putumayo, Casement commented: '*Urimaguas* leaves for Manaos at 2 pm with mails. I am not writing officially by her, as Arana goes on her & all letters might easily be opened.'38

On 7 September, after his interviews with the Barbadians, Casement wrote to John Harris at the Anti-Slavery Society to say that he had already 'found out a *great* deal – sufficient to amply justify our presence here ... There has been a conspiracy of evil here if ever there was one, and a very powerful one. I am glad I came, and more than grateful that your Society was able to convince Sir E. Grey. He has done splendidly in forcing this Commission to be appointed; and the result, I am already sure, can only be for good – whatever happens.'39 When Harris subsequently mentioned Casement's tale of atrocities to a FO official, it was felt at the FO that Casement should not be reporting directly to the Anti-Slavery Society and that he should be told to exercise the 'greatest discretion' in communicating with correspondents in England.40 A telegram was despatched to Casement to this effect.

After two weeks in Iquitos, the party left on 14 September for the Putumayo. La Chorrera, the company's main station and their first port of call, was 1000 miles away and the journey involved retracing their steps downriver, some 500 miles, back into Brazilian territory, before turning into the Putumayo River and steaming north-west towards the Igaraparaná and La Chorrera. Casement described the scenery in his diary: 'Lovely morning – passing a new palm, the Punchana pilot calls *Pona* – a lovely thing. Fox raving about it & well he may. Beside the assai it shoots up its graceful stem with from 6–12 magnificent fronds like those of a harts-tongue fern on top – & then a green bulging head to its long stem. Five lovely and quite different palms growing here close together & in enormous numbers.' The pilot, too, caught his attention: 'The young Quichua pilot on *Liberal* is named Simon Pisango – a pure Indian name – but calls himself Simon Pizarro, because he wants to be civilised! Just like the Irish Os and Macs dropping first their names or prefixes to shew their "respectability" & then their ancient tongue itself, to be completely Anglicised.'41

On the Igaraparaná they stopped at a small PAC station, Indostan: 'Found prisoner heavy chain ("Bolivar", a Boras boy) crime trying to escape. The "hands" absolutely miserable – starving. 2 girls in *dreadful* state & high fever. Gave Quinine. 2 lads also ill. Woman sleek & fat – the concubine.' They released Bolivar and took him with them. Before reaching La Chorrera, Casement interviewed Stanley Lewis and James Clark, two Barbadians who had avoided him in Iquitos: 'Interviewed Stanley S. Lewis again this morning & got the most disgraceful statements about Ultimo Retiro & J.I. Fonseca from him – murders of girls, beheadings of Indians and shooting of them after they had *rotted* from flogging. Asked if he wd. come with me he said yes only Fonseca had threatened to shoot him if he ever saw him again!'42

La Chorrera

They arrived at La Chorrera, the principal station on the Igaraparaná River, on the 22nd, and were greeted by Juan Tizon and Victor Macedo, the chief representatives of the company. '*Also 7 Boras Indians*, nude save for their bark covering, to carry our Baggage. *5 Barbadians there to drive them*. Three of the Boras show broad scars on their bare buttocks – some of them 1" or 2" broad – weals for life. This is their wealfare, their daily wealfare. All slaves.'43

Now, at the nerve centre of the PAC system, the seriousness of his situation came home to Casement. What would the likely consequences be of his planned interviews with the five Barbadians at La Chorrera? If their testimony inculpated the heads of sections, under whom they worked and who were still in command in the area, would they be in danger? Despite company avowals, there were no Peruvian magistrates or courts in the Putumayo; the company was supreme. What if the PAC agents denied the charges and reacted angrily? He decided to press ahead, with Tizon, but not Macedo, present. On the 23rd the five Barbadians, Donald Francis ('a liar'), Philip Lawrence ('said nothing'), Siefert Greenidge ('saw little'), James Chase and Stanley Sealy, were interviewed by Casement, with Barnes also present. In contrast to the first three, Chase and Sealy 'spoke out like men and told of dreadful things. They had flogged men and seen them flogged & killed too – often, & said so & maintained it. Tizon did not like it at all, but bore it and in evening began flattering me after dinner & saying nice things about me and how glad he was my Govt. had sent a man like me. Is it sincere or is it part of the game?'44

Another Barbadian, Joseph Dyall ('the man is a brute but has been employed by greater brutes'), arrived that evening and Casement interviewed him the following day: he 'accused himself of *five murders* in presence *Barnes* – atrocious crimes'. Casement was not happy with the commission members: 'Why have not the Commission themselves questioned anyone? They do nothing. They sit in their rooms and read, or are occupied in the purely commercial and economic aspects of the Station and the Company's affairs.'45 Anxious now to have the seriousness of the accusations accepted by the commission members and by Tizon, Casement brought all together and 'we had his Statement read over and confirmed & I then called Bishop and S. Lewis to confirm and they did and we thrashed the matter out. Tizon practically chucked up the sponge and admitted that things were very bad & must be changed.' After a lengthy session with Tizon himself, which lasted until after midnight, 'Tizon asked me to try & stop this & promised to carry out *sweeping reforms* & to dismiss all the incriminated men.' To copperfasten this private commitment Casement called another general meeting the following day. Since it had been agreed among them that it was wiser not to take the Barbadians with them to other stations to confront the accused station chiefs, Casement needed the depositions publicly accepted by Tizon: 'I insisted on acceptance of Barbadian testimony if the men did not accompany us to press their statements & *he made his promise in face of Commission*.'46

Though worried about what might happen subsequently, Casement cannot have been displeased with the outcome of his investigation so far. He sensed that a watershed had been passed: 'After yesterday's dreadful "field day" I feel tired out – but I have practically done all I *can* do now.' By his count, there were only nine more Barbadians left to interview, distributed through a number of stations.47 He had already learned a great deal about their involvement in the Putumayo and about the rubber system itself. The first, preliminary report he submitted after his return to London concerned the Barbadian workers and the most extensive section in the Blue Book itself comprised the detailed testimony of thirty Barbadians.

These reports described the history of some 196 Barbadians, recruited in 1904 and 1905 to work on the Putumayo. Some had withdrawn at Manaos, before reaching their destination, on hearing rumours of life on the Putumayo. Others, though desirous of doing the same, had been escorted on board ship by police guard. The first party of thirty men and five women arrived on the Putumayo in November 1904. While some were employed in general agricultural activities and clearing sites, most were quickly deployed in the task of forcing Indians to work for their white employers. For this they were armed and, Casement stated, 'all the men still remaining at the time of my visit were employed in guarding or coercing or in actively maltreating Indians to force them to work and bring in india-rubber to the various sections'.

Their own circumstances, however, were far from ideal. Many were themselves cruelly mistreated, often for trivial or even unwarranted reasons. In his preliminary report, Casement was to give details of four cases. Joshua Dyall, for example, was confined to the stocks or *cepo*, having been accused of 'having improper relations with the concubine of one of the white employees'. The leg-blocks on the stocks were inordinately small, even for the slighter-framed Indians:

> For an ordinary-sized European or negro the top beam could not close upon the leg without being forced down upon the ankle or shin bone, and this was what happened to Dyall. He and men who had witnessed his imprisonment assured me that to make the top beam close down so that the padlock could be inserted in the staple two men had to sit upon it and force it down upon his legs. Although more than three years had passed since he suffered this punishment, both his ankles were deeply scarred where the wood (almost as hard as metal) had bit into the ankle flesh and sinews. The man's feet had been placed four holes apart – a distance, I should say, of from 3 to 4 feet – and with his legs thus extended, suffering acute pain, he had been left all night for a space of fully twelve hours. When released next day he was unable to stand upright, or to walk, and had to reach his quarters crawling on his belly propelled by his hands and arms.

Casement also documented the system of debt bondage in operation. Most of the Barbadians were in debt to the company. A good deal of this was due to their need to purchase necessities from the company's stores. Many of the men had Indian 'wives', whom they looked after, and the company argued that the men must pay for the women's sustenance, even though they had been brought to the stations by force and performed a range of general services for the company. Casement estimated that prices at the stores were 1000 per cent over their cost price. A second cause of indebtedness was the pervasive practice of gambling, with winnings and gains being officially recorded on the stations' books by the bookkeepers. Casement persuaded the company to reduce all debts by 25 per cent and to terminate the system whereby the gambling of wages was virtually official company practice.[48]

In addition to what he learned about the Barbadians and their plight, Casement had begun to unravel the logistics of rubber collection and shipment in the Putumayo. No rubber was collected directly from La Chorrera; it was the administrative and shipping centre. It was located about 220 miles from the mouth of the Igaraparaná, immediately below rapids on the river. Launches operated above the rapids, to stations further upriver. At the time of Casement's visit, ten stations or sections, subject to La Chorrera, were actively engaged in rubber collection. Each was run by a chief of section, assisted by salaried staff, known as *racionales*, mostly Peruvians. There were 101 in all. Under these worked the *muchachos* or *muchachos de confianza*, young armed Indian men, generally deployed away from their own immediate kin groups. The *racionales* and the *muchachos* compelled the local Indians to collect rubber for the company – they did no work themselves. Rubber collecting was carried out in two stages. The first was the *puesta*, a period of two to three weeks, during which the Indians collected a prescribed amount of rubber. At the end of the *puesta*, the *racionales* or *muchachos* went out from the station to bring in the Indians and their rubber. Perhaps three times a year, the rubber collected over a number of *puestas* was transported to La Chorrera. This was the *fabrico*. No payment was made to Indians until the *fabrico*.

Casement collected detailed evidence on the ill-treatment of Indians under this system. Flogging was common and was quite horrific. Should an Indian not produce his quota of rubber, flogging was virtually automatic. Witnesses recounted how, the moment the scales registered a shortfall, the unfortunate victim would often lay himself out in anticipation of the whip. Twisted tapir hide was used and the lash cut into the flesh. Casement believed, from observation and questioning, that 90 per cent of the population had been flogged. Some died under flogging, others afterwards, when untreated wounds became maggot-infested. Dying victims were sometimes shot. It was not unknown for Indians to be flogged while imprisoned in the *cepo*, or when suspended from chains. Confinement in the stocks was common to every station and the *cepo* was usually visible in a prominent position. As already noted, the leg-holes were exceedingly small, and long confinement in such a forced position left victims virtually unable to walk. It was not unknown for women to be raped while confined in the stocks.

Sexual exploitation was endemic. Chiefs of section had virtual harems. 'A Chief of Section', wrote Casement, 'travelled in state. I met more than one *en route*, and, while the half-starved Indians staggered under enormous baskets of rubber, a troop of pleasant-faced girls and women, decently clad in long chemises or *cushmas* of bright cotton prints, sleek, shining and well fed, waited upon the Chief of Section, or possibly carried their infants and his.'[49] If desired, wives of Indians were, on occasion, appropriated. Bishop told of one of the worst cases of sexual cruelty, perpetrated by Elias Martinengui at Atenas. One night he discovered that an Indian girl he kept had venereal disease, so in the morning he had her tied up and flogged; then he made a young Indian boy 'insert firebrands into her body'. 'That girl', recounted Bishop, 'nearly died, but she got better in the end. She is at Occidente now.' The boy ran away and 'we never saw him again'.[50] Other forms of torture were also practised, such as deliberate starvation and immersion in water, just short of the point of drowning.

On the economic level, Indians were grossly cheated when it came to payment for their labour in collecting rubber. No fixed scale of remuneration existed; what was given depended on the mood of the chief of station. From inventories he took of station stores, Casement concluded that virtually worthless items were given in payment for substantial loads of rubber. A tin bowl was given to an Indian for an entire *fabrico* load – 70 to 80 kilos of rubber; the recipient threw it on the ground and left in disgust. Another accepted a puppy dog, a third four one-pound tins of 'roast beef'.

Occidente

Casement and the commission left La Chorrera in a launch on 27 September and travelled upriver, arriving at Occidente on the 28th. Occidente was held by Gielgud to be 'the best station of the Company', the one that gave the biggest output, fifty tons a year, perhaps a seventh of the Putumayo's total rubber crop. Its chief was Fidel Velarde. In preparation for the coming of the commission, Velarde had organized an Indian dance and, throughout the day, the big drums, the *manguaré*, beat out the message of invitation:

> Lots of Indians arriving from 11 am onwards ... Many of them whose limbs are bare show clear marks of flogging – one small boy, a child, quite recent *red weals* unhealed & many other small boys show marks of flogging. There will be near 1000 people here tonight, all the population of the district ... The dance a Success – these poor gentle creatures have few occasions like this. I photo'd a lot of them. I never saw anything more pathetic than these people. They move one to profound pity.51

While Casement watched, he was also busy, checking what had been written of Velarde: 'I sat up late at night hunting up the "record" of this man Velarde in my police news. Did not get to sleep till after 3 am, as I had to go all through the 240 pages of typed document. I find he is one of the "principal criminals" of the Putumayo ... '52 The morning after the dance, Bishop came to Casement with word that an Indian *capitán* (leader) had approached him, telling of machete beatings and of the more recent punishment of being held under the water and half-drowned. One Indian had drowned under such treatment within the past few months. Casement urged Bell to go and take the details of the man's story, which he did. 'In the afternoon an Indian *capitan* came and embraced me, laying his head against my chest, and putting his arm round my waist. He did the same to Barnes who was standing by. Both of us were touched. I knew quite well what it meant. I bathed in the river, and "Andokes" and Barnes caught butterflies. I was not well today, and turned in without dinner.'53

While in Occidente, Casement again interviewed Sealy. Sealy had been taken on a raid on Colombian territory towards the Caquetá River in 1908 by Augusto Jiménez, now chief of station in Ultimo Retiro, their next port of call after Occidente. Sealy's account was horrific: 'It reveals the most hideous crime I've almost ever heard of, absolutely hellish. I took down his statement almost word for word, and I shall never forget it. It was told with a simple truthfulness that would have convinced anyone in the English-speaking world, I think, of the man's absolute good faith and simplicity.'54 The worst incident was the burning of an old woman, whom Jiménez believed to have lied to him. He had her tied up and suspended so that her feet did not touch the ground: ' "Bring me some leaves – some dry leaves," he said, and he put these under the feet of the old woman as she hung there, her feet about a foot or so above the ground; and he then take a box of matches out of his pocket and he light the dry leaves, and the old lady start to burn. Big bladders (blisters) I see on her skin up here' (he pointed to his thighs). 'All was burned; she was calling out. Well, sir, when I see that, sir, I said "Lord have mercy!" and I run ahead that I could not see her no more.'[55]

With this evidence, Casement again called a meeting with Tizon and the commission: 'It was difficult to meet in the house. We were watched all round, and as every room is open, everything said can be overheard ... So I proposed the Indian house at the back of the station, and we wandered off there pretending to look at the plants, sugar cane etc., with butterfly nets, camera, etc. as if just off for a stroll. And this is the way the Commission sent by the Company and the Company's chief agents is forced to hold a meeting in one of the principal stations of the Company.' After Casement presented the evidence, there followed 'a veritable tussle – this time chiefly with Gielgud who opposed much. Tizon bewildered – after another battle Royal carrying Barnes & Bell absolutely with me (& Fox, of course) we agreed to accept Sealy & Chase & that Tizon should of course dismiss Jiménez. He is in despair – so am I'.[56]

While Casement interviewed and wrote, the commission members had gone to the forest to survey the rubber-gathering system. 'I stayed at home, writing and sleeping – not well – and trying to avoid my host, Fidel Velarde,' he wrote. He was not surprised at what the visitors found:

> There were no labourers – there was no industry on the Putumayo. It was simply a wild forest inhabited by wild Indians, who were hunted like wild animals and made to bring in rubber by hook or by crook, and murdered and flogged if they didn't. That was the system ... The whites in the station did not care a damn where the trees were, all they troubled about was where the Indians were – that is to see they did not 'escape'. It was evident, I pointed out, that the only system was one of sheer piracy and terrorisation, and if you lifted the lash you stopped the supply of rubber ... That the forest was gradually giving out its stock of rubber seemed almost apparent to me, as we found these 'sections' were continually changing their locality.[57]

Velarde, too, the commission members believed, was lying to them continually. They could get no satisfactory details of the section's records. Casement commented: 'Here are no books at all, they say, nothing but *blancos* lolling in hammocks, idle (often absent) *muchachos*, who go and come into the forest armed, but never a stroke of work of any kind done on this so-called factory. No one works.' The decision arrived at was that 'Velarde is to go'.[58] Casement worried increasingly about what would follow for the Barbadians and for the Indians from the unmasking of the main perpetrators. The problem for the Barbadians was the more immediate. Having told their stories, they now relied for protection on the British consul, but he had no power to provide it – there was no law, no authority. They were in some danger and could be accused of 'crimes' or even got rid of. He warned the Barbadians with him, therefore, to take precautions, and advised them to avoid complications over women; they were to be 'Galahads of negro virtue'. The problem for the Indians was longer-term;

should 'reforms' take place, involving the dismissal of the chiefs of section and the resignation of London directors, the ultimate effect could be the destruction of the Indians, as Arana and his henchmen could regain control: 'Arana returns to his vomit.'[59]

All told, he felt his work was coming to an end and that he would soon be leaving the commission to continue its work on its own: 'I go very soon, that is settled since our first field day at Chorrera, and they will then be alone and in a very trying position, trying to save what, morally speaking, should be destroyed, in the hope of "doing good" ...' He talked to Barnes about it, suggesting that he would soon leave, interview the remaining Barabadians at Chorrera and then take them with him; this would take pressure off the commission. Barnes agreed and they informed Tizon.[60] Casement wrote constantly, not only in order to keep a full and accurate record, but to help clarify his thoughts: 'I have been writing all day nearly. One has to, to keep sure of one's track.' On another occasion, he recorded: '[I] ... went to my room, and there thought over all that has happened in this amazing tangle of lies, deceit and half-told stories, none of which we were even to be permitted to test by the only test open, viz. to question employees of the Company openly.' When he had the opportunity, he measured the stocks and took an inventory of the store: 'Here at one of its chief trading stations it has not in store sufficient trade goods to meet the demand of a tenth-rate Banyan Store outside, say Delagoa Bay. Its rubber store, on the other hand, is vast.'

The strain of it all took a toll on his health: 'I am getting positively ill. My nightmare last night was a composite creature of all these criminals, a sort of Velarde-Jiménez-Aguero-Flores – indescribable and bleary-eyed, sitting at the door of my room *waiting* for me. That was all. Just waiting. No wonder I yelled in my horrid sleep, and roused the whole house!'[61] The Putumayo atrocities, he now agreed, were 'a bigger crime than that of the Congo, although committed on a far smaller stage and affecting only a few thousands of human beings, whereas the other affected millions'. Yet, despite the evidence all round, the commission members ('kindly Englishmen') needed persuading. No wonder, he commented,

> there were French Sheldons and Montmorres on the Congo, and Colonel Harrisons and even Boyd Alexanders! The world, I am beginning to think – that is the white man's world – is made up of two categories of men – compromisers and Irishmen. I might add, and Blackmen. Thank God that I am an Irishman ... and if these unhappy, these enormously outraged Indians of the Putumayo, find relief at last from their cruel burden, it shall be through the Irishmen of the earth – the Edward Greys, the Harris[es], the Tyrrells, and even the Hardenburgs and the Whiffens.[62]

Ultimo Retiro

The party left Occidente on 6 October and proceeded further upriver to Ultimo Retiro, stopping overnight on the way at Puerto Peruano. Casement's diary recorded their arrival:

> Arr Ultimo Retiro at 4 pm. Jiménez & his staff the greatest set of villians yet. Concubines everywhere. The stocks in place of honour amidships – the house built like a ship – a Pirate Ship ... The bows front river – the thick stockade of basement walls (16') rises 2' above Verandah & makes the bulwarks ... Warned Bishop & B[arbadian]s to sleep together & no girls! ... A sentry, I think pacing all night – someone certainly shaking the ship. Please God I'll shake this ship of state to its bilge.[63]

On the following day, they examined the stocks and the 'black hole, too, with its trapdoor'. As they looked at the stocks, a sturdy Huitoto, named Waiteka, burst into speech, showed them the weals on his thighs and buttocks, and told of many who had died in this *cepo*: 'The man had grasped the situation and it poured out. All were laughing, but in different ways. I was smiling with pleasure that this fearless skeleton had found tongue and the innocent-faced lad beside him, and that these two incontrovertible bottoms with the sign manual of "Case Arana" were being flaunted in the faces of the Commission.' As in Occidente, Casement took an inventory of the store: 'The "Commission" went there after questioning Jiménez, and I stood at the door and looked in. They merely glanced at the guns, handled one or two, and came away, but my searching eye and Sherlock Holmes soul did the rest ... There is not $5 worth of stuff all told, or anything like it, apart from the guns.'[64]

A good deal of the day was taken up by the examination of the only Barbadian based there, Edward Crichlow. Crichlow had been reluctant to testify and had been warned by Jiménez not to do so, but Casement sent him a counter-warning via Bishop about the possible implications of refusing. He agreed to talk. He described his experiences in a number of sections, under different chiefs, including Velarde, Fonseca and Alfredo Montt, now in charge at Atenas. He had seen Indians shot and kept in stocks and chains. He had been a participant, too, earlier that very year, under the leadership of Jiménez, in an expedition to the Caquetá in search of fugitive Indians. They had captured twenty-one Indians and three Colombian white men.[65] There was further evidence in Ultimo Retiro of the amount of work carried out by the forest Indians, without recompense: 'The path had indeed been smoothed for us – trees felled, saplings and trunks laid over wet spots, and bridges made over many streams with a liana rope banister to hold by. Over three traversings of a large river, a tributary of the Igaraparaná, we found very large trees felled, and a strong bridge thus made at great labour by these poor people.'[66] He later listed the various tasks carried out:

From building these huge houses (this one is fully 45 yards long and as strong as an old three-decker) clearing great tracts of forest, making plantations of yucca, mealy, sugar cane, &tc. constructing roads and bridges at great labour, for these men to more easily get at them – to supplying them with 'wives', with food, with game from the chase, often with their own food just made for their own pressing wants, with labour to meet every conceivable form of demand. All this the Indians supply for absolutely no remuneration of any kind, this entirely in addition to the India rubber which is the keystone of the arch.[67]

In Africa Casement had talked at times of the laziness of the people; in the Putumayo his comments were on the constant work of the Indians and of the laziness of the overseers. It was while he was in Ultimo Retiro, too, that the ideas of taking an Indian boy home with him and of a Christian mission to the Putumayo first came to him. 'I intend', he wrote on 9 October, 'taking a boy home to try and interest the Anti-Slavery people etc. etc. and the Missions, so that possibly some of the wealthy people, who are also good people, may, possibly – who knows? – it is a wild thought – take share in the company not to get rubber but to save Indians. If the Company goes, as I fear *must* be the case, then all is lost.' The following day, he developed the thought:

> If a Mission were started it might help a lot, but it can only come on two conditions – that the Company (I mean the English part of it) is strong enough to crush Arana and dismiss the gang of murderers, and put in decent men, and then that the Company itself will consent to carry on – even at a loss, as it must be for some years. Then a Mission here would be first rate, but a Mission with the present system would mean only more victims.[68]

Casement's eye problem, troubling him since early in the journey, now caused him a good deal of concern: 'My eye is very bad indeed, left eye and I have it bandaged with Boracic lotion & the Dr of *Hilary's* stuff. Turned in early with wet bandage over eyes.'[69]

Entre Rios

On the morning of 11 October they left Ultimo Retiro: 'Jiménez accompanied us to the beach to wave affectionate farewells with his white military cap. I raised mine to this thrice, triple murderer! And shook hands, too!'[70] They travelled downstream to Puerto Peruano and spent the night there. The following morning, with an entourage of some forty Indians ('literally starving') to carry their loads, they set off overland to Entre Rios, where the head of section was Andrés O'Donnell. They arrived mid afternoon: 'Entre Rios in midst of fine plantations, a circular clearing about $1^1/_4$ miles diameter, largely cleared & planted. O'Donnell far the best-looking agent of the Coy we've met yet, honest even & certainly healthy. Has been shot at often – even here on river bank bathing.'[71] On the trek, Casement had assessed the amount of Indian labour involved in maintaining the forest path; now he did the same for the plantation and the station house. 'The station house is a fine building ... Like the rest, it is entirely the work of the Indians. Not a nail used in construction. The big beams and trees of the uprights and rafters are peeled of their bark and lashed always with a tough liana ... The thatch is splendid – cool and dry and of immense extent.'[72]

The days at Entre Rios were busy. His eyes now improved, Casement wrote intensively. He interviewed James Chase again: 'took his Statement of all his term of service at Abisinia, the most awful things happening right up to three or four months ago. Perfectly atrocious. Took all morning at this'. The following day, he was 'busy writing all day'.[73] Part of what he wrote concerned his ongoing attempt to unravel the nature of the rubber system: he had the rubber 'sausages' in the store weighed; he assessed their value and the recompense to the Indians, the onerous task of conveying the loads to La Chorrera, the time consumed in so doing and loss of time to local food production as a result. Casement's anger is evident:

> The Indians who actually prefer their forest freedom to the whip, the *cepo*, the bullet and the raping of their children are spoken of in terms of reprobation as lazy, idle and worthless – and this by men who never leave their hammocks all day, and whose only 'work' is to work crime. They have not cultivated a square yard of ground or done one useful thing with their hands since they came here. Their only use – their sole purpose – is to terrorise and rob. And this is the function of the paid employees; the higher staff of a great English Company! Truly Mr Arana has planted a strange rubber tree on English soil![74]

He admired Indian resistance, mentioning on several occasions that of Katenere, a Boras *cacique* or *capitán*, who had led armed opposition in the area before himself being killed. And he now had an encounter with another brave witness, an old 'Captain of the Inonokomas ... a very intelligent looking man, with bright piercing eyes'. This man seized his opportunity during dinner and, pointing to his buttocks, let loose a tirade. Casement arranged with Bishop to have the man brought to him, using the pretext of buying a collar of leopard teeth: 'It was as I suspected; he was the spokesman for all. He had said that O'Donnell was working his people to death, that many had died, and now they were all being flogged for not bringing in the rubber put upon them, and they could not work harder than they did, and he wanted the flogging stopped to save his people.'[75] Later, another Indian, Hatima, the Muinanes chief, asked to look through Fox's field-glasses. He then 'caused an appalling silence' by remarking: 'I suppose you buy these with the rubber we produce.'[76]

One of the central events of the visit was an Indian dance, organized in the party's honour by O'Donnell: 'There is to be an Indian "ball" tonight – but it is raining & I don't think they will come. The *manguari* is beating its summons ... The Dance afterwards – about 500 Indians, O'D. says. I should say 350 at outside in to it.'[77] The dance gave Casement one of his few opportunities to observe something of an indigenous ceremony and he described it in some detail, including body-painting and the mode of arrival:

> The women and children tip lightly in, the men, with bunches of trees and ferns, palm fronds, or anything 'pretty' they may have plucked on the way, then assault the house with loud cries (firing off their guns as well) and as they pour in at the door they flog the low eaves and thatch and make a tumultuous eruption upon their hosts and the assembled guests. This sham fight is, I take it, to show their independence. They come to dance to-day in friendly gathering, but they *could* come if they liked as attacking warriors. The survival of an old past no doubt. The new-comers join the dance, and so it grows with each new party or 'nation' that comes on the scene.[78]

Despite the show of gaiety, Casement believed the underlying mood to be more sombre:

> Although dancing gaily and making these simulated attacks as they arrive, there is a pervading gloom about this festivity that never leaves human things on the Putumayo. Whatever it be, one sees and feels it. These rejoicing Indians are sad savages indeed ... One sees it in their eyes. You have only to speak suddenly to any man around, and an instant silence falls on him, and those near him who may perceive to whom you are speaking.[79]

Casement had mixed feelings about O'Donnell. He was attracted by his wide knowledge of Indian culture and questioned him about it. He had also to come to terms with O'Donnell's illustrious Irish surname. Before he had arrived in Entre Rios, he had commented: 'To think that a name so great should be dragged so low! That an Irish name of valour, truth, courage and high-mindedness should be borne by a Peruvian bandit, whose aim is to persecute these wretched Indians, his money for their blood.' But while O'Donnell had flogged, killed and terrorized Indians, his record was not as bad as those of other chiefs. O'Donnell's easy way with the Indians also impressed Casement and their gentle response led him to contrast them with Africans:

> Were these poor savage beings like the Africans, this paltry handful of filibusterers and pirates – for the whole gang numbers only about 150 – would have been swept away, after the first few murders. But the simplicity of the Indians and their fatal obedience have been their undoing, and their childish weapons, blow pipes and toy spears, thrown three at a time in their fingers, are a poor substitute for the African battle spear and axe. The African never feared blood; he liked its flow. These child-like beings, even in their wars, took life secretly and silently with as little flow of blood as is possible. The Winchester rifle in the hands of one desperado can overawe and subdue a whole tribe here, although they are not cowards. Their humble simplicity and humility are more dangerous to them than the weapons of their enslavers.[80]

Matanzas

The party left Entre Rios for Matanzas station, also known as Andokes, and, after a night in a Muinanes house on the way, they arrived in a downpour on 17 October. While the Indians used palm fronds and big leaves to keep dry, Casement made use of his Dublin 'brolley' – 'the first, I'll wager, ever used in these forests'. The chief of section, Armando Normand, arrived soon afterwards: 'A rifle shot & he came! A *loathsome monster* – absolutely filthy.' Casement avoided him until dinner: 'He came up, I must say, to all one had read or thought of him, a little being, slim, thin and quite short, say, 5' 7" and with a face truly the most repulsive I have ever seen, I think. It was perfectly devilish in its cruelty and evil.'[81] The evidence already collected indicated that Normand was among the worst of the Putumayo criminals and Matanzas among the worst of the stations: 'This place, along with Abisinia, are those which occur most often in the dreadful record of crime and horror compiled by Hardenburg, and Normand's name probably more often than that of any other. The Commission and myself have for some time now come to the conclusion that the Hardenburg document is true.' So negative and uncomfortable did Casement feel in Matanzas that he resolved to stay only as long as it took to interview the two Barbadians there, James Lane and Westerman Levine. This he did on the day after they arrived, starting with Lane: 'Again disgraceful things revealed & brutal murders. An Andokes man flogged to death last month at La China. Later on Westerman Levine who arrived – He is a blackguard, but I made him speak. He lied first & then admitted all. I told Tizon & brought him into the confrontation of the two, when Lane forced Levine to admit his lying. A disgusting day.' Part of the disgust was induced by the fact that, while Lane was recounting the death of an Indian captive only the previous month from flogging and confinement in the stocks, Normand ('the human beast') was telling the commission that he had not flogged for three years. More of the disgust came from finding the *cepo* concealed under palm thatch. Tizon, according to Casement, was dazed after the interviews with the Barbadians. ' "To think I am mixed up with this," was his cry.' He had decided that Normand had to go and that the stations at Matanzas, La China, Abisinia, and Morelia, and probably those at Sabana and Santa Catalina, ought to be closed.[82]

As their visit had coincided with a *fabrico*, later in the same day they witnessed numbers of Boras and Andokes Indians arriving with heavy loads of rubber:

> They came up the hill, men, women and children, largely the two last, staggering under perfectly phenomenal loads. I have never seen such weights carried on roads – and such roads! – in Africa or anywhere else ... I tried to carry one load of rubber, made Chase lift it and put it on my shoulder, Normand standing on. I could not walk three paces with it – literally and truly. My knees gave way and to save my life, I don't think I could have gone 50 yards.[83]

On the morning of 19 October, Casement set off on the return journey to Entre Rios. His journey coincided with that of a straggling line of Indians, taking loads of rubber down by Entre Rios to Puerto Peruano. 'On road found a "boy" of Matanzas with rifle lying on road in dying condition. Has been 12 days out without food to look for the "wife" of Negretti who had "run away". I tried to help him on & fed him, but he could not walk over 50 yards without falling. So I left him at last under shelter with my umbrella to keep off the rain & sent Sealy on to get 3 carriers to go back & help him on to Muinanes where I decided to sleep.' He then met an Andokes woman carrying a load of rubber, but in distress and unable to go any further. They stopped once more, took her load of rubber, gave her tea and helped her on: 'The woman could hardly walk, and that task of getting her on was a very slow one. She fell several times, and I gave her my walking stick to help her trembling legs. She gave way constantly at the knees and fell. I cried a good deal, I must confess. I was thinking of Mrs Green and Mrs Morel if they had been and could have seen this piteous being – this gentle-voiced woman – a wife and mother – in such a state.'[84]

They spent the night at the Muinanes House, where Casement fed the woman and dressed the scarred wounds of carriers who had arrived in twos and threes. After a night of little sleep, Casement continued on to Entre Rios the following morning. His thoughts were of Normand and the Indian rubber-carriers:

> For me, a famous walker once, and still pretty good on my legs, the route was excessively wearisome. I was bathed in perspiration half an hour after starting, and the constant ducking one's head, or balancing on a slippery pole, or falling over the ankles into the mud, wearied the mind and the attention more even than the body. Here were these men, many of them with loads far over a *cwt.* on the lightest diet man ever lived on, to get over this path, with no hope of relief before or behind them, and with this human devil and his armed *muchachos* behind to flog up the stragglers.[85]

They arrived at Entre Rios around midday and bathed and rested. Later, when the weary rubber-carriers came, Casement tried to get photographs: 'I begged Fox to observe them closely and to take some photos of the children with my camera.'[86] But the Indians were allowed no rest and driven on towards Puerto Peruano. During the following days, Casement thought out his strategy and did a good deal of retrospective writing up, since writing had been difficult during the days of journeying:

> What with taking down the depositions of the Barbadians, no light task in point of time, questioning them and trying to check their answers, then looking around me for confirmation or otherwise each day, leaves little time or energy, always with only the night for writing. At night I am very tired, and on the road it is almost impossible to write; the sandflies at Muinanes were a dreadful pest up to about 6 pm and then I had the sick Indians, and all my anxiety about the poor famished boy in the forest and the sick woman beside me. If only I could write

shorthand, never felt the need as now. So much depends on noting at the time and writing down at the time, leaving as little as possible to memory and the vague chances of recalling correctly, or not recalling at all. Much is lost in any case, and all I can do is try and record as promptly and as clearly as may be my thoughts, my perceptions of things and such facts as arise.[87]

Normand arrived from Matanzas on his way to the Igaraparaná with the *fabrico*, and he tried to engage Casement in conversation: 'Tried to talk to me to convince me of his gentle treatment of the Indians & to make me change my "assertions". I said, "I make no assertions".'[88] During the following days, when the Barbadian, Westerman Levine, failed to appear in Entre Rios and Normand defied Tizon's written note to return him, it became clear that Normand was plotting. Casement feared that Macedo, Normand and others might attempt to undermine the investigation by bringing charges against the Barbadians; should he, he wondered, take them downriver directly to Brazilian territory, returning on his own to Iquitos, to speak to the prefect? He decided to send Bishop down to La Chorrera to inform the Barbadians there of what was happening. Matters were not helped by the lack of purpose displayed by the commission. Fox felt this, too: 'He said that they were not proceeding properly at all and he bitterly regretted the absence of Col. Bertie. They needed a President and someone of greater experience to keep them together and collect their work. Barnes had no capacity for it and did nothing.' Casement agreed: 'There was no collective action it seemed to me, and no Secretary to take minutes of their proceedings, and no method in their enquiry.'[89]

Tizon and he teased out the situation in detail, once again. Tizon now felt isolated in the company; he was no longer *persona grata* with other employees. And, while they would not fight openly, they would engage in a campaign of intrigue and lying behind his back. Casement's thoughts turned to the weaponry of the company:

> A few good Boras armed with rifles, with the military force of Peru and a military magistrate behind them, would end the *correrias* and *commissions* of the Juanitos, Velardes, Montts and co. in a very short time. Something of the kind will have to be done ... I said, three weeks ago, at Occidente, when we had our last straight talk, that I should strongly urge him to write them for troops and a military magistrate – what in West Africa would have been a District Commissioner.

He later added, 'I would dearly love to arm them, to train them, and drill them to defend themselves against these ruffians.[90]

His thoughts for the Indians sparked wider comparisons: 'It is true that a very evil condition prevails, I believe, all through the Peruvian montaña and the Bolivian rubber districts as well, as described by Baron von Nordenskiöld (and other writers) – but the sum total of the poor outraged humanity suffering under it is less than two or three decent-sized African native tribes.'[91] While the depravity in the Putumayo was worse, millions had been affected in the

Congo; here one spoke of thousands. The North American pattern had been different, too:

> The inevitable disappearance of the North American Indian before an advancing stream of colonists who came to possess the soil and till it and found families, great cities and a mighty people, differed from the mere enslaving invasion of Latin exploiters who came *not* to till the soil, or possess it or found a great civilised people – but merely to grow individually rich on the forced labour of the Indians whom they capture and have held for centuries, in rapidly diminishing numbers, as perpetual and hereditary serfs.

Latin civilization had been a disaster for the Indians, he believed:

> The tragedy of the South American Indian is, I verily believe, the greatest in the world to-day, and certainly it had been the greatest human wrong for well-nigh the last 400 years that history records. There has been no intermission from the day Pizarro landed at Tumbes, no ray of a dawn to come. All has been steady, persistent oppression, accompanied by the most bloody crimes. A race once numbering millions, practising many of the arts, adapting itself to a wholly gentle civilisation imposed rather by precept and advice than by force of arms and conquest has been reduced to the wretched Andean serfs – the Cholos of Peru, a race 'without rights'.92

A solution to the oppression of the Indians would have to come from Europe rather than from North America. The Monroe Doctrine, which placed Latin America within the US sphere of influence, was, he believed, 'a stumbling block in the path of humanity. Instead of being the cornerstone of American Independence, it is the block on which these criminals behead their victims ... The blight in the forests of Peru and Bolivia would end to-morrow were it not for the Monroe Doctrine'.93

La Chorrera Revisited

While at Entre Rios, Casement visited Atenas on 26 October, before leaving on the 27th for Puerto Peruano. After an overnight stay, the party travelled downriver to La Chorrera. Here Casement was to remain several weeks, waiting for the arrival of the Peruvian Amazon Company steamer, the *Liberal*, to take him back to Iquitos. The interval was relatively busy, since he had arranged to have the remaining Barbadians brought to La Chorrera so that he might interview them. The taking of depositions occupied much of the last day of October and the first few days of November. On 2 November, for example: 'I interviewed Five Barbados men today. It took me all the day. Their statements cover a lot of ground and in some cases show grave ill treatment of themselves, particularly by Normand. Further infamous acts of cruelty against Normand and Aguero & the rest of these monsters & infamous treatment of Clifford Quintin by Normand. Wrote till 5 pm or later.'94 All the while, he was cross-checking the men's stories with those already obtained and compiling a more detailed dossier of criminal acts perpetrated by agents of the company. He began to put together a 'Black List' of the chief offenders.

Given that most of the Barbadians had testified about terrible abuses in the various stations, accusing their employers as well as themselves, and given that the worst agents of the company were being dismissed by Tizon, there was little future for the Barbadians in the Putumayo. Most decided to leave with Casement. He began to investigate the status of their accounts with the company. The majority were in debt to the company but, when he looked at the terms of their contracts, it was clear that the terms had not been complied with, concerning free food and medicines, for example. Moreover, indebtedness had been induced largely through gross overcharging in the company's stores: 'I went through a lot of the accounts of the Barbados men to-day and find the grossest overcharges. They have been robbed incredibly. 10/– for a tin of butter, 10/– for a pair of thin wretched carpet slippers (about 9d a pair at home) and food that should be supplied them charged at outrageous prices.'95 Macedo and Tizon quickly offered a 25 per cent reduction on the men's accounts, but while the men were delighted and willing to accept, Casement was perturbed. Was he mandated to accept such an offer on behalf of the men and, if he approved on their behalf, would his acceptance as British consul prejudice future action on foot of his report? He hesitated and looked for a sign:

Just as this thought raised itself, I looked up from the verandah to the eastern sky – and saw, to my amazement, an arc of light across the dark, starless heaven. For a moment I did not realise what it was – then I saw it – a lunar rainbow – a perfect arch of light in the night. The moon was in the West – with stars and a clear sky round her in the East, obscure sky and coming rain – and this wondrous, white, perfect bow spanning the dark. I called Fox, Bell, all of them – everyone came – none had ever before seen such a sight ... We watched it for nearly ten minutes – I take it to be a good omen – an omen of peace and augury of good – that God is still there – looking down on the sins and crimes of the children of men – hating the sin and loving the sinner. He will come yet to these poor beings – and out of the night a voice speaks. I shall not sell the great question of the Indians and their hopes of freedom for this mess of pottage for the handful of blackmen. These shall get their rights, too – but they shall come as rights – freely granted – and I shall not be the agent of silence, but I hope of the voice of freedom ... I have decided – or rather I do feel that this extraordinary sight, coming as it did, when my whole soul is seeking the right path, points the way. It was a direct answer to my question. I think it can only be read one way. Superstition, I suppose – yet are we not all children of a very ancient human mind that has sought in the heavens for its god and read His will in the clouds.96

In the event, he decided neither to agree nor disagree with the offer, treating it as a matter between the men and the company, to be accepted or rejected as the men saw fit. He also raised with Tizon the question of compensation for those men who had been seriously ill-treated, through flogging and confinement in the stocks, and the practice of semi-official gambling, which had further contributed to the indebtedness of the Barbadians. 'There is fear all round,' he commented in the charged atmosphere of La Chorrera. Edward Crichlow, who had decided to stay on to work in Ultimo Retiro, changed his mind, no longer feeling safe, and wrote to Casement, asking to be recalled. Three other Barbadians, who had gone back to Santa Catalina to collect their wives and their belongings, had turned back frightened, having been warned of a plot to attack them at night.

Following a period of little rain, the level of the river fell and Casement worried that the *Liberal* might not be able to come upstream. He swam and admired the young Indians: 'I bathed in river in morning. The Indian boys are swimming all afternoon. Lovely bodies out in the stream & the girls too, paddling logs across to the island & lying there awash by the hour. After dinner talked two Risigaros – muchachos – one a fine chap. He pulled stiff and fingered it laughing.'[97] It rained heavily at the beginning of November and the river rose steadily during the following days, allaying fears of being stranded. The pace of work and the mood varied from day to day: 'Did nothing all morning'; 'Heartily sick of the place'; 'Very busy day'; 'Lazy day'; 'A very anxious day'. There was a one-day trip to the station at Sur ('a wretched place') and, towards the end, a romp with the station dogs:

> Up very early at 5.20 and out on Verandah. Found a glorious morning looming, so out with all the dogs – the dear old Scots deerhound 'Duchess', 'Boff' the mediator of new smells, 'Blackie' of the Dugs, and the all-round 'Ladybird', the dog who attached herself to us up country at Entre Rios and now tries to attach herself to every male dog she sees. Had a delightful scamper in my pyjamas and French felt bath slippers – soaked – through the dewy grass and up the Sur hill, where the Hound and the dogs gave chase to the Company's with 'Lady' leading, of course.[98]

Hopes of bringing Indian boys to England also took concrete form during these weeks in Chorrera. He had thought of bringing them to the Anti-Slavery Society, to Charles Dilke, of using them to encourage support for a mission and of having Herbert Ward use them as models for one of his sculptures. Now, back in Chorrera, the choice was actually made:

> I picked one dear little chap out and asked if he would come with me. He clasped both my hands, backed up to me and cuddled between my legs and said 'yes'. After much conversation and crowding round of Indians it is fully agreed on, he will go home with me. His father and mother are both dead, both killed by this rubber curse – and his big brother – a young man – was shot by Montt … The Captain asked for a shirt and a pair of trousers which I gave him, and Macedo with great unction made me 'a present' of the boy. The child's name is Omarino …[99]

That same day, a second candidate materialized:

I had noticed him looking at me with a sort of steadfast shyness and as I gave him and others salmon his face flushed. He now came and eyed me in the same way and when I came out from my swim he followed me up to the house and begged me to take him away with me ... This youth is a bigger boy ... a married man of 19, probably, or 20 and would make a fine type for Herbert Ward in the group I have in my mind for South America ... This youth's name is Arédomi ... He has the fine long strong hair of the Indians, the cartilage of the nose and the nostrils bored for twigs and a handsome face and shapely body. I gave him a pair of pantaloons, and he stripped the old ones off, and stood in his *fono* – a splendid shape of bronze and I thought of Herbert all the time and how he would rejoice to have the moulding of those shapely limbs in real bronze.[100]

Journey To Iquitos

'My last hour in Chorrera,' he wrote on the morning of 16 November. He felt relieved to be going: 'Thank God! I left Chorrera and the Peruvian Amazon Company's "Estate" to-day. I am still their involuntary guest on their steamer *Liberal*, with the eighteen Barbados men, four Indian wives of these, and the children of John Brown, Allan Davis, James Mapp and J. Dyall.' As he looked back at the group waving farewell and beyond them the cataract, he reflected: 'My last view of the scene of such grim tragedy as I believe exists no where else on earth today.'[101]

The journey to Iquitos was to be a slow one, taking ten days. As elsewhere, his journal showed him to be a keen observer of his surroundings, natural and human. They steamed down the Igaraparaná, then the Putumayo, before reaching the Amazon on the 19th and turning upriver for Iquitos. On the night of the 16th, he saw an eclipse of the moon and woke, later, under a full moon:

I turned in early, but wakened at 2.30 with a glorious moonlight, and the lovely palm-crested forest slipping past silently and softly against a pale blue night sky. I looked long at it, and thought of the fate of the poor Indian tribes, who have been so shamefully captured and enslaved, and murdered here in these lovely regions, by this gang of infernal ruffians. I thought of Katenere, the brave Boras chief – of all the murdered Indians of these forests; of the incredible and bestial crimes of these infamous men, and wondered at the peace God sheds upon the trees. The forest, with its wild creatures, is happier far than the 'centres of civilisation' these Peruvian and Colombian miscreants have created and floated into a great London Company.[102]

He observed the inhabitants on the banks of the rivers, their houses and modes of livelihood. He noted with approval any signs of 'industry' they passed and was caustic about its absence anywhere rubber was relied on:

The rubber industry so-called, even when unattended by crime and oppression of the Indians, is on the Amazon – throughout Brazil or here in Peru – one of the most harmful pursuits a people could have given themselves up to. Every man has long since abandoned himself to this wretched rush for 'black gold', as some one has called it. All else neglected, not even thought of. Agriculture and the uses of the soil; the comforts of life; the joys of society, and the welfare of the community have been sacrificed in the rush to get rich. The demoralisation of the Spanish methods of dealing with a subordinate people has here reached a climax. Regular work, the great need of the region, the one thing that would have reclaimed the wild Indians from their irregular and fitful life has been entirely lost sight of.[103]

From his days in Brazil, he had begun to imagine a civilization in the Amazon that would tap its untold riches. Now, on this voyage, disillusioned further with the realities of the rubber industry, he elaborated his vision anew:

I am sure of this, that in a reorganised South America, when the Monroe Doctrine has been challenged by Germany and happily dispatched under her shot and shell, the valley of the Amazon will become one of the greatest granaries of the world. Also, too, I believe it will be peopled with a happy race of men. It supplies practically for the asking all the essentials of human existence, and this in a climate that for an equatorial latitude is superior to anything else in the world. All it needs is the touch of a vanished hand. The Portuguese (and Peruvians and others) have killed off in a shameful and cowardly fashion the aboriginal Indians, who, had the Jesuits gained the day over Pombal and the Colonists, would have today numbered millions. The murderers have put nothing in the place of those whom they destroyed, neither civilisation to replace savagery, nor white humanity to replace the copper – all they could do and have done was to pull down, not to build up or create. This mighty river, and far beyond its shores of this great continent, awaits the hand of civilisation. Four hundred years of the Spaniard at its sources, and 300 years of the Portuguese at its mouth have turned it first into a hell, and then into a desert. No sight could be pleasanter than the flag of Teutonic civilisation advancing into this wilderness. The Americans have got their part of America, and it will take them all their time to civilise themselves. Germany, with her 70,000,000 of virile men has much to do for mankind besides giving us music and military shows. Let loose her pent up energies in this Continent, and God help the rats who have gnawed at it for so long.[104]

He agreed with the entomologist Henry Walter Bates – one source, clearly, for some of his thoughts – that it was in the equatorial regions alone that the perfect race of the future would emerge; Casement believed that German immigrants would provide the needed human component.[105]

As the voyage continued and the tensions experienced in the Putumayo lessened, he seemed more alert to the physical attractions of young men: 'Very handsome Cholo sailors on board. One is a young half Indian *moço* of 18 or 19 – *beautiful* face & figure – a perfect dusky Antinous, would make a fine type for H[erbert]W[ard]'s statues of the Upper Amazon.' He was particularly taken by one of these sailors and was soon to learn his name – Ignacio Torres.[106] When they encountered some Yaguas Indians, he was struck by their demeanour and clothing:

One was tall, the other shorter, both young and handsome. The faces were exceedingly agreeable and shy and modest. Both looked down on the deck as we examined them. Their skins were coloured too, pink with annatto, I fancy. It looked like African cam wood powder. The taller young man might have stood for an Inca prince – regular features, soft gentle eyes, a beautiful mouth and downcast, pensive glance. I lifted his face twice to try and meet the eyes, but he smiled gently, and looked down again.[107]

Meanwhile, he visited some settlements they passed, read Harry Johnston's *Negro in the New World* ('which I like'),[108] played with a little chiviclis, which had been given him in La Chorrera, treated Arédomi for sandfly bites, and suffered his usual variations in health – worrying, in particular, about the onset of stomach symptoms similar to the attack that had laid him low in Pará. Once they entered Brazilian waters, his tensions concerning a possible threat to the Barbadians subsided somewhat. When they reached Esperanza, at the mouth of the Javari River, the Barbadian men disembarked, with the exception of Bishop, Brown and Lewis, who were to continue on with him to Iquitos. Casement purchased food from the *Liberal*'s stores for those disembarking and wrote letters for the captains of steamers and for the British vice-consul at Manaos, to facilitate the men's passage. Now there was Iquitos to face. 'Will it be peace or war?' he mused in his diary.[109]

Iquitos

His first sight, almost, when they reached Iquitos on 25 November, was the flag at Booth & Co.: 'Hurrah! I'll welcome the sight of the English flag ... since there is no Irish flag – yet.' The *Athualpa*, in which he planned to travel downriver, was already in port. He got medicine for his stomach from her doctor, arranged lodgings in the town for Bishop, Arédomi and Omarino, and then went to stay with Cazes. That evening, he had a long conversation with Cazes about affairs in the Putumayo. During this and later talks about the region, he came to the conclusion that Cazes had known a great deal more than he had earlier disclosed. When, a week later, Cazes suggested that Tizon had known everything months ago, Casement was clearly unimpressed: '... it is clear he knew just as much as Tizon. I told him so at lunch – and he got pretty scarlet'.[110]

On the following morning he made a formal call on the prefect, with Cazes as interpreter. Casement told him of the ill-treatment of the Barbadians and of the charges brought against the company agents. The prefect, in turn, informed Casement that a Peruvian Commission of Justice, under Dr Valcárcel, was about to leave for the Putumayo, to investigate conditions. He would telegraph Lima to say that he had met Casement and that the allegations in *Truth* had been confirmed. He begged that there be no publicity and that Casement not write a report for publication. In response, Casement explained that he was likely to compile two reports, one dealing with the narrower question of the relations between the Barbadians and the company, and a 'separate and confidential' report that would include 'very damaging charges against Peruvian citizens and implicate many individuals of that nationality'. While there would be no desire to wound a friendly country, he continued, some public response might have to be made should the Peruvian commission fail in its mission. He took the opportunity, too, of suggesting that the primacy of Mr Arana in the region should not continue. 'He was profoundly impressed,' remarked Casement, 'and again and again said that justice should be done.'[111]

After a picnic on the river on the following day, Casement plunged into the final phase of work prior to leaving Iquitos. 'Up at 6.30 and busy writing out a memorandum to aid the Prefect and the Judge in their work on the Putumayo,' he wrote on Monday morning. Later in the day, he commented, 'I am overwhelmed with work and no time for more diary.' He arranged with the Barbados men, Bishop, Brown and Lewis, to go and give statements to the prefect. He settled his account with the company. He wrote again to the vice-consul in Manaos, seeking his cooperation concerning the Barbadians. He collected information on shoddy treatment of the Dutch-French Colonizing Company by the local Peruvian authorities. When he got films back from an Iquitos photographer, he discovered that the one from Indostan, of 'Bolivar' in chains, had disappeared. At another meeting with the Frenchman, Vatan, the latter told him that 'it was only because I had come in an official character that I was allowed out alive!'[112]

There was time for resting and socializing. He went for walks to the village of Punchana, close to Iquitos, the home of the *Liberal* pilots, Manuel Lomas and Simon Pisango. He arranged that Ignacio Torres meet him for walks, and their parting was an emotional one for Casement: 'At length the parting & at Factoria Calle said Adios, for ever! He nearly cried I think ... He said *Hasta luego* [see you later]. I turned back & found him still standing at corner, looking straight in front. I to Fotografia & he crossed street. Last time I saw him was there standing and looking. Poor Ignacio! Never to see again.' At other times, he walked the streets in the evening: 'After dinner round Square very many times till near midnight & saw some types ...' He dined with Booth's staff and went to the 'Cinematograph' twice.[113]

Finally, the day of his departure arrived. He had gone to the *Athualpa* the day after his arrival in Iquitos and 'took my room No 1'. On 6 December, they steamed away, to farewells from Zumaeta and others:

> This is the last view I shall ever have of the Peruvian Amazon – of the Iquitos Indians and their pleasant cheerful faces – of the low line of houses fronting the wide, bold sweep of the Marañon as it comes down from its throne in the Andes – the mightiest river upon earth bathing the meanest shores ... My work is over on the Amazon. I have fought a stiff fight and so far as one man can win it, I have

won – but what remains behind no man can see. Anyhow, the party of English-men and myself have let daylight in to those dark wastes and, scheme how they may, we have broken the neck of that particular evil. The much bigger question remains – the future of the S. American Indians and Native people generally.[114]

The journey downriver was rapid and Casement's diary entries became more relaxed. He noted mostly the features of the passing landscape. When they reached Esperanza, he learned that the Barbadians had got a boat for Manaos only two days after they had landed there. Casement reached Manaos on the night of the 9th and went ashore the following morning. He discovered that most of the Barbadians had gone to work on the Madeira–Mamoré Railway, only five of them returning to Barbados. As they passed the Xingu River, the pilot told him stories of the Xingu Indians. Finally, on 13 December, he reached Pará. Having taken a room in the Hotel do Commercio, he went in search of sex: ' "Olympio" first at big Square, then Polvora & followed & pulled it out & to *Marco* when in *deep*.' Next day he met João '& he gave me a big bunch of flowers – very nice indeed.' There were social calls from Pogson, Pickerell and Kup. Let-ters from home awaited him, too, and he noted the December general election results: '518 seats filled with a Liberal-Labour-Irish majority so far of only 60. Conservatives 229 & the others all told only 289.' On the 15th and 16th he was not feeling well and stayed mostly in the hotel. Since Arédomi and Omarino were to go with Bishop to Barbados, prior to following on later to England, he wrote to Fr Frederick Smith SJ in Barbados to make arrangements for their sojourn.

On the 17th, he left for home on the *Ambrose*. With trade winds against them, the sea was rough for the first part of the voyage and many were seasick. There were deaths on board, too, one from yellow fever. 'Played Bridge again – impossible to write or do anything. Ship like a girl on a skipping rope, jumping & kicking.' He talked to M. Fabre of the Dutch–French Colonizing Company about affairs in the Putumayo and of an apparent attempt by Arana to sell his shares in the Peruvian Amazon Company. With calmer seas and colder weather, Casement thought ahead of Lisbon: 'I fear we shall be quarantined at Lisbon, but if not I hope to go on shore & see Agostinho & Antonio too!' By Christmas Eve he was 'very tired of this voyage', and Christmas Day was a 'stupid day'. When he did get to Lisbon and ashore, on the morning of the 28th, he recorded his sightings of young men: 'to Avenida where long-legged boy types & sailor ... & then Largo again & young soldier lad (18 or so) in grey twill – Splendid'. In the few hours he had, he went to The O'Neill's house and paid a visit to the British consul, Somers Cocks. That same day, they sailed north and called at Oporto and Vigo, before reaching Cherbourg on the last day of 1910.

13: *Putumayo Campaign, 1911–12*

From Cherbourg, Casement travelled to Paris, where he stayed until 4 January. As with 1910 he kept a diary for 1911, through which his movements can be followed in somewhat more detail than would otherwise be the case. From January to October he kept a cash ledger, whose day-to-day records of moneys spent allow further insights into his activities. In Paris he saw Dick Morten and the Wards, and had lunch with the British ambassador, Francis Bertie. On the evening of the 3rd, seeking sex on the streets, he was robbed: 'met Beast at Place de l'Etoile who got £2 gold & 30 fcs gold + 12 fcs silver = 92 fcs!'[1]

On the 4th he crossed to England with Dick Morten, and went on to his old lodgings at Philbeach Gardens. The following days were taken up with working on Putumayo matters and in meeting family and friends after his long absence. On the 5th he went to the FO. Tyrrell was at a wedding and Spicer away, but he met Mallet ('I like Mallet, he was full of sympathy for the Indians') and Sperling ('whom I don't like'). Next day, he caught up on letter writing and visited the Anti-Slavery Society, where he met Harris and Travers Buxton. During the coming days he met the journalists G.P. Gooch and John St Loe Strachey, spent time with the Lynds, dined with Colonel Bertie and met his old friend Cuibono ('who is being divorced by Mrs Cui'). With Nina he went to see *Tales of Hoffman* – 'not good or well done rather'.[2]

When he went to the FO on Saturday the 7th, he got a note from Mallet asking him to prepare a short preliminary report, 'to try to get some of the criminals hanged'. Mallet told him that he had been haunted by the stories Casement told him and had conveyed the gist of it to Grey, who asked to see him after the 16th.[3] He went home and began working on a report at once and 'did most of it before 7 pm when out for Nina'. The following day he completed it. In it he singled out the worst criminals in senior positions on the Putumayo:

Fidel Velarde, Alfredo Montt, Augusto Jiménez, Armando Normand, José Inocente Fonseca, Abelardo Aguero, Elias Martinengui and Aurelio Rodriguez.4 The puppet-master, Julio Arana, not listed here with the others, wrote to him on the 3rd and again on the 10th, asking for a meeting to discuss matters. Casement must have sought FO advice, for, when Mallet wrote to acknowledge receipt of the preliminary report, he suggested that such a meeting was not likely to do much good, but that, if Casement were to agree to one, he should have witnesses.5 In the event, Casement wrote to Arana, declining.6

As soon as the preliminary report was out of the way, he immersed himself in the task of documenting the experiences of the Barbados men and of producing a detailed expense account.7 From the 14th he worked all day, with the assistance of a typist ('He is an ass and cannot type or take down dictation either'). On the basis of his preliminary report, the FO telegraphed Des Graz in Lima, instructing him to inform the Peruvian government of the state of affairs in the Putumayo and asking that proceedings be taken immediately against those responsible. When Des Graz returned with the information that a Peruvian commission was to be sent to the Putumayo – information already known in London – the FO responded that the arrest of the criminals, many of them already gone from the Putumayo and some of them in Iquitos, needed to be effected. FO officials kept Casement informed of their actions throughout and sought his advice.8 Casement visited the FO on 30 January, and Mallet wrote the following day, saying he had been glad that Casement approved of their action. At the beginning of March, Mallet wrote again, commenting that, though the story was horrible, 'it is a comfort to think that your visit had done so much good'.9

Apart from his official duties, he engaged in a busy round of social engagements. Some stemmed from his Congo work, as when he met Gilmour, was in contact with Mrs Morel and Lady Margaret Jenkins, or went to visit the Norburys. He also saw Irish friends, visiting Mrs Green, her brother Colonel Stopford and the Lynds, and there were outings with Nina, Gertrude and Lizzie. Sidney Parry, a rubber investor and later to marry Gertrude, was part of his widening social circle: 'Out in Parry's motor with Mrs Green' is the ledger entry for 3 February. The Mortens were virtually relatives and, during January and February, Casement spent several weekends in their company in Denham.10

Ireland was never far from Casement's thoughts. He had written to Gertrude about an English–Irish dictionary, and he wrote to Bulmer Hobson renewing his offer of money to buy a farm and joking at the prospect of being a landlord. A few weeks later he advised Hobson against trying to combine a farm with his other pursuits.11 He expressed his anger to Gertrude, too, about an issue which exemplified British exploitation of Ireland: overtaxation.

Ireland can, and does, more than pay her way to-day, and half her revenue under the existing Treaty between the two Kingdoms is absorbed by England! That is to say, out of the £12,000,000 she raises, £6,000,000 is spent in Great Britain ... The robbery of Ireland since the Union has been so colossal, carried on on such a scale, that if the true account current between the two countries were ever submitted to any important tribunal England would be clapped in jail ...[12]

The belief that England systematically extracted Irish money had become a public issue around the turn of the century, when a special commission found that Ireland had been overtaxed, relative to her population. It was a matter for vigorous debate and protest.[13] For Casement it was another indication of the draining of resources desperately needed in Ireland and of England's bad faith. He was to come back to it from time to time in his writings:

> During the last century it is not too much to say that England drew over £1,000,000,000 from the 'poverty of Ireland' and that during the same period she forced or starved some 3,000,000 of Irishmen to toil as serfs in her mines, quarries, iron pits and ports or by 'voluntary enlistment' to fight her battles abroad.
>
> While a million Irishmen died of hunger on the most fertile plains of Europe, English Imperialism drew over one thousand million pounds sterling for investment in a world policy from an island that was represented to that world as too poor to even bury its dead. The profit to England from Irish peonage cannot be assessed in terms of trade, or finance, or taxation. It far transcends Lord MacDonnell's recent estimate at Belfast of £320,000,000 – 'an Empire's ransom', as he bluntly put it.[14]

In late February, he decided to take a few weeks' break in Dublin. He crossed on 21 February and lodged in the Gresham Hotel. It was not to be an auspicious visit: 'Ill with cold coming on,' he wrote on the 24th, and he was bedridden over the following days. In addition, his eyes were giving trouble, necessitating a visit to a doctor and getting spectacles. When he was up and about, he frequented bookshops. Hobson seems to have come south to visit him; he was also in contact with Agnes O'Farrelly, dined with Eddie Wilkinson and went 'to dinner Dr Sigerson (John Daly there)'.[15] And he took the usual pleasure in eyeing and describing a young man who took his fancy. On 6 March he headed for London by the ferry from Kingstown.

William Tyrrell had written on 4 March to report that Grey would like to see him, and Casement called to the FO immediately on his return to England. The day afterwards, his ledger recorded: 'Got letters from FO and very nice ones too.' The outcome was that he went directly to the Mortens' house in Denham and plunged into the writing of the full Putumayo reports. He was to remain at this for a month in the Morten's house, the Savoy, with occasional forays to London. After eight days' work he submitted his 'reports on methods of rubber collection and treatment of natives on the Putumayo', which would later be incorporated into the Blue Book. Several days later he submitted a second major instalment, the detailed statements of the Barbados men.[16] Spicer wrote on 30 March, gently suggesting 'toning down' the language of the report. There would be no problem if the report stayed within the walls of the FO but what if it went to the US? And to Peru? 'I venture to suggest that the report would in no wise lose in dignity or strength if some of the expressions used were a little softened ... The tale is ghastly and horrible enough whatever the language used.'[17]

The reports completed, he began putting together, at a more leisurely pace, an album of Putumayo photographs for Sir Edward Grey.[18] This he completed at the end of March and went to the FO to give it to Grey.

He took the train to Liverpool on 7 April and spent the next two days there working on the Morel testimonial, before going on to Manchester on the 10th. On Good Friday, 14 April, he crossed over to Belfast, where he and Mrs Green were to spend Easter with Francis Joseph Bigger. On Easter Sunday the three were 'At Ardrigh – To Lunch with Alec Herdman and family – & then up Ben Madogan with Mrs Green & A.H. & his daughter. Lovely day.' On Monday the tour took them to Cranfield via Shane's Castle demesne and on to Toome. He wrote to Gertrude about it: 'Yesterday we motored to Toome on the Bann and saw a lovely Holy Well on the way – a glorious spot.' He talked of a poem by Clarence Mangan, of Margaret Dobbs, and of Ada MacNeill.[19]

On Easter Tuesday he left Ardrigh for 105 Laburnum Terrace (Antrim Road), a rooming house run by Mrs Elizabeth Thomas. While in Belfast he worked hard on the Morel testimonial and on a scheme to sell copies of Mrs Green's new book, *Irish Nationality*. He told Hobson that he wanted her book sold by hand throughout Ireland – booksellers like Easons were afraid to order too many. Would Hobson act as an agent to sell it? It could be done by bicycle or motorcycle. He would send 500 copies to Tom Clarke; window displays could be used, and 'sandwich boys' in Irish kilts.[20] He sent off a subscription to Tom Clarke for *Irish Freedom*, the organ of the IRB.[21] And he noticed attractive young men: 'Gloriously beautiful type – one of loveliest ever saw in life – soft & auburn & *rose*.' From Belfast he made a day trip to Ballymena and a longer visit to Ballycastle and Cushendun. In Cushendun he renewed his acquaintance with 'Íde' (Ada) MacNeill and he was joined by Gertrude and Lizzie. Together they did some local touring, including to Murlough Bay.[22] He returned to Belfast on the 25th, where letters from two of his favourite partners awaited him: 'Letter from darling *Bernardino* at Rio – also card from Millar.' He met the latter on the following day and two of the entries for the following day in the cash ledger read: 'Lovely morning in Belfast – To sleep with Millar tonight', and 'At Carnstroan with Millar & Mrs G. *Entry* at 12.50 am.'[23]

He returned from Belfast to London, arriving on the 30th, and went straight to Alice Stopford Green's. At lunch there he met Lord Dunraven, Sir Anthony MacDonnell and Sir J. Solomon. On the following day, he worked on the Morel testimonial. In response to a wire from Barnes, home from the Putumayo, he went off to visit him in East Malling, in Kent, on 2 May. Back in

London on the 3rd, he went to the FO and, on the 4th the cash ledger noted: 'Return to Ireland today'.

He was to spend another fortnight in Belfast and its surrounds. He came down immediately with another of his bouts of illness: 'In house nearly all day cold and wretched. Thinking of Ignacio, Bernardino and *Mario*.' On Monday 8 May he 'heard from Millar suggesting he should call tomorrow evg. at 7. Replied yes'. He met Hobson for lunch and busied himself trying to make arrangements for the distribution of Alice Stopford Green's book in large numbers. On a day trip to Ballymena, the day being very warm, he went to a local swimming spot, which brought back memories of earlier days there: 'To old Turnpool by Braid and Devinish Burn of *Nov 1897!!!* Rippling in brown & swift & there too when I plunged across in Mch *1877!* Glorious boys of Erin – big & fair.' He and Millar decided to go to Newcastle together, where they spent the weekend of 13–15 May: 'Arr. Newcastle. Huge! In. *Bath*. Splendid. Millar into me!' And, 'At Newcastle with M. Into Millar! & then he came too ... Mist & rain. No go for Sl[ieve] Donard – so took car to Annalong along the "whin lit way".' The following day Casement left, arriving in 'Sasana' on the 17th.

His holidaying was now over and the next two and a half months were to be spent in London. He spent some days in a social round, visiting the Norburys in Carlton Park, the Mortens in Denham and the Blüchers in London, and attending the exhibitions in Crystal Palace and Earl's Court. On the 23rd, after lunching with the Putumayo commission, back from South America, he went for an overnight visit to Birmingham to the Cadburys and 'talked Putumayo'. He was in London again on the 25th, lunching with Nina for her birthday and visiting Mrs Green to discuss the Morel testimonial. Monday the 29th was the day of the Morel testimonial luncheon, and after calling at the FO, where he saw Dufferin and Mallet, he went to Picadilly for the Morel function. The following day he had another lunch with the members of the commission, before he took himself down to Denham and the hospitality of the Mortens.

The FO had sent Casement's report to Washington and Lima at the end of March, and in mid April, three months after they had first sought action from Peru, they again brought pressure to bear. Lucien Jerome, *chargé d'affairs* in Lima while Des Graz was away, forwarded what information he had been able to glean both locally and from Iquitos. Eleven of the PAC employees had been dismissed; most of the criminals had fled, some into Brazilian territory. A Peruvian commission, led by Dr Rómulo Paredes, had gone to the Putumayo and action was anticipated upon its return.[24] Jerome had an interview with the minister for foreign affairs in May and, when results were not forthcoming, in July sought and was given an interview with President Leguia, who promised to look into the matter himself. The FO thanked Jerome for his initiatives and urged action on two fronts. Firstly, 'you should urge that ... immediate steps be taken to compel the local authorities to arrest and punish the criminals whose names we have already communicated. This must still be possible, though it would, of course, have been easier had prompt action been taken in the beginning'. Secondly, they suggested the establishment of a religious mission in the Putumayo: 'They trust that the Peruvian Government would not only afford every facility to such a mission, but would give an earnest of their good intentions by granting it a substantial annual subsidy.'[25]

When he talked of a mission, Grey was, undoubtedly, building on Casement's suggestions in this regard. Casement had discussed the possibility with the Anti-Slavery Society and with Bertie soon after his return from the Putumayo. In June, Tyrrell wrote to say that he was in communication with the Archbishop of Westminster regarding papal assistance; this, he felt, was the best channel for getting action. By July, Casement was pursuing the matter with some energy. When talking to Cadbury about the future of the Putumayo, he listed possible lines of action: the reforming of the PAC; a lecture tour by himself, with the two Indian boys on the platform; and a mission. He wasn't very confident about the Catholic Church ('they did so little in the Congo'), but he thought that 'the appeal to them by Protestants and a Protestant Government would stiffen their hearts and would really be, in itself, an appeal to that wider, truer, better faith that to me is above Church or Creed or Dogma'. On the same day, he raised the matter with Spicer, saying that it must be publicized and funds raised: 'The Duchess of Hamilton with whom I was staying up to y'day promised to write to the Duke of Norfolk. The Duke is writing to Andrew Carnegie to try and interest that magnate in human beings as well as books.' In the latter part of July, he made calls on some influential Catholics, as the cash ledger indicates: on the 18th he 'Saw Ev. Fielding[26] at lunch, M'nr Bidwell at Cathedral'[27] and on the 25th, '*To Duke of Norfolk.* 11.15 am ... Lay down till 7.10 & then in Mrs G.'s motor to Archbishop's.' The Duke and Duchess of Hamilton took an active role in promoting the scheme. Hoste, the Duke's secretary, reported on 25 July: 'I have just written a long letter to Carnegie, sending him the report ... glad to hear that the RC Mission Scheme is catching on ... The Duchess wants a report to send to the Duke of Norfolk.' Lady Hamilton wrote telling him she was glad he was going to see the Duke of Norfolk about the mission. Her husband was pledging £100 (it would be more, she added mischievously, if a punitive expedition were being raised).[28]

In the meantime, now that the PAC commission members were back in England, contact between them and Casement had re-commenced. Barnes, and to an extent Bell, were anxious to work for reforms.[29] Casement now learned the details of their movements since he had left them in mid November. From La Chorrera, they had travelled overland to El Encanto, on the Caraparaná, the second headquarters of the company in the Putumayo region. There between late December and 22 February they had investigated company affairs in that region before returning to Iquitos early in March. Departing for Europe in April, they left Gielgud at Manaos, as company affairs there proved to be unsatisfactory. Their report, signed by Barnes, Bell and Fox, was submitted on 16 May. It was damning and fully corroborated Casement's findings:

> The general conditions that have obtained in the Company's territory can only be characterised as disgraceful. As has already been shown absolute power was put into the hands of men who recognised no responsibility save that of extorting rubber for their own benefit. Forced labour of the worst sort, that imposed by fear by private individuals for their own benefit, was the basis. The Indians were considered as possessing none of the ordinary rights of humanity, women in particular would be assigned to employees on their arrival in a Section and would often not be allowed to accompany them when removed to another post, even when desirous of so doing.[30]

Casement had some reservations about the report and shared them with the FO:

> This scheme of things takes no account whatsoever of the Indians as a native, or inhabitant of the territory the white or civilised man enters, with pre-existent native rights and long-established methods of existence that are to him of vital importance. If these be not considered, and the relation between the Indians and the trader are, at the outset, to be established on the assumption that the former belong to the latter it is impossible to prevent these relations degenerating into slavery.

Regarding a British company, he believed that

> its object should be to beget independence, to recognise that the Indian has rights over which it can exercise no jurisdiction and in the absence of any effective administration by an impartial governing authority to see that its dealings with the native populations shall be more and more founded on freedom of intercourse, mutually profitable, rather than on compulsion and supervision and allotted tasks which, however controlled, in such surroundings must degenerate into slavery. The Indian can and should be encouraged in many ways to improve his surroundings by those who have an interest in his welfare and the ability to assist him ... Before the white pirates came among them the wild Amazon Indians never lacked for food.[31]

In general, he felt that 'the history of slavery was written too soon – it took account of the overseas slave trade from Africa, but there is an internal slave trade that is more revolting still – because the victims of it are simpler, more defenceless and of gentler disposition than the native Africans'.[32]

With the commission members home and their report submitted, the directors of the Peruvian Amazon Company tried to address the question of reform. Bertie, though he had withdrawn from the commission before it began its work, still maintained an involvement. He requested that Casement be invited to board meetings, at which members of the commission would be present, and he told Casement that he wanted action and not *mañana*. The first meeting Casement attended was that of 1 June. Present were J. Russell Gubbins (Chair), H.M.

Read, Sir John Lister Kaye, Baron de Souza Deiro, and MacQuibban (for J.F. Medina). According to Casement's notes, the directors seemed 'at sea' and nothing was done. Bertie put his finger on the key problem, when he wrote to Casement: 'I am sure that Sir John will co-operate fully with you and the others in initiating reforms, but finance is the main difficulty and one which cannot be obscured or put off indefinitely.'[33]

Later in the month the name of Alan Boisragon was proposed as a travelling director of the company. On hearing this, Casement wrote to Spicer: 'Boisragon must be Alan Boisragon, a former Major, who was a colleague of my own in the Old Niger Coast Protectorate many years ago. He got into trouble over the Benin massacre – being one of the two survivors who escaped. I knew him well 16 years ago – and I shall make a point of meeting him now.' A week later, he referred again to Boisragon: 'It is 16 yrs. since I saw him on the Niger. He was told off to accompany me at the head of troops on a journey I made against refractory natives in Opobo which I settled without bloodshed or firing a hut – in February–March 1895 – and without calling into action a single rifle – to Boisragon's disgust at the time. I liked him then as a man and I am sure he is quite incapable of any dirty act or connivance at wrongdoing – but he is a weakling I fear.'[34]

Casement attended a second board meeting on 28 June. Arana, though in London, had not been invited, since it was thought that his presence would not be welcome to Casement. Casement urged that he be present in future.[35] Again, nothing was decided on Putumayo reforms. In Peru, Mr Dublé, one of the senior company figures, had made an unauthorized order that Indians who had been set to planting rubber trees go back to collecting wild rubber. Regarding the suggestion that Major Boisragon or another representative be sent out, it was stated that the company was 'quite without funds' and could not despatch him. When Casement raised the possibility of publicity due to their lack of action, there was 'agitation' among members and the confession that there was 'no money to carry on anything unless something turns up'. Casement wrote to Gubbins on 1 July, asking that a proposal be put to the next board meeting that the members raise among themselves enough money to send Boisragon. This would strengthen Tizon and show the 'deep personal concern' of the directors.[36]

The third meeting took place on 5 July. This time Arana was present. A draft letter to the FO was read out. Casement responded that it 'seemed to fall short of the needs of the situation' and again suggested that they take responsibility by putting up money personally to send an official representative. This was agreed, after much discussion, and Bell was to be invited to call on the board at an early date. The company's debts were listed: home liabilities of over £49,000, with no expectation of funds until the next shipment of rubber, not due till September. Arana offered to accept £100 per month as against the £2500 per year he had been receiving.

Next evening, 6 July, Casement received a letter from Gubbins, asking him to call on the 7th. Gubbins explained their financial plight. He didn't trust Arana – he had seen a letter from Arana to Zumaeta suggesting taking back control of the Putumayo. He felt £100,000 was needed to set the company on a proper footing and they were unlikely to get it.

The fourth and final meeting of the board attended by Casement took place on 17 July. There was a continuation of the financial discussion. The company had belatedly discovered an extra £60,000 liability to Mrs Arana. The powers of Zumaeta and Arana were to be cancelled. There was a danger of having all of their property seized by local creditors – everything would be gone, should this happen. Then there were the heavy expenses incurred: a costly commission had been sent out; thousands of pounds had been paid to dismissed employees, drawn on London, unknown to the directors; the new method of handling native labour meant a drop in production; there had been a sharp fall in the price of rubber.

Casement informed the board of talks he had had with friends regarding possible investment in the company. He was queried about their interests. What did they desire? Places on the board? A reduction in capital? Would they meet the board? Or send a representative? Casement responded very carefully, anxious to point out that he was acting in a personal capacity only. He stressed that the company must solve its short-term problems first. The original vendors (the two Aranas, Alarco, Zumaeta) must share in the sacrifice. His friends were interested in the commercial side, but there was also the humanitarian angle. The meeting ended with assurances that they would work on the task of getting extra capital. Otherwise, it seemed futile to send Bell while the company was threatened with liquidation.[37]

By the end of July, the interest of potential investors petered out. The cash ledger records: 'In city with Horner, Laidlaw & then Van Oppel. No go!' Perhaps William Cadbury captured the truth when he asked who would want to associate with discredited directors and suggested that it might be best that the company collapse; should it be patched up, there would be a danger that Casement's report would be withheld.[38]

Knighthood

While Casement was busy with the affairs of the Peruvian Amazon Company, his work on the Putumayo had another, unexpected outcome. On 15 June, his cash ledger recorded, cryptically, 'Letter from Sir E. Grey telling me of Knighthood. Alack!' The letter read:

My Dear Casement,
It gives me great pleasure to inform you that the King has been pleased, on my recommendation, to confer upon you a knighthood in recognition of your valu-

able services in connection with your recent Mission to the Putumayo district.
Yours sincerely,
    E. Grey.39

One source of his uneasiness became clear a little while later, when he responded to Alice Stopford Green's congratulations:

My dear Woman of the Good Woods,
Your congrats have been the best, for you alone have seen that there was an Irish side to it all. What you say is true – although few will believe it, can possibly believe, that I have not worked for this – for a 'distinction' and 'honour' – or whatever they call it, instead of, in reality, deeply desiring *not* to get it. In this case, it was like the CMg [Companion of the Order of St Michael and St George] – I couldn't help it at all – and could not possibly fling back something offered like that. Yes, it was Sir E. Grey – I had a charming letter from him telling me it was he who did it. But there are many in Ireland will think of me as a traitor – and when I think of that country, and of them, I feel I am.40

Whatever his qualms, he accepted and wrote a formal reply to Grey, the tone of fealty of which was to be used against him by the prosecution at his trial in 1916:

I find it very hard to choose the words, in which to make acknowledgement of the honour done to me by the King. I am much moved at the proof of confidence and appreciation of my services on the Putumayo, conveyed to me by your letter, wherein you tell me that the King has been graciously pleased, upon your recommendation, to confer upon me the honour of Knighthood. I am indeed grateful to you for this signal assurance of your personal esteem and support, and very deeply sensible of the honour done me by His Majesty. I would beg that my humble duty might be presented to his Majesty, when you may do me the honour to convey to him my deep appreciation of the honour he has been so graciously pleased to confer on me.41

When the honour was announced, congratulations came from friends far and near. Lucien Jerome, the consul general in Lima wrote and F.O. Lugard from Hong Kong. The latter wrote: 'It is many years since we last met, and you have probably forgotten my existence, but I take occasion to send you a line of congratulations on your appearance in the Coronation honours List. I do not lose touch with African affairs and I have followed with interest and appreciation your fearless championship of the Congo natives and I have seen also your more recent exposure of similar barbarities in South America.' Closer to home, letters came from Lord Dufferin, Mallet, Bertie and Eve Symons. Úna Ní Fhaircheallaigh, humorously reflecting Casement's own ambivalence, announced that she hadn't told Colm yet, for fear of another poem along 'die, traitor, die' lines.42 The cash ledger records the actual ceremony in a few words: 'To St James Palace to be knighted by George V.' That evening, he dined with Nina and Lizzie.43

South American Slavery and a 'Movement of Human Liberation'

Casement and Lucien Jerome began corresponding during this summer of 1911 and Jerome's letters were to keep Casement informed of events as seen from the Peruvian capital. More importantly, perhaps, they also showed him that serious abuses were taking place in other parts of Peru and Bolivia. In his first extant letter to Casement, Jerome noted that he had written 'endless despatches' to the FO about the treatment of natives by rubber companies. He mentioned two other London companies, the Inambari Pará Rubber Co. Ltd and the Tambopata Rubber Syndicate Ltd. He had information on yet more companies and was collecting data on the debt peonage system, known as *engancho*, which, he informed Casement, was perfectly legal in Peru. From Jerome, too, Casement began to learn about the Peruvian Sociedad Pro-Indigena, headed by Señor Capelo ('a rascal') and Dora Meyer ('earnestly sincere which is about all').44 Casement discussed the Inambari Rubber Company with the FO, writing to Spicer on 11 July:

> The Company works largely in what is termed the 'civilised' parts of Peru – in the hills where the people are not wild Indians at all, but domesticated Inca or Quichua Indians owning llamas and having farms – and yet even here one learns of gross oppression, of floggings and fraudulent debts and snared or crimped labourers captured by the local 'governors' and practically sold to various companies. This is what I term peonage in my despatches and is a matter of purely internal concern to the countries which tolerate it. It is disgraceful and cowardly – but the disgrace is theirs and I don't well see how any outsider can remonstrate.45

He discussed the Inambari Rubber Company and the Putumayo campaign in general with Travers Buxton, too, with whom he was in regular contact through the year. On 2 June, for example, he appealed for publicity: 'The real fighting is only now to begin I think and I hope you and your friends will now lose no opportunity of keeping the matter before the press – as a real live issue. The more publicity that can now be obtained will be all the better – both here and in Peru.'46

In 1911 Mexico became another focus of his attention, as the Mexican revolution spread, leading to the overthrow of President Diaz in May. He read *Barbarous Mexico*, by M.K. Turner: 'It is a terrible indictment – and makes my blood boil,' he wrote to Buxton. 'Please get it, and get others to get it too.' To Morel, he said: 'Diaz, the Autocrat of Mexico, is merely Leopold in the New World – a bit rottener perhaps in some things.' He went on:

> Slavery is spreading – the steamboat and steam engines and modern armaments and the whole scheme of modern government are aiding it – with the stock gambling and share market as pillars of the scheme. The *people* must fight for their lives and freedom always – and to root them in the soil and exalt agricul-

ture and debase landlordism must be their weapon. The land is at the bottom of all human progress and health of body and mind, and the land must be kept for the people.

He argued that no help could be expected from the United States: 'She is content to let them be, because they suit her personal ambitions.' He wrote again a week later, pleading: 'You *must* get that book and read every word of it ... Slavery dead!'47 Alice Stopford Green was another recipient of his enthusiasm for *Barbarous Mexico*, which, he told her, painted a 'dreadful picture of twentieth-century Mexico':

> Between Leopoldism on the Congo, Diazism in Mexico – and what I know of the Amazon rubber trade – there are more human beings held today in hopeless slavery, accompanied by the most inhuman cruelty than at the heights of the overseas slave trade. This is, I am convinced, a literal truth. Africa no longer exports slaves – her people are enslaved at home to European capitalists – and in South and Central America an *enormous* extension of the most disgraceful slavery has taken place in the last 25 years – induced by America and their capitalists and by the upward price of rubber ... International humanity is the only check to international financial greed.48

William Cadbury, himself caught up in a long controversy about the sources of his family firm's cocoa supplies in São Tomé and Principe, provided a sympathetic sounding board for Casement throughout the summer:

> You and I know that labour conditions in Angola are indeed slavery – they are 'debt' bondage and even purchased body bondage in fact – but they are in truth lawless forms of slavery ... The situation of thousands and thousands of labourers in Angola and scores and scores of estates [?] is that of slavery pure and simple – and the extension of this systematic enslavement of workers to the Cocoa islands of St Thomé and Principé was merely the wider application of an existing and time-honoured practice that has prevailed among the Iberian colonists of Africa – and of South and Central America – from their first landing among a primitive people.

Humanitarians, he continued, made two false assumptions: that slavery applied only to black or Negro races and that slavery had ended with the US Civil War and Brazilian abolition. He had reflected on the theme in his Putumayo Journal:

> Slavery is rampant today in many parts of the world – and I believe has taken on to itself a considerable expansion in recent years ... People ... write as if the excesses of Pizarro and Cortez ended 300 years ago. The principles (if piracy may be said to act on principles) of Pizarro govern a great part of South America today and rule the relations of *blancos* and *infieles* (the 'Infidels' God help them).

Now he concluded, 'I feel so lonely, in this matter of the Indians – It is so appalling and so hopeless.'49 He believed that the tragedy of the South American Indian was 'the greatest in the world today, and certainly it has been the greatest wrong for well nigh the last 400 years'.50 He attributed lack of development on the Amazon to '400 years of Spaniards at its source, 300 years of Portuguese at its mouth ... first hell, then, a desert'.[51]

He reflected on the roles of the United States and of Europe. 'I think the Monroe Doctrine is at the root of these horrors on the Amazon – it excluded Europe (the mother of Western civilisation with 500,000,000 people as against USA with less than 80m whites) from her proper correcting and educating place in the whole of South America.' South America, with nearly 7,000,000 square miles of territory, had only 40,000,000 inhabitants 'after nearly 400 years of occupation':

> Iberian civilisation is not Latin civilisation – and the coming of the Spaniards and Portuguese to South America with the resultant destruction of all the Inca, Aztec, Mayan and other Indian civilisations has been an unmitigated loss to the world – an invasion of barbarism destroying the growths of a gentler, kindlier mind. Northern Europe – especially Teutonic Europe – might redress the wrong – even today – but all effective European influence is shut out by the Monroe Doctrine – or its modern interpretation.[52]

To his growing opposition to the British Empire, Casement was now adding the continuation in Latin America of the evils of the Iberian empires. To his professional experience in Portuguese colonies in Africa, Lourenço Marques, Angola and Cabinda, he had added Brazil. Once the Putumayo investigation began, Casement began to reflect on the colonial history of Spanish America. His experiences, both in Portuguese colonies in Africa and, more especially, in South America led him to be extremely critical of Iberian colonization and empire. While immersed in the Putumayo investigation, he became sharply aware of the reality of conquest.

He was struck by the continuity in the process of colonization in Latin America. He cited evidence to show that the colonization of the Upper Amazon, including the Putumayo region, began about 100 years earlier, with slave raids from Portuguese Brazilian territory lower down the river. This, in turn, was a precursor to the first white settlements ('colonies') in the Putumayo itself in the 1890s, followed by the rubber boom and wholesale destruction of the Indians. The PAC representatives were in the direct line from Pizarro – they were 'conquistadores' whose aim was to conquer the Indians; they were 'pirates' and 'bandits' and the station buildings reminded him of pirate ships.

Some new social contacts contributed to Casement's conception of the almost limitless extent of human oppression; one was with the distinguished American black scholar and activist W.E.B. Du Bois, whom he met at this time. On 13 July, Travers Buxton wrote to him asking: 'Have you meet Prof. Du Bois, from Atlanta, who is one of the chief champions of his race in the Southern United States, and is over for the Universal Races Congress?' Casement responded, expressing interest in meeting Du Bois, and Buxton evidently arranged this. On 29 July, Casement wrote: 'I enjoyed so much meeting her

[Mrs Buxton] and the pleasure you gave me of meeting Dubois.'53 In addition Du Bois was present at a meeting of the Nationalities and Subject Races Committee conference held in Caxton Hall on 24 July, and the ledger indicated that Casement was present, though not impressed: 'To Caxton Hall in evening. Rotten performance.'54

Increasingly, Casement's associates tended to be from the radical wing of the political spectrum, including many in the Liberal Party. One such in the journalistic field was A.G. Gardiner, editor of the *Daily News*, Robert Lynd's employer and a friend of Alice Stopford Green's. Casement had published an anonymous piece about the Putumayo in the newspaper in December 1910 and wrote to Gardiner about it: 'The signature is wholly fictitious, a sort of hybrid corruption of my name ... You need not be afraid of libel suits if you print this. I'll see you through, that I can promise you, if anyone or the P.A. Directors dared to take action. But they won't – they'll only shiver in their skins for fear of what else may be coming.'55 The two met on a number of occasions during the summer of 1911, and shortly before he left for his second journey to the Putumayo Casement wrote: 'The *Daily News* has been a staunch friend in this dreadful crime and I hope between all the good influences at work we may bring effective changes for good.'56

Ricudo and Omarino

On 13 June, Casement had heard from Fr Smith in Barbados that Ricudo and Omarino were sailing for England the following day.57 While awaiting their arrival, he talked of them to his friends. He wrote to Patrick Pearse in Dublin, to see if Pearse would take Omarino into his educationally innovative school, St Enda's. Pearse replied: 'I shall be very glad to receive your young Indian at St Enda's. Indeed I think it will be a very interesting experiment for myself personally. I am sure he will be at home among our boys, if anywhere in this hemisphere, and we will all, boys and masters, do our best to make his school life here happy.' Pearse went on to discuss fees, which would include school cap, football suit and kilt for drill and scouting. He also offered to take Omarino to his cottage in the West for the summer, at a fee of £1-1-0 per week. 'I sincerely hope,' he concluded, 'that between us we shall make a great success of this young barbarian. It is work that appeals to me very much.'58

On 25 June, Casement travelled to Southampton to collect the two and returned with them to London the following day. Omarino went to stay with the Barnes family in East Malling. Anne Barnes wrote on 5 July: 'The little boy is quite good and happy now. I think he missed Ricudo at first – he enjoys doing his lessons.' The following day, her husband wrote: 'regarding the Sphinx of the woods I will bring him up by the train arriving at Victoria 10.43 – you might if possible send Ricudo and someone to meet him ... he can certainly return here if he will but he seems very anxious to get back to Ricudo as far as I can make out'.59 In London, Casement showed them off, bringing them to Fisher Unwin, Alice Stopford Green and others. William Rothenstein recounted in his memoirs how Casement approached him to have a portrait of the boys painted:

> Would I help? He wanted me to paint the two youths, which I readily did. Their bodies were a rich golden colour, and their dress simple – but a few brilliant feathers strung together. Such models were rare. While they sat, Casement would tell me stories of his adventures. He was full, too, of the wrongs of Ireland. 'As long as he only bothers about present conditions,' said [W.B.]Yeats, 'it doesn't matter; but Heaven help him if he fills his head with Ireland's past wrongs.' I was uneasy about Casement; he was excitable and restless ...60

The cash ledger recorded five sittings, Nina Casement accompanying the boys on a few of these visits. Rothenstein kept in contact with Casement about them. 'The boys', he wrote in his first letter, 'turned up happily, and put on their ornaments with care – almost with pedantry, with the help of combs, water and a looking glass, and then stood like rocks ... When the boys have done what I would like them to do in the way of sitting I will hand over fair wages to you, to invest for them as you think fit, so following your advice with regard to giving them no money personally.'61 The boys also sat for 'anthropological photos'.62

On 6 June, Casement brought Omarino and Ricudo with him when he went to see the Duchess of Hamilton, as he told Spicer: 'I dressed the big Indian up – or *undressed* him up – at the Hamiltons – in his bark loincloth, his yellow and crimson plumes and leopard's teeth. He looked splendid.' He was going to take them to the Archbishop of Canterbury, he told Spicer, and they were learning English fast.63 Then, there was a weekend of croquet at Denham; a day in the zoo with Nina, Dennett and the boys; dinner with Lady Caledon; and a visit to the Exhibition with Lord and Lady ffrench. He sent a gift of a rug to Mrs Green and £80 to his brother Charlie in Melbourne. Here and there, too, he recorded sightings of desirable male partners. One such took place on a weekend visit to Sir T. Fowel Buxton64: 'Lovely youth 18 there. Coalblack. Alexander Scot. Son of Master of Polwarth. *Magnificent* one. Huge. Bathed together in pond.'65

By May of 1911 it was known that some of the principal criminals from the Putumayo had fled to Brazil. The FO telegraphed the British legation in Petropolis on the 6th to give a précis of events, to alert them to the flight of criminals and to inform them that extradition would be sought. On its heels, they sent a second telegram, relaying information from HM representative in Lima, to the effect that extradition had been refused by Brazil. In addition, they explained that the diplomatic situation between Peru and Colombia was 'most critical', with conflict expected. Since the Peruvian Amazon Company was the only effective force on the Colombian border, the Peruvian government relied on Arana to defend Peruvian interests there.66 William E. O'Reilly, from the

British legation in Petropolis, replied on the 15th to say that they had had to pull back from making a planned application, on learning that Brazil had no extradition treaty with Peru. He again telegraphed on 27 June, saying: 'The arm of the Federal Government is not very long, and it is never certain that their orders will be faithfully obeyed on the Upper Amazon, but I see no sign of unwillingness on their part to go the full length of their powers in this matter.' He also informed the FO that a new extradition law had just been passed.[67]

By mid summer, then, there had been months of pressure for action, followed by regular reassurances and delaying tactics from the Peruvian authorities, and the flight of the wanted men. The British representatives in Lima and Petropolis were distant from the Amazon and pinned down by diplomatic niceties. At this point the decision was taken to send Casement back to the Amazon, though the purpose of his return is not clear. Perhaps it was felt that his experience could help in the apprehension of the criminals; it would be valuable, too, to meet Paredes, recently returned to Iquitos from the Putumayo; and, he could prepare the ground for the arrival of Consul Michell and his family. At any rate, Casement recorded in the cash ledger on 29 July: 'To Spicer at FO and offered to go out to Iquitos.' On 3 August, he noted: 'Marching orders to Putumayo again today from FO.'[68] As part of the response to the situation, it had been decided to appoint a permanent British consul. In June, Casement had been asked to advise on local and office allowances for the new post and, in July, he was informed that the appointee was to be George Michell, a former colleague in the Congo and, latterly, consul in Paris. Casement was asked to advise on the extent of the district to be covered by the consulate. Michell wrote on 24 July, thanking Casement for getting him the Iquitos job.[69]

Casement took one last, quick break in Ireland, crossing on Saturday 5 August and going to the Gresham Hotel in Dublin. There he had a letter from Millar, which elicited a response in the cash ledger: 'Good on for Tuesday. Hurrah! Expecting!' In Dublin he had several sexual assignations and made a number of social calls: he dined on several occasions with J. Nelson, a friend from Buenos Aires, visited Arbuthnot at the zoo,[70] went to Sandycove, where he had been born, and met 'Harrie and Annie', the Wilkinsons from Baronstown. On Tuesday, 8 August, he noted: 'Leaving for Belfast. To sleep with Millar' and, in the margin, 'About 11 pm I trust and shall thrust too! My last night with Millar was 12th. May at Newcastle. *In at once.* Turned and pushed on to it.' While in Belfast, there occurred the death of a Johnnie Bell, which deeply affected him: 'Oh! dear God to think of it. Dead and gone! Old father and mother and sisters.' He went up to Ballycastle, to visit Roger and Susie, before returning to Belfast, intending to leave for England on Saturday the 12th. But, getting a telegram from T.P. Gill, he travelled to Dublin instead and went with Gill to visit St Enda's and from there to Sarah Purser at Mespil House. He arrived in London on the 14th.[71]

Return to Iquitos

He had only a few days left before leaving for the Putumayo. He decided to take Ricudo and Omarino back with him; they had been in England little more than a month. Perhaps the fact that he was unexpectedly asked to return to Peru again and the difficulty involved in having them looked after in England led him to this decision; in any event, they had played only a very peripheral role in raising awareness of the Putumayo issue. He settled the accounts for himself and the two boys with Miss Cox, made the necessary arrangements for the voyage and engaged in a last round of social calls. He visited Louie Heath and dined with Barnes and Dick Morten. On the 16th the trio left Southampton on the *Magdalena*; they reached Barbados on 28 August.

There Casement met the Putumayo section head, Andrés O'Donnell. He wrote to Spicer, repeating earlier views that O'Donnell was the 'best of a bad lot' and 'I don't think he killed Indians for pleasure or sport – but only to terrorise for rubber – a thing he was appointed to do by his superiors ... his Indians seemed happier than any others I met – that is to say less miserable.'[72] He celebrated his forty-seventh birthday on the island.[73] Apart from visiting the Ursuline convent and Fr Smith, which he did on the 31st, he recorded little of the days he spent waiting in Barbados other than the physical attractions of young men. He was particularly taken by the young son of a clergyman he met at a local public bath: 'Teddy & "Budds" at 5.30. Latter lovely & *huge* one too – only 11 years old on 17 July!' At the same bath, on the following day, 'Clergyman there – told me was father of Beauty. Returned 11. & beauty came – glorious limbs, but *did not* show it. Alas. I love him.'[74] A second encounter was with a young man, named Stanley Weeks: 'Out to Light House & saw a nice boy. Asked him to bath & he came alone. Stanley Weeks. 20. Stripped. Huge one – circumcised – swelled & hung 9' *quite* & wanted it awfully ... His stiff and mine stiff. Then had to leave. Farewell to Stanley!'

He and the boys left on 5 September: 'On *Boniface* – a filthy tub. She has legal accommodation at N. York for 5 passengers, & has 16! A barefaced swindle. These Booths are blackguards.' On board he met a Dr Dickey, who, as the diary noted, 'was the doctor at El Encanto once – speaks Huitoto. Told me that Fonseca & Montt are at Sta Theresa about 7 hrs up Javari on Brazilian side – working under contract for a firm called Edwards and Serra.' Over the coming days, Dickey told more stories from his experience of the Putumayo, including ones of Normand's cruelty and Dublé's chicanery. Casement relayed this information to Mallet in London and included a rough map of the areas to which the fugitives had gone. When Casement detected Amazon waters far out to sea, he turned his thoughts forward to Pará and its pleasures: 'I'll go to Hotel do Commercio and after room & dinner will be out to Praça do *Palacio* where I hope almost at once to run across a good *big* one. Will grasp & off to Marco. It is delightful to think of Olympio & the others.'[75]

They arrived on the 10th and he did cruise the town after dinner, but without success. On the following day he wrote to the FO to say that Fonseca and Montt were at a small Brazilian town near Benjamin Constant on the River Javari, beside the Peruvian frontier. He asked that they be expelled by Brazil, while he would give notice to the Peruvian frontier magistrate to arrest them.[76] Meanwhile, he and his party were not to leave Pará until the 22nd, presumably waiting for a suitable vessel; in the interlude, Casement divided his time between socializing with other Europeans and seeking sexual outlets. He met João, who 'looked poor' and gave Casement roses. Another encounter is described on the 17th: 'In evening after rest, out at 7 to Palace Square & almost at once a beautiful *moço* in white looked and entered Kiosque. Met outside & invited to *passear* and away we went. Felt in darkness big head ... he stripped almost & in *furiously* – awfully hard thrusts & turns & kisses too & biting on ears & neck. Never more force shown. From Rio.'[77] He was to meet 'Rio' on other evenings, as well. He dined, too, with his consular colleagues Pickerell and Pogson. Meanwhile, Dr Dickey, Ricudo, Omarino and he waited for the same ship. An inspector of customs refused to release Casement's luggage and, when local representations failed to make an impact, he wired the legation for help; but even a telegram from there didn't work. On the 22nd, the day they left: 'Pogson down at 9.30 to report his utter failure to get my things out of Customs! The Inspector declined all recognition of telegrams or Governors. So I have to go up river with all my equipment & gear in the hands of Pará Customs!' The state of the *Hilda*, the boat they were to travel on, didn't improve his mood: 'A filthy pigsty – I am very sorry I came! What a fool I've been!' And, in the cash ledger: 'Left Pará about 2.30 am on Saturday after being 14 hours on this detestable craft there. God! How hopeless this people is!'[78]

He whiled away the time between Pará and Manaos doing a jigsaw. Ricudo and Omarino, he recorded, were very miserable, 'altho' I feel less sympathy for the latter who is a wee fox'. He bought four parakeets at one stop and arranged to send money to the Irish College at Cloghaneely. They arrived at Manaos on the 28th and the cash ledger noted on the following day: 'Sent to ask if Governor would see me – he said tomorrow only.' The governor had, in fact, just been contacted about the Putumayo fugitives. O'Reilly, in Petropolis, had written to Grey a few days earlier to explain Brazilian sensitivities about extradition to Peru – they resented European interference. But the foreign minister, the Baron de Rio Branco, telegraphed the governor at Manaos, instructing him to watch for and expel the fugitives.[79] Casement saw the governor and immediately wrote to O'Reilly; the governor would do all he could to catch Fonseca and Montt and was sending an officer with Casement on the *Hilda*. 'If Fonseca and Montt are collared,' he concluded, 'it will be an excellent day's work and you should congratulate the Baron de Rio Branco on having enabled his country to perform a distinct service to humanity.'[80]

These essential duties seen to, Casement indulged in a virtual orgy of sexual activity, particularly on Sunday, 1 October. Both diary and ledger gave details. The latter, matter-of-factly, listed three names and added: '3 lovers and two others wanted.' Referring to one of these partners, the diary noted: '*three* times he did it & three times from the two sailors. In all *six* times tonight.'[81]

The *Hilda* left for Iquitos on 3 October with the promised police officer on board. Dr Dickey came down with fever and Casement seems to have surrendered his cabin to him, sitting himself in a chair on deck. The weather was hot and he, too, began to feel 'seedy ... fear it is the old complaint of Lisbon *1904* & *1909*'. Progress was painfully slow and he noted, in exasperation: 'Stopped at several places again in night. There are 55 mail ports on our list from Manaos to Tabatinga! & 38 other passenger & cargo ports!! It is perfectly insane the way time is wasted. We are now 15 days out from Pará – with certainly a good fortnight yet before us to Iquitos.'[82] On the 8th, the diary recorded: 'Took candy – Enema broken I find – only ear syringe left. One week after event.' The event has to have been the sexual exploits at Manaos, now taking a physical toll.[83]

On 11 and 12 October the attempt to apprehend Fonseca and Montt fell apart. The police officer from Manaos and another picked up on the way, duly instructed in what to do, went ashore to arrest the two, got drunk and were apparently bribed. Fonseca and Montt, Casement learned, had slipped away.[84] His first attempt at arranging the arrest of two of the criminals had thus failed. The *Hilda* travelled on and they reached Iquitos on the morning of Monday, 16 October. Their arrival coincided with the funeral of Lionel Lilly, son of the trader John Lilly, who had succumbed to an outbreak of yellow fever. Casement noted: 'Prolonged dry weather. Fearful heat,' and added, again: '*Fearful heat* – atrocious. Nearly fainted.' The day was largely devoted to necessary social calls: breakfast with David Cazes, a sympathy call on John Lilly, talks with David Brown of Booth's and with Vatan.

In all, Casement spent a little short of two months in Iquitos on this visit, which convinced him, if convincing were necessary, that little could be expected of the local authorities. Two days after his arrival, the first indication came from a meeting with the prefect, whose performance was smooth:

> Called on Prefect who said the Putumayo mystery had been solved by me – the honour was mine. It had been a 'mystery' even here in Iquitos. Don Pablo [Zumaeta] was hidden here in Iquitos the Prefect says – waiting the result of his appeal against the Judge Dr Valcárcel's order of imprisonment. Dr Paredes' report covers 80 pages & goes to Lima 'next mail'! ... Got the order for Montt & Fonseca to go down by *Anastasia* with J. Lilly tomorrow.[85]

Some days later, Casement met Paredes, who 'complimented me mightily'. They met regularly and Paredes made a copy of his report available to Casement. He read it carefully and must have copied much of it, for he was to submit a detailed précis to the FO not long after his return to London early in 1912.

Casement wrote to the FO that he was not convinced by the prefect, who had had Paredes's report since July and had still not forwarded it to Lima. And Casement felt that the prefect was aware of Zumaeta's hiding place in Iquitos. He wrote to Spicer, too, sending a copy of Paredes's paper, *El Oriente*, and giving details about Ricudo and Omarino: 'My big Indian has gone to Putumayo on a Government launch with an order from the Prefect to find his wife and bring her to Iquitos. I shall then leave these Indians with Michell as they will end by being useful servants here. The ordinary Iquitian *won't* act as servant [at] all – and many people have no servant!'[86]

Almost from the moment of his arrival, Casement's health was poor. 'Very bad cold & sore throat,' he noted in the diary on the 17th; on the following day, he went to bed immediately after dinner with a '*fearful cold*' and 'in real pain'. He continued to refer to his indisposition over the course of the following weeks. In spite of his illness, page after page of his diary is devoted to descriptions of the physical endowments of young men whom he encountered during his daily rounds in Iquitos. He had been anticipating his arrival and listed in advance in the cash ledger some sixteen individuals, under the heading, 'To see (D.V.) in Iquitos in Oct. 1911'. These had to have been young men with whom he had been in contact when in Iquitos in 1910. Some he named – and the names are familiar – Ignacio Torres, Simon Pisango, 'Cajamarca'; others are described: 'Beautiful legs', 'Young big eyes', 'Office boy – Cazes', 'Soldier boy'. On this visit, after the names he added, varyingly: 'seen', 'gone', 'no sign', 'gone, I fear'. Ignacio Torres, for example, was not in Iquitos, much to Casement's disappointment.[87]

While there was much eyeing and physical description, some were more attractive and seen more often. One such was Alcibiades Ruiz, who appears in the diary on at least five occasions. Casement also engaged in a prolonged courtship with another youth, José Gonzales, whom he identified two days after his arrival as the 'young pilot of *Liberal*'. Casement begged him to come to his house the following morning at nine, which he did. 'Sat down & I stroked knee & gave 10/– & cgttes & photos. Would like it I am sure. Caressed hand too. His is a big one I know. To come on Saturday to *passear* with me & get his photo taken. He is beautiful.' Two days later José came again: 'New pants, showing much & bowed from street & then up to my room. I shut door & took his hat & almost at once I saw his getting stiff & bulging out sideways his pants. We sat down side by side & looked at Enock's book & I caressed and held hand & thigh & sometimes back. He blushed & hand hot & wanted *awfully* – leaning close to me & hand against my thigh.'[88]

Day after day they met, going frequently to nearby streams to bathe, looking at books and, towards the end, working on Spanish exercises. Despite his desire and their regular meetings, Casement held back; on one occasion, he took José to his room '& his got up too & he wanted awfully. His lovely face suffused with glorious Indian blood & eyes glistening. I refrained with enormous difficulty ...' A few days later, they went bathing again, providing another opportunity for physical admiration: 'after coming out mine under h'kf [handkerchief] got stiff & he did same with his h'kf & fingered it too & it got *huge*. I saw it swelling & at last under h'kf got glimpse of it & it was a tremendous one with red head. Nearly did it'. José called to Casement's house that afternoon 'and on till 5 stayed with me – mine huge & his up too stiff. He wants it! He is quite ready – but if I do it I must take him with me to Rio.' Neither of them, it seems, felt able to move beyond preliminary overtures: 'He came at 8.15 & sat beside me & after a minute to table. Till 10.20 but he persistently refused all my efforts. I tried hard – at end about 10 his got half up & I touched it once & felt its hard curve & he showed it too. He left at 10.30.' The day before Casement left Iquitos, he and José met for the final time and Casement recorded their parting with a terse, 'Bid José goodbye.'

The mere sight of a good-looking youth could set off infatuation: 'At wharf most *glorious* type of Indian purser *moço* on *Victoria*. I fell deep in love with him – perfectly divine face & limbs'. Or, when Alcibiades left on the *Liberal*: 'Adios! Adios! I love him & his beautiful face & body & mind.' The admiring was done discreetly, in such a way that it was unlikely to be observed; to one such description, for example, he adds: 'Harding with me all time.' Some viewing he did from the window of his residence, especially when he was ill. 'I hid behind window,' was his comment on one occasion. Having admired a strong young *cholo* pass his window and later return, he wrote: 'I saw him coming but hid. He glanced in window as passed but did not know I was there! and so I have again sacrificed love to fear.'

Throughout his stay, Casement was in regular contact with other members of the British community: the Cazes family, but to a lesser extent than in 1910; David Brown, of the Booth Shipping Line, who would later serve as British vice-consul for a short period; F.J. Harding, local manager for John Lilly & Co. From them he derived useful local knowledge and, as a result of his warm relations with Harding, he was invited to join the John Lilly steamer, the *Anastasia*, on a journey up the Javari River, where Fonseca and Montt were believed to be working. They left on 13 November, on a voyage of some 1600 miles. Casement had written to O'Reilly in Rio on 5 November, apprising him of the failure to apprehend Fonseca and Montt and telling him of his planned journey up the Javari. The fugitives were, he told O'Reilly, at a place called Boa Vista, about eight hours steaming above Benjamin Constant, and 'armed to the teeth'.[89]

On the 15th, from Nazareth, he informed O'Reilly that Campos, the Brazilian police officer, had waited four days before setting off upriver after Fonseca and Montt, the implication being that they were being given plenty of prior warning. There was precise information, too, as to their present whereabouts. Six days later, after they had gone 500 miles upriver and were on their way back, he wrote again: 'I passed in the night the place where Fonseca is working for Edwards & Serra.' Edwards, himself, had come on board. Casement was convinced by his local informants that the two police officers, Campos and Helm, had been bribed. 'I am full of wrath over the failure to lay hands on these two execrable ruffians – it could so easily have been done. Everything was in our favour.'[90]

They arrived once more at Iquitos on 25 November. The time remaining to him was now short. From the time of his first arrival on 16 October, he had been awaiting word from George Michell as to when he and his family would arrive to take up residence. In the meantime, he looked for a house for them, which would also serve as accommodation for himself in the interim. Having found and taken one, he moved in on 30 October, without enthusiasm: 'Packed up & got ready for flitting to new house ... Moved into House – horrid. José came with me & said w'd arrange a *peón* & water for tomorrow – *Peón* to clear out the filth at back.' He was even more negative the following day: 'New House is a pig stye – literally – It will never do for the Michells. Infested with mosquitoes & every noise & syllable next door heard.' The Michells did arrive, on 30 November, and Casement remained on for one week, seeing a good deal of them during that period.

Over the course of his final weeks he met Paredes regularly and discussed the general situation and the latter's report, given to him in confidence. The report was impressive, he felt, and he also heeded Paredes's warning about the dangers of involvement. 'He fears assassination & again warns me not to go to Putumayo. Says I will be attacked too – just like Hardenburg & if I go to Putumayo [I will be] in danger.' During one of his last nights he dreamed of his days in the Congo: 'I wakened with vivid dream 1887–1888 going up Mazamba Hill – oh! God – to think of it – "the fields of Heaven" from Congo dia Lemba – 24 years ago in the heyday & glowing flush of my youth & just 23 years old – more than half my life gone since then.' On 7 October, the diary recorded: 'Up early packed & off to Michells & Hardings. Paid bills & bid goodbye all round & then to *Ucayali* ... I don't suppose I'll ever see Iquitos again – altho' it is quite possible I may – but I do not want to.'[91]

Homeward

The journey downriver was rapid and he busied himself writing and copying despatches. In these letters, he told them of his voyage and of what was happening about the Putumayo culprits. He was to add more detail in a memo written shortly after he arrived back in England on 20 January. He had left England on 16 August, he wrote, after they had learned of Paredes's return from the Putumayo and of the impending arrest of many of the criminals. There had then seemed to be hopes of local reform of the system of exploitation employed in the collection of rubber. His first action on his journey, he reported, had been the unsuccessful attempt to arrest Fonseca and Montt, in Brazilian territory. Then, when he had arrived in Iquitos, he was informed by the prefect that only nine men had been arrested of a total of 237 for whom warrants had been issued. Of the nine, only Aurelio Rodriguez could be counted a significant figure. Pablo Zumaeta had been arrested but had succeeded in having the original order of arrest overturned by the Iquitos Supreme Court. He had actually gone on the offensive, attacking the reformers, standing as a candidate in municipal elections in Iquitos, and resuming his functions for the Aranas regarding rubber exports from the Putumayo. The superior court also ruled that charges against the nine held could not proceed until others charged were apprehended. While many of those charged had left the area, Casement continued, others had not and could easily be apprehended. The official who went to the Putumayo to apprehend them was Amadéo Burga, *comisario* or commissioner of the Putumayo, a paid employee of the PAC and brother-in-law of its managing director. Burga brought back only one minor personage, all the other accused, he claimed, having been in the forest when he arrived or having left a short time before his arrival. Some of these, Casement learned during his stay, had returned to their stations after Burga left. Punishment of wrongdoers at Iquitos, Casement concluded from his experiences, could not now be expected.[92]

It was the reformers who were under pressure: Judge Valcárcel had been dismissed; Paredes was being attacked; Tizon, who had written to him, was 'effective' but now 'highly unpopular'. He believed no serious reform steps were now likely to be taken in Iquitos and he worried about affairs on the Putumayo itself. The volume of rubber returns from the Putumayo suggested that there was no slackening of pressure on the Indians. All in all, he felt things were almost back where they started at the time of Hardenburg. His concrete suggestions to the FO centred on its taking steps to have the Paredes report brought into the open and acted upon.[93]

He stayed in Manaos for almost a week. On 15 December, he noted in his diary: 'Missed Arana Bros visit – thank goodness.' Leaving on 17 December, he was not well and 'lay down all day'. He looked forward to a letter from Tyrrell when he reached Pará, hoping to be redeployed from Rio to Buenos Aires. It was not to be: 'To Pogson & letter from Tyrrell saying B.A. is given to Mackie of Congo! Alack – alack – So I am done out of that. What a shame.' He embarked on 24 December for Barbados on the *Denis*, a 'fine boat' with only five passengers. Christmas day was spent 'reading mostly – old books and loafing'. They arrived in Bridgetown on the 28th and, finding that the SS *Terence* was due to go to New York, he left on her on the last day of 1911.

14: *Putumayo: Mission and Select Committee, 1912–13*

In the United States, Casement travelled to Washington, where he was granted meetings on the Putumayo issue with President Taft and US officials. How the detour came about is not clear. Casement gave one version in a letter to Charles Roberts, early in 1913:

> I went to Washington ... *entirely* off my own bat – without a hint that such a move was on ... I realised that we (the FO) could do no more and that it was time the USA were dragged in. So I went off to Washington without letting FO know and got the USA Consul appointed [to Iquitos] and the thing taken up from there by a sort of personal assault on Taft and the State Department. Grey was delighted when he knew and spoke in the warmest terms to me.[1]

James Bryce, British ambassador to the United States, gave another version in a despatch to the FO at the time: 'Having heard from Sir Roger Casement that he would be passing through New York this week on his way home from his mission to the Putumayo district, I asked him to be good enough to come and discuss the situation there with me, with special reference to the relations of the United States Government to the matter.' Bryce, anticipating that Casement's Putumayo report would be published, believed that a visit by Casement would help to bring US officials onside with HMG:

> The simplest and directest way of effecting this seemed to be to bring Sir Roger Casement into personal contact with those officials here who would be responsible for United States policy in the matter. And this seemed of sufficient importance to justify my requesting Sir Roger Casement to remain here until the next sailing, which allowed him three days in Washington, most of which he has spent in talking with various officials and President Taft ... he was able to create a personal interest in the matter among the higher authorities which had not previously existed.

It was a good moment, therefore, to suggest to the US a definite line of action that the two governments might take. Bryce agreed with Casement's suggestion that the appointment of a US consul in Iquitos would be a good thing.[2]

George Young, a member of the embassy staff in Washington, described the same events, but with added colour:

> President Taft was lured to dinner in the embassy and led away to a quiet corner where Casement was let loose on him. A queer picture they made – the tall Celt, haggard and livid from the Putumayo swamps, fixing with glittering black eyes the burly rubicund Anglo-Saxon. It was like a black snake fascinating a wombat. But Putumayo gave no further trouble in Washington.[3]

Upon arriving back in England on 20 January Casement put together several despatches outlining his experiences and reflections. One of these dealt with the investigations of Romulo Paredes, who had gone to the Putumayo on 15 March 1911 and returned to Iquitos on 15 July. During his investigation, he had visited every station of the company, interviewed witnesses intensively, including native Indians, and his findings had fully confirmed those of Casement's own report. He had amassed some 3000 pages of testimony and had also written a general report. Before going to the Putumayo he had been an Assistant Judge of First Instance, but after his return was no longer connected with the court. He had submitted his report to Valcárcel's successor, who was now studying it.[4] As well as discussing Paredes's report in detail, not long after his return Casement submitted a précis and part translation, informing the FO that it had been shown him in strict confidence. An FO minute stated: 'This is a most striking and courageous report by Dr Paredes, and Sir Roger Casement has compiled a most valuable summary of it.' It bore out, the minute added, all that Casement had written.[5]

Casement briefed the FO on reform of the public administration in the Putumayo. The prefect in Iquitos had assured him that measures were about to be taken, but, Casement pointed out, the only public officials in the Putumayo were a commissioner and a magistrate (*juez da paz*), both of whom were PAC employees. The only reform he could identify during his stay was the replacement of the existing incumbents with two others; but these, too, were employees of the company. As for the actual practice of rubber collection, he believed that the local representatives of the company had recovered from the shock of the investigations and were reverting to their traditional methods. Orders to plant rubber trees and to introduce more humane methods in dealing with the Indians had been reversed and the gathering of wild rubber recommenced. He related the volume and value of rubber collected since 1900 to the ravaged and declining population of Indians in the area and ended by reflecting on the overall impact of the rubber era in the Amazon on native life:

> With all it has given to the Amazon Valley of prosperity, of flourishing steamship communications, of port works, of growing towns and centres of

civilisation with electric light and tramways, of well-kept hospitals and drainage schemes, it may well be asked whether the rubber tree has not, perhaps, taken more away ... It may be long before a demoralisation drawing its sanction from so many centuries of indifference and oppression can be uprooted, but Christianity owns schools and missions as well as Dreadnoughts and dividends. In bringing to that neglected region and to those terrorised people something of the suavity of life, the gentleness of mind, the equity of intercourse between man and man that Christianity seeks to extend, the former implements of her authority should be more potent then the latter.[6]

In another major memorandum, submitted around the same time, Casement discussed a number of possible ways of bringing pressure to bear on Peru to instigate reforms. He argued that it was vital to publish the reports, as publicity was a sine qua non for success, and that US cooperation ought to be secured in whatever steps were taken. He then suggested four possible lines of action. The first was to bring to arbitration the boundary disputes in the Putumayo region. The pressure of such arbitration could force Peru to take seriously the treatment of the Indian inhabitants of the area. A second possible course of action would be to form a commission to oversee reforms, comprising the British, US and Brazilian consuls in Iquitos. An opening for such a commission, Casement believed, was to be found in a statement by the Peruvian president. Thirdly, the Brazilian government might be invited to take over the policing of Putumayo waterways. A good proportion of the journey from Iquitos to the Putumayo was through Brazilian waters and some 300 miles of the Putumayo itself was in Brazilian territory: 'Brazil has only to close the door at Tabatinga and Iquitos starves. She has only to close the Putumayo at its mouth ... and the Putumayo murderers starve.' Fourthly, Peru ought to be asked to put into effect the scheme of administrative reforms drawn up by Paredes. Indeed, should Peru be willing to do so, none of the other three courses would be necessary. This option, then, might be the first to be tried. Its advantages were 'that it involves no open break with Peru; that it carries the United States of America entirely with us; and that it still entrusts to Peruvian hands the needed reforms and policing, while ensuring by external influence on the spot that these reforms are honestly set going and are adequate'.7

The FO now pursued the tortuous path of diplomacy. Officials worked on several fronts: they attempted to pressurize Peru, through Des Graz and Jerome in Lima; they tried to persuade the US to use its influence with Peru; through Haggard and O'Reilly, they attempted to move a reluctant Brazil to lend its support. At home, the government had to respond to regular pressure from Parliamentary Questions and the lobbying of the Anti-Slavery Society. During the spring, despatches coming in to the FO were regularly marked 'Sir R.C. to see' and he responded by submitting observations, corrections and caveats on their content. In early March, feeling that the US minister in Lima, Clay Howard, was being lied to by the Peruvians and disbelieving Peruvian good intentions, Casement pressed once more for publication of his report, arguing that in publicity lay a major hope of improvement. Peru might respond to the 'compulsion of civilised communities', and possible British investors in similar ventures ('such coffin ships of finance') might be alerted to the dangers.

Another acquaintance he had made now contributed to his placing the Putumayo atrocities in a broader context. Regular letters began to flow from Mitchell Innes, counsellor at the British Embassy in Washington and a kindred spirit. Innes, who had worked for the FO in Egypt, sent Casement a copy of an article he had completed on the topic of colonial justice, arguing that colonial rule was doomed to fail because of a failure to understand the Oriental mind. Eastern and Western ideas of justice were diametrically opposed, the former being rooted in the local community, the village unit. These communities were 'to a remarkable extent popular, democratic, constitutional, decentralised', but had been replaced by a colonial state system, 'which is purely bureaucratic, despotic, centralised'. Ideal justice, Innes argued, combined the three elements of law, religion and custom, but, under the European system now imposed on the East, religion and custom 'dwindle to almost nothing, while law becomes a fetish to be worshipped for itself, because it is The Law'. And while in the West the weakness of religion and custom has to be made up for by 'an ever-increasing mass of statutes limiting the power of masters over their servants, of creditors over their debtors, of landlords over their tenants, of capital over labour', at the same time Europeans were imposing their law in the East, where religion was still a 'vital power'.[8] Innes had a practical suggestion to make:

> I have been thinking seriously over the question of how to bring organised influence to bear to obtain the doctrines which you and Morel and I and certainly many others hold on the subject of native government ... Could we not form a society for the study of existing native systems of administration, law and justice, and for the publication of articles on the subject, by men who have practical knowledge.[9]

'I like him immensely,' Casement told Morel, 'his gentleness of mind and largeness of view are fine in that diplomatic world.' And he shared Innes's goals: 'The feudal tyranny which upset so much in Europe is now represented by a commercial tyranny we call "western civilization" and we want some checks upon its dealings with the "undeveloped" peoples – particularly when these undeveloped ones have a system of their own like that made statutory by the Koran which preserves them in peace and well-governed village communities.' The task facing an organization of the type suggested by Innes would, he said, be big,

> for it has to tackle an *enormous thing*. 'Commercial interests' are practically modern Civilization itself. They make and remake Governments – and destroy peoples, just as they make war. They build battleships and incidentally sink liners too. 'Commercial interests' represent profits – and all men nearly are after prof-

its. Show them profits – and they won't trouble about making (or breaking) the welfare of peoples.

This was true, he felt, not only in Egypt, but in Ireland, where 'landlordism' was

> imposed on a people of local freedom – with a central state behind the land-lords to wage war on the village communities and the tillers of the soil. The Irish hatred of English 'law' had its source right here where the Egyptian hates it – because it spelt the upsetting of ancient custom which was just and a part of the life of the community and imposed a cold mechanical scheme of punishment that was inhuman to the Irish heart – and unjust too.[10]

In his despatches to the FO, Casement referred to the possible support of Brazil in actions regarding the Putumayo. He was encouraged by the recent establishment of the Brazilian Society for the Protection of Indians (SPI), believing it reflected an advance in Brazilian sensitivities. In his FO despatch of 30 January 1912 he wrote:

> Brazil could further be moved to act by appeals to her vanity on the ground that by her recent humanitarian action in creating a State department for the protections of the Indian race, and placing it under one of her most distinguished soldiers, Colonel Rondon, she was in the best position of all the South American States for ensuring the temporary protection of the neighbouring Putumayo Indians.[11]

Casement's references to Brazil rankled with the ambassador in Petropolis, and in March Haggard drew Mallet's attention, privately, to what he considered to be their deficiencies,

> especially in regard to those points on which my old friend Sir R. Casement has not lately had the same opportunities of information as I have here in Rio. At the same time, admiring as I do his enthusiasm in the good cause for which we are both working, I am unwilling to put permanently on official record inevitable minor disagreements, and I therefore send you privately the memorandum in which my remarks are contained, though of course for whatever use you may see fit to make of it.[12]

In contrast to what Casement had written, Haggard was pessimistic regarding the likelihood of Brazilian cooperation. To be flattered by an invitation to help would be the last thing that would occur to them, he believed: 'In point of fact, I take it that they are more inclined to suspect our motives and resent our interference with its implied comparison between South American and Congo civilisation, and they also fear that humanity may interfere with the satisfactory flow of rubber.' Should they cooperate, it would stem from a different motivation: 'The prospect of being pilloried before the world will doubtless be very unpleasant to Brazilian vanity, and may possibly yet prove sufficient to goad them into doing what we have asked, even though it mean trouble and expense and go sorely against the grain.' He believed, further, that a Brazilian blockade of the Amazon waterways would hurt innocent parties in Iquitos, including the

Michells and Booths.[13] Later that summer, after the publication of the Blue Book, Haggard reiterated his view that Casement had misjudged the Brazilians.[14] Casement became aware of Haggard's criticisms and responded to the FO on a number of occasions. He then made the mistake of writing two personal letters to Haggard, in which he discussed Brazil's role in a very unguarded way. 'Brazil', he said in the first,

> is very foolish not to take the opportunity so gracefully given her in the Blue Book to do a good thing for her name and fame. Her own hands are not at all clean of Indian blood and the more this ghastly tragedy of the Putumayo is probed, the worse it will be for all those near at hand. She may find herself the target before very long! There are people on the Amazon now who know a great deal about Brazilian methods of collecting rubber too – and I hope the flame of enquiry may spread and light some of those ruffians' quarters of Manaos firms too. The whole place is an infernal den of criminals – Brazilians, Peruvians and all the scum of Central [and] South America – men of every hue and no morals.

Three days later, having been sent another batch of Haggard despatches and telegrams, he wrote:

> I fear you and the others who say Brazil will do nothing *serious* are right. The Govt (& people) is so poor a show. Possibly the fear of being implicated may have more effect than appeal to higher motive – I had not thought of that – but you are clearly right in attributing lower motives than I did to the B[razilian]s. I had hoped (rather than believed) that an appeal to their better nature might have moved them. Well – let us see what some of the truth anent conditions in the Brazilian Amazon may do. They can throw few stones at the Peruvians![15]

Privately again, Haggard informed Spicer of the two letters and quoted some extracts, drawing attention to the discrepancy between these and Casement's official view as stated in the Blue Book. 'I am afraid that Casement, kindly and talented fellow as he is, is but a weak reed to lean on in founding a policy. He evidently wants now to attack Brazil. Has he the evidence to do this with and, if he has, what good would it do? ... One result of an attack would probably be a perfectly useless row which would at least destroy my influence here to the detriment of our great interests. As a matter of fact, Brazil could do nothing with Peru if she would.'[16]

Casement continued to pass on the latest information he had received from correspondents, one instalment, for example, to Spicer on 25 May from Cornwall, where he was holidaying with Nina. From Jerome in Lima he had learned that Paredes had gone there and made an impression in government circles. The Leguia government, Jerome reported, was on the way out and 'the financial position is as bad as any of the worst defaulting states of Central America: the whole body politic being sick to death and would not go on but for the subcutaneous injection of Monroe Doctrine serums'. From Iquitos he had heard from Harding and Michell, the former telling him about Valcárcel's dismissal and reinstatement and about the latest shipment of rubber from the Putumayo – eighty tons, one of the largest on record for a single period.

On the last day of May, from the Savoy, Casement submitted a full translation of the Paredes report.[17] But, increasingly, he had his doubts about Paredes: having been made a fuss of in Lima, 'he will return to the Putumayo a somewhat different man' and would now see things 'in a more official light'. If the Peruvian government were interested in reform, he concluded, it would welcome the publication of Casement's own report; instead, they were working to stall it.[18] Some time previously, Des Graz had reported what looked like another stalling attempt on the part of the Peruvian government – the decision to appoint a commission to study the defects of the existing system of administration on the Putumayo. Casement's scepticism was vindicated when it was announced some time later that the proposed commission was to be reorganized, that Paredes was to help in preparing a scheme for reforms and, finally, that a subsidiary commission was to be established at Iquitos. Definite proposals for reform were to be ready by the end of the year.[19] For Casement, all of this seemed a means of gaining time.

Despite the impact of Casement's visit in January, Washington was reluctant to sour relations with her chief South American ally, Peru, and had been prevaricating concerning the publication of Casement's report. On the more positive side, Bryce was able to announce the appointment of a US consul to Iquitos; the appointee, Stuart J. Fuller, was to arrive in Iquitos on 24 May.[20] During May and June the FO had been voicing increasing frustration at US advice to delay publication: 'I cannot postpone publication indefinitely,' exclaimed Sperling on 25 May. FO minutes on 6 June accused the US of 'very mean behaviour', stating, 'we are committed to publication'. On 9 July, an official noted that 'the Putumayo Blue Book will be distributed to the Press' on Saturday the 13th.[21] The report duly appeared. Inglis has described its impact: 'The report on the Putumayo created a sensation. *The Times* gave it two columns, and a long editorial: the horrors revealed, it claimed, "must stir the anger and compassion of all who are not utterly dead to the sense of humanity and of right ... Sir Roger Casement has deserved well of his countrymen and of mankind by the ability and the zeal with which he has investigated under very difficult conditions an appalling iniquity." '[22]

Morel wrote a glowing tribute, which was published in the *Daily News*, under the title 'The Bayard of our Consular Service'. Opening with a description of Casement's striking looks, he went on to refer to a quality 'of pure metal, of a soul almost primitive both in simplicity and in strength, set in the frame of an athlete, and seen through the outward trappings of a grave courtesy and perfect ease of manner. I have never known such personal magnetism emanate from any man'. Having summarized Casement's work in the Congo and Putumayo, he concluded dramatically:

To denounce crime at a distance is a relatively simple task. To track the criminal to his lair in the Equatorial forest; to rub shoulders with him round camp fires; to realise he knows it is only you that stands between him and immunity – you and a few inches of cold steel, which makes no noise ... to be enervated by fever, and maddened by the bites of stinging flies; to run short of food – and what food! to parch in thirst, to experience the lassitude of damp, moist heat which makes exertion a misery – this is different. And to retain, through all, your clearness of vision, capacity to weigh evidence, self-control and moral strength – this is to pass through the highest test of mental and physical endurance, to attain the most conspicuous of human achievement.[23]

To Gertrude, Casement exclaimed: 'The Putumayo Horror is out at last! I am bombarded with people trying to interview me!' And, in another letter: 'I've blown up the Devil's Paradise in Peru! I told you I should – and I've done it. It is a good step forward in human things – the abodes of cruelty are not so secure as they were and their tenants are getting very scared. Putumayo *will* be cleansed – altho' nothing can bring back the murdered tribes – poor souls.'[24] Horace Plunkett, with whom he dined shortly afterwards, was circumspect: 'Sir R.C. whom I had formerly met as a friend of Mrs J.R. Green dined. He is at the moment in the public eye, a report of his as to the treatment of the Indians by the British Rubber Co. in Peru having staggered humanity. Mrs Sellar and I both felt he would not be an altogether reliable chronicler of facts where emotion was significant.'[25]

Throughout the summer, Casement continued to monitor developments regarding the Putumayo. September, for example, saw a veritable flood of letters from him to the FO on Putumayo matters, some from Belfast and some from Falcarragh in Donegal, where he was visiting the Irish language college, Coláiste Uladh. Those concerned with bringing about reform, Casement among them, were exploring a number of possible approaches. Some focused on control of rubber exports from the Putumayo. Casement suggested that, if two competent inspectors were placed in the key rubber stations, methods of rubber extraction could be certified at source. More radically, should Peruvian cooperation not be forthcoming, it was again suggested that Brazil might play a part by monitoring rubber exports, since all Peruvian shipments had to travel through Brazilian territory. Reacting to one of these despatches, a FO clerk minuted: 'Sir R. Casement's despatches make one's head go round. They are so full of incident. I do not think there is anything very new in all this.'[26] In fact there was. His despatch was cogently argued and the FO minute reflects badly not on Casement but on the FO itself. It dealt with a raid by Peruvian Amazon Company employees on the Colombian settlement at La Union in January 1908, which was an important event. It happened after the company was incorporated in London, therefore the action was one by a British company; the rubber confiscated from it was sent to London as a PAC product; at another level, it showed how the PAC, through Arana, was the only effective Peruvian presence in this disputed border territory with Colombia. The perpetrators of this event were arrested, but then released. Casement's efforts were to document the event clearly and to try to assess conflicting Peruvian and Colombian versions.

In July, the same month as the publication of the Blue Book, George Michell had been instructed by London to visit the Putumayo. He and the US consul, Stuart Fuller, began their journey from Iquitos almost immediately, but word soon filtered back to the FO that they had been joined by Rey de Castro, Arana and Zumaeta. Throughout September and October, Casement worried about the effects of the chaperoning on the consuls' work.[27] After the completion of their tour, Michell submitted his report on 14 October, describing in it the attempts of the accompanying company officials 'not to let us see anything but the good side which it was wished we should see':

> No evidence of cruelties now being perpetrated came to our notice, the policy of the company under Señor Tizon's management having been changed for the better. But the dispositions of the Government for the securing of justice and good treatment have hitherto been entirely inadequate, and the new arrangements are not yet developed enough to be able to judge of their results. Consequently the fate of the Indians lies almost wholly in the hands of a commercial concern, the future of which is very doubtful, and whose action may have to change with its fortunes. The present fairly satisfactory state of things depends very largely upon the continuance of the policy of the company's present agents at La Chorrera and El Encanto, and on the development, faithful application, and maintenance of the new proposals of the Peruvian Government. The financial condition of the company, the poverty of the Putumayo district, the critical situation of the Amazon rubber market, and the financial and political exigencies of the administration at Lima are grave difficulties in the way of the practical carrying out of the reforms.[28]

Though he was soon to cooperate with the Parliamentary Select Committee on the Peruvian Amazon Company, Casement's active role in the campaign was winding down by the end of 1912. Overall, the campaign had less success than that on the Congo. Despite considerable investment, European involvement in Latin America was much less than in Africa, where all the major Powers were competing. There was no international agreement covering the Putumayo, for example, in the way the Berlin Agreement governed recognition of the Congo Free State. European Powers and Britain, in particular, deferred to US primacy in Latin America. Nor was the British government put under as sustained pressure regarding the Putumayo as it had endured in the case of the Congo. Despite the endeavours of the Anti-Slavery Society and others, they did not compare with Morel's campaign for the Congo; neither did the ASS have the missionary support available to Morel as a campaigning resource. The Putumayo, too, was geographically peripheral, even within Peru, and a disputed border territory; the system of abuses, awful though it was, was less clearly a policy of the state, though PAC control in the area suited Peruvian interests.

'A Colony of Compassion': A Catholic Mission

The establishment of a Catholic mission to the Putumayo was one initiative, independent of whatever reforms the Peruvian authorities were willing to implement, that appeared to Casement to offer positive hope of improvement. His reading of South American history had made him sympathetic to the work there of Catholic missionaries, such as the Jesuits and Franciscans. And his reading of the politics of Peru convinced him of the wisdom of working within the Catholic ethos of that country. In late January 1912, Msgr Bidwell, chancellor to the diocese of Westminster, wrote to him to say that he had got a reply in November from Cardinal Merry del Val regarding questions submitted to him by Bidwell, following a conversation with Casement. Could Casement, he wondered, call to discuss the issue?[29]

He reopened contacts, early in February, with Randall Davidson, the (Anglican) Archbishop of Canterbury. Writing on 6 February, the Archbishop told Casement that he had thought much about the matter and consulted others. He had grave difficulties regarding the suggested action on a Catholic mission and asked if Casement could call to discuss them.[30] An appointment was arranged and the two met at the end of February. Not long afterwards, Casement wrote saying that he appreciated the Archbishop's problems, but that the mission must be Catholic, though with humanitarian motivation – a 'colony of compassion', as he now tended to call it in the words of the Nonconformist leader, the Revd F.M. Meyer. 'I am hopeful that the main object in view, the betterment of the lot of the wild Indians in those regions, will commend itself warmly to all humane hearts in this country and in Ireland.'

Writing a second time he enclosed a copy of a letter from Dora Meyer of the Pro-Indigena Society in Lima. Though herself a Lutheran, she felt that a Catholic mission was the only possibility: 'If it can be linked an industrial scheme for bettering the Indian lot and character it is perhaps the most that Christian friends of these poor people can hope to obtain.' The Archbishop responded warmly, but was unable to discount the denominational dimension. 'I rejoice', he wrote, 'to think of the effect which has already been produced by your own competent and painstaking study of the question on the spot. I imagine that it is true to say that no one else now alive could have done quite what you have done.' He 'cordially and earnestly' endorsed the proposal for a Catholic mission, but that was different from being a promoter or a sponsor. The philanthropic aspect was fine, but there were 'larger religious and inter-ecclesiastical questions, which hamper one's freedom'. He was anxious, however, to be kept abreast of developments.[31]

The period following his return to England from South America had been extremely busy. Writing to Travers Buxton at the beginning of March, Casement indicated his wish to get away to Ireland for a month after St Patrick's Day.[32] He was still in London, however, in April and told John Harris that he had been laid up for some days with a 'severe cold and cough ... I have not been out of London – save to the margins – since my return from the Amazon'. In mid April he was instrumental in having a committee formed to organize the collection of funds for the planned mission. Percy H. Browne, whom Casement described to John Harris as 'a nephew of the Marquess of Sligo and an Irish Protestant', was appointed as secretary to the committee. Casement, apparently, drafted a mission appeal document, which he showed to Bidwell. Tyrrell in the FO advised that he saw no problem in Casement's signing such an appeal, as long as he did so in his private capacity, omitting his consular title after his name.33

In the second half of April Casement did succeed in going to Ireland, and his letters to Harris were addressed from Belfast and Larne. He was, he told Harris, moving through the country until 1 May or later and expected to be back in London about the 5th. The mission appeal would be launched, he told him, as soon as the Blue Book was published, 'and with a widely representative Committee ... of all churches we go a long way to secure a Christian pre-eminently Mission rather than a purely dogmatic or propagandish one. I drafted the appeal which states this, and *all* the RC members present agreed willingly and spontaneously to that view – including Msgr Bidwell of the Cathedral – so that we [are] already fairly non sectarian!'34 But, at this point, the mission appeal draft aroused denominational hostilities, reminiscent of what had happened in the Congo. The Protestant churches had been prominent in the Congo campaign, both as missionaries in the Congo and as pressure groups at home; there was a tendency for Catholics to see these actions as indications of hostility to Catholic Belgium. Now Protestants were suspicious of a Catholic endeavour. Like Casement, the Revd John Harris was prominent in both campaigns. He had been a missionary in the Congo before returning to England to take up a position with the Congo Reform Association; now he worked for the Anti-Slavery Society on the Putumayo case.

Harris was clearly unwilling to leave the field to the Catholics in Peru. At first Casement held his ground, writing to Harris on the 26th to argue his case. He ended the letter, saying that he saw nothing to alter in the appeal and that the PAC commissioners supported him in this, 'none of whom is an RC ... I shall, therefore, advise Mr Browne, despite your view, that I hold entirely to the appeal as drafted'.35 However, the opposition played on his mind and, a few days later, clearly disturbed, he wrote in great detail to both Travers Buxton and John Harris, elaborating on the reasoning behind the need, as he interpreted it, for the mission to be Catholic. On 28 April, Buxton received the first of these, on the topic of a possible Protestant mission in Peru. Casement drew attention to the official status of Catholicism in Peru, making for a very different situation than in the Congo and other parts of Africa:

> The use of the word 'mission' by the Protestants in Peru is, to my mind, quite misleading. It is on a par with the application of the word to the Bible or

Scripture readers who are maintained in Galway, Mayo, and other parts of Western Ireland and is really very offensive there as it implies that Roman Catholics are not Christians. Where the Bible readers and other Protestants are now settled in Peru they are in an entirely Roman Catholic country and their efforts are concentrated on getting the Bible into the hands of Roman Catholics.

To attempt to introduce a Protestant mission would set the cause of reform back: 'Not only would the local authorities interfere and prevent them going on, but local feeling would be worked up to the highest pitch of excitement (in which, doubtless, local priests of the Established Church of Peru would take an active part) and instead of the body of Protestant workers doing good they would be the innocent means of bringing about a wholly impossible situation.' Whatever hope there was lay with a Catholic mission.

A Roman Catholic Mission, if successfully founded on the Putumayo, could, and I believe would, do great good, and to protect the Indians I can think of no other external agency that can be trusted. The Putumayo is not like the Congo – it is not open by Treaty to all, but a closed demesne privately owned by a band of murderers and pirates and it will take all the power and authority of Rome working on the Lima Government and local hierarchy to get even a strictly Roman Catholic mission into the country.

He acknowledged his own role in drawing up the appeal – 'I am responsible for the wording of the appeal' – but the committee involved

were of opinion that we should have only laymen as the signatories. They agreed with me that it might be signed by members of various religious communities – so as to appeal to as many as possible ... Unfortunately, I fear, there are a lot of people who under no circumstances would view any effort directed from Rome or in conjunction with Roman Catholics as Christian effort and their objections I fear I can do nothing to meet. It is not likely any of those people would help our effort in any case.[36]

On the following day, John Harris got an equally long cry from the heart. Speaking of Protestant organizations already in Peru, he warned:

To transfer some of these men, or their definitely anti-Roman Catholic propaganda from the Andean or Coast regions of Peru into the heathen wilderness – the Putumayo – would not be to my mind to introduce a helping factor but to provide a situation of extreme difficulty and to beget, in addition to the powerful existing opposition of the *caucheros* or rubber pirates, the active resentment and hostility of organised Roman Catholic institutions on the Upper Amazon. These would join the Aranas in representing this intrusion of Protestantism as a foreign invasion – and all that is already said at Iquitos as to the campaign against the Aranas being due to foreign greed and English commercialism desiring to secure the 'rich' lands of the Putumayo for itself would then be enormously strengthened by the Established Church and clerics of the region joining the bandits.

I don't think, for a single instant, that a Protestant mission of that kind, or I fear of any kind, if sent as a mission on religious grounds would get into the

Putumayo – or within a 1000 miles of it. It might be possible to get an Industrial Mission, on purely industrial and wholly non-sectarian lines, into the Upper Amazon but even to that there would be great difficulty and certain delay. The fate of the Indians is pressing – their need is urgent. The *only* body in the world that can come to their help quickly is the Church of Rome. Of that I am profoundly convinced. It is – in Peru – the existing church of the country, the State and the people. It has unchallenged ecclesiastical control – granted that locally the Church has fallen away – or that its priests in Peru are very often not good men. That, if we put aside prejudice, has nothing to do with the case. It is not on those priests or the local backsliders the new mission will count. The Church of Rome has many good men – great humanitarians too – and it is prepared to put forward good men for this definite task ... The Head of that organisation, the Pope – a sincere and holy Christian surely – is profoundly moved at the lot of these people and hears the call and is willing and anxious to help. My view is that all humane men irrespective of creed could and should help this organisation which is willing to tackle the evil ...

Peru is the most bigoted of all the South American republics. Her Government, once the Report is published, will clutch at any straw to obscure the truth and the real issue – and the opposition of Iquitos would take forms of violence that Lima would not attempt – but would surely encourage. The whole thing would end in disaster – and while the Protestants would certainly not get into the Putumayo they might very well defeat the Papal attempt to send good men there and begin a reform that may spell great things for the remaining Indian tribes of that unhappy region.

Even on this topic his thoughts turned to Ireland: 'If I could get three kindly Irish Catholics out on the Putumayo with the power of the Pope behind them, I'd back them against Julio Arana and Pablo Zumaeta and the whole gang!' He wondered how he could accommodate Harris's viewpoint: 'I have been thinking all the morning of how to draft another appeal inviting responses for a dual mission – but I don't know how to start it. My feeling is so strong that only one Church *can* tackle this thing that I don't know how I can help in asking Protestants to go in as Protestants. They are fish out of water there.' His attitude was bolstered by his reading on Latin American history: 'The Jesuits very nearly saved the Indian tribes of the Amazon – and were driven out because of their humanitarianism conflicting with the greed of the Portuguese slavers. Any similar band of resolute, good Catholics got into the Putumayo could, even now at the eleventh hour, save the remnant of the Indians I think – altho' it is almost a forlorn hope.' Unable to end his flow of thoughts, he added a postscript, in which he viewed the broader political situation of Latin America:

You know me quite well enough to know that I have no axe to grind. I only want the one thing – the easiest and readiest way of helping those poor, hunted people – of bringing *some* ray of hope into their lives. I see no other way than this one I have put before you in the appeal – none at all. The only other way is to challenge the Monroe Doctrine – proclaim the right of Europe to actively intervene in South American affairs, and invite Germany as the Mandatory of Humanity and European Civilisation to occupy the Amazon and Teutonise it –

which, incidentally, might mean to Protestantise it! Are you game for that? I am. As a man – but not as a British Consul. It wouldn't save the Indians either. It might be, and I believe would be, the right thing for Christian civilisation to adopt (and still more for British interests) but it could only begin to work, after much turmoil and many years of strife. Someday it may come – please God. Meantime, there are the unhappy Huitotos ('the spectres' of Dr Paredes' compassionate heart) the mutilated Boras, the burnt-alive Muinanes and all the other hopeless fugitive tribes, hunted, flayed alive, and outraged in every conceivable way. For God's sake let the Pope have a first try at it and *help* him too. That's my view. I see around me, here in Ireland, some of the best and kindliest and most Christian men on earth, with hearts aflame at cruelty, among the priests of the Church of Rome and I cannot see why the organisation that has such servants cannot find and send to the Putumayo men – like them, to help and encourage and fearlessly face the murderers and ruffians.

Later the same day, the matter clearly troubling him a great deal, Casement wrote a second time to Harris, toying (though clearly reluctantly) with the possibility of a dual appeal, one component being for a Catholic mission, which could be activated quickly, and a second for a non-sectarian industrial or medical mission to be organized as soon as feasible. Two sets of sponsoring signatories could be attached. His fear was that they would fall between two stools, the Indians being the losers. He tried to make Harris aware of the hostility to any mission likely to be experienced in Iquitos:

> When I was in Iquitos in November last and spoke again to the Prefect about the possibility of a mission being sent by the Church of Rome with the Pope's blessing etc. etc. he preserved a stony silence – he never said a word but looked grim and forbidding. To give you an idea of what they *can* do in Iquitos – In 1910 when I was there a French-Dutch commercial expedition came with a steam launch to go on to Upper Amazon. They had the French Consul with them and letters of support even from the Peruvian Minister in Spain and ample bona fides and vouchers. They never got past Iquitos – and had to clear out of that inside of two months – under threats of being lynched and their steamer burnt. The officials took an active part in stirring up feeling against them and they lost practically everything and the company in Europe burst. All over jealousy and hatred of foreigners and suspicion that they were friends of Ecuador. Colombia is even more hated than Ecuador and an anti-Arana mission run by English influence on the Putumayo would be denounced as friendly to Colombia – and that would be enough. The Lima Government would not show their hand at all – but the Upper Amazon ruffians and their press in Iquitos would probably act even in despite of Lima.

But at the end of this second letter, Casement was clearly uneasy with the dual appeal idea and indicated a preference to proceed with the Catholic appeal, even if that meant some signatories being unable to attach their names. He concluded: 'When men begin talking about "their Church" I feel a sense of despair – and resign myself to the blessed paganism of my Irish forefathers, who denounced Patrick and his "bell ringing" as the first authentic grievance ever wrought on Erin.'[37] Upon his return to London from his visit to Ireland in April, he left immediately for a holiday with Dick Morten in Germany. They visited Strasbourg, Lake Constance, Nurenberg, Coblenz, Rottenburg, Wiesbaden, Heidelberg and Frankfurt.[38]

After his return to England, Casement talked about Germany to Ernest Hambloch, who came to visit him at the Mortens and left an account of their conversation. 'I have just come from there,' said Casement, 'I have been spending some time there, motoring through the principal towns and studying their municipal organization. They put a car at my disposal. They are magnificent organizers. You English have nothing to compare with what they do. They are a fine race.' With that, according to Hambloch, Casement clammed up on the topic.[39] Afterwards, Casement went to Cornwall with Nina and wrote to Spicer on 25 May from the Green Bank Hotel, Falmouth.

Meanwhile, the Putumayo Mission Fund committee had been working away at its task, led by its secretary, Percy Browne. The committee had been set up to raise the necessary finance. Casement met Fr Genocchi, the papal delegate associated with the mission, in mid June. Casement and Harris agreed to differ on the denominational question: 'I fully understand the position of yourself and your friends in the matter,' but 'I must retain my own conviction and act as far as I can upon it.'[40]

After the publication of the Putumayo Blue Book, the mission appeal went public. Browne wrote to Casement on 13 July, enclosing a dossier he was sending out to newspaper editors. The appeal letter was signed by the Duke of Hamilton, W.H. Goschen, W. Joynson-Hicks, the Duke of Norfolk and E. Seymour Bell. Count Blücher and George Pauling were to be treasurers and trustees of the fund. The dossier included a long letter of explanation from Casement and three short letters, justifying the need for the Catholic nature of the mission, one each from Mallet in the FO, from Cazes in Iquitos (who identified himself as Jewish), and from the three PAC commissioners, Bell, Fox and Gielgud.

The denominational issue refused to go away, however, and, within days, the Archbishop of Canterbury wrote to Casement saying that he had an offer of £1000 for a Protestant mission and that other offers were likely. Was it, he asked, wise to leave it in Catholic hands – what had they done to date? Casement's reply pointed out that Catholic missions, though underfunded, *did* protest abuses in the Peruvian Amazon, a matter which was documented, including in the Blue Book. 'I feel', he wrote,

> that a heavy responsibility lies on all of us to help those weaker human beings, victims of the unscrupulous greed of the age, which is an international vice of our time and our material civilisation – and that to bring them speedy help by the readiest means to hand is the duty of all men calling themselves Christians ... If England, which is far more responsible than Ireland for the 'trade' conditions on the Putumayo, cannot make up her mind to help such a mission as this, then I

must see what can be done by a *national appeal* to the Irish heart and conscience, both in Ireland and the USA, to wipe out this stain on our common Christianity.

The intention was, he concluded, to send out Irish Franciscans, then working in the slums of Dublin.[41] With only £2000 in and £15,000 needed, he complained to Morel of lies from various Protestant bodies about the appeal. 'I think there is mighty little Christianity in any of the "*Churches*" – a good deal of severe Heathenism would be good for mankind.'[42]

In a memo to the FO of 1 August he pointed out that the Vatican would 'bear a large share of the permanent cost of the Mission', but, for the rest, the appeal to date had brought in only £2000, while they had hoped for enough to give a permanent annual income of not less than £400.[43] In mid September, Casement was able to inform the FO that five Franciscans had been selected, two from Liverpool and three from London; 'Two Irish missionaries', he specified, 'may be added.' A few days later he reported that the missionaries would sail in November. He wondered whether they would be allowed to establish a mission: 'I am inclined to think they will be so bitterly opposed at Iquitos (by the Arana faction and others) that they will not be able to set up a permanent settlement at La Chorrera.'[44]

Concluding that the Peruvian government response was a charade, he felt there was nothing left but to encourage the mission: 'It will be the sole guarantee of any civilised mind, or humane human nature being in contact with the Indians.' It didn't seem much in response to the 'enormity of the crimes committed and the horror of the whole regime', but 'it is the only alternative to leaving the Indian tribes entirely alone and defenceless with their exploiters'.[45] On 9 October he wrote to Mallet to say that the mission was 'the last string to our bow'; Brazil had failed and the US was unlikely to take strong action. 'So, there we are, with less than £3000 in hand and the Mission announced to go; and, as I say, with really the most practical part of our effort at doing good embarked in that small company of good men.'[46]

Ireland and the Ulster Crisis

During the summer of 1912, Casement, as usual, busied himself about Irish affairs. In May he had received a request for financial assistance for his old school, now the Ballymena Academy, from J.A. Fullerton, a master there. 'I hope', he addressed Casement, 'that as perhaps the most famous of all the old boys of the Diocesan School you may think the scheme worthy of support.'[47] Casement replied tartly:

I fear it is not in my power to give you any substantial help, for I am already committed by promise to aid several educational movements in Ireland of a distinctively *national* character, which must have the first claim upon my sympathy and support. These are a Training College in Donegal – an Irish school in Galway and a school in Dublin (St Enda's) where the course of teaching is Irish throughout – that is, a course devised primarily to interest boys in their own country and make them good and useful citizens of it. Now from my own recollection of the old Diocesan School and from what I know of similar establishments in Ireland, their aim is not so much to fit a boy to live and thrive in his own country as to equip him for export from it.[48]

Casement was, indeed, taking an active interest in Pearse's St Enda's, as two letters he received that summer illustrate. One came from Alec Wilson in June, when the school was facing a financial crisis. Wilson talked of the school's accounts; it was difficult, he felt, to guarantee solvency ten years ahead, but there had been rapid development and the present success showed that the school 'fills a much-wanted place'.[49] In early September, Hugh Law wrote in response to a letter from Casement on St Enda's. His own help, he said, was conditional on the possibility of permanent success, which seemed unlikely given the 'load of old debts'.[50]

During the summer, Casement commenced a correspondence with Lady Constance Emmott.[51] His opening letter, written from the Savoy, where he spent a lot of the summer, began with an excuse for not visiting: 'I have not been in London since I last saw you, save for a few scattered hours at times and have given up living there since April ... I am now on the wing for Ireland – to Rathlin Island and the Glens of Antrim, as soon as I can get away from my present duties – and shall not be in London any more except to go to [the] Foreign Office.' He talked of a book:

> I have been reading *Loch Dhuairg* and wondering where the beautiful picture is – as I did not go to the Academy ... I wonder if you have ever read Carleton's *Stories of the Irish Peasantry*. They are extraordinarily moving; often horrible, pitiless and depressing yet with a fearful sense of truth about them. He did not love the Ireland of the pre-famine days, but he knows it and has depicted it ruthlessly – and there is something of Carleton, to my fancy, in *Loch Dhuairg*.[52]

He wrote again on 10 July, once more declining an invitation. He was due to leave for Ireland and hoped to visit her later in Scotland: 'It will be far nicer to be free to go to Argyle ... when you are there, and to have a delightful glimpse of Inverary and the Highlands – parts of the Gaelic world I have never seen.'

He explained to her, too, that he was 'very busy on some South African matters that are causing me trouble'. He had been approached for help that summer by both of his brothers, Charlie and Tom. Tom and his first wife, Blanche, had divorced. With his new wife, Katje, he now sought capital to buy a mountain inn at Rydal Mount, Witsieshoek, in the Orange Free State. Casement approached friends, including Cadbury, to support the venture and he, himself, borrowed on his life insurance to send more than £300.

The Cadbury family had planned a holiday in Ireland and a suggestion was made that they meet Casement in Bundoran.[53] He now planned a stay in Ireland, which would combine a short visit with the Cadburys, a stay in Belfast and Antrim, and a visit to Coláiste Uladh in Donegal. He crossed to Belfast in late July. On 1 August, he wrote to Gertrude from Belfast, reporting that he was leaving for Dublin that night and from there to Galway, Bundoran and Falcarragh.54 His tour took him first to Tawin and then on to meet the Cadburys. He was in a poor physical condition, as William Cadbury was to recall in 1916, 'so weary and depressed with recurring attacks of malaria that often he would stay in his room the whole day hardly eating or sleeping'.55

On 20 August, he wrote to Lady Emmott from Cloghaneely: 'I am in the far Northwest of Donegal in a very Irish speaking district where I am glad to hear the Gaelic constantly, and to find it well taught. There is a college here that I helped to get started some years ago and I have come back after five years away to find it going splendidly and the Irish language far more generally spoken – and proudly spoken – than before.' He sent her a printed circular of

> my Rathlin school idea too – which is not so far from Cantyre – I don't send it to you for a subscription – please don't think that – but merely to show you how widespread and growing is the movement to revive Irish. Miss Gough, the secretary of our Rathlin effort – is a Protestant of course and a niece of Lord Gough's. So here, in Donegal ... we have Protestants with us and taking a yearly growing interest in the work of the Gaelic League.56

On 1 September he wrote from the Falcarragh Hotel to Eamon De Valera in Tawin saying that he was 'going about a good deal' and that he had been on Tory Island recently. 'Here ... there is plenty of Irish too and the College is doing well.'57 Schools were largely bilingual and he wished that that at Tawin was.58 He also wrote several letters to Travers Buxton of the Anti-Slavery Society. Responding to a request for a photo for use in the Putumayo campaign, he sent one taken in Tory: 'Everyone save myself in the picture speaks Irish as their mother tongue. The old men, the girl next to me and the young man on the opposite side (brother and sister) are all wonderful Irish speakers, singers and dancers.' Should Buxton make use of it, 'you must include all the rest of the group – and you must call it "Sir R.C. at home on Torry Island, off the Donegal Cost, Ireland".'59 He sent photos, too, to Gertrude, who, with her sister Elizabeth, had been at Coláiste Uladh: 'The photos from Tory have turned out *splendid*. I will send you copies, as soon as the full supply comes from Dublin. Everyone (except poor Bessie) has come out well – you and Eilís and lots of others as clear as the Sun could make yous [*sic*].'60

His health seemed to deteriorate in Donegal and he referred to it in apologizing to Constance Emmott for another postponement of his hoped-for visit to Scotland.61 To Spicer at the FO he complained of 'a bad attack of lumbago ... I hope every day to be able to write – but I can't manage to sit up long and the pain of moving is so great that I just lie quiet on a made-up bed before a huge fire – trying an old Irish remedy – to drive the devil out by his own element!'

On 14 September, he told Gertrude that he was leaving Cloghaneely, 'glad in one way too as I shall go straight to Lucan Spa Hotel and take the rheumatic baths there. I am tired of being so stiff and sore and I *won't* go to Wales or Sasana or any other foreign country'.[62] In fact, he went to Belfast first, where political tensions had been steadily mounting.

Lloyd George's Finance bill of 1909 (the 'People's Budget') had been rejected by the House of Lords in November of that year, forcing the Liberals to go to the country. Two general elections had followed in 1910, in January and December, with similar results: the Liberals and Conservatives won an almost equal number of seats. The Liberals, who remained in power with the support of the nationalist Irish Parliamentary Party and of Labour members, moved to introduce a measure of Home Rule for Ireland as the price for the former's support. The restriction on the veto powers of the Lords introduced by the Liberal government would also, of course, limit the power of the upper house to undermine a Home Rule Bill.

Unionists, sensing the threat, began to mount determined opposition to the projected introduction of a Home Rule Bill. Impassioned speeches were made; unionists began making arrangements for the purchase of arms; a commission was established to draw up a provisional constitution for Ulster, should a Home Rule Bill be passed. A bill was, in fact, introduced on 11 April 1912, a modest measure, spurring Arthur Griffith to remark: 'If this is liberty, the lexicographers have deceived us.' Nonetheless, in July, at a major rally at Blenheim Palace, the leader of the Conservatives, Andrew Bonar Law, threatened force: 'I repeat now with a full sense of the responsibility which attaches to my position, that, in my opinion, if such an attempt is made, I can imagine no length of resistance to which Ulster can go in which I should not be prepared to support them.'[63] Civil disorder erupted on a number of occasions in Ulster and in June 1912 a suggestion was made at committee stage in the House of Commons to exclude four Ulster counties from the measure.

As a climax to the opposition campaign, Saturday, 28 September 1912 was set aside as 'Ulster Day', at which a covenant would be signed, pledging adherents 'to stand by one another in defending for ourselves and our children our cherished position of equal citizenship in the United Kingdom and in using all means which may be found necessary to defeat the present conspiracy to set up a Home Rule Parliament in Ireland'. With the maximum of ceremony, Protestants signed in their thousands. It was estimated that, in Ulster, a total of 218,206 men signed the covenant and 228,991 women the accompanying declaration.

Casement observed the quickening events from Donegal. On 18 September, writing to Gertrude, he referred to the Ulster Unionist council leader Edward Carson as 'the ugly brute'. A few days later, by now in Belfast, he described a Protestant parade: 'The Church Parade has begun past my windows – how appalling they look, with their grim, Ulster Hall faces ... I tremble at the piety

of this realm – this Ulster so bathed in the tears of righteousness – self-right-
eousness, so washed in Papish blood ... How truly Christian and kindly a spirit
inhabits the "Ulster" breast!'[64]

He was in Belfast on Covenant Day, as was his friend Henry Nevinson. On
the following day, Nevinson met Casement at his lodgings on the Antrim road
and they proceeded to Bigger's house: 'C was steeped [?] in hope for Ireland and
contempt for all this circus show,' wrote Nevinson in his diary. 'But for a pre-
occupation with himself, he would be the finest man I know. I think he is.'[65] A
more detailed view of Casement's reactions can be derived from a number of
letters he wrote to C.P. Scott, editor of the *Manchester Guardian*.[66] Earlier in the
year, Scott had asked Alice Stopford Green to recommend a correspondent on
the Ulster question and she suggested Casement. Scott duly wrote to Casement
on 18 April to ascertain if he would be willing to send reports on Ulster. He
must have consented, though the first evidence of him sending a report doesn't
come until the autumn. On 2 October he sent an eight-page letter to Scott from
the Gresham Hotel in Dublin. In it he expressed the opinion that

> in some ways, it is as well that Carson and his gang of bigots and bullies are
> going the lengths they are going in unscrupulous misstatement. It cannot really
> win sympathy or support in the end in England, and when the fact comes home
> to the bulk of Englishmen and Scotsmen that the sole argument against Home
> Rule is that Irishmen in the majority are Roman Catholics and *therefore* have no
> right to govern their country or rule their own affairs, they must turn in disgust
> from such a doctrine.

He had another objection beyond the denial of Home Rule to the majority:

> These people would make eternal the differences that separate Irishmen and
> would, till the end of time, keep one people divided into two hostile camps. Irish
> Nationalists claim, and claim rightly, that we are one people and that the differ-
> ences due to religion are transitory and can be effaced by direct contact and con-
> verse[ly], Irish Unionism says that under no circumstances will I ever enter the
> same room with you or discuss on terms of equality with you the affairs of our
> common country. Rather than that I would be governed by Germany, by any
> country so long as *my* 'religion' prevails. The whole thing is grossly irreligious and
> is indeed what I call it – an outrage on Christian civilisation itself.[67]

The following day, he sent a telegram, asking that the letter not be published, and followed it up with a long explanation of his action. He was following the advice of a friend, conscious of his status as public servant: 'I much
regret that I am debarred from taking a public part in defending my fellow
countrymen in Ireland who are so outrageously libelled by Sir E. Carson and the
Ulster bigots.' He suggested repeatedly that the ordinary people for whom he
had nothing but 'affection and respect' were being misled. Belfast was pervaded
by an atmosphere of intimidation:

> I do not think the conditions in Belfast can be realised by any Englishman. A
> very large body of Belfast people – certainly much more than one fourth of the

population, possibly more than one third even – are either warmly in favour of Home Rule or certainly not opposed to it. They scarcely dare to express their opinion in public – save, of course, the Roman Catholic centre in West Belfast. Some men whom I know to be Home Rulers were actually on the platform on Friday night at the Carson meeting. There is something of a reign of terror – it is not safe for a Belfast Protestant to differ from the majority. He can be hurt in a variety of ways.

His harshest words were reserved for the Ulster Covenant:

> The Solemn Covenant is, I believe, a criminal document for under an oath to God it is committing these sincere and ignorant men to the policy of very insincere and very unworthy men. Riot and outrage will have the sanctions of 'loyalty' and fealty to leaders whose word or hinted word will now come clothed with the sanctity of a religious command. The whole thing fills me with grief – for I see Ireland thrown back again for years to the barren and stultifying agitations of the past.[68]

To these two letters of Casement's, Scott replied that they were 'sorry not to print your letter because it is an excellent letter and says things which need saying', but that they appreciated the advice of Casement's friend. Could they, though, quote 'some bits & pieces', as coming from a correspondent? 'We do this from time to time ... But, of course, I will not do this if you would rather not. There's a lot of insincere and superficial stuff written about this Ulster business & what you write is so much the reverse.'[69]

Casement responded graciously, restating his difficulty as a public servant: 'You are most welcome to publish any bits of my letters (both of them) and in any way you think fitting – saving of course the signature.' Expressing a wish that the *Manchester Guardian* might be pushed more in Ireland, he went on to talk of the character of newspapers in Ulster and recommending the journalist, James Windsor Good:

> It is indeed strange to contrast the democratic and liberal utterance of the *Irish News*, a Catholic organ, with the anti-democratic, anti-Christian anti-human narrowness of vision and selfishness of mind of the two Unionist papers – the *Newsletter* and the *Whig*. There is a man on the staff of the latter named Goode who is really a trained journalist and writes very good stuff (on the sly) for Nationalist organs. He is, of course, a Nationalist – and is wasted on such an organ of the bigoted ascendancy as the *Whig*. I should like to put him in touch with your paper, if it were possible.[70]

Not long afterwards he must have penned some scathing remarks about Carson to Mitchell Innes in Washington, which spurred Innes to protest:

> Steady on, my dear Casement, steady on with your denunciation of poor Carson. The accounts I hear of him from an intimate friend of mine at the bar who knows Carson and his work well, are very different from yours. *He* tells me of a man of the highest honour, who, though a strong fighter, is full of human feeling and sympathy, a man to be trusted in all things; while you call him a cross between a jackal and a bloodhound, dishonest, a Castle hack, a man who would

dip his hand in Irish blood, if briefed enough. You do not mean it all, of course; and Carson, no doubt, says similar things of you and your party which he too does not mean. But you lash yourselves with your own eloquence, till the pain makes you forget everything else. No one understands himself; how, then, can he understand others. That which to you is natural and right, to Carson is intolerable and wicked.[71]

War in the Balkans

On a very different front, mounting tensions erupted into war in the Balkans in late 1912. The Ottoman Empire was dissolving. While Turkey was preoccupied defending Tripoli against an invasion by Italy, the independent states of the Balkan region (Greece, Bulgaria, Serbia and Montenegro), newly united into the Balkan League, took the opportunity to attack the remaining Turkish territories in Europe. The Turkish armies crumbled rapidly, barely retaining the toehold of Adrianople, west of Constantinople. A peace brokered by the Great Powers was finalized in London in May 1913.

Casement's sympathies were more with the Turks than with their Balkan attackers. He shared his thoughts with C.P. Scott:

> The horrible state of things in eastern Europe by which 'Christianity' is being used for a cloak to unbridled action against a whole people whose chief sin is inefficiency fills me with disgust. I am profoundly sorry for the Turkish people and I do not think this dreadful appeal to wholesale murder has any sufficient justification in their misdeeds. If every Great Power were to be called on to pay for its sins of omission and commission as dearly as Turkey is being called on to pay for theirs – which would escape?

He agreed that it was inevitable that Turkish rule had to end, 'but I object to the method employed and the hypocrisy and mendacity accompanying it. The real criminals are far more the Great Powers – and when a man is down as Turkey is down it is a loathsome thing for onlookers to run in and kick him'.[72]

The Putumayo Select Committee

On 14 March 1912, a select committee of the House of Commons had been established with a double brief: 'to inquire whether any responsibility rests upon the British directors of the Peruvian Amazon Company in respect of the atrocities in the Putumayo district, and whether any changes in the Law are desirable to prevent the machinery of the Companies Acts being used in connection with similar practices in Foreign countries'. Charles Roberts MP was selected as chairman of the committee of fifteen. Between March 1912 and publication of its report on 5 June 1913 the committee held a total of thirty-six sittings (a number in camera) and interviewed twenty-seven witnesses. Because of the seriousness of the charges, evidence was taken on oath and some of the witnesses were represented by counsel.

Roberts instructed the members to distinguish between the periods before and after the appearance of the *Truth* articles, as their publication had brought the possibility of atrocities directly to the attention of all concerned. The final report, in fact, was to take the existence of atrocities as given, merely summarizing the general picture to provide context for the specific tasks of the committee. Atrocities had been authenticated, it held, not only by Casement's report, but by that of Dr Paredes and by earlier evidence, such as that of a US consul, Dr Eberhardt,[73] and that of Hardenburg, Whiffen and various publications on the Amazon region.[74]

Casement appeared before the committee on 13 November and on 11 December. He was questioned at length, most of the fifteen members present on the day participating. Roberts led off and, having clarified that Casement's expertise related to general matters rather than the two specific issues of the committee's brief, the questioning focused on the knowledge two of the PAC directors, Arana and Alarco, might have had of atrocities, subsequent to the company's incorporation in London in 1907. Casement pointed out that Arana was present on the Putumayo in 1908 during the raids on the Colombians; and that Eugenio Robuchon's book, published in 1907, contained evidence of the system of rubber production on the Putumayo, including the payment of commission to agents for the amount of rubber produced.[75] Evidence on *correrias*, slave-raiding expeditions to acquire Indian workers, was available, too. 'The system,' Casement stated, 'I should attribute to the company; the individual crimes were frequently excesses of degenerate men who were employed in a responsible capacity.'

He was less specific on the knowledge and culpability of the British directors; Giclgud, he felt, had been made a fool of, and may not have been fully aware of what was going on. Casement responded to questions on his attendance at Peruvian Amazon Company board meetings during the summer of 1911. He outlined the ideas he had had for PAC-led reforms in the Putumayo, though any possibility of these happening went by the board when the company went into liquidation.[76] Committee members also asked questions about the nature of the roles of the FO and British consuls and about possible changes in the consular system to make it more responsive to abuses of labour.

Casement was upset when newspapers misreported his comments on the cognisance of the British directors and, in his second appearance, on 11 December, he went into considerably more detail on issues discussed during his attendance at board meetings and he submitted his records of these meetings to the committee. To illustrate the exploitative quality of the labour system, he also displayed to the members a number of those items given to Indians in return for rubber. These he had brought back from his first visit: a single-barrelled shotgun, a hat, a pair of pantaloons, shirt, belt, machete, flask of powder, fish-hooks and some beads. 'They are all things', he pointed out, 'of very trifling prime cost indeed, and of very inferior quality.' To the charge brought against himself in a Peruvian journal that he had tried to blackmail the company, he responded: 'It is, of course, absolutely untrue, and an absurdity.' In both sessions, he gave some indication that abuses such as those found on the Putumayo could also be found in other parts of South America. 'I believe,' he said, 'there are very wrongful things taking place in that great forest in connection with getting rubber, and I would say wherever there are wild Indians the same methods are employed.' And, when asked whether the Indians had any civil rights, he retorted: 'These people have absolutely no human rights, much less civil rights. They are hunted and chased like wild animals.'[77]

Health And Leave

Casement's health continued to be in a very debilitated state throughout the autumn of 1912. He had got to Dublin in October and from 55 Lower Baggot Street informed Louis Mallet: 'This address will find me until I go over to London. I have come here to see a doctor and get some treatment.'[78]

A month later, in London between select committee appearances, his health had deteriorated again, as he wrote to Lady Emmott:

> ... I am stuck in London for the moment over official things – but I leave for Ireland on Saturday next I hope. This place is impossible – and *I* am impossible at present. I cannot see people at all – or talk civilly even – and am longing to be told by the FO that I am free to get away abroad altogether ... I am like a bear with a sore head and every evening I get into impossible attitudes with my feet on sofas and cushions – often on the hearth rug! – and simply wait for bed time with a heart and conscience at war with all mankind. Joking apart I don't think there is anything for it, in my case, but to go abroad to the sun as soon as I can.

Two days later, responding to Lady Emmott's persistent invitations to visit, he told her that he was in a depressed state of mind:

> ... should I come it would be in my day clothes, for owing to my abominable mood I do not change my clothes for dinner and have refused every single invitation involving 'civilised' man's starched garb at nightfall. There is first the chance of not being able to leave at all on Saturday for Ireland in which case I should hope to call on you on Monday afternoon at tea-time but you will find me a very forbidding guest – 'dour and litigious to a degree' as an old Antrim peasant once described the Scots to me in my boyhood ... This dreary cold and deep, forbidding gloom is the longest spell of cold I've had since I was a child.[79]

Statements made by friends on Casement's behalf days before his execution in August 1916 shed further light on his condition at this time. Alice Stopford Green made one of these, in which she wrote:

On his return from the Putumayo he was evidently extremely ill. He was constantly unable for days to leave his lodgings from excessive pain in the back. On other days he would crawl to my house almost bent double with pain, and I could scarcely arrange a position in which he could sit or lie with any ease, generally on two very large easy-chairs. I attributed his depression and nervous irritability to the pressure of constant and severe pain, and difficulty of movement.[80]

Sidney Parry testified similarly about Casement's condition in late 1912:

I have known Casement off and on for a period of 20 years. Whenever I met him I found him well-balanced and reasonable during those years. However, during the trial of the Putumayo Directors, I visited him in his rooms in Ebury Street, and I found him suffering from severe mental strain, in a highly nervous condition, and quite incapable of discussing anything but the horrors of his investigations with which he seemed to be obsessed.[81]

Dr Charpentier of Uxbridge also wrote in 1916, saying that he had attended Casement in December 1912: 'He was very ill, suffering from severe pains in the back and side.' Charpentier thought he had 'renal calculus' and referred him to Dr Thompson Walker. The x-rays showed an absence of calculus 'but the presence of spicules of bone – arthro-arthritis – which accounted for the pain'. Sir Lauder Brunton, Alice Stopford Green's brother-in-law, also examined him and explained (for the FO): 'I found him suffering from congestion of the liver, feeble circulation, gastro-intestinal catarrh, and so much irritation and tenderness over the appendix as to render it questionable whether he ought not to have the appendix removed.' Hearing of his illness, Henry Nevinson wrote in sympathy: 'I have never heard of this disease, and did not know it was possible. It sounds horribly painful and depressing. Do please let me hear at once when they know the result of the X-rays.' [82]

It is somewhat surprising, then, given his physical condition, that Casement should have written to the FO on 14 December, requesting permission to withdraw his application for sick leave. Algernon Law and Tyrrell both replied, the former to say that Grey concurred in his immediate return to Rio. Tyrrell repeated the message, adding that there was no offer of a change at present.[83] It is difficult to believe that Casement had any intention of returning at this point to Rio and he may merely have been trying to force the FO's hand to give him an alternative posting. At any rate, on the day after the FO replies were written, he wrote to Roberts, saying: 'I may be forced to go away in a few days and may not be able to see you again ... Make it this week, however – as I am getting seedier and seedier daily and *must* lie up very soon and sweep all this off my mind.' And, in a second letter on the same day:

I am not going back to Rio yet I think. It was not promotion or anything – merely notification that I was returning to the post I have filled for several years. However the doctors have intervened and I gather, so far, they will certainly not sanction my return to Rio, or any unhealthy climate, unless I wish to die there ... I have to be with two doctors tomorrow and probably Sir Lauder Brunton on Thursday. [84]

A few days later, he told Roberts the results of the doctors' examinations:

I got the two medical opinions this morning – the specialist on the kidney (Dr Thompson Walker), after full study of the 'skiagram' or X-ray photograph, says there is no trace of kidney trouble after all and he attributes my increasing pain to inflammation of the bony tissues of the spine caused as he judges by poor and insufficient food – which has brought on a great deal of indigestion and intestinal trouble. He is prescribing a certain course of treatment and diet etc. which of itself will preclude my return to the tropics ... Sir Lauder Brunton ... sticks to his appendicitis fear – and both of them entirely prohibit my going out to Rio. I shall now arrange with my own doctor, and if they do not prohibit it, I shall go to Las Palmas at once in the Canary Island. Dr Thompson Walker thinks the treatment alone will last for four months – and doubts somewhat if I shall find permanent cure – so that I may be laid up for a long time. I have felt this coming on me for some time, but I have been so strong (and reckless) I never gave heed to it.[85]

The FO, for its part, granted three months' extension of leave, subject to the provision of doctors' certificates.[86]

Obviously in an uncertain frame of mind about the future, Casement consulted John Hartman Morgan, a Welshman whom Casement had probably met through Dick Morten.[87] Morgan was professor of constitutional law at University College, London, and influential in Liberal circles; he took a keen interest in the Home Rule proposals for Ireland. 'I am in bad need of some friendly counsel – from one like yourself,' wrote Casement. 'My future depends on the decision I come to in the next few days – and I do not want to leap impetuously or follow my impulse alone ... I am in great doubt how to act – and in much trouble of mind.' He went on to discuss his poor health and asked if Morgan would come to lunch next day – Morel was already coming.[88] Whatever the outcome of their meeting, Casement pressed on with his plan to go to the Canary Islands. He wrote again to Morgan on Christmas Eve, 1913, saying he would be sailing for Las Palmas on 27 December.[89]

PART V
Ireland and Germany

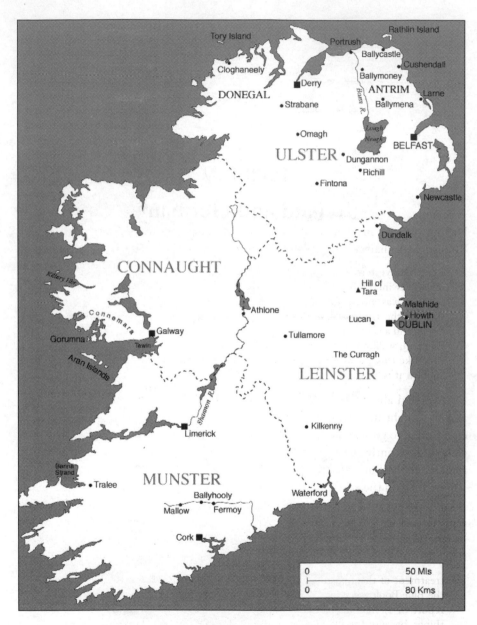

Map 8: Ireland

15: *Ireland, 1913–14*

Having arrived in the Canaries, Casement wrote a long letter to Charles Roberts MP, chairman of the select committee on the Putumayo atrocities:

> I got here yesterday after a bad enough voyage of 7 days from Dover – for this malady is increasing fast and I am now almost crippled. The earlier medical opinion was all wrong and the treatment wrong and it was only the x-rays showed the true source of my trouble. *Arthritis* of the hip and lower spine bones and a very painful thing indeed. I've been in bed practically since leaving England; walking is so painful. The doctor here thinks I may be a very long time like this and is not sure I shall be able to get rid of the disease – he says anyhow it is 'now or never' – for I have, by neglect, let it get a hold on me.

Worried about FO commitment to the Putumayo issue, he suggested that Roberts might introduce into his report 'an opinion that shall compel the Foreign Office to go further. If left to themselves they will let Putumayo drop gradually and decently', with 'assurances' from the Peruvian government. 'You must remember the Putumayo affair has been practically a one-man affair – my own. I must tell you the truth – so that you may understand – and you will acquit me I know from anything like boasting ... Grey was upset and troubled at the reports and sent me personally – but I *far* exceeded my instructions. I had *no* instructions to investigate the treatment of the Indians at all.' He pointed out that the sentence in his original instructions dealing with the

> treatment of the Indian labourers of the company was interpolated just before the Blue Book was issued in May 1912 so as to explain how I came to send in the report of 17 March 1911, which is the atrocity report ... Now I tell you these things, because I want you to fully realise that the carrying through of the Putumayo question was a personal thing and once the personal factor goes the matter will, of necessity, relapse into the ordinary routine methods of diplomatic effort.

He concluded: 'Remember I was not the FO's selection. I saw the list of names by chance that had been laid before Grey, departmentally, by the official in charge at FO & I was not on it. They fear my Congo record!'[1]

He was to remain a month in the Canaries, moving around the islands and keeping in regular touch with Roberts and the affairs of the select committee. On 27 January he sent Roberts his Putumayo Journal, the detailed handwritten day-to-day record of his investigation, which he had kept from 26 September to 6 December 1910:

> I had it with me, but have not read it for two and a half years! ... Naturally there is in it something I should not wish anyone to see – but then it is as it stands ... As a diary it must be read in conjunction with the evidence of the Barbados men, which ran concurrently with much of it. Also I have two notebooks in which are other portions of the diary and sometimes letters are to go in when I had left blanks. The value of the thing, if it has any value is that it is sincere and was written with (obviously) never a thought of being shown to others but for myself alone – as a sort of aide-memoire and mental justification and safety valve.[2]

From a distance, he followed carefully the examination of Gubbins, Lister Kaye and Read before the select committe, pointing up what he considered to be distortions when he found them. He was warm in his praise of Roberts: 'I must congratulate you warmly on your conduct of the latter examination. You have got out an enormous lot of evidence and information from the accounts of the Coy ... You already know *far* more about the P.A. Co. and its methods and finance in two or three months – than all the directors put together in four years.'[3]

While in the Canaries he also read Alice Stopford Green's *Old Irish World* and complained to her that, while all mediaeval conquerors had later apologized for their deeds, not so the English in Ireland:

> The Spaniards in Peru, for instance, even in the first heat of the conquest and enslavement of the Indians produced many historians and writers who, even then, saw the wrong inflicted and deplored it. Today, no Spanish Peruvian but, in speech, denounces the crimes of the conquest and uplifts the memory of the murdered Incas. He is proud to call himself by an Inca name – Huascar or Atahualpa – and to identify himself, so far as he can, with the past of the country.

The same was true in the Canaries, where the original inhabitants, the Guanchas, conquered in the fifteenth century, were now honoured.[4]

In another letter, his mind wandered over a wide range of topics: the Balkan war, the Derry election, the Irish Party and British politics, letters he had got from master and pupils in his old Ballymena school, Morel's silence. His thoughts on nationality led him to reflect on the Boers: 'I am sending lots of things out to the Dutch fighting in South Africa for their language,' he told her.[5] On 30 January, writing to Roberts, he returned to the topic of his health and the immediate future. He was 'getting better' and might go off 'on a voyage to the Cape to see my brother'. The local doctor warned that to go back to Rio 'will be my death' and that he should be shut up on a desert island for six months in the sun, with no post or letters. A few days later, on 2 February, his plans to go to South Africa began to firm up: 'I've practically made up my mind to got to the Cape this week ... this may be my last letter on Putumayo for some time.'6

Besides writing from the Canaries to Roberts and to close friends, he also maintained contact with the FO. On 14 January he complained to Tyrrell about being put on half pay, about the withdrawal of his local allowance and about the expenses he had incurred over the Putumayo.7 Perhaps in response to this, Dufferin wrote on 29 January enquiring about his health and informing him of a proposed increase of £350 in his office allowance. On 6 February he informed Roberts that he was leaving for the Cape the following day on the *Grantilly Castle*: 'Doctor approves warmly.'8

In the course of the voyage, he wrote to Alice Stopford Green for pamphlets on the Irish language and nationality for the Cape Dutch: 'I am giving a copy of your *Nationality* to General Hertzog.'9 Almost exactly a month later, having arrived in Cape Town, he resumed his concern with the affairs of the select committee. He wrote to Roberts, 'I am here a few days on my way to my brother's place in the Drakensberg in the Free State – I got the Minutes of Evidence (Nos. 16 & 17) of 29 & 30 Jany – the other day here.' After some comments on the content, he added: 'I was lunching y'day with the Gladstones at Govt. House & the talk was all the time on Putumayo and your Committee too and what would be the outcome. FO have given me leave till 31 May. I am much better since I landed in Cape Town. The sun and warm air are doing wonders together and I am beginning to feel quite my old self. It is very hot.'10 The following day he wrote to say he was going that day to Durban and on to his brother.11

He had learned on arriving in South Africa that Julio Arana was to go to London. If he had realized this, he told Roberts, he wouldn't have come to South Africa.12 Two days later he was analysing further pieces of testimony from the London hearings, including that of Parr, the young English accountant at La Chorrera, and that of Dr Dickey. He was caustic on the latter: 'Take Dr Dickey's letter in favour of Arana – you see how worthless it really is. Dickey is an unscrupulous rascal probably and wrote that letter for a consideration. His conversation with me was *entirely* against Arana and the whole system.'13

At the end of March, he told Roberts that he intended leaving South Africa in mid April and expected to be in London by May.14 Conditions in South Africa stimulated some comparisons with Ireland, which he shared with Gertrude. Hertzog, he felt, was 'the best of them out here. He is the Dutch Parnell of sorts – sees clearly what the English mean by "conciliation" (the giving up by the Dutch of everything while the English, of course, give up nothing)'. He talked to her, too, of the select committee and Arana's appearance:

'If *he* is whitewashed there is no one who cannot raid Indians and Niggers with impunity henceforth and for ever.'[15]

Early in April, Casement began his return journey to Europe. Back in London in May, he continued his correspondence with Roberts: 'Here I am back again – today only ... I am much better – but I fear unlikely to return to active service in Brazil. I do not feel equal to the drudgery of a Consulate office in that climate and surrounding and I doubt if the doctors will sanction my return. I am sure you must hate the name of Putumayo, so no more.'[16] By now somewhat restored in spirit and body, he was, nevertheless, quite unsure what course of action to take with regard to his future. In a letter to J.H. Morgan he revealed that his 'mind was still in fluctuation' about severing links with the FO, not only for himself, but 'for all the obligations I have contracted'. The traditional respectable alternative of directors' fees he rejected: 'One must *earn* what one takes – and it is occupation as much as money or more than money my mind seeks. If I could see clear what to *do* with myself once I am free from Consuling I'd go tomorrow.' He was toying with the possibility of touring his old haunts in Africa, 'to record en passant how I found Leopold'. But Ireland, too, beckoned: 'Now that I am back I am obsessed by Ireland! I've been on the wing for Ireland all through the week ... I hope tonight shall see me crossing the Irish Sea.'[17]

He did cross to Dublin shortly. Writing to Gertrude from 55 Lower Baggot Street, which was to be his base for a month, he talked of his work translating Victor Hugo's 'Feuilles d'automne' and of meeting Douglas Hyde.[18] While in Dublin, too, he had his portrait painted by Sarah Purser, who worked on a commission from William Cadbury. Some weeks later, the work was complete: 'The portrait is finished. Thank goodness – ten sittings is enough to break a heart – It is very good indeed.' A few days later, he enthused; 'The portrait by Miss Purser is a *great* success. She calls it *Columcille in Iona*! So I *am* an Irish saint you see after all.' He still thought he would 'go out to Africa for a long spell'.[19] During this month in Dublin, he also lunched with Major John McBride and, revealing how far his views had changed since the days of the Boer War, in some respects at least, he suggested to Alice Stopford Green that the story of the Irish Brigade 'was a fine fight and should be told'.[20]

In early June, from Dublin, Casement shared his uncertainties about the future with Charles Roberts: 'My plans are so uncertain, because I am still in doubt as to what I shall do with myself. I do not want to return to Rio de Janeiro and the alternative is to resign from the service. This I think is the thing I shall do and in that case I should go out to South Africa again almost at once – as my brother needs me there very urgently ... ' He would be in London for a few days only on leaving Ireland, 'for my present thought is that after a visit to some friends in Galway to go off to South Africa – saying goodbye to the public service in doing so'.[21] With the select committee report on the verge of publication, Roberts returned some of Casement's photos to him: 'I have kept back two of them of which there are duplicates, for I want the reproduction of them, if I may have them. And I can't send through the photo of the woman starved to death.'[22] Casement received his photos and the report on his return to Dublin from a journey to Connemara. He replied on the 11th in praise of Roberts's work: 'The *Irish Times* today had a good leader on your report. I handed the copy you kindly sent me yesterday to the editor ... I think the Report excellent – and I heartily congratulate you on the very effective ending to a most prolonged and exhaustive examination.'

He told Roberts he would go to London, and on to South Africa by the end of June, free from public service: 'I have made up my mind not to return to Rio and to retire altogether rather than go back to that horrid life – and useless life in that unpleasant Brazilian city. I shall probably end ... by becoming a Negro – a kaffir chief on the Drakensburg.'[23]

Fever in Connemara, May–June 1913

In May of 1913 a serious fever epidemic broke out in the Connemara islands region. On the 9th, on two different pages, the *Irish Independent* carried the news in bold headlines, with photographs: 'Stricken Connemara District', 'Epidemic of Fever. Western Scourge. Typhus and Typhoid among Poor Peasants'. The newspaper continued to report on the outbreak during May and June, opening a subscription list on 15 May. One reader who reacted quickly to the story was Casement's sister Nina. From Berkshire, she wrote to the newspaper on 10 May, describing the occurrence as an outrage and complaining of official apathy towards what was a recurring sickness.[24]

It seems likely that it was through her that Casement became aware of the problem. At any rate, he submitted a letter to the *Irish Independent*, which appeared on 20 May, under the heading 'This "Irish Putumayo" ', and attributed the 'appalling state of things in Connemara' to the 'absence of anything like civilised government in that part of the world. Were this, in truth, a "united kingdom" the Press of its capital would contain some reference to a state of things so near its doors, but I have not seen a single word in any London daily, from *The Times* to the *Globe* or *Daily News* to the *Westminster Gazette* of this dire need of our plague-pestered "fellow-subjects" of Connemara'. He enclosed £10 from Colonel J. Kennedy, to whom he had spoken about the outbreak, and £5 from himself.[25]

In Dublin he made contact with Dr Seamus O'Beirne on 24 May, asking that he come to see him before he consulted with 'some important people'.[26] He sounded satisfied when, a few days later, he wrote to Alice Stopford Green that

> my 'grave indiscretion' in likening Connemara to the Putumayo has, after all, done *only good*. That is clear. No one I find reproaches me and all were secretly

glad – some openly so and at any rate widespread public attention has been called to the evil and wicked plight of those poor people – a remnant of Cromwellian civilisation sitting in the embers of the hell or Connaught then decreed the doomed Irish race.[27]

After his consultations in Dublin, Casement travelled to Connemara. The visit tore at his emotions. Back in Dublin, he opened Charles Roberts's letter of 6 June and jotted in the margin: 'Recd. in Dublin, on return from Connemara, 9 June 1913 at 11 pm very wet cold and *tired* with today's glimpse of the Irish Putumayo. Mavrone! The *White Indians* of Ireland are heavier on my heart than all the Indians of the rest of Earth.'[28]

He appealed to friends for help and soon responses were coming in – from Margaret Dobbs, among others.[29] Francis Cowper in Lisbon was moved. He had received Irish newspapers with Casement's letters 'depicting the dreadful condition of the poor starving inhabitants of Connemara':

> Your description of the sufferings of those poor people is truly heartrending and most pathetic, and written in your usual brilliant style. Alas, poor Ireland! ... Your mission in this world seems to be to bring to the light of day and unmask the infamies and oppressions of brutal men exercised over defenceless human beings for – *auri sacra fames* ['accursed hunger for gold'] – first the accursed Congo atrocities – then the diabolical tortures at Putumayo, and now the sufferings of your own poor countrymen ... In truth you are fulfilling your altruistic mission nobly.[30]

Responses came from further afield, notably from Buenos Aires, where £871 had been raised by September.[31]

Using the money collected, Casement organized a food-distribution scheme for children in Connemara schools. To Gertrude he wrote in mid July: 'The Connemara party leaves Galway today for Carraroe etc. in two motor cars to visit the schools ... and begin my free meals daily. Strictly on the Irish language and it alone.'[32] On 13 December, he was to receive a long letter from Jane Tubridy, a teacher in St MacDara's Infant School, Carraroe. She thanked him for a letter of his, but said she would have preferred a visit, as he would have enjoyed seeing the children at their 'daily feast'. The conditions of the scheme – prayers etc. in Irish – were being adhered to.[33] The collection of funds to continue the scheme was, in fact, to continue after Casement's death and in his memory.[34]

Judging from later developments it seems likely that the 'important people' that Casement mentioned to Seamus O'Beirne were people active in the cooperative movement. One such was Harold Barbour, member of a family engaged in the linen business in Ulster since the late eighteenth century and occupied in the cooperative movement with Horace Plunkett. On 16 June, Barbour wrote to Casement saying that he was trying to get people 'to act', mentioning Sir Horace Plunkett, Mrs Green, Dr Costelloe of Tuam and Dr Bigger in Dublin. Casement and Plunkett probably discussed the matter at this time, too.[35] And

E.A. Stopford, another co-worker of Plunkett's, wrote three times to Casement, outlining an improvement project.[36]

Meanwhile, Barbour was organizing a visiting party for Connemara. He was planning to include Douglas Hyde in a preliminary trip, because of his knowledge of Irish. Visits did take place and by November Barbour was reporting to Casement that their report was completed. It was later published in May 1914 in *The Irish Review* as 'The Connemara Islands', under the signatures of Barbour, Mrs Green, Douglas Hyde and Alec Wilson.[37]

Retirement

After his Connemara efforts, Casement returned to England, where he spent most of July and August at the Savoy with the Mortens. A decision on his future could be postponed no longer. After his return from South Africa, he had sought further leave until the end of June, backed up by a certificate from Dr Sigerson in Dublin; this had been granted.[38] Still unsure what to do, he wrote to Morgan for advice. He could, he told him, easily retire '& spend the next ten years ... in doing just those things I like best to try to do ... I don't know that I am justified in pleasing myself, or following an inclination ... I've got a month still to think of it – & I don't worry about it. Things always come right in the end – the fatal optimism of an Irishman I feel!'[39] On 29 June, he took the momentous step and wrote formally to Algernon Law and William Tyrrell, asking permission to retire, citing ill health.[40] Both replied, Tyrrell expressing his regret and asking for a visit, Law pursuing the necessary formalities, which included provision of medical evidence.[41]

On 6 August, Travers Buxton wrote on behalf of the Anti-Slavery Society, offering a vice-presidency to Casement:

> At the last meeting of our Committee it was unanimously resolved that you should be asked to accept the position of a Vice President of this society. It is my pleasant duty to convey this invitation to you, with the hope that you will do us the honour of accepting the post. You have already done such notable service to the cause of freedom for native races that it seems only fitting that you should, if you will, be connected with our Society. I append a copy of the formal Resolution.[42]

Not unexpectedly, given Casement's attitude to honours and publicity, he hesitated. When he wrote to Spicer at the FO a little later, to talk of his retirement and the Putumayo, he told him of the offer: 'I have not yet replied and feel strongly indisposed to accept the honour, if I can do so on civil grounds.'[43] He replied to Buxton at the end of August:

> I have deferred answering it from uncertainty of movement and some doubt as to my future that must necessarily influence my decision. This uncertainty

still continues so that I find myself unable to do more today, while reserving a decision as to acceptance or otherwise of your invitation, than to thank you and the Committee of your Society for the honour they do me in asking me to become one of its Vice-Presidents. I much appreciate the invitation you have conveyed to me in such cordial terms and I trust I may soon be able to give you a definite answer to the formal Resolution you were so good as to forward with your letter.[44]

During August, the terms of his pension payment were clarified with Law and other FO officials. The initial Treasury arrangement would have left him one month without pay, which he sarcastically drew attention to: 'The Treasury, unlike Nature, does not abhor a vacuum.'[45]

He had been telling most of his associates of his intention to return directly to South Africa.[46] Gardiner was one of those; when Casement wrote to him in mid July, he said: 'Read inclosed – it gives you an idea of why there are strikes on the Rand and you may care to quote this case of how the Money bags tried to smash a Labour paper. I am going out to South Africa very soon to live there altogether.' His departure seemed imminent, and he promised that he would see Gardiner before leaving; he was, however, rushed, and had to get packed and off by the 26th.[47] In the event, early August found him in Paris, visiting the Wards: 'I am with Herbert Ward and Sarita,' he told Gertrude, giving details of his touring. Thinking, perhaps, of Cloghaneely, he reflected on the fate of the Irish language, commenting: 'I wonder, oh! I wonder if Irish will ever come back! I fear not – I fear it is a too difficult tongue to begin with to replace the easy, illogical, English.' But already, without his usual activity, he was bored: 'Everyone in life should have work that *must* be done.'[48] Thinking of his friend's future, J.H. Morgan wondered later in the month if he should put in a good word for Casement at the FO, or perhaps with Fitzmaurice? Casement, he felt, deserved 'a governorship of one of the Crown Colonies'.[49]

Ulster, Autumn 1913

The affairs of Ireland were very soon to fill the lacuna that had appeared in Casement's working life. Tensions in Ulster had been steadily mounting. In November 1912 the Home Rule Bill had passed through the House of Commons, for the first time, only to be defeated in the House of Lords in January 1913. In January, at the AGM of the Ulster Unionist Council, a decision was taken to combine local groups of anti-Home-Rule volunteers into a united Ulster Volunteer Force of some 50,000 men. By the summer of 1913 the military organization of the UVF was well advanced. Despite Unionist opposition, the Liberal government, with the full commitment of the nationalist Irish Parliamentary Party, led by John Redmond, pushed on with the Home Rule measure. In July, the bill passed its second reading in the House of Commons, to be again defeated by the Lords. The vehement opposition from a major section of the population of Ulster was a cause of alarm for the government, and on 9 September Lord Loreburn created a sensation when he publicly raised the possibility of separate treatment for Ulster. On 23 September, Ulster Unionist Council delegates approved the setting up of a provisional government for Ulster, should the Home Rule Bill be passed.

This was the developing scene facing Casement at the time of his retirement from the Foreign Office. Earlier in the summer, soon after his return from South Africa, he had expressed himself at some length to Morgan on Home Rule:

> The truth is nearly every Irishman one meets is now a Home Ruler of some sort – the Ulsterians worst of all. They go in for the Whole Hog of Sinn Féin – ourselves alone & war to the last bolt – and rivet – against compromise. What an extraordinary people we are. The 'Unionists' one meets often say 'if this were *real* Home Rule – a Colonial Parliament, we could accept it – but this bill is neither one thing nor another' – so that their objection to Home Rule is that they are not offered enough of it.
>
> Personally I am a Separatist – I want Ireland on her own – on her own pocket too. We want the grave responsibilities of life to be thrust on us – and I never fear that once we had to face the problem of doing for ourselves we should manage. The thing to fear is that under the present measure causes of friction between the two Parliaments will increase not diminish ... If I am still in Dublin I shall be delighted to hear your speech on the subject.⁵⁰

After his exertions over Connemara, Casement had spent a leisurely two months, most of it with the Mortens at Denham. Now, with events quickening in Ulster, he was drawn there. He wrote to Morgan at the end of August, telling him that he was anticipating a journey 'to "Ulster" for a few days to inspect the rebel troops'. Now that it was the season of mellow fruitfulness, 'our pens should all be dropping matured reflection. Mine, when it comes to Ulster will be found to have a wasp in it'.⁵¹

His identity as a Protestant was tested when he received an appeal from a Mrs Griffiths for a contribution to a Protestant Orphan Fund: 'I am afraid you have addressed me under a misapprehension as I am not a Protestant.' Referring to wealthy Protestants, he suggested that he had not 'the privilege to stand in this favoured class'. As it happened, he continued, he was helping two poor young men, 'who have done no wrong but have been driven from their work here in Belfast, because they are Irish and because they are Catholics ... No single clergyman of the Irish Protestant Church has said one word against this cruel and wicked conduct.'⁵² In fact, as he told Gertrude soon afterwards, he did not send this letter he had drafted, but sent five pounds instead.

He had seen one of the UVF marches and derided Smith and Carson. He loved, he proclaimed, the Antrim-Down Presbyterians, but they were

> *exploited* by that damned Church of Ireland – that Orange Ascendancy gang who hate Presbyterians only less than Papishes ... For they are Irish right

through really – and this perverted abominable creed that they are to remain colonists and settlers to the end of time in a land inhabited by Jebusites, Perizites and Hittites. I wish the Hittites would become the Hitouts and give them a hell of a drubbing, for their own good ... Failing that I pray for the Germans – and their coming ... then pray God the head of Europe step in and end this affront to the civilisation of the world.53

With no demands on his pen from the FO, he began to work at putting his thoughts on Ireland onto paper. Two articles were published in the autumn and, now out of the public service, he agreed to attach his name to them. In *The Nation*, he argued that the core of the claim of Irish Unionsts was that

Ireland is a Crown Colony, and must be governed accordingly from Downing Street. This, in a phrase, is the gospel of Carsonism – Ireland a Crown Colony, with no representative control from within, so that the garrison through an external authority may still dominate the white heathen who outnumber them physically, and, it is gravely feared, might surpass them intellectually if they once found their feet. To keep colonist and native from mingling in a common national life is the chief pre-occupation of the Crown Colonist – a pre-occupation derived in truth from a most ignoble fear ... Not forty General Elections will induce 'Ulster' to recognise the natives; rather than that, we are told, Ireland will be drenched in blood. A more baleful conception of duty to one's country it were hard to conceive ...

Ulster people, he believed, could not deny their Irishness. 'Despite feigned forgetfulness, Belfast cannot escape its parentage. Ulster cannot get away from Ireland.'54

In November's *Fortnightly Review*, he developed his theme further. In the face of the emergence of an Irish nation during the eighteenth century, a new method of perpetuating the conquest had to be found: the Act of Union of 1800. This time, withdrawal, not invasion, was the goal – to 'withdraw the one and a half million of Protestants from political life within their own country'. The Union, therefore, was conceived 'in no pious aspiration after union, but in an impious hope to make disunion perpetual'. To make it work, it was necessary to convince the mass of Irish Protestants and, in particular, Irish Presbyterians, to 'look across the water' and to view their Catholic fellow-Irishmen as a threat to Protestant institutions. Established Church opposition to non-conformity had to be abandoned: 'To maintain the Union, therefore, it became essential to identify Presbyterian with Churchman, and to weld these two differing elements of protest into an irreconcilably anti-Irish mass.' Every prejudice needed to bring this about was fostered. The effort succeeded and 'the rectory captured the manse'. Catholic efforts to win rights – as in the tithe war and the land war – were consistently 'represented as threats' to the Protestant community.

As a result:

After more than a century of a Union that was to unite Ireland and great Britain into one people, we find not only has the Union failed in this ... but

Unionists themselves assure us it has split Ireland irrevocably in two. Where it found one Irish people after a hundred and twelve years of resolute effort it now offers us two ... A separation of one people into two hostile bodies, artificially achieved in the face of nature, is to be regarded as a natural law, and enforced in defiance of reason, judgment, and religion.

Home Rule must be tried, he concluded, if for no other reason than to address the 'smaller area of reconciliation'.[55]

Ballymoney Meeting, 24 October 1913

In September 1913, the idea emerged of holding a protest meeting for Ulster Protestants who opposed Carsonism. Captain Jack White[56] seems to have been the first to broach the idea, when he contacted the Revd J.B. Armour of Ballymoney about the possibility.[57] He visited the town with his wife and talked to Armour and Dr Thomas Taggart, a local Liberal. Soon afterwards, and it seems independently, Casement wrote to Armour making a similar suggestion.[58] He had been staying with Bigger in Belfast and it is possible that the idea stemmed from their discussions.[59] He soon came from Belfast, lunched with Armour and had a meeting with 'some fifteen of the stalwarts'. The proposal to hold a meeting was discussed and agreed on, as was a list of possible speakers, a suitable chairman and the details of resolutions to be put.

White was angry on learning of Casement's initiatives, especially what he considered to be a change in the focus of the meeting from the theme of the 'lovelessness' to that of the 'lawlessness' of Carsonism. He described what followed:

I was indignant when I heard of Casement's action, and made an appointment to meet him in Belfast. I believe it was the first time we met. The interview was pretty stormy. Casement was, of course, far ahead of me in experience and influence, a man of kingly presence, courtly address. One can imagine his horror at being informed by an ebullient boy, 'We'll get on all right if you're honest.' 'I think you're most insulting,' he replied. But we got over that. In our long subsequent association the note of that first interview was often repeated, but affection and a humorous tolerance on his part of my rival messiahship formed a pleasant accompaniment.[60]

In the event, Casement was to play a larger role than White in the arrangements for the meeting. While two of his suggested speakers were rejected – Lord Ashbourne because he was a 'papish' and Bigger because he was 'a crank – a banner and pipe maniac' – it was he who arranged that Alice Stopford Green and, probably, Alec Wilson would speak.[61] He was responsible, too, for one of the two resolutions and for part of the second.

The Ballymoney committee busied itself in making local arrangements. These included finding a chairman (local rivalries played a part) and taking security precautions. Armour reported: 'The Tories here are in a state bordering on political insanity as they have a project in hand to summon from Coleraine and elsewhere a band of Orange rowdies with drums to drown the speakers or it may be to rush the hall the night before and keep it against all comers.' To address the latter danger, it was decided to issue tickets for the meeting and to request the police to allow only ticket-holders past the top of the street.

Meanwhile, during October, Casement wrote excitedly to friends, informing them of his impending debut as a public speaker.[62] As well as keeping Gertrude informed, he wrote to Morel and to Cadbury, who hoped he would circulate the reports of the meeting widely. He also wrote to his cousin Roger in Magherin-temple, wondering if he would come and, in the process, revealing how sporadic communications were between them.[63] Two days before the meeting, he told Morel that he was going the fifty-three miles to Ballymoney on the morrow – by motor car. 'It is my first appearance on a political platform – almost on any – and my first attempt to deliver a speech.' He had it fully written out.[64]

The meeting took place peacefully on 24 October, some 500 people attending. Armour described the proceedings in his correspondence: 'The speaking was high tone and earnest and everybody says it was the finest gathering ever held in the Town Hall. Captain White spoke well ... Mrs Green, Sir Roger, Alec Wilson and young Dinsmore made very fine harangues ... The platform was crowded by a large number of good looking women, Marion A[rmour] being not the less distinguished looking of the females.'[65] The two resolutions were put first:

(i) That this meeting of Protestant inhabitants of Ballymoney and the Route protests against the claim of Sir Edward Carson and the self-constituted Provisional Government of Ulster to represent the Protestant community of North-East Ulster in the policy they have announced of lawless resistance to the will of the Parliament of Great Britain and Ireland, and further hereby pledges itself to offer such opposition as the law permits or enjoins to the arbitrary decrees of an illegal and entirely non-representative body.

(ii) That this meeting disputes the narrow claim that differences of creed necessarily separate Irish men and women into hostile camps, affirms its belief that joint public service is the best means of allaying dissensions and promoting patriotism, and calls upon his Majesty's Government to pursue the policy of bringing all Irishmen together in one common field of national effort.[66]

Opening his own address, Casement asserted that he had no wish to add to the tensions of the day: 'I would seek only to point a way, not to conflict and further embitterment of feeling, but to peace with honour – and peace for Ireland as a whole and honour for Ulster as the first province of Ireland.' He went on to summarize the elements of dissension: talk of two Irelands, inevitably disunited; of Ulstermen being sold by political trickery; of arming and drilling against a perceived enemy. But 'the enemy they are being led against is no enemy at all', he declared. Citing his own knowledge of 'Catholic Ireland, Nationalist Ireland', he claimed that 'they desire no triumph over Ulster. They seek only the friendship, the goodwill, and I believe *even the leadership of Ulster*'.

This being true, what lay behind the animosity of Ulstermen? 'Well, I think the explanation is a two-fold one. Sectarian animosity is, as Lecky called it, the Master Curse of Ireland; and while sectarian animosity has blinded the eyes of Ulstermen in one direction, a misguided Imperialism has led their vision astray in another.' He continued:

There can be no healthy empire founded on loss, decay, and over-emigration at home. While the Empire has been expanding and consolidating, Ireland has been contracting and drawing apart. A hundred years ago there was only one Ireland. The Wexford Catholic and the Antrim Presbyterian were then equal rebels in the cause of that one Ireland; they fought and died in the selfsame camp, and the cause was that of a united Ireland. Where do they stand to-day? Disunited and severed, they stand far apart, and while the Ireland they died to make one has lost millions of her people to build up greatness abroad, she has been growing poorer in men, poorer in heart, more abject in spirit, until to-day it is actually hailed as a triumph of Unionism that here at the very heart of the Empire, here at the seat of rule, there are not one Irish people, but two, not one Irish nation, but two Irish nations, and that wherever else men may be united here they must always be disunited.

Briton and Boer may make peace, the British and American peoples may make peace:

There is to be peace across the Atlantic Ocean, but war across the Irish Sea ... An Empire built on the desertion of Ireland, on the abandonment of their country in its need by Irishmen, is an Empire of parricides and cannot last. If the British Empire is to endure and to be a great and healthy factor in human development, as I hope and believe it will, it must be founded on a free and healthy Ireland no less than on a free and healthy Britain.

The old order, he argued, was doomed to fall in Ireland; some form of self-government was inevitable. Ulstermen, then, rather than resisting it, should turn their talents and industry to building up the rest of Ireland, should take a position of leadership. Concluding, he begged:

Bend your pride, your strength to worthy uses, not to ignoble ends. Go out to conquer Ireland with greatness in your hearts, with gentleness in your minds, and with no poverty in your souls. If this be your task you will find not only Protestant Ulster behind you, but Catholic Ulster too, aye, and all Ireland behind you as well.

The meeting was well covered by the press, local and national. Friends wrote to congratulate Casement. Helen MacNaghten liked his speech, Erskine Childers thought it splendid and Gilmour agreed with it 'entirely'.[67] The London *Times* dismissed the meeting as representing only 'a small and isolated pocket of dissident Protestants', to which Casement responded with a rebuttal, suggesting that there were other places nearby where similar meetings could be held. He also reacted defensively to the newspaper's comment that he was a 'citizen of the world' and a 'romantic nationalist', by pointing to his Ulster roots. 'I have', he added, 'lived amongst Ulster people many years of my life, and in quiet and daily contact with them I have learned to know them well.'[68] An attempt was made to hold a second meeting, this time in Coleraine, but it had to be abandoned when the local council refused to rent the Town Hall.[69]

The Loyalists, he wrote to Gertrude from Cushendall, were 'at high water mark', and in a letter to Alice Stopford Green he recorded his depression at the mood in Ulster, her 'pulpits resounding with yells for a Holy War'.[70] He was pessimistic about the prospects for Home Rule, fearing a lack of resolve in England to proceed with the measure. Should not 'Ireland' take a lesson from 'Ulster' and Carson? If it was deemed admirable in England for Ulster to 'arm & drill against those who ... never hurt her', would it not be more admirable for Ireland to 'arm & drill against those who have always hurt her'?[71]

Casement spent a good deal of November and December 1913 in the home of Sidney Parry in 8 Onslow Gardens, London. Parry's appeal for clemency at Casement's trial revealed that, despite some improvement in his health due to his sojourn in South Africa, he was far from being a healthy man at this time: 'During his visit he was in an extremely excitable state, generally unbalanced and showing signs of great irritability. My guest, Mr Hugh Spender, complained to me of Casement's habit of facing his (the adjoining) room talking to himself aloud, and generally disturbing Mr Spender's rest.'[72] Parry's statement was corroborated by Spender's, who wrote that he saw Casement 'constantly for a fortnight' during December. He 'struck me as being in a highly nervous and excitable condition', and 'used to pace about at night. Although as a rule extremely courteous and amiable, he was sometimes extremely irritable and I took care not to cross him or contradict him. I particularly recall the fact that in the evening he would sometimes suddenly leave the room as if he could not bear himself any longer, and if music was played this was invariably the case.' Spender was convinced that he was on the verge of a nervous breakdown.[73] William Cadbury tried to soften Casement's sense of grievance:

> I met him in Dublin at the end of 1913, and went to the Abbey Theatre with him to see some historical plays. I remember saying that I thought the policy of always pressing upon the people the wrongs of the past and their old hatred of England was not the best way of securing Home Rule, and though he said nothing that evening, next morning he remarked that after consideration he felt sure that I was right and it was a mistake to dwell too much on the wrongs of the past.[74]

Irish Volunteers

Events in Ulster in opposition to Home Rule were becoming of increasing concern to nationalist supporters of the measure. Moderates and even pacifists like Owen Sheehy Skeffington began to talk of violence and arms. The establishment of volunteers to defend Home Rule began to be discussed and small volunteer groups emerged in different places. The youth group Na Fianna had been established in 1909 and, as a result of the bitter strike and lockout that began in Dublin in late August 1913, the Irish Citizen Army was established in November, its first commander Captain Jack White. Casement sent two supportive telegrams to be read at a public meeting. In one, to White, he said: 'Strongly approve proposed drill and discipline Dublin workers, and will aid that healthy movement, as I am also prepared to aid wider national movement to drill and discipline Irish National Volunteers throughout Ireland. Please read this at today's meeting.' In the second, addressed to Professor Collingwood, he wrote:

> I understand you begin movement drill and discipline Dublin workers. That is good and healthy movement. I wish to support, and I hope it may begin a widespread national movement to organize drilled and disciplined Irish Volunteers to assert Irish manhood and uphold national cause in all that is right. It is time drilled and disciplined Irishmen stood up all over the land to give the lie to those who say we are a Quaker Oats sort of people, who take everything lying down.75

An article published on 1 November by Eoin MacNeill, proposing the establishment of a national volunteer movement, proved the catalyst to the emergence of the Irish Volunteers. His article was noted by members of the secret revolutionary Irish Republican Brotherhood, who acted on the suggestion and helped set up a steering committee, which, in turn, organized a public meeting in Dublin's Rotunda on 25 November. A large crowd attended, Mac-Neill addressed them, a manifesto was read out and the Irish Volunteers came into existence. Casement was not present, but he became active from the beginning and helped draft the manifesto.76

He was to play a key role in the subsequent recruitment drive, travelling throughout the country, addressing public meetings. At an early stage he made the acquaintance of Colonel Maurice Moore of the Connaught Rangers, brother of the writer George Moore. Colonel Moore had been a prominent Gaelic Leaguer and was to become inspector general of the Volunteers. He later described his first meeting with Casement in London:

> It was very soon after I sent my adhesion to the Volunteers, that I first met Sir Roger Casement in London. He came to my club, and we had a long convers[at]ion on the Volunteers, and the Nationalist cause. A man of nobler character I never met, nor hope to meet; he moved about the world thinking nothing of his own advancement, and caring little how his actions might affect his prospects. His dark earnest eyes gazed out from the spare features of an enthusiast. He was handsome mainly because of the earnestness of his expression; he spoke eagerly and convincingly, and whatever plans he suggested were those of an idealist striving for a purpose that seemed to be far off, but still not beyond the reach of our honest endeavours.77

Casement's first recorded involvement was a speech at a recruitment meeting in Galway on 12 December. Casement wrote to Moore from the Railway Hotel:

The meeting last night was a great success, a very big crowd – far too many to get into the Town Hall. There is no doubt of the extreme desire of the youth of Galway to enrol – to 'enlist' in an Irish army, but there is no equipment, and no organisation here, or any human fibre (that I can see) with which to weave it. The students had made no serious preparation for enrolling, and the rush of 400 or 500 young men at the end overpowered them nearly.

Casement pointed out to Moore the need for money, instructors and, above all, 'a capable man who cared to lead and guide this untutored, but none the less real patriotism of the poor'.[78]

The activities of the Volunteers were closely monitored by the Royal Irish Constabulary (RIC), and from this point on Casement's own movements were observed and reported on. The RIC noted that on 9 December he visited University College Galway with MacNeill, Pearse and George Nicholls: 'On 10-12-13, accompanied by a torchlight procession and five local bands, he, MacNeill, and Pearse, attended a meeting at Town Hall in furtherance of Volunteer Movement.'[79] Casement left Galway on 12 December and travelled on to Cork, where he arrived on the 13th.[80]

MacNeill was the principal speaker in Cork and, in line with his general approach of being positive towards the Ulster Volunteers, he called for cheers for them. He had done so in both Dublin and Galway, but in Cork the call led to uproar. Unknown to MacNeill, Cork nationalists were riven into two factions, O'Brienites and Redmondites, both well-represented in the hall. The call was taken to be an endorsement of William O'Brien's position. According to Moore, Casement had some part in restoring order: 'He came on the stage at once and was well received: the meeting became quite calm, the speakers were heard, so that it turned out a success after all.' The RIC report of his visit noted that in Cork he 'associated with local suspects'. It continued: 'He visited Queenstown while in Cork in connection with proposal to make Queenstown a port of call for Hamburg–Amerika Line. He gave an interview to a reporter of *Cork Examiner* re this proposal, which was reported in *Cork Examiner* of 17-12-13.'[81]

The context for his involvement with the Hamburg–Amerika line lay in the decision of the Cunard Line to terminate its calls to the southern port of Queenstown (Cobh), first in 1910 for the eastward voyage and then in 1913 for the westward leg. The decline in the numbers of Irish emigrants to North America was given as the reason for the end of the service, but the impact on the port of Cork was considerable. Opposition was organized, with deputations going to Dublin, London and Washington.[82] When in Cork for the Volunteer meeting, Casement made the acquaintance of John J. Horgan, a young solicitor and follower of John Redmond, who became active on the shipping question. Ten days after the Volunteer meeting, on 22 December, Casement wrote to Horgan about the Hamburg–Amerika Line: 'I have seen a statement from the "headquarters staff" of the Coy that they positively mean to call at Cove [*sic*].' He advised keeping the welcome to the ship informal and to avoid publicity, hoping that the event would not be seen as anti-English. But he was concerned that the broader issue of English–German relations was affecting the shipping question. Was the FO being got at by Cunard and White Star? 'There is a very anti-German clique and bitterly anti-Irish gang in the FO'; 'Read inclosed pamphlet on Germany and Ireland – it is interesting. It is the last contingency – is indeed the likely one – if anything serious now [?] happens to John Bull. It is the pamphlet General von Bernhardi made such a fuss about lately and all Germany was talking of.' Ireland, he believed, was ceasing to be 'an island beyond an island'.[83]

The end of the year found him in Belfast, staying with Bigger, still pursuing the Queenstown matter. The first German ship to call, he told Horgan, would be the *Rhaetia*, due on 20 January.[84] Then, suddenly, there was a problem, recorded in a flurry of communications from Casement. The directors of the Hamburg–Amerika Line were alarmed, he wrote to Horgan, about the political implications, and therefore wished no formal welcome for the ship. There should be no fuss or public reception of any kind, he instructed in two further communications. He, himself, was coming to Cork on the following Sunday or Monday.[85] He sent a longer letter to Baron von Horst, the Hamburg–Amerika representative in London: 'I write you from my bed to say how sorry I am to learn of the decision of the Hamburg–Amerika Co. to forego the welcome that the public bodies of Cork naturally wished to extend to the first steamship of their line to call in that port.'

He regretted more, he continued, that the decision was made – as he understood it – because of fear that the visit would be exploited for 'political purposes' by those welcoming her. There was, he asserted, no foundation for this; the Mayor of Cork and other dignitaries were simply exercising 'proper civic pride'. In Brazil he had seen how public bodies welcomed new vessels and no question of political intent was ever raised. But, when anything beneficial to Ireland was projected, the accusation of 'political action' was made. He was, nevertheless, informing Cork of the requirements. Many would be discommoded – the Corporation, Harbour Board and others, including the youth: 'Tugs have been chartered – bands hired – they did so want to give a German ship a real kindly greeting!' He concluded, 'What a calamity it is to be an Irishman, either to have no country and so have no manhood; or to *have* a country – and to so have no home!'[86]

Worse news was to follow, with the cancellation of the *Rhaetia's* visit altogether. On 17 January 1914 Casement sent a cryptic telegram to Horgan: 'Sir Roger Casement thinks statement for press should appear promptly explaining guardedly steamers none call Tuesday.'[87] He followed this up a few days later, saying: 'I had a long letter from the Coy. yesterday from Hamburg explaining why the *Rhaetia* did not call – and reading between the lines the reason is not far to seek.' There was hope that the *Fürst Bismark* would call on 11

February and he appealed for 'no incautious words or acts' in the meantime.[88] But, by mid February, it was clear that no German ships would call; the endeavour was over.[89]

When he returned to Ireland from London he found a gloomy letter from Horgan, to which he replied: 'It moves me greatly – and I feel for you my Catholic countrymen, perhaps, more even than you feel for yourselves – I feel for Ireland – as John Mitchell [*sic*] felt for Ireland – the shame and ignominy of our race – the White Slave race of European peoples. But I don't despair because I feel with John Mitchell that the manhood of Ireland will outlast the British Empire.' He knew, his letter continued, that Carson would win, because he appealed to force, and a craven British government would not use force against Protestants or Loyalists – 'they are going to strip all the flesh off the Home Rule Bill – if we let them! Shall we?' The response should be to build up the Volunteers: 'Don't despair of the arms. I think we can get them.' Pressure had been building up in Volunteer circles to acquire arms to compete with the Ulster Volunteers, who had been steadily importing them since their formation. Casement clearly shared the goal. In addition, he indicated where his thoughts were turning to for finance and perhaps for the arms themselves; the Irish Americans, he told Horgan, would help. Regarding the Hamburg–Amerika Line, it was England that had objected 'on political grounds' and 'No British Government will ever willingly allow free foreign intercourse with Ireland ... The mere suspicion of foreign intercourse with Ireland drives England mad.' She wanted Ireland as a pocket Argentina, with Irishmen being the cattle: 'She holds Ireland in a grip of economic servitude but by a bond far more fatal – intellectual servitude. Most Irishmen are slaves in their outlook on life – England has made them so – by hideous cruelty and oppression in the past, carried on today by rigorous seclusion from contact with others and by the control of every means of advancement.'[90]

Casement had spent most of January 1914 with Bigger at Ardrigh, working on the Queenstown campaign. He did other work, too, and wrote to Gertrude, saying he was busy on important work for America, a reference perhaps to planning for a Volunteer-related visit to the US. Having spent a day in a library trying and failing to find a reference, he bemoaned not having access to his own materials: 'I have this in my own belongings – but these, mavrone, are scattered all over the "Empire" and I feel more and more I *must* get a house of my own, of some sort, and settle down – otherwise I cannot do the work that should be done before I go hence and leave no word behind for the Ireland yet to be.'[91]

He travelled to Limerick for a Volunteer meeting on 25 January. Lawrence Kettle had written on the 11th, to say that the Limerick men wanted Casement as principal speaker: 'Mr Pearse will be going down to the meeting.'[92] The RIC, once more, noted his movements. He stayed with James Daly; 'While in Limerick he associated with P.H. Pearse, Dublin, the Mayor of Limerick, Michael

O'Callaghan, D.C., Limerick.' At 8 pm on the 25th, the report continued, a meeting was held in the Atheneum 'to form a Volunteer Corps'.93 From Limerick Casement wrote to Joseph Plunkett: 'Tonight's meeting was a great success. Pearse spoke splendidly – a real orator.' The mayor had presided and it was the 'finest audience I've seen yet in Ireland … the Volunteers have been given a good start'.94

He next made a temporary base for himself at Malahide, on the coast just north of Dublin, taking rooms in a private house. He was busily producing articles for publication and continued his work for the Volunteers, which included a visit to England in February, where he may have begun arrangements for the importation of arms for the Volunteers.95 The RIC noted of his Malahide sojourn: 'He remained there for about four months. During this time he seemed to have few or no acquaintances. He did a lot of correspondence … He was absent on occasions for a week or so at a time. He made no speeches and attended no meetings while there. He has not since visited Malahide.'96

An article of his that appeared at this point involved the idea of a celebration of the anniversary of the Battle of Clontarf in 1014. In the first issue of the *Irish Volunteer*, he proposed 'a Volunteer review at Clontarf in April next, three months from now, to commemorate one of the really great events in our history of depression. The 23rd April, 1914, will be the nine hundreth anniversary of the Battle of Clontarf, a conflict not less memorable in European affairs than was the battle of Hastings that followed it half a century later'. At Hastings, the Anglo-Saxons under Harold went down before the invader, but, at Clontarf, the Irish under Brian overthrew him

> and the civilization of the West proved that heroic valour and great martial achievement were not incompatible with the strictest fidelity to the Christian Faith … Clontarf, Christian Clontarf, calls Ireland back to manhood; let Irish manhood and boyhood respond to that call. If 20,000, if 10,000 Irish Volunteers assemble in April next on that greatest field of Irish martial achievement, this year of 1914 may take its place beside 1782 and 1014 itself in the annals of European endeavour.

He also argued that Ireland should field its own team at the 'Olympic Games of the White Races' to be held in Berlin in 1916: 'Ireland should then be ranked among the free countries of the world. She will be, at least as free as Finland, or Alsace-Lorraine. While within the Empire, she will enjoy complete internal autonomy – just as Basutoland, for instance, does in South Africa – and she should enjoy the same right of participating in those games as an individual entity as Finland did in Stockholm in 1912.'97

From Malahide, he wrote to Daniel Enright on 18 February that he was

> awfully rushed – just back from *Sasana* … Look out for early developments and get *all* the Volunteers ready. Distribute these to good boys … Get the Volunteer song *sung*. We sang it at Limerick. Get Pearse's words out of the *Irish Volunteer*.

Two days later, he spoke pessimistically about political developments:

> On the Home Rule farce the Liberals are playing for own benefit. Well – now the
> *only* thing to do is to go on with the Volunteers early and late – man and child. If
> we don't – we shall get exactly the 'Home Rule' we deserve – and that will be a
> debating society on the banks of the Liffey. The Liberals will 'rat' before June.

And, on 27 February, still thinking of Queenstown:

> We'll have Ireland yet enjoying 'freedom of the seas', if not 'mastery' of them.
> That's going to be the great fight of the world yet – to release Ireland and
> return her to Europe and thereby restore to Europe the freedom of the Seas.
> For Ireland is, in truth, the Keeper of the Seas.[98]

Another large Volunteer meeting followed in Kilkenny, on 5 March. The
RIC reported that 'R.C. arrived on 5th with Thomas McDonagh ... At 8 pm a
torchlight procession was formed with three bands, and a meeting was held at
the Parade which was addressed by Casement who urged the Volunteer Movement. A movement was then made to the Town Hall where 300 Volunteers
were enrolled.' The two left on the following day, according to the report.[99]

By now, Casement was on the Provisional Committee of the Volunteers, a
position he owed to Moore's friendship, as the latter recounted: 'I was surprised
to find that Sir Roger Casement was not on the Committee; in the endeavour,
I suppose, to get men representing every section, the man who best represented all Ireland, was omitted. I immediately proposed his co-option, and this
was done unanimously. He was generally silent at the Committee meetings; he
had no heart for wrangling, and the contentions of a few caused him pain.'[100]
Around this time, members of the Provisional Committee had obviously felt
that something might be gained from Moore's going to talk to Colonel John
Seely, Secretary of State for War, to reassure him on the intentions of the Volunteers. One suggestion to be raised was the possibility of having the Volunteers recognized as a territorial army. On 15 March, Casement wrote to Moore,
having concluded that it was likely that both sets of Volunteers would be suppressed and that Moore's proposed visit to Seely would be useless. He was trying to assess how best to react in the case of suppression.[101]

On St Patrick's Day, 17 March, he was back in Limerick for another Volunteer function. The RIC reported: 'R.C. arrived on Patrick's Day and drove to
James Daly's house ... At 11.30 am he headed 600 City Volunteers and marched
with them to Ballinacurra, three miles, where he reviewed them. They then
marched back to City to Butter Market, where before dismissing them he
addressed them. On same night at 8.30 p.m he inspected 150 of the Limerick Boy
Scouts at their Drill Hall in Suspect J. Daly's yard.'[102] In positive mood, Casement described the events to Enright: 'I had a grand review at Limerick of 1000
Volunteers on Patrick's Day. Limerick has the finest turnout of Volunteers in Ireland – better than Dublin and they've taken it up more seriously too.'[103]

The Curragh Mutiny, March 1914

Meanwhile, tensions surrounding the introduction of Home Rule had continued to mount. By the end of 1913, there were signs of war in Ulster. The UVF Military Council had set up headquarters in the Old Town Hall in Belfast; arms were being imported in a piecemeal way and the argument was made for a large-scale arms coup. Beginning in January 1914, a British covenant was organized and was supported by such prominent figures as Lords Milner, Lansdowne and Roberts, Rudyard Kipling, Dicey and Elgar. Kipling donated £30,000, as did Waldorf Astor.

Early in March, Asquith proposed to the House the option of excluding six Ulster counties from Home Rule for a six-year period. The idea was rejected angrily by Carson, who dubbed it 'a stay of execution for six years'. During the same month, General Sir Arthur Paget, commander-in-chief in Ireland, received information on a threat to arms depots in Ulster and he was ordered to take steps to protect them. In London, a cabinet subcommittee met on 18–19 March and orders were given for troop movements to Ulster and for the deployment of ships to Belfast harbour. Warrants for arrests were also prepared. Saturday, 21 March was to be the target date for action. However, the UVF got warning of government intentions and mobilized.

On the 20th, in Ireland, various contingents of troops were moved northwards; naval forces, too, began to move. But that evening Paget sent several cables to the War Office reporting that the officers of various corps in the Curragh were tendering their resignations. On the same day Brigadier General Hubert Gough, commander of a cavalry brigade in the Curragh camp, having interviewed his officers, wrote to the War Office: 'But if the duty involves the initiation of active military operations against Ulster, the following numbers of officers by Regiments would respectfully and under protest prefer to be dismissed.' Almost all cavalry officers in Ireland had resigned, in what became known as the Curragh Mutiny. In the ensuing crisis, the plan to coerce Ulster ceased. There were sensational headlines the next morning, followed by high-level resignations, including that of Colonel Seely, Secretary of State for War. In the aftermath, alarmed at the possibility of civil war, both Liberals and Tories drew back somewhat and further attempts were made to seek a compromise. There were proposals from Unionists for a federation of the British Isles as an alternative to Home Rule.[104] Nationalists were appalled and Casement and MacNeill despatched a joint letter of protest to the *Irish Independent* on 27 March. For them, the lesson was that Home Rule was faced with the threat of force and the failure to enforce the rule of law; constitutional methods were being undermined. They drew attention to the militant remarks made by senior members of the British Establishment in the months prior to the 'Curragh Coup' and claimed that now 'the cat is out of the Irish bag'. Also, 'British Ministers and ex-Ministers will do their best to slur over the significance of recent events. They know well that military government will not be tolerated in Great

Britain; they know equally well that it is the only Government in Ireland.'[105]

Fiercely critical on one level of the actions of Ulster Unionists, Casement admired their determination in taking bold steps to oppose London. He conceived the idea of approaching Carson with a view to cooperation with the Irish Volunteers, specifically on his proposed celebration of the Battle of Clontarf. Maurice Moore later recalled:

> I remember one of his plans which took my fancy more especially: it was a proposal to celebrate the ninth centenary of the Battle of Clontarf by a big parade of Volunteers, to which the Ulster Volunteers should be invited to send a contingent. His idea was that Clontarf had been fought before the divisions which now separate Irishmen had begun and that such a true and national event might be celebrated by all. Coalition was not to be insisted upon, or even pressed, but if all met on that field, the seed of Irish sentiment might be sown in Orange hearts. These ideals may sometimes have been visionary, but they were the ideals of a noble mind not set on party purposes. I never heard him express any opinion that was commonplace or unworthy.[106]

Casement had been in Limerick in mid March, when tensions concerning the north of the country were building to their climax, and from there he travelled to Belfast 'to try and see Carson about Clontarf. However, the "plot" against Ulster intervened and he was surrounded by bayonets and guards, and it was, moreover, impossible to discuss friendly action with all that tomfoolery on foot – on both sides'.[107] The moment was not propitious for cooperation between the two sets of Volunteers. In a partial letter to an unidentified recipient, he referred again to his somewhat ambivalent attempt to approach Carson, then at Craigavon and anticipating imminent arrest:

> he was ringed around with bayonets and 'war correspondents'. Besides I could not lay myself open to a rebuff of that kind ... If Carson would see me he would know that the future of Ireland lies far more with this Volunteer spirit ... Carson is missing the greatest chance ever came to an Irishman. If he would only show some great spirited [?] love for Ireland and enlarge his Ulster patriotism into a wider patriotism he would sweep like a prairie fire across Ireland.[108]

Whether due to lack of courage or the impossible circumstances, he pursued the matter no further. After Belfast, he visited Connemara. As well as conducting Volunteer business with prominent local activists and seeing to the implementation of his school meals project, he was accompanying Oskar Schweriner, a journalist from Berlin, who was to write on the poverty of the western islands. The Schweriner connection indicates one of Casement's sources of information regarding the failure of his efforts to get Hamburg–Amerika Line ships to call at Queenstown, but also reveals another link with Germany prior to Casement's journey there in late 1914. The RIC was observing and compiled two accounts:

> He arrived [in Galway] at 10.34 am from Dublin on 1-4-14 and put up at the Railway Hotel. Oscar Schmernier [*sic*], a German, arrived at Hotel at 9 pm from Limerick on previous night. About 1.45 pm Casement, Schmernier, Doctor S.

O'Beirne, and Professor O'Malley (Galway), a prominent Sinn Feiner, left Galway by motor for Connemara. They visited National Schools at Carraroe, and called on Father Healy, PP. They later called on Mr Tubridy, N. Teacher, Carraroe. The German here alleged that the failure of Hamburg–Amerika Line boats to call at Queenstown was due to the action of British Government. The party then motored to Hotel of the Isles via Polam Head, and stayed the night there. On 2-4-14 they visited National Schools at Lettermullen, Frabane, and Tiernea and called at Carraroe at 12 noon – their alleged object being to see the children at lunch. The German was represented as a Berlin newspaper correspondent who took an interest in the kelp business. They then called at Derrynea Courthouse and returned to Galway at 9.15 pm. Casement on their arrival went into Gaelic League Rooms and watched Volunteers drill for ten minutes. On 3-4-14 Casement and Schmernier left Galway for Dublin and were seen off at Railway Station by George Nicholls and Brian Cusack. Casement never made any public speeches in County Galway.[109]

The second RIC report, in which the party was driven by Mr Stornmouth, owner of a hotel in Galway, adds further detail on the second day's activities. After their visits to schools, it has them travelling on to 'Kilmilken near Lenane where Patrick O'Malley, brother of the Professor T. O'Malley resided'.[110] Years later, Sinéad Ní Mháille, sister of Professor Tomás Ó Máille (the Professor T. O'Malley, above) recalled the Leenane (Muintir Eoin) section of the tour:

Shortly before the beginning of the 1914 war she entertained to dinner at Muintir Eoin, Sir Roger Casement and Zweinreinger [sic], the Editor of the 'Berlin Tablet'. She recalled that on that occasion, Zweinreinger prophesied complete freedom for Ireland if Germany won the war, provided she lent her support, and she believed that this influenced Casement in his subsequent actions.[111]

Not long after the Connemara visit, further light was shed on the story by an article which appeared in the Irish Independent on 27 April 1914, under the heading: '"Irish Wilderness: Nothing but Stones" – An Eminent German on Gorumna Island'. The story was a translation from an article that had appeared on 6 April in the Berlin newspaper Vossische Zeitung, by 'one of the journal's editorial staff', Herr Oskar Schweriner. The introduction stated: 'Herr Schweriner's articles on Ireland have been widely read throughout Germany and elsewhere abroad, and have attracted much attention. One of them furnished the subject matter for the weekly article in the Kreuz Zeitung of Professor Schiemann, who is a personal friend of the German Emperor. We are indebted to Sir Roger Casement for the translation.'[112]

On 8 April Eoin MacNeill wrote to Maurice Moore, who seems to have expressed worry over Casement's lack of discretion:

Casement is all right. In conversation he is the deadly enemy of the existing order, as we all are, only that we do not let ourselves go to the same extent. In all matters of action, he is wise and careful, and worthy of the fullest confidence. I certainly think he ought to meet Redmond, and have a good talk with him, or to see Devlin, if he cannot see Redmond.[113]

Casement himself addressed Moore's worries in another letter on the 9th:

> I am sorry my letter has alarmed you so much. You have completely failed to grasp my meaning – a failure doubtless due to my writing in haste, and not carefully weighing each word before use. I will try in future to be very precise, and leave no room for misapprehension. For the moment I would merely reassure you that I am not a 'revolutionary' and 'idealist' beyond the limit of most of my countrymen, or anxious for a 'rebellion'. Pray put such thoughts out of your head, for they are entirely irrelevant to anything I have in view, or intend to convey.[114]

The Irish Volunteers and the Irish Parliamentary Party

By now, the leaders of the Irish Parliamentary Party, who had been suspicious of and aloof from the Irish Volunteer movement, realized that it had become a significant force and became convinced of the necessity of bringing it under their control. Formal contacts between the leaders of the Party and of the Volunteers began. On 13 April, MacNeill wrote to Moore, telling of a planned meeting with Joe Devlin on the 15th, to which he had invited Tom Kettle and Casement. When the meeting took place, Devlin informed them that Redmond must control the Volunteers. 'Casement remained after MacNeill left,' wrote Moore, 'and said that he had been very much impressed by Devlin's sincerity of purpose.'[115]

Casement continued making public appearances at Volunteer meetings, and his speeches began to reflect the need to avoid sectional divisions. He went to Tullamore on 19 April and his speech was recorded in the *Irish Volunteer*:

> Sir Roger Casement, who was loudly cheered, said he came from the North of Ireland and was a Protestant. He had been most of his adult years an officer in the British service, but neither the fact that he was an Ulsterman and a Protestant and once a British officer had impaired the primeval fact that he was first of all an Irishman (cheers). The volunteers stood, he said, for an independent Ireland as did the Volunteers of 1782. 'An independent Ireland is a threat to no other country. On the contrary, I believe that in Irish independence will be found the ultimate guarantee of British safety and of the common weal of all British people throughout the world, for I do not believe that the British Empire can continue to endure as a permanent fact by holding down one people at the heart of the Empire' (cheers). He went on to claim that the present volunteer movement was, in one major respect, a happier one than that of 1782, in that it was more democratic – it came from below, from the people, and not from above.
>
> At last they were beginning to realise that they had a country, and he believed in a few weeks – certainly in a few months – they should have a Constitution with an Irish Parliament. He did not think that anything now could prevent it. But now they had seriously to consider what might come after the passing of the Home Rule Bill. They were within sight of constitutional effect

being given to their efforts. They had played the game constitutionally, and according to the rules drawn up by their enemies. They played the game loyally and faithfully, and were within sight of winning; but now their enemies said they were not going to play it that way at all. There was an appeal to force. But two could appeal to force (cheers), and the first duty of the Irish Volunteers might be to protect and safeguard an Irish Parliament on the soil of Ireland (cheers). They had got to make it impossible to be deprived by trick or artifice of what they had won by law, and if they could keep their Parliament they could keep their nationality. He looked upon the Irish Volunteers as perhaps the surest form of national insurance.[116]

On the night of 24–5 April, in a boldly executed operation, the UVF imported over 216 tons of arms into Ulster, mainly through the port of Larne. The move was carried out under cover of a general mobilization of the force and made use of a large fleet of motorized vehicles. The arms were quickly distributed to arms dumps throughout the province. British newspapers were full of the story during the succeeding days. According to Alice Milligan's biographer,

> In old age Alice recounted to a friend how she and Roger Casement – two years her senior – had taken a walk round Larne harbour in the spring of 1914. It was just after the April night when the Unionist Ulster Volunteer Force had landed 35,000 rifles and five million rounds of ammunition at the port and distributed them by car to every corner of Ulster in a highly organised gun-running operation. As they viewed the scene Casement turned to Alice and said: 'We'll have to do something like this.'[117]

He had time at the beginning of May to write a letter to Dick Morten, warm in tone, but strong in its political attitudes:

> If they think – as they do – that any hypocritical sham called 'Federalism' is going to settle the 'Irish Question' – the question they both made – they are clearly mistaken. *Before I die*, please God, I'll raise the *English Question* – and make *its* solution the *chief care of Europe* ...
>
> Ireland can go out again into the wilderness – for 40 years – and bide her time. They will not dish Ireland – they may dish Redmond. But Redmond is not Ireland. However trusted he may be and is, this country and people have a faith, ability [?], assurity no political trickery of any English party will destroy. The vital question for England, if she only knew, is to secure Irish friendship and goodwill on terms of equality. She wants to keep Ireland as a piece of real estate and thinks it *belongs* to her – instead of to its own people. Well – we'll live on and hope on and work on.
>
> The [Home Rule] Bill may or may not pass – most of us don't care a damn *now*. We knew all along it was a makeshift – but we were prepared to take it and make it work. Now, with this fresh development it is plain that all that will be left for Ireland under this Bill will be the bones. The flesh will be divided between the two English parties – and of course, 'Ulster' will accept, or sanction or allow anything that means the undoing of a *national* settlement ...
>
> I may be in London next week possibly – on my way abroad. I'm not quite sure yet. I'm awfully busy – if I can get an *Entente Cordiale* up between my volunteers and the Ulsterites will join hands and put John Bull back in England –

his proper place. He is finished dealing with only half of one province of Ireland – if we can join up all four it is a new day for the world. It will come sooner or later – that junction and union of parts – and then we'll have Home Rule and much more ...[118]

May saw the beginning of tense and protracted negotiations between the Irish Party and the Volunteers over control of the movement. It had been agreed by the Provisional Committee that MacNeill and Casement would go to London to consult with Redmond. MacNeill reported to Moore on the outcome of the meeting, which probably took place on Saturday, 9 May: 'Casement made a statement of some length embodying the views of the Volunteers, as I have already stated them, and giving assurances that they were not anti-party.' Casement then left, leaving detailed discussions in MacNeill's hands.[119]

On the following day, MacNeill and Casement attended a meeting in Alice Stopford Green's house, which set in motion plans to import arms for the Irish Volunteers. Darrell Figgis, also present, described the occasion:

> ... looking outward before the window-curtains, stood Roger Casement, a figure of perplexity, and the apparent dejection which he always wore so proudly, as though he had assumed the sorrows of the world. His face was in profile to me, his handsome head and noble outline cut out against the lattice-work of the curtain and the grey sky. His height seemed more than usually commanding, his black hair and beard longer than usual. His left leg was thrown forward, and the boot was torn in a great hole – for he gave his substance away always, and left himself thus in need, he who could so little afford to take these risks with his health. But as I spoke he left his place by the window and came forward towards me, his face alight with battle. 'That's talking,' he said, throwing his hand on the table between us; and I remember the whimsical thought crossing my mind that language had wandered far from its meaning when one man could say to another that he was talking, when his appreciation and brevity betokened an end of talking.[120]

A committee to organize the acquisition of arms had already been established. According to the historian F.X. Martin, 'an Anglo-Irish committee was privately formed in London, with Mrs Alice Stopford Green as chairman, and Mrs Erskine Childers as secretary ... The committee was an informal circle of friends. On it were Lord Ashbourne, Lady Alice Young of Formosa Place, Mary Spring Rice and her cousins, Conor and Hugh O'Brien'. Money was needed if guns were to be purchased; several members of the committee themselves subscribed.[121] Mary Spring Rice conceived the plan of how to bring arms by boat. The group was to succeed in buying 1500 Mauser rifles and 45,000 rounds of ammunition in Germany and in landing them in Ireland; Erskine Childers on the *Asgard* and Conor O'Brien on the *Kelpie* played key roles. The main landing took place in Howth on Sunday, 26 July, by which time Casement was in the United States.

On 8 May, while in London, Casement gave testimony before the Royal

Commission on the Civil Service. During this brief sojourn in England, he took the opportunity to visit Wilfrid Scawen Blunt, a letter from whom had just been published in Ireland. Casement wrote on 12 May: 'My name may be known to you – either as a friend of Mr Dryhurst and the late *Egypt* – or perhaps in connection with Congo and later Amazon rubber crimes. Now I am only out to end the Irish crime – and I write you on that account.'[122] Blunt responded positively and, the following day, Casement visited him at his home at Newbuildings, Sussex. Blunt described his visitor in his diary:

> Sir Roger Casement came to lunch and to talk over the Volunteer movement in Ireland, of which he is one of the chief organizers ... He is an interesting man of the same Irish type as was Michael Davitt, only much bigger and better looking, still very like him; an Ulsterman, he tells me, and a Protestant, but his mother was a Catholic, and he now is of no religious complexion, only a strong Nationalist. He is not in favour with Redmond, who considers him a dangerous revolutionist, being anti-imperialist, and opposed to the Parliamentary alliance with the English Radicals. He holds Dillon greatly responsible for this, and that it is demoralizing Irish patriotism. Hence his zeal for the Volunteer movement.[123]

Casement wrote a note of thanks on 14 May and, on the 16th he sent a copy of an essay he had written, 'a most treasonable pamphlet called the "Elsewhere Empire". Read it if you are not shocked, for it is not polite literature but a crude appeal to nationality versus Imperialism. It is an instance, a poor one perhaps, of the new Ireland – an Ireland reverting to '48 and '98 – when Irishmen preached not freedom for themselves alone but freedom for all others.'[124]

Back in Ireland, Casement set off on a punishing round of Volunteer meetings. On 23 May he was in Greencastle, on the 24th in Carrickmore and Sixmilecross, on the 25th in Omagh, in Derry on the 26th and 27th, in Strabane on the 28th, before reaching Cushendall on the 31st. During the tour, he had time for a letter to Daniel Enright: 'May the Teuton sit in her gates and play the Meistersinger as the long walls of London collapse. We preached nationalism versus Imperialism yesterday to the hillside men of Tyrone – and faith it went well. E. MacNeill was grand.'[125]

In the weeks that followed the meeting with Redmond in London early in May, there were intense negotiations between the leaders of the Parliamentary Party and those of the Volunteers. Negotiations essentially concerned the nature of a proposed new governing body for the Volunteers, which the Party wished to control. As the Home Rule Bill passed its final reading on 25 May, Redmond's negotiating hand was very strong.[126] Casement commented to Moore: 'By the way, Redmond proposed J. Devlin and young Michael Davitt to come on our governing Committee; Devlin may be all right, altho' I hae ma doots – but the other will not do, and can't be accepted. He denounced and derided the Volunteers from the first, and did all he could to discourage them in the National University.'[127]

He continued his tour, visiting Dungannon and Belfast on 5 June and Fintona and Dundalk on the 7th. Then came the crisis. As negotiations over representation on the new governing board of the Volunteers continued, Redmond and his close associates grew increasingly frustrated with the existing Volunteer leaders, especially MacNeill. On 6 June, *The Irish Times* expressed some sympathy with the latter and criticism of Redmond's efforts. Three days later, on 9 June, Redmond issued a public press statement defining his approach. He stressed the importance of the Volunteer movement and of the need for its governing body to be fully representative; the existing Provisional Committee of twenty-five, he stated, was self-elected and Dublin-based. He recommended that the existing committee 'should be immediately strengthened by the addition of 25 representative men from different parts of the country, nominated at the instance of the Irish Party, and in sympathy with its objects and aims'. The Provisional Committee met that night and drafted a conciliatory reply, which was published the following day. It welcomed the new-found interest of the Parliamentary Party in 'a work which the nation has spontaneously taken in hand' and looked forward to cooperation. At the same time, it tried to implement its own plan for extending representation by issuing a general order, which set in motion the election of county representatives.

Casement had hurried to Dublin for the meeting and had played a part in it. Late that night, he also wrote a conciliatory letter to Redmond, anxious to avoid a split. Searching for a mechanism to unite both parties, he felt that to identify and appoint a good military commander for the Volunteers, acceptable to all, would qualify as such a unifying deed. He suggested General Kelly-Kenny, who had served with distinction in the Boer War.[128] He wrote again on the following day, expressing a wish for cooperation. He had, he said, come especially from Belfast to put the suggestion about county committees to the Provisional Committee: 'I shall not be able to stay here, and must at once put myself on the sick list and take a complete rest.'[129] After this, he returned to Belfast.

On 12 June Redmond issued a second ultimatum: 'unless the Committee sees its way to reconsider the decision, and adopt the proposal I have made, I must appeal to all supporters of the Irish Party in the Volunteer movement to at once organise County Committees, and to maintain that form of organisation quite independent of the Dublin Provisional Committee till it is sufficiently complete to make it possible to hold a representative convention to elect a permanent governing body'. The impact on the Provisional Committee can be imagined. The leading members of the committee gathered in Buswell's Hotel in Dublin. Moore described the scene:

Casement was with me at Buswell's, and in his bedroom we discussed the matter with MacNeill, I lying on a spare bed, sick almost to the last stage of physical incapacity ... It was much less strange that Casement, who had constant bad health from fevers, the result of long residence in tropical climates, was also ill at this moment, but not so utterly helpless as myself. When most other men would have remained inert, his mental energy continued unabated.[130]

All were anxious to avoid a split. Casement, at first, felt they should resign and MacNeill agreed. Hobson disagreed and recommended accepting Redmond's terms. The others came round to his view and they drew up a statement to be put to the committee. 'It was written in the main by Casement, but MacNeill had a good hand in it, and Hobson also,' wrote Moore. After a long justification, the document stated that

> the Committee, under a deep and painful sense of responsibility, feel it their duty to accept the alternative, which appears to them the lesser evil. In the interests of National unity, and in that interest only, the Provisional Committee now declares that, pending the creation of an elective governing body by a duly constituted Irish Volunteer Convention, and in view of a situation clearly forced upon them, they accede to Mr Redmond's demand to add to their number twenty-five persons nominated at the instance of the Irish party.[131]

The committee met on Wednesday, 16 June and, after a full debate, all but eight voted to accept Redmond's ultimatum. In two letters to an unidentified friend, Casement described his role in the events. In the first, he talked of the positive contribution of the Volunteer movement and of his suspicions of the Party, especially over Home Rule: 'They are out solely for office I believe – otherwise they would never have consented to this wretched Bill.' The Volunteers, he continued, 'are out for Ireland – north and south – for a true Union among Irishmen. We have laid the foundations sure and deep. Eoin MacNeill and I (the Antrim papish and the Antrim Protestant) have brought the gospel of the gun to Ireland – and it is the Gospel of patriotism and good will. An armed Ireland will be a friendly Ireland'.[132]

In his second letter, written on the day of the Provisional Committee meeting, he stated that their decision had been 'carried with heavy hearts (almost with tears)'. It was justified for the sake of unity:

> A new Parnell split would have swept the country. I was asked to be the new Parnell – and I refused. To have divided national Ireland into two warring factions over the control of the Volunteers would have been a crime. The Resolution was mine and Prof. MacNeill's – the two leading Irish Volunteers I presume and the two who have made the Gospel of Goodwishes for 'Ulster' the outstanding feature of the Irish Volunteers. We do not surrender that – and shall not.

He believed that, in making their decision, they had not surrendered control of the Volunteers: 'We shall still guide the vessel I believe.'[133] He complained to Gertrude on the 21st: 'I think Carson will win!'[134] On the same day, Erskine Childers, involved in the plan to import arms for the Volunteers, arrived in Dublin and wrote to his wife, Mary, describing what he found:

> I ought to say that last night on arrival I found Casement staying here and also Colonel Moore, the latter a rather embarrassing factor as he knows nothing ...

I had had a long talk already with Casement in his bedroom as to our view of their recent action and communicate what Mrs G[reen] said ... Casement looks ill – bad cold – He is burning himself up, I think. He told me a lot about the negotiations which was new to me.[135]

Casement soon left Dublin and travelled north. He was in Cushendun on 28 June, the day on which the Archduke Franz Ferdinand of Austria was assassinated in Sarajevo. On 30 June Casement wrote a long letter to Enright in Cork. He made negative comments about the Redmond group. 'Once the rifles come into Ireland,' he continued, 'the hand that holds the rifle will be much mightier than that dipping the pen.' He urged him to keep drilling and to go to Mitchelstown and to the review of the Galtee Regiment. He had been invited himself and wanted to go, 'for the sake of the brave Galtee boys'. He had had to cry off attending a review at Athenry. 'However, I did go to Shane O'Neill's Carn (but that was quite close and only a stone's throw from my cousin's house where I'm spending this Sunday) and there I harangued in a cracked voice.' Presumably responding to a comment on Enright's part about him leading the country, he lamented:

> I am too old dear youth – and besides I have no personal ambition – but I feel convinced a new Ireland will find, or make, a new chief like Parnell – or Owen Roe – or Hugh O'Neill – better a fighting chief. Were I twenty years younger I'd plunge *in media res* – but my life has been spent in the vilest climates and for nearly 30 years I've been a sort of militant Columcille fighting (in the name of Ireland) against slavers and slave kings too – for the poor of the black lands. Now in my old age I come home to Ireland to give a helping hand – no more than that at the utmost – to those I love best of all – the gentle, kindly Irish of the Irish.[136]

Soon after, he took a boat to Glasgow, from where he sailed, incognito, to the United States via Canada.

16: *Towards Berlin: The United States and Norway, 1914*

Casement left Ireland for Glasgow on 2 July. Two days later he boarded the *Cassandra*, bound for Montreal, as a second-class passenger under the name of 'Mr R.D. Casement'. On 5 July, he saw to the south the 'jagged precipices and towers' of Tory Island and beyond them 'rose in blue lines Muckish, Errigal and the hills of my heart'.[1] The voyage was a pleasant one and he marvelled at the sight of icebergs near Newfoundland. The island of St Pierre brought back memories of the Congo campaign and his period of unemployment in 1905; a suggestion had been made at the time that he go there as consul. Montreal appalled him, 'belching forth the blackest smoke in the world'. After a one-night stay, he wrote to John Devoy, the leading figure in the Irish-American nationalist organization Clan na Gael, before taking the train to New York.[2]

While Casement was still in transit, Eoin MacNeill sent him a letter to facilitate his fund-raising work in the US. Though recognizing that he was already a member of the Provisional Committee, MacNeill felt that it would help if he were 'in a special position to act on our behalf' while in America: 'I therefore request you to act as accredited representative of the arms sub-committee.' Arms and, possibly, experienced officers were the two items MacNeill felt Irish-Americans could help the Volunteers with.[3] Bulmer Hobson had already written directly to Devoy, announcing Casement's journey. Now, Casement introduced himself to the ageing leader of Irish-American opinion:

> Our mutual friend Hobson has probably told you of my journey across. I hope to be in New York by end of this week at latest and shall call on you on arrival. I shall probably stay a night or two in some hotel – probably at the Belmont, as I see it is near the station – until I can get a private apartment somewhere. It is possible you may not be in New York now – as I see by the papers there is great heat there and thousands are leaving the city. There are things to discuss with you, and one or two more of interest, and I propose staying a few weeks

in USA with New York my headquarters. I don't mind heat very much. Looking forward to the pleasure of seeing you very soon.4

As the train took him south, the landscape around Lake Champlain reminded him

> of the days when Mohicans and the Six Nations had here a hunters' paradise. Poor Indians! you had life – your white destroyers only possess things. That is the vital distinction I take it between the 'Savage' and the civilized man. The savage is – the whiteman has. The one lives and moves to be; the other toils and dies to have. From the purely human point of view the savage has the happier and purer life – doubtless the civilized toiler makes the greater world.

On his arrival in New York on the evening of 18 July he checked in at the Belmont Hotel, where he was heartened by Irish voices and Irish faces. Afterwards, out for a stroll on Broadway, 'a young Norwegian sailor spoke to me – and I befriended and told him to see me next morning'. The young man's name was Eivind Adler Christensen, aged 24, from Moss, Norway.5 What Casement did not reveal in his diary was that he had known Christensen previously, in South America; their relationship almost certainly had a sexual component. And it is clear that the two now remained in contact while Casement was in the US, though the diary again fails to mention it.6

Casement and Devoy met on the evening of the 20th. Devoy made it clear how strongly opposed he was to the 'surrender' of control of the Volunteers to Redmond and how the Clan leaders blamed Hobson for it. He also suggested that it was having a negative effect on fund-raising. 'Casement', Devoy later wrote, 'listened attentively to all I said and then in a calm and very friendly manner undertook to persuade me that I was mistaken.' This he did in a long letter to Devoy, written on the morrow, in which he summarized in detail the events of early June: 'The whole truth is simply that *something* had to be done, and done at once, and that of all the evils before us we chose the one we thought, and I firmly believe, was the least of the evils threatening the Volunteer team.'7 The leaders of Clan na Gael, while maintaining their own interpretation of the events, were impressed by 'the downright sincerity of the man' and agreed to use Casement in collecting funds for the Volunteers.

In the following days he met two other leaders of Irish-American opinion, John Quinn[8] and William Bourke Cockran,[9] both lawyers and more conservative than the Clan na Gael men. Soon he travelled to Philadelphia to meet another of the key figures in Clan na Gael, Joe McGarrity, who was to become his closest associate in America.[10] From Philadelphia he wrote to Poultney Bigelow, who had invited Casement to visit him in upstate New York. He couldn't come immediately, he said, as he had engagements in Philadelphia and Virginia and was, that evening, going to Long Island: 'When I get back to this address (my headquarters pro tem) I'll come along to you up in your Lonesome Forest lair.'[11]

The Howth Guns

Casement's dash back to New York was in preparation for the annual meeting of the Ancient Order of Hibernians (AOH), being held in Norfolk, Virginia. In Quinn's car, they collected Bourke Cockran and rushed to catch the night train to Norfolk. Casement and Bourke Cockran spoke at the AOH meeting on 24 July, after which Casement returned to McGarrity's home in Philadelphia. Here he waited for news of the Howth gun landings, which he knew were due to be landed on 26 July. While they waited, he wrote of his expectation to Alice Stopford Green: 'My dear Woman of the Ships! If all goes well, today should be a happy day at home for the Volunteers. We are praying for it! I am staying with a splendid character here, and he knows all ... I am waiting hourly for a telegram ... to say the picnic has been held or prevented or broken up. Today was the day of Fate.' He commented, too, on the approaching war in Europe: 'This War that has come like a bombshell from the Almighty Arsenal may throw *everything* into the fire. If Germany is involved as seems most likely, John Bull *will have* to face the music – whether he likes it or not. And then ...'[12]

His diary recorded the tense period of waiting for news of Howth: 'That Sunday I spent at McGarrity's in great anxiety and on tenterhooks. It was a very hot day. At 7 pm Joe and I walked down the fields in front of his house until full twilight fell and darkness came. We lay on the grass and talked of Ireland.'[13] Eventually they learned that the guns had been landed safely. It later emerged that, in Dublin, on its way back to the city, the convoy of Volunteers had been challenged by police and a contingent of The King's Own Scottish Borderers. The Volunteers succeeded in outmanoeuvring their challengers, getting away the bulk of the arms. Events later took a turn for the worse: as the troops returned to barracks, they were jeered by a crowd on Bachelors' Walk; in response, some of the troops used bayonets and some opened fire, killing three and wounding thirty-eight. In Philadelphia, there was elation at the arms landing but anger at the killings. Casement became the focus of press attention. He wrote immediately to Bourke Cockran in New York:

> This massacre in Dublin is taking up my time. Everything has gone as we expected ... the only thing wherein we failed was in not having our cartridges ready to meet fire with fire ... Last night at the first receipt of the news ... two companies of Irish Volunteers here in Philadelphia put up, there and then, 3000 Dollars – from about 160 or 200 poor men – for arms for Ireland ... I hope you will help us too ... Please remember that money sent to Redmond for arming the Volunteers is money in doubt – He has no official right or even connection with the Volunteers ... This gun-running ... was entirely & absolutely ours – Redmond knew nothing of it – I planned it with three others before I left ... It is only the first effort – and we have not failed ...[14]

Two days later, he shared his feelings of exultation with Alice Stopford Green: 'I was in anguish first – then filled with joy – and now with a resolute pride in you all.' There had been press coverage in the US, though less than might otherwise have been the case, because of the threat of war in Europe. As to his own role, 'The Irish here would make me into a demi-god if I let them. In Philadelphia they have christened me, a deputation told me, "Robert Emmet"! They are mad for a Protestant leader. At the Hibernian Convention when I opened the ball and said I was a Protestant they cheered and cheered and cheered until I had to beg them to hear me.' He was sorry not to be closer to the events: 'My grief is that I was here, and not on the Howth Road last Sunday – and my blood is hot with wrath when I think of that bayoneting and bulleting.' He signed himself 'The Fugitive Knight'.[15]

On 30 July he wrote to Quinn requesting letters of support for his mission from himself and Bourke Cockran:

> Everything looks like war, with John Bull pulled in; and, if so, I think we should lose no chance to arm the Volunteers so that we may be able to repeat 1782 over again. Bull will want our help, and it should be given *only* on terms that we get freedom at home, and if we have the men armed we can ensure a greater measure of respect for our claims.[16]

On the 31st he gave details to Devoy of a hectic schedule – Philadelphia, Chicago, Baltimore, Buffalo. He reported, too, that Quinn had sent $250 and a 'fine letter' and that Bourke Cockran was set to do likewise. On Sunday, 2 August a protest meeting was held in Philadelphia over the Bachelors' Walk incident, at which Casement was the principal speaker. When Devoy and Casement were photographed in an open carriage, Casement tried to hide his face, fearing, as Devoy later put it, 'that it would lessen his chances of escaping detection by the English in case he wanted to go on any mission unknown to them. He was evidently, even then, thinking of going to Germany, although he had not mentioned it up to that time'.[17]

War in Europe

In Europe the worst-case scenario was unfolding. On 30 July Russia ordered a general mobilization, as did Germany, in response, on the 31st. France followed, upon which Germany declared war on her, and, in a drive towards French territory, invaded Belgium on 4 August. That same day, Britain declared war. These events had a shattering effect on Casement. He revealed his state of agitation when he wrote to Bigelow on 10 August, from John Quinn's residence in New York:

> This awful Calamity in Europe has upset everything – all my plans & movements & thoughts & hopes. It is the Crime of all the ages – and I blame not the Kaiser or Germany – but chiefly England who has plotted and planned it from the days of the first big German battleship. I am staying with John Quinn (the Lawyer) an Irish friend, and seeing various Irishmen & others to interest them

in the Irish Volunteers – but what *can* one say or do with this welter of blood & horror & crime in Europe. I pray day & night, 'God save Germany'!

Yesterday I called on Col. [Theodore] Roosevelt ... and exchanged ideas. I meet Mayor Mitchel to-morrow & do the same – & day by day I collect funds to arm my Irish boys at home – some day, who knows? – to fight a fight for Ireland.[18]

For several years Casement had been thinking and writing of the inter-related issues of the historical oppression of Ireland, the denial of her proper role within Europe, and the relevance to this of England's Empire and her control of the seas and of trade. He had been watching, too, the growing international tensions within Europe and saw Germany as a defender of European civilization, as a key player likely to challenge Britain's dominance, and as the provider of hope for Ireland.

He saw Germany as a rising nation, France and Britain as declining ones.[19] Essays which he had been writing mainly in 1913 and early 1914 revealed how he saw and interpreted the direction of German development:

The laws of progress demand that efficiency shall prevail. The crime of Germany has been superior efficiency, not so much in the arts of war as in the products of peace.

During the first six months of 1914, German export trade almost equalled that of great Britain. Another year of peace, and it would certainly have exceeded it, and for the first time in the history of world trade Great Britain would have been put in the second place. German exports from January to June had swelled to the enormous total of £1,045,000,000 as against the £1,075,000,000 of Great Britain. As war against such figures could not be maintained in the markets, it must be transferred to the seas.

Europe reproduces herself yearly at the present time at the rate of about five million souls. Some three-fifths of the number are to-day absorbed into the life of the Continent, the balance go abroad and principally to North America, to swell the English-speaking world. Germany controls about one-fifth of Europe's natural annual increase, and realising that emigration to-day means only to lose her people and build up her antagonist's strength, she has for years now striven to keep her people within German limits, and hitherto with successful results far in excess of any achieved by other European States. But the limit must be reached, and that before many years are past. Where is Germany to find the suitable region, both on a scale and under conditions of climate, health and soil that a people of say 90,000,000 hemmed in a territory little larger than France, will find commensurate to their needs? No European people is in such plight.[20]

In contrast, Casement saw France as being in decline. We find him, in the same essays, writing such phrases as: 'her stagnant population of 40,000,000'; 'Her life blood is dried up'; 'France as a great free power is gone'; she was in decline; 'France, far from needing outlets, increases not at all, and during 1911 showed an excess of close on 40,000 deaths over births. For France the day of greatness is past.'[21] On top of his growing hostility to England because of events in Ireland, Casement saw England, too, as a declining nation, due to the related phenomena of the degeneration of her urban population and general population decline. On the question of population decline, he contrasted Germany's population of 66,000,000, 'the vast majority of them of German blood', with the British Empire's 59,000,000 'made up of various national and racial strains'. With her own population in decline, she relied more and more on the peoples of the Empire for her manpower.[22]

Now, when Casement shared his views with Poultney Bigelow, whose politics were very different, his friend reasoned with him: 'Why do you pray for the enemy who sought the harm of the US in 1898 – Germany. Why not pray for the success of my mother country – the only country that represents Liberty of Conscience and Freedom of Trade – England, the mother of Free Colonies.' He urged Casement to avoid Irish-American politicians who would use and discard him. He should help America against priestly interference in schools, against popery and Irish Bosses. He ended with the petition: 'come into my mountains and breathe pure air ...'[23]

Meanwhile, the war had affected fund-raising, Casement wrote to Alice Stopford Green: 'Things one could rightly say in peace cannot be said publicly to Irish audiences here now.' But he had already raised $6000 or $7000 in the previous three weeks. 'Poor Germany! – my heart bleeds for those poor people beset by a world of hatred, envy and jealousy. Their crime is their efficiency. England is playing an atrocious part ... She wins, perhaps, today by the sword of Russia and France – not by her own manhood! – and the sword she has hired to slay German commerce and industry will yet be turned against her in the East.'[24]

Quinn was later to comment on this period: 'Casement stopped with me three weeks before the war. I knew he was going to Germany. I tried to persuade him against it; but he wouldn't see anything but "the poor Kaiser" and the hand of England causing the war. Utter absurdities, both of them!'[25] John Butler Yeats, father of the poet, who was in New York at this time and in contact with Quinn, met Casement and corroborated the general picture of his despondency. Yeats sent his daughter Lily a pen sketch of Casement:

> Sir Roger over here to promote the cause of the Nationalist Volunteers – in great trouble over war, all his sympathies for Germany, partly because he really likes Germany but chiefly because he hates England ... He is very high strung and over six feet. Quinn is in high tension about him ... He talks all the time against England and is about sick with grief over 'poor Kaiser' ... He is well-educated and talks agreeably even though so much on one subject.

He likened Casement to 'a very nice girl who is just hysterical enough to be charming and interesting among strangers and a trial to his own friends'. Quinn thought Casement 'seriously ill' and had a doctor examine him. The latter's report was: 'I have given Sir Roger a great deal of advice which he won't take.' John Yeats commented: 'As you may guess, Sir Roger is not a man open to advice on any subject.' He added, however: 'He is a very fine gentleman ... a prince of courtesy.'[26]

Another Irish visitor who observed and left an account of Casement in New York was Mary Colum:

> One day my husband and I went down to William street to see the old Fenian editor of the *Gaelic American*, John Devoy ... While waiting in the outer office we saw the tall figure of Casement in earnest conversation with one of the editors, a captain Freeman. Devoy himself had his own distinction of appearance, a powerful head with thick grey hair that gave him a strong resemblance to Sigmund Freud, but beside the aristocratic figure and face of Roger Casement, all the people in the office except the extra-ordinary Freeman looked plebeian. In fact Casement was so different in mind, body, and life experience that he roused their suspicions to the extent that some of the Irish organizations had him trailed by a detective, who found everything he did quite aboveboard, as the editor of another Irish paper, the *Irish World*, told us. Indeed he was spied upon by all sides wherever he went.[27]

German–Irish contacts in the United States

During the summer of 1914, radical Irish-American nationalist leaders and German representatives were in contact with one another, though the German ambassador, Count Johann von Bernstorff, was on holiday in Germany. Soon after the outbreak of the war, the nationalist leadership in Ireland and in the United States decided to use the opportunity to attempt to overthrow British rule in Ireland. Since his visit to the US coincided with this development, Casement was drawn into discussions on the matter, though he was a member of neither the IRB nor Clan na Gael. Out of the German–Irish discussions in which he now participated emerged his decision to travel to Germany.

He was introduced to two Germans, George von Skal, an active propagandist, and the military attaché, Captain Franz von Papen.[28] Shortly after the Bachelors' Walk protest and the outbreak of war, von Papen wrote to the German Foreign Office:

> The leader of all Irish associations in America, Roger Casement, has contacted me for the purpose of cooperation with Germany. At the mass meeting this evening very strong declaration of protest against England on account of destruction of Germanic culture. It is certain that the largest part of the Irish people are ready to free themselves. The movement will influence public opinion in America favourably and can mean assistance for Germany. Leader ready to land arms for fifty thousand in Ireland with own means. It is the view of the leader that the movement can be successful only if German Government declares or causes to be declared that after victory it would favour liberation. Irish organization so strong that success probable even if Government itself would not take position. Press campaign would suffice but one would have to see to it that it become known here. Leader declares that

declaration of sympathy necessary for mass movement. Special success hoped for with the Irish regiments.[29]

The first meeting of the Clan leaders with the German ambassador, von Bernstorff, back from his summer vacation, was on 24 August at the German Club in Manhattan.[30] It seems likely that Casement was well informed of the details, since two documents from his hand, relating to German–Irish relations, date from the following day, the 25th. In the first of these, the objectives outlined were essentially those of his forthcoming mission to Germany. One was the procurement of arms and ammunition to support 'a war of independence that may greatly impair England's offensive power on the Continent'. His memo stated that 'Rifles and ammunition could be got into Cork, Kerry, Limerick, Galway, etc. and a number of Irish-American officers could be introduced at once to prepare for a military *coup de main*.' Two other objectives concerned the issuing by the German government of a statement of positive intent towards Ireland, and the formation of a brigade from the ranks of Irish prisoners of war held in German camps:

> In the event of capture of British prisoners by the German armies, the German War Office should discriminate between Irish soldiers and ordinary British regulars. The Irish regiments, and even individual soldiers of Irish birth, should as far as possible be kept in separate confinement from other British prisoners. A military proclamation should be issued that Germany recognised that Irishmen, being without a Government of their own, and not free agents in this war were now, as in the case of the Boers, unwillingly driven to attack a people with whom they had no quarrel. German Catholic Priests should be introduced among the Irish prisoners to aid in pointing out that Germany was fighting for Irish freedom, and that Catholic Irishmen had nothing to fear from a land that contained 25,000,000 Catholics enjoying (so differently from what English rule had established in Ireland!) complete political equality with German protestants.
> Germany, it should be pointed out, would free Ireland if victorious; and, therefore, every Irish soldier taken was given the option of obtaining freedom at once by joining the 'Irish Brigade' to be formed in the German army, whose specific purpose should be to aid in the restoration of Irish independence.[31]

On the same day he produced a formal address to the Kaiser, Wilhelm II. The text was written by Casement and adopted and signed by the members of the Clan na Gael Executive, though John Devoy later gave it as his opinion that they would have 'worded some portions of it differently'. The address claimed to 'give voice to the feeling of Irishmen in America', and began by expressing sympathy and admiration for Germany,

> assailed at all points by an unnatural league of enmity, having only one thing in common, a hatred of German prosperity and efficiency. We feel that the German people are in truth fighting for European civilisation at its best and certainly in its less selfish form. We recognise that Germany did not seek this war, but that it was forced upon her by those jealous of her military security, envious of her industrial and commercial capacity, and aiming at her integrity as a

Great World Power that was capable, if peace were maintained, of outdistancing the competition of all her rivals.

War was the only solution for those unable to compete in peace.

The address went on to draw the Kaiser's attention to the significance of Ireland in the war. Britain's strength rested on her control of the seas and this, in turn, depended on her continued subjection of Ireland.

> It is by sole possession of Ireland that Great Britain has been able for two centuries to maintain an unchallengeable mastery of the seas and by this agency to convert a small trading community into the wholly arbitrary judges of war and peace for all mankind ... We are profoundly convinced that so long as Great Britain is allowed to control, exploit and misappropriate Ireland and all Irish resources – whether of men, material wealth, or strategic position – she will dominate the seas. Thus the freedom of Ireland becomes of paramount, nay, of vital importance to the larger question of the freeing of the seas.

The address concluded with a plea to the Kaiser not to forget Ireland and a wish for a German victory.[32]

Soon afterwards, on 1 September, his birthday, he wrote to Gertrude: 'I don't like the USA. The more I see of it the less I like it – but it is a great country. The people are ignorant and unthinking and easily led by anything they read in their rotten papers. The press is the worst in the world.'[33] On 12 September, Casement received a letter from Alice Stopford Green which reassured him about Nina and brought him news of Volunteer affairs. 'My dear Watchman of the Night,' she opened, 'In what calamities we are! I go back in thought to the war before the Union. God preserve us all.' His sister, about whom he was worried, was in good spirits and with friends in Ballycastle. Hobson, too, was all right, but, with regard to Volunteer affairs, a bad organiser. The 'Volunteer War Office' was in chaos and Childers and Barton were sent to organize it. Figgis, she told him, was erratic and had enlisted. She ended with a prayer of hope: 'Some day you will come to stay with me in Ireland and see a country in which good men and a good spirit will still be left.'[34] Casement responded two days later, in a despondent mood, probably with news of the French counter-attack at the Marne on his mind. Germany, he now felt, would 'go down for 40 to 50 years', and England would be left supreme. If he came home now, he didn't think he could keep quiet and would be 'in jail within a week, or in a Concentration Camp or in flight to the hills'.[35]

During September the polemical essays he had been writing over the preceding few years were collected and published for propaganda purposes under the title of *Ireland, Germany and the Freedom of the Seas: a Possible Outcome of the War of 1914*. The booklet was to be widely circulated in American-Irish circles and, later, in Germany, appearing in a second edition as *The Crime Against Europe*.[36] In mid September, too, Casement penned an 'Open Letter to Irishmen', a manifesto which challenged the call for Irishmen to join the British army and fight

Germany as a response to the promise that Home Rule would be implemented at the end of the war. The British Liberal Party, Casement argued, 'now offers to sell, at a very high price, a wholly hypothetical and indefinite form of partial internal control of certain specified Irish services, if, in return for this promissory note (payable after death), the Irish people will contribute their blood, their honour and their manhood in a war that in no wise concerns them. Ireland has no quarrel with the German people or just cause of offence against them'.

Turning to the current state of Ireland, he pleaded: 'Ireland has no blood to give to any land, to any cause but that of Ireland. Our duty as a Christian people is to abstain from bloodshed; and our duty as Irishmen is to give our lives for Ireland. Ireland needs all her sons. In the space of sixty-eight years her population has fallen by far over 4,000,000 souls, and in every particular of national life she shows a steady decline of vitality.' Even if Home Rule were granted tomorrow, 'it would be the duty of Irishmen to save their strength and manhood for the trying tasks before them, to build up from a depleted population the fabric of a ruined national life ... If this be a war for the "small nationalities", as its planners term it, then let it begin, for one small nationality, at home.'[37]

Casement proceeded to draw up another statement and, on 18 September, sent a copy to Devoy, with a note saying: 'I had intended sending this out to press today, but J. Quinn and Bourke Cockran strongly deprecate my doing so. They say it will do harm not good! What do you think?' In his *Recollections*, written years later, Devoy commented that Clan members were alarmed at Casement's taking Quinn and Cockran into his confidence, as both were 'honorable men, but neither of them was in agreement with our policy'. The incident, presumably, contributed to his more general assessment of Casement:

> While a highly intellectual man, Casement was very emotional and as trustful as a child. He was also obsessed with the idea that he was a better judge than any of us, at either side of the Atlantic, of what ought to be done (though he was too polite and good natured to say so), and he never hesitated to act on his own responsibility, fully believing that his decisions were in the best interests of Ireland's Cause. This created many difficulties and embarrassments for us.[38]

In Ireland on 19 September John Redmond precipitated a crisis for the Irish Volunteers when he gave a speech at Woodenbridge, Co. Wicklow, calling on the Volunteers not only to defend Ireland but to fight 'wherever the firing-line extends'. Within days, most of the members of the original Provisional Committee joined in issuing a statement repudiating Redmond's position. A split ensued: the bulk of the Volunteers, some 170,000, remained with Redmond and became the National Volunteers; a much smaller number, perhaps 11,000, though the more active and militant, retained the name of Irish Volunteers and set up a new organization.[39]

On 5 October, Casement's 'Open Letter to Irishmen' was published in the *Irish Independent*. Its very public challenge to the British government was to elicit a neutrally-worded, yet ominous, response from the Foreign Office. Arthur Nicolson wrote to Casement:

> The attention of the Secretary of State has been called to a letter dated New York, September 16th [sic] which appeared in the *Irish Independent* of October 5th over your signature. The letter urges that Irish sympathies should be with Germany rather than with Great Britain and that Irishmen should not join the British army. As you are still liable, in certain circumstances, to be called upon to serve under the Crown I am to request you to state whether you are the author of the letter in question.[40]

Meanwhile, negotiations between Clan members and German representatives were progressing; they included arrangements for Casement's journey to Berlin. On 5 October, McGarrity penned the following coded note:

> New York at Judge Cohalan's 7.15 pm. J. Devoy, Sir R.C. and Judge agreed on $3.000 [$3000] for Sir Roger's trip to Berlin; agreed on interview with Von Bernstorff. Positive declaration must be made, if we are to do the work here we are capable of doing. Dan's [Cohalan] suggestion about land tenure mistake. Republic declaration expect from William [Emperor Wilhelm II] a mistake. Independence covers the matter agreed to arrange meeting of J.D. – Sir R.C. and Dan, possibly another. Hope it comes off. R.C. to leave by way of Norway.[41]

On 10 October another German–Irish meeting took place in New York, with the ambassador in attendance. The clipped record is again McGarrity's: 'Cohalan's house. Rory [Casement], John Devoy, Schuylkill [McGarrity]. 7–8.15. German Club 9. Captain Von Papen, Dr Dernburg, Bernstorff, Rory, Cohalan, McGarrity, John Devoy. One hour and thirty minutes. Very satisfactory interview. Democratic appreciative.'[42]

On the 12th Casement wrote to Gertrude:

> I sorrow for the Belgians – but I cannot blame the Germans. They offered fair terms, and did it openly and above board. If England had refused to co-operate with France and Russia the war would *never* have come – that is the grief of it all … I feel despair often … I cannot bear to think of Ireland in this cauldron of hatred and murder … Mavrone, mavrone. Ireland will never be the same again – nor can I be ever the same again.[43]

Von Bernstorff, meanwhile, penned an official introduction for Casement to the Imperial Chancellor, Theobald von Bethmann Hollweg: 'I am honored to warmly recommend to Your Excellency the bearer of this letter, the frequently mentioned Sir Roger Casement. I may repeat obediently that according to views here it would be desirable to consider the proposals of Sir Roger.'[44] Some days later, he wrote to the German Foreign Office:

> I am being pressed constantly by Casement and other Irish that the Imperial Government should declare that in case of victory it would support the Irish. Casement himself wants to travel to Germany this week. An Irish leader who just returned from Ireland declared with certainty that the Irish were disloyal and declining to offer volunteers [for military service]. During the Battle of

Mons an Irish regiment is said to have taken shots at the British intentionally. Looked at from here, nothing could be said against a [German] declaration in the way the Irish wish it. Moreover, the mood against us in England appears to be so thoroughly embittered that it can't get any worse. German declarations for the Irish, the Poles, the Jews, the Finns etc. could only have a positive effect here ...45

On 13 October the Clan gave Casement $2500 to cover the costs of his journey.46 With the help of the Austrian Embassy, tickets had been purchased for Adler Christensen and himself on the Norwegian vessel, the *Oskar II*, due to sail for Christiania (Oslo) on the 15th. When and why Casement decided to take Christensen with him is not known. They were travelling via Norway and he may have considered Christensen's being Norwegian helpful; Christensen also spoke some German. It is difficult, however, to discount the motive of companionship.47 To conceal his departure, Casement changed hotel, registering in the new one as 'Mr R. Smythe'. On the 15th, before sailing, he penned a number of farewell letters. To Devoy, he wrote: 'My Dear Old Friend, I cannot go without a farewell word and grip of the heart. Without you there would be nothing, and if success come, or even a greater hope for the future, it will be due to you and your life of unceasing devotion to the most unselfish cause on earth ... Good-bye and *au revoir* where we both hope that meeting may be.'48

His mood in a letter to Dick Morten was despondent:

Your note last night! I am still here and not likely to get off for long. The war has upset and changed everything – including my heart. It is a crime. Grey and Asquith are *greatly* to blame. *England* could have *prevented* this war altogether had she wanted to – but *she* wanted to get Germany down and could not resist the chance that came – as the direct result of her own planning and contriving with France and Russia ... Now England will pay dearly and bitterly in the end – but God knows all will pay – It is a monstrous crime and calamity and will ruin half the world ...

I fear, oh dear old Dick, a terrible evil will fall on us all – the Germans will never forgive England and I think Grey did his country the greatest wrong ever done it – for this war could have been prevented. It was that evil gang at F.O., who ran Grey, plotted it with their *entente* and anti-German 'understandings' when they could have had a good, strong honest understanding with Germany and that would have kept the peace of the world. I am very wretched and despondent – my brother is ruined in South Africa and I feel old and broken hearted.49

Immediately prior to his departure, in order to disguise himself, he shaved his beard, lightened his complexion with buttermilk and boarded the ship in the name of James E. Landy (the real Landy being a Clan member). The *Oskar II* attempted to avoid the British Atlantic blockade by taking a northerly route.50 But on the 24th they were intercepted by HMS *Hibernia*, boarded by a prize crew and escorted to Stornoway on the island of Lewis in the Outer Hebrides. Passengers had been tense during the voyage, some believing Casement to be a

British spy, as he later discovered. From his own narrative, it seems likely that others on board saw through his disguise, an Austrian diplomat and a German consul, for example. When they reached Stornoway, the cliffs and rocks in the entrance to the harbour mouth reminded Casement of shark's teeth – 'it felt just as if we were really going into a shark's jaws. I had that feeling'. Six German passengers were taken off for internment, but Casement went unnoticed.

The 'Findlay Affair'

Having continued its voyage, the *Oskar II* sailed into Christiania at midnight on 28 October. Casement and Christensen went ashore, taking rooms in the Grand Hotel; Casement wired New York with word of his safe arrival.[51] It would seem that the British legation in Christiania rapidly became aware, through Christensen, of Casement's presence. Two versions of what happened survive: Casement's, derived from Christensen, and that contained in documents from the British side. According to the British legation account, Christensen had presented himself at the door of the legation, intimating that he had information on a well-known 'Englishman' involved in an 'Irish-American-German conspiracy'. Francis Lindley, the First Secretary, was the first official to interview Christensen. While cautious, he was willing to hear more, and asked his visitor to return the following day. Christensen did so and was met by a man who proved to be the Minister, Mansfeldt de Cardonnel Findlay. He revealed both Casement's identity and his alias and handed over documents given him by Casement for safekeeping during the encounter with HMS *Hibernia*.[52]

Casement's version painted a very different picture. According to it, early in the afternoon of 29 October, Christensen was approached by a stranger in the hall of the hotel and taken by car to a large house, which Casement later ascertained to be the British legation; here he was questioned about his master. Casement may have been predisposed to believe the story, as, on leaving the hotel himself, he had observed a man following him. After Christensen had given this version of what had taken place to Casement, they agreed to play the British officials along. Over the course of three visits, Christensen's hosts, Findlay and Lindley, quizzed him about his master, whose identity legation officials were very interested in. Christensen told Casement, for example, that Findlay had suggested that 'if someone knocked Casement on the head, he would get well-paid'. On his part, Christensen claimed to have driven a hard bargain and to have, ultimately, extracted a promise of £5000 in gold for delivering Casement. The latter believed his associate's account, was outraged at such behaviour by diplomatic officials in a neutral country, and allowed the issue to become a virtual obsession over the course of the following months.[53] Christensen, it seems likely, was playing a double game, seeing possible advantages for himself, especially financial gain, on both fronts. Subsequent knowledge of him reveals him to have been a man who lived on his wits.

During his encounters with Christensen, Francis Lindley received from him information on Casement's homosexuality: 'He implied that their relations were of an unnatural nature and that consequently he had great power over this man who trusted him absolutely.'[54] Findlay returned to this matter in despatches to the FO in February and March of 1915, enquiring in one if it was the reason for Casement's retirement from the service. 'Was it sodomy?' he asked.[55] In addition to Christensen's hints to Lindley and Findlay, the latter subsequently acquired corroborating information from a Norwegian, who was willing to come forward only 'if *absolutely* necessary'.[56] In the event, after Casement's capture in 1916, a number of Norwegian witnesses made sworn affidavits relating to the sexual nature of Casement's and Christensen's relationship (see Appendix).

Casement had visited the German legation immediately after his arrival in Christiania in order to arrange his onward journey to Berlin. He presented a letter written for him by von Bernstorff in Washington to the minister, von Oberndorff. The latter asked him to return the following morning but, following the events of what Casement was to dub 'the Findlay Affair', Casement wrote to and again called on von Oberndorff, impressing on him the urgency of the matter, in the light of the perceived threat to himself. Von Oberndorff promised to act as soon as word came from Berlin. It came on the following morning and so, too, did Richard Meyer, an employee of the Foreign Office, to accompany Casement on his journey.[57] Christensen claimed to have told Findlay that they were travelling by train via Copenhagen and, late in the afternoon of 30 October, the party boarded the Copenhagen section of the train, having been accompanied to the station by some 'sturdy friends' provided by the German legation. When the two sections of the train separated, they quickly changed from the Copenhagen section to the one going on for Trälleborg and the ferry to Sassnitz in Germany. Meyer's presence was needed in negotiating passage through the German frontier and to assuage the hostility of passengers who heard Casement speaking English.[58]

Map 9: Germany

17: *Imperial Germany, 1914–16*

They arrived in Berlin on the evening of 31 October. Casement and Christensen checked into the Contintental Hotel, Casement under the name of 'Mr Hammond' of New York. Meyer warned the two men not to leave the hotel until arrangements for their safety could be made. 'At last in Berlin!' wrote Casement in his diary, with seeming relief. 'The journey done – the effort perhaps only begun! Shall I succeed? – Will they see the great cause aright and understand all it may mean to them, no less than to Ireland? Tomorrow will show the beginning.'[1] They remained in the hotel all the following day; Meyer called to announce that the Undersecretary of State for Foreign Affairs, Arthur Zimmermann, would see Casement the next day.[2] Before leaving for the meeting the following morning, Casement drafted a memorandum outlining the context of his mission. With the formation of an Irish Brigade in mind, he suggested that Irish Catholic prisoners of war, most likely to be nationalist at heart, be separated out from others and that appeals be made to their patriotism. They had probably joined the army, he suggested, out of poverty or the attraction of fighting itself. He went on to a second issue, the importance to the British government of recruitment in Ireland and the propaganda campaign being waged to encourage enlisting. For example, the German invasion of Catholic Belgium was being portrayed as an example of what might happen to Catholic Ireland should Germany defeat Great Britain. Casement proposed the issuing of a German declaration to 'nail this lie to the counter'.[3]

When he met Zimmermann later that morning, Casement liked the man: 'He was warm-*hearted* as well as warm-handed.' They talked of the events in Christiania and of the idea of a German declaration. Zimmermann approved. Next, Casement was introduced to Count Georg von Wedel, head of the English Department at the Foreign Office. The two talked mostly of the scheme to organize a brigade from Irish prisoners of war. 'If you do that,' exclaimed von Wedel, 'it is worth ten *army corps* to us!'⁴ On a more immediate and concrete matter, von Wedel visited the head of the secret police to arrange a pass for Casement. Meyer duly delivered this to the hotel that afternoon. It read: 'Mr Hammond of New York, presently living in the Continental Hotel, is not to be troubled by the police.' Following these first positive contacts with their guest, the German Foreign Office informed its embassy in Washington: 'Sir Roger Casement has arrived. His proposals are being carefully gone into. Zimmermann.'⁵

Casement reported back to his contacts in the US. He sent a message to Judge Cohalan:

> They are ignorant true purpose my coming Germany, but seek evidence at all costs. Here everything favourable, authorities helping warmly. Send messenger immediately to Ireland fully informed verbally. No letters on him. He should be native born American citizen, otherwise arrest likely. Let him despatch priest here via Christiania quickly. German legation there will arrange passport. Also let him tell Bigger, Solicitor, Belfast conceal everything belonging to me.⁶

Early in his stay in Berlin, Casement made the acquaintance of Professor Theodor Schiemann, through whom he met Kuno Meyer, who, in turn, introduced him to his brother, Eduard, a professor of ancient history and also a man of some influence in official circles.⁷ Soon afterwards he wrote a warm letter to Meyer, who was still in Berlin but due to travel to the US to undertake German propaganda work; in his letter, Casement advised Meyer on US contacts, recommending Quinn, Devoy, McGarrity and a Philadelphia priest, Gerald Coghlan. He should get Quinn to arrange a lecture tour – 'your Irish Literature course will appeal most strongly to Irish nationalists' – and he could quote from Casement's own essays, 'Seas' and 'Crime'. 'Politics', he advised, 'would have to be avoided, that is *present-day* politics, but one can always illuminate the present with the shadow of the past! – when it is Ireland you speak of.' He gave a blow-by-blow account of the Christiania incident and suggested that, when proof was available, Meyer could publicize it.⁸

After he arrived in the US Meyer wrote to Alice Stopford Green to assure her of Casement's safety:

> Our friend the Knight of the Ships had safely though after great dangers arrived in Berlin, where we met repeatedly. He has burned his ships behind him and is embarked on a new course, or rather one as old almost as the Old Woman herself, at least since she has fallen upon evil days. He will get every assistance that he and she stand so much in need of. Everybody is interested in him. He spent an evening at the Schiemanns' and wished you had been there with us. By a curious coincidence Schiemann had just translated his last pamphlet which showed that wonderful insight into coming events.

Green responded on 15 December, distancing herself from Meyer's political opinions before referring to Casement: 'Nor can I discuss with you the subject of my friend Sir Roger Casement though your references to him force me to express the profound and heartful sorrow I feel at the political course he has been unhappily led to adopt wholly unknown to me.'9 Her response was a sharp reminder that a parting of the ways had come between Casement and many of his former friends and supporters; even one as close to him as Green, who had participated in the arming of the Volunteers, strongly disapproved of his German enterprise. She remained loyal, however, and was to be one of his main supports during his imprisonment in 1916.

The German Declaration

The German authorities acted rapidly with regard to the segregation of Irish prisoners. The Secretary of State at the Foreign Office, Gottlieb von Jagow, having received Zimmermann's report, responded on 7 November to say that the chief of staff of the army had given instructions for bringing Irish prisoners together in one camp:

> Once these measures have been carried out there would be no reservations against Sir Roger Casement or Irish priests establishing contact with the prisoners and the discussion of the idea of organising an Irish legion. The reservations against actually carrying out the idea are evident. The military results would be small, possibly even negative, and it would be said that we had violated international law. However, it would suffice to have it known that the Irish prisoners were quite ready to fight against England on our side.

He was more hesitant about a proclamation, suggesting that to publicize an interview between Casement and Zimmermann might suffice.[10]

Casement was unhappy with this more limited measure. A week later, on 14 November, when Zimmermann forwarded the text of the interview between Casement and himself to the Imperial Chancellor, Theobald von Bethmann Hollweg, he relayed Casement's dissent: 'It is his opinion that in order to reach that effect it would instead be necessary to clearly express during the interview that I was speaking to him officially representing your Excellency.' The Chancellor gave his consent and, on 20 November, the German statement, including an official declaration, was released to the press. Contrary to stories being circulated in Ireland concerning the pillage that would result from the invasion of a successful German army, the declaration set out to reassure Irish people as to the positive disposition of Germany. It included the following statements:

> The German Government repudiates the evil intentions attributed to it in the statements referred to by Sir Roger Casement and takes this opportunity to give a categoric assurance that the German Government desires only the welfare of the Irish people, their country and their institutions with whom Germany has no cause to quarrel.

The Imperial Government formally declares that under no circumstances would Germany invade Ireland with a view to its conquest or the overthrow of any native institutions of that country.

Should the fortune of this great war, that was not of Germany's seeking, ever bring in its course German troops to the shores of Ireland they would land there not as an army of invaders to pillage and destroy, but as the forces of a Government that is inspired by good will towards a Country and a people for whom Germany desires only national prosperity and freedom.[11]

The declaration was a valuable first step, but it fell short of support for the cause of Irish independence and Casement continued to seek a fuller statement of German commitment. In this he was destined to be disappointed.

The number of government departments involved in arrangements regarding Irish prisoners – Foreign Office, War Office and army general staff – meant that progress was slow. On 16 November, Casement was called to the headquarters of the general staff in Berlin and told he must go to the military headquarters at Charleville on the French front. He set off the following day, accompanied by Richard Meyer and a young Prussian nobleman, taking the train as far as Cologne, where a military staff car was provided. They drove, in intense cold, the 270 kilometres to Charleville, passing scenes of military destruction in Belgium on the way. The first person Casement met in Charleville was Baron Kurt von Lersner, who talked of the proposed brigade and of the difficulty in distinguishing Irish Catholics from other prisoners of war. After a spartan sojourn in a hotel that night, the head of the Political Department of the general staff, Baron von Stumm, talked over the practicalities of the enterprise with Casement.

While returning, he was moved on hearing of the execution of 350 Belgian men in retaliation for an attack: 'I nearly wept as I looked at these pitiable evidences of a sorrow that is now, perhaps, the chief national asset of the Belgian people ... I feel that there may be in this awful lesson to the Belgian people a *repayment*. All that they now suffer and far more, they, and their King, his Government and his officers, wreaked on the well-nigh defenceless people of the Congo basin.'[12] When Casement arrived back in Berlin on 20 November, von Wedel passed on the contents of a telegram received that day from Rome, stating that two priests, an Augustinian, Fr Canice O'Gorman, and a Dominican, Fr Thomas Crotty, were prepared to travel to Germany immediately to minister to the Irish prisoners: 'Both Irish patriots,' the telegram stated, 'full of the sentiment desired by us.' Fr O'Gorman was only available for a period of two months, while Fr Crotty could stay indefinitely. The two, probably reflecting Vatican instructions, were to remain politically neutral and to devote themselves to ministering to the spiritual needs of prisoners. They could play no part, therefore, in recruiting for a brigade.[13]

The next day, General Erich von Falkenhayn, chief of staff, circulated a memo summarizing the proposals that Casement had made in his visit to Charleville: that Catholic Irish prisoners be separated and brought to one location; that Casement would visit them, once the process was under way; that copies of the German declaration be circulated among them; that select prisoners be freed for propaganda purposes; that Casement would attempt to form a regiment or brigade from among the prisoners, who would be led by officers from Germany and from the US; that Egypt might be a suitable arena to use such a brigade; and that, at the end of the war, no members of such a group would be extradited to England. Von Falkenhayn concluded: 'I herewith order that Lieutenant of the Reserve, Ret. Nadolny will take over from the Deputy General Staff the handling of this matter and for this purpose will contact the Foreign Office and the War Ministry. He will further inform the Chief of the General Staff of the Army (Section P) on the continuing development of the Irish matter.'[14] Thus entered the picture Count Rudolf von Nadolny, head of general staff's political section, who, of those who played a central role in Casement's affairs from 1914 to 1916, seems to have had the least sympathy for Casement personally.

Following the publication of the declaration and feeling himself in need of help with the Irish Brigade enterprise, Casement tried to contact Eoin Mac-Neill in Dublin. He forwarded a copy of the declaration, asking MacNeill to have it circulated in Ireland and reiterating the goodwill of Germany towards Ireland.[15] After less than one month in Germany, his mood was still positive:

> Send to me here in Berlin, by way of Christiania, if possible, one or two thoroughly patriotic Irish priests – young men best. Men like Father Murphy of Vinegar Hill – *and for the same purpose* ... Tell all to trust the Germans – and to trust me. We shall win everything if you are brave and faithful to the old cause. Try and send me word here to Berlin by the same channel as this. Tell me all your needs at home, viz. rifles, officers, men. Send priest or priests at all costs – one not afraid to *fight* and die for Ireland. The enemy are hiding the truth.
>
> The Germans will surely, under God, defeat both Russia and France and compel a peace that will leave Germany stronger than before. They already have 550,000 prisoners of war in Germany, and Austria 150,000, and Russia has been severely defeated in Poland. India and Egypt will probably both be in arms. Even if Germany cannot reach England to-day, we can only gain by helping Germany now, as with the understanding come to, Ireland will have a strong and enlightened friend to help to ultimate independence.[16]

When his arrival and actions in Germany became known, the security services in Britain and Ireland began to gather all available information about Casement. In December, circulars were sent from Dublin Castle to Tullamore, Limerick, Kilkenny, Belfast, Dundalk, Galway, Londonderry, Cork, Tyrone, Dublin, Lisburn, Antrim and Down. RIC reports filtered back to the chief secretary's office and the Special Branch in Dublin Castle, giving details, for example, of his earlier movements in Ireland in connection with the Volunteers. His family connections were documented and newspaper coverage meticulously monitored.[17]

The Findlay Affair, Phase Two

Through all of this time, the events of Christiania had never left Casement's mind and he was now to spend considerable energy in an effort to entrap Findlay, but also to confuse the British authorities as to the nature of German–Irish plotting. In all of this he was losing sight of the key goals of his mission. He had come for a number of purposes. He sought, in the first place, official German support for the independence movement in Ireland and in this he was already partly successful with the declaration. Secondly, and related to this diplomatic aim, he intended to engage in a propaganda campaign partly aimed at sensitizing influential German opinion to the Irish question and partly at influencing Irish-American opinion regarding Germany. Thirdly, there was the scheme to form an Irish Brigade from the ranks of Irish prisoners of war in Germany. And, lastly, there was the goal of supporting an Irish struggle for independence with a supply of arms or, should circumstances allow, with a military invasion of Ireland as part of the war effort. In the light of these the Norwegian enterprise was a distraction and Casement's persistence in pursuing it raises serious questions about his judgment. It did have some propaganda potential, but its main contribution was probably to alienate his German hosts.[18]

Soon after his arrival in Berlin, he had decided to pursue the Findlay matter and, toward that end, planned to send Christensen back to the Norwegian capital. He drafted a number of false letters concerning Irish plotting, which Christensen would give to British legation officials, thereby sowing confusion. One was dated 1 November and began, 'My dear Joe'. In it he talked of not being spotted when their ship had been held up on the voyage from America; of having been followed in Christiania and covering his traces; of Christensen ('The man I brought was very useful and is absolutely faithful to me'); and he talked, in transparent code, of arms: 'The *Sanitary Pipes* will be furnished and on a big scale, with plenty of stock of *disinfectants*. Enough for 50,000 health officers at least.' The second letter was enclosed in another, a short note to Fr Gerald Coghlan of Philadelphia, asking him to forward it 'to our good friend Pat'. It was dated 14 November and opened with, 'Dear Patrick'. Exuding optimism and jauntiness, it read:

> The German–Irish alliance will beat the *Entente* yet! ... So far as I can see up to this all will be ready here by end of December. The enemy only know that we are moving – they have no idea of the extent of our resources or of the heartiness of the cooperation of our friends here. They will be *very* sorry, before long, they so wantonly plotted this war against Germany ... But it is getting plainer every day that our friends will and can dispose of the Russian bear and the French tiger cat and then have their strong hands free to tackle the Sea Serpent. Meantime we must perform our part of the compact and 'carry the war into Africa' ... So, have all our men ready for early in January ... They have over half a million prisoners of war now in Germany alone – to say nothing of Austria with 100,000.

He talked, too, of a German plan to mine British waters.[19]

Christensen set out for Norway on Sunday 22 November, carrying the false letters and some 'stolen' pages from Casement's diary. He was to be away almost a month, returning to Berlin on 15 December. After he was gone a week, Casement wrote to Christensen, his letter filled with tenderness. 'I am looking forward very soon to hearing from you. I miss you very much ... Don't forget me – and be sure I don't forget you. I shall be very glad to hear from you; and to see you again back with me once more. My beard and moustache have grown a lot since you left – and I look very nearly the same as ever ... Write soon to me, dear Adler. I think very often of you and will be glad to see you again and clasp your hand ...'[20]

The first communication Casement got from Christensen in Norway came on 1 December, in the form of a note and a letter dated 26 November. To aid in his entrapment of Findlay, or so he told Casement, Christensen asked for another false letter, listing the types of items he wished included in it, to convey the impression of some military-type scheme being organized by Casement.[21] The latter duly obliged with a false letter for Findlay's eyes, dated 1 December. The letter instructed Christensen to charter a schooner and hold it in readiness for a shipment Casement had ready, and also expressed negative feelings about Britain, her empire and the conduct of the war.[22]

When Christensen returned from his stay in Norway, he and Casement spent several days going over Christensen's version of what had transpired between Findlay and himself. According to Christensen, he met Findlay twice on this visit, once on 26 November and again on 12 December. Casement summarized what his companion told him:

> Adler spun a delightful web of lies! He talked vaguely, he says, of the 'Secret Society' in the USA, of its wide-spread organization, of the wealthy accession to its ranks of late, since the war, of the rich Irish-American with his big steam yacht ready; of my commission to him, Adler, to charter two sailing yachts in Norway to meet me on the coast of Schleswig at an early date; of my complete system of intelligence, how I got 'word from Ireland three hours after anything happened there'; how I had agents 'in the Navy itself' and how I was certainly going to get into Ireland with the American contingent in the yacht at an early date – probably he said, I intended the Norwegian chartered boats for transhipment 'at sea'.

Adler graphically described the effect of all of this on Findlay, pale and perspiring as he paced the room.[23]

Christensen's visit to Christiania gave rise to communications between the legation and London. The British were interested in apprehending Casement and were prepared to pay for it. On 27 November a minute from Sir Edward Grey read: 'We should authorize Mr Findlay to go up to £5000.' This decision was forwarded to Findlay by Arthur Nicolson.[24] Details of Casement's doings were also passed on to other branches of government in London. An FO minute recorded, in relation to the Casement file, that 'all the papers are with Mr

McKenna or at Scotland Yard',[25] and another that a telegram from Findlay be sent to Captain Hall.[26] Copies of the German-produced English-language propaganda newspaper, *The Continental Times*, with information on Casement and an edition of his political essays, *The Crime against Europe*, also made their way to the FO files.[27] The combination of these various types of information on Casement, including the false material, was to lead to an overestimation of his importance in the movement towards rebellion in Ireland.

While Christensen was away on his mission, Casement began to realize that his German hosts had developed grave doubts about his friend's personality, the veracity of his accounts of what had transpired between himself and Findlay and the wisdom of Casement's course of action. Schiemann had called on 1 December 'with disquieting statements about Adler that were unwarranted and malicious'. These were added to by his old friend Prince Blücher, whom Casement found to be in Germany with his wife, stranded by the war.[28] From Blücher, Casement learned that the German Foreign Office did not trust Christensen 'on account of his rather loose habits'. Blücher, too, had 'gossiped' about the events, although Casement was trying to keep them private until such time as he acquired definitive proof of Findlay's perfidy. He was even more perturbed when he learned from Blücher that von Jagow was of similar mind and, worse, that Casement should not 'hope for any full declaration of German policy about Ireland ... Jagow had told him this – They (the German Government) were not going to "make themselves ridiculous" and say things they had no intention of carrying out or attempting.' When Bernhard Dernburg, a member of the German propaganda team in the US, spoke of Germany's support for small nations, omitting Ireland from the list, Casement's suspicions were deepened further, and soothing remarks from von Wedel failed to reassure him. He was beginning to glimpse the reality: German support for Irish agitation was based less on idealistic considerations than on a hard-nosed assessment of its potential to weaken the British war effort. Casement's confidence in the German authorities was never to recover.[29]

Despite German doubts about Christensen, Casement was determined to press ahead with his attempt to unmask Findlay. 'I then discussed with von Wedel the possibility of the Navy getting something out of Findlay's insane projects against myself, as reported by Adler. All is fair in war, and, if these fine gentlemen will stick at nothing to catch me, why not take advantage of their trap and use it for our common interest.'[30] Von Wedel did go to the Admiralty and, surprisingly perhaps, they took up the idea. The plan that emerged involved leading Findlay to believe that Casement was to embark on a boat at Gothenburg on 8 January to make a rendezvous at sea with an American yacht, before proceeding with an expedition to Ireland. It was anticipated that Findlay would arrange to have British ships intercept Casement, while, in turn, German submarines would be waiting. Casement's main contact in the Admiralty for all of this was Captain Walther Isendahl, the 'Chief of Department N of the Admiralty, responsible for espionage, counter-espionage and agents stationed abroad'.[31] The Admiralty prepared two maps for Christensen, showing mythical minefields on each end of the Irish Sea to further confuse the British.

Before Christensen left, yet again, for Norway, Casement noticed a change in his behaviour. This, Casement believed, was partly due to Christensen's new admiration for Findlay and partly to his resentment at the Germans, who had harassed him at the border on his last exit and whose police had filed a negative report about him (Casement had informed him of it). 'His face is changed,' remarked Casement. 'The old boyish eyes and smile are gone and he does not look at me openly in the face.' Reflecting on all of this, he commented: 'Knowing now all I do of his character, of its extraordinary complexity, I should feel gravely disposed to mistrust his fidelity in a matter, whence German ships were the issue as against British ships. I should even, now, be indisposed to trust myself to his schemes!'[32] Nevertheless, the plan went ahead and Christensen left for Norway on Christmas Day, but was not given full details of the Admiralty's plan. Casement spent the evening 'quietly in Berlin with Countess Hahn'.[33]

On 30 December Casement departed for Limburg, where Irish prisoners were being collected, and he remained there until his return to Berlin on 23 January 1915. On 5 January he got a letter and a telegram from Christensen saying that he was arriving in Berlin with some 'good news'. After the 5th, though in communication with the Foreign Office in Berlin, Casement was told nothing of events in Christiania and he began to feel that he was being deliberately kept in the dark. In exasperation, he exclaimed: 'The German FO are very peculiar people – and one never knows where one is with them.'[34]

He did not learn the details of what had happened until after his return to Berlin on 23 January, almost a month after Christensen had left for Norway. Then, in discussions with Meyer, von Wedel and Christensen (himself back in Berlin), he was told the story. Christensen had visited the British legation a number of times, but the plot to trap British vessels had fizzled out.[35] But, on the matter of pressing Findlay to give a written guarantee of payment for apprehending Casement, Christensen was successful. In colourful terms, he described what had transpired: there had been heated words, Findlay offered his word of honour, to be told, 'You go and – – – – yourself!' by Christensen, who several times stormed out. In the end, Findlay sat down and wrote the guarantee, on formal legation stationery:

> On behalf of the British Government I promise that if, through information given by Adler Christensen, Sir Roger Casement be captured either with or without his companions, the said Adler Christensen is to receive from the British Government the sum of £5000 to be paid as he may desire. Adler Christensen is also to enjoy personal immunity & to be given a passage to the United States should he desire it. M. de C. Findlay, HBM Minister.[36]

It was mainly to deliver this document that Christensen had returned to Berlin early in January, where he had handed it over to Meyer. The Foreign Office had not informed Casement of its arrival; when he returned to Berlin, he was shown it, enclosed in their files as a 'State Paper'. 'They have', he wrote, 'wilfully kept me in ignorance of a fact of supreme importance to myself and the cause of Ireland and have taken possession of a document they have no more right to than to my purse!'[37] A grudging promise, extracted from von Wedel, that it would be returned to him when he needed it did little to mollify him. Much later, he was to claim that German actions in this sequence of events 'made me feel that I had made an awful fool of myself in ever believing that this Government would help Ireland. I never recovered faith in them.'[38]

When Christensen made contact with the British legation in Christiania, despatches again began to flow from there to London. In one, Findlay sent details of the location of the supposed minefields – one to the north of Tory Island. In another, he sent a description of Christensen: 'Has a fleshy, dissipated appearance, has been wanted by the police in N.Y. as a dangerous type of a Norwegian-American criminal.' Since Christensen had told him that he was interested in £20,000 in Casement's possession, Findlay was afraid that Christensen might 'rob Casement and bolt'. In a third despatch, he told of the tempestuous interview between himself and Christensen, with the latter demanding £1000 down or threatening to warn Casement.[39]

Meanwhile in London, on the basis of the (false) information that Casement was going to set out on an expedition, with its destination assumed to be Ireland, Captain Hall of naval intelligence and Basil Thomson of Scotland Yard together hatched a plot to capture him. They hired a yacht, the *Sayonara*, and in mid December sent it on a voyage along the west coast of Ireland, it purported to be part of Casement's plot and, at various points along the coast, attempted to collect information on his plans. When information was eventually received that he had never left Germany, the *Sayonara* was recalled.[40]

In Berlin, Casement's attention turned to publicly unmasking Findlay and the British system. He had contemplated doing this in the form of an open letter to Sir Edward Grey, and he had begun working on it while in Limburg:

> I propose writing this letter while here at Limburg and sending the original from Berlin, through the American Ambassador, to London, and handing copies formally to the Ambassador himself for transmission to his Government as well as complimentary copies to the Norwegian Government, the German and the Austro-Hungarian and also getting one to the Pope. Doubtless when the House of Commons meets early in February the enemy will announce his 'sensible punishment' of me. It will be well to let him and the world know first that his base attempt against me was known from the first.[41]

The 'sensible punishment' to be meted out to him derived from an exchange in the House of Lords late in 1914, where, in response to a question from Lord

Curzon on what was to be done about Sir Roger Casement, Lord Crewe had responded that 'very sensible punishment' was due.[42] A second line of action which Casement contemplated, linked to the writing of the letter, was to go personally to neutral Norway and publicly challenge Findlay's actions in the courts there.[43]

Plans were made for Casement and Christensen to travel to Norway on 31 January to confront Findlay. Meyer organized three detectives to accompany and protect Casement. On the 26th, 27th and 28th, Casement worked on the letter to Grey and got copies typed and photographs made of the Findlay guarantee.[44] On the 31st, the party went to the station in Berlin only to find that, due to wartime changes, their planned train would miss the Sassnitz ferry. They set off again that evening, more apprehensive now, because the Admiralty had warned that a British submarine could stop the mailboat. They had to overnight at Stralsund, where Casement went 'to bed in my clothes greatly upset and wondering how best to proceed'. It was not the submarine he feared, but the might of the British government: 'To go out, single-handed to thus challenge the mightiest Government in the world and to charge them publicly with infamous criminal conspiracy through their accredited Representative is a desperate act. I have no money; no friends; no support; no Government, save that of the One bent on destroying me, to appeal to.'[45] Next morning they travelled on to Sassnitz and, while waiting for the boat, debated the wisdom of proceeding. Contemplating his meagre financial resources, the likely British response and what he took to be lack of German cooperation, Casement hesitated. Finally, he lost his nerve and they decided to return to Berlin. 'Spent a miserable day,' he noted in his diary.[46]

A direct confrontation in Norway now aborted, Casement concentrated on sending out the letter to Grey from Berlin. Anticipating that there would be questions about him when Parliament resumed at the beginning of February, he was intent on stealing their thunder by making the Findlay affair public before that. He began his letter by referring to Lord Crewe's suggestion that he merited 'sensible punishment'. What of the secret punishment that was attempted on him, Casement asked. 'I was prepared to face charges in a Court of Law; I was not prepared to meet waylaying, kidnapping, suborning of dependants or "knocking on the head" – in fine, all the expedients your representative in a neutral country invoked when he became aware of my presence there.' He described, in detail, the sequence of events, as he perceived it, and the attempts to manipulate his 'faithful follower'. 'Your object', he continued, '... was to take my life with public indignity – mine was to expose your design and to do so through the very agent you had yourselves singled out for the purpose and had sought to corrupt to an act of singular infamy.' His own actions, over time, had been honourable, he argued: 'I served the British Government faithfully and loyally as long as it was possible for me to do so, and when it became impossible, I resigned. When, later, it became impossible for me to use the pension assigned to me by law, I voluntarily abandoned that income as I had previously resigned the post from which it was derived, and as I now proceed to divest myself of the honours and distinctions that at various times have been conferred upon me by His Majesty's Government.' He concluded the letter by formally renouncing his CMG and knighthood.[47]

Though the letter was dated 1 February, Casement was still adding finishing touches on 3 February. Late that afternoon he got it to Meyer, who promised to have it despatched immediately to Holland, where it would be posted the following day. Copies were typed and sent out to a list of embassies in Berlin. He sent a copy to Devoy and three to Rome – to Monsignor O'Riordan, Dr O'Hagan (Vice-Rector of the Irish College), and Fr O'Gorman.[48] Casement now made arrangements to go into seclusion for a short period, 'to be quiet and away from press reporters'. He approached his old friends from Brazil, the Nordenflychts, for a room, but did not go to them; he and Christensen tried Potsdam: 'But it was wretched and at the Palast Hotel where Klicks the Manager of the Continental told me to stay I got such a rude reception when they found I spoke only English that I returned to Berlin in despair.' Finally, on 10 February, he went to a sanatorium in Grunewald, where he wrote up his diary for the preceding weeks ('Nearly three weeks since I wrote in my diary'). While there he was approached by an agent of the secret police, who asked for his military pass. The record of this incident was to be his last regular entry in his German diary. 'I stopped that diary', he later wrote, 'when I became clear that I was being played with, fooled and used by a most selfish and unscrupulous government for its own sole petty interests. I did not wish to record the misery I felt or to say the things my heart prompted.'[49]

The results of his campaign cannot have enhanced his mood. Because of the delay, he was late for the opening of Parliament in London and the attendant publicity he had hoped to attract. On 5 February he got word that, in reply to questions in the House of Commons, Grey ('the public liar!') had said that 'he did not know whether Sir Roger Casement was in Germany or not'!!![50] Elsewhere, the letter received little attention. The Portuguese minister returned it, saying that it exceeded the legal rights of his legation to forward it. Word began to filter back from Norway that the government there was not allowing newspapers to publish any more on the Findlay affair. Casement made further efforts, writing to the Norwegian minister of foreign affairs and to the representative in Berlin, but to no avail.[51] Rome, too, yielded nothing: Dr O'Hagan replied, thanking him for the letter and calling his pamphlet 'splendid', but, as regards action, he felt it was 'inopportune' to tell the Holy Father at present – 'he must appear neutral'.[52] In the United States the story was not much better. Devoy records: 'The *New York American* was the only paper which gave it space. The other New York newspapers, having already openly taken sides with England in the war ...

either took no notice of the incident or sneered at it as "German propaganda". In Ireland, not a word pertaining to the Findlay–Christensen matter was allowed to pass the English censor.'53

An Irish Brigade

Meanwhile, a location near the town of Limburg had been chosen as the 'concentration camp' for Irish prisoners of war. One of those prisoners, Michael Kehoe, was later to describe the town as 'snugly slumbering in the lower reaches of the valley, and sentinelled by the spire of St Killian's Cathedral, with its 300 feet of graceful masonry towering heavenwards ... Surely the fruitful seed of Irish Catholic missionary labours had taken firm root in the Lahn valley.'54 The camp lay on a hill to the south of the town. The process of identification, selection and transportation of prisoners had commenced by the last weeks of November 1914. Towards the end of November, Casement met the two priests, Frs Crotty and O'Gorman, who had just arrived in Berlin from Rome. On the 30th, Meyer brought news that some 400 prisoners had already been collected in Limburg and Casement resolved to travel there and prepare the ground for the two priests. On 2 December he travelled by train to Frankfurt, where General de Graaff, commandant of the Frankfurt region, made arrangements to take him to the camp the day after. In the town of Limburg they had a discussion with General Exner, the camp commandant.

After a walk through the camp with the two generals and their staff, Casement talked to the Irish prisoners, first to a group of some twenty NCOs and, afterwards, to the rest of the men.55 He outlined his position and distributed newspapers and pamphlets. This was the first of several meetings he had with the men over a few days. The views he recorded of the men were mixed, suggesting that his own predispositions were ambivalent, even contradictory. On the one hand, he believed that the men embodied his vision of Irish manhood, noble and likely to be moved by appeals to nationhood; on the other hand, because they had enrolled in the British army, after the foundation of the Irish Volunteers, they could be seen as representing the lowest rung of Irish society, 'the scum of Ireland', as he phrased it. He was certainly taken aback at their miserable condition, compared with that of the neat and sturdy French prisoners in the camp.56 Two men showed particular interest, Corporal Timothy Quinlisk from Wexford and Sergeant MacMurrough from Belfast, and he left them notebooks to record the names and regiments of all the men. When he returned, they gave him a list of 383 names. Casement returned to Frankfurt for another meeting with General de Graaff, at which he requested items for the men – soap, shaving equipment, tobacco – and broached his idea of using the Brigade in Egypt. By now he had a severe cold with a racking cough and, back in Limburg, had to call a doctor and spend a day in bed. Up again, he took Quinlisk and Mac-Murrough into the town and bought them food and some clothing. He was not much impressed by them – 'Both look rogues' – nor were they hopeful of volunteers for the Brigade; they found the men very anti-German.57

His mood while in Limburg was one of loneliness and depression. He was upset by what he perceived to be the lack of German sympathy in Berlin for his campaign against Findlay in Norway. In Limburg, though recruitment for the Brigade had scarcely begun, he was not confident of success, remarking: 'I despair of any patriotic act coming from such men.' He also felt that the German authorities needed to take the matter of Ireland and the Brigade more seriously, before he could accept responsibility for placing volunteers in a treasonable position. On 7 December he wrote from Limburg to von Wedel, broaching the need for fuller endorsement: 'I have little doubt the men will do all I suggest – It will lie with me and how far I go – they will follow. Before committing them, however, I should like to see the Secretary of State, or the Chancellor who are both, I understand, now in Berlin.'58

He returned by train to Berlin on 10 December and his conversation the following day with Count Blücher helped deepen his negative mood. Blücher had offered to arrange a meeting with the Secretary of State, von Jagow, but now revealed that von Jagow had indicated to him the limited German intentions towards Ireland. This led to words between the friends and a deepening of Casement's suspicions. On 18 December Casement met von Wedel, who informed him that his conditions for the formation of a brigade had been accepted and then took him to see the Chancellor himself. They spoke for half an hour, Casement in English and von Bethmann Hollweg in French. Casement talked of his hopes for Irish freedom and of the importance of Germany's developing a clear policy in support of that goal. He also sketched out the details of the events in the Findlay affair.

Following his meeting with the Chancellor, Casement drew up a formal document proposing the formation of an Irish Brigade; it comprised ten articles, listing the conditions of formation. The Brigade's aim was to be 'the national freedom of Ireland' and it should fight solely in that cause; its members should have a distinctive uniform and be led, when available, by Irish officers; it should be supplied and armed by the German government, but with unpaid, volunteer members; in the event of a German naval victory, it should be transported to Ireland with adequate German military support and, should military operations in Ireland result in the overthrow of British authority, Germany should recognize and support an independent Ireland; should a German naval victory not come about, the Brigade might be employed 'to assist the Egyptian People to recover their freedom by driving the British out of Egypt'; to bring this about, Germany should help transport the Brigade to Constantinople and seek Turkish recognition of it as a Volunteer Corps to assist its army to expel the British from Egypt.[59] On 28 December, Casement received word of German assent from Zimmermann: 'I have the honour to inform you that the Imperial German Government agrees to your proposal.'[60]

With this agreement or 'Treaty' formally accepted and with a much larger number of Irish prisoners now in Limburg, Casement set off south for a second visit to the camp. He left Berlin by train on 30 December but, suffering from a bad cold, took to his bed in Frankfurt for several days before travelling on to Limburg on 3 January 1915. He spent two days in the town, meeting the Irish priests and Fr Berkessel of Balduinstein, a warm-hearted old German priest who had spent time in Ireland in the 1880s. On the afternoon of 5 January he made his way out to the camp. The reception was hostile; he seems to have been jostled and to have needed protection from his German guards. The thoughts he put on paper that night showed his dejection: 'I *very* soon saw, from the manner of the men, that all hope of an Irish Brigade from such a contemptible crew ... must be entirely abandoned. Some of them insulted me – but all showed clearly the utter slothful indifference of that type of debauched Irishman to any appeal but to his greed.' He was despondent at 'the revelation of Irish depravity I had witnessed among those 2200 so-called "Irishmen" '.[61] When faced with a return visit in March, he was to comment: 'I will not return to Limburg to be insulted by a handful of recreant Irishmen. I cannot meet them on *that* ground. I cannot meet insults from cads and cowards with insults. I can only avoid the cads and cowards.'[62] Casement's discomfort on this occasion was observed by a young Irishman, Bryan Kelly, who had just come to the camp at Casement's insistence. Kelly had been studying at the University of Marburg and had been interned following the outbreak of the war. He had been moved from place to place between August and December and ended up in the civilian detention camp at Ruhleben, near Berlin. Having sent a postcard to Kuno Meyer, to which he received no reply, he was suddenly summoned to see von Wedel on 18 December. Having interviewed him, von Wedel asked him to go to meet Casement and the two met on 19 December at the Eden Hotel. Kelly later described the encounter in a statement he gave after his release and return to Ireland:

> I saw Sir Roger Casement the following morning at 11 am at the Eden Hotel near the Zoological Garten. He seemed in an extreme 'fidget', and impressed me as a very impulsive excitable man. He gave me his book, 'England's Crime', to read while he dressed. He found I knew Irish, talked about the Gaelic League; about Kerry; told me he thought he could get me out of Germany. He then entered into a long invective against the British Empire: England was the enemy of Europe; the ruthless destroyer of Peace; Germany was the nation of the future; she was Ireland's natural friend. For himself, he had burnt his boats behind him: he was trying to save Ireland from falling with the ruins of the British Empire.[63]

Casement went on to outline his plans for the formation of an Irish Brigade. He suddenly asked the young man, 'Will you help me?' After Kelly gave a non-committal answer, Casement's plan for him began to emerge. He should go to Limburg to see the Irish camp and, having returned to Ireland, help spread the good word there. Kelly did go to Limburg and was to leave a description of the town and the camp, the propaganda material lying around (including Casement's), the work of the two priests, and the contrast between the British and French prisoners. He was there when Casement arrived:

> On the evening of 5th January, Sir Roger Casement came to the Camp and talked to the men. A crowd gathered about, and there were cheers for Redmond. One man asked: 'How much are the Germans paying you?' Sir Roger called the man a scoundrel and left the Camp.

Kelly was released from the camp on 7 January and told to see Casement in the town of Limburg. His account continued:

> I saw Sir Roger Casement at his hotel. He told me he did not think he should try to do anything with 'these men up there' and spoke of them as the very last men he would think of were he engaged in raising an Irish Brigade in Ireland. Pointing to a large green flag which lay on the sofa he said he had intended to give them that but did not think he should do so now. He might send for one hundred youngsters and do something with them; but, as for the whole lot, he would not like to take the responsibility for them on his shoulders. He had obtained permission from Berlin to bring the Irish down to Mass in the Cathedral at Limburg every Sunday, and he did not know if even that would be wise.

Casement and Kelly travelled to Frankfurt, where the latter was given a passport. He returned to Berlin, while Casement went back to Limburg. Allowed to return to Ireland, Kelly made a statement about his experiences to the Undersecretary for Ireland, Sir Matthew Nathan.[64]

After the unpleasantness of his visit to the camp on 5 January, Casement spent the next two days in the Nassauer Hof, a quiet hotel in Limburg. On the 8th, the day after he had taken Bryan Kelly to Frankfurt, Timothy Quinlisk provided him with another negative picture of the soldiers' reactions: they threatened to inform on Quinlisk, after the war, as Casement's agent and a traitor. Uncertain what to do, Casement remained on in Limburg, mulling over developments in the Findlay affair and working on an early draft of the letter of denouncement he planned to send to Sir Edward Grey.[65] On 23 January, he returned to Berlin.

Casement had first visited the internment camp at Ruhleben on 29 December 1914 with a view to seeking the release of Irish people being held in detention. Such releases could produce dividends in the propaganda war. Richard Meyer provided him with a list, inviting him to indicate those whom he considered ought to be released. A total of 163 were identified as 'Catholic' and 'Irish'.[66] Professor Macran of Trinity College Dublin and his wife were soon to join Bryan Kelly in freedom.[67] In March, three more were to be added: John Bradshaw from Ballymoney, Patrick Coyne from Ballyhaunis and Thomas Hoy from Dungannon.[68] On his return home, the last of these was to give a statement to the intelligence services in which he claimed to have been in Germany since 1912 and to have been close to the authorities there. For them, Ireland was the keystone of the Empire: 'The Empire without India or Australia or Africa or Canada is wounded, without Ireland the Empire is dead.' He had met and become friendly with Casement, he claimed: 'He said that he was compelled to hide himself in Berlin as he had information that British agents were preparing against his life. He is guarded by a German Secret Agent by whom one is examined before being allowed to pass.'[69]

Perhaps the most intriguing of those whose release Casement secured was George Chatterton-Hill, a former professor of sociology in Geneva. Chatterton-Hill wrote to and met Casement in mid March, shortly after which he was released. In his letter of 16 March, he protested that: 'As a Catholic and an Irishman I swear solemnly before God and on my word of honour that I am true to the national cause of Ireland ... I recognize without hesitation that England is the only Enemy of Ireland ...'[70] Chatterton-Hill quickly became active in propagandist work. Not long after his release, however, he seems to have played a role in spreading what Dr Curry termed 'the various scandalous reports circulated in Berlin on the authenticity of the Findlay affair'. When Casement learned of this, he confronted Chatterton-Hill, who immediately retracted, pleading that he had been told 'many disagreeable things' about Christensen by people of authority in Berlin.[71]

The well-known professor of sociology from Kiel, Ferdinand Tönnies, met Casement through his efforts to assist Chatterton-Hill. He recorded his impression of Casement:

> He gave the impression of a sombre man who was very embittered. He did not in the least give the impression of one inspired by hope. I had the feeling that he was a lonely man, a recluse, who sought a path with integrity and honesty and who ended up in a cul-de-sac, from which he did not know how to get out.[72]

In February and March, after the stress of the Findlay affair and his visit to Limburg, Casement sought some relaxation in short visits to Hamburg. He found his host, Madame Behrens, to be very kind. Having lived in hotels since the previous May, he found that a few days 'in a private house is quite an experience'. He wrote to Countess Hahn: 'I hear that the *Lusitania* brought two American Submarines for the English on her last voyage, *under the American flag too!* That is a queer manner of being "neutral".' The news from Hindenburg on the Eastern Front he felt to be the best since the war began.[73]

Fr Nicholson, Captain Boehm and Joseph Plunkett

A second phase in the attempt to establish an Irish Brigade soon began with the arrival from the United States of Fr John T. Nicholson. It would seem that plans to send a priest from the US had been discussed before Casement left for Germany, and in his letter to Judge Cohalan in early November he had requested, with apparent urgency: 'Let him despatch priest here via Christiania quickly.' McGarrity was probably responding to this with his comment that 'Padre I hope will soon be on his way.'[74] The German Embassy in Washington informed Berlin in mid December: 'Revd John T. Nicholson, of Philadelphia, is on sick leave now and ready to start. First available vessel sails for Netherlands December 18th. Arranged to have pass for Italy and Switzerland. Is in every way qualified. Speaks Irish well. Has visited Germany and is in full sympathy with the work we want done. Born in Ireland, but is American citizen.' Some days later Richard Meyer passed on this information to Casement and, in mid January, let him know that Nicholson had arrived in Rome and would leave for Berlin on 19 December 1914.[75]

After a delay in Rome, Nicholson arrived at the end of January 1915. On 27 January, Casement made his apologies to Eduard Meyer for not attending his birthday celebration, 'owing to the presence in Berlin of a friend from America'.[76] The friend was Nicholson, as the diary recorded on Wednesday 27 January: 'Father Nicholson left for Limburg this morning. I spent most of yesterday with him – and on Monday he was with me the greater part of the day and at six I took him to the Foreign Office to von Wedel to let him see the Findlay Document.'[77]

Nicholson was to stay four months in Limburg and his work was to be very different in character from the spiritual ministry of Frs Crotty and O'Gorman. During February and March, he directed his energies at recruitment into the Brigade, keeping Casement apprised of his experiences. On 9 February and on the 23rd he sent assessments of the situation, which were broadly negative. One of the obstacles for him was where to begin, 'especially as I was accused of being pro-German ... My work must be all indirect as otherwise it would be an express violation of neutrality'. Since the future of potential volunteers after the end of the war would be a difficult one, he raised the question of getting them to the US and possibly into the US army. He reported on German cruelties towards prisoners and made suggestions for the amelioration of conditions. Indeed, German handling of his own presence left something to be desired: he spoke of having been arrested at the camp when a prisoner was seen handing him a question to answer on a piece of paper. The prisoners could be divided, he felt, into four classes: those with houses in England, those with families, those nearing pension entitlements and those who were no good for anything. Among the questions needing answering were: what positive good for Ireland would the Brigade do and what prospects were there of employment in the US? The men raised concerns relating to the prospect of Home Rule and the treatment of Belgium. In addition, they disbelieved a lot of the material in *The Continental Times* and *The Gaelic American*, John Devoy's nationalist paper.[78]

On 1 March, Nadolny sent Captain Hans W. Boehm, of the Admiralty Staff, a specialist in propaganda and espionage,[79] and Anthony J. Brogan, an Irish

American journalist associated with the *Irish World*, to visit Casement at the Continental Hotel. Brogan's presence, though brief, was to prove embarrassing for Casement, since Brogan was not trusted by Clan na Gael members in America. Devoy, in his *Recollections*, wondered 'which of the German departments or agents of departments consented to the sending of Brogan', and added that 'we became morally certain of his identity as one who had given much trouble to the Embassy here by meddling in matters that were already in capable hands'.[80] Devoy had written to Casement warning him of Brogan's arrival with the comment that he was 'wholly untrustworthy and unreliable'.[81] Casement, aware of Brogan's German military contacts and of the Clan's views, discussed the matter with 'the authorities', who assured him of Brogan's usefulness. Casement then confronted Brogan with the Clan's reservations about him and was convinced by his response. Brogan travelled to Limburg, visited the camp on 17 March, and reported on his visit to Casement. The latter informed Fr Nicholson: 'The man who went Limburg brought back pretty hopeless picture of possibilities. Might have to give up on whole plan.'[82]

In mid March Casement was forced to devote part of his energies to responding to a hurtful report in the *New York World*, which alleged that he was in receipt of large sums of German money to instigate rebellion in Ireland. On 15 March he wrote to von Wedel asking for help in identifying the *World's* Berlin correspondent and enclosing a cable he wanted sent to John Quinn, whom he wished to initiate libel proceedings. In due course Quinn replied, listing his reasons against taking a libel case: the libel laws were unsatisfactory; it would be a costly business; there was the old legal maxim, *inter arma silent leges*; his doubt about the nature of the remarks. 'It would be no crime for Sir Roger to have been paid by Germany. It does not reflect upon his integrity or his honour or his personal reputation. He is acting for Germany. He is doing it openly and not secretly.'[83]

Despite Quinn's opinion, Casement determined to plough on. He said so to Thomas St John Gaffney, US consul general at Munich, whom he had come to know and who supported him in taking the libel case. He was, he said, determined 'to go on with the matter whatever Quinn says'.[84] But he could make little headway, beyond sending a sharp letter to Quinn drawing attention to 'some extraordinary statements in your letter'. Since the US was neutral, Quinn's legal maxim did not apply, he pointed out. But, the real hurt in Quinn's letter had been the imputation that he worked for Germany: 'I should have thought it was abundantly clear that I was acting not "for Germany" but for Ireland. No action of mine since I arrived in Europe has been an act for Germany – anymore than, say, to cite a very notable case, Wolfe Tone acted "for France" when he tried to get French help for Ireland in a previous great continental war.'[85]

After Brogan's visit to Limburg, Casement received a letter from Michael Kehoe, who was an enthusiastic recruit to the Brigade there. He drew Casement's attention to the presence in the camp of 'so many Cockney speaking

Irishmen', prisoners who, he claimed, had perjured themselves to get better terms.[86] Casement immediately wrote to von Wedel, remonstrating that nothing had been done to implement an agreement arrived at with General Exner in January 'that the English born and pro English men in the camp should be separated from the others'. Neither was censorship of letters effective, as false information was getting through to the men. He asked that 500 copies of *The Gaelic American* be photographed and sent to Limburg. Finally, he asked that Quinlisk and Kehoe be brought to Berlin, and quietly ('no one inside the camp need know why they disappear for a day or two').[87]

On the following day, having received a letter from Fr Nicholson, in which the latter made a number of complaints about the German regime in the Limburg camp – guards, for example, were striking prisoners – Casement again wrote to von Wedel protesting: 'It is to my mind not only an act of ill will, but an act of cowardice for armed men to strike unarmed men under their guard; and unless I receive clear assurance that it shall be instantly stopped I shall be compelled to desist from all further effort.'[88] He also wrote to Fr Nicholson, telling him of his letter to von Wedel and indicating that he was considering bringing Kehoe and Quinlisk to Berlin. He said that he would like to talk to Nicholson himself.[89] Nicholson came to Berlin, where Casement sent him to brief von Wedel on affairs in the camp, after which he returned to Limburg. Quinlisk, Kehoe and Joseph Dowling also came, but they were to remain for some considerable time. The handling of their departure from the camp angered both Nicholson and Casement; it was, in the latter's terms, 'not done discreetly'.[90] The three corporals from Limburg had brought a list of sixty-six 'undesirables', which Casement forwarded to von Wedel, requesting that they be removed to some other camp 'on the grounds that they are either Englishmen, pure and simple, or wholly pro-English and, therefore, hostile to the effort to form an Irish Brigade'. The three corporals should be kept in Berlin until this was done.[91]

Casement shared his frustrations with Captain Hans Boehm, who was now beginning to take an active interest in the affairs of the Brigade. 'I am not disposed to go on with the idea of the Irish Brigade unless more serious efforts at co-operation are displayed by those who could derive the chief benefit – both moral and material – from the step I should be responsible for.' The benefits to Germany he believed to be, firstly, bringing about Irish-American influence in keeping the US out of the war and, secondly, impeding recruiting in Ireland. It had been said to him the previous day that the German government 'have no interest in Ireland at all'. He concluded that 'A man in doubt is a bad worker; and I have been in this doubt for some time now, and I fear the doubt increases.'[92]

In another letter on the same day, Casement told Boehm: 'I saw Nadolny today. He said he would have you sent to Limburg.' Two days later, his mood had brightened. After a further talk with the corporals, he said he was convinced that a brigade could be formed 'if you are given over on the lines we talked ... Without you I should not go on – with you I may, if I am convinced on the two points I raised yesterday in our conversation.'[93] Part of the task was to weed out problem soldiers; the sixty-six undesirables had already been removed and 'a 67th to go – a Sergeant named MacMorrough'. He agreed, too, with Fr Crotty that 'the idea of a band too will take tremendously'. And the corporals 'must have the freedom they insist on for interviewing all likely men outside the prison lager'.[94] Nevertheless, he expressed frustration at the slowness of German decision making: 'It is four weeks tomorrow since the 3 corporals arrived here from Limburg! ... They will have plenty of enemies soon enough – God knows! Why be so chary of making friends.' But, on the same day, Boehm reported: 'I have just come from the War Office. There is no doubt about the matter being "settled" and that the order will be given.' The delay, he explained, had been caused by the fact that three offices were dealing with it – the general staff, the Foreign Office and the War Office. A few days later, Kehoe wrote to Casement announcing Boehm's arrival in Limburg and telling him that he had started work the previous morning, weeding out undesirables.[95]

Casement's somewhat more hopeful mood was reflected in letters he wrote to John Devoy in the first part of April. His opinion on 6 April was that

> things are improving ... There is a chance of a move there – but nothing can be said openly yet. The day I cable 'publish text' you will know that the men have responded and that the Treaty of Alliance and recognition may be proclaimed. The first need is officers. Something must be done to have these available, for as you see from the Treaty no *active* operations can be undertaken until our own Nationality is in command. That was an essential condition – one without which I could not have got the assent to my conditions. My chief difficulty has been being single handed. I needed, and need, others to work below me and do the things I cannot do. The work of recruiting *has* to be done by others ... Today, however, I begin to see some hope, and *some* of the dejection I have experienced for so long is breaking up.[96]

Just as negotiations for sending Boehm to Limburg were being completed, another visitor came to Berlin. At 8.30 on the morning of 20 April, Joseph Mary Plunkett arrived on a mission from the leaders of the insurrectionist movement in Ireland.[97] He went to the Foreign Office and was received by von Wedel. From there he rang Casement at the Eden Hotel, 'who said to come round'.[98] Though tired from his journey, on this first day he also met Captain Boehm and an Indian, Virendranath Chattopadhyaya. Next day Casement brought the three members of the Brigade, Quinlisk, Kehoe and Dowling, who were still in Berlin; at lunch Plunkett met the Countess Blücher; in the afternoon he met Boehm, Richard Meyer and Adler Christensen, before going for a long talk with von Wedel ('quite satisfactory').[99] From the 22nd to the 27th he stayed with Casement at the Eden Hotel. During these days there were further meetings and discussions with Professor Schiemann, Nadolny, Kehoe, Quinlisk, Dowling and, of course, Casement. On the 27th he moved to an apartment. Plunkett had brought Casement news of military planning in Ireland:

> In April 1915 came P. from Ireland with his great tale of the planned revolution there. I discounted all that – and sat on it and him as vigorously as was possible. I told him just what I had often told Wedel at the FO that no rebellion or rising in Ireland could possibly succeed of its own unaided effort. The *sine qua non* of a successful military movement in Ireland, today far more than in 1798, 1690, 1641 or 1598–1601 was the military (and naval) support of a great Continental power. To attempt a Rising in the streets of Dublin in 1915 I held was worse than folly – it was criminal stupidity.

But, if the planners persisted, he went on, he would 'come and join you' and 'stand and fall beside you'; it would, he felt, be a fight, 'an act, a deed – and not talk, talk, talk'.[100] Indeed, Casement and Plunkett collaborated in producing and submitting a memorandum to the German government, outlining the situation in Ireland, including the disposition and strength of British forces there, and detailed plans for an insurrection. Crucial to the latter was the sending of a German expeditionary force of 12,000 soldiers and 40,000 rifles for the Volunteers.[101] On 7 May Plunkett set off for Limburg, with Boehm, Quinlisk and Dowling. Here he met and talked with Fr Nicholson. Nicholson reported progress on Brigade recruitment: of the first sixty interviewed, there were seventeen recruits, including 'the champion four mile runner of Ireland'.[102]

On 12 May Casement arrived in Limburg from Berlin, his first visit since his unhappy experience in January.[103] On the following day, Ascension Thursday, when Plunkett seems to have paid his first visit to the camp itself, there were lengthy consultations. On Friday Casement went to Frankfurt and back, before visiting the camp again on Saturday. On Sunday Plunkett and Casement went by train to visit Fr Berkessel. On 24 May Plunkett dropped Casement a note, in which he commented on two events of broader significance: the entry of Italy into the war on the side of Britain and her allies ('news of Italy's accomplished treachery') and the formation of a new coalition war cabinet in Britain.[104] Plunkett departed for Berlin on 1 June. There he had further meetings with Nadolny, Richard Meyer and von Wedel, and visited the Brigade members.

Casement arrived back from Limburg early on 8 June and, on the 10th, Boehm, Plunkett and Casement held a council of war. At some time during his visit Plunkett requested arms of the Germans in connection with a planned uprising; the response, according to Casement, was negative. He talked of 'furious interviews' between the military and FO people, at which Plunkett was present:

> He asked ... for arms for Ireland. These were contemptuously refused by Nadolny who said that they had plenty of goodwill for Ireland (his very words!) but would give no arms. Arms must be provided by the Irish in America ... P. was raging – and asked me if I could obtain him an interview with the Minster of War!!! I laughed and said you might as well ask to see the Emperor.[105]

The two finally parted on 20 June and, when he had got as far as Berne in Switzerland, Plunkett discussed his further movements and sent his thanks to Casement: 'Love to Adler and yourself (but you need not give it to Herr Ass. M[eyer]. P.P.S. Respects and kind regards to the Nordenflychts.'[106]

Zossen

While Casement, Plunkett and Boehm were in Limburg, Richard Meyer wrote to report the transfer of fifty of the Irish prisoners who had signed up for the Brigade to temporary quarters in a military camp at Zossen, just south of Berlin.[107] This represented a significant step and one must assume that it followed on the complaints and suggestions made by Nicholson, the negative report by Brogan and the recent involvement of Boehm.[108] At this point, Fr Nicholson returned to the United States. 'I feel', he wrote to Casement, after four months' work, 'that our wrestling here was not so much against present conditions as against the disintegration of the last twenty years. If it goes on there will soon be no Ireland left. I still hope that Ireland's hour has not struck in vain.'[109] Casement sent a farewell greeting, asking him to tell McGarrity and Devoy of the 'great importance of backing up the handful of men in arms', and concluding with a tribute: 'whatever success exists is due to you and your unselfish, unstinting efforts'.[110]

Casement seems to have wished to mark the move of the first group of volunteers to Zossen and the formation of the first company, with the publication of the agreement with the German government, drawn up the previous autumn. However, von Wedel responded negatively on 15 June. He had, he wrote, spoken to the acting Secretary of State, the secretary of the American Department, the head of the Political Department and the military authorities. The conclusion of all was that it was not expedient at present, because 'the total number of the Irish Brigade is as yet too small to justify its attaining publicity'. There was a danger of its being called a failure or 'German bluff'. He also suggested that Irish-Americans needed to show greater interest 'in the cause of their fellow-countrymen ... Our hopes put into an active support on the part of Irish-Americans has as yet scarcely been realised'.[111]

Casement wrote to Joe McGarrity in dejection:

Meetings in the US don't influence them indeed they never hear of them. Beside they don't value 'public opinion' or fear it, or court it. They regard only force and organization and rely on these. We offer none of these ... Could the Brigade have been formed we had an Alliance and a Treaty committing to active effort & help. Without the Brigade there is nothing between us & I am wholly useless here ... I tried all I could ... We have failed ... Let me go back. They don't care a fig for our cause by itself; they know nothing of us or it or our country

... They will not help us with arms or anything ... They said in effect 'get them yourselves you have millions of your people in USA & they should do that'...[112]

Hans Boehm must have sensed Casement's despair. In a memo to the authorities on 24 June he pleaded:

If we don't wish to turn even the Irish into enemies, then we must treat those people who volunteered for the Irish Legion exactly as planned originally. Above all they should not be housed in a prison camp. The men must be removed immediately from the Half Moon Camp where their presence is disturbing anyway ... If Casement and Brogan go back to America as our enemies they will cause us enormous damage.[113]

Casement's withdrawal to the environs of Munich at this point was symbolic of his general attitude to Brigade affairs and to Germany. In August, Gaffney wrote to Zimmermann, asking that some way be found to facilitate Casement's return to the US, perhaps 'on the warship of some (friendly) neutral power'. Some days later, von Wedel wrote to a GFO colleague, Count Adolf von Montgelas, on the matter: 'I am decidedly in favour of helping him get to America. As matters stand with the Irish Legion at this point, he cannot be of use here to either the Irish or the German side. In America he can at least be active in an anti-British way provided that he makes it across and is not hanged before by the British.'[114]

Indeed, there was a hint of farewell, some time previously, in a note that von Wedel sent Casement thanking him for a photograph sent: 'it will always remind me of the hours I spent with you in these great times, and of a friend whose heroic efforts in struggling against fearful odds in the interest of his country I shall never cease to admire'.[115] With departure on his mind, Casement communicated with Meyer in the German Foreign Office on the details of acquiring a passport. In a way, the move of prisoners to Zossen had only added to the tribulations of the Brigade project. There were now two separate locations to be looked after. Efforts to enrol further recruits continued: by Boehm, and, it would appear, by the new Irish activists. Kehoe sent a note to Casement on 12 June about the need for further recruits 'for completion of 1st Coy + prospect of 30 more'. He presumed that Boehm, who had just left for Berlin, would have explained things regarding the 'present slow and unsuccessful method of recruiting'. It might help to publish pictures of the men at Zossen, he believed, and letters from Zossen to friends in Limburg would also help.[116]

From the summer of 1915 on, Casement was to spend most of his time in southern Germany, mainly in Munich and its surrounds. His sojourn there was partly linked with the friendships he formed with the Gaffneys and with Dr Charles Curry,[117] but it also had something to do with his feeling more at ease with Bavarians than northern Germans and, specifically, with a desire to distance himself from Berlin officialdom. He stayed on the Amersee, a small lake not far from Munich (at Riederau, Diessen and Feldafing), and visited nearby Andechs and Augsburg. In Munich he stayed at a modest hotel called the Basler Hof.

A German author, Franz Rothenfelder, visited these areas after Casement's execution, interviewing those who knew him, mostly in a social capacity. The picture painted by them is consistent with what we know of him in other contexts.[118] He was recognized as an idealist or dreamer and as a man who kept much to himself. As elsewhere, his eyes drew attention: 'What his mouth did not utter, his eyes said. These eyes had unlimited things to say.' When in his hotel in Munich, according to staff, he remained largely unknown to the guests, working in the mornings and forenoon (including during morning prayers, customary in Christian hostels). Hotel staff believed him not to be in good health. He drank up to eight cups of coffee at a time and even worked during meals, on which he placed little value – he ate what was put in front of him. He drank, smoked heavily and played cards (always returning his winnings). His abstemiousness over money was also observed: it was never requested nor accepted; if offered, it was returned as not necessary.

More endearing traits were noted. He was not taciturn by nature and chatted to people in fluent French. Casement's love and knowledge of nature was also observed. Of a visit to the Munich Botanic Gardens, one friend commented: 'He knew every flower, every shrub.' Music, too, he loved, and he impressed on the few occasions on which he sang. On the Amersee, he enjoyed swimming and rowing and loved walking barefoot.

Meanwhile, in Zossen, progress was being made. On 10 July, von Wedel informed Casement that the men were due to be moved to barracks, while Richard Meyer wrote that 'it can be hoped that you will see the men in uniform before long'.[119] Nevertheless, when Kehoe wrote on 17 July, his letter conveyed unease. Dowling, Quinlisk and he, he wrote, 'are quite in the dark at turn of events at present'. He wanted an explanation and requested an interview with Casement. Pay arrears was one issue of concern.[120] In early August Kehoe complained that the men's morale 'is terrible here with the Darkie soldiers of all descriptions ... It is no easy task to keep the men together, their position is so disheartening'. He urged sending men to recruit in Limburg.[121] Boehm wrote from Berlin on 10 August, expressing his belief that everything was being done by the general staff to expedite matters. Delay was due to friction between different offices, none of which was anxious to handle the matter. He had made appointments among the men: Kehoe was colour sergeant; Quinlisk, quartermaster sergeant; Dowling, Michael O'Toole[122] and Beverley [Daniel Bailey], sergeants.[123]

Shortly after the move of one company to Zossen, Boehm was joined by some new German officers. Franz Zerhusen was one; he had written to Casement on 5 July, giving references and requesting transfer to the Irish Brigade. Robert Monteith, who was later to meet Zerhusen, described him in his diary as 'one of the interpreters attached to the Brigade – find he is the husband of an Irish lady, his home is in Hamburg – and unfortunately his business is ruined by the War, consequently his love of England is intense and fervent'.[124]

Boehm and Zerhusen worked at improving conditions for the men. Zerhusen was trying to get funds for football outfits, drums, pipes and so on. Boehm, too, told of Zerhusen's efforts to get 'bagpipes, drums and fifes, also material for instruction in German and Geography etc. It seems he is getting along splendidly with them'. Casement promised to visit, once the men were in their new quarters.[125] But, despite a move to a new barracks, problems of discipline remained. One factor was that the Brigade members were still treated as prisoners. Early in September, Kehoe gave the details. There was still, he wrote, wire fencing and a sentry; the NCOs couldn't visit the canteen without Zerhusen or an *Unterofficier*, and word of their enrolling had got home and there were fears that payments to relatives would stop.[126] Both Kehoe and Boehm reported on the unpleasant case of Corporal Mahoney, who engaged in bad conduct, including stealing, and was to be stripped of rank.[127]

Casement was exercised by the problem of how to make use of the Irish Brigade, now that there was stalemate on the Western Front and little prospect of getting the Brigade to Ireland. The possibility of employing the Brigade on the Eastern Front had been envisaged in its constitution, in its references to Egypt. This seemed more appealing to Casement by the the autumn of 1915. During the summer, the Central Powers had made remarkable advances against the Russians; now, in the autumn, they turned to the Balkans, where Serbia was soon overcome. An overland path to Turkey was becoming a reality. Just before leaving Munich for Berlin, Casement shared his thoughts with Boehm. The only thing he could think of was the employment of the Brigade

> in some military effort – and it is to this end I have adopted the idea of going to Turkey. If that can be carried through, the thing is, after all, not such an *abject* failure as is otherwise the case. They will have done something, struck a tiny blow at the enemy, as fighting men and have justified, so far as they can, as Irishmen, their 'treason'. But to have committed the treason all in vain, and be penned up in a camp or compound waiting for the war to end is to them (and to me) the extremity of misery.

He was hoping for a breakthrough in Serbia and the opening of a road to the East. This would give them activity, to avoid 'the mental death of idleness'.[128] Boehm replied, saying that he was now 'out of the race'. The Foreign Office didn't want him any longer and he would be going back to his regiment. He knew that Casement would be disappointed. Duke Adolf Friedrich of Mecklenburg, he went on, was in Turkey, 'looking over the ground with regard to certain enterprises'; if he succeeded, it would be 'just the thing for your men'.[129]

Casement's vision regarding the East was a broadly anti-colonial one. In November 1914 he had written:

> If Turkey breaks through the Canal [Suez] as I trust she may do, it may indeed bring about the downfall of the British Empire ... With the Canal gone, Egypt goes – and with both gone I look for such an outbreak in India as must tax 'the

Empire' to its limit, and with Germany at the gates of Calais, the Irish Declaration out, I do not think Master John can spare many men, ships or guns for India – to hold India he will *have* to appeal to Japan – and that spells his own sure and certain eviction from Asia later on. Once India falls the whole house collapses – for it is chiefly on India and its plunder the Colossal scheme of robbery depends.[130]

When he came to Berlin, Casement raised the matter with a Turkish friend, Halil Halid, who wrote to him on 29 September asking that Casement let him know when he decided definitely on going to Constantinople. It would be better, Halil Halid advised, to write to the Turkish minister. He would like to give Casement a letter of introduction to the 'Chef de Cabinet' of the minister of the Interior, an excellent man, who spoke English and would, no doubt, facilitate him.[131] Casement, who had returned quickly to Munich, replied saying that he had been advised by the Foreign Office not to attempt a journey through Romania – he was likely to be handed over to the British. He would wait till a road through Serbia was opened by force: 'Of course I should always be delighted to know that you had apprised Enver Pacha of my idea and to learn that his Excellency welcomed it.' He hoped that, by then, more Irish soldiers would be available.[132]

Casement had travelled to Berlin on the evening of Tuesday 21 September, arriving on Wednesday morning. A few days later, Hans Boehm reported to the general staff on conditions:

> The Irish are housed in a very good, well furnished barrack, which – located inside the area of the work detachment – has been specially fenced off. Food is good and plentiful. As a consequence of various transgressions it has been found necessary to tighten up on discipline. Greater liberty has been held out to them for good behaviour. All concerned offices showed full and far-reaching understanding of the situation, and I find the measures taken to be thoroughly fitting. The men have no justified cause to complain.[133]

Some days later, he largely concurred with Boehm's assessment in a letter to Richard Meyer:

> I was out at Zossen yesterday – the men are *very* well cared for, very well treated – and I am sincerely grateful to you for the kindly way in which you are fulfilling your promises. On the other hand there is no use concealing the fact that they are unhappy and feel themselves useless – also that they are without personal liberty at all.[134]

He went on to urge Meyer to visit the camp with him and he made some requests for the men. 'Books they want badly – also a *couple of* sets of running costumes, and running shoes for two of the men who were famous athletes in Ireland – one a champion I believe.' A sewing machine, too, would be greatly appreciated.

A statement in the name of the Brigade NCOs was also published while Casement was in Berlin, the wording of which bears his stamp. It was apparently directed at negative propaganda against the Brigade and drew attention to the existence of parallel units among the Allies: 'In this, too, we are only doing what many other soldiers of the "small nationalities" are doing or are being asked to do by the Allied Governments of England, Russia, France and Italy.' And, 'If these things be loyal and right for the Allied Sovereigns to do, and to enrol soldiers of the Austrian or German armies in corps pledged to fight against Austria and Germany, then how much more right is it for Irishmen to volunteer to fight for Ireland and for that cause alone?'[135]

After his brief sortie to Berlin and Zossen, Casement returned to Munich. In a letter to Mrs Boehm, he gave an indication of his pursuits: 'I went to Tannhauser in the evening to hear Maud Fay – a charming American – as Elizabeth ... I sent you "The Sickman" and I wrote another Fable the other day – also some other more serious things – on Sir E. Grey and Viscount Bryce.' He sent regards to her father and mother-in-law 'and love to the children' and promised to visit when he came to Berlin.[136] A few days later he was in correspondence with Frau Elsa Douglas, thanking her for her rapid typewriting of his article on Lord Bryce, forwarding payment, apologizing that he could not help her financially from his own slender resources, and hoping that her circumstances would improve.[137]

Casement's ire had been aroused by a report by Lord Bryce into atrocities allegedly perpetrated by the Germans during their defeat of Belgium. Casement refused to accept the validity of the accusations:

> I have investigated more *bona fide* atrocities at close hand than possibly any other living man. But, unlike Lord Bryce, I investigated them on the spot, from the lips of those who had suffered, in the very places where the crimes were perpetrated, where the evidence could be sifted and the accusation brought by the victim could be rebutted by the accused; and in each case my finding was confirmed by the Courts of Justice of the very States whose citizens I had indicted.

Not so with Bryce's report, he argued: 'Was there ever in history a more shockingly conceived attempt at the moral assassination of a people?' Unlike Bryce, he had been to Belgium since the war began. He explained the devastation he saw there as 'that which a sea in storm hurls upon the shore', the result of the clash between invading and defending armies. He suggested that the true authors of 'Belgian atrocities' were those responsible for the war, namely Britain.[138]

From June onwards most of the Irish prisoners remaining in Limburg seem to have been either sent to work on farms in the surrounding districts or dispersed to other camps. On 15 June, Crotty wrote to say that he had seen two hundred in Giessen and that they would prefer to be back in Limburg.[139] A further source of tension arose when Fr Crotty became the target of criticism with regard to his supposed political views. One source of the criticism would appear to have come in a letter from George Freeman to Professor Schiemann, dated 12 July, which was also to cause grief to Casement himself. Casement informed

Crotty of the charges on 17 August – that he was a 'Redmondite' and not a true nationalist. Casement had denied the charges and recalled the terms of service that he had discussed with Frs Crotty and O'Gorman when he first met them in Berlin in November 1914: 'I said – "All I ask you both is that you will not be agents of the British Government".' Both had then assured him that they had been sent on religious duties only, which Casement never doubted for a moment. But, he went on, he was now being blamed for bringing them into Germany. It was claimed that, under Crotty's chairmanship, 'God Save the King' had been sung at a concert. Casement defended Crotty to Richard Meyer: 'Fr Crotty is not a "Redmondite" as I see he has been so ignorantly termed in a letter written to Dr Schiemann by a correspondent in New York (who is not an authority); but a very whole-hearted Irishman; and a very sincere and whole-hearted friend of Germany and the German cause.'140

Replying in a long letter, Crotty defended his neutrality and spiritual ministry: 'The English and Canadian soldiers too whom I have met in the course of my duties have found in me, I believe, a priest and no politician.' These included Protestants, Catholics and Irishmen of every opinion. In reality, he had instructed that 'God Save the King' not be sung in future, 'as we were not now in England'.141

Robert Monteith

With Casement in dejection and the affairs of the Brigade tottering on, help finally arrived from the United States in the person of Robert Monteith. The absence of Irish officers had long nagged at Casement. Devoy, aware of the need, addressed the question in a letter to him on 21 May 1915. An officer could only be sent from the US if there was no trouble between America and Germany. 'I am confident', he wrote, 'of getting a fully qualified man, who held the rank of Lieutenant-Colonel, has seen plenty of service and is a West Pointer, for the job. I think we could also get a few commissioned officers and that we could get about 150 smart sergeants, retired from the Regular Army, to go over – if they could get over. But there's the rub. How could such a number get over?'142 When Fr Nicholson returned to the US in June, he, too, was committed to trying to get recruits there. In July, Casement hoped that Zerhusen's arrival would 'in many ways make up for the dreadful lack of officers of their own'. And he enthused about the possibility of capturing for the Brigade Henry J. Reilly, correspondent of the *Chicago Tribune*. Reilly was of Irish descent, had served in the US army and, on learning of the Brigade, had told Gaffney that 'he would be prepared to join it as an officer. This would be splendid indeed. He is just the man wanted'. Casement maintained contact with Reilly, but the would-be volunteer eventually decided that his best contribution lay elsewhere.143

Upper Igaraparaná River. Indostan Station

Young boy on Putumayo showing
scars from flogging

'Volley on departing'. Group departing from rubber
station on march

Indians on Putumayo

Muchachos de confianca; armed
Indians on a Putumayo rubber
station, with a Barbardian

Casement and Juan Tizon at La Chorrera
during the Putumayo investigation

William Rothenstein's portrait
of Arédomi and Omarino,
the two youths whom Casement
brought from the Putumayo
to England to draw attention
to the campaign

Casement and the Putumayo Commissioners.
From left to right: Juan Tizon, Seymour Bell,
H.L. Gielgud, Walter Fox, Louis Barnes, Roger Casement

Youth posing in front of wall.
Photograph possibly by Casement

Two stylish young men photographed
by Casement (his shadow is visible in
the foreground)

Alfred Emmott (1858–1926)

Emmeline and William Cadbury
with parrot and children, c.1909–10

John Holt (1842–1915), Liverpool trader
and humanitarian campaigner

Sir Arthur Conan Doyle (1859–1930)

Sir John Harris (1874–1940) Congo
missionary and campaigner, later
secretary to the Anti-Slavery and
Aborigines Protection Society

Travers Buxton (1873–1944), honorary
secretary of the newly amalgamated
Anti-Slavery and Aborigines Protection
Society, in 1909

Casement with John Devoy (1842–1928)
in New York, August 1914

Casement in consular
uniform, in his forties

Postcard portrait of Eoin MacNeill
(1867–1945)

Senator Colonel Maurice Moore
(1854–1939)

Postcard portrait of Joseph
Mary Plunkett (1887–1916)

Adler Eivind Christensen (b. 1890)

The Irish Brigade in Germany, *c.*1915

Count Rudolf von Nadolny (1873–1953)
of the German Army General Staff

Captain Robert Monteith
(1879–1952)

Richard Meyer of the
German Foreign Office

Sir Roger Casement having tea with Mr and Mrs St John
Gaffney and other friends in Munich (September 1915).
Gaffney is second from left; Mrs Gaffney is seated centre

Casement during his trial, 1916

Serjeant Alexander Martin Sullivan
(1871–1959)

Postcard of the leaders of the 1916 Rebellion; Casement's portrait on the wall
suggests his peripheral position in the proceedings

Towards the end of October, Adler Christensen was despatched to Copenhagen 'to meet the first batch of volunteers from the States', but none arrived. In their letters to Casement both Devoy and McGarrity referred to efforts made to get officers or volunteers to travel to Germany. There had been difficulties in getting passports and, even when these were acquired, some men were turned back.[144] Devoy's later account lists another problem: Christensen's perfidy. The Clan had been making preparations to send across a number of recruits, 'mostly men of the Irish Volunteers in this City, all members of Clanna-Gael'. Christensen, he continued, journeyed from Germany to help with their travel, but 'he proved himself a trickster and a fraud, with the result that we were compelled to abandon the project and to summarily dismiss him'.[145] More fundamental, perhaps, was Devoy's conviction that action in Ireland was more important than the affairs of the Irish Brigade: 'Any number of successes elsewhere would not compensate for inaction there.'[146]

Two recruits did get through: Robert Monteith and, later, John McGoey.[147] On 21 September word had been sent by a German representative from New York that a thirty-six-year-old Irishman, Robert Monteith, was being sent to work with the Brigade. The message contained a biographical sketch: Monteith was 'formerly sergeant major of the royal riding artillery in the English army. Participated in Boer War and Indian border wars, served in Egypt, and was wounded twice'. His nationalist activities, including his involvement with the Irish Volunteers, had caused him to fall foul of the authorities and he soon left Ireland for the United States: 'The Irish leaders recommend him as captain of the first Irish company and advocate free communication with the prisoners.'[148]

Adler Christensen helped Monteith travel across the Atlantic and the latter succeeded in reaching Berlin on 22 October 1915. He learned that Casement was in Munich, wired him and told Richard Meyer that he would do nothing 'until I report to Sir Roger Casement and receive orders from him'. For the following day, his diary records: 'Left Berlin by night train for Munich to see Sir Roger. Reached his hotel about 9 am. Wandered round Munich until evening ... Returned to Berlin by night train – Sir Roger accompanying us. Sir Roger looked very ill, despondent and nervous, and in a state of fretfulness.' On the 25th, Casement visited the War Office to obtain permission for Monteith to visit Zossen. The following day, the two men and Major von Baerle of the War Office travelled to Zossen: 'The men were paraded (no. on parade 50). SRC [Sir Roger Casement] spoke to them informing them that in future I was to be regarded as their commanding officer (or until such time as a senior officer arrived from America). I also said a few words to them.'[149]

While all of this was happening, Casement had other worries. One concerned the dismissal of his friend Gaffney as US consul general in Munich. On 1 November, he sent a long, formal letter to Gaffney recounting how the latter had been 'charged, among other things, with having given a "dinner" in my honour at which "anti-British speeches" were made', incredulous that 'this alleged act is cited as one of the justifications for your recall'. Casement denied the allegations, the 'deliberate lie', and recalled Gaffney's kindnesses and courtesy. He talked, too, of meeting and dining with Mr Lay, the US consul in Berlin, and of rejecting overtures from Mr Gerard, the ambassador: 'I came to Germany for one thing only, to help the cause of Ireland, and I did not need the help or intervention of the American Embassy to effect my object ... For your friendship to me, a lonely man, far from friends and with so many doubts, anxieties and perplexities to make my way dark, I thank you from the bottom of my heart ...'

To an acquaintance he commented: 'I wept at G's departure – a true, staunch friend – and a faithful Irishman. I shall not forget his loyalty to me.'[150]

Another source of worry was the current of criticism directed at his own role from both sides of the Atlantic. The criticisms dated from the summer period, but Devoy now took steps to defend Casement, making a formal statement and having it forwarded to Berlin. Casement had complained of a letter from Freeman to Professor Schiemann in which it was stated that 'everyone regrets that Casement was sent over'. Lest the German government give credence to such an assertion, Devoy stated that 'my colleagues have requested me to give an emphatic and categorical contradiction to the said statement. We have the fullest confidence in Sir Roger Casement'. After reinforcing these sentiments of praise, he turned to the detractor: 'Mr George Freeman, whose work for Germany we fully appreciate, is not a member of our organization, has no authority to speak for it ... and his statement ... has no foundation whatever.'[151]

Meanwhile in Berlin it was decided that, after a short rest, Monteith should go to Limburg, accompanied by Zerhusen and two of the Irish sergeants, to try to convince more of the prisoners there to join the Brigade. Casement wrote to von Wedel, updating him on events and, once more, pleading for certain concessions for the men. 'If only I had an Officer to take command most of my difficulties would disappear – but Mr Monteith will do very well in most respects ... to keep the Camp in order. I am appointing him pro tem "Commanding Officer" of the Irish Corps.'[152] On Monday, 1 November, Monteith, with O'Toole, Beverley and Zerhusen, took the train to Limburg, where he threw himself into the recruiting task immediately. He was to spend only three weeks there. Already, on the 2nd, he reported to Casement:

> Up to the present we have nothing to show for our work. I have interviewed 70 men about 10 of whom I intend to see again. The first 25 men were inclined to be a little rusty and insolent, but I managed to smooth their ruffled feathers and part with them on good terms; the men whom I saw today were in a far better frame of mind and reasoned out the matter squarely, and I think we stand to get 8 or 10 of them.[153]

Over the next few weeks, as Monteith recorded in his diary, the small team interviewed the men: 'Men seem indifferent. A lot of them are absolutely impossible'; 'A little hostility today'; 'One man sent to Zossen y'day, he is of the right sort'; 'We now manage to get through about 50 men per day'; 'Two more men for Zossen'. The German authorities were supportive, but there were problems. Monteith was still 'Mr Monteith', without permission to wear uniform. On 13 November, he told Casement, he had 'selected 52 men who will in all probability join us', but feared the way they were being handled by the Germans: 'It seems to be the way of the German people to have things their way – which is wrong. The men selected by me are to be separated into separate rooms, consequently they will be under suspicion of every man in the camp, Irish, Russian and French. It will spoil everything – The German soldier is not tactful.'[154] Kehoe arrived after a week and was impressed by the work: 'The men in camp have taken a different attitude towards us this time, they listen attentively, quietly and are never insulting, it is much easier to work with them.'[155]

On the basis of Casement's letters, Monteith observed in his diary that '*SRC is not well*. I do not think he is mentally fit and I am afraid to ask him to see a doctor. Last time I saw him he was simply quivering like a leaf.'[156] Affairs at Zossen soon cut short Monteith's recruiting at Limburg. In his diary for 16 November he recorded: 'I am wanted back to Zossen; things are not going well there, men are out of hand and SRC thinks it would be advisable for me to return as early as possible.'[157]

On the evening of 23 November, Monteith, Zerhusen, Kehoe and Beverley set off for Berlin, leaving Michael O'Toole behind to continue interviewing potential recruits. Monteith's encounter with Casement was a sobering one:

Reach Berlin 10 am. See SRC ... SRC on verge of collapse, disappointment of his hope time after time has almost killed him – I am seriously afraid he contemplates self destruction – Zerhusen and I go to War Office and see Major von Baerle, who has charge of our affairs. He is unable to give me permission to go to Zossen or to wear uniform and requests me to stay in Berlin for a few days until the necessary authority is given by the General Officer commanding.[158]

Despite Casement's state of health, he was working hard on plans for the Brigade. Early in December the prospect of the Brigade's going to the East began to take on a more concrete form. On 3 December he wrote to von Wedel, discussing his plan to travel to Constantinople and enclosing a memorandum that he intended to present to the Turkish minister of war there. In the memo he referred to the Agreement of 28 December 1914 and its clauses on the possible use of the Brigade in 'assisting the Ottoman forces to expel the British from Egypt'. Though small in size, the force 'might have a moral effect and be of political value ... out of all proportion to their actual number'. The one stipulation was that 'we should be recognised as a band of Irish nationalists in arms, fighting England where we found her assailable, and combating, as allies, in the common cause to free others from the imperial yoke of Britain that threatens alike the Eastern and Western peoples'.[159]

A week later he sent von Wedel a second memorandum on the same topic, a copy of which he had given to Nadolny. It was now clear that German aid could not be furnished directly to Ireland: 'the few men armed there are insufficient in number and inadequate in organization and have far too little equipment to make any successful fight. It would be not only hopeless, but a crime to urge them to an armed effort'. Action in the East could inspire those nationalists fighting against England in India, Persia and Afghanistan. Finally, because the men had never been prisoners of the Turks, they would be received there as honourable volunteers fighting in a common cause.[160] The general staff took a hand in facilitating the process, though their sense of deep frustration with the whole Irish Brigade endeavour is captured in a memo from Nadolny at the beginning of January 1916:

> The request first has been presented for a reaction to the Military Attaché in Constantinople. He replied that both Enver and Dschemal Pascha [Djemal Pasha] agreed to use the men as a machine gun detachment in the latter's campaign in Syria. It need not be emphasized that the deployment of the men would be a relief [*Enlastung*] for us. There is hardly a danger of desertion because the British are informed about their joining the Irish Brigade and they know it.[161]

Meanwhile, in Zossen, with Monteith's return, the Brigade members were being prepared for this eventuality. The Ministry of War agreed to the appointment of Monteith as commanding officer and on 27 November, with two feet of snow on the ground, he had travelled to Zossen to meet the men: 'All prisoners, no leave allowed, no arms, no overcoats – men in an ugly humour in consequence – return to hotel.' A few days later he was able to move into the camp: 'Move into officers quarters ... Have a parade of the men, inspected clothes, boots, quarters, ascertained wants, which include everything imaginable. Boots, clothes, overcoats, blankets, football, melodeon, sewing machine for tailor, glass for windows, broken through horseplay, etc. etc.'[162] On 1 December, Monteith's diary recorded:

> Parade the men and explain that it is hardly probable that the invasion of British Isles will take place – But ask them to think over the idea of striking a blow at England by going to the Eastern theatre of war and joining the army for the invasion of Egypt and helping to free another small nationality which England strangely enough omits to free – nobody seems very enthusiastic about the prospect.[163]

Training followed, rifles were issued, parades took place and passes were granted. On the 3rd, Monteith and Casement interviewed the men on the question of going to Egypt: '38 of 56 volunteer. I am disappointed, very disappointed.' Casement was now staying at the Hotel Golden Lion in Zossen and joined the Brigade in some marches. His depressed state was evident in the few private letters he wrote at this time. To Antonie Meyer he apologized for not visiting her and her brother and reflected on Christmas, Christianity and the war:

Certain it is no people today is Christian, for if the war has done nothing else, it has killed Christianity in the life of nations ... Were men Christians today – were Governments Christian, or inspired by any ray of that Gospel – peace would come tomorrow ... I do not like to think of the future – it is all dark and hopeless and forbidding – and I think the dead are best.

The countless dead appalled him: 'And this is what our boasted Civilisation ends in! – an orgie of Hatred, Lying and organized Murder! The Middle Ages were better – the dark Ages even.'[164] On the same day, he wrote to Eduard, her brother, with apologies: 'I cannot wish anyone in these war-stricken lands a happy Christmas – it is not possible – I wish I could say even a peaceful Christmas. Everything looks dark and dreary and with the exception of Mr Ford's "Peace Ship" (!) there is no sign of peace anywhere.'[165]

Similar observations poured out in a letter to his old friend Fritz Pincus, whom he had last met in February in Berlin:

Since then I have had many worries, trials and vexations of soul. I have not for a long time felt inclined to go about and see people ... *Like everyone* I am waiting for the war to end. It is a shocking Calamity to the Whole Earth and my heart is sick at it – It is no longer a war but a massacre. Today I walked near 20 kilometres through the Mark of Brandenburg and saw the empty closed factories, and smokeless chimneys and the houses everywhere half shut up – all men folk gone to the war – gone to their Death. And I see no daylight. No way out. The Robber of the Seas cannot be reached – by water anyhow – and until *She* wants peace none will come to the world ... I wish you a very – no I *can't* say happy Christmas – it is not possible – but I wish you a hopeful Christmas. More one cannot say today. I have no hope.[166]

Christmas 1915 he spent in Dresden in a despondent mood. 'Dresden was very gloomy and sad – and so was I,' he told Pincus afterwards, 'I feel worse every day.'[167] An incident described by a friend, Frau Küntzelmann, must date from this visit. She described his reaction to hearing 'Silent Night' sung. His ears pricked up and then he disappeared from the room: 'I looked for him and found him in the doorway of another room. His eyes were glazed with tears. He did not speak. I took him by the hand and steered him back to the company. There, he soon came to himself again.' Frau Küntzelmann also talked of his return for the New Year, when he sang Irish songs in a magnificent voice: 'I have never seen a look on a human face as that one, while he sang the Irish songs. His eyes were fascinating. One of the songs he sang he wrote down: it was Thomas Moore's "Come Rest in this Bosom".'[168]

He wrote a long, despairing letter to Eduard Meyer early in the new year:

I return to dreary, deadly dull Zossen tomorrow – but shall not stay there much longer. It is too dreadful a place and too lonely. I have been so unwell of late – my heart troubling me – that I have not been able to write or do anything but *brood*. And that is very bad – I want to move and do something in the open air – as of old in Africa where the happiest days of my life were spent.

He spoke of the prospect of conscription in Ireland and in England:

> I fear every evil for Ireland. But I think the Cabinet will be driven (by fear of the consequences) to leave Ireland out of the Conscription Bill. It would meet with double resistance – that of Redmond and Co. and his 84 supporters in Parliament – and that of the remaining Irish Volunteers some 25,000 (more or less armed) men ... These Tory powers hate the English 'lower classes' – they want to reduce them to servitude – a servitude that shall be perpetual and endure after the War. The fight for Conscription in England is really the old issue of privilege versus the people. The aristocracy of wealth want the people numbered – like the Israelites of old – ticketed, put to specified tasks and 'kept in their place'.

And, in a final outburst of emotion: 'I would to God I were in Ireland – were I there today I would make it the last act of my life to see that the resistance was offered with every ounce of strength and courage we still possess in the hearts of Irishmen. Maybe I shall go by submarine!'[169]

A few days later, on 7 January 1916, Monteith commented on Casement's condition: 'SRC is ill, nervous and depressed.' By the 12th, he was positively alarmed:

> No arms have yet arrived, usual parades. SRC very ill. I am afraid his mind is going, disappointment after disappointment has broken him. Have tried to get him to see a mental specialist, wire for his doctor and go to Berlin to see some people, friends of his to whom I make known his condition. Go to General Staff, who promise to hurry our departure for the front – also call at Foreign Office – wire for Father Crotty to come to Zossen as I think SRC would like to see him, this was done entirely on my own responsibility.[170]

Two days later, on 14 January, Casement went to see a specialist and met Monteith on his return to Zossen: 'He arrives about 8 pm. Looks wretched. The specialist Dr Oppenheim has ordered him to a sanatorium – This means that all devolves upon me. *I am not up to my job.*'[171] After making necessary arrangements with Monteith, Casement retired to a Kuranstalt in Munich.

Almost immediately, Fr Crotty sent a coded message about Casement's condition to McGarrity in the United States: 'He may *or may not* recover. C. is unable to do his part of the work. Perhaps you may wish, & will send some one to take Claxton's [Casement] place ...'[172] Within days, it appeared as if Crotty's own long sojourn in Germany was to come to an end. He informed von Wedel on 22 January that he had received a letter from his superior general requesting his return to Rome as soon as possible.[173]

Casement, in the sanatorium in Munich, wasn't completely out of touch with events. Monteith kept in contact and responded encouragingly on the 24th to a letter from Casement. 'As your body is fit, you may also get your mind in the same condition, and be ready to join us as we pass through Vienna on our way to the front. I am sure we will go this time.'[174] A week later, Monteith wrote again, sending on materials, but adding a word of caution: 'I am afraid you are going to start writing again and if I was sure of it I should not send on these things, a spade and a garden rake would be better ...'[175]

Before leaving for Ireland in April, Monteith committed to paper his version of events in Zossen:

> Sir Roger Casement went to Munich to a rest house under the care of Dr Rudolf van Hoesslin and I took over charge of Brigade affairs. Things went badly, the men wanted new clothing and boots which I repeatedly asked for – to one application I was told the men's boots and clothing were worn out 'through their playing football in them' and, as I did not want to see the men playing football in their nakedness, I did not forbid the awful practice. It must be explained that the men had only one suit of uniform – The men were still kept as prisoners, no leave granted. This ... exasperated the boys so much that 24 out of 38 who had volunteered for service in the East withdrew their names. Of this I informed the General Staff at Berlin through Capt. Nadolny who went into a towering rage and said *he would send them all to the Western front*. I said you cannot and will not do so, and to his question why? I said, 'because I will prevent it. My men will do as I say'.

He wrote to the general staff shortly after this, asking for clarification regarding the deployment of the men and was called to the general staff:

> This I did and after some talk in which I put the men's case pretty strongly, Lt. Frey sharply and curtly informed me that the German Government had not asked me to come to Germany (although this is covered by a para[graph] in the agreement entered into by the Imperial Government and Sir Roger Casement). I therefore said if you talk to me in that way I have nothing more to say! I will hand my sword to General Schneider in the morning, then you can put me over the border, or if you so wish it hand me to the English. I took up my cap and books and was about to go, on which his manner changed immediately, he tried all he knew to pacify me, and implored me to discuss the matter fully. This we did and I outlined a scheme by which the men might be set free on police pass, and earn their own living. I was promised on more than one occasion that efforts were being made to meet my wishes.[176]

At the end of January, the commander of the army barracks at Zossen, General Schneider, sent a report to Berlin, complaining of the Irishmen's lack of discipline:

> With but a few exceptions, the Irish have no sense of honour, no military ethos, and no good-will that would help adjust themselves to the situation they are in. Almost everyone is lying, most of them have taken to drink, hanging about or other excesses. Exhortations and punishments do not make any impression. Their continuing presence, under the current circumstances, is highly detrimental to our [German] soldiers, with whom they pick fights easily. Wherever they show up, they make a very poor example for our soldiers.[177]

Indicative of wider suspicion at the highest level of the German military system concerning Casement's whole German project were the words of General Löwenfeld in early February: 'I cannot have any great measure of confidence in someone like Sir Roger Casement who brings charges of such severity against the very Government he has served for so many years; even more so since I cannot rule out the possibility that this propagandist could be guided by more sinister intentions.'[178]

Towards the Easter Rising

On 17 February, Count Bernstorff in the Washington Embassy sent a telegram to the German Foreign Office: 'Irish leader John Devoy informs me that revolution shall begin Easter Sunday Ireland. Requests arms between Good Friday and Easter Sunday Limerick, West coast of Ireland. Longer waiting impossible, request wire reply whether I may promise help from Germany.'[179] Nadolny, at the general staff, was informed and consultations began between the German Foreign Office, the general staff and the Admiralty. Agreement was reached and details worked out, which Nadolny communicated to the GFO on 1 March:

> Between April 20 and 23 in the evening two or three fishing trawlers could land about 20,000 rifles and 10 machine guns with ammunition and explosives at Fenit Pier in Tralee Bay. Irish pilot boat is to expect trawlers before dusk ... at entry Tralee Bay ... Unloading has to be effected in a few hours. Please wire whether necessary steps can be arranged in Ireland by Devoy.[180]

On the same day, Lieutenant Frey sent for Monteith and informed him that something was about to happen in Ireland and that rifles and ammunition were being asked for. Monteith, in turn, wrote to Casement, asking that he come to Berlin.

Unable to travel, because of his illness, the latter requested that Monteith come to Munich, which he did. Arriving on 7 March, they discussed the matter, and Casement drew up two memoranda advising on the landing of arms, which Monteith delivered to the general staff.[181] On the 15th, Casement followed Monteith back to Berlin, where the news that awaited him was to be very different from that which he expected. At 10 am on the morning of 16 March, he met with Captain Nadolny and two colleagues, to be told that the shipment of arms was no simple arming of the Irish Volunteers but was in support of a planned 'outbreak' or 'rising' in Ireland'. He was shown a copy of Devoy's letter of 16 February, asking for 100,000 rifles and some artillery, together with German officers and trained artillerymen. The German decision was to send 20,000 rifles, ten machine guns and 5,000,000 cartridges. This, his informants suggested, now provided a suitable military opportunity for himself, Monteith and the members of the Irish Brigade. 'For the most part,' Casement recorded,

> I remained silent, listening to what I held to be absurd views ... The whole project took my breath away. I had come prepared to discuss the best means of landing arms in Ireland and I found myself confronted with a proposal for a 'rebellion' in Ireland I believed to be wholly futile at the best, and at the worst something I dreaded to think of.[182]

The next day, 17 March, Casement had an appointment at the German Admiralty. He now found himself more or less committed, he realized, to sail for Ireland about 8 April with 'Lt. Monteith and a handful of the Irish prisoners of war who had not been consulted, on a journey that involved the gravest personal risks and that *might* involve appalling consequences for Ireland'.[183] He impressed on the Admiralty officers the importance of sending a messenger to Ireland to give accurate details of the coming shipment and to make necessary arrangements, and suggested John McGoey's name. Surprisingly, perhaps, they consented and made arrangements to have McGoey sent across the frontier in Denmark. While Casement was genuine with regard to this aspect of McGoey's mission, he had an added purpose: 'he goes really to try and get the heads in Ireland to call off the rising and merely try to land the arms safely and distribute these'.[184] McGoey left on 19 March but seems unlikely to have reached Dublin.

At this point, Casement returned to Munich to think matters over and attend to personal affairs. He later explained his quandary to von Wedel. Part of his problem was his isolation. It had been 'eleven months since I had had direct communication from Ireland and over three months since I had received any news from America'. While he supported the sending of arms to Ireland, he was strongly opposed to any armed outbreak 'unless backed with strong foreign military help'. What was being offered was far short of that and he feared the consequences. While he brooded over these issues and wrote his farewell 'memo' for Dr Curry, he received word from Monteith that the men of the Brigade had just been issued with machine guns and were starting drill.[185]

Casement returned to Berlin on 29 March 'the victim of grave doubt and a prey to extreme anxiety'. Events of the following days were not destined to lessen his tension. He went first to the Admiralty and learned more of the evolving transport plans. The fishing vessels, which were originally to carry the arms, had been replaced by a 1228-ton steamer, formerly the British Wilson-Linc *Castro*, but detained in Germany upon the outbreak of war and renamed *Libau*; she was now disguised as a Norwegian vessel and named *Aud*. Casement also registered his objections to taking the men. There followed a meeting with Nadolny and general staff colleagues, which 'soon developed into an acrimonious controversy'. He was, by his own account, accused 'in terms of extraordinary discourtesy' of an 'underhand trick' in sending McGoey and threatened that, should he not agree to the conditions outlined, a telegram would be sent to Devoy stating that, because of his (Casement's) opposition, no arms would be sent and the whole enterprise undermined: 'I left the General Staff in a state of still deeper perplexity as to how I should act in the very trying situation in which I was being put.'

The discussion continued, more courteously but no less firmly, the following morning. Nadolny stated that the outbreak had been planned in Ireland and that the German government was responding with assistance to the best of its means. The general staff 'were not inspired by an "idealistic" interest in Ireland and were only sending the rifles in the hope that they should be at once used. In other words, "no revolution no rifles" '. Under such pressure Casement accepted reluctantly, but only for himself. His instinct, he told von Wedel, pressed him to be with his countrymen, while his reason and judgment pressed him to oppose the project. But if he opposed it, he would bring hurt to many of his friends in Ireland and his name would 'be cursed by future generations of my countrymen ... I do not think any man in this world was ever put in a more atrocious position'. The ship, he finally concluded, should go and he, alone, go with it: 'This seems the best I can decide. While it is not all I should wish it at least will leave my character as an Irishman safe on the final facts of my public career; and it will in no wise damage or weaken the enterprise in Ireland or endanger the German vessel and her gallant crew.' In a separate note, Casement recorded his opinion of this meeting and of Nadolny and his role: 'Went & he again tried to blackmail me into full acquiescence with his plan. I think him a complete and perfect scoundrel & he knows I do. He is but the instrument of a policy of scoundrels.'[186]

The arrival at this point of a copy of the *Irish World*, containing a speech of John Devoy's, helped reconcile Casement, somewhat, to his participation in the coming rebellion in Ireland. Despite having excluded Ireland from the Conscription Bill, Devoy said, largely because of the presence of the Irish Volunteers, the British government was now preparing to destroy the Volunteers and introduce compulsory service. This the Volunteers had always pledged to oppose, by force if necessary, and all the American Irish could do was to support the action of the Irish. In this situation, Casement felt: 'I will very gladly go to Ireland with the arms and do all I can to sustain and support a movement of resistance based on these grounds. For in this case it is better for Irishmen to fight at home and resist conscription by force than to be swept into the shambles of England's continental war and lose their lives in an unworthy cause.'[187]

On the following day, 3 April, he was asked to go to the general staff, where two officers, von Haugwitz and von Hülsen told him of the plans for sending arms and ammunition. In addition – to intimidate him, he thought – they showed him a letter of Devoy's from December 1915 'recording Christensen's perfidy' in the US. When the two were finished, Casement informed them that he was firm in his decision not to take the Brigade members with him to Ireland. At this point Nadolny appeared and the conversation became 'more infamous than before'. Nadolny claimed that a brigade had not been formed, that the Agreement of December 1914, therefore, was dead and that Casement had now no right to claim the men were under his authority: 'He [Nadolny] could do as he pleased with the soldiers at Zossen and send them to Ireland if he chose and they agreed. I said laconically. 'Try it".' They argued on, Nadolny terming the men 'deserters' and suggesting that Casement had no feeling for the military requirements:

> The only gentleman on their side was young von Haugwitz. He agreed with me on all points, except that the military necessity of the case required the men as gunners. I said I should let no plea of military necessity or any other necessity override my sense of honour. They said – collectively – 'You argue for a theory – a principle – we, as soldiers, for a vital military need. Do you wish the thing to succeed or fail?'[188]

The general staff succumbed and, on the following day, Casement and Monteith were told that the men would not go. He, Monteith and Julian Beverley would travel: 'We took Beverley at Monteith's wish. Poison arranged for all!'[189] In a distraught state, he called on the Princess Blücher. Her account told of receiving a telephone call from him, asking to visit, urgently. He came, 'like one demented'; he was in trouble: a prisoner in Germany, a noose round his neck in England. He sat down, sobbed like a child and hinted at his activities but refused to give details – it would endanger the lives of many. The solution, he felt, was to kill himself. He gave her 'a bundle of farewell letters to be opened after his death' and asked to see her again. She refused, claiming that she was being watched, 'like everyone else here!'[190]

On the following day, Casement went to see the men in Zossen: 'Spent day at Zossen talking to men a word of farewell. Breaking heart. I have been crying all the morning.'[191] He went there, he said,

> ostensibly with the Priest who confessed the men, really to bid them goodbye. At least I have saved them! The whole thing appals me as a piece of the most ghastly folly – or rather one of the most criminal attempts ever perpetrated ... On all grounds by which we may consider it, it is a scheme that can only bring failure – and probably something far worse than failure – disaster: Let us – let me put down these grounds as I perceive them. This is a record of my mind and understanding – and I want it to live after me.

He went on to assess the enterprise on military, political and moral grounds, finding it wanting on all three. Militarily, it might pass if it were a gun-running enterprise by an arms firm: 'But for the G.G. Staff of the greatest military power in the world it is an astonishing adventure ...' He and Monteith, disguised as sailors, carrying poison, and bringing 20,000 rifles were 'to invade a Kingdom'. Politically, he acknowledged the strength of John Devoy's argument, but the political risks were tremendous. Law-abiding and peace-loving Irishmen 'will bitterly resent bloodshed and civil strife in Ireland – forced on, as will then seem apparent, by a filibustering expedition launched from Germany for that purpose', in what, for Germany, was merely a 'diversion'. The result, he feared, would be a backlash, and the danger that 'the British recruiting sergeant will get the reward – not the German military machine'.

Morally, too, he felt the action wrong, not least for how he was being used:

'Advantage is certainly being taken of me in a wholly unfair and even cowardly way, and if (the inevitable!) I am captured by the British, this will be made clear.' But, after his capture and vilification as a 'traitor', Britain would turn the vilification towards Germany, accusing them of making him a 'sacrificed dupe'. He felt alone and his dejection was total. 'I am so completely in the dark as to what is being really planned in Ireland, in America, that I dare not accept the responsibility – And no one here will accept any responsibility. They put it all on me.' He felt weighed down by his responsibilities towards the members of the Brigade: 'It is time I died – for if I looked them in the face again I could not say what I wrote just now – "all is lost but honour". I feel that *all* is indeed lost and the sooner my life is taken from me the better.'[192]

At this moment, on 5 April, the German minister in Berne informed the GFO that Count George Plunkett had arrived and that a letter to Casement was being forwarded. The minister's note made the following points: that the Rising was timed for Easter Sunday; that arms should be sent to Tralee Bay not later than the evening of Easter Monday; that German officers were absolutely necessary; that a submarine was necessary for Dublin harbour. Nadolny dictated the reply, sending confirmation on the first two points, but a negative response on the other two.[193]

On the morning of the 7th Casement wrote up his diary. The *Aud* was due to sail and there were many things to be done and he would make 'a last fight for the submarine'. His request to be sent ahead of the arms ship on a submarine had been rejected, but he was still intent on pursuing the matter: 'Today is really my last day – and I shall be hunted and driven all day. It is still early. I told that faithful, splendid Monteith last night that I should be glad to go even to death on the scaffold – to an English jail, to get away from Germany and these people I despise so much. He said "Indeed I think I would, too".'[194] A message arrived asking him to go to the general staff, where he discussed Count Plunkett's letter, telegraphed a reply and gave von Haugwitz a letter to be sent to Berne: 'It was brought back at 7.45 pm in the evening.' Plunkett was to send another letter, dated 11 April, which, however, only arrived after Casement's departure for Ireland. In it Plunkett asked Casement to press the Germans on the questions of officers and a submarine for Dublin harbour: 'The effect of the presence of German officers, and of a German submarine (which otherwise might not seem so important) in Irish waters, assisting us, would be very great. I may add that the Supreme Council of the Irish Volunteers desire to associate Germany, in this marked way, with the liberation of Ireland.'[195]

In the meantime, in a final attempt to get a submarine, Casement had approached an associate, Jacob Noeggerath, an influential German-American, whom he described as 'a confidential agent of the FO'. On the afternoon of 7 April, after a flurry of contacts, Captain Heydell [Heidel] phoned, asking Casement to come to the Admiralty at 4 pm – it was 'over the submarine'. Casement waited there for two hours, reading. 'Then came Heydell in great excitement to say they had had a full dress debate and the thing was settled. I was to go by submarine.'[196]

Two days later, on 9 April, one of the Brigade members, Sean Francis Kavanagh, was summoned to the Hotel Saxonia, Friedrichstrasse, to meet Casement and Monteith.[197] Kavanagh was left alone with Casement, who had 'a nervous and worried look upon his face'. 'I sent for you,' he said,

> to entrust to your care this envelope, which contains the pay for the Brigade, a letter to Mr Zerhusen, and a document which I wish him to hand to the local Chaplain, with instructions that he is to read it to the men when we are gone. I am setting out on a mission and may never see any of you again. It is for our own interests that I cannot take all the men with me, but tell them to carry on with their training, for the time may come when they will be required to fulfil their promise.

Casement then asked Kavanagh to name those men he considered most reliable for a dangerous mission. The interview came to an end in an atmosphere of heightened emotion. 'Walking quickly to the door he opened it, and looking back raised his right hand in salute, whilst the word "Courage" floated to me across the room as if it had been pronounced in a whisper. He had gone – Gone to his death – and he knew it.'[198]

Casement's remaining major concern was for the welfare of the Brigade members being left behind. On 11 April, the day before the submarine party left, he wrote to the Imperial Chancellor, von Bethmann Hollweg, arguing the case for the men. He reminded Bethmann Hollweg of their meeting in December 1914 and of the agreement subsequently drawn up, covering Brigade affairs: 'These men remain a charge confided to the honour of the German Government and German people. They are guests of Germany in the highest sense of the word and are entitled to the scrupulous fulfilment of the terms of the Agreement under which they threw off their allegiance and entered into rebellion.' Now, he had been told that the agreement was null and void and that the men were deserters or prisoners of war. He dissented profoundly, he said, from this view and appealed for the Chancellor's support.[199] He sent another letter to von Wedel, explaining some details regarding the men, telling him, as he had the Chancellor, that he had asked St John Gaffney to look after the affairs of the Brigade. He enclosed a full list of names of the men remaining at Zossen.[200]

Finally, he wrote a letter of farewell to the Brigade members, which was signed also by Monteith and Beverley. It apologized for their sudden and secretive departure, referring to the dangers of the mission:

> We are sure that all of you would have gladly faced those dangers seeing that it is in the Cause of Ireland that we go, but we have decided it was unfair to you to appeal to your courage in a matter where all the elements of danger are very apparent and those of hope entirely wanting. You must, therefore, forgive us

for going in silence from you and leaving you to the continued inactivities that have already been so harmful to you and contrary to your hopes when you volunteered for the Service of Ireland.[201]

On 12 April, Casement, Monteith and Beverley left Wilhelmshaven by submarine for Ireland. Richard Meyer noted their departure with a memo.[202] While Casement had been anxious to travel to Ireland ahead of the arms ship in order to warn the planners of the Rising about the meagreness of German help, the fact that ship and submarine were now to rendezvous in Tralee Bay would seem to indicate that the Germans were not going to risk that outcome. They may have felt, though, that he had a better chance of evading capture in travelling by submarine.

18: *Capture, Trial and Execution, 1916*

From Berlin to the Tower of London

The arms ship *Aud*, under the command of Captain Karl Spindler, sailed from Warnemünde on 10 April, having a rendezvous date with Casement's submarine for midnight of 20 April in Tralee Bay.[1] During the voyage, she had several encounters with British vessels, but was not boarded. Despite Spindler's subsequent accounts to the contrary, it seems likely that he made an error with regard to the location of the rendezvous point and was not where he should have been on the night of 20 April. On Good Friday, the 21st, the ship's adventure moved to a close when, after a period of shadowing by a number of British vessels and a brief chase, the *Aud* was apprehended by the *Bluebell* in the late afternoon. Under escort to Queenstown, her crew scuttled her on the morning of Saturday 22 April.

On 12 April, a few days after the *Aud* had left Germany, Casement, Monteith and Beverley began their journey from Wilhelmshaven on the submarine U-20. Mechanical difficulties forced the submarine back; the party switched to U-19 at Heligoland, from which they embarked again on 15 April. Under the command of Captain Raimund Weisbach, aiming for their rendezvous with the *Aud*, they sailed round the north of Shetland. They ran into very heavy seas and Casement suffered a good deal from seasickness. On the evening of 20 April they reached Tralee Bay and, at 12.10 am on the 21st, the rendezvous point. Neither the *Aud* nor a pilot boat was to be found and Weisbach, conscious of the vulnerability of his craft, made arrangements to put his Irish passengers ashore.[2] Around 2.15 am on the 21st, Casement, Monteith and Beverley set off for the shore in a small boat, 'three men in a boat – the smallest invading party on record', as Monteith later put it wryly. Monteith did most of the rowing, despite a damaged hand. Close to shore they were overturned by a large wave and thrown into the water; forced to swim ashore, they reached dry land at Banna Strand, exhausted:

I do not think that Casement was even conscious. He was lying away below high water mark, the sea lapped his body from head to foot, his eyes were closed and in the dim moonlight his face resembled that of a sleeping child. I dragged him to his feet, and chafed his legs and hands as best I could, while the water ran from his hair and clothing; then, I made him move about to restore his circulation.[3]

After some time, having buried most of their equipment, Monteith and Beverley set off for Tralee, while Casement remained in 'McKenna's Fort', a local rath or ring fort at Curraghane, where he rested. From prison, he described his feelings to Nina:

When I landed in Ireland that morning (about 3 am) swamped and swimming ashore on an unknown strand I was happy for the first time for over a year. Although I knew that this fate waited on me, I was for one brief spell happy and smiling once more. I cannot tell you what I felt. The sandhills were full of skylarks, rising in the damp, the first I had heard for years – the first sound I heard through the surf was their song as I waded in through the breakers, and they kept rising all the time up to the old rath at Currahane where I stayed and sent the others on, and all round were primroses and wild violets and the singing of the skylarks in the air, and I was back in Ireland again ...[4]

Early though it was, the presence of a party of strangers in the quiet shore-land did not go unnoticed for long and local people observed their movements. They were later called to testify at Casement's trial: Mary Gorman, a servant girl, Michael Hussey, a labourer, John McCarthy, a local farmer and Martin Collins, a youth. McCarthy, who claimed that he had been visiting a holy well, came upon the boat on the shore and, with the help of a neighbour, pulled it above the high-water line and sent word to the RIC at nearby Ardfert. Shortly after 1 pm that afternoon, Casement found himself facing the gun of RIC constable, Bernard Riley. As he was being taken away, Martin Collins noticed him tearing and dropping pieces of paper behind his back, which the youth later collected and took to the RIC; pieced together, the sheet was discovered to contain a code to be used for further communications with Germany. After being taken to Ardfert by Riley and Sergeant Thomas Hearn, Casement was soon transferred to Tralee.

While in custody here, he succeeded in speaking to a local doctor, Michael Shanahan, and to a Dominican priest, Fr F.M. Ryan, telling them who he was and asking Ryan, at least, to get a message to Eoin MacNeill in Dublin, advising him to postpone the Rising because of the inadequacy of German help. Monteith, meanwhile, had made contact with Austin Stack, local commandant of the Volunteers, who went by car in search of Casement, unaware that he was already in custody. Stack was himself detained after his return to Tralee. With the Rising planned to start and the German arms ship expected to arrive on the following Sunday, no attempt was made to rescue Casement. In the event, he was quickly taken to London, travelling on Saturday via Killarney, Mallow and

Dublin, where he was roughly stripped and searched at Arbour Hill barracks. He travelled by night boat to Holyhead and arrived in London early in the morning of Easter Sunday, 23 April. He was escorted from Euston Station to Scotland Yard by Inspector Joseph Sandercock.[5]

Interrogation at Scotland Yard

At Scotland Yard, Casement was interrogated each day from Sunday, 23 April to Tuesday the 25th. Present on the 23rd were the assistant chief commissioner, Basil Thomson; Captain Reginald Hall, chief of naval intelligence at the Admiralty; and Superintendent Quinn. Major Frank Hall, an MI5 officer involved in tracking Casement, was also present.[6] Casement asked immediately to see 'a friend', Sir William Tyrrell, not for himself, he declared, but because it might affect other people. During the course of the interview, he indicated to his interrogators the predicament he felt himself to be in regarding the planned Rising:

> I have committed perhaps many follies in endeavouring to help my country according to what I thought was best, and in this last act of mine in going back to Ireland, I came with my eyes opened wide, knowing exactly what I was going to. Knowing that you were bound to catch me. Knowing all the consequences, and I came from a sense of duty, which, if I dared tell you the facts, you will be the first to agree with me. The difficulty now is whether it is my duty to tell you now or wait. If I told the truth, I may involve other men, and may be accused of treachery to them or my country. You see my difficulty. I am in terrible difficulties.

Asked if he believed Germany sincere in her goodwill towards Ireland, he responded that she had been, a year previously. 'It may not be so good today. Germany as a power is fighting a very desperate battle for itself. It is not quite so well to think of the life of someone else, if he is fighting for himself.' As to whether he was pro-German, he replied: 'No, I am not. Germany wanted to help my country. I didn't feel that they were going to do anything for Ireland alone.'[7]

On the following day, Lieutenant Serocold, of Reginald Hall's staff, and Quinn probed again on his role in the Rising. He didn't, he told them, know 'Collins': 'I wasn't a member of any secret body at all. I did not know any. I was a member of the governing body of the Volunteers, an open organization, and although my intentions were to get as many arms into Ireland and to arm these men, I had no ulterior aim of any kind.' He gave details of how he had learned of the planned Rising from German officials:

> I said I have been here for a year and a half and begged you again and again to send rifles to Ireland and you refused always. Now you spring it at my head at the eleventh hour, when I have long given it up, of hoping to arm my countrymen. At last you have come with this offer of the belated help, and it synchronises with what I can only regard as a hopeless rising in Ireland where my

countrymen will be shot down. Obviously I think it is cowardly, dastardly and I go alone. They wanted me to take all my Irish boys. Those young men ... We had a terrible fight and I won the day. I shall not have it said that I handed these men over to hang them.[8]

As Casement was being interrogated on this second day, the planned Rising began in Ireland. The military authorities had had intelligence concerning a possible landing of arms on the south-west coast and the RIC had been put on alert there and in the capital. But, after the sinking of the *Aud* on 22 April, Casement's capture and the issuing of a countermanding order for Volunteer exercises by Eoin MacNeill, published in the *Sunday Independent*, the attention of the authorities lulled a little. Casement, too, was believed to be more important than he was. Plans had been made to round up the ringleaders, but had not yet been put into effect. Despite the setbacks, the IRB leaders were determined to go ahead with the planned Rising, though there was by now utter confusion among Volunteers nationally. As a result, when the Rising did take place, a total of less than 1600 men participated and the action was confined mainly to Dublin, where a number of key buildings were seized on Easter Monday, 24 April. A proclamation of an Irish Republic, signed by representatives of the provisional government, was read at the General Post Office; present were Patrick Pearse, Tom Clarke, Sean McDermott, Joseph Plunkett and James Connolly.

On Tuesday the 25th Casement was interrogated again by Thomson and Hall. Thomson told him of the Rising in Ireland: 'Since I saw you yesterday what we thought would happen has happened. There has been more or less a rising in Dublin, and a good many have been killed, and that is all the good that has proceeded from your expedition.' Asked about the likelihood of the arrival of another German ship, he replied: 'They would not come unless I telegraphed for them.' He traced for his interrogators the history of his own involvement. To Thomson's query, 'When did you become a nationalist?', he responded: 'I have been a nationalist all my life but not so extreme.' 'But your father was a Protestant?' 'I am now – or was,' replied Casement.

> I went abroad and what morally, and intellectually, brought me back to Ireland to become a red hot nationalist were two things: the Boer War, in which I took part, and the Congo. I started in the Boer War, feeling I was doing the right thing, but I felt shame on myself going against these people afterwards. I have the medal for the Boer War but I have never worn it. I refused the CMG that was offered me for the Congo.

'You could have refused the decorations altogether,' Thomson pressed. 'Only by retiring from the service and that I could not afford to do.' The Germans, he told them,

> could not understand me. They sometimes called me a dreamer but they were quite willing to profit by my foolishness ... I went over to America to arm the Irish Volunteers just as Carson came here to get money for the Ulster Volun-

teers. The only people that could help us was the Irish-Americans. Then the war came and upset all the plans. The Irish did not want to fight for England. I said I will go to Germany and try to get the arms there.

During the conversation, Thomson asked: 'Have you got some trunks at 50 Ebury Street? I propose having them down and examined.' Casement is recorded as replying, 'There's nothing in them.'9 While the authorities deliberated on whether Casement should undergo a military or civil trial, he was confined in the Tower of London, where little attempt was made to afford him basic comforts and where he was deprived of outside contact. While in isolation and in a mood of deep despair, he made two attempts at suicide. He first tried to introduce the poison he had brought with him into his bloodstream, by cutting his finger with a broken spectacle lens; then he swallowed nails, which he had taken from the firewood left in his cell. In addition, he was refusing food. On 3 May, one of the guards whispered news of the executions of the leaders of the Rising in Dublin. 'I was then very ill and thought I was dying,' Casement wrote afterwards of these days.10

On 25 April Casement's arrest was announced in the press. His cousins, Gertrude and Elizabeth, had been staying at Frinton-on-Sea for their Easter holidays when, on Tuesday the 25th, Elizabeth returned from a walk 'white-faced and scared', by Gertrude's later account. 'There is bad news on the posters,' Elizabeth announced. Gertrude, ill with a severe cold, got out of bed and packed her things, and the two of them set off for London.

> We stopped at the Wilton Hotel near Victoria Station. The same evening I went to see Mrs A.S. Green at her house in Grosvenor Road, S.W., to ask her advice. We had few friends in London, none of them influential. Our first wish was to get into communication with Roger, and I thought Mrs Green (who knew so many people in London) could advise.11

There followed what Gertrude termed ten days of cruelty, during which they visited the Home Office, the Secretary for War, Scotland Yard and the Treasury. Denied information, but knowing that he was in the Tower, 'my sister and I went down and wandered round the Tower, trying to make our thoughts penetrate to Roger'. Mrs Green introduced Gertrude to the solicitor George Gavan Duffy, son of the Young Ireland leader Sir Charles Gavan Duffy, who consented to act for Casement and wrote to him on 1 May. His first request to visit Casement and consult him about his defence was refused, but he was admitted to see his client early in May. His description of the encounter horrified the cousins and Mrs Green:

> He said that he was not sure that it was really Roger (though he knew him well), that he was terribly changed, that his clothes were dirty, his face unshaven (he had shaved his beard off in Germany and it was half grown) and his eyes red round the rims and bloodshot; his manner hesitating, and he was unable to remember names or words. His tie, bootlaces and braces had been taken away

from him and his boots were hanging round his ankles; he was collarless and he had to hold up his trousers. I discovered afterwards that his cell in the Tower was verminous, and his poor arms, head and neck were all swollen with bites.[12]

Gavan Duffy raised Casement's treatment with the Director of Public Prosecutions, Sir Charles Mathews, and Alice Stopford Green wrote in protest to Asquith. About the same time, the two cousins met Major Arbuthnot of the Life Guards, who took steps to help:

> At last we saw a certain Major Arbuthnot who showed sympathy. He said it was really the Governor of the Tower to whom application must be made and when I told him I had written to the Governor and received no reply he said, 'I will write personally'. He then told us he had seen Roger. He said he needed clothes and suggested we should send in some.[13]

A few days after Gavan Duffy's visit, Gertrude and Elizabeth were allowed to see their cousin:

> The interview was terrible. Roger thought he was to be shot and that was why we had been brought to say good-bye. We told him that we had been trying from April 25 till that day, May 5, every day to see him. He had not been told this; in fact, he had been deliberately told that none of us had made any effort to see him as we were all disgusted at his 'treachery'. Damn all those people who told him those lies and tried to break his heart.[14]

Gertrude was bitter about the circumstances of the interrogation by Thomson and Hall – 'these two high-minded, chivalrous English gentlemen' – while Casement remained 'collarless, unwashed, unshaven', in clothes hard and sticky after his ditching in the sea. In the Tower, he told them that two soldiers were with him day and night. This was the only visit allowed the sisters before Casement's first court appearance: 'We did not see him again until we went to Bow Street on May 15 for his preliminary trial before the magistrate. By that time he was shaved and clean-looking but was wearing the clothes we had sent in which were hopelessly bad.'

By now the decision had been made to subject Casement to a public, civil trial by jury rather than to a court martial, and the prosecution began assembling its documentation and witnesses. The latter included civilians and RIC members from Kerry, some technical witnesses and, most importantly, a number of former internees from Limburg, who had arrived home some time previously as part of a prisoner exchange.[15] On 10 May, the day on which a civil trial was decided on, word came to the FO from the US that Adler Christensen had made an offer to testify against Casement and, on the same day, Arthur Nicolson at the FO sent a dossier on Casement to the Attorney General, F.E. Smith.[16] Led by Gavan Duffy and Green, Casement's friends began casting around for a defence team and for the finances to pay for it. There were several refusals and, with the first round of the contest imminent, in the shape of an inquiry at the police court, the brief was offered to Mr Artemus Jones, a

Welsh barrister, who had come to prominence in a well-known libel case. Casement's friend, John Hartmann Morgan, an expert in constitutional law, offered his services free of charge.

The magisterial inquiry was held at Bow Street Police Court from 15 to 17 May. Presiding was Sir John Dickinson, with Sir Charles Mathews, the Director of Public Prosecutions. For the Crown appeared the Attorney General, Sir F.E. Smith, with Mr Archibald Bodkin and Mr Travers Humphreys; for Casement, Artemus Jones and J.H. Morgan, instructed by Gavan Duffy.[17] Superintendent Quinn represented the police. Also present in the court were Reginald Hall and Sir Horace Plunkett. The small court, which held about fifty people, was packed. Among this group were the Bannister sisters. Casement and Daniel Bailey (Beverley by now having reverted to his real name) sat in the dock. Casement appeared nervous and fidgety, but followed the proceedings intently, taking copious notes. The Attorney General opened with a lengthy statement, summarizing Casement's career, making play of the loyal and courtier-like tone of his letter to Grey accepting his knighthood. He read a statement given by Bailey while in police custody, describing events in Limburg and his subsequent association with Casement. Smith went on to describe the capture of the *Aud* and the items found on Casement when he was arrested.

After Inspector Parker gave evidence of Casement's transfer to the Tower, a number of the ex-prisoners of war told of what they knew about the Irish Brigade. These were followed by the witnesses from the Banna Strand area, who had seen Casement on the morning he landed. They were followed by RIC members involved in the arrest and detention of Casement and Bailey. A clerk for the FO, giving details on Casement's pension, concluded the Crown's evidence. Artemus Jones, for the defence, requested adequate time to prepare for a trial, while Humphreys, for the Crown, asked that it be 'at the earliest possible moment'. At the end of proceedings, Sir John Dickinson charged Casement and Bailey with high treason and committed them for trial 'at a place and time to be fixed hereafter'.[18] It was later fixed to commence on 26 June.

Brixton, 15 May–29 June

Once the civil proceedings commenced, Casement was moved to Brixton Prison. Gertrude described the change in his circumstances:

> Here conditions were much better. He was put into the Prison Hospital and given hospital diet and his friends were allowed to send him in occasional gifts. He was allowed to see visitors. The warders were decent and courteous. One of them told me that the Governor told them to try to imagine themselves in the position of the prisoners and as far as possible to treat them as they would wish they had been treated if they were there instead.

His head, which had become infested with lice in the Tower, was treated with insecticide. He was allowed to write and receive letters and to have visits. Among those to call on him, according to Gertrude, were Mrs Green, Morten, Robert Lynd, Nevinson, Parry, Morgan and one or two others: 'His solicitor, Mr Gavan Duffy, saw him constantly and so did Mrs Green and myself and my sister, but we always had two warders in the room.' Green wrote to the Home Secretary on 15 and 19 May, asking for permission to visit (Casement had expressed a wish to see her) and about the number of visits allowed. Herbert Samuel, now Home Secretary, replied that the prisoner was entitled to one *visit* a day, which was not necessarily limited to one *person*. It was up to Casement to specify whom he wanted to see. A minute to his note added: 'I have spoken to Sir Charles Mathews about this. He regards Mrs G[reen] as practically an accomplice of Casement and does not like his communication with her.' But it was felt that the presence of a warder would make it impossible for her to pass papers or poison to him or receive any papers from him. Moreover, since the governor of Brixton had heard of Casement's suicide attempt while in the Tower, he was now under constant supervision.[19]

Henry Nevinson was one of those who visited Brixton. Drawing on his diaries, he later wrote of the encounter:

> ... after waiting long I was shown into a largish, scantily furnished room, and Casement was soon brought in by an old warder, who was polite. R.C. looked much aged, wrinkled and careworn; his hands at first worked nervously, sometimes being passed quickly over his face and eyes, to hide or suppress emotion and even tears, that seemed to come especially when I mentioned his cousin, Gertrude Bannister, and Mrs N.F. Dryhurst, and gave their messages. But his eyes were straight and frank and blue as ever, his manner charmingly polite, speaking to the warder as a friend, and hoping our three-quarters hour conversation was not keeping him too long.[20]

Emmeline Cadbury visited, too, and asked: 'Roger, why did you do it? Why did you not come to Wast Hills instead?' 'How I wish that I had, Emmeline!' was the reply, 'But I had to go to Germany. I was sure that they would win, and I had at all costs to stop them from doing cruel things to the Irish ... don't grieve for me, whatever you do.' When conversation turned to his landing in Ireland, he said: 'I wanted to go to Carraroe, Emmeline, if only they had landed me at Carraroe, things might have gone differently! They were waiting for me at Carraroe – armed men who would have protected me and hidden me. But the Germans chose instead to land me on an open beach at Tralee.'[21]

One of Casement's friends who did not visit was Edmond Morel. Responding to a request from Gertrude Bannister, he wrote to Mrs Green, giving his reasons for not doing so: 'If I obeyed my own personal feelings I should at once respond, and apply for permission to pay the visit, but I cannot act only on my personal feelings.' He went on to talk of the movement with which he was associated – the Union for Democratic Control – and the negative use that would be made of any association between him and Casement at this point. He was already being castigated for his earlier words of praise for Casement and charges had been made that the Congo campaign had been fought in the interests of Germany. 'Of course neither he nor she [Gertrude] can realise the position in which his actions have placed me, and I would not for the world add to the terrible burden which he is now bearing, by giving him this further source of trouble.' He concluded with the hope that she not consider him a 'moral coward' for the stance he was taking.[22]

On the other hand, Casement declined a visit from the Revd John Harris of the Anti-Slavery Society.

> It is very kind of you to write and suggest coming to see me – but I know not how to fit it in with the visits of near relatives that are booked and down for all the spare time I can give to visitors – There would be no chance of any intimate conversation between us – as you could see me for only a few minutes and in the presence of a warder – and I fear the interview would be uninteresting to you – and perhaps painful. Will you then accept all my thanks and gratitude for your kindly thought to come and see me – it assures me that the same kind heart still dictates your actions. I am thank God, much better in bodily health than I have been for a long time – and surrounded with comforts![23]

Attention among Casement's friends had turned to the question of a defence team for his trial. Casement wanted to defend himself, but was dissuaded by his friends, who doubted his ability to do so in his fragile mental and emotional state. One sympathetic onlooker who agreed with him, however, was George Bernard Shaw. In her diary, Beatrice Webb described the circumstances of Shaw's involvement: 'A painful luncheon party: Mrs Green and the Bernard Shaws to consult about the tragic plight of Roger Casement. Alice Stopford Green has made herself responsible for the defence of her old friend. He has no money and only two relatives in England – cousins who are school-teachers.' She went on to tell of how Green had got Gavan Duffy as solicitor, of his partners having repudiated him, of Mrs Green's putting up £300 and of the difficulty in getting a first-rate lawyer.

In these circumstances Beatrice Webb approached the Shaws ('Charlotte is a wealthy Irish rebel').

> But GBS as usual had his own plan. Casement was to defend his own case and make a great oration of defiance which would 'bring down the house'. To this Mrs Green retorted tearfully that the man was desperately ill, that he was quite incapable of handling a court full of lawyers, that the most he could do was the final speech after the verdict. 'Then we had better get our suit of mourning,' Shaw remarked with an almost gay laugh. 'I will write him a speech which will thunder down the ages.' 'But his friends want to get him reprieved,' indignantly replied the distracted woman friend. The meeting turned out to be a useless and painful proceeding ...[24]

Several English barristers turned down the brief and Gavan Duffy turned to his brother-in-law in Ireland, Serjeant Alexander Martin Sullivan, son of the nationalist MP and historian A.M. Sullivan. While he was a senior counsel in the Irish courts and had been called to the English bar, his status there was that of a junior and he could not take his place on the front benches with other leading counsel.

Having conferred in Ireland about the appropriateness of accepting the brief, Sullivan agreed to do so. Gertrude Bannister later commented: 'A most unfortunate choice, as Serjeant Sullivan was entirely out of sympathy with Roger and his ideals ...' Casement and perhaps Sullivan would have agreed with her. In his two autobiographical monographs, Sullivan wrote about Casement: 'Casement was a man of supreme energy, great physical courage, and of intelligent audacity. He had undermined his mental balance. His vanity was inconsistent with reason, and it was this weakness that wrecked what might have been the most daring project of the Great War.'[25] And, again: 'Casement was a very remarkable man ... I do not think that he said anything beyond what he believed, and his principal belief was in his own importance. He had that touch of megalomania which is associated with mental aberration of a more unpleasant kind ...'[26]

Sullivan was busy in Ireland and could not come to London for some time. Gavan Duffy briefed him through the post and Casement began to send regular sets of reflections from Brixton. On 2 June, in a memo to Gavan Duffy on what he had concluded to be the best line of defence, Casement wrote:

> I have come to a conclusion on this I believe to be right from every point of view, and one I shall not depart from nor permit my Counsel to depart from. The best defence is to admit one's full responsibility and accept all the consequences. This involves not only responsibility for the rising in Ireland which was, without question, based on my prior teaching, on my pro-Germanism, on my presence in Germany and on the hope of help from that country derived from my being there and the knowledge that the German Government had entered into an agreement with me; but it involves also my responsibility *vis-à-vis* the German Government and my duty to defend them.[27]

Having been far removed from the plotting of the IRB leaders in Ireland, Casement clearly had an exaggerated opinion of his role in bringing about the Rising, one ironically shared by the British authorities. But his suggested line of defence – involving admitting his responsibility – was not much different from that put forward by Shaw. Sullivan's main approach, however, was to be based on an interpretation of the ancient statute for treason. Advocate and accused had their first meeting in Brixton on 12 June. Casement wrote to Gavan Duffy the following day:

> My objection to the line he proposes is based on principle. He calls it 'sentiment'. We are, as he says, 'poles apart', and at the end of a defence of his making I should find myself without a case, and debarred from the only defence

possible, viz., my own plan and that of GBS. I owe it to Ireland, to the Irish in the USA, who so loyally helped, and to Germany, and even to my own wretched self to adopt the only course and conduct my case myself. I should be in a far less false position, and could at least make my position clear, leave it on record, justify the cause of Ireland before the world and leave the British government to do what it pleased.[28]

He was persuaded, however, by friends to accept Sullivan's approach and reminded that he could put the broader case in a statement from the dock. In the weeks before the trial, both defence and prosecution prepared for the contest. In late May Gavan Duffy had had to get a writ against the *Graphic*, which had published a photograph with the caption 'The Traitor Casement'.[29] On 13 June the American lawyer Michael Francis Doyle arrived in London to help with the case.[30] Meanwhile Casement, with few illusions as to the likely result of his trial, availed of the freedom allowed to write letters to friends and family. When his cousin Roger, in Magherintemple, with whom he had had comparatively little contact for some years, sent a generous contribution of £25 to Gavan Duffy, he sent a warm letter, full of nostalgia:

> My dear Roger,
> I heard yesterday of an act of yours that I much appreciate – and which I think shows a very good heart – I know quite well how you feel on the points where we differ so profoundly and so I can appreciate all the more your action – and the real good feeling that prompted it ... I am much better here than in the Tower – and have improved in health enormously.[31]

With his brother Tom away fighting in East Africa, he wrote a letter to Tom's second wife, Katje, asking that she pass it on:

> Tell him I often thought of him and particularly of the last look I had of him at the railway station the day he drove me across the veld to catch my train. It was a pity I ever left you both that day! It is more than three years ago now – and the world has gone to wreck and ruin since then. I hope you may soon have Tom back with you in peace and with all this dreadful nightmare gone from you and the world.[32]

On 3 June Casement renewed contact with Richard Morten, opening his letter whimsically: 'I am beginning to think you are a Myth! I shall be so glad to see your dear honest old *English* face again! (You know I don't like all English faces but a good many are v. near my heart – & none so more than yours.)' He suggested that Morten come to visit either with Gertrude or with Sidney: 'You'll be as welcome as the flowers of May.' His thoughts returned to their holiday together in Germany in 1912, to Coblenz, the Moselle, Trier: 'This time last year we had the most glorious weather by the Rhine and the country looked like a great field of Paradise – full of grain and flowers – I heard the nightingale (for the first time in my life!) there just this very day last year in the garden of an old Catholic priest who had been many years in Ireland and spoke English with a brogue.' The war had brought sorrow to others, including to their mutual friends Herbert and Sarita Ward. When Casement was ill in hospital the previous January, he had read in *The Times* of the death of their son Charlie. 'I am grieved for Sarita – and Herbert – God comfort them.' Another mutual friend was J.H. Morgan, who had appeared in Bow Street: 'It was indeed kind of 'Jackie M.' to come stand beside me the way he has done – seeing how poles apart we stand on the one thing that brings him to my side – the war. There we see with different eyes – but, remember, Dick, there *are* two sides to every question and all we read, *and believe too*, is not for all that true.' As he wrote, his own circumstances impinged: 'It is so cold here today I can hardly write.'33

A few days later Morten did visit (Morgan was present for some of the time); the meeting must have been an emotional one and Casement responded to it on 8 June:

Dear Dick,
I am sorry you came. It upset us both – me more than I can tell you. Please dismiss from your mind all that was said – rub it out for ever – I shall not see you again I fear – not in this life – but you are often – indeed ever – in my thoughts as one of the truest friends a man ever had – and one of the most sincere and loveable of men.

I am *very* sorry at Herbert's & Sarita's loss – deeply grieved for them, and the boys – For May I feel the deepest sympathy – God help her and bless her. *Don't* worry about me – I did what I conceived to be right and my duty under the circumstances. No man can think for another man – or substitute his understanding for the other man's. Things that are dark to you are very clear to me – and vice versa – The real difference lies in something quite outside ourselves – that we belong to different countries, to different beliefs on right and wrong in national issues – and to differing claims of duty ...

Goodbye, dear old Dick – for you always my truest affection and remembrance, and may the days go happily with you to the end that awaits us all sometime – somewhere – somehow. It has been one of the true joys of my life to have had you for a friend so many years – and one of the bitter griefs to lose you. Goodbye and may it all rest in peace between us for ever and ever – Your loving friend,
Roddie.34

Others wrote to him, including Cathal O'Byrne from Belfast, who addressed him as 'Friend of my Heart', told him he had prayed much for him during a pilgrimage to Lough Derg, and sent a statuette of Our Lady to have near him. 'There is no need to tell you of the love and reverence in which you are held. These things could never have been said face to face, but it is different now, for there are times when "the kindly word unspoken is a sin" and this is one of them.'35

Alice Stopford Green worked for her friend on a number of fronts, including making a plea to General Louis Botha in South Africa. 'I desire to plead for your sympathy in the matter of Sir Roger Casement,' she wrote, 'whose present situation is known to you ... In the course of the last troubled six weeks your name has been constantly invoked here, and your example cited on the side of clemency ... I cannot doubt that no voice would be so powerful as yours in its effect on turning the public mind to clemency and generosity.' She outlined Casement's career, laying stress on his broken health after his second visit to the Putumayo. She mentioned the parallel with Professor Masaryk, then a refugee in England and charged with high treason at home.[36] She described the shoddy treatment of Casement after his capture and the pressure his supporters were now under with little time and little money to organize a defence. She concluded by saying that 'all the dice are loaded in a very singular degree against the prisoner. I have therefore ventured to appeal to you if you could give your word at the critical moment on behalf of mercy. No influence would be so powerful with this people'.[37]

Others intervened in a less welcome manner, one being Poulteney Bigelow in the United States, who published Casement's 1914 letters to him in the *New York Times*. Bigelow traced the history of his links with Casement, but then went on to say: 'Casement commenced his career of madness through a too strenuous study of Irish mythology masquerading under the name of history. Little by little he became a victim to that species of autointoxication which culminates in the orator who delights a St Patrick's Day banquet by frothing at the mouth as he portrays an imaginary Paradise converted into a howling wilderness by the cruelty of Saxon domination.'[38] He followed this with a letter to the paper on 24 May, in which he said:

> Roger Casement has himself claimed distinction as a traitor to his country in her hour of need. He has helped the Hun to enter at our gates; for every sane American knows that Prussian rule in Ireland would be followed by a Prussian raid across the Atlantic. Only a madman could have conceived what Roger Casement attempted to carry out under German auspices. His letters to me prove him a paranoiac who should be confined in a safe place. When I kill a man I expect to be punished according to the law. Why should murderers be exempt whenever they claim to be murdering in the name of Ireland? Casement asks no favors, which shows that in this matter he is not a normal Irishman. And I have permitted these letters to be published because by this means the world may be convinced that his is the act of a deranged mind, and that the best thing for him and for the British Government would be to exile him to Berlin or Potsdam until pronounced cured of his Prussianism. It would not be a long exile.[39]

His old adversary Julio Arana wrote to him on 14 June: 'You tried by all means to appear a humanizer in order to obtain titles fortune [*sic*], not caring for the consequences of your calumnies and defamation against Peru and myself doing me enormous damage. I pardon you, but it is necessary that you should be just and declare now fully and truly all the true facts that nobody knows better than yourself.'[40] From London, Basil Thomson wrote to Horace Plunkett at the beginning of June, seeking help for the prosecution case. Plunkett, who had served as a Unionist MP but become a convert to Home Rule, was clearly not in sympathy with Casement's German adventure or with the Rising. Thomson referred to a visit of Plunkett's to London and to a discussion they had on Casement's case, in which Plunkett had given some details of Casement's contacts in Ireland: 'I find that the evidence for the Prosecution is meagre as regards the period in 1913 after he had taken his pension in August, and his departure for America some time in 1914. Are any details procurable about his movements during this period? I ask this because we understand that evidence is being brought for the Defence over from America, and it is clear that they intend to spring something on the Prosecution.' Plunkett reported a blank, having had enquiries made through the RIC and the Dublin Metropolitan Police.[41]

Trial, 26–9 June

The trial took four days, opening on 26 June in the Royal Courts of Justice, before the King's Bench Division.[42] Three judges presided: the Lord Chief Justice, Viscount Reading; Mr Justice Avory; Mr Justice Horridge. Four counsel appeared for the Crown: the two seniors were the law officers, the Attorney General, Sir F.E. Smith, and the Solicitor General, Sir George Cave; the two juniors were Mr A.H. Bodkin and Mr Travers Humphreys, assisted by Mr G.A.H. Branson. The defence was led by Serjeant Sullivan, assisted by Artemus Jones and Professor Morgan. Michael Francis Doyle sat with George Gavan Duffy at the solicitors' table.

Since no knight of the realm had been tried for treason for several centuries, the case attracted wide attention and the courtroom was packed. Casement's appearance was much improved and a suit of his clothes had been acquired from a trunk in Bigger's house. Gertrude later described the appearance of her cousin in court:

> Roger looked wonderfully tall and dignified and noble as he stood in the dock. He seemed to be looking away over the heads of the judges and advocates and sightseers, away to Ireland – probably his mind's eye was fixed on some well-known spot such as Fair Head or Murlough Bay – certainly he had no look of one who was conscious of his awful and sordid surroundings ... A small band of his friends were in the Court – Mrs Green (best and truest of friends), myself and my sister, Miss Ada McNeill, Miss Eva Gore-Booth, Miss [Esther] Roper, Mrs Lynd, Mr Henry Nevinson and perhaps a few more. Mrs Gavan Duffy sat at the solicitors' table with her husband.

Although the prisoner could not talk to them, the presence of friends was a support. Gertrude, who had asked Eva Gore-Booth to attend, described the effect of her presence:

> While she sat in the gallery looking down at him, Roger suddenly raised his head and turned and looked full at her and smiled. Eva smiled back, and Roger waved his hand. It was as if a flash had passed between them, and from that

moment those two people who had never met, never spoken to each other, formed a real friendship. On several occasions when I visited him in Pentonville Roger asked, 'What does Eva say, or think, about this? What is Eva doing?' Always he spoke of her thus, simply by her Christian name, and until her death, she too thought and spoke of him as if he had been her intimate friend all her life.

Henry Nevinson, too, told how he and Casement bowed when they noticed each other across the courtroom.[43]

The case opened with mediaeval ceremony, followed by the reading of the indictment by the King's Coroner. Among the six counts listed were alleged acts of treason committed during a state of war between the King and the German emperor, including the attempt to suborn prisoners of war and to land arms in Ireland as part of a military expedition. Immediately, Serjeant Sullivan rose 'and moved to quash the indictment on the ground that no offence known to the law was disclosed by the indictment as framed'.[44] He was interrupted by Lord Reading and informed that procedure dictated that such a motion would have to wait until the end of the prosecution's case. Asked how he pleaded, Casement then replied, 'Not guilty.' Following the selection of the jury, during which process Sullivan challenged many of the names proposed, the Attorney General opened for the prosecution. His language, though restrained, was full of subtle irony, calculated to present the defendant in a bad light. He sketched out the course of Casement's career and his services to the Crown, suggesting that his disloyalty was of quite recent origin.

To heighten this point he made play of the letter accepting the knighthood in 1911: 'Such a man writes in terms of gratitude, a little unusual, perhaps, in their warmth and in the language almost of a courtier, to express his pleasure at the title with which his Sovereign had rewarded his career.' Yet how did he act a few years later, when his country was struggling for survival? 'It will be my task now to acquaint you with the method in which he carried out his humble duty in times dark enough to test the value of the unsolicited professions he was so forward in making.'[45] He spoke of Casement moving freely through wartime Germany, of his attempts to 'seduce and corrupt' the prisoners, of their contemptuous response to him, with hisses and even blows. Since Irish Brigade numbers were insignificant to the Germans from a military point of view, 'The inference will probably be drawn by you that it was intended then that such men as could be seduced from their allegiance should form the first-fruits of a body which should be actually used for the purpose of raising armed insurrection in Ireland against the forces of the Crown, and of acting as a trained and instructed nucleus round which the disaffected section of the population might rally and grow.'[46]

He then described the arrival and apprehension of the *Aud* and Casement's arrest in Kerry:

I have, I hope, outlined these facts without heat and without feeling. Neither in my position would be proper, and fortunately none is required. Rhetoric would be misplaced, for the proved facts are more eloquent than words. The prisoner, blinded by a hatred to this country, as malignant in quality as it was sudden in origin, has played a desperate hazard. He has played it and he has lost it. Today the forfeit is claimed.[47]

After details were supplied by two government officials on Casement's Foreign Office career and pension, the evidence of eight former prisoners of war was taken.[48] They described Casement's visits to Limburg and the circulation through the camp of a printed appeal to fight for Ireland, and they succeeded in portraying the sense of a depressing and failed endeavour. The soldiers were followed by witnesses from Kerry, whose evidence took up the first part of day two of the trial; they described the items found in connection with the landing – Casement's 'itinerary', a railway sleeper ticket from Berlin to Wilhelmshaven and, of special significance, the code for communicating with Germany. In cross-examining the POW John Robinson, and District Inspector Britten of Tralee, Sullivan attempted to draw into the record details concerning the history of the Home Rule controversy, of the formation of the Ulster and the Irish Volunteers and the tense state of the country before the war. Further evidence followed on day two concerning the *Aud* and her cargo, before the prosecution case concluded.

Now Sullivan rose to put his case. The indictment charged that the defendant had committed treason 'by adhering to the King's enemies elsewhere than in the King's realm', namely in Germany. It was based on a statute of 1351, originally in Norman French, which defined treason as 'levying war against the King or being adherent to the King's enemies in his realm giving them aid or comfort in his realm or elsewhere'. The statute was without punctuation and Sullivan's challenge was based on an interpretation of the wording which limited treason to acts 'in his realm', taking the rest of the phrase ('giving them aid or comfort in his realm or elsewhere') as a qualification of that.

Given that Casement was not in the realm, but in Germany, when the allegedly treasonable actions took place, the defence believed it might succeed. However, were the statute taken to define as treason acts committed 'in his realm ... or elsewhere', Sullivan's interpretation would fall. During the latter part of the second day, he spent almost two hours arguing his position, citing numerous precedents, and Morgan continued the line the following morning, day three of the trial. The Attorney General then gave his interpretation and, after some brief remarks by Jones, the three judges ruled on Sullivan's objections. They were unanimous in rejecting them.[49] Since Sullivan had decided to call no witnesses, his turn now came to address the jury.

Before he did so, Casement was allowed to make a brief statement. In a nervous and barely audible voice, he availed of the opportunity to correct a number of points. He focused, in particular, on two matters: the 'horrible insinuation' that he had been instrumental in having the rations of those who refused to join the Irish Brigade reduced and the accusation that he had taken 'German gold'. On this latter he pointed out: 'Money was offered to me in Germany more than once, and offered liberally and unconditionally, but I rejected every suggestion of the kind, and I left Germany a poorer man than I entered it.'[50]

Sullivan then addressed himself to the jury.[51] 'The trial,' he told them, 'is a trial for the life of a man. It is more than that. You represent your country ... The prisoner is not a countryman of yours. He is a stranger within your gates. He comes from another country where people, though they use the same words perhaps, speak differently; they think differently; they act differently.' Appealing to their sense of fair play in coming to a decision, he proceeded to argue that, in all his actions in Germany, Casement did not 'adhere to the King's enemies' there, but sought to recruit men to fight for Ireland: 'You have to try the man for his intentions; you have to judge of his motives; and there is no task so difficult as judging of the motives or intentions of a man who is not of your race and is not one of yourselves. Now the intention of the prisoner is the whole substance of the offence of treason. It is his view of his own acts which must justify him or condemn him.' He continued: 'If the object was to have in Ireland at the close of the war men in arms and skilled in arms for the purpose of protecting what were the rights of the people of Ireland against unlawful tyranny, no matter in whose name it was sought to be exercised, that is not treason.' He went through the evidence given by the former prisoners in Limburg to demonstrate that it was all consistent with his argument.[52]

He then shifted to the evidence concerning conditions in Ireland, and it was here that he ran into difficulties with the bench. There was nothing in the indictment, he pointed out, concerning Casement's actions in Ireland. If there was anything illegal in these actions, it was not treason and was matter for a different tribunal. He again worked on the jury to press home the difference between Ireland and England:

> Sir Roger Casement was not in the service of England, Sir Roger Casement was in the service of the United Kingdom; he was in the service of His Majesty in respect of the whole Empire of his Majesty's Dominion. In Ireland you have not only a separate people, you have a separate country. An Irishman's loyalty is loyalty to Ireland, and it would be a very sorry day for the Empire when loyalty to one's own native land should be deemed to be treason in a sister country.

He cited the example of the Ulster Volunteers in the north of Ireland to oppose Home Rule:

> There was in the north of Ireland an armed body of men ostensibly marching about, as Robinson proves, in Belfast, deliberately originated with the avowed object of resisting the operation of an act of Parliament which had the approval of the rest of the country. They armed and nothing was said to them; they

drilled and nothing was said to them; they marched and countermarched; the authorities stood by and looked at them.

How, he asked, was one to react to such a situation, where the goals won after long labours were thus threatened and the police and military proved inadequate? 'You may lay down under it, but if you are men, to arms; when all else fails defend yourself.' As he proceeded to tease out the details of the situation in Ireland, the Lord Chief Justice became restive and then intervened: 'Where is the evidence for this?' To this the Attorney General added: 'I was most loath to intervene, but I have heard a great many statements which are wholly uncorroborated.' The Chief Justice addressed Sullivan: 'We have allowed you very great latitude. I confess for myself I have found it rather difficult not to intervene on several occasions, and I intervene at this moment because I think you are stating matter which is not in evidence or which I have no recollection of being stated in evidence ...' Sullivan apologized, tried to readjust his argument, continued for a little time, paused, then faltered and confessed: 'I regret, my Lord, to say that I have completely broken down.' The trial was adjourned until the following morning.

On the morning of the fourth day, Thursday 29 June, Sullivan did not reappear in court. Artemus Jones explained: 'My Lords, I regret to say that my learned leader is in a condition this morning which does not permit of his appearance in Court. I have just seen him. He is in consultation with his medical adviser, and the effect of the advice is that he must not go on.' Jones asked for and was granted permission to conclude the presentation for the defence. Contending with challenges from the bench and from the Attorney General, he attempted to continue Sullivan's line of argument. Trying to draw on evidence given to the court, he reviewed Casement's work for the Irish Volunteers and his addresses to prisoners in Limburg, and argued: 'I ask you to form this opinion upon the evidence as it stands, that Sir Roger Casement's object when he addressed these prisoners of war in Germany was precisely the same object that he had in mind when, long before the war broke out, he addressed that meeting in Cork to form the National Volunteer movement.' Casement was acting for Ireland, not Germany. And, if there were a charge for importing arms into Ireland, 'that act would be a charge framed under the Defence of the Realm Act. The point I make on that is that that is not high treason or adhering to the enemies of the King within the Empire of Germany'.[53]

The Attorney General responded: 'Had the acts for which the prisoner stands arraigned been committed before the war took place, had they been committed at the time when the acts which he alleges on the part of the Ulster Volunteers were taking place, these words might have been a good defence or a bad defence, but they would indeed have had great relevance in those days.' One fundamental fact had changed things dramatically. What was that fact?

It was that the greatest military power which the world had ever known was trying to destroy this country and trying to make an end of this Empire. Since these controversies arose, who was thinking or talking of whether or not there might be resistance to the Home Rule Bill at the time? From the moment that Germany made that tiger spring at the throat of Europe, I say from that moment the past was the past in the eyes of every man who did not seek to injure this country ...54

Now came Lord Reading's summing-up for the jury. Treason, he pointed out, was 'a most odious charge' in normal times, but in time of war it was 'almost too grave for expression'. Referring to the defence's attempts to sketch the divided and tempestuous conditions in Ireland before the war, he suggested that 'it was found that however deep the gulf might be between the north of Ireland and other portions of Ireland [in] times of peace, when war came against the British Empire there was a union of forces which would resist any attack which would be made upon the Empire'.55 He told the jury:

> I direct you as a matter of law, that if a man, a British subject, does an act which strengthens or tends to strengthen the enemies of the King in the conduct of the war against the King, that is in law the giving of aid and comfort to the King's enemies. Again, if a British subject commits an act which weakens or tends to weaken the power of the King and of the country to resist or to attack the enemies of the King and the country, that is, in law, the giving of aid and comfort to the King's enemies.

Introducing arms into Ireland in order to start a rebellion would constitute such an act. He added that finding the prisoner guilty of any one of the six alleged acts would mean a guilty verdict.

Lastly, he told the jury that they 'must be satisfied before you convict the prisoner of the intention and purpose of the act':56

> If he knew or believed that the German authorities were taking the steps they did in collecting the Irish prisoners into one camp, distributing literature amongst them, forming an Irish Brigade and providing them with uniforms, etc., for their own purpose, and to serve their own ends in the war, and he in concert with them was promoting the enterprise, then he was contriving and intending to assist the enemy, though he had another purpose to serve. If he knew or believed that the Irish Brigade was to be sent to Ireland during the war with a view to securing the national freedom of Ireland, that is, to engage in a civil war which would necessarily weaken and embarrass this country, then he was contriving and intending to assist the enemy.57

After a trial lasting four days, the jury retired on Thursday 29 June at 2.53 pm and returned at 3.48 pm with a verdict of 'Guilty'. Before sentence was passed, Casement was extended the customary privilege of addressing the court. With a degree of nervousness, he opened by protesting against the jurisdiction of the court and telling his listeners that the comments he was going to make were 'addressed not to this Court but to my own countrymen'. He reflected on the irony of his, an Irishman's, condemnation by the ancient statute of a king who was not King of Ireland, though he had lands in France. To be tried by one's peers was, he argued, a fundamental right in England and he claimed the same right – to be tried before an Irish court:

> This Court, this jury, the public opinion of this country, England, cannot but be prejudiced in varying degree against me, most of all in time of war. Place me before a jury of my own countrymen, be it Protestant or Catholic, Unionist or Nationalist, Sinn Feiners or Orangemen, and I shall accept the verdict and bow to all its penalties ... If they adjudge me guilty, then guilty I am. It is not I who am afraid of their verdict; it is the Crown. If this be so, why fear the test? I fear it not, I demand it as my right.

Gaining in confidence as he spoke, he turned from his own case to that of Ireland and her people's persistence in facing oppression in the face of many failures: 'The cause that begets this indomitable persistency, the faculty of preserving through centuries of misery the memory of lost liberty, this surely is the noblest cause men ever strove for, ever lived for, ever died for. If this be the case I stand here today indicted for, and convicted of sustaining, then I stand in a goodly company and a right noble succession.' He said that nationalists

> welcomed the coming of the Ulster Volunteers, even whilst we deprecated the aims and intentions of those Englishmen who sought to pervert to an English party use, to the mean purpose of their own bid for place and power in England, the armed activities of simple Irishmen. We aimed at winning the Ulster Volunteers to the cause of a united Ireland. We aimed at uniting all Irishmen in a natural and national bond of cohesion based on mutual self-respect.

He defended the right to arm the Irish Volunteers under the circumstances, and for this purpose he himself travelled to the United States. 'If, as the right honourable gentleman, the present Attorney-General, asserted in a speech at Manchester, Nationalists would neither fight for Home Rule nor pay for it, it was our duty to show him that we knew how to do both.' The war had upset all Casement's calculations: 'War between Great Britain and Germany meant, as I believed, ruin for all the hopes we had founded on the enrolment of the Irish Volunteers.' He addressed the question put by the Attorney General to the jury: why had he gone to Germany?

> A constitutional movement in Ireland is never far from a breach of the constitution, as the Loyalists of Ulster had been so eager to show us ... We had seen the working of the Irish constitution in the refusal of the army of occupation at the Curragh to obey the orders of the Crown. And now that we were told the first duty of an Irishman was to enter that army, in return for a promissory note payable after death – a scrap of paper that might or might not be redeemed – I felt over there in America that my first duty was to keep Irishmen at home in the only army that could safeguard our national existence. If small nationalities were to be the pawns in this game of embattled giants, I saw no reason why Ireland should shed her blood in any cause but her own, and if that be treason beyond the seas I am not ashamed to avow it or to answer it here with my life.[58]

Implicitly included in his references to the interventions of English politicians in the Ulster crisis was the person of F.E. Smith, the Attorney General. Now he became more explicit, comparing their paths:

> The difference between us was that the Unionist champions chose a path they felt would lead to the woolsack; while I went a road I knew must lead to the dock. And the event proves we were both right. The difference between us was that my 'treason' was based on a ruthless sincerity that forced me to attempt in time and season to carry out in action what I said in word, whereas their treason lay in verbal incitements that they knew need never be made good. And so, I am prouder to stand here today in the traitor's dock to answer this impeachment than to fill the place of my right honourable accusers![59]

Irishmen, he continued, were encouraged to lay down their lives in the present war, but if they dared to lay them down for the freedom of Ireland, they were termed traitors:

> If we are to be indicted as criminals, to be shot as murderers, to be imprisoned as convicts because our offence is that we love Ireland more than we value our lives, then I know not what virtue resides in any offer of self-government held out to brave men on such terms ... Ireland, that has wronged no man, that has injured no land, that has sought no dominion over others, Ireland is treated today among the nations of the world as if she was a convicted criminal. If it be treason to fight against such an unnatural fate as this, then I am proud to be a rebel, and shall cling to my 'rebellion' with the last drop of my blood ...[60]

Once Casement had finished, the Chief Justice then declared: 'The duty now devolves upon me of passing sentence upon you, and it is that you be taken hence to a lawful prison, and thence to a place of execution, and that you be there hanged by the neck until you be dead.'[61]

Pentonville

Gertrude's account of this last phase of Casement's life described what then happened:

> After the trial Roger was not taken back to Brixton but was taken to Pentonville and put into the condemned cell. He was dressed in a blue convict's dress and given a dreadful cap – 'A felon's cap the brightest thing an Irish head can wear,' he quoted to me the first time I was allowed to visit him and saw him thus clothed ... Visitors were not allowed frequently. No one, of course, ever saw him alone except Father Carey, Canon Ring and the Catholic Chaplain, Father McCarroll. He was allowed to read letters but not allowed to keep them. By some manner of means he managed to keep one or two ... I saw him in all five times. Mrs J.R. Green saw him twice. Mr Gavan Duffy, of course, saw him, and also Mr J.H. Morgan, as they decided to appeal against the sentence.

On 30 June, the day after the trial ended, Casement was stripped of his knighthood. Ten days later, on 11 July, the prison governor reported to the

Undersecretary of State that certified copies of letters had been handed to the prisoner, degrading him from his knighthood and removing him from the Order of St Michael and St George. On 1 July, Gertrude made a personal and impassioned plea to Casement's former employer, Sir Edward Grey:

> May I intrude again upon your forbearance to write once more about my cousin Roger Casement. Throughout this long & ghastly tragedy, when his deed has been painted in the blackest hues that journalistic power could mount, & when stealthy slander has been insidiously disseminated to ruin him in the eyes of those who might otherwise have sympathised, no voice has been raised to point to his past great record of selfless devotion to the cause of suffering humanity.

Grey, she pointed out, knew that record very well and she appealed for his intervention. 'Roger Casement', she concluded, 'injured no man, has taken no man's life, even the deed for which he is to die brought no weakening to England and no strength to Germany. He still stands as the man who helped to right those who suffered wrong & who fed the hungry.'[62]

Others were intent that the verdict should not be overturned. On 10 July, Basil Thomson wrote to Sir Ernley Blackwell, legal advisor to the Home Office, arguing against reprieve: 'It has come to my knowledge from various sources that if Casement is reprieved there is an intention both in Ireland and amongst the Indian revolutionarists to turn the matter to great account.'[63] Blackwell and Sir Edward Troup, Permanent Undersecretary of State at the Home Office, had drafted a memo some days previously on the disposition of Casement's prison papers. Casement wanted to see Gavan Duffy about them, but the two Home Office officials were suspicious and opposed to handing them over. There was a danger, they argued, that Casement wanted Gavan Duffy to publish the material after his death 'to establish his Irish martyrdom'.[64]

Though an appeal had still to be made, Casement began writing farewell letters to friends, certain that execution was his fate. He wrote to Dick Morten, his closest friend, other than Gertrude, on 8 July. He worried about the lack of understanding of his actions: 'Don't mind what anyone says about me, Dick – it is easy to pelt the man who can't reply – or who is gone – but remember no story is told till we've heard all of it – and no one knows anything about mine – including those who think they know all. Even I don't know all! But I know most ...' He hadn't changed, he hadn't gone mad, and didn't

> believe in lies and hatred anymore now than I did when 'The Turk' was the enemy. You remember I didn't accept the popular verdict then that Ferdinand of Sofia was a Crusader – any more than I accept him as one now. If he is a villain now – what was he then? The truth is man and nations and Kings and Kinglets fight always for one thing only – self-interest. If they have that right – so have others ... Talk about tyrannies and the Church, Dick – there never was any Church tyranny equal to some of the tyrannies of your modern Devil God – 'Democracy'.

He ended with a farewell wish: 'Well, dear old Dick, goodbye and may God bless you and keep you long – you and May – to grow old together and grow nearer as you grow older. We shall never meet again – but I shall often meet you in my heart – often think of you as of old in the sunny days when we bathed together.'[65]

He sent a nostalgic note of thanks to Brigid Matthews, Francis Bigger's housekeeper:

> Do you remember the 'Cradle Song' I liked so much? Get Cathal to sing it for me, and give him my love and thanks from my heart, also to Colm, if he is ever near you, and Dinny and Seaghan Dhu, whenever they come to you and the old room again. I dreamt last night I was lying before the fire in it, and the boys were telling stories, and you standing at the door with the pipes... I have thought of you often, and of the garden, and of the last time I saw you, and the message I gave you. Do you remember? ... And so farewell – and may God's blessing rest on you and yours and be with you in your work – and may the heartfelt thanks of one in much sorrow and affliction of soul be part of your reward for your affection.[66]

Lady Constance Emmott wrote to a Protestant minister:

> Whether it is possible for you to convey a message to Sir R. Casement under present circumstances, I do not know. But having known him in former years, it is a painful thought that anyone in such circumstances should think him or herself forgotten by former friends – so, if it is possible, or in your judgement advisable to convey to him merely the message that I have remembered him daily in intercession throughout these weeks, I ask you to do so – and that I shall continue to so remember him whatever the future has for him to endure. Remind him of a picture he liked of the hills. By this expression of sympathy in *suffering* he will not, of course, and could not, imagine that I have felt anything but the deepest regret and horror that he should have acted as he did. What I ask you to tell him is wholly apart from that – and lies beyond and beneath human judgements and human actions and human sin and error. Just an assurance of remembrance when and how remembrance can always help. If he is being ministered to by the Roman Catholic Chaplain I leave it with you to pass on this message as you consider best.[67]

Anther who tried to reach Casement was a Congo associate, A. Werner, who wrote to Nevinson:

> Do you know of anyone who can communicate with R.C. just now? I think there are some relatives, but I am not sure of their names or how to get at them. If you can, would you be so kind as to let them have the enclosed? ... I am afraid all the old Congo comrades are gone – Deane – Glave – Swinburne – Skagerstrom – surely they would have come forward – I think Coquilhat would too, if he had been alive.[68]

Petitions

After Casement was found guilty, friends and supporters turned to the task of organizing petitions for a reprieve from the death sentence. In addition, individuals made personal and private representations on his behalf. An early set of representations argued that Casement had actually come from Germany not to lead but to try to stop the planned Rising. A letter to this effect from Henry Nevinson appeared in the *Daily News* on 12 July.[69] Eva Gore-Booth followed on the same lines sending a letter and supporting documents to Herbert Gladstone, a leading Liberal statesman and son of the former Prime Minister: 'May I venture to beg you to use your influence to avert this terrible tragedy.' Gladstone responded unsympathetically noting that Casement may simply have wished to delay the rebellion until a more opportune moment.[70] She also appealed to Alfred Emmott and James Bryce, who, in turn, brought the matter to the attention of the Home Secretary.[71]

Some days later, Gore-Booth again wrote to Gladstone, arguing strongly that there was *no* connection between Casement's landing and the landing of arms by the ship: 'It was *The Times* on Tuesday that put the two absolutely separate events together in a way calculated to make everyone think that Casement was with the ship.'[72] Blackwell countered such arguments in a memo to the cabinet:

> ... it is impossible to believe that he came to Ireland for the purpose of stopping the rising. He looked on the rising as hopeless [when plans miscarried] but, if all had gone well, there can be little doubt that Casement would have taken an active part in the rising, notwithstanding that he had sense enough to know that, while it might serve the Germans' purpose to some extent, it must inevitably end in dismal failure.[73]

He suggested that stories should be fed to the press on the proximity of the *Aud* to Casement's submarine and on Casement's possession of a code for military operations and of a green flag.[74]

Gertrude Bannister worked tirelessly collecting signatures on a petition. Among those who signed were Mary Childers, W. Cadbury, A.R. Dryhurst, Duncan Grant, G.P. Gooch, Francis W. Hirst, L.T. Hobson, J.A. Hobhouse, R.D. Holt, Francis Meynell, Ottoline Morrell, Arnold Rowntree and Lytton Strachey.[75] Ottoline Morrell, who had met Casement at Mrs Green's and who was moved by the trial, sought support among her acquaintances: 'I wrote to all the influential people that I knew, Asquith, Violet Bonham Carter, Bernard Shaw, Nevinson, Crompton Llewellyn Davies among others, and Philip worked very hard in the House of Commons and elsewhere to help him. I could not believe it possible that they would hang a man who had done such noble and self-sacrificing work for humanity as he had.'[76]

One of the weightiest petitions was that organized by Arthur Conan Doyle and Clement Shorter. On 1 July Doyle wrote to Shorter: 'Personally I believe his mind was unhinged, and that his honourable nature would in a normal condition have revolted from such an action.' He was against the execution 'on grounds of expediency', acknowledged Casement's guilt and the justice of the sentence, but urged 'the political wisdom of magnanimity. It should be signed as far as possible by men who have shown no possible sympathy for Germany or pacific leanings'. He enclosed a rough draft.77 They approached Gavan Duffy for support, but he replied that, as Casement's solicitor and confidant, he couldn't participate, because he knew that his client 'welcomes the death sentence and that he would not ask the Government for any favour'. But he was delighted as a friend that 'strenuous efforts are being made for him' and would put Shorter in touch with Mr Llewellyn Davies, 'in whom the general movement for reprieve is centred'. He also disagreed with the introductory sentence of the text regarding Casement's sanity. 'I have found no warrant for the assumption in the many conversations I have had with him during the past month.'78

The Doyle-Shorter appeal cited three grounds for clemency. It referred, firstly, to the 'violent change which appears to have taken place in the prisoner's previous sentiments towards Great Britain', attributing a resulting 'abnormal physical and mental state' to the 'severe strain' brought about by his two humanitarian investigations. Secondly, it suggested that execution would only help Germany and harm British interests in the US and elsewhere, while magnanimity would soothe opinion in Ireland and throughout the Empire. Lastly, it referred to the aftermath of the US Civil War, where reconciliation between north and south was hastened by a policy of no executions.

By 21 July, the collecting of signatures was completed and the results submitted. The response had been illuminating. Many people of stature signed, among them Jerome Jerome, John Masefield, Sir Sydney Olivier, Revd Thomas Phillips (president of the Baptist Union), C.P. Scott, Clement Shorter, Ben Tillett, Beatrice and Sidney Webb, Rt. Revd Bishop of Winchester, Israel Zangwill and G.K. Chesterton.79 The motives for signing varied. Sir Clifford Allbutt, Regius Professor of Physic at Cambridge, noted: 'one doesn't hang freaks'. H[all] C[aine] commented: 'I went to look at C. at Bow St. and found him bad, not mad, and therefore deserving of death'; but he was convinced by the wording of the petition. Sir James Frazer wrote: 'My dear Shorter, I gladly sign the petition, with which and the reasons assigned for clemency I cordially concur.' Alice B. Gomme was a little more dubious: if only, she said, he had given up pension and title before his actions, a large number would be in favour of altering his sentence – 'but his action with the imprisoned Irish soldiers goes so terribly against him'. Thomas Phillips commented: 'I feel strongly that Casement is not fully responsible. Our missionaries say he was one of the best Christians that ever came to Congo land.'

Negative responses were equally varied. Among those who refused were J.B. Bury, J. St Loe Strachey ('quite impossible'), Rudyard Kipling, G.E. Buckle,

George Trevelyan and Mary A. Ward ('not as it stands'). Some felt obliged to keep their representations private; James Bryce replied: 'I have done all I can privately to urge H.M.G. not to have R.C. executed', and he would continue to do so; R.B. Haldane agreed with the wording, but said he must not sign and that he had expressed his opinion privately. A number of journalists preferred to use the medium of their newspapers, including J.L. Garvin (*The Observer*) and J.A. Spender (*New Statesman*). A.C. Haddon felt: 'I can understand patriotism, even if misguided – and for most of the recent Irish "rebels" I felt more pity than anger – but Casement tried to tempt British soldiers to join the enemy, and he played into the hands of Germany – for this he deserves no mercy.' H.G. Wells barked, 'Certainly not. He ought to be hung.'

W.B. Yeats, writing from Normandy, informed the petitioners: 'I have already written at the request of Miss Bannister and Henry Nevinson to the Home Secretary, and sent a copy to Mr Asquith. I wrote as strongly as I could. I think your form of words excellent for English men to sign, but this as an Irishman I could not sign. Clause 1: An apology for Casement's "without going so far as to urge complete mental irresponsibility" is one that I feel he would resent if it came from his own countrymen'. Another Irish respondent, Albinia Broderick, an Irish nationalist and sister of Lord Midleton, refused, saying: 'I do not believe Sir Roger to be in any sense irresponsible.' She linked her refusal to the deficiencies of the Home Rule Bill: 'You probably realise that the suggested arrangement is repugnant to all except the extreme section of the Orange party ... Irishmen at large hate and distrust the whole Bill.'[80]

From Ireland, too, came petitions. The largest was coordinated by a committee, on which two of the initiators were Agnes O'Farrelly and Maurice Moore. On the committee with them were Lord ffrench, Rt. Revd Msg Ryan PP, Revd Matthew MacGuire PP, Douglas Hyde, Lorcan Sherlock (Late Lord Mayor of Dublin), F.J. Allen Esq., Mrs Hutton, Mrs O'Nolan, Miss [Ella] Young (Queen's Co.). This petition was also submitted on 21 July. Among the signatories were six bishops, twenty-three MPs and forty-two representatives of universities. The clergy included Cardinal Logue, Abbot Justin McCarthy, of the Cistercian Abbey at Roscrea, and Revd J.C. Whitty, superior general of the Christian Brothers; among the politicians were Joe Devlin, William O'Brien, Tim Healy and Stephen Gwynn.[81]

In Ulster, Alice Milligan sought support and submitted a petition on 22 July. Its three-page covering letter pointed up the anomaly of the situation in the light of the recent history of the Ulster Volunteers. Her petition made clear that the signatories had no sympathy for his German actions and represented Ulster Liberals.[82] Yeats made a personal plea to the Home Secretary. 'I have never before written to an English minister on an Irish question, but I am convinced that the execution of Sir Roger Casement will have so evil an effect that I break this habit of years.' Young men and women he had worked with believed that the Rising was put down with harshness and were 'less likely to be restrained by fear than excited by sympathy'. 'There is', he concluded, 'such a thing as the vertigo of self-sacrifice.'[83]

Hanna Sheehy Skeffington, whose own pacifist husband had been tragically executed during the Rising, wrote to the Prime Minister, 'conscious that I am speaking in the name of my murdered husband ... As the wife of one whose life was taken by the military wrongfully and without trial during the recent rising'. She pleaded that 'you will exercise wisdom and humanity'.[84] Canon Lindsay of Malahide wrote to the Home Secretary:

> He lived in my parish for several months in 1914, and I had various opportunities of conversing with him and observing his character. The impression left on me was that with much quick-witted intelligence, culture and experience of life, he was a crack-brained fanatic, and with such a distorted mind as to be scarcely responsible for his actions. He seemed to possess some strange psychic power which fascinated and almost paralysed the minds of those whom he sought to influence, and my wife thought him the most interesting and charming man she had ever met. But he had the habit of walking the roads bareheaded and swinging his arms in the air, so that the people thought him mad.

He closed by raising the question of insanity in Casement's family.[85]

From the United States the Negro Fellowship League organized a petition and pleaded: 'There are so few heroic souls in the world who dare to lift their voices in defence of the oppressed who are born with black skins, that the entire Negro race would be guilty of the blackest ingratitude did we not raise our voices on behalf of the unfortunate man who permitted himself in an evil hour to raise his hands against his own Government ...'[86] From Miami, a prominent black doctor, Alonzo Holly, took another initiative 'on behalf of the colored citizens of this Great Commonwealth, and also on that of British subjects of African descent'.[87]

The Diaries and the Appeal

On 22 June, Inspector Parker and Superintendent Quinn of the Special Branch, CID, Metropolitan Police, had submitted a report giving details of the various addresses at which Casement had stayed between 1906 and 1914. Their sources of information were Casement's bank, William Deacons Bank, and the Paymaster General's Office. One of the addresses proved to be highly significant:

> During the month of May 1914 Casement deposited with Mr Germain of 50, Ebury Street, Pimlico, S.W. some boxes containing books, etc. These books which included three diaries for the years 1903, 1910 and 1911, a ledger, an address book and a memorandum book were brought to New Scotland Yard by Mr Germain on the 25th April, 1916.[88]

When the possible uses of the diaries were recognized, it seems likely that the process of reproducing them began. At any rate, two months after they were found, shortly before the opening of the trial, Inspector Parker reported that copying of the diary and ledger for 1911 had been completed and he suggested that sections be forwarded to the Director of Public Prosecutions.[89] But long before the typing was completed, extracts from the diaries were being shown to representatives of the press and to influential figures in London. The process appears to have commenced a little over a week after the diaries were found; Reginald Hall played a prominent part in organizing the showings. Two American journalists attested to the fact that the showings commenced in early May at the regular press briefings held by Reginald Hall.[90] Among the English journalists who were shown the diaries were Clement Shorter of the *Sphere*, Robert Donald of the *Daily Chronicle* and Henry Massingham. The diaries were also shown in London clubs and in the House of Commons, and were reportedly viewed by King George V.[91] F.E. Smith, too, had access to the diaries and, before the trial, offered them to the defence team, who declined to use them.[92]

The showings of the diaries continued after the trial. On 30 June, the day after the trial ended, the taunt of 'moral degeneracy' was hurled at Casement in the *Daily Express*. Its headline read: 'Paltry Traitor Meets His Just Deserts. Death for Sir Roger Casement. The Diaries of a Degenerate'. On 2 July, Mrs N.F. Dryhurst wrote to Sir Sydney Olivier asking him to make representations about 'an abominable slander' which had appeared in the *Daily Express* the previous Friday and which had, up to that point, 'only been whispered or hinted at in secret about Roger Casement'. She went on to say: 'I saw a leading American journalist yesterday who told me that a month ago every American and English journalist had been shown certain documents purporting to be diaries or letters of Roger Casement's admitting unnatural practices. We Irish naturally concluded that they were the usual forged documents that have hitherto been used in every Irish political trial, but they were not produced.' Citing the Revd John Harris in support, she went on to suggest that the diary descriptions probably related to some of the unspeakable Putumayo atrocities that Casement had recorded. Sir Sydney wrote immediately to Basil Thomson, who replied on 7 July. 'What the American journalist told her,' he countered, 'is absolutely untrue. No journalist, American or otherwise, has seen the diaries, nor as far as I am able to ascertain, even copies of them, but, as I told you yesterday, I have heard indirectly that copies were shown to the defending Counsel. I quite agree with Mrs Dryhurst that it is very desirable that the facts should be brought into the open, but I do not see how this can be done unless Casement's friends make the first move.' He went on to mention that he had just learned of police evidence in Christiania of Casement's actions there while on his way to Germany.[93] Between the trial and the appeal, the *News of the World* claimed that nobody who saw the diaries 'would ever mention Casement's name again without loathing and contempt'. On 23

July, the appeal over, the *Weekly Dispatch* proclaimed: 'Why Casement must Hang; the Horrible Confessions of his own Diary'.[94] Friends of the condemned man began to object. Alice Stopford Green approached Sir John Simon and Lord Haldane, who, in turn, made representations.[95]

While he had been busy with his petition, Conan Doyle had called to the Foreign Office regarding Casement. There he was told of Casement's 'several offences' and of 'a diary of his in proof of it'. He told Shorter that he had heard of it previously and did not let it deflect him, as it was beside the point. 'None the less it is of course very sad, and an additional sign of mental disorder.'[96] On 14 July, Randall Davidson, the Archbishop of Canterbury, following various approaches to him, wrote to the Home Secretary to make a private representation in the case. He spoke of his knowledge of and admiration for Casement's work in the Congo and Putumayo: 'At each of these times I saw something of Casement and was always impressed by his capacity, his enthusiasm, and his apparent straightforwardness. I find it difficult not to think that he has been mentally affected, for the man now revealed to us in the evidence which has been made public seems a different creature from the man whose actions I knew and watched.' He then raised 'the accusations which are current against him respecting unnatural vice'. On this he claimed no means of forming a judgment, but referred to that of the Revd John Harris, which he respected. 'He has assured me, and probably has assured you, that from intimate knowledge of Casement's life in the close intercourse which Casement and Harris had during the Congo days he is able to say without hesitation that at that time he was one of the purest of men at a time when opportunity of vice was not only easy but was commonly yielded to.'[97]

On the same day, the Archbishop wrote to Harris, who was organizing a petition of his own, to say that 'I do not sign documents of this sort' but that he had written to the Home Secretary and giving details of the contents of his letter.[98] Harris wrote to Samuel, telling him of a petition he was preparing, but primarily drawing attention to 'the other charge' being circulated: 'I am absolutely convinced *and with solid reason*, that Casement is innocent of moral depravity and think I could give you good ground for saying this if you would allow me to come and see you for a few minutes.' He appended a memo on Casement's 'alleged depravity', arguing against its likelihood.[99]

Blackwell saw Harris on the 19th – the day after the appeal ended – and showed him the diaries. The result was dramatic. On the following day Harris wrote to thank Blackwell for his 'kind consideration under the extremely painful circumstances of yesterday afternoon' and to enclose a letter he had just written to the Archbishop of Canterbury. In this latter he stated that 'I must admit with the most painful reluctance that the Roger Casement revealed in this evidence is a very different man from the one up to whom I have looked as an ideal character for over fifteen years.' The only consolation, he added, was that 'there appears to be no certain evidence that these abominable things were practised in the Congo – it may be that our presence checked them'. Harris felt obliged to write to those who had offered their signatures, informing them of the new circumstances.[100]

On 5 July the cabinet had taken steps to assess the legal potential of the diaries by submitting them for assessment to two alienists, the equivalent of today's psychiatrists. They submitted their report on 10 July: 'They contain definite evidence of sexual perversion of a very advanced type in the writer ... Consequently, it is our opinion that the writer must be regarded undoubtedly as a mentally abnormal individual.' The alienists couldn't make a diagnosis of 'certifiable insanity', but the writer's 'absorption in the subject' and his conduct 'suggests much more mental disorder than is usually met with in a person who is suffering only from a perverted instinct'.[101]

Soon afterwards, in two memos submitted to the cabinet, immediately before Casement's appeal, Blackwell assessed the arguments for granting a reprieve. Addressing the imputation of insanity, he wrote:

> Casement's diary and his ledger entries covering many pages of closely typed matter, show that he has for years been addicted to the grossest sodomitical practices. Of late years he seems to have completed the full cycle of sexual degeneracy and from a pervert, has become an invert – a 'woman' or pathic who derives his satisfaction from attracting men and inducing them to use him. The point is worth noting, for the Attorney-General had given Sir E. Grey the impression that Casement's own account of the frequency of his performances was incredible and of itself suggested that he was labouring under hallucination in this respect. I think that this idea may be dismissed. I believe the diaries are a faithful and accurate record of his acts, thoughts and feelings just as they occurred and presented themselves to him ... No one who had read Casement's report to the Foreign Office on the Putumayo atrocities (at a time when his sexual offences were of daily occurrence), his speech from the dock ... his private letters to friends ... could doubt for a moment that Casement intellectually at any rate is very far removed from anything that could properly be described as insanity. His excesses may have warped his judgement and in themselves they are of course evidence of disordered sexual instincts, but they have not in my opinion any relevance in consideration of his crime, such as drunkenness, sexual excesses, jealousy, revenge, provocation, etc. have in the case of crimes of violence ...

On the second ground for reprieve, the question of expediency, he made the following observations:

> The Foreign Office from the start appear to have taken the view that in order not to alienate more Irish-American sentiment, we could not safely hang Casement unless we first published the fact of his private character as disclosed in his diaries. There are obviously grave objections to any sort of official or even inspired publication of such facts while the man is waiting trial or appeal, or even waiting execution. I see not the slightest objection to hanging Casement, and *afterwards* giving as much publicity to the contents of his diary as decency permits, so that at any rate the public in America and elsewhere may know

what sort of man they are inclined to make a martyr of. His private character is by this time pretty generally known in London. The *Daily Express* on three occasions has openly stated that he is a moral degenerate, addicted to unmentionable offences, and has cited his 'diaries' in proof.[102]

Following the guilty verdict at the trial and discussion between Casement, his legal team and friends, notice of appeal had been lodged on 3 July. The main ground was the same as in the trial, namely 'that Casement's acts as charged did not constitute an offence within the meaning of the Statute of Treason'.[103] Sullivan, still unwell after his collapse, requested time to recuperate; a delay of a fortnight was consented to. The appeal was set for 17 July. In the intervening period, Casement composed a lengthy statement aimed at helping his counsel. In the course of this he drew attention to what he considered to be the political dimension of treason trials:

> I could cite innumerable cases of recent years of flagrant cases of 'High Treason', in the fullest sense of the term too, where either the Crown has not prosecuted (where it would have been *politically* inconvenient to prosecute) or has remitted the sentence because the political needs of the country called for remission. If this be so – and it is clearly so – 'High Treason' becomes not the 'greatest crime' at all, but merely a political offence to be proceeded against or not proceeded against according to the political complexion of the times or the passion or fury of the times.

He cited the cases against Colonel Lynch and Major MacBride, who had fought against the British during the Boer War.[104]

The appeal was heard in the Court of Criminal Appeal on 17 and 18 July. Mr Justice Darling presided with four other judges. Addressing himself to the meaning of the statute of 1351, Sullivan re-argued at great length that Casement had committed no treasonable act within the meaning of the statute. Contrary opinions by legal experts he held to be incorrect. When he sat down on the morning of the second day, the judges retired to confer. On their return, before proceeding to reject Sullivan's arguments, the presiding judge announced that there was no need for the Attorney General to reply. A man charged with treason, he said, 'is the King's liege wherever he may be ...' inside or outside the realm. The appeal was dismissed.[105]

Only two possibilities for avoiding execution now remained: reprieve, through the exercise of royal prerogative, which needed the recommendation of the Home Secretary; or an appeal to the House of Lords, which required a certificate of fiat from the Attorney General. Casement's supporters attempted both avenues. George Gavan Duffy wrote immediately to Sir F.E. Smith requesting the necessary certificate for an appeal to the Lords. After reflection and consultation with his colleagues, the Attorney General refused the application.[106] With regard to reprieve from the king, Casement's friends redoubled their efforts in organizing petitions. The execution had been set for 3 August; they had only sixteen days left.

Herbert Samuel, the Home Secretary, deferred to the cabinet in coming to a decision about reprieve. The cabinet discussed Casement's case at a number of its meetings, twice before the court appeal (5 and 12 July) and three times afterwards (19 and 27 July, and 2 August). Before the meeting on 19 July, Samuel circulated memos from Ernley Blackwell and Sir Edward Troup, both of whom argued strongly in favour of execution.[107]All of the various arguments were discussed: that Casement had come to stop the Rising; his unique humanitarian contributions and the serious decline in his health; the contention, advanced by Michael Francis Doyle, that his defence had been interfered with by a refusal to allow witnesses to be brought from Germany; the likely effect on US opinion. This last was of considerable importance, given British desire for war support from the United States. Cecil Spring-Rice, the British ambassador in Washington, took great pains to alert the Foreign Office to the danger of alienating American opinion. In addition to petitions arriving from the US, a flow of representations was arriving at the White House and a number of resolutions passed in the Senate.[108] After consideration of Casement's case, 'it was the unanimous decision of the Cabinet that he should be hanged'.[109]

On 18 July, when Casement's appeal was rejected, Inspector Parker again referred in a report to the whereabouts of the diaries. He stated that he called on Mr Guy Stephenson, Assistant Director of Public Prosecutions, who had in his possession 'Casement's diary and ledger for 1911, which the Director of Public Prosecutions had asked for on Saturday last, 15th instant, for information of the Attorney General and for use at the Court of Appeal if necessary'. While Parker was present, 'Sir Ernley Blackwell, C.B. Legal Advisor to the Home Office, asked Mr Guy Stephenson to send him the diaries of Casement.' Parker took the diary and ledger, 'together with typewritten copies of the entries which he had to Sir E. Blackwell'. Blackwell wished to show them to 'a native of the Congo,' who 'had some influence over the natives in the Congo' and who had declared that Casement was 'morally clean'. Blackwell feared that his Congo visitor 'might attempt to create a rising amongst the natives in the event of Casement paying the extreme penalty of the law'.[110]

Towards the end of July the campaign of denigration continued. On the 26th, Basil Thomson informed Blackwell that he had shown the 'diary' to Dr Page, the US ambassador, and 'pointed out the innocuous passages that identified the writer as well as the filthy part ... I left photographs of two pages with him. He said that he considered the matter of international importance in view of the pressure that was being brought to bear on the President, and of Doyle's propaganda. But he wd tell everything to the President and he felt sure that he would be in time'.[111] With this letter and another on the following day, he sent Blackwell copies of statements 'sworn and unsworn', which had been made in Norway about the sexual relations between Casement and Christensen.[112]

Last Weeks

After his appeal was dismissed and 3 August set as the date of execution, Casement made his final farewells to those close to him. Nina received a tender and guilt-ridden set of reflections:

> My dearest, dearest Nina,
> This may be, probably it will be the last letter I shall write you. I have put off writing, because the things I wish to say to you are so hard to say [and] for others to read. I had hoped that a chance might yet come before I died to tell you with my lips what now I can say only in this way. It wrings my heart to leave you, beyond all else on earth, and to leave you thus, without being able to show you all I feel for you, and all the keen and bitter sorrow I feel at having left you, neglected you, and gone from you without a word.

He went on to talk of cutting things he had said to her and for which he had not apologized, because of pride and cowardice:

> Especially have I reproached myself – always and always – for that day in Berkshire when I said such unkind things to you in your cottage. Oh! dearest of my heart, forgive me forgive me and believe that I have bitterly repented – not once – not to-day only but a hundred times. Often and often in Germany the memory of that day came upon me, and my heart nearly suffocates me with pain. You said once I was all that you had to love, and I left you without a word and now you are alone and I can never see you again to tell you how much I loved you even when I scolded you ... Now dearest do you know what I feel for you? My eyes are blinded with tears and I can scarcely write. All my selfishness has passed away, and I see you plain and clear – your face – your eyes – your heart, and I can only sob and say that you are more to me than all else on earth, and to undo, and to aid you and to comfort you there is nothing I would not do, but alas! alas! it is all too late and I must go from you without a word. The bitterness of death has been upon me now these many days, but nothing like to-day and the bitterness is in this vain remorse at all my neglect of you and leaving you alone in the world when you had only me to help you and protect you. God may forgive me my sins – I can never never forgive myself this sin of neglect and coldness – and I loved you all the time – there is the mystery of transgression – we wound what we love and shun what we long for and go on our cold and lonely path, thinking there is plenty of time to go back to the loved one – and Death comes and cuts us down.
> Now that I have only these few days to live – that a cruel fate has brought me to the grave so far from you I bow my head in your lap, as I did when a little boy, and say Kiss me and say Goodnight ... I prayed for death often and often in Germany, I was so unhappy and months before I started to return to Ireland, coming as I knew straight to death, I was fixed on it and begging for death. For I had lost all hope, something had broken in me, and I walked about as if in a dream and every day the future whispered here's but death. I was so lonely, and I could do nothing and go nowhere. Often I tried to get away. All last year I was trying, again and again. Twice I tried in the spring and winter. In January I set out for Norway at the end but had to turn back. In March and April I planned another route, but could not carry it through ... And then in July I actually again set out and got a passport to go but had to return to stand by those poor chaps and help them altho' it was not I recruited them or

'tempted' them at all. I never saw one of them (or only one of them) in my life until I found them enrolled by others, and I could not help it or do anything but take all responsibility on my own shoulders. In September an appeal was made to a certain quarter (a high one) to help me to get away – but it failed ...

Long ago, years ago, I wrote these lines of another – but they are my own – my epitaph on my own fate perhaps more than on that of the man I penned them of – 'In the mystery of transgression is a cloud that shadows Day, For the night to turn to Fire – showing Death's redeeming way.' Will Death bring for me the redeeming way? I sought it thus – and now I stand on the shore, wondering, with clasped hands and blinded eyes, and no path opens in the waters and my heart is cold with sorrow and pain and numb with longing for a peace that will not come ... Some unknown friend sent me from the Court House at Bow Street a little book, *The Imitation of Christ*. You know it – with a beautiful inscription from the unknown friend. I will leave it to go to you with the priest here, and will ask for it to be allowed – also my Crucifix that Brigid sent me. And now, I must tear myself away – it is God's will, dearest Nina – I am going to lie down, it is late and my last thought to-night will be of you. Charlie I hope is coming home, and I have left a letter for him and begged him to see you if possible before he returns.

Goodbye, Goodbye and may the friendship of Christ be yours, may His blessing be yours and His pardon and peace be mine and bring us together in the land where He dwells and where pardon comes to the sorrowful. Your loving brother – loving you, I hope, far more deeply hereafter, when the grace of God has cleansed his heart, than he ever did on earth, but loving you now with his best heart beats and so to the end.

Roddie – or as you always called me – Scodgie.[113]

He wrote, too, to William Cadbury, thanking him and Emmeline for their kindnesses and asking them to help the school children at Carraroe. The letter was heavily censored. When Cadbury wrote to the Home Office on 7 August, asking for a letter Casement wrote him in the last days of life, Sir Ernley Blackwell wrote to Sir Edward Troup: 'I think this letter should be suppressed. It contains a great deal that is false and which Casement might have said on oath and did not.' He was afraid Cadbury might use the contents. Part of the letter was sent. Casement's letters to some others were destroyed, one to Agnes O'Farrelly, for example, on the grounds that it might help make a martyr of him ('it is treasonable as well ... This kind of stuff would go down with people unacquainted with his other writings and the most engrossing pursuit of his life.') A letter to his brother, Tom, was also destroyed, as were some of his prison writings. A HO minute stated: 'I think that the whole of these documents which have been sent up now from the Prison *should be destroyed forthwith* [margin, 'done, EB, 16/8/16']. We clearly cannot admit any right in Executors to have handed over to them the writings of a pr[isoner] while in prison or any letters etc. which he may have been allowed to receive.'[114]

Dick Morten got a second farewell letter, written on 28 July. Casement talked of the trial and appeal, making negative comments about Sullivan and positive ones about Morgan, before continuing:

By the way, you remember the day I wrote a certain polite letter, and how long I hesitated? Don't you? Well *don't* forget it. You know the truth about that and some day my ghost may call on you, and demand a recollection. You'll hear me clanking up the Avenue, because I'll be in armour of course – look at the date: 1351! – and I'll ask (in Norman-French) if one Dick de Morten lives there, and demand his memory or head – and it won't be the slightest use you stammering and putting it off on May (or Jacky M.). It's you and only you I'll call as a witness.

Since I saw you at Brixton, I have thought of you often and often and longed to see you again. There was something I forgot to say to you that day, and now I can't say it, and I'm afraid you'll never know ... I made awful mistakes, and did heaps of things wrong, confused much and failed at much – but I *very near* came to doing some big things ... on the Congo and elsewhere. It was only a shadow they tried on 26 June; the real man was gone. The best thing was the Congo, because there was more against me there and far cleverer rascals than the Putumayo ruffians ... The whole world is a sorry place, Dick, but it is our fault, our fault. We reap what we sow – not altogether, but we get our desserts – all except the Indians and such like. They get more than they deserved – they never sowed what 'civilisation' gave them as the price of toil.[115]

Some days before the execution, Gertrude paid her last visit to her condemned cousin:

On Thursday, July 27, I went to see him alone. He had had an interview with the Governor which had upset him, the Governor having told him that he felt it right to tell him how abhorrent his action had been. Also he had tried to get his oldest friend, Herbert Ward, to send him a message (he had asked one of his counsel to try) and he had had a rebuff. He was for the first time broken and sorrowful. We both tried to keep cheerful on the surface. Then he said, 'What will you do, Gee, when it is all over?' I cried, 'Don't don't, I can't think of that.' He said, 'Go back to Ireland, and don't let me lie in this dreadful place – take my body back with you and let it lie in the old churchyard in Murlough Bay.' I said, 'I will,' and then I broke down, I couldn't help it, it was the only time I was in tears when I was with him. He, too, wept and said, 'I don't want to die and leave you and the rest of you dear ones, but I must.'

Afterwards, she was brusquely ushered out of the prison:

I wanted to shriek and beat on the gate with my hands. My lips kept saying, 'Let him out, let him out.' I staggered down the road, crying out loud, and people gazed at me. I got home somehow. Now, writing it down, I cry and want to scream out, but what's the good. I can't see now to write any more today – he was inside waiting for death, such a death. I was outside and wanted to die.

Casement begged Alice Stopford Green also that his body be treated with dignity after his death: 'Do not, please, desert me in this.' He would like, he begged, a Christian burial.[116]

On 2 August, the day before the execution, Gertrude made a final effort to stave off the inevitable. She submitted the list of petitions she had elicited from friends, all of whom attested to the perilous state of Casement's health after his Putumayo endeavours. She forwarded a report from Sir Lauder Brunton, as well as testimonies directed to Asquith, dated 1 August, from Mrs Green, Sydney Parry, H.F. Spender, Dr Charpentier and Louie Heath. Gertrude hoped that the documents and letters 'from intimate friends' would prove sufficient to persuade the Cabinet to spare 'the life of a man who spent himself for 19 years in unhealthy climates, doing great public service, and slaving to mitigate the lot of the helpless black races suffering from horrible oppression'. He brought, she added, no army to fight against England.[117] From the US came a blunter telegram from Nina: 'If you execute my brother it is murder.'[118] The Cabinet met on the 2nd and, again, gave detailed consideration to the case; it concluded, however, 'that no ground existed for a reprieve'.[119]

Casement had been preparing spiritually for his death for some time. Fr Thomas Carey, a Limerick man and a Catholic chaplain to Pentonville Prison, was informed on 29 June that Casement was lodged in Pentonville and that he had registered as a Catholic. He immediately visited him. Carey was one of a number of priests with whom Casement came into contact during the following weeks. Fr James McCarroll, a Scot, who shared Carey's address and ministered in the prison, also came to know Casement well. So, seemingly, did Canon T.J. Ring, a native of Kerry. Denis Gwynn described Ring as 'a man of great energy and enthusiasm', but 'inclined to see himself as a central figure in important events'. He saw Casement in prison several times, but Fr McCarroll later said that Casement 'found Canon Ring too excitable, and asked to have some other spiritual adviser instead'.[120]

When he was in Brixton, Casement had taken steps to be instructed in the Catholic faith. On 16 July he wrote to Fr Edward F. Murnane, who was stationed in Bermondsey, concerning doubts he had about conversion to Catholicism:

> The trouble is: *am I convinced?* or do I only *think* I am? Am I moved by love? or fear? I can only accept in my soul from love – never from fear – and part of the appeal *seems* at times to be my fear – the more I read the more confused I get – and it is not reading I want, but companionship – I am sure you understand. And then I don't want to jump, or rush or do anything hastily just because time is short. It must be my deliberate act, unwavering and confirmed by all my intelligence. And alas! to-day it is not so. It is still, I find, only my heart that prompts from love, from affection for others, from association of ideas and ideals, and not yet my full intellect. For if it were thus the doubts would not beset me so vigorously as they do. I am not on a rock – but on a bed of thorns.[121]

On one of Gertrude's visits to Pentonville, the topic of his becoming a Catholic arose: 'On my third visit to him he said, "I want to be a Catholic, but they are trying to make me betray my soul. They have put my body in bonds but I cannot betray my soul." I was entirely in the dark as to what he meant, and did not dare to question him because of the warders. Afterwards, when I told the chaplain of this, he said it was "the paper they tried to make him sign".' Because it had been discovered that Casement had been baptized a Catholic as a child, it was only necessary to reconcile him to the Church, but permission had to be secured from Cardinal Bourne. It seems that the Cardinal insisted on some form of 'recantation'. Gwynn has suggested, with some plausibility, that Bourne must have come under pressure arising from the degeneracy charges and would have been conscious that the admission of Casement to the Church would be interpreted as excusing treason and immorality. In the event, Casement declined to sign. There was considerable anger among Irish priests in London at the Cardinal's action, and they found a mechanism under Canon Law, whereby the last rites could be given to a person on the point of death (*in articulo mortis*).[122]

Fr Carey was to describe the hours before the execution:

> I know you will be glad to learn that your friend Roger Casement was reconciled to the Church and made his first Confession on last Wednesday evening, and made his first and last Communion on the morning of his execution, on last Thursday. He died with all the faith and piety of an Irish peasant woman ... I gave him the Holy Father's Blessing, with Plenary Indulgence attached, shortly before his execution, and for an hour before he followed me in fervent and earnest prayer. He marched to the scaffold with the dignity of a prince, and towered straight over all of us on the scaffold. He feared not death and he prayed with me to the last ... He sobbed like a child after his confession, and his contrition for any sins he may have committed was intense.[123]

After Mass and Holy Communion on the day of his execution, the prisoner had breakfast and prayed with the chaplain. At nine the governor arrived and Casement, dressed in ordinary clothes, was led to the scaffold. On Thursday, 3 August 1916 Roger Casement was hanged in Pentonville Prison. According to his executioner, 'Roger Casement appeared to me the bravest man it fell to my unhappy lot to execute.'[124]

Appendix: *The Black Diaries*

Since the authenticity of the so-called 'Black Diaries' has been repeatedly challenged, I believe it necessary to present the reasons why I take them to be genuine and have treated them as such in the present work. The diaries are the major, though not the only, sources providing evidence of Casement's sexual thoughts and actions.[1]

The Black Diaries Described

The term 'Black Diaries' is applied to a group of five volumes: a 1901 War Office Army Book, a Letts's Pocket Diary for 1903, a 1910 Dollard's Diary, a 1911 Letts's Desk Diary and a 1911 Cash Ledger.[2] Though not strictly a diary, the 1911 Cash Ledger contains the record of day-to-day spending from January to October of that year and, since it also contains material of a sexual nature, its authenticity has been disputed as has that of the three diaries proper. The War Office Army Book is very different from the other volumes, containing only a small number of notes and sketches pertaining to the Congo in 1901–2. It contains no sexual material and is not central to the forgery controversy; its authenticity has not been challenged. The argument about authenticity, then, concerns four volumes. These coincide with only a few years in Casement's life, the years 1903, 1910 and 1911; in 1903, the year of the first of them, Casement was almost forty years old. Only two uncontroverted Casement diaries have survived. The first is the account he kept while in the Putumayo between 26 September and 6 December 1910. This is a very different type of document from the Black Diaries; it is a lengthy narrative of Casement's investigation, written in a discursive style on loose foolscap sheets of paper. For those convinced of the forgery of the Black Diaries, here is an undisputed private Casement diary with no evidence of homosexual activity; for others it is a detailed aide-memoire, compiled on the spot by Casement to aid in the later compilation of his Putumayo report and possibly destined for public use. It has been termed the 'Putumayo Journal' by Mitchell and a 'white' diary by him and by Sawyer. Casement made it available to Charles Roberts MP for his use during the Parliamentary Select Committee on the Putumayo, for which purpose Roberts had it typed. When writing to Roberts about this document, Casement commented: 'Remember it is less a diary than a reflection – a series of daily and weekly reflections.'³ The second undisputed diary is one which Casement kept fitfully during his stay in Germany and which he intended as a public record of the events in which he participated. According to Charles Curry, before Casement departed for Ireland, he 'left me various written instructions chiefly regarding his diaries and their publication upon the close of the war'.⁴ Though the term has not been applied to it, the German diary might equally be termed a 'white' diary, as it too is devoid of explicit sexual content.⁵

There is some evidence, though it is by no means conclusive, that other Casement diaries may have existed but were destroyed by his friend Francis Joseph Bigger. In an interview conducted by René MacColl in November 1954, a 'well-known resident of Cork', informed him of a conversation he had had with a nephew of Bigger's. The nephew told how he had been informed by his uncle that Casement had left in his house a tin trunk containing his papers, which Bigger had opened after Casement's execution:

> What he discovered inside gave him a staggering shock for he, presumably, like so many of Casement's intimate friends, had not the slightest inkling of his sex inclinations. There lay a voluminous diary, full of homosexual notations and reminiscences; and there was also a large quantity of letters from various young men, the contents of which left no doubt as to the nature of their relations with Casement. Biggar [*sic*] then did what Casement ought to have done, not only with these but with the sorry records which he left behind in Ebury Street – burned them.⁶

Casement's later biographers, Inglis, Reid, Sawyer and Dudgeon, who accept the authenticity of the diaries, are all inclined to believe this story. Opponents are not. MacColl later identified his Cork informant as John J. Horgan. None of the protagonists in the controversy has referred to Horgan's own comments, published in his 1948 recollections. Having pointed to some character weaknesses in Casement, he continued: 'Yet no one who knew him could believe the vile, and entirely unproved, suggestions which, with diabolical cleverness, were later made against his moral character by British propagandists.'⁷ It is, of course, conceivable that Horgan relayed the nephew's story to MacColl but did not believe it or that he heard it after the above words were published in 1948. Recent research has shed further light on the testimony of Bigger's nephew, Professor Joseph Warwick Bigger, which tells of uncle and nephew finding and burning the threatening materials.⁸ Whatever the truth of the story, only the four contentious Black Diaries have survived.

The diaries are written in what Dr Letitia Fairfield termed 'jerky sentences', making them difficult to read.⁹ Two examples, both from the 1903 Diary, should convey a sense of the writing style. The entry for Saturday, 14 February is the first surviving entry in the diary and shows the writer preparing to leave for the Congo:

> Writing in morning – Labelling G.B.'s heads for Club. Then to 53 Chester Square to lunch. Mortens there – with them to Paddington 3.35. Then to Nina to tea then to studio (H.W. gone). Then to Club – H.W., Collis, Cui & I. Then to Collis' to dinner. Did not wire Dick Morten as agreed. Home early on bus. 10.15 to Nina. She still seedy. To bed at 11.10. Slept very long. No letters. Very interesting articles in 'West Africa' about Burrows' book.¹⁰

The second example is from Wednesday, 25 March, which places the writer in the Canary Islands in the course of his voyage:

> {[*Just above day/date,which are bounded on each side by an* 'x'] 'Mucho amigo'}
> Not at all well. Very bad night between 'John' and dysentery. Lying down nearly

all day. Dr Otto advised going to bed and not leaving for Congo. In afternoon slightly better – so decided to go. Phillippeville in all day – sailed for home at 5 pm. After dinner went to Olsen's to pay for dinner of Monday 3/5. To waiter. In street & to Avenida. Juan. 20. mu nu ami diaka Nsono. 18p. 20 years. Back to Olsens – Pepe 17 bought cigarettes – mucho bueno – diaki diaka – moko mavelela mu mami mucho bueno – fiba, fiba, x. p.16.

The physical appearance of the diaries and the handwriting in them are also noteworthy. B.L. Reid provides a good sense of their character: 'bits erased or scratched out or corrected, bits cramped in at top or bottom or side of an entry, change of ink or pen, change from pen to pencil, variations in size or weight of script, oddities in sequence of events, "out of character" sentiments, and so on'.[11]

The content of the diaries, whether genuine or forged, follows the life of a British consul through the course of the three relevant years, incorporating a lot of detail on aspects of Casement's Congo and Putumayo investigations. The mechanics of ocean travel is a prominent theme, with details of travel to and from Africa and South America. The names of ships and of some of their officers are given, as are records of weather conditions and of daily progress; the author reads to while away the boredom of journeys. The diaries track regular communications with the Foreign Office in London and with a wide range of friends and relatives. They follow the day-to-day activities of a consul in situ, including his patterns of socializing. They follow his round of activities when on leave in Britain and Ireland. While generally matter-of-factish and cryptic, expressions of love, frustration and condemnation are occasionally expressed.

Sexual thoughts and activities appear from time to time: the writer regularly admires the bodies of young men and comments on their sexual attributes, frequently, for example, recording the penis sizes of those he admires. Late evening walks are a common feature, as he cruises the streets for sexual partners. He generally pays for sex and, while most of the encounters are casual, a recognizable cast of individuals appears in locations where he remained for some time. Travel brings back memories of earlier conquests and the anticipation of coming pleasures. It appears that the protagonist feels no shame in recording such intimate details of his sexual life. There is a marked increase in the level of indulgence between 1903 and 1911, with sexual material becoming quite dominant in the latter year.

Ernley Blackwell believed the diaries to be genuine and, in what B.L. Reid termed 'clinically if cruelly accurate' terms, described the nature of the author's sexual preferences: 'Casement regularly had intercourse with other men, usually younger men or youths; it was usually anal intercourse, though sometimes it was oral and sometimes only a matter of manual manipulation; more often than not he functioned primarily as the receiving or female partner.'[12]

History of the Controversy

Extracts from what were claimed to be Casement's diaries first appeared in 1916, while he was in prison in London, and were shown to journalists and influential members of society to undermine sympathy for him and to counter the efforts being mounted to win a reprieve. Afterwards they were quietly withdrawn and it became Home Office policy 'not to make any official statement as to the existence or non-existence of these diaries'.[13] Subsequent accounts of the physical character of the documents shown suggest a mixture of manuscript, photograph and typed matter. In 1921, during the Anglo-

Irish Treaty negotiations, Lord Birkenhead showed diaries to two members of the Irish delegation, Eamonn Duggan and Michael Collins. The latter is said to have accepted the handwriting as Casement's.[14] In 1922 a British journalist, Peter Singleton-Gates, acquired copies of the diaries, almost certainly from Basil Thomson, but, on attempting to publish a book based on them in 1925, he was threatened with prosecution under the Official Secrets Act, as were British publishers. In the same year, Scotland Yard's Casement file was moved to the Home Office.[15] Confusion about the provenance of the diaries was added to when Basil Thomson, in various publications, gave four different versions of how they came into Scotland Yard's possession and of what they comprised.[16] Forgery proponents have interpreted this confusion as an indication of chicanery, while authenticity proponents have taken it to be the result of carelessness and/or defective memory. Suspicions were added because of Thomson's arrest in Hyde Park in 1925 on an indecency charge.

As a clearly identified set of volumes, the Black Diaries only became publicly known for the first time in 1959. On 23 July of that year the British Home Secretary, R.A. Butler, informed the House of Commons in London that five volumes had been 'found in a trunk which the landlord of Casement's lodgings in London handed to the police at their request on 25 April 1916, two days after Casement had arrived in London under arrest'.[17] The five volumes, in the possession of the Home Office, were to be transferred to the Public Record Office where they would be available for study by serious scholars. The Home Office admission had been forced by the publication in Paris of *The Black Diaries* by Singleton-Gates in collaboration with the publisher Maurice Girodias; their edition included the diaries for 1903 and 1910 and the 1911 Cash Ledger.[18]

The year 1959, then, marked a watershed in the history of the diaries controversy. For the first time the diaries were clearly listed and made available for study by accredited researchers in the Public Record Office in London. Most of them were more widely available for perusal in the edition by Singleton-Gates & Girodias, though this, it is now clear, contained numerous errors.

Studies on Casement's life written between 1916 and 1959 were made, therefore, without access to the Black Diaries and judgments as to the authenticity or falsity of the diaries before 1959 were made in complete ignorance of their number, general structure and content. This is true of the two earliest biographies by Gwynn and Parmiter and, more interestingly, perhaps, of two major contributions to the forgery debate, William J. Maloney's *The Forged Casement Diaries*, published in 1936, and Alfred Noyes's *The Accusing Ghost*, which appeared in 1957. Maloney's book, produced two decades after 1916, marked the real beginning of a forgery school. Though it failed to convince George Bernard Shaw, it did draw a poem from William Butler Yeats, thereby giving prominence to the issue.[19] One of the earliest theses of the forgery proponents was that Casement had collected detailed evidence of the sexual depredations of the Putumayo criminal, Armando Normand, and that this formed the substance of the forger's or forgers' interpolations into genuine Casement diaries. This 'Normand defence' failed to recognize that the sexual element of Normand's brutal and sadistic behaviour was decidedly heterosexual and bears no resemblance to that of the protagonist in the Black Diaries. Neither does it account for such locations of sexual activity as Dublin, Belfast, London, Paris, Madeira and so on.[20]

From 1959, with the publication of the Singleton-Gates edition and the placing of the diaries in the Public Record Office in London, the debate entered a new phase. Scholars had now to assess diaries from 1903, 1910 and 1911 and a cash ledger from 1911. On one side of the argument, an early and serious challenge to their authenticity came from Professor Roger McHugh. Dr Herbert Mackey, too, who had written about the diaries before 1959, continued his campaign alleging forgery. On the other hand, three post-1959 biographers, Inglis, Reid and Sawyer, accepted that the diaries were genuine.[21]

In a BBC radio programme in September 1993, Dr David Baxendale, a forensics expert, after a brief examination of the diaries and of uncontroverted examples of Casement's handwriting, gave it as his opinion that the writing in the diaries, though variable, was Casement's.[22] From the mid 1990s, in pursuance of a British 'open government' programme, the Public Record Office began to release a significant number of Casement documents: in 1994 restrictions on access to the diaries were eased and between 1995 and 2000 a large number of hitherto closed files was made available to researchers, including some MI5 files. In 1997 the appearance of Mitchell's and Sawyer's editions of the diaries for the year 1910 served to fan the flames of the controversy once more, when they took opposite sides on the authenticity question.[23] Following an initiative taken by the Irish Taoiseach, Bertie Ahern TD, the Royal Irish Academy held a symposium in May 2000, which discussed all aspects of Casement's life, including the diaries. Debates there generated were added to by McCormack's critical analysis of the background to the production of William J. Maloney's book, and by the results in 2002 of a careful analysis of the disputed documents by Dr Audrey Giles of the Giles Document Laboratory, which found the diaries to be Casement's work.[24] Dudgeon's biography, with its heavy focus on the diaries and Casement's sexuality, was published in 2002, while Mitchell's edition of Casement's 1911 documents (Black Diaries excepted), and one of the 1903 Congo diary by Ó Síocháin and O'Sullivan both appeared in 2003.

The Case for Forgery Analysed

Few of those who allege that the Black Diaries are forged have specified what, precisely, they mean by forgery. One can identify three different models from the contributions of proponents, who may hold one or all at the same time. The first model would involve the *simple interpolation of fabricated sexual material* and it is based on the assumption that the extant Black Diaries are genuine Casement diaries to which have been added false homosexual content. In this case, all of the content and handwriting of the diaries, other than the sexual material, would be Casement's. The forgery theorist focuses either on variations in the handwriting, believed to provide evidence of the hand(s) of the forger(s) or, alternatively, on manipulations of innocent words and passages in the originals to create fictitious sexual partners and episodes. The search for discrepancies is confined, then, to the sexual material – believed to be straight interpolation or distortion of some elements of genuine Casement material. Mackey's work is a prime example of this approach.[25] McHugh also argues for interpolation, summarizing his argument by stating: 'My own view ... is that the "black diaries" are not authentic but have been faked by the interpolation of indecencies into gapped and partly pencilled volumes.'[26] The oldest variant of this interpolation theory is that the forgery was based on the diary of the Putumayo miscreant Armando Normand.[27]

The second model of forgery, involving the *interpolation of fabricated sexual material and the rewriting of the whole text*, is also based on the assumption that there were genuine Casement diaries and that the forger had possession of them. It suggests that the forger, having acquired suitable blank diaries, inserted false sexual incidents into original Casement material and then wrote out the total documents afresh. This would have been necessary, it is suggested, because of lack of space in the genuine diary to interpolate new matter. Mackey, again, provides an example of this model of forgery theorizing, with reference to the 1911 Diary:

There is every reason to believe that this series of entries was constructed by the counterfeiter from the diarist's genuine diary and many notebooks and memorandum books dealing with the period, which gave the correct time and place; and that the whole was then transcribed on to a new diary-book interior specially printed for enclosing in the old cover ... An experienced forger copied in the prepared material in a handwriting forged skilfully to imitate Casement's ... The penmanship was done on the pages of a newly printed copy of a 1911 diary – identical with that removed. This new 'diary' was thus substituted for the real one by putting it into the original and authentic cover; the authentic diary for that year having been skilfully removed from the cover. Thus the only thing genuine about what is now shown as the '1911 diary' is the cover.[28]

At one point Mitchell comes close to a similar position, when he suggests that a deep study and thorough contextualization of the diaries 'may lead to the conclusion that the diaries are in fact rewritten versions of existing journals'. And: 'It is not hard to envisage that from those diaries they either interpolated existing diaries or manufactured a new set with the sex-centred narrative.'[29] Needless to say, an enormous degree of creativity would have been needed to portray the patterns of sexual activity depicted for 1903, 1910 and 1911 and to falsify Casement's handwriting through all the diary volumes.

The third model involves the *fabrication of the sexual and non-sexual content* of the diaries. In it the sexual content is, again, false, but the rest of the content is also fabricated, though from genuine Casement sources. This would be necessary either because the authorities did not have access to genuine Casement diaries and were forced to construct the day-to-day, non-sexual content from Casement's despatches and private correspondence or because, if they did have genuine Casement diaries (e.g. the Putumayo Journal), the forgers merely mined them to create their own new narrative. As with the two other forgery models, handwriting might be considered important here, but a new argument has recently been made: that the literary style of the diaries is quite distinct from that in undisputed Casement documents.[30] A further approach taken is to argue that, though the general matter in the Black Diaries was constructed from genuine Casement writings, in the process of abstracting it and creating totally new texts, a large number of discrepancies was produced, detectable by the forgery sleuth. This option must also mean that the forgers had to acquire blank diaries, fill them and make sure they looked authentic. Even more than in the case of the second model, it is difficult to imagine how a forger could produce the necessary degree of creativity and coherence to produce a day-to-day diary in this manner. Casement's despatches to the Foreign Office would have contained none of the personal detail found in the Black Diaries. [31]

Of the three models of forgery, the first, involving simple interpolation, effectively ceased to be sustainable after the release of the diaries in 1959 (*pace* McHugh). Though many sexual entries do appear at the end of the day, many do not and could not have been interpolated.[32] In addition, the Giles tests have judged the writing in the diaries to be that of Casement, with no evidence of interpolation. Scientific tests had previously been carried out – handwriting tests by Drs Wilson Harrison and David Baxendale and an ultra-violet-ray test – but either the secrecy or limited nature of these tests had led sceptics to question them. The results of new tests on the five documents carried out by Dr Giles of the Giles Laboratory in 2002 constitute an important milestone in the debate. A significant sample of uncontested Casement material – from his letters to E.D. Morel and from the Putumayo Journal – was used for comparison. In her summary statement of findings relating to all of the disputed documents, she concludes that: 'It is clearly the case that the handwritings in the questioned documents ... are a single population and that the vast majority of the handwritings can be identified conclusively as those of Roger Casement. There is, therefore, no evidence to support the proposition that these documents ... are wholesale simulations.' In addition, she assessed what she terms 'contentious entries': 'I have been requested as part of my instructions to consider the authorship and authenticity of entries of a sexual nature. I refer to these as the "contentious" entries. In examining these entries I have not only considered the detail of the handwritings but how these entries relate to other entries of an innocuous and general nature throughout the document [1903 Diary].' Referring to these entries, she concludes:

> The questioned documents ... contain contentious entries. Where they do occur they are often entirely consistent with innocuous entries. I found no significant differences in these contentious entries when compared with the writings of Roger Casement, even though the entry may be restricted in quantity. On this basis there is no evidence to support the proposition that entries have been added by someone else into genuine Diaries and documents written by Roger Casement.33

The results of the Giles tests equally undermine the second forgery model, that of interpolation-cum-rewriting by a forger.

While models one and two assume the bulk of the content of the diaries to be genuine Casement material, not so with the third. Again, the Giles tests counter this position, as do the weaknesses of the suggested 'discrepancies' found in the diaries. Some examination of these is necessary here. Various writers – Mackey, McHugh, Ó Máille, Mitchell – have concentrated on alleged discrepancies between elements in the Black Diaries and uncontroverted Casement documents. The most sustained recent argument for forgery has been that of Mitchell; he devoted the whole of the introduction to his *Amazon Journal* (pp. 15–56) to 'The Diaries Controversy', and he has added a further general statement in 'The Riddle of the Two Casements'.34 His intense work on Casement's Putumayo investigation in 1910 convinced him that the Black Diary for the same year was forged. The year 1910 was unique in that it has left us two diaries, the Black Diary for the full year and a much more detailed diary, the Putumayo Journal, which only covers the period from 23 September to 6 December, when Casement was in the Putumayo region.35

In his introduction to *The Amazon Journal*, Mitchell sets out the broad dimensions of his argument, but his claims rest on a long list of supposed discrepancies and contradictions, some forty in all, between material in the Amazon Journal and items in the Black Diaries; such errors, he suggests, reveal the forger's hand. Most of the alleged discrepancies fall into a number of recognizable categories: omissions from the 1910 Black Diary, discrepancies in handwriting, in spelling and in dates, measurements and so on. 36 In addition, he selects what he takes to be two telling examples, the one dealing with Casement's weak eyes, the other with an observation by Casement on his celibacy.37 Lying behind these more technical discrepancies is an imputed lack of fit between the personality of Casement reflected in the Amazon Journal and in the Black Diary.

Most of the 'discrepancies' dissolve under analysis. Take, for example, the case of Casement's eye trouble during 1910. Mitchell introduces the topic at length: 'From the outset of the voyage Casement began to suffer a chronic eye infection which he referred to with mounting concern in his correspondence with friends and Foreign Office colleagues as he journeyed up river.' The first of these references was on 11 August:

> Over the next two months the problem continued until the night of Wednesday 12 October when he was forced to bandage both eyes and was rendered momentarily blind, albeit at night. In all he mentions his eye problem on more

than fifteen separate occasions in his correspondence and journals – and at times at some length. By contrast, the *Black Diary* avoids any mention of the eye infection until eighty days after the outset of the journey when it is rather nonchalantly mentioned in the entry for 10 October.[38]

The argument Mitchell derives from Casement's eye problem is twofold. One is the omission from the 1910 Black Diary of all mention of it until 10 October.[39] The second is its implication for Casement's writing capacity: why would he have written two diaries in the circumstances and how could he have written the Black Diary in a neat hand and in fine ink, when, for all his other correspondence at the time, his weak eyes forced him to use a pencil and showed a shaky hand?

On the alleged effect on Casement's writing, Mitchell offers the following reflections:

> The handwriting in Casement's genuine journal is quite clearly affected by his increasing eye problem and his pages of pencilled script become unusually untidy and scrappy during this journey through the forest when his vision was impaired by his ocular infection. The corresponding entries in the Black Diary for 12–13 October are neatly written in black ink – the tightly-packed script shows no signs whatsoever of the shakiness evident in Casement's own hand. Future handwriting experts seeking to make a judgment about the Black Diaries should begin with a comparison of these days. On the strength of handwriting analysis alone of these parallel entries, it becomes extremely difficult to believe that the same man wrote both journals.[40]

One can respond directly by showing that an expert examination has judged the handwriting on these days to be Casement's. The Giles Report has stated:

> It has been suggested in *The Amazon Journal of Roger Casement* edited by Angus Mitchell that 'the pencil scrawl of 12th October of the Putumayo Journal is not mirrored in the corresponding diary entry where the hand is deliberate and in pen'.
> ... the section of the Putumayo Journal which I have examined, which included entries for 9th to 14th October is all written in large fluent handwriting, suggesting that it was rapidly executed and may have been written in sections. The writing, however, is not scrawled – the character forms are identifiable and the writing is perfectly readable. If indeed the entry of 12th October in the Putumayo Journal was written on that date, then Roger Casement's writing does not appear to have been unduly affected by his eye problems.
> The entry of 12th October in the Dollard's Office Diary ... is written in smaller writing, such as might happen when there is only restricted space available to make an entry in the diary. The writing is fluent and shows no significant differences from the writings of Roger Casement. Furthermore, there are no significant differences between this writing and the writing of the previous entry dated 11th October where the eye problem is referred to.[41] *

Further counter-evidence can be offered. Firstly, there is the contrast between pen and pencil. Casement alternated regularly between the two and the choice was not determined by the state of his eyes. In his 1903 Diary there is a great deal of pen–pencil alternation unconnected with any eye problem. Writing to Francis Cowper in 1914, having broken his pen, he finished his letter in pencil and commented, 'I must run out for a box of nibs.' But, more often, he seems to have used pencil when writing large amounts or when writing in awkward situations, such as when moving about, on board ship, or in bed. Inglis comments on Casement's prodigious output in early September 1912, up to four to five thousand words per day, writing in pencil. In 1915, when in Germany, he asked Richard Meyer to 'forgive pencil but I have a lot to write today and pen and ink are so much slower'.42 For purposes of his Putumayo investigation, he was recording large volumes of information depositions, day-to-day observations and reflections on events. This was done on loose foolscap pages. Whatever the state of his eyes, it is not surprising that he wrote in pencil.

Secondly, the 1910 Black Diary entries had to fit into the restricted spaces allocated to each day in a formal diary. If one desired detailed entries, fine writing was called for, which would be facilitated by the use of pen. But, thirdly, one must ask: did the volume of Casement's writing decrease as a result of his troublesome eyes? Mitchell suggests that one effect of Casement's eye infection was that 'it forced him to be as economic with his writing as possible and avoid unnecessary strain'.43 He uses this statement to question the likelihood of Casement's keeping two diaries. But, compare two of Casement's own statements at the time his eye problem was worst. On 10 October, he wrote: 'My eye is getting very bad, and I have to do all my writing now with one eye – the right – the left is carefully bandaged up.' On 13 October, one of the dates on which Mitchell finds the Black Diary writing suspicious, Casement noted: 'Up early and a very heavy day. Eye better and took bandage off and started writing hard right away.' The pattern of intense writing continued thereafter.44 Even when his eyes were at their worst, Casement generated substantial amounts of writing. There was no let-up. The 1910 Black Diary entries were insignificant in volume compared with his overall production.

It has been suggested by forgery proponents that Black Diaries exist only for the years 1903, 1910 and 1911 because, being the years of the Congo and Putumayo investigations, adequate materials would have been available to forgers for their fabrications. While the coincidence of the years is strange, the argument is not sustainable because no amount of official Casement papers could have provided the wealth of detail concerning his personal activities contained in the Black Diaries. And the only occasion where the 1910 Black Diary is paralleled by a second day-to-day narrative is the period in late 1910 covered by the Putumayo Journal, when Casement was conducting his inquiry. No equivalent parallel text exists for 1903, 1911 or the remainder of 1910. The two 1910 documents differ in nature: the Black Diary commenced in the beginning of the year, when Casement was in Brazil and when he was as yet unaware of his future role in the Putumayo; the Putumayo Journal was kept only for the period when Casement was in the Upper Amazon engaged in his investigation. It does not come as a surprise that he kept a lengthy account of the progress of his investigation on that occasion or that, while doing so, he should have continued with a private diary he had been keeping since the year's beginning.45

As regards the ease with which 'contradictions' are found in the diaries, it is important to be aware of Casement's habits in writing up his diaries. While most of the diary entries were probably written at the end of each day, this was not always so. At times, several days were written up at one sitting; at other times, a single day's entry was written at several sittings, some of them quick jottings. One example of the latter is the entry for 29 September 1910, where part of the entry, perhaps written in the afternoon, talked of 'tonight's dance' and of lots of Indians arriving from 11 am onwards. The reference was to a planned Indian dance. Towards the end of the day's entry, he remarked: 'The dance a success', clearly written after the event, possibly late at night.46 Sometimes he made only the most cursory entries, e.g. during the voyage to South America in 1911; sometimes the pages are left totally blank for periods of time; and sometimes the day's spaces are very systematically filled in, day by day. There are changes, too, in script, even within a single day. On occasion, he made and later corrected errors, as on Thursday, 21 December 1911, where he wrote: 'See yesterday's entry – in error under Wednesday. I only landed today at 8.30 am.' If one examines his private correspondence, one can find parallel practices, as, for example, when he gave as his address one he expected to be at some days later, or when he used hotel notepaper for letters, though not in the vicinity at the time.47 Occasionally he made errors in dates, for example, putting down the old year in early January.

The complex nature of the diaries' construction and the likelihood of variations between concurrently running texts has aided some forgery proponents in their unceasing search for 'contradictions'. Some such characteristics have been taken as indications of forgery; in all likelihood, they are rather signs of authenticity. My own conclusion on the many suggested 'contradictions' is that, in virtually all cases, the arguments made for them are tendentious and that they fail to stand up to critical analysis.

Alleged Contradictions Regarding Casement's Sexuality and Personality

Two factors contributed significantly to the development and simmering of the forgery thesis for almost a century. One was the secrecy and uncertainty surrounding the existence and nature of the diaries between 1916 and 1959. The veil of secrecy has been slowly lifted, notably with the release of the diaries themselves and then of a significant number of ancillary documents. The second factor is the apparent surprise and shock experienced by many of those close to Casement, when the homosexual accusations were first made. Many refused to believe it. This, combined with strong moral disapproval of active homosexual behaviour, has led to a similar refusal up to our own day. Adrian Weale has captured the position well:

> Those people who admired Casement as a humanitarian were uncomfortable that he should be revealed to have been paying poor, young native men and boys for sex; whilst those who admired him as an Irish Republican revolutionary hero have, for the most part, shared the morally conservative Catholicism which has traditionally underpinned mainstream Republicanism, in which the practice of homosexuality is widely regarded as aberrant if not an abomination. The revelations of Casement's sexuality which the diaries presented do not sit well with either standpoint and, over time, partisans of both of these essentially positive views of Casement have tended to look for evidence which would exonerate 'their' man.48

We are inevitably brought back to the interpretation of Casement's personality and of the connection between morality and sexuality when we address the Black Diaries issue. Most commentators, forgery theorists in particular, have found the contrast between the author of the Black Diaries and the Casement of other writings to be quite marked. This is very clear in the case of Roger McHugh in his meticulous study of the diaries' controversy.49 His conclusion, after comparing the two 1910 diaries, was as follows:

> Were there then two Casements? The Casement of the fuller diary has the ring of an integrated personality, a strict sense of morality, a sensitivity to human suffering and an intelligence and dedication in his mission which make a coherent impression on the reader. The diarist of the shorter diary is at once capable of moral judgements and of complete immoral comments; of contempt for

homosexual behaviour and of secret addiction to it. This impression of discrepancy is caused by a small percentage of indecencies scattered throughout the shorter diary. Could a personality so split as this have kept its secret? Or is it to be explained by the theory that this shorter diary which, unlike the fuller diary, had been through police hands, was doctored by the insertion of scattered indecencies?[50]

Having assessed the 1911 Diary, where the number of sexual incidents is considerably higher than in the 1910, McHugh concluded more strongly: 'The total effect of these passages is to create the impression of a dull degenerate who has reached the last stages of abnormality, who has no moral scruples and who is under such a compulsive or obsessive neurosis that he is driven to write down a very detailed record of his thoughts and actions which establishes clearly his psychopathic condition during that period.'[51]

Mitchell's viewpoint is similar and the language is, at times, even more intemperate. Writing about one of Casement's letters from September 1910, he comments: 'The figure of Roger Casement who emerges from it is so different in general attitude and moral values from the Casement portrayed by the Black Diaries as to be totally irreconcilable.' The purpose of the forgeries, according to him, was 'to portray Casement and homosexuality as a sickness, perversion and crime'. The 1911 Diary is 'the most explicit and pornographic in its content'; 'By this account the diarist did little on this journey except fantasize and seek out willing sexual partners or seduce under-age boys at every opportunity.' And, 'it unequivocally portrays Casement as both a pederast and obsessive fantasist'. He believes that the diaries are not genuine homosexual products.

> They were manufactured in an age when acts of homosexuality were considered sexually degenerate. Whoever wrote the diaries had a desire to portray Casement and homosexuality as a sickness, perversion and crime for which a person should suffer guilt, repression, fantasy, hatred and, most of all, alienation and loneliness. These are not the confessions of a Jean Genet or Tennessee Williams, W.H. Auden or Oscar Moore. Rather than sympathizing with the struggle of the homosexual conscience, they are clearly homophobic documents.[52]

More recently, Mitchell summarizes the impact he believes the Black Diaries have had on Casement's place in history:

> The Black Diary narrative trivialises Casement to a level of low-life, bad health and bitterness; the type of petty-minded consular status that Casement despised and spent his life deliberately rising above. It constructs the type of man the British felt justified in executing in 1916 ... They destroy his mystical role as both imperial knight and the moral standard-bearer of advanced nationalism. He is turned from being the investigator of the system into the exploiter, the sexual coloniser, the crude fantasist. It is impossible to champion Casement's worth as a human rights campaigner and, in the same hand, uphold the diaries as the master narrative in the telling of the key moments of his human rights campaign.[53]

The belief that the diaries are homophobic is not shared by members of the gay community who have taken an interest in them, including some who have studied Casement's life closely. The sexual life depicted in the Black Diaries is of a recognizable type. Dudgeon has observed that: 'Casement showed himself to be an early exemplar of what is now fairly standard in the gay community', while O'Sullivan, writing of the Giles tests, commented: 'So the diaries are genuine after all and their contents reveal their author as a proselytising homosexual with a penchant for rough trade.'[54] The 'homophobic documents' (Mitchell) and the 'dull degenerate' (McHugh) seem to be in the eyes of the beholders.

Ironically, both forgery theorists and those who take the diaries to be genuine have described something similar to McHugh's 'two Casements', but the former reject the one Casement as being the forger's creation, while the latter interpret the duality (if such it be) as part of Casement's character. They talk of his 'ambivalence', 'dividedness', 'schizoid personality' and 'compartmentalisation'. A number of responses is possible to the 'two Casements' in so far as it relates to his sexuality. One is that practising homosexuals were, indeed, forced to lead double lives, as the practice of 'buggery', 'sodomy' or 'gross indecency' were crimes, punishable by terms of imprisonment with hard labour.[55] It is hardly surprising that friends and acquaintances of Casement's would have been unaware of this guarded life of his. Prosecution would have meant an end to his consular career.

A second response to the perceived contradiction in Casement's character comes, to my mind, from a misinterpretation of his moral attitudes. In general, his actions and language resound with moral content: concern with good and evil, kindliness and compassion, lies and selfishness. Moreover, despite his religious ambivalences and his regular criticisms of the various Christian denominations in his writings, his general attitude to Christianity was positive, as reflected, perhaps, in his conversion to Catholicism before his death. Given that homosexual behaviour was both illegal in the eyes of the law and immoral in the eyes of the Christian churches in his day, can one believe that the Casement we know from general sources is the same man who wrote the diaries? The answer has to be yes. One can reasonably assume that practising homosexuals would not have agreed with the condemnatory attitudes prevalent at the time or with the terms used to characterize it by McHugh and Mitchell. In this context, one must carefully note the spheres of life to which Casement's moral terminology was applied: it was invariably applied to human behaviour he deemed exploitative of other human beings. Personal sexual behaviour is rarely mentioned. One example where it was is worth reflecting on, the case of Mrs Meyer in the Congo, who was a victim of State injustice. In summarizing for the Foreign Office the sequence of events in her case, Casement reported on an interview he had had with the Governor General on 30 June 1903:

> His Excellency then sought to make light of Mrs Meyer's character, as of her complaint to me, saying he knew her well, that for years she had been in trouble with the local tribunals and that she and her two daughters led immoral lives. To this I replied that it was not Mrs Meyer's morals that were at issue but that of the Luki garrison, and that I must decline to pursue the conversation on that line since I was about to place H.E. in possession of my views in writing ...
>
> The question of Mrs Meyer's morals or those of her daughters is one that has no tangible relation to the very definite charges of assault and robbery she brought against the Congo soldiers and I should not touch upon it save that the Governor General himself at the first mention of these charges sought to belittle their importance by assuring me that Mrs Meyer's record was not unimpeachable. This woman had in fact lived some ten or twelve years on the Congo, and her life was probably every bit as edifying during that period as the lives of the majority of Europeans.[56]

A third source of the 'divided Casement' theme derives from the (mis)interpretation of a small number of passages in the Black Diaries. A striking example can be found in the Amazon Journal for 4 October 1910. Casement wrote: 'Even the table boys go their hammocks at 9 am and lie down three deep playing with each other.' Not unexpectedly,

Mitchell argues that this innocent phrase has been twisted to give it a sexual meaning in the 1910 Black Diary, which reads:

> At 9 to bath and found 'Andokes', the light boy & a little boy in hammock outside bathroom, all doing what Coudenhove once said of the boys of Rome, & Johnston of the Nyasaland Boys, without concealment! The other servants looking on practically while these three boys played with each other, with laughter and jokes! A fine beastly morality for a Christian Co. at 9 am with three of the domestic servants.[57]

Two things are important about this quotation. Firstly, it is inconceivable that a forger could have conjured up these very specific references to homosexual play from two sources who happened to have been associates of Casement: Coudenhove, either Richard or Hans, friends of his since Lourenço Marques days, and Harry Johnston, whom he had known from the time of the Congo campaign. Rather, the reference suggests Casement's awareness of the phenomenon of homosexuality in different cultural settings. Secondly, there is the matter of interpretation. For two of Casement's biographers, Reid and Sawyer, this is a key passage indicating the alleged dividedness or compartmentalization of Casement's personality. Sawyer writes: 'Casement was appalled because servants, looking on while two young boys "played with each other", found the spectacle amusing. His reaction is distinctly puritanical; surely these lines expressing his disgust would have been erased/written over/modified by a forger wishing to give the impression that the diarist was himself addicted to similar practices.'[58] Reid goes even further, turning the phrase 'A fine beastly morality for a Christian Co.' into a chapter heading and suggesting that Casement reacted to the scene 'with a surprising conventional censoriousness'. He continued: 'But Casement's reaction to the scene presents one with the same problem as his response to the suicide of Sir Hector Macdonald and can only be explained in the same way as illogical and self-deceiving, in fact schizoid.'[59] In contrast, I take Casement's response as more humorous than puritanical and the phrasing to represent his characteristic irony, particularly because of the use of his characteristic exclamation mark and the structure of the last sentence, including the phrase 'fine, beastly morality'. This is one of a handful of key quotations contributing to conclusions about dividedness or forgery. Arguably, misinterpretation of the passage has contributed to a major misinterpretation of Casement's personality.

If one accepts the existing evidence from outside the diaries for Casement's homosexuality, deriving largely from the Norwegian evidence (see below); if one accepts that the type of homosexual lifestyle depicted in the diaries conforms to what today is a recognizable variant; and if one accepts that Casement directed his moral wrath not at sexual behaviour but at individuals or institutions he considered to be oppressive of individuals or communities, then we begin to see many of the references to Casement's 'dividedness' in a new light. Claims that the author of the diaries is 'sub-human', 'moronic', 'schizoid', can then be seen for what they are: reflections of the moral positions of those making the judgments rather than of Casement's morality.

Further Evidence for Authenticity

One of the key elements in feeding the forgery argument since 1916 was the unavailability of relevant evidence. But the import of the gradual release of fresh documentary evidence has been to strengthen the case for authenticity substantially. Firstly, the diaries themselves came into the public arena in 1959 and, secondly, a significant body of supportive documentation from 1916 was made available in stages from the mid 1990s onwards.

On the one hand there are the diaries themselves, four documents of considerable scale and complexity. The day-to-day record contained in them so matches Casement's actions, movements and contacts over extended periods of time and in diverse locations as to make total fabrication (model three) out of the question. The diaries contain such a wealth of detail that no forger or forgers could possibly have fabricated. The sources available to a potential forger – Casement's despatches to and his personal correspondence with the Foreign Office, together with material found in his trunks (such as letters to him from friends and acquaintances and other miscellaneous materials, but not his letters to others) – could not have provided the detail to create the intricate texture of the diaries in the Public Record Office.[60] The same would hold for a second scenario (models one and two), suggested by some forgery proponents – the interpolation of sexual material into otherwise genuine Casement documents. The creation of so many personalities, sexual encounters, expressions of longing and remembrance could not have been sustained by any forger. Reid's formulation is hard to surpass:

> The forgery theory will not wash and the reason is one not only of details but of basic size or scale in the diaries, and of their texture, the feel of the fabric ... the larger point is that the case for forgery grows physically and psychologically incredible in terms of scale and texture. I think it is impossible for a forger to have tailored the homosexual details into this big convincing fabric without destroying the homogeneity of it: he would have had to weave the whole fabric, and the whole fabric is not invented; it is Casement's. This matter of wholeness or homogeneity cannot be demonstrated by piecemeal analysis, it has to be felt in one's own experience of a total texture.[61]

If one examines the two entries from the 1903 Diary, cited earlier, one can begin to get a sense of the implausibility of forgery. The entry for Saturday, 14 February contains a whole cast of Casement's family and friends: Nina, his sister, two close friends, Dick Morten and Herbert Ward (H.W., whose address was 53 Chester Square and whose studio is also mentioned), and a few other friends, Collis, Cui Bono and George Brown (possibly a sexual acquaintance). It also refers to his club (the Wellington Club) and to a recent work on the Congo by Guy Burrows. Paddington was the station for travelling to the Mortens' house near Uxbridge. The entry for Wednesday, 25 March, from the island of Tenerife, mentions his dog, 'John', which he had just collected, and tells of an illness and the travel advice of a local doctor; and it refers to the departure of the *Philippeville*, one of the Elder Dempster steamers which plied the Congo run. It is one of a few entries, too, which contain some phrases in Kikongo, some command of which Casement had gained in the Congo. Is it conceivable that any forger could have replicated the Kikongo phrases incorporated into the diary, phrases which have a sexual reference?[62] Similar lists of authentic references occur in page after page of the diary. The bulk of this material could not be fabricated nor could the coherence of the total narrative.

Add to this three specific examples. In the diary entry for 20 April, the writer records: 'Reading Gertrude's present of the *Reminiscences of an Irish RM*. They are delicious.' The book was a well-known novel by Edith Somerville and Martin Ross. On the same day, 20 April, Casement wrote to his cousin, Gertrude, thanking her for the present of the book, which he said he found delightful and spent all night reading.[63] The only forgery scenario which would account for this reference in the diary and its corroboration in a Casement letter not available to a forger would be one that posited the existence of genuine Casement diaries which were subsequently tampered with, i.e. an interpolation model. A second example relates to the diary entry for 10 March, when the writer was in Madeira. It appears in the Singleton-Gates edition as: 'Joe McV. on shore at noon'. The entry should read: 'Joe MP [Joseph Chamberlain] on shore at noon' and refers to the visit to Madeira of the British Colonial Secretary, Joseph Chamberlain, who was returning from a visit to South Africa. His visit is corroborated by Madeira newspapers of the time. It is clear that neither Singleton-Gates nor the source of his copy, the Scotland Yard typists, understood the reference. Can one seriously claim that such an entry was forged?

Thirdly, the Kikongo examples in the 1903 Diary are paralleled by some in Irish in that for 1910. For Monday 6 June, failing completely to decipher the text, Singleton-Gates reads: 'Dod Uscubitsig called on way to Kerf naglesum.' Sawyer's more recent edition renders this as: 'Hugh Duffy [written in Irish] called on way to Glenshesk [in Irish].' I read the manuscript entry as follows: 'Aodh Ua Dubhthaigh called on way to Feis na nGleann.'[64] Ua Dubhtaigh was on his way to the Feis, a cultural festival, and not to Glenshesk. If all commentators up to the present have had difficulty with the language and the script, how can it be claimed that such entries were forged? There are at least two references to Ua Dubhtaigh in the Casement correspondence. In September 1907 Casement told Mary Hutton of a motor journey he had made in his company, describing him as a Gaelic League Organizer; in 1908 Ua Dubhthaigh, signing himself as Hugh O'Duffy, wrote to Casement, thanking him for a 'princely donation'.[65]

To all of this one would have to add the 'when', 'how' and 'why' questions. Is it credible that the British authorities would have begun forging such a corpus as early as 1914, when they got a first indication of Casement's homosexuality, but in the absence of any indication of the likely progress of the war or of his subsequent movements?[66] Could they possibly have forged such elaborate documents in the short time between the date given for the confiscation of his trunks in 1916 and the circulation of diary material? Is it at all conceivable that the process of forgery continued up to 1959, long after Casement's execution, as has been claimed by a few?[67] Is it credible that limited resources would have been allocated to such a complex enterprise at any of the times mentioned?

The documentation released since the mid 1990s provides a number of pieces of crucial evidence from 1916 on the provenance of the diaries and on the official responses to Casement's sexuality. A report from the Special Branch of the Metropolitan Police in Scotland Yard, dated 22 June 1916, indicated that the police had pieced together a list of Casement's addresses from 1906 to 1914, mainly with the help of his bank, William Deacons. His last London address was 50 Ebury Street and the police report stated that: 'During the month of May 1914 Casement deposited with Mr Germain of 50, Ebury Street, Pimlico. S.W. some boxes containing books, etc. These books which included three diaries for the years 1903, 1910 and 1911, a ledger, an address book and a memorandum book were brought to New Scotland Yard by Mr Germain on the 25th. April, 1916.'[68] After Casement was found guilty on 29 June, a list of his property was compiled, which included all the contents of the boxes brought by Mr Germain. Included were '3 diaries. 1 ledger. 1 address book. 1 memorandum book.'[69] The same police reports attest to the typing up of the 1911 diaries at this time.

A second piece of evidence now available shows that, prior to Casement's execution, the Foreign Office was asked to corroborate selected references from the 1911 Diary and cash ledger. A Home Office minute of August 1916, conscious of the possibility of forgery, summarizes what happened:

A number of entries in these books refer to visits paid by Casement to the Foreign Office, and to correspondence with that Department – incidents which would not be known to anyone contemplating the production of a forgery. Lists containing some of these entries were sent by Sir Ernley Blackwell to the Foreign Office with an inquiry whether they could be verified from Foreign Office records. A number of them were verified – see lists within and Foreign Office notes thereon thereby affording independent evidence of the authenticity of the Diary and Ledger.

The Foreign Office letter returning the annotated entries to Blackwell was written by Rowland Sperling on 2 August, the day before Casement's execution.[70] And there was a related process of verification or reference to the same process. A Scotland Yard Special Branch report, of 17 August 1916, stated that Casement documents on the Putumayo, which came into the possession of the police after his arrest, had been examined: 'During the examination of Casement's diaries and documents nothing has been ascertained to shew that he obtained second hand information and afterwards made to appear as first hand information.'[71]

A third piece of evidence from 1916 is now available and shows attempts at corroboration. This was the identification of one of the sexual partners mentioned in the Black Diaries; the figure of 'Millar', whose name Mackey suggested was the forger's manipulation of 'Bigger', Casement's known friend F.J. Bigger. From diary references, including one in the 1911 Cash Ledger for 3 June, recording the payment of £25 to Cyril Corbally for a motorbike for 'Millar', British intelligence was able to trace the sale and identify the recipient as Joseph Millar Gordon, aged 26, a clerk in the Donegall Square branch of the Belfast Bank, who lived with his mother in Belfast.[72] Thus, one of Casement's sexual partners from the diaries was identified.

Fourthly, we now know that at a 1916 cabinet meeting, which discussed Casement, it was decided to submit the diaries to two alienists (psychiatrists) for an opinion on the writer's mental condition. Drs. R. Percy Smith and Maurice Craig reported on 10 July, giving their opinions on diary materials, which had been shown to them:

> We have read and considered the copies of the diary dated 1st January to 31st December 1911 and of the ledgers [sic] 1st January to 31st October 1911. They contain definite evidence of sexual perversion of a very advanced type in the writer ... There appears to be no evidence of delusion or general intellectual defect, but that he should permit himself to write such compromising and obscene matter in his diary and ledger indicates that the writer was a man whose disordered instinct and feelings influenced and out-weighed his judgement ... Consequently it is our opinion that the writer must be regarded undoubtedly as a mentally abnormal person ... We cannot say that the condition amounted to certifiable insanity, as the facts before us are too meagre, but we are of opinion that his absorption in the subject and at times his conduct suggest much more mental disorder than is usually met with in a person who is suffering only from a perverted instinct.[73]

The significance of the alienists' opinion is not in their, by now, dated judgment on Casement's mental state, but in the fact that copies of the 1911 Diary and ledger were made available to them while Casement was in prison.

Two further pieces of evidence from 1916 have come to light, which support the preceding ones; they relate to Casement's sexuality rather than to the diaries. The first derives from his passage through Christiania in late 1914, when the British representatives at the Christiania legation were made aware of Casement's sexual relationship with Adler Christensen. Further evidence concerning this episode arrived in London in July

1916 as part of the prosecution's preparations for the trial. Among the papers released to the Public Record Office in 1994 was a series of affidavits, eight in all, taken in Christiania in July 1916, which testified to Casement's homosexual behaviour in October 1914. The affidavits were forwarded to London and sent by Thomson to Blackwell on 26 and 27 July 1916. The statements were taken between 11 July and 21 July and the last witness, Gustav Olsen, was, in fact, interviewed in Scotland Yard by Inspector Sandercock, who showed him a photo of Casement, which Olsen identified as that of G.E. Landey [*sic*], who had stayed in the Grand Hotel, Christiania, on 28 October 1914. Olsen stated that he had been employed in the hotel as chief reception clerk; that Casement and Christensen had engaged rooms nos. 442 and 443, which adjoined one another; that the German naval attaché, who was resident in the hotel, had enquired for them about two hours after their arrival. 'I went to room No. 442, allotted to Landey,' his account continued, 'knocked and opened the door without waiting for an answer, and found Landey and Christensen half-naked and in a suggestive position over the bed.'74

The second piece of evidence regarding Casement's sexuality derives from the results of a physical examination carried out by Dr Percy Mander immediately after his execution. Dr Mander reported the results to his superior, Sir Herbert Smalley:

I made the examination which was the subject of our conversation at the Home Office on Tuesday, after the conclusion of the inquest today, and found unmistakeable evidence of the practices to which, it was alleged, the prisoner in question had been addicted. The anus was at a glance seen to be dilated and on making a digital examination (rubber gloves), I found that the lower part of the bowel was dilated as far as the finger could reach. The execution went off without a hitch and prisoner was dead in 40 seconds from leaving the cell. The vertebrae were completely severed and spinal cord also, so that death was absolutely instantaneous.75

As with the opinion of the alienists, the physical examination is significant not in the results as in the fact that it points to the concern of the authorities to try to verify Casement's homosexuality.

Together, therefore, the foregoing materials provide us with: evidence from 1914 and 1916 of Casement's homosexual behaviour during his passage through Christiania; evidence as to how and when the diaries – and all of the now-extant volumes are listed – came into the possession of the authorities in 1916; evidence of the care taken in the Home and Foreign Offices to authenticate the diaries by cross-checking individual entries; an MI5 agent's identification of Casement's Belfast partner, Millar; the submission of the 1911 volumes to two alienists and their judgment on his sexual practices; and the result of a physical examination after his execution. While one may wish to be cautious in interpreting aspects of these materials, overall they lend weight to the case for authenticity. To challenge them would necessitate casting the forgery net wider, to encompass materials other than the diaries, and to suggest that certain branches of the British establishment were themselves taken in by the forgery.

In conclusion, the various pieces of evidence, positive and negative, suggest that the Black Diaries are the work of Roger Casement. When old 'discrepancies' or 'contradictions' have been found to be no longer sustainable, the forgery school has continued to reinvent itself by discovering new ones. Most are either tendentious or amenable to more straightforward explanation; a few remain puzzling. In contrast, it is impossible to imagine how a forger could have produced many entries in the diaries (e.g. Kikongo or Irish language examples), unless genuine Casement diaries existed prior to interpolation. Interpolation, though, seems impossible because of the position in the text of many 'contentious' entries and because of the forensic evidence of the Giles Report. The overall content of the diaries fits comfortably with Casement's movements during the relevant years. And the contrast between the telegrammatic style of the diaries and Casement's more discursive formal style is not surprising: indeed, there are many indications of his imprint in the diaries. The patterns of sexuality revealed in the volumes, though causing shock to many, are familiar to gay observers. Finally, the evidence of documents released in the 1990s and of the Giles Report support a verdict of authenticity.

Notes

PREFACE

1. Rebecca Solnit, 'The butterfly collector' in *A Book of Migrations: Some Passages in Ireland* (London: Verso 1997), p. 29.

2. B.L. Reid, *The Lives of Roger Casement* (New Haven: Yale University Press 1976), p. 8. The period is covered by him on pp. 6–16; by Brian Inglis, *Roger Casement* (London: Coronet Books/Hodder & Stoughton 1974 [1973]), on pp. 24–32; and by Roger Sawyer, *Casement: the Flawed Hero* (London: Routledge 1984), on pp. 20–4.

3. Conrad to Cunninghame Graham, 26/12/1903. For Conrad's letters, see Frederick R. Karl & Laurence Davies (eds.), *The Collected Letters of Joseph Conrad*, vol. 3, 1903–7 (Cambridge: CUP 1988). For Conrad in the Congo see Chapter 2.

4. The term is incorporated into the title of his excellent study by D.C.M. Platt, *The Cinderella Service: British Consuls since 1825* (London: Longman 1971). The discussion in this section draws on Platt's treatment. The consular service had three main divisions, the Far Eastern, the Levant and the General Service. Casement belonged to the last of these. Roger Sawyer was the first biographer to give due weight to Casement's consular role; see, for example, 'Appendix A: Consular Functions in Casement's Day' in Sawyer, *Flawed Hero*, pp. 149–55.

5. I have sketched some patterns in Casement's thinking in Séamas Ó Síocháin, 'Roger Casement's vision of freedom' in Mary E. Daly (ed.), *Roger Casement in Irish and World History* (Dublin: Royal Irish Academy 2005), pp. 1–10.

6. Sir Roger Casement CMG 'Chivalry', *Fianna Handbook* (issued by the Central Council of Na Fianna Éireann for the Boy Scouts of Ireland 1914), p. 75. The notions of chivalry and knighthood reflect Victorian and Edwardian values; the influence of Standish James O'Grady may well be present. Casement drew a different lesson from history in comparing the contest between Germany and England with that

between Rome and Carthage: 'England relies on money. Germany on men. And just as Roman men beat Carthaginian mercenaries, so must German manhood, in the end, triumph over British finance. Just as Carthage in the hours of final shock, placing her gold where Romans put their gods, and never with a soul above her ships, fell before the people of United Italy, so shall the mightier Carthage of the North Sea, in spite of trade, shipping, colonies, the power of the purse and the hired valour of the foreign (Irish, Indian, African), go down before the men of United Germany.' Quoted in Herbert O. Mackey (ed.), *The Crime against Europe: Writings and Poems of Roger Casement* (Dublin: Fallon 1958), pp. 27–8.

7. Martin Daly (pseudonym of Stephen McKenna), *Memories of the Dead: Some Impressions* (Dublin: Powell Press n.d. [1917?]), p. 4.

8. Fred Puleston, *African Drums* (London: Gollancz 1930), pp. 278–9. See also Chapter 2.

9. Reid, pp. xvi, 454; for the theme of dividedness see also Sawyer, *Flawed Hero*, p. 145.

10. Quoted in Reid, p. 15. This is unduly harsh; one can assess it, for example, in light of the 1910 and 1911 writings of Casement published by Mitchell.

11. *Ibid.* pp. 134, 136 and 138.

12. Eduard Meyer, 'Personal Memories', BBAW NL Eduard Meyer 357.

13. Martin Mansergh, 'Roger Casement and the idea of a broader nationalist tradition: his impact on Anglo-Irish relations' in Daly, p. 190.

14. William Roger Louis, 'Roger Casement and the Congo', *Journal of African History*, 5 (1964), 99.

15. Sawyer, *Flawed Hero*, pp. 146–7, and *Roger Casement's Diaries: 1910: The Black and the White* (London: Pimlico 1997), p. 2. For a balanced assessment of Casement's humanitarian contribution, see Andrew Porter, 'Sir Roger Casement and the international humanitarian movement' in Daly, pp. 11–25.

16. Mansergh, p. 192.

17. Lucy McDiarmid, 'The posthumous life of Roger Casement' in A. Bradley and M.G. Valiulis (eds.), *Gender and Sexuality in Modern Ireland* (Amherst: University of Massachussets Press 1997), p. 131. Mary Daly also draws attention to the considerable amount written about him and comments: 'Angus Mitchell's claim that Casement was written out of history until recent times is not borne out by the facts.' Daly, pp. v, vi.

1: EARLY LIFE

1. Roger Casement (RDC) to Gertrude, 1/9/1909, NLI MS 13074(6/i).

2. See Casement Family: Selected Genealogy, p. 4. Among the distinguished Casements were Major-General Sir William Casement KCB (1778–1844), a member of the Supreme Council of India, and Rear-Admiral John Casement of Cushendall

(1854–1910). Roger David Casement refers to both in his correspondence. At a time when he was feeling despondent about affairs in Ireland, he referred to other antecedents, who had fought on the Royalist side in the English Civil War of the 1640s: 'The people are sleeping ... it may be a lost cause – it probably is. I fight with despair in my heart. That matters nothing – it even makes you keener – my ancestors fought Cropredy Bridge for King Charles I and fought as keenly there and then as at Edgehill and Marston – when the cause was not a lost one.' NLI MS 13089(5), partial, undated letter. Edgehill (23/10/1642) and Cropredy Bridge (29/6/1644) were Royalist victories, but Marston Moor (2/7/1644) was a defeat. An extremely valuable source of information on the Casement family is the set of genealogical notes compiled by Hugh Casement and titled 'The Family of Casement of Magherintemple, Ballycastle, Co. Antrim', 1992 (to be cited hereafter as 'Hugh Casement'). The term 'a leading county one' is used of the Casement family in the Royal Irish Constabulary (RIC) dossier on Casement, which was opened in 1914 (PRO CO 904/195). The most thorough use of this and other sources for Roger Casement's family background can be found in Jeffrey Dudgeon, *Roger Casement: The Black Diaries, with a study of his background, sexuality, and Irish political life* (Belfast: Belfast Press 2002).

3. RDC to Edmund Morel (EDM), n.d.[*c*.1905], NLI MS 13080(6/ii).

4. Hugh Casement, p. 19. Roger David entered his grandfather's address in his poem book as 'Castle Casement, Hollywood, Co. Down', NLI MS 12114.

5. Details and sources are given in Peter Singleton-Gates and Maurice Girodias, *The Black Diaries: An Account of Roger Casement's Life and Times with a Collection of his Diaries and Public Writings* (Paris: Olympia Press 1959), p. 38.

6. For more detail, see Séamas Ó Síocháin and Thomas Kabdebo, 'Hungary and the two Roger Casements' in Thomas Kabdebo, *Ireland and Hungary: A Study in Parallels* (Dublin: Four Courts Press 2001), pp. 73–9.

7. NLI MS 13077(3).

8. Dudgeon, p. 52, corrects the hitherto accepted account of a Paris wedding.

9. RDC to Louisa Jephson-Norreys, 1/6/1895, reprinted in Maurice Denham Jephson, *An Anglo-Irish Miscellany; Some Records of the Jephsons of Mallow* (Dublin: Allen Figgis 1964), pp. 295–6.

10. RDC to Louisa Jephson-Norreys, 10/6/1895, *ibid.* p. 261.

11. Brigadier Maurice Denham Jephson to Roger Sawyer, 20/9/1967, quoted in Sawyer, *Flawed Hero*, p. 6. Sawyer stresses the mixed religious and social origins as one source of Casement's divided personality. For further probing see Dudgeon, pp. 53–8.

12. Roger Casement Sr. to John Casement, 24/1/1871, PRONI T3787/1. John was Roger Sr.'s uncle, though younger than him, as Roger of Harryville (see Casement Family: Selected Genealogy, p. 4) had married twice and fathered children to a late age. Following the death in 1863 of Hugh Casement, Roger Sr.'s father, it took many years for his estate to be distributed.

13. Details can be found in the Monteith Papers, Allen Library, Dublin: box 1, fol. 2.

14. Reid, p. 356; PRONI T3072/13.

15. NLI MS 17594 (Nina). Accounts of Casement's early life were written after his death by his sister Agnes (Nina) and by his cousins Gertrude and Elizabeth Bannister. These are to be found in NLI MSS 5588 (Gertrude), 9932 (Nina), 13079 (Gertrude) and 17594 (Nina, Elizabeth, Gertrude). The present account draws heavily on them.

16. Dónall Ó Luanaigh, 'Roger Casement, senior, and the siege of Paris (1870)', *The Irish Sword*, XV (1982–3), 33–5. In Ó Luanaigh's opinion, the letter to Gambetta was not sent, nor were the newspaper letters published. The letter had a London address. The documents are to be found in NLI MS 13077.

17. 'Brief to Counsel', NLI MS 13088(1/iii).

18. TCD Early Printed Books. The books are strongly moralistic in tone, and provide a small clue to the type of value formation that Casement received.

19. Elizabeth Bannister, 'Recollections of Roddie', NLI MS 17594(2). Casement's familiar name appears as 'Roddie' and 'Roddy' (and, sometimes, as 'Scodge'); I have adopted the first form throughout.

20. NLI MSS 9932 (Nina) and 17594 (Gertrude). Giovanni Costigan makes the following observation: 'The existing lives of Casement do not explore the childhood origins of his passionate self-identification with the sufferings of others, although a clue is perhaps afforded by the casual remark of one biographer that his father was so strict a disciplinarian that he would thrash his children for the least breach of rules, and that Roger as a child had resented this.' Giovanni Costigan, 'The treason of Sir Roger Casement', *American Historical Review*, lx (1955), 299. The biographer referred to is Geoffrey de C. Parmiter.

21. RDC to Alfred Emmott, 12/11/1906, Emmott Papers, Nuffield College, Oxford.

22. RDC to Gertrude, Autumn 1913, quoted in René MacColl, *Roger Casement* (London: Four Square Edition 1965 [1956]), p. 96. He was to make similar comments on the need for discipline in the Irish College in Donegal and on the desirability of Germany's applying the rod to South America.

23. NLI MS 9932 (Nina).

24. RDC to Nina, 25/7/1916, NLI MS 13600 (copy).

25. NLI MS 17594 (Elizabeth).

26. NLI MS 13079 (Gertrude).

27. From this evidence Dudgeon (p. 46) deduces that she was an alcoholic: 'Her death certificate ... provides a melancholy explanation both for the silence surrounding her life and the mysteries developed after her death.'

28. Roger Casement Sr. to John Casement, 8/12/1873, PRONI T3787/3. He had aspirations at this time to make his living by writing.

29. NLI MS 13077. Roger Sawyer cites evidence that Casement Sr. held seances in a Ballymena hotel after his wife's death.

30. The dissent had occurred also in the generation before that of Casement's father, in the life of young Hugh in 1798 and after (see n. 45).

31. Roger Sr.'s siblings were not available. He had had one brother and two sisters: Hugh had died in Melbourne in 1861; Agnes and her husband, Dr Thomas Aicken, had emigrated to New Zealand; Eleanor, described as 'a discontented person', married the Revd Somerville Hugh Lampier. She is said to have died c.1865 in New Zealand when staying with the Aickens, while the Revd Lampier is believed to have died by 1878.

32. See Hugh Casement. Katie Pottinger and Anne Coulson were first cousins of Casement's father (Casement Family: Selected Genealogy p. 4). Casement's diaries record him visiting the Pottingers on 29 December 1903 and on 14 June 1910.

33. The 'father's stepbrother' might refer to the Revd Lampier, who did exercise guardianship over the orphaned children. However, he was the husband of Eleanor, Roger Sr.'s sister.

34. Hugh Casement; details of the estate settlement can be found in PRONI T3787/3. Certain sums were also paid to Revd Lampier to repay 'the sums of money he had paid for the maintenance and education of the boys since the death of their father and in providing the two elder boys with suitable outfits for sending them to sea and paying any premium that might be necessary for apprenticing them'. There is also a letter to Charlie and Tom Casement in NLI MS 12114, giving details of New Zealand properties from their grandfather's estate and advising them to sell.

35. The Ballymena Diocesan School was later to become Ballymena Academy. For short histories see the pamphlet by W.H. Mol, *The Ballymena Academy 1828–1978* (Ballymena, privately printed 1978).

36. The Revd Robert King (1815–1900) was born in Cork, educated in Trinity College, Dublin, and ordained in 1841. He was headmaster in Ballymena for forty-two years. He published scholarly work on both religious and Irish themes (including an Irish translation of the Book of Common Prayer). He was a friend of the scholars William Reeves and John O'Donovan. He married Harriette, daughter of the Revd A.G. Stuart, Rector of Kilcoole, Co. Louth, who played an active role in running the school. Casement's 1903 and 1910 diaries record visits to the King family (31 December and 13 June, respectively); see Boyd.

37. NLI MS 17594 (Nina).

38. I take this to be the person whose address has appeared in various accounts of Casement's life as 'Lisnavarna' or 'Lismore'. Casement writes 'Lisdoron', while Slater's Directory for 1894 has 'Lisdoran, Galgorm Road, Ballymena'. I have not been able to determine if she is related to the Youngs of Galgorm Castle.

39. PRO CO 904/195/22989.

40. I am grateful to the Wilkinson family for their help with identifications.

41. RDC to EDM, n.d. [c.1905], NLI MS 13080(6/ii).

42. NLI MS 17594(2) (Elizabeth).

43. The history of Rome was to provide some of the raw material for Casement's later thinking on empire and freedom. With regard to literature in English, Gertrude Bannister preserved, from an old 1881 Smith's Diary of Casement's, a list of his

favourite plays. They include several by Shakespeare (*Merchant of Venice*, *Much Ado about Nothing*, *As You Like It*, *The Comedy of Errors*, *A Midsummer's Night Dream*) and others, such as *Richelieu*, *The Colleen Bawn* and *Arrah na Pogue* (McMullan Papers, Cushendall, Co. Antrim).

44. The letter is reproduced in Geoffrey de C. Parmiter, *Roger Casement* (London: Arthur Barker 1936), pp. 93–5. For Dr King as a Gaelic scholar see Pádraig Ó Snodaigh, *Hidden Ulster: Protestants and the Irish Language* (Belfast: Lagan Press 1995), p. 81. Casement later wrote of King: 'My own old master, the late Revd Robert King ... spoke and knew Irish well – and often preached in Irish in his *Protestant Church* of the Six Towns up in the Derry hills above Maghera and Magherafelt in the '40s.' Undated article, Santos, NLI MS 10880.

45. NLI MS 9932. With reference to the 1798 Rebellion, she tells of a great-grand-uncle of theirs, Dr Casement of Larne, Co. Antrim, 'a bigoted loyalist ... instrumental in sealing the fate of William Orr'. This was Surgeon George Casement (*c*.1745–*c*.1828), who 'narrowly escaped being murdered by rebels'. Significantly, a son of George's (and brother to Major-General Sir William Casement), Hugh (1784–1804), is said to have run away and joined the insurgents. Having then gone to India in the British army, in Ceylon he supported 'the king of Kandy who was holding out against the English'. He was arrested, failed in an escape attempt, and was pardoned because of his youth only to die of fever (Hugh Casement, p.15).

46. RDC to Roger Casement (Magherintemple), 6/6/1916, PRONI T3787/19.

47. If Anne Casement was a music teacher, it is not surprising that she communicated her love for music to the children. In the notes preserved by Gertrude Bannister, Roddie listed his favourite operas; they included *Carmen*, *Mignon*, *Faust*, *Maritana*, *Les Cloches de Corneille* and *Il Trovatore*. And, having met Nina and Roger Casement at a social occasion in Dublin before the First World War, J.R. Clegg wrote that Nina 'sang charmingly, several selections to her own piano accompaniment'. NLI MS 21536.

48. Eva appeared later in Casement's correspondence as Eva Symons, her married name. See Dudgeon, p. 4 and *passim*.

49. Quoted in Inglis, p. 23.

50. NLI MS 9932 (Nina).

51. Not all the poems in Casement's MSS have dates, but it is clear that historical Irish themes were important in 1882 and 1883. In addition to his focus on the sixteenth and seventeenth centuries, there are such poems as 'Cathal More' ('of the wine-red hand', king of Connaught in the thirteenth century), and 'Grattan', referring to Henry Grattan (1746–1820), leader of the Irish Parliament at the end of the eighteenth century. For a detailed analysis, which argues that to understand Casement's local and national identity and his political evolution, his early poetry notebooks must be put at the centre of his story, see Margaret O'Callaghan, ' "With the eyes of another race, of a people once hunted themselves": Casement, colonialism and a remembered past' in Daly, pp. 46–63. She argues (p. 49) that 'the relation-

ship between Casement's British consular career, his mounting anti-imperialism, and his increasingly more self-conscious nationalism, is complicated and dialectical, not linear and sequential'.

52. Reprinted in Mackey, *Crime Against Europe*, p. 201. Casement's later poem on the Ndebele king, Lobengula, is very much in the same genre.

53. *Ibid.* p. 203. The poem begins: 'Och! Portglenone House is the place for the grouse'. Notes to the poem record: 'Written by me when a boy at Portglenone in February, 1883' and 'Record of that day's shooting: seven guns ... 20 pheasants, 2 woodcock, 87 hares, 13 rabbits, and three owls by the keeper.' Portglenone House had been built *c.*1810 by Bishop Alexander. There were close ties between the Alexanders and the Casements; Roddie's uncle Julius is recorded as living there in the mid 1850s. John Alexander may have helped with Casement's early appointments – he is referred to in a letter to John Casement, 2/7/84, PRONI T3787. See Nina's reference, NLI MS 17594. The house seems also, at one point, to have belonged to Miss Annie Young of Galgorm, another friend of the Casements. Mary Alice Young, of Galgorm, wrote: 'Annie Young had gone there at the end of a romance with two old Alexander bachelors. Instead of leaving the place to their next of kin, who fully expected it, they left it to her and she used to have shooting-parties. One day ... we got twenty-three pheasants and thirteen woodcock. She always gave an excellent luncheon and everyone enjoyed going there.' Eull Dunlop (ed.), *The Recollections of Mary Alice Young née Nacnaghten (1867–1946) of Dundarave and Galgorm, Co. Antrim* (Ballymena: Mid-Antrim Historical Group 1996), p. 45.

54. Roger Casement, 'Introduction', *Some Poems of Roger Casement* (Dublin: Talbot Press 1918), p. xi.

55. For his poem on Parnell's death, see NLI MSS 12114 and 12115; it is reproduced in Mackey, *Crime Against Europe*, p. 171.

56. Quoted in Risteárd Giltrap, *An Ghaeilge in Eaglais na hEireann* [*The Irish Language in the Church of Ireland*] (Baile Átha Cliath: Cumann Gaelach na hEaglaise 1990), pp. 60–2. The letter was written in April 1914.

57. Tom Casement to Gertrude Bannister, 5/10/1917, McMullan Papers.

58. NLI MS 17594 (Nina). Singleton-Gates and Girodias, p. 43, suggests that, while in the employ of the Elder Dempster Company in Liverpool, the young man had come close to dismissal by his employer, Sir Alfred Jones. Sir Alfred Lewis Jones (1845–1909) was a prominent businessman and partner in the shipping company of Elder Dempster. He helped found the Liverpool School of Tropical Medicine in 1898 and was knighted in 1901. He was to become a major defender of King Leopold's regime in the Congo and, as such, was vigorously opposed by both Casement and Morel.

59. *New York Times*, 25 April, 1916, quoted in W.M. Maloney, *The Forged Casement Diaries* (Dublin: Talbot Press 1936), p. 126.

60. Ada (or Íde) MacNeill (1860–1959) was born in London, of Protestant parents. Her paternal grandfather was a native Irish-speaker and she became interested in the

language herself. She was to be a key person in the Feis of the Glens and in the founding of Coláiste Uladh, the Irish-language college in Donegal, established in 1906. She was a watercolourist of talent and exhibited in Belfast in 1913.

61. 'Recollections of Ada MacNeill', 1929, McMullan Papers. The following extracts are all taken from this source.

62. In addition to the presence of a significant library on Irish matters, the changing, at some point, of the family seat's name from Churchfield to Magherintemple (Machaire an Teampaill, 'the plain/field of the temple/church') suggests an engagement with the Irish past among the Casements.

63. RDC to John Casement, 20/6/1884, PRONI T3787.

64. RDC (from the *Bonny*) to John Casement, 2/7/1884, PRONI T3787.

2: THE CONGO FREE STATE, 1884–91

1. Henry Morton Stanley (1841–1904) was born John Rowlands and brought up in a Welsh workhouse. He ran away to the US in 1859, where he was adopted by and took the name of a New Orleans merchant. He was, successively, a Confederate soldier during the Civil War, a seaman and a journalist; the *New York Herald* sent him to Africa to find Livingstone and the two met at Ujiji on 10 November 1871.

2. Quoted in Frank Pakenham, *The Scramble for Africa, 1876–1912* (London: Weidenfeld & Nicolson 1991), p. 12.

3. Leopold II (1835–1909) was king of the Belgians from 1865 until his death. For his colonial ambitions, see Jean Stengers, 'King Leopold's imperialism' in Roger Owen & Bob Sutcliffe (eds.), *Studies in the Theory of Imperialism* (London: Longmans 1972), pp. 248–76.

4. For general surveys of the history of the Congo Free State see, for example, Pakenham, *Scramble for Africa*; S.J.S. Cookey, *Britain and the Congo Question: 1885–1913* (London: Longmans 1968); Peter Forbath, *The River Congo* (London: Secker & Warburg 1978); Ruth Slade, *King Leopold's Congo* (Oxford: OUP 1962); Adam Hochschild, *King Leopold's Ghost: A Story of Greed, Terror and Heroism in Colonial Africa* (London: Macmillan 1999 [1998]).

5. I use the terms Lower and Upper Congo to refer to the river below and above Leopoldville/Kinshasa, respectively, rather than the terms Lower, Middle and Upper, sometimes employed. I have used placenames current among Europeans at the time, which appear in variable spellings.

6. Forbath, p. 15.

7. E.J. Glave, *Six Years of Adventure in Congo-Land* (London: Sampson Low, Marston & Co. 1893), p. 32; Herbert Ward, *A Voice from the Congo: Comprising Stories, Anecdotes and Descriptive Notes* (London: Heinemann 1910), pp. 119–22 and 187–92.

8. Sir Francis De Winton (1835–1901) entered the Royal Artillery and served in the Crimean War, in North America and various part of Africa, before becoming

administrator general of the Congo from 1885 to 1886. In 1887 he became secretary of the Emin Pasha Relief Committee. He was sent to Swaziland as commissioner in 1889 and retired from the army in 1890.

9. Henry Shelton Sanford (1823–91), entrepreneur and diplomat, founded the town of Sanford, Florida, and served in St Petersburg (1847), Frankfurt (1848) and Paris (1849). He was minister resident in Belgium for seven years (from 1861), became a member of the executive of the IAA and was an associate delegate at the Berlin Conference, where he furthered Leopold's cause.

10. The figures are from Sigbert Axelson, *Culture Confrontation in the Lower Congo: From the Old Congo Kingdom to the Congo Independent State with Special Reference to the Swedish Missionaries in the 1880s and 1890s* (Studia Missionalia Upsaliensia XIV, Falköping, Sweden: Gummesons 1970). See also C.H. Stuart, 'The Lower Congo and the American Baptist Union to 1910' (Ph.D. dissertation, Boston University Graduate School 1969), and Wyatt MacGaffey, 'Ethnography and the closing of the frontier in the Lower Congo, 1885–1921', *Africa*, 56 (3) (1986), 263–79, and his *Custom and Government in the Lower Congo* (Berkeley: UCP 1970). Axelson and Stuart have good treatments of the transport system and its problems.

11. MacGaffey, 'Ethnography', p. 266.

12. Axelson, p. 257.

13. *Biographie Coloniale Belge* (*BCB*), 1 (Bruxelles: Institut Royal Colonial Belge), cols. 220–1.

14. RDC to EDM, 27/6/1904 and 15/3/1905, LSE MP F8/17 and F8/18.

15. W.G. Parminter (1850–94) joined the British army in 1876 and served with distinction in southern Africa. When he went to the Congo, he served with Stanley and the Congo State and carried out De Winton's functions in the latter's absence. He later joined the Sanford Exploring Expedition as one of its directors, and afterwards the Société Anonyme Belge.

16. RDC to Fritz Pincus, 5/4/1899, TCD 827.

17. On his final journey through the Congo, Glave wrote a diary which included criticisms of the State policies. It was published and afterwards included in H.R. Fox Bourne's *Civilization in Congoland: a Story of International Wrong-doing* (London: P.S. King and Son 1903).

18. 'We are willing to enlist Mr Ward on the same terms which we now impose on all our candidates. These terms are as follows: £72 to £80 a year, with promise of promotion if we are satisfied with them.' Quoted in Sarita Ward, *A Valiant Gentleman – being the biography of Herbert Ward, Artist and Man of Action* (London: Chapman & Hall 1927), p. 41. Sidney Pawling, a fellow pupil at Mill Hill School in the 1870s, described Ward (1866–1938) as 'a well-knit figure, with unusually deep chest and broad shoulders, deep-set blue eyes wide apart, and a remoteness, almost shyness, of manner bespeaking a reticence not perhaps in accord with the accepted convention of public school life'. Before arriving on the Congo, Ward had spent three years in the 'university of life' as a sailor, kauri-gum digger, coal and gold miner,

sailmaker, gymnast in a travelling circus and stock-rider. Herbert Ward, *Mr Poiliu: Notes and Sketches with the fighting French* (London: Hodder & Stoughton 1916). Ward became a very successful sculptor afterwards and moved to Paris.

19. Ward, *Voice from the Congo*, pp. 206–7.

20. NLI MS 9932 (Nina), p. 120. I take this description to apply to their shared period on the caravan road with the Sanford Exploring Expedition, but it could also apply to this first employment.

21. Puleston, pp. 278–9.

22. *Ibid.* p. 40. A slip of paper in the Casement Papers, Farmleigh House, Dublin, tells that Casement was called *Mbendi*, 'a spotted rat', in the Congo, 'because he walked so fast and disappeared'; he was also called *Matota*, 'the man who picks up something owing to his peculiar way of picking up carriers'.

23. RDC to Dandelman, 10/5/1915, NLI MS 5459. The article Dandelman sent was 'Der Bankrott der Kongoakte', *Deutsche Reveu*, Mai 1915. Hermann von Wissmann (1853–1905) made several extended explorations of Central Africa. His second expedition started from Loanda in January 1884, explored the Kasai region and followed its course to the Congo river. He reached Leopoldville in the spring of 1885. After recuperating in Madeira, he returned to the Congo in February 1886. It is at this point that Casement is likely to have met him. *BCB*, 1, col. 973.

24. RDC (Rio) to Major Berry, 9/9/1909, Casement Papers.

25. The following account of the history of the SEE is taken from James P. White, 'The Sanford exploring expedition', *Journal of African History*, VIII (2) (1967), 291–302, and Joseph A. Fry, *Henry S. Sanford: Diplomacy and Business in Nineteenth Century America* (Reno: University of Nevada Press 1982), pp. 156–63.

26. At this time there were three settlements adjacent to one another at Stanley Pool: Ndolo, Kinshasa and Leopoldville.

27. Emin Pasha (1840–92) was a German explorer and scientist. Born Eduard Schnitzer, he made a career in the Sudan, where he was appointed governor of Equatoria province in southern Sudan. When he was cut off by the Mahdist revolt and believed to be in danger, an expedition was mounted to rescue him. Somewhat reluctantly, he left with the rescuers, but was murdered by Arab slave traders in 1892. The fate of the expedition itself was disastrous.

28. Taunt to Sanford, 22/8/1886, Sanford Papers (SanP), box 28, fol. 1.

29. Taunt to Stanford, Matadi, 12/9/1886, SanP, box 28, fol. 1.

30. Taunt to Sanford, 24/9/1886, SanP, box 28, fol. 1.

31. Parminter to Sanford, 14/10/1886, SanP, box 26, fol. 7.

32. Swinburne to Sanford, 17/11/1886, SanP, box 27, fol. 14. He asked if representations could be made in Brussels to improve matters.

33. Taunt to Sanford, 15/2/1887, SanP, box 28, fol. 3.

34. Weber, 23/4/1887, SanP, box 23, fol. 9. See also Parminter, 26/6/1887, SanP, box 26, fol. 7.

35. James P. White, 298.

36. RDC to Richard Morten, 28/7/1916, quoted in Reid, p. 437. The complete letter is reproduced in H. Montgomery Hyde, *Famous Trials: Roger Casement* (Harmondsworth, Middlesex: Penguin 1964 [1960]), pp. 147–9.

37. Herbert Ward, *Voice from the Congo*, p. 131. Georg Schweinfurth (1836–1925) carried out extensive explorations in north-east Africa, especially in the Sudan. His most famous book was *The Heart of Africa: Three Years' Travels & Adventures in the Unexplored Regions of Central Africa from 1868 to 1871*, 2 vols. (London: Sampson Low, Marston, Low & Searle 1873).

38. Rothkirch to Parminter, 10/3/1887 (continued on 13/3 and 14/3), SanP, box 26, fol. 14.

39. Dorothy Middleton (ed.), *The Diary of A.J. Mounteney Jephson, Emin Pasha Relief Expedition 1887–89* (Cambridge: CUP 1969), pp. 87–8. Arthur J. Mounteney Jephson (1858–1908) published *Emin Pasha and the Rebellion at the Equator* (1890) and an edition of native folk tales; he was appointed Queen's messenger in 1895. The Mounteney Jephsons were an English branch of the Jephson family of Mallow.

40. Walter George Barttelot, *The Life of Edmund Musgrave Barttelot*, 3rd edn. (London: R. Bentley & Sons 1890), p. 85.

41. Barttelot, pp. 86–7; Middleton, p. 91.

42. Middleton, pp. 91–2.

43. Frank McLynn, *Stanley: Sorceror's Apprentice* (London: Constable 1991), pp. 171, 174. Casement was to write to Stanley on 28 June 1890 sharing his impressions about changes in the Congo and expressing optimism about the prospects for an English trading company there: Stanley Papers (unclassified), Brussels, Tervuren.

44. RDC to Dandelman, 10/5/1915, NLI MS 5459.

45. RDC, Memo to FO, 14/1/1904, PRO FO, 10/807. Emile Francqui (1863–1935), born in Brussels, was an officer, consul, banker and liberal politician. He explored Katanga, fought the Mahdists and went to China, before returning home to become involved in finance. He was Belgian minister for finance in 1926.

46. Weber to Sanford (?), 17/4/1887 and 6/7/1887, SanP, box 23, fols. 9 and 10.

47. Swinburne to Weber, 30/5/1887, 16/7/1887 and March 1888, SanP, box 27, fol. 14.

48. Weber to Sanford (?), 6/7/1887, SanP, box 23, fol. 10.

49. RDC to EDM, 27/6/1904, LSE MP F8/17.

50. RDC to FO, 14/1/1904, PRO FO 10/807. Casement also referred to this encounter in a letter to Farnall of the FO on 18/7/1903 (NLI MS 13080 6/i), in which he stated that van Kerckhoven was an Inspecteur d'État. Van Kerckhoven is also mentioned in a memo on atrocities by Mr de Bernhardt, PRO FO 10/754, 28/10/1900. He later led an expedition to the Upper Nile, where he was accidentally shot dead on 4 October 1892 (Pakenham, *Scramble for Africa*, pp. 435–6).

51. See Chapter 8. The references are in the 1903 Diary and in the Congo Report: see PRO HO 161/2, and Séamas Ó Síocháin and Michael O'Sullivan (eds.), *The Eyes of Another Race: Roger Casement's Congo Report and 1903 Diary* (Dublin: UCD Press 2003).

52. Glave to Sanford, 30/12/1887, SanP, box 24, fol. 19.

53. Weber to ?, n.d. (with reference to a letter from Major Parminter of 10/2/88), SanP,

box 23, fol. 11. The second letter was written on 16/2/1888: 'Swinburne and Casement went up the Kassai, Casement to take over Luebo – Swinburne to try the rivers.'

54. RDC to EDM, 27/6/1904, LSE MP F8/17.

55. *Ibid.*

56. RDC to Sanford, 27/8/1888, SanP, box 22, fol. 5.

57. Herbert Ward, *Five Years with the Congo Cannibals* (London: Chatto and Windus 1890), pp. 94–102; cf. Glave, pp. 245–6.

58. For this section I have drawn on Axelson and Stuart as well as on Ruth Slade, *English-Speaking Missions in the Congo Independent State (1878–1908)*, (Brussels: Académie Royale des Sciences Coloniales 1959). The phrase 'missionary scramble' is from Axelson, p. 206.

59. H. Grattan Guinness (1835–1910), minister and author, was born in Kingstown (Dún Laoghaire), near Dublin. He became an evangelical minister and preached extensively in Britain, Ireland, continental Europe and North America. He founded the Livingstone Inland Mission in 1878 as well as other missionary organizations, all of which were amalgamated into the 'Regions Beyond Missionary Union' in 1899.

60. Slade, *Missions*, pp. 49 and 80–5. Grenfell published a chart of the Congo River for the Royal Geographical Society in 1887.

61. *Ibid.* p. 231.

62. Notebook 1, 1/6/1888, 'Journals of A.D. Slade', Baptist Missionary Society Archives (to be cited hereafter as BMSA), (Oxford 1907).

63. Notebook 1, 26/8/1888, Journals of A.D. Slade', BMSA. Slade died on 20 December, before Casement took up his duties. Michael Richards, another missionary friend of his, had died on 19 August.

64. Bentley described his own experiences in *Pioneering on the Congo*, 2 vols. (London: Religious Tract Society 1900), and in *Life on the Congo* (London: Religious Tract Society n.d.) He went to the Congo in 1879, as one of the pioneer missionaries, and was later stationed at Wathen, 'where he did considerable translation and linguistic work, as well as missionary duties'. Glasgow University gave him a DD in 1905. He died the same year (*Baptist Handbook*, BMSA, p. 447).

65. The reference is to A.J. Mounteney Jephson, though any relationship with Casement would have been extremely distant.

66. Bentley to Baynes, 29/11/1888, BMSA A/31. Theodore Hoste was to become a close friend of Casement's. It was a letter from him that stimulated the writing of Casement's poem 'Lost Youth'; see Mackey, *Crime against Europe*, p. 168. According to Casement, Hoste had been a lieutenant in the British navy and gave up his commission to become a missionary in the Congo (LSE MP F8/16, 18/1/1904). He was one of the last batch of Livingstone Inland Mission members to be sent in 1884, when the LIM handed over the Lower Congo to the American Baptist Missionary Union (ABMU). It seems that he arrived in order to serve as captain of the steamer *Henry Reed*. But, in fact, he became senior missionary at Lukunga and

played a number of key roles there, particularly in education and transport. He was a dominant personality and reversed the earlier heavy reliance on outside support for the station by attempting to make it more self-sufficient. After a continuous service of twelve years, he departed the Congo in July 1896, being in his own words 'a broken-down man'. In the absence of his strong leadership, Lukunga declined after his departure (Stuart, pp. 289–91).

67. Bentley, Journal, 30/12/1888, BMSA A/30; letter to wife, Margo, 28–31/12/1888, BMSA A/34.

68. Bentley, Journal, 6/1/1889, BMSA A/30: 'Oran and Casement to Ewombe (35–60), Nkuku Kimbanda, Ntetela – Limoresu [?], Kindingu (10) and Manteva (10).'

69. RDC to Bentley, n.d., BMSA A/34.

70. Bentley to Baynes, 29/4/1889, BMSA A/31. Many years later, in the year of Bentley's death, Casement recalled his stay at Wathen in a letter to Bentley: 'I hope Mrs Bentley and your family are with you and that you are all well and happy. I often think of the pleasant days at Ngombe in your hospitable kindly home – and I beg that when you return to Africa you will bear a word of greeting from Matota to all his old friends – white and brown.' RDC to Bentley, 23/8/1905, BMSA A/34.

71. RDC to EDM, 27/6/1904, LSE MP F8/17.

72. *Ibid.*

73. NLI MS 12114.

74. RDC to Gertrude, 23/10/1889, NLI MS 13074 (1/i). A later comment suggests he visited Baronstown, Co. Meath, in November 1889.

75. Reid, p.16. On his voyage to the US, Ward met Sarita Sanford, whom he would soon marry. Sarita Ward, pp. 124–5. She was the daughter of C.H. Sanford of New York, no relation of General Sanford's. Of her future husband's lecturing at home, she wrote that there was 'not a town of any size or importance in England, Scotland, Wales or Ireland that he did not visit', *ibid.* p. 136.

76. Charles E. Curry (ed.), *Sir Roger Casement's Diaries: His Mission to Germany and the Findlay Affair* (Munich: Arche Publishing Co. 1922), p. 25.

77. Taunt to Sanford, 13/11/1889, SanP box 28, fol. 5.

78. NLI MS 5463.

79. RDC to EDM, 27/6/1904, LSE MP F8/17.

80. *Ibid.* Albert Thys (1849–1915) participated in the planning of many of the IAA's expeditions to the Congo, before going to the Congo himself in 1887. He played a key role in the many ventures of the Compagnie du Congo pour le Commerce et l'Industrie and later founded the Société Anonyme Belge. Thysville was named after him in 1904.

81. RDC to FO, 30/6/1902, PRO FO 403/327. Reginald Heyn (1860–92), Nina writes, was the 'only son of a wealthy Belgian merchant whose wife, strange to say, came from Carrickfergus. Young Heyn was a charming man and a devoted friend. Years later when he persisted in returning to the Congo against doctor's orders, he died in my brother's arms, of malarial fever' (NLI MS 9932, p. 120). However, the date

of Heyn's death is elsewhere given as 2 June 1892, when Casement was not present on the Congo. *BCB*, 1, col. 508.

82. Teodor Josef Konrad Korzeniowski (1857–1924) was born in Poland of an aristocratic family and went to sea as a young man, joining first the French, and later the British, merchant marine. He became a ship's master in 1886 and voyaged to the Malay archipelago in 1886 and 1887, before taking a position as steamer captain on the Congo. He gave up the sea in 1894 to write full-time. He became one of the most famous English novelists of his day. *Almayer's Folly* (1895) was followed by *Lord Jim* (1900), *Nostromo* (1904) and *The Secret Agent* (1907). *Heart of Darkness*, based on his Congo experience, was published in 1902.

83. Zdzislaw Najder (ed.), *Congo Diary and Other Uncollected Pieces by Joseph Conrad* (Garden City, NY: Doubleday 1978), p. 7.

84. Karl and Davies, vol. 5, 1912–16, pp. 596–7.

85. Conrad to Graham, 26/12/03, Karl and Davies, pp. 100 ff.

86. After he reached Stanley Pool, Conrad left immediately for the upper river on the *Roi des Belges*. He returned at the end of September, ill, to Kinshasa, where he remained until abandoning his Congo venture in early December. It is conceivable, but unlikely, that he met Casement in that latter period. His account, in any case, creates a false impression.

87. RDC to Gertrude, 4/9/1890, NLI MS 13074 (1/i).

88. 'Au cours de ce troisième terme, Casement déploie une grande activité; il établit une factorerie à Kimpese, puis à Luvituku, organise les transports dans la région des chutes et se fait classer par les dirigeants de la Société comme "agent exceptionnel".' *BCB*, 1, col. 219.

89. RDC, undated article, Santos, MacNeill Papers, NLI MS 10880. He further added that in 1889, in the Inishowen Peninsula, he heard only Irish, indicating that he had visited the area that year also.

90. NLI MSS 12114, 12115 and 13082 (2/i–vii) contain Casement's poems, only some of which are dated. His comment from 1916 is found in his 'Brief to Counsel', NLI MS 13088 (1/iii).

91. NLI MS 12114 has two poems on Montreux, dated 14/3/1892 and 21/3/1892 (signed, 'R.C. Montreux and Les Avants, March 21 1892'). See 'Evening and Night: Montreux' in Mackey, *Crime Against Europe*, p. 214.

92. Ward to RDC, 16/5/1892, NLI MS 13073 (46/xviii).

3: THE NIGER COAST PROTECTORATE, 1892–5

1. List of Officers, PRO FO 403/200, Inclosure 158, p. 283. Casement had not yet begun to build up that circle of friends with whom he would later carry on a vigorous correspondence, so, as with his first years in the Congo, we have compara-

tively few letters of his from this period. But, because he was in the employ of the British government, some of his activities can be traced in the official archive material in the Public Record Office (PRO) in London. Most interestingly, these records give details of various exploratory journeys he made while a member of the protectorate Survey Department. The extent and detail of those journeys has hitherto not been appreciated, and a series of maps based on them has scarcely been referred to at all.

2. RDC to EDM, 26/4/1904, MP F8/17. Casement's superior in the Niger Protectorate was Sir Claude MacDonald (1852–1915), who entered the army (74th Highlanders) in 1872, and retired in 1891. He was appointed HM Commissioner for West Coast of Africa in December 1888 and sent on a special mission to the Niger Territories in June 1889, following which he was appointed commissioner and consul general of the Oil Rivers Protectorate in 1891. He became envoy extraordinary and minister plenipotentiary to the emperor of China in 1896 and organized the defence of the legation at Peking during the Boxer Rebellion in 1900. He was made minister to Tokyo in 1900 and ambassador from 1905–16.

3. For the history of the period see J.C. Anene, *Southern Nigeria in Transition, 1885–1906* (Cambridge: CUP 1966); Arthur Norton Cook, *British Enterprise in Nigeria* (London: Frank Cass 1964); Michael Crowder, *West Africa under Colonial Rule* (London: Hutchinson, 1968).

4. Anene, p. 112.

5. Crowder, p. 121. Sir Harry Johnston (1858–1927), explorer, administrator and scholar, was vice-consul in the Niger Delta, 1885, and later held a series of colonial appointments in Central and East Africa. He had wide scientific and artistic interests, and his studies spanned the areas of natural history, geography, ethnology and linguistics. Among his many publications were: *The River Congo, from its Mouth to Bolobo* (1884); *The Uganda Protectorate: an attempt to give some description of the physical geography, botany, zoology, anthropology, languages & history of the territories under British protection in East Central Africa*, 2 vols. (1902); *The Living Races of Mankind* (1905); *The Negro in the New World* (1910); *A Survey of the Ethnography of Africa: and the former racial and tribal migrations in that continent* (1913); *A Comparative Study of the Bantu and Semi-Bantu Languages*, 2 vols. (1919). He was to be become an acquaintance of Casement's, mainly concerning the Congo campaign.

6. MacDonald to Rosebery, 12/1/1893, PRO FO 2/51 p. 12. Archibald Philip Primrose, the 5th Earl of Rosebery (1847–1929), was a statesman, notable orator and racehorse owner. He was a liberal imperialist, Secretary of State for Foreign Affairs in 1886 and 1892 and he succeeded Gladstone as Prime Minister in 1894. His government only lasted fifteen months. In 1896, he resigned the leadership of the Liberal Party.

7. *Ibid*. p.14.

8. Sir Claude MacDonald, Annual Report for 1894–5, 25/7/1895, PRO FO 403/216, no. 57 p.114. Captain Alan Boisragon was head of the protectorate military force. Later, as one of only two Englishmen to survive the event, he was to publish *The*

Benin Massacre (London 1897); see Crowder, p. 123. Boisragon was to reappear in Casement's life in 1911.

9. RDC to Gertrude, 28/7/1892, NLI MS 13074 (1/i), Lagos Roads. It was on this voyage that he met Miss Louisa Jephson-Norreys, of the Jephson family of Mallow Castle, in 'the Hotel at Las Palmas'. He was to write to her subsequently, in 1895, enquiring about his mother's connections with the Jephsons of Mallow (see Chapter 1 and below). On 26 August, he sent a hurried note from Old Calabar to his Aunt Charlotte in Magherintemple, asking her to read and forward a letter to his uncle, Jack (RDC to Charlotte Casement, 26/8/1892, PRONI T 3787/6). Kru or Kroo was an ethnic category from the Liberian coast area and there are frequent references in Casement's writings to Kroomen or Krooboys working along the coast of West and Central Africa.

10. MacDonald, Annual Report for 1891, PRO FO 84/2194.

11. PRO FO 84/2194.

12. *Ibid*.

13. RDC to John Casement, 27/1/1893, PRONI T3787/8. He addresses it from 'H.B.M.'s Vice-Consulate, Old Calabar'. The wedding of (Rear Admiral) Jack Casement and Maria (Mya) Young, of Galgorm Castle, Ballymena, took place on 23 December 1892.

14. S.A. Bill, Diary, Aug. 1891–Aug. 1894, PRONI D3301/CA/7, entries from 24–8 October 1892; Qua Iboe Mission 'Occasional Paper', May 1893, p. 46.

15. Bill, Diary, entries from 17 to 25/12/1892, 29/12/1892, 4 and 18/1/1893, and 13/2/1893, PRONI D3301/CA/7.

16. Revd William Marwick, Pocket Diary, 1892, UE, Marwick 768/3.

17. Elizabeth Marwick, Diary (Old Calabar), 1893, UE, Gen. 768/7.

18. RDC to William Marwick, 24/4/1893, NLS MS 2984 f107.

19. UE, Gen. 768/7.

20. RDC to Gertrude, 2/9/1893, NLI MS 13,074 (1/i).

21. RDC to John Casement, 10/10/1893, PRONI T3787/9.

22. RDC to John Casement, 11/10/1893, PRONI T3787/10.

23. RDC to Gertrude, 6/11/1893, NLI MS 13074 (1/i). Reginald Heyn had died in the Congo in June 1892; this visit would have been to the family. In his letter to Gertrude, he also launched into a series of sarcastic comments on 'the graces of German civilisation and character', interesting in the light of his later pro-German views.

24. Leander Starr Jameson (1853–1917) was born in Edinburgh, took an MD in London in 1877 and went to Kimberley in 1878, where he formed a friendship with Cecil Rhodes. He represented the British South Africa Company in negotiations with Lobengula (1889–90) and was part of the force sent against him in 1893. He led the famous raid across the Transvaal border in support of the *Uitlanders* in December 1895; after his capture, he was sent to England for trial and imprisoned, but quickly released. He entered the Cape parliament as member for Kimberley (1900), became Prime Minister of the Cape Colony (1904–8) and entered the first Union

parliament (1910). He was made baronet in 1911 and retired in 1912. For the Jameson Raid see Chapter 4.

25. Mackey, *Crime against Europe*, p. 178.

26. RDC to John Casement, 14/12/1893, PRONI T3787/11.

27. NLI MS 13082 (1/i). While the date of his visit to Fernando Po is uncertain, this is the likeliest occasion for it to have taken place. Stephen Gwynn, in his *Life of Mary Kingsley* (London: Macmillan & Co. 1932), cites her acknowledgment that Casement had been one of those to climb another mountain in the region, the Peak of Cameroon (Mungo), before she did. That he did climb it seems corroborated by lines in Casement's poem 'The Peak of the Cameroons': 'For thus, by the Dualla, art thou seen,/Home of a God they know, yet would not know;/But I, who far above their doubts have been/Upon thy forehead hazardous ...' (Mackey, *Crime against Europe*, p. 165).

28. In his 'Brief to Counsel', in May 1916, Casement used the term 'travelling commissioner' of his position in the protectorate. It appears to be his term; official lists include him as a member of the Survey Department. NLI MS 13088 (1/iii).

29. PRO FO 2/50, p. 14.

30. *Ibid.* pp. 23, 278.

31. The sketch maps are to be found in PRO MPK 141, 1–3 and PRO FO 2/64, fols. 30A, 30B, 72; the lithograph versions are in FO 925/621, 622 and 623. They are also referenced in the following: A. Crispin Jewitt, *Maps for Empire; The First 2000 Numbered War Office Maps 1881–1905* (The British Library 1992), nos. 1054–6; *Maps and Plans in the PRO*, vol. 3, Africa (1982), nos. 2090–2; R.V. Tooley, *A Dictionary of Mapmakers Part II* (Map Collectors Series no. 28 1979). To observe how Casement's work was incorporated into later maps, see, for example, *Map of the South-Eastern Portion of the Niger Coast Protectorate*, compiled by Captain C.F. Close RE, 1895, Bodleian Library, Oxford, Maps 20752 a.22.

32. *Report on the Administration of the Niger Coast Protectorate, August 1891 to August 1895*, Africa no. 1 (1895), London: HMSO, Inclosure 18, p. 43.

33. RDC to John Casement, PRONI T 3787/7. This letter is dated 2/1/1893, but I am sure the year is 1894 – an error by Casement.

34. *Report on the Administration of the Niger Coast Protectorate, August 1891 to August 1895*, Africa no. 1 (1895), London: HMSO, pp. 27–8. Billington's observations are in Inclosures 11 to 13. The report was printed and presented to both Houses of Parliament and, since it incorporated two of his accounts, it brought Casement to the attention of a wider audience. The report is also contained in FO 403/200.

35. Casement's account, written on 10 April, became Inclosure 17 in MacDonald's 1891–4 Report to the Foreign Office. It and the third journey were included in the version presented to Parliament.

36. Casement's account, written on 2 May, became Inclosure 18 in MacDonald's 1891–4 Report.

37. Though the journey was in May and Casement's report dated 6 June, MacDonald

seems to have received it too late to be incorporated into his 1891–4 Report, which he submitted in August. He subsequentely forwarded it to the FO on 22/9/1894, as Inclosure 135 in MacDonald No. 45. On 10 October, a FO official wrote to Mac-Donald, indicating that he was 'directed by the Earl of Kimberley' to acknowledge receipt of the report and continuing that 'I am to state that the interesting report by Mr Roger Casement of his journey from Okoyon to Okurike therein contained has been read with interest', PRO FO F2/62. Available as a 'Confidential Print', it would have been seen by senior officials in the FO and other government departments.

38. MacDonald to FO, 12/10/1893, PRO FO 403/187, p. 245.

39. PRO FO 881/6546 and FO 2/64. Casement wrote his account on 4 July and Mac-Donald forwarded it to the FO on 13/9/1894. It also became a Confidential Print. The death of Lalor from wounds was reported on 6 September that same year.

40. A map in P. Amaury Talbot, *The Peoples of Southern Nigeria* (London: Humphrey Milford 1926), first published in 1913, shows that by that date a road had, in fact, been constructed between Oron and Eket.

41. These are Casement's first recorded comments on rubber, a crop that was to be of immense significance in his life.

42. Henry Richard Fox Bourne (1837–1909), social reformer and author, was born in Jamaica and served as secretary of the Aborigines Protection Society from 1889 until his death. He also wrote lives of Sir Philip Sidney (1862) and John Locke (1876).

43. RDC to Fox Bourne, 7/2/1894, Brit. Mus. Add. MS 46,912M (NLI n. 1154, p. 1355). In a postscript, he reminded Bourne that he had written from St Thomas's Hospital, London. He had hoped, but found it impossible, to visit and talk to Bourne after his release from hospital. This would have been in October 1893.

44. MacDonald to FO, 6/12/1894, PRO FO 403/215.

45. RDC to MacDonald, 24/11/1894, PRO FO F2/64.

46. *Ibid.*

47. RDC to MacDonald, 4/12/1894, PRO FO 2/64. MacDonald reported the episode to the FO on 6 December and the action taken was approved by the FO on 19/1/1895 (FO 403/215).

48. NLI MS 13082 (i/i). I would judge the article to have been drafted not too long after Casement's Niger employment.

49. MacDonald's Annual Report for 1891–4, pp. 7–8, draws specific attention to the 'evils' of cannibalism, putting to death of twins, human sacrifice (usually crucifixion) at the death of chiefs, trial by ordeal (usually poison) and witchcraft. To these he added the 'evils of the liquor traffic'.

50. A.C. Douglas, *Niger Memories* (Exeter: John Townsend & Sons 1927). Quotations are from pp. 18–27. He used 'Nemo' as a nickname for himself. The account, of course, was written many years after the events.

51. George C. Digan is given as 'Assistant to Vice-Consul' and 'Consular Agent' in listings from 1894.

52. A photograph survives of the party, with Casement and other consular staff. There are a few scattered references to Mary Kingsley in Casement's writings; in 1905, for example, she figures in an exchange of letters with Sir Harry Johnston: Johnston to RDC, 3/4/1905, NLI MS 13073 (30/ii). Her thinking ('Kingsleyism') had a considerable influence on Casement's friend E.D. Morel, and it is interesting to speculate whether it had any on Casement himself; see Catherine Cline, *E.D. Morel 1873-1924: The Strategies of Protest* (Belfast: Blackstaff Press 1980).

53. Maloney, p. 127.

54. RDC to William Cadbury, 19/2/1912, NLI MS 8358. I do not know if Casement's 1901 letter has survived.

55. Sir Ralph Moor (1860–1909) was appointed commandant of the constabulary in the Oil Rivers Protectorate in 1891, vice-consul in 1892 and consul in 1896. He served as commissioner and consul general of the newly formed Niger Coast Protectorate from 1896 to 1900 and as first high commissioner of Southern Nigeria from 1900 to 1903.

56. In a letter to Casement in 1904, J. Frederick Roberts, British consul general in Barcelona and a former associate of Casement's in the protectorate, wrote: 'Moor I have not seen since I left the Coast. I never liked him ...' He suggested that Moor served his own ends, turned MacDonald against him (Roberts) and was 'jealous of my popularity among the natives and traders in the Protectorate'. Roberts to RDC, 19/12/1904, NLI MS 13073 (14). Casement commented that 'Moor was often a hard-hearted chief – and where he took dislike he was a relentless pursuer of his prey.' RDC to EDM, 14/1/1905, MP F8/20. For the historical background, see Crowder, and Anene.

57. 'Brief to Counsel', NLI MS 13088 1/iii. Reid (pp. 20–1) identifies this missionary as Theodore Hoste, and the identification seems plausible, but ABMU records suggest that Hoste only left the Congo, reluctantly and after a long service, in July 1896. Stuart; ABMU Records, 1817–1959: Miscellaneous Correspondence 1880–1900: Revd T.H. Hoste 1884–9. I do not know how to explain the contradiction, though Hoste may have been going home on leave (I owe this suggestion to Roger Sawyer).

58. *New York Ledger* to RDC, 26/6/1895, NLI MS 13073 (12/i). Casement's manuscript poems are found in NLI MS 13078 (2/i–viii).

59. Reid, p. 21. Casement and Joseph Conrad may have met again during this leave. In 1916 Conrad gave details of their various encounters to John Quinn, beginning with the first in 1890: 'Next time we met was in 1896 in London, by chance, at a dinner of the Johnson Society. We went away from there together to the Sports Club and talked there till 3 in the morning.' Quoted in Frederick Karl, *Joseph Conrad: The Three Lives* (London: Faber & Faber 1979), p. 289, note and pp. 786–7. Since Casement was not home in 1896, the meeting could have been in 1895.

60. NLI MS 13078 (2/ii).

61. RDC to Ward (n.d., partial), NLI MS 13078 (1). I do not know who 'Leslie' was.

The letter was probably written in late February or March 1894. J. Rose Troup had been an associate of Casement's in the Congo; he was one of those who joined the Emin Pasha Relief Expedition; see J.B. Lyons, *Surgeon-Major Parke's African Journey 1887–89* (Dublin: The Lilliput Press 1994).

62. Jephson, pp. 259–62. While working for the protectorate, Casement had some contact with another member of the family, Sir Alfred Jephson, who acted as agent-general for the protectorate in London; see FO 403/200 (1894).

63. RDC to Cowper, 15/6/1901, NLI Acc. 4902 (5). Cowper was consul in Lisbon and Casement was to maintain a steady correspondence with him. Henry St George Foley became a FO clerk in 1888 and précis writer to a succession of Foreign Secretaries (Rosebery, 1892; Kimberley, 1894; Salisbury, 1895; Lansdowne, 1900). He was promoted to assistant clerk in August 1902 and died on 13 April 1903.

64. RDC (Matadi) to Foley, 20/6/1901, PRO FO 2/491. The Hon. Armine Wodehouse CB, MP, was second son of John Wodehouse, Lord Kimberley. Born in 1860, he married the daughter of Matthew Arnold in 1889 and was elected Liberal MP for Essex North in 1900. He died on 1 May 1901. He served as private secretary to his father in several of the latter's capacities, including that of Secretary of State for Foreign Affairs, 1894–5.

4: LOURENÇO MARQUES, 1895–7

1. 'Brief to Counsel', NLI MS 13088. John Wodehouse, 1st Earl of Kimberley (1826–1902) was Secretary of State for Foreign Affairs in 1894–5.

2. FO to RDC, 27/6/1895, PRO FO 63/1297. There were also British consuls at Inhambane and Beira.

3. FO to RDC, 28/6/1895; RDC to FO, 9/9/1895, PRO FO 63/1297.

4. For a detailed treatment see Philip R. Warhurst, *Anglo-Portuguese Relations in South-Central Africa 1890–1900* (London: Longmans 1962).

5. Roger Sawyer was the first of Casement's biographers to address the topic of consular functions in a systematic and perceptive manner. I have benefited significantly from his treatment: see, in particular, Sawyer, *Flawed Hero*, pp. 31, 53–5 and 149–55. For discussions of the British Foreign Office at the time, see Ray Jones, *The Nineteenth-Century Foreign Office: An Administrative History* (London: Weidenfeld & Nicolson 1971), and *The British Diplomatic Service 1815–1914* (London: Colin Smythe 1983); D.C.M. Platt, *The Cinderella Service: British Consuls since 1825* (London: Longman 1971).

6. RDC to FO, 14/1/1896, PRO FO 63/1316.

7. RDC to John Casement, 2/3/1896, PRONI T3787/12.

8. RDC to FO, 27/1/1896, PRO FO 63/1316. What happened was that, when the Jameson Raid began, the German consul in Johannesburg had telegraphed Berlin for armed protection. The German Imperial Government, in turn, requested per-

mission of Portugal to land marines in Delagoa Bay. Portugal refused and no guns were landed, but international tensions were heightened by the events.

9. RDC to Foley, 3/4/1896, TCD Misc. Photocopy 89–90. Foley was clearly impressed by this letter and sent it on to the Colonial Office, where H.T. Wilson brought it to Chamberlain's attention. Chamberlain minuted 'very good letter' on 31/5/1896. Joseph Chamberlain (1836–1914) was a member of a screw-manufacturing firm in Birmingham but became interested in social reform and entered politics. He became active in the Liberal Party and served in the Gladstone cabinet in the 1880s. He resigned because of his opposition to the Home Rule Bill and led a Liberal Unionist group into alliance with the Conservatives. He joined the Salisbury cabinet as Secretary of State for Colonies in 1895. He was accused of complicity in the Jameson Raid, soon after taking up office.

10. RDC to FO, 29/5/1896, PRO FO 63/1316. Pfeil was a noted explorer and friend of Dr Karl Peters (Warhurst, p. 136).

11. RDC to FO, 30/5/1896, PRO FO 63/1316. Dr Leyds was Secretary of State for the Transvaal and General Piet Joubert a veteran Boer leader.

12. RDC to FO, 7/3/1897, PRO FO 63/1336. Majuba was the location of a British defeat in 1881, during the First Anglo-Boer War.

13. RDC to FO, 17/10/1896, PRO FO 63/1317. Pfeil was jostled on another occasion, when he caused offence by failing to remove his hat during a religious procession (Warhurst, p. 136).

14. RDC to FO, 16/6/1896 (tel.); 18/6/1896, PRO FO 63/1317.

15. RDC to FO, 26/6/1896 and 63/1336, 20/3/1897, PRO FO 63/1317.

16. RDC to Foley, 11/11/1896; 28/11/1896; 3/2/1897; 15/2/1897, Hatfield House, Salisbury Papers (HH SalP), 3M/A98/90–6. Casement's letter of 3 February 1897 was initialled by Salisbury and minuted, 'The writer is Consul at D[elagoa]B[ay] and an excellent official' and 'seen by Mr Chamberlain, Mr Balfour and Undersecretaries'.

17. RDC to FO, 17/10/1895 and 23/10/1895, PRO FO 63/1297; 11/7/1896, PRO FO 63/1317.

18. RDC to FO, 21/11/1896, PRO FO 63/1336; 24/4/1897, PRO FO 63/1317. The poor state of the lighthouse is also referred to in this context: RDC to FO, 4/12/1896, PRO FO 63/1317.

19. RDC to FO, 6/3/1896, PRO FO 63/1316.

20. RDC to FO, 9/5/1896, FO 63/1316; 7/8/1896, 17/10/1896, 31/10/1896, PRO FO 63/1317. Among the categories of goods listed in the last of these reports as coming through Lourenço Marques are 'ammunition', 'railway goods' and 'distilled drinks'.

21. RDC to FO, 16/11/1895, PRO FO 63/1297.

22. Other countries were involved, notably France, but not to the same extent. For French involvement see RDC to FO, 22/8/1896 and 12/9/1896, PRO FO 63/1317, 9/1/1897 and 20/3/1897, PRO FO 63/1336.

23. For this discussion of the railway I draw heavily on Philip Warhurst's excellent study.

24. RDC to FO, 25/10/1895, PRO FO 881/6915.

25. RDC to FO, 6/3/1896, PRO FO 63/1316; and see RDC to FO, 14/11/1896, PRO FO 881/6915.

26. Warhurst, p. 125.

27. *Ibid.* pp. 125–6, 146.

28. RDC to Foley, 15/2/1897, HH SalP, 3M/A98/90–6.

29. RDC to FO, 27/3/1897, PRO FO 63/1336; it was acknowledged by the FO on 19/5/1897, PRO FO 63/1336. The trade report is: FO 1897 Annual Series, Diplomatic and Consular Reports on Trade and Finance, Portugal, Report for Year 1896, Trade and Commerce of Lorenzo Marques, 1897.

30. RDC to FO, 6/3/1896, PRO FO 403/231.

31. RDC to FO, 18/5/1896, PRO FO 403/231.

32. RDC to FO, 18/5/1896, PRO FO 63/1316 and 6/6/1896, PRO FO 63/1317.

33. RDC to FO, 5/9/1896, PRO FO 63/1317.

34. RDC to FO, 18/5/1896, PRO FO 63/1316.

35. RDC to FO, 18/5/1896, PRO FO 63/1316 and 2/9/1896, 5/9/1896, 10/9/1896, 24/10/1896, 20/11/1896, 17/12/1896 etc., PRO FO 63/1317.

36. RDC to Foley, 11/11/1896, HH SalP, 3M/A98/90–6.

37. Quoted in Inglis, p. 41. According to Reid, p. 50, Bigelow (1855–1944), though a trained lawyer, made his career as a traveller, journalist and semi-professional historian. Bigelow refers briefly to his meeting with Casement in Lourenço Marques in volume two of his autobiography, *Seventy Summers* (London: E. Arnold 1925). The two remained in contact and Bigelow was to play a role in the final months of Casement's life.

38. The overthrow of Gaza is discussed in Malyn Newitt, *A History of Mozambique* (London: Hurst 1995) and in Warhurst.

39. RDC to FO, 9/9/1895, PRO FO 63/1297.

40. *Ibid.* The Foreign Office reply was not sent until 5 November, showing how slow communications with London were at this time.

41. RDC to FO, 3/10/1895, PRO FO 63/1297.

42. RDC to FO, 26/11/1895, PRO FO 63/1297.

43. RDC to FO, 30/11/1895, PRO FO 63/1297.

44. RDC to FO, 7/1/1896, Telegraph, PRO FO 63/1316.

45. RDC to FO, 12/3/1896 and 8/5/1896, PRO FO 63/1316. Junod later devoted a great deal of his energies to ethnographic studies of native Mozambiquan society, the results of which were included in his classic study, *The Life of a South African Tribe* (London: David Nutt 1912). He attributed the awakening of his interest in ethnography to a conversation he had with James Bryce, when Bryce visited Lourenço Marques in 1895.

46. RDC to FO, 12/3/1896 and 8/5/1896, PRO FO 63/1316.

47. RDC to FO, 8/5/1896, PRO FO 63/1316. The language bears a striking resemblance to that which Casement was to use years later in relation to the Franciscan mission sent to the Putumayo.

48. RDC to FO, 9/10/95; FO to RDC (tel.), 2/1/1896, PRO FO 63/1315. The territory of the Tonga people lay on both sides of the colonial borders.

49. The details are described in the following Casement despatches: on the Portuguese edict, FO to RDC, 19/12/1895 and RDC to FO, 24/10/1895, PRO FO 63/1297; on Nguanasi, RDC to FO, 25/1/1896, 5/2/1896, 7/2/1896, 15/2/1896, and 7/3/1896, PRO FO 63/1315. For more detail on Nguanasi see W.S. Felgate, *The Tembe Thonga of Natal and Mozambique: an Ecological Approach* (Durban: Department of African Studies, University of Natal 1982), pp. 19 ff.

50. RDC to FO, 7/2/1896, PRO FO 63/1316.

51. RDC to FO, 17/12/1896, PRO FO 63/1317.

52. RDC to FO, 9/4/1897, PRO FO 63/1336. Casement drew his figures from an analysis of the Table of Finances of Gazaland for 1896–7 taken from the official gazette. He was here engaged in the type of probing that later helped him assess the pattern of exploitation in the Congo Free State.

53. RDC to FO, 6/3/1896, PRO FO 403/231.

54. RDC to FO, 4/8/1896, PRO FO 63/1317 and 9/4/1897, PRO FO 63/1336.

55. *Royal Commission on the Civil Service, Appendix to Fifth Report* (to be cited hereafter as *Royal Commission*), Minutes of Evidence, 29 April 1914–16, July 1914, Q. 38,555, p. 81.

56. RDC to FO, 10/1/1896, PRO FO 63/1316 and 11/11/1897, PRO FO 63/1336.

57. FO to RDC, 1/10/1895, PRO FO 63/1297; RDC to FO, 16/11/95, PRO FO 63/1317, 11/6/1896; FO to RDC, 6/3/1897, PRO FO 63/1336.

58. RDC to John Casement, 2/3/1896, PRONI T3787/12.

59. RDC to Gertrude, 23/10/1896, NLI MS 13074 (1/i).

60. RDC to FO, 7/5/1896, PRO FO 63/1316.

61. *Royal Commission*, Q. 38,558, p. 81.

62. RDC to FO, 24/4/1897, PRO FO 63/1336.

63. RDC to FO, 31/3/1896, PRO FO 63/1316.

64. RDC to FO, 7/5/1896, PRO FO 63/1316. The FO, while sanctioning the leave and replacement, observed that it was unusual for a clergyman to act as consul. Casement informed them that the Revd J. Bovill was the only suitable Englishman available.

65. RDC to FO, 5/3/1897, PRO FO 63/1336. The FO was sympathetic to his suggestion that a vice-consul or consular agent be appointed and minuted that it would be considered.

66. RDC to FO, 4/8/1896, PRO FO 63/1317 and 22/8/1896, PRO FO 63/1317.

67. RDC to FO, 4/8/1896, PRO FO 63/1317 and 403/232.

68. *Ibid.*

69. RDC to Foley, 28/11/1896, HH SalP 3M/A98/188–91; RDC to FO, 18/4/1897, PRO FO 63/1336 (and see 63/1317, 17/10/1896 for a brief reference).

70. R. Coudenhove to RDC, 29/7/1912, NLI MS 13073 (46/xvii). Richard Coudenhove-Kalergi (1867–1934) belonged to a landowning family with roots in Flanders (Coudenhove) and Greece and Italy (Kalergi). He started out as a professional

officer in a regiment of Hussars in Hungary. After his father's death he left the army and lived on the proceeds of an estate that was sold. He was an easy-going man, enjoyed the pleasures of life and was well liked by his friends. He went twice on shooting trips to Eastern Africa. He was involved in music and art and his house in Vienna became a well-known salon, frequented by such as Furtwängler, Schalk, Bruno Walter, Alma Mahler, Franz Werfel and many others (Barbara Coudenhove-Kalergi, private communication). Casement also came to know Richard's brother, Hans, during this period.

71. Quoted in Inglis, p. 43. The original is in Prince Gebhard von Blücher, *Memoirs*, ed. Evelyn, Princess Blücher (London: John Murray 1932), p. 178.

72. RDC to Foley, 11/11/1896, HH SalP 3M/198/90–6. Blücher was great-great-grandson of Marshal Blücher, Prussian field marshal, who had played a key role in the Battle of Waterloo (1815).

73. The Lord ffrench in question was Charles Austen ffrench, 6th Baron, born 1868; he married Mary Corbally in 1892 and succeeded to the title in 1893. Lord Ennismore was Viscount Richard Granville Hare, born 1866, the eldest and only surviving son of the 3rd Earl of Listowel; he served in the Second Anglo-Boer War in 1900 and married in 1904.

74. A note of welcome to Bryce from Casement survives: 'I hope you will be able to come on shore, and to bring Mrs Bryce, this afternoon. I could get a rickshaw and have it sent down to the pier to meet you, if you cared for it – and if you would tell me when I might expect you. I shall be delighted to see you any time after 4 o'clock – before which hour you might find it too hot.' RDC to Bryce, 30/10/1895, BOD, MS Bryce 48, fols 91–9. James Bryce, Viscount (1838–1922) was a jurist, historian and statesman. He was Regius Professor of Civil Law at Oxford from 1870 to 1893 and a Liberal MP from 1880 to 1906. He was to be chief secretary for Ireland (1905–6) and ambassador at Washington (1907–13). He presided over a commission on alleged German atrocities in Belgium in September 1914.

75. RDC to Pincus, 8/1/1899; 5/4/1899; 21/3/1900, TCD MS 827.

76. RDC to Pincus, 1/6/1896, TCD 827.

77. RDC to Pincus, 3/5/1897.

78. RDC to FO, 5/3/1897, 24/4/1897 (and FO minutes), PRO FO 63/1366; FO to RDC, 15/4/1897.

79. RDC to FO (tel.) and FO to RDC, 7/6/1897, PRO FO 63/1336.

80. RDC to FO, 2/11/1897, 3/11/1897, PRO FO 63/1336. Rejecting the request to pay Parminter, in a testy response, the FO pointed out that Casement had already received 'specially favourable treatment' both by being on full pay himself from 10 June to 14 October and by not having to pay Parminter from 10 June to 12 September (his official leave). He would have to pay Parminter himself from 12 September to 14 October.

81. Parminter to FO, 23/11/1897, PRO FO 63/1336.

82. RDC to FO, 18/1/1898, PRO FO 63/1353. A local directory shows Lambourn Place

to have been occupied by Herbert Ward in 1899. Long demolished, it has been described as a large mansion with extensive grounds. In his letter of 18/1/98, Casement also thanked the FO for a raise and for the appointment of a vice-consul.

83. FO to RDC, 4/2/1898, PRO FO 63/1353.
84. RDC (Lambourn Place) to R.Morten, n.d., NLI ACC 4902.
85. RDC to FO, 16/2/1898 and 17/2/1898, PRO FO 63/1353. The certificate is from 'P.M. Laffan MO, Physician and Surgeon, Royal College, Dublin'.
86. RDC to Gertrude, 18/3/1898, NLI MS 13074 (1/i); RDC to FO, 12/3/1898, PRO FO 63/1353.
87. RDC (115 Lr Baggot St. Dublin) to Morten, 9/3/1898, NLI Acc. 4902.
88. RDC to FO, 30/3/1898, PRO FO 63/1353.
89. RDC to FO, 27/5/1898 and FO to RDC, 28/5/1898 (tel.), PRO FO 63/1353.
90. RDC to Morten, 27/5/1898, NLI Acc. 4902. The centenary of the 1798 Rebellion was being commemorated during this year; the rebel cry 'Erin go Bragh' is the only hint of that celebration fact that I have found in Casement's writings.
91. RDC to FO, 3/6/1898, 11/7/1898 and FO to RDC, 1/7/1898, 29/7/1898, PRO FO 63/1353.
92. RDC to F. Bertie, 16/7/1898, PRO FO 63/1352. Francis Bertie was head of the African and Asian Departments and Assistant Undersecretary from 1894 to 1903; he was ambassador in Rome from 1903 to 1905 and in Paris from 1905 to 1918.
93. RDC to Gertrude, 5/9/1898, NLI MS 13074. The Battle of Omdurman took place on 2 September 1898. It was the key battle in the defeat of the Mahdist forces in Egypt. See Pakenham, *Scramble for Africa*.

5: ST PAUL DE LOANDA, 1898–9

1. The Gaboon (Gabon), earlier a Portuguese colony, had been taken over by the French in the mid nineteenth century. Its capital was Libreville.
2. RDC, 1899 Notebook, NLI MS 12116. A second note on the poem was added later: 'And finished 8 a.m. on 20th June 1901 – the last 20 verses having been composed chiefly on 19th June. Was not this Queen Victoria's Accession Day?'
3. Note to poem, quoted in Mackey, *Crime against Europe*, p. 208. Another poem of the same name, with what appears to be clear homosexual content, is also attributed to Casement; for a lengthy discussion of it, see Dudgeon, pp. 568–80.
4. Acting Governor General Fuchs was to write to Casement on 19 December to congratulate him formally on his appointment: Fuchs to RDC, 19/12/1896, NLI MS 13981 (3/i).
5. RDC to FO, 18/12/1896, PRO FO 63/1352.
6. RDC to FO, 18/12/1898, PRO FO 63/1352. Casement sent two letters to the FO on this date, just as he was leaving to continue his journey to Loanda.
7. RDC to FO, 21/12/1898, PRO FO 63/1352. The FO minutes indicate that their

priority was to open a full consulate at Leopoldville, retaining only an unpaid vice-consul at Boma.

8. RDC to Pincus, 9/1/1899, TCD 827.

9. RDC to Pincus, 5/4/1899, TCD 827.

10. RDC, 1899 Notebook, NLI MS 12116, and Reid, p. 25, who adds: 'Casement's habit of admiring the muscular bodies of young men grows more visibly ominous as time passes.' This is another indication from Casement of his sense of passing youth, though he was only in his mid thirties. There may be a link between his experience of ageing and his sexual attraction to youths.

11. RDC to FO, 15/1/1899, PRO FO 2/230. The tone of this request seems that of a neutral observer and hadn't yet taken on the crusading tone of his later communications.

12. Quoted in Inglis, p. 50.

13. RDC to FO, 26/1/1899, PRO FO 2/230. For the Stokes affair see Cookey, p. 31, and Pakenham, *Scramble for Africa*, pp. 407, 415, 417–18 and *passim*.

14. Cookey, p. 5. The development of the Leopoldian system in the Congo Free State has been graphically described in Neal Ascherson, *The King Incorporated: Leopold the Second and the Congo* (London: Granta Books 1999 [1963]); and Hochschild. Jules Marchal provides comprehensive coverage of the later phase, which includes a chapter on Casement, in *E.D. Morel Contre Léopold II: L'Histoire du Congo 1900–1910*, 2 vols. (Paris: Éditions L'Harmattan 1995). For a recent brief overview, see Marchal, 'Roger Casement in the Congo: reactions in Belgium' in Daly, pp. 26–35.

15. Details of Leopold's expenditure are taken from Pakenham, *Scramble for Africa*, pps. 155, 161, 244, 320, 397–9 and 524–5. See, also, Axelson.

16. See Hochschild, pp. 158–9 and Robert Harms, 'The end of red rubber: a reassessment', *Journal of African History*, xvi (i) (1975), 73–88.

17. For details of exports see Pakenham, *Scramble for Africa*, p. 524 ff.

18. Axelson, pp. 209–10.

19. Cookey, p. 16. The ABIR quickly became an exclusively Belgian affair. The Anversoise was the Société anversoise du commerce du Congo, its territory being the basin of the Mongala River.

20. For Bannister, see Cookey, pp. 27–9, Marchal, vol. 1, pp. 153–69, and Dudgeon, pp. 77–85. A quick-tempered man, he overstepped the mark when he pushed an official while investigating the contract terms of a group of British subjects. He was convicted of assault by a Congo court and the FO agreed to remove him.

21. *The Times*, 18/11/1895. See Slade, *Missions*, p. 244; Cookey, p. 40.

22. Cookey, p. 40.

23. Arthur to FO, 20/7/1896, quoted in Cookey, p. 39.

24. For details, see Slade, *Missions*, Cookey, and William Roger Louis and Jean Stengers (eds.), *E.D. Morel's History of the Congo Reform Movement* (Oxford: Clarendon Press 1968).

25. RDC to FO, 11/3/1899, PRO FO 629/4.

26. RDC to FO, 10/4/1899, PRO FO 629/5. All quotations above are from this report.

Casement was to spend some time in Lake Mantumba on his 1903 investigation; this despatch shows that he was aware of atrocities there in 1899.

27. RDC to FO, 31/3/1899, with enclosures, PRO FO 10/731.

28. RDC to FO, 25/4/1899, PRO FO 10/731.

29. RDC to FO, 15/9/1899 and 9/10/1899, PRO FO 10/731.

30. RDC to FO, 1/9/1899, PRO FO 375/5 (Register of Correspondence); *Report for the Years 1897 and 1898 on the Trade and Commerce of Angola*, Diplomatic and Consular Reports, Portugal, no. 2363, Annual Series, London: HMSO, 1899. All quotations are from this report.

31. RDC to Morten, 12/10/1899, NLI ACC 4902 (1).

32. The treatment of labour on the two islands was to become a major issue in later years, involving two men with whom Casement was to develop close links: William Cadbury and H.W. Nevinson.

33. From this point on, references to sleeping-sickness appear regularly in Casement's reports, notably in his 1904 Congo Report. They attracted the attention of medical specialists: see Sir Philip Manson Bahr, *Patrick Manson* (London: Thomas Nelson 1962), p. 180.

34. On German colonial practice in Cameroon, Casement commented: 'The Germans are successfully solving the problem in their colony of Cameroons; slowly it is true, but still with a thrifty purpose that has already converted nearly 100 miles of once wild forested coastline (and that only 10 years since) from the Rio del Rey to the mouth of Cameroon river, into a series of flourishing cocoa plantations.' (p. 7)

35. RDC to Pincus, 5/4/1899, TCD 827.

36. RDC to Pincus, 2/5/1899, TCD 827.

37. RDC to Morten, 2/7/1899, NLI Acc. 4902 (1).

38. RDC to Morten, partial, n.d., NLI MS 13080 (6/ii).

39. RDC to Morten, Autumn 1899, NLI MS unclassified, quoted in Reid, p. 29.

40. Roger Casement (1850–1928) married Susanna ('Susie') Beatty of Dublin in 1877. She was born *c.*1852–3 and died in Magherintemple on 10 February 1915. Their eldest son, John ('Jack', 1880–1944), joined the Royal Navy in 1894. He is the 'youthful' Jack RN of this letter.

41. RDC to Roger Casement (Magherintemple), 26/9/1899, PRONI T3787/13. He commented also on the Dreyfus case in France: 'On the 16 August every paper in the World – not French – seemed to consider his entire acquittal an absolute certainty – and certainly the Evidence against him seemed daily growing more trivial ...' The first book he requested in this letter was: Revd George Hill, *An Historical Account of the MacDonnels of Antrim* (Belfast: Archer & Sons 1873). The second work was the famous *Annála Ríoghachta Éireann*, popularly known as the Annals of the Four Masters, compiled in the 1630s under the direction of the Franciscan Mícheál Ó Cléirigh. Rose Young (1865–1947) was another of the Youngs of Galgorm House, Ballymena, with whom the Casements had strong links. Rose became immersed in Irish language studies; for an excellent general picture, see Diarmaid Ó Doibhlin, *Womenfolk*

of the Glens of Antrim and the Irish Language (Belfast: An tUltach Trust c.1994).

42. RDC to Morten, 2/7/1899, NLI ACC 4902 (1). He also refers to the Dreyfus case in this letter.
43. RDC to Pincus, 7/9/1899, TCD 827.
44. RDC to Morten, 12/10/1899, NLI Acc. 4902 (1).
45. FO to RDC, 17/10/1899, PRO FO 63/1365. In August, Casement had requested permission to travel to the Upper Congo before returning to Europe on leave: 'I wish to avoid remaining in Loanda during another hot season – the period from January to May.' RDC to FO, 5/8/1899, PRO FO 63/1365.

6: THE BOER WAR: SPECIAL COMMISSIONER, 1899–1900

1. Nina's Recollections, NLI MS 9932.
2. RDC to Foley, 25/12/1899, HH SalP, 3M/A98/229–40. The letter was minuted: 'I think Mr Balfour should see this' and initialled by St John Brodrick, A.J. Balfour, Mr Chamberlain and Lord Salisbury. In 1917, Tom Casement wrote of their meeting during the war, when he was invalided to Cape Town: 'Roddie was on the Pier to meet me. He then went off on a special mission to Delagoa Bay ...' Tom Casement to Gertrude, 5/10/1917, MacMullen Papers.
3. Chamberlain to Milner, 20/12/1899, PRO CO 879/56, Tel. no. 646, p. 483. Alfred, Viscount Milner (1854–1925) served as Undersecretary for Finance in Egypt from 1889–92 and as high commissioner for South Africa from 1897–1905. He tried unsuccessfully to resolve the dispute between Boers and Britons and to reach agreement before the Boer War. Later, his policy of importing Chinese labourers led to severe criticism in Britain and contributed to the fall of the Conservative government. He opposed Home Rule for Ireland, served as a member of Lloyd George's War Cabinet from 1916–19 and as colonial secretary from 1919–21.
4. Milner to Chamberlain, 22/12/1899, PRO CO 879/56, no. 650, p. 485.
5. Chamberlain to Milner, 24/12/1899, PRO CO 879/56, no. 655, p. 487. Salisbury was both Prime Minister and Foreign Secretary at this time.
6. Chamberlain to Milner, 25/12/1899, no. 657, p. 494 and 29/12/1899, no. 666, p. 496; Milner to Chamberlain, 26/12/1899, no. 662, p. 494 and 30/12/1899, no. 673, p. 501, PRO CO 879/56. Cohen was a trader in Lourenço Marques.
7. RDC to FO, 1/2/1900, PRO FO 2/368.
8. RDC to FO, 1/3/1900, PRO FO 2/368.
9. Milner to Chamberlain, 17/2/1900, no. 310, p. 99, and Chamberlain to Milner, 6/3/1900, no. 425, p. 136, PRO CO 879/63.
10. RDC to FO, 5/2/1900, PRO FO 2/368.
11. RDC to FO, 24/2/1900, PRO FO 2/368.
12. RDC to FO, 5/3/1900, PRO FO 2/368. The Irishman alluded to is almost certainly Major John MacBride, who helped organize a pro-Boer brigade during the war. See

Donal P. McCracken, *The Irish Pro Boers, 1877–1902* (Johannesburg: Perskom 1989).

13. RDC to FO, 5/7/1900, PRO FO 2/368.

14. RDC to Foley, 24/4/1900, HH SalP, 3M/A98/90–6, fols. 229–40.

15. Cecil Headlam (ed.), *The Milner Papers (South Africa), 1899–1905*, 2 vols. (London: Cassell & Co. 1933), vol. II, p. 89. Forbes is mentioned again at this time in two letters from Roberts to Milner. Buller's opposition is also to be inferred from the advice of Roberts to Forbes that 'in the event of Buller questioning him, he should reply that he is employed on a secret service by my orders'. *Ibid.* pp. 75 and 90. Buller had remained in service in South Africa after being superseded as chief of staff.

16. RDC to FO, 5/7/1899, PRO FO 2/368.

17. RDC to FO, 5/7/1900, PRO FO 2/368. Though based on a less than adequate understanding of the detailed sequence of events, there has been a tendency on the part of biographers to judge negatively Casement's role during the Boer War. MacColl, p. 23, is the most extreme in suggesting that his actions 'gave a foretaste of the kind of fiasco with which his path was to be littered as the years wore on'. Inglis, p. 54, referring to the bridge episode, felt that it 'was another example of how hard he found it to preserve detachment about ventures in which he was involved'. Reid, p. 27, muses that 'Casement's involvements in enterprises of such kind, now and later, and the disorderly course they tended to run, keep revealing a strange amateurishness in British conduct of public affairs in late Victorian and Edwardian times – full of whim and happenstance and flaccid wisdom by hindsight.'

18. NLI MS 13082 (2/vii), 8/5/1900, and MS 12116. In a note at the end of the poem, Casement wrote: 'The Fingoes were a Kafir tribe expelled from their country by the invading hordes of Iska [Shaka] the Zulu king. They came into the Dutch Colony begging – and the Kafir chiefs claimed and kept them as slaves, calling them Fingoes or pedlars. Finguza, i.e. to peddle – until British suzerainty established their freedom.' For the Fingo (Mfengu), see John Selby, *A Short History of South Africa* (London: New English Library Mentor 1975); Thomas Pakenham, *The Boer War* (London: Weidenfeld & Nicolson 1979), pp. 396, 402 and 410.

19. *South African News*, 26/5/1900, p. 4.

20. RDC to Pincus, 5/3/1900, TCD 827.

21. RDC to Pincus, 21/3/1900, TCD 827.

22. RDC to Pincus, 18/5/1900, TCE 827.

23. RDC to Foley, 24/4/1900, HH SalP, 3M/A98/990–6, fols. 229–40.

24. RDC to Gosselin, 30/4/1900, PRO FO 403/304.

25. The 'high official of the Congo Government' who had written to him seems to have been Richard Dorsey Mohun, who was, in general, an apologist for the State: Marchal, vol. 1, p. 50.

26. I have chosen to go ahead here of the general narrative of Casement's life in order to highlight the role of Africa in his changing political allegiances from the period of the Boer War onwards.

27. RDC to Foley, 3/8/1900, PRO FO 63/1375.

28. 'Brief to Counsel', NLI MS 13088 (1/iii).

29. RDC to Alice Stopford Green (ASG), 20/4/1907, NLI MS 10464 (3). Green (1847–1929) was born in Co. Meath, daughter of a Church-of-Ireland archdeacon. She married the English historian John Richard Green in 1877 and worked with him in the revision of his work, until his early death in 1883. Later, she helped found the Africa Society in 1901 ('for promotion of African studies'), to keep the ideas of her friend, Mary Kingsley, alive. Her house in London became an intellectual centre – among her friends being Florence Nightingale, John Morley, R.B. Haldane, H.A.L. Fisher and Winston Churchill. She was a founder member of the School of Irish Studies in 1903. She was to become a considerable historian in her own right; her works included *The Making of Ireland and its Undoing* (1908); *Irish Nationality* (1911); *The Old Irish World* (1912); *History of the Early Irish State to 1014* (1925). She was made an Irish senator in 1922.

30. In November 1900, in a Cabinet reshuffle, Lord Lansdowne succeeded Salisbury as Foreign Secretary. He held the position until December 1905. Henry Charles Keith Petty-Fitzmaurice, Marquess of Lansdowne, was born in 1845 and succeeded as Marquess in 1866. Before becoming Foreign Secretary, he had held a number of government positions: he was Undersecretary of State for War, 1872–4, and for India, 1880; Governor General of Canada, 1883–8, and viceroy, 1888–93.

31. William Tyrrell (1866–1947) was to become Casement's closest associate in the FO. He became 1st Baron Tyrell and served successively as private secretary to Sanderson, 1896–1903; secretary to the Committee of Imperial Defence, 1903–4; précis writer to Sir Edward Grey, 1905–7; private secretary to Grey, 1907–15; head of the Political Intelligence Department, 1916; Permanent Undersecretary, 1925–30. He was later ambassador to France and president of the Board of Censors.

32. RDC to FO, 14/6/1901; RDC to Tyrrell, 16/6/1901; RDC to Foley, 20/6/1901, PRO FO 2/491. RDC to Pincus, 18/2/1903 (which encloses RDC to Reuters, 28/10/1901); TCD 827. The FO response was to refer the matter officially to the Intelligence Division (minute to Casement's of 14/6/1901). In 1903, Casement told Pincus he was glad that the campaign of vilification was over: 'I regret it very keenly not because it injured you so much as that it struck at my own countrymen's sense of fair play.'

33. RDC to Pincus, 20/10/1901, 18/2/1903, 9/6/1903, 25/8/1903, TCD 827.

34. Tom Casement to RDC, 8/1/1904 and 3/12/1904, NLI MS 13076.

35. Selby, p. 178.

36. Pakenham, *Scramble for Africa*, pp. 646–7.

37. RDC to Morten, 2/1/1905, NLI MS 13600. Unfortunately, the letter breaks off as Casement is discussing the Chinese question. Interestingly, Casement seems to have held out some prospect of being included in a possible Labour Commission to be sent to South Africa. His friend Alfred Emmott MP commented that, if there were to be one, Casement would be eminently suitable (A. Emmott to RDC,

3/2/1906, NLI MS 13073 (29/i)). I take W. Tyrrell's letter of 24/1/1906, NLI MS 13073 (43)) to be about the same issue. He stated that the likelihood of 'sending out a Commission' was doubtful, but 'Lord Elgin's Private Secretary has made a note of your wish to serve on it'. Alfred Emmott (1858–1926), 1st Baron Emmott, was a cotton spinner and Liberal politician. In 1899 he won a parliamentary seat from the Conservatives in Oldham, which he held until raised to a peerage in 1911. He became chairperson of several committees in the House of Commons in 1906 under Campbell-Bannerman. He became an active member of the Congo Reform Association and was supportive of Casement.

38. Selby, pp. 182–3; Pakenham, *Scramble for Africa*, pp. 648–9.

39. RDC to Gertrude, 14/7/06, NLI MS 13074 (3/ii).

40. RDC to EDM, 21/8/1906, LSE MP F8/22. Edmond Dene Morel (1873–1924) was to be Casement's closest confidant in the Congo campaign. He was born in Paris to a French father and English mother and educated in England after the early death of his father. He worked as a clerk in Liverpool for the Elder Dempster Company and, after a period, became an energetic critic of the Congo State. He established the *African Mail* in 1903 and the Congo Reform Association in 1904. In the lead-up to the First World War, he heavily criticized Britain's 'secret diplomacy', helped establish the Union for Democratic Control and suffered a six-month imprisonment in 1917. He was elected Labour MP for Dundee in 1922.

41. RDC to EDM, 3/12/1906, LSE MP F8/22; RDC to ASG, 21/9/1906, NLI MS 10464. McCallum is, presumably, Colonel Sir Henry Edward McCallum, born 1852, who was governor of Natal from 1901 to 1907.

42. Pakenham, *Scramble for Africa*, pp. 649–50. See also Monica Wilson and Leonard Thompson (eds.), *The Oxford History of South Africa* (NY: OUP 1975 [1971]), vol. 2, 1870–1966, pp. 345–6 and 351.

43. RDC to EDM, n.d. [late 1907?], LSE MP F8/22.

44. RDC to EDM, 23/6/1909, LSE MP F8/23. The Danishway incident has been described as follows: 'A fracas between *fellahin* and pigeon-shooting British officers at the delta village of Danishway ... led to the more or less accidental death of one officer and the injury of several others, and became the occasion for a display of judicial terror. After a scandalously summary trial before a special tribunal, four sentences of hanging, and fourteen of flogging, were carried out in public at Danishway. To all politically-conscious Egyptians, Danishway was profoundly shocking and humiliating ... After Danishway ... [i]t was no longer possible for any Egyptian group overtly to support the occupation.' G.N. Sanderson, 'The Nile basin and the Eastern Horn, 1870–1908' in R. Oliver and G.N. Sanderson (eds.), *The Cambridge History of Africa*, vol. 6, 1870 to 1905 (Cambridge: CUP 1985), p. 626; and see M.W. Daly, 'Egypt' in A.D. Roberts (ed.), *The Cambridge History of Africa*, vol. 7, 1905 to 1940 (Cambridge: CUP 1986), pp. 743–4. George Bernard Shaw wrote on two occasions about Danishway, in prefaces to *John Bull's Other Island* and to a Hall Caine novel; see Dan H. Laurence and Daniel

J. Leary (eds.), *Bernard Shaw: the Complete Prefaces* (Allen Lane, Penguin Press 1993), vol. 1, 1889–1913, pp. 225–39 and 312–15.

45. RDC (Rio) to EDM, 31/7/1909, LSE MP F8/23.
46. RDC to EDM, 15/9/1909, LSE MP F8/23.

7: THE CONGO FREE STATE, 1900–2

1. RDC to FO, 7/8/1900, PRO FO 63/1375.
2. RDC to Foley, 3/8/1900, PRO FO 63/1375.
3. RDC to FO, 7/8/1900, PRO FO 63/1375.
4. FO to RDC, 20/8/1900, PRO FO 10/739.
5. RDC to Pincus, 11/8/1900 and 8/9/1900, TCD 827. His 'charming rooms' were at 12 Aubrey Walk, Kensington; this was the address of his friend, Blücher.
6. Sawyer, *Diaries*, p. 48, n. 14. Tyrrell had married Urquhart's sister. Casement had, of course, visited Switzerland previously, in 1892.
7. His 'Address and Memorandum Book' of 1901 contains references to source books on Italy, which he may have used during the course of his travels. Reid, p. 28, n. 1, draws attention to the sexual implications of a note at the end of a poem written by Casement after his Italian sojourn: 'Casaldo's friend – R.C./Naples, 3 September 1900/ Written going to lunch at Naval & Military/on Saturday, Sept. 22/1900 – Oh Sad! Oh! grief stricken.'
8. RDC to FO, 12/9/1900, PRO FO 2/336.
9. RDC to FO, 19/9/1900, PRO FO 63/1375.
10. RDC to FO, 14/10/1900, PRO FO 2/336. Casement's memo on the conversations was submitted from 12 Aubrey Walk, Kensington. Constantine Phipps, the British envoy in Brussels, asked for copies, which Casement agreed to send. The FO minuted Casement's report: 'The King ought to have been a lawyer perpetually retained for the criminal.' On 19/10/1900 Casement was thanked for his memo ('which His Lordship has read with much interest').
11. FO to Nightingale, 15/10/1900, PRO FO 63/1375.
12. RDC to FO, 20/10/1900, PRO FO 10/739.
13. RDC to Cowper, 5/11/1900, NLI Acc. 4902 (5). Francis Henry Cowper was born in 1843. His consular postings were: Porto Rico (1862), Cuba (1868), Santos (1878) and Lisbon (1890). He retired on 1/3/1905. Dudgeon, p. 592, suggests that Taormina was a popular pilgrimage spot for gay men at this time.
14. The report for the Niger Coast Protectorate for 1891–4 lists Roberts as having organized the Treasury there, based in Old Calabar.
15. RDC to Morten, 26/11/1900, NLI Acc. 4902 (1). He was writing from the SS *Cazengo*, Praiya, Cape Verde Islands.
16. Details can be found in a series of despatches beginning on 31/12/1900 and into the early part of 1901, PRO FO 10/739 and 10/751.

17. FO, 20/8/1900 and RDC to FO, 20/10/1900, PRO FO 10/739.

18. RDC to Susan Casement, 2/3/1901, PRONI T3787/14. Susan (née Beatty) was wife of Roddie's uncle, Roger Casement (son of John). Details of Casement's journey to the Pool can also be found in the War Office Army Notebook of 1901, PRO HO 161/1.

19. RDC to FO, 26/2/1901, PRO FO 2/491. He later submitted his expenses: RDC to FO, 21/3/1901, PRO FO 10/751. The War Office Army Book contains a sketch map of the proposed consulate in Kinchassa; see Paul Hyland, *The Black Heart: A Voyage into Central Africa* (London: Gollancz 1988), p. 108.

20. RDC to FO, 17/7/1901, PRO FO 2/491. Richard Edward Dennett (1857–1921) was a trader, but also a keen ethnographer, who produced a long list of publications, initially on the Fjort/Fiote of the French Congo and later on Nigeria. He was a strong opponent of the injustices of the colonial system in Central Africa. He was an associate of Mary Kingsley and it was he who suggested that Casement should contact Alice Stopford Green.

21. RDC to FO, 13/6/1901, PRO FO 2/491. A Foreign Office minute suggested that this might be an infraction of free trade, but felt that nothing could be done unless a trader took a case.

22. RDC to FO, 7/5/1900 and 26/5/1900, PRO FO 2/491.

23. RDC to FO, 4/6/1901, PRO FO 2/491. A FO minute to this despatch noted the unequal treatment but added, 'we can take no action'.

24. RDC to FO, 15/6/1901, PRO FO 2/491. He was forwarding a set of regulations for the Upper Congo Marine Service (the State had a 'large number of steam vessels' on the Upper Congo) and, in doing so, went on to give figures for rubber exports.

25. RDC to FO, 27/7/1901, PRO FO 2/491.

26. RDC to FO, 13/6/1901, PRO FO 2/491.

27. RDC to FO, 11/7/1901, PRO FO 2/491. A FO minute on this recommends that Constantine Phipps, HM Representative in Brussels, should bring this matter before the Congo government, with reference to the Game Convention, but commented sarcastically: 'he will no doubt be told that the small ivory has been confiscated by zealous officers anxious to stop wrongful slaughter'.

28. Casement regularly received FO telegrams instructing him to monitor the contents of named vessels and the destination of those contents. For example: 'SS *Stanleyville* left Antwerp 30 ult. for Congo w. large no. of bales of rifles described as arms of precision. Watch landing and report destination of this and similar cargoes.' FO to RDC, 1/5/1901, PRO FO 2/491. Similar instructions came on the following dates: 20/7/1901, 9/8/1901, 19/8/1901, 9/9/1901 and 1/10/1901. His replies were often forwarded to the Intelligence Division of the War Office.

29. RDC to FO, 4/12/1901, PRO FO 2/491.

30. *Ibid.* This despatch was initialled by Farnall, Bertie, Gosselin and Sanderson, and copies were to be sent to Lord Percy and to Phipps.

31. RDC to FO, 9/12/1901, PRO FO 2/491.

32. RDC to FO, 28/6/1901, PRO FO 403/305. During 1901 he handled the case of some

70–80 Ugandans who had settled temporarily in Boma, having been engaged in cable laying in the Eastern Congo. In one of his despatches dealing with the case, he referred to 'speaking to one or two of the men in KiSwahili (a language with which I am very imperfectly acquainted)'. RDC to FO, 7/5/1901, PRO FO 2/491.

33. One of the key publications in the Congo campaign was to be Edmond Morel's *Red Rubber* (1906).

34. RDC to FO, 28/6/1901, PRO FO 403/305.

35. RDC to FO, 26/7/1901, PRO FO 2/491. The Revd Aaron Sims was a Scottish doctor who had gone out to the Congo in 1882. He had many contacts with government officials and was something of a State apologist, at one point suggesting that missionaries on the Upper Congo should be warned not to make propaganda against the State.

36. RDC to FO, 12/6/1901, PRO FO 2/491.

37. RDC to FO, 13/6/1901, PRO FO 2/491 and 12/7/1901, PRO FO 2/491.

38. RDC to FO, 7/6/1901, PRO FO 2/491. Casement referred once more to his hope to travel in the Upper Congo: 'I hope to do one or two longish journeys up the Congo and its tributaries before coming home for a spell next year ...' RDC to Foley, 20/6/1901, PRO FO 2/491. Reid writes (p. 32) regarding 1901: 'Whenever he could get free from routine consular duties, Casement moved restlessly about in the interior, in the basin of the great river and its tributaries.' This statement seems to be based on ignorance of both the geography of the region and of Casement's real movements. It may well be based on the following similar passage in MacColl, p. 28: 'Through the spring and summer of 1900 Casement was hard at work, travelling almost incessantly, afoot, by donkey and sometimes by Congo steamer.'

39. RDC to FO, 28/8/1901 and 26/7/1901, PRO FO 2/491. Shipping was, of course, one of the concerns of consuls and, during this stint, Casement did deal with a number of incidents concerning ships. In one case, involving stranding, litigation and salvage, he advised the captain 'without the help of any of the legal books usually available in such cases'. The captain won his case. RDC to FO, 5/6/1901, PRO FO 10/751.

40. RDC to FO, 7/5/1901, 27/5/1901 and 24/6/1901, PRO FO 10/751. A FO minute wondered how they might guard against 'accidents' like this; it was suggested that all letters with confidential material should be sealed.

41. RDC to Susan Casement, 2/3/1901, PRONI, T3787/14.

42. RDC to Cowper, 9/3/1901, NLI Acc. 4902 (5).

43. RDC to FO, 30/4/1901, PRO FO 10/751.

44. RDC to Foley, 20/6/1901, PRO FO 2/491.

45. RDC to Susan Casement, 2/3/1901, PRONI, T3787/14.

46. RDC to Cowper, 9/3/1901 and 15/6/1901, NLI Acc. 4902 (5).

47. RDC to Susan Casement, PRONI T3787/14. She was also treated to a long, humorous passage on consuls having no legal existence after the death of the Queen. Queen Victoria died on 22 January 1901.

48. RDC to Cowper, 9/3/1901, NLI Acc. 4902 (5). He had been at Stanley Pool 'looking for ground for New Consulate'.
49. RDC to Susan Casement, 2/3/1901, PRONI T3787/14.
50. RDC to FO, 22/8/1901, PRO FO 10/751.
51. RDC to Gertrude, 28/08/1901, NLI MS 13074 (1/ii).
52. RDC to Pincus, 20/10/1901, TCD 827; RDC to Gertrude, 18/10/1901, NLI MS 13074 (1/ii). Foley wrote from Bristol (20/10/1900), 'Alas! on cure for lung problem on Mendip Hills' – he was to die in April 1903 – Foley to RDC, 20/10/1901, NLI MS 13073 (6/i).
53. RDC to Reuters, 28/10/1901, TCD 827.
54. RDC (Northern Counties Hotel, Portrush) to Cowper, 22/10/1901, NLI Acc. 4902 (5). The name of Mr E.R. Parkinson appears on FO correspondence in 1904; he took temporary charge of the Lisbon consulate towards the end of that year.
55. RDC to Morten, 31/10/1901, NLI Acc. 4902 (2).
56. RDC on Sir Edward Grey, *The Continental Times*, 18/10/1915.
57. RDC to FO, 13/11/1901 and FO to RDC, 23/11/1901, PRO FO 10/751. Dean's letter was dated 12/11/1901.
58. RDC to PRO, 23/11/1901, PRO FO 2/491.
59. Fisher Unwin to RDC, 19/11/1901, NLI MS 13073 (23/i).
60. For Casement's collection of poems, readers' comments and Casement's response, see NLI MS 13082 (2/i–vii) and 13089 (1); RDC to PRO FO 403/305, 28/6/1901. Casement also received indirect advice from Fr Matthew Russell SJ, who wrote from St Stephen's Green in Dublin to say that he agreed with pleasure to give his ideas on 'your forthcoming volume'. He suggested that Casement name himself, since he hated anonymity. Matthew Russell to ? [RDC], 28/11/n.y. and 7/12/n.y., NLI MS 13078 (3). Russell (1834–1912) was born near Newry, Co. Down. In 1873 he established the *Irish Monthly*, which he edited for nearly forty years and published many volumes of poetry. See also Reid's negative assessment of Casement as a writer on pp. 32–4 of his biography.
61. RDC to Cowper, 3/11/1901, NLI Acc. 4902 (5).
62. RDC to Cowper, 14/11/1901, NLI Acc. 4902 (5).
63. RDC to Morten, 9/12/1901, NLI MS Acc. 4902 (1). The date given is 1902, but I think incorrectly; from its content I would place it in 1901.
64. RDC to Gertrude, 31/1/1902, NLI MS 13074; RDC to Cowper, 17/2/1902, NLI Acc. 4902 (5).
65. RDC to Cowper, 6/3/1902, NLI Acc. 4902 (5).
66. RDC to FO, 25/2/1902, PRO FO 2/626. The FO acknowledged the contribution, saying a copy would be sent to the Secretary of State for the Colonies, FO to RDC, 8/3/1902, PRO FO 2/626. When back in the Congo in 1902, Casement forwarded another £10, RDC to FO, 24/7/1902, PRO FO 2/626.
67. RDC to FO, 1/4/1902, written from Lisbon, PRO FO 10/765. He had written to Cowper earlier to say that he hoped to leave on the 28th on the *Thames* or, if not,

the following week. RDC to Cowper, 21/3/1902, NLI Acc. 4902 (5).

68. RDC to Cowper, 7/4/1902, NLI Acc. 4902 (5).

69. RDC to Roger Casement, Magherintemple, 12/4/1902, PRONI T3787/15. He closed with, 'Your affectionate Cousin, Roddie Casement'.

70. Sir Bernard Eric Edward Barrington KCB was senior clerk in the Foreign Office, who served under both Salisbury and Lansdowne. He was born in 1847 and joined the FO in 1867. In 1906 he was to become Assistant Undersecretary for Foreign Affairs, before retiring in 1907.

71. RDC to Cowper, 28/4/1902, NLI Acc. 4902 (5).

72. RDC (on board the SS *Anversville*, near Sierra Leone) to Barrington, 28/4/1902, PRO FO 629/9.

73. RDC to Gosselin, 16/5/1902, PRO FO 629/9.

74. *Ibid.*

75. RDC to FO, 21/6/1902, PRO FO 10/773 and 6/7/1902, PRO FO 629/9. He brought up the matter again several times, at one point indicating that he was investigating a 'Portuguese option'. Casement gives the following sketch of Hezekiah Andrew Shanu: 'Mr Shanu is a native of Lagos and is probably the oldest member of the British Colonial Native Colony in the Congo State. He was for many years a servant of the Congo Administration at HQs at Vivi and Boma – and is now a very respectable member of the local mercantile community, with two houses in Boma and one in Banana.' RDC to FO, 23/7/1902, PRO FO 2/626. For Shanu, see Hochschild.

76. For Morel, see Hochschild; Cline; Marchal.

77. RDC to FO, 16/5/1902 and 17/5/1902, PRO FO 403/327. Casement refers to an expedition of Major Wissmann in 1881–2 for population estimates on the Kasai.

78. RDC to FO, 30/6/1902, PRO FO 2/626.

79. RDC to FO, 4/10/1902, PRO FO 2/626.

80. RDC to FO, 22/7/1902, PRO FO 403/327.

81. RDC to FO, 10/8/1902, PRO FO 2/626.

82. RDC to FO, 10/7/1902, PRO FO 403/327.

83. RDC to FO, 2/6/1902, PRO FO 629/9.

84. RDC to FO, 29/6/1902, PRO FO 403/327.

85. RDC to FO, 10/7/1902, PRO FO 403/327.

86. RDC to FO, 10/8/1902, PRO FO 2/626.

87. RDC to FO, 2/6/1902, PRO FO 629/9.

88. RDC to FO, 28/6/1902, PRO FO 403/327. After retiring from the British army in 1888, Captain Guy Burrows took service in the *Force Publique* of the Congo State. In 1898 he published *The Land of the Pygmies* (London: C.A. Pearson). Following his retirement, he published *The Curse of Central Africa*, which appeared at the beginning of 1903 and made a public impact, but also led to a libel case against him. Casement's diary for 1903 recorded his reading Burrows's book on 25 August. I do not know what the report referred to here comprised.

89. RDC to FO, 29/7/1902, PRO FO 403/327.
90. RDC to FO, 16/5/1902, PRO FO 403/327.
91. RDC to FO, 10/7/1902, PRO FO 403/327. The significance of sleeping sickness as opposed to colonial oppression as key factors in causing population decline was and has remained a topic of debate. Casement was quite conscious of both factors, as were missionaries on the Congo. For the debate, see Louis and Stengers.
92. RDC to FO, 21/7/1902, PRO FO 403/327.
93. RDC to FO, 22/7/1902, PRO FO 403/327. The three Cs (civilization, commerce, and Christianity) were claimed to be the major benefits brought by European colonialism.
94. RDC to FO, 4/10/1902 and 22/7/1902, PRO FO 403/327.
95. RDC to FO, 10/8/1902, PRO FO 2/626.
96. RDC to FO, 10/7/1902, PRO FO 403/327.
97. RDC to FO, 29/6/1902, PRO FO 629/9; RDC to FO, 21/7/1902, PRO FO 2/626.
98. RDC to FO, 18/7/1902, PRO FO 403/327, 629/9 and 10/773.
99. RDC to FO, 30/6/1902, PRO FO 10/765 and 26/9/1902, PRO FO 2/626.
100. Regarding Matadi visits, see RDC to FO 22/7/1902 and 22/8/1902, PRO FO 10/765. For Banana, RDC to FO, 10/8/1902, PRO FO 2/626. The security of post continued to be a problem and he requested a supply of canvas despatch bags. Because he believed that post was opened, he now sent it in the care of private individuals. RDC to FO, 21/7/1902, PRO FO 10/765.
101. RDC to FO, 8/8/1902, PRO FO 2/626.
102. RDC to FO, 9/7/1902, PRO FO 629/9.
103. RDC to FO, 7/8/1902, PRO FO 2/626. This information he had got from a local official. The FO sent it to the Commercial Deptartment, Imperial Institute, Kew Gardens.
104. RDC to Cowper, 27/6/1902 and 3/7/1902, NLI Acc. 4902 (6).
105. RDC to Pincus, 24/9/1902, TCD 827. As he anticipated being home soon, he gave his address as c/o King & Co., 45 Pall Mall, London.
106. RDC to FO, 21/7/1902, PRO FO 403/327; 22/8/1902, PRO FO 2/626; FO to RDC, 26/8/1902, PRO FO 2/626.
107. RDC to FO, 5/9/1902, PRO FO 2/626, and 3/10/1902, PRO FO 10/765. John Casement, of Magherintemple, died on 13/10/1902; I do not know if Casement's journey home had any connection with this event.
108. RDC (SS *Bornu*) to Cowper, 20/10/1902, NLI Acc 4902 (6).
109. RDC (SS *Bornu*) to Cowper, 13/11/1902, NLI Acc 4902 (6). This letter is, I think, wrongly dated 13/10/1902.
110. RDC (c/o King & Co.) to Cowper, 24/11/1902, NLI Acc. 4902 (6).
111. RDC to FO, 13/12/1902, and FO to RDC, 27/12/1902, PRO FO 2/626.
112. RDC to FO, 7/1/1903, PRO FO 403/338.
113. RDC to FO, 7/1/1903 and 15/1/1903, PRO FO 10/803. In the latter letter, he also commented on the appearance of Fox Bourne's book – 'seems fair and impartial enough'. The book was *Civilization in Congoland*.

114. RDC to FO, 21/1/1903, PRO FO 2/764.

115. RDC to FO, 15/2/1903, PRO FO 403/338.

116. FO minutes to RDC, 15/2/1903, PRO FO 2/764. Harry de la Rosa Burrard Farnall, CB, CMG, became one of the Foreign Office staff closest in sympathy with Casement's work. He was born in 1852 and became a FO clerk in 1873, assistant clerk in 1894, and senior clerk in 1900; he also served as secretary to various delegations.

117. RDC to Gertrude, 1/1/1903, 29/1/1903 and 20/2/1903 (N.W. Hotel, Liverpool), NLI MS 13074 (1/ii).

118. RDC to Cowper, 18/2/1903, NLI Acc. 4902 (7).

119. 1903 Lett's Pocket Diary, PRO HO 161/2. It is reproduced, with many obvious errors, in Singleton-Gates and Girodias. A new edition is now available in Ó Síocháin and O'Sullivan. It has been suggested that the entries from 1 January to 13 February were torn out of the original in 1916, to be selectively shown to figures of influence in London.

120. Baron Nisco was an Italian lawyer and senior judge of the Congo Court of Appeal. He was later to play a significant part in the investigation of Congo atrocities.

121. 'Denham' is Morten's address; 'Uxbridge', the train station for Denham; 'Aubrey' is 12 Aubrey Walk, Kensington, Casment's London address during this leave; 'H.W.' is Herbert Ward; 'G.B.' is probably George Brown, who is referred to on a number of occasions in the 1903 Diary (the intials would also be correct for Blücher).

122. In 1897 Casement was in Lourenço Marques; granted leave early in June he arrived back there on 1 November. In September, therefore, he could have passed through Madeira. In February 1885, he was in the early days of his first period in the Congo. While he may have taken leave early in the year and visited Madeira, I have found no record of such a trip.

123. For Will Reid of Reid's Hotel see Sawyer, *Diaries*, p. 62. For Hughes see Chapter 10.

124. RDC (*Anversville*, Tenerife) to Cowper, 24/3/1903, Tenerife, NLI Acc. 4902 (7). *The Curse of Central Africa* was by Guy Burrows (see n. 88, Chapter 7).

125. The word *fiba* means 'to suck, to kiss': Professor Wyatt MacGaffey (personal communication).

126. Casement was collecting his dog John, which he had left with Parkinson on his way home. From this and other references, it would seem also that on this leave Casement travelled with his black servant, Charlie.

127. I can only speculate as to why Casement should have spent these two weeks in Cabinda and not gone directly to Boma. He may have wished to avoid the oppressive inland heat as long as possible; with Nightingale gone to Europe, he may have been looking after the coastal area of the consulates. Or, aware of the growing tensions over the Congo regime and of his own forthcoming journey, he may have wished to limit his contact with Belgian officials.

1. RDC to Gertrude, 20/4/1903, NLI MS 13074 (1/i).
2. Friday, 17 April. On the following day, he wrote: 'The foregoing is Saturday's entry', which suggests that he may not have written his diary every day and opens up the possibility of error in some of his diary entries. Sir Hector Macdonald had had a distinguished military career in India and during the Boer War. For a thoughtful commentary on this entry in Casement's diary, see Dudgeon, pp. 121–4.
3. RDC to FO, 8/5/1903, PRO FO 10/803.
4. RDC to FO, 22/5/1903, and FO minutes thereon, PRO FO 10/804.
5. Quoted by Cookey, p. 82, from Hansard. Herbert Samuel (1870–1963), first Viscount Samuel, was a liberal politician, administrator and philosopher. He was to become Undersecretary of State at the Home Office in 1905 and Home Secretary in 1916, which position he held during Casement's trial. He resigned later in the same year, when Lloyd George replaced Asquith.
6. RDC to FO, 26/5/1903, PRO FO 403/338.
7. RDC to FO, 2/6/1903, PRO FO 10/804.
8. RDC to Farnall, 28/5/1903, PRO FO 10/804. Gustave-Marie Rabinek was an Austrian trader in the Congo, who was arrested in 1901 for trading in rubber, despite the fact that the area he worked in was officially a free-trade area. He was given the right to appeal, which, however, entailed a long journey downriver to Boma. Before embarking, he smuggled out a letter, indicating worries that he might not reach Boma alive. He didn't. He died suspiciously shortly before reaching Stanley Pool and was buried beside the river. The case caused widespread indignation in several countries, in Britain partly because it was claimed (and proved) that he had been arrested on a British vessel while in international waters (Lake Mweru). Casement had been requested by the FO to collect information on the case. See Inglis, pp. 62, 71, 126, 147.
9. RDC to cousin Roger, 28/5/1903, PRONI T3787/16 and 1903 Diary.
10. *Ibid.* and 1903 Diary, 26/5/1903.
11. RDC to FO, 4/6/1903, PRO FO 10/804.
12. Reid, p. 42, mistakenly has Casement travelling on foot from Matadi to Stanley Pool. See Hyland, p. 82.
13. RDC to FO, 30/6/1903, PRO FO 10/804.
14. RDC to FO, 10/6/1903, PRO FO 10/804.
15. *Ibid.*
16. *Ibid.*
17. RDC to FO, 15/6/1903, PRO FO 10/804.
18. RDC to FO, 11/6/1903 and 20/6/1903, PRO FO 2/764.
19. 1903 Diary, 18/6/1903 and RDC to Gertrude, 24/6/1903, NLI MS 13074 (1/ii).
20. RDC to Pincus, 9/6/1903, TCD 827.
21. RDC to FO, 1/7/1903, PRO FO 10/805.

22. Casement also gave the daily departure times, steaming times and distances for the Leopoldville–Chumbiri leg of his journey at the beginning of the 1903 Diary.

23. Congo Report, pp. 4–5, PRO FO 10/806. Casement's report was published as *Correspondence and Report from His Majesty's Consul at Boma respecting the Administration of the Independent State of the Congo*, PP 1904 (Cd. 1933) LXII. His initial report, submitted on 11 December 1903, contained the names of individuals and places, which were excised from the published version. For this reason, I have generally drawn on the December version (hereafter referred to as Congo Report). See Ó Síocháin and O'Sullivan.

24. Congo Report, p. 6.

25. RDC to FO, 16/7/1903, PRO FO 2/764.

26. RDC to FO, 18/7/1903 and 19/7/1903, PRO FO 2/764. The BMS letter had been sent on 27/5/1903 and was signed by John Howell, A.E. Scrivener, J.A. Clark, C.T. Williams, D. Dron and Miss L. de Hailes.

27. Congo Report, pp. 6–8.

28. The Revd D.J. Danielson accompanied him as engineer.

29. PRO FO 629/10, 20/7/1903. The FO approved his action and stated that he was to be relieved of personal responsibility – it was essential that he be able to move around freely. PRO FO 10/805, 20/7/1903, minute.

30. Congo Report, p. 37.

31. *Ibid.* pp. 9 and 39–41. Scrivener named the main culprit as Massard, who had been in the district from 1898 to 1900. His successor, Auguste Dooms, was horrified at what he found.

32. *Ibid.* p. 9. Casement's Lake Mantumba is today's Lake Ntomba.

33. RDC to FO, 3/8/1903, PRO FO 403/338. One of the enclosures to Casement's report gave the details of the case of Mola Ekulite, the young man whose hands had been beaten off. The enclosure included a letter that Clark had sent about it in 1901. As he left Lake Mantumba, Casement brought it to the attention of the Commandant of the Fort at Irebu, who took action immediately. For Fiévez, see Hochschild.

34. Congo Report, Bikela's Statement, p. 50. In the diary for 12 August, Casement wrote: 'Declarations of some few of the Mission girls as to how they became orphans & entered the Mission. Dreadful.'

35. *Ibid.* p. 14.

36. *Ibid.* p. 13. Wauters told Clark that, while he had stopped flogging some months previously, he still put men in blocks.

37. RDC to FO, 3/8/1903, PRO FO 10/805. Sjöblom, Clark and Banks, all ABMU, had done far more to protect natives and protest at abuses, said Casement, 'than any and all of the members of this Commission'. On 5 August the diary gave the Revd Stapleton's opinion: 'the Mission has been too quiet ... he does not approve of Grenfell's acquiescence in State rule and methods ...'

38. RDC to FO, 4/8/1903, PRO FO 2/764. His diary had recorded meetings with

Hansen on 11/7/1903, 15/7/1903 ('Captain Hansen called to bid goodbye and made some strange remarks on Belgian officers') and 16/7/1903.

39. RDC to FO, 5/8/1903, PRO FO 10/805.

40. RDC to Gertrude, 9/8/1903, NLI MS 13074 (1/ii).

41. RDC (Lake Mantumba) to Cowper, 3/8/n.y. [1903], NLI Acc. 4902 (6).

42. The Marquess of Lansdowne to Sir E. Monson *et alii* ['Note to the Powers'], no. 147. Africa, 8/8/1903, PRO FO 10/805. The results were to be disappointing; no support was forthcoming.

43. Congo Report, p. 15.

44. *Ibid.* p. 19. 'Brass rods', known locally as *mitakos*, were lengths of copper and brass wire used as a currency.

45. *Ibid.* p. 15.

46. RDC to FO, 21/8/1903, PRO FO 629/10.

47. Congo Report, p. 19.

48. *Ibid.* p. 22.

49. *Ibid.* p. 24.

50. *Ibid.* p. 20.

51. *Ibid.* p. 27. The Revd Edgar Stannard was one of the missionaries and his case became a celebrated one, some years later, after he was arrested by the State.

52. *Ibid.* p. 28.

53. RDC to FO, 5/9/1903, PRO FO 10/805.

54. RDC to FO, 6/9/1903, with enclosure of 4/9/1903 (RDC to Governor General), PRO FO 403/338.

55. The settlement is variously called Ekanza, Ikanza, Ikanza-na-Bosunguma, or Bosunguma. Details of the incidents are in the Congo Report, pp. 30–5, and in a letter to the FO on 15/9/1903, PRO FO 10/805.

56. Congo Report, p. 34. The Epondo case comprises enclosure 5 in no. 1 in this report, pp. 44–6. It was witnessed by the Revds W.D. Armstrong and D.J. Danielson and the interpreter, Vinda Bidiloa. In its challenge to Casement's report, the Congo State was later to focus on this case: see Chapter 9.

57. Commandant Steevens was the second-in-command in Coquilhatville.

58. Revd John Weeks (1861–1924) had been in the Congo since 1881 and had founded the BMS missionary station of Monsembe; he later began to protest against abuses, using Morel as an outlet. He was a keen folklorist and ethnologist, publishing in the journals *Folklore* and the *Journal of the Royal Anthropological Institute*; among his books were *Congo Life & Folklore* (1911); *Among Congo Cannibals* (1912); *Among the Primitive Bakongo* (1914). See Marchal.

59. RDC to FO, 15/9/1903, PRO FO 10/805.

60. PRO FO 403/338, 15–16/9/1903.

61. PRO FO 403/338, RDC To FO, 16/9/1903 with enclosures. Whitehead's letters were to be included in the 1904 report; see Ó Síocháin and O'Sullivan, pp. 128–40.

62. RDC to FO, 30/9/1903, enclosing RDC to Fuchs, 12/9/1903, PRO FO 403/338.

63. PRO FO 10/805, minutes of 17/10/1903, 18/10/1903 and 19/10/1903.
64. PRO FO 10/805, minutes on despatches of 15/9/1903, 17/10/1903, 18/10/1903 and 19/10/1903.
65. Arthur Nightingale, the consul, was in Europe at the time.
66. FO to RDC, 16/10/1903; RDC to FO, 17/10/1903 and 19/10/1903, PRO FO 10/806. His diary referred to this correspondence on 16 and 17 October.
67. RDC to EDM, 23/10/1903, MP F8/16. The first extant letter from Casement to Morel was written on 23 October. I take this to be the letter which the diary records as having been written on the 20th; Casement often wrote letters over several days and the date on this could be that on which he finished the letter.
68. FO to RDC, 20/10/1903, PRO FO 10/806.
69. RDC to FO, 7/10/1903, PRO FO 629/10. Casement suggested that the type of abuses listed by Dorbritz were 'entirely unknown' in British colonies.
70. RDC to Pincus, 28/10/1903, TCD 827.
71. RDC to FO, 31/10/1903 and 4/11/1903; FO to RDC, 3/11/1903, PRO FO 10/806.

9: CONGO REPORT AND CONGO REFORM, 1903–13

1. RDC to Gertrude, 1/12/1903, NLI MS. 13074 (1/ii). While he was in London, he stayed at Herbert Ward's house, while the Wards were away. The present chapter focuses on Casement's work concerning the Congo, including his involvement with Congo affairs until the dissolution of the Congo Reform Association in 1913. The early part of this chapter should be taken in conjunction with the following one, which deals with Casement's interests in Ireland and his posting to Lisbon. The latter part moves ahead of the general narrative of his life.
2. Conrad to RDC, 1/12/1903, NLI MS 13073 (27/ii). The letters are printed in Karl and Davies.
3. RDC to Cowper, 3/12/1903, NLI Acc. 4902 (7).
4. Henry (Harry) Grattan Guinness, MD, BD (1861–1915) was the son of the founder of the Livingston Inland Mission and the Congo Balolo Mission (also Henry Grattan Guinness). For some time he was ambivalent with regard to atrocity reports from the Congo, but later swung in behind the reformers.
5. Quoted in Cline, p. 38.
6. Morel later described the meeting in his manuscript history of the CRA. This was finally edited and published by W.R. Louis and J. Stengers as *E.D. Morel's History of the Congo Reform Movement*, *op. cit.* The quotations are from pp. 158–62.
7. RDC to Clarke, 11/12/1903, PRO FO 10/806, and Congo Report (Confidential). Edward Clarke, born in 1860, became a FO clerk in 1881, acting senior clerk for the African Department on 20 April 1904 and senior clerk in 1906.
8. RDC to Bigelow, 13/12/1903, NLI MS 13080 (1/ii).
9. Before his execution, individual letters of petition were submitted by a number of

people; they included one by Louie Heath, who described herself as 'formerly Local Scholarship Examiner to the Royal College of Music and correspondent to the *Musical Times*'. I assume that it is she who is mentioned in the 1903 and 1910 diaries.

10. Conrad to RDC, 17/12/1903, NLI MS 13073 (27/ii).
11. Conrad to RDC, 21/12/1903, NLI MS 13073 (27/ii).
12. RDC to EDM, 1/1/1904, LSE MP F4/1.
13. RDC to FO, 28/12/1903, PRO FO 10/807.
14. Conrad to Cunninghame Graham, 26/12/1903, in Karl and Davies, vol. 3, pp. 100–2. Robert Bontine Cunninghame Graham (1852–1936) was a flamboyant figure, a traveller, scholar, Scottish nationalist and socialist; he rode with the *gauchos* in Spanish America and was equally at home in Spain, Morocco or Scotland. He was Liberal MP for North-West Lanarkshire from 1886–92, was imprisoned in 1887 after a Trafalgar Square riot, and became first president of the National Party of Scotland in 1928. His works include studies of old Spanish life and the *conquistadores*, and volumes of stories, essays and sketches.
15. Conrad to RDC, 29/12/1903, NLI MS 13073 (27/ii).
16. RDC to FO, 2/1/1904, PRO FO 10/807. This was minuted to the effect that the right of consular jurisdiction had been obtained in a convention with the International Association in 1884 and, though Britain had agreed subsequently with the Congo State not to exercise it, 'we carefully reserved power to do so'. A FO memo on consular jurisdiction on 9/1/1904 shows that the FO was seriously considering this option or the threat of it. Under this arrangement, a consul could hold consular court, 'and shall exercise sole and exclusive jurisdiction, both civil and criminal, over the persons and property of British subjects'.
17. David Lloyd George (1863–1945) was already a well-known politician at this point. Brought up in Caernarvonshire, he qualified as a solicitor in 1884 and became known as a fearless advocate. He was elected Liberal MP for Caernarvon Burroughs in 1890 and became a leading political figure in Wales. He became notorious for his opposition to the Boer War and had had to flee a mob in Birmingham in 1901. He was a champion of Welsh causes.
18. RDC to Cunninghame Graham, 5/1/1904, Cunninghame Graham Correspondence, NLS, box 1, 2C.
19. FO memorandum and minutes, 21/1/1904, PRO FO 10/807.
20. Farnall to RDC, 1/2/1904, NLI MS 13073 (22/ii). Removing the names had varying effects on the text's readability. One example from Casement's main document reads: 'These people were at once followed by two men of M**, situated, they said, close to K**, and only a few miles distant. They brought with them a full-grown man named AA, whose arm was shattered and greatly swollen through the discharge of a gun, and a small boy named BB, whose left arm was broken in two places from two separate gun shots ... On returning to M** they found that CC, the sentry, had shot dead two men of the town named DD and EE, and had tied up this man AA and the boy BB, now before me, to two trees.' (Congo Report, pp. 54–5.)

21. RDC to FO, 2/2/1904, 7/2/1904, 11/2/1904 and 20/2/1904, PRO FO 10/807.

22. For publication and press coverage, see Inglis, pp. 86 and 91.

23. RDC to FO, 21/3/1904, and Barrington to RDC, 27/3/1904, PRO FO 10/789.

24. Ennismore to RDC, 27/4/1904, NLI MS 13073 (30/i), and RDC to Cowper, 15/4/1904, NLI Acc. 4902 (8).

25. Louis and Stengers, p. 162.

26. *Ibid.* p. 163.

27. *Ibid.* p. 164. The location of the meeting is left blank in Morel's manuscript, in Louis and Stenger's published edition of his *History*, and in Catherine Cline's biography of Morel.

28. Note, LSE MP F4/2.

29. RDC to EDM, 23/3/1908, LSE MP F8/23.

30. RDC to EDM, 25/1/1904, MP F8/16. W.T. Stead (1849–1912) was a supporter of Morel's. He was a journalist and author, assistant editor and later editor of the *Pall Mall Gazette*; he started the *Review of Reviews* (1890). He was drowned in the *Titanic* disaster. Barbara Tuchman described him as 'the most ebullient and prolific journalist of an age rich in his kind' and as 'a human torrent of enthusiasm for good causes. His energy was limitless, his optimism unending, his egotism gigantic'. Barbara Tuchman, *The Proud Tower* (NY: Bantam Books 1966), p. 286.

31. RDC to EDM, 1/2/1904, LSE MP F8/16.

32. RDC to EDM, 13/2/1904 and 18/2/1904, LSE MP F8/16.

33. RDC to ASG, 24/4/1904, NLI MS 10464 (2).

34. RDC to EDM, 24/3/1904, LSE MP F8/16.

35. Although it involves moving ahead of the general narrative, the remainder of this chapter will summarize Casement's involvement with Congo affairs until the dissolution of the Congo Reform Association in 1913. While he played an active part in only a very limited way, he followed events carefully and constantly encouraged Morel over the years. Full accounts of the campaign itself can be found in Cookey, Marchal, and Hochschild. The main narrative of Casement's life will resume in Chapter 10.

36. W.R. Louis, 'Morel and the Congo Reform Association, 1904–1913' in Louis and Stengers, pp. 170–220.

37. 'Notes on the Report of Mr Casement, Consul to His Britannic Majesty, of the 11th December, 1903', Brussels, 12 March 1904. The document is contained in *Further Correspondence Respecting the Administration of the Independent State of the Congo*, Africa no. 7 (1904).

38. Quoted in Cookey, p. 114; see Inglis, pp. 91–3.

39. Sir Edward Grey (1862–1933), 3rd Baronet and Viscount Grey of Fallodon, served as private secretary to Sir Evelyn Baring (1884), Liberal MP for Berwick-on-Tweed (1885–1916), and Parliamentary Undersecretary at the Foreign Office (1892–95). His support for the Boer War caused distrust among radical members of the party. He was Foreign Secretary from 1905–16, during which time he continued Lans-

downe's policy of friendship with France and of treating Germany as the greatest threat to European peace; this was reflected in his handling of the Agadir crisis in 1911, when it was indicated that Britain would fight, should Germany attack France. He was responsible for the Anglo-Russian Agreement in 1907, which also contributed to Germany's sense of encirclement. He resigned in December 1916.

40. Edmond George Petty-Fitzmaurice was brother of Lord Lansdowne, though they served in different political parties. He was born in 1846 and served as Parliamentary Undersecretary of State for Foreign Affairs in 1883 and in 1905. He was raised to the peerage as Baron Fitzmaurice of Leigh (Wilts) in 1906, became Privy Councillor in 1908 and resigned in June 1909.

41. For details see Cookey, Inglis, Marchal, and Hochschild.

42. Quoted in Inglis, p. 103; see also Galen Broeker, 'Roger Casement: background to treason', *Journal of Modern History*, XXIX (1957), 237–45. A pamphlet Harrison wrote introduced him as 'a country gentleman of absolutely independent mind, a sportsman and a traveller, and a familiar figure in London social and political circles', quoted in Hochschild, p. 239. For Harrison, see also Marchal, vol.1, pp. 256–62.

43. RDC to EDM, 27/6/1904, 12/4/1905, 29/4/1905, 19/7/1905, 28/8/1905, 27/9/1905 etc., LSE MP F8/18–20.

44. Cline, p. 44. Morel visited the US in September 1904 and helped found a branch of the CRA, in which the young sociologist Robert Park was involved.

45. RDC to EDM, 14/12/1904 and an undated letter of the same period, LSE MP F8/17.

46. Details can be found in Cookey, pp. 130–1; Cline, p. 46; Hochschild, pp. 220–1; Marchal, vol. 1, pp. 296–303.

47. RDC to EDM, 1/12/1904, 3/12/1904, 13/12/1904, 15/12/1904 etc., LSE MP F8/17.

48. RDC to EDM, 14/12/1904, LSE MP F8/17.

49. Nightingale to RDC, 21/1/1905, NLI MS 13073 (22/i). Beauchamp and Farnall also discussed protection.

50. Marchal, vol. 1, pp. 330–2; Hochschild, pp. 220–1; Cline, p. 46. In two letters in September, presumably when he got the news, Casement referred to this: 'Poor Shanu! – it is a brutal shame! I am very sorry indeed – this last news of Harris about the son going off his head is damnable. What a swinish lot of pigs are these, dear Bulldog.' RDC to EDM, 4/9/1905 (and see 8/9/1905), LSE MP F8/20.

51. Colonel John George Beresford Stopford entered the British army in 1859 and retired with the rank of colonel; he became the first treasurer of the African Society, established in memory of Mary Kingsley.

52. RDC to EDM, 15/12/1904, LSE MP F8/17.

53. RDC to EDM, 27/2/1905, 9/3/1905, April 1905, LSE MP F8/18.

54. RDC to EDM, 13/12/1904, LSE MP F8/17 and 15/3/1905, LSE MP F8/18.

55. Quoted in Inglis, p. 122, and Hochschild, p. 238. For her role, see Marchal, vol. 1, especially pp. 303–10.

56. Nightingale to RDC, 24/9/1904, NLI MS 13073 (35); RDC to EDM, 15/3/1905,

23/5/1905, LSE MP F8/18; see Hochschild, p. 237. Mountmorres later published *The Congo Independent State: A Report on a Voyage of Enquiry* (London: Williams and Norgate 1906). See Marchal, vol. 1, *passim*.

57. Henry Wellington Wack was one of the Congo State propagandists in the US. He published *The Story of the Congo Free State* in 1905. In it he stated of the Congo that: 'It is ... the story of a great colonizing undertaking founded upon modern social science.' Referring to the testimony of the Congolese, he commented: 'It is to be regretted that Mr Casement was not put on his guard against the statements of the blacks.' A good deal of the pro-State propaganda writing was shown subsequently to have been paid for by Leopold.

58. RDC to EDM, 13/12/1904, 14/12/1904, 15/3/1905, 27/1/1905, 24/5/1905, LSE MP F8/18.

59. For *La Vérité sur le Congo*, see RDC to EDM, 10/3/1905. Morel did publish the account of Casement Sr.'s ride in the *West African Mail*, 24/3/1905, p. 1234: LSE MP F8/25 (for details see Chapter 10).

60. RDC to EDM, 14/12/1904, LSE MP F8/17.

61. RDC to EDM, 2/2/1905, LSE MP F8/18.

62. RDC to EDM, 15/3/1905, LSE MP F8/18.

63. Cookey, p. 77, described Phipps thus: 'A conceited and conservative man with limited imagination, he was charmed by Brussels and could not bring himself to believe that the genial Belgians among whom he moved could be responsible for the atrocities revealed by Casement.' And Inglis, p. 107, observes: 'Casement was right about Phipps. His despatches from Brussels were full of almost hysterical resentment at the Congo reform movement in general, and Casement's contribution in particular.'

64. RDC to Cadbury, 7/7/1905, NLI MS 8358.

65. For Leopold's use of the sectarian issue, see Slade, pp. 299–305.

66. RDC to EDM, n.d. [Santos, 1907], LSE MP F8/17.

67. Hyde to RDC, 12/9/1905, NLI MS 13073 (27/i).

68. RDC to EDM, 21/4/1905, LSE MP F8/18.

69. RDC to EDM, 1/11/1905, LSE MP F8/20.

70. In April 1904, Mrs Green 'wrote to Redmond ... arranged for Dillon to be sent a concise memorandum and ... arranged for Casement to have a talk with a nationalist MP, who "was converted"'. R.B. McDowell, *Alice Stopford Green: Passionate Historian* (Dublin: Allen Figgis 1967), pp. 74–5. See RDC to ASG, 24/4/1904, NLI MS 10464 (2).

71. RDC to EDM, 12/4/1905, LSE MP F8/18. Hugh Alexander Law was born in 1872, second son of Hugh Law, Lord Chancellor of Ireland, 1881–3. He was educated at Rugby School and University College, Oxford, and became MP for the West Donegal Division of Co. Donegal (1902–18).

72. RDC to EDM, April 1905, LSE MP F8/18.

73. RDC to EDM, 1/3/06, LSE MP F8/22.

74. RDC to EDM, 3/4/1905, LSE MP F8/18.

75. RDC to Law, 12/4/1905, NLI MS 13080 (1/ii).
76. William Brabazon Lindsay Graham-Toler (1862–1943) was the 4th Earl of Norbury. Two of his sisters, Margaret and Charlotte, were in regular contact with Casement at this time. Lady Margaret married Edward Boycott Jenkins, while Charlotte did not marry.
77. RDC to EDM, 27/4/1905 and later letters, LSE MP F8/18.
78. William A. Cadbury (1867–1957) entered the family chocolate business in Bournville in 1887; he married Emmeline Wilson (1883–1966) in 1902 and they regularly holidayed on the west coast of Ireland. From 1901 to 1908 he became involved in investigating conditions of virtual slavery in the production of cocoa in the islands of St Thomé and Principe; the Cadbury firm was, in turn, accused by the conservative *Standard* of complicity, but took legal action, which it won (Edward Carson appeared for the defendants). Cadbury was active in the civic life of Birmingham, including a term as Lord Mayor (1919–21), and was a member of the Society of Friends. He and Emmeline were to give warm support to Casement.
79. John Holt was a Liverpool trader and campaigner for just colonial administration. Having lived in West Africa for some years as a young man, he built up a thriving trading business with the area and became a leading spokesman for Liverpool traders. His humanitarianism was stimulated by his friendship with Mary Kingsley and then with Edmond Morel; he played an active role in opposing abuses in the Congo State and in the French Congo. A man of great moral courage who disliked publicity, his gruff exterior concealed a deep kindliness and sympathy. He helped found the Royal African Society, to honour Mary Kingsley, and the School of Tropical Medicine in Liverpool; he died in June 1915 at the age of seventy-four.
80. RDC to EDM, 8/5/1905, LSE MP F8/19.
81. Mark Twain lent his support to the Congo campaign in the US and in 1905 wrote *King Leopold's Soliloquy: a Defence of his Congo Rule*, in the form of an ironic monologue by Leopold. Before seeing it, Casement told Gertrude that he heard it was 'excruciating' and then sent her a copy. Later in 1905 he commented to Morel that it 'should do immense good', but in an undated letter registered a negative judgment about it: 'I don't like it – it is *not* funny or witty – and is *not* Leopold at all. It may suit American tastes but will not bring in any converts over here I am sure.' RDC to Gertrude, 6/5/1905 and 8/5/1905, NLI MS 13074 (2/ii); RDC to EDM, 27/4/1905, LSE MP F8/18, 10/5/1905, F8/19, 8/9/1905, F8/20, and n.d., F8/25. For Mark Twain, see Marchal, vol. 2, pp. 131–4.
82. Sir Henry Seaton-Karr was Conservative MP for St Helen's, Lancashire, 1885–1906; he contested Berwick, 1910.
83. Frederick Courteney Selous (1851–1917) was born in London, where his father was chairman of the London Stock Exchange. He went to Africa in 1871, where he became a professional ivory hunter and trader, museum collector and gold prospector; he was involved with Rhodes in the occupation of Matabeleland. He traveled later in Asia Minor, Canada and Iceland and was killed in action in January 1917.

84. John Burns (1858–1943), labour leader and politician, represented Battersea in parliament, 1892–1918. He believed that the First World War could have been averted, resigned, and took no further part in public life.

85. Lord Beauchamp later became a Liberal cabinet minister. According to Dudgeon, p. 156, he led an increasingly open homosexual lifestyle and had to flee the country in 1931.

86. RDC to EDM, 22/5/1905 and subsequent letters, LSE MP F8/19. A lot of Casement's correspondence at this time is addressed from 7 Trebovir Rd., Colonel Stopford's home.

87. RDC to EDM, 12/5/1905, 26/5/1905 and 1/6/1905, LSE MP F8/19.

88. RDC to Holt, 27/5/1905, RHO Holt Papers, MSS Afr. s. 1525.

89. RDC to Holt, 8/6/1905, RHO Holt Papers, MSS Afr. s. 1525. On 7 June 1905 the Norwegian parliament refused to recognize the Swedish king and declared independence from Sweden. Soon after this, Casement got to know Arthur Conan Doyle, who was becoming interested in the Congo issue: see RDC to Holt, 16/6/1905, RHO Holt Papers, MSS Afr. s. 1525, where he refers to their having met.

90. Cookey, p. 137.

91. Johnston to RDC, 18/5/1905, NLI MS 13073 (30/ii). W.R. Louis has suggested that Johnston exercised a moderating influence on the reformers. Perhaps an example of this 'moderation' was his objection to having a 'Lagos negro' speak at the meeting: he would, on the one hand, be too 'verbose' and, on the other, 'he might introduce theories of self-government for the negro for which – unfortunately – the negro is not yet ripe'. Johnston to RDC, 6/6/1905. See Louis, 'Morel', pp. 171–220.

92. The Holborn meeting is often described as a CRA meeting. The whole genesis of the meeting suggests to me that it was an independent venture, though clearly part of the broader movement.

93. (Sir) John Harris (1874–1940) and his wife Alice Seeley Harris spent some years as missionaries in the Congo and became involved in the fight against abuses; they returned to England and worked energetically with Morel in the campaign: 'In 1910, when a large amount of success had been obtained in carrying through the campaign, Harris accepted an invitation to become Parliamentary Secretary to the Anti-Slavery and Aborigines Protection Society ...' He had 'a flair for publicity, and through his efforts the society gradually grew in numbers, and especially in political influence'. He stood for parliament as a Liberal on several occasions and was elected for North Hackney in 1923, but lost the seat in the next election; he later worked for the League of Nations; he was 'a man of strong physique, active disposition, keen mind, wise judgement and great capacity for work' (Obituary, July 1940, *Anti-Slavery Reporter and Aborigines' Friend*).

94. Nightingale to RDC, 28/11/1904, 8/1/1905 and 19/2/1905, NLI MS 13073 (35). For some details of the Commission's work, see Slade, pp. 287–93; Hochschild, pp. 250–5; Marchal, vol. 1, ch. 14 and vol. 2, chs. 24 and 26.

95. Cookey, p. 148.

96. Casement informed Morel on 10 November that he had got a copy of the report, without a covering letter, though he recognized Baron Nisco's hand. He had not yet read it. RDC to EDM, 10/11/1905, LSE MP F8/20.

97. As editor of the *Morning Post*, Thomas Lennox Gilmour (1859–1936) had been providing sympathetic coverage of the Congo campaign; Casement came to know him in 1904. He was educated at Edinburgh University and became private secretary to Lord Rosebery (1885–1903). He was managing director for the Mozambique Company in London (1904–13); member of the War Savings Committee (1916) and assistant director in the Department of Information (1916–17). He had been engaged in journalism since 1880.

98. RDC to EDM, n.d. [early July], 4/7/1906, 10/7/1906 (misdated, I believe, as 10/1/1906), 17/7/1906, LSE MP F8/21. The *Daily Chronicle* expressed an interest in partly funding the enterprise: 16/7/1906, LSE MP F8/21.

99. David Arnold, *Britain, Europe and the World, 1870–1955* (London: Edward Arnold 1966).

100. Cuibono to RDC, 22/1/1905, NLI MS 13073 (46/xviii); Stead to RDC, 30/1/1905, NLI MS 13073 (14).

101. RDC to Gertrude, 15/03/1905, NLI MS 13074 (2/ii); RDC to EDM, 12/04/1905, LSE MP F8/18, and 08/09/1905, LSE MP F8/20; 'Quo Vadis', n.d., NLI MS 13159.

102. RDC to EDM, 14/12/1905, and 24/1/06, LSE MP F8/20 and F8/22. Within the Liberal Party, Grey belonged to the group of Liberal Imperialists ('Limps'), as opposed to the 'Little Englanders' or Radicals.

103. RDC to FO, 12/12/1905, NLI MS 13081 (2/i).

104. RDC to EDM, 14/12/1905, LSE MP F8/20, and 24/1/1906, F8/22.

105. Tyrrell to RDC, 24/1/06, NLI MS 13073 (43); Emmott to RDC, 3/2/1906, NLI MS 13073 (29/i).

106. For accounts, see Cookey, ch. 5, and Marchal, vol. 2, pp. 202–10.

107. Quoted in Inglis, p. 151.

108. RDC to EDM, 4/7/1906, LSE MP F8/21.

109. Tyrrell to RDC, 5/7/1906, NLI MS 13073 (43); Emmott to RDC, 15/7/1906, LSE MP F8/21; Gilmour to RDC, 9/7/1906, NLI MS 13073 (46/ix); RDC to Morten, 10/7/1906, quoted in Parmiter, p. 47.

110. Louis, 'Morel', p. 211.

111. RDC to EDM, 19/9/1906, LSE MP F8/22. He also mentioned Hoste to John Holt at this time and his own 'interest in the Tea Company': RDC to Holt, 19/9/1906, RHO, MSS Afr. s. 1525.

112. RDC to EDM, 12/10/1906, LSE MP F8/22.

113. RDC to EDM, 3/12/1906, LSE MP F8/22. The 'brave man' at Lukolela was the Revd John Whitehead.

114. RDC to EDM, 27/12/1906 and 4/1/1907, LSE MP F8/22.

115. RDC to EDM, 2/4/1907, LSE MP F8/22.

116. RDC to EDM, 1/8/1907, LSE MP F8/22.

117. RDC to EDM, 10/8/07, LSE MP F8/22. Casement had actually broached the idea

of a Memorial to Morel in 1906: see RDC to EDM, 17/7/1906, LSE MP F8/21.

118. RDC to EDM, 13/9/1907 and 21/9/1907, LSE MP F8/22; Cadbury to RDC, n.d. (r. 8/9/1907), NLI MS 13073 (26/ii); Emmott to RDC, 5/9/1907, NLI MS 13073 (29/i).

119. RDC to EDM, 16/10/1907, LSE MP F8/22.

120. RDC to EDM, 22/11/1907, LSE MP F8/22.

121. RDC to EDM, 29/6/1909, LSE MP F8/23.

122. RDC to EDM, 31/7/1909, LSE MP F8/23. Morel had challenged Grey's vacillation in a letter to the *Morning Post* in June 1909: see Cookey, p. 247.

123. RDC to EDM, 19/11/1909, LSE MP F8/23. See Marchal, vol. 2, pp. 415–21 and, for a poster, Hochschild, pp. 244–5.

124. RDC to EDM, 15/12/1909, LSE MP F8/23.

125. RDC to EDM, 30/11/1909 and 25/12/1909, LSE MP F8/23.

126. RDC to EDM, 30/1/1910, LSE MP F8/23. Relations between Morel and Harris had been edgy, since the latter had joined the CRA in 1906. Morel was in Liverpool and Harris in London, closer to the centre of power. In October 1908 Morel moved the headquarters of the CRA, and his family, from Liverpool to London. After the Anti-Slavery Society and the Aborigines Protection Society amalgamated, Harris left the CRA in 1910 to become the Parliamentary Secretary to the new organization.

127. RDC to EDM, 7/6/1910, LSE MP F8/23.

128. RDC to EDM, 12/7/1910 and 15/7/1910, LSE MP F8/23.

129. Arthur Conan Doyle (1859–1930) studied medicine at Edinburgh University, and became famous for his series, *The Adventures of Sherlock Holmes*, which started in 1891. He served as a physician in the Boer War (1899–1902) and was knighted in 1902. He became interested in spiritualism in his later years.

130. Quoted in Pierre Nordon, *Conan Doyle* (London: John Murray 1966), p. 72.

131. *Ibid.* pp. 77–8. Interestingly, Cardinal Bourne, the Archbishop of Westminster, refused Doyle's invitation to help. Having been educated at Louvain in Belgium, he was suspicious of the reformers. He read Doyle's book, *The Crime of the Congo*, and responded: 'the perusal has strengthened me in my distrust of the methods of the Congo Reform Association, and in my reluctance to see Catholics identified with it in any way'. Quoted in Nordon, p. 77.

132. RDC to EDM, 29/6/1910, LSE MP F8/23.

133. Sawyer, *Diaries*, p. 57; RDC to Gertrude, 26/6/10, NLI MS 13074 (6ii); RDC to EDM, 29/6/10, LSE MP F8/23. According to Cline, p. 82 and n. 43. Casement and Morel had discussed the possibility of a testimonial in May; Doyle to RDC, 3/7/1910, NLI MS 13073 (28/i).

134. Beauchamp to RDC, 1/7/1910, NLI MS 13073 (22/i); RDC to Holt, 3/7/1910, RHO MSS Afr. s. 1525; Cadbury to RDC, 5/7/1910, NLI MS 13073 (26/ii).

135. RDC to Holt, 15/7/1910, RHO, MSS Afr. s. 1525; 1910 Diary, 12, 21 and 25/7/1910. His contributions came from Emmott, Dick Morten, Mrs Green, Elizabeth Bannister, Ferdinand Ware and Will Reid. He was to get a letter and contribution from his former vice-consul in Rio, Bosanquet, now posted in Moscow: Bosanquet

to RDC, 31/7/1910, NLI MS 13073 (46/iii); another letter came from Colonel Stopford, 18/7/1910, NLI MS 13073 (40).

136. Holt to RDC, 30/3/1911, NLI MS 13073 (26/i).

137. 1911 Cash Ledger, 3/4/1911 and 6/4/1911, PRO HO 161.

138. RDC to ASG, 8/4/1911 and 9/4/1911, NLI MS 10464 (4).

139. Cadbury kept in touch, too. On the 10th, he wrote that Morel had a very small circle of 'warm-hearted followers', but that he was too outspoken to please many, for example, Sir Edward Grey, the Church Missionary Society, the anti-liquor party and the Conservatives; consequently, a small number of very wealthy supporters would be the best bet. Two days later, he expressed satisfaction at the impression Casement was making 'in the north'; he asked him whether he would like to visit at Easter, a family occasion, or later, more quietly. Cadbury to RDC, 10/4/1911 and 12/4/1911, NLI MS 13073 (26/ii).

140. On 1 May Holt wrote and talked of a visit from Casement and their conversation regarding Morel; he hoped for success and enclosed a cheque for £200 – to be from an 'anonymous donor' – Holt to RDC, 1/5/1911, NLI MS 13073 (46/x). On the 6th Casement contacted Hoste also about the testimonial: RDC to Hoste, 6/5/1911, Hamilton Papers, bundle 2772.

141. RDC to Holt, 25/5/1911, RHO, MSS Afr. s. 1525. With the Congo campaign winding down, Morel now sought new outlets for his energies. He began to turn to politics and at this time William Cadbury agreed to sponsor him financially in a bid for the Liberal seat of Birkenhead.

142. A copy of the programme can be found among the Cadbury Papers in Birmingham (Cadbury 227); see also Cline, p. 91.

143. RDC to EDM, 26/5/1911, LSE MP F8/24. According to Gertrude in her notes on his life, 'he hated publicity and loathed being "shown off" '. NLI MS 17594 (Gertrude). This point is also made by Nina.

144. RDC to Mrs Holt, 2/6/1911, RHO, MSS Afr. s. 1525. Ann Barnes, wife of Louis Barnes of the Putumayo Commission, wrote on the 2nd thanking him for an invitation to the luncheon; Vandervelde, she commented, spoke splendidly. Ann Barnes to RDC, 2/6/1911, NLI MS 13073 (19).

145. For details, see Cline, pp. 82–7; Marchal, vol. 2, pp. 448–51; Cookey, pp. 276–8.

146. EDM to RDC, 12/4/11, LSE MP F8/24.

147. RDC to EDM, 13/4/11, LSE MP F5/3.

148. RDC (105 Antrim Road) to EDM, 22/4/1911, LSE MP F8/24. Casement was contacted soon afterwards by a representative of Lever Brothers to arrange a meeting, but there is no evidence that anything came of it. Lever Brothers to RDC, 25/7/1911 and 26/7/1911, NLI MS 13073 (10/i).

149. RDC to EDM, 29/2/1912, LSE MP F8/24.

150. RDC to EDM, 11/6/1912, LSE MP F8/24. Within a month of writing this letter Casement was telling Morel of his intention of writing a book about the Putumayo. RDC to EDM, 27/7/1912, LSE MP F8/24.

151. RDC to EDM, 13/6/1912, LSE MP F8/24.
152. RDC to EDM, 24/7/1912, LSE MP F8/24. Morel's article was titled 'Roger Casement: The Bayard of our Consular Service'. For the Intelligence Bureau, see Charles Watney to RDC, 17/7/1912 and 19/7/1912, NLI MS 13073 (16/ii). Watney apologized for publishing Casement's photograph; he was, he said, helping Percy Brown and the Putumayo Mission Fund; he also said that he had met Casement at Lady Margaret Jenkins's some years previously.
153. RDC to EDM, 5/6/1913, LSE MP F8/25.
154. RDC to EDM, 11/6/1913, LSE MP F8/25.
155. *Ibid.*

10: IRELAND: A NEW COMMITMENT, 1904–6

1. RDC to ASG, 20/4/1907, NLI MS 10464 (3).
2. Arthur Griffith (1872–1922) worked as a journalist in the Transvaal, 1896–9, and founded *The United Irishman* with William Rooney in 1899; he took the position that Irish self-government could not be attained through parliamentary action at Westminster. He formed Cumann na nGaedheal in 1900, the National Council in 1903, and began elaborating the Sinn Féin ('Ourselves') policy in late 1905, a policy of self-reliance, incorporating the economic ideas of Friedrich List. *The Resurrection of Hungary: a Parallel for Ireland* sold 30,000 copies. In 1907–8 these earlier organizations and the Dungannon Clubs coalesced to form the Sinn Féin League. In 1907 *The United Irishman* went out of business and was followed by the weekly *Sinn Féin*, which for a time became a daily paper. Griffith married Maud Sheehan in 1910, opposed Irishmen joining the British army during the First World War but took no part in the rebellion of 1916. He was imprisoned several times from 1916–21, was one of the plenipotentiaries who negotiated the treaty of 1921 with the British government, and was president of Dáil Éireann in 1922.
3. Bulmer Hobson (1883–1969) was born at Holywood, Co. Down, of Quaker stock, and was educated at the Friends' School, Lisburn. He was a founder member of the Ulster Literary Theatre in 1904, became secretary of the first Antrim board of the Gaelic Athletic Association and, with Countess Markievicz, established Na Fianna Éireann, a nationalist youth movement, in 1909. He was active in the Irish Republican Brotherhood (IRB), founding and editing its paper, *Irish Freedom*, from 1911 to 1914; he was also prominent in the Irish Volunteer movement, but opposed the 1916 Easter Rising. From 1922 to 1928 he held a position in the Revenue Commissioners. He was author of several books, including studies of Wolfe Tone and William Orr, as well as his autobiography, *Ireland: Yesterday and Tomorrow* (1968).
4. As a young man Denis McCullough (1883–1968) was active in the Gaelic League and GAA, and became a member of the IRB of which he was later to become a leading member, involved in preparations for the 1916 Easter Rising.

5. The quotations are from RDC to ASG, 10/2/1911 and 24/12/1912, NLI MS 10464 (5) and 27/6/1907, NLI MS 10464 (3).

6. This letter is reproduced in full in Séamus Ó Cléirigh, *Casement and the Irish Language, Culture and History* (Baile Átha Cliath: Clódhanna Teoranta 1977). The record of Casement's meetings with John Hughes in Madeira is in the 1903 Diary for 4, 5 and 11 March.

7. Both Ennismore and his father, Lord Listowel, gave support to the Congo Reform Association. Casement was in Mallow on 1 February 1904 and gave Convamore as his address for most of the following week in his communications with the FO. He was back in Antrim by 11 February. It is also conceivable that he visited the nearby Jephson residence in Mallow Castle during this trip.

8. RDC to Morten, 10/7/1906, NLI Acc. 4902 (2). George Henry, 5th Earl Cadogan (1840–1915), was Lord Lieutenant of Ireland from 1895 to 1902. He married Lady Beatrix Jane Craven (1865–1907), fourth daughter of the 2nd Earl of Craven. Louisa Farquharson's maternal grandmother was Lady Louisa Craven, hence there was a family link with the Cadogans. Members of the Hare family of Convamore were among the friends Louisa Farquharson made in Ireland. The address appears on items of her correspondence held in Invercauld Castle, Braemar, Scotland.

9. Louise Farquharson's letters to RDC are in NLI MS 13073 (31/i) and (46/viii). Casement's 'Brief to Counsel' is in NLI MS 13088 (1/iii). See also Sawyer, *Flawed Hero*. In 1905 a lecture she gave in London was published in pamphlet form, as *Ireland's Ideal* (Gaelic League Pamphlets no. 31). In describing those participating in the new movement in Ireland, Farquharson wrote: 'In one case, a man who served His Majesty ably in a responsible position in a distant land, ready to throw up everything in order to help on this great – this wonderful thing; for he had left Ireland, he said, asleep, and had returned to find her awake.' This man was Casement.

10. Quoted in Ó Cléirigh, p. 20, and see Mackey, *Crime against Europe*, p. 170. Clark wrote a tribute to Casement in August 1916, using his pen-name, 'Benmore': 'In Memoriam – Roger Casement', NLI P2275.

11. *Feiseanna* (pl.) were local festivals, associated with the Irish cultural revival.

12. Casement's letter to the *Irish News* is referred to by J.C. O'Boyce.

13. Quoted in Michael Tierney, *Eoin MacNeill: Scholar and Man of Action 1867–1945*, ed. F.X. Martin, (Oxford: Clarendon Press 1980), p. 84. Tierney states that MacNeill and Casement met at the Feis and became friends subsequently. MacNeill (1867–1948) was born in Glenarm, Co. Antrim, and educated in St Malachy's College, Belfast, and the Royal University of Ireland. One of the founders of the Gaelic League in 1893 and first editor of its paper, *An Claidheamh Soluis*, he became professor of early Irish history in University College, Dublin. He was the catalyst for the formation of the Irish Volunteers in 1913 and was sentenced to life imprisonment after the 1916 Easter Rising. He was minister for education in the first Free State cabinet, 1922–5, but departed from public life in 1927, following controversy over the Boundary Commission, and devoted himself to scholarship and cultural

activities. He was author of *Phases of Irish History* (1919) and *Celtic Ireland* (1921).

14. The history of the Feis of the Glens has been documented in detail in Séamus O'Cléirigh's lovingly compiled book, *Feis na nGleann* (n.d., privately published). I have drawn on it for some of the detail here, as I have on the *clár* (programme) and the report for the 1904 Feis, in the NLI. Further detail is now available in Eamon Phoenix, Pádraic Ó Cléireacháin, Eileen McAuley & Nuala McSparran (eds.), *Feis na nGleann: A Century of Gaelic Culture in the Antrim Glens* (Belfast: Feis na nGleann & Stair Uladh/Ulster Historical Foundation 2005).

15. RDC to Gertrude, 9/3/1904, 24/3/1904 and 2/5/1904, NLI MS 13074 (2/i).

16. Twice in 1905, when he himself was in financial straits, he collected money for her. He also remarked on the callousness of her brother-in-law, Dr Dunlop, for not being willing to help: 'Some of the north-of-Ireland hearts are not Irish at all – and do not please confound those basaltic compositions imported from Scotland or God knows where with anything native to the Irish temperament ...' (2/1/1905). It later emerged that she sought and received help from a number of sources. RDC to M. Causton, 1/3/1902, 2/3/1904, 16/3/1904, 16/4/1904, 23/4/1904, 2/1/1905, 5/11/1905, 22/12/1905, 20/1/1906 and 26/2/1906, NLI MS 18574.

17. Douglas Hyde (1860–1949) was born in Frenchpark, Co. Roscommon, son of a Church-of-Ireland rector. He engaged in literary work on the Irish language and published several volumes, e.g. *The Love Songs of Connacht* (1893) and *An Sgéalaidhe Gaedhealach* (1901). He is especially noted for his influential lecture in 1893, 'The Necessity of De-Anglicising Ireland'. He was one of the founder members of the Gaelic League in 1893, but always argued for the separation of the language move-ment and political allegiances; he campaigned for the recognition of Irish in the educational system at all three levels. He was appointed professor of modern Irish in University College, Dublin, in 1909 and became first president of Ireland under the 1937 Constitution.

18. O'Boyce (Seaghan Ua Buaidhe/Seaghan Michil) to RDC, 8/4/1904, NLI MS 13073 (13/i). Later that year Casement had to seek his friend Mary Hutton's help in trans-lating a card in Irish from O'Boyce (RDC to Hutton, 15/12/1904, NLI MS 8612). The second teacher, P. Magill, wrote in April: Magill to RDC, 28/4/1904, NLI MS 13073 (10/ii). The only evidence I have of the date of Casement's visit is his com-ment to Morel on 24 March that he was back from Donegal (RDC to EDM, 24/3/1904, MP F8/16). Hyde's first letter to Casement was written on 19 June 1904. In it he acknowledges Casement's cheque for £5 for the Training College in Ballingeary, Co. Cork, which Hyde had forwarded to Liam de Róiste. The college was formally opened on 4 July. See Diarmaid Ó Murchadha, *Liam de Róiste* (Baile Átha Cliath: An Clóchomhar Teoranta 1976), p. 36 ff.

19. Francis Joseph Bigger (1863–1926) came from a prosperous business family; he qualified and practised as a solicitor, but his passions were history and archaeol-ogy. He revived and was editor of the *Ulster Journal of Archaeology*, restored castles and churches, encouraged Irish music, song and economic development. He pub-

lished many articles and pamphlets. Casement became a close friend and frequently stayed at his house near Belfast. Dudgeon, pp. 181–98, provides a valuable sketch of Bigger's life and of his circle.

20. Reprinted in Ó Cléirigh, pp. 61–2. The Cathal to whom Casement refers is Cathal O'Byrne, who evocatively recalls one such evening in 'Roger Casement's ceilidhe', *The Capuchin Annual* (1946–7), 312–13. O'Byrne's name was drawn into the diaries debate by Reid, p. 487; on this, see Séamus O'Neill, 'Note: Roger Casement, Cathal O'Byrne and Professor Reid', *Studies* (Spring/Summer 1979), 117–21; and Dudgeon, pp. 584–90.

21. Joseph Campbell, 'Northern Autobiography', no. 4, TCD MS 10189/270. Campbell (1879–1944) was born in Belfast and became active in literary affairs in Ulster. He published several books of poetry and song. Casement was to write letters of recommendation for Campbell in 1906 and to discuss his case with William Tyrrell at the FO: see RDC to Campbell, 2/7/1906, NLI MS 5459.

22. Robert Gordon John Johnstone Berry (1870–1947) retired with the rank of colonel, after a military career in which he served in the Boer War and in West Africa. He was an active antiquarian and amateur archaeologist and became a life member of the Royal Irish Academy in 1905; he was also active in the Royal Society of Antiquaries of Ireland and in The Belfast Natural History and Philosophical Society. He published many articles, including reports of excavations and papers, on the Celtic Mother Goddess and the 'Sierra Leone Cannibals'. He lived for some years in Richhill Castle, near Lurgan, Co. Armagh, where Casement visited the family. For Casement's letters to him, see Casement Papers, 9. IX, E2.

23. Margaret Dobbs (1871–1962) came from a comfortable and staunchly Unionist family. She set about learning Irish in her teenage years and became involved in the planning for the first Feis and remained active on the Feis committee until the end of her life. She was a Celtic scholar, with a considerable list of publications. She is reported as saying of Casement: 'Roger was my friend. He used to stay here weekends after his return almost broken in health from Putumayo ... I have always had the highest admiration for Roger. He was a gentleman, humanitarian, poet and patriot. Not only was he my friend but he was a friend of all the Irish people. But I have not the same admiration for his judgements.' Jack McCann, 'Margaret Dobbs', *The Glynns: Journal of the Glens of Antrim Historical Society*, 11 (1983), 41–6.

24. Alice Milligan (1866–1953) was born in Omagh, Co. Tyrone, and educated at Methodist College, Belfast; Magee College, Derry; King's College, London. She was active in organizing the 1798 centenary celebrations, served as a Gaelic League organizer for some years, as a member of Inghinidhe na hÉireann ('Daughters of Ireland') and of Sinn Féin. She established the journal *Shan Van Vocht* ('The Poor Old Woman' i.e. Ireland) with Anna Johnston ('Ethna Carbery') and wrote a good deal of poetry, for which she is primarily known. See Sheila Turner Johnston, *The Harper of the Only God: A Selection of Poems by Alice Milligan* (Omagh: Colourpoint Press 1993), and *Alice: A Life of Alice Milligan* (Omagh: Colourpoint Press 1994).

25. Stephen Lucius Gwynn (1864–1950), grandson of William Smith O'Brien (a leader of the 1848 Rebellion), was educated at St Columba's College and at Oxford. He became Nationalist MP for Galway city from 1906 to 1918, was an active member of the Gaelic League and sent his son Denis (Casement's biographer) to Pearse's Scoil Éanna. He enlisted in the Connaught Rangers in the First World War and left public life after the war for scholarship and writing. He was author of many books, including his autobiography, *Experiences of a Literary Man* (1926).

26. Sir Horace Plunkett (1854–1932), educated at Eton and University College, Oxford, became a cattle rancher in Wyoming (1879–89) and a key figure in the cooperative movement in Ireland from 1889. He was vice-president of the Department of Agriculture and Technical Instruction for Ireland, 1899–1907. He was Unionist MP for South County Dublin from 1892–1900, but converted to Home Rule.

27. Evelyn Gleeson (1855–1944) studied painting in London and also developed an interest in tapestry and weaving; she became secretary of the Irish Literary Society in London. In 1902 she established the Dún Emer Guild, through her friendship with Augustine Henry and in association with the Yeats sisters, Lily and Lolly. It aimed at producing Irish crafts and providing employment, and had a number of departments, including carpet-making, embroidery, printing, tapestry-weaving and bookbinding. See Sheila Pim, *The Wood and the Trees: Augustine Henry – A Biography* (Kilkenny: Boethius Press 1984), and William M. Murphy, *Family Secrets: William Butler Yeats and his Relatives* (Dublin: Gill & Macmillan 1995).

28. Quoted in Inglis, pp. 119–20.

29. Alice Milligan, 'Events of Easter Week', *Catholic Bulletin*, vi (Jan.–Dec. 1916), 573–5.

30. Benmore, 'In Memoriam – Roger Casement', August 1916, NLI P2275. The Feis was not all sweetness and light. In his first letter to Bigger, Casement noted that 'Miss McDonnell has been unhappy, I think.' RDC to Bigger, 27/5/1904, NLI MS 21531. She resigned at the end of the year and, in a letter to Casement, she remarked that 'I fear you and I should never agree on certain points tho' it is possible that you might think differently were you living among the people or belonged to them as I do ... I thank you for informing me of the incompetence of my self and my neighbours. I do not hold the same view of them – tho' if you alluded to our Hon. Sec. I should not contradict you.' McDonnell to RDC, 1/12/1904, NLI MS 13073 (11).

31. He gave the details, retrospectively, in a telegraph to FO: RDC to FO, 16/8/1904, PRO FO 10/789; and see his letters to Cowper, 14/6/1904 and 22/6/1904 ('sorry to hear you are so ill'), NLI Acc. 4902 (8).

32. RDC to Bigger, 15/7/1904, NLI MS 21531. There is correspondence between Jorge O'Neill and Bigger in the Bigger Collection in Belfast Central Library. A card there is addressed, 'J. O'Neill, His Excellency The O'Neill, Prince of Tyrone'. Casement told Mary Hutton that he was a direct descendant of Brian Ballagh O'Neill, that his ancestor had left Ireland after the Siege of Limerick (1691) and that he had 'an Irish heart and sympathies still': RDC to Hutton, 15/12/1904, NLI

MS 8612. He was a subscriber to the first Feis na nGleann.

33. Farquharson to RDC, 7/7/1904, 17/7/1904 and 6/8/1904, NLI MS 13073 (31/i). Casement seems to have had time for at least one sexual encounter in Lisbon. The entry for 28 February in the 1910 Black Diary records: 'Lovely, young & glorious. Biggest since Lisbon July 1904 & as big. Perfectly huge.' Sawyer, *Diaries*, p. 43.

34. RDC to FO (Cockerell, Barrington), 16/8/1904, PRO FO 10/789.

35. J. O'Neill to Bigger, 22/8/1904, Belfast Central Library, F.J. Bigger Collection.

36. RDC to Bigger, 26/8/1904, NLI, MS 21531.

37. On 8 September Casement had also written from London to Nightingale in the Congo to say that he had returned ill after two months in Lisbon. RDC to Cowper, 17/9/1904, NLI MS 14100. Cowper had an Irish connection: he was married to Mary Flanagan, first cousin of Sinéad Flanagan, Éamonn de Valera's wife.

38. Tom O'Flaherty, *Aranmen All* (Dublin: Three Candles 1934), pp. 157–8. O'Flaherty (1890–1936) emigrated to Boston at the age of twenty-one and became active in socialist and trade union circles. He wrote in the *Daily Worker* and the *Labour Defender* but was expelled from the Communist Party in 1928 for Trotskyite ideas; he returned to Ireland in 1932 and was editor of *An t-Éireannach* for some time.

39. RDC to Hutton, 21/11/1904, NLI MS 8612. Mary Anne Hutton (1862–1953) was daughter of a Unitarian minister and married Arthur Hutton, a wealthy coach-builder. She learned Old Irish and corresponded with Kuno Meyer from 1900. The first edition of her major work, *The Táin*, was published in 1907 and was well-received. She lectured in Middle Irish in Belfast and Dublin. Her husband being dead, she moved to Dublin in 1910 and became a Catholic in 1911. She was a financial supporter of Pearse's Scoil Éanna.

40. Ó Ceallacháin to RDC, 3/1/1905, NLI MS 13078 (4); Nic Néill to RDC, n.d., NLI MS 13078 (2). Her letter was in Irish. Ó Ceallacháin (*c*.1853–1937) was an important influence in the early life of Liam O'Flaherty, who based the character of the teacher in his novel *Skerret* on him; he later lost his teaching position after a serious disagreement with the local parish priest. See Breandán Ó hEithir, *An Chaint sa tSráidbhaile* (Baile Átha Cliath: Comhar Teoranta 1991), pp. 161–2.

41. He saw the play on Friday, 30 September, travelled to Tawin on Saturday and attended Mass in the chapel on Sunday, where he met Fr Kean. Séamus O'Beirne (1881–1935) was born in Tamhain, qualified as a doctor in 1905 and worked in the Connemara area, where he initiated a programme of community education on tuberculosis. He helped establish a summer college in Tamhain, which Casement was to visit.

42. RDC to Hyde, 4/10/1904 (Tawin Appeal), NLI MS 8612. He added: 'I think were I to live in Tawin or Kilmurvy in Aran for three months I should be able to speak the language a bit, and certainly to read it. I can pick up fairly quickly, and in Tawin I found myself able to follow something of what was said around me. Oh! if it could only be made again a living tongue!'

43. Patrick H. Pearse (1879–1916) was born and educated in Dublin and was called to

the Bar in 1901. He joined the Gaelic League in 1896 and became editor of its journal, *An Claidheamh Soluis*, 1903. He opened Scoil Éanna (St Enda's), an innovative school for boys, in 1908. He was a speaker at the inaugural meeting of the Irish Volunteers on 25 November 1913, joined the IRB shortly afterwards and was involved in the planning of the 1916 Easter Rising. As chairman of the Provisional Government of the Republic, he read the Proclamation on Easter Monday; he was executed on 3 May 1916.

44. The appeal was launched in *An Claidheamh Soluis* on 5 November, with the publication of Casement's letter. Casement contributed £20, Hyde 2 guineas and the editor, Pearse, 1 guinea. There was an enthusiastic response; the fund reached £47–12–00 by 19/11/1904 and £133–17–00 by 3/12/1904, when it was closed. Among the contributors were Dr William Walsh, Catholic Archbishop of Dublin (who also wrote a supportive letter); Edward Martyn; The O'Neill; Stephen Gwynn; Lady ffrench. *An Claidheamh Soluis*, 19/11/1904, 26/11/1904 and 3/12/1904. Hyde and Casement maintained links with Tawin chiefly through Seamus O'Beirne, who was just completing his medical studies in Dublin.

45. RDC to Hutton, 2/11/1904, NLI MS 8612.

46. RDC, draft article on Mandeville memorial, n.d. [*c.*1904] NLI MS 13082 (3). The eleven-page incomplete document is undated. Interestingly, a statue of Mandeville was erected and stands today in the centre of Mitchelstown. Closer to home, Casement also gave strong support to the effort to bolster Irish on Rathlin island, Co. Antrim. From 1904 on he made regular payments to the Rathlin Teacher's Fund.

47. RDC to FO, 20/9/1904, PRO FO 10/789.

48. RDC to Cowper, 9/10/1904 and 3/11/1904, NLI Acc. 4902 (9).

49. RDC to FO, 24/11/1904; RDC to Cockerell, 25/11/1904; FO to RDC, 6/12/1904, PRO FO 10/789.

50. RDC (c/o King & Co.) to Cowper, 13/12/1904, NLI Acc. 4902 (9). To Cowper he also added: 'I have a dog here who was out 10 years ago with me up to the top of Cameroon Mountain!' And he sent some lottery tickets, hoping Cowper would win, and a letter for O'Neill, as well as speculating on who would be Cowper's successor – would it be Mackey [Mackie], Churchill or young McD[onnell]?

51. Ennismore to RDC, 8/10/1904 and 27/11/1904, NLI MS 13073 (30/1). Ennismore was, he said, nervous as the wedding approached, 'at my time of life' (he was approaching forty at the time).

52. Blücher to RDC, 30/12/1904 and 31/1/1905, NLI MS 13073 (46/ii). He wrote again in February and in March.

53. O'Neill to RDC, 6/1/1905, NLI MS 13073 (12/ii). He wrote again in March, talking of Gosselin's death, poetry and his history of the O'Neills.

54. RDC to EDM, F8/16, 10/1/1905. Casement incorrectly dated the letter 1904, misleading earlier biographers.

55. Hutton to RDC, 20/1/1905, NLI MS 13078/4 ('good to see you looking better the other afternoon').

56. RDC to EDM, 27/1/1905, MP F8/18.

57. RDC to Hutton, 30/1/1905 and 1/2/1905, NLI MS 8612.

58. RDC to Cowper, 14/2/1905, NLI Acc. 4902 (10).

59. NLI MS 13073 (46/xiv).

60. Troup to RDC, 20/10/1904, NLI MS 13073 (46/xviii).

61. RDC to Hutton, 15/12/1904, NLI MS 8612.

62. Blücher to RDC, 20/2/1905, NLI MS 13073 (46/ii). The reference is to Richard Coudenhove.

63. Morel published it again in the *West African Mail* the next month (see Chapter 9).

64. RDC to Gertrude, 15/3/1905, NLI MS 13074.

65. NLI MS 13080 (6/iii), 23/1/1905.

66. Jenkins to RDC, 1/2/n.y. [1905], NLI MS 13073 (46/xi). She was also glad to hear that he was doing well after his operation and four weeks on his back.

67. Milligan, 574. Her poem 'The Man on the Wheel' was based on the incident: 'A man goes by on a wheel with the rain on his face,/Against the way of the wind, and he not caring;/Goes on through the winter night toward a lonesome distant place,/For his heart is hot with the glow of the ancient hero-daring.'

68. RDC to EDM, 25/2/1905 and 9/3/1905, MP F8/18. His mood while recovering from his operation cannot have been helped by news of Sir Martin Gosselin's death. He told Cowper: 'I am more grieved than I can tell you at the news of poor Sir Martin's death. It is a real deep grief. I liked him more than anyone I had dealings with in official life – save, perhaps, poor Henry Foley – Foley died in 1902 – and now poor Sir Martin!' He recalled their last meeting in Lisbon, when 'we looked at each other for a long time'. He died, said Casement, of his own old complaint, 'intestinal haemorrage [*sic*]'. RDC to Cowper, 28/2/1905, NLI Acc. 4902 (10).

69. RDC to EDM, 4/5/1905, MP F8/19; 21/8/1905, F8/20. He wasn't the only one in his circle in financial difficulties; he was approached in April by J. Rose Troup for an advance of £400. It seems unlikely that he could have met it – Troup to RDC, 5/4/1905, NLI MS 13073 (46xviii).

70. Reproduced in Mackey, *Crime against Europe*, pp. 112–16.

71. *Ibid*. pp. 95–101.

72. RDC to EDM, 15/3/1905, MP F8/18. I do not think the article was published. He wrote similarly to Colonel Berry, saying: 'I am writing a much longer and more exhaustive article for a Dublin Review dealing with Irish life in the middle ages.' RDC to Berry, 28/3/1905, Casement Papers, 1864/2.

73. 'The Irishman as soldier – glimpses at the Irish Annals', *Freeman's Journal*, 16/9/1905 and 23/9/1905. The two-part article was unsigned. Angus Mitchell has identified other Casement writings at this and other periods in 'John Bull's other empire: Roger Casement and the press, 1898–1916' in Simon J. Potter (ed.), *Newspapers and Empire in Ireland and Britain: Reporting the British Empire, c.1857–1921* (Dublin: Four Courts Press 2004).

74. RDC, 'Lecture on the Irish Language', draft, n.d., NLI MS 13082 (4).

75. *Ibid.*

76. *Uladh*, May 1905. The poem is reproduced in Mackey, *Crime against Europe*, p. 161, as 'The Heart's Verdict'.

77. RDC to Gertrude, 15/3/1905, NLI MS 13074 (2/ii).

78. 'Redistribution', *United Irishman*, vol. 13, no. 315 (11 March 1905), 6.

79. RDC to Gertrude, 15/3/1905, NLI MS 13074 (2/ii).

80. RDC to Morten, 2/1/1905, NLI MS 13600.

81. This is the only reference of his to Montesquieu that I have found, but it is revealing. Montesquieu described the love of liberty in the Roman Republic and Rome's decline under the Empire as being due, at least partly, to softness. He touched on other issues, which may well have had an influence on Casement, such as a negative attitude to the Spanish Empire, the attribution of a spirit of liberty to the Germans, and a notion of *esprit general*, akin to Casement's sense of national character. If, as I suspect, Casement studied this work as a school text, we have here one source for a set of views, which would remain with him (though further developed) throughout his life. See Robert Shackleton, *Montesquieu; a Critical Biography* (Oxford: OUP 1961), pp. 156–170. Casement, who could not remember the precise title of the *Considerations*, comments to Morten: 'it is years since I looked at the delightful book'.

82. T.P. Gill (1858–1931) was born in Nenagh, Co. Tipperary and educated at Trinity College, Dublin. He served as editor of the *Catholic World* magazine, New York, and associate editor of *North American Review* (1883–5). He served as MP for South Louth (1885–92) and as secretary of the Department of Agriculture and Technical Instruction for Ireland.

83. RDC to Gill, 29/3/1905, TCD 4733/4 and 31/3/1905, TCD 4733/5.

84. Lansdowne to RDC, 29/06/1905, NLI, MS 13081(3/i).

85. The quotation from Hobson is from MacColl, p. 52; Argyll to RDC is in NLI MS 13073 (1); Baillie-Hamilton to RDC, 13073 (2/i) and RDC to Baillie-Hamilton, 13080 (1/i); details from Reid, pp. 70–3. Casement also wrote to Barrington, discussing the possibility of declining the honour: RDC to Barrington, 12/07/1905, NLI MS 13080(1/i).

86. RDC to Clarke, 20/07/1905, quoted in Reid, pp. 71–2; Clarke to RDC, 30/07/1905, NLI MS 13073 (46/v).

87. He did have a problem with his hand, as his letters to Morel show. On 23 November he wrote: 'My hand is still in bandages – and I cannot get on with my writing at all'. RDC to EDM, 23/11/ 1905, LSE MP F8/20. And, a little later: 'I am (happily) not going to the Investiture on Monday as my health is not up to the mark – and it wd be a great pity to go limping and halting and bandaging into the King's presence'. RDC to EDM, 14/12/ 1905, LSE MP F8/20.

88. Tyrrell to RDC, 29/11/1905, NLI MS 13073 (43). And see Tyrrell to RDC, 13/12/1905, NLI MS 13073 (43).

89. RDC to Morten, 3/7/1905, NLI MS Acc. 4902 (2). He may also have attended the Toome Feis that year; Alice Milligan later told how he had taken the time there to

help a drunken man. During this summer, Ada MacNeill seems to have had her own problems. On 1 June she wrote to Casement saying that things had changed in her home and that she wasn't sure she could stay. Could he suggest anything she could do in Ireland? Bigger was always thoughtless on such issues, but 'you have been most kind to me more so than anyone I ever met before or since'. 'Mac' to RDC, 1/6/1905, NLI MS 13073 (46/xii). Around this time, too, Louisa Farquharson probably introduced him to William J. Pirrie, head of the shipbuilding company Harland and Wolff, and an active politician. The purpose was twofold: to get his support for the Industrial Section of the Feis and to get his support for the Congo campaign. See Farquharson to RDC, 26/4/n.y. [1905?], 5/5/1905 and 14/5/1905, NLI MS 13073 (31/i). The following year Casement asked Morel to send Pirrie a copy of the Belgian debate on the Congo: RDC to EDM, 29/5/1906, LSE MP F8/22.

90. See Sawyer, *Flawed Hero*, p. 48 and p. 168, n.15. Hobson wrote: 'A four-page leaflet was issued and very widely distributed. In its first draft it was written by Alice Stopford Green; Roger Casement added a bit, and I added more.' Bulmer Hobson, *Ireland Yesterday and Tomorrow* (Tralee: Anvil Books 1968). 'Irishmen and the English Army' was published as Dungannon Club Publication no. 1. The text of the pamphlet is reproduced in Hobson's book, pp. 99–102, from which the above quotations are taken.

91. RDC to Morten, 8/7/1905, NLI MS Acc. 4902 (2). I suspect that this is also the pamphlet referred to by E.A. Stopford in the following guarded terms: 'I notice in the *Irish Times* that the police have found the District flooded with literature which they don't approve of and are making active search about it ... The little book you know of is selling well and quite a large circulation will bring a very nice little profit!' E.A. Stopford to RDC, 25/8/1905, NLI MS 13073 (40). Also see Law to RDC, 7/8/1905, NLI MS 13073 (10/i). Hobson later wrote: 'Francis Joseph Bigger, although he did not appear as solicitor in the case, took charge of the defence, and Roger Casement made himself responsible for the expense. As was his custom, he collected what he could among his friends and then made up the balance himself', Hobson, p. 24. See RDC to Berry, 19/7/1905, where he says, 'Please send this to Bigger. a subscription to help Stephen Clarke to pay his costs – some £70 is being raised [?] here', Casement Papers, 1864/4.

92. Plunkett, Diaries, 29/7/1905 and 30/7/1905. Monteagle was an associate of Plunkett's in cooperative work.

93. R. Barry O'Brien (1847–1918) was called to the Irish Bar in 1874 and to the English in 1875. He gave up practice for literature and politics. He was editor for a time of *The Speaker* and was one of the founder members of the Irish Literary Society, serving as its chairman and president. He wrote many books, including a history of Ireland and biographies of Parnell and John Bright. He used to tell how, as a young law student, he was imbued with the physical-force ideas of the Fenians, until he was converted to the constitutional path on hearing the speeches of John Bright and Gladstone.

94. O'Brien to RDC, 3/8/1905, NLI MS 13073 (46/xiv).

95. RDC to O'Brien, 22/8/1905, NLI MS 13080 (3/i).

96. RDC to Hutton, 29/8/1905, NLI MS 8612.

97. RDC to Hobson, 10/8/1905, NLI MS 13158 (2). Among the papers relating to Casement in the Public Record Office in Northern Ireland, there is a copy of Hobson's 'Irish National Chart', relating to intellectual, material, physical and financial dimensions of self-government: PRONI D2711.

98. Nevinson, Diaries, 21/9/1905, Bodleian Library, Oxford, MS Eng. misc. e. 613/1. Henry Wood Nevinson (1856–1941) was an influential crusading journalist and served as war correspondent in several major conflicts. At the time he came to know Casement, he was beginning his investigation of labour exploitation in the Portuguese islands of São Tomé and Principe, off the coast of Angola. He was the author of many books, including the autobiographical *More Changes, More Chances* (London: Nisbet 1925) and *Last Changes, Last Chances* (London: Nisbet 1928). Nevinson had travelled to West Africa in 1904 and heard positive reports of Casement's investigation there.

99. RDC to ? n.d., incomplete, NLI MS 13080 (6/iv).

100. R. Donovan to RDC, 16/1/1906, NLI MS 13073 (5), and R. Donovan to RDC, 25/9/1905, NLI MS 13073 (5).

101. RDC to EDM, 29/9/1905 and 6/11/1905, MP F8/20.

102. Hoste to RDC, 29/12/1905 and 4/1/1906, NLI MS 13073 (25/i).

103. RDC to Ward, 28/12/1905, NLI MS 13080 (3/ii); (a) RDC to Morten, n.d., partial, NLI Acc. 4902 (4) and (b) RDC to Morten, n.d., partial, no signature, NLI Acc. 4902 (14).

104. Gilmour to RDC, 11/11/1905 and 12/11/1905, NLI MS 13073 (46/ix).

105. RDC to EDM, 8/3/1906, LSE MP F8/21.

106. FO to RDC, 5/1/1906, PRO FO 369/51.

107. Barrington to RDC, 4/4/1906, NLI MS 13073 (21).

108. RDC to Tyrrell, 5/4/1906, NLI MS 13080 (5).

109. RDC to EDM, n.d.[early July], LSE MP F8/21.

110. Tyrrell to RDC, 10/5/1906, NLI MS 13073 (43).

111. Tyrrell to RDC, 29/5/1906 and 7/6/1906, NLI MS 13073 (43). Tyrrell seems to have had an Irish connection, judging by his remark, 'Give my love to the old country', and by his comments on getting Barry O'Brien's *History* from Casement.

112. RDC to EDM, 16/7/1906, 17/7/1906, n.d.[early July], LSE MP F8/21; 16/6/1906, F8/22. In September 1906 Casement, in a letter to Holt, said he had hoped 'to have introduced my friend Mr Hoste, of the Tea Company to you' and that he was 'retaining my interest in the Tea Company and hope its custom may extend'. RDC to Holt, 19/09/1906, RHO, Holt Papers, MSS Afr. s.1525.

113. RDC to Morten, 30/6/1906, NLI MS Acc. 4902 (2).

114. RDC to Gertrude, 31/5/1906, NLI MS 13074 (3/i).

115. Nevinson, Diaries, 1/6/1906, Bod. MS Eng. misc. e. 613/3.

116. Louis Mallet (Rt. Hon. Sir Louis Mallet, GCMG, CB) was private secretary to Sir

Edward Grey, 1906–7. He had entered the FO in 1888 and was précis writer to Lord Lansdowne, 1902–5. He was later Assistant Undersecretary, 1907–13, and ambassador to Constantinople, 1913–14.

117. Mallet to RDC, 25/7/1906 and 30/7/1906, NLI MS 13073/32.

118. Tyrrell to RDC, 3/8/1906, 9/8/1906, 10/8/1906, 15/8/1906, 22/8/1906, NLI MS 13073/43. Pará loomed already, as Frank Gritton of the FO passed on Rhind's (consul at Pará) suggestion that Casement might like to exchange with him and go to Pará, where he might explore the Amazon. Gritton to RDC, 25/8/1906, NLI MS 13073 (7/ii).

119. RDC to EDM, 19/9/1906, PRO F8/22.

120. RDC to Gertrude, 21/9/1906, NLI MS 13074 (3/ii).

121. Acting Consul Thomas Thornton did indeed hand over to Casement on the 10th. The FO minute on Thornton was rather caustic: 'I don't think we need thank. He probably made something by it.' FO minute, 5/11/1906, PRO FO 369/5.

122. RDC to Gertrude, 23/9/1906, NLI MS 13074 (3/ii). A.M. Sullivan (1830–84), from west Cork, was a nationalist MP and popular historian. He was owner of *The Nation*, an opponent of the physical-force Fenians and one of the initiators of the first Home Rule movement. He was father of Casement's counsel in 1916 (also A.M. Sullivan). During Fenian actions of 1867, an attempt to rescue a Fenian leader led to the accidental shooting of a police guard; three young Irishmen, Allen, Larkin and O'Brien, were executed for the deed and became emotional symbols in nationalist thinking, known as the 'Manchester Martyrs'.

11: BRAZIL, 1906–9

1. *Report for the Years 1905–6 on the Trade of Santos* (to be cited hereafter as *Trade of Santos*), FO Diplomatic and Consular Reports, Brazil, no. 3952 Annual Series, London: HMSO 1908, pp. 3, 8 and 11–12.

2. *Ibid.* p. 12, and RDC to EDM, 12/10/06, LSE MP F8/22. The rail journey to São Paulo, he pointed out to Morel, took 2.5 hours in a train that was pulled by ropes part of the way, because of the gradient.

3. RDC to Gertrude, 9/10/1906, NLI MS 13074 (3/ii).

4. RDC to EDM, 12/10/1906, LSE MP F8/22. One assumes that he felt the effect of this keenly, because of his lack of income in 1905 and 1906, his borrowings and his need to repay loans to friends.

5. RDC to Hutton, 24/10/1906, NLI MS 8612.

6. RDC to Cowper, 7/11/1906, NLI Acc. 4902 (10).

7. RDC to EDM, 12/11/1906, LSE MP F8/22.

8. RDC to Emmott, 12/11/1906, Emmott Papers, box 3, fols. 371–82.

9. RDC to FO, 20/10/1906, PRO FO 369/4.

10. RDC to FO, 24/12/1906 (quoting an earlier letter of 3/12/1906) and 7/1/07 (quoting

one of 15/12/1906), RDC to FO, PRO FO 369/4.

11. RDC to FO, 15/12/1906, 25/3/1907, 14/?/1907, 28/1/1907 and 1/7/07, PRO FO 369/63.

12. Appeal dated 12/12/1906, PRO FO 369/63. The amounts are in Brazilian dollars.

13. RDC to FO, 17/11/1906, PRO FO 369/5. See also RDC to FO, 17/12/1906, 15/1/1907, PRO FO 369/63; 28/11/1906, PRO FO 128/308; 29/4/1907, PRO FO 128/315 (regarding what Casement deemed a severe and unfair fine on the *Dawn* over a breach of customs regulations. 'The Inspector of Customs here is an ignorant, ill-mannered boor' and it was time that he be informed of the normal rules of courtesy).

14. 'Notes on Military and Political Conditions etc. in the State of São Paulo', 10/5/1907, War Office Paper: Casement Papers.

15. RDC to FO, 29/1/1907 and minutes thereon, PRO FO 369/63. Rowland Arthur Charles Sperling was born in 1874, became a FO clerk in 1899, acting 3rd secretary in 1903 and assistant clerk in 1907.

16. RDC to FO, 9/3/1907 and Sperling minute, PRO FO 369/63.

17. RDC to Gertrude, 1/4/1907, NLI MS 13074 (4/i).

18. RDC to Cowper, 15/5/1907, NLI Acc. 4902 (10).

19. One of Casement's cheque stubs records Ross's name on 17 March. Ross wrote to Casement later that year wondering would Casement, should he retire from the service, draw public attention to their conditions of employment: Ross to RDC, 11/9/1907, NLI MS 13073 (4/i). During this visit to Buenos Aires, Casement also met William Warden, with whom he maintained contact in later years: see Warden to RDC, 16/5/1907, NLI MS 13073 (16/ii).

20. RDC to FO, 24/3/1907, PRO FO 369/63; RDC to Haggard, 26/3/1907, PRO FO 128/315. Haggard replaced Colville Barclay at the legation in December 1906. Casement probably had a visit from his friend, Major Berry, shortly after his return from this leave; Berry was orchid-hunting in Brazil. For their correspondence, see the Casement Papers.

21. RDC to Berry, 16/4/1907, and 20/5/1907, Casement Papers, 1864/6 and 1864/7. For Guarujá, see Sawyer, *Flawed Hero*, pp. 63 and 74.

22. *Trade of Santos*, p. 8.

23. *Ibid.* pp. 32, 34.

24. *Ibid.* p. 36. In one of his despatches, he requested the FO to produce a circular asking consuls for details of imports from Ireland: 'I wish to make some remarks about Irish imports here.' RDC to FO, 17/11/1906, PRO FO 369/5.

25. *Ibid.* pp. 11, 13.

26. RDC to ASG, 20/4/1907, NLI MS 10464 (4).

27. RDC to ASG, 27/6/1907, NLI MS 10464 (4).

28. RDC, undated draft article, Santos, MacNeill Papers, NLI MS 10880.

29. RDC to Hobson, 30/5/1907, NLI MS 13158 (2). The reference is to the Irish Council Bill, an attempt by the Liberal government to introduce a small measure of self-government to Ireland. The bill received a frosty reception in Ireland and, ultimately, the Irish Party rejected it. See F.S.L. Lyons, *Ireland since the Famine*

(London: Fontana 1973 [1971]), pp. 264–6, and McDowell, pp. 88–93.

30. RDC to Gertrude, 3/10/1906, NLI MS 13074 (3/ii).

31. RDC to Gertrude, 3/10/1906 and n.d., NLI MS 13074 (3/ii); RDC to Gertrude, 12/01/1907, NLI MS 13074 (4/i). Casement told Cowper that he had 'an Irish stow-away boy now as my servant cleaning my uniform – and a tiny Brazilian kid of 13 as office boy' – the two were fighting to clean his uniform for a grand review on 15 November: RDC to Cowper, 7/11/1906, NLI Acc. 4902 (10). Sawyer, *Flawed Hero*, p. 63, n. 30 provides further detail on this stowaway. I suspect that this youth is the author of a letter thanking Casement and the Keevils; see P. Hayes to RDC, 27/6/1907, NLI MS 13073 (8/ii).

32. RDC to Grey, 4/3/1907, NLI MS 13081/2 (i).

33. Tyrrell to RDC, 14/2/1907, NLI MS 13073 (43).

34. RDC to Gertrude, 22/7/1907, NLI MS 13074 (4/ii).

35. See Jonathan Bardon, *A History of Ulster* (Belfast: Blackstaff Press 1992), pp. 427–30, and Emmet Larkin, *James Larkin* (London: NEL Mentor 1968 [1965]), pp. 23–4.

36. RDC (Ballycastle) to EDM, 1/8/191907, LSE MP F8/22.

37. RDC to Gertrude, 14/8/1907, and 23/8/1907, NLI MS 13074 (4/ii). In 1906, plans to open an Irish-language summer training college came to fruition and Coláiste Uladh was opened in Ardaidh Bhig in Cloghaneely, Falcarragh, Co. Donegal. The college was under the auspices of Dáil Uladh, an all-Ulster committee of the Gaelic League. Friends of Casement's were active in the Dáil and in Coláiste Uladh. Íde Nic Néill (Ada MacNeill) became secretary and general administrator; Margaret Dobbs became treasurer and gave lectures, as did Mary Hutton. The first head lecturer, Úna Ní Fhaircheallaigh (Agnes O'Farrelly), was to become a friend.

38. RDC to Hutton, 11/8/1907, NLI MS 8612.

39. RDC to Gertrude, 28/8/1912, 2/9/1912, NLI MS 13074 (4/ii).

40. RDC to Hobson, 2/9/1907, NLI MS 13158 (2). He later sent him the college prospectus for 1908, RDC to Hobson, 24/10/1907, NLI MS 13158 (2).

41. RDC to Hutton, 19/9/1907, NLI MS 15535.

42. For example, £25, 15/8/1908; £30, 14/10/1909; £31, 20/7/1910, NLI MS 15138 (1).

43. RDC to Hobson, 12/8/1907 and 24/10/1907, NLI MS 13158 (2, 3), 'Ireland at the Olympic Games', NLI MS 13159. He suggested names for the committee, including Plunkett, Hyde, Colonel Moore and Talbot Crosbie.

44. RDC to Hobson, 28/10/1907, NLI MS 13158 (3). Casement discussed Hobson's employment in all of his letters to him at this time.

45. RDC to Hobson, 27/3/1908, NLI MS 13158(4).

46. Emmott to RDC, 24/8/1907, NLI MS 13073 (29/i).

47. Vansittart to RDC, 22/10/1907, NLI MS 13073 (16/i).

48. Quoted in Inglis, pp. 162–3.

49. RDC to Tyrrell (not sent), 19/11/1907 NLI MS 13080 (5). Terence John Temple-Blackwood, 2nd Marquess of Dufferin & Ava (1866–1925), entered the FO in 1890. He became acting senior clerk in 1907 and senior clerk in 1909.

50. FO (Langley) to RDC, 2/12/1907, NLI MS 13081 (3/i); Deeds of Appointment: E. Grey to 'Roger Casement, Esquire, a Companion of Our Most Distinguished Order of St Michael and St George', 2/12/1907, NLI MS 13081 (4). Casement did put his complaints to Tyrrell in early December: RDC to Tyrrell, 5/12/1907, 13080/5.

51. W.A. Churchill to RDC, 15/12/1907 and 21/12/1907, NLI MS 13073 (4/ii).

52. RDC to Hutton, 25/11/1907, NLI MS 15535. He told her in an earlier letter that he thought poorly of the sketches in her book: 'most of heroes of Seaghan Mac Cathmhaoil [John Campbell] look as if they have digestive problems'. Would she not leave them out if the book went to a 2nd edition, as he felt it would? RDC to Hutton, 11/8/1907, NLI MS 8612.

53. RDC to Gertrude, 4/1/1908, NLI MS 13074 (5/i); RDC to Hobson, 14/12/1907, NLI MS 13158 (3).

54. RDC to Hobson, 19/12/1907 and 1/1/1908, NLI MS 13158 (4).

55. RDC to Gertrude, 4/1/1908, NLI MS 13074 (4/ii, 5/i).

56. RDC to Hobson, 19/12/1907, NLI MS 13158 (3).

57. RDC to FO, 5/3/1908, PRO FO 369/123. His request to have his Madeira stopover sanctioned retrospectively was not warmly received at the FO. It was, the minutes noted, irregular and to be discouraged. But, aware of Casement's general disposition towards Brazil, it was remarked that 'he may possibly have retired before he gets this dispatch'. He had just passed through Lisbon when the king of Portugal and his heir were assassinated. 'You must have been horrified,' he commented to Cowper, 'I was in Madeira when those dastardly crimes occurred.' RDC to Cowper, 18/3/1908, NLI Acc. 4902 (10). Francis Villiers, who had been appointed ambassador in Lisbon in 1906, and whom Casement clearly met on his way through, wrote: 'What a tragedy since you were here! It seems impossible to realize what has happened.' Villiers to RDC, n.d. (r. 1/3/1908), NLI MS 13073 (46/xvi). Casement also met The O'Neill on his way through Lisbon: RDC to Bigger, 27/3/1908, NLI MS 21531.

58. RDC to Morten, 22/1/1908, NLI Acc. 4902 (2). He enclosed £30, presumably a repayment on money borrowed, and promised the rest by Easter; he was sorry it had taken so long, but others needed money more urgently.

59. RDC to EDM, 23/3/1908, LSE MP F8/23.

60. RDC to Gertrude, 27/2/1908, NLI MS 13074 (5/i).

61. RDC to Rio Legation, 3/4/1908, PRO FO 128/324.

62. RDC to Dufferin, 6/3/1908, PRO FO 369/123.

63. RDC to Cowper, 18/3/1908, NLI Acc. 4902 (10); FO 743/22; Sawyer, *Flawed Hero*, p. 65 and p. 169, n. 1.

64. *Royal Commission*, answer to Q. 38,633, p. 85. For the London Bank's objections to the consulate, see RDC to FO, 2/6/1908, PRO FO 369/124.

65. *Royal Commission*, answer to Q. 38,558, pp. 81–2.

66. Minute on RDC to FO, 14/3/1908, PRO FO 369/123; RDC to FO, 12/3/1908, PRO FO 369/12. He gave an example of the cost of furnishings: 'As an instance of the

dearness of things in Pará, an American roll top desk, sold in London for £8, pays on import into Pará £22–10–0 in duty and is sold locally for £37.' RDC to FO, 14/3/1908, PRO FO 369/123.

67. RDC to FO, 13/4/1908, PRO FO 369/123; two FO minutes exclaimed, 'all this change in 6 weeks!' and 'no man should be kept long in Brazil unless it is wished to ruin him in health and pocket'; 'Memorandum on Care of Confidential Archives at Pará by Roger Casement, HM Consul', 7/10/1908, PRO FO 743/22.

68. FO summary of Casement's letter of 12/3/1908, PRO FO 369/123.

69. RDC to EDM, 23/3/1908, LSE MP F8/23.

70. RDC to FO, 2/6/1908 and 21/10/1908, PRO FO 369/124.

71. RDC to Dufferin, 4/3/1908, NLI MS 13080 (4).

72. RDC to Dufferin, 6/3/1908, PRO FO 369/123.

73. RDC to Cowper, 18/3/1908, NLI Acc. 4902 (10).

74. RDC to Cheetham, 15/5/1908, PRO FO 128/324. Milne Cheetham was to serve as *chargé d'affaires* in the British legation at Petropolis, when Casement was consul general in Rio.

75. RDC to Gertrude, 3/7/1908, 13074 (5/ii).

76. RDC to FO, 1/4/1908, PRO FO 369/124; 10/4/1908, PRO FO 128/324. On the 21st he told them he expected to leave on the 23rd.

77. RDC to FO, 3/6/1908, PRO FO 369/124.

78. RDC to Gertrude, 16/5/1908, NLI MS 13074 (5/i). He also mentioned the trip to Morel (RDC to EDM, 15/5/1908, LSE MP F5/3) and to Churchill (RDC to Churchill, 1/6/1908, NLI MS 13073 (4/ii)). During 1908, Casement presented two ring-tailed coatis and one red and yellow macaw to the Royal Zoological Gardens, Dublin, and was made a Corresponding Member of the Society. Early in his stay he must have sent an animal to Reid's Hotel, Madeira, as Louise C. Reid wrote to him: 'I was so delighted to get that dear little beastie, it has already got quite tame … It really was so kind of you to trouble about my small zoo before you are really well settled.' Louise Reid to RDC, 30/3/1908, NLI MS 13073 (14). In November, he suggested that Hobson should go and visit his sister Nina, then in Dublin, and go 'also to the zoo to see my two animals' (he signed himself 'Ruairí'): RDC to Hobson, 7/11/1908, NLI MS 13158 (4).

79. RDC to FO, 11/5/1908, PRO FO 128/324.

80. RDC to Gertrude, 25/5/1908, 13/6/1908, 27/6/1908, NLI MS 13074 (5/i–ii); *Report for the Year 1907 on the Trade of Pará*, FO, Diplomatic and Consular Reports, Brazil, Annual Series no. 4111 (C.3727–194), CIX, 1908.

81. RDC to Cheetham, 4/11/1908, PRO FO 128/324.

82. RDC to FO, 4/6/1908 and 27/6/1908, PRO FO 128/324. He enclosed an article from the *Provincia do Pará* of 4/6/1908.

83. RDC to Gertrude, 15/4/1908, 25/5/1908, 27/7/1908, NLI MS 13074 (5/i–ii).

84. See, for example, NLI MS 13087 (23/ii) (31/iv), and MS 13089 (6).

85. RDC to Gertrude, 13/6/1908, 27/6/1908 and 27/7/1908, NLI MS 13074 (5/ii).

86. RDC to Hobson, 27/3/1908, 20/8/1908, 9/9/1908, NLI MS 13158 (4). Hobson had, by now, moved to Dublin. After the problems in Cushendall, Casement thought of Hobson's welfare; writing to Bigger, he asked: 'How could he be helped now that the Co-operation Scheme at Cushendall has ended. Ms McD. is furious with me – what for, only she knows!' RDC to Bigger, 27/3/1908, NLI MS 21531. For remittances, see his cheques in NLI MS 15138 and Hugh O'Duffy (Ó Dubhthaigh) to RDC, 9/6/1908, NLI MS 13073 (12/ii).

87. RDC to Hobson, 9/9/1908, NLI MS 13158 (4).

88. RDC to EDM, 15/5/1908, MP F5/3; RDC to Cheetham, 15/5/1908, PRO FO 128/324.

89. RDC to FO, 16/7/1908, PRO FO 369/124. When Casement reported in June how expenditure had exceeded income, the FO successfully requested an extra £100 temporary local allowance for him; a FO minute added: 'Not only do we consider Pará at present the most expensive but its climate the worst in Brazil', RDC to FO, 18/6/1908, PRO FO 369/124.

90. Emmott to RDC, 16/7/1908, NLI MS 13073 (29/i).

91. RDC to Gertrude, 28/7/1908, NLI MS 13074 (5/ii).

92. RDC to Hobson, 20/8/1908, NLI MS 1158 (4).

93. RDC (Barbados) to FO, 5/8/1908, PRO FO, 369/124.

94. RDC to FO, 18/9/1908, and minutes, 18/9/1908, PRO FO 369/124; RDC to Cheetham, 4/11/1908, PRO FO 128/324.

95. RDC to Gertrude, 1/9/1908, NLI MS 13074 (5/ii).

96. RDC to FO, 3/10/1908, PRO FO 369/124.

97. RDC to EDM, 4/12/1908, LSE MP F8/23.

98. RDC to Gertrude, 7/12/1908 and 11/12/1908, NLI MS 13074 (5/ii).

99. RDC to Gleeson, 21/12/1908, TCD MS 10676/17/53.

100. RDC to FO, 7/12/1908, PRO FO 369/124.

101. RDC to Berry, 7/12/1907, Casement Papers.

102. RDC to Hobson, 10/2/ 1909, and 1/2/1909, 7/2/1909, 12/2/1909, 23/2/1909 (Lisbon), 5/3/1909, NLI MS 13158 (5).

103. RDC to Hutton, 1/2/1909, NLI MS 8612.

104. FO, 31/12/1908, PRO FO 369/125; RDC to FO, 30/1/1909, PRO FO 369/125.

105. RDC to FO, 5/2/1909, PRO FO 369/197.

106. RDC, cheque stubs, NLI MS 15138 (1): cheques on 9/2/1909 (Emmott and Ward); 22/12/1908, 31/12/1908, 26/1/1909 (*The Peasant*); 14/4/1909, 25/8/1909 (*Sinn Féin*); during this leave, he also bought a writing case for 'Millar', 18/12/1908. Millar has subsequently been identified as Joseph Gordon Millar and the references to him in the diaries became a focus of contention in the authenticity debate; for an extensive treatment, see Dudgeon, especially Chapter 13, 'Millar Gordon', pp. 383–401.

107. RDC to FO, 6/1/1909 and 30/1/1909, PRO FO 369/196. The leave was granted, FO to RDC, 4/2/1909, NLI MS 13081 (3/i).

108. RDC to Cowper, 22/2/1909, NLI Acc. 4902 (10).

109. RDC to FO, 29/3/1909, PRO FO 369/196.

110. Bosanquet, however, went on leave at the beginning of May and did not return until September, while Pullen, too, seems to have been ill from August: 1/5/1909, 4/5/1909, 138/334; 17/1/1910, 128/343, FO 369/197. Sawyer, *Flawed Hero*, p. 71, notes that Pullen was a failed businessman, but an extremely efficient clerk.

111. There is, though, a record of disagreement between Casement and his predecessor, Chapman, over furniture. Casement thought the £50 asked of him by Chapman for office furniture too much. See 28/2/1910, FO 369/277. Casement's submission of detailed accounts of office expenditure for April to October, 1909, drew an interesting observation in the FO minutes: 'The salaries of the Chief Clerk and the Second Clerk are very high, but Mr Casement seems to leave a great deal to the Chief Clerk which he might do himself.' 25/10/1909, FO 369/198.

112. RDC to FO, various, PRO FO 128/334 and 128/343.

113. RDC to FO, 1/5/1909 and 6/12/1909, PRO FO 128/334.

114. RDC to FO, 6/8/1909, PRO FO 369/198.

115. RDC to FO, 2/8/1909, PRO FO 128/33; there was a subsequent hiccup. Barry changed his mind and withdrew his name but then, with the threatened closure of the vice-consulate, reconsidered: RDC to FO, 30/8/1909, 31/8/1909, 1/11/1909, and Barry letter of 18/10/1909, PRO FO 369/198.

116. RDC to FO, 20/9/1909, PRO FO 369/198. Sir Harrry Johnston wrote twice to Casement at this time seeking help with a book he was writing on the 'Negro in the New World'. When it appeared, it contained material on the Botocudo Indians. Johnston to RDC, 26/8/1909 and 17/10/1909, NLI MS 13073 (30/ii).

117. Sawyer, *Flawed Hero*, without citing a source, suggests that relations between Casement and Haggard were cool (p. 72) and of having fallen out with him (p. 76). While Haggard was later negative towards Casement, I have found no evidence of a rift between the two.

118. RDC to Legation, 17/1/10, PRO FO 128/343.

119. FO minute, 7/10/1909, FO 372/148.

120. Ernest Hambloch, *British Consul: Memories of Thirty Years' Service in Europe and Brazil* (London: Harrap 1938), p. 72.

121. RDC to FO, 13/4/1909 and 19/10/1909, PRO FO 369/198; RDC to Gertrude, 1/9/1909, NLI MS 13074 (6/i), 1/9/1909; Hambloch, pp. 74–5 and 93.

122. Hambloch's treatment of Casement was not sympathetic, and his book betrays signs of being anti-German. He was to send Casement a rather sharp letter in 1913: Hambloch to RDC, 26/10/13, NLI MS 13073 (8/i). But most of his stories about Casement would seem to have the ring of truth about them. Freiherr Ferdinand von Nordenflycht (1850–1931) was born in Berlin and, after a legal training and practice, entered the consular service of the German Foreign Office. He served in a number of locations in the US, before being appointed consul general in Rio de Janeiro in 1908; he was then transferred to Montevideo in 1910 and appointed minister there in 1912. He served in a number of European countries during the First World War.

123. RDC to Gertrude, 31/3/1909, NLI MS 13074 (6/i).

124. RDC to Cowper, 21/4/1909 and 2/6/1909, NLI Acc. 4902 (10).
125. RDC to Roger, 15/8/1909, PRONI T3787/17. He talked, too, of Tom in South Africa and of Roger's wife, Susan, and sons Bertie and Jack Jr.
126. RDC to Gertrude, 1/9/1909, NLI MS 13074 (6/i).
127. Emmott to RDC, 25/7/1909, NLI MS 13073 (29/i).
128. RDC to Morten, 14/9/1909–10/11/1909, NLI Acc. 4902 (2).
129. RDC to Hobson, 7/9/1909, NLI MS 13158 (6).
130. RDC to Hobson, 25/5/1909 and 23/12/1909, NLI MS 13158 (6).
131. RDC to Hobson, 7/9/1909, NLI MS 13158 (6). Casement's cheque stubs show two payments to the O'Hickey testimonial, £5 on 14/9/1909 and £2–10–0 on 14/10/1909, NLI MS 15138 (i).
132. RDC to Hobson, 7/9/1909, NLI MS 13158 (6).
133. RDC to Gertrude, 1/9/1909, NLI MS 13074 (6/ii).
134. RDC to Gertrude, 2/8/1909, NLI MS 13074 (6/ii). He was all the time in touch with events at home: 'Poor old Nina has been very ill at Lucan', he commented in one letter. He attacked Dillon, Redmond and the Irish Party, while praising Hyde and Agnes O'Farrelly ('I like her'). He composed sarcastic aphorisms about imperialists, referring to a newspaper article, which suggested that the south and west of Ireland were 'as bad as any district in darkest Africa'.
135. RDC to Morten, 14/9/1909–10/11/1909, NLI Acc. 4902 (2).
136. See his letters to Hobson and Gertrude at this period.
137. RDC to Cowper, 11/1/1910, NLI Acc. 4902 (10).
138. RDC to Morten, 11/1/1910, NLI Acc. 4902 (2).
139. Sawyer, *Diaries*, p. 42. References to the 1910 Diary in subsequent pages are to this edition. I have made slight changes in the text drawing on the manuscript diary, PRO HO 161/3. The early part of the 1910 Diary is quite spare in its entries.
140. RDC to FO, 26/11/1909, PRO FO 369/198; 25/1/1910, 4/2/1910, 16/2/1910, 2/3/1910 and 31/3/1910, PRO FO 369/277. Hambloch only knew Casement for one month in Rio, though they did meet briefly afterwards.
141. Sawyer, *Diaries*, p. 46, Sunday, 3 April. Ramon's name reappears on a number of later occasions. According to the 1910 Diary, Casement wrote to him on 20 May and on 29 December; in the 1911 Cash Ledger, his name is given as Ramon Tapia, together with an address in Buenos Aires.
142. Katherine Parnell was Mrs Bill Moule. Dudgeon, p. 266, observes that Katie Moule never used the name Parnell, though she was his daughter and not Captain O'Shea's.
143. Captain L.C. Arbuthnot was superintendent of the Zoological Gardens in Dublin, to whom Casement had sent animals from Brazil. The entry in the 1910 Diary for 22 May reads, in my opinion: 'At Tara with Harrie[tte] and family' and refers to the Wilkinson family and not to the Revd John Harris; similarly, with the identification on 23 May (Sawyer, *Diaries*, p. 51). Presumably, it was members of the family who attended the party.
144. Sawyer, *Diaries*, p. 53.

145. Sawyer, *Diaries*, p. 54, 31/5/1910; Hyde to RDC, 4/6/1910, NLI MS 13073 (27/i).

146. Sawyer, *Diaries*, pp. 56 and 57, 17 June and 23 June.

12: THE PUTUMAYO INVESTIGATION, 1909–10

1. Parliamentary Question no. 36366, 29/9/1909, PRO FO 371/722. The *Truth* articles began on 22/9/1909; Sidney Paternoster was editor of the journal.

2. Sir Charles Louis Des Graz KCMG was born in 1860 and served as a diplomat in various parts of Europe and the Near East before being appointed envoy extraordinary and minister plenipotentiary to Bolivia, Ecuador and Peru (and consul general) in September 1908. He was transferred to Belgrade in 1916.

3. David Cazes, a trader, had been appointed vice-consul at Iquitos in February 1902 and consul for Loreto in 1903; a paid consulate was to be established on 7 December 1911. Cazes died in the UK in 1915.

4. Draft autobiography of Sir John Harris, RHO, Anti-Slavery Papers (ASS), MSS Brit. Emp. S353 fol. 32. The year given in the manuscript for this event is, incorrectly, 1910. The autobiography exists in very rough draft only and was never published. Hardenburg's work later appeared in print, edited with an introduction by Reginald Enock, as *The Putumayo: The Devil's Paradise* (London: Fisher Unwin 1912). He wrote a short piece for the anthropological journal *Man* in 1910, 'The Indians of the Putumayo, Upper Amazon', *Man*, 10, nos. 80–1 (1910), 134–8.

5. Travers Buxton, a barrister by training, was active in the anti-slavery movement from early manhood, including in the Congo campaign; he became honorary secretary of the newly-amalgamated Anti-Slavery and Aborigines Protection Society in 1909.

6. Whiffen Report, 21/10/1909, PRO FO 371/722. For Whiffen (1878–1922), see Michael Taussig, *Shamanism, Colonialism, and the Wild Man: A Study in Terror and Healing* (Chicago: University of Chicago Press 1987); Angus Mitchell, *The Amazon Journal of Roger Casement* (Dublin: The Lilliput Press 1997). When Whiffen's military career had ended after a serious injury during the Boer War, he went on an exploratory expedition to the north-west Amazon in 1908; he published an account in *The North-West Amazons: Notes of Some Months Spent among Cannibal Tribes* (London: Constable 1915). He also published a short account in the journal *Folklore* in 1913.

7. Bryce to FO, 3/11/1909, PRO FO 371/722.

8. FO memo, 24/11/1909, PRO FO 371/722.

9. For Julio Arana, see Howard Karno, 'Julio César Arana, Frontier Cacique in Peru' in Robert Kern (ed.), *The Caciques* (Albuquerque: University of New Mexico Press 1973), pp. 89–98.

10. FO memo, 24/11/1909, PRO FO 371/722.

11. FO minutes on PAC to FO, 30/12/1909, PRO FO 371/722. A FO minute said of one

PAC letter: 'The tone of this letter is somewhat truculent and does not hold out much prospect of the Co. being ready to listen to reason.' PAC to FO, minute, 8/3/1910, PRO FO 371/967.

12. ASS to FO, 15/12/1909 (PRO FO 371/722), 11/5/1910, 7/7/1910 and 12/7/10 (PRO FO 371/967); Resolutions, 2/6/1910, 6/6/1910, 14/6/1910, 13/7/1910, PRO FO 371/967 and 968.

13. Gielgud to ASS, 11/4/1910, ASS S22 G322. Gielgud's visit to the Putumayo had been as an accountant; he recorded no observations on abuses.

14. Quoted in Reid, pp. 98–9.

15. Hardenburg to ASS, 28/6/1910, ASS S22 G322.

16. Josiah Clement Wedgwood, 1st Baron Wedgwood (1872–1943), was a naval architect and served in the Boer War. He was MP for Newcastle-under-Lyme from 1906 to 1942; he changed from the Liberal to the Labour Party in 1919 and was devoted to causes including Indian independence and a Jewish homeland.

17. Sawyer, *Diaries*, 17, 18 and 23 June, pp. 56 and 57. Noel Edward Buxton (1869–1948), politician and philanthropist, was a son of Sir T.F. Buxton. As an MP he also moved from the Liberal to the Labour Party. He worked for peace settlements during both World Wars. Casement seems to have developed close links with him. Wedgwood and Buxton had strong links with the anti-slavery movement.

18. Casement familiarized himself with a range of materials on the Putumayo and referred to them regularly during his investigations there. In addition to the work of Hardenburg, they included a report by Lieut. William L. Herndon of the US Navy, who had visited the Amazon in the 1850s; an account by Lieut. Henry L. Maw, RN, who had journeyed across northern Peru in 1828; Eugenio Robuchon's *En El Putumayo y sus afflluentes* (Lima 1907).

19. Gerald Sydney Spicer was born in 1874 and became a FO clerk in 1894; he later served as private secretary to two Permanent Undersecretaries for Foreign Affairs, Sir T. Sanderson (April 1903–January 1906) and Sir C. Hardinge (February 1906). He became assistant clerk in 1906 and senior clerk in 1912.

20. Sawyer, *Diaries*, 11–13 July, pp. 59–63. For Will Reid, see Sawyer, *Diaries*, p. 62, n. 60. The year 1910 is unique in that it has left us two Casement diary-like texts, the Black Diary for the full year and a much more detailed daily chronicle, written on loose foolscap pages and covering only the period from 26 September to 6 December, the actual period Casement was in the Putumayo region. In contrast to the Black Diary, this second document, the 'Putumayo Journal', dubbed a 'White Diary' by Angus Mitchell, contains no explicit sexual material. It is in the NLI in two forms: a manuscript version, MS 13085–6, and a typewritten version, MS 1622–3. In addition, Mitchell has compiled other documents written by Casement covering his movements from the time he left London in August until he returned in December; the overall narrative, comprising the 'Putumayo Journal' and extra documents, he has called the 'Amazon Journal of Roger Casement'. I follow his usage, and quotations from Casement's 'Amazon Journal' are taken

from his edition, Angus Mitchell (ed.), *The Amazon Journal of Roger Casement* (Dublin: The Lilliput Press 1997). Discussion of the forgery question can be found in the Appendix.

21. Tyrrell to ASS, 13/7/1910, ASS S22 G322.

22. FO to RDC, 21/7/1910, PRO FO 371/968; *Correspondence respecting the Treatment of British Colonial Subjects and Native Indians Employed in the Collection of Rubber in the Putumayo District*, Miscellaneous, no. 8 (1912), London: HMSO, 1912, p. 1. This is generally known as the Putumayo Blue Book and referred to henceforth as 'Blue Book'.

23. The record of the meeting with Grey, dated 13 July 1910, is at NLI MS 13080 (6/iii) and can be found in Mitchell, *Journal*, pp. 61–2, from which the quote is taken. As he left, Casement requested that John Brown, Whiffen's 'boy', be made available, now that no representative of the Barbadian government was to be present. The FO promised to try, but word came that Brown was ill and doubts were expressed as to whether he could be contacted in time.

24. Sawyer, *Diaries*, pp. 65-6, 23/7/1910–12/8/1910. RDC to Gertrude, 8/8/1910, NLI MS 13074 (6/ii); RDC to Hobson, 8/8/1910, NLI MS 13158 (7). Both letters are given in full in Mitchell, *Journal*, pp. 68–9.

25. RDC to EDM, 2/8/1910, LSE MP F8/24, quoted from Mitchell, *Journal*, p. 66; RDC to Spicer, 11/8/1910, PRO FO 371/968 (the full letter is given in Mitchell, *Journal*, pp. 70–1). Cândido Mariano da Silva Rondon (1865–1958) attended Military School in Rio; he studied engineering and came under the influence of Auguste Comte's social evolutionary positivism, which he used to interpret Indian societies. In 1890 the Brazilian government commissioned him to carry out a series of military and scientific expeditions to the unexplored interior regions of the country, for which he became renowned. In 1910 Rondon and other sympathetic officers persuaded the Government to create a special agency for the protection of Indian tribes; he was appointed first director of this agency, the SPI; with a motto of 'Die if necessary, but kill never', it set out to convince fearful or hostile Indians of its positive intentions by leaving gifts and patiently waiting for contact. In 1913 he accompanied former US President Theodore Roosevelt on his famous geographical expedition through the wilderness regions of Brazil. See Shelton Davis, *Victims of the Miracle: Development and the Indians of Brazil* (Cambridge: CUP 1977). Mitchell, *Journal*, p. 71, n. 72.

26. RDC to Tyrrell, 14/8/1910, quoted from Mitchell, *Journal*, p. 72, who gives the letter in full, from PRO FO 800/106.

27. RDC to Grey, 16/8/1910, PRO FO 371/968, and quoted in Mitchell, *Journal*, pp. 74–5. In the Congo, he had guaranteed his independence by hiring a missionary steamer.

28. Mitchell, *Journal*, pp. 75–81, 'Notes of a talk with Mr Victor Israel etc.', 24/8/1910, NLI MS 13087 (26/i). Casement, the ship's captain and the doctor discussed Israel and his concession afterwards, all wondering about the reasons for his success: *ibid.* p. 86.

29. Mitchell, *Journal*, pp. 81–5, 'Notes on the Peruvian Frontier etc.', 26/8/1910, NLI MS 13087 (24).

30. Mitchell, *Journal*, pp. 87–90, 'Early morning August 28th 1910 etc'.
31. David P. Werlich, *Peru: A Short History* (Carbondale: S. Illinois UP 1978), pp. 122–3.
32. Sawyer, *Diaries*, pp. 73–4, 31/8/1910. In Peruvian usage, the term *cholo* was a racial category between Indians and mestizos.
33. Mitchell, *Journal*, pp. 92–6, 31/8 to 2/9/1910; Sawyer, *Diaries*, pp. 73–5.
34. RDC to FO (Spicer), 13/9/1910, PRO FO 371/968. As well as that from Bishop, statements were taken in Iquitos from the Barbadians Nellice Walker, Norman Walcott, Preston Ford, Joseph Jones and Joseph Labadie. All of these statements were subsequently included in the Putumayo Blue Book (nos. 1–7, pp. 53–62). Significantly, Casement also enclosed one from Juan Garrido, a Peruvian who had served in the Putumayo; it is the only one not included in the Blue Book. He was not a British citizen and he subsequently refused to repeat his allegations, having, Casement believed, been 'got at'.
35. Mitchell, *Journal*, pp. 95–102, 8/9/1910, 9/9/1910, 12/9/1910 and 14/9/1910; Sawyer, *Diaries*, pp. 77–80.
36. Sawyer, *Diaries*, pp. 77–9, 9/9/1910 and 12/9/1910.
37. RDC to Tyrrell, 12/9/1910, quoted in Mitchell, *Journal*, pp. 105–6.
38. Sawyer, *Diaries*, p. 79, 12/9/1910.
39. RDC to Harris, 7/9/1910, ASS D 2/1 1910.
40. FO minute, 24/10/1910, PRO FO 371/968.
41. Sawyer, *Diaries*, pp. 81–2, 19/9 and 17/9/1910.
42. *Ibid.* pp. 83–4, 21/9/1910 and 22/9/1910.
43. *Ibid.* p. 84, 22/9/1910.
44. Mitchell, *Journal*, pp. 120–4, 23/9/1910; Sawyer, *Diaries*, p. 85. Their depositions are nos. 10–14 (pp. 67–83) in the Blue Book.
45. Mitchell, *Journal*, p. 133, 26/9/1910.
46. Sawyer, *Diaries*, pp. 85–6, 24/9/1910 and 25/9/1910; Mitchell, *Journal*, pp. 124–132.
47. Sawyer, *Diaries*, p. 86, 26/9/1910.
48. RDC, 'Reports on treatment of Barbados men employed by Peruvian Amazon Company', 31/1/1911, Blue Book, pp. 7–24.
49. RDC, 'Reports on methods of rubber collection and treatment of natives on the Putumayo', 17/3/1911, Blue Book, pp. 25–52; the quotation is from p. 46.
50. Bishop's evidence, Blue Book, p. 58.
51. Sawyer, *Diaries*, p. 88, 29/9/1910.
52. Mitchell, *Journal*, p. 141, 29/9/1910.
53. *Ibid.* pp. 146–8, 30/9/1910. Confusingly, Andokes was the name of a person, as here, an ethnic group and a company station.
54. Mitchell, *Journal*, p. 149, 1/10/1910.
55. Blue Book, p. 81.
56. Mitchell, *Journal*, p. 153, 3/10/1910; Sawyer, *Diaries*, p. 90, 3/10/1910.
57. Mitchell, *Journal*, pp. 149–50, 3/10/1910.
58. *Ibid.* pp. 166 and 168, 4/10/1910.

59. *Ibid.* pp. 163 and 169–70, 3/10/1910 and 4/10/1910.

60. *Ibid.* p. 167, 4/10/1910.

61. *Ibid.* pp. 162, 166, 168 and 185, 3/10/1910, 4/10/1910 and 5/10/1910.

62. *Ibid.* pp. 183–4, 5/10/1910.

63. Sawyer, *Diaries*, p. 93, 7–8/10/1910.

64. Mitchell, *Journal*, p. 192, 8/10/1910.

65. Blue Book, pp. 87–92.

66. Mitchell, *Journal*, pp. 198–9, 9/10/1910.

67. *Ibid.* pp. 198–9 and 208–9, 9/10/1910 and 10/10/1910.

68. Mitchell, *Journal*, pp. 203 and 208, 9/10/1910 and 10/10/1910.

69. Sawyer, *Diaries*, p. 95, 10/10/1910.

70. Mitchell, *Journal*, p. 221, 11/10/1910.

71. *Diary*, 12/10/1910, Sawyer, *Diaries*, p. 96.

72. Mitchell, *Journal*, p. 224, 12/10/1910.

73. Sawyer, *Diaries*, pp. 95–6, 13/10/1910 and 14/10/1910.

74. Mitchell, *Journal*, p. 250, 15/10/1910.

75. *Ibid.* p. 239, 14/10/1910.

76. Mitchell, *Journal*, pp. 251–2, 15/10/1910.

77. Sawyer, *Diaries*, p. 97, 14/10/1910. The entry for this day was clearly done at two sittings, before and after the dance.

78. Mitchell, *Journal*, p. 236, 14/10/1910.

79. *Ibid.* pp. 241–2, 14/10/1910.

80. *Ibid.* pp. 196 and 245, 8/10/1910 and 14/10/1910.

81. Sawyer, *Diaries*, p. 98, 17/10/1910; Mitchell, *Journal*, p. 256, 17/10/1910.

82. Mitchell, *Journal*, pp. 255 and 262, 17/10/1910 and 18/10/1910; Sawyer, *Diaries*, p. 98, 18/10/1910. The depositions from Lane and Levine are in the Blue Book, nos. 17 and 18, pp. 92–9.

83. Mitchell, *Journal*, p. 263, 18/10/1910.

84. *Ibid.* p. 270, 21/10/1910; Sawyer, *Diaries*, p. 99, 19/10/1910.

85. *Ibid.* p. 274, 20/10/1910.

86. Casement's camera has survived and is held by the National Museum of Ireland.

87. Mitchell, *Journal*, p. 279, 20/10/1910.

88. Sawyer, *Diaries*, p. 99, 20/10/1910. The conversation took place during the afternoon of the 21st. Both of Casement's diaries show retrospective writing at this point.

89. Mitchell, *Journal*, p. 282, 22/10/1910.

90. *Ibid.* pp. 305, 307–8 and 310, 24/10/1910 and 25/10/1910.

91. *Ibid.* p. 295, 23/10/1910. Baron Erland Nordenskiöld (1877–1932) was a Swedish ethnographer who travelled widely in parts of South America; he wrote to the Anti-Slavery Society in 1910 regarding ill-treatment of the indigenous population in parts of Peru and Bolivia. Casement was made aware of this through his contacts with the society.

92. *Ibid.* pp. 295 and 312, 23/10/1910 and 25/10/1910.

93. *Ibid.* pp. 313–14, 25/10/1910.
94. Sawyer, *Diaries*, p. 106, 2/11/1910. The depositions from Evelyn Batson, Sidney Morris, Preston Johnston, Augustus Walcott, James Mapp, Alfred Hoyte, Reuben Phillips, Clifford Quintin, Allan Davis, Joseph Minggs and Armando King can be found in the Blue Book, nos. 19–29, pp. 99–139.
95. Mitchell, *Journal*, p. 351, 3/11/1910.
96. *Ibid.* pp. 362–3, 6/11/1910.
97. Sawyer, *Diaries*, p. 104, 29/10/1910.
98. Mitchell, *Journal*, pp. 396–7, 14/11/1910.
99. *Ibid.* p. 340, 31/10/1910.
100. *Ibid.* pp. 341–2, 31/10/1910.
101. Sawyer, *Diaries*, p. 113, 16/11/1910; Mitchell, *Journal*, pp. 408 and 410, 16/11/1910.
102. Mitchell, *Journal*, p. 412, 16/11/1910.
103. *Ibid.* p. 441, 23/11/1910.
104. *Ibid.* pp. 433–4, 21/11/1910. Sebastião Marquês de Pombal (1699–1782) became Portuguese chief minister for foreign affairs and war in 1750 and Prime Minister in 1756. He believed the Church had too much power and, in 1759, expelled the Jesuits from Portugal and her South American colonies. At this time, Casement was becoming increasingly convinced of the Church's historical role as a defender of the indigenous population.
105. Henry Walter Bates (1825–92) was author of *The Naturalist on the River Amazons* (1863), based on eleven years of research on the river. Casement possessed a copy to which he referred regularly in his writings, for example, in his Pará Trade Report.
106. Sawyer, *Diaries*, pp. 114–18, 17/11/1910 to 25/11/1910.
107. Mitchell, *Journal*, 23/11/1910, p. 445.
108. According to Casement, Johnston had sent him 'the first copy (so he says) and I find it interesting in the extreme and well done'. Johnston acknowledged Casement's help in the book, which contained a photo lent by him. See Johnston to RDC, 16/7/1910, NLI MS 13073 (30/ii).
109. Sawyer, *Diaries*, p. 117, 24/11/1910.
110. Mitchell, *Journal*, pp. 454–7 and 478, 26/11/1910 and 2/12/1910.
111. *Ibid.* pp. 459 and 461, 26/11/1910.
112. *Ibid.* p. 471, 29/11/1910; Sawyer, *Diaries*, 25/11/1910–6/12/1910.
113. Sawyer, *Diaries*, p. 122, 5/12/1910.
114. *Ibid.* p. 118, 26/11/1910; Mitchell, *Journal*, pp. 486–8, 6/12/1910.

13: PUTUMAYO CAMPAIGN, 1911–12

1. 1911 Diary, 1/1/1911. The diary is a Letts's Desk Diary; both documents are to be found at PRO HO 161. The cash ledger was published in some editions of Singleton-Gates and Girodias and page references to the ledger are from this source.

I am grateful to Roger Sawyer for a typescript copy of the 1911 Diary. Dudgeon contains an abridged edition of both diary and ledger. Sir Francis Bertie was ambassador in Paris (1905–18); he had previously been head of African and Asian Departments in the FO, Assistant Undersecretary (1894–1903), and ambassador in Rome (1903–5).

2. 1911 Diary, *passim*. G.P. Gooch was editor of the *Contemporary Review*; John St Loe Strachey was on the executive of the CRA and was editor of *The Spectator*.

3. 1911 Diary, 7/1/1911; Mallet to RDC, 7/1/1911, NLI MS 13073 (32). Angus Mitchell's compendium of Casement's 1911 writings and of letters to him contains the full text of documents (the diary and ledger excluded) and is an invaluable source: Angus Mitchell, *Sir Roger Casement's Heart of Darkness: The 1911 Documents* (Dublin: Irish Manuscripts Commission 2003). The context of quotations in the present chapter can be found there. It opens with Casement's announcement to Sir Edward Grey of his return to London.

4. RDC to FO, 7/1/1911 (r. 9/1/1911), PRO FO 371/1200. It was incorporated into the Blue Book, pp. 1–5.

5. Mallet to RDC, 10/1/1911, NLI MS 13073 (32).

6. Arana to RDC, 3/1/1911, 10/1/1911 and RDC to Arana, 11/1/1911, ASS S22 G344a.

7. 'Reports on treatment of Barbados men employed by Peruvian Amazon Company', Blue Book, no. 8, pp. 7–25.

8. Communications between the FO and Des Graz can be found in the Blue Book, no. 3 ff., 16/1/1911 etc.; FO (Mallet) to RDC, 21/1/1911, 30/1/1911, 24/2/1911, 3/3/1911, NLI MS 13081 (3/ii); Langley to RDC, 4/3/1911, NLI MS 13081 (3/ii). His visit to the FO on 30th is dated 31/1/1911.

9. Mallet to RDC, 1/2/1911 and 1/3/1911, NLI MS 13073 (32); 1911 Cash Ledger, 30/1/1911, p. 544.

10. 1911 Cash Ledger, January and February 1911.

11. RDC to Gertrude, 20/1/1911, NLI MS 13074 (7/i); RDC to Hobson, 28/1/1911 and 11/2/1911, NLI MS 13158 (7).

12. RDC to Gertrude, February 1911, quoted in Parmiter, pp. 326–7.

13. For discussion on the topic of the overtaxation of Ireland, see R.D. Collison Black, *Economic Thought and the Irish Question, 1817–1870* (Cambridge: CUP 1960), p. 148 n. 5; Phillip Marcus, *Standish O'Grady* (Lewisburg: Bucknell University Press 1970), pp. 70–4; F.S.L. Lyons, *John Dillon; A Biography* (London: Routledge 1968), pp. 158–9 and 174–8; Inglis, pp. 131–2.

14. Mackey, *Crime against Europe*, pp. 134 and 24.

15. 1911 Cash Ledger, 22/2/1911, 26/2/1911, 2/3/1911. Dr George Sigerson (1836–1925) was born in Strabane, Co. Tyrone, graduated as a doctor of medicine in 1859, built up a reputation as a neurologist and became professor of botany and biology in the Catholic University and later in the National University of Ireland. He learned Irish and published many studies on historical and literary topics, including *History of the Land Tenures and Land Classes of Ireland* (1871), *The Last Independent*

Parliament of Ireland (1918), and *Bards of the Gael and Gall* (1897). Dora Sigerson Shorter was one of his daughters.

16. Blue Book, no. 9, 17/3/1911, pp. 25–52; no. 10, 21/3/1911, pp. 52–142.
17. Spicer to RDC, 30/3/1911, NLI MS 13073 (39).
18. Searches have failed to unearth these albums or the bulk of Casement's Putumayo photographs.
19. RDC (Belfast) to Gertrude, 18/4/1911, NLI MS 13074 (7/i). For Cranfield, see Dudgeon, p. 274.
20. RDC (105 Antrim Road) to Hobson, 19/4/1911, NLI MS 13158 (7).
21. According to Lyons, 'The paper ... was managed by Hobson and O'Hegarty. From the outset, until its suppression by the government in 1914, it took an advanced republican line, advocating, as Hobson has lately recalled, 'the independence of Ireland by every practicable means, including the use of physical force'. F.S.L. Lyons, *Ireland*, p. 319. Born in 1858, Tom Clarke had spent fifteen years in prison for revolutionary activities; he was a senior member of the IRB and a key player in planning the 1916 Easter Rising, after which he was executed.
22. Casement writes 'Muirbolg', the Irish name of the bay (1911 Cash Ledger, 24/4/1911); see 26/4/1911, 'Domnail óg de Muirbholg' ('young Donal of Murlough').
23. Carnstroan, Myrtlefield Pk., is given in Belfast Street Directories as the home of Mrs Gordon, who was the mother of 'Millar', Joseph Millar Gordon: see Dudgeon for the Gordon family.
24. Paredes was a judge in Iquitos and editor of a local newspaper; he left for the Putumayo in March 1911 and returned to Iquitos in July.
25. Grey to Jerome, 21/7/1911, Blue Book, no. 22, pp. 146–7. Lucien Jerome FRGS was born in 1870 and took up the first of his FO positions in 1891. He was appointed consul general in Callao in 1907 and was in charge of the legation at Lima from 6/3/1908 to 30/11/1908 and 8/10/1909 to 12/11/1909. He was in charge of the consulate at La Paz from 29/3/1910 to 25/11/1910 and again of the legation in Lima from 21/2/1911 to 6/11/1911. He was transferred to Quito in 1913 and retired in 1919.
26. Casement described Fielding to Morel as 'a sort of leader of Catholic opinion' and a brother of Lord Denbigh, one of the leading Catholic peers. RDC to EDM, 1/8/1907, LSE MP F8/22. Fielding sent a contribution to Casement for the Mission in 1912: Fielding to RDC, 9/8/1912, NLI MS 13073 (6/i).
27. Rt. Revd Mgr Manuel Bidwell DD was born in 1872 at Palma, Mallorca; he took the degree of B. ès Sc. in Paris 1890, and then went through a course in the Applied Science Department at King's College, London. He was educated for the priesthood at the French Seminary in Rome, and at the Academy of Noble Ecclesiastics, where he was ordained in 1898. He became secretary and archivist to the diocese of Westminster in 1904 and chancellor in 1907. He served in the Papal Secretariat of State, Rome, in 1908, and became Domestic Prelate to His Holiness, the Pope, in 1911.
28. Tyrrell to RDC, 14/6/1911, NLI MS 13073 (43); RDC to Cadbury, 11/7/1911, NLI MS

8358; RDC to Spicer, 11/7/1911, PRO FO 371/1202; 1911 Cash Ledger, 18/7/1911 and 25/7/1911; Hoste to RDC, 25/7/1911, NLI MS 13073 (8/ii); Lady Hamilton to RDC, 25/7/1911, NLI MS 13073 (8/i). Carnegie was not forthcoming with help, see Hoste to RDC, 1/8/1911, NLI MS 13073 (8/ii).

29. Their letters to Casement are to be found in NLI MS 13073: Bertie (23/ii); Barnes (20/i–ii); Bell (17); Fox (6/ii); Gielgud (24/i) and (7/i).

30. The general portions of the report were published as part of the Proceedings of the Parliamentary Select Committee in 1912, RHO ASS S22 G335.

31. RDC to FO, 20/6/1911, PRO FO 371/1201.

32. RDC to FO, 22/6/1911, PRO FO 371/1201.

33. RDC, Minutes of Board Meetings, RHOASS S22, G335 and 344a. Casement arranged that notes of these meetings be taken by a shorthand typist: Bertie to RDC, 26/5/1911 and 9/6/1911, NLI MS 13073 (23/ii).

34. RDC to Spicer, 17/6/1911 and 22/6/1911, PRO FO 371/1201.

35. Arana wrote to Casement on 31 May and 27 June. In the first, he wrote that: 'I most respectfully thank you for your assistance in anticipation and feel quite sure that same will be of the greatest advantage to all concerned and especially to the natives of that region.' Casement added an exclamation mark to this and the word 'Liar' to another remark. Arana to RDC, 31/5/1911 and 27/6/1911, RHO ASS S22 G344a.

36. RDC to Gubbins, 1/7/1911, RHO ASS S22 G344a.

37. The company did go into liquidation in September, after Casement had again left for Iquitos.

38. J. Stuart-Horner to RDC, 15/7/1911–2/8/1911 (seven letters), NLI MS 13073 (41); Hobson to RDC, 20/7/1911–31/7/1911 (four letters); 1911 Cash Ledger, 14/7, 26/7, 317 and 1/8; Cadbury to RDC, 3/7/1911 and 13/7/1911, NLI MS 13073 (26/iii). His main contacts seem to have been J. Stuart-Horner and J.J (?) Hobson. In their correspondence, the names of Sir Robert Laidlaw, Gilbert Jennings and Baron von Opell appear as interested parties. What is clear is that all were being cautious, attempting to gain an understanding of the company's situation.

39. 1911 Cash Ledger, 15/6/1911; Sir E. Grey to RDC, June 1911 (r. Denham 15/6), NLI MS 13081(3/iii). See, also, Meiklejohn (10 Downing St) to RDC, 20/6/1911, informing Casement of the king's intention to knight him. NLI MS 13073 (46/xiii). And FO to RDC, 3/7/1911 (r. 17 July), NLI MS 13081 (3/iii), enclosing 'a Medal to be worn in commemoration of the Coronation of their majesties King George V and Queen Mary'.

40. RDC to ASG, 21/6/1911, quoted in Inglis, p. 194; the full text is given in Mitchell, *1911 Documents*, pp. 397–8.

41. RDC to Grey, 19/6/1911, PRO FO 95/776; the full text is given in Mitchell, *1911 Documents*, p. 386.

42. See, for example, in NLI MS 13073: Symons to RDC, 4/8/1911 (46/xvi); Lugard to RDC, 28/7/1911 (46/xi); Ní Fhaircheallaigh to RDC, 22/6/1911 (12/ii). Sir Frederick Lugard (1858–1945), soldier and colonial official (associated with the development

of the policy of 'indirect rule'), served in many parts of Africa, including in the Niger area in 1894–5. He was later high commissioner in the protectorate of Northern Nigeria and governor of Hong Kong (1907–12).

43. 1911 Cash Ledger, 6/7/1911.

44. Jerome to Casement, 9/6/1911, NLI MS 13073 (29/iii). There is enthusiasm and warmth in Jerome's letters to Casement, due, no doubt, to his clear commitment to reform and to his Irishness (they were, he said, 'both paddies').

45. RDC to Spicer, 11/7/1911, PRO FO 371/1202.

46. RDC to Buxton, 2/6/1911, RHO ASS S19 D2/2.

47. RDC to EDM, 8/4/1911 and 13/4/1911, LSE MP F5/3.

48. RDC to ASG, April 1911, NLI MS 10464 (4).

49. RDC to Cadbury, 26/5/1911, NLI MS 8358.

50. RDC, Putumayo Diary, NLI MS 1622, pp. 220–1.

51. *Ibid*. pp. 351–2.

52. RDC to Cadbury, 6/6/1911, NLI MS 8358.

53. Buxton to RDC, 13/7/1911, NLI MS 13073 (45/i); RDC to Buxton, 22/71911 and 29/7/1911, RHO ASS S19 D2/2. William Edward Burghardt Du Bois (1868–1963) was a prominent Afro-American academic, writer and political activist. In 1909 he was involved in the planning for the National Association for the Advancement of Colored People and in 1910 founded *Crisis*, its monthly organ. In 1911 he was joint secretary of the US delegation at the Universal Races Congress in London.

54. One of Casement's associates was Mrs Nannie Dryhurst, who was secretary to the Nationalities and Subject Races Committee. His friend Robert Lynd had married Sylvia Dryhurst, daughter of Alfred Robert Dryhurst, administrative secretary of the British Museum and an early Fabian, and of Nannie Dryhurst, née Robinson: 'NFD, as she was known, was artistic, supplementing her income by selling *objects d'art* and hand-painted Christmas cards. She was a suffragette, an anarchist, founder with Gordon Craig, Ellen Terry's son, of the Purcell Operatic Society – very much the Shavian New Woman.' Robert Lynd, *Galway of the Races – Selected Essays*, ed. Sean McMahon (Dublin: The Lilliput Press 1990), p. 25.

55. RDC to Gardiner, 23/12/1910, quoted in Stephen Koss, *Fleet Street Radical: A.G. Gardiner and the Daily News* (London: Allen Lane 1973), p. 128.

56. RDC to Gardiner, 16/8/1911, LSE GP, 1/6 (A).

57. Smith to RDC, 21/3/1911, 2/5/1911 and 13/6/1911, NLI MS 13073 (38). Smith had bought clothes and arranged English classes for them. They were both slow at English, he reported, Omarino being the better. During his stay, Ricudo (also called Arédomi) had got restless, indicating a wish to return to the Putumayo.

58. Pearse to RDC, 15/6/1911, NLI MS 13073 (13/iii).

59. A. Barnes to RDC, 5/7/1911, NLI MS 13073 (19); L. Barnes to RDC, 6/7/1911, NLI MS 13073 (20/i).

60. William Rothenstein, *Men and Memories* (London: Faber and Faber 1932), vol. II, 1900–1922, pp. 170–1. He added: 'I remember George Moore meeting Casement

and Mrs Green at dinner with us. George Moore and Casement got on well together, but George Moore couldn't abide Mrs Green.' Rothenstein, p. 171.

61. Rothenstein to RDC, 15/7/1911, NLI MS 13073 (37).

62. RDC to Cadbury, 19/7/1911, NLI MS 8358.

63. RDC to Spicer, 11/7/1911, PRO FO 371/1202. While the boys were in England, Nina seems to have carried a good deal of the burden of minding them, while her brother busied himself with his other interests.

64. Sir Thomas Fowell Buxton, 3rd Baronet (1853–1915), served as Liberal MP for King's Lynn, 1865–8 and as governor of South Australia, 1895–8.

65. 1911 Cash Ledger, June and July; the Buxton weekend was from 29–31 July.

66. Grey to Goodhart, Petropolis, 6/5/1911, PRO FO 128/361.

67. O'Reilly to Grey, 15/5/1911, 27/6/1911, PRO FO 128/361.

68. 1911 Cash Ledger, 29/7/1911 and 3/8/1911.

69. Dufferin to RDC, 23/6/1911 and 26/6/1911, NLI MS 13081 (3/iii); Gritton to RDC, 22/7/1911, NLI MS 13073 (24); Michell to RDC, 24/7/1911, NLI MS 13080 (2/i).

70. Captain L.C. Arbuthnot was director of the Dublin zoo.

71. 1911 Cash Ledger, 5/8/1911 to 13/8/1911. For Johnnie Bell, see Dudgeon, pp. 300–4.

72. RDC to Spicer, 29/8/1911, PRO FO 371/1202.

73. 1911 Diary, 1/9/1911. This recommenced, with brief entries, during August, becoming fuller from September until the end of the year. For September and October, there is an overlap between it and the ledger, which continues until the end of October.

74. This boy is the youngest recorded in the diaries to attract Casement's admiration; it is almost certainly one of the entries giving rise to the suggestion of paedophilia. It should be noted that admiration only is involved.

75. 1911 Diary and 1911 Cash Ledger, 4/9/1911 to 10/9/1911; RDC to Mallet, PRO FO 371/1203 and NLI MS 13080 (1/ii). Herbert Spencer Dickey wrote of his experiences as a doctor in several South American countries in *The Misadventures of a Tropical Medico* (London: Bodley Head 1929). For further detail on Dickey, see Mitchell, *1911 Documents*.

76. RDC to Grey, 11/9/1911, PRO FO 128/361.

77. 1911 Diary, 17/9/1911.

78. *Ibid.*, 22/9/1911; 1911 Cash Ledger, 22/9/1911.

79. O'Reilly to Grey, 26/9/1911, PRO FO 128/361.

80. RDC to O'Reilly, 30/9/1911, PRO FO 128/361.

81. 1911 Cash Ledger, 1/10/1911; 1911 Diary, 1/10/1911.

82. 1911 Diary, 7/10/1911.

83. In 1904 Casement had suffered from diarrhoea and piles, which he had then described as 'my old African complaint'. He also suffered from anal bleeding, which, presumably, was linked to his sexual activity.

84. 1911 Diary, 11–12/10/1911.

85. 1911 Diary, 18/10/1911.

86. RDC to FO, 23/11/1911, PRO FO 128/361 and NLI MS 13081 (2/ii); RDC to Spicer, 24/10/1911, PRO FO 371/1203.

87. The cash ledger ends after 31 October, and the list of names is given with his summaries of expenditures at the end of the month.

88. Casement had taken two books by Reginald Enock with him to the Amazon in 1910, *Peru* and *The Andes and the Amazon*. He claimed that Enock had not visited the rubber regions, but was aware of conditions there from his reading. RDC to FO, 17/9/12, PRO FO 371/1453.

89. RDC to O'Reilly, 5/11/1911, PRO FO 128/361. The Javari marked the boundary between Peru and Brazil; the fugitives were on the Brazilian side.

90. RDC to O'Reilly, 15/11/1911 and 21/11/1911, PRO FO 128/361; the meeting with Edwards is recorded in the diary, under 20/11/1911.

91. 1911 Diary, October–December.

92. Regarding Fonseca and Montt, Casement felt that there was no point urging further steps except that pressure might act as a deterrent: 'As a matter of fact, I have for some time now given up all hope of seeing any of the criminals punished.' He related the farcical episode of the police going to arrest Fonseca and Montt on board John Lilly's steamer, the *Anastasia* (with Mr Lilly on board). The two culprits had arrived in a canoe, requesting a tow, and, when asked if they knew Fonseca and Montt, had jumped back into their canoe and made off. The police refused Lilly's offer to use his steamer to apprehend them; indeed, the officer refused any action. Memo, RDC to FO, 27/1/1912, PRO FO 128/361.

93. RDC to FO, 24/11/1911, 17/11/1911 and 9/12/1911, PRO FO 128/361.

14: PUTUMAYO: MISSION AND SELECT COMMITTEE, 1912–13

1. RDC (Grand Canary) to Roberts, 4/1/1913, RHO ASS S22 G344c.

2. Bryce to Grey, 12/1/1912, PRO FO 128/361. At the time Bryce was also addressing the boundary dispute between Colombia and Peru.

3. George Young, *Diplomacy Old and New*, quoted in Inglis, p. 204. Young's wife, Helen, wrote to Casement in February from the *Lusitania*, offering advice about the campaign in England, including advice on *Times* journalists, and suggesting family help. Casement must have indicated the possibility of returning to the US later, as she wrote: 'Do come over in April and let us know', and 'I do hope your blue parrot will cheer you up soon – if she doesn't you must bring her across to Washington with you in April.' Helen Young to RDC, 18/2/1912, NLI MS 13073 (16/iv).

4. RDC to FO, 5/2/1912, PRO FO 881/9977.

5. RDC to FO, 13/2/1912, PRO FO 371/1451. The document comprises 17 pages in the Confidential Print.

6. RDC to FO, 5/2/1912, PRO FO 881/9977.

7. 'Memorandum by Sir R. Casement Respecting Suggested Steps to Follow Publica-

tion of Putumayo Reports', RDC to FO, 30/1/1912, PRO FO 128/361.

8. The article was soon to be published, as 'Love and the law: a study of oriental justice', *The Hibbert Journal*, XI (Oct. 1912–Jan. 1913), 273–96.

9. Innes to RDC, 20/3/1912, NLI MS 13073 (28/i).

10. RDC to EDM, 21/3/1912 and 29/4/1912, LSE MP F8/24. The reference to liners
    sinking was, presumably, to the *Titanic*, which had sunk on 15 April 1912.

11. RDC to FO, 30/1/1912, FO 128/361.

12. Haggard to Mallet, 18/3/1912, PRO FO 128/361.

13. Haggard to FO, 18/3/1912, PRO FO 128/361. By the mechanism of the private let-
    ter, Haggard, Casement's superior in Brazil, was able to make his criticism but not
    have it registered as an official one.

14. Haggard to FO, 30/8/1912, PRO FO 128/361 and PRO FO 371/1453.

15. RDC to Haggard, 6/9/1912 and 9/9/1912, PRO FO 128/36. He also asked if Haggard
    could do anything to help raise funds for the Putumayo mission.

16. Haggard to Spicer, 1/10/1912, PRO FO 371/1454.

17. RDC to FO, 31/5/1912, PRO FO 371/1451. The text comprises 30 pages and repre-
    sents a considerable amount of work on Casement's part.

18. RDC to FO, 18/6/1912, PRO FO 371/1451. FO minutes to his memo, including
    Grey's, expressed their agreement with his arguments.

19. Des Graz to FO, 4/4/1912 and 28/5/1912; RDC, note, 11/4/1912; FO minute, 5/6/1912,
    PRO FO 371/1451.

20. Bryce to FO, 1/3/1912 and FO note, 1/7/1912, PRO FO 371/1451.

21. FO minutes, 25/5/1912, 4/6/1912 and 9/7/1912, PRO FO 371/1451.

22. Inglis, p. 208.

23. EDM, *Daily News*, 20/7/1912.

24. RDC to Gertrude, 2?/7/1912 and 25/7/1912, NLI MS 13074 (7/ii). Further publicity
    was drawn to the Putumayo case after the publication of the Blue Book, when
    Canon Hensley Henson, of Westminster Abbey, preached about the atrocities and
    wrote to *The Times*. In one sermon, he named the three English directors of the
    Peruvian Amazon Company and, having received solicitors' letters, had all the cor-
    respondence published. See Herbert Hensley Henson, *Retrospect of an Unimportant
    Life*, 3 vols. (Oxford: OUP 1942–50), vol. 1, 1863–1920, pp. 114–20. The events are
    referred to in Casement's correspondence.

25. Plunkett, Diaries, 2/8/1912, fol. 255.

26. RDC to FO, 9/9/1912, FO minute, PRO FO 371/1453. Casement's report com-
    prised eleven foolscap pages and two enclosures of a further eight foolscap hand-
    written pages.

27. See, for example, RDC to FO, 7/9/1912, and RDC to Spicer, 9/10/1912, PRO FO
    371/1453.

28. Michell to Grey, 14/10/1912 (r. 5/12/1912), pp. 1, 4.

29. Bidwell to RDC, 24/1/1912, NLI MS 13073 (24/ii).

30. Cant. to RDC, 6/2/1912, NLI MS 13073 (46/vii).

31. Cant. to RDC, 26/2/1912 (per J.V. Macmillan, Chaplain), NLI MS 13073 (46/vii) and 15/3/1912, NLI MS 5463; RDC to Cant., 13/3/1912 (two draft letters), NLI MS 13073 (46/vii). The Revd F.B. Meyer, referring to the proposed mission, enquired: 'have you done anything more with respect to the colony of compassion[?]' and continued: 'tho' I dread to trust the RCs – better they than nothing'. Meyer to RDC, 12/3/1912, NLI MS 13073 (10/ii).

32. In February, Conan Doyle invited him down to the Grand Hotel, Lyndhurst and, a little later, wrote to say that 'your visit was a real pleasure'. He was quite solicitous about Casement, writing: 'I hate to think of you seedy and alone. If you came to us here you should have rooms of your own and never emerge if you didn't want to. You have done so much good in your life that no shadow should in justice come near you. If you come, now or later (with your macaw) you *can't* come amiss.' Doyle was also getting interested in the Home Rule issue, mentioning Erskine Childers, among others. See Doyle to RDC, 12/2/1912, n.d. (r. 16/2/1912), 4/3/1912, n.d. (r. 25/3/1912), NLI MS 13073 (28/i).

33. RDC to Buxton, 2/3/1912, ASS S19 D2/3; RDC to Harris, 6/4/1912, ASS S19 D4/1; Bidwell to RDC, 16/4/1912, NLI MS 13073 (24/ii); Tyrrell to RDC, 16/4/1912, NLI MS 13073 (43).

34. RDC to Harris, 18/4/1912, 26/4/1912, 29/4/1912, RHO ASS S19 D4/1.

35. RDC to Harris, 26/4/1912, RHO ASS S19 D4/1.

36. RDC to Buxton, 28/4/1912, RHO ASS S19 D2/3.

37. RDC to Harris, 29/4/1912, RHO ASS S19 D4/1.

38. RDC to Gertrude, 3/5/1912, 9/5/1912 and 13/5/1912, NLI MS. 13074 (7ii). They were accompanied by a German friend, Heini, who seems to have been interned in Ceylon during the First World War: see NLI Acc. 4902 (2), 15/10/1914.

39. Hambloch, p. 145.

40. RDC to Harris, 20/6/1912, RHO ASS S19 D4/1.

41. Cant. to RDC, 20/7/1912, and 3/8/1912, NLI MS 13073 (46/vii); RDC to Cant., 30/7/1912 (draft), NLI MS 13073 (46/vii).

42. RDC to EDM, 31/7/1912, MP F8/24. Emmott wrote to say that Beauchamp couldn't stomach making a direct subscription to a Catholic mission, but that he might send something to Casement directly, to do with as he wished. Emmott to RDC, 1/8/1912, NLI MS 13073 (29/i). Conan Doyle sent £5 for the mission, but added: 'I fear the RCs did not do much good in the Congo. Give me a half-educated flat-footed Baptist for such work. Besides, what an awful example of intolerance that no other creed is recognised.' Doyle to RDC, n.d. (r. 19 July [1912?]).

43. RDC to FO, 1/8/1912, PRO FO 371/1452.

44. Browne to RDC, 2/9/1912, NLI MS 13073 (25/ii); RDC to FO, 14/9/1912, PRO FO 371/1453; RDC to FO, 17/9/1912, PRO FO 371/1453. Four Franciscans of the English Province went to Peru: Fathers Leo Sambrook, Cyprian Byrne, Frederick Furlong and Felix Ryan. Fr Sambrook, the Superior, had been professor of moral and dogmatic theology at Forest Gate, London, and editor of the *Francisan Monthly*. He

was to send regular letters reporting on the progress of the mission. A photograph appeared in the *Freeman's Journal* on 9 September 1912.

45. RDC memo, September 1912, PRO FO 371/1453.

46. RDC to Mallet, 9/10/1912, PRO FO 471/1453.

47. J.A. Fullerton (Ballymena Academy, Co. Antrim) to RDC, 6/5/1912 (r. in Germany), NLI Acc. 4902 (12). Enclosed was a printed appeal, signed 'Rt. Hon. John Young, P.C., D.L, Chairman'. This was John Young of Galgorm Castle, who himself gave £50.

48. RDC to Fullerton, quoted in Parmiter, pp. 93–4. Fullerton replied with a refreshingly human letter in which he confessed, from his own experience as a Presbyterian, to having some appreciation of Casement's criticisms: 'I have quietly enjoyed the heaviest of your "hits".' The school had changed, he pointed out, enclosing the previous week's history sheets to show that 'pupils have to know something of their native land'. He concluded by saying, 'I would feel no qualms whatever about accepting help for the Academy building fund from the most pronounced Nationalist that ever lived. As for the Governors it would be presumption for me to speak. If you sent them a cheque accompanied by some home truths for the Ulster ascendancy they would probably have enough humour to pocket the subscription and chuckle over their spoliation of the Egyptian.' Fullerton to RDC, 16/6/1912, NLI Acc. 4902 (12).

49. Alec Wilson (Belvoir Park, Newtonbreda, Co. Down) to RDC, 10/6/1912, NLI Acc. 4902 (12). Wilson was a successful chartered accountant, who was active in the Gaelic League; he gave generous financial support to St Enda's and acted as accountant and adviser to Pearse. The school was in constant financial difficulties. See Ruth Dudley Edwards, *Patrick Pearse: The Triumph of Failure* (Dublin: Poolbeg Press 1990 [1977]), pp. 144–51.

50. Law to RDC, 4/9/1912, NLI MS 13073 (10/i).

51. Lady Constance Emmott (1864–1922) was the daughter of the 8th Duke of Argyll and widow of Charles Emmott Esq (d. 1910), brother of Alfred Emmott. She was a professional landscape painter in oil and watercolours; she exhibited at the Royal Academy in 1912 and 1914, also at the Royal Scottish Academy, Edinburgh, 1917. She was a contributor to various magazines and reviews and had a residence in London and at Tighan-Rudha, Inverary, Argyll.

52. RDC (Savoy) to Lady Emmott, 21/6 1912, PRONI T3072/1.

53. Cadbury to RDC, 16/7/1912, NLI MS 13073 (26/iii).

54. RDC to Gertrude, 25/7/1912 and 1/8/1912, NLI MS 13074 (7/ii).

55. Statement by William Cadbury, January 1916, Cadbury Papers, Cad. 181, p. 2.

56. RDC (Cloghaneely) to Lady Emmott, 20/8/1912, PRONI T3072/4. Enclosed was a printed circular from the Rathlin Irish Teaching Scheme.

57. Eamonn De Valera (1882–1975) participated in the 1916 Easter Rising and subsequently went on to become Taoiseach and president of Ireland.

58. RDC to De Valera, 1/9/1912, NLI MS 14100. He had earlier sent £5 for prizes for the Tawin Feis or Sports ('Proviso – Irish in competitions and judging, if possible'),

RDC to De Valera, 14/8/1912, NLI MS 14100. He wrote twice to Mrs O'Beirne, Dr Seamus O'Beirne's mother, firstly to thank her for her hospitality and later regarding a gift he had sent: RDC to Mrs O'Beirne, 20/8/1912 and 4/11/1912 ('I am glad that Robert Emmet reached you safely and not broken').

59. RDC to Buxton, 8/9/1912, ASS S19 D2/3; he also wrote on 2/9/1912, 6/9/1912 ('I am at present ill in bed'), and 7/9/1912.

60. RDC to Gertrude, 16/9/1912, NLI MS 13074(7/iii). 'Torry' and 'yous' are Ulster idiom. Casement's visit to Tory also led to correspondence from Séamus Mac an Bháird (Seumas Ward) asking advice on the building of a pier on the island: see Mac an Bháird to RDC, 15/9/1912, McMullen Papers, and 24/11/1912, NLI MS 13073 (16/i).

61. RDC (Falcarragh) to Lady Emmott, 6/9/1912 and 16/9/1912, PRONI T3072/5–6.

62. RDC to Gertrude, 14/9/1912, NLI MS 13074 (10/ii).

63. Quoted in Bardon, p. 436.

64. RDC (105 Antrim Rd.) to Gertrude, 22/9/1912, NLI MS 13074 7/iii). In this letter he sent more photos of Donegal, with glimpses of Magheroararty and Muckish.

65. ND, 28/9/1912 and 29/9/1912, BLO MSS Eng. misc. e.617/3.

66. Charles Prestwich Scott (1846–1932) was a liberal journalist and editor of the *Manchester Guardian* from 1872 to 1929; he was an MP from 1895 to 1905. He made the paper a leading moral voice on world issues and was a critic of Grey's foreign policy.

67. RDC to Scott, 2/10/1912, Scott Papers, A/C25/4.

68. RDC (Gresham Hotel) to Scott, 3/10/1912, Scott Papers, A/C25/7a.

69. Scott to RDC, 6/10/1912, Scott Papers, A/C25/8.

70. RDC (Gresham Hotel) to Scott, 7/10/1912, Scott Papers, A/C25/9a. James Windsor Good (1877–1930) was a highly regarded journalist, who worked as a reporter with the *Northern Whig*. He later moved to Dublin, where he became a leader-writer for the *Freeman's Journal*, before joining the *Irish Independent*. He was author of *Ulster and Ireland* (1919) and *Irish Unionism* (1920).

71. Innes to RDC, 22/11/1912, NLI MS 13073 (28/i).

72. RDC to Scott, n.d. [1912] (two letters), Scott Papers, A/C25/11a and 12a.

73. Eberhardt's 1907 report was later published in a US government publication on the Putumayo, entitled *Slavery in Peru*. This publication included the whole of Casement's Putumayo report, Consul Fuller's reports, and a range of official correspondence. *Slavery in Peru*, Washington, House of Representatives, Document no. 1366, 7 Februray 1913.

74. Fisher Unwin wrote to Casement several times in November and December about the publication of Hardenburg's Putumayo material. Among other things, he requested Putumayo photographs from Casement and promised that the first copy he could put his hands on would be sent to him. Fisher Unwin to RDC, 23/7/1912, 4/11/1912, 7/11/1912, 8/11/1912, 12/11/1912, 4/12/1912, NLI MS 13073 (23/i). The book was published, with an introduction by R. Enock, as Walter E. Hardenburg, *The Putumayo: The Devil's Paradise: Travels in the Peruvian Amazon Region and an Account of*

the Atrocities Committed upon the Indians Therein (London: T. Fisher Unwin 1912).

75. Eugenio Robuchon was a French explorer and ethnologist. Commissioned by the Arana Company in 1904 to explore the Putumayo, he disappeared without trace in the process, rumoured to have been murdered by the company, when his sympathies changed. His notes were edited and published in 1907 by Carlos Rey de Castro, Peruvian consul in Manaos and a close associate of Julio Arana's, as *En el Putumayo y sus Afluentes*. The book was used as propaganda to sustain Peruvian claims to the area. Casement brought a copy with him to the Putumayo, which is now housed in the NLI; his notes on the book can be found in ASS S22 G344a. He brought its significance to the attention of Charles Roberts, who responded: 'I am much obliged for the Robuchon Book and for your notes on it. I quite realise the importance of the publication.' Roberts to RDC, 8/11/1912, NLI MS 13073 (36/i). For Robuchon, see Mitchell, *Journal*, and Taussig.

76. The company had gone into voluntary liquidation in September 1911 and appointed Arana as liquidator; his appointment was subsequently legally challenged and the case was finally heard in March 1913 at the High Court of Justice before Justice Swinfen Eady. He concluded his fifteen-page judgment thus: 'I am quite satisfied upon the whole of the case, both with regard to the manner in which the operations of the Company were conducted in the Putumayo district and in Brazil and with regard to the way in which the financial transactions in this country have been concerned, that it is a case in which there ought to be a compulsory order to be followed by the fullest investigation and that Senor Arana is the last person to whom the conduct of that investigation ought to be allocated.' RHO ASS S22 G332.

77. Select Committee on Putumayo Atrocities, 1912, Minutes of Evidence, Wednesday, 13/11/1912 and 11/12/1912, ASS S22 G 336 (Part I).

78. RDC to Malet, 9/10/1912, PRO FO 371/1453.

79. RDC (Ebury St.) to Lady Emmott, 19/11/1912, 21/11/1912, PRONI T3072/8–9.

80. ASG Statement, 1/8/1916, McMullen Papers.

81. Sidney Parry, Statement, 1/8/1916, McMullen Papers.

82. Charpentier, Statement, 1/8/1916, McMullen Papers; Brunton's letter is quoted in Inglis, p. 217; Nevinson to RDC, 19/12/1912, is quoted in Reid, p. 165.

83. RDC to FO, 14/12/1912, NLI MS 13081 (2/ii); Law to RDC, 16/12/1912, NLI MS 12081 (3/iv); Tyrrell to RDC, 16/12/1912, NLI MS 13073 (43). Law had earlier written to notify Casement that the area of the Rio consulate was being extended to include the State of Goyas. Casement responded with a somewhat facetious letter on the inaccessibility of the new area; deputies, he said, left three years in advance to arrive in Rio and he himself might never reappear if he visited there. A. Law to RDC, 2/12/1912, NLI MS 13081 (3/iv); RDC to FO, 18/12/1912, NLI MS 13081 (2/ii).

84. RDC to Roberts, 17/12/1912 (two), RHO ASS S22 G344c.

85. RDC to Roberts, 22/12/1912, RHO ASS S22 G344c.

86. Law to RDC, 23/12/1912, NLI MS 13073 (46/viii), 31/12/1912, MS 13081 (3/iv).

87. John Hartman Morgan (1876–1955) was born and educated in Wales and worked for the *Daily Chronicle* (1901–3) and the *Manchester Guardian* (1904–5). He was called to the Bar in 1915, served as professor of constitutional law in London University and as reader in constitutional law at the Inns of Court. He served with the rank of brigadier general in the Inter-Military Control Commission in Germany after the First World War and in the War Crimes Commission after the Second. In that war he also advised Sir Winston Churchill on constitutional law. In 1914, Horace Plunkett wrote that he was 'important at the moment as the Cabinet consults him as an authority on Constitutional Law. He is a young opinionated person. He is of books not affairs. But he has the ear of men who ought to be both.' Plunkett, Diaries, 21/3/1914.

88. RDC to Morgan, 18/12/1912, quoted in Sawyer, *Flawed Hero*, p. 109. These letters are not available to researchers at present.

89. Sawyer, *Flawed Hero*, p. 109.

15: IRELAND, 1913–14

1. RDC (c/o British Consulate, Las Palmas, Grand Canary) to Roberts, 4/1/1913, RHO ASS S22 G344c. Casement may have had no written instructions in 1910 to investigate the treatment of Indians in the Putumayo, but, by his own account, he had discussed it with Grey: see Chapter 12, pp. 273–4.

2. RDC (Quiney's English Hotel, Las Palmas) to Roberts, 27/1/1913, RHO ASS S22 G344c.

3. RDC to Roberts, 30/1/1913, RHO ASS S22 G344c.

4. RDC (c/o British Consulate, Tenerife) to ASG, 24/1/1913, NLI MS 10464 (6).

5. RDC (British Consulate, Las Palmas) to ASG, 1/2/1913, NLI MS 10464 (6).

6. RDC (c/o British Consulate, Las Palmas) to Roberts, 28/1/1913, 30/1/1913, 31/1/1913, 1/2/1913, 2/2/1913, 5/2/1913, RHO ASS S22 G344c. Roberts wrote to Casement on 1 February, telling him of the raid he had organized on the PAC offices, which yielded revealing documentation to the select committee: 'The documents have thrown some new light. The main point is that the "design of conquest", "reduction of the Indians", "conquering them or rather attracting them to work and civilisation", is frequently referred to in the correspondence and accounts. These phrases turn up again and again.' He also thanked Casement for 'the very clear account of peonage' and added: 'Some of your photographs haunt me, like the child with the load of rubber.' Roberts to RDC, 1/2/1913, NLI MS 13073 (36/iii).

7. RDC to Tyrrell, 14/1/1913, NLI MS 13080 (5). Dufferin to RDC (r. Cape Town 28/2/1913), 29/1/1913, NLI MS 13081 (10).

8. RDC (Las Palmas) to Roberts, 6/2/1913, RHO ASS S22 G344c.

9. RDC to ASG, 17/2/1913, NLI 10464 (6).

10. RDC (c/o Union Castle, Cape Town) to Roberts, 3/3/1913, RHO ASS S22 G344c.

Herbert Gladstone (1854–1930), youngest son of William Gladstone, was the first Governor General and high commissioner of the Union of South Africa between 1910 and 1914. He had become a Liberal MP in 1880, after which he held a number of important government posts, including Secretary of State for Home Affairs, 1905–10.

11. RDC (c/o Union Castle Coy, Cape Town) to Roberts, 4/3/1913, RHO ASS S22 G344c. He acknowledged Roberts's long letter of 1 February.

12. RDC to Roberts, 14/3/1913, RHO ASS S22 G344c. The letter is on paper from the Royal Hotel, Harrismith.

13. RDC (Rydal Mount, Witzies Hoek, OFS) to Roberts, 16/3/1913, RHO ASS S22 G344c. On 8/1/1910, Dickey had penned a spirited denial of abuses on the Putumayo, accusing Hardenburg of pure imagination: 'Nor have I seen', he wrote, 'a single Indian bearing the scars of flogging upon his back.' RHO ASS S22 G335.

14. RDC to Roberts, 30/3/1913, RHO ASS S22 G344c. In this letter he enclosed a letter from Baron von Nordenskjold to the Anti-Slavery Society, and a translation of an article about Indian hunts in the Acré in 1905 and 1906.

15. RDC (in Rydal Mount with Tom and Katye) to Gertrude, 21/3/1913, 13074 (8/i).

16. RDC (Ebury St.) to Roberts, 10/5/1913, RHO ASS S22 G344c.

17. RDC to Morgan, 20/5/1913, quoted in Sawyer, *Flawed Hero*, p. 110.

18. RDC ('dear dirty Dublin') to Gertrude, 21/5/1913 and 29/5/1913, NLI MS 13074 (8/i). Under the signature of 'The Poor Old Woman', Casement published an article entitled 'Victor Hugo, Victoria, and Ireland' in *Irish Freedom*, April 1914, in which the translation appears. It is reproduced in Mackey, *Crime against Europe*, p. 176, and begins, 'I hate oppression with a hate profound …'

19. RDC to Gertrude, 4/7/1913 (which I take to be an error for 4/6/1913), 24/6/1913 and 26/6/1913, NLI MS 13074 (8/i). Sarah Purser had competed with Dermod O'Brien for the commission and, in fact, painted two portraits of Casement. See John O'Grady, *The Life and Work of Sarah Purser* (Dublin: Four Courts Press 1996), pp. 116–18 and 258–9. William Cadbury wrote of this: 'He was at all times supremely indifferent to his own personal comfort and welfare; I remember when his portrait was being painted by a lady in Dublin, he said he thought the blue serge coat suited him best, and she laughingly replied "I am quite sure you haven't got another".' Cadbury Statement, January 1916, Cadbury Papers, 181–2.

20. RDC to ASG, 30/5/1913, NLI MS 10464 (6).

21. RDC (55 Lr Baggot St.) to Roberts, 2/6/1913, RHO ASS S22 G344c. One presumes that his brother Tom was experiencing continuing difficulty with his mountain lodge in Witzies Hoek.

22. Roberts to RDC, 5/6/1913, RHO ASS S22 G344c.

23. RDC (Baggot St.) to Roberts, 11/6/1913.

24. *Irish Independent*, 9/5/1913, pp. 3 and 5; Agnes Newman (Nina) to *Irish Independent*, 10/5/1913; it was published on the 13th, p. 5. She wrote two further letters to the newspaper, published on 23/5/1913 and 29/5/1913, in tones of increasing condemnation. For

another treatment of this episode see Angus Mitchell, ' "An Irish Putumayo": Roger Casement's humanitarian relief campaign among the Connemara islanders 1913–14' *Irish Economic and Social History*, XXXI (2004), 41–60.

25. *Irish Independent*, Tuesday 20/5/1913, p. 5. As is evident from later responses, Casement wrote to other newspapers as well. Lieut. Colonel R.J. Kennedy had been in contact with Casement about Putumayo affairs. See, for example, RDC to Kennedy, 27/7/12, NLI MS 10464 (6); Kennedy to RDC, 20/10/12, NLI MS 13073 (46/xi), and 27/7/12, enclosed in RDC to Roberts, 20/1/1913, RHO ASS S22 G344c.

26. RDC (55 Lr Baggot St.) to O'Beirne, 24/5/1913, NLI MS 14100.

27. RDC to ASG, 30/5/1913, NLI MS 10464 (10).

28. Roberts to RDC, 6/6/1913, RHO ASS 22 G344c.

29. Maighréad M.C. Dobbs to RDC, 2/7/1913, NLI MS 13073 (5): 'I have been intending for some time to send you the enclosed for the school-children or any other use you like to put it to in Gorumna.'

30. Cowper to RDC, 10/7/1913, NLI MS 13073 (13/ii).

31. William Warden to RDC, 13/8/1913, 26/9/1913, 19/10/1913, 26/12/1913, NLI MS 13073 (16/ii); John Nelson to RDC, 3/10/1913, 6/10/1913, 21/11/1913, NLI MS 13073 (12/i).

32. RDC to Gertrude, 19/7/1913, NLI MS 13074 (8/i).

33. Tubridy to RDC, 13/12/1913, NLI MS 5463. She also expressed thanks to William Cadbury. She went on to say that she had established the first school there, twenty-five years previously, and had introduced what had since become the bilingual programme. Referring to the National Board, she continued: 'I never adhered to their barbarous rules in dealing with the little Irish-speaking children committed to my care.' Two Connemara schoolchildren of the time were later to record their memories of Casement's visits: see Colm Ó Gaora, *Colm* (Baile Átha Cliath: Oifig an tSoláthair 1969), which is also referred to in Máiréad Ní Chinnéide, *Máire de Buitléir: Bean Athbheochana* (Baile Átha Cliath: Comhar Teoranta 1993), p. 129. Similarly, Peadar Neillí Ó Domhnaill recalled the illness and poverty of the time, Casement's visits, the teachers, Pádraig and Sinéad Ní Thiobraide, Casement's politics, the Putumayo comparison and the continuing food-aid afterwards. See Peadar N. Ó Domhnaill, 'Ruaidhrí Mac Éasmuint', *Ar Aghaidh*, Lughnasa (August), 1946, 1. He wrote elsewhere of the events, as well. (I am indebted to Éamonn Ó Ciosáin for supplying me with this reference.)

34. See *An Claidheamh Soluis*, 5/1/1918 and 19/1/1918, for example. Details of the amounts collected appeared in these and subsequent issues. Details of the scheme are given in Ní Chinnéide, p. 130; it was organized by Máire de Buitléar (Mary E. Butler) with the help of Úna Bean Uí Dhiosca (Mrs McClintock-Dix).

35. Plunkett to RDC, n.d., NLI MS 13073 (46/xv).

36. Stopford to RDC, 12/6/1913, 14/6/1913, 20/6/1913, NLI MS 13073 (40). I do not know if anything became of this scheme.

37. Barbour to RDC, 14/11/1913, 22/11/1913, 27/11/1913, NLI MS 13073 (18). In the letter of 22/11 he added that he was sad at the news that fever had broken out again in

Connemara. A.S. Green, H. Barbour, D. Hyde, A. Wilson, 'The Connemara islands', *The Irish Review*, May 1914, 113–27. The practical success of the enterprise can be judged by an editorial note, which reads: 'At the suggestion of Sir Roger Casement, whose personal experiences on the Islands had convinced him of the urgent need for reform, the following Report, based upon visits and enquiries on the spot, was drawn up for submission to the Congested Districts Board. No notice of the Report, other than a formal acknowledgement of its receipt, was taken by the Board, and no attempt seems as yet to have been made by them to deal with the problem here presented. Further comment is needless – at present. A.W.' The article was divided into two parts, 'descriptive' and 'constructive', and presented a concise and coherent analysis of the bleak conditions and of economic and social possibilities.

38. RDC (Ebury St.) to Grey, 19/5/1913, NLI MS 13081 (1), applying for extension; Law to RDC, 27/5/1913, NLI MS 13081 (1), granting leave.

39. RDC (55 Lr Baggot St.) to Morgan, 26/5/1913, quoted in Sawyer, *Flawed Hero*, pp. 110–11.

40. RDC to Law, 29/6/1913, NLI MS 13081 (1); RDC to Tyrrell, 29/6/1913, NLI MS 13073 (5).

41. Tyrrell to RDC, 7/7/1913, 13081 (1); Law to RDC, 30/6/1913, 7/7/1913, 12/7/1913, NLI MS 13081 (1). The last of these includes a copy of Dr Charpentier's certificate of 1 July (in Casement's hand); RDC (Savoy) to Law, 14/7/1913, which includes a note by Casement and a copy of a standardized certificate – by Charpentier – which responded to certain questions, e.g. Q. 3 'What has been the state of his health during the last five years?' A. 'In the five years 1911 was the only year in which he was not seriously ill. In 1912 he was ill to my knowledge almost all the year.' Q. 4 'Nature of malady?' A. 'Arthritis chiefly in the spine and sacroillae joints, and to some extent in the knees.' It suggested the danger of his becoming permanently crippled.

42. Buxton to RDC, 6/8/1913, RHO S19 D1/13.

43. RDC (Savoy) to Spicer, 22/8/1913, NLI MS 13081 (1).

44. RDC (Savoy) to Buxton, 28/8/1913, RHO ASS S19 D2/4. Buxton's letter of 6 August had reached him in France, he explained.

45. Law to RDC, 23/8/1913, 26/8/1913, NLI MS 13081 (1); RDC to Spicer, 26/8/1913, NLI MS 13080 (3/ii); FO (Montgomery, for Tyrrell) to RDC, 27/8/1913, NLI MS 13081 (1); Paget to RDC, 10/9/1913, NLI MS 13081 (10).

46. Following his retirement, he was approached by a few acquaintances to write a book. Fisher Unwin was to repeat an earlier request in November: 'the time is surely ripe for you to give me a great and good book to publish'. Casement declined, saying he was too unsettled. Fisher Unwin to RDC, 1/8/1913, NLI MS 13073 (23/i). A little earlier, Harris had suggested that Casement take a trip through Africa and write a book about it. Casement replied, giving three reasons for not doing so: he might not be free to make the trip or all of it; 'Next, even if I go and follow the itinerary I propose, I might, for many reasons, not ever write a book

upon the journey or feel disposed to do so. I have made many long journeys in my time in interesting countries and have never yet written spontaneously of them or of the things I have seen, and this predilection for abstention may rule me to the end'; and thirdly he cited his need for *freedom* – not to take on new responsibilities. RDC to Harris, 25/7/1913, NLI MS 13080 (1/i).

47. RDC to Gardiner, 11/7/1913, LSE Gardiner Papers.

48. RDC (Rolleboise) to Gertrude, 5/8/1913 and 7/8/1913, NLI MS 13074 (8/ii).

49. Morgan (Pas de Calais) to RDC, 24/8/1913, NLI MS 13073 (46/xiii). The letter was a humorous one, beginning, 'My dear Potentate'. Morgan later went on to say, 'I agree with you about the Turk. The Balkan peoples remind me of Hobbes' state of nature – "nasty, poor, brutish and short".' He talked of his article, due to appear in the following month's *Nineteenth Century*, 'How Ireland is Governed', using new documentation. He was, too, reading Renan's *Souvenirs de mon Enfance* on his Breton childhood, and found the work beautiful.

50. RDC to Morgan, 26/5/1913, quoted in Sawyer, *Flawed Hero*, pp. 110–11.

51. RDC to Morgan, 21/8/1913 and 29/8/1913, quoted in Sawyer, *Flawed Hero*, pp. 112–13.

52. RDC to Mrs Griffiths, 27/9/1913, NLI MS 13080 (1/i).

53. RDC (Belfast) to Gertrude, n.d., Monday, NLI MS 13074 (8/ii). Given these views on the Church of Ireland, in which he had been brought up, it is not surprising that he expressed ambivalent attitudes when invited to the launch of the Cumann Gaelach na hEaglaise (Church Gaelic Society) in April 1914. See Giltrap, pp. 60–2.

54. Roger Casement to the editor, 'The Irishry of Ulster', *The Nation*, 11 October 1913, 100–1.

55. Roger Casement, 'Ulster and Ireland', *Fortnightly Review*, 1 November 1913, 799–806. To Gertrude he wrote that *The Times* was 'raging' with him about his 'rather savage' attack on 'Irish Protestants': RDC to Gertrude, 4/11/1913, 13074 (8/ii).

56. Captain Jack White (1879–1946) of Whitehall, Ballymena, was the son of Field-Marshal Sir George White, hero of the British defence of Ladysmith during the Boer War. Jack, after a brief army career, took to mysticism and then socialism; in 1913 he helped found the Irish Citizen Army.

57. James Brown Armour (1841–1928) was born in Ballymoney, Co. Antrim, and became a Presbyterian minister in 1869. He was a strong liberal, a supporter of Home Rule, the Tenant Right movement, the proposal for a Catholic university and the teaching of Irish. He served on the senate of Queen's University, Belfast, and retired from the ministry in 1925.

58. For a detailed account see J.R.B. McMinn, *Against the Tide: A Calendar of the Papers of Revd J.B. Armour, Irish Presbyterian Minister and Home Ruler 1869–1914* (Belfast: PRONI 1985).

59. Bigger had been restoring Castle Seán in Ardglass, Co. Down, and had opened it to the public, with great pageantry. Casement now described a similar event at the castle to Gertrude: RDC to Gertrude Bannister, 23/9/1913, NLI MS 13074 (8/ii). Alice Green devoted a chapter in her *The Old Irish World* to a history of the castle,

in which she described Bigger's restoration and the opening.

60. Captain J.R. White, *Misfit: an Autobiography* (London: Jonathan Cape 1930), p. 185. Casement and White subsequently cooperated together in addressing meetings of the Irish Volunteers in the north of Ireland.

61. McMinn, pp. lv, 131. Armour vetoed the participation of any Catholic at the meeting.

62. RDC (Ardrigh) to Gertrude, 5/9/1913, 16/9/1913, 23/9/1913, 10/10/1913, 15/10/1913, 18/10/1913, NLI MS 13074 (8/ii); RDC to ASG, 24/9/1913, 26/9/1913, 29/9/1913, NLI MS 10464 (7).

63. Cadbury to RDC, n.d. (r. 29/9/1913), NLI MS 13073 (46/iv); RDC to Gertrude, 10/10/1913 and 15/10/1913, NLI MS 13074 (8/i); RDC to Roger Casement (Magherintemple), 7/10/1913, PRONI T3787/18. He commented to his cousin, Roger, 'of course, I don't know what precise views you have, if any, on the chief political events of the day'.

64. RDC (Ardrigh) to EDM, 23/10/1913, LSE MP F8/25. In this letter he gave his assent to Morel's writing about his role in the founding of the CRA, given that he had now left government service.

65. Armour to J.B.M. Armour, n.d. [October?] 1913, in McMinn, pp. 134–5.

66. 'A Protestant Protest', Ballymoney, 24 October 1913, p. 8, Cadbury Papers, 182.

67. MacNaghten to RDC, 19/11/1913, NLI MS/ 13073(11). She was an Antrim Protestant lady, with strong sympathies for the Irish language: see Ó Snodaigh, p. 91. Childers to RDC, 29/10/1913, NLI MS 13073(4/i); Gilmour to RDC, 2/11/1913, NLI MS 13073(46/ix). Gilmour added that it would be difficult for anyone in ten years' time 'to understand how the madness of Carsonism found a lodgement in the minds of so many people'.

68. Quoted in Inglis, p. 250.

69. The details are given in a letter to the press by Hugh Eccles and Robert Hunter, 24/11/1913, NLI MS 13089 (8). See also Hunter to RDC, 29/11/1913, NLI MS 13073 (9); Thomas Taggart to RDC, 7/11/1913 and 14/11/1913, NLI MS 13073 (15).

70. RDC (Cushendall) to Gertrude, 11/11/1913, NLI MS 13074 (8/ii); RDC to ASG, 11/11/1913, NLI MS 10464 (7).

71. RDC to ASG, 11/11/1913, NLI MS 13074 (7), quoted in Reid, pp. 182–3.

72. Sidney Parry to Asquith, 1/8/16, McMullen Papers.

73. H.F. Spender, Statement, 1/8/16, McMullen Papers.

74. Cadbury, Statement, January 1916, Cadbury Papers, 181.

75. The two telegrams are given without dates in White, p. 254. F.X. Martin suggests that Casement had talked of a volunteer movement to White in September. See F.X. Martin, 'MacNeill and the foundation of the Irish Volunteers' in F.J. Byrne and F.X. Martin (eds.), *The Scholar Revolutionary: Eoin MacNeill, 1867–1945, and the Making of the New Ireland* (Shannon: Irish University Press 1973), pp. 134–5. For a recent overview of Casement's involvement with the Volunteers see Michael Laffan, 'The making of a revolutionary: Casement and the Volunteers, 1913–14' in

Daly, pp. 64–73. The account is unsympathetic, stressing Casement's mood swings, immoderate language and lack of political judgment.

76. See RDC to Daniel Enright, NLI MS 5611. As part of the process of establishing a Volunteer group in Cork, a 'Provisional Committee' was established, among whose members is listed Daniel Enright, described as a student in UCC. UCC records list a Daniel Enright who passed his final medical exams in 1912. This is likely to be Casement's correspondent and presumably Casement met him during his visit to Cork in mid December: Gerry White and Brendan O'Shea, 'Baptised in Blood': The Formation of the Cork Brigade of Irish Volunteers 1913–1916 (Cork: Mercier Press 2005), p. 27.

77. Colonel Maurice Moore, 'History of the Irish Volunteers', *The Irish Press*, January–March 1938.

78. RDC to Moore, 11/12/1913, in Moore, 4/1/1938.

79. RIC, Dublin Castle, 26/11/1914, Crime Special: Sir Roger Casement, PRO CO 904/195.

80. He wrote to Gertrude en route from Athlone: RDC (Prince of Wales, Athlone) to Gertrude, 12/12/1913, NLI MS 13074 (8/ii). Referring, presumably, to the Galway meeting, Edward Martyn had written declining to come, saying he believed the 'Volunteers will kill Home Rule'. Martyn to RDC, 10/12/1913, NLI MS 13073 (11).

81. RIC, Crime Special. For further details of the Cork visit, see White and O'Shea; David Hogan, *The Four Glorious Years* (Dublin: Irish Press Ltd 1953); J.J. Horgan, *From Parnell to Pearse: Some Recollections and Reflections* (Dublin: Brown and Nolan 1948); Ó Murchadha; Tierney.

82. Details can be found in Horgan, and in Casement's letters to him (NLI P4645). Matters were exacerbated in February, 1914, when the White Star Line decided to end its mail contract. In March there was an all-Ireland protest meeting in Dublin and a decision to send a deputation to the Prime Minister ('Sir Roger Casement suggested that independent lines of communication should be established between this country and America'). On 25 March, the Prime Minister received a deputation and in May–June an inquiry was held in London.

83. RDC (8 Onslow Gardens, London) to Horgan, 22/12/1913, NLI D4645 N4657. *Documents relative to the Sinn Fein Movement* (London: His Majesty's Stationery Office 1921), p. 2, states that: 'In 1912 the first-mentioned of C's articles was sent by him to von Bernhardi. It was translated and widely circulated in Germany and attracted considerable attention and discussion in the German press.' General Friedrich von Bernhardi (1849–1930) had himself written an influential propaganda piece in 1912 entitled 'Germany and the next War'.

84. RDC (Ardrigh) to Horgan, 31/12/1913, NLI D4645 N4657.

85. RDC (Ardrigh) to Horgan, 12 /1/1914 (two) and 13/1/1914, NLI D4645 N4657.

86. RDC (Belfast) to Baron L. von Horst, Charing Cross, W.C., 13/1/1914, PRONI D2711/1–4.

87. RDC (Grand Hotel, Malahide) to Horgan, 17/1/1914, telegram and card, NLI D4645.

88. RDC (Grand Hotel, Malahide) to Horgan, 20/1/1914, NLI D4645. He was, himself, writing to *The Irish Times* and *Freeman's Journal*.

89. The sequence of events and the communications from the Hamburg–Amerika Line would indicate that Anglo-German political sensitivities were a major factor. Tensions between the two countries were mounting; Albert Ballin, head of the German company, had been playing a leading role in diplomatic efforts to avert a war. See Parmiter, pp. 117–18 and 127–9.

90. RDC (Malahide) to Horgan, 16/2/1914, NLI D4645.

91. RDC (Ardrigh) to Gertrude, 6/1/1914, NLI MS 13074 (9/i).

92. Kettle to RDC, 11/1/1914, NLI MS 13073 (9); he also had a telegram from MacNeill regarding Limerick, MacNeill to RDC, 15/1/1914, NLI MS 13073 (11).

93. RIC, Crime Special. John Daly (1845–1916) had spent twelve years in penal servitude for Fenian activities; he subsequently established a prosperous business in Limerick and served as mayor of the city. He was struck by a serious illness in 1908, from which he never recovered, and he died in June 1916. After this visit in January, a short correspondence ensued between Casement and Daly: see University of Limerick, Daly Papers, fols. 46 and 47.

94. RDC (Limerick) to Plunkett, n.d. [Sunday night], NLI MS 5459. Joseph Mary Plunkett (1887–1916), son of Count Plunkett, was one of the founders of the Irish Volunteers and a member of the IRB. He was to be director of military operations in 1916. A poet and editor of *The Irish Review*, he suffered from continuous ill health. In this letter, Casement referred to his own article on the 'Coffin Ship', which was to appear in *The Irish Review* in March 1914 (reprinted in Mackey, *Crime against Europe*, pp. 102–10), and enquired how much it would cost to print 1500–2000 copies.

95. See pp. 374–80 and Reid, p. 189. On 4 February, from Malahide, he told Hobson that he was going to Belfast, back to Dublin and on to England and gave the following enigmatic message: 'Could you have the Elizabethan drama papers and the two actors with you by 6.30 – as I want to get back here fairly soon.' RDC to Hobson, 4/2/1914, NLI MS 13158 (8).

96. RIC, Crime Special: Sir Roger Casement, PRO CO 904/195.

97. Roger Casement, 'From Clontarf to Berlin: national status in sport', *Irish Volunteer*, 1, no. 1, Saturday, 7 February 1914, 2.

98. RDC (Malahide) to Enright, 18/2/1914, 20/2/1914 and 27/2/1914, NLI MS 5611. In the last, he recommended the Volunteer march, 'Searlus Óg' – 'it is one of the finest Irish airs in the world'. His comments included reference to the titles of two of his propaganda articles, 'The Keeper of the Seas' and 'The Freedom of the Seas' (reprinted in Mackey, *Crime against Europe*). He was engaged in a flurry of such writing from 1912 to 1914.

99. RIC, Crime Special: Sir Roger Casement, PRO CO 904/195.

100. Moore, 7/1/1938.

101. RDC to Moore, 15/3/1914, Moore, 8/1/1938.

102. RIC, Crime Special. Casement had written to Daly on 11 March saying he hoped to visit Limerick around St Patrick's Day and hoped to see a turnout of the Volunteers and Na Fianna: UL, Daly Papers, Typescript biography of John Daly, Chapter 15.

103. RDC to Enright, 28/3/1914, NLI MS 5611.

104. Events surrounding the Home Rule controversy were of considerable interest to Germany. A.T.Q. Stewart refers to the presence during the Curragh crisis of a correspondent from the *Vossische Zeitung*: A.T.Q. Stewart, *The Ulster Crisis: Resistance to Home Rule, 1912–1914* (London: Faber and Faber 1979 [1967]), p. 167. A.P. Ryan cites a letter to *The Times* from two German professors, Kuno Meyer and Theodor Schiemann, which attacked the 'hope and belief' expressed by Ulster Covenanters, that 'in the case of Home Rule becoming law, Germany might be induced to interfere in the cause of Protestantism in Ulster'. A.P. Ryan, *Mutiny at the Curragh* (London: Macmillan 1956), p. 166.

105. The letter is contained in Mackey, *Crime against Europe*, pp. 110–12; Reid fails to mention the Curragh Mutiny at all.

106. Moore, 4/1/1938.

107. RDC to Moore, 5/4/1914, quoted in Moore, 14/1/1938.

108. RDC to ?, partial, n.d., NLI Acc. 4902, fol. 14.

109. RIC, Crime Special. Local observers had difficulty with the name of the German journalist, which I take to be Schweriner. Casement had written to John Daly about Schweriner in late March, referring to him as editor of the *Vossische Zeitung*, who was in Ireland 'in quest of the "Irish Question" from the great German paper'. 'I want you to put him in the way of seeing the true nationalist of Limerick – not the shoneens.' UL, Daly Papers, Typescript Biography of John Daly, Chapter 15; and RDC to Daly, 24/3/1914, fol. 46.

110. 'The Movements of Sir Roger Casement', RIC, Crime Special. This report was submitted on 6/6/16 from the District Inspector's Office, Oughterard.

111. 'Death of Noted Galway Woman', *Irish Press,* 11/11/47. Also, Tomás Ó Máille, *An t-Iomaire Ruadh* (Baile Átha Cliath: Comhlucht Oideachais na hÉireann 1939), pp. 4, 6. I would like to thank Professor Ruairí Ó hUiginn for this reference.

112. On 4 May Casement sent John Daly '6 of the 8 articles on Ireland the little German wrote': RDC to Daly, 4/5/1914, UL, Daly Papers, fol. 46.

113. MacNeill to Moore, 8/4/1914, quoted in Moore, 13/1/1938. Commenting, Laffan, p. 69, observes that 'MacNeill was considered often a poor judge of character'.

114. RDC to Moore, 9/4/1914, quoted in Moore, 14/1/1938. Casement told Dr Enright that 'half my letters are tampered with'. RDC (Belfast) to Enright, n.d., NLI MS 5611.

115. MacNeill to Moore, 13/4/1914, quoted in Moore, 14/1/1938. In this letter, MacNeill again reassured Moore about Casement: 'I am afraid that you have taken alarm at Casement's forcible expression of his sentiments. Personally I find him very cautious with regard to policy, and especially he is in agreement with me, that any line of action tending towards futile political divisions should be strongly discounte-

nanced. He ought to be in our confidence and in our councils.' For another account of Casement's meeting with Devlin, see Tom Clarke to John Daly, 29/4/1914, UL, Daly Papers, fol. 47.

116. 'Progress of the Movement – Tullamore – Speech of Sir R. Casement', *Irish Volunteer*, I, no. 12, 25/4/1914, 13.

117. Johnston, *Alice*, pp. 122–3. Henry Nevinson noted in his diary on the 27th: 'Had another long letter from Casement too about instructions to the army in Ireland.' ND, 27/4/1914, BLO Nevinson Papers.

118. RDC (Malahide) to Morten, 1/5/1914, PRONI T3072/9.

119. Moore, 20/1/1938. Tierney suggests that the meeting took place on 9 May, Tierney, p. 142.

120. Quoted in F.X. Martin (ed.), *The Howth Gun-Running and the Kilcoole Gun-Running 1914* (Dublin: Browne and Nolan 1964), p. 32.

121. *Ibid.* p. xiv; he also gives a list of subscribers to the gun-running fund, p. 35. According to him, p. xv, 'In Dublin the project was a secret between MacNeill, The O'Rahilly and Bulmer Hobson; Sir Roger Casement was chosen as their liaison officer with the committee in London ... A final plan was then agreed upon, known in its entirety only to Childers, MacNeill, Casement, and Hobson.'

122. RDC (50 Ebury St.) to Blunt, 12/5/1914, Wilfred Scawen Blunt, *My Diaries: Being a personal narrative of events, 1888–1914* (London: Martin Secker 1919–20), vol. II, pp. 455–7.

123. Blunt, vol. II, pp. 424–5. Blunt met John Dillon on 11 June and recorded the latter's view of Casement: 'Dillon says: "The Volunteer business is a VERY serious one. Sir Roger Casement is, I have no doubt, an excellent and able man, but he knows no more of Irish politics than I do of the Congo, and Irish politics are no more safe for amateur idealists to play about it than a powder magazine for children" ' (pp. 426–7).

124. RDC (50 Ebury St.) to Blunt, 14/5/1914, 16/5/1914 (RMS *Ulster*), in Blunt, vol. II, pp. 455–7. On the same day he wrote to Edward Martyn, trying to set up a meeting; the note suggests that they were well acquainted. RDC to Martyn, 14/5/1914, NLI D4645 (Horgan Letters). Casement's essay, 'The elsewhere empire', was written in December 1913 and published in *Irish Freedom*.

125. RDC to Enright, 25/5/1914, NLI MS 5611.

126. For accounts of the negotiations, see Tierney; Denis Gwynn, *The Life of John Redmond* (London: Harrap 1932); F.S.L. Lyons, *Dillon*.

127. RDC to Moore, 2/6/1914, quoted in Moore, 21/1/1938. The nomination of Michael Davitt, son of the Land League leader, was strongly resisted by the Volunteer leaders, as he had not been at all sympathetic to the movement; his name was subsequently withdrawn.

128. RDC to Redmond, 9/6/1914, text in Denis Gwynn, *Redmond*, pp. 319–21. Commentators have pointed out the impractical nature of the suggestion, since the General was paralysed in both legs and his political sympathies were not known.

129. Text in Denis Gwynn, *Redmond*, pp. 321–2.

130. Moore, 26/1/1938.

131. *Ibid.*

132. RDC (Ardrigh) to 'A chara dhíl', 14/6/1914 (Sunday), NLI Acc. 4902 (14). On 14 June he declined an invitation to attend a lecture organized by the Church-of-Ireland Gaelic Society on the grounds of indisposition: 'I am ill in bed (in a friend's house) in Belfast – too much "volunteering" of late and cold night winds in Tyrone.' Quoted in Giltrap, p. 63.

133. RDC to 'A chara dílis', 16/6/1914, NLI Acc. 4902 (2).

134. RDC to Gertrude, 21/6/1914, NLI MS 13074 (9/i).

135. Erskine Childers to Mary Childers, 21/6/1914, quoted in Martin, *Howth Gun-Running*, p. 49.

136. RDC (Belfast) to Enright, 30/6/1914, NLI MS 5611. He told him that 30,000 Volunteer manifestos had been printed: 'it goes out from the Provisional Committee they have formed'. He said he had written most of it and Eoin MacNeill had done the rest.

16: TOWARDS BERLIN: THE UNITED STATES AND NORWAY, 1914

1. Curry, p. 21. Curry's is a selection from Casement's German diaries, which can be found at NLI MSS 1689–90 and 5244 ('A Last Page'). Casement's German diaries comprise: (i) a retrospective narrative, covering the period from his departure from Ireland in July up to his first day in Berlin in early November; it was written on 7 November 1914; (ii) a narrative, with some gaps, covering the period from November 1914 to 11 February 1915, at which point Casement ceased to keep a diary; (iii) a retrospective summary of events from 11 February 1915 to the end of December 1915, written under the entry for 28 March 1916; (iv) a retrospective summary of events from the beginning of 1916, written under the entry for 17 March; (v) a narrative of events from 27 March to 8 April 1916. Unless otherwise indicated, German diary quotations are taken from Curry.

2. John Devoy (1842–1928) was born in Kill, Co. Kildare; he coordinated Fenian activity within the British army and was sentenced to fifteen years' penal servitude in 1866, serving five. He went into exile in the United States, where he worked in journalism and became a leading figure in Clan na Gael. He founded *The Gaelic American* in 1903 and became a key figure in American-Irish support for Irish causes.

3. MacNeill to RDC, 7/7/1914, cited in Reinhard R. Doerries, *Prelude to the Easter Rising: Sir Roger Casement in Imperial Germany* (London: Frank Cass 2000), p. 43. Doerries's selection of documents, mainly from the archives of the German Foreign Office, constitutes a new and invaluable source for Casement's German period. For Casement in the US, a useful source is Charles Callan Tansill, *America and the Fight for Irish Freedom, 1866–1922* (New York: Devin-Adair 1957).

4. RDC (Montreal) to John Devoy [JD], 14/7/1914, quoted in John Devoy, *Recollections of an Irish Rebel* (New York: Charles P. Young 1929), p. 410.

5. Curry, p. 25.

6. See Dudgeon, pp. 432–58, for a masterly account of Christensen and his relationship with Casement.

7. RDC to JD, 20/7/1914, quoted in Devoy, pp. 410–13. On the following day, Casement wrote to Hobson, telling him of the damage that Redmond was doing to the fund-raising effort: 'the belief is held that the real intention is not to get money for the Volunteers, but to prevent us getting it!' RDC to Hobson, 21/7/1914, NLI MS 13158 (8).

8. John Quinn (1871–1924) was a successful Irish-American lawyer, both of whose parents had been born in Ireland. He had an international reputation as a collector of books, manuscripts and contemporary art. He supported many Irish causes and was particularly generous to the Yeats family.

9. William Bourke Cockran (1854–1923), orator, statesman and lawyer, was born in Co. Sligo. He was educated in Ireland and France and went to the US in 1871, where he was admitted to the Bar in New York in 1876. He won a national reputation through noteworthy speeches in the Democratic National Conventions of 1884, 1892 and 1920; he represented NY constituencies in the 50th, 52nd, 53rd, 58th, 59th, 60th and 67th Congresses.

10. Joseph McGarrity (1874–1940) was born in Carrickmore, Co. Tyrone, and emigrated to the US at the age of sixteen, where he was to become a key figure in Irish-American politics. He was one of the three members of the Directory of Clan na Gael (with Devoy and John Keating of Chicago) and helped maintain links between the IRB and Irish America.

11. RDC (Philadelphia) to Bigelow, 23/7/1914, PRO FO 95/776.

12. RDC to ASG, 26/7/1914, quoted in Martin, *Howth Gun-Running*, p. 127.

13. Curry, pp. 27–8.

14. RDC to Bourke Cockran, 27/7/1914, quoted in Doerries, *Prelude*, p. 44.

15. RDC to ASG, 29/7/1914, quoted in Martin, *Gun-Running*, pp. 172–3, and Doerries, *Prelude*, p. 45.

16. RDC to Quinn, 30/7/1914, quoted in Reid, p. 202. When France and Spain declared war on Britain in the late 1770s, siding with the American revolutionaries, a volunteer movement came into being in Ireland to defend the island, by then denuded of troops. There followed a political shift in which the armed volunteers began to demand various reforms, including – at a convention held in Dungannon in 1782 – legislative independence.

17. Devoy, pp. 416–17.

18. RDC (Central Park West, NY) to Bigelow, 10/8/1914, PRO FO 95/776. The address is that of John Quinn. Following Casement's interview with former President, Theodore Roosevelt, the latter wrote to Bainbridge Colby: 'Sir Roger Casement was charming': Roosevelt to Colby, 12/8/1914, NLI MS 14100.

19. German growth rates were, in fact, remarkable: 'By the year 1906, 25 years after the founding of the Empire in 1871, the Reich's population had grown from about 41 million to 62,863,000. National income had risen from the early 1890s, when it stood at 22,638,000,000 marks, to 39,919,000,000 marks by 1906 ... The transformation of the German Empire from an agricultural to an industrial society was rushing ahead. In 1871, 63.9% of the population had lived in rural areas; 40% did so in 1910 ... Between 1897 and 1906 hard coal extraction had risen from 91 to 136 million tons, pig iron production had doubled, and German foreign trade had risen in value from 8,455,000,000 Mk to 14,582,000,000 Mk ... Germany's industrial base and population were already larger than that of the United Kingdom and she had become a serious threat in trade and finance, activities hitherto dominated by British enterprise.' Jonathan Steinberg, 'The German background to Anglo-German relations, 1905–1914' in F.H. Hinsley (ed.), *British Foreign Policy Under Sir Edward Grey* (Cambridge: CUP 1977), p. 193.

20. Mackey, *Crime against Europe*, pp. 13, 12 and 45, respectively.

21. *Ibid.* pp. 10, 13, 14, 20 and 46.

22. *Ibid.* pp. 65–7.

23. Bigelow to RDC, 11/8/1914 (r. in NY City, 14/8/1914), NLI MS 14100.

24. RDC (58 Central Park West) to ASG, 15/8/1914, quoted in Doerries, *Prelude*, pp. 47–8.

25. Quinn to T.W. Rolleston, 8/2/15, quoted in Doerries, *Prelude*, p. 48.

26. William M. Murphy, *Prodigal Father: The Life of John Butler Yeats (1839–1922)* (Ithaca: Cornell U.P. 1978), p. 41 and notes. The letter to Lily was written on 17 August.

27. Mary Colum, *Life and the Dream* (Dublin: Dolmen Press 1966 [1958]), p. 188. She recounted two incidents, which seemed to corroborate the spying charge, and also added: 'As we parted he gave us a book on Conrad by a man called Richard Curle.'

28. For a clear discussion of these contacts see the 'Introduction' in Doerries, *Prelude*.

29. German military attaché [Franz von Papen] (New York) to GFO, 9/8/1914, quoted in Doerries, *Prelude*, p. 46. As the British authorities were to overestimate Casement's role in planning the 1916 Easter Rising, so von Papen overestimated his leadership role at this stage.

30. *Ibid.* pp. 2–3, and Devoy, p. 403.

31. RDC memo, 25/8/1914, quoted in Joachim Lerchenmueller, ' "The wretched lot" – a brief history of the Irish Brigade in Germany 1914–1919' in *Yearbook of the Centre for Irish-German Studies*, 1998–9, 96 and notes 4 and 5. The memo is held in the Political Archive of the German Foreign Office.

32. Address to the Kaiser, 25/8/1914. The text is given in full in Devoy, pp. 404–6; see also Doerries, *Prelude*, p. 4, n. 17. Casement had taken a train to Chicago on 24 August. On the same day John Keating, who, with Devoy and McGarrity, was one of the three key Clan leaders, wrote from Chicago to Devoy, approving the Casement document. See William O'Brien and D. Ryan (eds.), *Devoy's Post Bag, 1871–1928* (Dublin: Fallon 1953), vol. II, 1880–1928, p. 466.

33. RDC to Gertrude, 1/9/1914, NLI MS 13074 (9/i) and quoted in Reid, p. 204.

34. ASG (5 Sandford Terrace, Dublin) to RDC, 29/8/1914 (r. 12/9/1914, Brooklyn), NLI MS 14100.

35. RDC to ASG, 14/9/1914, quoted in Reid, p. 205.

36. Roger Casement, *Ireland, Germany and the Freedom of the Seas: a Possible Outcome of the War of 1914* (NY and Philadelphia, Irish Press Bureau September 1914); *The Crime Against Europe* (Berlin: *The Continental Times* 1915). Copies were acquired by the FO and included in their dossier on Casement: see PRO FO 95/776.

37. RDC, 'Open Letter to Irishmen', 17/9/1914, Curry, pp. 17–19. See Doerries, *Prelude*, p. 5 and n. 19, p. 26.

38. RDC to Devoy, 18/9/1914, quoted in O'Brien and Ryan, p. 467; Devoy's assessment is given in Devoy, p. 406.

39. For a general account see Charles Townshend, *Easter 1916: The Irish Rebellion* (London: Penguin Books 2006), pp. 62–71; F.S.L. Lyons, *Ireland*, pp. 329–30, and Devoy, p. 414.

40. Nicolson to RDC, 26/10/1914, quoted in Curry, p. 15. Sir Arthur Nicolson was born in 1849 and became a FO clerk in 1870. He served as ambassador to St Petersburg 1906–10 and was Permanent Undersecretary from 1910–16. He was unlikely to be sympathetic to Casement: 'Nicolson was a vehement Ulsterman ... [He] believed that Liberal policy in Ireland would provoke a civil war, weaken the army and undermine British influence in Europe. As Ulster became the dominant issue of the day during the spring of 1914, personal relations with Grey became increasingly strained.' Zara Steiner, 'The Foreign Office under Sir Edward Grey, 1905–1914' in Hinsley, p. 52.

41. McGarrity, note, 5/10/1914, quoted in Doerries, *Prelude*, pp. 49–50. *Prelude*, p. 2, n. 9, describes Daniel F. Cohalan as 'an influential and well-connected New York judge', born in 1865 in Middletown, New York, of Irish parents.

42. McGarrity, note, 10/10/1914, quoted in Doerries, *Prelude*, p. 50. Bernhard Dernburg was 'former chief of the German Colonial Office' and directed German propaganda efforts in the US during the war; see Doerries, *Prelude*, pp. 2–3.

43. RDC to Gertrude, 12/10/1914, NLI MS 13074 (9/i).

44. Bernstorff to Bethmann Hollweg, 13/10/1914, quoted in Doerries, *Prelude*, p. 50.

45. Bernstorff to GFO, 15/10/1914, quoted in Doerries, *Prelude*, p. 51.

46. Devoy, p. 418; Reid, p. 209.

47. Dudgeon suggests that Adler was 'a lame duck, sex partner and son all rolled into one' (p. 438) and that he was 'butch, bisexual and closer to the rough trade' than Casement appreciated (p. 437).

48. RDC to Devoy, 15/10/15, quoted in O'Brien and Ryan, p. 468.

49. RDC to Morten, 15/10/1914, NLI Acc. 4902 (2), Philadelphia. He talked, too, of a letter from Heinrich [Heini], a German friend, who had accompanied them on their German tour in 1912 and who had now been seized in Ceylon and held in a concentration camp, with little money; 'Tell Sidney', he begged Morten.

50. Casement's account is given in a letter (never sent) to his sister, begun off Norway on 28 October and completed in Berlin on 1 November. In the letter he wrote as

an American lady and described Christensen as 'that poor Norwegian girl of mine'. Curry, pp. 31–9. For a brief discussion of this letter, see McDiarmid, 'Posthumous life', pp. 127–8.

51. Curry, p. 45.
52. See Findlay to Grey, 31/10/1914, PRO FO 95/776.
53. Details of the events as described by Casement can be found in RDC, 'Memorandum dealing with my arrival and stay in Christiania 28–29 October to 30 October 1914', 16/11/1914, Curry, pp. 45–55. Christensen, too, drew up a sworn statement about the events, dated 9 April 1915, which is reproduced in Curry, pp. 55–64.
54. Findlay to Grey, 31/10/1914, PRO FO 95/776; see Inglis, p. 289 and Reid, p. 214.
55. Quoted in Reid, p. 217.
56. *Ibid.* p. 212.
57. Richard Meyer was an employee of the German Foreign Office and had a legal qualification, being regularly addressed as 'Assessor'. He was to be Casement's regular contact in the GFO for day-to-day affairs. According to Doerries, he 'was one of the few Jews working in the Berlin Foreign Office' and was allowed to leave Germany for Sweden in 1939 (Doerries, *Prelude*, pp. 26–7). He was not a brother of Kuno Meyer, as is frequently stated.
58. See Reid, Chapter 16.

17: IMPERIAL GERMANY, 1914–16

1. Curry, pp. 68–9.
2. Arthur Zimmerman, when later German foreign minister, was to send a coded telegram to the German representative in Mexico suggesting a German–Mexican alliance. In the event of war between the US and Germany, Mexico would receive territory in Texas, Arizona and New Mexico. The message was intercepted by British naval intelligence and the United States informed; the event helped push the US towards entering the war.
3. Text in Doerries, *Prelude*, pp. 52–6.
4. The events that took place from 31 October to 2 November, as recorded in Casement's diary, can be found in Curry, pp. 65–74.
5. FO Berlin to Washington Embassy, 3/11/1914, *Documents relative to the Sinn Fein Movement*, p. 3.
6. RDC to Cohalan, n.d., [November], Doerries, *Prelude*, p. 57; a version dated 6/11/1914 can also be found in *Documents relative to the Sinn Fein Movement*, pp. 3–4.
7. Eduard Meyer, 'Personal Memories', BBAW NL Eduard Meyer 357. Casement also came to know Antonie Meyer, sister to Kuno and Eduard. Theodor Schiemann (1847–1921) was professor of history at the University of Berlin, and he was active during the war as a propagandist and political agent. He had earlier studied the Ulster question carefully, believing that the threat of civil war there would deter

Britain from becoming involved in hostilities on the continent. Reid, p. 227.

8. RDC (Continental Hotel, Berlin) to Kuno Meyer, 12/11/1914, NLI MS 5459; and see Seán Ó Lúing, *Kuno Meyer, 1858–1919: A Biography* (Dublin: Geography Publications 1991), p. 187. Among Casement's published works were 'The Crime against Europe', 'The Keeper of the Seas', and 'The Freedom of the Seas'.

9. K. Meyer (SS *Rotterdam*, Atlantic Ocean) to ASG, 17/11/191914, quoted in Ó Lúing, p. 176; ASG to Meyer, 15/12/1914, Ó Lúing, p. 177. Meyer replied with a virtual apology, but noted: 'The man who in 1911 wrote "Ireland, Germany and the next war" was bound to go to Berlin as he did.' Meyer to ASG, 1/1/1915, Ó Lúing, p. 178.

10. Von Jagow to Zimmermann, 7/11/1914, Doerries, *Prelude*, p. 58.

11. Zimmermann to von Bethmann Hollweg, Doerries, *Prelude*, p. 59; text of German statement, pp. 60–1. Doerries records the changes made to the text of the declaration for the final version. Eduard Meyer claimed that Kuno Meyer worked with Casement on the text of the declaration before Kuno left for the US. Eduard Meyer, 'Personal Memories', BBAW NL Eduard Meyer 357.

12. NLI MS 1689, fol. 64.

13. On this point see, for example, RDC to von Wedel, 13/1/1915, Doerries, *Prelude*, pp. 77–9; J. Plunkett to RDC, 12/5/1915, NLI MS 13085 (26).

14. Von Falkenhayn to Nadolny, 21/11/1914, Doerries, *Prelude*, pp. 63–5. According to Doerries, most of those from the general staff dealing with Irish affairs were attached to Section IIIb, dealing with intelligence matters.

15. When Devoy wrote the following January, he commented: 'The Declaration was all that could be expected in the present military and naval situation.' Devoy to RDC, 1/1/1915, NLI MS 13073 (44/i).

16. RDC to Eoin MacNeill, 28/11/1914, *Documents relative to the Sinn Fein Movement*, pp. 4–5. The 'channel' Casement used here for getting letters through was not as reliable as he thought, since his letter to MacNeill was intercepted. For his references to it see NLI MS 1689, fols. 24 and 18.

17. Roger Casement dossier, PRO CO 904/194/46, 23/11/1914; 'Case of Sir Roger Casement, 1913–1920', PRO CO 904/195.

18. According to Devoy, pp. 431–2, there were three objects to Casement's mission: to secure military help, to educate German opinion on the Irish situation and to organize Irish prisoners of war into a military unit. 'Casement did his best in all these things, but did the first ineffectively, succeeded admirably in the second, and failed badly in the third.'

19. Findlay to Nicolson, 4/12/1914, PRO FO 95/776, in which he enclosed the three letters. The letters were later included in *Documents relative to the Sinn Fein Movement* and may have been accepted as genuine, when received. They are reproduced, too, in Curry, pp. 79–84.

20. RDC to Christensen, 30/11/1914; Curry, pp. 100–2. On his way to Norway, Christensen was held up by the Germans in Sassnitz and Casement had to act to help get him released.

21. Christensen to RDC, 26/11/1914; Curry, pp. 97–100.
22. Casement to Christensen, 2/12/1914, enclosing the false one dated 1/12/1914; Curry, pp. 109–13.
23. RDC, Geman Diaries, 16/12/1914; Curry, p. 125. Casement wrote up the account on 17 December as 'Adler's Report on his second Interviews', Curry, pp. 127–30.
24. FO minute, 27/11/1914 (copies to Birrell, McKenna, War Office, Admiralty, Kitchener and Churchill) and A. N[icolson] to Findlay, 28/11/1914, PRO FO 95/776.
25. Reginald McKenna (1863–1943) was Secretary of State at the Home Office, 1911–15. A Liberal MP, 1905–18, he was first lord of the Admiralty, 1908–11, during which period a substantial number of Dreadnoughts were constructed.
26. FO minute, 25/11/1914 and note on Findlay to Nicolson, 28/11/1914, PRO FO 95/776. From this point on, Captain, later Admiral, Reginald Hall, chief of naval intelligence, was in a position to monitor Casement's activities. He was to play a key role in Casement's interrogation in 1916 and in the selective showing of the diaries. Hall (1870–1943) entered the navy in 1884 and became director of the Intelligence Division in the Admiralty, 1914–18, which helped decipher German naval and international messages.
27. *The Continental Times* was published three times a week in Berlin and 'was aimed predominantly at demonstrating to an American readership that their neutrality had been 'contaminated' by "slander and calumny" ' (Mitchell, 'John Bull's other empire', p. 230). Mitchell has expanded our knowledge of Casement's publications in this and other outlets. Casement did not have a high opinion of *The Continental Times*, dubbing it 'that awful paper' in one comment: RDC to Blücher, 26/1/16, Blücher Collection, Clare Archives, PP/1/24.
28. Evelyn, Princess Blücher, in an attempt to distance herself from Casement, left a very negative and distorted account of their relations with him in Germany. One example refers to this period: 'My husband went to see him shortly after his arrival and tried to show him what a false position he had put himself in, and that he had better leave the country as quickly as possible, but it was no use. So after that we refused to see him or have anything more to do with him.' Her remarks do not square with the record as found in Casement's diaries and the correspondence with the Blüchers in the Clare Archives. Evelyn, Princess Blücher, *An English Wife in Berlin* (London: Constable 1920), p. 43. For a critical assessment, see G. Barry Gifford, 'Princess and Patriot – Sir Roger Casement and the Princess Blücher', NLI MS 13091.
29. RDC, German Diaries, *passim* from 3/12/1914 to 18/12/1914; Curry, pp. 107–38. The GFO had a police report on Christensen, of which Casement was aware: Curry, p. 135.
30. RDC, German Diaries, 18/12/1914; Curry, p. 133.
31. Doerries, *Prelude*, p. 18 (Admiral Behnke and Captain Heidel were also involved); RDC, German Diaries, 18/12/1914–24/12/1914; Curry, pp. 131–44.
32. RDC, German Diaries, 18/12/1914; Curry, pp. 134–6.
33. RDC, German Diaries, 8/1/1915; Curry, p. 145.

34. RDC, German Diaries, 14/1/1915, 15/1/1915, 18/1/1915; Curry, pp. 150, 151, 153. The letter he received from Christensen on 5 January had been written on 27 December, just as contacts with Findlay were being resumed.

35. For the details, see Curry, pp. 153–67.

36. There is a facsimile copy in Curry, p. 170.

37. RDC, German Diaries, 24/1/1915; Curry, p. 153.

38. RDC to Curry, 26/3/16, quoted in Curry, pp. 178–81.

39. Findlay to Nicolson, 27/12/1914, 3/1/1915, 14/1/1915, PRO FO 95/776.

40. Inglis, pp. 297–8, 304, 331.

41. RDC, German Diaries, 13/1/1915; Curry, p. 149.

42. Reid, p. 270. Robert Offley Asburton Crewe-Milnes, the 1st Marquess of Crewe (1858–1945) was a highly respected senior Liberal politician; he had been Lord Lieutenant of Ireland, 1892–5, Secretary of State for the Colonies, 1908–10, Secretary of State for India, 1910, and Lord Privy Seal, 1912.

43. See Curry, pp. 154, 162 and 173–4.

44. On 30 January, he told Eduard Meyer that he had to defer the pleasure of seeing him as 'strange happenings call me again away from Berlin on a very sudden journey … You will understand the reasons later on. I have been kept very busy and with a *very* heavy strain upon me since I got back to Berlin and apart from the work I was not disposed for any visits'. RDC (Hotel Esplanade, Berlin) to Eduard Meyer, 30/01/1915, BBAW NL Eduard Meyer 357.

45. RDC, German Diaries, 31/1/1915; Curry, p. 178.

46. Casement left an account of his feelings to Charles Curry. RDC to Curry, 26/3/16, in Curry, pp. 178–81.

47. RDC to Grey, 1/2/1915; Curry, pp. 184–91. 'It is as we feared. The informer was playing a double game all the time', read the minute in London, on receipt of the letter. Minute on Casement's letter of 1/2/1915, PRO FO 95/776. 'It is an extraordinary mixture of truth and falsehood', commented Findlay of the letter. Findlay to Nicolson, 17/2/1915, PRO FO 95/776. If Casement's statement is true, he had stopped collecting his pension before the FO suspended it. On 1 December 1914, Sir Edward Grey wrote: 'I gave instructions some time ago that his pension was to be stopped. I assume this had been done.' Reid, p. 240.

48. The embassies were those of Norway, the US, Italy, Austria-Hungary, Spain, Sweden, Denmark, Holland, Portugal, Switzerland, Greece and Romania. Curry, pp. 193–4.

49. RDC, German Diaries, 17/3/16; Curry, p. 195. At the beginning of February, he had written: 'Then to the Nordenflychts at 6 and stayed to supper with them. Told them I wanted to stay with them and they offered me a room there' (German Diaries, 4/2/1915; Curry, p. 192). In the latter part of March, he did stay with them for several weeks.

50. RDC, German Diaries, 5/2/1915; Curry, p. 193.

51. See Curry, Chapter 11, for details.

52. J. O'H. to RDC, 15/2/1915, NLI MS 13085 (15).

53. Devoy, p. 431.

54. Michael McKeogh, 'Roger Casement, Germany and the World War', *Catholic Bulletin*, 18 (1928), 397. McKeogh used the name 'Kehoe' while in Germany and I use the latter form throughout. See also Michael McKeogh Papers, UCD Archives, P128.

55. Devoy later criticized Casement for his method: 'Instead of approaching the men individually, he had them all assembled at a meeting at which he delivered an address that went over their heads. The good and the bad, the Orangeman and the Catholic, the half decent fellow and the blackguard, were all there to listen to his high patriotic sentiments, and what was still worse, old Reserve men – whose wives were receiving subsistence money from the British Government and who naturally would think of the interests of their families before and above all else – were present.' As well as reflecting Devoy's shrewdness and experience in recruiting during the Fenian period and Casement's lack of judgment regarding men, two other observations seem relevant: firstly, that the German authorities maintained a strict control over the process and, secondly, that Casement did not envisage his role as an on-the-ground recruiter – it is likely that he was replicating the methods he had used in Ireland when addressing potential recruits for the Irish Volunteers.

56. MS 1689, fol. 104 ff. After his first day in the camp, Casement commented: 'I left the camp with a sense of despair.'

57. MacMurrough was later one of over sixty men removed from the camp because they were deemed 'undesirables' and hostile to the Brigade effort.

58. RDC to von Wedel, 7/12/1914, Doerries, *Prelude*, pp. 67–8.

59. RDC to Zimmermann, 23/12/1914, Doerries, *Prelude*, p. 71; the full text is given on pp. 72–4. There has been a tendency to scoff at Casement's interest in taking the Brigade to Egypt. Given that the approaches to Ireland were cut off, making that theatre an impossibility, and that a path to the Near East was to be opened up, the desire had a logic to it. 'If Turkey breaks through the [Suez] Canal as I trust she may do it may indeed bring about the downfall of the British Empire – as Wilfrid Blunt prayed for it in May. With the Canal gone Egypt goes – and with both gone I look for such an outbreak in India as must tax "the Empire" to its limit, and with Germany at the gates of Calais and the Irish Declaration out I do not think Master John can spare many men, ships or guns for India – to hold India he will have to appeal to Japan – and that spells his own sure and certain eviction from Asia later on. Once India falls the whole house collapses – for it is chiefly on India and its plunder the Colossal scheme of robbery depends.' RDC, German Diaries, 27/11/1914, NLI MS 1689, fol 27.

60. Quoted in Reid, p. 265.

61. NLI MS 1690, fol. 62.

62. RDC to Fr Nicholson, 18/3/1915, NLI MS 13085 (8).

63. Kelly was born in Killarney, Co. Kerry, in 1889 and educated at Clongowes, Blackrock and Trinity College, where he took a BA Mod. in 1911 and an LLB in 1913. He took a great interest in Irish, throughout. A promising student, he proceeded to

spend a year at the University of Paris, before going to Marburg. Later in his life he was to play a key role in advising Tomás Ó Criomhthain during the writing of *An tOileánach* (*The Islandman*). He was appointed schools inspector by the Department of Education, but there is some mystery about the latter part of his career and it is speculated that his report on Casement may have worked against him. He died in 1936, in his mid forties, in Split, Yugoslavia. His career is fascinatingly traced and the text of his statement on Casement given in Muiris Mac Conghail, 'Brian Ó Ceallaigh, Tomás Ó Criomhthain and Sir Roger Casement', *Journal of the Kerry Archaeological and Historical Society*, 22 (1993), 190.

64. For Kelly's report, see Nathan to Undersecretary of State for Foreign Affairs, 11/2/1915, PRO FO 95/776. Sir Matthew Nathan (1862–1939) was Undersecretary for Ireland from 1914 to 1916; he had entered the Royal Engineers in 1880 and been governor of a number of colonial territories from 1900 to 1909.

65. On 8 January he wrote in his diary: 'It is nearly 2 weeks since I wrote in my diary. I have been ill and greatly upset at failure of my hopes.' Curry, p. 145.

66. For details, see Reid, pp. 265, 272.

67. Through Macran Casement tried to get word to friends at home: to Gertrude, Alice Green, Eoin MacNeill, F.J. Bigger and Ada MacNeill. He also sent money for Nina.

68. See Doerries, *Prelude*, pp. 85–6 and 95.

69. Hoy, Statement to DID/Admiralty, 12/5/1915, PRO HO 144/1636 ... 3A.

70. Chatterton-Hill to RDC, 16/3/1915, quoted in Doerries, *Prelude*, p. 96.

71. See Curry, pp. 219–26 for details, including correspondence between Casement and Chatterton-Hill. Unsympathetic to Chatterton-Hill, Curry suggests (p. 219) that he was 'born in Ceylon of an Irish father but native mother and never ... put foot on Irish soil'. Chatterton-Hill later became active in the German-Irish Society.

72. Quoted in Franz Rothenfelder, *Casement in Deutschland* (Augsburg: Reichel 1917), p. 110.

73. RDC (Hamburg) to Countess Hahn, 22/02/1915, NLI MS 13085 (9ii).

74. McGarrity to RDC, 31/11/1914, NLI MS 13085 (18).

75. Bernstorff to GFO, 14/12/1914, Doerries, *Prelude*, p. 69; a copy can also be found in *Documents relative to the Sinn Fein Movement*, p. 6; R. Meyer to RDC, 17/12/1914 and 16/1/1915, NLI MS 13085 (23). Fr Nicholson was from Philadelphia and was close to McGarrity. For an interview with him, see the *Catholic Bulletin*, 18 (1928), 749–53.

76. RDC (Hotel Esplanade, Berlin) to Eduard Meyer, 27/01/1915. He sent his best wishes, on the Emperor's birthday, 'and for the speedy triumph of the righteous cause in which the German people are engaged in defending'.

77. Curry, p. 174. Fr O'Gorman left Limburg on 18 January 1915 to return to Rome: see RDC, German Diaries, NLI MS 1690, fol. 9.

78. Nicholson to RDC, 9/2/1915 and 23/2/1915, NLI MS 13085 (25). Kehoe suggests that there was some opposition in the camp to Nicholson, including an attempted boycott of his Mass, because of the blend of his religious and political roles. McKeogh, 512.

79. For Boehm, see Doerries, *Prelude*, pp. 147 and 154.

80. Freeman to Schiemann, 19/2/1915, NLI MS 13085 (9/ii); RDC, note on meeting with Boehm and Brogan, 1/3/1915, NLI MS 13085 (19); Devoy, p. 444.

81. Devoy to RDC, 19/2/1915, NLI MS 13073 (44/ii). Letters from Devoy took up to a month to reach Casement.

82. Nicholson to RDC, 18/3/1915, NLI MS 13085 (25); Kehoe to RDC, 20/3/1915, NLI MS 13085 (21); RDC to Nicholson, 21/3/1915 NLI MS 13085 (8); Brogan to Nicholson, 22/3/1915, NLI MS 13085 (8). When Casement received a subsequent letter of warning from Devoy, he sat down, in early April, and wrote a memo explaining the circumstances of the case. Devoy, pp. 444–8. For Brogan's report, see Lerchenmueller, 102.

83. RDC to von Wedel, 15/3/1915, quoted in Doerries, *Prelude*, p. 93; Quinn to Bernstorff, 22/3/1915, Doerries, *Prelude*, pp. 102–3.

84. RDC to Gaffney, 1/4/1915, NLI MS 8605. In this letter, Casement talked of going to Munich; his interest in the city probably derived from his acquaintance with Gaffney.

85. RDC to Quinn, 29/4/1915, Doerries, *Prelude*, pp. 120–1.

86. Kehoe to RDC, 20/3/1915, NLI MS 13085 (21). In his articles, Kehoe refers in a number of places to the existence of 'secret cliques' among the prisoners, working against the formation of a brigade (e.g. pp. 399–400). One of Brogan's recommendations was the segregation of nationalist from non-nationalist prisoners: see Lerchenmueller, 102.

87. RDC to von Wedel, Doerries, *Prelude*, pp. 99–100 and NLI MS 13085 (9/iii). Kehoe talks of the emergence of a 'Council of Seven' working in Limburg for the Brigade: Fr Nicholson, himself, Dowling, Kavanagh, O'Toole, McGrenaghan and Delamore: McKeogh, 514.

88. Nicholson to RDC, 18/3/1915, NLI MS 13085 (25); RDC to von Wedel, 21/3/1915, Doerries, *Prelude*, pp. 100–1.

89. RDC to Nicholson, 21/03/1915, NLI MS 13085 (8).

90. RDC to von Wedel, 25/3/1915, NLI MS 13085 (9/iii); Nicholson to RDC, 29/3/1915, NLI MS 13085 (25); RDC to Nicholson, 4/4/1915, NLI MS 13085 (8).

91. RDC to von Wedel, 6/4/1915, Doerries, *Prelude*, pp. 108–11. The full list of the sixty-six has been included by Doerries. Referring to the clearly organized opposition among prisoners to the whole recruitment effort, Casement told von Wedel: 'The British flunkeys in the Camp are furious and endeavouring more than ever to terrorise those over whom they can exercise any control.'

92. RDC to Boehm, 8/4/1915, UCD P127/5.

93. RDC to Boehm, 8/4/1915 and 10/4/1915, UCD P127/5 and P127/6.

94. RDC to Boehm, 15/04/1915, UCD P127/7. Presumably this was the same MacMorrough whom Casement had met on his first visit to Limburg.

95. RDC (Eden Hotel, Berlin) to Boehm, 24/4/1915, UCD P 127/8; Boehm to RDC, r. 24/4/1915, NLI MS 13085 (19); Kehoe to RDC (Eden Hotel, Berlin), r. 30/4/1915, NLI MS 13085 (21).

96. RDC to Devoy, 6/4/1915, quoted in Devoy, pp. 436–7.

97. See Geraldine Plunkett, 'Joseph Plunkett's diary of his journey to Germany in 1915', *University Review*, 1(11) (1954), 32–48. Plunkett's diary, a valuable source, covers the period from 17 March 1915, when he left Dublin, to 17 June, when he was still in Germany. The language is exceedingly cryptic, virtually in code, and from 1 May he switched to Irish (of a very unidiomatic variety), all of which makes the text difficult to decipher. The editor's identifications in the notes are extremely useful.

98. Casement appears as 'E', presumably because he was staying at the Eden Hotel when Plunkett arrived.

99. Amusingly, Christensen was rendered in Plunkett's diary as 'Iolair bán ['white eagle' = Adler] MacGiolla Chríost'.

100. NLI MS 1690, fol. 47.

101. For details see Michael Foy & Brian Barton, *The Easter Rising* (Stroud, Gloucestershire: Sutton Publishing 1999), pp. 12–20; Townshend, pp. 106–7.

102. Nicholson to RDC, 9/5/1915, NLI MS 13085 (25).

103. While he was in Limburg, Casement received a letter from Mrs Dryhurst: 'A chance has come to send you a few words of undying friendship and affection ... If I did not believe that we shall see you back one of these days, I should lose half my courage to go on facing the complications and cross-currents of life. For we shall want you badly to lead us to the better state of things.' She told him that Alice Stopford Green had got two of his messages. Dryhurst to RDC, 29/4/1915 (r. 15/5/1915), NLI MS 13073 (46/vii).

104. Plunkett to RDC, 24/5/1915, NLI MS 13085 (26). Among the Conservative politicians in the new coalition were Lord Newton (Undersecretary of State in the Foreign Office); A. Bonar Law (Colonies); W. Long (Health and Local Government); Lord Lansdowne (Minister without Portfolio). Sir Edward Carson became Attorney General, but was succeeded in the post in November by Sir F. Smith. The changes were not to strengthen Casement's case after his capture in 1916.

105. NLI MS 1690, fol. 56. For an assessment of the German response, see Foy and Barton, p. 19.

106. Plunkett to RDC, 24/6/1915, NLI MS 13085 (26).

107. R. Meyer to RDC, 22/05/1915, NLI MS 13085 (23).

108. On 10 June, shortly after arriving in Limburg, Boehm submitted his own report, in which he recommended transferring the Brigade members to Zossen, where they should be treated as 'legionnaires' and not as 'prisoners'. Lerchenmueller, 103–4 and n. 43.

109. Nicholson (Limburg) to RDC, 9/6/1915, NLI MS 13085 (25).

110. RDC (Limburg) to Nicholson, 7/6/1915, NLI MS 13085 (8). See also Nicholson to Wedel, 5/6/1915, quoted in Doerries, *Prelude*, pp. 126–7. Lerchenmueller, 105, seems to suggest that Nicholson left after a mid July crisis, having been blamed by Casement and Boehm for the failure of Brigade affairs. Nicholson actually left in early June and this explanation does not seem to me to ring true. Lerchenmueller cites

a report by Professor Bresien, submitted in July, as the source of his interpretation. Casement described Bresien as 'the chief interpreter of the camp', and as 'dreadfully officious' but 'well meaning'. NLI MS 1689, fol. 110. Reid, p. 245, says he was an elderly school-teacher. The matter needs further investigation.

111. Wedel to RDC, 15/06/1915, NLI MS 13085 (27).

112. RDC to McGarrity, 20/6/1915, Doerries, *Prelude*, p. 130. Devoy vigorously defended the efforts being made by Irish-Americans in a letter to Casement: Devoy to RDC, 22/8/1915, NLI MS 13073 (44/vi).

113. Boehm, memorandum, 24/6/1915, Doerries, *Prelude*, p. 131. It seems that, in Zossen, the men were at first housed in another prisoner camp rather than in a military barracks.

114. Gaffney to Zimmermann, 6/8/1915, Doerries, *Prelude*, p. 138; von Wedel to Montgelas, 10/8/1915, Doerries, *Prelude*, p. 141.

115. Von Wedel to RDC, 10/7/1915, NLI MS 13085 (27).

116. Kehoe (Limburg) to RDC, 12/6/1915, NLI MS 13085 (21).

117. Kehoe suggests that Curry was an 'Irish-American professor of Munich University', who had a summer residence on Lake Amersee, and that his brother, Laurence, 'superintended the extensive farm attached to the villa'. McKeogh, 833.

118. The following summary in the text is based on Franz Rothenfelder. While there was, presumably, a propaganda dimension to the book, the observations on Casement ring true.

119. Von Wedel to RDC, 10/7/1915, NLI MS 13058 (27); R. Meyer to RDC, 13/7/1915, NLI MS 13085 (23). In December Casement had described the uniform being prepared as 'a pale grey with a touch of green running through the warp'. NLI MS 1690, fols. 25–6.

120. Kehoe to RDC, 17/7/1915 (r. Lake Ammersee 22/7), NLI MS 13085 (21).

121. Kehoe to RDC, 4/8/1915, NLI MS 13085 (21).

122. In a thoughtful but undated letter, O'Toole introduced himself to Casement as a former branch secretary of the Gaelic League. O'Toole (Limburg) to RDC, n.d., NLI MS 13085 (21). Lerchenmueller, 109, describes him as 'the cleverest and best educated of the Brigade', who was later employed by the Department of Local Government and Public Health in Ireland. He was to give a detailed account of the Irish Brigade to British Intelligence in 1921: 'Statement of Private Michael O'Toole', 11/6/21, KV/10.

123. Boehm to RDC, 10/8/18, NLI MS 13085/19. Daniel Bailey, alias W. Julien Beverley (or Beverly), was to accompany Casement and Monteith to Ireland, by submarine, and to be captured and brought to London for trial. The choice of Bailey was made by Monteith, but Casement described him as 'an old friend'.

124. Zerhusen to RDC, 5/7/1915 and 18/7/1915, NLI MS 13085 (28); Monteith, Diary, 1/11/1915, Allen Library, Dublin. Monteith kept a diary from the time of his arrival in Germany until shortly before he left for Ireland with Casement.

125. Zerhusen to RDC (r. Feldafing), 25/08/1915, NLI MS 13085 (28); Boehm to RDC (r.

Feldafing), 26/08/1915, NLI MS 13085 (19); RDC to Kehoe, 16/8/1915, NLI MS 13085 (28).

126. Kehoe to RDC, 4/9/1915 (r. Diessen 11/9), NLI MS 13085 (21).

127. Kehoe to RDC, 7/9/1915, NLI MS 13085 (21); Boehm to RDC, 17/9/1915, NLI MS 13085 (19). A report on the circumstances of the Brigade in Zossen made its way to British Intelligence files at this time: see KV/9 20/8/1915.

128. RDC (Diessen) to Boehm, 12/09/1915, NLI MS 13085 (21).

129. Boehm to RDC, 15/09/1915, NLI MS 13085 (19).

130. NLI MS 1689, fol. 27.

131. Halil Halid to RDC, 29/9/1915, NLI MS 13085 (17).

132. RDC (Hotel Baseler Hof, Munich) to Halil Halid ('Dear Halil Halid Bey'), 5/10/1915, NLI MS 13085 (17).

133. Boehm to ? General Staff, 24/9/1915, Doerries, *Prelude*, p. 146.

134. RDC to R. Meyer, 28/9/1915, Doerries, *Prelude*, p. 147.

135. Quoted in Devoy, p. 440; the statement was dated 24 September. On the same date, Casement made out a detailed financial statement for Devoy and McGarrity, in which he accounted for all monies received from the US and all his expenditure. O'Brien and Ryan, pp. 477–80.

136. RDC to Mrs Boehm, 18/10/1915, UCD P127/15. These were probably German translations of his article. Earlier in the month he had sent Blücher German translations of both: RDC to Blücher, 5/11/1915, Blücher Collection, Clare Archives, PP/1/15.

137. RDC (Hotel Baseler Hof, Munich) to Frau Elsa Douglas, 20/10/1915, 22/10/1915, 23/10/1915, NLI MS 5459.

138. The essay is reproduced in Mackey, *Crime against Europe*, pp. 121–30, as 'The Far-Extended Baleful Power of the Lie'. For a detailed analysis of the facts and myth-making surrounding these 'Belgian atrocities', see John Horne & Alan Kramer, *German Atrocities, 1914: A History of Denial* (New Haven: Yale University Press 2001). The authors conclude: 'For the first time ... we have confirmed the wartime official estimates that some 6,500 civilians were killed in Belgium and France from August to October 1914' (p. 419). Their assessment of the Bryce Report, published in early May 1915, is that, while its figures were in the main broadly correct, 'some of the witness evidence cited by Bryce on the fate of women and children was fantasy' (p. 234) and that the Bryce Committee 'exemplified the loss of critical perspective which accompanied wartime mobilization' (p. 236). Ironically, one of the mythic elements concerned 'severed hands'. Another irony, perhaps, was that Casement's friend, Professor J.H. Morgan, conducted part of the investigation.

139. Crotty to RDC, 15/6/1915, NLI MS 13085 (20).

140. RDC (c/o US Consulate General, Munich) to Crotty, draft, 17/8/1915, NLI MS 13085 (20). He was, he noted, not in Munich itself, but some miles away in a small village with friends. RDC to R. Meyer, 17/8/1915, Doerries, *Prelude*, p. 143. For reference to Schiemann's letter, see John Devoy, 12/11/1915, Doerries, *Prelude*, pp.

160–1. Lerchenmueller, 100 and 105, draws attention to another source of criticism, the report, dated 30/7/1915, submitted by Professor Bresien.

141. Crotty to RDC (r. at Feldafing 22/8), 20/8/1915, NLI MS 13085 (20).

142. Devoy to 'Dear Friend' [Casement], 21/5/1915, enclosed in RDC to von Wedel, 8/6/1915, Doerries, *Prelude*, pp. 127–8.

143. RDC to von Wedel, 15/7/1915, Doerries, *Prelude*, pp. 134–5. And see Reilly to RDC, 5/9/1915, NLI MS 13085 (18). It seems likely that Reilly was one source of British knowledge of affairs in Limburg; his papers came into the possession of the French War Office: see KV 2/6, 9/10/1915.

144. For Christensen's journey see RDC to von Wedel, 'Tuesday afternoon' [26/10/1915], Doerries, *Prelude*, pp. 151–2, and 28/10/1915, pp. 152–4; McGarrity to RDC, 9/11/1915, Doerries, *Prelude*, pp. 156–9.

145. Devoy, p. 441. See, also, Devoy to RDC, 19/12/1915, NLI MS 13073 (44/vii), and McGarrity to RDC, 16/12/1915, NLI MS 13073 (31).

146. Devoy to RDC, 21/11/1915, NLI MS 13073 (44/vii). In August he had commented: 'It is military considerations which must determine our relations and we think we can show that we can do things of infinitely more value than forming a Brigade although that too will count.' Devoy to RDC, 22/8/1915, NLI MS 13073 (44/vi).

147. McGoey arrived in Copenhagen on 26 November. Casement took him out to Zossen on 1 December: for his part, see Doerries, *Prelude*, pp. 150, 156–7, 162, 165, 171, 188–9, 195 and 198.

148. *Ibid*. pp. 145–6, unspecified German representative in New York to Berlin, 21/9/1915. Doerries suggests that the representative was likely to have been Wolf von Igel.

149. Monteith, Diary, 23/10/1925, 24/10/1915 and 26/10/1915.

150. RDC (Hospiz am Brandenburger Tor, Berlin) to Gaffney, 1/11/1915, NLI MS 8605; RDC to Karstensen, 17/11/1915, NLI MS 8605.

151. Devoy, statement, 12/11/1915, quoted in Doerries, *Prelude*, pp. 160–1. The US side was conscious of the danger of Casement's vulnerability to criticism. See McGarrity to Devoy, 1/8/1915, quoted in O'Brien and Ryan, p. 473. Schiemann seems to have made his own complaints about Casement directly to Kuno Meyer in the US. See Meyer to Devoy, 2/9/1915, Doerries, *Prelude*, p. 475.

152. RDC to von Wedel, 28/10/1915, Doerries, *Prelude*, pp. 152–4.

153. Monteith to RDC, 2/11/1915, Doerries, *Prelude*, p. 155.

154. Monteith, Diary, 3/11/1915 to 23/11/1915; Monteith to RDC, 5/11; 8/11; 10/11/1915, NLI MS 13085 (24).

155. Kehoe to RDC, 10/11/1915, NLI MS 13085 (21).

156. Monteith, Diary, 6/11/1915.

157. *Ibid*., 16/11/1915.

158. *Ibid*., 24/11/1915.

159. RDC to von Wedel, 3/12/1915, text in Doerries, *Prelude*, pp. 166–8.

160. RDC to von Wedel, 11/12/1915, Doerries, *Prelude*, pp. 171–4.

161. Nadolny to Dept. P., 7/1/1916, Doerries, *Prelude*, pp. 176–7. Halil Halid had relayed

the advice to Casement that, 'if he wishes to display the Irish Flag in any part of the Eastern seat of war, and contribute actively to the cause of Irish Independence, a personal visit to Constantinople rather than correspondence will do much more to complete arrangements'. Halil Halid Bey to RDC, 26/12/1915, NLI MS (13085/11).

162. Monteith, Diary, 27/11/1915, 30/11/1915; Ministry of War to GFO, 27/11/1915, Doerries, *Prelude*, p. 163. His rank was to be lieutenant sergeant [*Feldwebelleutnant*].

163. Monteith, Diary, 1/12/1915.

164. RDC (Zossen) to Antonie Meyer, 20/12/1915, NLI MS 5459.

165. RDC to Eduard Meyer, 20/12/1915, BBAW NL Eduard Meyer 358.

166. RDC (Hotel zum 'Goldenen Löwen', Zossen) to Pincus, 16/12/1915, TCD 827. He enclosed two articles, one written in Philadelphia the previous September, the second published in German in *Deutsche Rundschau* in June.

167. RDC (Zossen) to Pincus, 30/12/1915, TCD 827.

168. Rothenfelder, p. 90.

169. RDC (Hotel Europaeischer Hof, Dresden) to Eduard Meyer, 04/01/1916, BBAW NL Eduard Meyer 358.

170. Monteith, Diary, 7/1/1916 and 12/1/1916.

171. *Ibid.*, 14/1/1916.

172. W. Scott [Crotty] to 'Dear Friend' [McGarrity], 19/1/1916, quoted in Doerries, *Prelude*, p. 177.

173. Crotty to von Wedel, 22/1/1916, Doerries, *Prelude*, p. 177. It would appear that the negative attitude of the German military authorities was responsible for this; Crotty was to get a reprieve and remain in Germany for some further period. Extra detail has been shed on the matter with the discovery of the Blücher Collection in Ennis, Co. Clare.

174. Monteith to RDC, 24/1/1916, NLI MS 13085 (24).

175. Monteith (Zossen) to RDC, 1/2/1916, NLI MS 13085 (24).

176. Monteith, Diary, retrospective entry, 10/4/1916. Though the details of what transpired are somewhat unclear, see also, Monteith to Nadolny, 24/1/1916, quoted in Doerries, *Prelude*, p. 178, and Nadolny to GFO, 26/1/1916, p. 179. Zerhusen offered his loyalty to Casement at the end of January: 'I am quite willing to go with you anywhere, but of course I am not my own master, and it would therefore depend if you could arrange this with the authorities.' Zerhusen to RDC, 31/01/1916, NLI MS 13085 (28).

177. Schneider, Report, 29/1/1916, quoted in Lerchenmueller, 107 and 112, n. 66.

178. Löwenfeld, Deputy General Command, Report, 10/2/1916, quoted in Lerchenmueller, 107 and n. 68.

179. Bernstorff to GFO, 17/2/1916, text in Doerries, *Prelude*, p. 185. The telegram arrived in Berlin on 20 February. Two earlier communications had been sent by the embassy, on 10 and 16 February, giving details of the planned rising, but they did not reach Berlin until 7 and 8 March, respectively, i.e. some time after the telegram of 17 February. That of 16 February was from Devoy and gave considerable detail

on the military situation in Ireland. Doerries, *Prelude*, pp. 180–4.

180. Nadolny to GFO, 1/3/1916, Doerries, *Prelude*, p. 186.

181. RDC to von Wedel, 30/3/1916, Doerries, *Prelude*, pp. 192–203. According to Casement, Monteith reported him on 11 March that the recipients 'seem more than pleased with your proposals'. *Prelude*, p. 194.

182. RDC to von Wedel, 30/3/1916, text in Doerries, *Prelude*, pp. 194–5.

183. Curry, pp. 168–9.

184. *Ibid.* p. 195; Diary notes by RDC, n.d., Doerries, *Prelude*, p. 189; McGoey's farewell to his Comrades, 18/3/1916, Doerries, *Prelude*, p. 188; McGoey, 19/3/1916, NLI MS 13085 (24), in which McGoey listed twenty of the 'surest men' to take from among those at Zossen. McGoey's fate is clouded in mystery: some believe he was captured and executed by the British, some that he was working for British intelligence. For sources, see *Prelude*, pp. 30–1.

185. Monteith to RDC, 24/3/1916, Doerries, *Prelude*, p. 190 and NLI MS 13085 (24).

186. RDC, Notes, 30/3/1916, Doerries, *Prelude*, p. 203.

187. RDC to von Wedel, 2/4/1916, Doerries, *Prelude*, pp. 204–5. On conscription, see Townshend, pp. 77–8.

188. All quotations from RDC's Diary, 3/4/1916, as found in 'Dilemma in Berlin: from Casement's last diary', Roger McHugh (ed.), *Dublin 1916* (London: Arlington Books 1966), pp. 3–16, pp. 4–7. The original is contained in RDC, 'A Last Page', NLI MS 5244.

189 RDC, Notes, Doerries, *Prelude*, p. 206.

190. Blücher, Prince Gebhard von, p. 130. The date was 4 April. In 1919 three letters Casement had given the Blüchers came into the possession of the British authorities. PRO HO 144/1637/ ... 194A.

191. Additional diary entries and notes by Casement, 28 March–5 April, NLI MS 17587 (2).

192. RDC, Diary, 5/4/1916, McHugh, *Dublin*, pp. 7–13.

193. German Minister, Berne, to GFO, 5/4/1916, Doerries, *Prelude*, pp. 206–7 and Nadolny to GFO, 6/4/1916, p. 207.

194. RDC, Diary, 7/4/1916, McHugh, *Dublin*, p. 13.

195. Plunkett to RDC, 11/4/1916, Doerries, *Prelude*, pp. 208–9. Since Plunkett was still in Berne at this point, the implication is that the general staff officers did not allow Casement's letter to go.

196. RDC, Diary, 7/4/1916, McHugh, *Dublin*, pp. 1–16. For Noeggerath, see Doerries, *Prelude*, pp. 21 and 30; and see Noeggerath to RDC, 10/3/1916, NLI MS 13085 (18).

197. Sean Francis Kavanagh, 'The last historic interview with Roger Casement in Berlin', *Roger Casement Commeration* (Conradh na Gaedhilge, Craobh Rudhria Mhic Easmuinn, Murlough, Co. Antrim 1953), pp. 11–16.

198. Kavanagh records how Monteith later found a waiter listening outside the door and how he, himself, took a roundabout train journey back to Zossen, to avoid being followed.

199. RDC to Bethmann Hollweg, 11/4/1916, Doerries, *Prelude*, pp. 209–10.

200. RDC to von Wedel, 11/4/1916, Doerries, *Prelude*, pp. 211–14. There are fifty-five names on the list, together with the men's ranks and pre-war occupations.

201. The letter is given in Kavanagh, pp. 15–16 and in McKeogh, 735.

202. R. Meyer, memorandum, 12/4/1916, Doerries, *Prelude*, pp. 214; p. 215–20 also includes a number of significant documents relating to the shipment of arms and the lead-up to the Easter Rebellion.

18: CAPTURE, TRIAL AND EXECUTION, 1916

1. I take this account from John de Courcy Ireland's careful analysis in *The Sea and the Easter Rising* (Dún Laoghaire, Co. Dublin: Maritime Institute of Ireland, revised edition 1996 [1966]). The ship was without radio and had already sailed when the leaders of the Rising requested that it delay its arrival until after the Rising, planned for 23 April, had started. Unaware that their message had not been communicated to the ship, those on the Irish end did not expect her until the night of 23 April, Easter Sunday. Karl Spindler left an account, *The Mystery of Casement's Ship* (Tralee: Anvil Books 1965), which also has a valuable 'Foreword' by Florence O'Donoghue (pp. 7–27) on the Irish side of the planning. Spindler's book had originally been published in German in 1931. For a general account of the voyage and events in Kerry, see Townshend, pp. 126–31.

2. For details, see de Courcy Ireland, pp. 35–44. Monteith left a short description of the voyage in Robert Monteith, *Casement's Last Adventure* (Chicago, privately printed 1932).

3. Monteith, p. 131.

4. RDC to Nina, 25/7/1916, NLI MS 13600 (copy). For further discussion of the various objects associated with the landing on Banna Strand, see Gerard L. Lyne, 'New light on material concealed by Roger Casement near Banna Strand', *Journal of the Kerry Archaeological and Historical Society*, no. 21 (1987), 94–110, and Lucy McDiarmid, 'Secular relics: Casement's boat, Casement's dish', *Textual Practice*, 16, no. 2 (2002), 277–302.

5. When Casement was later transferred to Brixton prison and allowed to write letters, his first was to Sandercock, whom he thanked for 'your unfailing manliness and kindness to me' and for treating him 'in a wholly chivalrous and high-minded way'. Hyde, pp. 65–6.

6. For this discovery, see Dudgeon, pp. 481–4. Hall was from Ulster and had been military secretary of the UVF after its formation. He was involved in the landing of arms in Larne in April 1914.

7. Shorthand notes from Monday, 23/4/1916 at New Scotland Yard, PRO HO 144/1636/ ... 3A.

8. Interrogation of 24/4/1916 at New Scotland Yard. Lieut. Serocold (DID's office) and Quinn, PRO HO 144/1636 ... 3A.

9. *Ibid.*, excerpt from conversation between RDC, the assistant chief commissioner and Hall, 25/4/1916.

10. Hyde, p. 51. Sawyer, *Flawed Hero*, pp. 128–9, gives details of Casement's suicide attempts, derived from an interview with Corporal A.E. King, who was one of Casement's guards at the time.

11. Gertrude Parry [Bannister], 'The last days of Roger Casement' in McHugh, *Dublin*, pp. 289–305, from which all subsequent quotations from Gertrude's account are taken.

12. Sawyer, *Flawed Hero*, p. 127, inspected the accommodation itself and observed that 'prior to, and after, occupation by prisoners, the rooms in the Casemates were used to accommodate warders' and that in the one occupied by Casement, Number 2A, 'the original floor remains and it is difficult to accept that the cell was ever verminous or even damp'.

13. For an account of this episode involving Major Arbuthnot, see the passage by his son-in-law, Claude Cockburn, in *I Claude* (Harmondsworth: Penguin 1967), pp. 278–82.

14. There is some confusion in existing accounts about when Gavan Duffy and the Bannisters first saw Casement in the Tower. Most accounts put Gavan Duffy's first visit at 9 May and the Bannisters' at 11 May.

15. Owen Dudley Edwards, 'The trial of Roger Casement: a study in theatre management' in Daly, p. 173, suggests that the return of these prisoners was deliberately contrived by Germany to ensure Casement's death and thereby influence US opinion in their favour.

16. Acting Consul General, Philadelphia, to Nicolson, 10/5/1916, PRO FO 95/776, and 5/6/1916, KV 2/9. On Nicolson's dossier, see Reid, pp. 369 and 380.

17. Three reflective, informed, and insightful essays on Casement's trial can be found in the proceedings of the Royal Irish Academy Casement Symposium: Frank Callanan, 'Between treason and blood-sacrifice: the trials of Roger Casement', pp. 121–37; Conor Gearty, 'The Casement treason trial in its legal context', pp. 138–48; Owen Dudley Edwards, 'The Trial', pp. 149–77; all in Daly. See also Owen Dudley Edwards, 'Divided treasons and divided loyalties', *Trans. Royal Historical Society*, 32 (1982), 153–74. Here Edwards provides useful pen-pictures of the various members of the prosecution team for Casement's trial; not all took part in this preliminary phase.

18. Hyde, pp. 64–5. There was a further court hearing, on 25 May, when the indictment drawn up by the DPP was presented to the Grand Jury of Middlesex. Hyde, p. 69, and Reid, p. 379.

19. ASG to Home Secretary, 15/5/1916, 19/5/1916, PRO HO 144/1636/ ... 7A; Samuel to ASG, 19/5/1916, PRO HO 144/1636/ ... 7A.

20. Nevinson, *Last Changes*, p. 104.

21. Quoted by MacColl, p. 193, from an interview.

22. EDM to ASG, 25/5/1916, quoted in Cline, pp. 152–3. The Union of Democratic

Control was established at the beginning of the war 'to work for parliamentary control of foreign policy and a moderate peace settlement' (Cline, p. 100). Morel remained a stern critic of British foreign policy and was handed a six-month jail sentence in 1917 on a trivial charge (Cline, pp. 111–12). In a letter he wrote to the Home Secretary, however, defending himself against the charge of being a 'German Agent', Morel stated that 'Casement's defection was a sad blow to all his friends, myself among them, and his friends in this country included many men of distinction and public position.' EDM to Samuel, 3/4/1916, LSE MP.

23. RDC (Brixton) to Harris, 1/6/1916 [or 11/6?] BL MSS Add. 46,912 fols. 30–1.

24. Norman and Jeanne MacKenzie (eds.), *The Diary of Beatrice Webb* (London: Virago 1984), vol. 3, pp. 255–7 (21 May 1916). Contributions to Casement's defence fund, many of them small, came from his close friends. Among those who contributed were Mrs Green, Conan Doyle, Cadbury, Gertrude and Elizabeth, Roger Casement (Magherintemple), Margaret Dobbs, Robert and Sylvia Lynd, Agnes O'Farrelly, Nevinson, Sidney Parry and Mrs Fisher Unwin. An American contribution raised by Devoy was brought by Michael Francis Doyle. Reid p. 368 and note c; MacColl, p. 181; O'Brien and Ryan, pp. 495–8.

25. A.M. Sullivan, *Old Ireland: Reminiscences of an Irish K.C.* (London: Thornton Butterworth Ltd 1927), pp. 187–8.

26. A.M. Sullivan, *The Last Serjeant* (London: MacDonald 1952), p. 267.

27. Quoted in Hyde, p. 72.

28. *Ibid.* p. 77. Callanan, who characterizes Sullivan as 'archaically conservative by disposition' (p. 125), offers several cogent reasons in support of the line taken by Sullivan (pp. 122–5).

29. For details, see Hyde, pp. 66–7.

30. Michael Francis Doyle (1876–1960) was an international lawyer practising in Philadelphia. He was a friend of St John Gaffney's and an associate of members of Clan na Gael. In 1915 he had represented Casement in his action against the *New York World*. For many years he served as a member of the Permanent Court of International Arbitration at the Hague, and he assisted in the drafting of the Constitution of the Irish Free State in 1922.

31. RDC to Roger Casement (Magherintemple), 6/6/1916, PRONI T 3787/19. For the gift see Dudgeon, pp. 498–9.

32. RDC to Katje, 11/6/1916, quoted in Reid, p. 391. He commiserated, too, at their losing the farm.

33. RDC to Morten, 3/6/1916, NLI Acc. 4902 (3).

34. RDC to Morten, 11/6/1916, NLI MS 13600. Part of Casement's upset may have been due to a reference by Morten to the rumours that had begun to circulate about Casement's diaries.

35. O'Byrne to RDC, 22/6/1916, NLI MS 14100.

36. Casement himself had cited the case of Thomas Masaryk, whose actions during the war on behalf of the Czech people against Austria were parallel to Casement's

on behalf of Ireland. Masaryk got a declaration in favour of the Czech people from the Asquith government: see Inglis, pp. 343–4 and 413–14.

37. ASG to Botha, 16/6/1916, quoted in O'Brien and Ryan, pp. 499–502. Louis Botha (1862–1919) had a distinguished military career during the Boer War, finally submitting at the Treaty of Vereeniging in May 1902; he took a leading position in the new Union of South Africa from 1910 on. He gave full support to Great Britain during the First World War and helped defeat German forces in South-West Africa.

38. Bigelow in *New York Times*, 21/5/1916. It is difficult to agree with Reid, p. 370, when he claims that Bigelow's intention was to save Casement's life. Casement himself commented: 'I saw Poultney Bigelow's act of "friendship"! I will not call it by the name it deserves.'

39. Bigelow to *New York Times*, 24/5/1916 (appeared 25/5).

40. Arana to RDC, 14/6/14, quoted in Reid, p. 392.

41. Thomson to Plunkett, 1/6/1916, Plunkett Papers, THO 2; Plunkett to Thomson, 8/6/1916, Plunkett Papers, THO 3. Thomson had written to Plunkett a month earlier, shortly after Casement's arrest. He had talked of the situation in Dublin and of Casement's statement during interrogation that the Germans had cynically 'let him down'. With the likely effect on Irish-American public opinion in mind, he asked Plunkett to let him know if he learned of similar views among the revolutionaries. Thomson to Plunkett, 1/5/1916, Plunkett Papers, THO 1. The tone of their letters suggests that the two were well acquainted.

42. The official record of the trial can be found in PRO HO 144/1636/ ... 33.

43. Nevinson, *Last Changes*, pp. 112–13. Eva Gore-Booth, a poet, was one of the two sisters from Lisadell House, Sligo, made famous by W.B. Yeats. Her sister was Constance Markievicz.

44. PRO HO 144/1636/... 33, p. 3.

45. *Ibid*. p. 12.

46. *Ibid*. p. 15.

47. *Ibid*. p. 17. Callanan, p. 126, describes Smith as 'glitteringly cynical, and an advocate of immense ability', and this opening speech as 'succinct and artfully prejudicial'.

48. They were John Cronin, Daniel O'Brien, John Robinson, William Egan, Michael O'Connor, Michael Moore, John Neill and James Wilson.

49. Henry Nevinson's response to this line of defence was: 'The whole prolonged argument, though the plea was legally justified, only confirmed me in my previous resolve never to accept legal defence upon a political charge, or any other charge involving questions of principle. To slip through the legal loophole of a comma, as was argued in this case, would I hope, appear to me an unworthy escape even from death on the gallows.' Nevinson, *Last Changes*, p. 109.

50. *Ibid*. p. 161.

51. Sullivan's speech, with interventions from the bench, *ibid*. pp. 162–80.

52. The only exception was the testimony of John Neill, but Neill had contradicted himself in the course of giving evidence.

53. PRO HO 144/1636/ ... 33, p. 189.

54. *Ibid.* p. 194.

55. *Ibid.* p. 206.

56. *Ibid.* p. 209.

57. *Ibid.* p. 210. Addressing the question of whether Casement got a fair trial, Gearty, p.144, concludes: 'The facts meant that they [the judges] could be as grandly committed to the rule of law as they desired, and still deliver the result that the state required.' The trial, however, was an exercise in 'the carefully controlled passion of the powerful against the weak' (p. 147). From Casement's point of view, Callanan, p. 137, termed it 'an ordeal of powerlessness'.

58. PRO HO 144/1636/ ... 33, p. 225–6.

59. *Ibid.* p. 226. The woolsack, the official seat of the Lord Chancellor in the House of Lords, was a large square sack of wool covered with scarlet. At this reference of Casement's, Smith is said to have smiled and murmured: 'Change places with him? Nothing doing.' He then got up and 'ostentatiously walked out of Court with his hands in his pockets'. Hyde, p. 121.

60. *Ibid.* p. 226. His biographer described how Wilfrid Scawen Blunt was moved by Casement's speech: 'When Blunt read the speech from the dock he was lifted into a state of prolonged exaltation. A magnificent pronouncement, the noblest apologia ever made by a political prisoner before his judges in the whole history of Irish or any other national war for freedom. It moved me to a stream of tears ...' Elizabeth Longford, *A Pilgrimage of Passion: The Life of Wilfrid Scawen Blunt* (London: Weidenfeld and Nicolson 1979), pp. 402–3.

61. *Ibid.* p. 227.

62. Gertrude Bannister to Grey, 1/7/1916, quoted in Reid, pp. 413–14.

63. Thomson to Blackwell, 10/7/1916, PRO HO 144/1636/ ... 44.

64. Blackwell and Troup, 4/7/1916, Memo, PRO PCOM 9/2326.

65. RDC to Morten, 8/7/1916, NLI Acc. 4902 (3).

66. RDC to Brigid Matthews, 14/7/1916, quoted by Eva Gore-Booth, in Parmiter, p. 355.

67. Lady Emmott to 'Revd. and dear Sir', 11?/7/1916, PRONI T3072/11 (copy). Casement did not receive her message. See Fr McCarroll to Miss Cooper, 9/8/1916, PRONI T3072/13.

68. Werner to Nevinson, 31/7/[1916], NLI MS 13078 (3).

69. Nevinson to *Daily News*, 12/7/1916, PRO HO 144/1636/... 42.

70. Gore-Booth to Gladstone, 13/7/1916, BL Gladstone Papers, Add. MSS 46083, fols. 10–11.

71. Lord Emmott to Home Secretary, 14/7/1916, PRO HO 144/1636 /... 46. He sent letters by Eva Gore-Booth (n.d.) and Alice Green (10/7), who also sent a printed petition from Miss Bannister. Bryce to Samuel, 15/7/1916, PRO HO 144/1636/ ... 51, enclosing Eva Gore-Booth's letter. Sir Ernley Blackwell consulted Basil Thomson on the matter and the latter gave his interpretation (18/7/1916) of what Casement had said during his interrogation at Scotland Yard: 'Throughout his various

statements to us Casement made it clear that he had started from Germany with the idea of heading a rebellion, though he believed it hopeless; except once, when he remarked that when he knew the Germans had refused to send men, he felt it his duty to come and warn the rebels that a rising would be hopeless.'

72. Gore-Booth to Gladstone, 21/7/1916, BL Gladstone Papers, Add. MSS 46083, fols. 14–16. Minna O'Conor (widow of Sir Nicholas O'Conor) also wrote to Gladstone to plead for Casement, citing his work in the consular service. She enclosed a copy of a letter from Fr Ryan OP (12/7/1916): Minna O'Conor to Gladstone, 29/7/1916, BL Gladstone Papers, Add. MSS 46083, fol. 20.

73. Blackwell memo, 21/7/1916, PRO HO 144/1636/... 53.

74. One of the items buried at Banna Strand and later recovered was a green flag, which Casement had brought from Germany: see Reid, pp. 349, 355.

75. Gertrude Bannister Appeal, 21/7/1916, PRO HO 144/1636/... 58. Wilfred Scawen Blunt supported Casement's position, 'But I cannot bring myself to petition for his life to ... Asquith. It would be doing your hero too great a wrong.' He referred to Irish history, to moral right and to the analogy with Wolfe Tone. Blunt to Gertrude Bannister, 10/7/1916, McMullen Papers.

76. Ottoline Morrell, *Ottoline at Garsington: Memories of Lady Morrell, 1915–1918*, ed. Robert Gathorne-Hardy (London: Faber 1974), p. 113.

77. Doyle to Shorter, 1/7/1916, BL Add. MSS 63596 [1981–5 Acq.] vol. 40A, Casement Petition Papers: correspondence of Sir A.C. Doyle and Clement K. Shorter, ed. *The Sphere*, *re* their petition to government to reprieve RDC: partly printed. fols 176. The petition can also be found at PRO HO 144/1637/ ... 79.

78. Gavan Duffy to Shorter, 5/7/1916, BL Add. MSS 63596, fol. 10.

79. John Masefield wrote to Nevinson: 'I will back you against any prelate, home or colonial ... if they decide against R.C. (I don't think they will) for we must fire a hot shot in that case.' J.M. to Nevinson, 15/7/n.y. [1916], NLI MS 13078 (2).

80. Henry Nevinson organized and submitted a small petition, which was signed by William A. Albright, Emery Walker, Arnold S. Rowntree, Arthur G. Symonds, Joseph King, G.P. Gooch and Arthur Lynch. Nevinson Petition, PRO HO 144/1636/ ... 64

81. Other notables included Bertram Windle, Æ, R. Macalister, Miss Evelyn Gleeson, E.A. Stopford. Petition of Irish Notables, 21/7/1916, PRO HO/144/1637/ ... 70.

82. The names included N.N. Boyd; C.M. Legg JP (Chair, Carrickfergus Urban Council), John Denison Jr. (?) (Co. Councillor, Antrim), J.H. Scott JP, Hugh Eccles, Henry H. Graham, John McVeigh. Alice Milligan petition, 22/7/1916, PRO HO 144/1637/ ... 68. Alice Milligan and Elizabeth Bannister had travelled to Ireland to make contact with those in sympathy with Casement. Other petitions came from Mt St Benedict, Gorey, from Derry and Donegal (including the signature of John Boyce of Portsalon) and from Conradh na Gaeilge (the Gaelic League) in London.

83. W.B. Yeats to Home Secretary (copy to Asquith), 14/7/1916, PRO HO 144/1636 /... 45.

84. Hanna Sheehy-Skeffington to Asquith, 21/7/1916, PRO HO 144/1637/ ... 74.

85. J.S. Lindsay BD, Canon of Christchurch, Dublin (The Rectory, Malahide) to Home Secretary, 22/7/1916, PRO HO 144/1637/ ... 67.

86. Quoted in Inglis, pp. 379–80.

87. Holly to Bryce, 6/7/1916, BOD Bryce Papers.

88. Parker and Quinn, Special Report, 22/6/1916, MEPO 2/10672. Casement himself mentioned having left trunks in 50 Ebury St. and at Allisons, the London shipping agents he used. RDC, 'A Private Note for my Solicitor', 14/6/1916, NLI MS 10764.

89. Parker, memos of 23/6/1916 and 24/6/1916 and typed copies of 1911 Diary and Cash Ledger, PRO HO 144/1637/ ... 139. The typed copies have occasional crayon markings on the margins, drawing attention to particular entries. In one, the diary entry for 18 September, the word 'Photo' appears on the margin, suggesting that this passage may have been photographed.

90. Reid, pp. 382–4, gives the most detailed account of the showing of the diaries. Mary Boyle Reilly, a US news agency representative, supplied Gavan Duffy with details on 3 June. Admiral Sir W.M. James, author of a biography of Hall, wrote (*Spectator*, 23 Dec. 1955, p. 859): 'As some American papers were championing Casement, Thomson had some pages of the diary photographed and showed them to Dr Page, the American Ambassador ... Some hard things have been said of Hall for his part in disclosing the contents of the diary. In retrospect it seems unworthy of him, but the war was at a critical stage ... and neither Hall nor the majority of his countrymen was in the mood to deal lightly with traitors.'

91. For Shorter see Sawyer, *Flawed Hero*, p. 140; for Massingham and George V see Inglis, p. 373.

92. Sullivan, *Serjeant*, p. 271, claimed that while he was still in Dublin, both the Home Office and the Attorney General wrote, urging him to come and view the diaries, an offer he refused.

93. N.F. Dryhurst to Sir Sydney [Olivier], 2/7/1916; Olivier to [Thomson], 5/7/1916; Thomson to Sir Sydney [Olivier], 7/71916, MEPO 2/10672.

94. Quoted in MacColl, p. 211–12; Inglis, p. 374; and PRO HO 144/1636 ... /38.

95. Reid, pp. 384.

96. Doyle to Shorter, 13/7/1916, Casement Petition Papers, fol. 17.

97. Cant. to Samuel, 14/7/1916, PRO HO 144/1636/ ... 3A. The letter was acknowledged on 18/7/1916, HO to Cant., PRO HO 144/1636/... 3A.

98. Cant. to Harris, 14/07/1916, PRO HO 144/1636/ ... 3A.

99. Harris to Samuel, 17/7/1916, PRO HO 144/1636/ ... 49.

100. Harris to Blackwell, 20/7/1916, PRO HO 144/1636/ ... 3A; Harris to Cant., 20/7/1916, PRO HO 144/1636/ ... 49. Blackwell minuted the memo from Harris indicating how the latter had changed his mind.

101. R. Percy Smith MD, FRCP, and Maurice Craig MD, FRCP, 10/7/1916, PRO HO 144/1636/ ... 40. The 1911 Diary and Cash Ledger had been referred to them: CAB 41/37/25, 5/7/1916.

102. Blackwell, memos, 15/7/1916 and 17/7/1916, Cabinet Papers, PRO HO 144/1636/ ...

53 and Hyde, p. 200. He makes no comment on how such information came into the possession of the press. Blackwell's memos appear to be responding to the grounds cited in the Conan Doyle/Shorter appeal.

103. Hyde, p. 125.

104. *Ibid.* p. 127.

105. The full transcript can be found in Court of Criminal Appeal: Rex v. Roger David Casement, 17/7/1916, PRO HO 144/1636/31164333, pp. 1–74. For a summary see Hyde, pp. 130–2.

106. Hyde, pp. 132–4.

107. For details, see Bernard Wasserstein, *Herbert Samuel: A Political Life* (Oxford: Clarendon Press 1992), pp. 182–7. Wasserstein comments (p. 184) that 'Samuel's role in this affair was not impressive ... he sheltered behind the Cabinet and behind civil servants who, at least in the case of Blackwell, seemed almost as much concerned with asserting the prerogatives of the Home Office as with reaching a sensible political decision.'

108. For an account of events in the United States, see Tansill, pp. 202–14; Reid, pp. 419–24, provides good detail on the communications of the British ambassador, Cecil Spring-Rice.

109. CAB 41/37/25, 19/7/1916.

110. Parker, Special Report, 18/7/1916, PRO MEPO 2/10672.

111. Thomson to Blackwell, 26/7/1916, PRO HO 144/1637/ ... 140.

112. Thomson to Blackwell, 27/7/1916, PRO HO 144/1637/ ... 140. They had been forwarded by the British vice-consul, H. Charles Dick (see Appendix).

113. RDC to Nina, 25/7/1916, NLI MS 13600 (copy).

114. RDC to Cadbury, 26/7/1916, PRO HO 144/1637/ ...166; W. Cadbury to Home Office, 7/8/1916, PRO HO 144/1637/ ... 166; PRO HO 144/1636/ ... 182; PRO HO 144/1636/ ... 176.

115. RDC (Pentonville) to Morten, 28/7/1916, quoted in Hyde pp. 147–9. The 'polite letter' is likely to have been that accepting his knighthood.

116. RDC to ASG, 29/7/1916, PRO HO 144/1637/ ... 108.

117. G. Bannister, Statement, 2/8/1916, McMullen Papers.

118. Agnes [Nina] Newman (Atlantic City), PRO HO 144/1637/ ... 154. Charles Curry from Munich made a last-minute plea via the Vatican, as did Fisher Unwin in London.

119. CAB, 41/37/25, 3/8/1916 on the meeting of the previous day.

120. Denis Gwynn, 'Roger Casement's last weeks', *Studies*, 54 (Spring 1965), 63–73. Gwynn was told by Fr Crotty that 'Casement had told him of his desire to become a Catholic' when in Limburg. Gwynn found Crotty's testimony on other questions to be unreliable.

121. RDC to Fr Murnane, 16/7/1916, NLI MS 14100 and Denis Gwynn, 'Last weeks', 63–4. He told Murnane that he had had a letter from Fr O'Gorman, who was prohibited from visiting him again in the Tower. He was glad of news about the Fran-

ciscans in the Putumayo – the Franciscans were loved in Peru of old, he claimed. Denis Gwynn, 'Last weeks', 65.

122. The matter is discussed in Dennis Gwynn, 'Last weeks', 68–70.

123. Fr Carey to Parry, 5/8/1916, quoted in Gwynn, 'Last weeks', 69. A further account can be found in Milligan, 513–7.

124. Details in Hyde, pp. 157–8. After the execution, J.H. Morgan and Philip Morrell requested the release of the body. Morgan wrote: 'But Casement has now paid the full penalty – he has not only died a felon's death on the scaffold but before dying he was publicly degraded of all his honours, a step for which I believe there is no precedent in any treason case in the last 300 years. The law has therefore exacted its uttermost ... Roger Casement ... [is] now beyond the reach of human vengeance; it cannot matter to him whether his body remains in a felon's grave in Pentonville or not. But it matters a great deal to this unhappy lady sorrowing under a sorrow almost too grievous for any man or woman to bear. I cannot conceive of any petition which it would be easier for the authorities to grant and harder for any humane person to refuse.' Morgan to Samuel, 4/8/1916, PRO HO 144/1637/ ... 163. Morrell requested the body for private burial. The relatives, he said, gave an undertaking that the funeral would be private, with no demonstrations. Philip Morrell MP to Samuel, 4/8/1916, PRO HO 144/1637/ ... 164.

APPENDIX: THE BLACK DIARIES

1. Mansergh, p. 200, argues that 'the onus of proof ought to be on those who are convinced that the 'Black Diaries' are genuine'. Since I believe the diaries to be Casement's work, I refer to them as such in much of what follows.

2. They are held in the Public Record Office, Kew, classified as HO 161/1–5.

3. RDC to Roberts, 27/1/1913, quoted in Mitchell, *Journal*, p. 37, n. 36.

4. Curry, p. 9. And see NLI MS 1689, fol. 1.

5. Given that only two undisputed diaries exist in addition to the Black Diaries, suggestions that Casement was a habitual diarist may seem surprising. Sawyer opened his edition of the 1910 diaries with the words: 'Compulsive diary writing was a fairly common phenomenon in Edwardian times, but Roger Casement's compulsion was exceptional.' Yet on the same page he writes: 'Extant diaries are few.' Sawyer, *Diaries*, p. 1. And Mitchell has written: 'From looking at the nature and provenance of the various diaries it becomes clear that Casement conscientiously kept diaries or journals during large parts of his life ...' Angus Mitchell, 'Casement's Black Diaries: closed books reopened', *History Ireland* (Autumn 1997), 36–41, 38. Mackey actually accused the British Government of the illegal seizure of thirteen diaries (from 1900 to 1913) and cash ledgers for these years. Mackey, *Roger Casement: Forged Diaries* (Dublin: Fallon 1966), p. 14.

6. MacColl, p. 224.

7. Horgan, p. 240. See Inglis, p. 439; Reid, p. 472; Sawyer, *Diaries*, pp. 4–5.

8. Dudgeon, pp. 553–7. He also tells of the attempt by the IRA in 1937 to silence the professor, as does W.J. McCormack, *Roger Casement in Death or Haunting the Free State* (Dublin: UCD Press 2002), pp. 77–9. Roger Sawyer, 'The Black Diaries: a question of authenticity' in Daly, p. 91, cites evidence from the Casement family of its having destroyed some of Sir Roger's belongings.

9. Letitia Fairfield, review of Noyes and letter, *The New Statesman and Nation*, 4/5/1957 and 25/5/1957. Letitia Denny Fairfield CBE, MD, DPH was a pathologist, barrister and member of the Fabian Society, who became a convert to Catholicism in 1923. She had a keen interest in the Black Diaries question.

10. See the edition of the 1903 Diary by Ó Síocháin and O'Sullivan for this and the following extract. Ó Síocháin and O'Sullivan, *op. cit.*

11. Reid, p. 479.

12. *Ibid.* p. 465.

13. Quoted in Sawyer, *Diaries*, p. 11.

14. For an accurate account of this, see Deirdre McMahon, 'Roger Casement: an account of his reinterment in Ireland', *Irish Archives*, 3 (1) (Spring 1996), 3–12.

15. For details, see Sawyer, *Diaries*, pp. 10 and 13–16. Thomson had been dismissed from his post as assistant police commissioner in 1921.

16. For accounts, see Singleton-Gates and Girodias, pp. 21–5; Reid, pp. 475–6; Eoin Ó Máille, *Roger Casement: The Forged Diaries Exposed* (Dublin: M. Payne 1993), p. 12; Sawyer, *Diaries*, pp. 8–10; Mitchell, *Journal*, p. 31.

17. Quoted in Sawyer, *Diaries*, p. 16.

18. Singleton-Gates and Girodias. Singleton-Gates and Girodias did not publish the 1911 Diary. Montgomery Hyde published short extracts from it in his book on Casement's trial and Dudgeon has published an abridged edition (*The Black Diaries*). I do not know when the term 'Black Diaries' originated, but it predated the Singleton-Gates' volume. It is used, for example, in 1957 on the dust cover of Alfred Noyes, *The Accusing Ghost or Justice for Casement* (London: Gollancz 1957).

19. Denis Gwynn, *The Life and Death of Roger Casement* (London: Jonathan Cape 1936 [1930]); Parmiter; Maloney; Noyes. Noyes had been shown diary material in 1916. One positive contribution made by early forgery proponents was to begin to reconstruct the reprehensible pattern of use made of the diaries in 1916.

20. For an exhaustive treatment of the forgery debate, including the 'Normand defence' see McCormack. A more succinct account can be found in McDiarmid, 'Posthumous life', pp. 127–58.

21. Herbert O. Mackey, *The Life and Times of Roger Casement* (Dublin: Fallon 1954); *Crime against Europe, Forged Diaries*; Roger McHugh, 'Casement: the Public Record Office manuscripts', *Threshold*, 4 (1) (Summer 1960), 28–57. To the biographers who accepted the authenticity of the diaries must be added René MacColl, who got access to copies while preparing his biography but was circumscribed in his freedom to use them: MacColl.

22. BBC Radio 4, 23 September 1993. Sawyer (*Diaries*, pp. 18–19, 22; 'The Black Diaries', (pp. 95 and 97–8) gives details of two other occasions when the diaries were tested, a handwriting test by Dr Wilson Harrison and an ultra-violet ray test (witnessed by Letitia Fairfield). The results, however, were never made publicly available.

23. Sawyer, *Diaries*; Mitchell, *Journal*.

24. Audrey Giles, *Examination of Casement Diaries* (The Giles Document Laboratory, Amersham, Bucks February 2002). The tests were carried out in accordance with a brief from a supervising committee led by Professor W.J. McCormack of Goldsmiths College, London. The proceedings of the Royal Irish Academy symposium have now been published and the Giles report has been included in Daly, pp. 202–37.

25. Mackey, *Forged Diaries*, pp. 55–73.

26. McHugh, 'Manuscripts', p. 56.

27. See Maloney, pp. 198–200; Reid, pp. 479–80, where he discusses three versions of the interpolation approach; Sawyer, *Diaries*, p. 17.

28. Mackey, *Forged Diaries*, p. 56, on the 1911 Diary. Reid comments: 'But Mackey's argument is so incoherent and so full of errors, of illogic and misprision, that it is better dismissed out of hand' (p. 463, and see pp. 484–5).

29. Angus Mitchell, 'The riddle of the two Casements?' in Daly, pp. 105, 106.

30. For an example of the handwriting argument, see Mitchell, *Journal*, p. 349, n. 244. Eoin Ó Máille and his collaborators have concluded that 'Handwriting Examination has lost any authority it might claim' and have turned instead to a series of comparisons between undisputed Casement documents and the Black Diaries. Finding striking contrasts between the style of Casement's formal writings and that in the diaries, they conclude that they are not the work of the same author or that they lack Casement's distinctive 'linguistic finger-print' and 'deep-structure' patterns. Eoin Ó Máille, M. Uí Callanán and M. Payne, *The Vindication of Roger Casement: Computer Analyses & Comparisons etc.* (privately published 1994); Ó Máille, *Exposed*.

31. One should note that Casement writings in the possession of the authorities would not include any of his letters to friends, unless he had kept drafts or copies.

32. It has been pointed out that late evening is a typical time for sexual cruising and that sexual matter in the diaries would tend, therefore, to be placed at the end of each day's entry.

33. Giles, 'Report', p. 3 and p. 26.

34. Mitchell, 'Riddle', pp. 99–120. He has been more cautious in his edition of the 1911 documents, publishing them without suggesting discrepancies. In the Introduction (*1911 Documents*, p. xxvi) he writes: 'One intention of this volume is to allow a knowledgeable contextualising of the two contested diaries for 1911 so that a more balanced and less opinionated assessment of their authenticity might eventually be made using scientific methods of history.'

35. But, in order to test the authenticity of the 1910 Black Diary, Mitchell filled out the record of Casement's movements from the time he left London in August until he returned in December by drawing on other documents written by the latter.

This longer narrative he calls the 'Amazon Journal' of Roger Casement.

36. Mitchell, 'Riddle', p. 115, writes that 'there are 42 footnotes in *The Amazon Journal of Roger Casement* highlighting discrepancies which suggest another hand at work'. I have looked at these 'discrepancies', and find them unconvincing, in Séamas Ó Síocháin, 'Ruarí Mac Easmainn: an dubh agus an bán' ('Roger Casement: the black and the white'), *Oghma*, 10 (1998), 57–66.

37. On 29 September, Casement wrote in the Putumayo Journal: 'I swear to God, I'd hang every one of the band of wretches with my own hands if I had the power, and do it with the greatest pleasure. I have never shot game with any pleasure, have indeed, abandoned all shooting for that reason, that I dislike the thought of taking life. *I have never given life to anyone myself, and my celibacy makes me frugal of human life*, but I'd shoot or exterminate these infamous scoundrels more gladly than I should shoot a crocodile or kill a snake.' Mitchell suggests that those 'who believe in the "authenticity" of both "black" and "white" diaries should ask themselves exactly what Casement means by this reference to his "celibacy"'. In response, one might suggest that when referring to celibacy in this quotation, he speaks of never giving life to anyone, i.e. not fathering a child. This usage is confirmed in a similar passage elsewhere, when he talks of the exploiters on the Putumayo: 'These lords and masters, the undisputed *givers of life (they all have harems of ravished girls and women)* and death, they all murder ...' Again, the contrast is between the giving of life and the taking of life; he is celibate in the sense that he has never given life. This is consistent with dictionary usage, where one can find two possible meanings: unmarried or sexually chaste. Mitchell has chosen the latter, but Casement's own usage is different. Indeed, one could take Casement's usage as a hint regarding his homosexuality.

38. Mitchell, *Journal*, p. 44.

39. With regard to the first of these lines of argument it can be suggested that, if two parallel diaries (of different purpose) were being kept, it is unreasonable to expect total replication of content in each or to take variations between content as evidence of forgery. And with regard to Casement's eye problem, it can be argued that Mitchell's presentation is couched in language that exaggerates the phenomenon and the contrast between the two types of source. An examination of the narrative of Casement's journey reveals that he had mentioned his eyes only four times before the first Black Diary reference, twice (close together) in private letters to the Foreign Office, on 11 August (to Spicer) and 14 August (to Tyrrell), and twice (again close together), on 12 September (to Tyrrell) and 13 September (to Spicer). In other words, Casement was particularly conscious of his eyes in mid August and mid September. Note, too, Mitchell's language: 'mounting concern', 'momentarily blind', 'fifteen separate occasions', 'rather nonchalantly mentioned' (what, for example, is 'nonchalant' about the 10 October entry?). One might also note that the 1911 Cash Ledger contains at least eight references to Casement's problem with his eyes: 24 February, 1, 3, 11 March, 7, 13, 14 June and the end of June summary.

40. Mitchell, *Journal*, p. 222, n. 169. Mitchell included photographs of pages from the respective diaries between pp. 256 and 257 of his book. The reader is invited to compare the handwriting.
41. Giles, 'Report', p. 44.
42. RDC to Meyer, 8/3/1915, quoted in Doerries, *Prelude*, p. 87; RDC to Cowper, 6/1/1914, NLI Acc. 49902 (10); Inglis, p. 213. See, also, Sawyer, *Flawed Hero*, p. 112, where Casement wrote a pencilled letter to J.H. Morgan with a longer ink postscript.
43. Mitchell, *Journal*, p. 44.
44. *Ibid.* pp. 211, 222, 223 and 230.
45. As with the 1910 Diary, the 1903 Diary starts at the beginning of the year; it is hard to argue, therefore, that Casement intended it as a record of his Congo investigation. The survival of diaries coinciding with the Congo and Putumayo investigations may suggest that Casement stored items related to these two major public episodes in the same place.
46. Another example can be found in the Black Diary for 9 September 1910, concerning the launch *Argentina*, which is one of Mitchell's Black Diary contradictions (*Journal*, p. 97, n. 105 and pp. 102–3, n. 112).
47. An example of the former is his letter to Hobson of 7/2/1909, giving as his address Ward's address of Ave. Malakoff in Paris and adding, 'going next week Paris'.
48. Adrian Weale, *Patriot Traitors: Roger Casement, John Amery and the Real Meaning of Treason* (London: Viking 2001), p. 246. The term 'nationalist' would be more appropriate than 'republican'.
49. McHugh, 'Manuscripts'.
50. *Ibid.* p. 38.
51. *Ibid.* p. 41. McHugh uses the terms 'moronic', 'pathic', 'insanity', 'sub-human' etc.
52. Mitchell, *Journal*, pp. 9, 26, 27, 35 and 42. For the present author, the terminology used to characterize the sexual content of the diaries raises a number of issues. First, I believe it distorts the actual record of the diaries; the protagonist is not 'pederast', 'sexual predator' and 'perverter of the innocent', he sought sex in the public domain from others on a similar quest, youths included. Second, though forgery advocates deny that the protagonist in the diaries is Casement, the issue does raise the question of the moral responsibility of the scholar in employing such language.
53. Mitchell, 'Riddle', p. 112.
54. Dudgeon, Royal Irish Academy Address, 6 May 2000; Michael O'Sullivan, 'Case closed', *Gay Community News*, May 2002, p. 12. Mitchell accepts Casement's homosexuality, while still maintaining that the diaries were forged: 'He was always an embarrassment to Catholic Ireland. Even today, most of those who feel the diaries are forged deny that he was homosexual, and that is untenable.' Quoted in Nigel Jones, 'The Killing of Roger Casement', *The Guardian*, 28 February 1998, p. 6. Edwards, 'Trial', pp. 174, 175, suggests that 'Casement was probably homosexual in nature, though not necessarily in performance', and he names Frank Ezra Adcock as a 'good candidate' to be the forger.

55. See H. Montgomery Hyde, *The Other Love: an Historical and Contemporary Survey of Homosexuality in Britain* (London: Heinemann 1970), p. 5.

56. RDC to FO, 25/5/03, PRO FO 10/804.

57. Mitchell, *Journal*, pp. 168–9 and Sawyer, *Diaries*, pp. 90–1. Mitchell (wrongly) has Condenhor for Coudenhove and he does not include the final clause of the sentence ('at 9 am ...') in his Black Diary quotation.

58. Sawyer, *Diaries*, p. 91.

59. Reid, p. 109. For a reflective discussion on another passage – the case of Sir Hector Macdonald – see Dudgeon, pp. 121–4.

60. The only possible exception is the short period in the Putumayo, when Casement kept two journals.

61. Reid, p. 479.

62. While the manuscript readings are uncertain in places and therefore the original meanings, it seems certain that the phrases do have a sexual content. See Ó Síocháin and O'Sullivan.

63. RDC to Gertrude, 20/4/1903, NLI MS 13074/5. For a long list of items from the 1903 Diary, which he is convinced could not be known to a forger, see Daniel Vangroenweghe, 'Casement's Congo Diary, one of the so-called Black Diaries, was not a forgery', *Revue belge d'histoire contemporaine*, xxxii, 3/4 (2002), 321–50. Vangroenweghe is an anthropologist, who has conducted extensive research in the Congo.

64. The script in the original is the older Irish one, for which I have substituted the present-day romanized script A further example can be found under 'Tuesday 14 June 1910', which both Singleton Gates and Sawyer render as: '... up by Parcmoft car to Ballymena ...' The manuscript has 'Parc-mór' (*mór* = 'big'), corresponding to Parkmore in English. Dudgeon, p. 218, identifies this as Parkmore railway halt above Cushendall.

65. RDC to Mary Hutton, 19/9/07, NLI MS 15, 535; O'Duffy to RDC, 9/6/1908, NLI MS 13073 (13/i).

66. For a realistic assessment of British intelligence capabilities at the time, see Christopher Andrew, 'Casement and British Intelligence' in Daly, pp. 74–87. Andrew (p. 74) remarks: 'We need to approach the myth-encrusted history of British intelligence and Sir Roger Casement, like that of some other British intelligence operations in Ireland, with more than usual care.'

67. Mitchell, 'Riddle', p. 115, writes: 'Since the diaries were not independently identified in the physical condition we now know then [*sic*] until 1959 the authorities had 43 years to perfect the forgery.'

68. This material was part of a selection of documents released at a Royal Irish Academy Seminar in May 2000, some of which adds crucial new information on the manner in which the diaries came into the possession of the authorities. The conference was informed that these documents were due to be released to the PRO in the near future.

69. However, some caution is also needed in assessing these statements. Other evidence

indicates that, by January 1915, intelligence sources had discovered some of Casement's addresses, including Allisons and Mr Germain's at 50 Ebury St. The lodgings could have been searched at any time after that. See Frank Hall to Lloyd, 15/1/1915, PRO KV 2/6.

70. PRO HO 1637/311643/139 ref. 20261. See Sawyer, *Diaries*, p. 24. Because all of this material derives from official British sources, believers in forgery (if not ignoring it) tend to treat it with suspicion. It is, of course, conceivable that forgers could have concealed their forgery from, for example, FO officials.

71. Documents released for RIA Symposium, May 2000.

72. PRO HO 1636/ ... /7A ... 235, and PRO HO 144/1637/311643/139, ref. 20261. For 'Millar' in the 1910 Diary, see Sawyer, *Diaries*, pp. 52–3. Major Frank Hall was the MI5 officer who reported on the identification. Dudgeon, in *The Black Diaries*, has probed further into the background of Joseph Millar Gordon.

73. Dr R. Percy Smith and Dr Maurice Craig (87 Harley St.), 10/7/1916, PRO HO 144/1636/311643/40.

74. Statement of porters Russ and Suck, 11/7/1916; Statement of G. Gatti (who had been head waiter), 12/7/1916; Statement of H. Degeraud (gentleman), 17/7/1916; Statement of Henriette Christensen (Adler's mother), 18/7/1916; Statement of Mr Korth (porter at the Victoria Hotel), 19/7/1916; Statement of E.W. Jacobsen (Inspector of Taxes), 19/7/1916; Statement of Gustav Olsen (chief reception clerk), 21/7/1916. PRO HO 144/1637/311643/140 ref. 20261. Because these and the following pieces of evidence derive from official British sources, forgery advocates tend to be suspicious of them. Some, however, have come to accept, on the basis of the Norwegian evidence, that Casement was homosexual, while still maintaining that the diaries were forged.

75. Dr Percy R. Mander (Medical Officer, Pentonville Prison) to Sir Herbert Smalley (Medical Commissioner of Prisons), 3/8/1916, PRO HO 144/1637/311643/141 ref. 29261. The instruction to Dr Mander to carry out this examination itself points to the desire to provide evidence on Casement's sexuality.

Bibliography

PRIMARY SOURCES

The Allen Library, Christian Brothers, North Richmond Street, Dublin
Monteith Papers and Diary.

Baptist Missionary Society Archives, Regent's Park College, Oxford
Congo/Angola: Bentley letters and Journal; Journals of A.D. Slade, A/30, A/31, A/34.

Belfast Central Library
Francis Joseph Bigger Collection: Casement Correspondence.

Berlin-Branderburgische Akademie der Wissenschaften
Eduard Meyer, 'Personal Memories', NL Eduard Meyer 357.
RDC to Eduard Meyer, NL Eduard Meyer 358.

British Library
RDC to Fox Bourne, 1894, Add. MSS 46912 fols. 24–9.
RDC to John Harris, Add. MSS 46912 fols. 30–1.
Gladstone Papers, vol. XCIX May 1916–Dec. 1917, Add. MSS 46083 fols. 13, 22.
Sir Arthur Conan Doyle, 'A Petition to the Prime Minister on behalf of Roger Casement'.
Casement Petition Papers, Add. MSS 63596.

British Library of Political and Economic Science (London School of Economics)
Morel Papers, Letters of RDC: F5/3; F8/4; F8/16–25; F8/53; F8/67.
A.G. Gardiner Papers: 1/6A, RDC to Gardiner, 1911–13.

Central Library, Birmingham
Cadbury Archive, MS 466; MS 466a/561.

Central Library, Liverpool
Holt Collection.

National Library Of Ireland
MS 1622–3 Typescript, Putumayo Diaries.
MSS 1689–90 German Diaries, 7/11/1914– 28/3/1916.
MS 5244 'Last page of my diary, Berlin', 17/3/1916–8/4/1916.
MS 5459 Casement to Elsa Douglas, Miss Doyle, Plunkett, Miss A. Meyer etc.
MS 5462 Correspondence with Gaffneys etc., 1915–16.
MS 5463 Correspondence, 1911–14.
MS 5611 Letters to Dr Enright, Cork, 1914.
MSS 7982–4 Henry Papers.
MS 8358 Letters to William Cadbury, 1905–16.
MS 8605 Letters to St John Gaffney, 1915–16.
MS 8612 Letters to Mary Hutton, 1904–14.
MS 9932 Cuttings and Notes by Mrs Green, & Life of RDC by Mrs Newman, 1890–1918.
MS 10880 Eoin MacNeill Papers: Casement.
MS 10464 Alice Stopford Green Papers, 1904–16.
MS 10763–65 Documents of George Gavan Duffy: briefs, notes, correspondence.
MS 10999 J.M. Plunkett Papers, correspondence, 1911–15.
MS 12114–15 Poems by RDC, 1882–3.
MS 12116 Journal & Note Book of RDC, 1899.
MS 12117 Address & Memo Book of RDC 1901.
MS 13073 Various letters to RDC, 1895–1916.
MS 13074 Letters to Gertrude Bannister, 1889–1915.
MS 13076 Family letters to RDC, 1900–15.
MS 13077 Items on Casement family, 1850–1916.
MS 13078 Letters from and to RDC.
MS 13079 RDC's life: Gertrude Bannister.
MS 13080 Letters to and from RDC, 1901–14.
MS 13081 RDC to FO, 1898–1913.
MS 13082 Articles, poems etc. by and about RDC.
MS 13085 Letters concerning Germany and Irish Brigade, 1914–16.
MS 13086 Miscellaneous: Congo, CRA, Morel, 1903–12.
MS 13087 Brazil and Putumayo correspondence, 1907–12.
MS 13088 Trial, prison, execution, burial, 1916 (including 1916 'Brief to Counsel').
MS 13089 Miscellaneous, Africa, Peru, Ireland, Germany, 1901–45.
MS 13091 G. Barry Gifford, 'Princess and Patriot – Sir Roger Casement and the Princess Blücher'.
MS 13100 Letters concerning Irish Brigade.
MSS 13158–75 Bulmer Hobson Papers.
MS 13600 Photocopies of letters of RDC & associated documents.
MS 14100 Eamon de Valera's collection of letters. Seven letters: RDC to Alice Green, 1916.
MS 15138 Cheque stubs, vouchers, a/c statements, mainly 1910–11.
MS 15535 Mary Hutton to RDC.
MS 17587 Germany: additional diary pages, April 1916.
MS 17594 Short biographies by Nina [Agnes] Casement, Elizabeth and Gertrude Bannister.
MS 17595 Five Casement pedigrees.
MS 18574 RDC to Mary Causton.
MSS 21530–1 F.J. Bigger Papers and correspondence (Tawin).
MS 21536 F.J. Bigger Papers.
Acc. 4902 RDC to Richard Morten, Francis Cowper and others.

Microfilm:
P 4645 N 4657 Letters to J.J. Horgan, 1913–14.
P 1355 N 1154 British Museum Add. MS 46,912M, RDC to Fox Bourne.
P 6830 N 6102 Sanford Exploring Expedition.

National Library of Scotland
RDC to Revd W. Marwick, 24/4/1893, Creek Town. MS 2984 fol. 197.
RDC to R.B. Cunninghame Graham, 1904. Deposit 205, Correspondence and Literary
   Papers of R.B. Cunninghame Graham, box 1/2C.

National Register of Archives, Scotland
Hamilton Papers: Miscellaneous letters of T.H. Hoste, bundles 2772–3.
Farquharson of Invercauld Papers.

National University of Ireland, University College Dublin, Archives
RDC to Captain Hans Boehm, UCD P. 127.
Michael McKeogh Papers, UCD P. 128.

National University of Ireland, Maynooth
C.P. Scott Correspondence: Casement Correspondence, A/C25/1–20.

Plunkett Foundation for Co-operative Studies, Long Hanborough, Oxford
Papers and Diaries of Sir Horace Plunkett.

Public Record Office, London (Kew)
Oil Rivers, 1892–5
   FO 403: Africa, Confidential Print: 403/171, 1891–2, Oil Rivers Protectorate: Corre-
      spondence: print no. 6351; 403/187, 1893, Niger Territories: Correspondence: Print
      no. 6471; 403/200, 1894; Print no. 6572; 403/215, 1895 Jan.–June; Print no. 6697;
      403/216, 1895 July–Dec., Niger Territories: Correspondence; Print no. 6783; 403/217,
      1895, Chiefs of Brass, Print no. 6668.
   FO 2: 2/50, 1893, Niger Coast/Oil Rivers Protectorate; 2/52, 1893; 2/62, 1894; 2/63, 1894
      Jan.–Aug.; 2/64, 1894 Sept.–Dec.
   FO 84 Niger Coast 1891–3 – Slave Trade: 84/2193, drafts, 1892 (vol. 2), 229; 84/2194,
      despatches, 1892 (vol. 3), 229; 84/2195, telegrams & paraphrases, 1893 (vol. 4), 229.
   PRO MPK sketch maps: 141/1–3 and FO 2/64, ff. 30A, 30B, 72; lithograph versions: FO
      925/621–3.
Lourenço Marques, 1895–8
   FO 403: Confidential Print: 403/223, 1895–6, Correspondence, Delagoa Bay Railway
      Co.; 403/231, 1896 Jan.–June, Affairs South of Zambesi, Correspondence. 403/232,
      1896 July–Dec., *ibid.*; 403/247, 1897, *ibid.*; 403/257, 1897, Delagoa Bay Railway Co.;
      403/266, 1898, Affairs South of Zambesi; 403/276, Delagoa Bay Railway Co.
   FO 63: Portugal – Diplomatic, Consular, Commercial: 63/1297, 1895; 63/1315, 1896;
      63/1316, 1896; 63/1317, 1896; 63/1318, 1896; 63/1336, 1897.
St Paul De Loanda, 1898–9
   FO 63: Portugal: 63/1352, 1898, General Correspondence – Portugal. Consuls; 63/1353,
      1898, *ibid.*; 63/1365, 1899, *ibid.*; 63/1375, 1900, *ibid.*
   FO 2: Portugal – consuls at Loanda: 2/230, 1899, General Correspondence – Africa;
      2/368, 1900, Portugal – consuls at Loanda – Casement.

FO 629: Belgium, Congo Free State – Embassy & Consular Archives: 629/5, 1899 (St Paul de Loanda, Vice-Consulate).

FO 375: Loanda (Portugal) – Embassy & Consular Archives: 375/5, 1891–1905, Register of Correspondence.

FO 425: Confidential Print: 425/237, 1897–8, Commercial Negotiations between Great Britain & Portugal – Confidential Print, 7215; 425/243, 1899, *ibid.* Confidential Print, 7421; 425/252, 1901, *ibid.* Confidential Print, 7820.

South Africa, 1899–1900

FO 2: 2/365, 1900; 2/366, 1900 (I); 2/367, 1900 (I); 2/368, 1900; FO 63/1375, 1900 Aug.–Oct.

CO 879: 879/56, 1899, Confidential Print – Telegrams: Milner to Chamberlain; 879/61, 1899; 879/63, 1900, *ibid.*; 545/10, 1900.

Congo Free State, 1900–3

FO 2: 2/217, 1899, Belgium – Telegrams; 2/336, 1900, Congo – Casement; 2/491, 1901; 2/626, 1902, consuls for Congo State; 2/764, 1903, Congo – Casement.

FO 10: 10/721, 1895–9; 10/751, 1901; 10/754, 1900–1; 10/773, 1902; 10/789, 1904; 10/803, 1903 Jan.–May 20; 10/804, May 21–June; 10/805, July–Sept. 18; 10/806, Sept. 19–Dec. 14; 10/807, Dec. 15 1903–Feb. 10 1904; 10/808, Feb. 11–Mar. 1904; 10/809, Apr.–May; 10/810, June–July; 10/811, Aug.–Sept.; 10/812, Oct.–Dec.; 10/813, Jan.–Apr. 1905; 10/814, May–Sept.; 10/815, Oct.–Dec..

FO 629: Belgium, Congo Free State – Embassy & Consular Archives: 629/9, 1902, Roger Casement – Congo Atrocities; 629/10, 1903, Protection of Natives, Baptist Mission; 629/11, 1903, Congo Atrocities; 629/12, 1903, *ibid.*

FO 403: Confidential Prints: 403/304, 1891–1900; 403/305, 1900–1; 403/327, 1902; 403/338, 1903; 403/351, 1904; 403/364, 1905; 403/372, Jan.–Mar. 1906; 403/373, Apr.–June; 403/374, July–Dec.; 403/387, Jan.–June 1907; 403/388, July–Dec.; 403/399, Jan.–June 1908; 403/400, July–Dec.; 403/409, Jan.–June 1909; 403/410, July–Dec.; 403/417, Jan.–June 1910; 403/418, July–Dec.

Brazil, 1906–10

FO 128: Rio Legation Records: 128/308, 1906, Consuls; 128/315, 1907, Consuls; 128/324, 1908, Consuls; 128/334, 1909, Consuls; 128/343, 1910, Consuls; 128/361, 1911–12, Putumayo.

FO 369: General Correspondence, Consular: 369/4–5, 1906, Brazil, Consular; 369/51, 1906–7, Santos; 369/ 63, 1907, *ibid.*; 369/64, *ibid.*; 369/123, 1908, Pará; 369/124, *ibid.*; 369/125, *ibid.*; 369/196, 1909, *ibid.*, Rio; 369/197, *ibid.*; 369/198, *ibid.*; 369/276–8, 1910, *ibid.*; 369/355–6, 1911, *ibid.*; 369/446–8, 1912, *ibid.*

FO 743: General Correspondence, Consular: 743/2, 1903–7, Correspondence Register of Rio Consuls General, 743/3, 1908–10, *ibid.*; 743/4, 1910–14, *ibid.*; 743/5, 1911–14, *ibid.*; 743/22, 1908, Pará.

Putumayo, 1910–12

FO 371: 371/367, 1907, Miscellaneous Files 11255–22794; 371/368, *ibid.* 23992–42260; 371/722, 1909–10, Peru, Bolivia, Ecuador; 371/967, 1910, *ibid.*; 371/968, *ibid.*; 371/1200, 1911; 371/1201, *ibid.*; 371/1202, *ibid.*; 371/1203, *ibid.*; 371/1451, 1912, *ibid.*; 371/1452, *ibid.*; 371/1453, *ibid.*; 371/1454, *ibid.*; 371/1732, 1913, *ibid.*; 371/1733, *ibid.*; 371/1734, *ibid.*; 371/2081, *ibid.*; 371/2082, *ibid.*

FO 177, Consul, Iquitos: 177/375, 1912; 177/386, *ibid.*

Ireland and Germany, 1914–16

CO 904: 904/194/46, 1914, Chief Secretary's Office, Ireland; 904/195, Ireland, Sir Roger Casement, 1913–20.

PCOM (Prison Commission and Home Office): 9/2317; 9/2326; 9/2330.

FO 95/776.

HO 144/1636/311643/3A; .../32A; .../38; ...7A–235; 144/1637/311643/67–166; .../194a.

HO 161/1–5: War Office Army Book for 1901; Casement Diaries for 1903, 1910, 1911 and Cash Ledger for 1911.

CAB Cabinet Papers: 37/151/8, 13, 35; 37/152/, 1, 4, 13, 18, 29, 32; 41/37/25–9.

KV Records of the Security Service: 2/6–10.

Public Record Office, Northern Ireland

D2711/1–4: RDC to Baron von Horst; Bulmer Hobson, 'Irish National Chart'.

D3301/CA/7: Qua Iboe Mission Papers. S.A. Bill, 'Diary, Aug. 1891–Aug. 1894'; Qua Iboe Mission, 'Occasional Paper', May 1893.

T2646/10: RDC to Miss O'Rourke.

T3072: fifteen documents, June 1912–Aug. 1916, mainly RDC to Lady Constance Emmott.T3787/1–19: transcripts of nineteen letters (1871–1916), Casement family, including Roger Casement.

Sanford Memorial Library and Museum, Sanford, Florida

Correspondence of Sanford Exploring Expedition, box 28, fols. 1–5.

University of Birmingham

Cadbury Papers, Cadbury; pamphlet: 'A Protestant Protest', Ballymoney, 24 October 1913; Public Testimonial to E.D. Morel.

University of Dublin, Trinity College

RDC to Henry Foley, 34/96, TCD Misc. Photocopy 89.

RDC to Fritz Pincus, 1896–1915, TCD Misc. Box XXXVII.

RDC to Henry W. Farrell, TCD Misc. Autograph 304.

RDC to T.P. Gill, Gill Autograph, TCD 4733/3–5.

RDC to Liam de Róiste, TCD 10539/363.

RDC to Evelyn Gleeson, TCD 10676/17, 53, 66, 94, 159–60.

Kilteragh Guest Book, TCD 9923.

Joseph Campbell, 'Northern Autobiography', 4, TCD MS 10189/261–75.

University of Edinburgh

William Marwick Papers: Gen. 768/1, Correspondence; Gen. 768/3, Pocket Diary, 1892; Gen. 768/4, Pocket Diary, 1894; Gen. 768/2, 1–30; Gen. 768/5, Elizabeth Marwick (neé Hutton), Diary, Duke Town, Old Calabar, 1891; Gen. 768/6, *ibid.*, 1892; Gen. 768/7, *ibid.*, 1893; Gen. 768/8, *ibid.*, 1894.

University of Oxford, Bodleian Library

Bryce Papers, RDC to Bryce; ASG to Bryce etc., MS Bryce 48, fols. 91–9; MS Bryce 72, fols. 112–70.

Nevinson Diaries, MSS Eng. misc. e. 610–28.

University of Oxford, Rhodes House

Holt Papers: RDC to John Holt, MSS Afr. s. 1525.

Papers of the Anti-Slavery Society: MSS British Empire S19 D1/13, Travers Buxton (out), 1/7/1913–10/3/1914; S19 D2/1, Harris (in), 1910; S19 D2/2, Buxton (in), 1911; S19 D2/3, Buxton (in), 1912; S19 D2/4, Buxton (in), 1913; S19 D4/1, Harris (in), Jan.–July 1912; S19 D4/2, Harris (in), July–Oct. 1912; S19 D4/3, Harris (in), Nov. 1912–Apr. 1913; S19 D4/4,

Harris (in) 1913–15; S19 D4/5, Harris (in) 1913–14; S22 G32, Congo: Dennett; S22 G317–24, Peru, Pro-Indigena Association; S22 G330–48, Putumayo Enquiry; S22 G822–24, Putumayo, 1961–71 Acquisitions; S24 J28 and 49 Putumayo, 1912–14, press cuttings; S353, Lady Harris, draft biography of Sir John Harris.

University of Oxford, Nuffield College, Oxford
Emmott Papers: RDC to Alfred Emmott, box 3, 1906, fols. 371–82, 391; box 4, 1909, fols. 258–62.

Private Papers
Farmleigh House, Dublin
  Casement Papers, 9. 1X, E2.
Hatfield House, Salisbury Papers
  Casement to Lord Salisbury/Henry Foley, 3M/A98/90–6, 1895–1900.
Oliver McMullan Papers, Cushendall, Co. Antrim
  Miscellaneous Casement Papers.

British Government Papers
Report on the Administration of the Niger Coast Protectorate, Aug. 1891–Aug. 1894, PP 1895 (Cd. 7596) LXXI.
Report on the Administration of the Niger Coast Protectorate, 1894–5, PP 1895 (Cd. 7916) LXXI.
Report for the Year 1896 on the Trade and Commerce of Lorenzo Marques, FO, Diplomatic & Consular Reports on Trade & Finance, Portugal, Annual Series, no. 1904, 1897 (C. 8277–122) XCII.
Report for the Year 1899 on the Trade and Commerce of Angola, FO, Diplomatic and Consular Reports, Portugal, Annual Series, no. 2555, 1901.
Correspondence and Report from His Majesty's Consul at Boma respecting the Administration of the Independent State of the Congo, PP 1904 (Cd. 1933), LXII.
Further Correspondence Respecting the Administration of the Independent State of the Congo, PP 1904 (Cd. 2097), LXII.
Report for the Years 1905–6 on the Trade of Santos, FO, Diplomatic and Consular Reports, Brazil, Annual Series, no. 3952, 1908.
Report for the Year 1907 on the Trade of Pará, FO, Diplomatic and Consular Reports, Brazil, Annual Series no. 4111 (C.3727–194), CIX, 1908.
Correspondence Respecting the Treatment of British Colonial Subjects and Native Indians Employed in the Collection of Rubber in the Putumayo District, Miscellaneous, no. 8, 1912.
Royal Commission on the Civil Service, Appendix to the Fifth Report, Minutes of Evidence, PP 1914–16 (Cd. 7749), 1914 (the 'Putumayo Blue Book').
Documents Relative to the Sinn Féin Movement (Cd. 1108), XXIX (London: His Majesty's Stationery Office, 1921).

US Government Papers
Slavery in Peru, Washington, House of Representatives, Document no. 1366, 7 Feb. 1913.

Selected Publications by Roger Casement
Casement, Roger, 'Redistribution', *United Irishman*, vol. 13, no. 315 (11 March 1905), 6.
—, 'The Irishman as Soldier – Glimpses at the Irish Annals', *Freeman's Journal*, 16/9/1905, 8 and 23/9/1905.

—, *Irishmen and the English Army* (with Alice Stopford Green and Bulmer Hobson), Dungannon Club Publications no.1, n.d.[1905].

—, 'The Putumayo Indians', *Contemporary Review*, 102 (1912), 317–28.

—, 'The Irishry of Ulster', *The Nation*, 11 October 1913.

—, 'Ulster and Ireland', *Fortnightly Review*, 1 November 1913.

—, 'Chivalry', *Fianna Handbook* (issued by the Central Council of Na Fianna Éireann for the Boy Scouts of Ireland, 1914), pp. 75–86.

—, 'The Romance of Irish History' in Joseph Dunn and P.J. Lennon (eds.) *The Glories of Ireland* (Washington D.C.: Phoenix Ltd 1914), reprinted in Ó Cléirigh, pp. 42–53.

—, 'From Clontarf to Berlin: national status in sport', *Irish Volunteer*, 1, no. 1 (1914), 2.

—, 'Why I Went to Germany' [1916], reprinted in Mackey (ed.), *Crime against Europe*, pp. 144–8.

Gertrude Bannister [Parry] (ed.), *Some Poems of Roger Casement* (Dublin: Talbot Press 1918).

For further writings by Casement see Curry; Doerries (*Prelude*); Dudgeon; Mackey (*Crime against Europe*); Mitchell (*Journal, 1911 Documents*); Ó Síocháin and O'Sullivan; Sawyer (*Diaries*); and Singleton-Gates.

SELECTED SECONDARY SOURCES

Ajayi, J.F., Ade, *Christian Missions in Nigeria 1841–1891* (Evanston: Northwestern UP 1969).

Andrew, Christopher, 'Casement and British Intelligence' in Mary E. Daly (ed.), *Roger Casement in Irish and World History* (Dublin: Royal Irish Academy 2005), pp. 74–87.

Anene, J.C., *Southern Nigeria in Transition 1885–1906* (Cambridge: CUP 1966).

Arnold, David, *Britain, Europe and the World, 1870–1955* (London: Edward Arnold 1966).

Ascherson, Neal, *The King Incorporated: Leopold the Second and the Congo* (London: Granta Books 1999 [1963]).

Axelson, Sigbert, *Culture Confrontation in the Lower Congo: From the Old Congo Kingdom to the Congo Independent State with Special Reference to the Swedish Missionaries in the 1880s and 1890s* (Studia Missionalia Upsaliensia XIV, Falköping, Sweden: Gummesons 1970).

Bahr, Philip Manson, *Patrick Manson* (London: Thomas Nelson 1962).

Bardon, Jonathan, *A History of Ulster* (Belfast: Blackstaff Press 1992).

Barttelot, Walter George, *The Life of Edmund Musgrave Barttelot*, 3rd edn. (London: R. Bentley & Sons 1890).

Bentley, William Holman, *Life on the Congo* (London: Religious Tract Society n.d.).

—, *Pioneering on the Congo*, 2 vols. (London: Religious Tract Society 1900).

Bigelow, Poultney, *Seventy Summers*, 2 vols. (London: E. Arnold 1925).

Biographie Colonial Belge, vols. 1–5 (Bruxelles: Institut Royal Colonial Belge 1948–58).

Black, R.D. Collison, *Economic Thought and the Irish Question, 1817–1870* (Cambridge: CUP 1960).

Blücher, Evelyn Princess, *An English Wife in Berlin* (London: Constable 1920).

—, *Memoirs*, ed. Evelyn, Princess Blücher (London: John Murray 1932).

Blunt, Wilfrid Scawen, *My Diaries: Being a personal narrative of events, 1888–1914*, 2 vols. (London: Martin Secker 1919–20).

Bourne, H.R. Fox, *Civilization in Congoland: a Story of International Wrong-doing* (London: P.S. King and Son 1903).

Bower, Peter, 'Appendix: paper history & analysis as a research procedure' in Mary E. Daly (ed.), *Roger Casement in Irish and World History* (Dublin: Royal Irish Academy 2005), pp. 243–52.

Broeker, Galen, 'Roger Casement: background to treason', *Journal of Modern History*, XXIX (1957), 237–45.

Byrne, Francis J. and F.X. Martin (eds.), *The Scholar Revolutionary: Eoin Mac Neill 1867–1945* (Shannon: Irish University Press 1974).

Callanan, Frank, 'Between treason and blood-sacrifice: the trials of Roger Casement' in Mary E. Daly (ed.), *Roger Casement in Irish and World History* (Dublin: Royal Irish Academy 2005), pp. 121–37.

Casement, Hugh, *The Family of Casement of Magherintemple, Ballycastle, Co. Antrim* (mimeographed 1992).

Catholic Bulletin, 'Events of Easter Week' [Roger Casement], 6 (1916), 513–7.

Clarke, Séamus (Séamus Ó Cléirigh), *Feis na nGleann: A History of the Festival of the Glens* (privately published n.d.).

Cline, Catherine Ann, *E.D. Morel 1873–1924; The Strategies of Protest* (Belfast: Blackstaff Press 1980).

Cockburn, Claude, *I Claude* (Harmondsworth: Penguin 1967).

Collier, Richard, *The River that God Forgot* (London: Collins 1968).

Colum, Mary, *Life and the Dream* (Dublin: Dolmen Press 1966 [1958]).

Colum, Padraic, *The Road Round Ireland* (London: Macmillan 1926).

—, 'In vindication of Roger Casement', *Current History* (Sept. 1931), 819–26.

—, 'The career of Roger Casement', *The Dublin Magazine*, 6(4) (Oct.–Dec. 1931), 20–35.

Conrad, Joseph, *Heart of Darkness* (Harmondsworth: Penguin 1989 [1902]).

Cookey, S.J.S., *Britain and the Congo Question: 1885–1913* (London: Longmans 1968).

Coquery-Vidrovitch, Catherine, 'French colonialism in Africa to 1920: administration and economic development' in L.H. Gann & P. Duignan (eds.), *Colonialism in Africa: 1870–1960* (Cambridge: CUP 1969), vol. 1, pp. 165–98.

Cornevin, Robert, *Histoire du Congo* (Paris: Berger-Levrault 1966).

Costigan, Giovanni, 'The treason of Sir Roger Casement', *American Historical Review*, LX (1955), 283–302.

Cronin, Seán, *The McGarrity Papers* (Tralee: Anvil Books 1972).

Crowder, Michael, *West Africa under Colonial Rule* (London: Hutchinson 1968).

Curle, Richard (ed.), *Joseph Conrad, Last Essays* (NY: Dent 1926).

Curry, Dr Charles E. (ed.), *Sir Roger Casement's Diaries: 'His Mission to Germany and the Findlay Affair'* (Munich: Arche Publishing Co. 1922).

Daly, Martin, *Memories of the Dead: Some Impressions* (Dublin: Powell Press n.d. [1917?]).

Daly, Mary E. (ed.), *Roger Casement in Irish and World History* (Dublin: Royal Irish Academy 2005).

Daly, M.W., 'Egypt' in A.D. Roberts (ed.), *The Cambridge History of Africa*, vol. 7, 1905 to 1940 (Cambridge: CUP 1986), pp. 743–4.

Dandelman, U. von, 'Der Bankrott der Kongoakte', *Deutsche Reveu* (1915, Mai), 198–213.

Dangerfield, George, *The Damnable Question; A Study in Anglo-Irish Relations* (London: Constable 1977).

Davis, Shelton, *Victims of the Miracle: Development and the Indians of Brazil* (Cambridge: CUP 1977).

Devoy, John, *Recollections of an Irish Rebel* (NY: Charles P. Young 1929).

Doerries, Reinhard R., *Imperial Challenge* (Chapel Hill: University of N. Carolina Press 1989).

—, *Prelude to the Easter Rising: Sir Roger Casement in Imperial Germany* (London: Frank Cass 2000).

Douglas, A.C., *Niger Memories* (Exeter: James Townsend & Sons 1927).

Dudgeon, Jeffrey, *Roger Casement: The Black Diaries, with a study of his background, sexuality, and Irish political life* (Belfast: Belfast Press 2002).

Dunlop, Eull (ed.), *The Recollections of Mary Alice Young née Nacnaghten (1867–1946) of Dundarave and Galgorm, Co. Antrim* (Ballymena: Mid-Antrim Historical Group 1996).

Edwards, Owen Dudley, 'Divided treasons and divided loyalties', *Trans. Royal Historical Society*, 32 (1982), 153–74.

—, 'The trial of Roger Casement: a study in theatre management' in Mary E. Daly (ed.), *Roger Casement in Irish and World History* (Dublin: Royal Irish Academy 2005), pp. 149–77.

Edwards, Ruth Dudley, *Patrick Pearse: The Triumph of Failure* (Dublin: Poolbeg Press 1990 [1977]).

Felgate, W.S., *The Tembe Thonga of Natal and Mozambique: An Ecological Approach*, ed. E.J. Krige (Durban: University of Natal, Department of African Studies 1982).

Fischer, Fritz, *War of Illusions: German Policies from 1911 to 1914* (London: Chatto and Windus 1975).

Forbath, Peter, *The River Congo* (London: Secker & Warburg 1978).

Foy, Michael and Brian Barton, *The Easter Rising* (Stroud, Gloucestershire: Sutton Publishing 1999).

Frank, Katherine, *A Voyager Out: The Life of Mary Kingsley* (London: Corgi 1988).

Friedman, K. Ekholm, *Catastrophe and Creation: the Transformation of an African Culture* (Reading: Harwood 1991).

Fry, Joseph A., *Henry S. Sanford; Diplomacy and Business in Nineteenth Century America* (Reno: University of Nevada Press 1982).

Gearty, Conor, 'The Casement treason trial in its legal context' in Mary E. Daly (ed.), *Roger Casement in Irish and World History* (Dublin: Royal Irish Academy 2005), pp. 138–48.

Giles, Audrey, *Examination of Casement Diaries* (The Giles Document Laboratory, Amersham, Bucks February 2002).

—, 'Report of Dr Audrey Giles' in Mary E. Daly (ed.), *Roger Casement in Irish and World History* (Dublin: Royal Irish Academy 2005), pp. 202–37.

Giltrap, Risteárd, *An Ghaeilge in Eaglais na hÉireann* [*The Irish Language in the Church of Ireland*] (Baile Átha Cliath: Cumann Gaelach na hEaglaise 1990).

Glandon, Virginia E., *Arthur Griffith and the Advanced Nationalist Press, Ireland 1900–1922* (NY: P. Lang 1985).

Glave, E.J., *Six Years of Adventure in Congo-Land* (London: Sampson Low, Marston & Co. 1893).

Green, Alice Stopford, *The Making of Ireland and its Undoing* (London: Macmillan 1908).

—, *Irish Nationality* (London: Williams and Norgate 1911).

—, *The Old Irish World* (Dublin: Gill 1912).

—, H. Barbour, D. Hyde and A. Wilson, 'The Connemara Islands', *The Irish Review* (May 1914), 113–27.

Gwynn, Denis, *The Life of John Redmond* (London: Harrap 1932).

—, *The Life and Death of Roger Casement* (London: Jonathan Cape 1936 [1930]).

—, 'Roger Casement's last weeks', *Studies*, 54 (Spring 1965), 63–73.

Gwynn, Stephen, *Experiences of a Literary Man* (NY: Holt 1926).

— (ed.), *Letters and Friendships of Sir Cecil Spring Rice*, 2 vols. (London: Constable 1929).

—, *The Life of Mary Kingsley* (London: Macmillan & Co. 1932).

Hambloch, Ernest, *British Consul: Memories of Thirty Years' Service in Europe and Brazil* (London: Harrap 1938).

Hardenburg, Walter E., 'The Indians of the Putumayo, Upper Amazon', *Man*, 10 (1910), 134–8.

—, *The Putumayo: The Devil's Paradise. Travels in the Peruvian Amazon Region and an Account of the Atrocities Committed upon the Indians Therein* (London: T. Fisher Unwin 1912).

Harms, Robert, 'The end of red rubber: a reassessment', *Journal of African History*, XVI(1) (1975), 73–88.

Hawkins, Hunt, 'Joseph Conrad, Roger Casement and the Congo Reform Movement', *Journal of Modern Literature*, 9(i) (1981–2), 65–80.

Headlam, Cecil, *The Milner Papers*, 2 vols. (London: Cassell & Co. 1931).

Hemming, John, 'Roger Casement's Putumayo Investigation' in Mary E. Daly (ed.), *Roger Casement in Irish and World History* (Dublin: Royal Irish Academy 2005), pp. 36–45.

Henson, Herbert Hensley, *Retrospect of an Unimportant Life*, 3 vols. (Oxford: OUP 1942–50), vol. 1, 1863–1920, pp. 114–20.

Hill, (Revd) George, *An Historical Account of the Macdonnells of Antrim* (Belfast: Archer 1873).

Hinsley, F.H. (ed.), *British Foreign Policy Under Sir Edward Grey* (Cambridge: CUP 1977).

Hobson, Bulmer, *Ireland Yesterday and Tomorrow* (Tralee: Anvil Books 1968).

Hochschild, Adam, *King Leopold's Ghost: A Story of Greed, Terror and Heroism in Colonial Africa* (London, Macmillan 1999 [1998]).

Hogan, David, *The Four Glorious Years* (Dublin: Irish Press Ltd 1953).

Horan, James J., 'Review of the Giles Report on the Casement Diaries' in Mary E. Daly (ed.), *Roger Casement in Irish and World History* (Dublin: Royal Irish Academy 2005), pp. 238–42.

—, *From Parnell to Pearse: Some Recollections and Reflections* (Dublin: Brown and Nolan 1948).

Horne, John & Alan Kramer, *German Atrocities, 1914: A History of Denial* (New Haven: Yale University Press 2001).

Hutton, Mary, *The Táin*, 2nd edn., illustrated by Seaghan MacCathmhaoil (Dublin: Talbot Press 1924 [1907]).

Hyde, H. Montgomery, *Famous Trials 9: Roger Casement* (Harmondsworth: Penguin 1964).

—, *The Other Love: an Historical and Contemporary Survey of Homosexuality in Britain* (London: Heinemann 1970).

Hyland, Paul, *The Black Heart: A Voyage into Central Africa* (London: Gollancz 1988).

Inglis, Brian, *Roger Casement* (London: Coronet Books/Hodder & Stoughton 1974 [1973]).

Innes, A. Mitchell, 'Love and the law: a study of Oriental justice', *The Hibbert Journal*, XI (Oct. 1912–Jan. 1913), 273–96.

Ireland, John de Courcy, *The Sea and the Easter Rising*, revised edn. (Dún Laoghaire, Co. Dublin: Maritime Institute of Ireland 1996 [1966]).

Jephson, Maurice Denham, *An Anglo-Irish Miscellany: Some Records of the Jephsons of Mallow* (Dublin: Allen Figgis 1964).

Jewitt, A. Crispin, *Maps for Empire; the First 2000 Numbered War Office Maps 1881–1905* (The British Library 1992, nos. 1054–56).

Johnston, Sheila Turner, *The Harper of the Only God: A Selection of Poems by Alice Milligan* (Omagh: Colourpoint Press 1993).

—, *Alice: A Life of Alice Milligan* (Omagh: Colourpoint Press 1994).

Jones, Ray, *The Nineteenth-Century Foreign Office: An Administrative History* (London: Weidenfeld & Nicolson 1971).

—, *The British Diplomatic Service 1815–1914* (London: Colin Smyth 1983).

Karl, Frederick R., *Joseph Conrad: The Three Lives* (London: Faber & Faber 1979).

— and Laurence Davies (eds.), *The Collected Letters of Joseph Conrad* (Cambridge: CUP, vol. 3, 1903–7 [1988] and vol. 5, 1912–16 [1996]).

Karno, Howard, 'Julio César Arana, Frontier Cacique in Peru' in Robert Kern (ed.), *The Caciques* (Albuquerque: University of New Mexico Press 1973), pp. 89–98.

Kavanagh, Sean Francis, 'The last historic interview with Roger Casement in Berlin', *Roger Casement Commeration* (Conradh na Gaedhilge, Craobh Rudhria Mhic Easmuinn. Murlough, Co. Antrim 1953).

Kennedy, Kieran F., 'Official secrets, unauthorized acts', *Irish Literary Supplement*, 17(1) (Spring 1998), 26–27.

Kilfeather, Siobhán, 'Remembering pleasure and pain: Roger Casement's diaries', *Perversions, the international journal of gay and lesbian studies*, 2 (1994), 5–22.

Koss, Stephen, *Fleet Street Radical: A.G. Gardiner and the Daily News* (London: Allen Lane 1973).

Laffan, Michael, 'The making of a revolutionary: Casement and the Volunteers, 1913–14' in Mary E. Daly (ed.), *Roger Casement in Irish and World History* (Dublin: Royal Irish Academy 2005), pp. 64–73.

Larkin, Emmet, *James Larkin* (London: NEL Mentor 1968 [1965]).

Lerchenmueller, Joachim, ' "The wretched lot" – a brief history of the Irish Brigade in Germany 1914–1919' in *Yearbook of the Centre for Irish-German Studies* (University of Limerick 1998–1999), 95–113.

Longford, Elizabeth, *A Pilgrimage of Passion: The Life of Wilfrid Scawen Blunt* (London: Weidenfeld and Nicolson 1979).

Louis, William Roger, 'Roger Casement and the Congo', *Journal of African History*, 5 (1964), 99–120.

—, 'Morel and the Congo Reform Association, 1904–1913' in William Roger Louis and Jean Stengers (eds.), *E.D. Morel's History of the Congo Reform Movement* (Oxford: Clarendon Press 1968), pp. 171–220.

Lynch, Diarmaid, *The I.R.B. and the 1916 Insurrection: a record of the preparations for the Rising*, ed. Florence O'Donoghue (Cork: Mercier Press 1957).

Lynd, Robert, *Galway of the Races – Selected Essays*, ed. Sean McMahon (Dublin: The Lilliput Press 1990).

Lyne, Gerard L., 'New light on material concealed by Roger Casement near Banna Strand', *Journal of the Kerry Archaeological and Historical Society*, no. 21 (1987), 94–110.

Lyons, F.S.L., *John Dillon; A Biography* (London: Routledge 1968).

—, *Ireland Since the Famine* (London: Collins/Fontana 1973 [1971]).

Lyons, J.B., *Surgeon-Major Parke's African Journey 1887–89* (Dublin: The Lilliput Press 1994).

McCann, Jack, 'Margaret Dobbs', *The Glynns: Journal of the Glens of Antrim Historical Society*, 11 (1983), 41–6.

McCartney, Donal, 'Gaelic ideological origins of 1916' in O. Dudley Edwards and Fergus Pyle (eds.), *1916: The Easter Rising* (London: MacGibbon & Kee 1968), pp. 41–9.

—, 'The Sinn Féin Movement' in Kevin B. Nowlan (ed.), *The Making of 1916, Studies in the History of the Rising* (Dublin: Stationery Office 1969), pp. 31–48.

MacColl, René, *Roger Casement* (London: Four Square Edition 1965 [1956]).

Mac Conghail, Muiris, 'Brian Ó Ceallaigh, Tomás Ó Criomhthain and Sir Roger Casement', *Journal of the Kerry Archaeological and Historical Society*, 22 (1993), pp. 175–96.

McCoole, Sinéad, *Hazel: A Life of Lady Lavery 1880–1935* (Dublin: The Lilliput Press 1996).

McCormack, W.J., *Roger Casement in Death or Haunting the Free State* (Dublin: University College Dublin Press 2002).

McCracken, Donal P., *The Irish Pro Boers, 1877–1902* (Johannesburg: Perskom 1989).

McDiarmid, Lucy, 'The posthumous life of Roger Casement' in A. Bradley and M. G. Valiulis (eds.), *Gender and Sexuality in Modern Ireland* (Amherst: University of Massachusetts Press 1997), pp. 127–58.

—, 'Secular relics: Casement's boat, Casement's dish', *Textual Practice*, 16(2) (2002), 277–302.

—, 'The afterlife of Roger Casement: memory, folklore, ghosts, 1916–' in Lucy McDiarmid, *The Irish Art of Controversy* (Dublin: The Lilliput Press 2005), pp. 167–210.

—, 'The afterlife of Roger Casement' in Mary E. Daly (ed.), *Roger Casement in Irish and World History* (Dublin: Royal Irish Academy 2005), pp. 178–88.

McDowell, R.B., *Alice Stopford Green: Passionate Historian* (Dublin: Allen Figgis 1967).

MacGaffey, Wyatt, 'Ethnography and the closing of the frontier in the Lower Congo, 1885–1921', *Africa*, 56(3) (1986), 263–79.

—, *Custom and Government in the Lower Congo* (Berkeley: UCP 1970).

Mac Giolla Choille, B., *Intelligence Notes 1913–1916, preserved in the State Paper Office* (Baile Átha Cliath: Oifig an tSoláthair 1966).

McHugh, Roger, 'Casement: the Public Record Office manuscripts', *Threshold*, 4(1) (Summer 1960), 28–57.

—, 'Dilemma in Berlin: from Casement's last diary' in R. McHugh (ed.), *Dublin 1916* (London: Arlington Books 1966), pp. 3–16.

—, 'The last days of Roger Casement: memoir of his cousin, Gertrude Parry' in R. McHugh (ed.), *Dublin 1916* (London: Arlington Books 1966), pp. 289–305.

—, 'Casement and German help' in F.X. Martin (ed.), *Leaders and Men of the Easter Rising: Dublin 1916* (London: Methuen 1967), pp. 177–87.

MacKenzie, Norman and Jeanne (eds.), *The Diary of Beatrice Webb*, vol. 3, 1905–1924 (London: Virago 1984).

McKeogh, Michael, 'Roger Casement, Germany and the World War', *Catholic Bulletin*, 17 (1927), 1267–80; 18 (1928), 63–76, 165–77, 282–7, 396–402, 505–15, 613–22, 727–39, 833–45, 942–53, 1042–6, 1155–64, 1281–92.

McLynn, Frank, *Stanley: Sorcerer's Apprentice* (London: Constable 1991).

McMahon, Deirdre, 'Roger Casement: an account of his reinterment in Ireland', *Irish Archives*, 3 (1) (Spring 1996), 3–12.

McMinn, J.R.B., *Against the Tide: A Calendar of the Papers of Revd J.B. Armour; Irish Presbyterian Minister and Home Ruler 1869–1914* (Belfast: PRONI 1985).

MacNeill, Eoin, *Early Irish Laws and Institutions* (Dublin: Burns Oates and Washbourne 1935).

—, *Phases of Irish History* (Dublin: Gill & Son 1968 [1919]).

Mackey, Herbert O., *The Life and Times of Roger Casement* (Dublin: Fallon 1954).

— (ed.), *The Crime against Europe: Writings and Poems of Roger Casement* (Dublin: Fallon 1958).

—, *Roger Casement: The Forged Diaries* (Dublin: Fallon 1966).

Maloney, William J., *The Forged Casement Diaries* (Dublin: Talbot Press 1936).

Mansergh, Martin, 'Roger Casement and the idea of a broader nationalist tradition: his impact on Anglo-Irish relations' in Mary E. Daly (ed.), *Roger Casement in Irish and World History* (Dublin: Royal Irish Academy 2005), pp. 189–201.

Marchal, Jules, *E.D. Morel contre Léopold II: L'Histoire du Congo 1900–1910*, 2 vols. (Paris: Édition L'Harmattan 1996).

—, 'Roger Casement in the Congo: reactions in Belgium' in Mary E. Daly (ed.), *Roger Casement in Irish and World History* (Dublin: Royal Irish Academy 2005), pp. 26–35.

Marcus, Phillip, *Standish O'Grady* (Lewisburg: Bucknell University Press 1970).

Martin, F.X. (ed.), *The Irish Volunteers, 1913–1915* (Dublin: J. Duffy 1963).

— (ed.), *The Howth Gun-Running and the Kilcoole Gun-Running 1914* (Dublin: Browne and Nolan 1964).

—, '1916 – myth, fact, and mystery', *Studia Hibernica*, 7 (1967), 7–126.

— (ed.), *Leaders and Men of the Easter Rising: Dublin 1916* (London: Methuen 1967).

—, 'The 1916 Rising – a *coup d'état* or a "bloody protest"?' *Studia Hibernica*, 8 (1968), 106–37.

—, 'MacNeill and the foundation of the Irish Volunteers' in F.J. Byrne and F.X. Martin (eds.), *The Scholar Revolutionary: Eoin MacNeill, 1867–1945, and the Making of the New Ireland* (Shannon: Irish University Press 1973), pp. 99–179.

Meyers, Jeffrey, 'Conrad and Roger Casement', *Conradiana*, 5(iii) (1973), 64–9.

Middleton, Dorothy (ed.), *The Diary of A.J. Mounteney Jephson, Emin Pasha Relief Expedition 1887–89* (Cambridge: CUP 1969).

Milligan, Alice, 'Events of Easter Week: Roger Casement as an Irish-Irelander', *Catholic Bulletin*, vi (Jan.–Dec. 1916), 573–5.

Mitchell, Angus, 'Casement's Black Diaries: closed books reopened', *History Ireland* (Autumn 1997), 36–41.

— (ed.), *The Amazon Journal of Roger Casement* (Dublin: The Lilliput Press 1997).

— (ed.), *Sir Roger Casement's Heart of Darkness: The 1911 Documents* (Dublin: Irish Manuscripts Commission 2003).

—, *Casement* (London: Haus Publishing 2003).

—, ' "An Irish Putumayo": Roger Casement's humanitarian relief campaign among the Connemara islanders 1913–14', *Irish Economic and Social History*, XXXI (2004), 41–60.

—, 'John Bull's other empire: Roger Casement and the press, 1898–1916' in Simon J. Potter (ed.), *Newspapers and Empire in Ireland and Britain: Reporting the British Empire, c.1857–1921* (Dublin: Four Courts Press 2004), pp. 217–33.

—, 'The riddle of the two Casements?' in Mary E. Daly (ed.), *Roger Casement in Irish and World History* (Dublin: Royal Irish Academy 2005), pp. 99–120.

Mol, W.H., *The Ballymena Academy 1828–1978* (pamphlet, privately printed, Ballymena 1978).

Monteith, Robert, *Casement's Last Adventure* (Chicago, privately printed 1932).

Moore, Colonel Maurice, 'History of the Irish Volunteers', *The Irish Press*, January–March 1938.

Morrell, Ottoline, *Ottoline at Garsington: Memories of Lady Morrell, 1915–1918*, ed. Robert Gathorne-Hardy (London: Faber 1974).

Murphy, William M., *Prodigal Father: The Life of John Butler Yeats (1839–1922)* (Ithaca: Cornell U.P. 1978).

—, *Family Secrets: William Butler Yeats and his Relatives* (Dublin: Gill and Macmillan 1995).

Najder, Zdzislaw, 'Conrad's Casement letters', *Polish Perspectives*, XVII (Dec. 1974), 25–30.

— (ed.), *Congo Diary and Other Uncollected Pieces by Joseph Conrad* (Garden City, NY: Doubleday 1978).

Nevinson, H. W., *More Changes, More Chances* (London: Nisbet 1925).

—, *Last Changes, Last Chances* (London: Nisbet 1928).

Newitt, Malyn, *A History of Mozambique* (London: Hurs 1995).

Ní Chinnéide, Máiréad, *Máire de Buitléir: Bean Athbheochana* (Baile Átha Cliath: Comhar Teoranta 1993).

Nordon, Pierre, *Conan Doyle* (London: John Murray 1966).

Norton Cook, Arthur, *British Enterprise in Nigeria* (London: Frank Cass 1964).

Nowlan, Kevin B. (ed.), *The Making of 1916, Studies in the History of the Rising* (Dublin: Stationery Office 1969).

Noyes, Alfred, *The Accusing Ghost or Justice for Casement* (London: Gollancz 1957).

O'Brien, William and D. Ryan (eds.), *Devoy's Post Bag, 1871–1928* (Dublin: Fallon 1953), vol. II: 1880–1928.

Ó Broin, Leon, *Dublin Castle and the 1916 Rising* (Dublin: Helicon 1966).

—, *Revolutionary Brotherhood: the Story of the Irish Republican Brotherhood, 1858–1924* (Dublin: Gill and Macmillan 1976).

—, *Protestant Nationalists in Revolutionary Ireland: The Stopford Connection* (Dublin: Gill and Macmillan 1985).

Ó Buachalla, Séamus, *The Letters of P.H. Pearse* (London: C. Smyth 1980).

O'Byrne, Cathal, 'Roger Casement's ceilidhe', *The Capuchin Annual* (1946–1947), 312–13.

O'Callaghan, Margaret, ' "With the eyes of another race, of a people once hunted themselves": Casement, colonialism and a remembered past' in Mary E. Daly (ed.), *Roger Casement in Irish and World History* (Dublin: Royal Irish Academy 2005), pp. 46–63.

Ó Cléirigh, Séamus, *Casement and the Irish Language Culture and History* (Baile Átha Cliath: Clodhanna Teoranta 1977).

Ó Doibhlin, Diarmaid, *Womenfolk of the Glens of Antrim and the Irish Language* (Belfast: An tUltach Trust c.1994).

O'Flaherty, Tom, *Aranmen All* (Dublin: Three Candles 1934).

Ó Gaora, Colm, *Mise* (Baile Átha Cliath: Oifig an tSoláthair 1969 [1943]).

O'Grady, John, *The Life and Work of Sarah Purser* (Dublin: Four Courts Press 1996).

Ó hEithir, Breandán, *An Chaint sa tSráidbhaile* (Baile Átha Cliath: Comhar Teoranta 1991).

Ó Luanaigh, Dónall, 'Roger Casement, senior, and the siege of Paris (1870)', *The Irish Sword*, XV (1982–3), 33–5.

Ó Lúing, Seán, *Kuno Meyer, 1858–1919: A Biography* (Dublin: Geography Publications 1991).

Ó Máille, Eoin, *Roger Casement: The Forged Diaries Exposed* (Dublin: M. Payne 1993).

—, M. Uí Callanán and M. Payne, *The Vindication of Roger Casement* (pamphlet, privately printed 1994).

Ó Máille, Tomás, *An t-Iomaire Ruadh* (Baile Átha Cliath: Comhlucht Oideachais na hÉireann 1939).

Ó Murchadha, Diarmaid, *Liam de Róiste* (Baile Átha Cliath: An Clóchomhar Teoranta 1976).

O'Neill, Seamus, 'Note: Roger Casement, Cathal O'Byrne and Professor Reid', *Studies* (Spring/Summer 1979), 117–21.

O'Rahilly, Aodogán, *Winding the Clock: O'Rahilly and the 1916 Rising* (Dublin: The Lilliput Press 1991).

Ó Síocháin, Séamas, 'Roger Casement, ethnography and the Putumayo', *Éire–Ireland* XXIX(2) (1994), 29–41.

—, 'Evolution and degeneration in the thought of Roger Casement', *Irish Journal of Anthropology*, 2 (1997), 45–62.

—, 'Ruarí Mac Easmainn: an dubh agus an bán' ('Roger Casement: the black and the white'), *Oghma*, 10 (1998), 57–66.

—, 'Teanga agus tuath: Ruairí Mac Easmainn agus iarthar na hÉireann' ('Language and country: Roger Casement and the west of Ireland'), *Bliainiris 2000* (Baile Átha Cliath: Carbad), 35–60.

— and Thomas Kabdebo, 'Hungary and the two Roger Casements' in Thomas Kabdebo, *Ireland and Hungary: A Study in Parallels* (Dublin: Four Courts Press 2001), pp. 73–9.

— and Michael O'Sullivan (eds.), *The Eyes of Another Race: Roger Casement's Congo Report and 1903 Diary* (Dublin: UCD Press 2003).

—, 'Roger Casement's vision of freedom' in Mary E. Daly (ed.), *Roger Casement in Irish and World History* (Dublin: Royal Irish Academy 2005), pp. 1–10.

Ó Snodaigh, Pádraig, *Hidden Ulster: Protestants and the Irish Language* (Belfast: Lagan Press 1995).

O'Sullivan, Michael, 'Case closed', *Gay Community News*, May 2002.

Pakenham, Thomas, *The Boer War* (London: Weidenfeld & Nicolson 1979).

—, *The Scramble for Africa, 1876–1912* (London: Weidenfeld & Nicolson 1991).

Parmiter, Geoffrey de C., *Roger Casement* (London: Arthur Barker 1936).

Phoenix, Eamon, Pádraic Ó Cléireacháin, Eileen McAuley and Nuala McSparran (eds.), *Feis na nGleann: A Century of Gaelic Culture in the Antrim Glens* (Belfast: Feis na nGleann & Stair Uladh–Ulster Historical Foundation 2005).

Pim, Sheila, *The Wood and the Trees: Augustine Henry, a Biography* (Kilkenny: Boethius Press 1984).

Platt, D.C.M., *The Cinderella Service: British Consuls since 1825* (London: Longman 1971).

Plunkett, Geraldine, 'Joseph Plunkett's diary of his journey to Germany in 1915', *University Review*, 1(11) (1954), 32–48.

Porter, Andrew, 'Sir Roger Casement and the international humanitarian movement' in Mary E. Daly (ed.), *Roger Casement in Irish and World History* (Dublin: Royal Irish Academy 2005), pp. 11–25.

Puleston, Fred, *African Drums* (London: Gollancz 1930).

Reid, B.L., *The Lives of Roger Casement* (New Haven: Yale University Press 1976).

Robbins, K.G., 'Public Opinion, the press and pressure groups' in F.H. Hinsley (ed.), *British Foreign Policy Under Sir Edward Grey* (Cambridge: CUP 1977), pp. 70–88.

Rothenfelder, Franz, *Casement in Deutschland* (Augsburg: Reichel 1917).

Rothenstein, William, *Men and Memories*, vol. II, 1900–1922 (London: Faber and Faber 1932).

Rudkin, David, 'The chameleon and the kilt', *Encounter*, XLI(2) (August 1973), 70–7.

—, *Cries from Casement as his Bones are Brought to Dublin* (London: BBC 1974).

Ryan, A.P., *Mutiny at the Curragh* (London: Macmillan 1956).

Sanderson, G.N., 'The Nile basin and the Eastern Horn, 1870–1908' in R. Oliver and G.N. Sanderson (eds.), *The Cambridge History of Africa*, vol. 6, 1870 to 1905 (Cambridge: CUP 1985).

Sawyer, Roger, *Casement: the Flawed Hero* (London: Routledge 1984).

—, *'We Are But Women': Women in Ireland's History* (London: Routledge 1993).

— (ed.), *Roger Casement's Diaries: 1910: The Black and the White* (London: Pimlico 1997).

—, 'The Black Diaries: a question of authenticity' in Mary E. Daly (ed.), *Roger Casement in Irish and World History* (Dublin: Royal Irish Academy 2005), pp. 88–98.

Scannell, M.J.P. and O. Snoddy, 'Roger Casement's contribution to the ethnographical and economic botany collections in the National Museum of Ireland', *Éire–Ireland*, 3(4) (1968), 46–54.

Schweinfurth, Georg, *The Heart of Africa: Three Years' Travels & Adventures in the Unexplored Regions of Central Africa from 1867 to 1871*, 2 vols. (London: Sampson Low, Marston, Low & Searle 1873).

Selby, John, *A Short History of South Africa* (London: New English Library/Mentor 1975).

Shackleton, Robert, *Montesquieu: a Critical Biography* (Oxford: OUP 1961).

Sherry, Norman, *Conrad's Western World* (Cambridge: CUP 1971).

Singleton-Gates, Peter and Maurice Girodias, *The Black Diaries: An Account of Roger Casement's Life and Times with a Collection of his Diaries and Public Writings* (Paris: The Olympia Press 1959).

Slade, Ruth, *English-Speaking Missions in the Congo Independent State (1878–1908)* (Brussels: Académie Royale des Sciences Coloniales 1959).

—, *King Leopold's Congo* (Oxford: OUP 1962).

Solnit, Rebecca, 'The butterfly collector' in *A Book of Migrations: Some Passages in Ireland* (London: Verso 1997), pp. 28–43.

Spindler, Karl, *The Mystery of the Casement Ship* (Tralee: Anvil Books 1965).

Steinberg, Jonathan, 'The German background to Anglo-German relations, 1905–1914' in F.H. Hinsley (ed.), *British Foreign Policy Under Sir Edward Grey* (Cambridge: CUP 1977), pp. 193–215.

Steiner, Zara, 'The Foreign Office under Sir Edward Grey' in F.H. Hinsley (ed.), *British Foreign Policy Under Sir Edward Grey* (Cambridge: CUP 1977), pp. 22–69.

Stengers, Jean, 'The Congo Free State and the Belgian Congo before 1914' in L.H. Gann and P. Duignan (eds.), *Colonialism in Africa: 1870–1960* (Cambridge: CUP 1969), vol. 1, pp. 261–92.

—, 'Morel and Belgium' in Roger Owen and Bob Sutcliffe (eds.), *Studies in the Theory of Imperialism* (London: Longmans 1972), pp. 221–51.

—, 'King Leopold's imperialism' in Roger Owen and Bob Sutcliffe (eds.), *Studies in the Theory of Imperialism* (London: Longmans 1972), pp. 248–76.

— and Jan Vansina, 'King Leopold's Congo, 1886–1908' in R. Oliver and G.N. Sanderson (eds.), *The Cambridge History of Africa* (Cambridge: CUP 1985), vol. 6, pp. 315–58.

Stewart, A.T.Q., *The Ulster Crisis: Resistance to Home Rule 1912–1914* (London: Faber and Faber 1967).

Stuart, Charles H., 'The Lower Congo and the American Baptist Mission to 1910' (Ph.D. dissertation, Boston University Graduate School 1969).

Sullivan, A.M., *Old Ireland: Reminiscences of an Irish K.C.* (London: Thornton Butterworth 1927).

—, *The Last Serjeant* (London: Macdonald 1952).

Tansill, Charles Callan, *America and the Fight for Irish Freedom, 1866–1922* (New York: Devin-Adair 1957).

Taussig, Michael, *Shamanism, Colonialism, and the Wild Man: A Study in Terror and Healing* (Chicago: UCP 1987).

—, 'Culture of terror – space of death: Roger Casement's Putumayo report and the explanation of torture', *Comparative Studies in Society and History*, 26 (1984), 467–97.

Taylor, A.J.P., *The Trouble Makers: Dissent over Foreign Policy, 1792–1939* (London: Hamish Hamilton 1957).

Thompson, Brooks, 'A letter of Roger Casement (1888) in the Sanford Collection', *English Historical Review*, LXXVII (January 1962), 98–102.

Tierney, Michael, *Eoin MacNeill, Scholar and Man of Action 1867–1945*, ed. F.X. Martin (Oxford: Clarendon Press 1980).

Tooley, R.V., *A Dictionary of Mapmakers Part II* (Map Collectors Series no. 28 1979).

Townshend, Charles, *Easter 1916: The Irish Rebellion* (London: Penguin Books 2006).

Tuchman, Barbara, *The Proud Tower* (NY: Bantam Books 1966).

Twain, Mark, *King Leopold's Soliloquy* (Berlin: Seven Seas Books 1961 [1905]).

Ward, Herbert, *A Voice from the Congo: Comprising Stories, Anecdotes and Descriptive Notes* (London: Heinemann 1910).

—, *Five Years with the Congo Cannibals* (London: Chatto and Windus 1890).

—, *Mr Poiliu; Notes and Sketches with the Fighting French* (London: Hodder & Stoughton 1916).

Ward, Sarita, *A Valiant Gentleman – being the biography of Herbert Ward, Artist and Man of Action* (London: Chapman & Hall 1927).

Warhurst, Philip R., *Anglo-Portuguese Relations in South-Central Africa 1890–1900* (London: Longmans 1962).

Wasserstein, Bernard, *Herbert Samuel: A Political Life* (Oxford: Clarendon Press 1992).

Wauters, A.J., *Stanley's Emin Pasha Expedition* (London: J.C. Nimmo 1890).

Weale, Adrian, *Patriot Traitors: Roger Casement, John Amery and the Real Meaning of Treason* (London: Viking 2001).

Weeks, John H., *Among the Primitive Bakongo* (London: Seely, Service & Co. Ltd 1914).

Werlich, David P., *Peru: A Short History* (Carbondale: S. Illinois UP 1978).

West, Trevor, *Horace Plunkett: Co-operation and Politics, an Irish Biography* (Gerrards Cross, Bucks.: Colin Smythe 1986).

Whiffen, Thomas, *The North-West Amazons: Notes of Some Months Spent among Cannibal Tribes* (London: Constable 1915).

White, Gerry and Brendan O'Shea, *'Baptised in Blood': The Formation of the Cork Brigade of Irish Volunteers 1913–1916* (Cork: Mercier Press 2005).

White, Jack, *Misfit: an Autobiography* (London: Jonathan Cape 1930).

White, James P., 'The Sanford exploring expedition', *Journal of African History*, VIII (2) (1967), 291–302.

Wilson, Keith, 'Grey' in K. Wilson (ed.), *British Foreign Secretaries and Foreign Policy: From Crimean War to First World War* (London: Croom Helm 1987), pp. 172–97.

Wilson, Monica and Leonard Thompson (eds.), *The Oxford History of South Africa* (NY: OUP 1975 [1971]), vol. 2, 1870–1966.

Index

and Lever proposal, 208–9; decision not to visit Casement in prison, 446–7; testimonial appeal for, 203–4, 206–8, 267, 303, 304
Morel, Mary, 188, 208, 301
Morgan, Revd Hope T., 156, 158
Morgan, John Hartman, 348, 354, 357, 358, 359, 450, 472; acts for Casement's defence at trial, 445, 452, 454; appeals against sentence, 459; visits Casement in prison, 446
Morley, John, 190
Morrell, Ottoline, 462
Morrison, William, 138, 146, 154
Morten, Richard, 88, 89, 99, 102, 104–5, 118, 126, 135, 136, 149, 184, 202, 207, 213, 226, 228, 231, 233, 247, 262–3, 265, 300, 301, 302, 304, 316, 337, 348, 375, 392, 449; farewell letter from Casement, 460–1, 472–3; visits Casement in prison, 446, 450
Moule, Katie, 266
Mountmorres, Lord, 193
Mozambique Company, 231
Murnane, Fr Edward F., 474
Murphy, J.B., 96–7

Na Fianna, 365
'Nameless One', 91
Nathan, Sir Matthew, 411
National Council, 212
Nationalities and Subject Races Committee conference, 313
National Literary Society, 212
Negro Fellowship League, 465
Nelson, J., 315
Nevinson, Henry Wood, 230, 233, 342, 347, 461, 462, 464; attends trial, 452, 453; visits Casement in prison, 446
Nicholson, Fr John T., 412–13, 414, 415, 417, 418, 424
Nicolson, Arthur, 391, 402, 444
Ní Fhaircheallaigh, Úna, see also O'Farrelly, Agnes, 309
Niger Coast Protectorate, 44, 45, 46–66, 126; Benin massacre, 307; cannibalism, 54; Casement acting vice-consul in Opobo, 59–63; ethnography, 54; German atrocity (1894), 59; human sacrifice, 60–1; missionaries in, 49;

overthrow of King JaJa of Opobo, 47; punitive expeditions, 64; surveying work, 46, 48, 51–9
Nightingale, Arthur, 92, 125, 145, 150, 179, 193–4, 199
Ní Mháille, Sinéad, 373
Ní Mháille, Tomás, 373
Nisco, Baron Giacomo, 149, 192
Noeggerath, Jacob, 436
Norbury, Lord, 196, 197, 198, 301
Norfolk, Duke of, 190, 305, 337
Normand, Armando, 289, 290, 291, 292, 301, 316

O'Beirne, Seamus, 219, 355, 356, 372–3
O'Boyce, J.C., 215
O'Brien, Barry, 229
O'Brien, Conor, 376
O'Brien, Hugh, 376
O'Brien, Revd Lucius, 229
O'Brien, R. Barry, 213
O'Brien, William Smith, 229, 366, 464
O'Byrne, Cathal, 450
Ó Ceallacháin, Daithí, 219
O'Callaghan, Michael, 368
O'Connor, Thomas Power, 258, 265
O'Donnell, Andrés, 286, 287, 288, 316
O'Donnell, Red Hugh, 13
Ó Dubhthaigh, Aodh, 245, 255
O'Farrelly, Agnes (Una), 245, 267, 302, 464, 472
O'Flaherty, Liam, 218
O'Flaherty, Tom, 218–19
O'Gorman, Fr Canice, 399, 408, 413, 424
O'Grady, Standish James, 211, 212
O'Hegarty, P.S., 258, 263
O'Hickey, Fr Michael, 263
Oil Rivers Protectorate see Niger Coast Protectorate
Ó Laoghaire, tAthair Peadar, 212
'Oliver Cromwell', 14
Olivier, Sir Sydney, 463, 466
Olympic Games article, 245
Olympic Games of the White Races, 369
O'Malley, Patrick, 373
O'Malley, T., 373
Omarino, 294, 297, 299, 313–14, 316, 317, 319
O'Neill, Jorge, 217, 218, 220, 221
O'Neill, Owen Roe, 13–14, 213
'Open Letter to Irishmen', 389–91